CURRENT RESEARCH IN PHOTOSYNTHESIS

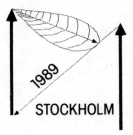

Current Research in Photosynthesis

Volume IV

*Proceedings of the VIIIth International Conference on Photosynthesis
Stockholm, Sweden, August 6–11, 1989*

edited by

M. BALTSCHEFFSKY

*Department of Biochemistry,
University of Stockholm,
Stockholm, Sweden*

KLUWER ACADEMIC PUBLISHERS
DORDRECHT / BOSTON / LONDON

Library of Congress Cataloging in Publication Data

International Congress on Photosynthesis (8th : 1989 : Stockholm,
  Sweden)
    Current research in photosynthesis : proceedings of the VIIIth
International Congress on Photosynthesis, Stockholm, Sweden, August
6-11, 1989 / edited by M. Baltscheffsky.
      p.   cm.
    ISBN 0-7923-0587-6 (set)
    1. Photosynthesis--Congresses. 2. Photosynthesis--Research-
-Congresses.   I. Baltscheffsky, Margareta.   II. Title.
QK882.I55   1989
581.1'3342--dc20   89-48127

ISBN 0-7923-0588-4 (Vol. I)
ISBN 0-7923-0589-2 (Vol. II)
ISBN 0-7923-0590-6 (Vol. III)
ISBN 0-7923-0591-4 (Vol. IV)
ISBN 0-7923-0587-6 (Set)

Published by Kluwer Academic Publishers,
P.O. Box 17, 3300 AA Dordrecht, The Netherlands.

Kluwer Academic Publishers incorporates
the publishing programmes of
D. Reidel, Martinus Nijhoff, Dr W. Junk and MTP Press.

Sold and distributed in the U.S.A. and Canada
by Kluwer Academic Publishers,
101 Philip Drive, Norwell, MA 02061, U.S.A.

In all other countries, sold and distributed
by Kluwer Academic Publishers Group,
P.O. Box 322, 3300 AH Dordrecht, The Netherlands.

Printed on acid-free paper

GENERAL CONTENTS

CONTENTS TO VOLUME IV

15. Respiration and Photosynthesis

16. Regulation of Chloroplast Metabolism

X

17. Adaptation Mechanisms

18. CO_2 Concentration Mechanisms

19. Stress and Photosynthesis

XVIII

PREFACE

These four volumes with close to one thousand contributions are the proceedings from the VIIIth International Congress on Photosynthesis, which was held in Stockholm, Sweden, on August 6-11, 1989. The site for the Congress was the campus of the University of Stockholm. This in itself was an experiment, since the campus never before had been used for a conference of that size. On the whole, it was a very sucessful experiment. The outcome of a congress depends on many contributing factors, one major such factor being the scientific vigour of the participants, and I think it is safe to say that the pariticipants were vigourous indeed. Many exciting new findings were presented and thoroughly dicussed, indoors in the discussion sessions as well as outdoors on the lawns. For the local organizing committee it was very rewarding to participate in these activities, and to watch some of our younger colleagues for the first time being subjected to the impact of a large international congress. The stimulating effect of this event on the local research atmosphere has been substantial.

As was the case with the proceedings from both the 1983 and 1986 Congresses these proceedings have been compiled from camera ready manuscripts, and the editing has mainly consisted of finding the proper place for each contribution and distributing the manuscripts into four volumes with some internal logic in each. In this I have had the invaluable help from Dr. Åke Strid, to whom I am indeed very thankful. The professional and unfailing support of our publisher, Ir. Ad. C. Plaizier, is also gratefully acknowledged.

The scientific programme for the Congress was put together by the Swedish Organizing Committee, with important input from the International Committee on Photosynthesis, and I thank my fellow-organizers for their competent and valuable work. The practical arrangements for the Congress were very well handled by Congrex AB, and I would like to specially mention Anette Lifors and Christel Bomgren for their enthusiastic help. The Congress would not have functioned without strong local support, foremost that of Professor Bertil Andersson and Dr. Stenbjörn Styring from the Department of Biochemistry, but also from all the students who were most helpful in uncounted numbers of ways, before, during and after the Congress.

Finally I thank all those who financially contributed to the Congress. Without their support there would not have been any Photosynthesis Congress in Sweden.

Stockholm in October 1989   Margareta Baltscheffsky

ACKNOWLEDGEMENTS

The Swedish Organizing Committee wishes to thank the following sponsors for their financial Support of the Congress.

Sponsors

Astra AB, Sweden
Pharmacia AB, Sweden
Scandinavian Airlines System, Sweden
Sparbankernas Bank, Sweden
Stiftelsen Kempes Minne, Sweden
Stiftelsen Lantbruksforskning, Sweden
Strålfors AB, Sweden
Swedish Council for Forestry and Agricultural Research
Swedish Natural Science Research Council
The City of Stockholm
The Nobel Foundation, Sweden

Exhibitors

ADC. The Analytical Development Company Ltd, UK
BIOMONITOR SCI, Sweden
HANSATECH Ltd., UK
LI-COR Inc., USA
QA-DATA, Finland
SKYE INSTRUMENTS LTD, UK
TECHTUM INSTRUMENT AB, Sweden
WALZ, Mess-und Regeltechnik, FRG

Swedish Organizing Committee

Chairperson: Margareta Baltscheffsky, University of Stockholm

Per-Åke Albertsson	Lund University
Bertil Andersson	University of Stockholm
Carl-Ivar Brändén	The Swedish University of Agricultural Sciences
Petter Gustafsson	Umeå University
Anders Kylin	Lund University
Christer Sundqvist	Gothenburg University
Jan-Eric Tillberg	University of Stockholm
Tore Vänngård	Gothenburg University
Gunnar Öquist	Umeå University

International Committee on Photosynthesis

C. Arntzen	USA
M. Baltscheffsky	Sweden (Chairperson)
J. Biggins	USA
G. Farquhar	Australia
G. Forti	Italy
R. Van Grondelle	The Netherlands
H. Heldt	FRG
P. Horton	UK
R. Malkin	USA
P. Mathis	France
I. Ohad	Israel
K. Satoh	Japan
Y.K. Shen	PR of China
V. Shuvalov	USSR
R. Vallejos	Argentina

SPEECH HELD AT THE OPENING OF THE VIIIth INTERNATIONAL
CONGRESS ON PHOTOSYNTHESIS STOCKHOLM, AUGUST 6th, 1989

BENGT GÖRANSSON
MINISTRY OF EDUCATION, 103 33 STOCKHOLM, SWEDEN

I consider it a great honour to extend to the delegates to this
congress the greetings of the Government of Sweden. Welcome to
Sweden and welcome to our capital. I would like to take this opportunity to share with you a number of personal reflections.

Photosynthesis is a good example of a science which enjoys rapid
development and whose practical application extends to ever wider
areas. It provides, to my mind, evidence of the role which highly
qualified and at the same time highly theoretical research plays in
changing and developing our lives and our society. Earlier societies
were much more static in character, the individual relied on well
established patterns for economic activity and survival. Ways of
life, attitudes, values and interests all built on traditions established by earlier generations. Today we live more like the sailor
who when he sails on open sea, must rely on the discoveries made by
the researcher/navigator on the basis of his experience and knowledge.

The researcher is to a very great extent our navigator, our path-
finder. The fact that he is also more and more of a theoretician is
of no small importance - this makes for greater demands on basic
theoretical education. It also calls for greater effort in providing
the wider public with sufficient popularized knowledge in order to
ensure that the insights and directions developed by the theoretical
researcher can be usefully exploited.

I would like to be concrete on this particular point. With mounting
concern I have observed how here in Sweden, as in many other countries, while basic schooling for the majority of our citizens has
improved there has been an increase in various types of what can
only be described as occult trends. A lack of faith in the future
together with a strong mistrust not only in the political establishment but also in the intellectual establishment to which the world
of research belongs, - these are far from uncommon today. To put it

more provocatively I might say that only those who know next to
nothing about the subject they express their opinions on, are
accepted as authorities.

A lack of faith in the future is dangerous for mankind. It is
dangerous because it is, paradoxically enough, often combined with
an unlimited exaggeration of the level of development we now enjoy
and of the capacity of the human brain that we judge ourselves to
possess. Those who do not think that we can solve the different problems we face today with tomorrow's discoveries and with the help of
tomorrow's people appear to believe that we in our own time, have
reached the final frontiers of knowledge.

Just as dangerous is the naive belief in the future or in progress,
especially that which is based on the belief that development is
automatic, that we have no cause to worry. In reality development
and change come about through the persistant pursuit of knowledge,
through the demanding job of fitting together various bits of knowledge, of matching ideas to ideas. The foundations of a positive
and productive belief in the future are to be found in the belief
that there are always new possibilities combined with the hard work
of winning new knowledge.

In creating a positive and productive belief in the future we have
good reason to consider more closely the research being carried out
in the field of photosynthesis. The experience gained in this field
gives us hope that we will be able to solve the global problems
affecting our environment, our future production of the necessities
of life and the possibility of finding a cure for serious diseases.
The global solutions will also be solutions to the problems faced by
the individual. The importance of the results of research in the
field of photosynthesis go far beyond the confines of the
researcher's world. Those aspects of research on photosynthesis
which have a bearing on the question of energy lead to an increased
interest on the part of government bodies and of business interests.
The nature of research calls for interdisciplinary cooperation and
important contributions are made by such groups as programmers and
technicians to the work of the researcher. This means that the need
to promote the exchange of ideas and experiences, such as take place
at congresses and conferences, is very great. The fact that representatives for science and research from university departments and
research institutions all over the world meet and confer, becomes an
event of decisive importance. I would therefore like to express my
gratitude and appreciation to you all for attending this congress.
I am of course delighted at the fact that our Swedish representives
in this field of scientific research have been entrusted with the
task of organizing the congress.

I would like to pursue my line of thinking further. In pointing to the paradoxical conflict between highly qualified and highly developed research on the one hand and the trend towards more occult interests on the other, I have done so because I think it is of vital importance that we combat the latter. Getting the researcher to step outside his isolation in the world of "interdisciplinary science" is not enough. It is vital that a broad section of the public should be given the opportunity to share the knowledge gained by research. A society in which the reseacher is isolated because of his research and knowledge and possibly regarded as a "deus ex machina", a wizard who can do things we others cannot do, such a society will never liberate itself from the threats posed by occultist movements. These threats are all the more dangerous because of the effects that they can have on wider relationships in society. A democratic social order rests ultimately on the fact that the citizens know enough about what happens in their community to feel secure. The ignorant and insecure citizen, who through lack of understanding is manipulated or feels manipulated becomes all too easily a victim of antidemocratic forces and campaigns. This gives me special cause to appeal to you as representatives for a highly specialized science, to give some consideration to what is often called popular science. I trust that the exchange of experience at the congress will in some way be made available for larger sections of the public. A quick glance through a Swedish school book shows that photosynthesis is far from being among the easiest of scientific topics and I regret to add that any student who satisfies himself with the contents of the school book will hardly broaden his knowledge of photosynthesis. What is important is that this broader knowledge is accessible to the average interested member of the public. (In this context it would be interesting to speculate on the causes of the chlorophyll hysteria of the nineteen fifties - you all remember the toothpaste with chlorophyll - was it in part due to a lack of understanding of man's own capacity in the field of photosynthesis?)

My personal wish, if you allow me to voice it, is that this congress and its work will stimulate popular education to take up popular science in the best sense of the term.

I would like to wish you all a fruitful congress week, a week that will benefit your scientific endeavours and ultimately, benefit humanity. It goes without saying, though I very much enjoy saying it - that I wish each and every one of you a pleasant stay in our summer clad Sweden and in Stockholm which I trust will show you the very best it has to offer the visitor from home or abroad.

Dear guests and congress participants!
I have used my privilege as invited minister by making these comments. I now turn to my official and ceremonial duty and declare the VIIIth International Congress on Photosynthesis opened.

TRANSFER OF REDOX EQUIVALENTS BETWEEN SUBCELLULAR COMPARTMENTS OF A LEAF CELL

H. W. HELDT, D. HEINEKE, R. HEUPEL, S. KRÖMER AND B. RIENS
INSTITUT FÜR BIOCHEMIE DER PFLANZE, UNIVERSITÄT GÖTTINGEN, UNTERE KARSPÜLE 2, 3400 GÖTTINGEN, F.R.G.

INTRODUCTION

In a plant cell the redox reactions involved in the photosynthetic assimilation of CO_2 and nitrate are located in four different compartments; the chloroplast stroma, the mitochondrial matrix, the peroxisomal compartment and the cytosol. The present report deals with the question in which way redox equivalents can be transferred between these different compartments and how the redox processes in the various compartments can be coordinated. The experiments shown in the following have all been carried out with spinach leaves grown in hydroponic culture in a 9 h light 15 h dark cycle.

RESULTS AND DISCUSSION

Redox state of subcellular pyridine nucleotide pools

In spinach leaves we found a NADPH/NADP ratio of 1.8 during illumination. We conclude that this high ratio mainly reflects the NADPH/NADP in the stroma, because Dietz and Heber (1) obtained the same NADPH/NADP ratio of 1.8 for chloroplasts from illuminated spinach leaves employing nonaqueous separation of chloroplasts from frozen spinach leaves. One may argue that the ratio of NADPH/NADP contents could differ from the ratio of the corresponding free concentrations. It has been shown that NADPH can be bound to ribulose-bisphosphate carboxylase (2), but this binding was found to be substantial only in the absence of RuBP, whereas in the presence of 4 mM RuBP there was practically no binding of NADPH observed (3). Since in illuminated leaves the RuBP concentration is about 8 mM, it is not to be expected that under these conditions the ratio of free NADPH/NADP will be dramatically different from the ratio of contents. It can be therefore concluded that in illuminated leaves the NADPH/NADP ratio in the stroma is in the order of 1.

Abbreviations: Mal, malate; OAA, oxaloacetate; MDH, malate dehydrogenase; GOT, glutamate oxaloacetate transaminase; 2-OG, 2-oxoglutarate; OH Pyr, hydroxypyruvate; Glc6P, glucose-6-phosphate; RuBP, Ribulose-1.5-bisphosphate

M. Baltscheffsky (ed.), Current Research in Photosynthesis, Vol. IV, 1–7.
© 1990 *Kluwer Academic Publishers. Printed in the Netherlands.*

TABLE 1. Subcellular content of aspartate, glutamate,
2-oxoglutarate and malate

Spinach plants were grown in a climatized chamber with a 9 h light/15 h
dark cycle and leaves were stopped in liquid N_2 after 8 1/2 h light. The
lyophilized leaves were fractionated in nonaqueous media as (7). The
results are mean values from two independent experiments.
*) The OAA concentration was calculated from the glutamate oxaloacetate
transaminase equilibrium.

	stroma	cytosol (mM)	vacuole
Glutamate	25.2	39.3	0.82
Aspartate	25.5	43.7	2.06
2-Oxoglutarate	0.16	0.58	0.025
Malate	3.0	1.0	26.7
Oxaloacetate*	0.025	0.098	
Mal/OAA	120	10	

Little is known about the NADH and NAD content of the cytosol. In order
to estimate the NADH/NAD ratio, the cytosolic contents of malate,
aspartate, glutamate and 2-oxoglutarate were determined by nonaqueous
fractionation of spinach leaves (Table 1). From these values the
NADH/NAD ratio was calculated on the reasonable assumption that the
reactions catalyzed by the cytosolic malate dehydrogenase and glutamate
oxaloacetate transaminase are near to equilibrium. Introducing the
equilibrium constants of these enzymes (K_{MDH} 2.8 . 10^{-5} at pH 7.0 (4), K_{GOT}
6.6 (4)), the NADH/NAD ratio is estimated as 1.2×10^{-3}, which in the
presence of 0.5 mM NAD corresponds to an NADH concentration of 0.6 µM.
This value is similar to the Km of spinach nitrate reductase for NADH
(1.4 µM (5)), and also similar to the NADH/NAD ratio found in the
cytosol of animal tissues, such as liver (6). From these findings we can
conclude that in the cytosol of illuminated leaf cells the NADH/NAD
ratio is in the order of 10^{-3}, which is about three orders of magnitude
lower than the NADPH/NADP ratio in the stroma. For spinach leaves data
on NADH/NAD ratios in the mitochondrial matrix are not available. In
mitochondria aqueously isolated from pea leaves we found in the steady
state of glycine oxidation in the presence of ADP and Pi an NADH/NAD
ratio in the order of 10^{-1} (Krömer, unpubl.).

Transfer of redox equivalents from the chloroplast to the cytosol

A specific transport of malate and oxaloacetate across the inner
envelope membrane enables a transfer of redox equivalents from the
chloroplast stroma to the cytosol (8). The translocator involved is half
saturated at very low concentrations of oxaloacetate (Km 9 µM). OAA
transport is insensitive to even high concentrations of malate (Ki 1.4
mM) as determined in spinach chloroplasts. The large redox gradient
between the NADPH/NADP in the stroma and the NADH/NAD in the cytosol,

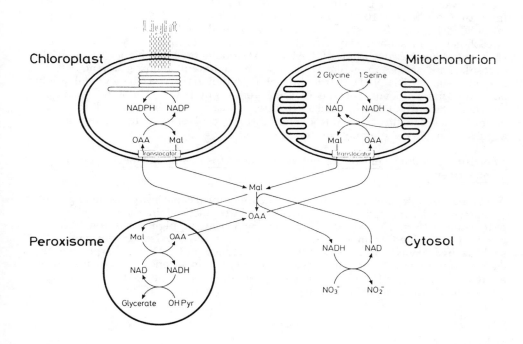

FIGURE 1.   Metabolic pathways of redox transfer between
subcellular compartments

discussed in the preceding, is in part maintained by the translocation step.
As shown in Table 1, the Mal/OAA ratio in the stroma appears to be about
one order of magnitude higher than in the cytosol. Additionally also the
stromal NADP-malate dehydrogenase contributes to the maintenance of the
redox gradient between the stroma and the cytosol. This enzyme is
strongly controlled in its activity by the stromal NADPH/NADP ratio (9).
The enzyme appears to function as a valve, allowing an export of redox
equivalents from the chloroplast stroma only if the stromal NADP system
is highly reduced. The capacity of the MAL-OAA shuttle from the
chloroplasts is very high (Vmax 52 µmol/mg chl.h), as determined in
spinach chloroplasts at 20°C (10).

Transfer of redox equivalents between the mitochondria and the cytosol

Plant mitochondria, in contrast to animal mitochondria, contain specific
translocators for malate and oxaloacetate operating as electrogenic
uniports (11). The uptake of OAA into mitochondria from spinach leaves

is half saturated at 6 µM OAA, and the maximal activity of the shuttle has been determined as 51 µmol/mg chl.h at 20°C (12). The transport of malate was found to be strongly inhibited by OAA at a concentration ratio of OAA/Mal = 10^{-3} (12). It is feasible that the OAA present in the mitochondrial matrix restricts the efflux of malate from the mitochondria in such a way that in the matrix the ratio of Mal/OAA and as a consequence also that of NADH/NAD could be kept higher than in the cytosol. This offers an explanation how the apparent redox gradient between the NADH/NAD in the mitochondrial matrix and the cytosol might be maintained. Because of the existing redox gradient a Mal-OAA shuttle between the mitochondrial and cytosolic compartment is expected to operate into the direction mitochondria to cytosol only, unless there is an unknown active element in this shuttle.

Transfer of redox equivalents between the cytosol and the peroxisomal compartment

A number of enzymic steps of the photorespiratory pathway, including the reduction of hydroxypyruvate to glycerate, are located in the peroxisomes (Fig. 2). For this reaction occurring at high rates the NADH has to be provided from outside the peroxisomes. Peroxisomal enzymes, such as hydroxypyruvate reductase, show latency (13). Recent experiments carried out in our laboratory have shown that this latency is not due to an impermeability of the peroxisomal membrane. It appears that the peroxisomal proteins form a dense matrix which is not affected by

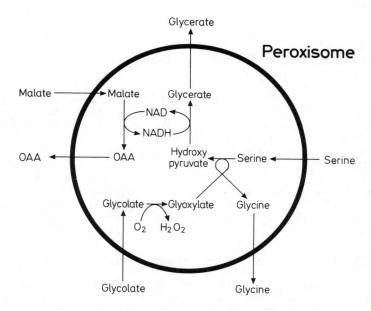

FIGURE 2. Reaction scheme of peroxisomal metabolism

TABLE 2. Glycerate formation by isolated peroxisomes in the presence of 15 mM serine and 2 mM glycolate.

For Method see (10,13). By using hydroxypyruvate reductase as marker enzyme, the activity obtained with the isolated peroxisomes was related to the chlorophyll content in a spinach leaf.

Reductant	Glycerate formation µmol/mg chl.h
NADH (0.2 mM)	50
Malate (20 mM) + NAD (1 mM)	33

osmotic shock and even persists to some extent after treatment with detergents. Our results suggest that due to the arrangement of the various peroxisomal enzymes of the photorespiratory pathway into a multienzyme complex, the intermediates of this pathway are transferred from one enzymic reaction to the next in the reaction chain without being released in between (Heupel unpubl). In the experiment of table 2 the rate of the glycerate formation from serine and glycolate was measured in isolated intact peroxisomes. The reduction of hydroxypyruvate can be accomplished by adding NADH or malate, the reduction rate with NADH being 50% higher than that with malate. It may be noted that an unphysiologically high concentration of NADH (200 µM) was employed in this experiment. For hydroxypyruvate reduction by intact peroxisomes the Km for NADH was determined as about 10 µM. Thus in the presence of 0.6 µM NADH as determined for the cytosol in the preceding, the rate of hydroxypyruvate reduction would be only 6% of the maximal activity, which is too low for a functioning of the photorespiratory cycle. For malate (Km~3 mM) a much higher rate can be obtained at physiological concentrations. It appears from these results that in peroxisomes, probably due to diffusion limitation, the cytosolic NADH because of its low concentration is unable to supply the peroxisomes with the redox equivalents required for hydroxypyruvate reduction directly. This implies that a Mal-OAA shuttle should also operate in peroxisomes.

Interaction of the redox transfer between compartments

The existing redox gradients suggest that in a leaf cell performing photosynthesis redox equivalents can be transferred from the chloroplast stroma and also from the mitochondrial matrix to the cytosol and the peroxisomes. In the photorespiratory cycle the amount of NADH formed from glycine oxidation is equal to the amount of NADH required for hydroxypyruvate reduction in the peroxisomes. The capacity of the existing Mal-OAA shuttles and the existing redox gradients make it possible that all the redox equivalents formed from glycine oxidation can be utilized in the peroxisomes for hydroxypyruvate reduction and are therefore not available for mitochondrial electron transport coupled ATP synthesis. But the demand of peroxisomal hydroxypyruvate reduction as well as the redox equivalents required for nitrate reduction in the cytosol could be also met by the chloroplasts. The spinach grown in our hydroponic culture showed under ambient CO_2 an average rate of CO_2 fixation of 120 μmol/mg chl.h. Taking into account a ratio of carboxylation/oxigenation of 2.5:1 (14), the rate of hydroxypyruvate reduction would have to be 29 μmol/mg chl.h. Assuming an assimilation ratio of CO_2/nitrate = 20, the NADH required for nitrate reduction would amount to 6 μmol/mg chl.h. The capacity of the Mal/OAA shuttle measured in isolated chloroplasts is clearly higher than the demand for the reduction of hydroxypyruvate and nitrate. Because of the accepted stoichiometry of noncyclic photosynthetic electron transport (NADPH/ATP = 0.75) and the stoichiometry of the Calvin cycle (NADPH/ATP = 0.66) there seems to be a surplus of NADPH in the chloroplasts. By Mal/OAA shuttle this could be utilized in the cytosol and in the peroxisomes.

Our present knowledge of redox gradients makes it seem unlikely that by Mal/OAA shuttle redox equivalents can be transferred from the chloroplasts to the mitochondria directly. But in C_3 plants photosynthesis is always accompanied by photorespiration. If the demand of the peroxisomes for redox equivalents to reduce hydroxypyruvate is served by the chloroplasts, it would be possible that an equivalent amount of NADH formed in the mitochondria from glycine oxidation is made available for mitochondrial oxidation. In this way, though indirectly, redox transfer by Mal/OAA shuttle from the chloroplasts could provide the redox equivalents for mitochondrial ATP synthesis to proceed at more than 50% of its maximal capacity. Such a cooperation of chloroplasts and mitochondrial metabolism appears to have the advantage of preventing an overreduction of photosynthetic electron transport and of improving the quantum yield of ATP formation. Whereas in cyclic photophosphorylation according to the accepted stoichiometry 2 quanta of lights are yielding 0.66 ATP, for noncyclic photophosphorylation connected with the oxidation of the formed redox equivalents by mitochondrial electron transport from 4 quanta of light about 4 moles of ATP can be formed, representing a three fold higher yield. In this way during photosynthesis the ATP demand in the cytosol can be very efficiently met.

On the function of mitochondrial ATP synthesis in photosynthesis metabolism

The above considerations make it seem probable that mitochondrial ATP synthesis has an important function to serve during photosynthesis the ATP demand of the cytosol. The essential function of mitochondrial ATP synthesis in photosynthesis metabolism has been demonstrated by its selective inhibition by oligomycin. Whereas the addition of low concentrations of this inhibitor did not affect the photosynthesis of isolated chloroplasts, photosynthesis of protoplasts was inhibited by up to 50% (16). As shown in table 3, the decrease of photosynthesis of whole protoplasts is accompanied by a marked increase of glucose-6-phosphate and a decrease of the ATP level specifically in the cytosol,

TABLE 3. Effect of oligomycin on subcellular levels of metabolites in barley leaf protoplasts.

For Methods see (15). The added oligomycin (0.05 µg/ml) inhibited the photosynthesis of the chloroplasts by 38%.

	Cytosol		Stroma	
	Control	+ Oligomycin	Control	+ Oligomycin
		(nmol/mg chl)		
ATP	12.1	6.8	17.4	12.0
ADP	8.3	11.0	17.5	19.9
ATP/ADP	1.5	0.6	1.0	0.6
Glc6P	70	125	36	21

whereas the stromal level of ATP is less affected. It appears from our results that the inhibition of photosynthesis of whole protoplasts by oligomycin is due to an inhibition of the transformation of the photosynthate into sucrose, caused by lack of ATP in the cytosol. These results demonstrate that during photosynthesis mitochondrial oxidative phosphorylation plays an important role in providing the cytosol with ATP.

Acknowledgement
This work was supported by the Deutsche Forschungsgemeinschaft.

REFERENCES
1. Dietz, K.J., Heber, U. (1984) Biochim. Biophys. Acta 767, 432-443
2. Badger, M.R., Lorimer, G.H. (1981) Biochemistry 20, 2219-2225
3. Ashton, A.R. (1982) FEBS Letters, 145, 1-7
4. Veech, R.L., Eggleston, L.V., Krebs, H.A. (1969) Biochem. J. 115, 609-619
5. Sanchez, J., Heldt, H.W. (1989) Botanica Acta, in print
6. Bücher, T., Klingenberg, M. (1958) Angew. Chemie 70, 552-570
7. Gerhardt, R., Heldt, H.W. (1984) Plant Physiol. 75, 542-547
8. Hatch, M.D., Dröscher, L., Heldt, H.W. (1984) FEBS Lett. 178, 15-19
9. Scheibe, R. (1987) Physiol. Plantarum, 71, 393-400
10. Ebbighausen, H., Hatch, M.D., Lilley, R.McC., Krömer, S., Stitt, M., Heldt, H.W. (1987) Plant Mitochondria (A.L. Moore, R.B. Beechey, eds.) Plenum Publishing Co. pp. 171-180
11. Zoglowek, C., Krömer, S., Heldt, H.W. (1988) Plant Physiol. 87, 109-115
12. Ebbighausen, H., Chen, J., Heldt, H.W. (1985) Biochim. Biophys. Acta 810, 184-199
13. Liang, Z., Huang, A.H.C. (1983) Plant Physiol. 73, 147-152
14. Sharkey, T.D. (1988) Physiol. Plant. 73, 147-152
15. Lilley, R.McC., Stitt, M., Mader, G., Heldt, H.W. (1982) Plant Physiol. 70, 965-970
16. Krömer, S., Stitt, M., Heldt, H.W. (1988) FEBS Lett. 226, 352-356

PHOTORESPIRATORY DEPENDENT LEAF MITOCHONDRIAL ATP PRODUCTION

Per Gardeström and Bosse Wigge, Dept Plant Physiol, Univ Umeå, S-901 87 Umeå, Sweden

1. INTRODUCTION

The cell functions metabolically as a unit, thus the interaction between different subcellular compartments is very important. Results obtained with isolated organelles must therefore be complemented with studies on the intact cell. Relatively few experimental approaches are availably for studies on the interaction between subcellular compartments, especially for investigations of photosynthetic metabolism.

Rapid fractionation of protoplasts by membrane filtration can be used for such studies (1,2). In this procedure the protoplasts are broken when forced through a nylon net, after which intact chloroplasts and mitochondria are removed from the filtrate by membrane filtration. The metabolic reactions in the resulting filtrates are quenched by denaturation of the proteins within about 0.1 s. An improved apparatus using these principles was recently described (3).

Measurements of adenylates using the rapid fractionating technique, have shown that in protoplasts incubated under conditions of limiting CO_2 the cytosolic ATP/ADP ratio is higher in light than in darkness (4). Since the CO_2 in air is limiting for C_3 plants this would reflect the normal physiological situation. From further studies involving inhibition of photorespiration it was suggested that the increase in the cytosolic ATP/ADP ratio was coupled to photorespiratory glycine decarboxylation in leaf mitochondria (3). Glycine decarboxylation will produce NADH in the mitochondrial matrix. A part of this NADH could be reoxidized via the respiratory chain and be coupled to oxidative phosphorylation. This would thus lead to a photorespiratory dependent mitochondrial ATP synthesis in the light. As the metabolic flux in the photorespiratory pathway is high this mechanism could have a big potential for ATP production. Under certain metabolic situations it could be an important source for cytosolic ATP in addition to the TP/PGA shuttle in the chloroplast envelope membrane (5).

---

*Abbreviations: AAN, aminoacetonitrile; PGA, 3-phosphoglycerate; TCA, tricloracetic acid; TP, triosphosphate

M. Baltscheffsky (ed.), Current Research in Photosynthesis, Vol. IV, 9–14.
© 1990 *Kluwer Academic Publishers. Printed in the Netherlands.*

Here we present results regarding the subcellular content of TP, PGA and the redox state of pyridine nucleotides. The results are discussed with respect to interaction between mitochondrial reactions and photosynthetic metabolism.

2.   MATERIALS AND METHODS
2.1. <u>Fractionation of protoplasts</u>. Protoplasts were isolated from 7 to 8 day old barley leaves (<u>Hordeum vulgare</u> var Gunilla, Svalöf) and fractionated by membrane filtration as described earlier (3).

2.2.   <u>Extraction of metabolites</u>. Since oxidized and reduced pyridine nucleotides has to be extracted in acidic and alcaline extraction medium respectively, the evaluation of the quenching time is difficult. We used the ATP/ADP ratio after TCA-quenching as a reference for the quenching time since TCA has been shown to stop the metabolism very quickly (3). TCA was inhibitory to the cycling systems and could not be used for determination of oxidized pyridine nucleotides. From experiments comparing ATP/ADP ratios after quenching in different acidic and alcaline media to TCA quenching it was concluded that 0.2 M HCl + 1% CHAPS (3- (3-Cholamidopropyl)dimetylammonio -1-propanesulfonate) and 0.2 M KOH + 0.08 % Triton-X-100 stopped the metabolism as fast as 5% TCA. These extraction media were used for the extraction of NAD(P) and NAD(P)H respectively. The acidic extract was also used for measurements of ATP, PGA and TP.

2.3. <u>Measurements of pyridine nucleotides</u>. Pyridine nucleotides were determined by enzymatic cycling (6). For NADPH and NADP, glutamate dehydrogenase and glucose-6-phosphate dehydrogenase was used in the cycling system. Cycling was performed at 38 ^{o}C for 1h and then stopped by boiling the samples. The 6-P-gluconolactone produced during cycling then decompose to 6-P-gluconate, which is used for NADPH production by 6-P-gluconate dehydrogenase. The NADPH formed was quantified by fluorescence emission at 460 nm with 365 nm as excitation wavelength. NADH and NAD were measured using the malate dehydrogenase-alcohol dehydrogenase system described by Kato et al. (7). The cycling was performed at 25 ^{o}C for 1.5 h. After boiling the samples, NADP-Malic enzyme was added to produce NADPH from malate and the NADPH formed was detected by fluorescence.

2.4. <u>Measurement of ATP and other metabolites</u>. ATP was determined by the firefly luciferase method as described elsevere (3). ADP was assayed after conversion to ATP by pyruvate kinase. PGA was assayed by coupling to ATP production by phosphoglyceromutase, enolase and pyruvate kinase. TP was coupled to ATP production by triosephosphate isomerase, glyceraldehyde-3-phosphate dehydrogenase and phosphoglycerate kinase.

3.   RESULTS AND DISCUSSION

3.1. Subcellular distribution of TP and PGA. In the total extract both
PGA and TP decrease considerably in limiting CO_2 as compared to
saturating CO_2 (Table 1). When the photorespiratory conversion of
glycine to serine was inhibited by the addition of AAN (8) in
limiting CO_2 only a small effect on the content of TP and PGA was
observed. With 20 mM Gald (which blocks the conversion of Ru5P to
RuBP in the Calvin cycle (9)) the PGA and TP levels falls under
the detection level (approx 2 nmol/mg Chl). In the total
protoplast extract the TP/PGA-ratio was higher in limiting CO_2
compared to saturating CO_2. This increase was also observed in
both the chloroplast and cytosolic fractions and was mainly due
to a greater decrease in PGA as compared to TP. In all conditions
the extrachloroplastic TP/PGA ratio was higher than the ratio
inside the chloroplasts. The amount and ratios of TP and PGA
agree well with reports on wheat protoplasts (10). We were not
able to detect a mitochondrial pool of TP and PGA. As the
mitochondria occupy a small fraction of the cell and the scatter
in the determinations are considerably we can hovewer not exclude
this.

TABLE 1. The subcellular content of TP and PGA in protoplasts incubated
in saturating light for 5-7 min under different conditions with respect
to photorespiration. In "limiting CO_2" the rate of photosynthetic O_2
production was 15-25% of the rate in saturating CO_2 (10 mM $NaHCO_3$). The
results are the mean $\pm$ SD from 3 to 4 experiments.

	Total extract			Chloroplasts			Cytosol		
	TP	PGA	TP/PGA	TP	PGA	TP/PGA	TP	PGA	TP/PGA
High CO_2	115	169	0.7+0.5	25	73	0.4+0.3	80	89	0.9+0.5
Limiting CO_2	61	36	1.8+0.4	19	18	0.9	42	27	1.9+1.5
Limiting CO_2+AAN	65	17	2.8+1.5	40	11	3.1	31	12	4.4+2.6

With respect to the TP/PGA shuttle to transfer ATP from the
chloroplast to the cytosol the content of the metabolites
involved is considerably lower in limiting CO_2 than in saturating
CO_2. Especially the PGA content in the cytosol is affected. This
might decrease the capasity of this shuttle for ATP export from
the chloroplasts to the cytosol in conditions with limiting CO_2.

3.2. Pyridine nucleotides. The NADPH/NADP ratio in extracts from
protoplasts incubated in saturating CO_2 was about 1 (Table 2).
When the Calvin cycle was blocked using Gald, a more reduced
state was observed for NADPH/NADP, whereas with PMS the pool was
almost totally oxidized. This shows that under extreme conditions
very different redox levels of NADPH/NADP can be detected. The

TABLE 2. NADPH/NADP ratios in the total extract from protoplast incubated for 5 min in saturating light with: Saturating CO_2, 20 mM glycolaldehyde (Gald) and with 60 µM Phenazinemethosulfate (PMS). Values are mean of two experiments.

	Saturating CO_2	Gald	PMS
NADPH/NADP	1.1	3.1	0.05

differences between the treatments is also in line with what can be expected. This indicates that the method can be used to estimate NADPH/NADP-ratios in different subcellular compartments. It is hovewer, important to remember that the results regarding metabolite levels after denaturation of proteins reflects the total pool, including both free and bound metabolites. The biggest problem due to such binding is perhaps with respect to the redox level of pyridine nucleotides. As these metabolites can bind strongly to native proteins (11) the results must be evaluated with great caution. On the other hand, a perfect method for the study of these factors in the photosynthetic cell does not exist. Therefore, this type of studies can still have its value, especially for comparative studies between different conditions of incubation.

The NADP(H)-content of the total protoplasts was 20-25 nmol·mg Chl^{-1} in all conditions of incubation tested. Most of this (70-80 %) was found in the chloroplasts except when Gald was present, then the chloroplast pool was only 45 % of the total NADP(H)-pool. Almost all of the extrachloroplastic NADP(H) was cytosolic, less than 2% was associated with the mitochondria. This was too low to allow changes between different experimental conditions to be detected in the mitochondria.

The NADPH/NADP ratio decreased sligthly in the cytosol and increased a little in the chloroplasts in limiting CO_2 as compared to saturating CO_2, although the effects were small (Table 3). The addition of AAN increased the reduction level slightly in both cytosol and chloroplasts. Gald had a more pronounced effect, here the NADPH/NADP-ratio increased to 6.6 in the chloroplasts. In the cytosol it was a more moderate increase, to 2.8. The large effect obtained with Gald indicates that the method can detect big changes when such occur. Thus the results indicate that the NADPH/NADP-ratio in both chloroplasts and cytosol is kept rather constant in the very different metabolic situations caused by saturating CO_2, limiting CO_2 and AAN inhibition. This suggests a strict control of the redox state in the chloroplasts. Scheibe and Stitt (12) used the activation level of NADP-MDH as an indicator of the redox state at the

TABLE 3. The redox level of pyridinenucleotides in subcellular compartments of barley protoplasts. Experimental conditions as in Table 1. The results are the mean ± SD from 3 to 4 experiments.

	Chloroplasts		Cytosol	Mitochondria
	$\frac{NADPH}{NADP}$	$\frac{NADH}{NAD}$	$\frac{NADPH}{NADP}$	$\frac{NADH}{NAD}$
High CO_2	1.0+0.2	0.4+0.1	1.8+0.4	0.07+0.06
Limiting CO_2	1.4+0.3	0.6+0.2	1.5+0.2	0.22+0.13
Limiting CO_2+AAN	1.6+0.7	0.3+0.04	2.0+0.1	0.08+0.11
Limiting CO_2+Gald	6.6+3.3	0.4+0.3	2.8+0.6	0.1 +0.08

acceptor side of photosystem 1. Their results indicated even a somewhat more oxidized state in limiting CO_2 as compared to saturating CO_2. Both of these results would be in agreement with results suggesting a down-regulation of photosystem II activity induced by restraints in carbon metabolism (13).

NADH/NAD results are only presented for the chloroplasts and mitochondria (Table 3) because a variable malate background was detected in the cytosol, possibly due to vacuolar malate. As the values for chloroplasts and mitochondria are obtained by taking the difference between two filtrates these will not be directly affected by a background in the soluble fraction. In the mitochondria there is an increase of the NADH/NAD ratio in limiting CO_2 as compared to saturating CO_2. This is expected since photorespiratory glycine oxidation will produce NADH in limiting CO_2 but not in saturating CO_2. 10 mM AAN which inhibit glycine oxidation and thus NADH formation reduced the mitochondrial NADH/NAD-ratio to the same level as in saturating CO_2. In the presence of Gald the ratio is low compared to the value in limiting CO_2. Glycine oxidation is certainly very low also in this condition since no photorespiratory substrate is present, as the supply of RuBP is stopped. In the chloroplasts the NAD(H)-pool is more reduced and changes in a way similar to the mitochondrial pool, although the changes between different conditions are smaller.

During photorespiration a varying fraction of the NADH produced by glycine oxidation can be reoxidized in the mitochondria resulting in ATP production. In the photorespiratory metabolism, phosphorylation of glycerate and NH_3 reassimilation by the GS/GOGAT system, both ATP consuming reactions, are localized to the chloroplast compartment of green cells (14). Thus, photorespiratory metabolism is directly involved in the distribution of energy within the leaf cell. Also, reducing equivalents can be exported from the chloroplasts to the cytosol and mitochondria utilizing malate/oxaloacetate exchange (15) and ATP and reducing equivalents can be exported on the phosphate translocator by TP/PGA exchange (5). Taken together photorespiration and shuttle mechanisms gives a high flexibility of the metabolism in a leaf cell. This allows adjustment of the metabolism to different availability and demands of energy and reducing power in the different parts of the cell. A great flexibility would be advantagous for the plant to meet the very different environmental conditions it encounters.

Acknowledgements: We are greatful to Gunilla Malmberg for technical assistance and to Monica Nilsson for typing the manuscript. Financial support was obtained from the Swedish Natural Science Research Counsil and the Carl Tryggers Research Foundation.

REFERENCES
1. Lilley, R. McC., Stitt, M., Mader, G. and Heldt, H.W. (1982) Plant Physiol. 70, 965-970
2. Stitt, M., Lilley, R.McC. and Heldt, H.W. (1982) Plant Physiol. 70, 971-977
3. Gardeström, P. and Wigge, B. (1988) Plant Physiol. 88:69-76
4. Gardeström, P. (1987) FEBS Lett. 212, 114-118
5. Flugge, U.I. and Heldt, H.W. (1984) Trends Biochem. Sci. 9:530-533
6. Lowry, O.H. and Passonneau, J.V. (1972). A flexible system of enzymatic analysis. Academic Press, New York.
7. Kato, T., Berger, S.J., Carter, J.A. and Lowry, O.H. (1973) Anal. Biochem. 53, 86-97
8. Gardeström, P., Bergman, A. and Ericson, I. (1981) Physiol. Plant. 53, 439-444
9. Sicher, R.C. (1984) in: Advances in Photosynthesis Research (Sybesma, C., ed.), Vol 3, pp 413-416, W Junk, The Hague
10. Stitt, M., Wirtz, W. and Heldt, H.W. (1983) Plant Physiol. 72, 767-774
11. Ashton, A.R. (1982) FEBS Lett. 145, 1-7
12. Scheibe, R. and Stitt, M. (1988) Plant Physiol. Biochem. 26, 473-481
13. Weiss, E. and Berry, J.A. (1987) Biochim. Biophys. Acta 894, 198-208
14. Wallsgrove, R.M., Turner, J.C., Hall, N.P., Kendall, A.C. and Bright, S.W.J. (1987) Plant Physiol. 83, 155-158
15. Ebbighausen, H., Hatch, M.D., Lilley, R.McC., Krömer, S., Stitt, M. and Heldt, H.W. (1987) in: Plant Mitochondria (Moore, A.L. and Beechey, R.B., eds.), pp 171-180, Plenum Press

PHOTORESPIRATORY METABOLISM AND PIGMENT CHANGES IN PHOTORESPIRATION MUTANTS

PETER J LEA, RAY D BLACKWELL, KAREN J LEWIS, ANDREW J YOUNG[1], GEORGE BRITTON[1], Division of Biological Sciences, University of Lancaster, Lancaster, LA1 4YQ, UK.
[1] Department of Biochemistry, University of Liverpool, L69 3BX, UK.

1. INTRODUCTION

Photorespiratory mutants have been obtained in five different C_3 species (1, 2, 3, 4), each deficient in enzyme activities associated with phosphoglycolate metabolism. These mutants survive only in atmospheres in which photorespiration is very slow, i.e. either enriched with CO_2 or depleted of O_2. In air, the rate of photosynthesis soon drops and these plants cease to thrive.

Of the eleven different lesions in the photorespiratory pathway detected to date, the work at Lancaster has characterised eight in barley, two of which have not been previously isolated. In addition, the first photorespiratory mutant of pea has also been identified. Four of the lesions, glutamine synthetase, hydroxypyruvate reductase (HPR), glutamate : glyoxylate aminotransferase (GGAT) and catalase have not been detected in Arabidopsis thaliana (1). Mutants have not been found lacking glycolate oxidase or glycerate kinase activities in any of the species studied, and only one lesion has been identified in a transport system (chloroplast 2-oxoglutarate uptake), although a transport mutant is implicated in one of the two glycine to serine conversion mutants isolated at Lancaster.

It had previously been suggested (1) that certain mutations (e.g. glycolate oxidase-deficiency) might not lead to obvious symptoms that could be picked out in the screen, but would merely slow down the rate of growth of the plant. It seems, however, from analysis of the mutants described here and elsewhere, that any lesion in photorespiratory carbon or nitrogen metabolism would eventually produce visible symptoms and ultimately kill the plant. Indeed, only a slight modification to the screen brought about the isolation of two mutants not previously discovered; HPR (5) and GGAT (6).

2. RESULTS AND DISCUSSION

2.1 Hydroxypyruvate reductase

An air-sensitive barley plant, LaPr 88/29, has been identified as having less than 5% of wild-type NADH-dependent HPR activity. In LaPr 88/29 there was an accumulation of serine and glycine, in fact

M. Baltscheffsky (ed.), Current Research in Photosynthesis, Vol. IV, 15–22.
© 1990 Kluwer Academic Publishers. Printed in the Netherlands.

they accounted for 86% of the total extractable amino acids after only 3 h exposure to air. When plants were fed $^{14}CO_2$ in air after photosynthetic induction, LaPr 88/29 accumulated almost four times as much $[^{14}C]$ in serine as the wild-type but at the same time the amount of $[^{14}C]$ in sucrose in LaPr 88/29 was 85% of the wild-type. When fed L-$[U-^{14}C]$serine, LaPr 88/29 was still able to metabolise 25% of the detected $[^{14}C]$ into sugars, as compared to a value of 41% obtained for the wild-type.

It has often been assumed that NADH-glyoxylate reductase (GR) and NADH-HPR are identical (7, 8). Evidence from Table 1, where NADH-GR activity in the mutant plant was reduced by only 20% as compared to the wild-type, would strongly suggest that the majority of NADH-GR activity is not catalysed by the same enzyme as NADH-HPR activity in crude extracts of barley.

Table 1. Activities of HPR and GR (nkat mg^{-1} protein) in crude leaf extracts of wild-type barley or LaPr 88/29 using either NADH or NADPH as a source of reductant.

Enzyme activity	Wild-type	LaPr 88/29
NADH-HPR	2.34	0.12
NADH-GR	0.51	0.40
NADPH-HPR	1.39	0.27
NADPH-GR	0.35	0.32

Although LaPr 88/29 lacked a photorespiratory enzyme, transfer from non-photorespiratory to photorespiratory conditions caused the rate of CO_2 fixation to fall by only 25% of the wild-type rate (see Fig. 1). Furthermore, when the oxygen concentration flowing over the leaves was increased to 50%, forcing more carbon through photorespiration, the CO_2 fixation rates of both wild-type and LaPr 88/29 fell but the mutant still maintained a fixation rate of 75% of the wild-type. The accumulation of ammonia was also little different in the wild-type and mutant plants. Clearly the disturbance to metabolism in LaPr 88/29 was not as great as has been shown for other mutant plants lacking key photorespiratory enzymes (2).

Studies were carried out with antibodies raised to spinach NADH-HPR (a gift from Drs L. Kleczkowski and C. Givan). Western blot analysis following SDS-PAGE revealed two cross-reacting bands for the wild-type and one band for the mutant. The bands corresponded to molecular weights of 42 and 38 kDa, for the mutant only the band at 38 kDa was present and was always more intensely stained. Using native PAGE, there were also two cross-reacting bands for the wild-type. We have constructed Ferguson plots and shown the molecular weights of the two bands to be approximately 95 and 72 kDa, which are similar to those shown for NADH and NADPH-HPR respectively (7, 9, 10). In LaPr

88/29 there was no evidence of the band at 95 kDa but the band at 72 kDa was clearly present and apparently at higher concentrations.

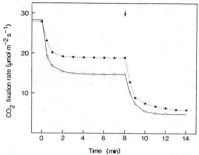

Figure 1. Rate of CO_2 fixation for detached leaves of wild-type (●) and LaPr 88/29 (○) after transfer to air at time zero and to 50% O_2 at the arrow.

The report that NADPH-HPR was located in the cytosol (11, 12) and the previous knowledge that hydroxypyruvate was able to 'leak' out of the peroxisome (13, 14) enhanced speculation that NADPH-HPR could have the same function as peroxisomal NADH-HPR. It would appear that the evidence collected from LaPr 88/29, the first reported mutant plant of any species lacking NADH-HPR activity, that these speculations may be correct and that the alternative NADPH activity may form a useful backup to the NADH-dependent enzyme. If in fact NADPH-HPR is present at higher concentrations in LaPr 88/29, it may explain some of the unusual characteristics associated with this mutant.

LaPr 88/29, provides a means for unrestricted study of the NADPH-dependent enzyme. From Table 1 it is possible to evaluate the contribution of the peroxisomal NADH-dependent enzyme to the total NADPH-dependent activity. It appeared that 81% of the total NADPH-dependent activity in wild-type barley, was due to the NADH-dependent enzyme, a figure that agrees with the earlier speculation of 75-85% (10), based on measurements of NADH and NADPH-dependent HPR in spinach.

2.2   Glycine to serine conversion
Two barley plants LaPr 85/55 and LaPr 87/30 have been isolated that accumulate glycine on exposure to air. The magnitude of this accumulation was different for the two mutants, but was at least 5 times the wild-type for the lesser of the two, LaPr 85/55. When $^{14}CO_2$ was fed to the mutants, after photosynthetic induction, almost 50% of the recovered [^{14}C] accumulated in glycine for LaPr 85/55 and 66% in LaPr 87/30. The inability of LaPr 87/30 to metabolise glycine was confirmed by the distribution of ^{14}C after [^{14}C]glycine feeding, where over 90% of the supplied radioactivity remained in glycine even after 2 h. Although LaPr 85/55 accumulated glycine after 40 min (82% of the total counts recovered), after 2 h most of the radioactivity was found

in the sugar fraction with only 15% in glycine. The probable explanation for this disappearance after 2 h, was that the mutation in LaPr 85/55 affected a glycine transport system (15).

The rates of serine transhydroxymethylase activity were similar for the mutants and the wild-type (4-5 nmol min^{-1} mg^{-1} protein). Glycine-bicarbonate exchange which can be used as a direct measure of glycine decarboxylase activity, showed that LaPr 87/30 had less than 15% of the wild-type activity, whereas LaPr 85/55 was able to convert up to 70% of the [^{14}C]bicarbonate into glycine. It was apparent from the measurements of bicarbonate exchange and from $^{14}CO_2$ release from [^{14}C]glycine feeding (less than 40% of the wild-type), that LaPr 87/30 lacked a wholly functional P or H protein (16). However, LaPr 85/55 had 70% of the wild-type rate of bicarbonate exchange and 80% of the wild-type $^{14}CO_2$ release from [^{14}C]glycine, it therefore seemed unlikely that the mutation in LaPr 85/55 was in either the P or H protein.

In LaPr 87/30, ammonia release in the presence of methionine sulphoximine was only 5% of the wild-type, a result which would be expected if there was mutation in either the P or H protein. Ammonia release from LaPr 85/55 under the same conditions was in stoichiometry with the $^{14}CO_2$ release. Ammonia production and $^{14}CO_2$ release from [^{14}C]glycine at less than wild-type rates for LaPr 85/55 would be consistent with a reduction in glycine transport into the mitochondria.

The rates of CO_2 fixation for both mutants in 1% O_2, 0.035% CO_2 was similar to those of the wild-type plant. In common with most photorespiratory mutants isolated thus far (2), the rate of both mutants fell to between 30-40% of that of the wild-type on transfer to conditions that promoted photorespiration. The possibility that the decline in the photosynthetic rate is caused by accumulation of amino groups in glycine (17), is strengthened by the run down of glutamate, an amino-donor for transamination of glyoxylate in the peroxisome, detected in both mutants in air.

There was no convincing evidence to support the view that in vivo a significant amount of CO_2 was evolved due to non-enzymatic decarboxylation of glyoxylate (18, 19), a reaction that has been demonstrated in isolated organelles and reconstituted systems (20). It has been shown (21) that oxidation of glyoxylate, either by reaction with H_2O_2, or by peroxidative action in the absence of catalase could evolve CO_2 and simultaneously generate C_1-tetrahydrofolate, which could combine with one molecule of glycine to synthesise serine. This pathway would bypass the glycine decarboxylase reaction and there would be no formation of ammonia or NADH. Other arguments in favour of this glyoxylate oxidation in photorespiration have been put forward (22), but it is the isolation of mutants such as those lacking glycine decarboxylase activity, which are unable to carry out normal photosynthesis when placed in air, that are conclusive proof that this is the only reaction which generates CO_2 during photorespiration. It is only in the absence of amino-donors for transamination that glyoxylate is oxidised to CO_2, which can be overcome by providing NH_3, serine or glutamate (23, 24). This has also shown to be the case for both the mutants described here, which when supplied with 40 mM serine, exhibited an increase in the CO_2 fixation rate to approximately 70% of the wild-type rate (6).

The sensitive technique of protein identification utilising ELISA has been used to study LaPr 87/30 and wild-type barley with antibodies to P and H proteins, (kindly donated by Drs R. Douce and M. Neuburger). Comparison of the ratios of antibody binding have shown that the binding of P and H protein in LaPr 87/30 was reduced compared to the wild-type, with H being more affected than P, indicating a possible mutation in the H protein. The reduction in binding of both P and H proteins shown using ELISA may imply a coordinated synthesis at the genetic level.

2.3   Changes in pigment content for some of the photorespiratory mutants on transfer to ambient CO_2 levels.

Mutant plants lacking phosphoglycolate phosphatase, catalase, SGAT, GS and glutamate synthase activities were grown in an atmosphere of 0.7% CO_2 prior to transfer to ambient air. A wide selection of mutants was chosen as other work has indicated different types of symptoms are expressed by mutants on exposure to ambient conditions. On transfer to air the plants were maintained in continuous light, supplemented at night to 150 µmol m^{-2} s^{-1}. Three replicates from each line were taken at each harvest up to day 9. Pigment extracts were made by homogenisation with redistilled ethanol and samples analysed by HPLC (25).

Following growth in high CO_2 all of the lines tested showed a similar pigment composition, with 4 major carotenoids being found; neoxanthin, violaxanthin, lutein and B-carotene. For brevity only the results for the wild type, GS and glutamate synthase deficient plants are shown.

2.3.1   Total Pigment content
Pigment levels in the wild-type remained constant for the first few days following transfer, then subsequently carotenoid and chlorophyll levels increased to approximately 150% of their initial values presumably a reflection increased light intensity (Fig. 2a). There was also a steady rise in the carotenoid/chlorophyll ratio suggesting a higher rate of carotenoid than chlorophyll synthesis. Both chlorophyll and carotenoid levels fell in the glutamate synthase deficient plant (LaPr 85/73) although the loss of chlorophylls was much more rapid than the loss of carotenoids (Fig. 2b). By day 2 over 40% of the chlorophyll and 30% of the carotenoid content had been lost. In contrast to LaPr 85/73 levels of chlorophylls in the GS deficient plant (LaPr 85/80) remained constant during the 9 days of

the experiment (Fig. 2c). Carotenoids were actually synthesised after transfer to air to peak around day 4 at 150% of the initial value.

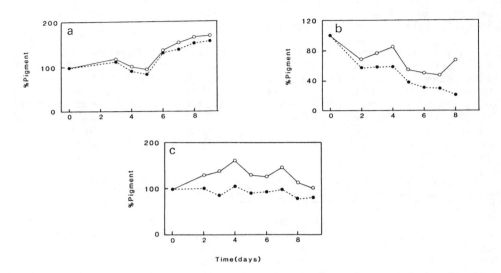

Figure 2. Total pigment content of the barley plants a) wild-type, b) LaPr 85/73 and c) LaPr 85/80 for carotenoids (○——○) and chlorophylls (●--●)

For all three plant lines there was no variation in the relative levels of chlorophyll a and b.

2.3.2 Carotenoids
In the wild-type the major change in the total carotenoid pool was caused by the violaxanthin cycle pigments, violaxanthin, antheraxanthin and zeaxanthin (Fig. 3a). The increase in the violaxanthin cycle pigments was largely due to an increase in the levels of violaxanthin itself (3-fold increase by day 9) with only a small increase in antheraxanthin and zeaxanthin detectable. LaPr 85/73 was characterised by a steady loss of individual carotenoids except the violaxanthin cycle pigments, which remained constant throughout (Fig. 3b). B-Carotene was lost much faster than either lutein or neoxanthin which behaved in the same way, and dropped by 40% over the 8 days of treatment. Again major changes in violaxanthin pigments were caused by the change in violaxanthin itself and it appeared that any decrease in violaxanthin synthesis was balanced by an increase in both antheraxanthin and zeaxanthin synthesis. In LaPr 85/80, B-carotene levels did not increase but fell to a value 75% of its initial value by day 8 (Fig. 3c). Lutein and neoxanthin increased for approximately 4 days but then fell to the same level as B-carotene. As in the WT,

increases in total carotenoid levels can be accounted for by increased synthesis of violaxanthin cycle pigments especially violaxanthin which rose 3-fold by day 4. At the same time both antheraxanthin and zeaxanthin increased, although these fell away after day 6.

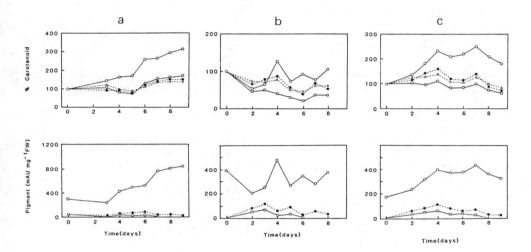

Figure 3. Top, Individual carotenoid levels; neoxanthin (●), violaxanthin pigments (○), lutein (△) and B-carotene (□), Bottom, Violaxanthin cycle pigments; violaxanthin (○), antheraxanthin (●) and zeaxanthin (□) for a) wild-type, b) LaPr 85/73 and c) LaPr 85/80.

2.3.3 Conclusions.
The function of the violaxanthin cycle has not been clearly demonstrated, although theories have been proposed that zeaxanthin can act as a super-quencher of excess excitation energy, thus protecting the photosynthetic apparatus from damage (26). In all of the plants studied violaxanthin was present in higher concentrations than zeaxanthin, a finding not completely consistent with the latter compound directly acting as a protectant, although changes in these components are are still to be measured in the first 48 h following transfer.

It appeared that damage to the mutants was probably related to the degree of inhibition of CO_2 fixation (LaPr 85/73 being more rapidly inhibited in air than LaPr 85/80, (27)). The accumulation of ammonia in the two mutants appeared not to influence the rate of pigment destruction and there was no reason to suggest that ammonia accumulation in LaPr 85/80, which was much higher than in LaPr 85/73, acted to exacerbate photoinhibition.
    Although all mutants exhibited one of the classical signs of senescence (that is chlorophylls degraded faster than carotenoids) the

type of damage as reflected by changes in pigment content, did not appear to be due simply to 'natural' senescence, rather it seemed to be a mixture of senescence and oxidative destruction.

REFERENCES
1   Somerville, C.R. (1984) in Oxford Surveys of Plant Molecular and
    Cell Biology (Miflin, B.J., ed.), Vol. 1, pp. 103-131, Oxford
    University Press
2   Blackwell, R.D. Murray, A.J.S. Lea, P.J. Kendall, A.C. Hall, N.P.
    Turner, J.C. and Wallsgrove, R.M. (1988) Photosynth. Res. 16, 155-
    176
3   Havir, E.A. and McHale, N.A. (1988). Plant Physiol. 87, 806-808
4   Suzuki, K. Marek, L.F. and Spalding, M.H. (1988). Plant Physiol.
    86, 51S
5   Murray, A.J.S. Blackwell, R.D. and Lea, P.J. (1989) Plant Physiol.
    (in press)
6   Blackwell, R.D. (1988) PhD. Thesis, University of Lancaster, U.K.
7   Kohn, L.D. and Warren, W.A. (1970) J. Biol. Chem. 245, 3831-3839
8   Tolbert, N.E. Yamazaki, R.K. and Oeser, A. (1970) J. Biol. Chem.
    245, 5129-5136
9   Kleczkowski, L.A. Randall, D.D. and Blevins, D.G. (1987) Progr.
    Photosynth. Res. 3, 565-568.
10 Kleczkowski, L.A. and Randall, D.D. (1988) Biochem. J. 250, 145-152
11 Givan, C.V. Tsutakawa, S. Hodgson, J.M. David, N. and Randall, D.D.
    (1987) Plant Physiol. 83, 63S
12 Kleczkowski, L.A. Givan, C.V. Hodgson, J.M. and Randall, D.D.
    (1988) Plant Physiol. 88, 1182-1185
13 Liang, Z. and Huang, A.H.C. (1983) Plant Physiol. 73, 147-152
14 Anderson, I.W. and Butt, V.S. (1986) Biochem. Soc. Trans. 14, 106-
    107
15 Walker, G.H. Sarojini, G. and Oliver, D.J. (1982) Biochem. Biophys.
    Res. Commun. 107, 856-861
16 Walker, J.L. and Oliver, D.J. (1986) J. Biol. Chem. 261, 2214-2221
17 Somerville, C.R. and Ogren, W.L. (1982) Biochem. J. 202, 373-380
18 Grodzinski, B. and Butt, V.S. (1976) Planta 128, 225-231
19 Grodzinski, B. and Woodrow, L. (1981) in Photosynthesis, Regulation
    of Carbon Metabolism. (Akoyunoglou, G., ed.), Vol. 4 pp. 551-559,
    Balaban International Science Services, Philadelphia
20 Walton, N.J. and Butt, V.S. (1981) Planta 153, 225-231
21 Shingles, R. Woodrow, L. and Grodzinski, B. (1984) Plant Physiol.
    74, 705-710
22 Singh, P. Kumar, P.A. Abrol, Y.P. and Naik, M.S. (1985) Physiol.
    Plant. 66, 169-176
23 Oliver, D.J. (1981) Plant Physiol. 68, 1031-1034
24 Somerville, C.R. and Ogren, W.L. (1981) Plant Physiol. 67, 666-671
25 Young, A.J. Barry, P. and Britton, G. (1989) Z. Naturforsch. (in
    press)
26 Demmig, D. Winter, K. Kruger, A. and Czygan, F-C (1987) Plant
    Physiol. 84, 218-224
27 Blackwell, R.D. Murray, A.J.S. Lea, P.J. and Joy, K.W. (1988) J.
    Exp. Bot. 39, 845-858

THE pH STAT OF CHLOROPLASTS IN RELATION TO RIBULOSE BISPHOSPHATE CARBOXYLASE ACTIVITY AND INORGANIC NITROGEN AND SULPHATE ASSIMILATION

Ivan R. Kennedy
Department of Agricultural Chemistry
University of Sydney, N.S.W. 2006
Australia

1. INTRODUCTION

In the leaf cells of C_3 plants there are at least five main compartments separated by membranes through which protons cannot freely pass. These are the thylakoid space and the stroma of the chloroplasts, the stroma of mitochondria and peroxisomes and the cytosol. As a result, achieving the correct pH in the separate compartments must be exerted metabolically, by the diffusion of gases such as carbon dioxide or by special pumps transporting species such as the bicarbonate ion. In the steady state, it is necessary that biochemical reactions producing alkalinity or acidity be compensated by some means, if pH is not to change.

The control of pH within the stroma of chloroplasts is clearly a significant factor in photosynthesis. The $[CO_2]$ available to ribulose bisphosphate carboxylase (Rubisco) kinetically determines its carbon dioxide fixing activity. In C_3 plants, $[CO_2]$ is controlled in the equilibrium reaction catalysed by stromal carbonic anhydrase:

$$CO_2 + H_2O \quad = \quad HCO_3^- + H^+$$

The dissociation constant (pK) for this reaction has recently been corrected[1] to 6.06 for the ionic strength of enzyme assay, indicating a Km value for dissolved carbon dioxide of about 8 micromolar. At the same time, the oxygenase activity of Rubisco associated with photorespiration in C_3 plants is also regulated, changing as the pH rises and bicarbonate replaces carbon dioxide.

It is generally considered that the stromal pH rises to about 8 when chloroplasts are illuminated, being around 7 in the dark. At this pH, the relative concentrations of bicarbonate and substrate carbon dioxide would be close to 100 to 1. This pH increase is consistent with the establishment of a proton-motive force across the thylakoid membranes as protons tend to be transferred out of the stroma by photoelectron transport. Incidentally, it shows that the stromal pH is not so strongly buffered as to be unresponsive to

M. Baltscheffsky (ed.), Current Research in Photosynthesis, Vol. IV, 23–30.
© 1990 *Kluwer Academic Publishers. Printed in the Netherlands.*

metabolic production of acidity and alkalinity. Too strong a buffering might mitigate against the role of the proton gradient.

2. SOURCES OF ACIDITY IN THE CHLOROPLAST STROMA

Apart from light, several other reactions contribute to the proton activity in the stroma. Both the carboxylase activity and the oxygenase activity of Rubisco generate two protons for each gas molecule consumed[2], together with either two molecules of phosphoglycerate or one of phosphoglycerate plus phosphoglycolate respectively.

Maximum rates of photorespiratory carbon dioxide formation in C_3 plants are of the order of 40 micromoles per hour per mg chlorophyll[2], corresponding to 80 microequivalents of protons and phosphoglycollate per hour per mg chlorophyll formed in the stroma. The lysis of water by photosystem II also theoretically produces two protons, but these cannot represent a net source of acidity in the chloroplast, other than extremely transiently, since two protons are simultaneously consumed there in the subsequent formation of NADPH and reduced carbon compounds in the stroma.

The buffering capacity of entire chloroplasts has been shown by titration[3], to be about one microequivalent per mg chlorophyll per pH unit in the physiological pH range. All of the protons produced by Rubisco carboxylase activity are required for either subsequent starch synthesis within the chloroplast or for sucrose synthesis in the cell cytoplasm (to where equivalent acidity must be transferred from the stroma). So none of the acidity generated by Rubisco would ever be expected to accumulate.

Nevertheless, in the absence of pH-correcting reactions in the stroma, the measured buffering capacity would plainly be insufficient to prevent significant changes in stromal pH in a matter of seconds when compared to the rate of metabolism in the stroma.

Whatever the source of inorganic nitrogen – nitrate, ammonium or dinitrogen – it is invariably delivered to the cytoplasm of plant cells as ammonium hydroxide[4]. In the case of nitrate, two equivalents of hydroxyls are produced for each ammonium formed[5].

$$NO_3^- + 8[H] \quad = \quad NH_4^+ + 2OH^- + H_2O$$

A similar alkalinity is involved in the assimilation of sulphate (although this is of less quantitative significance:

$$SO_4^{2-} + 8[H] + ROH \quad = \quad RSH + 2OH^- + 3H_2O$$

While this alkalinity is eventually neutralised by organic acid synthesis from sugar (glycolysis plus PEP carboxylase – ref. 4), the immediate effect is that two microequivalents of hydroxyl ions are produced in the chloroplast stroma for each microequivalent of nitrite or sulphate photoreduced via ferredoxin. The observed maximum rates of nitrate assimilation in leaves are about 5 microequivalents per mg chlorophyll per hour[3], producing 10 microequivalents of hydroxyl ions in the chloroplast stroma.

3.   THE pH STAT OF CHLOROPLASTS

Rubisco's oxygenase and inorganic nitrogen or sulphate assimilation obviously have opposing effects on the pH stat of chloroplasts.   According to the accepted scheme for the photorespiratory cycle in which glycerate is returned to the chloroplast stroma from mitochondria[3], four oxygen molecules would need to be consumed in the stroma with a further two consumed in the peroxisomes for each nitrite reduced.   This is because only one equivalent of alkalinity is left in the cytosol as bicarbonate in the first turn of the cycle.   The second equivalent of alkalinity is returned to the stroma as glycerate and more Rubisco oxygenase activity must occur to eventually export a total of two bicarbonates to the cytosol.

It seems inevitable, as there is no other obvious source of net acidity available in the stroma, that these two processes will counteract each other with respect to the pH stat of chloroplasts. Arguably, a proton-translocating ATPase or pyrophosphatase in the chloroplast envelope could maintain pH around 8 in the face of nitrite reduction by pumping into the stroma, or a bicarbonate pump could directly transport bicarbonate to the cytosol.   But if Rubisco's oxygenase is active and producing sufficient acidity, neutralisation of nitrite reductase activity is _fait accompli_, and achieved without any such consumption of energy.   Occam's razor dispels the suggestion of the need for such pH-correcting pumps.

Furthermore, to nitrite reduction as a source of stromal alkalinity, must be added the rate of ammonium uptake by chloroplasts in photorespiratory cycling and turnover of amino acids independent of photorespiration for reassimilation by glutamine synthetase and glutamate synthase.

An association between photorespiration and the metabolism in chloroplasts of ammonia from protein catabolism has been shown with the alga Chlamydomonas[6].   Evidence that increased oxygen stimulated this ammonia utilisation and carbon dioxide alone or anaerobiosis abolished it was obtained.   The results were consistent with a close link between Rubisco's oxygenase activity and protein catabolism releasing ammonia, which was then reassimilated in the chloroplast. Results suggesting a similar link when nitrate was utilised by the cells were also obtained.   Whether this link also exists in higher plants was not investigated.

Ammonium is normally exchanged with protons to balance charge in passing through each cell membrane, so that each ammonium absorbed and assimilated by chloroplasts has half the alkaline effect of each nitrite assimilation.   When taken together, the processes of nitrite and ammonium assimilation might therefore be of a similar order in terms of alkaline effect as the acidic effect of oxygenase activity of Rubisco.

There is little likelihood that the capacity of chloroplasts to maintain correct pH is ever seriously extended, even during maximum rates of nitrate assimilation.   Indeed, a more significant problem of pH control in the stroma may be the transport of the acidity of following the reactions in the peroxisome and the mitochondrion. This is followed by further oxygenase activity in the stroma involving reaction with half an oxygen molecule, and so on. Of course, fractions of molecules cannot be metabolised, so that such a scheme would really involve the assimilation of many nitrite molecules in each chloroplast.

Note that the alkaline product in the cytoplasm for the overall scheme is bicarbonate and not carbon dioxide gas. Thus this photorespiration could not be measured by a technique involving carbon dioxide efflux, since the alkaline effect of nitrite reduction does not allow this[7]. Nitrite reduction should be immediately slowed when the light is turned off.

The equation also balances charge, with nitrite (-1) from the cytosol exchanging for glutamate (-1) 2-oxoglutarate (-2) from the cytosol exchanging for two bicarbonates there and all other reactants and products balancing in the chloroplast stroma. The five excess protons are required for resynthesis of ATP from ADP and inorganic phosphate (six are needed for starch synthesis), when these are pumped with light energy into the thylakoid space. Expressed as ATP equivalents, the minimum energy cost for nitrite reduction and incorporation into glutamate when coupled in this way to photorespiration is 23ATP, compared to only 13 as usually calculated (3x3[2e]=9ATP for nitrite reductase + 4ATP for glutamine synthetase/glutamate synthase).

The advantage of this automatic link between the oxygenase activity and nitrite reduction would be one of minimising energy requirements to maintain a correct pH in the stroma. It is highly unlikely that protons could leak or be pumped from the cytosol into the stroma to relieve the alkaline stress, since this would tend to discharge the proton gradient across the thylakoid membrane.

If the alkaline stress theory is sustained experimentally, the claim that nitrate may be reduced in the leaf cells of plants with no energy cost when light is saturating using electrons from the photolysis of water therefore seems doubtful. In C_3 plants (which includes the legumes), photorespiratory cycling equivalent to nitrate reduction would need to be added to the cost of nitrate assimilation, as well as any photosynthate that might be required to store bicarbonate as organic acid anions.

In some plants - mainly grasses - bicarbonate may be transported to the roots as malate, and then excreted as bicarbonate in exchange for nitrate, so balancing charge and exporting alkalinity to the soil solution[4]. In other species, organic acid anions are stored in the leaf vacuoles, effectively storing the alkalinity of nitrate assimilation within the plant and perhaps providing cell turgor.

4. TESTS OF THE ALKALINE STRESS THEORY

This hypothesis was first formulated[4] without knowledge of the distribution of nitrate-assimilating enzymes in the C_4 plant species that do not carry out significant photorespiration. The hypothesis suggested that nitrate assimilation would logically occur in the mesophyll cells where its alkaline effect could be isolated from the

Rubisco's carboxylase activity to the cytoplasm when sucrose is synthesised there. In the case of starch synthesis in the chloroplast, this acidity is continuously consumed within the stroma.

The functioning of Rubisco's carboxylase and oxygenase activities must participate in the pH stat. Alkaline pH would favour the oxygenase activity, which automatically corrects the alkalinity by producing acidity. Rubisco's oxygenase activity should increase in response to nitrite reductase activity since this raises the pH increasing the relative proportion of bicarbonate relative to carbon dioxide in the carbonic anhydrase equilibrium. So a natural and almost instantaneous link between the two processes exists, neutralising the alkalinity of inorganic nitrogen (or sulphate) assimilation. This need not be disputed since it is inevitable from the known properties of the two systems.

An overall reaction that expresses this link between the oxygenase activity of Rubisco, the photorespiratory cycle and glutamate synthesis from nitrite and 2-oxoglutarate follows:

$$
\begin{array}{l}
\mathrm{CH_2OPO_3^{2-}} \\
|\ \\
\mathrm{C=O} \\
|\ \\
4\mathrm{CHOH} \\
|\ \\
\mathrm{CHOH} \\
|\ \\
\mathrm{CH_2OPO_3^{2-}}
\end{array}
\ +\ 6\mathrm{O_2}\ +\ \mathrm{NO_2^-}\
\begin{array}{l}
+\ 12\mathrm{Fd\cdot} \\
+\ 12\mathrm{H^+}
\end{array}
\ +\ 5\mathrm{ATPMg^{2-}}\
\begin{array}{l}
\mathrm{COO^-} \\
|\ \\
\mathrm{CH_2} \\
|\ \\
\mathrm{CH_2} \\
|\ \\
\mathrm{C=O} \\
|\ \\
\mathrm{COO^-}
\end{array}
$$

$$
\rightarrow 6
\begin{array}{l}
\mathrm{CH_2OPO_3^{2-}} \\
|\ \\
\mathrm{CHOH} \\
|\ \\
\mathrm{COO^-}
\end{array}
\ +\ 5\mathrm{ADPMg^-}\ +\ 7\mathrm{HPO_4^{2-}}
\begin{array}{l}
+\ 11\mathrm{H^+} \\
+\ 2\mathrm{HCO_3^-}\ +\ 12\mathrm{Fd}
\end{array}
\ +
\begin{array}{l}
\mathrm{COO^-} \\
|\ \\
\mathrm{CH_2} \\
|\ \\
\mathrm{CH_2} \\
|\ \\
\mathrm{CHNH_2} \\
|\ \\
\mathrm{COO^-}
\end{array}
$$

In this automatically coupled process, four molecules of ribulose bisphosphate are converted to six of phosphoglyceric acid plus two of bicarbonate. Three of the 2-electron reducing equivalents (6[H]) are required for nitrite reduction via photosystem I and ferredoxin and three further such equivalents for a re-iterated process of glutamate synthesis involving successive returns of diminishing amounts $(1+1/2+1/4+1/8+--- = 2.0)$ of ammonium to the chloroplasts in the photorespiratory cycle. This diminishing series follows from the stoichiometry of the cycle, in which the export of two molecules of glycollate from the chloroplast to the cytoplasm eventually result in one molecule of bicarbonate in the cytosol and the return of one molecule of ammonium and one of glycerate to the chloroplast stroma (see Fig. 1).

Balancing of pH then requires a single oxygen molecule to react with Rubisco, producing one molecule of glycollate for export resulting in one-half a molecule of both bicarbonate and ammonium,

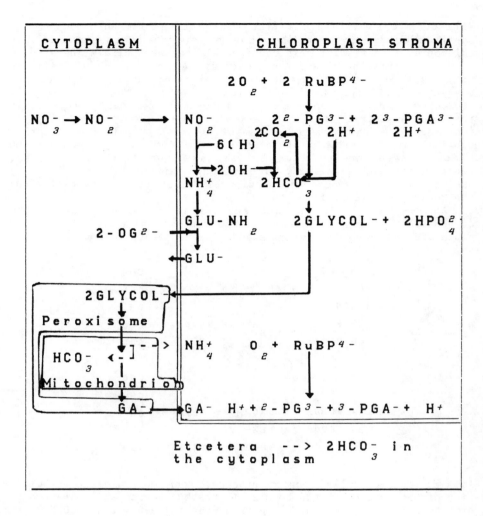

Figure 1. Coupling of nitrite reduction to photorespiration in C_3 chloroplasts. For coupled export of two bicarbonate molecules to the cytosol for each nitrite reduced, a sustained cycling process is necessary, since only one bicarbonate is formed in the first cycle (RuBP, ribulose bisphosphate; 3-PGA, 3-phosphoglycerate; GLYCOL, glycollate; 2-PG, 2-phosphoglycollate; GA, glycerate; 2-OG, 2-oxoglutarate).

Rubisco carboxylase activity in the bundle-sheath or Krantz cells. Determining whether this was the distribution therefore provided an experimental test.

A literature search revealed that the distribution of the enzymes of nitrate assimilation had been determined in one case[8] and was apparently as predicted by the theory. Nitrate and nitrite reductases were shown by isolation of mesophyll and bundle-sheath protoplasts to be predominantly in mesophyll cells. In addition, the enzymes of ammonium assimilation (glutamine synthetase and glutamate synthase) were also found mainly in these cells (see Edwards and Huber, ref. 9), rather than in the Kranz cells. No conclusions were drawn about the significance of such a distribution.

Whether sulphate reduction takes place only in the mesophyll chloroplasts of C_4 plants has not been determined.

The distribution of carbonic anhydrase is also in accord with the alkaline stress theory. This enzyme is highly active in C_3 chloroplasts[10] whereas it is absent from C_4 bundle-sheath chloroplasts conducting carboxlation[9] - nor is it needed there. Bicarbonate generated on nitrite reduction in the mesophyll chloroplasts could be transferred to the cytosol at a leisurely rate for PEP carboxylase activity there[9].

There is no clear-cut evidence directly linking the two processes of Rubisco's oxgenase activity and inorganic nitrogen assimilation in the chloroplasts of higher plants. As mentioned above, however, the results of experiments on an alga[6] can be interpreted to provide support for such a link. Other recent work with nitrogen-limited Selanastrum minutum has shown that ammonium assimilation is strongly linked to phosphoenolpyruvate carboxylase activity, with a major shift from carboxylation by Rubisco when assimilation was occurring in this C_3 organism[11]; oxygenase activity was not measured.

If the link between the two processes is obligatory, it could be expected that inhibiting photorespiration (as by growth with low oxygen pressure) might interfere with nitrogen assimilation and the growth of C_3 plants. But, since photosystem II evolves oxygen within the stroma it would be difficult to exclude Rubisco from some oxygenase activity. Further, in these conditions, nitrogen might be used with some economy, and the degree of ammonia metabolism by chloroplasts from protein turnover might vary, reducing the need for oxygenase activity and allowing a more economical use of oxygen.

As discussed by Lorimer and Andrews[2], none of the suggested roles for the oxygenase activity of Rubisco has a convincing logical basis or is supported by much evidence. The alkaline stress theory is presented as a possible explanation of its role, with a logical basis for the oxygenase activity as a means to relieve this stress. Should future experiments prove consistent with this proposed role, it would suggest further that at least part of the evolutionary pressure for the development of C_4 photosynthesis came from the advantage of removing photorespiration by separating Rubisco activity from nitrite reduction.

Clearly, there is a need for experiments specifically designed to test this alkaline stress theory that links inorganic nitrogen assimilation and photorespiration.

REFERENCES
1 Yokota, A. and Kitaoka, S. (1985) Biochem. Biophys. Res. Commun. 131,1075-79
2 Lorimer, G.H. and Andrews, T.J. in The Biochemistry of Green Plants (Hatch, M.D. and Boardman, N.K., eds.), Vol. 8, pp. 329, Academic Press, New York
3 Pfanz, H. and Heber, U. (1986) Plant Physiol. 81,597-602
4 Kennedy, I.R. (1986) "Acid Soil and Acid Rain: The Impact on The Environment of Nitrogen and Sulphur Cycling", Research Studies Press/John Wiley and Sons, Chicester, 1986.
5 Dijkshoorn, W. Nature, 194,165-7
6 Cullimore J.V. and Sims, A.P. (1980) Planta, 150,392-96
7 Kennedy, I.R. (1986) in The Eighth Australian Nitrogen Fixation Conference, (W.Wallace and S. Smith, eds.), AIAS Publn. 25, pp. 121-122, Australian Institute Agricultural science, Melbourne
8 Edwards G.E. and Huber, S.C. in The Biochemistry of Green Plants (Hatch, M.D. and Boardman, N.K., eds.), Vol. 8, pp.237, Academic Press, New York
9 Rathnam, C.K.M. and Edwards, G.E. (1976) Plant Physiol. 57,881-5
10 Graham, D., Reed, M., Patterson, B. and Hockley, D.G. (1984) Ann. N.Y. Acad. Sci. 429,222-37
11 Guy, R.D., Vanlerberghe, G.C. and Turpin, D.H. (1989) Plant Physiol. 89,1150-7

THE LIGHT RESPONSE OF CO_2 GAS EXCHANGE AND INTERNAL CO_2 CONCENTRATION SEPARATED FOR THE UPPER AND LOWER SIDE OF A MAIZE LEAF

W. Postl and H.R. Bolhar-Nordenkampf
Univ. of Vienna, Institute of Plant Physiology
Div. of Horticulture
Althanstraße 14, A-1090 Vienna

SUMMARY

The upper and lower surfaces of Zea Mays leaves show great differences in their photosynthetic rates (LONG, 1989). The differences in light response curves can be observed if the leaf is illuminated from the upper or from the lower side. In both cases differences in internal CO_2 (Ci) of the upper and lower substomatal cavities can be observed. The calculated internal CO_2 concentrations show differences, between the upper and the lower side of up to $30\mu l$ l^{-1} when illuminated from the top and of up to $140\mu l$ l^{-1} when illuminated from the bottom. The light response of photosynthesis in the upper mesophyll layer (UM) shows a hyperbolic increase and reaches 50% of the maximum rate at an illumination of $500\mu mol$ Photons m^{-2} s^{-1}. The light response curve of the lower mesophyll (LM) shows, after a shoulder, only a flat increase. After the 'crossing point' at a PFD of approx. $1500\mu mol$ m^{-2} s^{-1}, the CO_2 uptake of the lower mesophyll increases further, whereas photosynthesis of the upper mesophyll is light saturated. The gas exchange rates of the lower mesophyll reach saturation (after a considerably lower increase) at very high light intensities never occurring in the life of a plant. When the leaves are irradiated at the lower side, a very low photosynthetic CO_2 uptake and a small stomatal opening of the UM can be observed at very high light intensities (full sunlight) only. When irradiated at the lower side a great difference in Ci of the opposite substomatal cavities (up to $140\mu l$ l^{-1}) is shown. An inhomogenous light gradient within the maize leaf (LONG, 1989) seems to unfavour both the photosynthetic CO_2 uptake and the stomatal opening of the upper side under the above conditions.

MATERIAL AND METHOD

The fifth well developed leaf from field grown maize (Zea mays L. cv. 'Dea') was used in the experiments. In the middle of the leaf blade, 20 cm from the tip, leaf disks (∅ 6cm) were cut under water. They were dried with filter paper and mounted like a diaphragm into a thermostated leaf section chamber (HARRIS et al. 1983, LONG et al. 1989). The gas exchange from the upper and lower surfaces was separately measured with this set-up. Outside the chamber the cut edges of the leaf disks were watered with distilled water. In an open system the gas exchange was measured with an IRGA in differential mode (ADC). The relative air humidity was recorded by capacitive sensors (Testotherm). Leaf temperature was measured by an attached fine thermocouple (Dural). The leaf to air water vapor pressure deficit ranged between 0.9 and 1.8 kPa. The air temperature was 26±1.2°C. Beginning with 1900 μmol m^{-2} s^{-1} the light response curve was measured in 14 steps. A portable microcomputer (Epson HX-20) connected to a data acquisition system (LB-26) was used for recording and calculating the data.

RESULTS

A) UPPER SURFACE IRRADIATED

The 'light response curve' of the 'whole leaf' displays the 'normal' hyberbolic shape (Fig. 1). It represents the sum of the light response

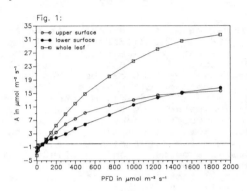

Fig. 1:

curves of the upper (UM) and lower side of the leaf (LM). The contribution of the upper and lower mesophyll layers to the whole leaf photosynthesis depends on the amount of intercepted light. At low light ($<200\mu$mol m^{-2} s^{-1}) the increase of both gas exchange rates is rather sigmoidal. At higher light intensities, the CO_2 uptake of the UM becomes hyperbolic. In contrast, the CO_2 uptake of the shaded LM increases rather linearly reaching the 'crossing point' at 1500μmol m^{-2} s^{-1}. Above this point, the CO_2 fixation of the UM is light saturated while the CO_2 uptake of LM further increases slightly. The stomata open well with increasing PFD at both surfaces (Fig. 2). The UM stomata in a 'hyperbolic' manner, the LM stomata in an 'exponential manner' according to the photosynthetic rates. The internal CO_2 in the upper and lower substomatal cavities drops with increasing PFD and rising CO_2 uptake (Fig 3). As pointed out by LONG et al. (1989), there is a significant c_i gradient between the c_i of the UM and LM illuminated from the upper side with $<1000\mu$mol m^{-2} s^{-1}. In most cases c_i is higher in the LM (Fig. 4). Only at the highest light levels, internal CO_2 concentrations of the substomatal cavities become comparable. At a very low PFD (100 and 150 μmol m^{-2} s^{-1}), c_i in the UM remains higher. Highest delta c_i values (approx. 28μl l^{-1}) were measured in the dark because of higher respiration rates in the UM. The same occurs at a light intensity of 300μmol m^{-2} s^{-1}.

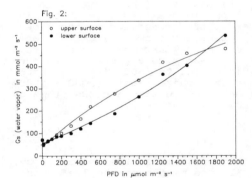

Fig. 2:

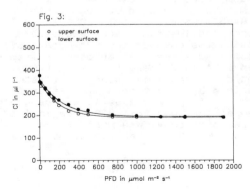

Fig. 3:

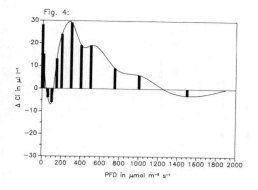

Fig. 4:

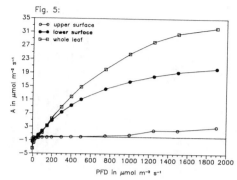

Fig. 5:

B) LOWER SURFACE IRRADIATED

When illuminating the leaf disk from the lower side the major contribution to the whole leaf photosynthesis comes from the UM (Fig. 5).

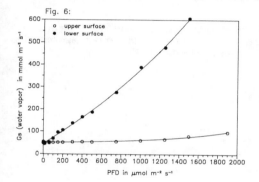

Fig. 6:

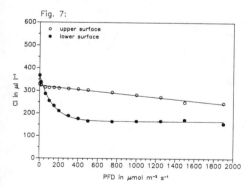

Fig. 7:

There is no reasonable CO_2 fixation in the UM up to $1200 \mu mol \ m^{-2} \ s^{-1}$. The stomata of the upper side remain closed up to the light intensities comparable with full sunlight (Fig. 6). In contrast, the stomata of the lower side show an almost linear opening with increasing PFD and higher photosynthetic rates. There are great differences in the internal Ci of the two mesophyll layers (Fig. 7). In contrast to a low photosynthetic rate, the Ci in the UM drops linearly from 329 to 245 $\mu l \ l^{-1}$. The reasons for reaction are the closed stomata (Fig. 6). In the lower epidermis the stomatal conductance is high as a consequence of the enhanced CO_2 uptake. Ci drops with increasing light intensity down to approx. $160 \mu l \ l^{-1}$. As a consequence of higher dark respiration rates the Ci of the LM reaches $+38 \mu l \ l^{-1}$ (Fig 8.). The highest difference in Ci (approx. $140 \mu l \ l^{-1}$) can be observed at $500 \mu mol \ m^{-2} \ s^{-1}$.

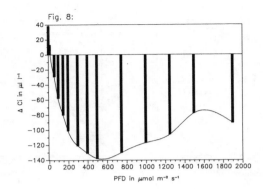

Fig. 8:

LITERATURE CITED:

Harris, G.C., Cheeseborough, J.K. and Walker, D.A. (1983) Measurements of CO_2 and H_2O vapour exchange in spinach leaf discs. Plant Physiol. 71, 102-107.

Long, S.P., Farage, P.K., Bolhar-Nordenkampf, H.R., and Rohrhofer, U. (1989) Separating the contribution of the upper and lower mesophyll to photosynthesis in Zea may L. leaves. Planta 177, 207-216.

USING WHOLE PLANT NET CO_2 EXCHANGE DATA FOR PREDICTING PRODUCTIVITY OF GREENHOUSE ROSES.

JIAO J., M.J. TSUJITA, and B. GRODZINSKI/ University of Guelph, Guelph, Ont., Canada. N1G 2W1

1. INTRODUCTION

The quantitative analysis of plant growth has been examined extensively since the beginning of this century (1-7). Most methods are based on destructive dry weight (DW) measurements taken at different time intervals over a relatively long growing period. These methods require very large populations of plants and are generally not sensitive enough to determine plant growth during a short period due to the small DW gained per plant.

Since the days of van Helmont in the early 17th century, it has been known that the weight of plants comes mainly from atmosphere. In the past few decades, many attempts have been made to increase crop productivity by improving leaf and canopy photosynthesis (8-10). Net CO_2 exchange has been used to estimate plant growth (11-16). Changes in absolute growth rate (ie. DW gain /time) and net assimilation rate (ie. DW gain/leaf area/time) of plants in response to changes in various ecological conditions can now be estimated quantitatively and nondestructively using the CO_2 exchange data (12).

In this report, we show how data of whole plant CO_2 exchange can be used to predict growth of 'Samantha' roses, and optimize the light, CO_2, and temperature environment not for leaf photosynthesis per se but for plant growth.

2. MATERIALS AND METHODS

Single stemmed Rosa hybrida 'Samantha' plants were propagated from cuttings and grown in PROMIX-BX in 13.8 cm diameter plastic pots under ambient greenhouse conditions (17). CO_2 exchange of plants at three stages of floral development was studied. At stage 1, the bud was not visible and the leaves reached about 30% of their final area. At stage 2, the bud was about 8 mm in diameter and leaf area was 80-90% of the final surface. At stage 3 the flower bud was about 20 mm wide with red-coloured petals visible. The leaves were fully expanded. Steady state net CO_2 exchange rate of individual leaves (L-NCER) as well as whole plants (P-NCER) was measured as described previously (12, 17). The respiration rates of flower buds, stems, and roots were measured similarly (18).

Daily carbon (C) gain of whole plants was equal to the day-time C gain minus the night-time C loss (8, 12, 14). The daily C gain was converted into DW by multiplying by a factor of 2.5 since the C content of 'Samantha' rose plant is 40% of its DW (12).

M. Baltscheffsky (ed.), Current Research in Photosynthesis, Vol. IV, 35–38.
© 1990 *Kluwer Academic Publishers. Printed in the Netherlands.*

3. RESULTS AND DISCUSSION

In a greenhouse when roses are grown as an indeterminant crop, flowering shoots can be found at all stages of development. To optimize the aerial environment for rose growth, the photosynthetic responses of leaves and plants at 3 stages of flower development were examined. Data in Table 1 indicate that L-NCER was saturated at irradiance of 400 μmol m^{-2} s^{-1} compared to 800-1000 μmol m^{-2} s^{-1} required to saturate P-NCER. Whole P-NCER of single stemmed 'Samantha' rose plants were similar at the 3 stages of flower development but P-NCER was higher on a plant basis at stage 3 due to the larger leaf area (Table 1). Photosynthesis and photorespiration in leaves of different ages were similar except in the youngest expanding leaf which had a lower net assimilation rate.

Table 1. Comparison between L-NCER and whole P-NCER of 'Samantha' roses at ambient CO_2.

		L-NCER (μmol m^{-2} s^{-1})		P-NCER (μmol m^{-2} s^{-1})		(μmol pl^{-1} min^{-1})	
Stage	% Leaf expansion	Irradiance (μmol m^{-2} s^{-1})					
		400	1000	400	1000	400	1000
1	32	-	-	3.1	6.1	3.9	7.7
2	90	-	-	2.8	6.2	10.4	23.1
3	100	9	9	3.0	6.2	11.9	24.6

As shown in Table 2, the respiratory loss of C from the major sinks of a rose plant contributes a significant amount to whole plant C economy. Due to varying light interception within the canopy and respiration of the sinks, production models based on L-NCER alone (19) tend to overestimate C fixation and plant growth. The whole plant net C gain data which takes into account mutual shading, sun-flecks, and respiratory loss from the sinks are therefore a much better basis for optimizing settings in greenhouses for rose growth (12, 17).

Table 2. Dark respiration of different parts of 'Samantha' roses at stage 3 of shoot development at 25°C. Numbers in brackets are percent of C loss from each part.

Source Leaf		Sinks			Total
(μmol m^{-2} s^{-1})	(μmol g^{-1} min^{-1})	Bud	Stem	Roots	
		(μmol g^{-1} min^{-1})			(μmol pl^{-1} min^{-1})
0.6	0.7 (23)	3.1 (32)	0.9 (20)	0.4 (25)	9.8 (100)

Data in Table 3 illustrate the use of our whole plant chambers for studying daily growth in a complex daily environment. Supplemental lighting during night even at low intensity has a great influence on daily growth. Rose production has been increased dramatically under 24 h lighting in winter months in the northern hemisphere (20). The extended radiation period is accompanied by an increase in the daily dose of radiant energy which results in more C assimilation. Interestingly, when the same total daily radiation energy input is maintained and only the duration of irradiation is varied, continuous irradiation still provides more growth in rose plants (Table 3). As long as the photoperiodic responses of the plants was not adversely affected an extention of the light period up to continuous irradiation also increased productivity of other crops (21). Table 3 also demonstrates the importance of controlling night-time temperature to minimize respiratory C loss for improved daily growth.

Table 3. Examples of nondestructive estimation of daily growth of 'Samantha' roses under ambient CO_2 and various day/night (12h/12h) irradiance and temperature regimes. Cd and Cn are net C gain and loss during day (D) and night (N), respectively.

D/N PAR (μmol m^{-2} s^{-1})	D/N Temperature (°C)	Cd	Cn (g C m^{-2})	Daily growth (g DW m^{-2})
515/0	22/22	2.48	-1.15	3.8
515/90	22/22	2.83	0.39	7.7
400/0	22/22	1.99	-1.03	2.4
200/200	22/22	0.87	0.89	4.4
700/0	27/27	2.69	-1.29	3.5
700/0	27/17	3.27	-0.79	6.2

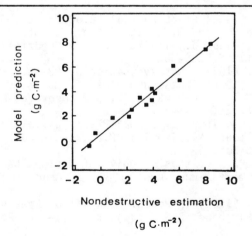

Fig. 1. Comparisons between the predicted values of daily growth and those measured nondestructively by means of gas exchange of whole plants exposed to different aerial environments.

Based on daily C gain, a model of plant growth of 'Samantha' roses was developed (18). This model includes two submodels, a P-NCER model as a function of irradiance, CO_2, and temperature, and a night-time respiration model as a function of temperature and day-time C assimilation.

The relationship between the predicted daily growth using our model and data obtained nondestructively from whole P-NCER measurements of roses grown in various aerial environments (eg. irradiance, duration of irradiation, CO_2 concentration, and D/N temperature regimes) is shown in Fig. 1. There is a good agreement between predicted values from the model and those obtained by experimentation. In summary, our approach to modelling and predicting optimal settings for rose production in a greenhouse environment is applicable to many other crops as well as to the study of many plant-environmental interactions in nature.

REFERENCES

1. Blackman, V.H. (1919) Ann. Bot. 33, 353-360.
2. Causton, D.R., and Venus, J.C. (1981) The Biometry of Plant Growth, Edward Arnold, London.
3. Erickson, R.O. (1976) Ann. Rev. Plant Physiol. 27, 407-434.
4. Evans, G.C. (1972) The Quantitative Analysis of Plant Growth, Blackwell Scientific Publication, Oxford.
5. Hardwick, R.C. (1984) Ann. Bot. 54, 807-812.
6. Hunt, R. (1978) Plant Growth Analysis, Edward Arnold, London.
7. Poorter, H. (1989) Physiol. Plant. 75, 237-244.
8. Coombs, J. (1983) Advances in Photosynthesis Research, IV. 85-94.
9. Gifford, R.M., and Evans, L.T. (1981) Ann. Rev. Plant Physiol. 32, 485-509.
10. Nelson, C.J. (1988) Plant Physiol. Biochem. 26, 543-554.
11. Bate G.C. and Canvin, D.T. (1971) Can. J. Bot. 49, 601-608.
12. Dutton, R.G., Jiao, J., Tsujita, J. and Grodzinski, B. (1988) Plant Physiol. 86, 355-358.
13. Heichel, G.H. (1971) Photosynthetica 5, 93-98.
14. McCree, K.J. (1986) Photosynthetica 20, 82-93.
15. Nilovskaya, N.T., Korzheva, G.F., and Bokovaya, M.M. (1973) Soviet Plant Physiol. 20, 464-470.
16. Peterson, R., Zelitch, I. (1982) Plant Physiol. 70, 677-685.
17. Jiao, J., Gilmour, M., Tsujita, M.J., and Grodzinski, B. (1989) Can. J. Plant Sci. 69, 577-584.
18. Jiao, J. (1989) Ph.D thesis, Univ. of Guelph, Canada.
19. Pasian, C.C. and Lieth, J.H. (1989) J. Amer. Soc. Hort. Sci. 114, 581-586.
20. Tsujita, M.J. (1987) in Roses, A Manual of Greenhouse Rose Production (Langhans, R.W., ed.), pp. 171-186, Roses Inc., Haslett.
21. Lisovskii, G.M., Sid'ko, F. Ya., Polonskii, V.I., Tikhomirov, A.A., and Zolotukhin, I.G. (1987) Soviet Plant Physiol. 34, 511-517.

PHOTOSYNTHESIS DARK RESPIRATION AND PLANT PRODUCTION IN *NICOTIANA TABACUM* GENOTYPES DERIVED FROM HAPLOIDS SELECTED BY LOW CO_2 SURVIVAL.

Delgado E, Azcon-Bieto, J.*, Medrano H.
Lab. de Fisiologia Vegetal. Dept. de Biologia i C.S.-Institut d'Estudis Avançats(UIB-CSIC).07071 PALMA DE MALLORCA. SPAIN.
*Lab. de Fisiologia Vegetal. Univ. de Barcelona. 08017 Barcelona, Spain.

1. INTRODUCTION

Leaf photosynthesis and dark respiration largely determine biomass accumulation by plants, so that both parameters has been used as a selection criteria to improve crop's yield (1, 2).

CO_2 compensation point reflects the balance between photosynthesis and respiration processes in the light (3, 4), and survival at CO_2 compensation levels has been suggested as an effective way to select genotypes of higher photosynthetic rate (5).

Tobacco haploids were selected by survival in a low CO_2 atmosphere chamber after a 45 days selection period (6). Survival haploids were diploidized by colchicine treatment and selfpollinated obtaining seeds (Selfpollinated genotypes, SP).

Because the selection criteria applied in the screening of haploid populations was clearly related to the carbon economy of entire plant, and also because the significant increase in dry matter production and leaf area per plant of selected genotypes on different field assays (7), the aim of this work was to characterize the photosynthesis and dark respiration of these genotypes in order to know the extent of possible physiological modifications which able them to survive in a low CO_2 atmosphere and to yield higher plant production in field conditions.

2. PROCEDURE
2.1 Material

Four selected genotypes, SP422, SP432, SP435, SP451 and the source cultivar from which haploids were obtained, Wisconsin-38 (W-38) as a control, were used in this experiment.

2.2 Methods

Seeds germinated in Petri dishes in growth room at 23 °C day / 20 °C nigth, 13 h./day photoperiod, and 300 μE m^{-2} s^{-1} (P.A.R.-Photon flux density) and 500-600 μl l^{-1} CO_2 air.

From the first growth stages, selected genotypes performed taller and bigger than the control (W-38) ones. Measurements were done on plants in vegetative stage, 11-12 weeks old after planting.

Photosynthesis, transpiration and dark respiration rates as well as stomatal conductance were taken with a portable gas exchange system (Li-Cor 6200) on attached full developed leaves at the growth

M. Baltscheffsky (ed.), Current Research in Photosynthesis, Vol. IV, 39–42.
© 1990 *Kluwer Academic Publishers. Printed in the Netherlands.*

conditions. Dark O_2 uptake was also measured on leaf slides with an O_2 electrode in a solution with 10 mM $CaCl_2$ at 25 °C.

For relative water content (RWC) measurements, fresh leaf discs were weighded before and after 3h period in destilled water. After, the discs were overdried at 80 °C for two days. RWC was obtained by

$$RWC = ((FW-DW)/FWmax-DW)) \times 100.$$

Chlorophyll content was also determined (8) in 80% (v/v) acetone leaf extracts.

Statistical analysis have been made between all genotypes at once (general comparison of means) with the Analysis of the vaiance, and also comparing between genotypes (Duncan Multiple range text).

3. RESULTS AND DISCUSSION
3.1 Photosynthesis and transpiration rates

As Table 1 shows, CO_2 Assimilation Rates (CER) showed significant differences among genotypes, but the variation range was only from 9,9 to 8,47 μmol CO_2 m^{-2} s^{-1}. Mean CER values of selected genotypes was 9% lower than the Control one. Nevertheless, the A versus Ci curve showed that they were only little non significative differences in which respects to CO_2 Carboxilation Efficiency and Amax, so these differences could be explained by conductance variations which also showed significative differences among genotypes. As Table 1 shows, all selected genotypes have mean conductance values lower than W-38. In this parameter, the selected genotypes average was 27% lower than Control. Stomatal conductance was 36% lower in SP422 and SP451 genotypes, showing a significative reduction even the relative water content (RWC) didn't show significative differences among genotypes (only a 3% of range of variation, Table 3).

Transpiration rates also showed significative differences. The biggest values were the W-38 ones (22% supperior to the selected genotypes average). Even though CER rates were higher in W-38, transpiration efficiency mean values were clearly lower (18%) with significative differences in respect to SP451. These data suggest that even selected genotypes have similar A/Ci response curve, they have better stomatal conductance regulation, which able them to save transpiration losses in a higher proportion than the CER reduction.

TABLE 1. Photosynthesis and transpiration rates. Mean values (=SE) of 6 to 14 replicates. S= Statistical significance according to the Analysis of the Variance. Values without a common subindex are significantly different at 0,95 level according to the Duncan Multiple Range Test.

Genotype	Photosynthesis Rate (A) μmolCO$_2$ m^{-2}s^{-1}	Stomatal Conductance (G) mol m^{-2}s^{-1}	Transpiration Rate (E)) mmolH$_2$Om^{-2}s^{-1}	Transpiration Efficiency μmolCO$_2$/mmolH2O
W38	9.78±0.29a	0.078±0.004a	1.4±0.5x10-4a	7.08±0.27a
SP422	8.61±0.32b	0.050±0.003d	1.0±0.6x10-4ab	8.74±0.33ab
SP432	8.48±0.15b	0.059±0.004c	1.1±0.7x10-4a	8.11±0.46ab
SP43	9.90±0.17a	0.069±0.009b	1.3±1.4x10-4a	7.62±0.90ab
SP451	8.47±0.27b	0.050±0.003d	1.0±0.6x10-4b	9.03±0.40b
	S	S	S	S

3.2 Dark Respiration Rates

Young leaves dark CO_2 release was similar among genotypes. Old leaves showed clear significative differences in this parameter both on leaf area and leaf dry weight basis (Table 2). Also in this parameter, SP451 genotype was clearly the better one with Dark Respiration Rates 27% and 36% lower on leaf area and leaf dry weigth basis respectivelly. Adult leaves slides showed a Dark Respiration Rate consistently lower than Control in selected genotypes (20% average reduction). Highest CER values were associated with highest dark respiration rates.

It was observed a negative correlation between O_2 uptake on a dry weight basis and Specific Dry Weight (SDW) in different genotypes . This suggest that lower respiration rate favours higher dry weight accumulation.

The rate of O_2 uptake in all tobacco genotypes mainly includes the activity of cytochrome pathway. The alternative oxidase does not seem to be active in the leaves givent that SHAM does not inhibit O_2 uptake. The capacity of the alternative oxidase is low in tobacco leaves because KCN inhibits very much respiration.

TABLE 2. Dark respiration rates of young and old tobacco leaves

	Dark CO_2 release in μmol m^{-2} s^{-1}		O_2 uptake by thin slides in μmol g-1 (DW) h-1	
Genotype	Young leaves	Old leaves	Young leaves	Old leaves
W38	1.07±0.09	0.51±0.04a	0.49±0.03	68.0±4.4a
SP422	1.11±0.07	0.51±0.05a	0.50±0.03	57.8±4.4a
SP432	1.11±0.08	0.65±0.05a	0.43±0.04	49.7±4.4a
SP435	1.08±0.05	0.56±0.10a	0.44±0.03	65.1±4.8a
SP451	0.99±0.06	0.37±0.04b	0.46±0.04	43.8±4.1b
	NS	S	NS	S

Dark CO_2 release. Values are means (SE) of 5 to 9 replicates.
O2 uptake. Values are means (SE) of 6 to 15 measurements.

3.3 Pigment content

Chlorophyll a+b content both refered to leaf surface or dry weight was significantly lower in SP451 genotype (mean values 10% and 24% lower than W38, Table 3). The rest of selected genotypes had mean values 3-17% higher than the source one (W-38). Chlorophyll a/b ratio didn't show any significative change among selected genotypes. Both in pigment content, Dark Respiration Rate, Specific Leaf Weigth and transpiration efficiency, SP451 showed the better values. The other selected genotypes were in general between SP451 and the source one for all these parameters From this and previously reported results (7), selected genotypes seem to have an association of higher leaf area per plant, lower dark respiration rate and superior transpiration efficiency. All these characteristics same to be possitively correlated with a higher plant production in the field. The way in which they could explain the low CO_2 atmosophere survival of these genotypes could be

related with the higher stomatal control, better carbon economy in the entire plant , and better leaf area ratio.
This performance on growth room conditions, and previously reported results on dry matter production, leaf area per plant and leaf nitrogen content in a field experiment (7), fortify the interest to study in depth the causes of higher yield and low CO_2 survival capacity of these genotypes.

TABLE 3. Leaf characteristics of adult tobacco leaves

Genotype	SDW (g m-2)	RWC (%)	Chl a+b mg m-2	mg g-1 DW	Chl a/b
W38	30.9±0.9a	79.9±0.8	330±10a	10.0±0.8a	3.78±0.11
SP422	34.6±0.9b	77.5±1.4	346±11a	11.0±0.6a	3.57±0.03
SP432	39.7±1.0c	76.6±1.0	340±28a	9.0±0.7a	3.55±0.04
SP435	32.6±1.4ab	79.6±1.0	361±13a	11.7±0.4a	3.72±0.08
SP451	42.9±1.4d	78.9±1.6	300±7b	7.6±0.6b	3.64±0.06
	S	NS	S	S	NS

SDW (Specific Dry Weight). Values are means (SE) of 11 to 22 measurements.
RWC (Relative Water Content). The values shown are means (SE) of 4 replicates
Chlorophyll determinations. Values are means (SE) of 4-6 replicates.

4. REFERENCES
1. Asay. K.H.; Nelson, C.J. and Horst, G.L. (1974) Crop Sci. 14, 571-574.
2. Wilson, D. (1982) Ann. Bot. 49, 303-312.
3. Azcon-Bieto, J. and Osmond C.B. (1983) Plant Physiol. 71, 574-581.
4. Azcon-Bieto, J. (1986) Plant Physiol. 81, 379-382.
5. Nasirov, Y.S. (1978) Annu. Rev. Plant Physiol. 29, 215-237.
6. Medrano, H. and Primo-Millo, E. (1985) Plant Physiol. 79, 505-508.
7. Medrano, H.; Pol, A. and Delgado, E. (1989) in Techniques and New Developmets in Photosynthesis. Plenum Press (481-484).
8. Lichtenthaler, H.K. and Wellburn A.R. (1983) Biochem. Soc. Transactions 603, 590-592.

ATP DEPRIVATION INDUCES STATE I TO STATE II TRANSITION IN THE DARK IN CHLAMYDOMONAS REINHARDTII

Pierre GANS*, Laurence BULTE[+], Fabrice REBEILLE* and Francis-Andre WOLLMAN[+]

*Service de Radioagronomie , Departement de Biologie, C.E.N. de Cadarache, 13108 Saint-Paul-Lez-Durance CEDEX, France.
[+]Service de Photosynthese, Institut de Biologie Physico-Chimique, 13 rue Pierre et Marie Curie, 75005 Paris, France.

INTRODUCTION

Depending of their state of phosphorylation, antenna proteins were shown to migrate reversibly between PSI and PSII, thus providing variations in the proportion of light excitation energy distributed to the two photosystems. This reorganization of the light harvesting complexes has been mainly understood as an adaptative mechanism by which plants and algae restore optimal photosynthesis in situation where the two photosystems would otherwise receive unbalanced light excitation. An alternative view has been developped by Horton et al. (1): state transitions would regulate the linear to PSI mediated cyclic electron flow in response to cellular variations in ATP demand. Here, we present results indicating that ATP deprivation caused by a block in the mitochondrial ATP synthesis in intact cells of *Chlamydomonas r.* leads to a reduction of the plastoquinone pool and to a genuine transition to state II in the dark.

MATERIAL AND METHODS

Chlamydomonas r. wild type 137 c was grown under continuous light at 2000 lx in minimal medium or at 300 lx on Tris-Acetate-Phosphate (TAP) medium. The FUD6 mutant a strain lacking the cytb_6/f complex (2) was grown in TAP medium under the same illumination. Cells were harvested in the mid-exponential phase of growth and resuspensed in fresh culture medium. For ^{32}P labelling of thylakoid membrane proteins, cells were resuspended in Tris-Acetate (TA) medium. Thylakoid membrane preparations were performed as in ref. 3 excepted that cells were broken through a French press in TA medium supplemented with 0.3 M sucrose, 10 mM EDTA, 200 μm PMSF[a] and 10 mM NaF. Fluorescence inductions, gel electrophoresis and autoradiography were performed as in ref. 3. Pyridine and adenine nucleotides were determined according to ref. 4. The 77 K fluorescence emission spectra were recorded after a rapid freezing in liquid N_2 of an aliquot of the cell suspension kept in dark well-aerated. State I was obtained by a 30 min incubation in darkness under strong agitation and State was obtained by a 30 min incubation under N_2 atmosphere.

RESULTS

In a previous paper, some of us have shown that inhibition of mitochondrial ATP synthesis induced changes in the fluorescence proper

M. Baltscheffsky (ed.), Current Research in Photosynthesis, Vol. IV, 43–46.
© 1990 *Kluwer Academic Publishers. Printed in the Netherlands.*

ties in *Chlamydomonas r.* in the dark (4). An increase in the stationnary fluorescence level was observed suggesting a reduction of some intermediate of the chloroplast electron transport chain. This was further studied by *in vivo* chlorophyll fluorescence induction kinetics of dark-adapted cells of the FUD6 mutant, blocked in plastoquinone reoxidation. The pool size of photosystem II electron acceptors may be measured by the area bounded by the fluorescence rise and its asymptotes (5). As shown in figure 1, the addition of AA plus SHAM or FCCP resulted in a marked decrease of this area indicating a partial reduction of the plastoquinone pool. A similar reduction occured in the wild type as indicated by an increased proportion of Q_B^- in the dark (result not shown). In these two strains, the addition of uncouplers or inhibitors of the mitochondrial oxidases led to a drop of the cellular ATP level (table I). The observed NADPH rise (table I) was presumably the result of a deregulation

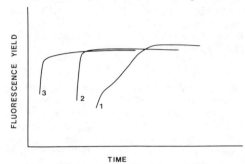

Fig.1 Fluorescence rise in FUD6 cells 1) control; 2) AA 1μM+SHAM 1mM; 3) FCCP 5μM; whole sweep 1.5 sec

of glycolysis (ATP controls tightly key enzymes of this pathway) and an increased carbon flow through the NADP glyceraldehydephosphate deshydrogenase. NADPH could be reoxidised by a NAD(P)H plastoquinone oxidoreductase, an enzyme bound to the thylakoid membrane and reported to initiate the chlororespiratory pathway (5), leading to a reduction of the plastoquinone pool.

TABLE 1. MAXIMAL FLUORESCENCE, ADENINE AND PYRIDINE NUCLEOTIDE LEVELS IN CHLAMYDOMONAS R.

	FUD6 mutant					wild type				
	Fmax	ATP	ATP+ADP	%NADPH	%NADH	Fmax	ATP	ATP+ADP	%NADPH	%NADH
Dark	100	165	200	10	n.d.	100	110	130	30	<5
AA+SHAM	98	90	160	40	n.d.	58	50	110	60	<5
FCCP	97	80	175	30	n.d.	59	35	95	55	<5

ATP and ATP+ADP were exprimed in nmoles.mg^{-1} Chl. NAD(P)H was exprimed in % of NAD(P)+NAD(P)H. AA was used at 1 μM, SHAM 1 mM, FCCP 5 μM. Fmax values were normalized to that in state I.

The Fmax in the wild type decreased after addition of AA plus SHAM or FCCP (table 1). The final level was very similar to that observed in state II (anaerobiosis)(3). The 77 K fluorescence emission spectra showed a marked decrease of the F_{685nm}/F_{715nm} ratio (respectively PS II and PS I fluorescence) after addition of either AA plus SHAM or FCCP (fig. 2) which was consistent with the occurence of a transition to state II. The kinetics of the fluorescence decrease in FCCP- or AA plus SHAM-treated cells are shown in figure 3. The half-time of the fluorescence changes were in the range of 130-150 sec after addition

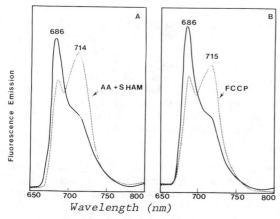

Fig. 2 Fluorescence emission spectra at 77 K. A: control and AA 1μM+ SHAM 1mM treated cells. B: control and FCCP 5μM treated cells.

of AA plus SHAM and 100-120 sec for FCCP. These half-time compared well with that of a transition to state II: 120 sec (6) and the observed decrease of the maximal fluorescence was possibly due to phosphorylation of PS II light harvesting complexes and migration towards PS I.

Fig. 3. Effect on the maximal fluorescence level of AA 1μM + SHAM 1mM (A) and of FCCP 1μM (a) and 5μM (b) (B). Light: 2000 lx. DCMU: 20 μM.

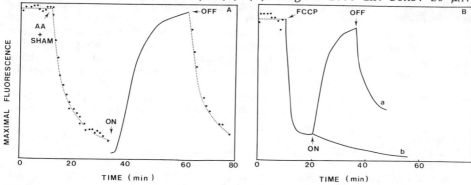

This was confirmed by measurements of proteins phosphorylations as shown in figure 4. When treated with AA plus SHAM or FCCP the algae displayed the same increase in phosphorylation of the LHC subunits as after an anaerobic incubation leading to State II (3). The ATP dependent fluorescence quenching (fig. 3) could be totally accounted for by a mere transition to state II, since the FUD6 mutant (devoided in the b_6/f complex and thus blocked in state I (7)) showed no fluorescence changes upon addition of either FCCP or AA plus SHAM.

We then tried to discriminate between a quenching effect under redox control of the PQ pool and specific quenching under ATP control per se. To this end, we attempted to revert the FCCP-induced and AA+SHAM-induced low fluorescence state by a white light illumination in presence of DCMU, a situation expected to reoxidise the PQ pool. As shown in figure 3 A, for AA+SHAM-treated cells, the Fmax level rose next to that in State I with a half time of 6 min, similar to that of a state II to state I transition: 330 sec (6). Similar results were obtained for FCCP-treated cells (fig.3) when the FCCP concentration uncouple the mitochondria, but not the chloroplast. In contrast, no

IV.15.46

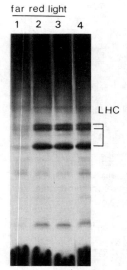

LHC

Fig. 4. Phosphorylation patterns of thylakoid membrane polypeptides from WT cells incubated in various conditions. 1: State I; 2: AA (1 μM) +SHAM (1 mM); 3: FCCP (5 μM); 4: State II (anaerobiosis). no reversion was observed when the chloroplast was also uncoupled (table 2). These observations are consistent with a specific control of either the ATP or the $\Delta\Psi$ on the transition from state II to state I. This point deserves further investigations.

CONCLUSION
The above results demonstrate that the fluorescence decrease upon addition of uncouplers or inhibitors of the mitochondrial oxidases can be attributed to a transition to state II : it occurs with similar kinetics , it is accompanied by a decrease in the ratio of F_{685nm}/F_{715nm} fluorescence emissions at 77K and an increased phosphorylation of the LHC subunits and it is not observed in $cytb_6/f$ mutants which are blocked in state I. The mechanism by which ATP controls the state transitions remains to be elucidated. We conclude that ATP deprivation causes a reorganization of the photosynthetic apparatus suitable for an increase in PSI-mediated cyclic photophosphorylation and favours ATP synthesis versus NADPH production

TABLE 2 TENTATIVE REVERSION FROM STATE II TO STATE I BY LIGHT AND DCMU

Wild type	Fmax	ATP	%NADPH	+DCMU/Light: Fmax	ATP	%NADPH
dark	100	110	30			
AA/SHAM	59	50	60	96	90	60
FCCP 1 μM	60	75	n.d.	91	75	n.d.
FCCP 5 μM	58	35	45	<60	25	60

ATP and ATP+ADP were exprimed in $nmoles.mg^{-1}$ Chl. NAD(P)H was exprimed in % of NAD(P)+NAD(P)H. AA was used at 1 μM, SHAM 1 mM. Fmax values were normalized to that in state I. DCMU 20 μM.

REFERENCES
1. Horton, P. (1985). In Photosynthetic Mechanisms and the Environment (J. Barber, N. Baker, Eds). 135-187. Elsevier, Amsterdam.
2. Lemaire, C., Girard-Bascou, J., Wollman, F. A. and Bennoun, P. (1986). Biochim. Biophys. Acta, 851, 229-238.
3. Wollman, F. A. and Delepelaire, P. (1984). J. Cell. Biol. 98, 1-7.
4. Rebeille, F. and Gans, P. (1988). Plant Physiol. 88, 973-975.
5. Bennoun, P. (1982). Proc. Natl. Acad. Sci. USA 79, 4352-4356.
6. Delepelaire, P. and Wollman, F. A. (1985). Biochim. Biophys. Acta, 809, 277-283.
7. Wollman, F. A. and Lemaire, C. (1988). Biochim. Biophys. Acta, 933, 85-94.

[a] Abbreviations: AA: antimycin a; SHAM: salicylhydoxamic acid; FCCP: carbonylcyanide trifluoromethoxyphenylhydrazone; DCMU: dichlorophenyl dimethylurea; PMSF: α-toluenesulfonyl fluoride.

EFFECT OF THE SALINITY ON THE ATPase ACTIVITY (CF1,F1)
ELECTRON TRANSPORT IN PHOTOSYSTEMS I,II AND RESPIRATORY
CHAIN IN Medicago sativa AND Amaranthus hypochondriacus

González, M.S., Vázquez, M.J., Quintanar, Z.R.
and Velasco, G.R. Lab. Bioquímica. UMF ENEP
Iztacala UNAM Apdo 314 Admon. Tlalnepantla
Edo de México México

In the plant salt adaptation, the ATPases are interesting because of their role in H^+ or ion transport (1,2).
However, little in known about the participation, and
similarities or differences between F1 ATPases and CF1
ATPases activities from higher plants in the resistance
to salinity ( )). Also, there is not conclusive –
information on the electron flow in PSI, PSII and respiratory chain in halophytes or glycophytes grown under different salinity conditions (3,4,5).
The present study examines and compares the effects
of NaCl in the growth medium and reaction mixture on the
ATPase activity in chloroplast (CF1) and mitochondria (F1)
and the electron transport in photosystems (PSI,PSII)
and respiratory chain from two species with different salt
tolerance, Amaranthus hypochondriacus and Medicago sativa.

MATERIALS AND METHODS

Alegría (Amaranthus h.) and alfalfa (Medicago s.) seeds
were surface-sterilized 15 min in a 1% sodium hypochlorite
solution and washed several times with water. The seeds
were germined at 30°C in the dark for 3 days in a lattice
of bronze inside of a special black acrilic cabinet. The
etiolated shoots in each lattice were transferred to plastic boxes containing Hoagland solution with 0, 50, 100 or
200 mM NaCl and maintained 5 days in the dark (samples for
mitochondria) orlight at 30°C, 4000 Lux and 12h photoperiod
Preparation of mitochondria was performed as described by
Bonner (6).
O_2 uptake in mitochondria was determined polarographically
using a Clark-type electrode in 1 ml of medium containing
0.3 M mannitol, 5 mM $MgCl_2$, 10 mM KH_2PO_4 and 10 mM KCl
brought to pH 7.2 with Trisma-base.
Protein was determined by the method of Bradford (7).

M. Baltscheffsky (ed.), Current Research in Photosynthesis, Vol. IV, 47–50.
© 1990 Kluwer Academic Publishers. Printed in the Netherlands.

The mitochondrial ATPase activity was determined by measuring Pi released at 30°C. Standard reaction mixture contained 20 mM Tris-HCl pH 7.5, 5 mM $MgCl_2$, 3 mM ATP. Other – additions are indicated under "Results". The reaction was started by the addition of 300 μg protein and arrested after 15 min with 0.5 ml of 30% trichloroacetic acid.
Pi release was measured according to the method described by Taussky and Shoor (8).
Isolation of thylakoid membranes was performed as described by Leegood and Malkin (9).
Thiol-modulation of CFo-CF1 was performed as described by Mills (9).
Assay of ATPase in pre-treated thylakoids was performed as described by Mills (9).
Electron transport through PSI and PSI-PSII was measured as oxygen uptake with a Clark electrode. Electron transport through PSI-PSII was measured after addition of methyl – viologen (0,1 mM), an PSI alone, after addition of ascorbate (5 mM) and DCPIP (10 μM) to inhibited thylakoids with 10 μM DCMU.

RESULTS

pH	mM NaCl in growth medium					
	0	100	200	0	50	100
	Amaranthus			Medicago		
6.5	5.8	4.6	3.0			
7.0	7.7	5.3	3.3	1.9	3.4	5.6
7.5	8.8	5.6	4.0	2.1	4.0	6.7
8.0	7.6	5.1	3.1	2.7	4.5	7.0
8.5	7.1	3.8	2.4	1.8	3.4	5.6
9.0	6.4	3.6	2.0	1.8	3.6	6.0

ATPase activity in mitochondria from Amaranthus and Medicago grown at different NaCl concentration.
Results are given as μ moles Pi/mg protein 15 min.

mM NaCl in reaction medium	mM NaCl in growth medium					
	0	50	100	0	50	100
	Amaranthus			Medicago		
0	144	171	222	159	177	194
25	138	138	200	162	163	178
50	134	133	192	147	158	166
100	130	126	194	139	147	155

ATPase activity in chloroplast from Amaranthus and Medicago grown at different NaCl concentration and with different NaCl concentration in the reaction mixture.

Results are given as μ mol Pi/20 μg Chl 6 min.

mM NaCl in reaction medium	mM NaCl in growth medium					
	0	50	100	0	50	100
	Amaranthus			Medicago		
0	102	102	114	239	271	170
50	78	124	114	257	244	174
100	142	148	88	266	244	161
0	46	102	114	147	170	115
50	36	124	108	126	142	105
100	36	28	18	138	142	92

Effect of NaCl in the growth medium and in the reaction mixture on the electron transport in PSI and PSI-PSII of Amaranthus and Medicago.

Results are given as n mol O_2/50 μg Chl min.

DISCUSSION

The present findings suggest that a qualitative difference
in the responses to NaCl exist between the mitochondrial
ATPase in Amaranthus and Medicago. The addition of NaCl
to the growth medium resulted in the stimulation of ATP
ase activity of Medicago, but induced an inhibition of this
activity in Amaranthus.
With respect to the ATPase activity in chloroplast, the
effect of NaCl in growth or reaction mixture was the same.
In both species there were stimulation exerted by NaCl in
the growth medium and inhibition by NaCl in the reaction
mixture.
The present study shows that a difference in the responses
to NaCl in growth medium exist between PSI in Amaranthus
and Medicago. The electron transport was inhibited only in
Medicago.
The rate of electron transport in PSI-PSII was stimulated
when both species were growing in saline medium with 50 mM
NaCl and inhibited with 100 mM NaCl.
The rate of the electron transport in mitochondria was
inhibited in both species grown in saline medium.
In conclusion, the present study shows that the variation
in salinity induce changes in the mitochondria and chloroplast of this two species with different salt-tolerance.

LITERATURE CITED

Vakmistrov, B.D. et al. (1982) Plant. Physiol. 55, 155-160
2.- Horovitz, C.T. and Waisel, Y. (1970)Experientia 26 941
3.- Livne,A. and Levine, N. (1967) Plant. Physio. 42, 407
4.- Ball, M.C. et al. (1984) Plant. Physiol. 76, 531-535
5.- Chritchley, C. (1982) Nature 298, 480-483
6.- Bonner, D.W. (1967) in Methods in enzymology(R.W.
     Estabrook ed.) vol X pp 126-133 Academic Press, N.Y.
7.- Bradford, M.M. (1976) Anal Biochem. 72, 248
8.- Taussky, H.H. and Shoor,E. (1953) J. Biol. Chem. 202,
     675
9.- Leegood, R.C. and R. Malkin (1986) in hptosynthesis
     energy transduction (Hipkins, M.F. and Baker, N.R eds.)
     pp 17-20 IRL Press Oxford England

INTERACTION OF THE PHOTOSYNTHETIC AND RESPIRATORY ELECTRON TRANSPORT CHAINS OF *RHODOBACTER SPHAEROIDES*

Simon Brown and Judith P. Armitage
Microbiology Unit, Department of Biochemistry, University of Oxford, South Parks Road, Oxford OX1 3QU, England

1. INTRODUCTION

Illumination inhibits respiratory electron transport in the photosynthetic bacterium *Rhodobacter sphaeroides* [1,2]. It is generally accepted that this is caused by an increase in the transmembrane electrochemical potential difference [2], although there is some evidence for a kinetic interaction via those components of the respiratory and photosynthetic electron transport chains which are common to them both [3].

The driving force for electron transport is determined by both the redox potential difference and the electrochemical potential gradient [4, 5]. Consequently, the rate of respiratory electron transport, in either the light or the dark, is determined by the imbalance between these factors. If the redox potential drop between the electron donor and the ultimate electron acceptor is greater than the transmembrane electrochemical gradient opposing it, then electron transport may operate in the forward direction.

2. PROCEDURE

Rhodobacter sphaeroides WS8 (wild type) was grown, as previously described [6], at 25°C under constant illumination. Cells were harvested and resuspended in either 10mM Hepes-NaOH (pH7.2) or, in the case of cells intended for the preparation of chromatophores, in 50mM NaCl, 8mM $MgCl_2$, 290mM sucrose, 50mM Tricine-NaOH (pH7.4). Chromatophores were prepared by the method described by Jackson and Nicholls [7].

Oxygen uptake was measured polarographically in the cell resuspension medium using a Clark-type electrode (Rank Brothers, Bottisham, UK). The carotenoid bandshift ($\triangle A_{523-510}$) was measured as previously described [8], except that the suspension was not sparged with N_2, and the photo-oxidation of P870 was assayed at 605-540nm [9]. In all measurements using whole cells the cell density was 10^9 cells ml^{-1} and chromatophores were used at 26µM BChl.

3. RESULTS AND DISCUSSION

The rate of oxygen uptake by whole cells was determined by their

M. Baltscheffsky (ed.), Current Research in Photosynthesis, Vol. IV, 51–54.
© 1990 *Kluwer Academic Publishers. Printed in the Netherlands.*

endogenous supply of substrates, but illumination almost completely
inhibited oxygen uptake (fig 1a). Addition of substrate, such as
succinate, to an illuminated suspension caused a resumption of oxygen
uptake which was only partly eliminated by doubling the photon flux
density (fig 1b). This suggests that the light-induced inhibition is
not simply due to an increase in the electrochemical potential, but
might be related to the redox balance of the respiratory chain.

The driving force for respiratory electron transport is more easily
manipulated using chromatophores, because they have no endogenous
supply of substrates. Addition of fumarate to a suspension of
chromatophores oxidising succinate caused inhibition of oxygen
uptake, both in the dark (fig 2a) and in the light (fig 2b).
Succinate alone caused an increase in the carotenoid bandshift
amplitude in both the dark (fig 3a) and in the light (fig 3b).
Subsequent fumarate addition had little effect on $\Delta A_{523-510}$, either
in the dark (fig 3a) or in the light (fig 3b). The stimulation of
respiratory electron transport in the light did not correspond to a
decline in $\Delta A_{523-510}$, and the inhibition following fumarate addition
was not accompanied by a significant increase in $\Delta A_{523-510}$.

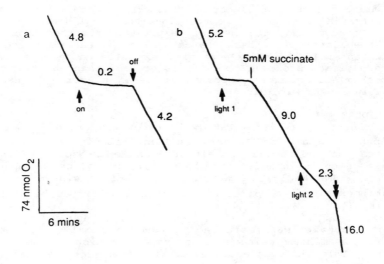

Figure 1. Respiratory oxygen uptake by whole cells in 10mM Hepes-NaOH
(pH7.2). Illumination was provided at 1000 μmoles photons m^{-2} s^{-1}.
Numbers on the traces are the rates of oxygen uptake in nmol O_2 min^{-1}
$(10^9$ cells$)^{-1}$.

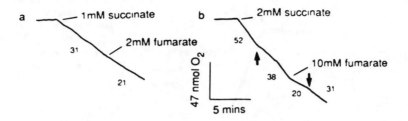

Figure 2. Oxygen uptake by chromatophores with different driving forces for respiratory electron transport in the dark (a) or the light (b). The numbers on the traces are the rates of oxygen uptake in μmol O_2 min^{-1} μmol^{-1} BChl.

The rate of P870 photo-oxidation is indicative of the rate of photosynthetic electron transport. In the presence of succinate, the rate of photo-oxidation was slightly lower (16.7 $\pm$ 0.4 ms^{-1}) than in it absence (18.8 $\pm$ 0.6 ms^{-1}). The amplitude of the signal was

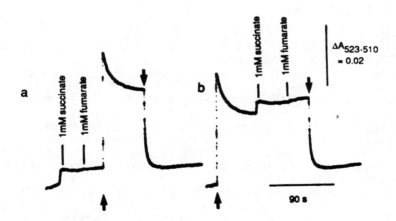

Figure 3. Effect of changing the driving force for respiratory electron transport in the dark (a) or the light (b) on the carotenoid bandshift ($\triangle A_{523-510}$).

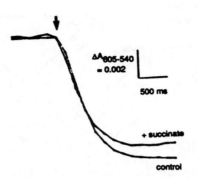

Figure 4. Effect 1mM succinate on the photo-oxidation P870 ($\triangle A_{605-540}$) under continuous illumination.

reduced from $8.5 \pm 0.1 \times 10^{-3}$ in the absence of succinate to $7.3 \pm 0.3 \times 10^{-3}$ in its presence (fig 4). This suggests either that the extent of light-induced oxidation of P870 was reduced in the presence of succinate or that P870 was more oxidised in the dark in the presence of succinate than in its absence, but the latter explanation is unlikely. It is more probable that the increased driving force for respiratory electron transport caused a decline in the rate of photosynthetic electron transport. This suggests that there is a direct interaction between the two chains even under continuous illumination and that there might be some limitation on the maximum rate at which electrons can flow through those carriers which are common to the two chains.

REFERENCES
1   McCarthy, J.E.G. and Ferguson, S.J. (1982) Biochem. Biophys. Res. Commun. 107, 1406-1411
2   Cotton, P.J., Clark, A.J. and Jackson, J.B. (1983) Eur. J. Biochem. 130, 581-587
3   Vermeglio, A. and Carrier, J.-M. (1984) Biochim. Biophys. Acta 764, 233-238
4   Mitchell, P. (1966) Chemiosmotic Coupling in Oxidative and Photosynthetic Phosphorylation, Bodmin, Glynn Research Ltd.
5   Brown, G.C. and Brand, M.D. (1985) Biochem. J. 225, 399-405
6   Armitage, J.P., Ingham, C. and Evans, M.C.W. (1985) J. Bacteriol. 161, 967-972
7   Jackson, J.B. and Nicholls, D.G. (1986) Meths. Enzymol. 127, 557-577
8   Poole, P.S. and Armitage, J.P. (1988) J. Bacteriol. 170, 5673-5679
9   Dutton, P.L., Petty, K.M., Bonner, H.S. and Morse, S.D. (1975) Biochim. Biophys. Acta 387, 536-556

THE EFFECT OF LOW INTENSITY BLUE LIGHT ON THE RATES OF RESPIRATION AND PHOTOSYNTHESIS, COMPOSITION AND GROWTH OF *LEMNA GIBBA*.

J. Gale[1], Gila Granot [2], M. Zeroni [2] and J. Reubeni [1].

Institute of Life Sciences, Hebrew University of Jerulsalem[1] and The Jacob Blaustein Institute for Desert Research, Ben Gurion University of the Negev[2], Israel.

1. INTRODUCTION

Low intensity blue light (BL) has been reported to increase the rate of respiration and metabolism of many lower plants, such as algae; this may be accompanied by a more rapid turnover of carbohydrates and synthesis of protein (1). While there are many and varied effects of BL on higher plants when given as extra lighting during the day period (2,3), there is very little information on the response of respiration (R), photosynthesis (P) and metabolism (M) when BL treatment is given at a low photon flux, during the night period only.

If BL does indeed increase the rate of R and M in the dark, this would suggest a practical application in controlled environment agriculture (CEA). Whereas CO_2 supplementation given in CEA usually increases yields, this is often accompanied by a reduced rate of P (per unit leaf area) when measured over time (4). This is considered to be the result of feedback product inhibition, a consequence of insufficient sink strength and too low rates of transport and metabolism. A low photon flux of BL, given at night, may therefore reduce this inhibition of photosynthesis and growth by stimulating the rates of R and M.

We have previously reported that on exposure of duckweed to conditions which induce high rates of P, the rate of P, at a given $[CO_2]$, falls within a few hours (5). In the experiments reported here we used duckweed, grown under long days with high $[CO_2]$, for studying the effects of low photon flux BL, given at night, on R and P and on growth and starch and protein composition.

2. MATERIALS AND METHODS

Growth and composition: Axenic cultures of *Lemna gibba* were grown in 250 ml erlenmeyer flasks. For 18h/d the culture received 300 μmol m^{-2} s^{-1} photosynthetic photon flux (PPF) from a mixture of fluorescent and incandescent lamps and were aerated with 1000 μmol mol^{-1} $[CO_2]$, in air.

For 6h/d the plants were irradiated with 50 μmol m^{-2} s^{-1} PF of either blue light (BL at 450 $\pm$ 25 nm, obtained via a filter of Rhom and Haas #2424 Plexiglass) or "white" light, as measured with a LiCor quantum probe. Temperature was held constant at 24 $\pm$ 1^{O}C. Initial fresh weight and fresh wt. / dry wt. ratios (for estimation of initial dry weight) were taken. After 5-6 days growth, dry weights were mwasured and the plants were assayed for protein (6) and starch (7) content. There were four replicates of each treatment and the experiment was repeated nine times, as there was considerable variability. Results were pooled and analyzed by the paired t test (Table 1).

Gas exchange measurements: Plants were placed in either horizontal erlenmeyer or flat plastic flasks with air inlet and outlet ports. The environmental controls and infrared CO_2 gas analysis based system and the calculation of rates of photosynthesis and repisration per unit dry matter with time, were essentially as described by Gale *et al.* (5) and by Gale, Macler, Smernoff and Reubeni (in preparation). Plants were irradiated during the night period with 20 µmols m^{-2} s^{-1} photons (PF) of either blue (450 ± 50 nm) or red (>550 nm) light, as measured with a LiCor quantum probe. Lower PF was used at night than in the growth wxperiments in order to reduce night period photosynthesis. Temperatures were held at 25 ± 1^OC. There were two replicates of each treatment and the experiment was repeated 7 times, with different day/night periods and ambient $[CO_2]$ concentrations.

3. RESULTS AND DISCUSSION
The effects of BL treatment on growth and on starch and protein content are summarized in Table 1.

Table 1 -   The Effect of Low Photon Fluence Blue Light on the Growth and on Starch and Protein Content of *Lemna gibba* Grown at High Ambient $[CO_2]$.

	Final D.Wt. mg		Growth Rate RGR		Starch Content mg g^{-1}		Protein Content mg g^{-1}		Protein Yield mg	
	BL	WL	BL	WL	BL	WL	BL	WL	BL	WL
Average of 9 experiments	67	56	0.525	0.49	152	182	249	225	17.6	12.9
BL/WL*100	120%		107%		84%		111%		136%	
Significance of difference*	P = 0.025		P = 0.001		P = 0.09		P = 0.069		P = 0.032	

BL - Blue light treatment   WL - White light   * - By paired t test (for details see text)

Fig. 1 - The Effect of Low Photon Fluence Blue Light at Night on the CO_2
Exchange Rate and Growth of *Lemna gibba* Grown at High Ambient [CO_2]
A. Photosynthesis and Respiration

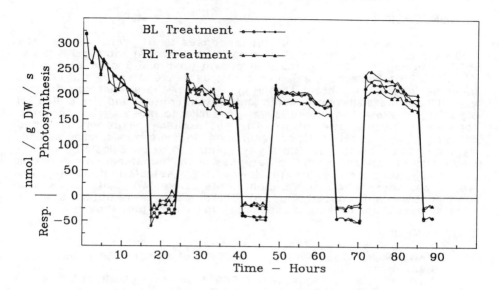

B. Calculated Dry Weight as a Function of Time

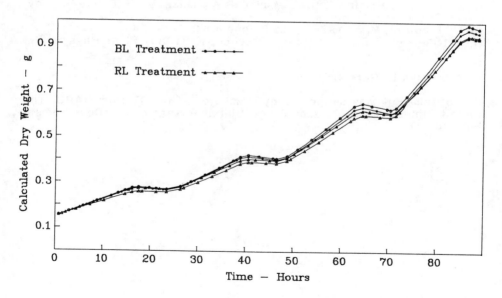

There was a consistent and large increase of nighttime respiration in the BL treated plants (Fig. 1A). There was also some, but inconsistent, evidence of a small increase of photosynthesis (Fig. 1A) and growth (Fig. 1B) in the BL treated plants.

4. CONCLUSIONS

The most consistent and significant responses to BL were a more than 100% increase in the net nighttime respiration (Fig. 1A) and the 7% larger RGR, resulting in a 20% increase in growth (in the 5-6 days of growth) (Table 1). This was accompanied by a 16% decrease in starch and an 11% increase in protein content (Table 1). However there was considerable variability in the analyses of starch and protein content and the statistical significance is low. These results are very similar to those already reported for algae and other lower plants. The gas exchange experiments, while showing a large effect of BL on respiration, indicate only a small and to-date insignificant effect on P/g dry wt. (Fig. 1A) or on calculated growth which may be related to small differences in the experimental conditions and the shorter periods of growth. However, it is notable that although dry weight was decreasing faster at night in the BL treated plants, dry weight increment was not reduced (Fig. 1B). Similar results were obtained in the other 6 replications of the gas exchange experiments (not shown).

5. REFERENCES

(1)   Kowallik, W. (1987) in Vol 1, pp 7-16 of Senger (Ed.) Blue Light Responses, CRC Press.
(2)   Laskowski, M.J., Briggs, W.R. (1989) Plant Physiol. 89: 293-298.
(3)   Assman, S.S. (1988) Plant Physiol. 87: 226-231.
(4)   Kramer, P.J. (1981) BioScience 31: 29-33.
(5)   Gale, J., Smernoff, D.T., Macler, B.A., MacElroy, R.D. (1989) Adv. Space Res. (in press).
(6)   Bradford, M.M. (1976) Anal. Biochem. 72: 248-254.
(7)   Sharkey, T.D., Berry, J.A., Raschke, K. (1985) Plant Physiol. 77: 617-620.

6. ACKNOWLEDGEMENT

Part of this work was supported by Grant No. I-1344-87 from BARD, The United States - Israel Binational Agricultural Research and Development Fund to J.G.

Glycine oxidation in green and etiolated tissue.

Per Gardeström, Dag Henricson and and Bosse Wigge

Department of Plant Physiology, University of Umeå,
S-901 87 Umeå, SWEDEN

ABSTRACT

The rate of glycine oxidation as compared to the oxidation of malate, succinate and NADH was measured in mitochondria from light- and dark-grown tissues. In etiolated wheat leaves the relative rate of glycine oxidation was similar to the oxidation of other substrates, comparable to the situation in green pea leaves. In etiolated pea leaves the relative rate of glycine oxidation was two to three times lower as compared to green leaves, but two to three times higher as compared to etiolated stalk tissue. In both green and etiolated leaf tissue serine hydroxymethyltransferase (SHMT) was almost exclusive mitochondrial. On the other hand, in spinach petioles SHMT was found to be about equally distributed between mitochondria and cytosol. It is suggested that, in addition to light induction of the glycine oxidation complex, it is also an important tissue specific development of the proteins involved in the conversion of glycine to serine in plant mitochondria.

INTRODUCTION

Photorespiration is a metabolic process in photosynthetic tissue in which phosphoglycolate produced from oxygenation of RuBP by Rubisco is metabolized (1). The photorespiratory production of serine in the mitochondria is catalyzed by two enzymes: glycine decarboxylase and serine hydroxymethyltransferase (SHMT). Glycine decarboxylase (2) and SHMT (3) have been isolated and characterized from leaf tissue, where the activity of both enzymes is high. The combined reaction of glycine decarboxylase and SHMT can be studied in isolated mitochondria as the capacity to oxidize glycine. In spinach glycine oxidation was high in mitochondria isolated from leaves, but low in mitochondria from roots, petioles or leaf veins (4). In etiolated leaf tissue the capacity for glycine oxidation has been reported to be considerably lower as compared to light-grown leaf tissue and induction of glycine decarboxylase by light is reported (5). In green leaf tissue SHMT is almost exclusively a mitochondrial enzyme (6). To our knowledge no study on enzyme level or intracellular localization of SHMT in etiolated leaf tissue has been reported. In the present study we have examined glycine oxidation in mitochondria, isolated from etiolated wheat leaves and from different parts of etiolated pea plants. Also, we have used protoplasts to study the localization of SHMT in green-, etiolated- and non-green tissue.

M. Baltscheffsky (ed.), Current Research in Photosynthesis, Vol. IV, 59–62.
© 1990 *Kluwer Academic Publishers. Printed in the Netherlands.*

MATERIAL and METHODS

Pea (*Pisum sativum*) was grown in greenhouse with supplementing artificial light at 20° C for about 10 days in commercial potting soil. Etiolated pea seedlings were germinated and grown in darkness at 20° C for 8 to 9 days. Etiolated wheat (*Triticum vulgare*) were germinated and grown in darkness for 7 days at 20° C.

The different parts of the pea plant were cut into ice cold grinding medium (0.3 M mannitol, 25 mm Hepes, 1 mm EDTA, 0.1 % BSA, 0.5 % PVP-40, 1 mM K_2HPO_4 and 4 mM Cysteine, pH 7.8) and were homogenized in 150 ml ice cold grinding medium for 3 s, filtrated through 4 layers of nylonet.

About 150 g of etiolated wheat leaves were cut into icecold wheat grinding medium (0.4 M mannitol, 20 mM Mops, 0.5 % PVP-4, 5 mM EDTA, 4 mM cysteine, 1 mM glycine, 0.1 % BSA, pH 7.2). The leaf pieces were homogenized in 200 ml wheat grinding medium filtered through four layers of nylon net.

A crude mitochondrial fraction was prepared from the filtrates essentially according to (4).

Respiration was measured at 25° C with a Hansatech O_2-electrode (Norfolk, Great Britain) in 0.4 ml respiration medium (0.3 M mannitol, 10 mM KH_2PO_4 and 0.1 % BSA, pH 7.2).

Preparation and fractionation of protoplasts were done according to (6). The activities of SHMT, Cytochrome c oxidase and fumarase were assayed according to (6).

RESULTS and DISCUSSION

In order to estimate the rate of glycine oxidation we compared the oxidation of glycine to oxidation of other substrates. The ratios of the glycine oxidation rate relative to the oxidation rates of malate, succinate and NADH in the presence of ADP, i.g. state III, are shown in Table I.

Table I. Glycine (Gly) oxidation in mitochondria from etiolated wheat leaves, green pea leaves, etiolated pea leaves and etiolated pea stalks in relation to oxidation of 10 mM malate (Mal), 10 mM succinate (Succ) and 1 mM NADH measured with oxygen electrode in respiration medium in the presence of ADP. For glycine, malate and succinate 1 mM NAD was present during assay and for succinate 100 nM ATP was also included. Values are based on 2 - 3 separate preparations from each source of material.

Source	Gly/Mal	Gly/Succ	Gly/NADH
Green pea leaf	1.2	0.95	0.55
Etiolated pea leaf	0.4	0.42	0.23
Etiolated pea stalk	0.25	0.15	0.10
Etiolated wheat leaf	0.75	1.4	0.55

Photorespiratory metabolism is occuring only in photosynthetic cells as phosphoglycolate is a product of the Rubisco reaction, and Rubisco is present only in these cells. In spite of this, we find substantial rate of glycine oxidation not only in mitochondria isolated from green leaves, but also in mitochondria from etiolated tissue. This is most pronounced in mitochondria isolated from etiolated wheat leaf tissue, where the oxidation of glycine as related to the oxidation of other respiratory substrates is similar to what is usually observed in mitochondria from green leaves. When the pea leaves had been grown in light the rate of glycine oxidation was similar to malate and succinate oxidation and about half of the NADH-oxidation. In the etiolated leaf mitochondria from pea the activity was about 40 % of the malate and succinate activity and about 20 % of the NADH oxidation. Thus, the relative glycine oxidation rate is two to three time higher in mitochondria from light grown leaves when compared to mitochondria from etiolated leaves.

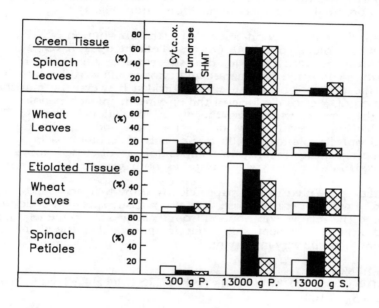

Figure 1. The distribution of cytochrome c oxidase, fumarase and SHMT in fractions obtained by differential centrifugation of broken protoplasts from green and non-green tissues. Both centrifugations were for 3 min. The values are the average of two determinations for each tissue. Values are % of recovered activity after fractionation.

Mitochondria from etiolated pea stalks showed about half the glycine oxidation activity of etiolated leaf mitochondria when the relative rates of glycine oxidation were compared. However, this difference might not reflect differences in individual cells but depend on different proportions between cells predestinated to photosynthetic and non-photosynthetic functions in the two tissues. This might also explain part of the difference between mitochondria isolated from green and etiolated leaves as the part of the plant used for preparations also contain the leaf petiole tissue. In green leaves on the other hand, the petioles make up a very small part of the total weight and are also excluded as much as possible from the preparation. In mitochondria isolated from etiolated wheat leaves the activity of glycine oxidation is similar to malate and succinate oxidation and about half the rate of NADH-oxidation (Table 1). This is similar to the relative oxidation rates for these substrates in green pea leaf mitochondria.

The localization of SHMT was studied in protoplasts from green tissue (spinach leaves and wheat leaves), from etiolated leaf tissue (wheat) and from non-green tissue (spinach petioles). In leaf tissue the distribution of SHMT in fractions obtained by differential centrifugation closely follows the distribution of the mitochondrial marker enzymes fumarase and cytochrome c oxidase (Fig 1).

Thus, most of the SHMT activity in green leaves is localized to the mitochondria. The distribution of SHMT in etiolated wheat leaf tissue also indicates a predominant mitochondrial localization (Fig. 1).

In spinach petioles, a non-green tissue, the distribution of SHMT is very different when compared to both green and etiolated leaf tissue. Most of the SHMT activity is recovered in the supernatant after the 13 000 g centrifugation compared to fumarase and cytochrome c oxidase activity. This indicates the presence of, about equally divided between the mitochondria and the cytosol, a cytosolic form of the enzyme in spinach petioles - a non-photosynthetic tissue where also the glycine oxidation is low (4). Thus it appears that high activity of glycine decarboxylase and mitochondrial SHMT are found only in photosynthetic tissue. This observation is in agreement with tissue specificity in enzyme composition as discussed above for the glycine oxidation capacity, which requires both glycine decarboxylase and SHMT.

The data presented in this paper clearly show that, in addition to light induction of glycine decarboxylase, it is also a tissue specific development of this activity. The relative contribution from these two components can not be evaluated from the present study, but it appears that the tissue specific component might be very important.

REFERENCES
1. Husic DW, Husic HD, Tolbert NE. (1987) CRC Critical Reviews in Plant Sciences 5, 45-100
2. Bourguignon J, Neuburger M, Douce R. (1988) Biochem. J. 255, 169-178
3. Henricson D, Ericson I. (1988) Physiol. Plant. 74, 602-606
4. Gardeström P, Bergman A, Ericson I. (1980) Plant Physiol. 65, 389-391
5. Walker JL, Oliver DJ. (1986) Arch. Biochem. Biophys. 248, 626-638
6. Gardeström P, Edwards GE, Henricson D, Ericson I. (1985) Physiol. Plant. 64, 29-33

UPSHIFT OF LIGHT INTENSITY ON SYNECHOCYSTIS 6714 CAUSES INCREASES IN GLYCOGEN, RESPIRATION, AND P700 REDUCTION

JACK MYERS, DEPARTMENTS OF ZOOLOGY AND BOTANY, THE UNIVERSITY OF TEXAS, AUSTIN, TEXAS 78712 USA

1.   INTRODUCTION

In cyanobacteria respiratory electron transport, measured in darkness as O_2 uptake, can also be measured in light in terms of turnover of P700. This is possible because

a)   Electron transport to O_2 uses some of the same carriers which provide for transport from PS2 to PS1 in light.

b)   Under a light 1 (as 440 or 680 nm) P700 is an effective competitor to cytochrome oxidase and becomes the acceptor for respiratory electrons. This gives rise to the Kok effect, a suppression of O_2 uptake.

c)   Under a light 1 rate of photoreaction 1 is limited by rate of electron supply.

I have used previously [1] the following simple model.

PHOTOREACTION 2 rate $v_2 = k_2 \, \alpha \, A \, I \, q$

where k_2 is the limiting quantum yield
α is the fraction of excitations available to Q
A is the fraction of incident quanta absorbed
I is the incident quantum rate
q is the fraction of PS2 centers Q open (oxidized).

PHOTOREACTION 1 rate $v_1 = k_1 \, (1-\alpha) \, A \, I \, p$

where p is the fraction of P700 open (reduced).

Also there is a

RETURN electron flow from low-potential donors (as ferredoxin, NADPH). The return flow may include

a)   "respiratory" flow from a kinetically buffered redox pool which is relatively constant and not linked to the prevailing v_1 rate. This component is called R.

b)   direct "cyclic" flow, a return electron flow closely linked and some fraction r of the v_1 rate.

M. Baltscheffsky (ed.), Current Research in Photosynthesis, Vol. IV, 63–66.
© 1990 *Kluwer Academic Publishers. Printed in the Netherlands.*

At steady state the photoreaction 1 rate must equal the sum of the several reducing rates

$$v_1 = k_1 \, (1\text{-}\alpha) \, A \, I \, p = k_2 \, \alpha \, A \, I \, q + r \, k_1 \, (1\text{-}\alpha) \, A \, I \, p + R$$

and

$$p = \frac{k_2 \, \alpha}{k_1 \, (1\text{-}\alpha) \, (1\text{-}r)} \bullet q + \frac{R}{k_1 \, (1\text{-}\alpha) \, (1\text{-}r) \, A} \bullet \frac{1}{I}$$

Hence I plot the steady state value of p vs $1/I$. At less-than-saturating intensities q is held close to one and the first term becomes constant. Then the slope Ip becomes a relative measure of R.

In a previous study [1] I compared changes in Ip with changes in dark O_2-uptake induced by added substrate and by dark starvation. I now report on the much larger changes induced by an upshift in light intensity.

2. PROCEDURE

Synechocystis 6714 grown in steady state culture under low light intensity (μ = 0.05 hr^{-1}). (I thank my colleague, J. Zhao, for providing this material.) Samples were transferred to a higher intensity under which the final growth rate was 0.14 hr^{-1} (35° C). As in other cyanobacteria, there was a characteristic growth delay of several hours. At various times during this period samples were removed for measurements of (1) dark O_2 uptake by O_2 electrode, (2) steady state % reduction of P700 (703/735 nm) vs actinic intensity at 440 nm, and (3) cell glycogen content assayed as glucose equivalents after NaOH digestion and enzymatic hydrolysis [2]. After two hours a fraction of the culture was transferred to darkness to observe kinetics of dark decay.

3. RESULTS AND DISCUSSION

Fig. 1 plots p vs $1/I$ at various times of the protocol. There are characteristic changes in Ip but relatively little change in the extrapolated intercept.

Fig. 2A plots the rate of dark O_2 uptake at various times of the protocol. A rate of 40 O_2/Chl•hr is a remarkably high 15% of the light-saturated photosynthetic rate and about 5X the rate supported by addition of glucose at zero time. Effect of added glucose at other times appeared to be constant and additive.

Fig. 2B plots the slopes Ip from several experiments such as that shown in Fig. 1. The ordinate scale is chosen so that relative changes in Ip are scaled to relative changes in O_2/Chl•hr. Then the same curve used in Fig. 2A is drawn upon Fig. 2B. It is evident that the upshift in light intensity increases both the rate of dark respiration and the value of Ip in a closely related fashion. Fig. 2A and 2B also show the effects of return to darkness after 2 h of high light. Effects on dark respiration and on Ip are qualitatively similar although less closely related in time.

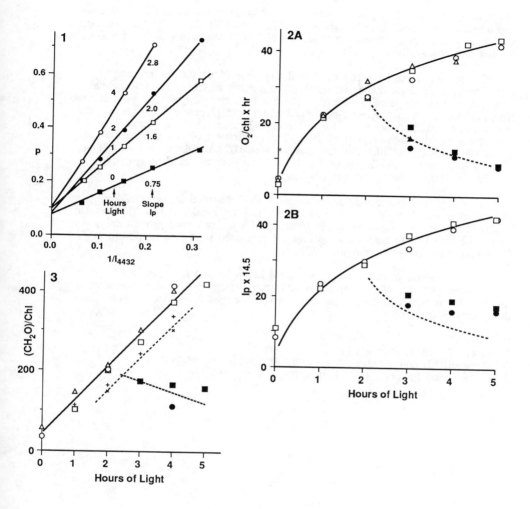

FIGURES 1-3. Effects of upshift in light intensity on Synechocystis 6714. Cells were held at 35°C with aeration by 0.5% CO_2 in air. Fig. 1, p, the fraction of P700 reduced, under actinic intensity I of 440 nm in nE $cm^{-2}sec^{-1}$. Fig. 2. Time course of electron flow rate measured by O_2-uptake and by Ip. Solid points describe cells transferred to darkness after 2 h high light. The curves for Fig. 2B are drawn as described in text. Fig. 3. Cell glycogen content. Data plotted x and + are for cells with added 20 mM NH_4^+. Solid points describe cells transferred to darkness after 2 h high light.

During the period of growth delay there is also a rapid synthesis of glycogen and a subsequent slow decay on transfer to darkness (Fig. 3). Glycogen synthesis was delayed but not prevented by 20 mM NH_4^+ so it seems not to be caused by a limited nitrogen availability.

The magnitude and kinetics of dark decay (Fig. 3) do not recommend glycogen as a substrate that is rate-controlling for the increased respiratory rate (Fig. 2A). However, conditions expected for a high rate of glycogen synthesis are high concentrations of glucose-1-phosphate, ATP, and glycerate-3-phosphate. The area under the dark decay curve for O_2 (Fig. 2A) measures the substrate pool responsible for the high respiratory rate. The substrate pool size is estimated at about 100 equivalents/Chl. The Chl content was 0.027 μmols/mg dry weight or about 5 mM on a wet cell volume basis. A large pool of readily respired substrate is formed during the growth delay.

All the phenomena described above were also observed in *Agmenellum quadruplicatum*. And the parallel changes in dark O_2 uptake and in Ip were also observed in *Synechococcus* 6301. In these species the observed growth delay was shorter (2 to 3 h). In both these species the estimated pool size supporting high O_2 uptake was 100 ± 20 equivalents/Chl.

As in previous work [1] the steady state behavior of P700 was simply interpretable in terms of a relatively steady return electron flow, the term R of the model. There was no evidence for any marked changes in a directly cyclic flow, the r term of the model.

REFERENCES
1 Myers, J. (1987) Photosyn. Res. 14, 55-60
2 Marshall, J.J. and Whelan, W.J. (1970) FEBS Lett. 9, 85-88
3 Levi, C. and Preiss, J. (1976) Plant Physiol. 58, 753-756

DOES NADH AVAILABILITY LIMIT NITRATE REDUCTION IN WHEAT GENOTYPES?
Division of Plant Physiology, Indian Agricultural Research Institute,
New Delhi 110012, India

M.Z. ABDIN, P.A. KUMAR AND Y.P. ABROL

1.   INTRODUCTION
Nitrate reductase (NR; EC 1.6.6.1) reduces nitrate to nitrite
utilizing NADH as a reducing power (1). The sources of reducing
power include triosephosphates (2), TCA cycle intermediate (3)
and glycine (4). It has been reported that nitrate reduction in
wheat and pearl millet is limited by NADH availability during
early stages of growth (5,6). Extensive studies carried out in
our laboratory revealed 2-3 fold differences in NR activity
among wheat genotypes. These genotypes were also found to
differ in nitrogen harvest and grain nitrogen(7).In this communication, we report the attempts made to ascertain as to whether
NADH availability influences the differences in NR activity
among the wheat genotypes.

2.   PROCEDURE
2.1   Materials and methods
      2.1.1 Plant material: Wheat (Triticum aestivum L.) seedlings
      were grown in pots (15 cm dia) containing sandy loam soil.
      For screening, the pots were kept in growth chambers
      ($25^o/18^oC$). 15 mM KNO_3 solution was added to each pot
      18 h before sampling. Light intensity in growth chamber
      was 350 uE m^{-2} sec^{-1}. For other experiments, the pots
      were kept in net house (light intensity 800-1200 uE m^{-2}
      sec^{-1}). First and second fully expanded leaf blades were
      used in all the experiments.
      2.1.2 Nitrate reductase activity assay: In vivo nitrate
      reductase activity was determined according to Klepper
      et al's method (2) with slight modification (8). In vitro
      activity was measured according to Hageman and Reed (9).
      Nitrite was estimated by the method of Evans and Nason
      (10). Metabolites were included in the assay medium prior
      to vacuum infiltration.
      2.1.3 NADH levels and in vitro oxidation: The amount of NADH in
      the leaf extracts of different wheat cultivars was
      determined according to Peine et al (11). In vitro NADH
      oxidation rates in the crude extracts from primary leaves
      of these cultivars were determined according to Mass (12).
      2.1.4 Photosynthetic rates: Photosynthetic rates in the third
      fully expanded leaf blades of wheat seedlings were

M. Baltscheffsky (ed.), Current Research in Photosynthesis, Vol. IV, 67–70.

determined with portable IRGA (ADC System, England) in the field.

3. RESULTS AND DISCUSSION

3.1 Forty genotypes of wheat were screened for NR activity (in vivo and in vitro) and were found to exhibit two to three fold differences in enzyme activity (data not shown). The differences persisted when the enzyme activity was expressed on the basis of fresh weight, dry weight and protein. Two high NR (cvs HD 1925 and HD 2204) and two low NR (cvs WH 147 and Safed lerma) genotypes were selected for the subsequent studies.

3.2 The difference in NR activity of the genotypes could be due to the limitation of substrate, reducing power or other biochemical characteristics. To examine the first possibility, the leaves were supplied with 15 mM KNO_3 for 15 h and tested for in vivo NR activity (Table 1).

TABLE 1. In vivo and in vitro NR activity

Cultivar	NR activity			
	in vivo		in vitro	
	(u mol g^{-1}dry wt h^{-1})		(u mol g^{-1} dry wt h^{-1})	(n mol mg^{-1} protein min^{-1})
	$-NO_3^-$	$+NO_3^-$		
HD 1925	43.68	65.85	61.56	2.14
HD 2204	50.73	75.28	90.91	2.79
WH 147	27.37	45.61	36.64	1.79
Safed lerma	14.86	22.50	20.73	1.30

There was considerable increase in the enzyme activity as a result of nitrate treatment to the leaves of the four genotypes. However, the activity differences persisted among both the categories.

3.3 A comparison of the two categories with respect to photosynthetic rate, endogenous NADH content and rate of NADH oxidation is shown in Table 2. The low-NR genotypes had low photosynthetic rates, low levels of NADH and high rates of NADH oxidation when compared to those of high-NR genotypes. These findings suggested that the enzyme activity is limited by the supply of NADH in the low NR genotypes.

3.4 To examine the above possibility, NADH was provided to the in vivo NR assay medium and infiltrated. While there was no increase in the enzyme activity in high-NR genotype (HD 1925), a 49.3 per cent increase was noticed in low NR genotype (Safed lerma) (Table 3).

TABLE 2. Photosynthetic rate, NADH levels and in vitro oxidation

Cultivar	Photosynthetic rate (mg CO_2 dm^{-2} h^{-1})		NADH (n mol g^{-1} fr wt)	NADH (Oxidation OD min^{-10} 340 nm)
	N_1	N_2		
HD 1925	29.38	33.94	35.0	0.099
HD 2204	30.81	35.58	35.8	0.133
WH 147	18.47	22.54	21.7	0.174
Safed lerma	25.11	21.35	11.7	0.180

TABLE 3. Effect of exogenous NADH on in vivo NR activity

NADH	In vivo NRA (u mol g^{-1} dry wt hr^{-1})	
	High NR^a	Low NR^b
0.0	48.56	23.49
0.2	31.03	33.15
0.4	42.16	35.07
0.6	44.23	27.99

a - cv HD 1925; b - cv Safed lerma

3.5 Glucose, glycine, fumarate and succinate, were also provided separately and their effects on in vivo NR were tested (Table 4, 5). Glucose and glycine enhanced the activity in the leaf blades of all the four genotypes. Maximum enhancement was noticed in Safed lerma, a low NR genotype.

TABLE 4. Effect of exogenous glucose on in vivo NR activity

Cultivar	NRA u mol g^{-1} fresh weight h^{-3}		
	Control	Glucose (10 mM)	Per cent change
High NR			
HD 1925	5.20	6.17	119
HD 2204	6.38	7.10	111
Low NR			
WH 147	4.00	4.78	120
Safed lerma	3.00	4.80	160

Despite the enhancement by NADH, glucose and glycine, the enzyme activity in low NR genotypes could not attain the level of activity exhibited by high NR genotypes. This revealed that NR activity is limited by biochemical characteristics other than NADH availability in wheat genotypes.

TABLE 5. Effect of addition of glycine and TCA intermediates on
in vivo NR activity

| Cultivar | Control | In vivo NRA ($u\ mol\ g^{-1}$ fresh weight h^{-1}) | | |
		Glycine (15 mM)	Fumarate (75 mM)	Succinate (10 mM)
High NR				
HD 1925	4.45	5.82 (131)	3.20 (72)	3.47 (78)
HD 2204	4.43	4.97 (112)	2.97 (67)	3.46 (78)
Low NR				
WH 147	2.62	3.40 (130)	2.15 (82)	2.07 (79)
Safed lerma	1.78	3.47 (195)	1.46 (82)	1.66 (93)

Values in the parenthesis are % increase in in vivo NR activities
over control

3.6 It was postulated that NR derives its reducing power from
triosephosphates (2), citric acid cycle (3) and glycine (4).
However, in the present study we did not obtain any enhancement
in NR activity by fumarate and succinate.

REFERENCES
1   Abrol, Y.P., Sawhney, S.K. and Naik, M.S. (1983) Plant Cell
Environ.6, 595-599
2   Klepper, L., Flesher, P. and Hageman, R.H. (1971) Plant Physiol.
48,580-590
3   Sawhney, S.K., Naik, M.S. and Nicholas, D.J.D. (1978) Biochem.
Biophys. Res. Commun. 81, 1209-1216
4   Kumar, P.A., Nair, T.V.R. and Abrol, Y.P. (1988) Plant Physiol.
88, 1486-1488
5   Brunetti, N. and Hageman, R.H. (1976) Plant Physiol.58, 583-587
6   Chanda, S.V., Joshi, A.K., Krishnan, P.N. and Singh, Y.D. (1987)
Aust. J.Plant Physiol. 14, 125-134
7   Abrol, Y.P., Kumar, P.A. and Nair, T.V.R. (1984) Adv.Cereal Sci.
& Tech. 6, 1-48
8   Nair, T.V.R. and Abrol, Y.P. (1973) Experientia 29, 1480-1481
9   Hageman, R.H. and Reed, A.J. (1980) Methods in Enz ymol.69,
271-281
10   Evans, H.J. and Nason, A. (1953) Plant Physiol. 28, 233-254
11   Peine, G., Hoffmann, P., Seifert, G. and Schilling, G. (1985)
Biochem. Physiol. Pflanzen, 180, 1-14
12   Mass, F.M. (1987) Ph.D. thesis, University of Groningen, The
Netherlands

THE EFFECT OF H_2O_2 ON THE PHOTOSYNTHETIC BIOCHEMISTRY OF *Pisum sativum*.

Ford,L., N.W. Pammenter, A.M. Amory and C.F.Cresswell.FRD/UN
Photosynthetic Nitrogen Metabolism Research Unit, Department of Biology, University of Natal, Durban, South Africa.

1.   INTRODUCTION

In higher plants hydrogen peroxide is produced in the peroxisomes and chloroplasts, during the oxidation of glycolate to glyoxylate, and when O_2 acts as an acceptor of PSI electrons, respectively (1).

Peroxisomal H_2O_2 may be enzymatically removed by catalase (2), or non-enzymatically by reaction with glyoxylate to form formate and CO_2 (3,4). In the chloroplasts the enzymes ascorbate peroxidase, dehydroascorbate reductase, glutathione reductase and Fd: $NADP^+$ oxidoreductase undergo a series of oxidation-reduction reactions which lead to the breakdown of H_2O_2 to O_2 and H_2O and the concomitant production of $NADP^+$ (5,6).

Enhanced H_2O_2 levels *in vitro* have been implicated in extensive ultrastructural damage (7) and derangements of chloroplast metabolism (8,9,10). This investigation examined the initial metabolic changes which occur as the H_2O_2 concentrations increase *in vivo*. The H_2O_2 concentration was increased by the addition of 3-amino-2,4-triazole, a catalase inhibitor (11), through the transpiration stream of pea seedlings.

2.   PROCEDURE

Aminotriazole (2mM) was applied through the transpiration stream of excised pea seedlings held in a water-jacketed glass cuvette. Rates of net CO_2 assimilation (A) and transpiration (E) were measured by conventional gas exchange techniques under different CO_2 and O_2 concentrations, with or without PGA added to the transpiration stream. Photosynthetic photon flux density (PPFD) was maintained at 500 μmol m^{-2} s^{-1}, temperature at 24 $\pm$ 2°C and atmospheric vapour deficit at 1 kPa. Results were normalized to steady state assimilation rates prior to commencement of treatment.

Assays were conducted on intact pea seedlings that had been maintained at similar conditions as for the gas exchange analyses. Catalase activity and H_2O_2 concentration were measured spectrophotometrically acccording to the methods of Macrae and Ferguson (12), and Smith (13), respectively.

M. Baltscheffsky (ed.), Current Research in Photosynthesis, Vol. IV, 71–74.
© 1990 *Kluwer Academic Publishers. Printed in the Netherlands.*

3.   RESULTS

Catalase activity was completely inhibited 300 minutes after the addition of aminotriazole (Figure 1a). This was accompanied by a decrease in the CO_2 assimilation rate (Figure 1b). However, contrary to expectations the H_2O_2 concentration remained unaffected (Figure 1a). This decrease appears not to be due to increased H_2O_2 levels resulting in oxidation of the PCR cycle enzymes as previously suggested (9,10).

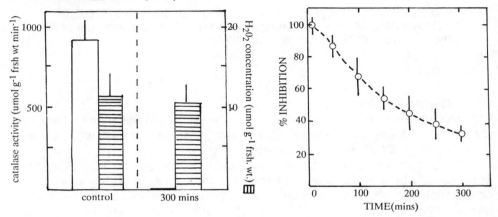

Figure 1. Effect of aminotriazole treatment on the H_2O_2 concentration and catalase activity (a) and assimilation rate (b) of pea seedlings.

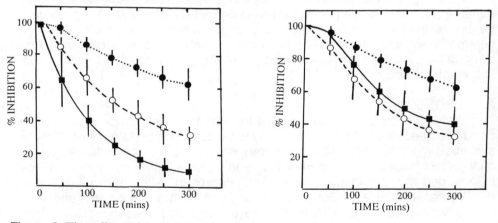

Figure 2. The effect of aminotriazole on the CO_2 assimilation rate at.
(a) 21%O_2 and 3 different CO_2 concentrations, 80 μmol mol^{-1} (——), 350 μmol mol^{-1} (– – –), 800 μmol mol^{-1} (·····), and (b) a constant CO_2:O_2 ratio, 800 μmol mol^{-1}:45%O_2 (——) and 350 μmol mol^{-1}:21%O_2 (– – –), and 800 μmol mol^{-1}:21%O_2 (·····).

The rate of inhibition of CO_2 assimilation was proportional to the rate of carbon flow through the photorespiratory cycle. The inhibition was greatest at low CO_2 concentrations and high O_2 concentrations (Figure 2a, b). Enhanced rates of photorespiration will result in increased rates of H_2O_2 production both in the presence and absence of aminotriazole. In the presence of aminotriazole the H_2O_2 must be metabolised by an alternative method. This appears to interfere with the mechanism of CO_2 assimilation.

CO_2 response curves (Figure 3a) show that both RuBP regeneration and the efficiency of the carboxylation reaction are affected by the aminotriazole treatment . These effects increased with time, but were initially alleviated by the addition of PGA (Figure 3b). It appears that the return of carbon to the PCR cycle is the first process to be affected in the short-term.

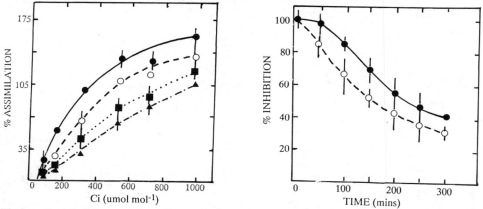

Figure 3. (a) CO_2 response curves of control plants and of plants treated with aminotriazole for 100 (– – –), 200 (·····) and 300 (– · –) minutes. (b) Effect of PGA (——) on the inhibition of the CO_2 assimilation rate by aminotriazole .

4. DISCUSSION

Aminotriazole inhibited the catalase activity but did not enhance the H_2O_2 concentration in the short term. This suggests that metabolic systems, other that those involving catalase, are able to cope with localized increases in H_2O_2 concentration. However, this appears to interfere with the CO_2 assimilation mechanism causing a decrease in both the RuBP regeneration rate and the efficiency of the carboxylation reaction. This is alleviated by PGA in the short term, which suggests that CO_2 assimilation initially decreases because of a reduction in the return of carbon to the PCR cycle.

REFERENCES
1   Gillham, D.J. and Dodge, A.D. (1986) Planta 167, 246-251.
2   Halliwell,B. (1974) New Phytol. 73, 1075-1086
3   Grodzinski, B. (1974) Plant Physiol. 63, 289-293

4   Amory,A.M. and Cresswell, C.F. (1986) J. Plant Phys. 124, 247-255.

5   Groden, D. and Beck, E. (1979) Biochem. et Biophys. Acta 546, 426-435

6   Nakano, Y. and Asada, K. (1981) Plant and Cell Physiol. 22, 867-880

7   Parker, M.L. and Lea, P.J. (1983) Planta 153, 512-517

8   Charles, S.A. and Halliwell,B. (1980) Biochem. J.189, 373-376

9   Kaiser, W.M. (1976) Biochim. et Biophys. Acta 440, 476-482

10   Kaiser, W.M. (1979) Planta 145, 377-382

11   Halliwell, B. and Gutteridge, J.M.C. (1985) in Free Radicals in Biology and Medicine (Halliwell, B. and Gutteridge, J.M.C., eds.), 20-65, Clarendon Press, Oxford

12   Macrae, E.A. and Ferguson, I.B. (1985) Physiol. Plant. 65, 51-56

13   Smith, I.K. (1985) Plant Physiol. 79, 1044-1047

USE OF COMPUTER SIMULATION AND NON-LINEAR REGRESSION IN PHOTOSYNTHETIC STUDIES

Amory, A.M., N.W. Pammenter and C.F. Cresswell. FRD/UN Photosynthetic Nitrogen Metabolism Research Unit, Department of Biology, University of Natal, Durban, South Africa.

1. INTRODUCTION

Biochemical models, based on the formulae below (1), have successfully been used to analyse whole leaf response to CO_2 uptake.

$$V_c = \frac{V_{cmax}}{1 + K_c (1 + Ox/K_o) / C_i} \qquad (1)$$

$$V_o = \frac{V_{omax}}{1 + K_o (1 + C_i/K_c) / Ox} \qquad (2)$$

$$A = (V_c - 0.5\,V_o) - Rd \qquad (3)$$

Photosynthetic capacity is limited by the ratio of total RuBP concentration to total enzyme sites. To model real data accurately *Eqn 3* is modified to:

$$A = (V_c - 0.5\,V_o)Q - Rd \qquad (4)$$

where Q is defined (2) as:

$$Q = P_m / (V_c + V_o) \quad \text{for} \ 0 \le Q \ge 1 \qquad (5)$$

and

$$P_m = \frac{\alpha\,PPFD\,P_{ml}}{(P_{ml}^2 + [\alpha\,PPFD]^2)^{\frac{1}{2}}} \qquad (6)$$

The objectives were to develop a software package that would analyse both laboratory and field photosynthetic gas exchange data and produce graphic output of such data, contain a simulation model based on *Eqn 1, 2, 4, 5* and *6*,

M. Baltscheffsky (ed.), Current Research in Photosynthesis, Vol. IV, 75–78.
© 1990 *Kluwer Academic Publishers. Printed in the Netherlands.*

enable comparison of real to simulated data, and be able to fit lines using non-linear regression to data applying *Eqn 1, 2* and *3*.

2.   PROCEDURE
The computer programme was written in Turbo Pascal. Algorithms used for gas exchange data analysis are based on the equations of Farquhar and Sharkey (3), photosynthetic simulation according to Weber *et al.* (2), non-linear regression by the Levenberg-Marquart method, and linear regression by singular value decomposition, including Pearson's correlation coefficient and Fisher's z-transformation (4).

To test the non-linear regression system photosynthetic rates were assimilated at three light intensities using the constants of Weber *et al.* (2) and the output was subjected to non-linear regression.

Two sets of data were subjected to non-linear regression. Using standard gas exchange techniques A:C_i plots of *Scaevola plumieri* (L.) Vahl., at different light intensities, were constructed. All data were collected from the upper leaf surface of a single leaf. The photosynthetic characteristics of *Poa cookii* Hook F. (a Sub-Antarctic tussock grass) as affected by the application of sea water was investigated. Plants were transplanted into plastic tubs, allowed to equilibrate for two days (day 0) and were subjected to 6% (day 1), 13% (day 5) and 30% (day 8) seawater.

3.   RESULTS AND DISCUSSION
The computer programme, POSSIM, allows gas exchange data to be analysed as A:C_i, A:temperature, A:light intensity and A:time plots, allows simulation of photosynthesis and comparison of simulated data. Non-linear

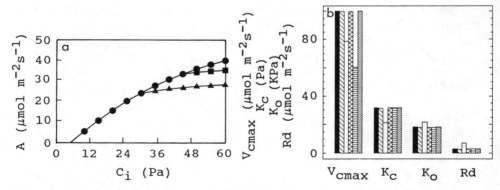

Figure 1. (a) Simulated photosynthetic rates at 800 (▲), 1200 (■) and 1800 (●) μmol m^{-2}s^{-1}. (b) Simulated (■) and estimated values of V_{cmax}, K_c, K_o and Rd of simulated data (▨ - 1800 μmol m^{-2}s^{-1}, $r=1.00$, $X^2 =0.01$; □ - 1200 μmol m^{-2}s^{-1}, $r=0.99$, $X^2 =3.59$; ▨ - 1200 μmol m^{-2}s^{-1*}, $r=1.00$, $X^2 =0.01$; ▤ - 800 μmol m^{-2}s^{-1}, $r=0.99$, $X^2 =0.11$; ▨ - 800 μmol m^{-2}s^{-1*}, $r=1.00$, $X^2 =0.001$)[* - limited data set].

regression can be applied to A:C_i plots and estimates V_{cmax}, K_c, K_o and Rd. Output is either graphical or as text.

Photosynthesis was simulated at 3 light intensities (Fig. 1a). The data output was regressed using the complete data set and using the portion of the data set where the concentration of RuBP was not limited. Successful regression was achieved with the data taken from the RuBP carboxylase limited portion of the curve (Fig. 1b).

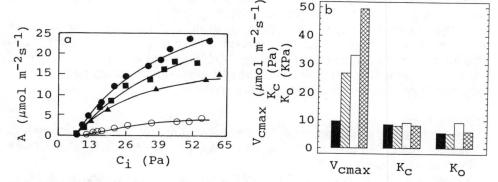

Figure 2. (a) Effect of light intensity ($\circ$ - 120, $\blacktriangle$ - 450, $\blacksquare$ - 650, $\bullet$ - 1550 μmol m^{-2}s^{-1}) on the A:C_i response of *Scaevola plumieri*. (b) Estimated values of V_{cmax}, K_c and K_o ($\blacksquare$ - 120 μmol m^{-2}s^{-1}, $r=0.99$, $X^2 =23.98$; $\boxbslash$ - 450 μmol m^{-2} s^{-1}, $r=0.99$, $X^2 =24.65$; $\square$ - 650 μmol m^{-2}s^{-1}, $r=0.99$, $X^2 =49.11$; $\boxtimes$ - 1550 μmol m^{-2}s^{-1}, $r=0.99$, $X^2 =7.22$).

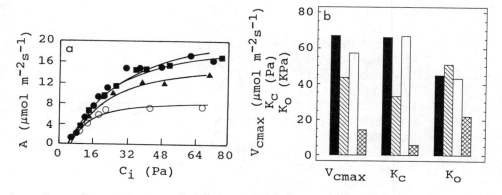

Figure 3. (a) Effect of salt application to the A:C_i response of *Poa cookii* ($\bullet$ - day 0, $\blacksquare$ - day 1, $\blacktriangle$ - day 5, $\circ$ - day 9). (b) Estimated values of V_{cmax}, K_c and K_o ($\blacksquare$ - day 0, $r=0.99$, $X^2 =13.45$; $\boxbslash$ - day 1, $r=0.99$, $X^2 =5.97$; $\square$ - day 5, $r=0.99$, $X^2 =5.25$; $\boxtimes$ - day 9, $r=0.99$, $X^2 =4.19$).

The photosynthetic rate of *Scivola tumbergia* was affected by different light intensities (Fig. 2a). Non-linear regression of the RuBP carboxylation limited portion of the curves showed little changes in K_c or K_o, while the V_{cmax} increased (Fig. 2b).

The application of seawater to *Poa cooki* decreased the photosynthetic rate (Fig. 3a). Non-linear regression showed that one day after salt application the photosynthetic parameters were affected (decreased V_{cmax} and K_c); by day five the system appeared to have readjusted, while continual salt stress lead to a decline the V_{cmax} and K_c, and increase in K_o (Fig. 3b).

The use of photosynthetic simulation allied with non-linear estimation of V_{cmax}, K_c K_o and Rd allows for rapid evaluation of the biochemical factors contributing to the photosynthetic processes. POSSIM offers an integrated environment for the analysis of all photosynthetic gas exchange measurements and for the fitting of non-linear regression lines to the data.

REFERENCES

1 Farquhar, G.D., von Caemmerer, S. and Berry, J.A. (1980) Planta 149, 78-90
2 Weber, J.A., Tenhunen, J.D., Gates, D.M. and Lange, O.T. (1987) Plant Physiol. 85, 109-114
3 Farquhar, G.D. and Sharkey, T.D. (1982) Ann. Rev. Plant Physiol. 33, 317-343
4 Press, W.H., Flannery, B.P., Teukolsky, S.A. and Vetterling, W.T. (1986) Numerical recipes, Cambridge University Press, Cambridge, New York, Melbourne

ABBREVIATIONS

α	-	initial slope of the PPFD response (mol mol^{-1})
A	-	photosynthetic rate (μmol m^{-2}s^{-1})
C	-	CO_2 concentration (Pa)
C_i	-	internal leaf CO_2 concentration (Pa)
K_c	-	Michaelis-Menton constant for CO_2 (Pa)
K_o	-	Michaelis-Menton constant for O_2 (KPa)
Ox	-	O_2 concentration (KPa)
P_m	-	CO_2-saturated photosynthetic rate (μmol m^{-2}s^{-1})
P_{ml}	-	PPFD and CO_2-saturated photosynthetic rate (μmol m^{-2}s^{-1})
PPFD	-	photosynthetic photon flux density (μmol m^{-2}s^{-1})
Q	-	'activation' factor
Rd	-	dark respiration occurring in the light
V_c	-	rates of carboxylation (μmol m^{-2}s^{-1})
V_o	-	rates of oxygenation (μmol m^{-2}s^{-1})
V_{cmax}	-	saturated rates of carboxylation (μmol m^{-2}s^{-1})
V_{omax}	-	saturated rates of oxygenation (μmol m^{-2}s^{-1})

PHOTOSYNTHESIS, PHOTORESPIRATION AND PARTITIONING IN LEAFLETS, STIPULES AND TENDRILS OF *PISUM SATIVUM*.

RICHARD CÔTÉ AND BERNARD GRODZINSKI, Department of Horticultural Science, University of Guelph, Guelph, Ontario, Canada N1G 2W1.

1. INTRODUCTION

The garden pea *Pisum sativum* is one of the most commonly studied plants, however the photosynthetic metabolism of each of the dominant parts of the pea leaf, the laminar structures (ie. the leaflets and the stipules) and the support structures (ie. the petiole, rachis and tendrils) have not been clearly established. Variability in leaf morphology in peas is under the control of two genes, the recessive gene "af" which transforms leaflets to tendrils and the gene "st" which reduces stipules to vestigial structures. Different combinations of these genes generate several plant phenotypes including conventional (AfAfStSt), semi-leafless (afafStSt) and leafless (afafstst) plants.

Differences in growth among pea lines have been related to differences in "leaf" photosynthesis. Pykes and Hedley (1) observed a consistent reduction in the rate of CO_2 uptake (expressed on a shoot dry weight basis) throughout the first week of seedling growth which appears to support the view that tendrils may be an inadequate photosynthetic replacement for leaflets (2). Based on gas exchange studies of individual leaves which included leaflets and tendrils but not stipules in each measurement, Harvey (3) showed that photosynthesis per unit area of the youngest leaf in the mutants was comparable to that of a conventional phenotype, while on a dry weight basis and at low light intensities the "leaf" of the leafless mutant was only 18% as active photosynthetically. More recently, Hobbs (4) pointed out that on a leaf area basis individual leaflets and tendrils of leafless mutants are similar. In the semi-leafless phenotypes 15-30% of total carbon fixation occurs in the tendrils (5) which is significant considering the low light interception capability and the reduced size of the tendrils (6). In addition,the photosynthetic contribution of the stipules can vary considerably (30 to 50%) depending on the cultivar (5).

The purpose of the present study was to measure photosynthesis, transpiration and respiration in the different leaf parts primarily in the leaflets, stipules and tendrils of a conventional phenotype *Pisum sativum* L. cv. Improved Laxton's Progress and a semi-leafless cultivar "Curly", and to provide primary information on the partitioning of newly fixed $^{14}CO_2$ within these structures.

M. Baltscheffsky (ed.), Current Research in Photosynthesis, Vol. IV, 79–82.
© 1990 *Kluwer Academic Publishers. Printed in the Netherlands.*

2. PROCEDURE

Peas (*Pisum sativum* L. cv. Improved Laxton's Progress and cv. Curly) were grown from seeds (Stoke's Seeds Ltd. Ont. Canada). Seeds were washed with 95% ethanol, rinsed with distilled water and soaked in distilled water for 24 hours before seeding in Promix. Plants were grown in a glasshouse under natural lighting for 4 weeks. Fertilizer 20:20:20 at 200 ppm nitrogen was applied weekly.

Leaf photosynthesis, photorespiration and transpiration were measured as described elsewhere (7). $^{14}CO_2$ was fed under steady state photosynthetic conditions for 10 min. and metabolites were analyses as previously described (8).

The part of the leaf which was enclosed in the cuvette was excised, traced onto paper for evaluation of the surface area with an area meter LI-3000 (LI-COR Inc. Nebraska, USA). Tendrils area was corrected to take into account cylindrical surface.

3. RESULTS AND DISCUSSIONS

Leaflets, stipules, and tendrils of *Pisum sativum* L. Improved Laxton's Progress, and cv. Curly a afila (semi-leafless) mutant have been assessed for their contribution to total plant gas exchange (Fig.1). Tendrils comprise 3% of the total fresh weight of the 3-4 week old conventional pea plant. The leaflets and stipules made up 63% and 34% of the shoot fresh weight and on this basis are responsible for 64% and 35% respectively of the total CO_2 fixed and the H_2O lost. On both a fresh weight and a chlorophyll basis leaflets and stipules have similar photosynthetic rates (219 µmol CO_2 g^{-1} FW.sec^{-1} and 133 µmol CO_2 mg^{-1} CHL.h^{-1}). Net photosynthesis of tendrils is 40% lower, but expressed on a surface area basis, tendrils are only 10-15% less efficient photosynthetically (Fig.1C). In tendrils transpiration rate and dark respiration are higher than in the

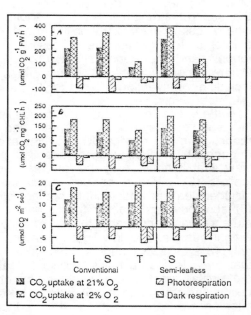

FIGURE 1. Gas exchange in leaflets, stipules and tendrils of *Pisum sativum* L. in conventional and semi-leafless phenotypes.

laminar organs, even though tendrils have a lower stomatal frequency and a higher chlorophyll content. In the afila phenotype of comparable age the stipules and tendrils contribute equally to total plant photosynthesis on area and chlorophyll basis (Fig.1). On a fresh weight basis, both cultivars show the same trend, although dark respiration was less in afila tendrils compared with the conventional cultivar.

TABLE 1. Distribution of ^{14}C-incorporated into ethanol insoluble and soluble fractions after a 10 min $^{14}CO_2$ feed under steady state photosynthetic condition.

Organ	Insoluble	Soluble		
		Neutral	Acidic	Basic
Conventional:				
Leaflets	27.8 ± 0.3	53.1 ± 2.1	6.2 ± 2.2	10.0 ± 0.1
Stipules	33.9 ± 5.0	42.8 ± 3.2	9.7 ± 3.0	13.7 ± 1.5
Tendrils	40.9 ± 6.8	32.5 ± 7.3	8.4 ± 3.6	18.3 ± 4.9
Semi-leafless:				
Stipules	40.2 ±10.1	48.1 ± 10.3	4.5 ± 1.2	7.2 ± 1.7
Tendrils	28.3 ± 5.1	42.7 ± 5.4	9.9 ± 3.7	23.2 ± 6.8

In all organs, leaflets, stipules and tendrils, the neutral fraction which consists mainly of free sugars contained most of the ^{14}C. The acidic fraction contained less than 10%. In the conventional pea, the basic fraction of leaflets and stipules contained 10.0% and 13.7% respectively, of the newly fixed ^{14}C. By comparison the basic fraction from the tendrils contained about 20% of the newly fixed ^{14}C in both the conventional and afila phenotypes.

TABLE 2. Percentage distribution of ^{14}C-incorporated into sugars in leaflets, stipules and tendrils of Improved Laxton's Progress. The pool sizes are expressed as $\mu mol \cdot g^{-1}FW$ in parenthesis.

	Leaflets	Stipules	Tendrils
Sucrose	27 (24.3 ± 5.6)	47 (26.6 ± 0.8)	54 (12.9 ± 1.0)
Glucose	44 (13.6 ± 4.0)	41 (4.0 ± 1.1)	29 (23.1 ± 2.5)
Fructose	29 (9.4 ± 4.4)	12 (1.1 ± 0.4)	17 (1.7 ± 0.2)

In the neutral fraction of leaflets and stipules, over 40% of the newly fixed ^{14}C was recovered in glucose. 29% of the label was present in glucose in the tendrils. The pool of glucose was greater in tendrils consistent with the high respiratory activity of these organs (Fig.1). In tendrils, over 50% of the newly fixed ^{14}C was in sucrose which may be either stored or exported.

Although proportionaly more of the newly fixed ^{14}C was incorporated into the basic fraction in tendrils compared to leaflets or stipules (Table 2), the pattern of distribution of ^{14}C among the amino acids was essentially the same in leaflets, stipules and tendrils (Fig.2). Over 50% of the newly fixed ^{14}C of the amino acids fraction is recovered in the serine pool (Fig.2). Other active pools include alanine and glycine which have also been implicated in nitrogen metabolism (9,10) and export during photorespiration (7,11,12).

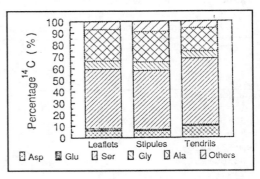

FIGURE 2. Distribution of ^{14}C into the amino acids fractions of pea leaflets, stipules and tendrils.

Current experiments with several conventional and mutant pea lines involve a closer examination of photorespiratory intermediates as intercellular metabolites.

4. REFERENCES

1 Pyke, K.A. and Hedley, C.L. (1985) in The pea crop: a basis for improvement. (Hebblethwaite, P.D., Heath, M.C. and Dawkins, T.C.K., ed), pp.296-305, Butterworth and Co. Ltd., London.
2 Harvey, D.M. and Goodwin, J. (1978) Ann. Bot. 42,1091-1098
3 Harvey, D.M. (1972) Ann. Bot. 36,981-991
4 Hobbs, S.L.A. (1986) Can. J. Plant. Sci. 66,465-472
5 Guillon, P., Cherbuin, A., Moutot, F., Cousin, R. and Jolivet, E. (1982) C. R. Acad. Sc. Paris, Série III, t-294,231-234
6 Heath, D.M., and Hebblethwaite, P.D. 1985. Ann. Appl. Biol. 107,309-318
7 Madore, M. and Grodzinski, B. (1984) Plant Physiol. 76,782-786
8 Côté, R., Bordeleau, L., Lapointe, J. and Grodzinski, B. (1989) Can. J. Bot. in press.
9 Housley, T.L., Schrader, L.E., Miller, M. and Setter, T.L. (1979) Plant Physiol. 64,94-98
10 Ta, T.C., Joy, K.M. and Ireland, R.J. (1985) Plant Physiol. 78,334-337
11 Grodzinski, B., Jahnke, S. and Thompson, R. (1984) J. Exp. Bot. 35,678-690
12 Grodzinski, B., Madore, M., Shingles, R.A. and Woodrow, L. (1987) in Progress in Photosynthesis Research, (Biggins, J. ed) III,645-652

EFFECTS OF GLUCOSE FEEDING ON PHOTOAUTOTROPHIC CELL
SUSPENSION OF <u>DIANTHUS</u> caryophillus

M.Helene AVELANGE, Frederic SARREY and Fabrice REBEILLE
Service de radioagronomie, Dept de Biologie, CEN-Cadarache,
13108 Saint-Paul Lez Durance CEDEX FRANCE.

1. INTRODUCTION

Among the numerous factors that modulate photosynthetic activity
(such as light , temperature , CO_2 and O_2 concentrations ...) the
partitioning and utilisation of the photosynthates within the plant
(i.e. the interactions of "source" and "sink") is often regarded as an
over-riding factor.(1.2). In this context, it was reported that
addition of sucrose or glucose in the external medium of
chlorophyllous higher plant cell culture inhibited photosynthesis and
chloroplast development (3,4,5) and that maximal rate of
photosynthesis were correlated with low cellular sucrose /glucose
content (6).In order to precise the cascad of events leading to the
photosynthesis inhibition we studied the effects of glucose feeding on
photosynthesis and respiration of photoautotrophic suspension culture
of carnation cells. The different gas exchange processes occuring in
the light were discriminated using ^{18}O and ^{13}C isotopes and a mass
spectrometry technique.

2. MATERIAL & METHODES
2.1 PLANT MATERIAL

Photoautotrophic air-grown cell suspension cultures of carnation
(*Dianthus caryophillus* L.) were routinely subcultured every four weeks
using the Murashige and Skoog medium, as previousely described (6).
Cells were harvested in the mid-log exponential phase of growth for
the experiments.
2.2 GAZ EXCHANGE MEASUREMENTS

Net O_2 exchanges were determined polarographically using a
Clark-type O_2 electrode. Unidirectional O_2 and CO_2 fluxes were
measured simultaneously with a mass spectrometry technique as
previously described (7). For O_2 and CO_2 exchange determinations, 2 ml
of $^{18}O_2$ and 0.15 ml of $^{13}CO_2$ (99% ^{18}O and 99 % ^{13}C) were bubbled in
the cell suspension before to close the reaction vessel. In these
conditions the initial O_2 and CO_2 concentrations were respectively 350
and 250 μM. Light intensity 800 $\mu E.m^{-2}.s^{-1}$. ; Temperature 25°c.

3. RESULTS
3.1.CARBOHYDRATE CONTENTS AND NET O2 EXCHANGE

When 20 mM glucose were added in the culture medium, there was,
during the ten first hours, a marked increase of the intracellular
carbohydrates (glucose, fructose, sucrose and starch) and
phosphorylated compounds (G6P, F6P and 3PGA) (results not shown).

M. Baltscheffsky (ed.), Current Research in Photosynthesis, Vol. IV, 83–86.
© 1990 *Kluwer Academic Publishers. Printed in the Netherlands.*

EFFECT OF GLUCOSE ON NET O₂ EXCHANGE

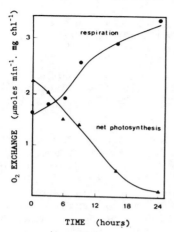 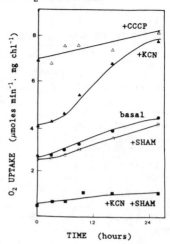

FIGURE 1: *Effect of glucose on photosynthesis and respiration.*
FIGURE 2: *Effect of glucose on the KCN insensitive respiration.*

These biochemical changes were accompanied by a decrease of net photosynthesis and a progressive increase of the respiratory rate recorded before illumination (fig. 1). The KCN insensitive respiration, suppressed by SHAM, was comparable to the uncoupled rate after 24 hours of glucose feeding (fig. 2).

The decrease of net photosynthesis could be the result of either the stimulation of mitochondrial respiration in the light or feedback inhibition through metabolic changes and "source-sink" interactions (8). In order to get a better insight of this phenomenon, we measured O_2 and CO_2 gas exchange under such conditions.

3.2. O_2 AND CO_2 GAS EXCHANGE IN THE LIGHT

O_2 and CO_2 gas exchange were undertaken in presence of a saturating level of CO_2 for photosynthesis. In light the rate of CO_2 uptake represented approximately 75% of the rate of O_2 evolution, indicating that at least 75% of the reducing power produced by the photosynthetic apparatus was diverted toward CO_2 fixation (fig. 4). This is a minimal value depending of the amount of respiratory CO_2 recycled within the cell. During a dark to light transition the O_2 uptake remained almost unchanged whereas the CO_2 efflux was strongly inhibited. It is not clear at the present stage whether this inhibition was representative of a decrease of substrate decarboxylations or the result of CO_2 recycling. This point is currently under investigation. As shown in figure 3, addition of glucose in the external medium resulted in an increase of both CO_2 release and O_2 uptake in the light. Such a result was indicative of a stimulation of the mitochondrial respiratory activity. As also indicated on this figure, the maximal CO_2 evolution rate was reached

MASS SPECTROMETRIC DETERMINATION OF GAZ EXCHANGE IN THE LIGHT

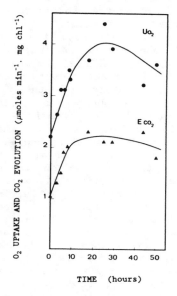 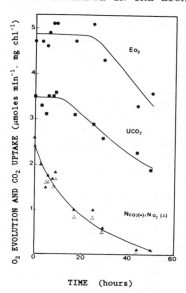

FIGURE 3: O_2 *uptake & CO_2 release*; FIGURE 4: CO_2 *uptake & O_2 evolution*
(*E=Evolution; U=Uptake; N=Net exchange*)

after 15-20 hours of experiment while the O_2 uptake rate increased further during the 10 following hours, before to decline (fig.3). After 8-10 hours of glucose feeding there was a progressive inhibition of the CO_2 uptake but not of the gross photosynthesis which remained constant during the first 24 hours following glucose addition (fig. 4). After this time the O_2 evolution rate started to decline. As expected from the tight coupling of these gas exchange processes, net O_2 and net CO_2 exchange curves were superimposed.

4.DISCUSSION

The rapid stimulation (up to two fold) of the respiratory rate after glucose supply was probably correlated with the intracellular accumulation of carbohydrates and glycolytic intermediates. Presumably the increasing level of phosphate ester compounds together with the enhancement of the overall cellular metabolism (the fresh weight of the culture increased faster than in standart conditions) would lead to a higher ATP consumption resulting in a rise the mitochondrial respiratory activity (9). The results obtained with KCN and SHAM are consistent with the presence of an alternative path capacity that seems to increase with glucose feeding.

Mass spectrometric measurements clearly established that, during the first hours of glucose feeding, the decrease of net photosynthesis was essentially due to an increase of respiration in light whereas the photosynthetic processes were almost not affected. After 10 hours, the rate of CO_2 fixation which was presumably representative of the Calvin cycle activity, started to decline, but the gross photosynthesis rate, which measured the rate of electron transfer in the chloroplastic chain, remained unchanged. The persistance of the gross in this condition, together with the fact that the O_2 consumption continued to increase when the CO_2 evolution had reached its maximum, strongly suggest that O_2 might replace CO_2 and serve as final acceptor for the photosynthetic reducing power. The precise nature of the O_2 consumption reactions possibly involved in this phenomenon, i.e: Mehler type reactions (10), chlororespiration (11) or transfer of reducing equivalents (NAD(P)H) from the chloroplast to the mitochondria and oxydation of these equivalents by the mitochondrial chain (12), remainsf to be determined. This process however was not sufficient to maintain a high rate of electron transfer for long times since both gross photosynthesis and O_2 uptake declined after 24 hours.

Several authors have suggested that the inhibition of the Calvin cycle activity following glucose or sucrose addition could be ascribable to a decrease of the cytosolic Pi concentration (8,13). In our experimental conditions, however, 1 mM Pi was present in the culture medium. Taking in account the high performances of the Pi translocator located on the plasmalema of higher plant cells (14), it is doubtfull that a cytosolic Pi depletion could alone explain our results. In addition no decrease of the total Pi pool could be detected in presence of glucose (result not shown). Variations of other metabolite concentrations, such as 3-PGA, or changes in the activity of some key enzymes of the Calvin cycle, could also be involved in this regulation.

REFERENCES
1. Foyer, C.H., Walker, D.A. and Latzco, E. (1982) Z. Pflanzen physiol. 107, 457-465
2. Stitt, M., Herzog, and Heldt, H.W. (1984) Plant Physiol. 75, 548-553
3. Pamplin, E.J. and Chapman, J.M. (1975) J. Exp. Bot. 26, 212-220
4. Dalton, C.C. and Street, H.E. (1977) Plant Sci. Lett. 10, 157-164
5. Chagvardieff, P. Pean, M. Carrier, P and Dimon, B. (1988) Plant Cell Tissue Organ Cult. 12, 243-251
6. Rebeille, F. (1988) Plant Sci. 54, 11-21
7. Rebeille, F., Gans, P., Chagvardieff, P., Pean, M., Tapie, P. and Thibault, P. (1988) J. Biol. Chem. 263, 12373-12377
8. Foyer, C.H. (1987) Plant Physiol. Biochem. 25, 649-657
9. Roby, C. Martin, J.B., Bligny, R. and Douce, R. (1987) J. Biol. Chem. 262, 5000-5007
10. Melher, A.H. (1951) Arch. Biochem. Biophys. 33, 65-77
11. Peltier, G., Ravenel, J. and Vermeglio, A. (1987) Biochim. Biophys. Acta 893, 83-90
12. Krmer, S., Stitt, M. and Heldt, H.W. (1988) FEBS Lett. 226, 352-356
13. Walker, D.A. and Sivak, M.N. (1986) Trends Biochem. Sci. 11, 176-178
14. Rebeille, F. Bligny, R. and Douce, R. (1982) Arch. Biochem. Biophys. 219, 371-378

AFFINITY LABELING OF PHOSPHORIBULOKINASE BY ADENOSINE
POLYPHOSPHOPYRIDOXALS

Henry M. Miziorko and Christine A. Brodt
Medical College of Wisconsin, Milwaukee WI 53226 U.S.A.

INTRODUCTION

Phosphoribulokinase (PRK; EC 2.7.1.19) catalyzes a key step in the
reductive pentose phosphate cycle, namely, production of the CO_2
acceptor, ribulose 1,5-bisphosphate.In recent years, substantial
structural information has become available for the spinach leaf
enzyme. For example, the primary structure has been deduced from the
cDNA sequence (Milanez and Mural, 1988; Roesler and Ogren, 1988). PRK's
cysteine residues have been examined in some detail. For example, the
identity of cysteines that participate in disulfide formation has been
determined (Porter et al., 1988). One of these cysteines (cys-16) has
been demonstrated to be located in the ATP binding domain (Krieger and
Miziorko, 1986; Krieger et al., 1987) although it is not essential for
catalysis (Porter and Hartman, 1988). It seemed that additional
structural information could be generated for PRK if ATP analogs that
have proven to be effective in modifying other classes of amino acids
in ATP-utilizing enzymes could be used to selectively modify this
enzyme. Recent results indicate that adenosine di- and triphosphopyr-
idoxals (Tamura et al., 1986) function as affinity labels of spinach
leaf PRK. The results of this protein modification work indicate the
existence of a reactive lysine within the ATP binding domain.

RESULTS and DISCUSSION

Inhibition of phosphoribulokinase by adenosine di- and
triphosphopyridoxal. While spinach leaf PRK loses activity in a time
dependent fashion when protein is incubated with adenosine di- and tri-
phosphopyridoxals (Fig. 1a,b), there are substantial differences
between the type of inhibition exhibited by these compounds and the
results usually obtained using affinity labels. For example,
borohydride reduction of the enzyme-inhibitor complex is required in
order to accomplish effective irreversible inactivation. In addition,
inactivation kinetics deviate from the first order pattern frequently
observed in affinity labeling studies. In this case, a plateau value
for residual activity is observed regardless of whether adenosine
diphosphopyridoxal (Ado-P_2-Pl) or adenosine triphosphopyridoxal
(Ado-P_3-Pl) is used for the inactivation experiment. Analysis of this
type of inactivation kinetics has been addressed by Chen and Engel
(1975). The plateau position indicates that equilibrium is established
between the noncovalent E*I complex and the covalent E-I complex in
which a Schiff's base adduct has formed between an enzymic amino group

and the aldehyde group of the inhibitor. Equilibrium and binding constant values (K_{eq} and K_d, respectively) can be extracted from the kinetic data if the residual activity (R) observed at the plateau (equilibrium) position is plotted as a function of inhibitor concentration (Tamura et al., 1986).When such an analysis is performed for the data obtained upon inactivation of PRK by Ado-P_2-Pl (Fig. 1a) or Ado-P_3-Pl (Fig. 1b), binding constants of 175 uM and 11 uM, respectively, are determined (Table I); these values are comparable to the recently reported affinity of PRK for another phosphorylated affinity label, the 2',3' dialdehyde derivative of ATP (oATP). As might be expected from the nature of the equilibrium established, there is not much difference between the equilibrium constants observed using either Ado-P_2-Pl or Ado-P_3-Pl (K_{eq} values of 10.4 and 8.5,respectively).

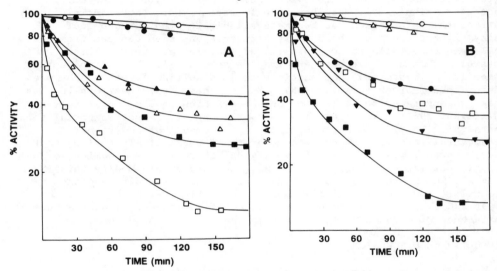

Fig. 1. Inactivation of spinach phosphoribulokinase by adenosine di- and tri-phosphopyridoxals. Activated enzyme was incubated in the dark for 5 min at 30°C in 100 mM HEPES (pH 7.5) containing 10 mM $MgCl_2$ and 0.5 mM DTT prior to addition of inhibitor. Aliquots were removed from the inactivation mixtures at the indicated times and quenched by addition of sodium borohydride (5 mM final concentration) prior to dilution (490 fold) into the assay mixture. In A, the curves are fit to data corresponding to the following concentrations of Ado-P_2-Pl: 0 (O), 25 (▲), 40 (△), 100 (■) or 180 uM(□). Protection against inactivation by ATP was evaluated by including 3 mM ATP in an inactivation mix that contained 180 uM inhibitor (●). In B, inactivation by Ado-P_3-Pl was investigated as described above; the panel depicts the data obtained using Ado-P_3-Pl at the following concentrations: 0 (O), 2.5 (●), 4 (□), 7(▼), or 25 uM (■). Protection against inactivation by ATP was evaluated by including 3.0 mM ATP in an inactivation mix that contained 25 uM inhibitor (△).

TABLE I

Inactivation of Spinach Leaf Phosphoribulokinase by ATP Analogs:
Summary of Kinetic and Binding Constants

Inhibitor	k_{inact}	K_i	K_{eq}
	(1/min)	(uM)	
Ado-P_2-Pl	-	175[a]	10.4[a]
Ado-P_3-Pl	-	11[a]	8.5[a]
oATP	0.07[b]	106[b]	-

[a]Values estimated by analysis of the data of Fig.1 a,b using the
method of Chen and Engel (1975).
[b]Values estimated from the inactivation kinetics data of Krieger and
Miziorko (1988).

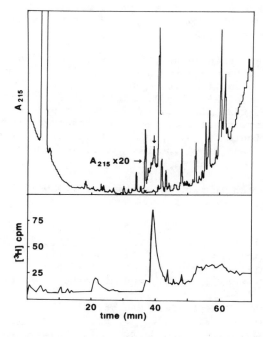

Fig. 2. Reverse phase HPLC fractionation of a tryptic digest of
Ado-P_3-[³H]Pl modified PRK. Sample (1.9 nmol)was loaded onto a
LiChrospher RP-18 column and eluted with a 0-70% gradient of CH_3CN in
0.1% trifluoroacetic acid. The top panel shows 215 nm absorbance, with
the inset depicting a 20-fold scale expansion to indicate (arrow) the
UV peak corresponding to the radiolabeled peptide. The bottom panel
shows the ³H profile measured using 10% of the column effluent.

<u>Affinity labeling of spinach leaf PRK by adenosine triphosphopyridoxal
results in selective modification of an active site lysine.</u> Specificity
of adduct formation is suggested by the ability of ATP to protect PRK
from inactivation (Figs. 1a, 1b) as well as by the stoichiometry of
inactivation. In experiments using the tight binding Ado-P_3-[^{3}H]Pl,
incorporation of 0.7 equivalents of radiolabeled inhibitor per site was
observed. Thus, a stable and specific adduct results from modification
of PRK with the adenosine polyphosphopyridoxals. Upon trypsinization
of the radiolabeled protein and mapping of the resulting peptides by
reverse phase HPLC, it is clear that one peptide is predominantly
radiolabeled (Fig. 2). Recovery of the radiolabeled peptide from the
HPLC effluent permits sequence analysis; the radioactively labeled
amino acid is recovered as the N-terminal residue of the isolated
undecapeptide. Comparison of the empirically determined peptide
sequence with the primary structure of spinach PRK (Milanez and Mural,
1988; Roesler and Ogren, 1988) indicates that the peptide corresponds
to residues 68-78, with lysine-68 being the target of the affinity
label. The occurrence of an arginine as residue 67 in PRK is compatible
with the sequence observed for this tryptic peptide. However, the
reason for the failure of trypsin to cleave after lysine-71 in the
modified enzyme remains unclear.

Lysine-68 is thirteen residues away from cys-55, but both of these
residues must be able to closely approach cys-16 in the native enzyme.
Cysteine-55 forms a disulfide with cys-16 to convert PRK into the
inactive form (Porter et al., 1988). Cys-16 and lys-68 are both targets
of adenosine analogs that affinity label PRK (Krieger et al., 1987;
this report) and must, therefore, be in reasonably close proximity.
These observations indicate that protein chemistry studies are steadily
improving our understanding of the PRK catalytic domain.

ACKNOWLEDGEMENT
This work was supported in part by a grant from USDA-CRGO.

REFERENCES

Chen, S.S. and Engel, P.C. (1975) Biochem. J. <u>149</u>, 627-635.
Krieger, T.J. and Miziorko, H.M. (1986) Biochemistry <u>25</u>, 3496-3501.
Krieger, T.J. and Miziorko, H.M. (1988) J. Cell Biol. <u>107</u>, 188a.
Krieger, T.J., Mende-Mueller, L.M., and Miziorko, H.M. (1987) Biochim.
  Biophys. Acta <u>915</u>, 112-119.
Milanez, S. and Mural, R.J. (1988) Gene <u>66</u>, 55-63.
Porter, M.A. and Hartman, F.C. (1988) J. Biol. Chem. <u>263</u>, 14846-14849.
Porter, M.A., Stringer, C.D., and Hartman, F.C. (1988) J. Biol. Chem.
  <u>263</u>, 123-129.
Roesler, K.R. and Ogren, W.L. (1988) Nucleic Acids Res. <u>16</u>, 7192 .
Tamura, J.K., Rakov, R.D., and Cross, R.L. (1986) J. Biol. Chem. <u>261</u>,
  4126-4133.

CATALASE IN AN AEROBIC PHOTOSYNTHETIC BACTERIUM, ERYTHROBACTER SP. OCH 114

MASAKAZU MORITA AND KEN-ICHIRO TAKAMIYA, DEPT. BIOL., FACL. SCI., KYUSHU UNIVERSITY, FUKUOKA 812, JAPAN

1. INTRODUCTION

Catalase, the enzyme which catalyzes the dismutation of hydrogen peroxide to molecular oxygen and water, is contained in both eukaryotes and prokaryotes. Most catalases isolated so far have common properties with respect to subunit composition, absorption spectra, pH dependence of the catalatic activity and inhibition by inhibitors. Recently catalases from a few bacteria, such as Rhodobacter capsulatus [1], Escherichia coli [2] and Comamomas compransoris [3], have shown to have different properties from those of typical catalases.

Erythrobacter sp. OCh 114 is an aerobic marine bacterium which has bacteriochlorophyll, reaction center complex and chromatophore structure, and shows photochemical reactions and photosynthetic ATP formation [4]. The latter two reactions take place either under aerobic conditions or under anaerobic conditions in the presence of auxiliary oxidants [4,5]. This suggests that optimal redox level for the photosynthetic electron transfer is maintained even under aerobic conditions. In this case peroxides such as hydrogen peroxide which may be produced under aerobic conditions must be enzymatically destroyed to avoid killing bacterial cells.

We purified a heme protein having catalatic activity together with cytochrome c peroxidase activity. Properties of the heme protein were similar to those from R. capsulatus, E. coli and C. compransoris.

2. MATERIALS AND METHODS

Purification of catalase

Aerobic photosynthetic bacterium, Erythrobacter sp. OCh 114 was grown in the light under aerobic conditions. Cells were collected and disrupted through French pressure cell. Disrupted cells were centrifuged at 300,000 x g for 3 h and the supernatant solution was obtained. From the supernatant solution, catalase was purified by ammonium sulfate fractionation (40-70 % saturation), DEAE-Sepharose CL-6B chromatography (about 0.2 M NaCl), Sephacryl S-300 gel filtration, butyl-TOYOPEARL hydrophobic chromatography (30→0 % saturation of ammonium sulfate) and cytochrome c-coupled Sepharose 4B affinity chromatography. The yield

M. Baltscheffsky (ed.), Current Research in Photosynthesis, Vol. IV, 91–94.

was about 3 % and catalase was purified about 170 folds.

3. RESULTS AND DISCUSSION

Physico-chemical properties

Purified catalase preparation showed a single band on polyacrylamide gel electrophoresis and sodium dodecylsulfate polyacrylamide gel electrophoresis (SDS-PAGE). Apparent molecular weight of catalase on SDS-PAGE was 75 kDa. Molecular weight estimated by HPLC of gel filtration was 145 kDa. These results indicated that the catalase was composed of two identical subunits as a dimer. This subunit composition was different from that of typical catalases which are usually composed of four identical subunits, combined molecular weight, 225,000 to 270,000. pI was 4.3. Figure 1 shows absorption spectra. Absorption maxima were at 280, 405, 500 and 630 nm at pH 8. Completely reduced form obtained by dithionite in an anaerobic cuvette had absorption maxima at 438 and 558 nm (Fig. 1). When the pH of the solution was incresed (pH~11) absorption bands of the reduced form became sharp (429, 553 and 562 nm). The reduced form was autooxidizable. Midpoint potential at pH 7 was -260 mV. α-Peak of pyridine ferrohemochrome was at 555 nm. These spectra indicated that catalase had a protoheme and iron atom of the heme was in the high spin state in the acidic and neutral pH range.

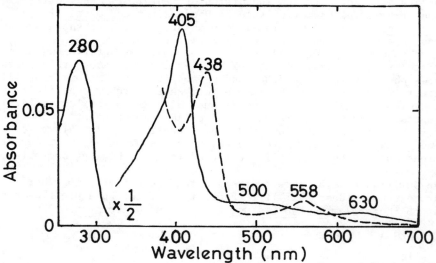

FIGURE 1. Absorption spectra of catalase of Erythrobacter sp. OCh 114. Catalase was dissolved in 50 mM Tricine-KOH buffer (pH 8.0). The concentration of the catalase was 0.59 μM. Dashed line, absorption spectrum of fully reduced form by dithionite in an anaerobic cuvette.

The addition of KCN to the catalase solution gave a spectrum with α-peak at 540 nm. CN-complexes of horse radish peroxidase and of cytochrome c peroxidase of yeast have absorption spectra with α-peak around 540 nm [6,7], whereas CN-complexes of typical catalases have α-peak at

554 nm. Thus catalase from this bacterium is different from the typical catalases with respect to the absorption spectrum of CN-complex.

Enzymatic properties

Catalase of this bacterium catalyzed O_2 production using H_2O_2 as a substrate. O_2 production was measured with a Clark type oxygen electrode at 25 °C. Catalase activity was determined by measuring the initial rate of O_2 production. pH Dependence of the activity is shown in Figure 2. Maximal activity was obtained around pH 8. Unlike typical catalases, whose activity was pH independent between pH 5 and 11, activity decreased below pH 7 and above pH 10. This pH dependence was similar to that of catalases from R. capsulatus [1], E. coli [2] and C. compransoris [3]. The catalatic activity was inhibited by CN⁻, N_3^- and NH_2OH. Some enzymatic properties of the catalase are summarized in Table 1. K_m value and molecular activity were similar to those of typical catalases.

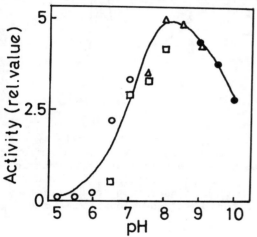

FIGURE 2. pH Dependence of catalase activity.

O , Mes-KOH; ☐ , Mops-KOH; △ , Tricine-KOH; ● , Ches-KOH. 5 of the relative activity corresponds to 5 mmoles O_2 produced per mg protein per min.

TABLE 1. Some enzymatic properties of Erythrobacter sp. OCh 114 catalase

		I_{50} (µM)	
pH optimum	8.0		
K_m for H_2O_2 (mM)	9		
Molecular activity		KCN	6
for H_2O_2	5.8×10^6	NaN$_3$	110
		NH$_2$OH	2.5

The catalase had a cytochrome c peroxidase activity (Fig. 3). In the time course (A), in the presence of both reduced horse heart cytochrome c (5.7 nmoles) and catalase, addition of H_2O_2 (500 nmoles) only partially (c and d) oxidized and finally (e) reduced cytochrome c. This indicated that added H_2O_2 was more rapidly consumed by catalatic activity than peroxidase activity. Exact value of peroxidase activity could not be determined because of the competitive utilization of H_2O_2 with catalase.

In conclusion, catalase of Erythrobacter sp. OCh 114 is different from typical catalases with respect to reducibility by dithionite, absorption spectrum of CN-complex, narrow pH optimum and cytochrome c peroxidase activity. These properties are similar to those of catalases of R. capsulatus, E. coli and C. compransoris. Thus catalase of Erythrobacter sp. OCh 114 may be classified to new type catalase as proposed previously [1].

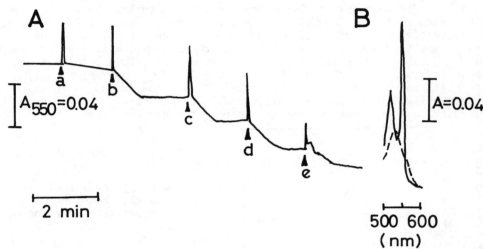

FIGURE 3. A. Time course of oxidation of cytochrome c by cytochrome c peroxidase activity. Reaction mixture contained 50 mM Tris-HCl buffer (pH 7.5), and 5.7 μM ferrocytochrome c. Arrow a indicates the addition of 500 nmoles of H_2O_2. b, addition of 1.5 μg of catalase. c,d and e, further addition of 500 nmoles of H_2O_2. B. Absorption spectra of the reaction mixture before (——) and after (----) addition of H_2O_2 and catalase.

REFERENCES

1 Nadler, V., Goldberg, I. and Hochman, A. (1986) **Biochim. Biophys.** Acta 882, 234-241
2 **Claiborne**, A. and Fridovich, I. (1979) J. Biol. Chem. 254, 4245-4252
3 Nies, D. and Schlegel, H.G. (1982) J. Gen. Appl. Microbiol. 28, 311-319
4 Okamura, K., Takamiya, K. and Nishimura, M. (1985) Arch. Microbiol. 142, 12-17
5 Takamiya, K., Arata, H., Shioi, Y. and Doi, M. (1988) Biochim. Biophys. Acta 935, 26-33
6 Keilin, D. and Hartree, E.F. (1951) Biochem. J. 49, 88-104
7 Yonetani, T., Wilson, D.F. and Seamond, R. (1966) J. Biol. Chem. 241, 5347-5352

ACKNOWLEDGEMENT

We are grateful to Professor M. Nishimura (Kyushu University) for valuable discussions and suggestions during this study.

IMMUNOCYTOCHEMICAL LOCALIZATION OF THE ELECTRON CARRIER PROTEINS FERREDOXIN-NADP$^+$OXIDOREDUCTASE AND CYTOCHROME c 553 IN THE N$_2$-FIXING CYANOBACTERIUM Anabaena variabilis

A.SERRANO, P.GIMENEZ, S.SCHERER and P.BÖGER
Lehrstuhl für Physiologie und Biochemie der Pflanzen, Universität Konstanz, Postfach 5560, D-7750 Konstanz (F.R.G.)

1. INTRODUCTION

The proteins ferredoxin-NADP$^+$oxidoreductase (FNR) and cytochrome c553 (cyt c553) are components of both the photosynthetic and the respiratory electron transport chains in cyanobacteria (blue-green algae). It is well established that the main physiological function of the flavoenzyme FNR is the reduction of NADP$^+$ using photosystem I reduced ferredoxin, being, therefore, the last component of the photosynthetic transport chain (1). However, it has been demonstrated very recently that this protein also operates in Anabaena variabilis as a respiratory NADPH-dehydrogenase coupled with KCN-sensitive phosphorylation (2). The cyanobacterial cyt c553 is a fairly abundant soluble non-autooxidizable c-type cytochrome of low molecular mass (about 11 kD) which seems to be widespread among the microalgae but is unknown in higher plants (3). With membranes of Anabaena both cyt c553 (from the same species) and horse heart cyt c effectively donate electrons to both P700 (in the light) and cytochrome oxidase (3,4). Using membrane preparations of Anabaena sp. 7119 Stürzl et al. (5) restored electron flow from water to NADP$^+$ in the light and from NAD(P)H to O$_2$ in the dark by adding Anabaena sp. 7119 cyt c553, which accepted electrons from the cytochrome b$_6$/f complex. Since an antibody against this cyt c553 inhibited not only photosynthetic but also respiratory electron transport in these membrane preparations (6), this protein could be considered the native donor for cytochrome oxidase. There are, therefore, common links between respiration and photosynthesis in cyanobacteria. But, whereas photosynthetic electron transport seems to be located exclusively in the thylakoids, there is still some controversy concerning the site of respiratory electron transport. In this report, the in situ location of the electron carrier proteins FNR and cyt c553 is investigated for the first time in a cyanobacterium using transmission electron microscopy and immunocytochemical techniques.

2. MATERIALS AND METHODS

2.1. Organism and growth. A. variabilis ATCC 29143 was growth under dinitrogen-fixing conditions at 30°C in continuous light as described (2) and harvested 2 days after inoculation (late logarithmic phase). Chlorophyll a was determined in methanol at 665 nm (2). Protein content was measured using the Bio-Rad (Munich, F.R.G.) protein assay.

2.2. Protein purification and antibody preparation. FNR from A. variabilis was purified to homogeneity using a procedure based on the use of

affinity chromatography on 2¦5'-ADP-Sepharose 4B (2,7). Polyclonal antibodies against the purified FNR were raised in rabbits (2). Polyclonal
antibodies against cyt c553 purified to homogeneity from Anabaena sp.
7119 were obtained as previously described (6). The antisera were used
either directly or after $(NH_4)_2SO_4$ fractionation with similar results.
2.3. Western blotting. Both FNR and cyt c553 from A. variabilis were detected immunologically, either in purified preparations or in cell-free
extracts, by Western blot analysis of SDS-PAGE (15% acrylamide) gels.
Cross-reactivity of the antibody against Anabaena sp. 7119 cyt c553
with the same protein from A. variabilis and specificity of both antisera were demonstrated.
2.4. Fixation, embedding and immunocytochemical labelling. A.variabilis
filaments were fixed in glutaraldehyde (2.5%;w/v), dehydrated in ethyl
alcohol (30-100%) and embedded in resin Epon 312. Upon sectioning, ul-
trathin sections were mounted on Formvard-coated gold or nickel grids
(200 mesh). The sections were etched in a 10% aqueous solution of H_2O_2
for 10 min; washed in PBS (20 mM phosphate buffer, pH 7.4, and 0.9%
NaCl); incubated for 1 h in PBS supplemented with 5% newborn calf serum,
0.2% Tween-20 and 0.5 M NaCl (PBS/ST); incubated for 2 h in the antiserum diluted 1:10 or 1:20 in PBS/ST; washed in PBS/ST; incubated for 2 h
in goat anti-rabbit IgG conjugated with 10 nm gold particles (Janssen,
Belgium) diluted 1:20 (v/v) in PBS/ST; washed in PBS/ST, in distilled
water and finally air-dried. Sections were stained with 4% aqueous uranyl acetate for 2 h and lead citrate for 5 min. The sections were studied with a Zeiss 9S TEM operating at an acceleration voltage of 60 kV.
2.5. Tris-EDTA treatment. The cells were harvested, washed twice in 50
mM Tris-HCl, pH 8, 30 mM NaCl and resuspended, at a chlorophyll concentration of 0.8-1 μmol/ml, in the same buffer containing 40 mM EDTA.Na$_2$,
0.5 M sucrose and 2 mM PMSF. During incubation with gentle agitation at
30°C aliquots were withdrawn and, after rapid centrifugation, supernatants were used for protein measurements and for the spectrophotometric
determinations of both phycocyanin (A_{620}) and -after $(NH_4)_2SO_4$ fractionation (70%)- cyt c553(5). Total content of cyt c553 in untreated cells
was estimated after disruption by ultrasonic treatment.

3. RESULTS AND DISCUSSION
It has been demonstrated that the antigenicity of the cyanobacterial
cell material is retained when using conventional Epon embedding (8).
Therefore, we have used this procedure to investigate the in situ location of the electron carrier proteins FNR and cyt c553 in both vegetative cells and heterocysts of the cyanobacterium A. variabilis using the
antibody gold technique carried out as a post-embedding immunoelectron
microscopy procedure. The results of the immunogold labelling experiments in the two cell types, namely vegetative cells and heterocysts,
present in N_2-fixing A. variabilis filaments are shown in Fig.1. Gold
labelling of FNR resulted in vegetative cells in a scattering of gold
particles in the thylakoid region, located in the cytoplasm periphery
and characterized by glycogen accumulations which are visible in thin
sections as electron transparent irregular dots (9)(Fig.1A). Few gold
particles are observed in the "centroplasm" which contains the DNA and
no label is located in the cytoplasmic membrane. The cellular localiza-

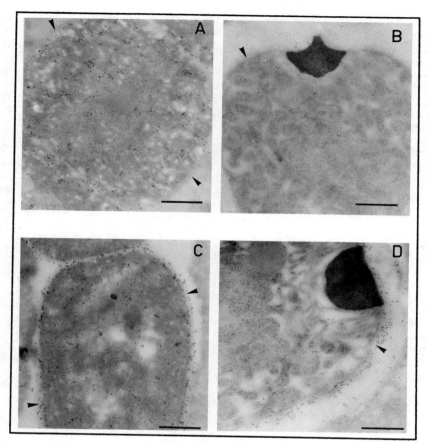

FIGURE 1. Immunogold labelling of FNR (A,B) and cyt c553 (C,D) in vegetative cells (A,C) and heterocysts (B,D) of A. variabilis. Note that
only in the case of cyt c553 a significant labelling is observed near
the cytoplasmic membrane and the periplasmic area (arrows). Bar markers
represent 0.5 µm.

tion of the FNR in A. variabilis vegetative cells is, as these results
suggest, consistent with the well established role of this enzyme in
photosynthesis. Comparatively, very little labelling is found in heterocysts (Fig.1B). Since in Western blots the antibody recognized specifically a polypeptide of 35 kD (apparent mol.mass of FNR) in extracts
of both cell types, it is probably the heterocystous environment, and
not the FNR protein itself, that makes this enzyme barely detectable in
situ. In this respect it is interesting to note that: 1)heterocysts do
not perform oxygenic photosynthesis but exhibit an intense respiratory
activity (3,4), and 2)only a very small inhibition of NADPH-dependent
O_2-uptake of Anabaena thylakoids is achieved with FNR antibodies (2).
Since we have obtained an intense specific labelling of heterocysts

using an anti-nitrogenase reductase serum (Reicher et al., unpublished) the existence of metodological problems with these cells can be ruled out. One can speculate that an special association of the FNR with other cell components, perhaps also involved in respiration, occurs in the heterocyst so that the in situ interaction with the antibody is severely restricted. In contrast, when using the anti-cyt c553 specific serum a clear distribution of gold particles near the cytoplasmic membrane and the periplasmic area is observed in both vegetative cells (Fig.1C) and heterocysts (Fig.1D) although vegetative cell thylakoids appear also labelled. As in the case of the FNR, specific labelling was absent when preimmune sera were used. Since it has been reported that most of bacterial cytochromes of c-type so far studied are located in the periplasmic area, we have applied a treatment with Tris and EDTA as a method to release periplasmic proteins (10). The selective release of most of the cell amount of A. variabilis cyt c553 during this treatment (60-70%, when only 1-2% of either total protein or phycocyanin was released) is consistent with a periplasmic localization of part of the cyt c molecules, being, therefore, in agreement with gold labelling experiments. The cyt c553 associated in situ with thylakoids should be involved in photosynthesis and probably also in respiration (3). The physiological role for periplasmic A. variabilis cyt c553 is more difficult to explain, but since a cytochrome oxidase has been recently reported to be located in the cytoplasmic membrane of this cyanobacterium (11), a role as electron donor for this enzyme cannot be ruled out. Finally, one can speculate on a role of periplasmic cyt c553 of heterocysts in the so-called respiratory protection of the O_2-labile enzyme nitrogenase, a protection that should be very efficient if the proteins involved in the process were located at the cell periphery, i.e. in the periplasmic area.

ACKNOWLEDGEMENTS. A.S. was recipient of a Research Fellowship of the A. v. Humboldt Foundation for a leave to the University of Konstanz. The authors thank Prof. W. Rathmayer for providing electron microscopy facilities. This work was supported by the Deutsche Forschungsgemeinschaft.

REFERENCES
1 Böger P.(1979)In Encyclopedia of Plant Physiology (Gibbs M. and Latzko E.,eds.), vol.6, pp.399-409, Springer-Verlag, Berlin
2 Scherer S.,Alpes I.,Sadowski H. and Böger P.(1988) Arch.Biochem.Biophys. 267,228-235
3 Scherer S.,Almon H. and Böger P.(1988) Photosynth.Res. 15,95-114
4 Peschek G.A.(1987)In The Cyanobacteria (Fay P. and Van Baalen C.,eds.) pp.119-161, Elsevier, Amsterdam
5 Stürzl E.,Scherer S. and Böger P.(1982) Photosynth.Res. 3,191-201
6 Alpes I.,Stürzl E.,Scherer S. and Böger P.(1984) Z.Naturforsch. 36c, 623-627
7 Serrano A. and Rivas J.(1982) Anal.Biochem. 126,109-115
8 Bergman B.,Lindblad P.,Petterson A.,Renström E. and Tiberg E.(1985) Planta 166,329-334
9 Stanier(Cohen-Bazire) G.(1988) Methods in Enzymology 167,157-172
10 Ferguson F.J.(1988)In Bacterial Energy Transduction (Anthony C.,ed.), pp.151-182, Academic Press, London
11 Wastyn M.,Achatz A.,Molitor V. and Peschek G.A.(1988) Biochim.Biophys.Acta 935,217-224

A SOLUBLE POLYSACCHARIDE FRACTION FROM HIGHER PLANTS: A POSSIBLE
PHYSIOLOGICAL SUBSTRATE OF THE CYTOSOLIC PHOSPHORYLASE ISOZYME

Yi Yang[1], Burkhard Greve[1], Martin Steup[1] and Elmar W. Weiler[2]
Botanisches Institut der Westfälischen Wilhelms-Universität Münster,
D-4400 Münster, FRG (1); Lehrstuhl für Pflanzenphysiologie, Ruhr-
Universität Bochum, D-4630 Bochum 1, FRG (2)

1. INTRODUCTION
    In higher plants several ∝-glucan metabolizing enzymes occur as
plastid- and cytosol-specific isozymes (1,2). The dual intracellular
location of these enzyme activities suggests that both the plastidic and
the cytosolic compartment contain a pool of polysaccharides. However,
until now a cytosolic starch-like polysaccharide which functions as the
physiological carbohydrate substrate of the cytosol-specific isozymes
has not been identified and, therefore, the metabolic function of these
enzyme forms remains enigmatic.
    The cytosolic and the plastidic forms of glucan phosphorylase (E.C.
2.4.1.1) differ strikingly in some kinetic properties, especially in
glucan specificities. The plastidic enzyme form has a high affinity towards low molecular weight glucans, such as maltodextrins, but its affinity towards highly branched polyglucans, such as glycogen, is extremely low. In contrast, the cytosolic phosphorylase isozyme has a relatively low affinity towards maltodextrins but its affinity towards high molecular weight glucans is high and exceeds that of the muscle phosphorylase (1). Based on these kinetic properties it is reasonable to assume that the in-vivo substrate of the cytosolic phosphorylase isozyme
is a high molecular weight compound.
    In this communication a water-soluble polysaccharide fraction is de-
scribed which has been isolated from photoautotrophic and from heterotrophic organs of Pisum sativum. This high molecular weight carbohydrate
fraction interacts strongly and preferentially with the cytosolic phosphorylase form. Interaction has been demonstrated by affinity electrophoresis, by kinetic studies and by ^{14}C-labeling experiments. For an
immunological characterization monoclonal antibodies directed against
the carbohydrate fraction were applied.

2. PROCEDURE
2.1 Materials and methods
    2.1.1. Plant material: Pea plants (Pisum sativum L. var. 'Kleine
           Rheinländerin') were grown under controlled conditions (3) or
           in the Botanical Garden of the Institute.
    2.1.2. Isolation procedures: The polysaccharide fraction was isola-
           ted from cotyledons of seeds or from fully expanded leaflets.
           The entire procedure consists of four steps: homogenization
           of plant material, deproteinization of the homogenate, de-
           ionization of the extract, and size fractionation. The poly-

saccharide fraction was stored frozen.
Cytosol- and plastid–specific phosphorylase isozymes from
Pisum sativum were purified as previously described (4).

2.1.3. Analytical techniques: The apparent molecular weight of the
isolated polysaccharide fraction was determined by gel filtration (HPLC). Dextrans were used as standards.
Following acid hydrolysis the monosaccharide composition of
the carbohydrate fraction was determined by HPLC or by thin-
layer chromatography.

2.1.4. Enzyme activity assays: Phosphorolytic activity of phosphorylase isozymes was determined as previously described (3).
Glucan synthesizing activity was monitored continuously as
orthophosphate liberation using a modification of the procedure of Fossati (5).

2.1.5. Electrophoresis: Affinity electrophoresis (discontinuous system, 7% w/v total monomer concentration in the separation
gel) was performed as previously described (6).

2.1.6. Immunological techniques: For production of monoclonal antibodies and immunoassays standard techniques were applied.

3. RESULTS AND DISCUSSION

A water–soluble carbohydrate fraction was isolated from cotyledons
of germinating pea seeds or from leaves. As determined by gel filtration
the apparent molecular weight was higher than 10^6. No low molecular
weight compounds were detectable in the preparation. Following acid
hydrolysis several monosaccharides, including glucose, were recovered.
Therefore, the polysaccharide fraction does not represent a homoglucan.

In order to investigate a possible physiological function of the
carbohydrate fraction its interaction with compartment–specific phosphorylase isozymes was studied by affinity electrophoresis and kinetic
measurements.

For affinity electrophoresis varying concentrations of a polysaccharide fraction which had been isolated from cotyledons were immobilized
in a polyacrylamide gel. Equal volumes of a pea leaflet extract were applied to each tube. Following electrophoresis and phosphorylase activity
staining, the migration distance of each phosphorylase form, relative
to that of bromophenol blue, was determined (Fig. 1). At increasing polysaccharide concentrations the migration velocity of the cytosolic phosphorylase isozyme decreased markedly whereas the retardation of the two
chloroplast isozymes was minor. This indicates that the cytosolic phosphorylase isozyme exhibits a much higher affinity towards the immobilized polysaccharide than the plastidic enzyme forms.

This conclusion was confirmed by kinetic measurements. Preparations
of purified cytosolic and plastidic phosphorylase isozymes from Pisum
sativum were adjusted to an approximately equal activity concentration
(as determined at saturating levels of soluble starch). Using these
isozyme preparations kinetic measurements were performed at varying
levels of the polysaccharide fraction. Orthophosphate or glucose 1–phosphate levels were saturating. The initial rates of phosphorolysis
(Fig. 2A) or of polysaccharide biosynthesis (Fig. 2B) were determined.

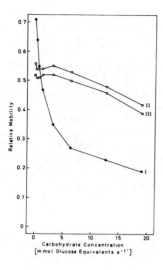

FIGURE 1. Affinity electrophoresis of
a pea leaflet extract. Separation gels
contained varying concentrations of a
polysaccharide fraction isolated from
cotyledons. For quantification, an aliquot of the polysaccharide fraction was
subjected to acid hydrolysis and the
monosaccharide content was monitored.
Cytosolic isozyme: I
Plastidic isozymes: II and III

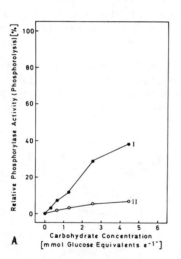

A

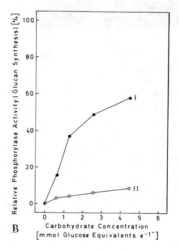

B

FIGURE 2A and 2B. Polysaccharide–dependent phosphorolysis (A) or
biosynthesis (B) catalyzed by purified cytosolic (I) or plastidic
(II) isozymes from Pisum sativum. Rates are given as percent of
the values obtained at saturatin concentrations os soluble starch.
Quantification of the polysaccharide concentrations as in Fig. 1

The polysaccharide fraction functioned as substarte for phosphorolysis and as primer for biosynthesis. However, for the cytosolic isozyme by far higher initial rates were obtained than with the plastid-specific enzyme form.

The priming capacity of the polysaccharide fraction was confirmed by labeling experiments. Incubation of the purified cytosolic phosphorylase isozyme with the polysaccahride fraction and ^{14}C-glucose 1-phosphate resulted in an effective incorporation of labeled glucosyl residues into the high molecular weight polysaccharide (data not shown).

For an immunological characterization monoclonal antibodies were produced using a polysaccharide from cotyledons as immunogen. Positive hybridoma cell lines cross-reacted with various polysaccharide preparations, including those from pea and spinach leaves. However, no cross-reaction with homoglucans, such as glycogen or starch, was observed (Fig. 3).

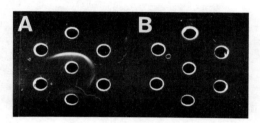

FIGURE 3A and B. Ouchterlony double diffusion assay of a serial dilution of a polysaccharide preparation (A) or soluble starch (B). Central hole: antibody.

These results were confirmed by ELISA and by competition experiments. These immunological data support the conclusion that the polysaccharide fraction which interacts preferentially with the cytosolic phosphorylase isozyme represents a non-starch like macromolekule although it contains α-1,4-linked glucosyl residues.

REFERENCES
1. Steup, M. (1988) Biochemistry of Plants 14, 255-296
2. Beck, E. and Ziegler, P. (1989) Annu. Rev. Plant Physiol. Plant Mol. Biol. 40, 95-117
3. Steup, M. and Latzko, E. (1979) Planta 145, 69-75
4. Conrads, J., van Berkel, J., Schächtele, C. and Steup, M. (1986) Biochim. Biophys. Acta 882, 452-463
5. Fossati, P. (1985) Analyt. Biochem. 149, 62-65
6. Steup, M., Schächtele, C. and Melkonian, M. (1986) Physiol. Plant. 66, 234-244

THE EFFECT OF PHOTOSYNTHESIS ON DIFFERENT STEPS OF DARK RESPIRATION

Natasha Mamushina, Helene Zubkova and Ludmila Filippova

Laboratory of Photosynthesis, Komarov Botanical Institute, 197022, Leningrad, USSR

INTRODUCTION

The physiological and biochemical studies of the interaction of photosynthesis and dark respiration in the light give conflicting conclusions. It should be stressed that the most of these investigations were carried out on different green plant material (algae, protoplasts or whole leaves), where oxidative pentose phosphate pathway (OPPP), glycolysis, Krebs cycle oxidative phosphorylation were studied separetely (1,2,3,4,5,6). No attempts have been made to consider the interaction of different steps of dark respiration during photosynthesis on the one plant under constant conditions. We have accordingly investigated the major dark respiration reactions – OPPP, glycolysis and Kreb cycle – on the leaves of different plants under conditions optimal photosynthesis by means of specific exogenous labelled substrates.

MATERIALS AND METHODS

Plant material. Barley seedlings (Hordeum vulgare L.) grown in a greenhouse under natural light during 9 days in pots with soil. The one part of barley grains prior to sowing were exposed to streptomycin (2.5 mg ml^{-1}) for 48 hr to obtain partially albinic leaves.

Ephemeroid (Ficaria verna Huds) and poplar (Populus balsamifera L.) were grown in the natural conditions in the Garden of Botanical Institute.

Experimental procedure. Investigation of OPPP, glycolysis and the Krebs cycle was undertaken by means of specific exogenous ^{14}C-substrates – 1,6 – ^{14}C-glucose (0,1 mM, 20 MBq), 1,4 – ^{14}C-malate or 2-^{14}C-pyruvate (0,1 mM-0,2 mM, 20 MBq, Firm "Isotop", USSR). This method is not a new one, but in our experiments we put the slices of leaf after the preincubation with ^{14}C-substrates in air with high concentration of CO_2 – 1% to avoid the external reassimilation of $^{14}CO_2$ in the light and to decrease the stomatal resistance. About the work of OPPP, glycolysis and the Krebs cycle we judged on the basis of the rate of $^{14}CO_2$ evolution during the oxidation specific substrate if the total uptake of substrate was identical in the light and in the darkness.Leaves were cut out into slices (about 1sm^{-2}) which were placed in flusks with 50 ml^{-1} soltuion of labelled$_2$ substrates and shaked during 10 min in the light 350wt/m^{-2},25 C.After that these slices were put into leaf chambers which were held in darkness or in the light.Air with 1% CO_2 was passed through the chambers at 30l/hour^{-1}. CO_2+$^{14}CO_2$ evolved was absorbed by 10% NAOH(three glass ab-sorbers in series,total volume solution 150 ml^{-1}).Comple-tness of $^{14}CO_2$ absorption was checked.After exposition the slices were washed carefully and fixed by ethanol.

Water-ethanol soluble substances were extracted from leaf material by (7),the insoluble material was fractio-nated into starch and residual components by (8).The to-tal summary of radioactivity of different fractions indi-cated on the value of uptake of ^{14}C-substrates by leaf.

The radioactivity of samples was measured by liquid scintillation with toluene+POPOP or with Triton X-100 (Isocap-300).Counting efficiencies,determined via the cha-nnel ratio method and quench correction curve,were suffi-ciently constant (about 70-80%).Gas exchange measurements of respiration of leaf were conducted by manometric tech-nique(9).It was found that the chosen concentrations of exogenous substrates had no effect on dark respiration of leaves studied plants.

All experiments were performed at least 3-4 times,and the analyses within experiment were made in triplicate.

RESULTS AND DISCUSSION

It was found that during oxidation of ^{14}C-glucose by green barly leaves the quantity of $^{14}CO_2$ evolved in the light was significantly less than that in darkness(Fig.1). The total uptake of ^{14}C-glucose by leaves in the light was some greater than in darkness.There could be three expla-nations of this fact:1) or a great part of evolved $^{14}CO_2$ in the light was reassimilated during photosynthesis; 2)or an inhibition of OPPP and glycolysis took place;3) iether the Krebs cycle was not limited and OPPP,glycoly-sis were inhibited in the light. If so, a question arises - the light per se or photosynthesis are responsible for limitations of these reaction of dark respiration? We tri-ed to give answer on this question by meanes of investi-gation of respiration and oxidation of ^{14}C-substrates on albino areas of primary bar-ley leaf. It was shown that uptake of ^{14}C-glucose and ^{14}C-malate in the albino party was stimulated.The rate of re-spiration was 1.5 times as great as that corresponding green areas of control leaves. The production of $^{14}CO_2$ at both

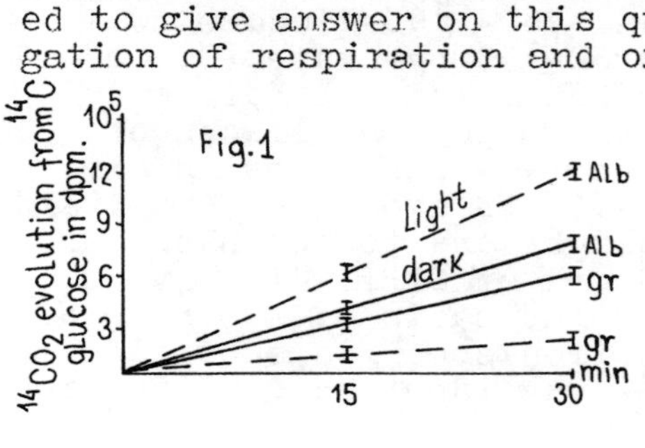

Fig.1

[14]C-glucose and ^{14}C-malate oxidation was greater in the
light than in darkness in albino part of leaves(Fig.1,2).

It is concluded that in albino tissues OPPP and glycolysis and the Krebs cycle are stimulated by the light,where-
as in the green tissues of the leaf OPPP and glycolysis
are depressed in the light,but the Krebs cycle works with
the same rate in light and darkness. On the basis of these investigations it is assumed that photosynthesis itself
but not light per se exersises a controlling influence on
these reactions of dark respiration.

It was discussed various mechanisms of inhibition of
OPPP and glycolysis during photosynthesis(1,10,11). We suggest that the main one is the competition in cytosol of
green cell for ADP,P_i,NAD,NADP between energy giving steps
of glycolysis,OPPP and specific shuttles of chloroplasts
which are responsible for transport enrggy equivalents.
The proplastids of albino tisaues have no capacity for
photophosphorylation that relives inhibition of glycolysis and OPPP in the light.

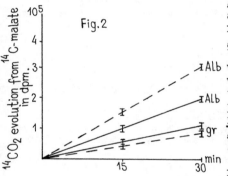

Fig.2

It is proposed also that a regulating influence of this mechanism on dark respiration depends on the level of labour in
green cell(11,12).Indeed it can
be admitted that during the growth of green leaf this mechanism
would not be worked.We checked
this idea on growing leaves of
poplar and the ephemeroid Ficaria verna which exercised the
growth programme during a very
short period in spring.

It is appeared that there is
no decrease of [14]CO$_2$ production
from ^{14}C-glucose in the light
in growing leaves of poplar,but
in the adult leaves we observe
another situation (Fig.3)

It let us to make a conclusion that there is no inhibition
of OPPP and glycolysis in the
light during the growth of poplar leaf.

As concerns with Ficaria verna (Table 1) it was found that
the rate of [14]CO$_2$ evolution from ^{14}C-glucose was the same in
the light and darkness,and there was a stimulation of [14]CO$_2$
production from ^{14}C-pyruvate in
the light during the all stages

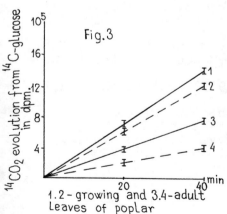

1.2 - growing and 3.4-adult
Leaves of poplar

Fig.3

Table 1

Date	^{14}C-glucose		^{14}C-pyruvate	
	light	darkness	light	darkness
26.04	6.5±0.3	6.0±0.1	6.6±0.5	5.3±0.5
18.05	3.7±0.4	4.3±0.2	14.0±0.8	6.2±0.6
5.06	4.3±0.2	3.7±0.6	4.8±0.7	2.1±0.3

(^{14}CO$_2$ in dpm.10^5, exposition 40 min)

of ontogenes- is of plant. It seems likely from these data that photosynthesis does not limite OPPP and glycolysis in leaves of <u>Ficaria verna</u>, moreover the Krebs Cycle is stimulated in the light. It is difficult to explain these facts, perhaps it is connected with the specific biology of ephemeroids. It should be stressed that the Krebs cycle was not limited in the light in each plants under investigation. It seems that continued operation of Krebs cycle is required in the light for the production of carbon intermediates which are not produce by chloroplasts.

In conclusion we should remark that it is not possible to give a general answer to the question about the inhibition of dark respiration and its different steps in the light. It depends on the type of plant or on the age of leaf.

REFERENCES

1 Graham, D. (1980) in The Biochemistry of Plants (Davis, D. ed.) v 2, pp.526-575, Academic Press, New York
2 Moyse, A. (1982) Bull.Soc.Bot.Fr., 129, Act.Bot., 53-72
3 Stitt, M., Lilley, R., Heldt, H. (1982) Plant Physiol., 70, 971-977
4 Singh, P., Naik, M. (1984) FEBS LETTERS, 65, 145-149
5 Gardestrom, P. (1987) FEBS LETTERS, 212, 114-118
6 McCachin, B., Cossins, E., Canvin, D. (1988) Plant Physiol., 87, 155-161
7 Bassham, J., Calvin, M. (1957) The path of carbon in photosynthesis. Prentice-Hall, NewJersey, 104p.
8 Voznesensky, V., Zalensky, O., Semikhatova, O. (1965) The methods of investigation photosynthesis and respiration of plants. Moskow. Hauka, 305p.
9 Semikhatova, O., Chulanovskaya, M., Metzner, H., (1971) in Plant photosynthetic production. Manual of methods. (Sestac, Z., ed.), Hague, 238-256
10 Ried, A., Setlik, I., Berkova, E. (1973) Photosynthetica, 7, 161-176
11 Raven, J. (1976) in The Intact Chloroplast (Barber, J., ed.), Vol.1, pp.403-443, Elsevier, Amsterdam
12 Fillipova, L., Mamushina, N., Zubkova, E., Miroslavov, E., Kudinova, G. (1986) Fisiol.Rast.(USSR), 33, 66-73

PHOTOSYNTHESIS AS A THERMAL PROCESS

G.G. Komissarov
Institute of Chemical Physics, Academy of Sciences
of the USSR, Moscow, the USSR

As it is generally known (see any textbook on photosynthesis) thermal energy is a useless waste of photosynthesis. Intensive process is characterised by accumulation, as the photosynthesis products, of but 0.5-5% of light energy absorbed while about 95% of energy is transformated into heat. Are these 95% necessary for the plant functioning? The photosynthetic organisms exist billions years on Earth. It is very difficult to suggest that they would not adapt themselves to the efficient light utilisation. The hypothesis has been put forward by the author in 1973 according to which thermal energy is an essential participant of the photosynthetic process / 1,2 /.

The present report summarises the data supporting this hypothesis. The initial substances which take part in photosynthesis (CO_2, H_2O) are chemically inert. Thus the ionisation potential of carbon dioxide (higher oxidation form of carbon) is 13.7 ev and the affinity to electron is 3.8 ev.

However it is necessary to take into consideration that photosynthesis proceeds in aqueous phase and besides the water is subjected to dissosiation (H_2O + 57.5 kJ $-\!-\!\rightarrow$ H^+ + + OH^-). This process requires thermal energy supply. It is necessary to note that the energy of water formation from elements is equal to 237 kJ/M and that for OH^- is equal to 158 kJ/M. Thus the energy required for the decomposition of hydroxyl ions would be by 80 kJ less than that for decomposition of H_2O_{liq}. Analogous situation holds for CO_2. So the reaction CO_2 + OH^- $-\!-\!\rightarrow$ HCO_3^- needs the activation energy of about 54 kJ/M.

Thus thermal energy is to be consumed at "preliminary" stages of photosynthesis to generate the corresponding ions which undergo light-induced transpormations.

According to contemporary data on the oxygen formation in physico-chemical systems and upon photosynthesis the pathway of oxygen formation in a chloroplast may be represent-

M. Baltscheffsky (ed.), Current Research in Photosynthesis, Vol. IV, 107–110.
© 1990 Kluwer Academic Publishers. Printed in the Netherlands.

ed as follows:

$$CH_a^- + p \longrightarrow OH_a^\bullet \quad (1) \qquad\qquad 2OH_a^\bullet \longrightarrow H_2O_{2a} \quad (2)$$

$$H_2O_{2a} \longrightarrow H_a^+ + HO_{2a}^- \quad (3) \qquad HO_{2a}^- + p \rightarrow HO_{2a}^\bullet \quad (4)$$

$$HO_2^\bullet \longrightarrow H^+ + O_{2a}^- \quad (5) \qquad\qquad O_{2a}^- + p \longrightarrow O_2 \quad (6)$$

The letter "a" means that the particles are connected with the pigment molecules by adsorption forces.
In accordance with this scheme four photons at least, each generation the electron-nole pair, are required to obtaine one molecule of oxygen. Due to spatial proximily and high recombination constant value for hydroxy-radicals ($\sim 10^{-9}$ l/M·s) the formation of the relatively "safe" compound (H_2O_2) is quite probable (see reaction 2) / 3,4 /. It follows from this scheme that there are both light reactions (1,4,6) and dark ones (2,3,5) with dark dissosiation of products obtained. It permits to explain the Joliot's / 5/ and Kok's / 6 / experiments without using the notions on the increase in the oxidation degree of a reaction centre. The important peculiarity of **the suggested scheme** ($OH^- \rightarrow$ $\rightarrow H_2O_2 \longrightarrow HO_2^- \longrightarrow O_2^- \longrightarrow O_2$) is the fact that IR-irradiation should affect the maxima position in the oxygen formation under pulsed illumination of the photosynthesising objects with white light. It was confirmed in our preliminary experiments / 7 /. The chlorella cells or chloroplasts were subjected to IR-illumination and then exposed to a series of 40 intensity-saturating white light flashes. Xenon lamp with glass filters for non-stop IR-illumination was used. Pulse lamp permits to obtain the intensity-saturating light flashes (flash duration is $2\,\mu s$). Oxygen was quantitated by pulse amperometric method (the sensitivity of the oxygen registration is 10^{-12} moles per flash). It was shown that a non-stop IR-illumination ($\lambda \geqslant$ 850 nm) results in the change of the kinetics of the pulse oxygen formation and the shift of the first maximum position by one time to the left.
As it is known from literature data, the temperature of the plant leaves may be by $10°$ and more degrees higher than ambient one. Hence the temperature of the chloroplast which in this case plays the role of the "heat element" for the leaf, would be even higher. How much higher? Attempts were made to estimate the temperature within the chloroplast and we found the temperature inside the selected volume to be 70-80°C. The solution of the thermal conductivity equation gives the relaxation time equal to $5 \cdot 10^{-6}$ s. If the leaf cell contains 10 chloroplasts it would be heated to 38°C according to our calculations. It is necessary to note that the temperature increase within the chloroplast may be connected with the recombination of radicals forming during the photosynthesis. What are the consequences of the temperature increase within chloro-

plast by several tens of degrees? First of all, it should
be noted that the temperature rise would substantially affect the degree of water dissociation as this process proceeds with considerable absorption of heat. The concentration of hydroxy and hydrogen ions would increase by more
than one order of magnitude in the region close to the reaction centre.
The temperature increase would also favour the dissociation of the water decomposition intermediates which require
thermal activation of the dissociation. For example the
dissociation $HO_2 \longrightarrow H^+ + O_2^-$ is characterised by $\Delta H = 17.5$
kJ and $\Delta Z = 27.3$ kJ. To cite yet another circumstance, it
is known from electrochemistry that the temperature increase by one degree would decrease the overvoltage in oxygen
and hydrogen release by 3 to 4 mV. For example, the temperature rise in the electrolyser from room temperature to
70-80°C would lead to a 40% decrease in overvoltage.
A temperature rise within chloroplast would accelerate
diffusion of both the photosynthesis products and the initial substances. It is a very important circumstance because an unmixed layer is formed on the solid liquid bord-
er. In other words, local heating would favour quicker
preparation of the given reaction centre for the reaction.
Dielectric constant of water changes with temperature in
accordance with the following empirical equation:
$\mathcal{E} = 87.74 - 0.4t°$, where t° - is the temperature in degrees
Centigrade. Thus the interaction of electric charges in
the water and consequently the conditions of the chemical
reactions would essentially be determined by the degree of
heating of the chloroplast or its individual parts.
The temperature increase also facilitates ions transport
across membranes. According to the known calculations the
energy required for the ion transport from the electrolyte
to the lipid membrane is 250 kJ/M. However the energy required for the ion transport across the chanell is much
less (about 20 kJ/M) / 8 /. The temperature increase in
the membranes gives rise to the appearance of the "glimme-
ring" sources of the overtemperature fluctuations. It may
change by more than one order the rate constants of corresponding reactions / 8 /.
And the last remark, which is of principal character in my
opinion. In terms of the proposed photoelectrochemical hypothesis of photosynthesis decomposition of water is considered as a process taking place in the molecular electrolyser. Its anode and cathode areas are on the same surface of the membrane and, under these conditions, electrolysis has "asymmetric" character.
The analysis testifies that in these conditions the thermodynamically necessary potential for water electrolysis
may he much less than 1.23 V. Under these conditions / 9 /
it was shown that "asymmetrical" water electrolysis may be

carried out in the cell supplied with electric and thermal energy. Evidently the chloroplast is a specific analogue of this unit. Hence the transformation of the light energy into thermal energy (when the photosynthesis proceeds intensely whereby the degree of light energy transformation is equal to 95%) can not be regarded as a useless process. The temperature increase contributes positively to a series of the processes (dissociation, diffusion, etc.) It is noteworthy that the temperature increase has the local character.

Therefore the original data and the review of the information available show that the overall equation of photosynthesis should contain both the light energy and the thermal one / 10,11 /.

REFERENCES

1 Komissarov, G.G. (1973) Problems of Biophotochemistry, in Transaction of the Moscow Society of Naturalist, Vol. XLIX, pp. 116-121, Moscow (in Russian)
2 Komissarov, G.G. (1980) The Chemistry and Physics of Photosynthesis, pp. 1-63, Moscow (in Russian)
3 Komissarov, G.G. (1973) Journal of Phys. Chem., Vol. 47, pp. 1633-1642, (in Russian)
4 Komissarov, G.G. (1971) Sov. Science Rev., pp. 285-290
5 Joliot, P., Joliot, A., Bonges, B. (1971) Photochem. Photobiol., Vol. 14, pp. 287-293
6 Kok, B., Forbursh, B., Mc Glin, M. (1971) Photochem. Photobiol., Vol. 14, pp. 307-315
7 Ptitsyn, G.A., Rjazantseva, S.V., Ilatovsky, B.A., Komissarov, G.G. (1987) Abstracts of the All-Union Conference "Photocatalytic Transformation of Solar Energy" pp. 44, Leningrad (in Russian)
8 Timashov, S.V. (1988) Physicochemistry of the Membrane Processes, pp. 16-17, 59, Moscow (in Russian)
9 Teschke, O., Zwanziger, M.G. (1982) Inter. J. Hydrogen Energy, Vol. 7, N 12, pp. 933-937
10 Komissarov, G.G. (1985) Proceedings of the First All-Union Workshop on Ecological Chemistry of Natural Waters, Kishinev, pp. 108-122, Moscow, 1988, USSR
11 Komissarov, G.G. (1989) Abstracts of the All-Union Conference "The Transformation of Light Energy in Photosynthesising Systems and Models", Puschino, pp. 9 (in Russian)

REGULATION OF LIGHT HARVESTING BY METABOLIC EVENTS

PETER HORTON, Robert Hill Institute, Department of Molecular Biology and Biotechnology, University of Sheffield, Western Bank, Sheffield, S10 2TN, U.K.

1. INTRODUCTION

The electron transport chain in plant chloroplasts operates at less than its full capacity. Metabolic capacity limits turnover of NADPH and ATP under high light, during induction following increases in irradiance and upon CO_2 deprivation. Under such conditions it would be expected that the stromal ATP/ADP and NADPH/NADP ratios would rise, ΔpH would increase, and the electron transport chain would become reduced, particularly on the acceptor side of PSII. However, observations show that none of these changes occur to any large or lasting extent; in the case of the thylakoid membrane the PSII acceptor Q_A stays remarkably oxidised at light saturation and P700 is increasingly oxidised, there being no evidence of accumulation of PSI acceptors in their reduced state. Similarly, stromal NADPH/NADP and ATP/ADP are fairly constant over a wide range of conditions. Clearly, photosynthetic electron transport is being regulated. The important questions are why and by what processes? In this paper some clear examples of thylakoid regulation are outlined, the mechanisms involved are discussed and finally, the central role of the thylakoid ΔpH in the control of the utilisation and dissipation of excitation energy is described.

MATERIALS AND METHODS

Simultaneous measurement of oxygen evolution, chlorophyll fluorescence and 9-aminoacridine fluorescence in aqueous phase systems used apparatus previously described (1,2). Chloroplasts were prepared either from spinach or pea by standard procedures (3,4). Chloroplasts were assayed at a concentration of 50µg chlorophyll/ml either as intact or after brief osmotic shock in 25mM MgCl. Cells of the green alga *Dunaliella C9AA* were grown as described by Gilmour *et al* (5) and assayed in buffered 2M NaCl. Spinach leaves were greenhouse grown and assayed in a Hansatech LD2 electrode, modified to accept the fibre optic of the Walz Chlorophyll Fluorometer. For pre-illumination experiments, leaves were cut at the petiole and floated on water at 25˚C for 30 minutes at a PFD of 1000µmole quanta/m^2/s before isolation of chloroplasts. Measurements of quantum yield are given in arbitrary units. Carotenoid compositions of chloroplasts and leaves were

M. Baltscheffsky (ed.), Current Research in Photosynthesis, Vol. IV, 111–118.
© 1990 *Kluwer Academic Publishers. Printed in the Netherlands.*

determined using HPLC by Dr A. Young at the University of Liverpool.

RESULTS AND DISCUSSION
     The quenching of chlorophyll fluorescence by photochemistry has
been qualitatively related to electron transport rate - changes in qQ,
determined by light saturation pulses or DCMU has been correlated with
O_2 evolution during induction (e.g. 6). Similarly, qQ was found to be
high in low light and low in high light (1,6). The quantum efficiency
of photosynthesis (Φs) declines in high light and associated with this
PSII reaction centres become progressively closed. In this sense, the
parameter qQ is also a measure of quantum efficiency. Using isolated
PSII particles it can be shown that qQ and Φs are linearly related over
a range of light intensities (Figure 1A), a relationship predicted from
models of the light-harvesting and electron transfer processes. The
ratio of Φs/qQ (referred to as Φp) is, in effect, a measure of the
intrinsic yield of the PSII reaction centres, Φs being corrected for
the proportion of closed centres. A major advance came with the
observation that *in vivo*, Φp is not a constant, but declines at high
irradiance (7); hence the decline in Φs was not only associated with
reaction centre closure but with a decline in efficiency of energy
capture by the reaction centres. *Regulation* of the primary
photosynthetic process had hence been discovered. Figure 1B shows data
obtained from *Dunaliella* cells illuminated at different irradiances.
The non-linearily of the relationship between Φs and qQ is clear and is
to be contrasted with Figure 1A. It can be seen that between 0 and 900
μmol quanta/m^2/s the value of qQ only changes between 0.95 and 0.65 in
a light range that sees Φs drop from 0.33 to 0.10, indicating a fall of
55% in the intrinsic yield of PSII (Figure 2).

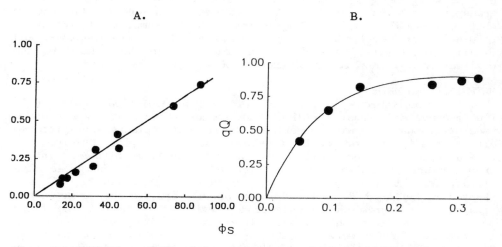

*Figure 1 Quantum yield of O_2 evolution and qQ upon illumination with
different PFD for (A) PSII "BBY" particles at pH 6.3 in the presence of
dichlorobenzoquinone and ferricyanide and (B) Dunaliella cells.*

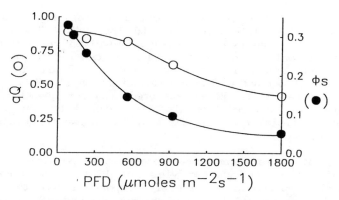

Figure 2   Dependence of quantum yield (●) and qQ (o) on PFD for Dunaliella cells

Decreasing the of temperature from 35˚ to 15˚C progressively reduces the rate of photosynthesis in *Dunaliella* (Figure 3). Despite the marked decrease in quantum yield, qQ stays constant. Thus, the efficiency of PSII is decreased as the capacity of utilisation of ATP and NADPH are decreased in exactly the same way as when irradiance is increased. The data in Figures 1-3 provide examples of the decrease in PSII efficiency in 'excess' light (*excess* is defined as any light level greater than that which can be used with *maximum* quantum efficiency).

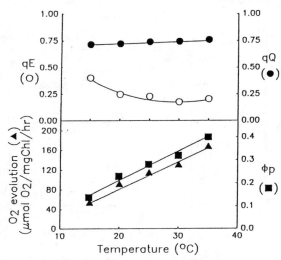

Figure 3   The effect of temperature on the rate of O_2 evolution, fluorescence quenching parameters qQ and qE, and the calculated intrinsic PSII yield, Φp for cells of Dunaliella illuminated at a PFD of 550µmole quanta/m^2/s

Suppression of the quantum yield of PSII can occur either due to dissipation of excitation energy or due to inefficient photochemistry. The quenching of chlorophyll fluorescence non-photochemically could be an indication of a dissipation of excitation that lowers quantum yield. Data obtained in leaves shows that Φp is well-correlated with qNP

(7-10). The major component of qNP is qE, quenching that results from changes in the thylakoid membrane due to the ΔpH. There is some controversy concerning the type of quenching involved *viz a viz* whether dissipation at the antenna or in the reaction centre is involved. It has recently been shown in an investigation of qE in isolated chloroplasts that it occurs in the antenna chlorophyll (11). Thus the quenching Fo in relation to qE was as predicted for quenching in the antenna. Moreover, the relationship was matched by the quenching induced by the artificial quencher DNB which is known to quench in the antenna chlorophyll.

Assuming that qE is an antenna process it is possible to predict the effects of qE on the quantum yield of PSII. The most simple prediction is that Φp should be directly proportional to the Fv/Fm at steady-state. A curved relationship between Φp and qE is predicted with large Φp (> 30%) changes only occurring at relatively high (> 0.8) qE. Some data in the literature are completely consistent with this relationship (e.g. 9,10). Conversely, other data (e.g. 7,8) show large Φp changes that are linearly related to qNP. Figure 4 shows examples of both these kinds of relationship, from *Dunaliella* cells and from spinach leaves; the latter are consistent with antenna quenching whilst the former are not. A definitive plot is the ratio Φp:Fv/Fm — for antenna quenching it is constant. In spinach leaves this ratio is constant over a wide range of light intensities but in *Dunaliella* it is not, suggesting that a mechanism other than antenna quenching contributes to the change in Φ_p (Figure 5).

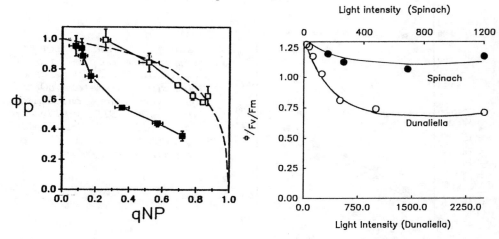

Figure 4   Relationship between Φ_p and qNP for spinach leaves (□) and Dunaliella cells (■) at different PFD

Figure 5   The ratio between Φ_p and the Fv/Fm value determined at steady state after illumination of spinach leaves and Dunaliella cells at different PFD.

The available data therefore suggests that there are two mechanisms contributing to the control of Φp. Experiments with isolated chloroplasts can clearly distinguish between the qE-dependent process and the second mechanism. Figure 6A shows the changes in Φp that result from illumination of chloroplasts in the presence of methylviologen at high $MgCl_2$ concentration. The decrease in Φp is biphasic – an initial rapid fall and a slower phase. The slower phase correlates with qNP formation, the Φp:Fv/Fm ratio being constant. The more rapid phase appears unrelated to qNP and the Φ_p:Fv/Fm ratio fell; this phase correlated well with the increase in ΔpH. In the presence of antimycin A, a qE antagonist which blocks all changes in Fv/Fm at low $MgCl_2$ (12), only this rapid Φp change was observed. The change in Φp in such conditions can be completely eliminated by addition of uncoupling agents (13,14).

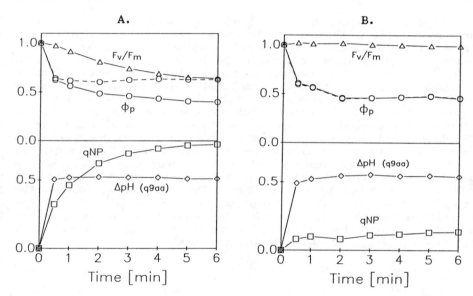

Figure 6 Time course for the development of the decrease in Φ_p, qNP, ΔpH as measured by the quenching of 9-aminoacridine fluorescence and Fv/Fm for isolated broken spinach chloroplasts in the presence of 30mM $MgCl_2$ (A) or 2mM $MgCl_2$ + 1μM antimycin A (B). The dotted line is the ratio Φ_p:(Fv/Fm).

ΔpH therefore has an important control function in chloroplasts – it determines the efficiency of light capture by PSII by controlling both the rate of thermal dissipation and also the photochemical rate. The former involves unknown changes in the antenna chlorophylls. The latter could involve the initiation of a cyclic flow of electrons around PSII that would give photochemical quenching but not O_2 evolution. Whilst this cycle is the best explanation for the *in vitro* data, photochemical dissipation of a different kind could be involved *in vivo* (e.g O$_2$ reduction *via* Mehler reaction); in this case the change in Φ_p might be triggered by a change in stromal redox state rather than ΔpH. However, a recent comparison between intact chloroplasts and leaves demonstrates very similar relationships between Φ_p and qNP when the chloroplasts are coupled but not when uncoupled, indicating that all the changes in Φ_p *in vivo* are ΔpH-dependent (15).

It is possible to explain the different relationships between Φ_p and qNP and the different levels of Φ_p change in saturating light by proposing that the relative extents of these two processes can vary. Thus, pK (cycle) might differ from pK (qE) and the size of the ΔpH would then determine the proportional effects of the cycle and qE on Φ_p. Uncoupler titrations of isolated chloroplasts indicate that the cycle is initiated at lower ΔpH than qE (16).

It is clear from Figure 6 that the Φ_p change due to the cycle occurs more rapidly than qE. The slow response of qE has been described *in vivo*, particularly when illumination is given after a period of dark adaptation of >10min. It is of interest therefore to examine the kinetics of Φ_p changes in an intact system. Figure 7 shows the results of an experiment with isolated barley protoplasts. The t½ for qNP is 2-3 minutes; however Φ_p fell to a low value (35% of the maximum) within 1.5 min, after which it steadily *increased*. In low light this rise brought the value of Φ_p to within 10% of the maximum, but in high light a peak value was followed by a fall to approx 40% maximum. The steady state values are the same as described previously (1) and can be largely accommodated by the steady state qE. The low values during the first few minutes of illumination can be explained by a PSII cycle promoted by a high ΔpH. The rise in Φ_p follows the kinetics of the rate of O$_2$ evolution, the increased rate of ATP consumption perhaps lowering the ΔpH. In isolated chloroplasts, it has been well-documented that a high ΔpH is built up during the early phase of induction but falls as O$_2$ evolution accelerates (2).

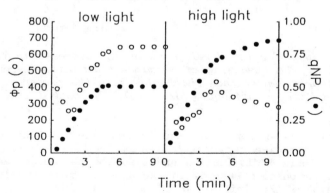

Figure 7 Kinetics of the changes in Φ_p and qNP is barley protoplasts illuminated with 150 (low) and 1500 (high) μmole quanta/m^2/s

It therefore seems that the direct effect of ΔpH on PSII is the major disipative process immediately following increases in irradiance, but that in the steady state, qE is probably more important. At 10°C the formation of qE is much slower and it was found that the minimum Φ_p values peristed for the first 3-4 minutes of illumination (data not shown). If this interpretation of the data in Figure 7 is correct, it is surprising that the steady state ΔpH is so low as to cause minimal effect on PSII and yet a high qE is present. In fact the key regulatory role for ΔpH discussed above is somewhat problematical. Data from isolated chloroplasts in which qE, Φ_p and electron transport rate are plotted against ΔpH indicates that high qE and low Φ_p require a relatively large ΔpH that would impose a large restriction on the rate of electron transport at the level of plastoquinol oxidation. Clearly, *in vivo* in high light when qE values as high as 0.85 and Φ_p decreases of more than 50% are observed, electron transport is occurring at high rates. According to Figure 8 a rate of 150 μmoles O_2/mg chl/hr would only occur at a q9aa of about 0.2 and a qE of <0.1. There must be some difference in these relationships *in vivo* and *in vitro*.

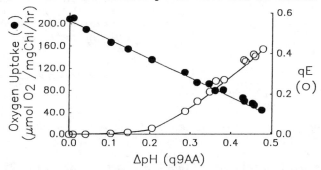

Figure 8   Titration of the rate of O_2 uptake and qE against ΔpH in isolated pea chloroplasts using small additions of nigericin and a saturating light intensity of 2000μmole quanta/m²/s.

Recently, it has been suggested that zeaxanthin formation may be necessary for qE (17). In isolated chloroplasts no zeaxanthin is formed, but qE values as high as 0.7 can be observed (data not shown). Illumination of leaves does induce zeaxanthin formation, giving a violaxanthin:zeaxanthin ratio of approx 1:1. Chloroplasts isolated from light treated leaves mostly maintain these zeaxanthin levels. If q9aa and qE are now titrated at constant irradiance with an uncoupler an important result is seen (Figure 9). The formation of qE now requires a much smaller ΔpH. This suggests that, *in vivo*, because of the presence of zeaxanthin, a high qE can be generated without requiring a ΔpH inhibitory to linear electron transport. Moreover, it is implied that the fine control of the xanthophyll cycle is central to the regulation of light harvesting. The rate of zeaxanthin formation appears to depend upon the supply of ascorbate and the ΔpH (18).

In conclusion, it appears that the control of light-harvesting and utilisation in the thylakoid membrane is complex. A combination of thermal quenching of excitation energy and photochemical dissipation can offset excess supply of light. ΔpH acts as the trigger signal. There is perhaps some variability between species or as a result of different growth conditions that alters the relative importance of these phenomena. At present, it is not clear how this variation arises but it is perhaps related to the factors which determine a) the sensitivity of the cycle and qE to ΔpH and b) the ΔpH that is necessary for a given rate of photosynthesis. The former may depend on the content of zeaxanthin or the phosphorylation state of PSII, whilst the latter may depend on the activation state of the ATP synthase or the levels of stromal metabolites or inorganic phosphate.

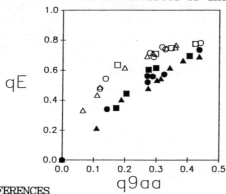

Figure 9 Relationship between the thylakoid ΔpH, assayed by 9-aminoacridine fluorescence, and qE obtained by uncoupler titration of broken spinach chloroplasts isolated from dark adapted (closed symbols) or pre-illuminated leaves (open symbols).

REFERENCES
1 Horton, P and Hague, A. (1988) Biochim. Biophys. Acta 932, 107-115.
2 Horton, P. (1983) Proc. R. Soc. Lond. B217, 405-416.
3 Walker, D.A. (1980) Methods in Enzymol. 69, 94-104.
4 Cerovic, Z.G. and Plesnicar, M. (1984) Biochem J. 223, 453-454.
5 Gilmour, D.J, Hipkins, M.F. and Boney, A.D. (1982) Plant Sci. Lett. 26, 325-330.
6 Quick, W.P. and Horton, P. (1984) Proc. R. Soc. Lond. B220, 371-382.
7 Weis, E. and Berry, J.A. (1987) Biochim. Biophys. Acta 894, 198-208.
8 Sharkey, T.D., Berry, J.A. and Sage, R.F. (1988) Planta 176, 415-424.
9 Peterson, R.B., Sivak, M.N. and Walker, D.A. (1988) Plant Physiol. 88, 158-163.
10 Genty, B., Briantais, J-M. and Baker, N.R. (1988) Biochim. Biophys. Acta 990, 87-92.
11 Rees, D., Noctor, G. and Horton, P. (1989) Photosyn. Res., in press.
12 Oxborough, K. and Horton, P. (1987) Photosyn. Res. 12, 119-128.
13 Horton, P., Crofts, J., Gordon, S., Oxborough, K., Rees, D. and Scholes, J.D. (1989) Phil. Trans. R. Soc. Lond. B323, 269-279.
14 Rees, D. and Horton, P. (1989), this volume.
15 Weis, E. and Lechtenberg, D. (1989) Phil. Trans. R. Soc. Lond. B323, 253-268.
16 Noctor, G.D. and Horton, P. (1989), this volume.
17 Demmig-Adams, B., Winter, K., Kruger, A. and Czygan, F-C. (1989) Plant Physiol., in press.
18 Yamamoto, H.Y. (1979) Pure & Appl. Chem. 51, 639-648.

REGULATION OF RIBULOSE BISPHOSPHATE CARBOXYLASE ACTIVITY BY RUBISCO
ACTIVASE: ASPECTS OF THE MECHANISM

A.R. PORTIS, JR.[a], S.P. ROBINSON[a,b], and R.McC. LILLEY[a,c],
U.S. DEPARTMENT OF AGRICULTURE/AGRICULTURAL RESEARCH SERVICE,
URBANA, ILLINOIS, USA[a]; CSIRO, DIVISION OF HORTICULTURAL
RESEARCH, ADELAIDE, AUSTRALIA[b]; DEPARTMENT OF BIOLOGY,
UNIVERSITY OF WOLLONGONG, WOLLONGONG, AUSTRALIA[c]

1. INTRODUCTION

Ribulose bisphosphate carboxylase/oxygenase (rubisco) is only
catalytically competent when its active site is completed by the
addition of CO_2 as a carbamate and Mg^{2+} (1). This may be achieved
spontaneously *in vitro* by preincubation of the enzyme with high CO_2 and
Mg^{2+} at alkaline pH. However the normal *in vivo* conditions of low CO_2
and the presence of RuBP do not permit the formation of fully active
enzyme without an additional protein factor called rubisco activase
(2,3). This was first shown clearly by the phenotype of the *rca* mutant
of Arabidopsis (4). The rubisco in this plant can be fully activated
by high CO_2 in the dark (5) or after the isolation of the enzyme (4).
However *in vivo* after several minutes under saturating light, the
activity of the enzyme is very low even at high CO_2 concentrations.
The *rca* mutant lacks two nearly identical polypeptides of about 45 and
41 kD (2,6). The ability to observe a rubisco activase dependent
activation of rubisco *in vitro* was followed by the rapid development of
procedures to purify the protein for detailed biochemical study (7) and
the cloning and sequencing of the rubisco activase gene (8).

It is clear that rubisco activase is an essential and probably the
primary factor in the regulation of rubisco activity. Now a detailed
understanding of the mechanism of activation by the protein is of major
concern in order to obtain a complete understanding of how rubisco
activity may be regulated *in vivo*. Some basic clues as to how rubisco
activase may be functioning to alter rubisco activity have been
obtained by investigating various features of the process *in vitro*.

2. RESULTS AND DISCUSSION

The presence of RuBP makes the rapid activation of rubisco
dependent on the presence of rubisco activase (Fig 1). The addition of
RuBP to the inactive form of the enzyme before CO_2 and Mg^{2+} are added
makes activation extremely slow. In contrast, the presence of rubisco
activase counteracts the inhibitory nature of RuBP allowing activation
to occur rapidly. The active enzyme obtained in this manner appears to
the same as that generated by the spontaneous process in the absence of

M. Baltscheffsky (ed.), Current Research in Photosynthesis, Vol. IV, 119–126.
© 1990 *Kluwer Academic Publishers. Printed in the Netherlands.*

RuBP in that it is also carbamylated (9) and appears so far not to be otherwise physically modified, e.g. phosphorylated.

Activation *in vivo* in the light (10) or *in vitro* with rubisco activase (3, Fig. 1.) occurs at lower CO_2 than that otherwise required by the spontaneous process. Starting with inactive enzyme, the addition of 10 μM CO_2 and 10 mM Mg^{2+} results in a final activity of only about 1/3 that obtained with much higher concentrations. In contrast the presence of RuBP and rubisco activase allows a much greater activity to be achieved. Under normal physiological conditions, the activity of the enzyme is thereby only limited by the Km of CO_2 for catalysis and not by the high CO_2 requirement for spontaneous activation. It is important to note that RuBP is essential in order to increase the activity of the enzyme with rubisco activase. Two possibilities, which are not mutually exclusive, to account for this requirement are that: (a) rubisco activase only interacts with rubisco with bound RuBP and (b) RuBP stabilizes the activated form of the enzyme which is generated by rubisco activase. The ability of RuBP alone to drastically retard the loss of activity (and by inference the loss of activator CO_2 and Mg^{2+}) when it is transferred to low CO_2 and Mg^{2+} conditions has been demonstrated (11). In this way RuBP can effectively trap the activated form of the enzyme generated by rubisco activase as long as the RuBP remains above the Km for catalysis.

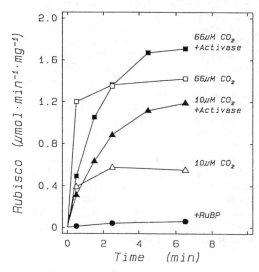

FIGURE 1. Activation of rubisco (100 μg/ml) in the presence and absence of rubisco activase (270 μg/ml) and/or RuBP (6mM) at high and low CO_2. An ATP regenerating system using creatine phosphokinase was also present. (A.R. Portis, unpublished)

Activation *in vivo* is increased by light (10). While the RuBP requirement suggests that this effect may be due to the absence of RuBP in the dark, other possible factors are the accompanying changes in redox potential (ie thioredoxin mediated activation) and phosphorylation potential (ATP/ADP regulation). The involvement of redox changes was shown to be unlikely by the observation that methyl viologen stimulates rubisco activation in contrast to its inhibitory effects on thioredoxin linked activities (5). In contrast, a requirement for ATP and an inhibition by ADP was found to be the basis for the requirement for illuminated thylakoids in the original rubisco activase assay (12). Subsequent studies (13) of rubisco activation in isolated chloroplasts demonstrated that changes in stromal ATP could regulate rubisco activation *in vivo*. Changes in ATP/ADP may be the basis for many of the observed effects of various imposed conditions on rubisco activation previously observed *in vivo*. The effects of ATP concentration and the potent inhibition by ADP on the ability of isolated rubisco activase to activate rubisco *in vitro* is shown in Fig. 2. In this assay system, an ATP/ADP ratio of only 10:1 is sufficient to inhibit rubisco activase activity by 50% but in the isolated chloroplast studies rubisco activation is reduced by 50% at ATP/ADP ratios of about 1:1. These values are not directly comparable however, because all of the factors affecting the relationship between rubisco activase activity and the resulting steady state rubisco activity are not yet clear.

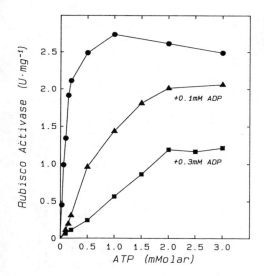

FIGURE 2. Effects of ATP and ADP concentration on rubisco activase dependent activation of rubisco (from ref. 14).

The ATP requirement for rubisco activase activity led to the finding that rubisco activase has an intrinsic ATP hydrolysis activity (14). The concentration dependence on ATP of the rubisco activation and ATP hydrolysis activities are identical (Fig. 3) and equally sensitive to ADP (not shown). However, the ATP hydrolysis activity is not strictly coupled to the activation of rubisco (Table I) and proceeds regardless of the presence of rubisco in various forms. On the other hand a loss of the ATPase activity by heating or various chemical inhibitors also causes a corresponding loss activation activity (14). Recently we have been able to reversibly alter the ATPase activity of the isolated protein and also change its apparent size on gel permeation columns by various treatments (Z.Y. Wang and

A.R. Portis, unpublished). The results seem to indicate that ATP hydrolysis may be linked to aggregation and/or disaggregation phenomena proceeding even in the absence of rubisco, but more work needs to be done to establish such a relationship.

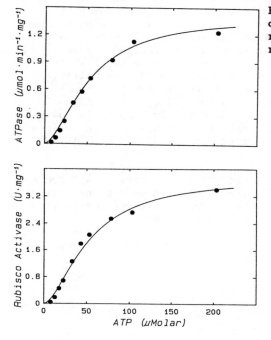

FIGURE 3. Effect of ATP concentration on ATPase and rubisco activation activities of rubisco activase (from ref 14).

TABLE 1. Lack of effect of rubisco on the rate of ATP hydrolysis by rubisco activase (from ref 14).

Condition	ADP release (% control)
No addition	100
+ CO_2 + RuBP	102
+ CO_2 + RuBP + ER (0.5 mg ml^{-1})	101
+ CO_2 + RuBP + ECM (0.5 mg ml^{-1})	115

Control activity was 1 μmol min^{-1} mg^{-1}.

In some plants, carboxyarabinitol 1-phosphate (CA1P) seems to be important in regulating rubisco activity (15). CA1P binds more tightly than RuBP to the activated form of the enzyme and thereby lowers the amount of catalytically active enzyme. CA1P does not seem to be an essential component in the regulation of rubisco since it is not found in all plants. Therefore it was somewhat surprising to find that rubisco activase promotes the release of CA1P from the inhibited enzyme (Fig. 4). RuBP without rubisco activase has a small effect which can be explained by competition with the released CA1P for rebinding. This effect of rubisco activase appears to account for the more rapid recovery of activity after illumination *in vivo* (17) than could be demonstrated by treatment of the inhibited enzyme *in vitro* with alkaline phosphatase to metabolize the CA1P (18). More importantly with respect to the mechanism, it was the first indication that rubisco activase was not specific for RuBP bound forms of the enzyme.

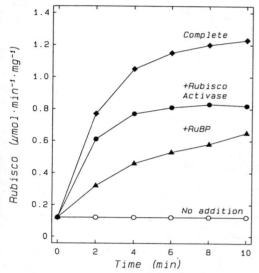

FIGURE 4. Reversal of CA1P inhibition of rubisco by rubisco activase (from ref 16).

We have further investigated the nature of the specificity of rubisco activase for rubisco by determining what effect rubisco activase has on the activation of the enzyme with CO_2 and Mg^{2+} in the presence of other phosphates known to be present in the stroma. PGA is normally present at the highest concentrations in the chloroplast stroma and has been termed a positive effector (11), meaning that it can increase the level of carbamate formation at suboptimal CO_2. Ribose 5-phosphate is a negative effector, while FBP was observed to be a very potent inhibitor of rubisco activation at low CO_2 concentrations even though it eventually acts as a good positive effector (11). As shown in Fig 5, activation was fairly rapid in the presence of PGA and rubisco activase addition had minimal effect on the kinetics. In contrast, rubisco activase greatly increased the rate and extent of activation of rubisco in the presence of FBP and ribose 5-phosphate. These results provide further support for a scheme in which rubisco activase, by alleviating the inhibitory effects of FBP, ribose 5-phosphate and RuBP on the forward spontaneous activation process, but not their inhibitory effects on the backward deactivation process, promotes the rapid attainment of a higher steady state activation level at low CO_2. However the effective catalytic activity of the enzyme after activation in the presence of high FBP or ribose 5-phosphate and low RuBP might not be as great as that with RuBP alone because of the competition for the activated form of the enzyme.

FIGURE 5. Activation of rubisco with rubisco activase in the presence of PGA, FBP, and ribose 5-phosphate at low CO_2 (R.McC. Lilley and A.R. Portis, unpublished).

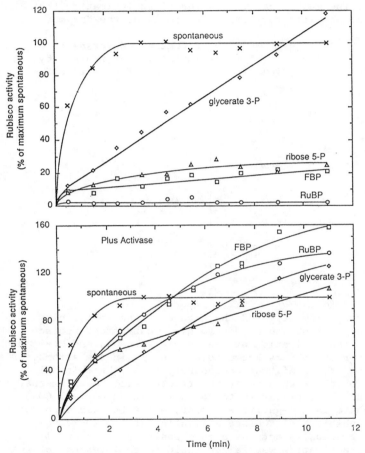

Isolated rubisco has the rather annoying characteristic of a slowly decreasing rate of catalysis after RuBP is added (19). The rather attractive possibility that this represented formation of the inactive rubisco-RuBP complex (20) was discounted by the finding that the enzyme remains carbamylated (J. Pierce, personal communication). Another possibility, that impurities in the RuBP cause the effect (21), also now seems very unlikely because the behavior can still be observed under a variety of conditions designed to minimize this possibility

(A.R. Portis, J. Pierce and S.P. Robinson, unpublished). Formation of an inhibitory bisphosphate from the ene-diol intermediate during catalysis seems to be the most likely explanation. Regardless of possible questions regarding the details of the mechanism responsible, the effect of rubisco activase on the behavior of the enzyme was of obvious interest. As shown in Fig. 6, the presence of rubisco activase (with ATP) eliminated the otherwise rapid decline in activity for a considerable time. The beneficial effect of rubisco activase provides yet another clue to its effect on rubisco in that it seems analogous to its effects with the other rubisco-sugar phosphate complexes shown previously. This is particularly true for CA1P, in which the enzyme is also carbamylated. By accelerating the release of the inhibitory compound and the subsequent competition with RuBP for rebinding, the level of inhibited enzyme can be kept low. Presumably this process also occurs *in vivo* and in that situation further metabolism of the compound would also be necessary to prevent the otherwise endless formation of the compound. However the increased understanding of the nature of the decline in activity has confused the situation with respect to how the enzyme becomes deactivated by reformation of an RuBP-enzyme complex without carbamate *in vivo* (23,24). Suitable conditions with rubisco activase *in vitro* where this also occurs instead of the formation of an inactive carbamylated enzyme have not been found as yet.

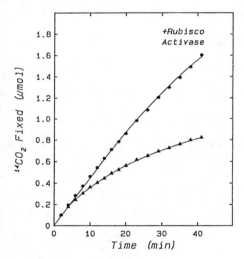

FIGURE 6. Time course of CO_2 fixation by rubisco in the presence and absence of rubisco activase (from ref. 22).

The experiments presented here provide some basic information with which one might begin to propose possible detailed mechanisms for the effect of rubisco activase on the activation of rubisco. Rubisco activase seems to recognize several different rubisco forms which presumably have some common conformational feature and appears to accelerate the rate of release of the bound sugar phosphate. While ATP hydrolysis seems to proceed in the absence of rubisco, it is nevertheless required for the activation process to occur. The lack of strict coupling between ATP hydrolysis and sugar phosphate release (measured thus far as an increase in rubisco activity) makes it difficult to determine their relationship. A role in either the formation or dissociation of a rubisco-rubisco activase complex is an attractive hypothesis for further work. More sophisticated means to explore the interactions between rubisco activase, rubisco, sugar phosphate binding, and ATP hydrolysis will be required to make further progress.

REFERENCES
1 Andersson, I., Knight, S., Schneider, G., Lindquist, Y., Lindquist, T., Branden, C-I., and Lorimer, G.H. (1989) Nature 337, 229-234
2 Salvucci, M.E., Portis, A.R. Jr., and Ogren, W.L. (1985) Photosynthesis Res. 7, 193-201
3 Portis, A.R. Jr., Salvucci, M.E., and Ogren, W.L. (1986) Plant Physiol. 82, 967-971
4 Somerville, C.R., Portis, A.R. Jr., and Ogren, W.L. (1982) Plant Physiol. 70, 381-387
5 Salvucci, M.E., Portis, A.R. Jr., and Ogren, W.L. (1986) Plant Physiol. 80, 655-659
6 Werneke, J.M., Chatfield, J.M., and Ogren, W.L. (1989) Plant Cell, in press.
7 Robinson, S.P., Streusand, V.J., Chatfield, J.M., and Portis, A.R. Jr. (1988) Plant Physiol. 88, 1008-1014
8 Werneke, J.M., Zielinski, R.E., and Ogren, W.L. (1988) Proc. Natl. Acad. Sci. USA 85, 787-791
9 Werneke, J.M., Chatfield, J.M., and Ogren, W.L. (1988) Plant Physiol. 87, 917-920
10 Perchorowicz, J.T., Raynes, D.A., and Jensen, R.G. (1981) Proc. Natl. Acad. Sci. USA 78, 2985-2989
11 Jordan, D.B., Chollet, R., and Ogren, W.L. (1983) Biochem. 22, 3410-3418
12 Streusand, V.J. and Portis, A.R. Jr. (1987) Plant Physiol. 85, 152-154
13 Robinson, S.P. and Portis, A.R. Jr. (1988) Plant Physiol. 86, 293-298
14 Robinson, S.P. and Portis, A.R. Jr. (1989) Arch. Biochem. Biophys. 268, 93-99
15 Salvucci, M.E. (1989) Physiol. Plant., in press.
16 Robinson, S.P. and Portis, A.R. Jr. (1988) FEBS Lett. 233, 413-416
17 Seemann, J.R., Berry, J.A., Freas, S.M., and Krump, M.A. (1985) Proc. Natl. Acad. Sci. USA 82, 8024-8028
18 Berry, J.A., Lorimer, G.H., Pierce, J., Seemann, J.R., Meek, J., and Freas, S. (1987) Proc. Natl. Acad. Sci. USA 84, 734-738
19 Laing, W.A. and Christeller, J.T. (1976) Biochem. J. 159, 563-570
20 McCurry, S.D., Pierce, J., Tolbert, N.E., and Orme-Johnson, W.H. (1981) J. Biol. Chem. 256, 6623-6628
21 Paech, C., Pierce, J., McCurry, S.D., and Tolbert, N.E. (1978) Biochem. Biophys. Res. Commun. 83, 1084-1092
22 Robinson, S.P. and Portis, A.R. Jr. (1989) Plant Physiol. 90, 968-971
23 Brooks, A. and Portis, A.R. Jr. (1988) Plant Physiol. 87, 244-249
24 Butz, N.D. and Sharkey, T.D. (1989) Plant Physiol. 89, 735-739

REDOX-REGULATION OF CHLOROPLAST ENZYMES: MECHANISM AND PHYSIOLOGICAL SIGNIFICANCE

RENATE SCHEIBE, Lehrstuhl für Pflanzenphysiologie, Universität Bayreuth, Box 10 12 51, D-8580 BAYREUTH, FRG.

1. INTRODUCTION

Light-activation of enzymes is known since more than 20 years (1) and the redox mechanism involved has been elucidated by the groups of L.E. Anderson (2), B.B. Buchanan (3), and others (4, 5). It has been argued that light/dark-modulation serves as an on/off-switch for the Calvin cycle in order to prevent the intermediate pools to become emptied in the dark. The occurrence of a lag phase of CO_2-fixation upon onset of illumination has been considered to result from the slow activation of Calvin cycle enzymes. Here an alternative interpretation of light/dark modulation is given and its prime role in meeting varying demands in the light will be demonstrated. In addition, the contribution of the described regulatory principle to the over-all regulation of chloroplast metabolism under in vivo conditions will be discussed.

2. METABOLIC SITUATION IN THE CHLOROPLAST

Light serves as an energy source for the photosynthetic reduction of CO_2, NO_2^- and SO_4^{2-}. In addition, other biosynthetic processes require ATP and/or NADPH. This machinery has to function under a variety of often unfavorable and fluctuating conditions. Therefore, poising of the NADPH/ATP ratio as well as flux control at key steps of the various pathways is necessary. Because such an adaptation cannot be accomplished by a simple on/off-switch, tuning of enzyme activities in the light is required which may result in a decrease of the activation state of one enzyme, while others need to be increased (e.g. malate valve versus CO_2-fixation when CO_2 increases). Consequently a regulatory system is required which is capable to regulate each key enzyme individually.

3. PRINCIPLE OF REDOX MODIFICATION

Due to the presence of oxygen in the illuminated chloroplast any enzyme that became reduced via the light-driven ferredoxin/thioredoxin system will be reoxidized within a few minutes or even less. This can be seen clearly upon darkening, when electron flow for reduction stops and only reoxidation is occurring. Hence the light-modulated enzymes are subjected to a continuous turnover with respect to their redox state. In Fig. 1 such a system (a) is compared with that of phosphorylated/dephosphorylated enzyme systems (b) which are known to occur in animal and bacterial cells (6). While in the latter case hydrolysis of ATP provides the energy for obtaining a system responding rapidly to changes in the metabolic requirements, electrons energized by light fulfill this function in the chloroplast stroma.

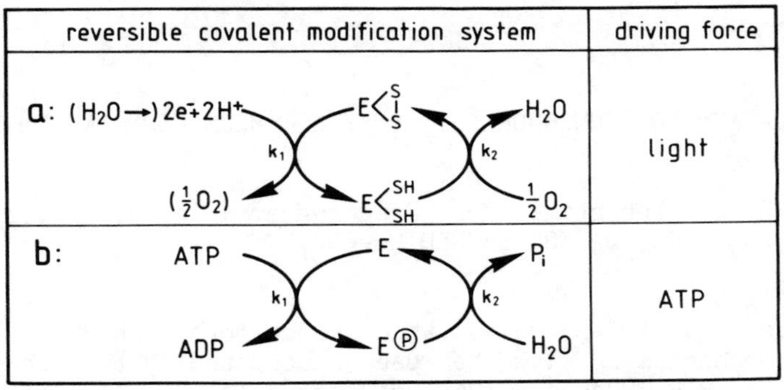

reversible covalent modification system		driving force

Fig. 1: Comparison of the regulatory principles in the illuminated
chloroplast stroma (a: redox modification by thioredoxins) and
in mammalian or bacterial systems (b: e.g. phosphorylation/de-
phosphorlylation by protein kinase/phosphatase).

In both cases effectors interfere with one or both modulation reactions
in order to adjust the ratio of active and inactive enzyme forms. Such
fine-tuning of the amount of active enzyme by both positive and negative effectors acting on the converter enzymes has been described in
detail for cyclic cascades in animal tissues and bacteria resulting in
an efficient signal amplification (6).

4. TUNING OF REDOX-MODIFICATION

Pronounced effects of metabolites on the reductive modulation of chloroplast enzymes have been demonstrated by several authors (8-12, 14,
16, 19). Key steps of CO_2-fixation that are under this type of control
are indicated in Fig. 2.
Results of experiments using the stromal fraction of isolated spinach
chloroplasts are presented. Incubation of a stroma extract with DTT in
the absence of O_2 allows to estimate the maximum rate of reductive
activation with the natural amounts of the respective thioredoxins. The
effect of metabolites on the rate of activation of some enzymes is summarized in Fig. 3. The types of regulatory strategy pertinent for the
individual chloroplast enzymes can be stated as follows:

4.1. NADP-Glyceraldehyde 3-phosphate dehydrogenase (NADP-GAPDH):

NADP-GAPDH is that enzyme for which activation by light has been shown
for the first time (1). The increase of specific activity upon illumination has been then studied in much detail and many factors (various
metabolites and/or reduced thioredoxin) can potentially influence the
rate of activation (8, 9, 10). As shown in Fig. 3, NADPH affects the
enzyme only in combination with the reducing agent DTT, while for ATP
as an effector, reduction is not required. However, ATP is only effective at concentrations beyond those availabe in the stroma. Inorganic
phosphate (up to 30 mM) and 3-PGA (up to 5 mM) are not effective at all
under the conditions used in these experiments (pH 8.0, 10 mM DTT)
(data not shown). However, 1,3-PGA when continuously generated in a

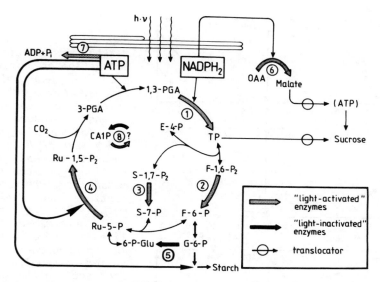

Fig. 2: Simplified scheme of regulation of CO_2-fixation by light.
The major uses of ATP and $NADPH_2$ are indicated. Key enzymes
with activation states under light- and/or metabolite control
are indicated by broad arrow. Products translocated into the
cytoplasm are triose-phosphate (TP) for sucrose synthesis and
malate which could provide ATP by dehydration and subsequent
oxidative phosphorylation. 1: NADP-GAPDH, 2: FBPase, 3: SBPase,
4: PRK, 5: G6PDH, 6: NADP-MDH, 7: ATPase, 8: CA1P-metabolizing
enzyme system.

system containing ATP at a constant concentration of 2 mM (regenerated
by pyruvate kinase and PEP) was most effective even at low concentrations (Fig. 3). This effect did not exhibit a significant dependence on
the presence of DTT. This suggests that the substrate 1,3-PGA alone is
capable of increasing NADP-GAPDH activity, thus promoting production of
carbohydrate without constraint even in the dark, when sufficient NADPH
is availabe. In conclusion, NADP-GAPDH at present turned out not to
belong to the redox-modulated chloroplast enzymes.

4.2. Fructose-1,6-bisphosphatase (FBPase): As shown previously (11, 12)
the reductive activation of chloroplast FBPase is largely stimulated by
FBP. On the other hand, the oxidized form exhibits activity only in the
presence of high concentrations of Mg^{++} (16 mM) and at an alkaline pH
(pH 8.8), conditions not likely to occur in vivo (13). Using chloroplast stroma extract, significant activation rates were obtained only
in the presence of Ca-FBP. Ca-FBP is not effective under these conditions without DTT. As a consequence chloroplast FBPase appears as
"classical" light-activated enzyme which is subjected to regulation by
redox-modification in a cyclic system and where the rate of reduction
is under the control of the positive effector Ca-FBP. It can regulate

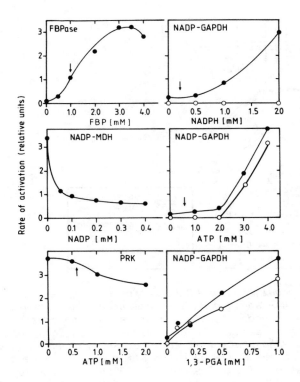

Fig. 3:
Metabolite effects on the activation of several enzymes in pea chloroplast stroma. Enzyme activity was measured at various times during preincubation without (o) and with 10 mM DTT (●) at pH 8 in the presence of increasing concentrations of the indicated metabolite. Protein concentration was 0.5 to 3.0 mg/ml. The activation rate was determined from the linear phase of activation. The concentration of the varied metabolite was kept constant in the assay. The arrows indicate the concentrations of the respective metabolites thought to be present in the chloroplast stroma in the light (7).

the C-flux through this irreversible step by readily being turned up (FBP increase) or down (FBP decrease) and hence can keep the FBP pool constant under any condition. Sedoheptulose-1,7-bisphosphatase (SBPase) appears to be regulated similarly by SBP (14).

4.3. Phosphoribulosekinase (PRK): The step responsible for the regeneration of the CO_2-acceptor Ru-1,5-P_2 is regulated using another strategy. Here, reductive activation is a prerequisite as it is for FBPase (15). However, the rate of activation is not influenced by any metabolite at least in the concentration range found in situ, e.g. 1 mM ATP decreases the rate of activation only by 10% (Fig. 3). On the other hand, the reduced enzyme appears to be less sensitive to oxidation than other light-modulated enzymes (16). This would result in a slower turnover of the active species which would be the prevailing form in the light. In addition, the activation state of PRK measured in intact chloroplasts and protoplasts was severalfold higher than the rate of O_2-evolution (17). Work from other laboratories (e.g. 18) has established that the activity of the already light-activated form is influenced by a variety of metabolites. However, the in vivo significance of all these effects is not yet fully understood. The reason behind this behaviour could be the most efficient conversion of any available pentose-P into CO_2 acceptor.

4.4. NADP-malate dehydrogenase (NADP-MDH): In C3-plants NADP-MDH has been shown to play a crucial role in poising the ATP/NADPH ratio during CO_2-fixation (5). NADP is a potent inhibitor of the reductive activation of NADP-MDH (19). Fig. 3 shows, that only 20-30% of the maximal rate of activation is obtained in the presence of NADP-concentrations as low as 0.05 mM. Hence, under most conditions in the light the conversion of this enzyme into the active form will be restricted by NADP levels present in CO_2-fixing chloroplasts (0.8 mM), thus keeping the malate valve under tight control. Only when no alternative electron acceptor is available and consequently the NADP-pool is overreduced, an extremely low NADP level will allow export of malate and thereby of reductive power. This can be observed e.g. during the induction phase in isolated chloroplasts (20) or upon sudden illumination of a darkened leaf disc (21).

4.5. Rubisco: Rubisco might be primarily responsible for limiting CO_2-fixation under certain conditions (22). However, the very complex modes of regulation of this key enzyme of CO_2-fixation still remain to be elucidated. Particularly the eventually light-dependent metabolism (23) of the recently discovered inhibitor carboxyarabinitol-1-P (24) (which is identical with hamamelonic acid-2'-phosphate (25)) might be a crucial site of regulation which is not yet understood at all.

4.6. Glucose-6-P dehydrogenase (G6PDH): The chloroplast isoenzyme of G6PDH has been characterized and compared with the cytosolic form (26). A redox dependent shift of the K_m for glucose-6-P resulting in apparent inactivation upon reduction under in vivo conditions is a unique property of the chloroplast form (27). The rate of inactivation is even enhanced in the presence of a high NADPH level (28) thus representing another example for the effector mediated type of redox-modulation. The cytosolic isozyme of G6PDH is not light/dark-modulated (28).

4.7. Other chloroplast enzymes: ATP hydrolysis catalyzed by the chloroplast coupling factor CF_1 is subjected to thiolmodulation (29), the target being the γ-subunit (30). Some enzymes involved in N- and S-metabolism might also be under redox control (31), although clearcut evidence for a certain type of regulatory principle has not yet been worked out. This might be due to the fact that dramatic changes of the activities of the respective enzymes may not become evident under all conditions due to tuning by metabolites. Thus only abrupt changes of supply or demand of the pathway under control by the key enzyme will show the full amplitude of activity changes. The adjusted steady-state will then be approached through oscillations as observed earlier for the photosynthetic O_2-evolution (32) and the malate valve (21).

5. STRUCTURE OF THE REGULATORY PEPTIDES
The amino acid sequence of several light-activated enzymes as compared with that of the respective non-regulatory counterparts reveals the presence of extra-peptides as a common structural feature (Fig. 4):

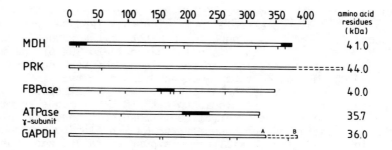

Fig. 4: Schematic view of the sequences of light/dark modulated enzymes with special indication of the non-homologous parts (black) and thiols (ı) thought to carry regulatory function (33 - 37, 39, 40).

Chloroplast FBPase has a 20 amino acids insert containing 3 thiol groups essentially involved in the redox-modification. Apart from the regulatory endopeptide the enyzme shows a high similarity to the mammalian FBPase (33, 34). A similar situation was found for the γ-subunit of CF_1 (35). The chloroplast NADP-MDH possesses two extrapeptides of together 50 amino acids at the N- and the C-terminus of an otherwise homologous MDH molecule (36, 37). This latter case, where the regulatory peptides are accessible to limited processing, allows to demonstrate the relative importance of various parts of these sequences for the regulatory and catalytic properties of the chloroplast enzyme. Apparently, the removal of the C-terminus causes a partial loss of the redox properties, but at the same time a drastic increase of the specific activity of the enzyme (38). Recent studies concerning the N-terminus show that progressive removal of amino acids results in active enzyme forms with changed properties (Kampfenkel et al., in preparation). Similar studies are not possible respective of PRK, since a sequence of an isoform not being under redox control has not been established, although the regulatory thioredoxin site is known (39). G6PDH has not yet been sequenced. A different situation becomes evident from sequence comparisons of GAPDH isoforms. No additional peptide could be detected in the chloroplast enzyme when compared with the cytosolic enzyme (40). This finding supports the view presented here, namely the lack of thiol dependence in the regulatory principle of the chloroplast NADP-GAPDH in situ.

6. DYNAMIC INTERACTION OF LIGHT-ACTIVATED ENZYMES WITH THE THYLAKOIDS
The differential binding of reduced and oxidized NADP-MDH to hydrophobic surfaces (plastic) and the specific interference of NADPH with such binding is used as a model system in order to introduce this feature as a new perspective in the in situ regulation of chloroplast key enzymes. Fig. 5 illustrates this fact showing that only the reduced and not the oxidized NADP-MDH attaches to the reaction vial and that the apparent loss of enzyme activity can be prevented specifically by NADPH

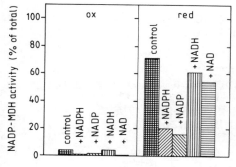

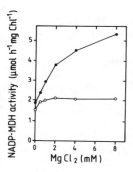

Fig. 5:
Apparent loss of oxidized (ox) and reduced (red) NADP-MDH in plastic vials. Incubation was at pH 8 for 80 min (30°C). All mixtures contained 250 mM PEG-600. Where indicated pyridine nucleotides (0.08 mM) were present in addition. The initial protein concentration was 0.5 µg/ml.

Fig. 6:
Association of oxidized (○) and reduced (●) NADP-MDH to thylakoid membranes as dependent on the concentration of $MgCl_2$. Spinach thylakoids washed once in lysing buffer (10 mM Tris-HCl, 10 mM $MgCl_2$, pH 8) were incubated for 30 min at the indicated $MgCl_2$-concentration in the presence of 250 mM PEG-600 and purified NADP-MDH (0.2 units per 50 µg chlorophyll in 0.1 ml). After a washing step in the same medium without enzyme, the thylakoids were solubilized in 0.05% Triton X-100 and assayed for adhering activity.

(and NADP). A similar effect was observed with washed thylakoids instead of a plastic surface. However, in the latter system the Mg^{++} concentration (and the pH) plays an additional role in the differential binding of the NADP-MDH forms (Fig. 6) (Rother and Scheibe, in preparation).

7. CONCLUSION

Light/dark modulation can be understood as a regulatory mechanism linking various chloroplast enzymes to the photosynthetic light reactions by furnishing a common (cyclic monocascade of covalently modified enzyme forms). However, independent control of each of the enzymes is provided by interference of metabolites with the degree of modification. Such a strategy is efficient in leading to i) maximal production of ATP by exporting excess NADPH via the "malate valve" if not required inside the chloroplast, and ii) maximal effectiveness and flexibility of the biosynthetic pathways producing reduced C-, N-, and S-compounds, under the varying endogenous and exogenous conditions encountered by the green plants. The regulatory principle described here involves as a basis, both the presence of O_2 and covalent thiol-disulfide changes of enzymes equipped with specifically evolved structures.

Acknowledgement: The financial support given by the Deutsche Forschungsgemeinschft for parts of this work is gratefully acknowledged.

REFERENCES

1 Ziegler, H. and Ziegler, I. (1965) Planta 65, 369–380
2 Anderson, L.E. (1985) in Advances in Botanical Research (Callow, J.A., ed.), Vol. 12, pp. 1–46, Academic Press, New York
3 Buchanan, B.B. (1984) BioScience 34, 378–383
4 Jacquot, J.-P. (1984) Physiol. Vég. 22, 487–507
6 Chock, P.B., Rhee, S.G. and Stadtman, E.R. (1980) Ann. Rev. Biochem. 49, 813–843
7 Wirtz, W., Stitt, M. and Heldt, H.W. (1980) Plant Physiol. 66, 187–193
8 Wolosiuk, R.A. and Buchanan, B.B. (1976) J. Biol. Chem. 251, 6456–6461
9 Wolosiuk, R.A. and Buchanan, B.B. (1978) Plant Physiol. 61, 669–671
10 Wolosiuk, R.A., Hertig, C.M. and Busconi, L. (1986) Arch. Biochem. Biophys. 246, 1–8
11 Chehebar, C. and Wolosiuk, R.A. (1980) Biochim. Biophys. Acta 613, 429–438
12 Hertig, C.M. and Wolosiuk, R.A. (1983) J. Biol. Chem. 258, 984–989
13 Schürmann, P. and Wolosiuk, R.A. (1978) Biochim. Biophys. Acta 522, 130–138
14 Nishizawa, A.N. and Buchanan, B.B. (1981) J. Biol. Chem. 256, 6119–6126
15 Wolosiuk, R.A. and Buchanan, B.B. (1978) Arch. Biochem. Biophys. 189, 97–101
16 Ashton, A.R. (1983) in Thioredoxins. Structure and Functions (Gadal, P., ed.) pp. 245–250, Editions du CNRS, Paris
17 Heber, U., Takahama, U., Neimanis, S. and Shimizu-Takahama, M. (1982) Biochim. Biophys. Acta 679, 287–299
18 Flügge, U.I., Stitt, M., Freisl, M. and Heldt, H.W. (1982) Plant Physiol. 69, 263–267.
5 Scheibe, R. (1987) Physiol. Plant. 71, 393–400
19 Scheibe, R. and Jacquot, J.-P. (1983) Planta 157, 548–553
20 Scheibe, R., Wagenpfeil, D. and Fischer, J. (1986) J. Plant Physiol. 124, 103–110
21 Scheibe, R. and Stitt, M. (1988) Plant Physiol. Biochem. 26, 473–481
22 Leegood, R. (1985) Photosynth. Res. 6, 247–259
23 Salvucci, M.E., Holbrook, G.P., Anderson, J.C. and Bowes, G. (1988) FEBS Lett. 231, 197–201
24 Servaites, J.C. (1985) Plant Physiol. 78, 839–843
25 Beck, E., Scheibe, R. and Reiner, J. (1989). Plant Physiol. 90, 13–16
26 Fickenscher, K. and Scheibe, R. (1986). Arch. Biochem. Biophys. 247, 393–402
27 Scheibe, R., Geissler, A. and Fickenscher, K. (1989) Arch. Biochem. Biophys., in the press
28 Scheibe, R. (1987) in Progress in Photosynthesis Research (Biggins, J., ed.) Vol. 3, pp. 233–240, Martinus Nijhoff Publ., Dordrecht
29 Mills, J.D. and Mitchell, P. (1982) Biochim. Biophys. Acta 679, 75–83
30 Moroney, J.V., Fullmer, C.S. and McCarty, R.E. (1984) J. Biol. Chem. 259, 7281–7285
31 Schmidt, A. (1983) in Light Dark Modulation of Plant Enzymes (Scheibe, R., ed.) pp. 124–128, University of Bayreuth
32 Walker, D.A. and Sivak, M.N. (1986) TIBS 11, 176–179
33 Raines, C.A., Lloyd, J.C., Longstaff, M., Bradley, D. and Dyer, T. (1988) Nucl. Acids Res. 16, 7931–7942
34 Marcus, F., Moberly, L. and Latshaw, S.P. (1988) Proc. Natl. Acad. Sci. USA 85,
35 Miki, J. Maeda, M., Mukohata, Y. and Futai, M. (1988) FEBS Lett. 232, 221–226
36 Fickenscher, K., Scheibe, R. and Marcus, F. (1987) Eur. J. Biochem. 168, 653–658
37 Metzler, M.C., Rothermel, B.A. and Nelson, T. (1989) Plant Mol. Biol., in the press
38 Fickenscher, K. and Scheibe, R. (1988) Arch. Biochem. Biophys. 260, 771–779
39 Porter, M.A., Stringer, C.D. and Hartman, F.C. (1988) J. Biol. Chem. 263, 123–129
40 Shih, M.-C., Lazar, G. and Goodman, H.M. (1986) Cell 47, 73–80

LIGHT/DARK-REGULATION OF C₄-PHOTOSYNTHESIS ENZYMES BY REVERSIBLE PHOSPHORYLATION

Raymond Chollet, Raymond J.A. Budde, Jin-an Jiao and Chrissl A. Roeske, Department of Biochemistry, University of Nebraska, Lincoln, NE 68583-0718 (USA)

This paper will present a brief overview of our ongoing research related to the light/dark-regulation of two maize mesophyll-cell enzymes by reversible covalent modification, chloroplastic pyruvate,Pi dikinase (PPDK) and cytoplasmic phosphoenolpyruvate carboxylase (PEPC). The reversible light-activation of both of these key C₄-photosynthesis enzymes is unique among the photoregulated carbon-fixation enzymes investigated in detail in that it involves the reversible phosphorylation of the two target proteins.

● PPDK

In the case of PPDK, an ADP-dependent threonyl-phosphorylation causes dark-inactivation, whereas a Pi-dependent phosphorolytic dephosphorylation results in light-activation (see **Fig. 1** and Refs. 1-4). The phosphorylated threonine group is one residue removed from an essential (phospho)histidine in the primary sequence (i.e., Thr-Glu-Arg-Gly-Gly-Met-*Thr(P)*-Ser-**His(P)**-Ala-Ala-Val-Val-Ala-Arg) (5), the latter of which plays a pivotal role in both regulatory phosphorylation/inactivation and catalysis (6). More specifically, the true protein substrate for this regulatory phosphorylation reaction is the phosphohistidyl form of the enzyme formed during partial catalysis with ATP plus Pi or phosphoenolpyruvate (PEP) (see **Fig. 1** and Ref. 6). Thus, the inactivation and catalytic mechanisms actually share and compete for this common phosphorylated enzyme intermediate (see **Fig. 1**). These complex and most unusual phosphorylation/dephosphorylation reactions are likely catalyzed by a single bifunctional regulatory protein (RP) (7,8) possessing two physically distinct active-site domains (9). We are presently in the process of purifying the maize leaf RP to apparent electrophoretic homogeneity by affinity chromatography on Blue A or Red A dyematrex gels and FPLC-based size-exclusion chromatography on Superose 12 for the dual purpose of unequivocally establishing its bifunctionality and producing monospecific polyclonal antibodies (C.M. Smith and R.

M. Baltscheffsky (ed.), Current Research in Photosynthesis, Vol. IV, 135–142.
© 1990 *Kluwer Academic Publishers. Printed in the Netherlands.*

Chollet, unpublished). These anti-RP antibodies will be subsequently used to screen maize leaf cDNA libraries for regulatory protein cDNA.

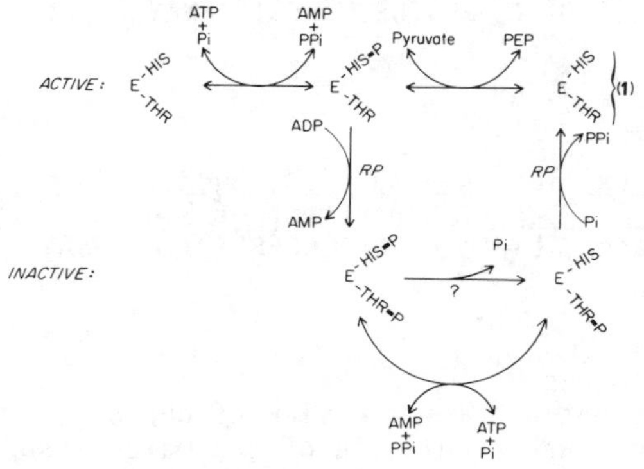

FIGURE 1. ADP-dependent threonyl-phosphorylation/inactivation and Pi-dependent dephosphorylation/activation of C_4 leaf PPDK (**E**) by the bifunctional regulatory protein (**RP**). The two-step catalytic reaction sequence of the maize leaf dikinase (10) is given by *Equation 1*.

Exactly why the threonyl-phosphorylation of PPDK causes complete inhibition of overall catalysis (1,3) is not known with certainty. However, given the close proximity of the threonine and essential histidine residues in the primary sequence (5), one can readily envision that regulatory phosphorylation of the former could cause conformational perturbation in the microenvironment of the catalytically essential phosphohistidine by a variety of possible mechanisms. For example, we (5) and Matsuoka et al. (11) have predicted the secondary structure of the maize regulatory-site peptide to be an α-helix from the methionine residue to the C-terminal arginine (**see above**). The two glycyl residues immediately preceding the methionine would likely disrupt the helical structure and allow increased flexibility. Given the α-helical structure of this region of the peptide and the general rule of approximately four residues per helix turn, the regulatory (phospho)threonyl residue would be situated on the opposite side of the helix from the essential His(P). This spatial separation of the histidyl and threonyl residues is possibly why the inactive Thr(P) form of the dikinase can still catalyze the partial reaction with the AMP/PPi or ATP/Pi substrate pairs at the (phospho)histidyl site (see **Fig.** 1 and Refs. 5, 12). Situated four residues away from the regulatory (phospho)threonine in the N-terminal direction is an arginyl residue. Between these two groups are the two glycyl residues which presumably destabilize the aforementioned α-helix. Perhaps phosphorylation of the regulatory threonyl residue creates a salt bridge between the arginine and the phosphothreonine, thereby extending and stiffening the helical structure (5). This decreased flexibility might preclude certain conformational changes from taking place, thereby rendering the dikinase inactive specifically with respect to the pyruvate/PEP partial reaction (12).

Although PPDK is activated by a light-dependent, DCMU- and photophosphorylation inhibitor-sensitive dephosphorylation process (4,13), the current model for the mechanism of activation/inactivation (see **Fig.** 1) shows no direct link with light (i.e., photosynthesis). One of the more likely possible modes of regulation of the dikinase regulatory cascade has been thought to be the availability of the RP's substrates [i.e., PPDK, ADP and Pi (see **Fig.** 1)] and various stromal "signal metabolites", including pyruvate, PEP and ATP (4,13,14). For example, the amount of PPDK-HisP, the requisite enzyme-form phosphorylated by the regulatory protein (6), available for inactivation could be decreased upon illumination by increasing the ratio of stromal [pyruvate] to [PEP] (see **Fig.** 1). Indeed, pyruvate has been shown to be a potent inhibitor of the regulatory phosphorylation (inactivation) reaction *in vitro* (14,15), consistent with its interaction with the requisite PPDK-HisP enzyme-intermediate during partial catalysis (see **Fig.** 1). However, the trends we recently observed for the **total** (i.e., free plus bound) concentrations of pyruvate, PEP, ADP and ATP in the maize mesophyll cell during the light/dark-regulation of PPDK activity *in vivo* (16) suggest that pyruvate and PEP do **not** play a major role in regulating the extent of light-activation (dephosphorylation) or dark-inactivation (ADP-dependent threonyl-phosphorylation) of dikinase by its bifunctional regulatory protein. While the twofold changes in [ADP] appear qualitatively consistent with a regulatory role for this metabolite in the reversible light-activation process, they are **not** of a sufficient magnitude to completely account for the tenfold change in PPDK activity observed *in vivo*. Along these same lines, Usuda (17) has recently reported that there is **no** significant correlation *in vivo* between the activation-state of dikinase and the total stromal levels of ADP, Pi, ATP/ADP or adenylate energy charge at various light intensities in nonaqueously purified maize mesophyll chloroplasts, the intracellular site of both PPDK and its regulatory protein. Thus, these recent metabolite-related data (16-18) suggest that another, as yet unidentified effector(s) or mechanism(s) is the major link between light and the activation-state of PPDK *in vivo*. Unfortunately, there is currently no supportive evidence for the differential regulation of the bifunctional dikinase regulatory protein by covalent modification, pH, [Mg^{2+}] or effectors (e.g., calcium/calmodulin, cAMP, cGMP) (8,15).

●**PEPC**

Evidence has accumulated from several research groups indicating that PEPC activity in illuminated C_4 leaves is about two- to threefold greater than that from darkened plants when assayed at suboptimal, but physiological levels of PEP and pH (19-25). In parallel with these light-induced changes in catalytic activity, the light-form enzyme is less sensitive to feedback inhibition by malate. Concomitant with these changes in enzymatic properties, C_4 PEPC undergoes changes in covalent phosphorylation-status upon light/dark transitions of the parent leaf tissue (22, 23, 26). We have reported that the differing catalytic and regulatory properties of maize PEPC purified from light- and dark-adapted green leaf tissue are related, at least in part, to the degree of covalent seryl-phosphorylation of the protein *in vivo* (23).

Related *in vitro* phosphorylation studies with maize, sugarcane (27) and sorghum (28) leaf extracts indicated the presence of an ATP-dependent soluble protein kinase(s) (PK) which modified crude PEPC exclusively on serine residues. In order to provide more definitive evidence in support of the role of covalent modification in the light-activation of PEPC, we have further developed a reconstituted system comprised of Mg·ATP, the electrophoretically pure target enzyme and a partially purified soluble protein kinase from dark- and light-adapted maize leaves, respectively, to perform detailed analysis of the effects of *in vitro* phosphorylation on the catalytic and regulatory properties of C_4-leaf PEPC (29). The direct correlation observed between the PK-mediated changes in the catalytic and regulatory properties and seryl-modification of the dark-form PEPC (29) provides the first unequivocal evidence in support of the view that the covalent seryl-phosphorylation of the target enzyme by an ATP-dependent soluble protein kinase is the mechanism to which the light-induced changes in catalytic activity and malate sensitivity of C_4-leaf PEPC observed *in vivo* are attributed.

As in the case of the dikinase regulatory cascade (see **Fig. 1**), little is known with certainty with respect to how light modulates the phosphorylation-status (activation-state) of cytoplasmic PEPC other than it, too, is dependent, either directly or indirectly, on photosynthetic electron transport and/or photophosphorylation (19, 20). Neither dithiothreitol-reduced spinach leaf thioredoxin *h* [Td_h (30)], PPi, fructose 2,6-bisphosphate (Fru 2,6-P_2), various combinations of EGTA/calcium/calmodulin (CaM) [see **Table 1** (Refs. 29, 31)] nor the CaM-antagonist calmidazolium (R. Chollet and J. Vidal, unpublished) has any significant effect on the regulatory phosphorylation and/or activation of purified dark-form PEPC in our reconstituted *in vitro* system. A one-hour preincubation of the dark-form PK with Mg·ATP is also without effect on its subsequent activation of PEPC. Thus, we currently have no supportive evidence for the regulation of the protein kinase by either various putative, light-modulated cytoplasmic effectors or autophosphorylation.

TABLE 1. Effectors of *In Vitro* Phosphorylation/Activation of Maize Dark-Form PEP Carboxylase

Addition(s)	Relative Activity (%)	
	Phosphorylation	Activation
Reconstituted System[*]		
None (Control)	100	100
Reduced Td_h (spinach)	-	105
PPi (2.5 mM)	-	109
EGTA (5 mM)	-	103
$CaCl_2$ (0.5 mM)	-	111
$CaCl_2$/CaM_s[**] (190 U)	-	114
EGTA (0.5 mM)	98	
EGTA/$CaCl_2$ (1 mM)	93	
EGTA/$CaCl_2$/CaM_b[**] (1000 U)	96	
Fru 2,6-P_2 (50 μM)	101	
Glu 6-P (5 mM)	70	
Malate (5 mM)	43	

[*] See Ref. 29.
[**] Calmodulin from spinach leaves (CaM_s) or bovine brain (CaM_b).

In contrast to these negative findings, several photosynthetically-derived metabolites have been recently implicated as possibly playing some role in the reversible light modulation of C_4 PEP carboxylase, including the PEPC activator glucose 6-P (Glu 6-P) and the inhibitor malate (see **Table 1**), the substrate PEP (20), and a Calvin cycle product(s) originating in the bundle sheath (20). This latter suggestion is based on the finding that D,L-glyceraldehyde, an inhibitor of Calvin cycle activity, suppresses the light activation of *Setaria* PEPC *in vivo* (20). This interesting observation is seemingly consistent with our repeated failure to detect light-activation of the maize enzyme *in situ*, in isolated mesophyll protoplasts (R. Chollet, unpublished). In contrast, the light-modulation of chloroplastic PPDK and NADPH-malate dehydrogenase is readily observed in such mesophyll-cell preparations (Ref. 3 and R. Chollet, unpublished).

In closing, it is noteworthy that several of the mesophyll cell-specific steps of the C_4 cycle are light-modulated in C_4 plants such as maize, including the transport of pyruvate across the chloroplast envelope-membrane (32) and the ensuing reaction sequence of pyruvate → PEP → oxaloacetate (OA) → malate catalyzed by stromal

PPDK, cytoplasmic PEPC, and stromal NADPH-malate dehydrogenase, respectively (see **Fig. 2**). Exactly why such a major portion of the C_4 cycle is light-modulated is not known, but perhaps it serves to coordinately regulate the activities of the mesophyll-specific carbon-assimilating reactions with those of the light-activated bundle sheath-specific enzymes of the Calvin cycle (e.g., Rubisco and the bisphosphatases) during C_4-photosynthesis. While the specific nature of the dark → light signal controlling the light-modulation of pyruvate transport and NADPH-malate dehydrogenase activity in the mesophyll chloroplast is thought to be the photosynthetic electron transport-induced changes in pH across the envelope-membrane (32) and in the redox-status of stromal thioredoxin and NADP (4, 13), respectively, little is known with certainty with respect to how light modulates the phosphorylation-status (activation-state) of the dikinase and PEPC (**see above**). The nature of this elusive light-dark "switch" must await further investigation.

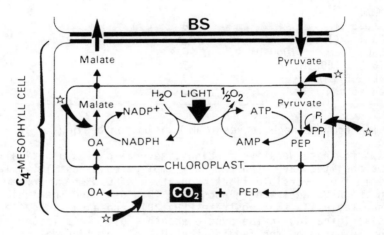

FIGURE 2. Reversible light-activation of several of the mesophyll cell-specific steps of the C_4 cycle (✮) in an NADP-malic enzyme-type C_4 plant such as maize (**see text for discussion**). BS, bundle sheath; OA, oxaloacetate.

ACKNOWLEDGMENT

The research from our laboratory summarized in this paper was supported in part by Grants DMB-8704237 and 85-CRCR-1-1585 from the National Science Foundation and the Competitive Research Grants Office of the U.S. Department of Agriculture, respectively.

REFERENCES

1. Ashton, A.R. and Hatch, M.D. (1983) Biochem. Biophys. Res. Commun. **115**; 53-60
2. Ashton, A.R., Burnell, J.N. and Hatch M.D. (1984) Arch. Biochem. Biophys. **230**, 492-503
3. Budde, R.J.A., Holbrook, G.P. and Chollet, R. (1985) Arch. Biochem. Biophys. **242**, 283-290
4. Edwards, G.E., Nakamoto, H., Burnell, J.N. and Hatch, M.D. (1985) Annu. Rev. Plant Physiol. **36**, 255-286
5. Roeske, C.A., Kutny, R.M., Budde, R.J.A. and Chollet, R. (1988) J. Biol. Chem. **263**, 6683-6687
6. Burnell, J.N. and Hatch, M.D. (1984) Arch. Biochem. Biophys. **231**, 175-182
7. Burnell, J.N. and Hatch, M.D. (1983) Biochem. Biophys. Res. Commun. **111**, 288-293
8. Burnell, J.N. and Hatch, M.D. (1985) Arch. Biochem. Biophys. **237**, 490-503
9. Roeske, C.A. and Chollet, R. (1987) J. Biol. Chem. **262**, 12575-12582
10. Jenkins, C.L.D. and Hatch, M.D. (1985) Arch. Biochem. Biophys. **239**, 53-62
11. Matsuoka, M., Ozeki, Y., Yamamoto, N., Hirano, H., Kano-Murakami, Y. and Tanaka, Y. (1988) J. Biol. Chem. **263**, 11080-11083
12. Burnell, J.N. (1984) Biochem. Biophys. Res. Commun. **120**, 559-565
13. Nakamoto, H. and Edwards, G.E. (1986) Plant Physiol. **82**, 312-315
14. Burnell, J.N., Jenkins, C.L.D. and Hatch, M.D. (1986) Aust. J. Plant Physiol. **13**, 203-210
15. Budde, R.J.A., Ernst, S.M. and Chollet, R. (1986) Biochem. J. **236**, 579-584
16. Roeske, C.A. and Chollet, R. (1989) Plant Physiol. **90**, 330-337
17. Usuda, H. (1988) Plant Physiol. **88**, 1461-1468
18. Usuda, H. (1988) Plant Physiol. **87**, 427-430
19. Karabourniotis, G., Manetas, Y. and Gavalas, N.A. (1983) Plant Physiol. **73**, 735-739
20. Samaras, Y., Manetas, Y. and Gavalas, N.A. (1988) Photosynthesis Res. **16**, 233-242
21. Huber, S.C. and Sugiyama, T. (1986) Plant Physiol. **81**, 674-677
22. Nimmo, G.A., McNaughton, G.A.L., Fewson, C.A., Wilkins, M.B. and Nimmo, H.G. (1987) FEBS Lett. **218**, 18-22
23. Jiao, J.-A. and Chollet, R. (1988) Arch. Biochem. Biophys. **261**, 409-417

24. Doncaster, H.D. and Leegood, R.C. (1987) Plant Physiol. **84**, 82-87
25. Rodríquez-Sotres, R. and Muñoz-Clares, R.A. (1987) J. Plant Physiol. **128**, 361-369
26. Guidici-Orticoni, M.-T., Vidal, J., Le Maréchal, P., Thomas, M., Gadal, P. and Rémy, R. (1988) Biochimie **70**, 769-772
27. Budde, R.J.A. and Chollet, R. (1986) Plant Physiol. **82**, 1107-1114
28. Echevarría, C., Vidal, J., Le Maréchal, P., Brulfert, J., Ranjeva, R. and Gadal, P. (1988) Biochem. Biophys. Res. Commun. **155**, 835-840
29. Jiao, J.-A. and Chollet, R. (1989) Arch. Biochem. Biophys. **269**, 526-535
30. Florencio, F.J., Yee, B.C., Johnson, T.C. and Buchanan, B.B. (1988) Arch. Biochem. Biophys. **266**, 496-507
31. Jiao, J.-A. and Chollet, R. (1989) Plant Physiol. **89** (Suppl.), 191
32. Ohnishi, J.-I. and Kanai, R. (1987) Plant Cell Physiol. **28**, 243-251

PURIFICATION AND CHARACTERIZATION OF PHOSPHORIBULOKINASE   FROM
N2 – FIXING CYANOBACTERIUM NOSTOC MUSCORUM

D.V.Amla, Plant Biotechnology Division,
NATIONAL BOTANICAL RESEARCH INSTITUTE, LUCKNOW-226001, INDIA

INTRODUCTION

Cyanobacteria are the photosynthetic procaryotes and like higher plants use water as the reductant to fix CO_2 via the Calvin cycle involving phosphoribulokinase (PRK , ATP D-ribulose 5-phosphate 1-phosphotransferase, EC 2.7.1.19) and ribulose -1, 5-bisphosphate carboxylase (Rubisco , 3-phospho-D-glycerate carboxylase, EC 4.1.1.39) as the key enzymes of carbon assimilation (1). The major role of PRK in reductive pentose phosphate pathway is to catalyse the biosynthesis of ATP dependent phosphorylation of ribulose 1, 5-bisphosphate which subsequently undergo carboxylation to produce phosphoglycerate. Therefore, extent of CO_2 assimilation in photosynthetic organisms is largely dependent on the activity of kinase enzyme. The enzyme PRK has been isolated and partially characterise from different photosynthetic organisms and activity of the enzyme is reported to be regulated by different intermediates of carbon and energy metabolism (2,3). In the present communication purification of the enzyme from N2-fixing cyanobacterium N. muscorum and activation with thioredoxins is described.

MATERIAL AND METHODS

N. muscorum UW (ATCC 29151) and Anabaena variabilis Kutz (ATCC 29413) were grown as described earlier(4). Thioredoxin m from A. variabilis was purified according to Rowell et al.(5) and thioredoxin f of spinach was a gift from Dr. P.Schurmann. Activity of PRK was monitored by coupling the formation of ADP to the oxidation of NADH at 340 nm (4). Cell free extracts of the cyanobacterium used for purification of enzyme employing ion-exchange, gel-filteration and affinity chromatography on Blue-Sepharose and reactive red agarose. Molecular weight of the enzyme was determined by gel filteration and SDS-PAGE(6).

RESULTS AND DISCUSSION

The enzyme was purified 178-folds with 90-95% homogeneity and showed a specific activity of 7 umol NADH oxidised $min-1$ $mg-1$ protein by emplying ion-exchange (DEAE cellulose, Mono Q), gel filteration (Sephacryl S-300) and two affinity column chromatography. The best separation of the enzyme protein was obtained with nucleotide analogue affinity ligand reactive-red 120 agarose. The enzyme

M. Baltscheffsky (ed.), Current Research in Photosynthesis, Vol. IV, 143–146.
© 1990 *Kluwer Academic Publishers. Printed in the Netherlands.*

yields during purification are summarised in Table 1. The elution profile and separation of different proteins in the last and final step of enzyme purification is shown in Fig. 1. Bulk of PRK enzyme was eluted with ATP containing buffer. One major band of protein of the purified enzyme was deteted on native PAGE. The subunit size of PRK is about 41.6 kD on SDS PAGE and on superose gel column molecular mass of the native enzyme estimated to be about 86 kD, suggesting dimeric structure of the enzyme. These values of molecular mass and structure of the enzyme are consistent with reports in higher plants (3,7).

Activity of the enzyme in crude and purified state was very low when assayed without any thiol or sulfhydryl reagents, but preincubation of enzyme with dithiothreitol (DTT) or DTT-reduced thioredoxins enhanced the activity to many fold. This agrees with previous reports in cyanobacteria(8) and also with light activation of photosynthetic enzymes in chloroplast(9). Activity of the enzyme was enhanced to several folds with preincubation of enzyme with reduced thioredoxins m or f over the control or DTT alone. Activation of enzyme with equivalent concentrations of thioredoxin f was 2-3 fold higher as compared to thioredoxin m. The rate of activation of the enzyme was of first order with respect to thioredoxin concentration. There are evidences for a non-regulatory form of PRK in higher plants (10) and cyano-bacterium C. fritschii(11) which does not respond to reduced thioredoxins. However, we could not detect two forms of the enzyme in N. muscorum. The activation of N. muscorum PRK by spinach thioredoxin f was significantly higher than the thioredoxin m of A. variabilis. This situation is similar to chloroplast system(9). Although it is difficult to explain precisely the specificity for higher activation with thioredoxin f, as the nature of active site residues and mechanism of their reduction is identical in both the thioredoxins. However, thioredoxin f possess little homology in the area surrounding the active redox sulfide bridge and activation process is independent of net reduction of S-S group on the enzyme molecule. Secondly thioredoxin f is detected exclusively in photoautotrophic plants. These characteristics of thioredoxin f may contribute for a greater affinity for enzymes of photosynthetic metabolism (5) while thioredoxin m precisely function as the hydrogen donor to ritonucleotide reductase in DNA systhesis(12).

ACKNOWLEDGEMENTS

This work was carried in the Laboratory of Prof. W.D.P.Stewart, Dept. Biological Sci, Univ. Dundee, Dundee,UK.

TABLE I — PURIFICATION OF PHOSPHORIBULOKINASE FROM N.MUSCORUM

Purification step	Total protein (mg)	Specific activity (units/mg protein)	Total activity (units)	Yield (%)	Purification (fold)
Crude extract	2137	0.039	83.34	100	1.0
DE cellulose	360	0.12	43.2	51.86	3.076
Sephacryl	310	0.13	40.3	48.3	3.34
Blue-Sepharose	8.4	1.29	10.83	13.0	33.07
Red agarose	1.2	6.96	8.35	10.02	178.46

One unit of enzyme catalysed the formation of 1 μmol of product min^{-1}.

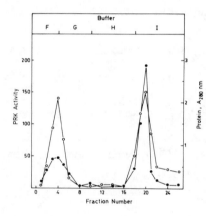

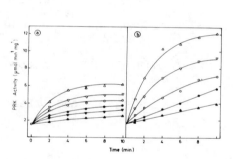

Fig. 1. Elution profile of total protein A280 (-O-) and PRK activity (-●-) from reactive red agarose affinity column. Buffer F-10mM, Hepes pH 8.0; G-10mM Hepes, 0.05% βME pH 6.8; H-10mM potassium phosphate, 0.05% βME pH 6.9; I-as for buffer H plus 1mM ATP pH 7.2.

Fig. 2. Response of preincubating the enzyme (6.2 μg protein) with different levels of (a) thioredoxin $\underline{m}$ 20ng (▼); 40ng (●); 80ng (0); 200ng (▽); 400ng (△) and corresponding levels of thioredoxin $\underline{f}$(b), control (▲) with 1mM DTT and no thioredoxin.

REFERENCES

1.   Stewart W.D.P. (1980) Annu. Rev. Microbiol. 34, 497-536.

2.   Tabita F.R. (1980) J. Bacteriol. 143, 1275-1280.

3.   Porter, M.A., Milanez, S., Stringer, C.D. and Hartman, F.C. (1986) Arch. Biochem. Biophys. 245, 14-23.

4.   Amla, D.V., Rowell, P., and Stewart, W.D.P. (1987) Arch. Microbiol. 148, 321-327.

5.   Rowell, P., Darling A.J., Amla D.V. and Stewart W.D.P. (1989) in Biochemistry of the Algae and Cyanobacteria (Rogers L.J. and Gallon, J.R. eds) Annu. Proc. Phyto. Soc. Europe. Vol. 28 pp. 201-216, Oxford University Press, England.

6.   Laemmli, U.K. (1970) Nature. 227, 680-685.

7.   Surek, B., Heilbronn, A., Austen, A. and Latzko, E (1985) Planta. 165, 507-512.

8.   Crawford, N.A., Sutton, C.W., Yee, B.C., Johnson, T.C., Carlson, D.C., and Buchanan, B.B. (1984) Arch. Micro-139, 124-129.

9.   Buchanan, B.B. (1980) Annu. Rev. Plant Physiol. 31, 341-374.

10.   Wara-Aswapati, O., Kemble, R.J. and Bradbeer, J.W. (1980) Plant Physiol. 66, 34-39.

11.   Marsden, W.J.N. and Codd. G.A. (1984) J. Gen. Microbiol. 130, 999-1006.

12.   Thelander, L. and Reichard, P. (1979) Annu. Rev. Biochem. 48, 133-158.

MOLECULAR MODELS OF 3-DIMENSIONAL STRUCTURES OF CHLOROPLAST AND CYTOPLASMIC PHOSPHOGLYCERATE KINASE FROM WHEAT.

[1]EILEEN M. McMORROW, [2] BRIAN J. SUTTON and [1] J. WILLIAM BRADBEER, [1]Biosphere Sciences Division, [2] Biomolecular Sciences Division;   King's College London, Campden Hill Road, LONDON W8 7AH, U.K.

INTRODUCTION
     The isoenzymes of phosphoglycerate kinase (PGK, EC 2.7.2.3) from barley leaves have been purified in this laboratory and used to raise antisera (1). These antisera were used to isolate the wheat cDNAs, specific for each isoenzyme, which have since been sequenced (2). The derived amino acid sequences have been used to build models for the structures of both isoenzymes on an Evans and Sutherland graphics station. The co-ordinates obtained from the x-ray crystallographic studies of the yeast structure, which have been deposited in the Brookhaven protein data bank, have been used as a template (3).
     The enzyme structure consists of two distinct domains each containing a 6-stranded β-pleated sheet surrounded by a-helices. The most interesting feature of the enzyme is the proposed model for the mechanism of catalysis which involves hinge-bending of the enzyme to form a closed structure around a hydrophobic catalytic centre (4 ,5). At the present time, although there is a large amount of evidence to support this mechanism, there is no available crystal structure for the closed form of the enzyme. The enzyme is highly conserved with the amino acid sequences of the wheat leaf isoenzymes having 82 % homology with each other and each having 52 % homology with yeast. There is a high degree of conservation of sequence homology for PGK from several sources (6). Crystallographic studies on the horse PGK revealed a very similar overall structure to the yeast enzyme (4). This conservation of structure has been further confirmed by more recent crystallographic studies on a thermophillic bacterial enzyme (7).

     The models described here represent the first models of PGK from a plant source and the first pair of 3-dimensional models for leaf chloroplast and cytoplasmic isoenzymes. The modelling was carried out to enable a closer comparison of these isoenzymes to try to explain differences observed in their regulation (see accompanying paper by McMorrow *et al.*).

     MATERIALS AND METHODS
     The preliminary alignment of the primary sequences was carried out with reference to known highly conserved homology blocks (H.C. Watson personal communication). These include those residues around the active site as defined for the yeast enzyme (see e.g. 6).   The 3- dimensional structures were built using the programme FRODO. Where the plant sequence contained an amino acid which could not

M. Baltscheffsky (ed.), Current Research in Photosynthesis, Vol. IV, 147–150.
© 1990 *Kluwer Academic Publishers. Printed in the Netherlands.*

be accommodated within the confines of the yeast structure, the position of the main chain of the plant model was moved to prevent close contacts of neighbouring atoms. The modelling procedure was initially carried out for the chloroplast isoenzyme. The cytoplasmic model was built using the chloroplast model as a template for most of the sequence except in instances where the cytoplasmic sequence was identical to that of yeast, where the yeast template was used.

RESULTS AND DISCUSSION

It is clear from Figure 1 that the chloroplast sequence fitted easily on the yeast template with most of the main chain alterations occurring in the N-terminal domain. The most obvious feature is the absence in the chloroplast model of a loop as seen in the top left-hand section of the figure which occurs at residues 128-141 of the yeast structure.. This has been shown to be absent in all the known prokaryotic PGK sequences (T. A. Littlechild, personal communication). This feature is also absent in the cytoplasmic isoenzyme, and coupled with the primary base sequence information, may indicate that recombination of the genes for these two isoenzymes has occurred (2).   For modelling of this major deletion, the sequences were aligned with reference to the secondary structural features, in order to maintain most of helix 4 . Other features which can be seen are the C-terminal extension of the chloroplast isoenzyme of 7 residues at the bottom left hand corner of the figure. The chloroplast sequence contains a 72 amino-acid N terminal extension which is thought to form the transit peptide(2). This will not be considered here.

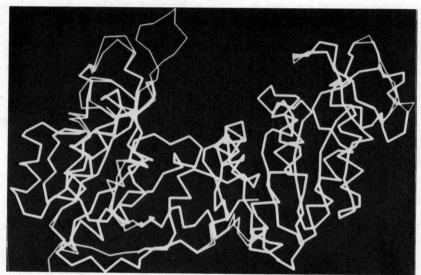

FIGURE 1. The a -carbon backbones of the chloroplast and yeast enzymes.   Areas where the backbones for the two models superimpose are seen as a broader line. Regions where the backbones differ are illustrated by divergence of the image to form two thinner lines.   The cytoplasmic a-carbon backbone is similar to that of the chloroplast.

More detailed analysis of the type and location of side chain residues is necessary to understand differences in the detailed structure and regulation of the isoenzymes.

This type of comparison is illustrated in Figure 2. The Mg^{2+} which forms part of the $MgATP^{2-}$ substrate can be seen clearly as a dot to the right of the centre portion of the figure. The ATP is buried in the C terminal domain beneath. To the left of the Mg^{2+} the PGA substrate, which interacts with the N terminal domain, is visible. There is a large amount of conservation of structure, particularly around the cleft region which encompasses the active site of the enzyme. Many differences in side chain residues can be observed of which some, of the surface changes are clearly visible here. Other changes which occur in the more central parts of the molecule are obscured in a monochromatic representation.

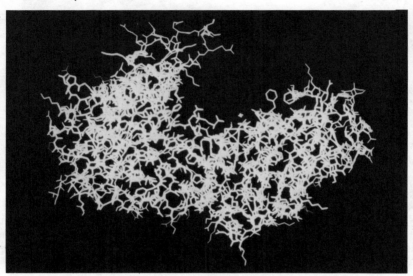

FIGURE 2 The models for the chloroplast and cytoplasmic isoenzymes superimposed on the yeast structure.

The possible anion binding sites on the enzyme are being examined by identifying the distribution of positively charged residues on the model, to try to explain differences observed in the effects of anions on the enzymic reaction. The chloroplast enzyme posseses 35 lysine and 10 arginine residues as compared with 42 lysines and 13 arginines for the yeast enzyme and 39 lysines and 9 arginines for the cytoplasmic enzyme. The study of anionic effects on the enzyme is discussed further in the accompanying paper.

Each of the three structures contain one cysteine, which could be important in protein-protein interactions. In the yeast and cytoplasmic enzymes this residue is conserved at the same position (residue 97 of the yeast sequence) whilst the chloroplast sequence substitutes a valine. In the chloroplast model the single cysteine is found on the surface at the position corresponding to residue 228 of the yeast sequence, with each of the yeast and cytoplasmic sequences substituting a valine at this point. Preliminary evidence suggests that some of the enzymes of photosynthetic carbon reduction may exist as a multi-enzyme complex(8). Other evidence in favour of this phenomenon has been provided by substrate channelling studies on the PGK-triosephosphate dehydrogenase pair(9). The space-filling model depicted in Figure 3 provides additional data about the surface of the molecule which could be important in the formation of a multi-enzyme complex.

A more detailed analysis of the structures will be described elsewhere utilising colour graphics (McMorrow *et al.*, in preparation).

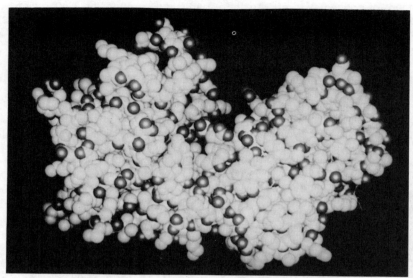

Figure 3. CPK space -filing model of the chloroplast isoenzyme Although the original coloured image was coloured by atom type, it is only possilble in this figure to clearly distinguish the oxygen atoms which are shown as darker images in contrast to the carbon,nitrogen and sulphur atoms.

REFERENCES

1 McMorrow E.M. and Bradbeer J.W. (1989) Plant Physiol.(submitted).

2. Longstaff , M., Raines, C.A., McMorrow, E.M. , Bradbeer, J.W. and Dyer, T.A.
      (1989) Nucleic Acid Res. (in press).

3. Watson, H.C., Walker, N.P.C., Shaw, P.J., Bryant, T.N.,. Wendell, P.L., Fothergill, L.A., Perkins, R.E., Conroy,S.C., Dobson,M.J., Tuite,M.F., Kingsman,A.J. and Kingsman S.M..(1982)   EMBO J. 1, 1635-1640.

4. Blake C.C.F., and Rice D.W. (1981) Phil. Trans. R.Soc. Lond. B, 293, 93-104.

5. Sinev, M.A., Razgulyaev, O.I., Vas,M., TimchenKo, A.A., and Ptitsyn, O.B. (1989)
      Eur.J.Biochem. 180, 61-66.

6. Mori,N., Singer-Sam,J. and Riggs, A.D. (1986)   FEBS Lett., 204, 313-317.

7. Littlechild, J.A., Davies,G.J., Gamblin, S.J. and Watson, H.C.(1987). FEBS Lett. 1,
      123-126

8 Gontero.B., Cardenas,M.L. and Ricard,J. (1988) Eur.J.Biochem.173, 437-443.

9 Macioszek, J. and Anderson, L.E. (1987) Biochim. Biophys. Acta, 892, 185-190.

(This work has been supported by AFRC grant Nº 29/49).

THE REGULATION OF SYNTHESIS OF CHLOROPLASTIC AND CYTOSOLIC ISOENZYMES OF PHOSPHOGLYCERATE KINASE IN BARLEY.

NISHITH SHAH and J. WILLIAM BRADBEER,
Division of Biosphere Sciences, King's College London, Campden Hill Road, LONDON, W8 7AH, UK.

INTRODUCTION
In photosynthetic eukaryotes distinct isoenzymes of phosphoglycerate kinase (PGK   EC 2.7.2.3) occur in chloroplasts and cytosol. The chloroplast isoenzyme is the second enzyme of the C_3 photosynthetic carbon pathway and is also considered to function in glycolysis by which substrates for fatty acid synthesis are produced. The cytosolic isoenzyme participates in both glycolysis and gluconeogenesis. Both isoenzymes are involved in the regulation of carbon partitioning between starch and sucrose and in the triose phosphate/phosphoglycerate shuttle by which phosphorylating and reducing power are transported across the chloroplast envelope via the phosphate translocator. Both isoenzymes are coded by the nuclear genome and synthesized on cytoplasmic ribosomes (1). In green barley leaves the plastid : cytosol isoenzyme ratio is 90 : 10 (2), but can vary from species to species and from tissue to tissue within a species. In this paper we describe the developmental changes in the activities of PGK isoenzymes during leaf growth.

PROCEDURE
Materials and   methods
Barley (Hordeum vulgare, cv golden promise) was grown on vermiculite at 22° C in incubators (for total dark growth)   or in continuous light in controlled environment cabinets. Barley seedlings were harvested at 8d after sowing, when the growth rate of the primary leaf was at its maximum. The seedling was cut at the leaf base and the coleoptile and the secondary leaf removed. The primary leaves were aligned at the leaf base on a chilled glass plate and 1.0cm sections cut from base to 9.0cm for transverse serial section analysis. For all other extractions leaves were aligned and only the section between 3 and 8 cm from base was taken. The sections were placed immediately in liquid N_2, ground to a powder and resuspended in 40mM TRIS buffer (pH 7.8) containing 5mM $MgSO_4$ and 1mM reduced dithiothreitol. After centrifugation an aliquot of the supernatant was taken to measure PGK activity and the rest applied to a DEAE-Sephacel (Pharmacia) column   equilibrated with extraction buffer. The column was thoroughly washed to allow complete removal of cytosolic PGK. Elution of chloroplastic PGK was carried out with a   0-0.4 M KCl linear gradient (2).
PGK was assayed, by measuring the consumption of NADH at 340 nm, in a linked reaction involving glyceraldehyde 3- phosphate dehydrogenase as described previously (2).

M. Baltscheffsky (ed.), Current Research in Photosynthesis, Vol. IV, 151–154.
© 1990 *Kluwer Academic Publishers. Printed in the Netherlands.*

RESULTS AND DISCUSSION

The two most common approaches to the investigation of chloroplast development involve either the illumination of dark-grown leaves or the study of serial sections of a monocotyledonous leaf in which there is a gradient of cellular and plastid development from the base to the apex of the leaf with the transformation from proplastid to plastid accompanied by qualitative and quantitative differences in protein composition (3, 4). Both approaches have been used in this study.

Figure 1 shows that the activities of both PGK isoenzymes increased in a sigmoidal fashion from the leaf base to tip of 8 day-old barley seedlings. Throughout the leaf the chloroplast isoenzyme accounted for 85-90% of total PGK activity and cytosolic isoenzyme for 10-15%. While there was some increase in cytosolic PGK activity, the majority of the increase was in the chloroplastic PGK. Most of the increase occured in sections 5-9 in which plastid replication has been reported to be complete in barley (5). Thus the 7-fold increase in chloroplastic PGK activity is not entirely due to an increase in chloroplast number. There appears to be synthesis (and import) of PGK after chloroplast division has stopped. Similar results have been reported for RUBISCO in barley (6) and the chloroplast isoenzyme of glutamine synthetase (GS) in wheat (7). In contrast the development of light - harvesting chlorophyll a/b protein in barley is complete in the lower half of the leaf (6). Although the first section of the leaf shows no photosynthetic CO_2 fixation (8) appreciable amounts of chloroplast PGK as well as RUBISCO and light - harvesting chlorophyll a/b binding protein are present (6). It would appear that the main function of PGK in this first section may be in lipid synthesis.

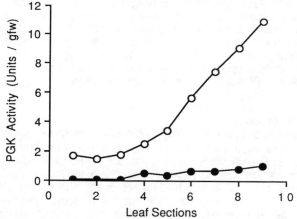

Figure 1. The chloroplast (o) and cytosolic (●) PGK in 1cm leaf sections of 8 day-old light grown barley seedlings.

The subsequent experiments were carried out in the 3-8 cm sections of the leaf (measured from the base). Plants were grown for 8 days in total darkness at 23° C prior to their transfer to continuous illumination of 80 μmoles m^{-2} s^{-1} at 22°C. Figure 2 shows that 8 day - old dark-grown plants had two peaks of PGK activities, confirmed as of cytosolic and chloroplastic origin using antibodies and thiol-reactive agents. These barley seedlings had a chloroplast : cytosolic PGK ratio of 67% : 33%, the activities of chloroplast and cytosolic isoenzymes respectively amounting to 11% and 50% of that in the same section of the light grown leaf (Fig. 1). Twenty-four hour illumination brought about a three - fold increase of chloroplast PGK, but there was no significant change in cytosolic isoenzyme (Fig. 2). Most of the chloroplast isoenzyme increase occurred in the first 6h of illumination.

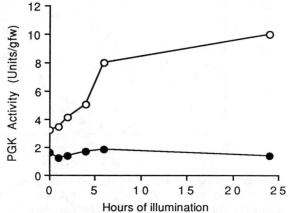

Figure 2. The effects of illumination on the chloroplast (○) and cytosolic (●) PGK content of the 3-8 cm leaf section of 8 day-old dark grown barley.

Figure 3 shows that the 2 : 1 ratio for chloroplast : cytosolic PGK occurred in all dark grown barley seedlings. The decrease in cytosolic PGK subsequent to continuous illumination may represent an inhibition in synthesis and/or an increase in degradation. In the course of continued leaf growth under illumination the cell population of the section has completely turned over after 13 days and therefore the sample represents a trough in PGK activity in those 13-day cells under continuous illumination. The rise in both PGK's after 22 days is probably related to senescence, the chloroplast increase being 33% and the cytosolic being about 600%. After 24 days the chloroplast : cytosolic ratio was 54% : 46%. These changes in the ratios occurred before any phenotypic changes associated with senescence were visible and certainly before there was any noticeable effects on the total protein and chlorophyll (results not shown). After 28 days the activities of both PGK isoenzymes had decreased substantially in barley. Similar increases have been recorded for the cytosolic isoenzymes of dihydroxyacetone phosphate (DHAP) reductase and GS, but in both cases there was a marked decrease in the activity of the chloroplast isoenzyme (9, 10). The decrease in GS activity was due to a reduction in the amount of protein suggesting that there was repression of the chloroplastic gene and stimulation of the cytosolic gene.

The physiological significance of an increase in the activity of cytosolic isoforms may relate to metabolic changes associated with senescence. During senescence there is breakdown of starch, nitrogenous compounds and membrane lipids hence the increase in cytosolic isoforms. GS assimilates NH_3 from degradation of cellular (and chloroplastic) proteins into amides for translocation. PGK would not only assimilate triosephosphates for export but (along with DHAP reductase) would be involved in the increased respiration and metabolic breakdown associated with senescence.

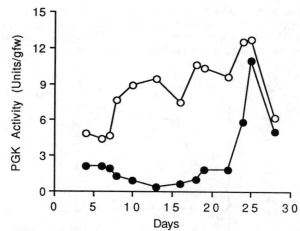

Figure 3. The chloroplast (o) and cytosolic (●) PGK content of the 3-8 cm leaf section of barley. The seedlings were grown in total darkness for 7 days at 23° C before transfer to continuous illumination.

In barley both PGK isoenzymes are synthesized in total darkness. The synthesis of chloroplast PGK being promoted by light, especially when light is supplied at an early stage of leaf development. The increased synthesis seems to be controlled by Pfr. The synthesis of the cytosolic PGK may be inhibited by light or its breakdown promoted by light. Thus it is clear that a number of factors govern the content of the two isoenzymes of PGK in leaf tissue. It would also appear that a number of isoenzyme systems may prove useful in the early detection of senescence.

This work was supported by the SERC (grant no:- GR/E 54505).

REFERENCES
1   Longstaff, M., Raines, C. A., McMorrow, E. M., Bradbeer, J. W. and Dyer, T. A. (1989) Nucl. Acids Res. (in press)
2   McMorrow, E. M. and Bradbeer, J. W. (1989) Plant Physiol. (Submitted)
3   Bradbeer, J. W. (1981) in The Biochemistry of Plants (Stumof, P. K. and Conn, E. E., eds.), Vol. 8, pp.423-472, Academic Press, New York
4   Dean, C. and Leach, R. M. (1982) Plant Physiol. 69, 904-910
5   Baumgartner, B. J., Rapp, J. C. and Mullet J. E. (1989) Plant Physiol. 89, 1011-1018
6   Viro, M. and Kloppstech, K. (1980) Planta 150, 41-45.
7   Tobin A. K., Ridley, S. M. and Stewart, G. R. (1985) Planta 163, 544-548
8   Baker, N. R. and Leech, R. M. (1977) Plant Physiol. 60, 640-644
9   Gee, R., Byerrum, R. U., Gerber, D. and Tolbert, N. E. (1989) Plant Physiol. 89,   305-308
1 0 Kawakami, N. and Watanabe A. (1989) Plant Physiol. 88, 1430-1434

A COMPARISON OF THE REGULATION OF YEAST PHOSPHOGLYCERATE KINASE WITH
THE ISOENZYMES OF BARLEY CHLOROPLAST AND CYTOSOL

[1]EILEEN M. MCMORROW, [1]J. WILLIAM BRADBEER, [1]PEDRO O. MONTIEL-CANOBRA
and [2]MÄRTHA LARSSON-RAŹNIKIEWICZ. [1]Biosphere Sciences Division, King's
College London, Campden Hill Road, LONDON W8 7AH, U.K. and [2]Department of
Chemistry, Swedish University of Agricultural Sciences, Box 7015, S-750 07,
UPPSALA, SWEDEN.

INTRODUCTION
Substantial investigations of the kinetics of phosphoglycerate kinase (PGK,
EC 2.7.2.3) from yeast have uncovered a complex mechanism of catalysis (see eg
1,2). Studies on the enzyme are seriously complicated by the observation that it
does not obey classical Michaelis-Menten kinetics and that it is activated and
inhibited by divalent metal ions(3). In green plants the regulation of PGK is very
poorly understood, but this is not surprising as leaves contain distinct isoenzymes
in chloroplast and cytosol (4). These isoenzymes have recently been isolated from
barley leaves (5) and this in turn has led to cloning and sequencing of cDNA from
wheat, the deduction of the amino acid sequence of the isoenzymes (6) and the
construction of three-dimensional models of the isoenzymes (see the accompanying
paper by McMorrow et al.) PGK structure is highly conserved in nature, which
would suggest that the enzymes from plants also should possess a complex
regulatory mechanism, as has already been demonstrated (7).
Most published accounts of the role of PGK in the regulation of
photosynthetic carbon metabolism maintain that the direction of flux of the enzymic
reaction in the chloroplasts is controlled by a simple mechanism of mass-action of
substrates and products (8). Although the enzyme equilibrium constant for this
reaction is the least favourable in the Calvin cycle, the high pool of 3-
phosphoglycerate (PGA) in the chloroplast has been implicated as the sole means of
regulating flux through this stage of carbon fixation. However, studies on the
isolated enzymes from barley suggest that the PGK isoenzymes from plant sources
have more distinct regulatory mechanisms when compared with the enzyme from
yeast and there are also differences between the plant isoenzymes (7). The results
for the plant isoenzymes suggest that such regulatory mechanisms would contribute
to the regulation of the rate of carbon fixation.
It has been shown previously that free Mg^{2+} behaves as an inhibitor of the
enzymic reaction for both isoenzymes with respect to both $MgATP^{2-}$ and PGA which
are the two true substrates for the reaction (7,9). The inhibition patterns
observed are complex and suggest that this could provide a means of slowing down
the rate of CO_2 fixation when the concentration of free Mg^{2+} exceeds the supply of
ATP (9) . In this paper we describe the effects of sulphate and nucleotides on the

M. Baltscheffsky (ed.), Current Research in Photosynthesis, Vol. IV, 155–158.
© 1990 *Kluwer Academic Publishers. Printed in the Netherlands.*

enzyme reaction from barley chloroplast and cytosol compared with the yeast enzyme.

PROCEDURE.
Materials and Methods.
    Barley leaf PGK isoenzymes were separated by DEAE Sephacel chromatography followed by purification on ATP Sepharose (5). The yeast enzyme was obtained from baker's yeast and the main electrophoretic component was used (10).
    All assays were performed under heavy-metal free conditions after extraction of heavy-metals and the acid treatment of glassware to remove contaminating heavy-metal ions. Except where stated otherwise, assays were carried out spectrophotometrically at 340 nm and 30°C in a 1 ml reaction mixture containing 50 mM Tris, pH 7.8, 0.14 mM NADH, 0.1 µg PGK and 40 µg glyceraldehyde-phosphate dehydrogenase. Concentrations of free Mg^{2+}, $MgATP^{2-}$, and PGA were calculated as described previously (11).

RESULTS AND DISCUSSION.
    Fig.1 shows the effect of SO_4^{2-} on the initial velocity of PGK from barley chloroplasts. Similar results have been obtained for the yeast enzyme, which is partly explained by the presence of strong anion-binding sites with activation occurring at low concentrations of anions and inhibition at higher concentrations (12). One fraction of wheat gave similar results while the other showed activation without inhibition(13). As stated above both of the PGK isoenzymes from barley have been found to resemble yeast PGK in their possession of non-linear kinetics (7).

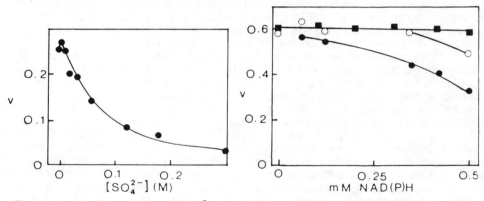

Figure 1.   The effects of SO_4^{2-} on the initial velocity of barley chloroplast PGK in 1 mM Mg ATP^{2-}, 2 mM PGA and 0.14 mM NADH.

Figure 2.   The effects of NADH (■●) and NADPH (○) on the initial velocity of PGK from yeast (■) and barley chloroplasts (●,○). Other conditions as in Fig.1.

    Comparative experiments with barley and yeast enzymes were complicated by differences in sensitivity to NADH concentration(14). It was found that the higher concentration of NADH (0.5 mM) used in the yeast assay had an inhibitory effect on the barley chloroplast isoenzyme, as shown in Fig.2. As the next enzyme in the Calvin cycle is NADPH dependent the effects of NADPH were also examined. The results indicate that NADPH was much less inhibitory. Fig.3 shows that NADH acted as a non-competitive inhibitor with respect to $MgATP^{2-}$, thus implying that it, for example, may bind to the previously suggested second nucleotide binding site (1,3). This does not appear to be an effect on the glyceraldehyde-phosphate dehydrogenase used in the linked assay .

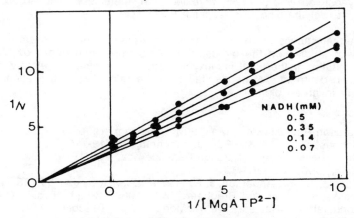

Figure 3.   The effect of NADH on the initial velocity of barley chloroplast PGK at varying $MgATP^{2-}$ and 2 mM PGA.

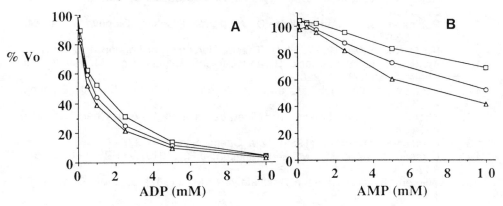

Figure 4.   The effects of (A) ADP and (B) AMP on the initial velocity of PGK from yeast,□; barley chloroplasts, Δ; and barley cytosol, o. The reaction mixture contained 3 mM $MgATP^{2-}$, 2 mM PGA and 1 mM Mg^{2+}. Initial velocity is expressed as % of rate observed in the absence of added ADP and AMP.

Studies on the effects of adenine nucleotides on the reaction for barley leaf PGK isoenzymes have revealed that these isoenzymes are not simply regulated by energy charge, but the nucleotides behave more as allosteric regulators. Fig.4 shows the effects of ADP and AMP on the reaction rates observed for the barley isoenzymes as compared with yeast. It can be seen that in all cases, the nucleotide analogues inhibit the rate of enzyme reaction to a greater extent in the plant isoenzymes as compared with the yeast enzyme and that the chloroplast isoenzyme showed most inhibition. Extensive studies on the effects of adenine nucleotides on the yeast enzyme (3,11,15) revealed that there appeared to be at least two different sites for the binding of adenine nucleotides.

Further studies on the regulation of the plant isoenzymes are in progress in parallel with studies on the structure (see accompanying paper by McMorrow *et al.*). The results for the plant isoenzymes suggest complex regulatory mechanisms which would contribute to the regulation of the rate of carbon fixation and carbon partitioning in green plants.

REFERENCES
1.   Larsson-Raźnikiewicz, M. (1967)   Biochim. Biophys. Acta, 132,33-40.
2.   Scopes, R.K. (1978)   Eur. J. Biochem. 91,119-129.
3.   Schierbeck, B. and Larsson-Raźnikiewicz, M. (1979)   Biochim. Biophys. Acta, 568, 195-204.
4.   Pacold, I. and Anderson, L.E. (1975)   Plant Physiol. 55,168-171.
5.   McMorrow, E.M. and Bradbeer, J.W. (1989)   Plant Physiol. (submitted).
6.   Longstaff, M., Raines, C.A., McMorrow, E.M., Bradbeer, J.W. and Dyer, T.A. (1989)   Nucleic Acids Research, 17 (in press).
7.   McMorrow, E.M. and Bradbeer, J.W. (1987)   in Progress in Photosynthesis Research (Biggins, J., ed.), Vol.III, pp.333-336, Martinus Nijhoff, Dordrecht.
8.   Robinson, S. P. and Walker, D. A. (1979) Biochim. Biophys. Acta, 545, 528-536.
9.   McMorrow, E.M. (1987)   Ph.D. Thesis, University of London.
10.   Arvidsson, L., Schierbeck, B. and Larsson-Raźnikiewicz, M. (1976) Acta Chem. Scand. B 30, 228-234.
11.   Larsson-Raźnikiewicz, M. and Arvidsson, L. (1971)   Eur. J. Biochem. 22,506-512.
12.   Khamis, M.M. and Larsson-Raźnikiewicz, M. (1987)   Acta Chem. Scand. B 41,348-355.
13.   Larsson-Raźnikiewicz (1983) Acta Chem. Scand. B 37, 657-659.
14.   Larsson-Raźnikiewicz, M. and Jansson, J.R. (1973)   FEBS Lett. 29,345-347.
15.   Wiksell, E. and Larsson-Raźnikiewicz, M. (1987)   J. Biol. Chem. 262, 14472-14478.

This work has been supported by AFRC grant PG 29/49, an OECD short-term fellowship, a grant from the King's College Research Strategy Fund and the Swedish Council for Forestry and Agricultural Research.

RELATIONSHIP BETWEEN THE PRIMARY STRUCTURE OF FERREDOXIN AND THIOREDOXIN AND THEIR REACTIVITY.

J.P. Jacquot, F. de Lamotte, M. Miginiac-Maslow, R. Peyronnet, J.B. Peyre, E. Wollman* and P. Decottignies . Physiologie Végétale Moléculaire. URA 1128. Bât 430, 91405 Orsay Cedex France and * Laboratoire d'Immunologie, IGR, 94805 Villejuif Cedex France.

1.   INTRODUCTION

Higher plants, algae and cyanobacteria possess a regulatory sytem. the ferredoxin- thioredoxin system , in which a light signal is converted into an electronic signal, which in turn generates the appearance of strongly reducing thiol groups. This system is able to photoregulate chloroplastic enzymes through thiol/ disulfide interchange reactions. In this regulatory chain, the ferredoxin- thioredoxin reductase is the only component restricted to photosynthetic cells.

On the other hand ferredoxin and thioredoxin are ubiquitous proteins present in bacteria, algae, plants and animals. This paper shows and discusses the effect of animal ferredoxin (adrenodoxin. ADX) and human lymphocyte thioredoxin (HTR) in several electron transfer reactions.

2.   MATERIALS AND METHODS

Corn leaf NADP- malate dehydrogenase (NADP- MDH), spinach ferredoxin. ferredoxin thioredoxin reductase and thioredoxin m were purified to homogeneity as described earlier (1). Pig adrenal ferredoxin was prepared as in (1). Human lymphocyte thioredoxin was cloned, overexpressed and purified from E coli as described in (2).

Ferredoxin dependent reactions:

Cyclic and pseudo cyclic photophosphorylation: In 100 μl the incubation medium contained 10 μmol HEPES NaOH buffer pH 7.8, 10 μmol sorbitol, .4 μmol Na phosphate containing 1.4 kBeq ^{32}P, 250 units catalase, freshly isolated pea thylakoids (10 μg chlorophyll) and spinach ferredoxin or pig adrenodoxin as indicated. After illumination for 15 min under white saturating light. the reaction was stopped and the radioactivity incorporated into the ATP determined.

Thioredoxin dependent reaction:

M. Baltscheffsky (ed.), Current Research in Photosynthesis, Vol. IV, 159–162.
© 1990 *Kluwer Academic Publishers. Printed in the Netherlands.*

DTT linked reduction of insulin: In a total volume of 1 ml, the reaction medium contained 100 μmol phosphate buffer pH 7, .13 μmol porcin insulin and thioredoxin as indicated. The reaction was initiated by adding .5 μmol DTT and the A 650 was recorded as described in (3).

Thioredoxin and ferredoxin dependent reaction:

Light activation of NADP- MDH: The activation medium (100 μl) comprised the following components: 100 μmol Tris HCl pH 8.0, 10 μmol ferredoxin, 10 μmol thioredoxin, 2 μmol ferredoxin thioredoxin reductase, .7 μmol NADP- MDH, 100 units catalase and pea thylakoids equivalent to 25 μg chlorophyll. When indicated, ferredoxin and thioredoxin were replaced by their animal counterparts (ADX and HTR). Photoactivation was performed under saturating white light and nitrogen. At appropriate times, aliquots were removed and used for the spectrophotometric determination of activity as in (1).

3.   RESULTS

Fig 1 shows the effect of pig adrenodoxin in cyclic and pseudo cyclic photosynthetic phosphorylations. Although these reactions are specific of photosynthetic organisms, the animal ferredoxin can replace plant ferredoxin with a rather good efficiency in the case of pseudocyclic photophosphorylation. On the other hand, adrenodoxin is unable to donate electrons in the cyclic pathway. These observations suggest that this animal ferredoxin can be photoreduced through PSI and the associated bound iron sulfur centers.

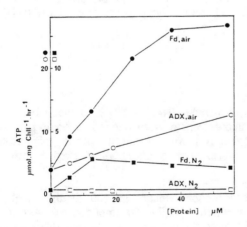

Fig 1: Effect of adrenodoxin in cyclic and pseudocyclic photophosphorylations

When photoreduced, adrenodoxin can be used as a substrate of ferredoxin thioredoxin reductase as seen by its capacity to promote the photoactivation of chloroplastic NADP malate dehydrogenase (Fig 2). It is however much less efficient than "authentic" plant ferredoxin since higher concentrations must be used (30 µM is optimal vs 10 µM) and the maximal level of activity is only 25% of the one obtained in the homologous system.

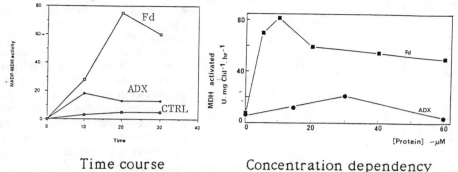

Time course   Concentration dependency

Fig 2: Effect of adrenodoxin in NADP- MDH light activation

The effect of human lymphocyte thioredoxin (HTR) is shown in two different assays: the DTT dependent insulin reduction and the photoactivation of NADP MDH. In the first reaction, HTR is slightly more efficient than spinach thioredoxin m (Fig 3) and as efficient than **E coli** thioredoxin, the protein with which the insulin reduction test was originally devised (data not shown).

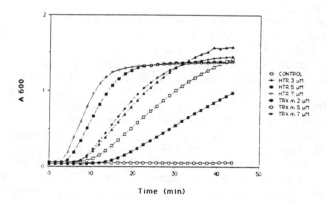

Time (min)

Fig 3: Effect of HTR in the DTT dependent reduction of insulin

As observed before with pig adrenodoxin. HTR is able to promote the light activation of NADP- MDH. Replacing the plant type thioredoxin m by an animal thioredoxin results in a decreased NADP- MDH light activation (30% compared to an homologous system). Moreover, the optimal concentration (around 40 µM) is higher than the one of spinach thioredoxin m (around 10 µM).

Fig 4. Effect of HTR in the NADP-MDH light activation

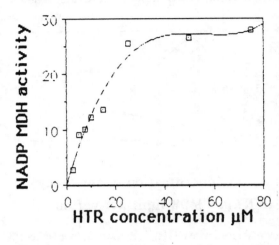

4.   CONCLUSIONS: The sequence homology betweeen pig adrenodoxin   and   spinach ferredoxin is very low. The cystein residues (involved in the iron sulfur binding) are not even conserved in the primary structure. Despite these marked differences, the proteins can be changed for one   another   in   several oxidoreduction reactions including pseudocyclic photophosphorylation and NADP MDH light activation. Other data not shown here indicate that ferredoxins can interact even with heterologous ferredoxin NADP reductases. The sequence data comparison together with the observed reactivity suggest that the iron sulfur center is involved in the protein protein interactions (1) and that plant and animal ferredoxins might present a common folding. The crystallographic structures obtained so far are too poor to allow an unequivocal answer to this question.

DTT reduced human thioredoxin is at least as efficient as spinach thioredoxin m in the reduction of insulin. HTR is also a very good substrate of **E coli** ribonucleotide reductase (data not shown). On the other hand, HTR is a poor substrate of ferredoxin thioredoxin reductase as shown by its lower efficiency in the NADP- MDH light activation. We also have evidence that HTR is even poorer for the DTT activation of FBPase and as a substrate of **E coli** NADPH thioredoxin reductase (unpublished results). Thus depending on the interacting enzyme, spinach thioredoxin m or HTR exhibit similar or very different kinetic behaviors. The comparison of the primary structures of both proteins is very interesting in this respect. While the sequence is well conserved around the active site it is very divergent in other parts of the molecule. Among the residues that are not conserved, tryptophane 33 of spinach thioredoxin m could play a very important role in determining the specificity. On the other hand, Asp 31 and Lys 96 of thioredoxin m are conserved in HTR and might be essential in determining the structure and function of these proteins.

5.   REFERENCES

1. Jacquot, J.P. et al. (1988) Eur. J. Biochem., **174**, 629- 635.
2. Wollman E. et al. (1988) J. Biol. Chem., **263**, 15506 - 15512.
3. Holmgren A. (1979) J. Biol. Chem., **254**, 9627- 9632.

IN VIVO SYNTHESIS AND IMMUNOLOGICAL RELATIONSHIP OF THIOREDOXIN *f* FROM PEA AND SPINACH.

Ana Chueca, Mariam Sahrawy, José L. Carrasco, Juan L. Ramos, Juan J. Lázaro, Rosario Hermoso and Julio López Gorgé. Department of Plant Biochemistry, Estación Experimental del Zaidín (CSIC), Granada, Spain.

1. INTRODUCTION

Thioredoxins are small proteins (typically 12 kDa m.w.) involved as cofactors in some oxidation-reduction processes, such as ribonucleotide reduction, reduction of sulfur-containing compounds, reductive activation of Calvin cycle enzymes (1,2). In addition, thioredoxin constitute an essential subunit of the DNA polymerase of bacteriophage T7 (3). Even though it has been mainly study in *E. coli* (4), this protein was isolated from a variety of prokaryotic and eukaryotic organisms. Those from *E. coli* (4), *Corynebacterium nephridii* (5), the cyanobacterium *Anabaena* 7119 (6), *Chromatium vinosum* (7), *Rhodospirillum rubrum* (8), bacteriophage T7 (9), and the *m*-type thioredoxins from spinach chloroplasts (10) have been sequenced. Except for that of bacteriophage T7, all the thioredoxins show considerable homology. The three dimensional structure of *E. coli* and T7 thioredoxins have been determined (11,12) and, in spite of large differences in amino acid sequences, both show many similarities in their terciary structures.

The light-induced reductive activation of chloroplast fructose-1.6-bisphosphatase (FBPase) is a property of one - the so-called thioredoxin *f* - of the multiple thioredoxin species so far isolated from plants (2,13,14,15), whereas the named thioredoxin *m* activates chloroplast malate dehydrogenase (15). Thioredoxins isolated from bacteria, yeasts or liver show in some degree activating capabilities of both chloroplast enzymes, adding these features to the apparently unlimited exchangeability of thioredoxins observed in reactions like ribonucleotide or sulfate reductions. However, green seedlings of soybean and wheat contain multiple thioredoxin-like proteins with all the typical thioredoxin properties, but ineffective in the activation of spinach FBPase (14).

In this work we describe the *in vivo* synthesis of spinach thioredoxin *f*, as well as the specificity of such a protein from spinach, pea and *E. coli* , by using polyclonal antibodies raised against spinach thioredoxin *f*. In addition, we have used the *E. coli* trxA gene as a probe for testing pea and spinach thioredoxin RNAs.

M. Baltscheffsky (ed.), Current Research in Photosynthesis, Vol. IV, 163–166.
© 1990 *Kluwer Academic Publishers. Printed in the Netherlands.*

2. MATERIALS AND METHODS

Spinach seeds were germinated in moistened vermiculite and grown in a growth chamber at 20-25°C. For *in vivo* labelling experiments leaves of 8 days grown seedlings were gently brush stroke with a ^{35}S-methionine (>1000 Ci/mmol) solution in 2% Tween 80, in proportion of about 1 µCi per seedling. These were illuminated for 1.5, 7, 20, 30 and 50 h before harvesting, and the leaves homogenized by hand in a chilled mortar with (1:3 p/v) 25 mM Tris-HCl pH 7.5, 5 mM MgCl$_2$, 5 mM 2-mercaptoethanol, 0.5 mM NaEDTA and 1 M phenylmethylsulfonyl fluoride. The homogenate was centrifuged at 12000 *g* for 30 min, and the supernatant collected for analytical determinations.

Thioredoxin f activity was assayed as Crawford et al. (15), thioredoxin protein by the ELISA method of Hermoso et al. (16), and the ^{35}S-labelling of soluble total protein according to Enger et al. (17). Finally, the ^{35}S incorporation in *de novo* synthesized thioredoxin f was determined by adding to a supernatant aliquot, 4 vol of PBS buffer containing 50 mM methionine and 10% Triton X-100. A sufficient quantity of spinach thioredoxin f antiserum was added to the mixture, and the Td-IgG complex sequestered by protein A-Sepharose. After short centrifugation, the pellet was 3 times washed with PBS buffer containing 10 mM methionine and 1% Triton X-100, and 2 additional ones with the same buffer but 10 mM methionine and 0.1% SDS. The thioredoxin f was separated by SDS-electrophoresis according to Laemmli (18), and visualized by fluorography at -70°C. The thioredoxin f labelled band was solubilized with H$_2$O$_2$, and counted in a liquid scintillator. Homogeneous thioredoxin f from spinach leaves was obtained according to Crawford et al. (15), and a specific antiserum against this polypeptide prepared from rabbits as described by Hermoso et al. (16).

Total RNA was isolated as Wallace (19), and poly(A$^+$)-RNA purified using oligo-dT-cellulose. Northern blot analysis were performed by electrophoresis of the RNA in formaldehyde-MOPS agarose, and blotted onto Gene Screen membranes. trxA gene labelled with ^{32}P-dCTP by nick-translation was used as a probe. Methods used for hybridization and washing of filters were those recommended by the manufacturers.

3. RESULTS AND DISCUSSION

The rate of light induction of thioredoxin synthesis was determined by experiments of *in vivo* synthesis with spinach seedlings leaf-supplied under illumination with a pulse of ^{35}S-methionine. Leaf extracts showed by immunoprecipitation with a specific antiserum raised against spinach thioredoxin f, a labelled polypeptide of about 12 kDa m.w. coemigrating in SDS-electrophoresis with spinach thioredoxin f. The amount of labelled protein increases in the first 20 h after labelling, and then decreases with the time. The ^{35}S incorporation in total protein was approximately 15% of the applied radioactivity, whereas after 20 h of ^{35}S-methionine application, just when both total protein and thioredoxin synthesis showed maximum rates, the level of labelled thioredoxin was about 0.03% of that of total protein. As deduced from Fig. 1, the thioredoxin f half-life could be estimated about 45 h.

As we can see in Table I, spinach FBPase is fully activated by the homologous thioredoxin f. However, spinach thioredoxin f appears completely inefective against the pea enzyme, which is in accordance with the earlier observed inactivity of thioredoxins from soybean and wheat in the spinach FBPase activation (14). In contrast, *E. coli* thioredoxin produces a similar activation of the spinach FBPase than that of the homologous polypeptide.

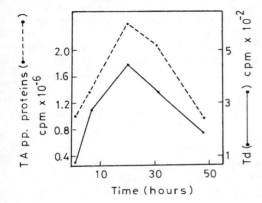

FIGURE 1. Patterns of ^{35}S incorporation in TCA precipitable total protein (- -) and chloroplast Td f (——), when etiolated pea plants were brush stroke with ^{35}S-methionine, and then illuminated for different times.

Even though it is well known that bacterial thioredoxins are unspecifics in heterologous assays, the finding that *E. coli* thioredoxin is closer to the spinach thioredoxin f than the pea one, raises the question if both higher plant proteins differ in structural properties. An antiserum raised against spinach thioredoxin f showed by ELISA (Table II) a cross reactivity with the

TABLE I. Stimulation of FBPase activity by different thioredoxins.

	FBPase activity (μmoles Pi/min)		
	+ spinach Td	+ *E. coli* Td[*]	– Td
Spinach FBPase	1.26	2.30	0.19
Pea FBPase	0.16	2.10	0.16
– FBPase	0.16	0.66	0.06

[*]*E. coli* lysate heated at 80°C for 1 h.

pea polypeptide of 18% of that obtained with the homologous thioredoxin f, whereas it was 30% against *E. coli* thioredoxin. This suggests that spinach thioredoxin f is closer in structural properties to the *E. coli* polypeptide than the pea one.

TABLE II. Immunological cross-reactivity (ELISA) of thioredoxins from spinach, pea and *E. coli*.

Source of thioredoxin (0.5 μg protein/well)	Cross reactivity (%)[*]
Spinach (leaf extract)	100
Pea (leaf extract)	18
E. coli (lysate)	30

[*]Antiserum (rabbit) against spinach thioredoxin f.

trxA gene of *E. coli* was used as a probe to detect thioredoxin mRNAs from pea and spinach, grown under different light conditions. mRNAs isolated from green or illuminated pea plants were detected by the heterologous probe under low stringency hybridization conditions (30% formamide), while no mRNA from etiolated pea seedlings was detected. This suggests that thioredoxin mRNA is synthesized or stabilized under illumination. Under similar conditions of hybridization thioredoxin mRNA was not detected (or only detected after prolonged exposure time) in the isolated spinach mRNA. This indicates that thioredoxin mRNA from spinach is less abundant, or that its nucleotide sequence exhibits a lower homology with the *E. coli* heterologous probe than the corresponding one from pea.

Acknowledgements. This work was supported by the grant PB87-0431 of DGICYT (Spain).

REFERENCES
1 Holmgren,A. (1985) Trends Biochem.Sci. 6,26-29
2 Buchanan,B.B. (1980) Ann.Rev.Plant Physiol. 31,341-374
3 Mark,D.F. and Richardson,C.C. (1976) Proc.Natl.Acad.Sci.USA 73,780-784
4 Hoog,J.O., Von Behr-Lindstrom,H., Josephson,S., Wallace,B.J., Kushner,S.R., Jornvall,H. and Holmgren,A. (1984) Biosci.Rep. 4,917-923
5 Meng,M. and Hogenkamp,H.P.C. (1981) J.Biol.Chem. 256,9174-9182
6 Gleason,F.K., Whittaker,M.M., Holmgren,A. and Jornvall,H. (1985) J.Biol.Chem. 247,8063-8068
7 Johnson,R.S. and Biemann,K. (1987) Biochemistry 26,1209-1214
8 Johnson,T.C., Yee,C.B., Carlson,D.E., Buchanan,B.B., Johnson,R.S., Mathews,W.R. and Biemann,K. (1988) J.Bacteriol. 170,2406-2408
9 Sjöberg,B.M. and Holmgren,A. (1972) J.Biol.Chem. 247,8063-8068
10 Maeda,K., Tsujita,A., Dalzoppo,D., Vilbois,F. and Schürmann,P. (1986) Eur.J.Biochem. 154,197-203
11 Soderberg,B.O., Sjöberg,B.M., Sonnerstam,U. and Branden,C.I. (1978) Proc.Natl.Acad.Sci.USA 75,5827-5830
12 Holmgren,A., Soderberg,B.O., Eklund,H. and Branden,C.I. (1975) Proc. Natl.Acad.Sci.USA 72,2305-2309
13 Jacquot,J.P. (1984) Physiol.Véget. 22,487-507
14 Häberlein,I., Schimpff-Weiland,G. and Follmann,H. (1985) Biochem. Biophys.Res.Commun. 127,401-406
15 Crawford,N.A., Yee,B.C., Hutcheson,S.W., Wolosiuk,R.A. and Buchanan B.B. (1986) Arch.Biochem.Biophys. 244,1-15
16 Hermoso,R., Chueca,A., Lázaro,J.J. and López Gorgé,J. (1987) Photosynth.Res. 14,269-278
17 Enger,M.D., Rall,L.B. and Hildebrunt,C.E. (1979) Nucleic Acids Res. 7,271-278
18 Laemmli,U.K. (1970) Nature 227,680-685
19 Wallace,D.M. (1987) Methods Enzymol. 152,33-41

PRIMARY STRUCTURES OF REGULATORY PROTEINS OF THE FERREDOXIN-THIOREDOXIN SYSTEM OF SPINACH CHLOROPLASTS.

PETER SCHÜRMANN, LAURA GARDET-SALVI, Laboratoire de Biochimie végétale, Université de Neuchâtel, CH-2000 NEUCHATEL, Switzerland

MASAHARU KAMO, KEIICHI YANO, AKIRA TSUGITA, Research Institute for Biosciences, Science University of Tokyo, 2669 Yamazaki, Noda-City, Chiba, 278, Japan

1. INTRODUCTION

The ferredoxin/thioredoxin system is an important regulatory system switching on and off certain key chloroplast enzymes like fructose 1,6-bisphosphatase, sedoheptulase 1,7-bisphosphatase, phosphoribulokinase, ATP-synthetase, NADP-malate dehydrogenase and glucose 6-phosphate dehydrogenase in response to light [1]. Light reversibly switches on photosynthetic enzymes and turns off degradative enzymes thus preventing the concurrent operation of assimilatory and dissimilatory pathways within the chloroplast.

The light signal, produced by the thylakoids, is transmitted via several proteins: ferredoxin, ferredoxin-thioredoxin reductase (FTR) and thioredoxins to the target enzymes.

Chloroplasts contain one type of FTR, composed of two nonidentical subunits, and two different types of thioredoxins, thioredoxin m and f, which interact very specifically with their respective target enzymes [2].

Whereas the primary structure of thioredoxin m is known [3], only limited structural information on thioredoxin f [4] and none on FTR are available. However, in order to get a better understanding of the regulatory mechanism, structural information on the proteins involved is essential. We are therefore studying the primary structures of two key proteins of the system, FTR and thioredoxin f and report here the complete primary structure of thioredoxin f and some structural information on FTR subunit B.

2. MATERIALS AND METHODS

Thioredoxin f was purified from spinach leaves and analysed by conventional sequencing as described elsewhere [5]. FTR was purified essentially as described earlier [6] substituting a Fd-affinity column for the last two chromatographic steps. The subunits of FTR were separated by SDS-polyacrylamide gel electrophoresis and after Coomassie blue staining extracted and purified according to [7]. The sequences were determined by conventional methods as described elsewhere [8].

3. RESULTS

Thioredoxin f is a protein containing 113 amino acids adding up to a calculated molecular mass of 12 564 Da. Its primary structure is shown in Fig.1. Apart from the active site sequence -Cys-Gly-Pro-Cys-, conserved in most thioredoxins, its primary structure is quite

```
Met-Glu-Ala-Ile-Val-Gly-Lys-Val-Thr-Glu-Val-Asn-Lys-Asp-Thr-Phe-Trp-Pro-Ile-Val-
                    10                                                    20
Lys-Ala-Ala-Gly-Asp-Lys-Pro-Val-Val-Leu-Asp-Met-Phe-Thr-Gln-Trp-Cys-Gly-Pro-Cys-
                    30                                                    40
Lys-Ala-Met-Ala-Pro-Lys-Tyr-Glu-Lys-Leu-Ala-Glu-Glu-Tyr-Leu-Asp-Val-Ile-Phe-Leu-
                    50                                                    60
Lys-Leu-Asp-Cys-Asn-Gln-Glu-Asn-Lys-Thr-Leu-Ala-Lys-Glu-Leu-Gly-Ile-Arg-Val-Val-
                    70                                                    80
Pro-Thr-Phe-Lys-Ile-Leu-Lys-Glu-Asn-Ser-Val-Val-Gly-Glu-Val-Thr-Gly-Ala-Lys-Tyr-
                    90                                                    100
Asp-Lys-Leu-Leu-Glu-Ala-Ile-Gln-Ala-Ala-Arg-Ser-Ser
                    110
```

FIGURE 1. Amino acid sequence of chloroplast thioredoxin f from spinach

different from that of the companion thioredoxin m [3]. In addition, a third Cys residue is present at position 64 in the C-terminal half of the protein. This third Cys is easily accessible to thiol reagents which may indicate, that it is exposed at the protein surface. A modification of the residue with N-ethylmaleimide reduces the activity of thioredoxin f by about 60% when tested in the activation of fructose 1,6-bisphosphatase. This result could mean that Cys-64 is somehow involved in the interaction with the target enzyme tested. Another feature of thioredoxin f is its blocked N-terminus. Our present results suggest that most probably acetyl-Met is at the blocked N-terminus. However, we can not rule out the possibility, that formyl-Thr-Gln-Glu-Met- constitutes the blocked N-terminus of the protein.

When the primary structure of thioredoxin f is compared with that of thioredoxin m then only 27 residues (24%) out of the 113 are found at identical positions. However, secondary structure predictions according to Chou and Fasman [9] indicate that, despite the differences in primary structure, thioredoxin f may be very similar to thioredoxin m or thioredoxin from E.coli. The apparent spatial similarity contrasts with the pronounced specificity of thioredoxin f towards its target enzymes. Further experiments will be needed to find the unique structural features responsible for the specificity of this protein.

The FTR is composed of two nonidentical subunits with apparent MW of 17 200 for subunit A and 15 400 for subunit B. We have separated them and determined the amino acid composition of each subunit and the amino acid sequence of subunit B containing the redoxactive disulfide bridge [10]. The results in Table 1 compare the amino acid compositions of the subunits with that of the whole protein as well as that derived from the preliminary sequence of subunit B. They provide good evidence that the native FTR is composed of equal amounts of subunits A + B and that the two subunits must have quite different primary structures.

Since FTR contains a redoxactive disulfide and an Fe-S cluster [10,11], it is of interest to know how many Cys residues there are per subunit and where they are located in the subunits. Three Cys residues are found in subunit A, five in subunit B. The preliminary primary structure of subunit B suggests the positions of its five Cys.

TABLE 1. Amino Acid Composition of FTR and its subunits from spinach

	A	B	B (Seq)	A+B (Sum)	Whole	Whole [Ref.11]
Asp	14	16	14	30	32	28
Thr	4	7	8	11	11	12
Ser	20	8	8	28	22	20
Glu	19	16	16	35	33	34
Cys	3	5	5	8	8	10
Pro	15	8	8	23	20	18
Gly	10	6	6	16	14	14
Ala	3	7	7	10	10	12
Val	16	11	10	27	28	26
Met	1	5	5	6	5	6
Ile	5	4	8	9	10	10
Leu	10	8	7	18	17	18
Tyr	6	4	5	10	6	8
Phe	5	6	8	11	12	12
Lys	19	13	12	32	28	28
His	2	3	2	5	6	8
Arg	4	7	7	11	12	10
Total	156	135	136	291	276	274

Two Cys are found in the N-terminal part of subunit B in the sequence -Cys-Arg-Lys-Ser-Cys- which is similar to -Cys-Lys-Lys-Ser-Cys- found in a ribonucleotide reductase [12] and in several metallo-thioneins [13]. Two more Cys are clustered in the sequence -Cys-Pro-Cys-Arg-Glu- at one third from the N-terminus and the fifth Cys is at two thirds from the N-terminus [14]. Our present results dont allow us to decide which Cys are part of the disulfide bridge and which are linked to the Fe-S cluster [10].

4. CONCLUSION

We present the first primary structure of a f-type thioredoxin from plants. This protein which has a blocked N-terminus shows only 24% residue identities with spinach thioredoxin m or _Escherichia coli_ thioredoxin. A third Cys present may have some function in the interaction between thioredoxin f and target enzyme.

The amino acid compositions of the two nonidentical subunits of FTR and a preliminary primary structure for subunit B have been determined. The results allow us to position five Cys present in subunit B.

5. AKNOWLEDGEMENTS

This research is supported by the Swiss National Science Foundation and by Grants in-Aid for Scientific Research from the Ministry of Education, Science and Culture of Japan.

REFERENCES

1 Cséke, C. & Buchanan, B. B. (1986) Biochim. Biophys. Acta 853, 43-63
2 Schürmann, P., Maeda, K. & Tsugita, A. (1981) Eur. J.Biochem.116, 37-45
3 Maeda, K., Tsugita, A., Dalzoppo, D., Vilbois, F. & Schürmann, P. (1986) Eur. J. Biochem. 154, 197-203
4 Tsugita, A., Maeda, K. & Schürmann, P. (1983) Biochem. Biophys. Res. Commun. 115, 1-7
5 Kamo, M., Tsugita, A., Wiessner, Ch., Wedel, N., Bartling, D., Herrmann, R. G., Aguilar, F., Gardet-Salvi, L. & Schürmann, P. (1989) Eur. J. Biochem. 182, 315-322
6 Schürmann, P. (1981) In: Photosynthesis IV. Regulation of carbon metabolism (G.Akoyunoglou Ed.) Balaban Intern. Sci. Services Philadelphia. Pa. , 273-280
7 Tsugita, A., Ataka, T. & Uchida, T. (1987) J.Protein Chem. 6, 121-130
8 Tsugita, A., Yano, K., Gardet-Salvi, L. & Schürmann, P. (1989) to be submitted
9 Chou, P. Y. & Fasman, G. D. (1978) Annu. Rev. Biochem. 47, 251-276
10 Droux, M., Miginiac-Maslow, M., Jacquot, J.-P., Gadal, P., Crawford, N. A., Kosower, N. S. & Buchanan, B. B. (1987) Arch. Biochem. Biophys. 256, 372-380
11 Droux, M., Jacquot, J.-P., Miginiac-Maslow, M., Gadal, P., Crawford, N. A., Yee, B. C. & Buchanan, B. B. (1987) Arch. Biochem. Biophys. 252, 426-439
12 Davison, A.J., and Scott, J.E. (1986) J. Gen. Virol. 67, 1759-1816
13 Winge, D.R., Nielson, K.B., Zeikus, R.D., and Gray, W.R. (1984) J.Biol.Chem. 259, 11419-11425
14 Yano, K., Tsugita, A., Gardet-Salvi, L. & Schürmann, P. (1989) to be submitted

REGULATION OF PHOTOSYNTHESIS: PHOTOSYNTHETIC CONTROL AND THIOREDOXIN-
DEPENDENT ENZYME REGULATION

DOROTHEA LECHTENBERG, BETTINA VOSS & ENGELBERT WEIS,
Institute of Botany, University of Düsseldorf, 4000 Düsseldorf 1, FRG

1. INTRODUCTION

When CO_2-fixation is limited by light the apparent quantum yield
of 'light-reaction' of photosynthesis is high. Obviously, this
requires optimal activation of ATP- and $NADPH_2$-consuming 'dark-
reactions' of carbon-fixation [1]. *Reductive activation* of enzymes
via the ferredoxin(Fd)-thioredoxin system [2,7] is thought to play an
important role in optimizing these reactions. However, when CO_2-
fixation is limited by CO_2-uptake (as, e.g., during water stress), a
high ΔpH is built up and feeds back to e^--transport (photosynthetic
control, 'PC'). As a consequence, PS1-activity is controlled by e^--
donation from PQH_2, rather than by consumption of $NADPH_2$ and its
center, P_{700} and acceptor, Fd accumulate in the oxidized form [3,4].
Hand in hand with this effect of PC on PS I the photochemical
efficiency of PS II is downregulated ('high-energy quenching' [3,8]).
We present evidence that such feedback control of PS1 causes gradual
oxidative inactivation of enzymes. A different control-pattern is
seen when photosynthesis is limited by consumption of triosephosphates. We propose a *feedback-cycle* which adjusts both, light-
reactions and enzyme-activation to the rate of carbon-flux.

2. MATERIALS AND METHODS

Gasexchange of attached leaves of *Phaseolus vulgaris* and 820 nm
absorbance changes, monitoring the redox state of P_{700} were measured
simultaneously as in [4]. To supress photorespiration O_2 was reduced
to 2% when CO_2 was low and net e^--transport (from H_2O to PGA) was
calculated from CO_2-uptake. Intact chloroplasts were isolated from
Spinacia oleracea. For determination of the activation state of
enzymes their activity was measured immediately after osmotic rupture
of chloroplasts as in [5].

3. RESULTS AND DISCUSSION

During light-limited photosynthesis in leaves, the apparent
quantum yield for electron transport, $\Phi_s = J_e/I$ (where $J_e = e^-$-
transport from gas-exchange; I = light-flux) is close to its maximal
value. Under such conditions, most PS1 centers are in the active

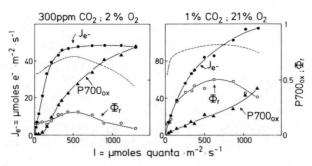

<u>Fig.1</u> *Light response of e^--transport (from gas-exchange), fraction of tot. P_{700} in the P_{700}^+-form and Φ_r, measured with attached bean leaves in 2% O_2 plus 300 ppm CO_2 ($C_i \approx 200$ppm) or 1% CO_2. Φ_r was calculated from e^--transport and 820 nm absorbance changes (see text).*

('open') state and only a small fraction of P_{700} accumulates in the photochemically inactive oxidized form, P_{700}^+. However, when photosynthesis reaches light-saturation and Φ_s decreases, the steady state level of P_{700}^+ increases. We observed that more than 50% of P_{700} could accumulate in the oxidized form. This photoaccumulation of P_{700}^+ is thought to be a thermodynamic consequence of PC: when the pH is high and the inner-thylakoid H^+-concentration exceeds a certain threshold, re-oxidation of PQH_2 at the cyt b/f complex is inhibited by a control-mechanism which is not yet well understood. PS1-activity is then limited by e^--donation from PQH_2 and P_{700}^+ accumulates [3,4]. The radical-form, P_{700}^+ is known to act as an efficient non-photochemical ('thermal') trap for excitation energy [6], i.e., energy reaching centers with P_{700}^+ is dissipated by non-photochemical mechanisms. Therefore, the fraction of P_{700}^+ is directly proportional to the quantum yield for 'thermal' energy dissipation at PS1, Φ_d. The largest part of non-oxidized P_{700} is thought to participate in net (linear) e^--transport to the carbon fixing cycle. Some non-oxidized PS1 centers might, however, contribute to cyclic or pseudo-cyclic reactions or might be 'closed' by accumulation of reduced Fd, i.e., the fraction of non-oxidized P_{700} is not necessarily proportional to Φ_s. Adding Φ_d and Φ_s we can define a 'residual' quantum yield, $\Phi_r = 1 - (\Phi_s + \Phi_d)$ [eq. 1] which corresponds to non-oxidized P_{700} that does not participate in net e^--transport. The value for Φ_r depends on the balance between e^--donation to PS1 and e^--consumption by dark-reactions. Fig.1 shows that Φ_r extrapolates to about 0.1 in the dark and very low light, respectively. This may reflect a small 'resistance' for electrons between PS1 and e^--consuming dark-reactions. Such a resistance, indicated by Φ_r may control the partitioning of electrons between the FNR (and other e^--consuming enzymes) on one hand and the thioredoxin system on the other hand. When e^--transport was limited by CO_2 (Fig. 1a) Φ_r stabilized at very low values, indicating a nearly complete control

of PS1 activity by PC and little resistance by e⁻-consuming reactions. In high light and saturating CO_2, however, $\bar{Q}_r$ stabilizes at
significant higher values. This indicates co-limitation of PS1-
activity by PC and additional control on its acceptor side. With
regard to the redox-gradient between the primary acceptors of PS1 and
the NADP/NADPH₂ couple even large
accumulation of NADPH₂ is not
expected to cause significant
'redox-backpressure' to PS1. However, investigating the connecting
enzyme, the ferredoxin-NADP-oxido-
reductase (FNR) *in situ*, we found
very efficient inhibition of the
light-driven NADP-reduction by
NADPH₂ (Fig. 2). This may indicate
a very sensitive allosteric feedback from the Calvin cycle to the
acceptor side of PS1: even a minor
increase in [NADPH₂] would convert
part of the FNR to an inactive
state. As a consequence, PS1-
acceptors would accumulate in the
reduced form and electrons could
be diverted to alternative pathways (increase in $\bar{Q}_r$).

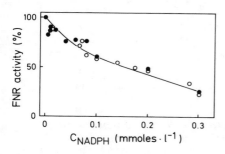

Fig.2 *The inhibitory effect of
NADPH₂ on FNR activity was measured in mildly broken chloroplasts. (o): 1 mM NADP⁺;
(•) 1 mM [NADP⁺ +NADPH₂]. 100% =
160 μmoles NADPH₂ mg⁻¹chl h⁻¹.*

The reduction state of the PS1 acceptor, Fd and of the thioredoxin-
system can be monitored by the activation state of the NADP-dependent
Malate-Dehydrogenase (MDH) which is mainly under the control of the
thioredoxin-system [2]. Fig. 3 shows a light-response of MDH-
activation and $\bar{Q}_r$ during steady state assimilation in isolated
chloroplasts. Up to $\bar{Q}_r$ =0.2 the enzyme activation increases linearly
with $\bar{Q}_r$ until it is saturated at still moderate values of $\bar{Q}_r$. At low
light, far below saturation for electron transport, $\bar{Q}_r$ increases with
light while no P_{700}^+ accumulates and thioredoxin-dependent enzyme
activation increases. Above 200 μE m⁻²s⁻¹ $\bar{Q}_r$ stabilizes at about 0.3
while P_{700}^+ increases with light indicating that PC comes into
effect. Enzyme activation remains at its high level or somewhat
decreases. Up to values of about 0.2, increase in $\bar{Q}_r$ was correlated
to thioredoxin-activation (Fig. 4). We observed, that thioredoxin-
dependent activation of other stromal enzymes such as FBPase, PRK and
GAPDH followed the same pattern as MDH-activation. Thus, in a first
approximation, $\bar{Q}_r$ may indicate to which degree the acceptor side of
PS1 is reduced and thioredoxin-dependent enzyme activation is in
effect. We used the curve in Fig. 4 (obtained from chloroplasts) to
calculate thioredoxin-dependent enzyme activation in leaves (Fig.
1a,b); dotted line). The curve suggests that thioredoxin-regulated
enzymes are down-regulated, when assimilation is strictly limited by
CO_2 (high I, low C_i; Fig. 1a). (We are aware that the enzymes of the
carbon-fixing cycle are modulated by many other factors. However, we

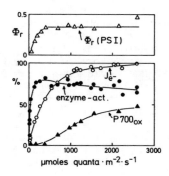 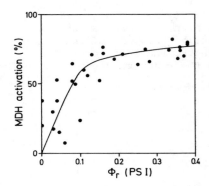

Fig.3 *Light-response of e^--transport (calc. from CO_2-dependent O_2-evol.), MDH activation, steady state level of P_{700}^+ (%) and $\tilde{Q}_r$ in intact chloroplasts. '100%' e^- transp. (during light-saturated assimilation) = 560 μmoles e^- $mg^{-1} chl\ h^{-1}$.*

Fig.4 *NADP-MDH activation versus $\tilde{Q}_r$, obtained from various experiments with chloroplasts.*

may regard the thioredoxin-system as a master-switch which determines a basic level of active enzymes of carbon metabolism). Since the redox-state of P_{700} is determined from farred-absorbance changes and $\tilde{Q}_s$ can be calculated from fluorescence [3], eq. 1 opens the possibility to use a pure non-invasive 'optical' approach to monitor the basic activation state of the carbon-fixing cycle in intact plants *in situ*.

REFERENCES

1   Heber, U., Neimanis, S., Dietz, K.J., Viil. J. (1986) Biochim. Biophys. Acta 852, 144-155.
2   Buchanan, B.B. (1980) Plant Physiol. 31, 341-374.
3   Weis, E., Ball, J.T., Berry, J. (1987) In: Progress in photosynthesis research, vol.2 (ed. J. Biggins), pp.553-556. Dordrecht: Martinus Nijhoff.
4   Weis,E. & Lechtenberg, D. (1989) Phil. Trans. R. Soc. Lond. B 323, 253-286.
5   Heber, U., Enser, U., Weis, E., Ziem, U. & Giersch, C. (1979) In: UCLA-Symposia (ed. D.E. Atkinson) pp. 113-137. New York: Academic Press.
6   Nuijs, A.M., Shuvalov, V.A., van Gorkom, H.J., Plijter, J.J., Duysens, L.N.M. (1986) Biochim. Biophys. Acta 850, 310-318.
7   Scheibe, R. (1987) Physiol. Plant. 71, 393-400.
8   Weis, E., Lechtenberg, D., Krieger, A., (1989) Proc. 8th Int. Congr. on Photosynthesis (in press). Dordrecht: Martinus Nijhoff

FUNCTION OF TWO DISSIMILAR THIOREDOXINS IN THE CYANOBACTERIUM, ANABAENA SP. 7120

FLORENCE K. GLEASON, Dept. of Plant Science, Univ. of Minnesota, ST. PAUL, MN 55108 U.S.A.

INTRODUCTION

The activities of enzymes involved in carbon dioxide fixation in photosynthetic organisms are regulated by a variety of physiological factors such as substrate and effector levels, intracellular pH and ion concentration, and redox control (1). Redox control can be effected through $NADP^+$/NADPH ratios, glutathione, or thioredoxin. Thioredoxin is a small disulfide-containing protein which has been implicated in the regulation of a number of processes in plant metabolism, including carbon dioxide fixation, sulfate metabolism, and deoxyribonucleotide synthesis. Two thioredoxin fractions occur in chloroplasts of higher plants which can modulate different enzymes although with some overlap of specificities. Thioredoxin in photosynthetic organisms can in turn be reduced by either ferredoxin or NADPH. Like higher plant chloroplasts, two dissimilar thioredoxins occur in the cyanobacterium, Anabaena sp. strain PCC 7120. The cyanobacteria provide a simple model system for investigating processes occurring in the chloroplast. We have been successful in cloning the two Anabaena thioredoxin genes into E. coli and producing large quantities of the proteins. We are currently characterizing these with respect to structure and activity.

One of the Anabaena thioredoxins (T-1) is abundant in cyanobacterial cells as determined by enzymatic assay and Western blotting. It also exhibits a high degree of structural homology to other bacterial thioredoxins and spinach chloroplast thioredoxin m. The second cyanobacterial thioredoxin (T-2) constitutes less than 5% of the total thioredoxin activity measured in vivo. It shows little structural homology to any known thioredoxins except for the active site region. Both cyanobacterial thioredoxins are effective reducing agents in ribonucleotide reduction and exhibit protein disulfide reductase activity with spinach chloroplast enzymes.

M. Baltscheffsky (ed.), Current Research in Photosynthesis, Vol. IV, 175–178.
© 1990 Kluwer Academic Publishers. Printed in the Netherlands.

However, the differences in activity indicate that each protein has a unique physiological function.

PROCEDURE
Materials and methods
   Genes for T-1 (from Anabaena 7119) and T-2 (from Anabaena 7120) were isolated and cloned into E. coli strain BH2012 which lacks thioredoxin. Both genes were spliced into pUC type plasmids and proteins were produced after induction with IPTG. Both proteins were purified by chromatography on DEAE Sepharose, Sephadex G-50 and Mono Q (2,3). T-1 activity was determined by monitoring the reduction of DTNB in the presence of E. coli thioredoxin reductase and NADPH (4). T-2 activity was determined by observing the thioredoxin-catalyzed reduction of insulin by DTT (5).
   E. coli thioredoxin reductase was purified on 2',5'-ADP Sepharose (4). E. coli ribonucleotide reductase was a generous gift of B-M. Sjoberg, Stockholm. Ribonucleotide reductase from Anabaena 7119 was purified as previously described (6). NADP-malate dehydrogenase and fructose-1,6-bisphosphatse were partially purified from spinach chloroplasts (7). Thioredoxins m and f were homogeneous preparations from spinach chloroplasts (8).

RESULTS AND DISCUSSION
   Both cyanobacterial thioredoxins were expressed in E. coli. One gram of bacteria yielded approximately 20 mg of thioredoxin. T-1 was able to restore the wild type phenotype in E. coli strains lacking thioredoxin except for the growth of T7 phage (2). T-2 was not effective in the bacterial system (3).
   T-1 is reduced by NADPH and the flavoprotein thioredoxin reductase from E. coli. T-2 is not reduced by the bacterial reductase, nor does it inhibit reduction of T-1 in a mixed system, indicating that it does not bind to the E. coli protein.

TABLE 1. Interaction of thioredoxins with E. coli thioredoxin reductase

THIOREDOXIN	Km (μM)	k_{cat} (min^{-1})
E. coli	2.0	2330
T-1	17.0	2330
T-2	not reduced	
Spinach m	22.0	2200
Spinach f	not reduced	

Assays were done by method 1 in (4).
Both cyanobacterial thioredoxins were able to function as

reducing agents for ribonucleotide reductase from either E. coli or Anabaena 7119. Both T-2 and spinach thioredoxin f exhibit higher K_m values suggesting that they do not have a major function in deoxynucleotide metabolism in vivo.

TABLE 2.   Thioredoxins as reducing agents for E. coli ribonucleotide reductase

THIOREDOXIN	K_m (μM)	k_{cat} (min^{-1})
E. coli	2.0	130
T-1	2.0	130
T-2	22.0	173
Spinach m	2.2	140
Spinach f	5.0	86

CDP reduction was monitored in the presence of 1 mM DTT as described (3).

TABLE 3.   Thioredoxins as reducing agents for Anabaena ribonucleotide reductase

THIOREDOXIN	K_m (μM)	k_{cat} (min^{-1})
E. coli	2.2	35
T-1	2.0	36
T-2	12.5	31
Spinach m	2.5	40

CTP reduction was monitored in the presence of 1mM DTT and dATP as described (3).

Both cyanobacterial thioredoxins can function as protein disulfide reductases in a model reaction using insulin as substrate (5). Five micrograms of either protein will catalyze the precipitation of 1 mg of insulin by DTT in approximately 15 min. Spinach chloroplast thioredoxins were equally effective in this reaction.

Reduced Anabaena T-1 will activate spinach chloroplast NADP-malate dehydrogenase after pre-incubation for a minimum of 10 min (7). Approximately 0.1 μg/ μg MDH produced a 2-3 fold stimulation of activity. E. coli thioredoxin was equally effective in this system. Reduced T-2 was completely ineffective. In this respect, it resembles spinach thioredoxin f.

Reduced Anabaena T-1 interacts poorly with spinach chloroplast fructose bisphosphatase. After 5 min pre-incubation, approximately 1 μg T-1/ μg FBPase produces a doubling of phosphatase activity. E. coli thioredoxin yields slightly lower activity. In contrast, 0.2 μg of T-2 per μg FBPase produces a 2-3 fold stimulation of phosphatase activity. While not as active as spinach Tf in the heterologous system, T-2 is apparently an "f" type thioredoxin.

Anabaena T-1 and spinach chloroplast Tm are the most abundant thioredoxins in vivo. They exhibit approximately 50% sequence homology to thioredoxins from other non-photosynthetic organisms (9). They can be reduced by NADPH and the flavoprotein-type reductase (10). Presumably they have intracellular functions which are common to thioredoxins in all living organisms, such as deoxynucleotide synthesis and sulfate metabolism.

Anabaena T-2 and spinach chloroplast Tf are unusual. They are not especially abundant in vivo. They exhibit less than 30% sequence identity to other thioredoxins although the overall tertiary structure may be conserved. They cannot be reduced by NADPH which suggests that the ferredoxin-dependent system (11) is the primary source of electrons. The evidence indicates that these thioredoxins have functions which are unique to photosynthetic organisms such as activation of enzymes in the carbon dioxide fixation cycle. Since the primary structures of these two thioredoxins do not appear to be similar, it may be that the cyanobacterial thioredoxin has diverged and may also have functions unique to cyanobacteria.

REFERENCES
1 MacDonald, F.D. & Buchanan, B.B. (1987) in Photosynthesis (Amesz, J., ed.) pp. 175-197, Elsevier, Amsterdam
2 Lim, C-J., Gleason, F.K. & Fuchs, J.A. (1986) J. Bacteriol. 68, 1258-1264
3 Alam, J., Curtis, S., Gleason, F.K., Gerami-Nejad, M. & Fuchs, J.A. (1989) J. Bacteriol. 171, 162-171
4 Luthman, M. & Holmgren, A. (1982) Biochemistry 21, 6628-6633
5 Holmgren, A. (1979) J. Biol. Chem. 254, 9627-9632
6 Gleason, F.K. & Frick, T.D. (1980) J. Biol. Chem. 255, 7728-7733
7 Whittaker, M.M. & Gleason, F.K. (1984) J. Biol. Chem. 259, 14088-14093
8 Wolosiuk, R.A., Crawford, N.A., Yee, B.C. & Buchanan, B.B. (1979) J. Biol. Chem. 254, 1627-1632
9 Gleason, F.K. & Holmgren, A (1988) FEMS Microbiol. Rev. 54, 271-298
10 Gleason, F.K. (1986) in Thioredoxin & Glutaredoxin Systems (Holmgren, A., Branden, C-I., Jornvall, H. & Sjoberg, B-M., eds.) pp. 21-30, Raven Press, NY
11 Droux, M., Jacquot, J-P., Miginac-Maslow, M., Gadal, P., Huet, J.D., Crawford, N.A., Yee, B.C. & Buchanan, B.B. (1987) Arch. Biochem. Biophys. 252, 426-439

EFFECT OF HETEROTROPHIC GROWTH ON THE THIOREDOXINS OF
WILD TYPE AND y-1 *CHLAMYDOMONAS REINHARDTII*

Heather C. Huppe and Bob B. Buchanan, Department of Plant Biology,
University of California, Berkeley, CA, USA, 94720
Jean-Pierre Jacquot, Physiologie Végétale Moléculaire, Université de Paris-
Sud, 91405 Orsay Cedex, France

1. INTRODUCTION
    Linking carbon metabolism to the presence of light via the ferredoxin-
thioredoxin (FT) system enables plants to both synthesize and degrade
starch within the chloroplast (1). Under photosynthetic growth conditions
the green alga, *Chlamydomonas reinhardtii*, has a photosynthetic
thioredoxin system similar to that of higher plants consisting of two types of
thioredoxins, m and f, and a ferredoxin-thioredoxin reductase (FTR) (2).
Unlike higher plants,*Chlamydomonas* is able to grow heterotrophically in
prolonged dark periods. Although the cells remain green they use
exogenous carbon (acetate, for example) rather than fixing CO_2. During
heterotrophic growth *Chlamydomonas* cells can increase their starch
reserves if excess acetate is present (i.e., 0.2% acetate) (3,4), a behavior
reminiscent of nonphotosynthetic storage tissues such as seeds. The
thioredoxins of seeds differ from those of the chloroplast in that they are
reduced via NADP-thioredoxin reductase (NTR), and no f-type thioredoxin
has been found (5).
    Is the ferredoxin-thioredoxin system of *Chlamydomonas* effected by
heterotrophic conditions? To investigate the relationship between growth
conditions and thioredoxins we examined the thioredoxins of
Chlamydomonas under light and dark growth in both the wild type and the
y-1 mutant. *Chlamydomonas* y-1 differs from the wild type in that it
requires light to green.

2. MATERIALS AND METHODS
    Cells: *Chlamydomonas reinhardtii* cc 124 mt+ and cc 400 y-1 were
obtained from Dr. Elisabeth Harris (Duke University). Cells were grown as
described previously (6) except that the media for dark growth was
supplemented with 2 g/L sodium acetate.
    Methods: Methods were as described previously (6,7) except for the
second method used to assay thioredoxin m which was done as follows: the

M. Baltscheffsky (ed.), Current Research in Photosynthesis, Vol. IV, 179–182.
© 1990 *Kluwer Academic Publishers. Printed in the Netherlands.*

sample is incubated for 15 min. in a 20 μl volume containing 50 mM Tris HCl (pH 7.9), 5 mM DTT; 1 μg of corn MDH, and then 10 μl of this mixture was added to a 1 ml cuvette containing 100 mM Tris-HCl (pH 7.9), OAA and NADPH. Method 2 uses much smaller amounts of the sample, a longer incubation time, and has less background oxidase interference than the first method we used. Proteins were divided into non-adherent (NA or m1) and adherent (Adh or m2) fractions after chromatography on DEAE Cellulose (pH 7.9).

3. RESULTS

Thioredoxins of Heterotrophically Grown WT: We initially examined the effect of prolonged darkness on *Chlamydomonas*. The thioredoxin activity profiles for light and dark grown culture extracts on DEAE Cellulose (pH 7.9) were qualitatively the same. *Chlamydomonas* cells maintain both their thioredoxin m and f while growing heterotrophically.

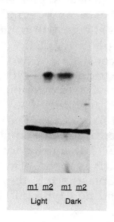

m1 m2   m1 m2
Light   Dark

In Western blot analysis, thioredoxins corresponding to m1 and m2 from heterotrophic and photoautotrophic cells reacted similarly with antibodies to corn thioredoxin m and all proteins appeared to have similar molecular weights (Fig. 1).

Fig. 1: Demonstration of antigenic and size similarity of m thioredoxins from light and dark grown *Chlamydomonas*. Proteins were standardized according to their ability to activate corn NADP-MDH.

Characterization of the Thioredoxins of y-1: Investigations of carrot tissue culture suggested that there was some difference between green and yellow callus tissues (8), but the situation with physiological tissues is less clear. We investigated the thioredoxins of *Chlamydomonas* y-1 to address the question of whether the presence of thioredoxin m or f was correlated with the presence of chlorophyll.

The thioredoxins of light grown y-1 cultures were found to be similar to the wild type cells, indicating that the y-1 mutation does not affect the thioredoxins in photoautotrophically grown cells.

When the pale yellow-green cells from the dark grown y-1 culture were extracted, we found that thioredoxin f was present but, strong oxidase activity interfered with the analysis of the thioredoxin m in these cells. We combined the adherent (m2) and non-adherent (m1) fractions from the DEAE Cellulose column to test their reactivity with antibodies to

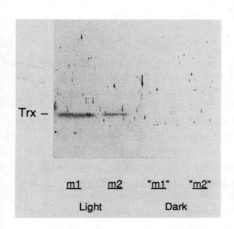

thioredoxin m. Similar quantities of proteins from the light and dark grown y-1 cell extracts were used.Whereas the samples from the light growncultures showed a reaction with the antibody to corn thioredoxin m, there was no significant reaction with the samples from the dark grown cultures (Fig. 2).

Trx —

m1   m2   "m1"   "m2"

Light   Dark

Fig. 2: Immunological analysis of m type thioredoxins from y-1 Chlamydomonas grown in the light and dark. Approximately 100 μg of each sample was used.

Another Thioredoxin in Chlamydomonas: It seemed possible that high oxidase activity early in purification was masking some thioredoxin activity. An NADP-linked thioredoxin (NT) system has been found in another green alga, Chlorella (9), and recent work has shown that the NT system is present in green spinach leaves (10), However, we had not found an NADP-linked thioredoxin in Chlamydomonas.

When we employed a method to assay NADP-MDH activation which eliminated much of the oxidase background, we found two adherent peaks of thioredoxin m type activity in extracts from Chlamydomonas wt chromatographed on DEAE Cellulose. On SDS-PAGE, the new protein was smaller than the Chlamydomonas thioredoxins m purified previously. In that previous study, crude extracts contained only a single band which crossed reacted with antibodies to higher plant thioredoxin m. Western blot analysis of the two adherent proteins confirmed that this new protein does not cross react with the antibodies to higher plant thioredoxins.

Table 1: Activation of Target Enzymes by Extracts from Chlamydomonas
WT and y-1 Cells[1]

	FBPase Activation (μm Pi/min/ml)	NADP-MDH Activation (μmNADPH/min/ml)
Wild Type	3.8	4.7
y-1 Mutant	1.6	1.4

Using the Method 2 assay for thioredoxin $\underline{m}$, we have reanalyzed the extracts from y-1 cells grown in the dark and have found some thioredoxin $\underline{m}$ activity in the extracts (Table 1). Western blot analysis of these samples, however, showed no significant cross reaction with antibodies to thioredoxin $\underline{m}$.

CONCLUSION

Chlamydomonas wt retains both thioredoxin $\underline{m}$ and $\underline{f}$ when grown heterotrophically. Thioredoxin $\underline{f}$ is present in y-1 mutant cells lacking chlorophyll, however there appears to be a reduction of the amount of thioredoxin $\underline{m}$. Earlier studies of y-1 found that mature chloroplasts are not a prerequisite to the formation of soluble photosynthetic enzymes in y-1 cells (3), so the change in $\underline{m}$ thioredoxins in heterotrophic y-1 cells is unexpected and further investigation of this may help improve our understanding the role of thioredoxin $\underline{m}$ in the chloroplast. There appears to be two types of thioredoxins in *Chlamydomonas* which are able to activate corn MDH. One of these is present in two isoforms which have the same molecular weight and antigenicity, but separate on anion exchange. The other protein has a smaller molecular weight and is not antigenically similar to the thioredoxin $\underline{m}$ from higher plants. Is this the thioredoxin $\underline{h}$? The answer to that question is under investigation.

REFERENCES

1. Buchanan, B. B. (1984) BioScience 34: 378-383.
2. Huppe, H. C., Buchanan, B. B., Christophe de Lamotte-Guéry, F., and Jacquot, J.-P. (1987) in Progress in Photosynthesis Research, Vol. III (Biggins,J., ed.), pp. 443-446.
3. Ohad, I., Siekevitz P., and Palade, G. E. (1967) J. Cell Biol. 35: 521-552.
4. Sager, R., and Granick, S. (1956) Ann. N. Y. Acad. Sci. 56: 831-838.
5. Berstermann, A., Vogt, K., and Follmann, H. (1983) Eur. J. Biochem. 131: 339-344.
6. Huppe, H. C. and Buchanan, B. B. (1989) Z. Naturforsch.44: 487-494.
7. Crawford, N. A., Yee, B. C, Hutcheson, S. W.,Wolosiuk, R. A., and Buchanan, B. B., (1986) Arch. Biochem. Biophys. 244, 1-15.
8. Johnson, T. C., Cao, R. Q., Kung, J. E., and Buchanan, B. B. (1987) Planta 171: 321-331.
9. Tsang, M. L.-S (1981) Plant Physiol. 68: 1098-1104.
10. Florencio, F. J., Yee, B. C., Johnson,T. C. and Buchanan, B. B. (1988) Arch. Biochem. Biophys. 266: 496-507.

(Supported by a grant from the NASA)

Regulation of Pyruvate,Orthophosphate Dikinase From Maize Leaves.Magnesium-dependent Dimer-tetramer Interconversion.

Hitoshi Nakamoto, Dept of Biochemistry, Faculty of Science, Saitama University, Urawa, Saitama 338, Japan

1. Introduction

Pyruvate, orthophosphate dikinase(PPDK, EC 2.7.9.1.), a key enzyme in the C4 pathway of photosynthesis, catalyzes the formation of phosphoenolpyruvate(PEP) as follows:

Pyruvate + MgATP + Pi = PEP + AMP + MgPPi

The amount of magnesium ion required for the reaction appears to be much more than that required for the formation of MgATP and MgPPi complexes(1). The plant enzyme is a homotetramer and dissociates to inactive dimer or monomer in the absence of magnesium ion or under cold treatment(1).

In the present study with maize dikinase, the effect of magnesium on the quaternary structure and the activity of the enzyme were examined. We provide evidence with gel filtration (HPLC) technique that in the absence of magnesium it dissociates to a dimeric form. The dissociated enzymes were reassociated to a tetramer by the addition of magnesium. Absence of magnesium also decreases the activity of the enzyme. The specific activity of the dimeric form seems to be a half of that of the tetramer form.

2. Materials and Methods

PPDK was purified to homogeneity (based on SDS-polyacrylamide gel electrophoresis, also see Fig.1A for the HPLC elution profile of the tetramer form of PPDK) from maize as described previously (2). The specific activity of the isolated enzyme was 2.0 u/mg protein. The enzyme solution was dissolved in the incubation mixture which contained 50 mM Tris-HCl (pH 8.0), 10 mM $MgCl_2$, 100 mM KCl, and 1 mM dithioerythritol(DTE).

The enzyme solution was concentrated with Millipore Mol-CutII and 50 µl(20 µg) applied to a TSK-gel G3000SW(7.5x60cm, Fig.1A) or a G3000SWXL(7.8x30cm, Fig.2) HPLC column equipped with a TOSOH HPLC system consisting of a CCPD computer controlled dual pump, a UV8000 and a CP-8080 data analyzer. The column was equilibrated and eluted at 20C with the basic buffer which contained 50mM Tris-HCl, pH 8.0, 100mM KCl, 1mM DTE.

PPDK was assayed in the reverse direction with the reaction mix-

M. Baltscheffsky (ed.), Current Research in Photosynthesis, Vol. IV, 183–186.

ture which contained 100mM Tris-Cl pH 8.0, 5mM $MgCl_2$, 2 mM DTE, 50 mM NH_4Cl, 0.5 mM PEP, 0.1 mM AMP, 0.5 mM PPi, 0.1 mM NADH, 5 units/ml of lactate dehydrogenase at 30C.

3. Results and Discussion
3.1. State of oligomerization of the enzyme in the presence of various concentrations of magnesium ion.

The enzyme was incubated for 5 min(within 5 min complete dissociation takes place. See Fig.3) in the presence of various concentration of $MgCl_2$ which was made by the addition of appropriate amount of EDTA and $MgCl_2$ and applied to a HPLC column equilibrated with the basic buffer containing the same concentration of $MgCl_2$ as used for the incubation. The flow rate was one ml/min. As shown in Fig.1A, at the concentrations of $MgCl_2$ examined (0 - 10 mM), there are only two peaks detected (at 13.4 min and 15.0 min), which correspond to the tetrameric form and the dimeric form of PPDK, respectively. Therefore, the tetrameric form dissociates to dimers, not to monomers in the absence of magnesium. The area of each peak of an elution profile was determined and plotted against a magnesium concentration present in the incubation mixture of the enzyme and equilibration and elution buffer of the column. As shown in Fig.1B, in the absence of $MgCl_2$, more than 80% of the total enzyme protein was in the dimeric form. As the $MgCl_2$ was increased, tetrameric form of the enzyme increased reaching almost 100 percent at 5mM.

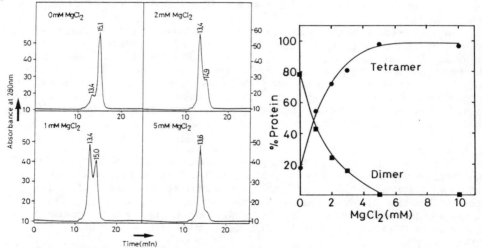

Fig.1A(Left). HPLC (gel filtration) elution profiles of PPDK. The concentration of magnesium included in the incubation mixture and equilibration and elution buffer for the column is shown in each profile. The number above each peak show the elution time. The elution times for PEP carboxylase (Mr. 400,000), catalase (Mr. 240,000) and aldolase(Mr.158,000) were 12.3 min, 14.9 min and 15.6 min respectively.
Fig.1B(Right). Effect of $MgCl_2$ on the quaternary structure of PPDK.

3.2. Reassociation of the dissociated enzyme after the addition of magnesium.

PPDK dissolved in the incubation mixture containing 10 mM $MgCl_2$ was added to the equal volume of the incubation mixture containing no $MgCl_2$ and 11mM EDTA to remove $MgCl_2$. After incubation for 10 min, the enzyme was applied to HPLC equilibrated with the basic buffer containing no $MgCl_2$. The flow rate was 0.4 ml/min at 20 C. After the gel filtration all the protein fractions were collected (from 16.5min to 21min in Fig.2A). It was concentrated and $MgCl_2$ was added at 10mM (total volume of the incubation mixture was 60 µl). After 10 min of incubation, 40 µl was applied to HPLC equilibrated with the basic buffer containing 10mM $MgCl_2$. As shown in Fig.2B, the dimer form(Fig.2A) was almost completely (88% of the total enzyme protein) reconstituted to the tetramer form.

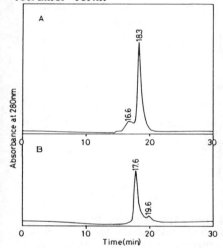

Fig.2A. HPLC elution profile of PPDK in the absence of magnesium in the incubation mixture and equilibrium and elution buffer of the column. The elution times for PEP carboxylase and catalase were 16.2 min and 18.4 min, respectively.

Fib.2B. HPLC elution profile of PPDK after bringing back the dissociated PPDK to the incubation mixture which contained 10 mM $MgCl_2$ and applying to HPLC column equilibrated with the basic buffer containing 10 mM $MgCl_2$. The elution times for PEP carboxylase and catalase were 16.7 min and 20.1 min, respectively. Note the delay of the proteins in the presence of magnesium in the basic buffer.

3.3. Relationship between the quaternary structure and the activity.

In order to clarify the relationship between the quaternary structure and the activity, PPDK activity was followed after the removal of magnesium ion by the addition of EDTA to the incubation mixture. Then, an aliquot(20µl) of the reaction mixture was taken at various times to assay the enzyme activity. As shown in Fig.3, the activity rapidly decreased and within 5 min, it reached the plateau. The specific activity of the enzyme decreased to a half of the initial activity.

Fig.4 shows the effect of varying the concentration of $MgCl_2$ on the activity of PPDK. As $MgCl_2$ in the PPDK assay mixture was increased, the activity of the enzyme increased, reaching a maximum at 5mM(closed circles). Then the calculated response of PPDK at varying concentrations of $MgCl_2$ was plotted, assuming that either dimer is completely inactive (Fig.5, open triangles) or 50% inactive as discussed above(Fig.5, open circles), respectively. The ratio of the amount of tetramer to dimer at varying concentrations of magnesium was taken from Fig.1B. When the dimer retains 50% of the initial activity, the activities are quite well fitted to the data (open circles). On the other hand, When the dimer is completely inactive, it does not fit (open triangles). The reason why the experimental activity at 0mM MgCl$_2$ is zero is because magnesium is required for the formation of MgPPi in the reaction.

When the tetramer dissociates to dimers, the number of the dimer is twice as many as that of the tetramer. The specific activity of the dimer(units/mg protein) was half of the tetramer. Therefore, the activity retained in the dimer might be 25% of the tetramer per mole. This interconversion is reversible.

It is thought that magnesium concentration in chloroplast stroma increases from 1 mM to 3 mM upon illumination. In that range, PPDK exists as a mixture of tetramers and dimers(Fig.1B). The magnesium dependent dimer-tetramer interconversion might affect the activity along with changes of pH and the adenylate energy charge in a chloroplast(2).

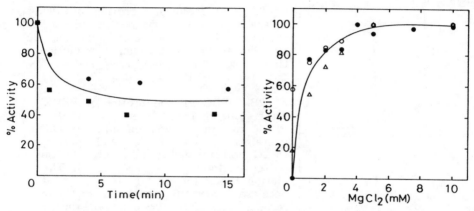

Fig.3. PPDK activity after removal of MgCl$_2$ from the incubation mixtures which contained 0.29 mg/ml of PPDK (closed circles) and 0.17 mg/ml of PPDK (closed squares).

Fig.4. The experimental (closed circles) and calculated (open circles and triangles) response of PPDK at varying concentrations of magnesium.

4. References

1 Edwards,G.E., Nakamoto,H., Burnell,J.N. and Hatch,M.D. (1985) Ann.Rev. Plant Physiol. 36, 255-286.
2 Nakamoto,H. and Edwards,G.E. (1987) Biochim.Biophys.Acta 924,360-368.

SEPARATION AND CHARACTERIZATION OF FRUCTOSE-1,6-BISPHOSPHATASES AND SEDOHEPTULOSE-1,7-BISPHOSPHATASES FROM LEAVES OF <u>PISUM SATIVUM</u> L.

DIRK NOTHNAGEL, JOACHIM HOFFSTÄDT, and ERWIN LATZKO,
Botanisches Institut, Universität Münster, 4400 Münster, FRG

1. INTRODUCTION

Chloroplast and cytosolic Fructose-1,6-bisphosphatase (FbPase) and Sedoheptulose-1,7-bisphosphatase (SBPase) have been investigated mainly from spinach leaves (1,2,3). We present data which show significant differences for these enzymes from pea leaves.

2. PROCEDURE

2.1. Material and methods

See legends of respective figures.

3. RESULTS AND DISCUSSION

3.1. Separation of chloroplast FbPase and SbPase from pea chloroplasts by high performance anion exchange chromatography

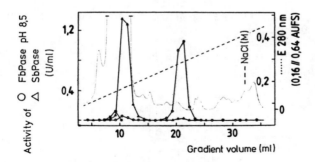

FIGURE 1. Sample: stromal extract from intact pea chloroplasts purified by Percoll centrifugation. Flow rate: 1 ml/min (0,7-0,8 MPa). Gradient: 50-500 mM NaCl in 50 mM HEPES-NaOH, 0,5 mM EDTA, pH 7,5 in 40 min. Apparatus: LKB HPLC system. Column: LKB GlasPac TSK DEAE 5-PW (0,5 cm^2 . 7,5 cm). Performance at 6-9°C.

M. Baltscheffsky (ed.), Current Research in Photosynthesis, Vol. IV, 187–190.

Chloroplasts from pea leaves exhibit, as well as shown for several other species (see 3), two different proteins for specific hydrolysis of FbP and SbP. We neither have indications for these enzymes to be interconvertible (4) nor for the existence of an 'alternate phosphate' (5).

3.2. Separation of cytosolic and chloroplast FbPase from leaf extract by DEAE anion exchange chromatography

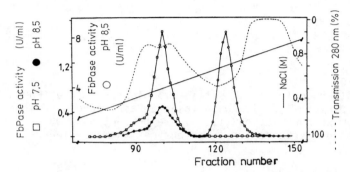

FIGURE 2. Sample: ammonium sulfate fractionated leaf extract (40-70 % saturation). Gradient elution: 500 ml 100-1000 mM NaCl in 20 mM Na-phosphate, 10 mM DTT, 0,4 mM EDTA, 0,5 mM FbP, pH 7,5. Column: Sephadex DEAE-A50 (5,3 cm^2. 28 cm). Fraction volume: 4,5 ml.

In contrast to previous results obtained with chloroplast FbPase from spinach the enzyme from pea chloroplasts is not active at pH 7,5 although the chromatographic separation was performed in presence of DTT (1,6).

3.3. Electrophoretic separation of FbPase and SbPase activities from leaf extracts by native PAGE

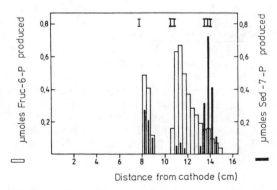

FIGURE 3. Electrophoretic conditions: continuous Tris-boric acid

system (cathode buffer contained FbP) with linear gradient from 6-12 % polyacrylamide. I) cytosolic FbPase, II) chloroplast FbPase, III) chloroplast SbPase. For detection of activity two lanes were cut from the gel and sliced into segments. Segments from one lane were incubated in 0,1 M Tris-HCl pH 8,2, 0,5 mM EDTA, 10 mM DTT, 10 mM $MgCl_2$, and 1,2 mM FbP. The segments from the second lane were incubated in the same medium however with 1,0 mM SbP instead of FbP. The activity was stopped by heat denaturation and the formed F6P and S7P were determined enzymatically.

The cytosolic FbPase was completely separated from the chloroplast bisphosphatases. The cytosolic enzyme exhibits activity with both FbP and SbP even in absence of DTT. This property is maintained throughout the purification.
When the gel was analyzed by activity staining for FbPase and for SbPase in absence of DTT chloroplast FbPase still remains slightly active with SbP whereas chloroplast SbPase is completely inactive.

3.4. Kinetic parameters of chloroplast and cytosolic bisphosphatases

	Chloroplast FbPase	Chloroplast SbPase
$S_{0,5}$ (FbP)	0,36 mM (pH 8,5) 0,14 mM (pH 8,5; plus DTT)	1,9 mM
$S_{0,5}$ (SbP)	2,2 mM (pH 8,5; plus DTT)	0,1 mM
pH optimum	8,8-9,3 8,5 (plus DTT)	8,2

For cytosolic FbPase the following parameters were obtained:
K_m (FbP) = 5,3 µM, K_m (SbP) = 30,3 µM; $S_{0,5}$ (Mg^{2+}) = 1,0 mM at 60 µM FbP, pH 7,5 and 1,3 mM at 1 mM SbP, pH 7,5; pH optimum 8,0 for FbP and 8,2 for SbP.

The chloroplast bisphosphatases exhibit activity with FbP and SbP however the affinity for the bisphosphates differs at least by an order of magnitude. Therefore hydrolysis of FbP and SbP under in vivo conditions is assumed to be catalyzed almost exclusively by the respective protein. For cytosolic FbPase from green leaves we have demonstrated a high specificity for SbP as well. This property has been reported to be a common feature of FbPases from microorganisms and mammalian tissues (7,8). The in vivo function of this activity in leaf cytosol remains obscure.

3.5. Effect of AMP and Fruc-2,6-P$_2$ on the activity of cytosolic FbPase

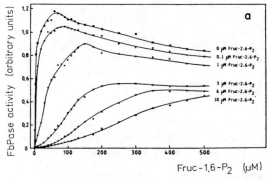

FIGURE 4a. FbP saturation in presence of different Fruc-2,6-P$_2$ levels. For assay of activity a FbP regenerating system was used with 5 mM Mg^{2+} and pH 7,5.

FIGURE 4b. FbP saturation in presence of 1 mM AMP and different Fruc-2,6-P$_2$ levels. For assay system see 4a.

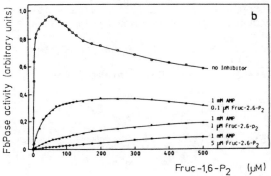

Inhibition of cytosolic FbPase by AMP even at mM levels never exceeds 40 % (data not shown). Fruc-2,6-P$_2$ however causes very severe inhibition at the observed physiological levels (3-20 µM). The combined action of both inhibitors decreases cytosolic FbPase even at the lowest so far observed Fruc-2,6-P$_2$ levels to negligible activity. We assume that in vivo Fruc-2,6-P$_2$ has to be partially bound in order to enable cytosolic FbPase to operate. These results confirm the role of AMP and Fruc-2,6-P$_2$ in regulating cytosolic FbPase activity (e.g. 9,10).

REFERENCES
1 Zimmermann,G., Kelly,G.J. and Latzko,E. (1976) Eur.J.Biochem.70,361-367
2 Zimmermann,G., Kelly,G.J. and Latzko,E. (1978) J.Biol.Chem.253,5952-5956
3 Cadet,F., Meunier,J.-C. and Ferté,N. (1987) Biochem.J.241, 71-74
4 Buchanan,B.B., Schürmann,P. and Wolosiuk,R.A.(1976)Biochem.Biophys. Res. Commun. 69, 970-978
5 Gontero,B., Meunier, J.-C. and Ricard, J. (1984) Plant Sci.Lett. 36, 137-142
6 Cadet.,F., Meunier,J.-C. and Ferté,N.(1987)Eur.J.Biochem.162,393-398
7 Tejwani,G.A.(1983)Adv.Enzymol.Relat.Areas Mol.Biol.54,121-195
8 Gerbling, K.-P., Steup M. and Latzko, E. (1986) Plant Physiol. 80, 716-720
9 Herzog,B., Stitt,M. and Heldt,H.W.(1984)Plant Physiol.75,561-565
10 Stitt,M., Herzog,B. and Heldt,H.W.(1985)Plant Physiol.79,590-598

CONTROL OF STROMAL FRUCTOSE 1.6 BISPHOSPHATASE AND SEDOHEPTULOSE 1.7 BISPHOSPHATASE BY METABOLITE LEVELS

D. SCHIMKAT, D. HEINEKE, H. W. HELDT
INSTITUT FÜR BIOCHEMIE DER PFLANZE, UNIVERSITÄT GÖTTINGEN,
UNTERE KARSPÜLE 2, 3400 GÖTTINGEN, F.R.G.

INTRODUCTION

During photosynthesis a fine control of enzymes is required for the Calvin cycle to operate at the variable environmental conditions, a plant leaf is exposed to. We have shown earlier that the stromal FBPase is controlled in its activity by its product Fru-6-P (1). This effect is very specific, Sed-7-P has no marked effect on the enzyme. The question arose whether such a feedback control also applies to SBPase.

METHODS

From isolated spinach chloroplasts SBPase and FBPase were partially purified similarly to the method of Cadet et al. (2) employing anion exchange chromatography (DEAE-TSK fractogel, Hr 10/10, Merck, Darmstadt). SBPase and FBPase were completely separated from each other. Prior to activity measurements both enzymes were activated in a medium containing 10 mM $MgCl_2$, 5 mM DTT and 100 mM Tris-HCl (pH 8). SBPase activity was assayed by colorimetric measurement of the release of inorganic phosphate (3) and FBPase activity was determined via enzymic assay of Fru-6-P (4).

RESULTS

Effect of metabolites on SBPase activity

In order to identify possible effectors of SBPase we tested the effect of major metabolites of the Calvin cycle and the photorespiratory pathway on SBPase activity when added at physiological concentrations. This sreening revealed that Sed-7-P and glycerate were strong inhibitors. Ru-1.5-P_2 was also inhibitory, causing 40% inhibition at a concentration of 10^2 mM. It may be noted that in a leaf performing

---

Abbreviations: FBPase, fructosebisphosphatase; SBPase, sedoheptulose bisphosphatase; Ru, ribulose; Fru, fructose; Sed, sedoheptulose; Ru-5-P, ribulose-5-phosphate; Ru-1.5-P_2, ribulose-1.5-bisphosphate; Fru-1.6-P_2 etc. accordingly.

M. Baltscheffsky (ed.), Current Research in Photosynthesis, Vol. IV, 191–194.
© 1990 *Kluwer Academic Publishers. Printed in the Netherlands.*

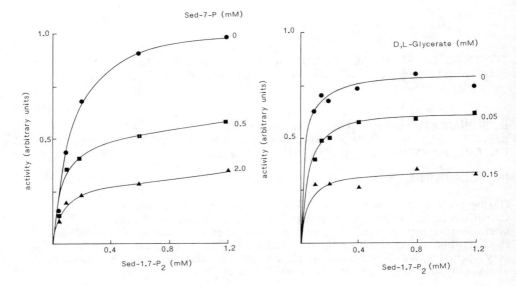

FIGURE 1.   Effect of Sed-7-P (A) and of D,L-glycerate (B) on the
            concentration dependence of SBPase activity.

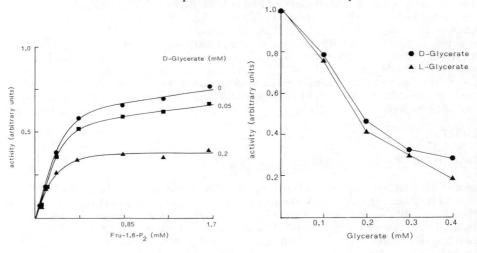

FIGURE 2.   Effect of D-glycerate on the concentration dependence
            of FBPase activity.

FIGURE 3.   Effect of D- and L-glycerate on FBPase activity assayed
            in a crude stromal extract of spinach chloroplast.
            Fru-1.6-P_2 conc. 1 mM.

photosynthesis under air the Ru-1.5-P$_2$ concentration in the stroma is about 10 mM (5). As shown in Fig. 1, the inhibition of SBPase by both Sed-7-P and glycerate is due to a decrease of the Vmax. The inhibitory effect of Sed-7-P is rather specific, Fru-6-P at a concentration of 0.5 mM inhibited SBPase by only 8%.

Effect of glycerate on FBPase activity

We also made a screening of the effect of intermediates of the photorespiratory pathway on the activity of stromal FBPase. Only glycerate had an inhibitory effect. As shown in Fig. 2, low concentrations of glycerate markedly decrease the Vmax of the enzyme. We checked the effect of D- and L-glycerate on FBPase activity separately (Fig. 3). Both stereoisomers had the same inhibitory effect on the enzyme.

DISCUSSION

Our results show that SBPase is strongly inhibited by its product Sed-7-P. Since the stromal Sed-7-P concentration can be estimated as about 2 mM, our findings indicate that during photosynthesis the activity of SBPase is strongly controlled by the concentration of

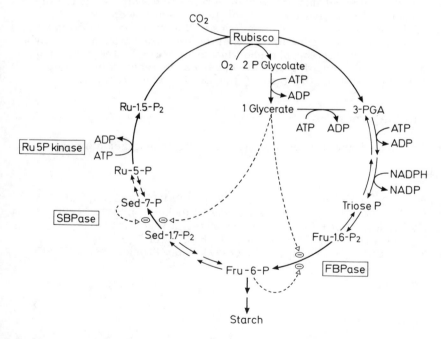

FIGURE 4. Schematic diagram of the fine regulation of SBPase and FBPase by metabolites.

Sed-7-P. This control makes it possibe that the irreversible hydrolysis of SBP can be adjusted in its rate to the demand of Sed-7-P. Similarly, also the activity of stromal FBPase is controlled by its product Fru-6-P (1). But there is a clear difference in the mode in which the two phosphatases are inhibited by their respective substrates. Whereas in the case of SBPase, Sed-7-P decreases the Vmax, with FBPase the presence of Fru-6-P results in a sigmoidal shift of the saturation curve towards higher concentrations without changing the maximal velocity. Thus, at high concentrations of $Fru-1.6-P_2$, as can be observed in the stroma under certain conditions, the inhibitory effect of Fru-6-P can be reversed (1). This inhibition characteristic makes it possible that independently of the regulation of the carbon flux through the Calvin cycle, an increased concentration of triosephosphate being in equilibrium with $Fru-1.6-P_2$ leads to an increasing activity of stromal FBPase. In this way the flux of surplus carbon into starch can be facilitated. Since SBPase is only involved in the regenerative part of the Calvin cycle, it seems plausible that the control of this enzyme by its product is more rigid as compared to the more flexible control of FBPase.

The inhibitory effect of glycerate on FBPase and SBPase may constitute a way to prevent that the photorespiratory pathway from glycolate to glycerate could be blocked due to lack of ATP. A moderate increase of glycerate concentration indicating ATP shortage might lower the formation of ribulose-5-phosphate from triose phosphate via inhibition of FBPase and SBPase. By reducing the metabolite flow through the Calvin cycle, the ATP demand for the phosphorylation of Ru-5-P, the reduction of 3-PGA and the recovery of glycolate could be decreaed. This may provide a way for adjusting the rate of the Calvin cycle to the ATP supply.

ACKNOWLEDGEMENT

This work has been supported by the Deutsche Forschungsgemeinschaft.

REFERENCES

1. Gardemann, A., Schimkat, D., Heldt, H.W. (1986) Planta 268, 536-545
2. Cadet, F., Meunier, J.-C., Ferte, N. (1987) Biochem. J. 241, 71-74
3. Itaya, K., Ui, M. (1966) Clin. Chim. Acta 14, 361-366
4. Baier, D., Latzko, E. (1975) Biochim. Biophys. Acta 396, 141-148
5. Gerhardt, R., Stitt, M., Heldt, H.W. (1987) Plant Physiol. 83, 399-407

INTERACTION OF CHLOROPLAST FRUCTOSE-1,6-BISPHOSPHATASE WITH MICELLES OF TRITON X-114

Gonzalo Prat-Gay, Roberto Rodriguez-Suarez, and Ricardo A. Wolosiuk

Instituto de Investigaciones Bioquímicas (Fundación Campomar, IIBBA-CONICET, FCEN-UBA), Antonio Machado 151, (1405) Buenos Aires, Argentina

INTRODUCTION

In chloroplasts of higher plants the ferredoxin-thioredoxin system links light-triggered events in thylakoid membranes with the regulation of enzymes in the stroma (1,2). If the conformation of enzymes changes because of modulators action then the surface exposed to the solvent will be different from the native state (3). As a consequence, interactions of modified enzymes with supramolecular structures (membranes, protein complexes) will differ respect to native forms. Since thylakoid membranes are complex structures they are not adequate for uncovering molecular mechanisms that participate in protein interactions(4). In this respect, the well-defined structure of micelles of non-ionic detergents constitute model compounds for the analysis of hydrophobic interactions in proteins (5,6). We report herein that chloroplast fructose-1,6-bisphosphatase interacts with micelles of Triton X-114 in a pH-dependent process.

EXPERIMENTAL PROCEDURES

Materials

Triton X-114 and all other biochemicals were purchased from Sigma Chemical Co (St.Louis, MO). Na^{125}I (17 mCi/mg.) was obtained from New England Nuclear (Wilmington, DE).

Chloroplast fructose-1,6-bisphosphatase was purified from frozen spinach leaves by the procedure previously reported (7).

Methods

Iodination of chloroplast fructose-1,6-bisphosphatase: Chloroplast fructose-1,6-bisphosphatase (120 ug) was incubated at 24ºC in a solution containing (in umoles): Tris-HCl buffer (pH 7.9), 50; fructose 1,6-bisphosphate, 1.6; CaCl$_2$, 0.25; final volume: 0.5 ml. After 45 minutes the solution was transferred to a tube coated with 20 ug of 1,3,4,6-tetrachloro-3α,6α-diphenylglycouril (Iodogen, Pierce Chemical Co., Rockford, IL) (8). After 25 minutes at 23ºC, suspended particles were centrifuged off and the supernatant was loaded on a Bio-Gel column (1 x 18 cm) and eluted with 30 mM Tris-HCl buffer (pH 7.9). Fractions eluting in the void volume were pooled and dialyzed overnight against 25 mM Na acetate buffer (pH 5.5). The dialyzate (^{125}I-chloroplast fructose-1,6-bisphosphatase) was stored at -15ºC and discarded after one week.

M. Baltscheffsky (ed.), Current Research in Photosynthesis, Vol. IV, 195–198.
© 1990 *Kluwer Academic Publishers. Printed in the Netherlands.*

Temperature-induced phase separation of Triton X-114: Temperature-induced phase separation of Triton X-114 was carried out as described (9,10) with minor modifications. ^{125}I-chloroplast fructose-1,6-bisphosphatase was incubated in 50 mM Tris-HCl buffer (pH 7.9) (final volume: 0.2 ml). After 30 minutes at 24°C, 0.02 ml of 50% Triton X-114 was injected and the solution was vortexed. The enzyme solution was incubated for 30 minutes at 0°C, and subsequently layered over a cushion of 0.75 M sucrose. Tubes were kept for 10 minutes at 30°C, and centrifuged for 5 minutes at room temperature. The amount of radioactivity was estimated in the detergent-rich phase formed at the bottom of the tube.

RESULTS AND DISCUSSION

Since binding of non-ionic detergents was a sensitive method for estimating protein hydrophobicity (5,6), several procedures were developed for the separation of protein-detergent complex from unreacted species (10-12). In our studies the experimental procedure was based in that solutions of Triton X-114 are clear at low temperature whereas large micellar aggreagates are formed at temperatures higher than 22°C (cloud point). Following centrifugation at room temperature, proteins - depending on their hydrophobic characteristics- partition between the upper (hydrophilic) and lower (hydrophobic) phases. Therefore, we analyzed the capacity of ^{125}I-chloroplast fructose-1,6-bisphosphatase to interact with micelles of Triton X-114 by (i) incubating the iodinated-enzyme with the detergent at 0°C, (ii) raising the temperature to 30°C, and, (iii) centrifuging the turbid suspension formed upon warming. Radioactivity in the detergent-rich (lower) phase constituted an estimation of protein-micelle interaction. Fig. 1 shows that above the critical micelle concentration (0.009%) the binding of ^{125}I-chloroplast fructose-1,6-bisphosphatase was directly related to the concentration of the detergent (13). In comparison to membrane proteins binding of chloroplast fructose-1,6-bisphosphatase to micelles of Triton X-114 was low (14); however, this result was expected because the enzyme is a stromal -operationally soluble- protein.

pH variations did not alter micelles of non-ionic detergents. Accordingly, any pH-mediated change in the amount of the enzyme bound to micelles would be indicative of modifications in the protein surface . As shown in fig. 2, the binding of ^{125}I-chloroplast fructose-1,6-bisphosphatase to micelles of Triton X-114 was stimulated 4-fold by lowering one unit the pH of the solution. From this findings it appeared that, the acidification of the milieu enhanced the hydrophobic characteristics of the surface of chloroplast fructose-1,6-bisphosphatase.

The above experiments indicated that chloroplast fructose-1,6-bisphosphatase had the potential for interacting hydrophobically with other structures. Moreover, this capacity was modified by factors -e.g., pH- which cause structural changes of the enzyme (15,16). In this context, the action of activity modulators on the interactions of chloroplast fructose-1,6-bisphosphatase with supramolecular structures emerged as an interesting analysis for the future (17).

ACKNOWLEDGEMENTS:This work was supported by grants from the Consejo Nacional de Investigaciones Científicas y Técnicas (CONICET) and the Universidad de Buenos Aires.

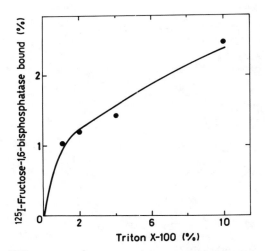

Fig.1. Binding of ^{125}I-chloroplast fructose-1,6-bisphosphatase to Triton X-114 as a function of detergent concentration. ^{125}I-chloroplast fructose-1,6-bisphosphatase was incubated at 0ºC for 30 minutes in a solution of 40 mM Tris-HCl buffer (pH 7.9) containing Triton X-114, as indicated. Phase separation of Triton X-114 and estimation of radioactivity was carried out as described under Experimental Procedures.

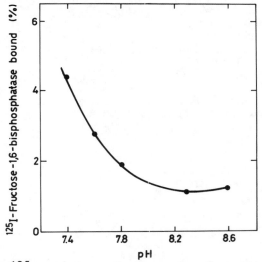

Fig.2. Binding of ^{125}I-chloroplast fructose-1,6-bisphosphatase to Triton X-114 as a function of pH. ^{125}I-chloroplast fructose-1,6-bisphosphatase was incubated at 0ºC for 30 minutes in a solution of 90 mM Tris-HCl buffer -pH as indicated- containing 4.6% of Triton X-114. Phase separation of Triton X-114 and estimation of radioactivity was carried out as described under Experimental Procedures.

REFERENCES

1.- Buchanan, B.B., Wolosiuk, R.A., and Schurmann,P. (1979)
   Trends Bioch. Sci. 4, 93-96
2.- Anderson, L.E. (1979)
   Encycl. Plant Physiol. 6, 271-281
3.- Chothia, C. (1984)
   Ann. Rev. Biochem. 53, 537-572
4.- Quinn, P.J. and Williams, W.P. (1983)
   Biochim. Biophys. Acta 737, 223-266
5.- Clarke, S. (1977)
   Biochem. Biophys. Res. Commun. 79, 46-
6.- Makino, S., Reynolds, J.A. and Tanford, C. (1973)
   J. Biol. Chem. 248, 4926-4932
7.- Stein, M. and Wolosiuk, R.A. (1987)
   J. Biol. Chem. 262, 16171-16179
8.- Fraker, P.J. and Speck, J.C. (1978)
   Biochem. Biophys. Res. Commun. 80, 849-857
9.- Bordier, C. (1981)
   J. Biol. Chem. 256, 1604-1607
10.- Pryde, J.G. (1986)
   Trends Bioch. Sci. 11, 160-163
11.- Stieger, S., and Brodbeck, U. (1984)
   in Enzymes, Receptors and Carriers of Biological Membranes (Azzi, A. et al.,
eds.), pp. 13-19, Springer Verlag, Berlin.
12.- Boquet,P., Silvermann,M.S., Pappenheimer,A.M. and Vernon,B.W. (1976)
   Proc. Natl. Acad. Sci. USA 73, 4449-4453
13.- Rosenthal, K.S. and Koussale, F. (1983)
   Anal. Chem. 55, 1115-1117
14.- Holm, C., Fredrikson, G. and Belfrage, P. (1986)
   J. Biol. Chem. 261, 15659- 15661
15.- Lazaro, J.J., Chueca, A., Lopez-Gorge, J. and Mayor, F. (1975)
   Plant Sci. Lett. 5, 49-55
16.- Buchanan, B.B., Schurmann, P. and Wolosiuk, R.A. (1976)
   Biochem. Biophys. Res. Comunn. 69, 970-978
17.- Stein, M., Lazaro, J.J. and Wolosiuk, R.A. (1989)
   Eur. J. Biochem. in press

THE IN VIVO FUNCTIONING FORMS OF RIBULOSE 1,5-BISPHOSPHATE CARBOXYLASE/OXYGENASE IN PLANTS

AKIHO YOKOTA,[1] TOMOAKI TAIRA,[2] HIDEAKI USUDA,[3] and SHOZABURO KITAOKA,[1] [1]Dept. Agric. Chem., and [2]Dept. Horticul. Sci. Agron., Univ. Osaka Pref., Sakai, Osaka 591, Japan, and [3]Fac. Med., Teikyo Univ., Hachioji, Tokyo 192-03, Japan

1. INTRODUCTION

Ribulose 1,5-bisphosphate carboxylase/oxygenase (RuBisCO) changes its functioning form depending on the concentration of ribulose bisphosphate (RuBP) in the in vitro assay (Fig. 1) [1,2]. The specific activity of the carboxylase reaction is very different among the three forms. Binding of RuBP to the regulatory sites of RuBisCO has been inferred to cause the change of the form. It is important that the concentrations

[RuBP] (mM)	Functioning form of RuBisCO	Relative specific activity
< 0.08	ECMRs	1.0
	↑↓	
0.1 - 1.0	RrECMRs	0.5
	↑↓	
2.0 - 5.0	Rr^{n}ECMRs	0.8

FIGURE 1. Relationship between the proposed functioning forms of plant RuBisCO and the concentration of RuBP. E, RuBisCO; C, CO_2; M, Mg^{2+}; Rs, RuBP bound to the substrate RuBP-binding sites; Rr, RuBP bound to the regulatory sites.

of RuBP that cause RuBisCO to have different forms with different specific activities are within the range of the concentrations observed in situ [3,4]. In this study, we tried to identify the in vivo functioning forms of RuBisCO in spinach and radish leaves in steady photosynthesis at various concentrations of CO_2.

2. MATERIALS AND METHODS

Previous studies with purified RuBisCO have shown that the functioning forms of RuBisCO in the primary carboxylase reaction can be deduced from the curve of the progress of the second reaction in the presence of 0.5 to 1.0 mM RuBP (Fig. 2) [1,2]. The leaves of spinach and radish were freeze clamped at liq. N_2-temperature after reaching steady photosynthesis in an atmosphere containing various concentrations

M. Baltscheffsky (ed.), Current Research in Photosynthesis, Vol. IV, 199–202.
© 1990 *Kluwer Academic Publishers. Printed in the Netherlands.*

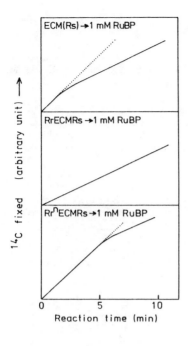

FIGURE 2. Progress curves of the carboxylase reaction of the different forms of RuBisCO transferred to the assay mixture containing 1 mM RuBP.

of CO_2 under illumination at 1500 uE/m^2/s at 25 °C. Frozen leaf segment was ground in liq. N_2 with a mortar and pestle for 5 min. As soon as liq. N_2 evaporated, part of leaf powder was put directly into the carboxylase-assay mixture containing 1 mM RuBP and protease inhibitors for direct assay. To measure the activated, total activity, RuBisCO in the powder was incubated for 12 min before adding 1 mM RuBP to start the reaction. These assay were done at 30 °C. RuBP in the leaf powder was extracted with formic acid [3], and measured with purified spinach RuBisCO [5]. The substrate RuBP-binding sites of RuBisCO were measured with ^{14}C-carboxyarabinitol bisphosphate [6].

3. RESULTS AND DISCUSSION
    The contents of the substrate RuBP-binding sites were 79.3 ± 13.2 and 90.5 ± 7.1 (n = 3) nmol/mg Chl in the spinach and radish leaves, respectively, used in this study. Figure 3 shows the progress of the direct and activated carboxylase reactions of RuBisCO "extracted" at liq. N_2 -temperature from leaves in steady photosynthesis at various CO_2 concentrations. The direct reactions of the "extracts" of the leaves at 1000 and 3000 ppm CO_2 showed large inflections a few min after the start of the reaction, and were similar to those of the activated "extracts" and of Panel A in Fig. 2, indicating that RuBisCO was functioning as the form of ECMRs under such CO_2 conditions. The RuBP content of the same leaf powder was 200 to 265 nmol/mg Chl. RuBisCO

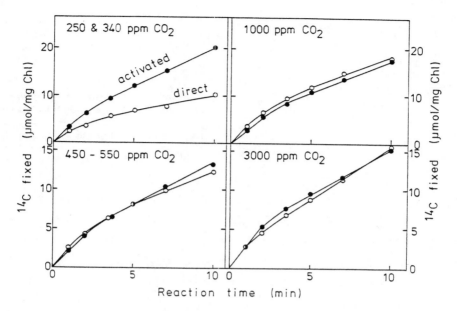

FIGURE 3. Progress curves of the direct and activated carboxylase reactions of RuBisCO "extracted" at liq. N_2-temperature from segments of spinach leaves in steady photosynthesis at various concentrations of CO_2.

from spinach leaves photosynthesizing at 450 to 550 ppm CO_2 showed similar progress of the carboxylase reaction in the direct assay to those at 1000 and 3000 ppm CO_2, although the linear progress of the reaction as shown in Panel B in Fig. 2 was obtained in the direct assay at similar CO_2 concentrations with radish leaves in some cases (data not shown). This may be because RuBisCO functions as the form of RrECMRs in a very narrow range of CO_2 concentration around 500 ppm. The content of RuBP was 290 to 350 nmol/mg Chl under these conditions. At 250 and 340 ppm CO_2 where the RuBP content in the spinach leaves exceeded 380 nmol/mg Chl, the activity in the direct assay decreased greatly with reaction time (Fig. 3). Such a progress curve has not been experienced in the in vitro assay with purified RuBisCO (Fig. 2), and the reason is not clear. Some unexpected factor(s) may have participated in the function of RuBisCO when the RuBP content exceeded 380 nmol/mg Chl. Similar results were obtained with radish leaves (data not shown).

Combination of these results and the properties of purified RuBisCO from spinach and radish plants [1,2] lead us strongly to a conclusion that RuBisCO changes its functioning form depending on the concentration of RuBP in chloroplasts. as shown in Fig. 4. RuBisCO senses total 14 mM RuBP (350 nmol/mg Chl) as less than 0.1 mM free RuBP in situ,

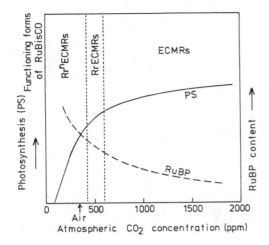

FIGURE 4. Relationship between ambient CO_2 concentration, RuBP content and the functioning forms of RuBisCO in plants.

and functions as the form of ECMRs. RuBisCO is not converted to the Rr^nECMRs form until the total RuBP concentration exceeds 15.2 mM (380 nmol/mg Chl). The RrECMRs form occurs only at the transition phase between ECMRs and Rr^nECMRs forms near 14 mM total RuBP (350 nmol/mg Chl). Since the specific activities of these functioning forms of RuBisCO are greatly different (Fig. 1), it should be noted that the **in vivo** maximum carboxylase activity of RuBisCO also changes largely depending on the form occurring at the given CO_2 concentration.

Furthermore, our results suggest that the concentration of free RuBP effective for RuBisCO as the substrate may not exceed 2 mM until total RuBP content in chloroplasts does 380 nmol/mg Chl (15.2 mM). Most of the total RuBP may be masked by non-specific binding to thylakoids and other proteins, and binding to the regulatory sites of RuBisCO itself.

REFERENCES
1. Yokota, A., and Kitaoka, S. (1989) Plant Cell Physiol. **30**, 183-191
2. Yokota, A., and Kitaoka, S. (1989) Submitted
3. von Caemmerer, S., and Edmondson, D. L. (1986) Aust. J. Plant Physiol. **13**, 669-688
4. Kobza, J., and Seemann, J. R. (1988) Proc. Natl. Acad. Sci. USA **85**, 3815-3819
5. Yokota, A., and Canvin, D. T. (1986) Plant Physiol. **80**, 341-345
6. Yokota, A., and Canvin, D. T. (1985) Plant Physiol. **77**, 735-739

STRUCTURAL ANALYSIS OF THE TRIOSE PHOSPHATE-3-PHOSPHOGLYCE-
RATE-PHOSPHATE TRANSLOCATOR FROM SPINACH CHLOROPLASTS

ULF INGO FLÜGGE, KARSTEN FISCHER AND ARMIN GROSS, INSTITUT
FÜR BOTANIK UND PHARMAZEUTISCHE BIOLOGIE, MITTLERER DALLEN-
BERGWEG 64, D-8700 WÜRZBURG, F.R.G.

1. INTRODUCTION
    The phosphate-triose phosphate-3-phosphoglycerate
    translocator, in short phosphate translocator is loca-
    ted in the inner membrane of the chloroplast envelope
    and catalyzes a strict counterexchange of the above
    mentioned substrates. Its main function during CO_2
    fixation is to export the fixed carbon in form of
    triose phosphate from the stroma to the cytosol for the
    synthesis of sucrose. The inorganic phosphate formed
    during biosynthetic reactions is shuttled back into the
    chloroplasts where it is used for the formation of ATP
    catalyzed by the thylakoid ATP synthase.
    As revealed by SDS-PAGE the translocator protein has a
    molecular weight of 29 kd and in its functional state
    it is built up of two identical subunits. It is coded
    for by nuclear genes and synthesized in the cytosol as
    a precursor protein (M_R 40 kd) (1). Recently we have
    succeeded in sequencing the cDNA encoding the entire
    spinach phosphate translocator precursor protein (2).
    Based on the deduced amino acid sequence a structural
    analysis of the translocator protein is presented.

2. RESULTS AND DISCUSSION
    The coding region of the cDNA clone encoding the spi-
    nach phosphate translocator precursor protein consists
    of 1212 bp corresponding to 404 amino acid residues
    with a molecular weight of 44 234 which is higher than
    that determined by SDS-PAGE (40 kd). Since the amino-
    terminal residue of the translocator was found to be
    blocked and could not be determined by Edman degrada-
    tion we do not know yet the exact start of the mature
    part of the protein. But several observations including
    the comparison between the primary sequences of the
    spinach phosphate translocator and that of pea chloro-
    plasts indicate an unusual high molecular weight of 10-
    11 kd for the presequence suggesting that the mature
    protein starts at amino acid positions 85-97 (2,3).
    The amino acid composition of the precursor form indi-
    cates that this protein is highly hydrophobic with a
    polarity index of only 36% being even lower for its

M. Baltscheffsky (ed.), Current Research in Photosynthesis, Vol. IV, 203–206.
© 1990 *Kluwer Academic Publishers. Printed in the Netherlands.*

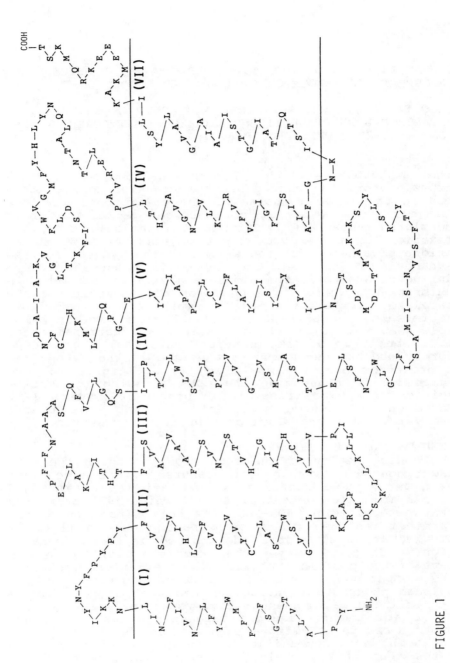

FIGURE 1

Predicted folding pattern of the chloroplast phosphate translocator in the inner envelope

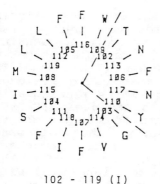

102 - 119 (I)

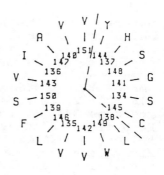

134 - 151 (II)

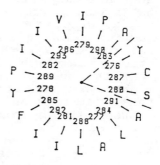

175 - 192 (III)

276 - 293 (V)

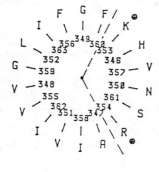

346 - 363 (VI)

FIGURE 2

Helical wheel projection of the
transmembrane segments I, II, III, V and VI
of the spinach chloroplast phosphate
translocator.

Hydrophilic regions and charges are
indicated

mature part. The hydrophobicity distribution analysis calculated with an 11 amino acid residue span (4) revealed that the mature part of the protein contains seven membrane-spanning segments: I, amino acid residues 99-119; II, amino acid residues 132-153; III, amino acid residues 170-192; IV, amino acid residues 216-238; V, amino acid residues 275-294; VI, amino acid residues 344-365 and VII, amino acid residues 369-390. Each of these transmembrane segments could have an α-helical conformation. On this basis, the following arrangement of the polypeptide chain of the phosphate translocator in the membrane is suggested (Fig 1). The seven membrane-spanning -helices are labeled I-VII. Whereas α-helices IV and VII have an hydrophobic nature continuing through the whole sequence, the other α-helices (I-III, V, VI) show an alteration between hydrophilic and hydrophobic residues every third or fourth residue i.e. at the frequency with which an α-helix turns around its central axis. This is demonstrated by drawing these segments in an helical wheel projection i.e. in an end-on view of an 18-residue α-helix (Fig 2). Obviously these α-helices have a strongly amphiphatic structure. It can be speculated that the hydrophilic sides of the amphiphatic helices might be directed towards the inside of the protein thus forming an hydrophilic translocation channel whereas the hydrophobic sides may interact with the lipid bilayer.

We have shown earlier that two cationic amino acid residues (most probably an arginine and a lysine residue) are involved in binding the twice negatively charged substrate molecules to the translocator (1). Interestingly, only two positive charges (lysine-353 and arginine-354, α-helix VI) are present in that part of the mature protein which is embedded in the membrane. It appears feasible but still has to be proven that lysine-353 and arginine-354 are both located at the substrate binding center.

REFERENCES
1   Flügge, U.-I. and Heldt, H.W. (1984) Trends Biochem. Sci. 9, 530-533
2   Flügge, U.-I., Fischer, K., Gross, A., Sebald, W., Lottspeich, F., Eckerskorn, C. (1989) EMBO J. 8, 39-46
3   Flügge, U.-I., Fischer, K., Gross, A., Willey,D.L., Link,T.A.(1989) 8th International Congress on Plant Membrane Transport Elsevier, North Holland, in press
4   Kyte, J. and Doolittle, R.F. (1982) J. Mol. Biol. 157, 105-132

BINDING OF THE LIPOPHILIC TERTIARY AMINE AND 'SELECTIVE' UNCOUPLER
DIBUCAINE TO THYLAKOID MEMBRANES

GABRIELE GÜNTHER AND HENRIK LAASCH, BOTANISCHES INSTITUT,
HEINRICH-HEINE-UNIVERSITÄT, D-4000 DÜSSELDORF 1, FRG

1. INTRODUCTION

Lipophilic tertiary amines (t-amines) are effective inhibitors of photophosphorylation (1-3). Bound up with the inhibition, light-induced uptake of (^{14}C)-methylamine and quenching of 9-aminoacridine (9-AA) fluorescence disappear. This indicates that inhibition of ATP synthesis may be related to a decline of the transthylakoid proton gradient, $\triangle$pH (4). Intriguingly, a strong pH-dependent control of electron flow was maintained in the presence of t-amines (3,5), despite of the low $\triangle$pH. Therefore, t-amines were termed 'selective' uncouplers (1).

In this paper, we characterized the binding of a fluorescent t-amine to thylakoid membranes in order to cast further light on the mechanism of selective uncoupling. The different binding classes obtained were related to the inhibitory effects of the t-amine used, as described in ref. (3). The binding of fluorescent amines to thylakoid vesicles has already been studied in detail with 9-amino-substituted acridines (e.g. 9-AA), since these compounds may serve as easy-to-handle reporters of the thylakoid membrane 'energization' (4,6). The results presented here will also be discussed in terms of the still continuing debate on the mechanisms underlying the 'energy'-dependent quenching of 9-AA fluorescence upon 9-AA binding to thylakoids.

2. PROCEDURE

2.1. Materials and Methods

Chloroplasts were isolated from spinach leaves, following the method in ref. (1). The t-amine used was 2-butoxy-N-(2-(diethylamino)-ethyl)-4-quinolinecarboxyamide (dibucaine). Electron transport was mediated by 50 µM DCIPH$_2$ / 2mM Na-ascorbate and 5µM methylviologen, in the presence of 10 µM DCMU. 0.5 µM nigericin served as uncoupler. Dibucaine binding to chloroplasts under equilibrium conditions was assayed by incubation of chloroplasts at pH 8, in the light (2500 µE/m^{2}s, PAR) or dark, with dibucaine for 1 min and subsequent sedimentation of the chloroplasts by centrifugation in the light or dark. The amine concentration in the supernatant was determined fluorometrically at excitation and emission wavelengths of 325 nm and 403 nm and served for calculation of bound dibucaine by subtraction of free from total amine.

3. RESULTS AND DISCUSSION

3.1. Binding of dibucaine in the dark

Two classes of dibucaine binding in the dark were discernable. First, a partitioning of dibucaine between membrane lipids and the aqueous suspension medium (Fig. 1). Partitioning was indicated i) by the linear dependence of bound vs. free amine over a wide range of concentrations and ii) by the concurrence of experimentally observed and theoretically calculated 'unloading' of dibucaine after a suspension of 'preloaded' membranes in a dibucaine-free medium (not shown). Theoretical calculations based on the Nernst-law of partitioning, $C_B=p^*C_F$ (C_B, C_F = concentrations of bound and free dibucaine, p = partition coefficient), by which this class of binding could be quantitatively described. Assuming a lipid phase volume of 2.8 µl/mg Chl (7), a partition coefficient for dibucaine of 1050 was calculated from our data. Partitioning of amine was unaffected by the metal cation concentration in the assay (Fig. 1). Following recent data on a correlation of amine lipophilicity and competence for inhibition of ATP synthesis , it seems that partitioning is essential for inhibition of ATP synthesis (3).

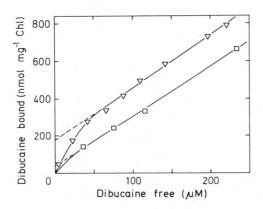

Fig.1: Binding of dibucaine to chloroplasts in the dark, under low-salt (10 mM KCl, ∇) and high-salt (10 mM KCl, 50mM $MgCl_2$, $\square$) conditions. The medium additionally contained 0.3 M sorbitol, 1 mM EDTA, 10 mM Hepes and 100 µg Chl/ml. Both functions of bound vs. free amine have linear phases with similar slopes. The extrapolated linear phases reflect the fractions of salt-dependent binding. The data were averaged from 3 independent measurements.

A second class was identified by its sensitivity against cations. In the presence of only 10 mM KCl, a pronounced hyperbolic component was superimposed on partitioning of dibucaine (Fig. 1). Under 'high-salt' conditions, this binding class vanished. A subtraction of partitioning from total binding and a linearization of the obtained hyperbola revealed a maximum concentration of cation-dependent sites (S) of S= 280 nmol/mg Chl and an apparent binding constant of 35 µM (Fig. 2).

From the data in Figs. 1,2 it appears, that dibucaine screens negative charges on the membrane surfaces via electrostatic binding. In this, dibucaine resembles 9-AA (6). The assumption of charge screening is supported by the coincidence with the number of negative charges per mg Chl on the outer thylakoid surface, $1.3;10^{17}$ (thylakoid surface, 1.67 m^2/ mg Chl (8); charge density, 0.012 C/m^2 (9)), and the number of dibucaine molecules bound per mg Chl, $1.7 \cdot 10^{17}$. It appears that the thylakoid membrane surface may be almost completely 'discharged'.

3.2. Binding of dibucaine in the light

During illumination in the presence of dibucaine, light-dependent binding occurs (Fig. 3). A PSI electron transport system was chosen,because it was not inhibited even by high dibucaine concentrations. In

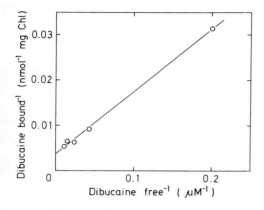

: Determination of the concentration of salt-dependent binding sites and the apparent affinity of dibucaine binding. 'Pure' salt-dependent binding under low-salt conditions (see Fig. 1) was linearized in a double reciprocal representation.

our experiments we found that partitioning of dibucaine in the light was unaffected as compared to binding in the dark (similar slopes of the related straightlines). An isolation of 'pure' light-dependent binding (total 'light-binding' minus 'dark-binding') showed a saturation of light-dependent binding at a concentration of about 25µM free amine.

Fig 3: Dibucaine binding in light and dark in dependence of the dibucaine concentration present. The reaction medium contained 1 mM MgCl$_2$, 10 mM KCl and 1 mM MnCl$_2$ in addition to the medium in Fig. 1. Chl concentration, 80 µg/ml. Light-dependent binding (- - -) was obtained by subtraction of binding in the dark (●) from total binding in the light (○). The fraction of dibucaine bound, reflecting partitioning is indicated by (- — -).

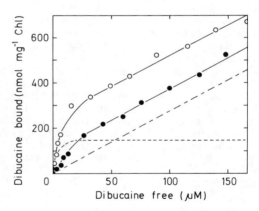

The maximum concentration of light-dependent binding sites was about 150 nmol/mg Chl. Light-dependent binding was maintained up to 250 µM free amine. Assuming that this binding is produced by a thylakoid membrane energization, this finding points out that energization is preserved even at dibucaine concentrations which completely inhibit ATP synthesis and ΔpH, as indicated by 9-AA and methylamine. When an uncoupler was added, light-dependent binding of dibucaine vanished (not shown). Hence, this binding is proton-dependent.

If dibucaine were accumulated in the light in the thylakoid lumen like methylamine (4), the amount of dibucaine bound should rise with

Fig. 4: Dependence of light-induced dibucaine binding on the Mg^{2+} concentration present. The total dibucaine concentration was 50 μM, the Chl concentration 80 μg/ml. The experimental conditions were as in Fig. 3.

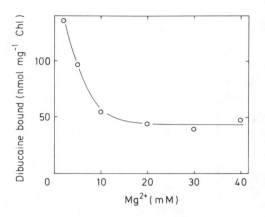

rising intrathylakoid volume, i.e., with a decrease of the reaction medium osmolarity. We did not find such increase of binding in the range of 0.07 to 550 mosmol/l (not shown). We conclude that a pH-dependent accumulation of dibucaine in the lumen is of minor importance for its binding to chloroplasts.

On the other hand, light-dependent binding proved to be cation-dependent (Fig. 4). The amount of dibucaine bound could be reduced to about 40 % of control values. Although the degree of competition between the t-amine and Mg^{2+} varied somehow in dependence on the chloroplast preparation, we may say that electrostatic binding of the amine to negative membrane charges is of major importance for the light-dependent binding. A comparison of the saturation points of light-dependent binding and inhibition of ATP synthesis, nevertheless, shows that this binding class may not be solely responsible for the inhibition of ATP synthesis. Summarizing the presented data, it appears that t-amine binding in the light may be similar to the energy-dependent binding of substituted 9-aminoacridines. A study of t-amine effects may thus help to a further understanding of thylakoid membrane energization and the related problems of energy coupling in photosynthesis (6).

This work was supported by the Deutsche Forschungsgemeinschaft (DFG).

REFERENCES
1 Laasch, H. and Weis, E. (1988) Biochim. Biophys. Acta 936, 99-107
2 Laasch, H. and Weis, E. (1989) Photosynth. Res., in press
3 Laasch, H. (1989) Planta, in press
4 Rottenberg, H., Grunwald, T. and Avron, M. (1972) FEBS Lett. 13, 41-44
5 Janowitz, A., Günther, G. and Laasch, H. (1989) In: Proc. 8th Int. Congr. on Photosynthesis, Martinus Nijoff, Dordrecht, in press
6 Kraayenhof, R. and Arents, J.C. (1977) In: Electrical Phenomena at the Biological Membrane Level, Roux, E. ed., 493-503, Elsevier
7 Douce R., Holtz B. and Benson A, (1973) J. Biol. Chem. 248,7215-7222
8 Barber, J. (1972) Biochim. Biophys. Acta 275, 105-116
9 Nobel, P.s. and Mel, H.C. (1966) Arch Biochem. Biophys. 113, 695-702

LOCALIZED PROTON DOMAINS IN pH-DEPENDENT CONTROL OF PHOTOSYNTHETIC
ELECTRON TRANSPORT UNDER THE INFLUENCE OF LIPOPHILIC TERTIARY AMINES

ANGELA JANOWITZ, GABRIELE GÜNTHER AND HENRIK LAASCH
BOTANISCHES INSTITUT, HEINRICH-HEINE-UNIVERSITÄT,
UNIVERSITÄTSSTR. 1, D-4000 DÜSSELDORF 1, FRG

1.   INTRODUCTION

Photosynthetic electron transport is under control of the intrathyla-koid proton potential, $\tilde{\mu}H_I$ (1,2). When $\tilde{\mu}H_I$ increases in the light, with the build-up of a transthylakoid proton gradient ($\triangle \tilde{\mu}H$), electron flow is decelerated. Two major sites of μH_I-dependent feed-back control have been discussed: the reduction of the primary photosystem (PS) II accep-tor Q_A (2) and the oxidation of plastohydroquinone at the cytochrome b/f complex (1). Under condition of photophosphorylation / $\tilde{\mu}H$ decreases and flow control is partly released. Recently, lipophilic tertiary ami-nes were shown to be effective inhibitors of ATP synthesis and of the build-up of $\triangle \tilde{\mu}H$ (3-5). The inhibition of a $\triangle \tilde{\mu}H$ rise, as indicated by 9-aminoacridine (9-AA) fluorescence quenching (6) or (^{14}C)-methylamine uptake (7), appeared to be determinant for the decline of photophos-phorylation. In this, the effects of lipophilic amines resemble 'clas-sical' uncoupler effects. Nevertheless, the pH-dependent flow control was preserved in the presence of tertiary amines despite of the low $\triangle \tilde{\mu}H$ observed. Control mechanisms were active although $\tilde{\mu}H_I$ appeared to be low. This is in apparent contradiction to the theory of pH-dependent flow control.

In this paper, we investigate pH-dependent electron flow control in the presence of the lipophilic tertiary amine dibucaine (2-butoxy-N-(2-(diethylamino)ethyl)-4-quinolinecarboxyamide). Artificial electron acceptors and donors were applied to locate the sites of control in the presence of dibucaine. Furthermore, we studied to what extent the hypo-thesis of uncoupler-like effects of tertiary amines may be tested by direct measurements of the light-induced proton uptake by thylakoids.

2.   Procedure
2.1. Materials and Methods

Chloroplasts were isolated from spinach leaves as described in ref. (3). Electron flow from H_2O to methylviologen (MV, 5 µM), from $DCIPH_2$ (10 µM) / Na-ascorbate (1 mM) to MV (5 µM) was measured as O_2 consumption, that from H_2O to phenyl-p-benzoquinone (PPBQ, 0.25 mM) as oxygen evolution. If required, 2 µM DBMIB and 2 µM 2-heptyl-4-hydroxy-quinoline-N-oxide (HQNO) were added. 0.2 µM nigericin plus 0.4 mM methylamine served as uncoupler. Electron flow was driven by red light (1200 µE/ (m^2s), PAR). The Chl concentration was 15 µg/ml The reaction medium was as in ref. (5). 9-aminoacridine (9-AA, 5 µM) fluorescence quenching was quantified as qAA=$\triangle$F/F ($\triangle$F= light-dependent fluorescence quenching, F= fluorescence remaining in the light). Proton uptake was measured with a glass electrode at a Chl concentration of 40 µg/ml, in a medium containing 0.5 mM Hepes, pH 8, and salt concentrations as stated in Fig 3. Dibucaine binding to chloroplasts was studied simultaneously to proton uptake, as in ref. (8).

3. RESULTS AND DISCUSSION
3.1. Electron transport in the presence of dibucaine

When electron flow from H_2O to MV (PSII+I) and the related qAA signal were measured in the presence of dibucaine, electron flow was low and pH-dependent control was not released until qAA had completely disappeared, thereby indicating a decline of $\triangle \tilde{\mu} H$ (Fig. 1). The data of 9-AA fluorescence were corroborated by methylamine uptake (not shown). Proton dependent control was apparently preserved in the absence of a strong $\triangle \tilde{\mu} H$, i.e., both amines appear to be no indicators for the proton potential in charge of flow control in the presence of dibucaine.

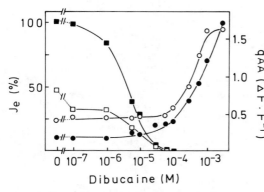

Fig.1: Photosynthetic electron flow, Je (o,●) and qAA (□,■) in the presence of increasing dibucaine concentration. Je and qAA were driven by PSII+I(●,■, H_2O to methylviologen) or PSI (ō,□, DCIPH$_2$ to methylviologen 100 % Je corresponds to the maximum electron flow in the presence of uncoupler plus the dibucaine concentration indicated.

A comparable effect was observed when PS I driven electron flow (DCIPH$_2$ to methylviologen) was investigated: Flow rates did not increase before qAA had completely declined (Fig. 1). In concentrations > 0.1 mM, dibucaine acted like a 'classical' uncoupler and released the proton-dependent flow control. It appears that dibucaine in concentrations < 0.1 mM had a specific effect on the proton potential difference underlying qAA (and driving ATP synthesis, see refs. 3,4), while the proton potential exerting flow control is unaffected. At concentrations > 0.1 mM, the dibucaine effects were similar to the effects of 'classical' amine-type uncouplers, e.g., ammonia. This points out the existence of functionally distinct proton domains at the thylakoid membrane.

In Fig. 2, PSII-driven electron transport from H_2O to PPBQ and the related qAA values are displayed in dependence of the dibucaine concentration. The reduction of PPBQ was only slightly affected by additions of DBMIB and HQNO. Hence, the cytochrome b/f complex was not decisively involved in this electron flow system (9). This may be the reason why pH-dependent control is lesser than in electron flow, as displayed in Fig. 1. Contrary to the data in Fig. 1, pH-dependent flow control was decreased in the range of dibucaine concentration where qAA disappeared. The protons exerting control at PSII were released by dibucaine in line with those, creating the $\Delta \tilde{\mu} H$ which is indicated by qAA. We conclude that electron flow control under the influence of dibucaine is predominantly preserved at the level of the cytochrome b/f complex. Proton-dependent control at PSII may be less sensitive to a decrease of 9-AA-indicated $\Delta \tilde{\mu} H$ by dibucaine than by 'classical' uncouplers (see ref 4), but under the present condition declines in the range of dibucaine concentration < 0.1 mM, i.e., of specific dibucaine effects.

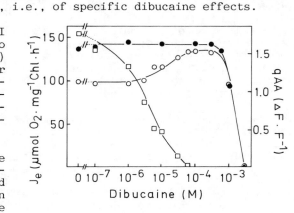

Fig. 2: Dependence of PSII driven electron flow (H_2O to PPBQ), in the presence ($\bullet$) and absence of uncoupler ($\circ$), on the dibucaine concentration present. The values of qAA ($\square$) were measured in the presence of dibucaine only.

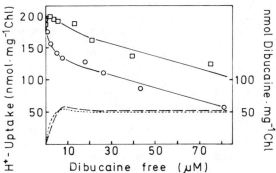

Fig. 3: Light-induced uptake of protons by thylakoid vesicles, under high ($\circ$) and low-salt ($\square$) conditions, in dependence of the dibucaine concentration present. Low-salt condition: 350 mM sorbitol, 20 mM KCl and 2 mM $MgCl_2$; high-salt condition: 250 mM sorbitol, 100 mM KCl and 20 mM $MgCl_2$. The salt-dependent differences of proton uptake are shown by a dotted line ($\cdots$). Salt-related differences in light-dependent thylakoid binding of dibucaine, as obtained from Fig. 4, are presented by the broken line ($- -$).

3.2. Proton uptake and amine binding to thylakoids

The proton uptake by thylakoid vesicles in dependence of the dibucaine concentration present, under low- and high-salt conditions, is shown in Fig. 3. The 'free' dibucaine concentration, i.e., total minus bound amine, was determined in a simultaneous binding experiment (Fig. 4). Proton uptake in the absence of amine was comparable under both salt regimes. Under low salt, proton uptake rised beyond the control level in the range of low dibucaine, then declined with increasing amine concentration. Under high salt, proton uptake decreased with increasing amine. The salt-dependent proton uptake is shown (Fig. 3).

Thylakoid binding of dibucaine in the light and dark and in dependence of the salt regime is pictured in Fig 4. The total dibucaine concentration varied from zero to 100 μM, where ATP-synthesis and 9-AA-

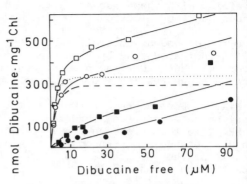

Fig. 4: Influence of salt concentrations in the reaction medium
on binding of dibucaine to thylakoids in the dark (●,■) and in
the light (○,□). High salt
(○,●) and low salt conditions
(□,■) were as in Fig. 3. Light-
induced binding of dibucaine under high-salt (———) and low-salt
condition (·······) were obtained by
substraction of the amounts of
amine bound in the dark from the
total amounts of amine bound.

indicated $\Delta\tilde{\mu}H$ were completely inhibited (5). The amounts of dibucaine
bound in the light were calculated by subtraction of 'dark binding'
from 'total binding' (see also ref 8). Fig 4 shows that light-dependent
binding is stronger under low-salt than under high-salt conditions. The
difference in light-dependent binding is plotted in Fig 3. It obviously
matches the salt-induced difference in proton uptake (Fig. 3). From the
data we conclude that salt-dependent binding is related to proton uptake from the reaction medium via a protonation of previously uncharged
amine (pK of dibucaine = 9.1). Binding of protonated amine is likely to
occur to negative charges on the membrane surfaces (see ref. 6).

Further analysis of proton uptake under high-salt condition shows
a biphasic dependence of proton uptake on the dibucaine concentration
present, one phase saturating at about 20 μM free dibucaine, the other
proceeding with higher amine concentrations. There is no correlation
between these concentration ranges and the ranges where inhibitory effects on qAA or ATP synthesis occur. Summarizing, we may say, that a
verification of the 9-AA and (14C)-methylamine-indicated decrease of
$\Delta\tilde{\mu}H$ in the presence of lipophilic amines, with the help of direct pH
measurements appears to be not feasible at present. Nevertheless, measurements of light-dependent proton uptake may be helpful for a characterization of tertiary amine binding to thylakoids (see ref. 8) and
thus for an elucidation of the mode of action of tertiary amines.

REFERENCES
1 Siggel, U. (1974) In: Proc. 3rd Int. Congr. on Photosynthesis, Avron
  M. ed., 645-654, Elsevier, The Hague
2 Weis, E. and Berry, J. (1987) Biochim. Biophys. Acta 894, 198-208
3 Laasch, H. and Weis, E. (1988) Biochim. Biophys. Acta 936, 99-107
4 Laasch, H. and Weis, E. (1989) Photosynth. Res., in press
5 Laasch, H. (1989) Planta, in press
6 Schuldiner S, Rottenberg H and Avron M (1972) Eur J Biochem.25,64-70
7 Rottenberg H, Grunwald T and Avron M (1972) Eur J Biochem. 25, 54-63
8 Günther, G. and Laasch, H. (1989) Proc. 8th Int. Congr. on Photosynthesis, Kluwer, Dordrecht, in press
9 Trebst, A. (1985) In: Coenzyme Q, pp. 257-284, Lenaz, G. ed., John
  Wiley & Sons

OSCILLATIONS OF PHOTOSYNTHESIS IN INTACT ISOLATED PEA CHLOROPLASTS IN THE PRESENCE OF DCMU AND ANTIMYCIN A

Sonja Veljović[1], Zoran G.Cerović[2] and Marjana Plesničar[3], Institute of Pesticides and Environmental Protection[1], P.O. Box 46 Banatska 31b, Institute of Botany[2], University of Belgrade, 11000 Belgrade, Institute of Field and Vegetable Crops[3], Novi Sad, Yugoslavia

1. INTRODUCTION
    The study of photosynthetic induction in intact isolated chloroplasts can contribute to a better understanding of photosynthetic regulatory mechanisms. In that respect, study of induced oscillations is of prime importance because they are an indication of the presence of regulated feed-back mechanisms. Oscillations of photosynthesis in intact isolated spinach chloroplasts were observed during the induction period, in non-optimal conditions, when the transport of phosphates was limited (1,2). Oscillations in both chlorophyll fluorescence yield and the rate of O_2 evolution were also induced when intact isolated pea chloroplasts were re-illuminated at 27°C (3). Under these conditions, the kinetics of fluorescence quenching and the rate of O_2 evolution were dependent on the length of the dark period, concentrations of bicarbonate, orthophosphate and Calvin cycle intermediates (3). The aim of the present work is to examine the effect of a deliberate change in the ratio of noncyclic and cyclic electron transport on fluorescence kinetics during oscillations. For that purpose, addition of DCMU and antimycin A, in catalytic amounts, was used.

2. PROCEDURE
2.1. Materials and methods
    Intact isolated chloroplasts (94-96%) were prepared from 13 days old pea shoots as described previously (4).Oxygen evolution and chlorophyll fluorescence (695 nm) were measured simultaneously using a DW2 O_2 electrode assembly (Hansatech Ltd., U.K.). Experiments were performed at 27°C in reaction mixture containing 330 mM sorbitol, 10 mM KCl, 1 mM EDTA, 50 mM HEPES pH 7.9, 3 mM $NaHCO_3$, 1 mM ATP, 5 mM $Na_4P_2O_7$, 2000 U catalase and 20 μg chloroplast chlorophyll in final volume of 1 ml. The intensity of actinic light was 2800 μmol quanta $m^{-2}s^{-1}$ at the surface of the light guide. The differential of the oxygen signal was produced using a passive RC network.

3. RESULTS AND DISCUSSION
    When intact isolated chloroplasts, that have attained the maximum rate of O_2 evolution at 27°C, are re-illuminated following a brief dark period (20 s), O_2 evolution resumes immediately and rises to a maximum value within a few seconds (fig. 1.). Oscillations in the

M. Baltscheffsky (ed.), Current Research in Photosynthesis, Vol. IV, 215–218.
© 1990 *Kluwer Academic Publishers. Printed in the Netherlands.*

chlorophyll fluorescence yield and the rate of O_2 evolution follow for a period of approximately 40 seconds. These oscillations have a much smaller amplitude and period than the one observed in leaves. The differences in fluorescence kinetics upon successive re-illuminations after short dark periods confirm the fact that the conditions surrounding the chloroplasts are continuously changing during prolonged illumination of isolated chloroplasts (fig. 1.).

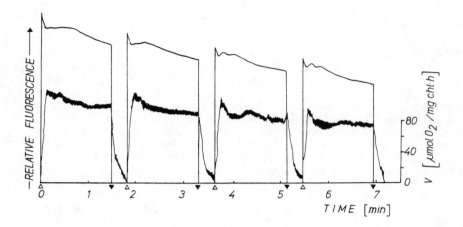

FIGURE 1. Induction of oscillations in chlorophyll fluorescence yield and the rate of O_2 evolution by successive re-illuminations of intact isolated pea chloroplasts. Conditions as in Methods. The maximum rate of oxygen evolution was 100 μmol O_2 mg^{-1}chl h^{-1}.

The effect of different substances was examined in the second light period (first after a 20 s dark period). Addition of catalytic amounts of PGA abolished the secondary maximum in fluorescence yield and the corresponding minimum in the rate of O_2 evolution (fig. 2.). Upon re-illumination in the presence of DCMU and antimycin A complex kinetics of both signals were induced again. DCMU and antimycin A were used to modulated the cyclic electron flow by redox poising of the components of the electron-transport chain. DCMU increased fluorescence quenching and decreased the rate of O_2 evolution (fig. 3.). The decrease in the rate of O_2 evolution after an abrupt burst during the first seconds, was associated with a slight relaxation of fluorescence quenching. The maximum in the rate of O_2 evolution preceded the minimum in fluorescence yield. Antimycin A, a specific inhibitor of cyclic electron flow at low concentration, had an opposite effect in decreasing fluorescence quenching and even slightly increasing the rate of O_2 evolution (fig. 4.) (5).

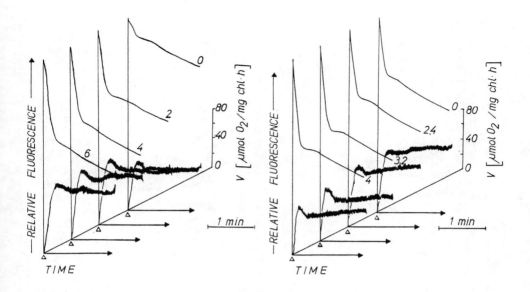

FIGURE 2. Effect of PGA on fluorescence kinetics and the rate of O₂ evolution. The concentrations of added PGA (x 10⁻⁵ M) are indicated along the traces..

FIGURE 3. Effect of DCMU. DCMU is added at concentrations (x10⁻⁸ M) indicated along the traces in the presence of 0.1 mM Pi and 0.01 mM PGA.

A secondary maximum in fluorescence yield is induced by re-illumination with no corresponding changes in the rate of O₂ evolution. The maximum of the rate of O₂ evolution is delayed in respect to the minimum of fluorescence yield.

In the presence of both DCMU and antimycin A, the secondary maximum induced by re-illumination is accentuated (fig. 5.). This might be a consequence of a decrease in the rate of O₂ evolution (effect of DCMU) under the conditions of a decreased energization of chloroplasts (effect of antimycin A).

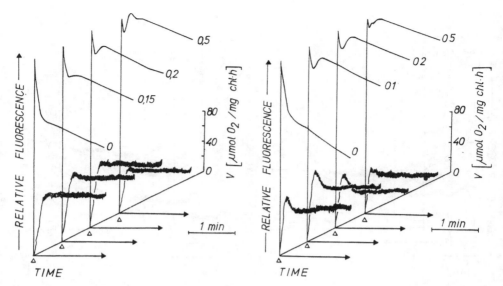

FIGURE 4. Effect of antimycin A. Antimycin A is added at concentrations (μM) indicated along the traces in the presence of 0.1 mM Pi and 0.01 mM PGA.

FIGURE 5. Combined effect of DCMU and antimycin A. The concentration of DCMU is 3.2×10^{-8} M and concentrations of antimycin A (μM) are varied as indicated.

These results confirm the notion that cyclic electron flow is involved in the oscillations occurring during the photosynthetic induction (6,7). Both the date on metabolite additions (PGA) and the effects of inhibitors indicate that the oscillations during photosynthetic induction are the consequence of readjustment of fluxes during a transients imbalance in the rate of ATP and NADPH turnover.

REFERENCES

1 Carver, K.A., Horton, P. and Anderson, A.S. (1982) In: Annual Report of the ARC Research Group on Photosynthesis. University of Sheffield, pp 50-52
2 Nakamoto, H., Sivak, M.N. and Walker, D.A. (1987) Photosynth. Res. 11: 119-130
3 Veljović, S. (1989) Masters degree thesis, Belgrade University.
4 Cerović, Z.G. and Plesničar, M. (1984) Biochem. J. 223: 543-545
5 Plesničar, M. and Cerović Z.G. (1985) Proc. Roy. Soc. Lond. B 226: 237-247
6 Quick, W.P. and Horton P.(1984) Proc. Roy. Soc. Lond. B 220: 361-370
7 Fejzo, J., Plesničar, M. and Cerović Z. (1986) Proc. Roy. Soc. Lond. B 228: 471-482

PHOTOSYNTHETIC METABOLISM IN BARLEY LEAVES INFECTED WITH POWDERY MILDEW

Julie Scholes, Pam Lee, Peter Horton and David Lewis. Robert Hill Institute, Department of Molecular Biology & Biotechnology, University of Sheffield, Sheffield S10 2TN.

INTRODUCTION
    Rusts and powdery mildews are biotrophic fungal pathogens which infect a wide variety of economically important plants. The powdery mildews are ectoparasites forming dense white mycelia on the leaf surface, with haustoria in epidermal cells. In the early stages of infection the nutrient fluxes characteristic of an uninfected plant may be sufficient to sustain fungal growth. However, as the mass of fungus increases a redirection of host assimilates to the pathogen occurs. This is accompanied by a number of other changes ; in some host/pathogen interactions gross photosynthesis (per unit chlorophyll) may be enhanced initially (1), however, in most systems net photosynthesis then decreases and chlorophyll is lost from the tissue as the disease progresses (2).
    Although these general effects are well documented the precise sequence of events and the mechanisms underlying these changes remain unclear. It is not known whether the pathogen initially causes changes in the rate of photosynthesis by directly affecting some aspect of photosynthetic electron transfer as has been suggested for powdery mildew of sugar beet (3), or whether the pathogen acts indirectly by altering carbon assimilation or the activity of enzymes of the Calvin cycle as has been reported for powdery mildew of barley and sugar beet (4). Part of this controversy is likely to result from the fact that experiments are usually carried out fairly late during the infection cycle when symptoms are visible and at this stage it is impossible to distinguish primary from secondary events.
    In this study we use the technique of the simultaneous measurement of chlorophyll fluorescence and O_2 evolution to examine changes in photosynthetic electron transfer and indirectly in carbon assimilation (during steady state photosynthesis and during induction) very early after infection by the pathogen, before symptoms are visible, to determine whether the primary changes in the rate of photosynthesis are due to changes in electron transfer or carbon assimilation.

PROCEDURE
    Seeds of barley (*Hordeum distichum* L.) cv Marris Otter were grown in John Innes compost no. 2. in a growth chamber at 18^0C under

M. Baltscheffsky (ed.), Current Research in Photosynthesis, Vol. IV, 219–222.
© 1990 *Kluwer Academic Publishers. Printed in the Netherlands.*

fluorescence and tungsten lamps (300 μmol m^{-2} s^{-1}) with 16 h light and 8 h dark cycles. Barley leaves were inoculated on the abaxial surface with spores of *Erysiphe graminis* when the first leaf was fully expanded (7 days after sowing) and experiments carried out 30 h later. Chlorophyll a fluorescence (from the adaxial surface) and O_2 evolution were measured simultaneously using a leaf disc O_2 electrode (Hansatech) and modulation fluorimeter. Experiments were carried out at $20^0C \pm 1^0C$ and at saturating CO_2 to minimise any changes in stomatal conductance and photorespiration. White actinic light for photosynthesis (400 – 700nm) was provided by a Schott lamp and photon flux density altered by means of neutral density filters. Saturating pulses of white light (3000 μmol m^{-2} s^{-1}) were provided by a Volpi lamp. Quenching co-efficients (qQ and qNP) were calculated according to (5).

RESULTS AND DISCUSSION

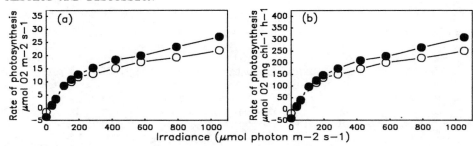

Fig 1. *Change in the rate of photosynthesis as a function of irradiance. (a) μmol O_2 m^{-2} s^{-1} ; (b) μmol O_2 mg chl^{-1} h^{-1}).* ($\bigcirc$) *control ; ($\bullet$) mildewed barley leaves*

Fig 1. shows the rate of photosynthesis of control and mildewed tissue as a function of irradiance, expressed per unit chlorophyll (Fig 1b) and per unit area of leaf (Fig 1a). In both cases at low irradiances (up to 200 μmol m^{-2} s^{-1}) the rate of photosynthesis was identical in control and mildewed leaves indicating that quantum yield (the rate of photosynthesis / absorbed photons (Φs)) remained unchanged. However, as irradiance increased to saturating values the rate of photosynthesis was significantly higher in mildewed tissue. At this stage of infection the concentration of chlorophyll and the ratio of chlorophyll a:b was the same in control and mildewed leaves. This initial increase in both <u>net</u> and <u>gross</u> photosynthesis has been observed in other host/pathogen interactions, notably rust of barley (1) but the basis of the increase has remained obscure.

The effect of the mildew on the functioning of photosystem 2 (PS2) was examined during steady state photosynthesis and during induction using the technique of chlorophyll fluorescence together with the simultaneous measurement of the rate of photosynthesis. Fig. 2. shows the light saturation curves of photochemical (qQ) and non-photochemical (qNP) quenching as a function of irradiance. In both control and mildewed leaves qQ, an indicator of the redox state of QA, fell as irradiance increased owing to a progressive reduction of QA. However there was <u>no</u> significant difference between the redox state of PS2 in

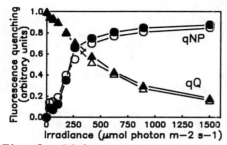

Fig. 2. *Light saturation curves*
of photochemical (qQ) (△) and non -
photochemical (qNP) (○) quenching
as a function of irradiance.
(△○) control ;(▲●)mildewed leaves.

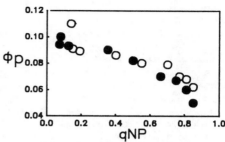

Fig. 3. *The relationship*
between intrinsic yield
(Φp) and non-photochemical
quenching (qNP). (○)
control ; (●) mildewed leaves

mildewed and control leaves. In 1987 Weis & Berry modified the traditional concept of quantum yield (Φs)(6). As qQ is a measure of the proportion of light energy absorbed by the pigments of PS2 that is used for photochemistry, they suggested that dividing Φs by qQ would give a measure of the intrinsic yield or quantum yield of functional PS2 reaction centers (Φp). If no regulation of electron transfer from H_2O to QB occurred Φp should be constant as a function of light intensity. However it has been shown that Φp decreases as irradiance increases indicating a regulation of intrinsic quantum yield, and this has been correlated with the extent of qNP quenching.

In both control and mildewed leaves there was a 40% decrease in Φp as qNP increased from 0 to 0.85 showing that the extent of the regulation of Φp was unchanged by the disease (Fig 3). In addition the relationship between Φp and qNP was the same shape in both types of tissue suggesting that the mechanism underlying the regulation (possibly quenching in the antenna) remained the same. During photosynthetic induction the extent of oxidation of QA, Φs and Φp were again unchanged by the presence of the mildew (Fig 4). These results demonstrate clearly that electron transfer is not affected by the mildew in the early stages of infection.

qNP is composed of a number of quenching processes ; qE, associated with the build up of the ΔpH, is the dominant process under most physiological conditions. The other quenching processes are attributable to a state transition, qT, and to photoinhibitory damage, qI. At low irradiances (up to 200 μmol m^{-2} s^{-1}) steady state qNP was lower in mildewed than in control leaves but as light became saturating qNP attained the same values in both types of tissue (Fig 2). During photosynthetic induction in low irradiance qNP was always lower in mildewed than in control leaves (Fig 4A & B). However, at saturating irradiance qNP built up more slowly in mildewed tissue but reached the same steady state value as control leaves (Fig 4C & D).

There are 2 possible explanations for these observations. Firstly, qNP would be lower in mildewed tissue if the disease had caused the thylakiod membranes to become "leaky", resulting in partial dissipation of the proton gradient. This is not consistent with an <u>increase</u> in the rate of photosynthesis and an unchanged capacity for electron transfer through PS2. An alternative explanation is that the pathogen either directly or indirectly has created an increased demand for and utilization of ATP such that only at high light intensities where light energy is in excess can the proton gradient be maintained. This also suggests that changes in C assimiltion and general metabolism occur rapidly after infection.

Further evidence that C assimilation is affected by the disease is provided by the alteration in the timing and amplitude of the secondary oscillation observed on turning on both low and high intensity light (Fig 4). Secondary dapmning oscillations are thought to be due, at least in part, to the build up of pools of metabolites of the Calvin cycle and the activation of enzymes (7). In mildewed leaves the oscillation occurred earlier and was smaller in amplitude than in control leaves (Fig 4). At present experiments are being carried out to characterize the oscillation with respect to changes in the concentration of Calvin cylce metabolites.

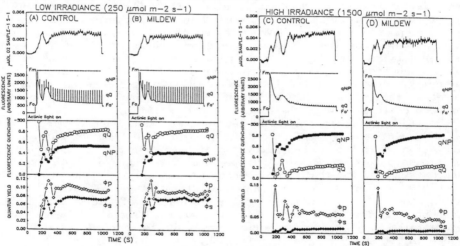

Fig 4. Characteristics of photosynthetic induction in low (A control and B mildewed leaves) and high irradiance (C control and D mildewed leaves) following a period in the dark.

REFERENCES
(1) Scholes, J.D., & Farrar, J.F. (1986) New Phytol. 104, 601-612.
(2) Scholes, J.D., & Farrar, J.F. (1987) New Phytol. 107, 103-117.
(3) Magyarosy, A.C. & Malkin, R. (1978) Physiol. Plant Path. 13, 183-8
(4) Gordon, T.R. & Duniway, J.M. (1982) Plant Physiol. 69, 139-142.
(5) Schreiber, U., Schliwa, U. & Bilger, W. (1986) Photosyn. Res. 10, 51-62.
(6) Weis, E. & Berry, J.A. (1987) Biochim. Biophys. Acta 894, 198-208
(7) Walker, D.A. (1981) Planta 153, 273-278.

THE RELATIONSHIP BETWEEN THE DEVELOPMENT OF HAUSTORIA OF *ERYSIPHE GRAMINIS* AND THE ENERGY STATUS OF LEAVES.

Derek P. Wright[1,2], Julie D. Scholes[1], Peter Horton[1], Brian C. Baldwin[2], M. Claire Shephard[3], Robert Hill Institute, Sheffield University, Sheffield, S10 2TN, U.K.[1], ICI Agrochemicals, Jealott's Hill Research Station, Bracknell, Berkshire, RG12 6EY[2], University of Reading, Reading, Berkshire, U.K.[3]

INTRODUCTION

Powdery mildews are obligate pathogens. The fungus grows externally on leaf tissues and forms haustoria only in host epidermal cells. The haustorium is believed to be the absorptive organ through which the fungus acquires photosynthates for growth. The intimate interface established between fungus and host and subsequent alterations made to the region of the host plasmalemma in direct contact with the haustorium [1] may aid this function.

It is generally agreed that pathogens such as powdery mildews cause a decline in net photosynthesis [2] and a reduction in chlorophyll concentration. However the precise mechanisms underlying such changes are unclear. Proposed mechanisms include ; increased host [3] and/or fungal respiration [4], destruction of chloroplasts [5], inhibition of photosynthetic electron transfer [6] and fungal sequestration of inorganic phosphate from the host cytoplasm [7].

The apparent confusion can be attributed to a number of factors. Firstly different research groups work on different host pathogen systems and there is no reason to assume all biotrophic pathogens affect photosynthesis similarly. Secondly different infection densities, different stages in pathogenic development and different growth conditions will all affect results obtained. Finally whole leaf studies use material which is highly heterogeneous, consisting of cells directly affected by, or closely associated with fungal mycelium and areas removed from the mycelium. Hence results will be a mean of infected and uninfected tissues.

This study identifies some of the major changes in photosynthetic metabolism of wheat infected with powdery mildew using a combination of chlorophyll a fluorescence analysis and light microscopy.

MATERIALS AND METHODS

Plants of wheat (*Triticum aestivum* L. cv.Rapier) were grown and their first leaf infected using spores of *Erysiphe graminis* f. sp.

M. Baltscheffsky (ed.), Current Research in Photosynthesis, Vol. IV, 223–226.
© 1990 *Kluwer Academic Publishers. Printed in the Netherlands.*

tritici when fully expanded. Infection was confined to the first leaf.

Chlorophyll *a* fluorescence (from abaxial surface) and O_2 evolution were measured simultaneously using a leaf disc oxygen electrode and modulation fluorometer. Experiments were carried out at 20 ± 1°C and at saturating CO_2 to minimise alterations in stomatal conductance and photorespiration.

Epidermal strips were prepared [8], stained using cotton blue/lactophenol for 5 minutes and mounted in lactophenol. Total haustorial counts for each epidermal strip were made and results expressed per unit leaf area.

Values for dark respiration are included in all calculations of photosynthetic rates to account for the potentially high rate of fungal respiration from infected leaf tissue which will occur in the light. Statisical analysis is by use of means and standard errors as appropriate.

RESULTS AND DISCUSSION

Over a period of 3-7 days total chlorophyll showed a sharp decline in infected leaves compared to uninfected controls [Fig. 1]. A small decrease in total carotenoid concentration occurred over the same period. The chlorophyll a:b ratio was unaffected by the pathogen. The light saturated rate of photosynthesis per unit area was initially increased, over the first three days, and then decreased over the next four days [Fig. 2A]. However when expressed per unit chlorophyll the rate of O_2 evolution was greater in mildewed than control leaves [Fig. 2B]. The numbers of haustoria increased during the period of decline in total chlorophyll concentration and net photosynthesis (leaf area basis).

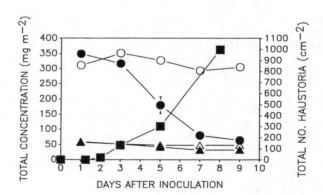

Figure 1. Changes in total chlorophyll (◯) and total carotenoid (△) concentrations with after inoculation. Control - open symbol, infected - closed symbols. Total number of haustoria per unit area(■)

The fluorescence measurements [Fig. 3] show that qQ, a measure of photochemical efficiency, increased slightly with infection under low light intensities (120μmol m^{-2} s^{-1}) but was unchanged at high light intensity (1100μmol m^{-2} s^{-1}). Non- photochemical quenching, qNP, here largely relates to high energy state quenching, qE, owing to the build up of the ΔpH. ATP synthesis is associated with discharge of the ΔpH and hence linked to qE and qNP. In mildewed tissues qNP decreased at low light intensity but was little changed at high light intensity.

The loss of chlorophyll from the mesophyll as the fungus infected the epidermal tissues was marked and suggested that the influence of the fungus extended well beyond the cells containing the haustoria. The fact that the rate of photosynthesis per unit chlorophyll increased while total chlorophyll content declined,indicated that the residual chloroplasts were fully functional.

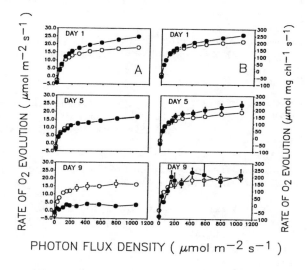

PHOTON FLUX DENSITY (μmol m^{-2} s^{-1})

Figure 2. Changes in the rate of photosynthesis expressed on a leaf area basis (column A) and unit chlorophyll basis (column B) as a function of photon flux density for control (◯) and mildewed (●) leaves on days 1,5 and 9 after inoculation. Standard errors of the means of three determinations are given for each photon flux density.

The slight increase in photochemical efficiency observed in mildewed tissue suggests that electron transfer through PS2 is unaffected by the disease in those chloroplasts that remain functional. The lower qNP values at low light intensity for mildewed tissue could reflect an increased requirement for ATP directly by the pathogen or result from pathogen induced changes to host metabolism. The alternative is an increase in basal uncoupling of photophosphorylation from proton efflux ie. pathogen induced "leakiness" of the thylakoid membrane. The results indicate that although the pathogen caused a

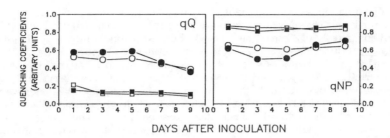

DAYS AFTER INOCULATION

Figure 3. Variation in quenching coefficients with days after inoculation.
○ - *low photon flux density (120μmol m⁻² s⁻¹)*
□ - *high photon flux density (1100μmol m⁻² s⁻¹)*
Control - open symbols. Infected - closed symbols.

loss of populations of chloroplasts in infected leaves, in chloroplasts that remained electron transfer appeared largely unaffected.

REFERENCES

1. Manners,J.M. and Gay,J.L. (1983) in Biochemical Plant Pathology (Callow,J.A.,ed.), 163-195, John Wiley. Chichester.
2. Owera,S.A.P.,Farrar,J.F. and Whitbread,R. (1981) Physiol. Plant Path. 18, 79-90.
3. Daly,J.M. (1976) in Physiological Plant Pathology, Encyclopedia of Plant Physiology, New Series, (Heitefuss,R. and Williams,P.H.,ed.), Vol.4, 459-479, Springer-Verlag Berlin.
4. Raggi,V. (1980) Physiol. Plant Path. 16, 19-24.
5. Ahmad,I.,Farrar,J.F. and Whitbread,R. (1983) Physiol. Plant Path. 23, 411-419.
6. Montalbini,P. and Buchanan,B.B. (1974) Physiol. Plant Path. 4, 191-196
7. Whipps,J.M. and Lewis,D.H. (1981) in Effects Of Disease On The Physiology Of The Growing Plant (Ayres,P.G.,ed.), 47-83, Cambridge University Press, Cambridge.
8. Silcox,D. and Holloway,P.J. (1986) Aspects Of Applied Biology 11, 19-28.

SYNTHESIS OF ALANINE FROM 3-PHOSPHOGLYCERATE BY INTACT BUNDLE SHEATH CELLS OF ZEA MAYS

ESTELA M. VALLE AND HANS W. HELDT, INSTITUT FÜR BIOCHEMIE DER PFLANZE, UNIVERSITÄT GÖTTINGEN, UNTERE KARSPÜLE 2, 3400 GÖTTINGEN, F.R.G.

INTRODUCTION
In a C4 plant, the mesophyll and bundle sheath (BS) cells are closely inter-connected by a number of plasmodesmata. Mechanical treatment of leaves of C4 plants by means of a blender results in a preferential disruption of the mesophyll cells. In this way bundle sheath strands (BSS) can be obtained, consisting of a segment of vascular bundle surrounded by BS cells of high functional integrity and metabolic competence (1). It has been recently shown that these BS cells have retained the plasmodesmata, which had been the connection to the now broken mesophyll cells (2,3). Due to these plasmodesmatic connections the intact BS cells are permeable for molecules up to a molecular weight of about 900 Dalton (2,4). This accessibility of highly intact cells to substrates added to the outside medium makes bundle sheath strands a very interesting object for metabolic studies.

In the phloem sap of maize leaves 28% of the total amino nitrogen was found in the form of alanine (5), which indicates that from the maize leaf cells a large portion of the assimilated nitrate is exported as alanine. In the present report we investigated whether bundle sheath cells have the capacity for a de novo synthesis of alanine from 3-phosphoglycerate as a product of photosynthesis.

MATERIALS AND METHODS
Plant growth. Zea mays was grown in soil under natural illumination supplemented with incandescent and cool white fluorescent lamps to provide 1 to 1.5 kW m^{-2} in a glasshouse at 25 to 30/15 to 18°C day/night temperature.

Preparation of bundle sheath strands. BSS were isolated from fully ex-panded leaves of 3 to 6 weeks old plants by blending 2 mm leaf segments in a polytron giving 1 sec (setting at 7) and 15 sec (setting at 5-6) bursts. The blending medium contained 0.35 M sorbitol, 20 mM Tricine (pH 8.2),

Abbreviations: BS, bundle sheath; BSS, bundle sheath strands, Pyr, pyruvate; PGA, phosphoglycerate; PEP phosphoenolpyruvate

M. Baltscheffsky (ed.), Current Research in Photosynthesis, Vol. IV, 227–230.
© 1990 Kluwer Academic Publishers. Printed in the Netherlands.

4 mM MgCl$_2$, 40 mM KCl, 2 mM KH$_2$PO$_4$ and 10 mM isoascorbic acid. After each burst, the crude homogenate was filtered through 1.3 and 1 mm sieves and 600 µm and 280 µm nylon nets. The BSS were collected by filtration on a 88 µm nylon mesh, washed, resuspended on 100 ml of resuspending medium (blending medium without isoascorbic acid) and filtered again. Finally, the BSS were washed off from the mesh, allowed to settle, resuspended in approximately 70 µg chlorophyll per ml resuspending medium and stored on ice.

Alanine synthesis from 3-PGA in the dark. Intact BSS (50 µg chlorophyll/ml) were incubated for two minutes with the additions indicated and the reaction was started by adding 3-PGA at 30°C. At various times, the reaction was stopped by 3% HClO$_4$ and after neutralizing with KOH metabolites were assayed spectrophotometrically (6) in the following sequence: pyruvate with lactate dehydrogenase, PEP with pyruvate kinase, 2-PGA with enolase and 3-PGA with phosphoglycerate mutase. Alanine was assayed according to ref(7).

Preparation of cell extract. BSS extracts were prepared by grinding BSS (200 µg chlorophyll) in a mortar and pestle with 2 ml extraction buffer (50 mM HEPES-KOH (pH 7.2), 10 mM DTT, 1 mM EDTA and 0.1% (w/v) PVP-40), filtering the homogenate through Miracloth and centrifuging the filtrate for 30 sec in an Eppendorf Microfuge. All operations were done between 0 and 4°C.

RESULTS AND DISCUSSION
In the experiment of fig. 1A BSS were suspended in a medium containing ADP and glutamate.Upon the addition of 3-PGA a rapid formation of 2-PGA, PEP, pyruvate and alanine is observed. The formation of alanine requires the existence of the intact cell structure. This is shown in the experiment of fig. 1B, where the BSS were disrupted prior to the incubation. With the cell extract the presence of 3-PGA, ADP and glutamate yielded only the formation of 2-PGA, PEP and traces of pyruvate, whereas the formation of alanine could not be detected. The experiment of fig. 1A was carried out with a 3-PGA concentration of 10 mM, which is near the 3-PGA concentration found in BS cells of intact maize leaves (13 mM (8)). In the experiment of table 1, the experiment was also carried out with 1 mM 3-PGA, similar to the concentration found in maize leaf BS cells in the dark (1.5 mM (8)). Although in this experiment the amount of total products formed was reduced by 50%, the amount of alanine synthesized was still 20% of the total products, as in the presence of high 3-PGA concentration.

In the experiment of table 2, the components of the incubation of BSS were varied. The results show that for the synthesis of alanine 3-PGA could be replaced by 2-PGA or PEP. When ADP or glutamate were omitted, 2-PGA and PEP were also produced, as to be expected, but there was not alanine synthesis observed. The formation of pyruvate from PEP in the absence of ADP, occurring at a low rate, reflects a PEP phosphatase activity of unknown origin. The results of table 2 confirm that the formation of alanine from 3-PGA in BSS proceeds via the glycolytic sequence.

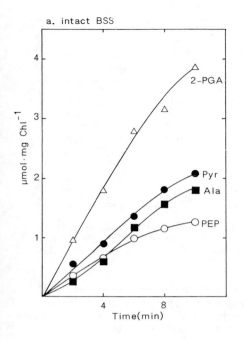
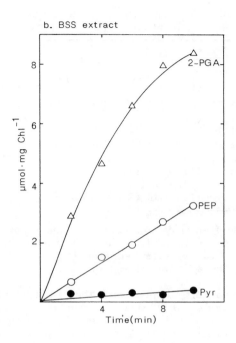

FIGURE 1. Synthesis of alanine from 3-phosphoglycerate by intact (A) and extract (B) of bundle sheath strands. BSS were incubated with 1 mM ADP, 5 mM Glu and reaction started by adding 10 mM 3-PGA. Metabolites concentrations were measured according to Materials and Methods.

TABLE 1. Formation of metabolites by intact BSS from maize leaves. BSS were incubated as in the expt. of fig. 1. The substrate concentrations were A) 1 mM 3-PGA, 2 mM ADP and 0.5 mM Glu, B) as in fig. 1, C) as B + 10 mM aspartate. Incubation time 10 min.

Metabolite	A 3-PGA (1 mM)	B 3-PGA (10 mM)	C 3-PGA (10 mM) Asp (10 mM)
	μmol/mg chl		
2-PGA	1.2	3.9	3.7
PEP	0.5	1.3	0.9
Pyr	1.8	2.1	3.2
Ala	0.9	1.8	2.5

TABLE 2. Formation of metabolites by intact BSS from maize leaves. Incubation time 10 min.

Additions (mM)		2-PGA	PEP μmol/mg chl	Pyr	Ala
3-PGA	(1), ADP (2); Glu (0.5)	1.2	0.5	1.8	0.9
3-PGA	(1)	1.1	0.8	0.6	n.d.
2-PGA	(1)	-	0.9	0.7	n.d.
2-PGA	(1), ADP (2); Glu (0.5)	-	0.9	2.1	1.0
PEP	(1)	-	-	3.6	n.d.
PEP	(1), ADP (2)	-	-	7.0	n.d.
PEP	(1), Glu (0.5)	-	-	2.8	0.4
PEP	(1), ADP (2), Glu (0.5)	-	-	6.7	1.0

The formation of alanine can be stimulated by the addition of aspartate, as shown in table 1. A decrease in the level of PEP and an increase in the level of pyruvate indicated that pyruvate kinase might have been stimulated by the addition of aspartate.

Our results demonstrate that isolated BSS from maize in the presence of physiological substrate concentrations are able to produce alanine from 3-PGA at a rate of about 15 μmol/mg chl.h. Thus, BS cells have more than enough of the capacity for de novo synthesis of alanine required for the export as a product of nitrate assimilation into the phloem system. Pyruvate kinase may be an important regulatory step in reaction sequence of alanine formation. Studies are now in progress to elucidate the regulatory properties of maize bundle sheath pyruvate kinase.

ACKNOWLEDGEMENT
This work has been supported by the Deutsche Forschungsgemeinschaft.

REFERENCES
1. Hatch, M.D., Kagawa, T. (1986) Arch. Biochem. Biophys. 175, 39-53
2. Weiner, H., Burnell, J.N., Woodrow, I.E., Heldt, H.W., Hatch, M.D. (1988) Plant Physiol. 88, 815-822
3. Valle, E.M., Craig, S., Hatch, M.D., Heldt, H.W. (1989) Bot. Acta, subm.
4. Burnell, J.N. (1988) J. Expt. Bot. 39, 1575-1580
5. Weiner, H., Blechschmidt-Schneider, S., Mohme, H., Eschrich, W., Heldt, H.W. (1989) Plant Physiol. subm.
6. Lamprecht, W., Heinz, F. (1984) In Methods of enzymatic analysis (H.U. Bergmeyer ed.) Verlag Chemie, Weinheim, Vol. VI, pp. 555-561
7. Graßl, M., Supp, M. (1985) in Methods of enzymatic analysis (H.U. Bergmeyer ed.) Verlag Chemie, Weinheim, Vol. VIII, pp. 345-349
8. Stitt, M., Heldt, H.W. (1985) Biochim. Biophys. Acta 808, 400-414

THE PRINCIPAL SCHEME OF PHOTOSYNTHETIC CARBON CONVERSION IN CELLS OF
ISOPRENERELEASING PLANTS
University of Stockholm, Sweden, August 6-11, 1989

G. A. Sanadze
Problem Research laboratory of Photosynthesis, Tbilisi State
University, Tbilisi, USSR

The interest to the study of biochemical mechanisms of the free isoprene
formation in the photosynthetic conversion of carbon arose immediately after
the discovery of the photobiological phenomenon named "isoprene effect" IE
(1-6). The first reports on the essential difference between the biochemical
pathways of carbohydrates and isoprene formation at photosynthesis were
obtained at the initial stages of the investigation of this phenomenon (7).
The evidence of this difference gradually increased and by the end of
sixties a hypothesis has been formulated that in isoprenereleasing plants
beside the known ribulosebisphosphatecarboxylase / oxygenase RUBP-C/O
another system of primary carboxilation must work, which somehow leads to
the formation of acetyl CoA (3, 4). This hypothesis has been further
ascertained by the study of the discribution of carbon atoms in an isoprene
molecule assimilated at photosynthesis (8, 9), the action of protein
synthesis inhibitors upon the photochemical activity, photosynthesis and
isoprene effect in protoplasts and isolated chloroplasts (10), the degree of
localisation of isoprene biosynthesis in chloroplasts (11), the dependence
of isoprene formation rate on the partial pressure of O_2 and CO_2 in the air
(12, 13), the extent of the dependence of IE upon temperature (5, 14, 15)
etc.

On the other hand, the evidence havs gradually been accumulated indicating
that IE like photosynthetic carbon reduction is closely connected with
chloroplast functioning (1, 4-6, 14-16), and in 1982 it was shown that
isolated poplar chloroplasts are capable of isoprene photobiosynthesis (17).

Thus, the available information points to the capacity of chloroplasts to
synthesize free isoprene and on the other hand to the essential difference
between the pathways conversion of carbon assimilated from CO_2 in
Benson-Canvin reaction cycles (BC) and IE.

In the present work an attempt has been made to find out the difference
between the pathways of carbon conversion in the chain of the above
mentioned reactions by means of D,L-glyceraldehyde(GA), recommended by
Stocks and Walker (18, 19) as a specific inhibitor of dark reactions of
photosynthesis, particularly in BC reaction cycle. The authors have shown

M. Baltscheffsky (ed.), Current Research in Photosynthesis, Vol. IV, 231–237.
© 1990 *Kluwer Academic Publishers. Printed in the Netherlands.*

that this compound practically does not affect the photochemical reactions of photosynthesis and they characterize it as a "darkness equivalent" of DCMU.

Methods

The experiments have been carried out on the protoplasts of 10-12 days old leaves (Populus deltoides Marsch) and celandine (Celadinum majus L).

The poplar was grown in the green-house at the natural light and temperature 25-30°C and celandine under conditions of artificial illumination (luminiscent lamp 40-4, illumination 5.10^3 lx) at the temperature 20-25°C. Physiologically ripe leaves from the middle layer of 2-3 year summer plants were applied.

Protoplasts were isolated by enzymic method using the technics of Edvards and coauthors (19). To provide good access of enzyme solution the leaves were cut in thin segments or their low epidermis was impaired by glass powder. Treated in such a way leaf material was placed into the media for the fermentation (A): sorbitol - 0.75 M, $CaCL_2$ - 1 mM, $MgCl_2$ - 2 mM, pH 5.5, depending on the investigation object, the concentration of enzymes has been modified: macerozim - R10 - 0.5%, Onozika - R10 - 2% (poplar) and macerozim R10 - 0.03%, onozuk R10 - 2% (greater celandine). incubation lasted 18-20 hours in the refrigerator at the temperature 8-10°C, but in the case of poplar 30 min. more at 20-22°C.

Protoplasts were isolated by shaking in the media for isolation and washing (B): mannitol - 0.8 M, HEPES - 5 mM, pH 7.2, $CaCl_2$ - 1 mM, $MgCl_2$ - 2 mM. The suspension of protoplasts was passed through kapron net (the size of pores 8 mm), centrifuged 20s at 300g and then the pellet was suspended and twice washed in B media (centrifuged in the same way). Protoplasts were kept in the dark 5-8 in the B media: sorbitol -0.8 M, tricin - 5 mM, pH 7. Before the determination of functional ability of protoplasts, the concentrated suspension was diluted by the reaction media (G): sorbitol - 0.8 M, tricin - 50 mM, pH 7.6 (the content of chlorophyll - 25 mkg/ml). At the estimation of the rate of Co_2 photosynthetic fixation after the preillumination of protoplasts (5-10 min), 10 mM $NaH^{14}CO_3$ was added to the media. The temperature was 25°C, illumination 2.10^4 lx, chlorophyll was determined according to Arnon (20). The rate of CO_2 absorbtion by leaves in light was measured on the infrared gas analyzer OA-5501, and in protoplasts radiometrically by the scintillation spectrometr "Multimat-1" ("Intertechnic", France), and of IE on the gas-liquid chromatograph (Fractovap 4200, Carlo Erba, Italy).

Each experiment was repeated 10 times. All of them indicated analogous results. The data of the typical experiment are shown on the graphs.

Discussion

On discussing the obtained data a working hypothesis was obtained about the existance of a close interconnection between the compartments of carbon photosynthetic transformation in Benson-Calvin cycle and in isoprene effect. Schematic expression (fig. 1) of the hypothesis is an attempt to generalize the results of IE study of many years. Though the work for giving a more precise definition of some details of this scheme has not been completed it may be used even in this simplified form to explain the results.

The central place in the scheme is occupied by the different pools of photosynthetic carbon conversion in chloroplasts, designated as BC and AcCoA.

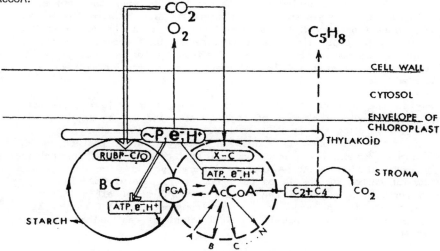

Fig. 1. Hipothesis of two interacting carboxylation systems in isoprens releasing plant photosynthesis. Designations: BC - pool of reactions of Benson-Calvin cycle; AcCoA - pool of acetyl-CoA and isoprene biosynthesis; RUBPC/O-ribulosebisphsphate C/O; X-C-unknown carboxylase leading to acetyl-CoA biosyynthesis; PGA-phosphoglyceric acid; PGAL-phosphoglyceric aldehyde; GA-D,L-glyceraldehyde; a,b,c...n-alternative pathways of acetyl-CoA use.

The first of them is supplied by the enzyme RUBP-C/O which catalyses the BC cycle reactions, the other one catalyses the reactions with the yet unknown enzyme x-carboxylase which leads to acetyl-CoA formation. Thus it is supposed that in chloroplasts of isoprenereleasing plants there are at least two compartments of light conversion of CO_2 carbon that comes to the leaves from the air, from two different carboxilation systems or from one system but along two channels. In fig.1 they are located in immediate vicinity. But the centres of carboxylation are separated, which is to be understood as a sign of the presence either of two different enzymes or two different carboxylizing centres of the same enzyme.

Both these pools are apparently supplied from the same sources of CO_2, and the primary products of photochemical reactions, occuring in the membrane of thylakoids. But judging by the isoprene production /14, 16/ the pool AcCoA, presumably is supplied by them in lesser degree than pool BC. Further it is supposed that the pool AcCoA, beside the main function - the biosynthesis of acetate which than is activated by coenzyme A functions as a supplier of phosphoglyceric acid in chloroplast (Ch) which can be synthesized from acetyl-CoA. Because of the spatial nearness of BC and AcCoA pools formed in that last PGA is a permanent source for BC pool. The existence of such source of FGA for the pool BC is indispensable, for example, in a lag phase of photosynthesis when it is necessary to attain a required autocatalitic level of intermediates of cycle for its starting.

The Benson-Calvin reaction having been started that is when the trigger mechanism has already been operated, the metabollic link between the BC and AcCoA pools remains preserved, but at the level at which the AcCoA is capable to supply BC pool with permanently changeable, corresponding and strictly regulated amount of PGA which is defined by the BC pool itself. As a whole the reaction must have the donor-acceptor interaction between closely located metabolism pools.

In this way in the chloroplasts of isoprenereleasing plants there supposedly exist two interconnected complexes of carboxylation induced by light in which RUBP-C/O supplies the pool BC with carbon, while x-carboxylase supplies pool AcCoA. The primary product of carboxylation of pool BC is FGA, and the reduced products are triozophosphates and carbohydrates. The primary product of carboxylation in AcCoA pool is unknown yet but the main product of reduction of carbon of Co_2 is to be considered as acetyl CoA. The coordinated functioning of these two pools depends first of all on their provision with CO_2, the products of electron-transport chain of chloroplasts and on the extent of their interaction which might be realized at the level of PGA exchange.

We judge of the functioning of these pools by means of the rate of absorption of CO_2 and isoprene emition. According to the available data by which the amount of carbon atoms, in IE is about 1-2% of the total amount of carbon atoms assimilated at photosynthesis of CO_2, it is evident that the participation of IE reaction in the light metabolism of isoprenereleasing plants is not great. Nevertheless these data can not be used for the quantitative estimation of carbon exchange of the whole pool AcCoA in which IE makes but a part of it. From the point of view of the above stated IE may be regarded as a cell reaction to the acetyl CoA conversion rate in chloroplasts, that is as a servosystem which reacts simultaneously on the ratio of the formation and realization rate of acetyl CoA in chloroplasts. But as IE is also in close reverse dependence on partial pressure of CO_2 in the air (rises with the decrease in partial pressure) /7, 12/ which means that isoprene synthesis in which acetyl CoA of chloroplast origin is used is obviously mediated by the connection with the reaction of photosynthetic carboxylation.

On the other hand as the amount of IE is estimated by the amount of released isoprene - the final product of carbon conversion in this process which begins with the light absorption of CO_2 by chlorophyll-containing cell it is possible by its help to estimate the extent of regulation of carbon metabolism in photosynthezing cell as well, depending in its turn on CO_2 pressure in the air. That is why IE must be regarded as one of the possible metabolic responses of chlorophyll-containing illuminated cell on the change of the partial pressure of CO_2 in the media surrounding chloroplast, that is as a result of the most general level of vital activity regulation in the hierarchic system of regulating mechanism in the autotrophic cell.

Proceeding from the above statements and using the logic of the presented scheme it is possible to suggest that GA (fig.2.) alters the rate of separate reactions of carbon metabolism of illuminated leaf and isolated protoplasts by inhibiting reactions of BC cycle, resulting from the suppression of the phosphoribulokinase activity /18, 19/, or by the products of these processes inhibition, or by competing with chloroplast ATP. Mainly all the existing possibilities of GA are realized.

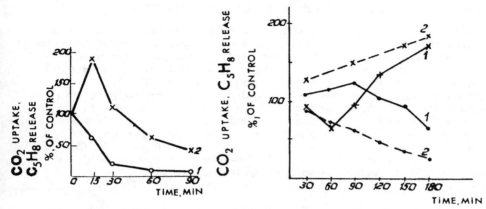

Fig. 2. The influence of 10 mM GA on photosynthesis (1) and isoprene effect (2) of protoplast of poplar leaves

Fig. 3. The action of Ca-salt of glucosaccharic acid at the concentrations of 0.25 mM (1) and 0.5 mM (2) on the photosynthesis (-.-) and isoprene effect (-x-) protoplasts.

Thus by means of GA it became possible to show that at the initial steps of the action of the inhibitor the rate of the photosynthetic CO_2 assimilation and formation free isoprene is changed in different ways. These facts show that the mechanism of carbon conversion in Benson-Calvin cycle differs from the one in IE and may be explained by the present scheme. The experimental data of the present paper with numerous references testify that in chloroplasts at least in isoprenereleasing plants beside the ribulosebis-phophat carboxylase/oxygenase another system of carboxylation works the primary product of which is not FGA but acetyl CoA.

In recent years papers appeared which show that there is close connection between carbon photosynthetic metabolism in chloroplasts and a number of compounds formed from acetyl-CoA, for example, fatty acids, polyprenols, carotenoids and etc. (20-22). As it is known the synthesis of the two latter groups of substances arises from isopentenilpyrophosphate (IPP) and dimethyallilpyrophosphate (DMAPP) (23). It is suggested that free isoprene in certain conditions may be synthesized from these precursors and as the calculations show the formation of isoprane molecule prasumably occurs as a result of elimination of pyrophosphate group of bridge nonclassical carbonium ion of DMAPP.The escape of proton from the bridge carbonium ion leads to the formation of isoprene. The reaction also may rapidly proceed unenzymatically if the reaction media is greatly protonized. There is a reason to suggest that in isoprenereleasing plants during the photosynthesis of chloroplasts acetyl CoA is formed because of the acetyl-CoA synthetase as well as pyruvatdehydrogenase complex localized there /22/.

To verify the hypothesis tests were carried out on the two groups of compounds which were suggested to inhibite fatty acids synthesis and photosynthetic assimilation of CO_2 and (by means of that) change the conditions of stationary exchange of acetyl-CoA in chloroplasts.

The influence of cerulenine, some phosphororganic compounds and synthetic analogues of natural carbohydrates upon the photosynthesis and IE of poplar protoplasts has been studied. The activation of IE and photosynthesis suppression affected by synthetic analoques of natural carbohydrates (fig. 3). Strong activation of IE and insignificant alterations of CO_2 assimilation rate was observed at the action of cerunine and phosphoorganic compounds (fig. 4-5). The expected in this case temporary excess of acetyl-CoA according the hypotheses increases the rate of formation and release of isoprene from protoplasts. The obtained data ascertain the validity of this suggestion. The action of this compound upon the CO_2 assimilation is also consistent with the statements of hypothesis of the regulation of light metabolism of photosynthetic cell.

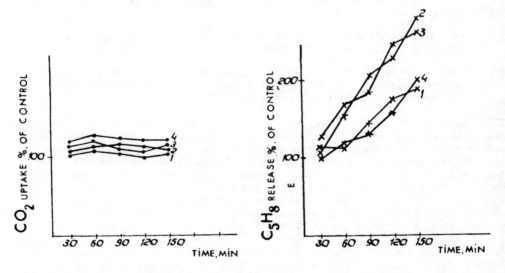

Fig. 4. The influence of cerulenine (1) and phosphoorganic compounds (phosphonacetic acid (2), γ-methyl-β-hydroxy-α-phosphonopropyl-phosphonate (3), bromphosphonacetic acid (4) on the photosynthesis of poplar protoplasts (0.5 mM).

Fig. 5. The influence of cerulenine (1) and phosphoroorganic compounds (phosphonacetic acid (2), γ-methyl-β-hydroxy-α-phosphonopropyl-phosphonate (3), bromphosphonacetic acid (4) on the isoprene effect of protopλasts (o.5 mM)

REFERENCES

1. Sanadze, G.A. (1959) Bullet. Acad. Sci. GSSR, 22, 449-454. (Engl. summ.)
2. Sanadze, G.A. (1966) Physiol. Rast. 13, 753-760. (Engl. summ.)
3. Sanadze, G.A. (1967) Biosynthesis and release of isoprene by leaves on the light, Doct. thesis. M. Plant. Physiol. Inst. Acad. Sci. USSR
4. Sanadze, G.A. (1969) In Progress in Photosynth. Res. Vol.2, 701-707
5. Rasmussen, R.A., Jones, G.A (1973) Phytochemistry, 12,15-21
6. Jones, G.A, Rasmussen, R.A. (1975) Plant Physiol. 55, 982-990
7. Sanadze, G.A. (1964) Physiol. Rast. 11, 49-52. (Engl. summ.)
8. Sanadze, G.A., Dzhaiani, G.I. (1972) Physiol. Rast. 19, 1082-1089 (Engl. summ.)
9. Sanadze, G.A., Dzhaiani, G.I., Baazov, D.I. (1976) Physiol. Rast. 23, 690-696. (Engl. summ.)
10. Mgaloblishvili, M.P., Litvinov, A.I., Kalandadze, A.N. (1982) Physiol. Rast. 29, 372-381. (Engl. summ.)
11. Mgaloblishvili, M.P., Chetsuriani, N.D., Kalandadze, A.N. (1978) Physiol. Rast. 25, 1055-1061. (Engl. summ.)
12. Tarchiashvili, G.M., Kalandadze, A.N., Sanadze, G.A. (1985) Bullet. Acad. Sci. GSSR, 119, 173-176. (Engl. summ.)
13. Sanadze, G.A., Tarchiashvili, G.M. (1986) Dokl. Acad. Sci. USSR, 286, 501-504
14. Sanadze, G.A., Kalandadze, A.N. (1966) Physiol. Rast. 13, 458-463. (Engl. summ.)
15. Tingey, D.T. , Manning, M., Grothaus, L.S. et al. (1979) Physiol. Plantarum, 47, 112-121
16. Tingey, D.T. (1981) Planta, 152, 565-572
17. Mgaloblishvili, M.B., Litvinov, A.I., Sanadze, G.A. (1981) Dokl. Acad. Sci. USSR, 259, 766-768
18. Stokes, D.M., Walker, D.A. (1972) Biochem. J., 128, 1147-1159
19. Edvards, G.E., Robinson, S.T., Tyler, N.J.C., Walker D.A. (1978) Plant Physiol. 62, 313-322
20. Klaus-Peter,H., Haus-Surgen, T. (1986) Proc. 7th Int. Symp. Plant Lipids, Davis, Calif. New York, L. Acad. Press, 1987, 505-509
21. Schulze-Siebert, D., Shultz, L. (1987) Plant Physiol. 84, 1233-1238
22. Schulze-Siebert, D., Heintze, A., Shultz, L. (1987) Z. Naturforch. 42, 570-580
23. Goodwin, T. W., Mercer, E.J. (1983) In The Introduction to Plant Biochemistry, Vol. 1, pp. 65-78, Pergamon Press, Oxford etc.

THE ENHANCEMENT EFFECT OF ISOPRENE EVOLUTION BY POPLAR LEAVES

D. I. Baazov, G. A. Sanadze. Problem Research laboratory of photosynthesis Tbilisi State University, Tbilisi, USSR

"The enhancement effect" (Emerson's 2nd effect), i. e. the increase of photosynthesis quantum yield in the far-red spectral region at simultaneous illumination of chlorophyll-containing cells with shorter-wave light, has been drawing attention of researchers for almost 30 years.

The purpose of this paper has been to elucidate the question – whether isoprene effect, by analogy with photosynthesis, is capable of enhancement. In the case of the positive answer it was intended to quantitatively compare photosynthesis enhancement effect by CO_2 assimilation and O_2 evolution with enhancement effects of isoprene evolution in poplar leaves. All the measurements were made with poplar leaves, (Populus deltoides Marsh), cultuvated in natural conditions.

In the experiments on determination of the enhancement of isoprene effect and photosynthesis beam 1 represented monochromatic light with the length 700 nm with intensity 6-12 wt/m^2, while beam 2- a shorter-wave monochromatic light of different wave length- from 400 to 675 nm. The beam intensity of every section of spectrum was chosen in such a way that the velocity of isoprene evolution or photosynthesis remained approximately equal. For this purpose the intensity of beam 2 in the experiment varied from 3 to 10 wt/m^2.

The enhancement effect of isoprene and photosynthesis is given in the Table below. It is clear from the Table that the enhancement effect of isoprene evolution is somewhat greater than that of photosynthesis by O_2 and especially by CO_2 assimilation for red (623-685 nm), as well as blue (420-450 nm) light. The enhancement effect of isoprene and photosynthesis for the red light is significantly higher than the enhancement values for the blue light.

M. Baltscheffsky (ed.), Current Research in Photosynthesis, Vol. IV, 239–241.
© 1990 *Kluwer Academic Publishers. Printed in the Netherlands.*

Table

The enhancement effect of photosynthesis and isoprene evolution for different wave lengthes of additional light to illumination with $\lambda = 700$ nm

wave length, nm	Enhancement of photosynthesis, %		Isoprene enhancement effect,%
	by assimilation CO_2	by evolution O_2	
420	14±3	18±3	36±3
435	22±3	30±5	41±3
450	21±3	27±4	44±3
623	29±5	39±5	90±6
650	25±4	34±4	78±6
675	60±4	70±6	96±7
685	32±4	66±6	88±7

In order to explain the obtained results on the enhancement effect of photosynthesis and isoprene given in the Table, it is first of all necessary to adopt the hypothesis that a nonadditive enhancement of all there processes is a consequence of the increase in effectiveness of ETC work in mixed radiation due to appearance of optimum conditions for charge separation and transfer. Besides the light other external factors, for example, Co_2 and O_2 air concentration, which are also the direct participents of photosynthesis, affect the creation of such conditions. A cell, in particular chloroplast, represents not only an arena, where all the events are acted out, associated with the transformation and movement of these substances, but also a single membrane structure with multiple feedbacks, controlling these processes. An example of this is the fact, that to some a degree there exists a stoichiometric dependance between assimilated CO_2 and O_2 evolution. This means that as a result of optimization of ETC functionich, CO_2, as well as O_2 assimilation and evolution should should be simultaneously enhanced, which actually takes place in the investigation of Emerson's effect has been shown in the Table. On the other hand, the enhancement effect of photosynthesis by CO_2 and O_2 quantitatively differs from one another. The reactions of water photolysis are compartmentalized in the membrane of tilakoids in close proximity from ETC, while reactional centres of carboxyliration are in the strom of the chloroplasts and, thus, should be at greater distance from ETC.

It should, therefore, be assumed that information on the change in ETC state should be more clear in water photolysis reactions than in carboxyliration. As a result, the enhancement effect of photosynthesis by O_2 actially surpass those by CO_2. Isoprene enhancement effect is higher than the enhancement effect of photosynthesis. This may serve as the evidence that the key reactions of isoprene photobiosynthesis are compartmentalized in immediate proximity of ETC and strongly depend on its activity.

Stabilizing energy, stored during the transformation from its short-living form (energy of light quantums) to a sufficiently longliving one as NADPH and

ATP molecules, may later be used in biochemical reactions of the plant cell. The main consumers of the formed molecules are commonly assumed to be the reactions, leading to the primary products of photosynthesis, including the predecessor of isoprene biosynthesis.

Since there are no processes competing with isoprene evolution, it should be thought that enhancement effect of isoprene is determined by two factors: 1) regulation of the rate of proceeding of two photochemical reactions by the distribution of excitation energy between photosystems and 2) enhancement of effectiveness of electron transfer by ETC.

REFERENCES

1. Myers, J. (1971) Annu. Rev. Plant Physiol., 22, 289-312
2. Sanadze, G.A., Baazov, D.J. (1982) Physiol. Rast., 29, 901-907,
     (Engl. summ)
3. Baazov, D.J., Sanadze, G.A. (1987) Phisiol. Rast., 34, 213-220,
     (Engl. summ)

REGULATION OF NADP-MALATE DEHYDROGENASE LIGHT-ACTIVATION BY THE REDUCING POWER. I FUNCTIONAL STUDIES.

M. MIGINIAC-MASLOW, P. DECOTTIGNIES, J-P. JACQUOT and P.GADAL, Laboratoire de Physiologie Végétale Moléculaire, URA 1128,Bât. 430, Université de Paris-Sud, 91405,ORSAY, France.

1. INTRODUCTION

NADP-malate dehydrogenase (MDH) light - activation via the ferredoxin-thioredoxin system requires a low light energy for saturation (1). Nevertheless, high light pretreatments which affect the functionning of photosystem II reaction centers were reported to inhibit enzyme light-activation in crude leaf extracts and in isolated chloroplasts (2,3). In the present work, we investigated the effect of photoinhibitory pretreatments on the different steps of the thiol-disulfide interchange cascade leading to MDH light-activation, in order to establish the relationship between the reduction state of the proteins of the system and the extent of activation of the target enzyme. For that purpose, a model system has been used, composed of isolated thylakoids and all the purified proteins of the ferredoxin-thioredoxin system at optimized concentrations.

2. MATERIAL AND METHODS

The different proteins: spinach ferredoxin (Fd), ferredoxin-thioredoxin reductase (FTR) and thioredoxin m (TRX) and corn NADP-MDH were purified to homogeneity by already published procedures (4,5). EDTA-NaCl washed thylakoids were used to avoid contamination by stromal proteins.The thylakoids were pretreated with high light (4000 µMol quanta.m-2.sec-1) for different lengths of time. All the proteins of the system and NADP-MDH were then added, and MDH activated for a few min under moderate light (300 µMol quanta.m-2.sec-1). The reconstituted system comprised, in 100 µl total volume: 100 mM Tris buffer, pH 7.9, thylakoids (20 µg chl), 10 µM Fd, 2 µM FTR, 10 µM TRX and 2.5 µM MDH. MDH activity and the thiol content of the different proteins of the mixture were then measured. Enzyme activity was measured by the decrease in absorbance at 340 nm in the presence of NADPH and oxaloacetate. Protein thiol quantitation was done by derivatization with 14C-labelled iodoacetate or iodoacetamide (6) and either TCA-precipitation of all the proteins, or HPLC separation of each of them. A special separation procedure was devised to recover the proteins from the reaction medium. It was done by molecular size exclusion on a TSK 3000 HPLC column and allowed a quantitative recovery of each of the proteins. The use of iodoacetamide as derivatizing agent and the addition of 300 mM NaCl to the elution buffer were necessary to obtain an efficient separation (7).

3. RESULTS

Preliminary experiments (8) showed that when studied in a reconstituted system, MDH light-activation was strongly inhibited by high light pretreatments, much more than NADP reduction, which requires much more energy. It could be restored by adding fresh thylakoids or a reductant (dichlorophenolindophenol + ascorbate, or dithiothreitol). Thus it was clearly impaired by the decrease in the photosystem II electron transfer capacity of the thylakoids which is known to be induced by high light pretreatments (9,10).

M. Baltscheffsky (ed.), Current Research in Photosynthesis, Vol. IV, 243–246.
© 1990 *Kluwer Academic Publishers. Printed in the Netherlands.*

This high sensitivity to photoinhibition might originate in a low TRX reducing capacity of the system if TRX is much less readily reducible than NADP. However, when the rates of thioredoxin reduction were measured in the presence of various amounts of NADP, it appeared that NADP was a poor competitor for thioredoxin reduction (Ki=2.3 mM) and that TRX was an efficient electron acceptor (result not shown).

When a photoinhibition experiment was run in parallel on TRX reduction (without MDH) and on MDH light-activation (complete system), it could be seen that the rate of TRX reduction was only moderately affected by the treatment: after an 8 min preillumination it was inhibited by about 50%, *i.e.* to the same extent as was NADP reduction after a similar pretreatment (Fig. 1). MDH light-activation was much more sensitive (full inhibition after 8 min).

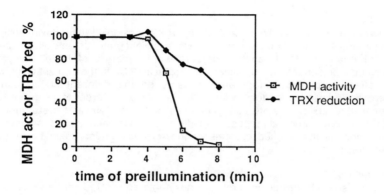

FIG. 1. Variation in the rates of either thioredoxin photoreduction or MDH light-activation as a function of the length of the photoinhibitory pretreatment of thylakoids. The assays were run on parallel samples, thioredoxin reduction being measured in the absence of MDH. In order to get linear rates, TRX reduction was measured 30 sec after its addition to the medium, and MDH activation after 4 min.

These observations were similar to those of Rébéillé and Hatch (11), obtained for MDH activation in the presence of dithiothreitol- reduced thioredoxin.These authors concluded that a high level of TRX reduction was necessary for MDH activation to occur ,due to the relatively high oxido-reduction potential of the disulfide bridge of the enzyme. As it is known that the activation of corn MDH is induced by the reduction of one disulfide bridge per subunit (5) and that the enzyme is very likely dimeric (7), it seemed interesting to check to what extent MDH reduction was impaired when the rate of TRX reduction was decreased. For this study, the different proteins of the light-activation system were separated at the end of the activation period, after derivatization (7). It can be seen (Fig. 2) that MDH reduction was affected to the same extent as was the rate of TRX reduction in Fig. 1 (*ca.* 50% decrease after an 8 min high light pretreatment). Its activation was much more affected (total inhibition after 8 min).

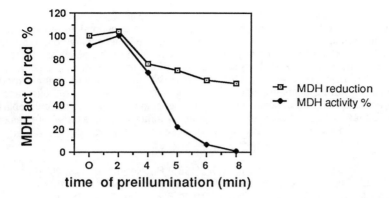

FIG. 2. Variations in the extent of MDH reduction and MDH activation as a function of the length of the photoinhibitory pretreatment (% of control). After activation for 4 min, activity measurement and derivatization, MDH was separated from the activation medium by HPLC.

The relationship between the extent of reduction of MDH molecule and its activity was investigated by activating MDH directly with dithiothreitol, without TRX. This can be done in the presence of a high Tris concentration (0.7 M). It could be seen that the activity appeared when more than 50% of the enzyme was reduced (result not shown).This observation suggested, in accordance with the results of Scheibe (12) obtained with pea MDH, that the enzyme was not active under a monomeric form, and that a full reduction of all its subunits was necessary to get an active form. When the results obtained in this last experiment were plotted together with the results obtained from different photoinhibition experiments (various times of photoinhibition and activation), in an attempt to correlate the activity of the enzyme to its reduction state, all the data *fitted the same curve*, which did not correspond exactly neither to the probability curve of a reduced dimer nor to the probability curve of a reduced tetramer being the active form of the enzyme. The sigmoidal shape of the curve rather suggested cooperative effects between the subunits (Fig.3).

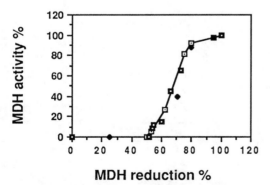

FIG. 3. Relationship between the reduction state of MDH and its activity (% of maximum).

4. CONCLUSION

Corn NADP-MDH activation state is strongly dependent on the reduction state of this probably dimeric protein : the reduction of all the subunits of the molecule is necessary to get an active form. This peculiarity, added to the already described inhibition of the activation by NADP (13,14) makes the enzyme very sensitive to small variations in the reducing power. As a consequence, it might be expected that NADP - MDH, which is involved in the export of reducing equivalents from the chloroplast to the cytoplasm, via the malate / oxaloacetate shuttle, can be active only under conditions where the reducing power inside the chloroplast is very high. This situation has actually been observed in intact chloroplasts where maximal activation of the enzyme was obtained only in the presence of uncouplers (15).

5. REFERENCES

1 Miginiac-Maslow, M., Jacquot, J-P. and Droux, M. (1985) Photosynth. Res. 6, 201-213
2 Powles,S.B.,Chapman, K.S.R.,and Whatley F.R. (1982) Plant Physiol. 69,371-374
3 Miginiac-Maslow,M., Cornic G. and Jacquot J-P. (1988) Planta (Berl.) 173,468-473
4 Droux,M., Miginiac-Maslow M., Jacquot J-P.,Gadal, P., Crawford, N.A.,Kosower N.S., and Buchanan, B.B. (1987) Arch. Biochem. Biophys.256,372-380
5 Decottignies, P., Schmitter, J-M., Miginiac-Maslow, M., Le Maréchal, P., Jacquot, J-P. and Gadal, P. (1988) J. Biol. Chem. 263, 11780 - 11785
6 Droux,M., Jacquot,J-P, Miginiac-Maslow,M., Gadal,P., Huet,J.C., Crawford,N.A.,Yee,B.C. and Buchanan, B.B. (1987) Arch. Biochem. Biophys. 256, 426-439
7 Le Maréchal, P., Decottignies, P., Jacquot, J-P. and Miginiac-Maslow, M. (1989) J. Chromatograph., in press
8 Miginiac-Maslow,M., Droux,M.,Jacquot,J-P.,Crawford, N.A., Yee,B.C. and Buchanan, B.B. (1987), Progress Photosynth. Res., III,3.241-3.247
9 Cornic,G. and Miginiac-Maslow, M. (1985) Plant Physiol. 78, 724-729
10 Cleland ,R.E., Melis,A. and Neale,P.J. (1986) Photosynth. Res. 9, 79-78
11 Rébeillé ,F. and Hatch, M.D. (1986) Arch. Biochem. Biophys. 249, 164-170
12 Scheibe,R. (1984) Biochim. Biophys. Acta 788,241-247
13 Scheibe,R. and Jacquot,J-P. (1983) Planta (Berl.)157, 548-553
14 Rébeillé ,F. and Hatch,M.D. (1986) Arch. Biochem. Biophys. 249,171-179
15 Scheibe, R., Wagenpfeil, D. and Fischer,J. (1986) J. Plant Physiol. 124, 103-110

REGULATION OF NADP-MALATE DEHYDROGENASE LIGHT-ACTIVATION BY THE REDUCING POWER: II. STRUCTURAL STUDIES.

P. Decottignies[1], J-M. Schmitter[2], M. Miginiac-Maslow[1], P. Le Maréchal[1], J-P. Jacquot[1] and P. Gadal[1].
[1] Laboratoire de Physiologie Végétale Moléculaire, Université de Paris Sud, Bâtiment 430, 91405 Orsay Cedex, France.
[2] Laboratoire de Biochimie, Ecole Polytechnique, 91128 Palaiseau, France.

1. INTRODUCTION

Chloroplastic NADP dependent malate dehydrogenase (NADP-MDH) is regulated by light via the ferredoxin-thioredoxin system (1). In vitro, light activation of NADP-MDH can be achieved using a reconstituted system, comprising thylakoid membranes, ferredoxin, ferredoxin-thioredoxin reductase and thioredoxin (2). The activation process can also be mimicked by thioredoxin in the presence of a reductant such as dithiothreitol (DTT) (3). It has been shown that the proteins of the ferredoxin-thioredoxin system undergo thiol/disulfide interchange reactions, during the light activation process (4). The critical disulfide bridge of spinach thioredoxin is now well characterized and its primary structure is known (5). However, the corresponding cysteinyl residues on NADP-MDH have not been identified yet. In this work, we studied the structure of the light-dependent regulatory site of NADP-MDH and we investigated the effect of NADP on the light activation of the enzyme.

2. PROCEDURE

Spinach ferredoxin, thioredoxin m, ferredoxin-thioredoxin-reductase and corn NADP-MDH were purified as previously described (4). Light activation of NADP-MDH, ^{14}C labeling of thiols and purification of the labeled protein were performed as described earlier (6).
Purification and sequencing of labeled peptides:
400 µg of ^{14}C carboxymethylated NADP-MDH were digested with 10 µg of trypsin at 37°C for 2h in 0.1 M ammonium bicarbonate pH 8.0. The tryptic digest was applied on a TSK 2000 SW column and the peptides eluted with 30% acetonitrile in 0.1% trifluoric acid. Radioactive fractions were further purified on an Ultrasphere ODS column with a linear 90 min gradient from 0 to 60% acetonitrile in 0.1% trifluoric acid. The radioactive peptides were submitted to sequence analysis using an Applied Biosystems model 470 A Sequencer. The phenylthiohydantoin (PTH) aminoacids were analyzed by the means of a High Performance Liquid Chromatographic (HPLC) system, and their radioactivity counted .

M. Baltscheffsky (ed.), Current Research in Photosynthesis, Vol. IV, 247–250.
© 1990 *Kluwer Academic Publishers. Printed in the Netherlands.*

3. RESULTS AND DISCUSSION

3.1. Structural studies of the light-dependent regulatory site of NADP-MDH.
First, NADP-MDH was activated by light in the reconstituted system as described in the Materials and methods and its activity measured. The light activated sample was 250 fold more active than a dark incubated sample. The thiol groups were derivatized by incubation with ^{14}C iodoacetic acid (IAA), then thylakoid membranes were removed by centrifugation and labeled NADP-MDH was purified from the incubation mixture by size exclusion HPLC, followed by affinity chromatography on a Ferredoxin-Sepharose column. The analysis of the recovered pure protein showed that, after light activation, NADP-MDH was about 100 fold more labeled than after dark incubation, corresponding to the appearance of 2.3 labeled SH/enzyme subunit (NADP-MDH is a dimeric enzyme). These values are in good agreement with those obtained for non isolated NADP-MDH after activation by light (4) or by thioredoxin+DTT (3). Then, ^{14}C carboxymethylated NADP-MDH was cleaved with trypsin and the fragmentation products purified first on a gel filtration column then by reverse phase HPLC. Radioactivity was recovered in 3 fractions. The major ^{14}C fraction (62% of total radioactivity) was subjected to sequence analysis. Its sequence was determined as:

Lys-Glu-^{14}CmCys-Phe-Gly-Val-Phe-^{14}CmCys-Thr-Thr-Tyr-Asp-Leu-Lys

In addition, the whole protein was light activated, then derivatized with ^{14}C iodoacetic acid and its N-terminus subjected to sequence analysis: two labeled carboxymethylcysteines (^{14}CmCys) were identified at cycles 10 and 15 (Table I).

			LIGHT	DARK	
Cycle	A.A.	PTH amount (pmol)	^{14}C cpm	A.A.	^{14}C cpm
1	Thr	56	980	Thr	45
2	Glu	143	235	Glu	28
3	Ala	162	338	Ala	36
4	Pro	106	279	Pro	24
5	Ala	150	275	Ala	28
6	Ser	62	381	Ser	34
7	Arg	56	252	Arg	29
8	Lys	75	247	Lys	25
9	Glu	87	584	Glu	39
10	Cm-Cys	62	2997	-(a)	62
11	Phe	68	1047	Phe	55
12	Gly	106	538	Gly	52
13	Val	94	454	Val	41
14	Phe	56	567	Phe	31
15	Cm-Cys	46	1952	-(a)	41
16	Thr	4	828	Thr	43
17	Thr				
18	Tyr				
19	Asp				
20	Leu				
21	Lys				
22	Ala				
23	Glu				
24	Asp				
25	Lys				

Table I: N-Terminal amino acid sequence of light activated or dark-treated NADP-MDH and radioactivity incorporated at each cycle.

(a): no peak was observed
1.5 nmol of NADP-MDH subunit, corresponding to 110,000 cpm (light activated) or 1,000 cpm (dark treated), was subjected to sequence analysis.

On the contrary, the sequence analysis failed to detect any residue at the same positions in the dark treated protein, as expected for non derivatized cysteinyl residues that are not stable during Edman degradation. It is obvious that the sequence of the major ^{14}C fraction fits the N-terminal sequence of NADP-MDH. Thus, light activation induces the appearance of two cysteinyl residues located at the N-terminus of the protein. Another experiment (not reported here) indicated that these two residues are linked in a S-S bridge and appeared after reduction and not following a conformational change.

Thus, it can be concluded that the site of regulation of NADP-MDH by light via thioredoxin is a disulfide bridge located at the N-terminus of the protein.

3.2. Effect of NADP.

It has been shown (7) that the activation of NADP-MDH in broken chloroplasts was inhibited by NADP. The question arose whether this inhibition was due to a competition between thioredoxin and NADP for the same site on the enzyme. Since the site for thioredoxin was now well characterized, it became possible to answer this question. First, we have investigated the effect of NADP on isolated NADP-MDH.

NADP-MDH was light activated in the reconstituted system, and its activity measured at different times, in the presence of 2 mM NADP. The activity was strongly inhibited (TableII), especially in the first ten minutes of incubation (data not shown). After activation ^{14}C iodo-acetamide was added, then NADP was removed and the protein components separated by size exclusion HPLC (Miginiac-Maslow et al, these proceedings). The radioactivity incorporated in the purified NADP-MDH was measured and the values obtained for 8 min. light activated NADP-MDH are given in Table II.

Table II: Light activation and ^{14}C labeling of NADP-MDH in the presence of 2mM NADP. Reversion by NADP removal.

Treatment	% of maximal potential activity		Incorporation of ^{14}C IAM (mole SH / mole subunit MDH)	
	Control	NADP	Control	NADP
8 min. light activation ↓	76	10	-	-
Derivatization of CYS* ↓	0	0	1.7	0.9
Reactivation by 1h incubation with 10 mM DTT in 0.7 M Tris.	36	70	-	-

NB. Activity of fully activated enzyme = -1,25 Δ uA_{340}. min.$^{-1}$

*Derivatization of cysteinyl residues was performed with 2.5 mM ^{14}C iodoacetamide (IAM) after 8 min. light activation. Thylakoids were removed by centrifugation then the protein components were separated by size exclusion HPLC and their radioactivity counted.

The extent of labeling decreased by about 50% when compared with the control. It is of interest to note that these values are in agreement with the relationship observed by Miginiac-Maslow et al. (these proceedings) between the activity of NADP-MDH and its extent of reduction, where 50-60% of reduction corresponded to a very low activity. After being derivatized the enzyme was totally inactive in both cases (control and sample with NADP). Both samples were then incubated in activation conditions (with DTT, at high Tris concentration) and their activity measured (Table II). The value obtained for the control was approximatively the one expected (about 30%), since the activity obtained in those conditions corresponds to the amount of enzyme previously not activated nor derivatized. In the case of the sample previously light activated in the presence of NADP, the value reached 70% of the maximal potential activity, indicating that the inhibition by NADP could be reversed. These results suggest that, during the light activation step, NADP binds to a site close to the site of regulation by thioredoxin. However, this result does not indicate the extent of reduction of each cysteinyl residue. Is only one subunit reduced per mole of enzyme or is one cysteinyl residue per disulfide protected on each subunit(in this case, the requirement of DTT to recover the full activity might be due to a non specific disulfide bridge)? To answer this question, it is necessary to determine how the radioactivity is distributed on each cysteinyl residue. Thus, the structural study (sequencing of the N-terminus) of NADP-MDH, after being incubated in the presence of NADP and derivatized, is under investigation.

4.REFERENCES
1. Buchanan, B.B. (1980) Annu. Rev. Plant Physiol. **31**, 341-374.
2. Jacquot, J-P., Gadal, P. Nishizawa, A.N., Yee, B.C., Crawford, N.A. and Buchanan, B.B. (1984) Arch. Biochem. Biophys. **228**, 170-178.
3. Wolosiuk, R.A., Crawford, N.A., Yee, B.C. and Buchanan, B.B. (1979) J. Biol. Chem. **254**, 1627-1632.
4. Droux, M., Miginiac-Maslow, M., Jacquot, J-P., Gadal, P., Crawford, N.A., Kosower, N.S. and Buchanan, B.B. (1987) Arch. Biochem. Biophys. **256**, 372-380.
5. Maeda, K., Tsugita, A., Dalzoppo, D., Vilbois, F. and Schürmann, P. (1986) Eur. J. Biochem. **154**, 197-203.
6. Decottignies, P., Schmitter, J-M., Miginiac-Maslow, M., Le Maréchal, P., Jacquot, J-P. and Gadal, P. (1988) J. Biol. Chem. **263**, 11780-11785.
7. Scheibe, R. and Jacquot, J-P. (1983) Planta **157**, 548-553.

LIGHT ACTIVATION OF MEMBRANE-BOUND FRUCTOSE-1.6-BISPHOSPHATASE FROM PEA LEAF CHLOROPLASTS.

Juan José Lázaro, Angeles Rodríguez Andrés, Ana Chueca, Rosario Hermoso and Julio López Gorgé.
Department of Plant Biochemistry, Estación Experimental del Zaidín (CSIC), Granada, Spain.

1. INTRODUCTION

Chloroplast fructose-1.6-bisphosphatase (FBPase) is one of the 13 enzymes of the Benson-Calvin cycle, all of them so far considered as solubles in the stromal space. However, the existence of some interactions with the thylakoid membranes has been reported in the last years concerning ribulose-1.5-bisphosphate carboxylase (1), FBPase (2,3), P-ribulokinase (4), and some other. In this context Kow and Gibbs (5) have obtained under mild conditions particulate preparations from spinach chloroplasts with low, but conclusive, CO_2 assimilation capability without addition of any soluble stromal enzyme. On the other hand, loose association between some enzymes of the Benson-Calvin cycle has been also described (6).

FBPase undergoes a reductive activation by accepting electrons from ferredoxin through the ferredoxin-thioredoxin system, which works as a link between the photosynthetic electron transport and enzyme regulation (7). The existence of non-covalent interactions of FBPase with the chloroplast membrane could improve the efficiency of its reductive light-activation. In this context the strong FBPase-thioredoxin interaction (8), the association between ferredoxin, thioredoxin and ferredoxin-thioredoxin reductase (9), the binding of ferredoxin to thylakoid membranes (10), and the existence of membrane-bound thioredoxins (11) may be relevant.

This work shows that membrane-bound FBPase, obtained from pea chloroplasts lysed under mild conditions, can be activated by light in a particulate preparation without addition of any soluble stromal component.

2. MATERIALS AND METHODS

Chloroplasts. Intact chloroplasts were isolated from pea (*Pisum sativum* L. var. Lincoln) leaves, grown in vermiculite, as described in a previous work (3). Chloroplasts showed at least 70% intactness, as determined by the ferricyanide assay (12), and were lysed for 15 min in 20 mM Hepes-KOH buffers pH 7.0, 7.6 or 8.0, containing 25 mM NH$_4$Cl, 0.025 mM CaCl$_2$, and increasing concentrations (0-100 mM) of KCl. Thylakoid membranes were separated from the stromal fraction as in (3),

M. Baltscheffsky (ed.), Current Research in Photosynthesis, Vol. IV, 251–254.
© 1990 Kluwer Academic Publishers. Printed in the Netherlands.

chlorophyll measured by the Arnon method, and FBPase protein determined in both fractions by the competitive ELISA technique described
by Hermoso et al. (13).

Light activation. Test tubes with 50 µl aliquots of lysates from
intact chloroplasts (25 µg Chl), or with thylakoid membrane suspensions (75 µg Chl), were illuminated at 20°C for 15 min. Tubes were removed and assayed for FBPase activity by addition of 450 µl of a reaction mixture containing 100 mM Tris-HCl buffer pH 7.9, 0.1 mM EGTA,
5 mM MgCl$_2$ and 0.4 mM fructose-1.6-bisphosphate. Samples were incubated for 15 min at 28°C, and the reaction stopped by adding 250 µl of
TCA. The precipitated protein was removed by centrifugation, and the
released P$_i$ determined in the supernatant using the phosphate reagent
described by Chen et al. (14).

DTT activation. Lysed chloroplasts obtained in the presence of 100
mM KCl were separated in stroma and thylakoid membranes, and both incubated in the dark for 5 min with 5 mM DTT. FBPase activity was determined as above.

Effect of pH on membrane-bound proteins. Pea chloroplasts were lysed as earlier described at pH 7.0 or 8.0, in the presence of varying
KCl concentrations (0-100 mM). Thylakoid membranes were separated from
the stromal fraction, and FBPase activity determined in non-activating
conditions according to Lázaro et al. (15). Proteins were measured by
Lowry.

3. RESULTS AND DISCUSSION

Light activation peculiarities of membrane-bound FBPase only have
been earlier studied in isolated thylakoids by Alscher-Herman (2), who
reported a ratio of 1.62 between the light and dark activities of the
FBPase bound to soybean thylakoids. Results of Fig. 1 show a FBPase
activity about 8 times higher than that of the dark control, when illuminated pea chloroplasts were lysed in 20 mM Hepes-KOH buffer pH 8.0
containing 100 mM KCl. However, lysed chloroplasts without KCl only
showed a scarce enzyme activation by light. In both cases the total
amount of enzyme, determined by ELISA, was the same, but in the former
the 40% of chloroplast FBPase was in the membrane-bound form, whereas
in the latter this amount was only about 6% (3).

When chloroplasts were lysed at pH 7.6 the enzyme activation by
light was low, and at pH 7.0 there was not activation at all (results
not shown). We have studied the % of membrane-bound enzyme and membrane-bound total protein at different KCl concentrations of the lysis
medium, both at pH 7.0 and 8.0. Both patterns were almost similar for
FBPase association, but there were sharp differences in the extent of
thylakoid-bound total protein at different pHs. This means that, at
least in the tested interval (7.0-8.0), pH can influence light activation, but not too much the enzyme association to the membranes (Fig.
2), which indicates some type of specificity in the FBPase binding.
It was noteworthy that the level of FBPase activation by light was
dependent of the extent of membrane-bound enzyme. Fig. 3 shows a good
linear correlation between the percentage of thylakoid-bound FBPase
and the light-induced activity. These light activation features of
photosynthetic FBPase in chloroplast lysates are also observed when

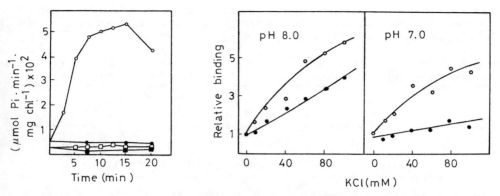

FIGURE 1 (left). Effect of light on FBPase activity of chloroplast lysates obtained with (o,●) or without (□,■) 100 mM KCl. Open symbols
are light-activated samples, and full ones the dark controls.
FIGURE 2 (right). Binding of FBPase (o) and total protein (●) to thylakoid membranes obtained in the presence of increasing concentrations
(0–100 mM) of KCl. An ordinate unit corresponds to a FBPase activity
of 0.021 µmoles of P_i.min^{-1}.mg^{-1} Chl, or to 0.264 mg protein.mg^{-1} Chl.

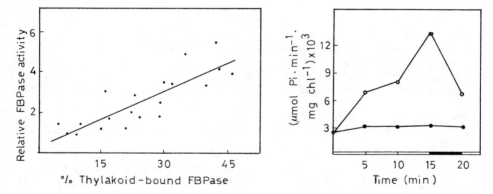

FIGURE 3 (left). Relationship between the % of thylakoid-bound FBPase
(ELISA) and its light activation. Data were fit using linear regression
least-squares analysis. Linear correlation coefficient was r=0.84 with
high significance (p<0.001).
FIGURE 4 (right). Effect of light on FBPase activity of isolated thylakoid obtained as described in Materials and Methods. Open symbols correspond to light-activated samples, and the full ones to dark controls.

thylakoids are previously isolated and tested without any stromal solution (Fig. 4).
  From these results we can speculate that, in addition to FBPase ac-

tivity, thylakoid membranes also support the ferredoxin-thioredoxin system (7), necessary for the enzyme activation. This conclussion has been also reported by Alscher-Herman (2) with soybean FBPase, and by

TABLE I. Effect of DTT (5 mM) on the FBPase activity of stromal and thylakoid preparations. Each value is the mean of 4 assays $\pm$ s.e.

	FBPase activity μmol P_i.min^{-1}.mg^{-1} Chl x 10^3	
	Control	+DTT
Stroma	13.2 $\pm$ 0.4	21.2 $\pm$ 0.5
Membranes	5.8 $\pm$ 0.1	31.7 $\pm$ 1.8

Shahak (10) with the thylakoid ATP synthase tentatively activated by the thioredoxin system (16). This is also corroborated because of a higher activation by DTT of the thylakoid-bound FBPase (about 5.5 times) than that of the soluble enzyme (1.6 times). It must be proba- bly due to the existence of membrane-bound thioredoxin (11), which acts as a link in the FBPase activation by DTT (Table I).

Acknowledgements. This work was supported by the grant PB87-0431 of DGICYT (Spain).

REFERENCES
1 Mori,H., Takabe,T. and Akazawa,T.(1984) Photosynth.Res. 5,17-28
2 Alscher-Herman,R.(1982) Plant Physiol. 70,728-734
3 Rodríguez Andrés,A., Lázaro,J.J., Chueca,A., Hermoso,R. and López Gorgé,J.(1987) Plant Sci. 52,41-48
4 Fischer,K.H. and Latzko,E.(1979) Biochem.Biophys.Res.Commun. 89,300- 306
5 Kow,Y.W. and Gibbs,M.(1982) Plant Physiol. 69,179-186
6 Gontero,R., Cárdenas,M.L. and Ricard,J.(1988) Eur.J.Biochem. 173,437- 443
7 Buchanan,B.B.(1980) Ann.Rev.Plant Physiol. 31,341-374
8 Plá,A. and López Gorgé,J.(1981) Biochim.Biophys.Acta 636,113-118
9 Ford,D.M., Jablönski,P.I., Mohamed,A.H. and Anderson.L.E.(1987) Plant Physiol. 83,628-632
10Shahak,Y.(1982) FEBS Lett. 145,223-229
11Ashton,A.R., Brennan,T. and Anderson,L.E.(1980) Plant Physiol. 66, 605-608
12Lilley,R.Mc., Fitzgerald,M.P., Rienits,K.G. and Walker,D.A.(1973) New Phytol. 75,1-10
13Hermoso,R., Chueca,A., Lázaro,J.J. and López Gorgé,J.(1987) Photo- synth.Res. 14,262-278
14Chen,P.S.Jr., Toribara,T.Y. and Wagner,H.(1956) Anal.Chem. 28,1756- 1758
15Lázaro,J.J., Chueca,A., López Gorgé,J. and Mayor,F.(1974) Phytochem- istry 13,2455-2461
16Mills,J.D., Mitchell,P. and Schürmann,P.(1980) FEBS Lett. 112,173- 177

HOW CAN THE C$_4$ STROMAL SYSTEM SENSE DIFFERENCES IN LIGHT INTENSITY TO ADJUST ITS ACTIVITIES TO THE OVERALL FLUX?

Hideaki Usuda
Lab. of Chem., Fac. of Medicine, Teikyo Univ., Hachioji, Japan

Introduction

The amount of light, the driving force of photosynthesis, that each leaf receives varies remarkably and the overall rate of photosynthesis changes significantly throughout the day. The rate at which photochemical reactions occur depends primarily on the intensity of the incident light, therefore,the ability of the stromal system to balance its activities to the overall flux under differing light intensities would seem to be of paramount importance. The means by which the stromal system senses different light intensities is not yet known, however. The main aim of this study was to approach the question of how the stromal system can sense different light intensities and accommodate its activites to the overall flux by evaluating a likely candidate that links PPDK regulatory cascade to light in maize (Zea mays L. variety Chuseishu-B) mesophyll chloroplasts and by estimating thermodynamically active ADP and ATP concentration in a reconstituted model of the stromal system.

Results and Discussions

PPDK activity is modulated in leaves in response to changes in light intensity. Regulation involves interconversion between an active non-phosphorylated form and an inactive phosphorylated form of the enzyme. The current model for the mechanism for modulating PPDK activity, however, shows no direct link with light (1). It has been suggested on the basis of in vitro studies that chloroplast adenylate energy charge, along with pyruvate (2), or the ADP concentration itself (3) may be responsible for controlling the activation/inactivation of PPDK. Table 1 clearly shows that the adenylate status (adenylate energy charge or stromal level of ADP or ATP/ADP ratio) was not solely responsible for regulating the activation and inactivation of PPDK in non-aqueously purified mesophyll chloroplasts of maize leaves under different light

Abbreviations: PPDK, pyruvate,Pi dikinase; AdN, adenine nucleotide; AEC, adenylate energy charge; CF$_1$, chloroplast coupling factor 1; PFK, phosphofructokinase; PK, pyruvate kinase; GK, glycerokinase; PMS, phenazinemethosulfate.

M. Baltscheffsky (ed.), Current Research in Photosynthesis, Vol. IV, 255–258.
© 1990 *Kluwer Academic Publishers. Printed in the Netherlands.*

Table 1. Influence of light intensity on the PPDK activity in maize leaves and the adenylate status in non-aqueously purified maize mesophyll chloroplasts. Maximum activity of PPDK was 188 μmol/mg Chl hr. For further details see (4).

Light intensity	PPDK activity	ADP/ΣAdN	ATP/ADP	AEC
$(\mu E/m^2 \cdot s)$	(% of maximum)			
0	7.8	0.392	1.05	0.606
75	22.5	0.263	2.55	0.799
200	52.9	0.288	2.19	0.771
400	77.7	0.307	1.98	0.756
800	100	0.263	2.53	0.811
1300	99.5	0.197	3.92	0.870

intensities. The concentration of ΣAdN in maize mesophyll chloroplasts was estimated to be about 1.4 mM assuming a stromal volume of 25 μl/mg Chl (see also 4). Under 1,300 $\mu E/m^2 \cdot s$ where PPDK is fully activated, the total concentration of ADP was 300 μM. Km of 52 μM ADP for inactivation of PPDK in vitro was reported (3). Thus, it seems that it is impossible to fully activate PPDK under high-intensity light, if all the ADP measured is thermodynamically active. Further, we estimated ADP binding site concentration by several proteins in maize mesophyll chloroplasts to be 680 μM using published results (see 4). Taken all together, it would appear that a large fraction of the ADP and ATP are associated with CF_1 and other proteins which utilize AdN in maize mesophyll chloroplasts and that with increasing light intensity, the H^+ flux into the intrathylakoid space from the stroma increased, thereby increasing the steady state levels of energized CF_1, and also the steady state amounts of ADP and ATP which, while being associated with CF_1, are not thermodynamically active (see Fig.7 in 4). The concentration of thermodynamically active ADP in maize mesophyll chloroplasts therefore decreases with increasing light intensity and is one component of the cascade from light to modulation of PPDK activity (4,5).

In order to assess the validity of this hypothesis, a reconstituted stromal system was designed and the concentration of thermodynamically active ADP and ATP in this system was monitored (Figure 1 and Table 2). ATP synthesized by photophosphorylation was instantaneously utilized by PFK to produce ADP and FBP. FBP was then broken into F6P and Pi by FBPase. After a while, a steady state ATP/ADP ratio could be attained, because only a small amount of ADP was added and it was turned over very rapidly. A small aliquot containing a small amount of GK and/or PK and a sufficient amount of glycerol and/or PEP was then added to the system. After 90s, the system was quenched by the addition of acid. PK (GK) activity in the system which was primarily dependent on the ADP (ATP) concentration was then determined by measuring the amount of pyruvate(glycerol-phosphate) produced. The dependency of PK (GK) activity on ADP (ATP) concentration was also determined using the same aliquot of PK (GK). Therefore, the concentration of thermodynamically active ADP (ATP) in the system sensed by the PK (GK) could be determined. The total amount of ATP and ADP was also measured by high per-

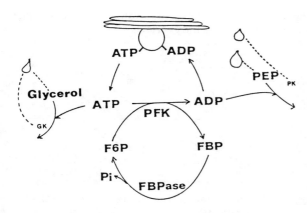

Figure 1. A reconstituted model of the stromal system designed to estimate the concentration of thermodynamically active ADP and ATP. Intact spinach chloroplasts were isolated by a conventional method (see, 5). Washed intact chloroplasts were suspended in a medium containing 0.05 M sorbitol, 2 mM EDTA, 1 mM MgCl$_2$, 1 mM MnCl$_2$, 50 mM HEPES-KOH, pH 7.6 to obtain thylakoids. Isolated thylakoids were washed and finally suspended in a medium similar to that mentioned above (0.33 M sorbitol instead of 0.05 M sorbitol). The reconstituted model system (50 µl) contained thylakoids (169 [97] µg Chl), added ADP (4.6 nmol), PFK (2.8 [1] U at 30 [1.6] µM ATP), FBPase (Vmax=7 U), Pi (5 mM), MgCl$_2$ (5.7 mM), sorbitol (0.23 M), EDTA (1.4 mM), MnCl$_2$ (0.7 mM), HEPES (35 mM)-KOH pH 7.6, F6P (5 mM), PMS (50 µM), and catalase (500 U). Photophosphorylation was carried out for 60s to 90s. An aliquot (8 µl) containing PK (Vmax=0.09 U, [6 mU at 1.8 µM ADP]), PEP (a final concentration: 1.73 mM), [GK (9 mU at 1.6 µM ATP)], and [glycerol 170 mM] was then added into the reconstituted system to monitor the concentration of thermodynamically active ADP and ATP. After an additional period of 90s, the reaction was quenched by the addition of HClO$_4$. After extraction of PMS from the mixture, the amount of pyruvate and [glycerolphosphate] produced were determined enzymatically using the neutralized reaction mixture. The two experiments shown in Table 2 were then carried out. Only alterations made in the Exp 2 shown in Table 2 are shown in the brackets above.

formance liquid chromatography. 13% and 4% (4%) of the total ADP (ATP) was monitored by PK (GK) in the reconstituted model system at a light intensity of 100 and 500 µE/m^2·s, respectively (Table 2). These results indicate that a substantial amount of ADP and ATP is bound to protein and is not thermodynamically active. Furthermore, the concentration of thermodynamically active ADP decreased with increasing light intensity in this reconstituted model system (Table 2). PK and GK activities in this reconstituted system were less than 5% of photophosphorylation activities. The small amount of PK added relative to the amounts of CF$_1$ and PFK in this reconstituted system resembles the situation of the PPDK regulatory protein in situ. This is because of the PPDK regulatory protein which has been proposed as the one that senses ADP concentrations is low in quantity compared to CF$_1$, PPDK, etc. in maize mesophyll chloroplasts.

One possible answer to the question of how the stromal system can sense differences in light intensity in order to adjust its activities to the overall flux, is that under high-intensity light a large amount

Table 2. Estimation of thermodynamically active ADP and ATP concentration in a reconstituted model of the stromal system.

	Dark		Light		
			$100 \mu E/m^2 \cdot s$ (nmol/sample)	$500 \mu E/m^2 \cdot s$	
	Exp 1	Exp 2	Exp 1	Exp 1	Exp 2
Total ATP	0.62[1]	0.70[1]	3.27	4.15	2.0
Total ADP	5.29[1]	5.0[1]	2.28	2.82	2.8
TA[2] ADP			0.29 (12.7%)[3]	0.12 (4.3%)[3]	0.099 (3.5%)[3]
TA[2] ATP					0.088 (4.4%)[4]

[1] ATP was not added. The amount of ADP added was 4.6 nmol. Thus, the ATP found and the difference between the amount of added ADP and detected ADP before commencement of the photophosphorylation could be attributed to the ATP and ADP associated with the thylakoids.

[2] Thermodynamically active.

[3(4)] Values in parentheses are the percentages of total ADP (ATP).

of ADP binds to CF_1 catalytically resulting in a decreased concentration of thermodynamically active ADP which is a crucial factor in the light-dark regulation of PPDK. It is these different levels of ADP which occur under differing light intensities that are then sensed by the PPDK regulatory protein. In line with this proposal, some interesting results reported recently show that substantial binding of ADP to rat liver cytosolic proteins solved the enigma of a physiological rate of gluconeogenesis occuring in the presence of an unfavorably high total ADP concentration in the liver (6).

Acknowledgements
    This work was partially supported by a grant from the Japanese Ministry of Education, Science, and Culture. Fresh spinach leaves were kindly provided by T. Saitoh.

References
1. Burnell, J.N. & Hatch, M.D. (1985) Trends. Biochem. Sci. 10, 288-291.
2. Nakamoto, H. & Edwards, G.E. (1983) Biochem. Biophys. Res. Commun. 115, 673-679.
3. Burnell, J.N. & Hatch, M.D. (1985) Arch. Biochem. Biophys. 237, 490-503.
4. Usuda, H. (1988) Plant Physiol. 88, 1461-1468.
5. Usuda, H. (1989) in Regulation of photosynthetic processes. (Kanai, R., Katoh, S., & Miyachi, S., ed.) in press, Botanical Society of Japan.
6. Morikofer-Zwez, S. & Walter, P. (1989) Biochem. J. 259, 117-124.

THE RELATIONSHIP BETWEEN THE EFFICIENCIES OF PHOTOSYSTEMS I AND II
AND THE CONTROL OF ELECTRON TRANSPORT

Jeremy HARBINSON[1], Bernard GENTY[2], Christine H. FOYER[3], and
Neil R. BAKER[2]

[1] John Innes Inst., Norwich, NR4 7UH, UK
[2] Dept. of Biology, Univ. of Essex, Colchester, CO4 3SQ, UK
[3] Laboratoire du Métabolisme, INRA, 78026 Versailles, France

Recently developed techniques that allow the estimation of the quantum efficiencies of photosystems I and II *in vivo* (1, 2, 3) have allowed us to adopt a quantitative approach to the analysis of the relationship between both photosystems and carbon assimilation (3, 4, 5). In this report we will describe the key findings of this and other related work which relates to the co-ordination of the quantum efficiencies of both photosystems, and the co-ordination of the thylakoids and the Calvin cycle activity.

For leaves in air, or for healthy leaves in a 2 % O_2 (350 ppm balance N_2) atmosphere the relationship between the quantum efficiency for electron transport of photosystem I (ϕ_{PSI}), the quantum efficiency for electron transport of photosystem II (ϕ_{PSII}), the excitation capture efficiency of PS II (ϕ_{exc}) and the coefficient for photochemical quenching of fluorescence (q_Q) is as shown in figure 1.

These results (fig. 1) show the importance of both ϕ_{exc} and q_Q in determining the efficiency of photosystem II. They also show the typical, linear relationship between ϕ_{PSI} and ϕ_{PSII} consistent with a predominant role for non-cyclic electron flow within the thylakoids under these conditions. Measurements of the half-time for P-700$^+$ reduction under similar conditions show it to be invariant (measured with an accurracy of ± 0.5 ms) with irradiance (6). A close linear relationship between ϕ_{PSI}, ϕ_{PSII}, and the quantum efficiency of CO_2 fixation (ϕ_{CO2}) has been demonstrates under conditions were competitive photorespiration has been minimized (2, 3, 5). Consequently large changes in both ϕ_{PSI} and ϕ_{PSII}, and ϕ_{CO2} occur with increasing irradiance and yet there is no change in the degree of "back pressure" exerted by the Benson-Calvin cycle over the kinetics of electron flow between photosystems I and II (IE no change in degree of photosynthetic control of the electron transport chain by the Benson-Calvin cycle).

M. Baltscheffsky (ed.), Current Research in Photosynthesis, Vol. IV, 259–262.
© 1990 *Kluwer Academic Publishers. Printed in the Netherlands.*

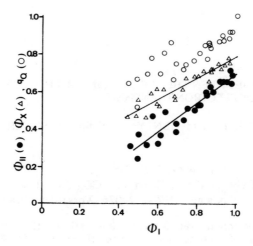

Figure 1. The relationship between ϕ_{PSII} (ϕ II),ϕ_{exc} (Φ X) and q_Q, and Φ PSI (ϕ_I) for pea leaves of variety "Finale" subjected to a range of irradiances (54-1260 μmol m^{-2} s^{-1}). All variables were measured under steady state conditions. Some leaves were then frozen in liquid N_2 prior to measuring NADP-MDH activity. Each datum point (ϕ_{exc}, ϕ_{PSII} and q_Q) was obtained from an individual leaf prior to freezing the leaf.

However changes in the kinetics of electron flow between the photosystems (IE the degree of photosynthetic control) can be produced by changes in CO_2 partial pressure (7, submitted) or photorespiratory activity (5). Therefore there is photosynthetic control of the electron transport chain, but the nature of this control is constant with regard to irradiance under normal conditions.

In response to increasing irradiance the NADPH pool of the stroma (as indicated by the activity of NADP-malate dehydrogenase (NADP-MDH), 8) increases with the increasing electron flux through either PS I or PS II (fig. 2). This indicates an increasing driving force for the Benson-Calvin cycle in direct proportion to the flux of reducing equivalents through the electron transport chain. However ever at the highest irradiance used (1260 μmol m^{-2} s^{-1}) the NADP-MDH is only 20 % activated. The increase in the NADPH pool might appear to contradict the implication from the kinetic studies that the regulated capacity of the electron transport chain appears to limit CO_2 fixation. However, the changes in the activation of NADP-MDH are small (fig. 2) and they indicate that under steady-state conditions, in the absence of stress, the stroma remains oxidized (9). This agrees with our observation that the restriction of photochemical oxidation of P-700 by a shortage of electron acceptor (eg ferredoxin, NADP) only occurs in air during photosynthetic induction.

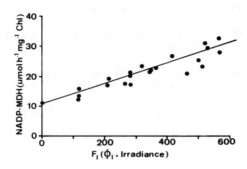

Figure 2. The relationship between the rate F1, which is the product of ϕ PSI (ϕ_I) and irradiance and which is therefore linearly related to electron flow through PS I, and the NADP-MDH activity of leaves sampled during the experiment shown in fig. 1. Maximum activity was 150 μmol h^{-1} mg^{-1} Chl. Maximum irradiance was 1260 μmol m^{-2} s^{-1}.

We conclude that in non-stressed leaves in air electron transport is predominantly non-cyclic and that changes in the degree of photosynthetic control of electron transport are generally not observed even though large changes in ϕ_{CO2}, ϕ_{PSI} and ϕ_{PSII} occur. The efficiency of PS II is strongly influenced by ϕ_{exc}, whose magnitude is normaly closely related to ϕ_I. The scale of the loss of PS II quantum efficiency is sufficient to prevent high levels of Q_A accumulation (q_Q remains high). The NADPH/NADP ratio of the stroma, as inferred from the NADP-MDH activation data remains low. These effects will serve to minimize oxidative stress due to oxygen radical formation (10) and reduce photo damage to PS II. Clearly *in vivo* electron transport is limited between PS II and PS I and the degree of this limitation is in most cases not influenced by increasing irradiance to values great enough to cause substantial changes in ϕ_{CO_2}. However the degree of this limitation can be modified, for example, by varying the CO_2 and O_2 partial pressures, and it is the analysis of this regulatory process which is fundamental to our understanding of the mechanisms of photosynthetic control.

REFERENCES

1 Harbinson J. and Woodward F.I. (1987) Plant Cell Environ., 10, 131-140
2 Weis E., Ball J.T. and Berry J. (1987) Progr. Photosynth. Res., 2, 553-556
3 Genty B., Briantais J.M. and Baker N.R. (1989) Biochim. Biophys. Acta, 990, 87-92
4 Harbinson J., Genty B. and Baker N.R. (1989) Plant Physiol., 90 (in press)
5 Genty B., Harbinson J. and Baker N.R. (1989) Plant Physiol. Biochem. (in press)
6 Harbinson J. and Hadley C.L. (1989) Plant Cell Environ. 12, 357-369
7 Foyer C., Furbank R., Harbinson J. and Horton P. (submitted) Photosynth. Res.
8 Scheibe R. and Stitt M. (1988) Plant Physiol. Biochem., 26, 473-481
9 Takahama U., Shimozu-Takahama M. and Heber U. (1981) Biochim. Biophys. Acta, 637, 530-539
10 Egneus H., Heber U., Mathiesen U. and Kirk M. (1975) Biochim. Biophys. Acta, 408, 252-268.

DIFFERENTIAL DIURNAL CARBON EXCHANGE AND PHOTOINHIBITION IN A psbA PLASTID GENE CHRONOMUTANT OF <u>BRASSICA</u> <u>NAPUS</u>

JACK DEKKER AND RONALD BURMESTER, Weeds Photobiology Laboratory, Department of Agronomy, Iowa State University, AMES, IOWA, 50011, USA

INTRODUCTION

S-triazine resistance (R) in higher plants was discovered in 1970 (1). Subsequent studies have led many to conclude that R mutants are inherently photosynthetically inferior to the susceptible (S) wild type (2). Previous work in our laboratory indicated a consistant, differential, pattern of variable chlorophyll fluorescence (F_T) between S and R over the course of a diel, i.e. R is a chronomutant (3). What remains unknown is the relationship of this differential pattern to terminal fluorescence and changes in carbon fixation during the diurnal. Therefore, we hypothesized that the mutation to the psbA plastid gene that confers s-triazine resistance also results in an altered diurnal pattern of photosynthetic carbon reduction relative to that of the susceptible biotype. We present data that supports this hypothesis.

PROCEDURES

<u>Growth environments</u>. Plants were established in a photoperiod of 16h light/8h dark; photosynthetic photon flux densities (PPPFD) under controlled environmental conditions was 120 umol quanta $m^{-2}s^{-1}$ at dawn and dusk with incremental increases and decreases either side of midday maxima of 1100 umol quanta $m^{-2}s^{-1}$. Several studies were conducted and then repeated; one at constant 25°C temperatures, a second at 35°C. A third study was conducted at 25°C with 1600 umol quanta $m^{-2}s^{-1}$.
<u>Plant material</u>. Two nearly isonuclear biotypes of oilseed rape (<u>B. napus</u>) were evaluated in these experiments: triazine-susceptible <u>B. napus</u>, cv. 'Tower'; and its triazine-resistant derivative, cv. 'OAC Triton' (Beversdorf et al., 1980).
<u>Gas exchange measurements</u>. Photosynthetic CO_2 gas exchange rate (CER) measurements were made with an ADC infrared gas analyzer. Carbon reduction rates for early (0600-0950 or 1000), midday (1000 or 0950-1700 or 1850 or 1900), late (1700 or 1850 or 1900-2150) and all day were calculated by integrating the CER area over that time period for the 9 plants of each biotype.

M. Baltscheffsky (ed.), Current Research in Photosynthesis, Vol. IV, 263–266.
© 1990 *Kluwer Academic Publishers. Printed in the Netherlands.*

RESULTS AND DISCUSSION
    These studies indicate a more complex model of photosynthetic
productivity than previously observed. The photosynthetic superiority
of S relative to R is a function of the time of day. Consistent with
previous reports (2), S had greater CER than R during the midday period
under optimal environmental conditions (Figure 1). Unlike previous

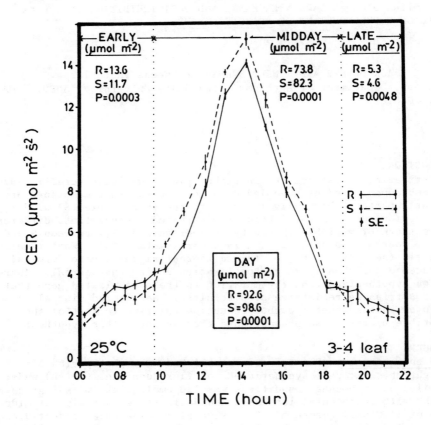

Figure 1.   Carbon exchange rate (CER)(umol $CO_2m^{-2}s^{-1}$) at $25^{o}C$ in 3-4
            leaf triazine resistant (R) and susceptible (S) <u>Brassica</u>
            <u>napus</u> plants through time (hour of the day) and cumulative
            carbon fixed (umol CO_2 per period) in three periods of the
            Diurnal: early, midday and late; S.E.=+/- standard error of
            the mean, n=9; R and S period means within a time period
            compared with an F-Test, associated significance
            probability level (P=probability).

studies, there appears to be times in the diurnal when R is photosynthetically superior to S: early and late in the day. Tese results
indicate that R may be better adapted to a range of unfavorable

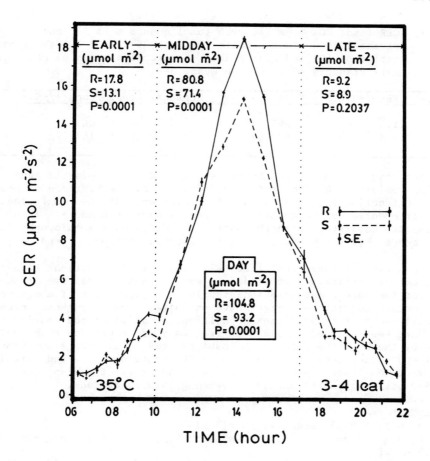

Figure 2. Carbon exchange rate (CER)(umol CO_2 $m^{-2}s^{-1}$) at $35^{o}C$ in 3-4 leaf triazine resistant (R) and susceptible (S) <u>Brassica napus</u> plants through time (hour of the day) and cumulative carbon fixed (umol CO_2 per period) in three periods of the diurnal: early, midday and late; S.E.=+/- standard error of the mean, n=9; R and S period means within a time period compared with an F-Test, associated significance probability level (P=probability).

environmental conditions that S; early and late in the day with lower available PPFD, and all day under hyperoptimal temperatures (Figure 2). The photosynthetic activity of S was less than that of R at hyperoptimal PPFD (Table 1). These results may indicate differences in photoinhibition, and temperature-dependent photoinhibition, between R and S.

TABLE 1.   CER (umol CO_2 $m^{-2}s^{-1}$), PPFD (umol quanta $m^{-2}s^{-1}$), and stomatal conductance (mol $m^{-2}s^{-1}$) at $25^{o}C$ in 3-4 leaf triazine resistant (R) and susceptible (S) <u>Brassica napus</u> plants; S.E. =+/- standard error of the mean, n=9.

Biotype	CER(+/-S.E.)	PPFD(+/-S.E.)	Stomatal Conductance(+/-S.E.)
R	21.4 (2.4)	1644 (78)	0.490 (0.06)
S	16.5 (1.2)	1629 (77)	0.305 (0.14)

These results support the hypothesis tested: psbA plastid gene mutation conferring R also confers a different diurnal pattern of photosynthetic function than that in S. They also provide important clues about differential photoinhibition responses between R and S. This work is also consistent with the pattern of differential chlorophyll fluorescence (F_T) early and late in the diurnal previously reported. (3).

It can be envisioned that there were ecological conditions before the advent of s-triazine herbicides in which R had an adaptive advantage over the more numerous S individuals in a population of a species. Under certain conditions R might have exploited a photosynthetic niche underutilized by S. Under these conditions, R survival and continuity could have been ensured at a higher frequency of occurrence than that caused by the mutation rate of the psbA plastid gene. These environmental conditions could have been the PPFD occurring early and late in the day or the lower light levels in the understory of a plant canopy; or under hot, high irradiance or crowded growth conditions.

REFERENCES
1 Ryan, G.F. (1970) Weed Sci. 18:614-616.
2 Holt, J.S., Stemler, A.J. and Radosevich, S.R. (1981) Plant Physiol. 67:744-748.
3 Dekker, J.H. and Westfall, B. (1987) Z. Naturforsch. 42c:135-138.
4 Beversdorf, W.D., Weiss-Lerman, J., Erickson, L.R. and Sousa Machado, V. (1980) Can. J. Genet. Cytol. 22:167-172.

PHOTOSYNTHESIS AND CHLOROPHYLL FLUORESCENCE QUENCHING IN AGING LEAVES
OF THREE SUNFLOWER (Helianthus annuus L.) GENOTYPES

Dejana Saftić, Marijana Plesničar, Inst.of Field & Vegetable Crops,
University of Novi Sad, 21000 Novi Sad, Yugoslavia.

1. INTRODUCTION
    In order to define phases in plant vegetation period which should
be used when comparing photosynthetic activities of different sunflower
genotypes, it is necessary to investigate changes of photosynthesis during plant and leaf development.
    Fluorescence measurement is a promising method on account of its
simplicity, rapidness and the possibility to be used in vivo. Quenching
analysis of fluorescence gives more information about the relation between this still qualitative indicator and the quantum efficiency of
CO_2 fixation. Up to now nonlinear and linear relations have been found
between quantum efficiency and q_Q; q_E; q_Q/q_E or between q_Q and the rate
of O_2 evolution (1,2,3 and 4).
    In this study we investigated changes of photosynthesis during leaf
development in different sunflower genotypes, the applicability of the
methods applied for the detection of differences between genotypes and
the relationship of fluorescence quenching components and steady state
O_2 evolution rate in a model system of developing leaf.

2. PROCEDURE
2.1. Materials and methods
    Two leaf position, 15 and 20 of the hybrid NS-H-43 (H), the mother
line OCMS-22 (♀) and the father line RHA-SNRF (♂) were examined during
leaf area development. The 15-th leaf appears and develops in the phase
of flower bud and the 20-th in the phase of flowering. Hansatech LD2
oxygen electrode and Hansatech Modulated Fluorescence Measurement System were used for simultaneous measurement of O_2 evolution and fluorescence yield. Photochemical and nonphotochemical components of fluorescence quenching were determined by pulse amplitude modulation technique according to (5). A high intensity light source according to Walker
(6) was adapted to be simultaneously used as a source of actinic light
$(600 \ \mu molm^{-2}s^{-1})$ and saturation pulses $(4500 \ \mu molm^{-2}s^{-1}, t=990 \ ms)$.
Having been cut, leaf disc received a 20-minute dark pretreatment, and
after that illuminated for 15 minutes until stady state photosynthesis.

3. RESULTS AND DISCUSSION
3.1. Induction phase
    Differences in fluorescence quenching between genotypes appeared
from 40 to 90 % A_{max} (Fig.1). The father line samples always had longer
lag periods in oxygen evolution.

M. Baltscheffsky (ed.), Current Research in Photosynthesis, Vol. IV, 267–270.
© 1990 Kluwer Academic Publishers. Printed in the Netherlands.

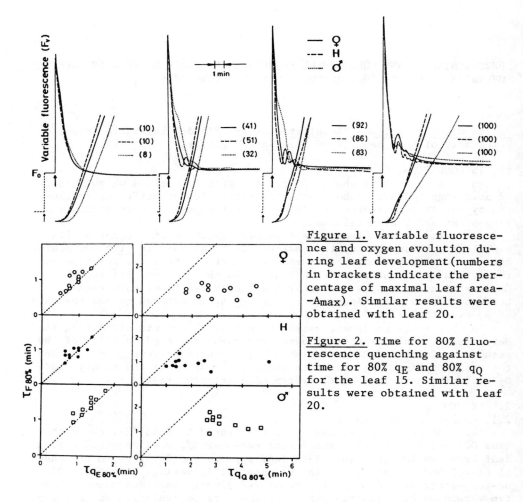

Figure 1. Variable fluorescence and oxygen evolution during leaf development (numbers in brackets indicate the percentage of maximal leaf area--A_{max}). Similar results were obtained with leaf 20.

Figure 2. Time for 80% fluorescence quenching against time for 80% q_E and 80% q_Q for the leaf 15. Similar results were obtained with leaf 20.

Results in Table 1. show that extended lag period was correlated with extended time for 80% fluorescence quenching, and that the leaves of the father line had longest lag phases in oxygen evolution and longgest respective time for 80% fluorescence quenching. At the same time, there were no differences in time for attaining maximal O_2 evolution rate. So, in intermediate phases of leaf development, differences in lag phase and time for 80% fluorescence quenching appeared, but the difference was lost when maximal O_2 evolution rate was achieved.

At the end of the lag period, q_E had already reached steady state value (90-100% q_{Ess}), while q_Q ranged between 30 and 80 % q_{Qss} (results are not shown). Thus, in our conditions, q_E was predominant fluorescence quenching component in the induction phase (in agreement with 6,7 and 8).

time	LEAF 15			LEAF 20		
(min)	♀	H	♂	♀	H	♂
T_{O_2}evol.	5.08	5.53	6.42	6.30	7.07	7.00
±S.E.	±0.31	±0.68	±0.48	±0.23	±0.61	±0.66
LAG	1.83	1.78	2.73	1.84	2.09	2.51
±S.E.	±0.18	±0.23	±0.38	±0.08	±0.05	±0.13
τ80%	0.91	0.81	1.93	0.92	1.10	1.39
±S.E.	±0.10	±0.05	±0.35	±0.06	±0.04	±0.09

Table 1. Average values of time for attaining maximal rate of O_2 evolution, lag period and time for 80% fluorescence quenching, for period of maximal leaf photosynthetic activity are represented.

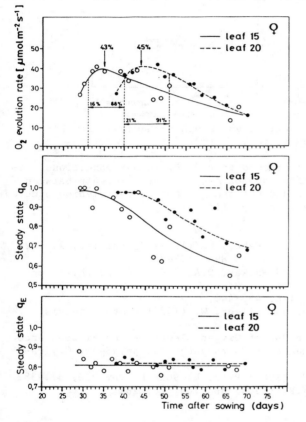

Figure 3. Steady state oxygen evolution rate, q_Q and q_E during leaf development. Numbers indicate the percentage of A_{max}.

The time for 80% fluorescence quenching was highly correlated with the time for 80% q_E and not q_Q (Fig. 2). Again it can be seen that the leaves of the father line had longer (τ80%) which was mostly caused by a slower q_E development.

3.2. Steady state photosynthesis
Steady state oxygen evolution rate increased during the development and reached the maximum when the leaves reached 40-50% of their maximum area. High rates were maintained, in the range from 20 to 90% A_{max}. Photochemical quenching had its maximum values up to 40-50% A_{max}, after that it decreased. In the same phases of development q_E values were higher, but later on they were distributed around 0.8. The decrease in O_2 evolution rates during the development is connected with the decrease of q_Q. Similar results were obtained for hybrid leaves. The father line had shorter leaf area duration, with longer period of high O_2 evolution rates (results are not shown).

The relationship between q_Q and oxygen evolution rate is shown in Fig. 4 . Results fit in the linear regression equation (according to 4) given in the figure. If values up to 40-50% A_{max} are omitted, the

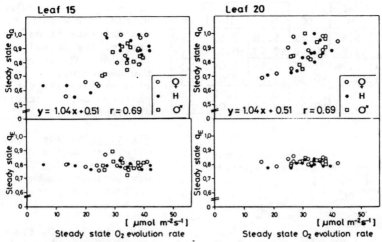

Figure 4. Plots of photochemical and nonphotochemical quenching against the rate of O_2 evolution.

correlation coefficient is increased to r=0.76. In our conditions, regardless of leaf position after 40–50% A_{max} the relationship between q_Q and oxygen evolution rate did not change, but no correlation occured between oxygen evolution rate and q_E (Fig. 4).

REFERENCES
1 Dietz, K.J., Schreiber, U. and Heber, U. (1987) Planta 166, 219–226
2 Weis, E. and Berry, J.A. (1987) BBA 894, 198–208
3 Peterson, R.B., Sivak, M. and Walker, D.A. (1988) Plant Physiology 88, 158–163
4 Furbank, R. (1988) Planta 176, 433–440
5 Schreiber, U., Schliwa, U. and Bilger, W. (1986) Photosynthesis Research 10, 51–62
6 Walker, D.A. (1988) in The Use of Oxygen Electrode and Fluorescence Probes in Simple Measurements of Photosynthesis, pp.48–49, Oxygraphics Limited, Chichester
7 Quick, W.P. and Horton, P. (1984) Proc. R. Soc. Lon.B. 220, 371–382
8 Bradbury, M. and Baker, N.R. (1984) BBA 765, 275–281

DEVELOPMENTAL VARIATION IN ASPARTATE-FAMILY AMINO ACID BIOSYNTHESIS BY ISOLATED CHLOROPLASTS

W. R. MILLS, S. F. CAPO, S. A. BERGH, and C. B. LASSITER, Division of Biological and Allied Health Sciences, UNIVERSITY OF HOUSTON, CLEAR LAKE, HOUSTON, TEXAS 77058-1062, U.S.A.

1. INTRODUCTION

In the last decade, it has become clear that the chloroplast is the main site, if not the sole site, for the biosynthesis of the nutritionally essential aspartate-derived amino acids (Fig. 1) in plant leaves [1,2]. For example, isolated intact chloroplasts carry out the light-driven synthesis of lysine, threonine, and isoleucine from labeled aspartic acid and malic acid [3]. This can be considered a photosynthetic process since ATP and NADPH produced in light are thought to be used directly (Fig. 1) to drive the synthetic reactions [3].

During the development of plant leaves, the requirement for amino acid production changes [4]. For instance, in the early stages of white lupin development (1-11 days) the young leaf serves as a net nitrogen sink, with the bulk delivered to the developing leaf as asparagine, glutamine, aspartic acid and gama-aminobutyrate. Nearly all of the other common amino acids must be synthesized *in situ.* Later in development (20-66 days) the lupin leaf becomes an overall nitrogen source. Because the demand for the aspartate-family amino acid production varies during leaf development, one might expect the ability of chloroplasts to synthesize these compounds to fluctuate accordingly. Here, we describe the use of intact chloroplasts as well as plastid extracts to examine developmental changes in essential amino acid biosynthesis.

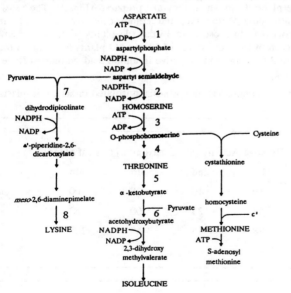

Fig. 1. Biosynthetic pathways for the essential aspartate-family amino acids. The numbers represent enzymes catalyzing the reaction: 1, aspartate kinase; 2, homoserine dehydrogenase; 3, homoserine kinase; 4, threonine synthase; 5, threonine dehydrogenase; 6, acetolactate synthase; 7, dihydrodipicolinate synthase; 8, diaminopimelate decarboxylase.

M. Baltscheffsky (ed.), Current Research in Photosynthesis, Vol. IV, 271–274.
© 1990 *Kluwer Academic Publishers. Printed in the Netherlands.*

2. PROCEDURE

2.1 Materials and Methods

2.1.1 *Chloroplast isolation and characterization:* Chloroplasts were prepared from 6-16 day old pea (*Pisum sativum* L.) leaves as described by Mills and Joy [5]. Chlorophyll and protein were determined as in [6] and [7] respectively; plastid numbers were estimated by hemacytometer counting. CO_2-dependent O_2 evolution was followed using a YSI O_2 electrode as previously described [5].

2.1.2 *Amino acid synthesis and analysis:* Isolated chloroplasts were incubated in light in the following medium: 300 mM sorbitol, 50 mM EPPS, 30 mM KCl and [^{14}C]aspartic acid [3]. For dark assays, tubes further contained ATP, NAD(P)H plus $MgCl_2$ at 10 mM each and were wrapped in aluminum foil. Plastid lysates were also studied; they were assayed as above except that Triton X-100 was added to give a 2% (v/v) final concentration. Reactions were stopped by addition of one-fifth volume 50% trichloroacetic acid. Following centrifugation to clarify the samples, the supernatants were mixed with amino acid standards and analyzed by two dimensional paper (Whatman 3MM) chromatography. The first dimension was run in butanol:acetone:water:diethylamine:triethylamine (10/10/5/1/1; v/v) for 14 hours and the second in isopropanol:water:formic acid (10/5/2; v/v) for 11 hours. After visualizing amino acids by spraying with ninhydrin, spots were cut out and radioactivity determined by scintillation spectrometry; counting efficiency was assessed by channels ratio. Radiolabel incorporated into lysine was estimated by one-dimensional paper electrophoresis as previously described [3].

3. RESULTS AND DISCUSSION

The ability of pea chloroplasts to synthesize lysine, threonine and the metabolic intermediate homoserine (which is made in unusually high amounts in peas [8]) from [^{14}C]aspartate is highly dependent on the age of the plants from which they are prepared (Fig. 2). The rates of incorporation of [^{14}C]aspartic acid into lysine, threonine, and homoserine were 2 to 10 times greater in plastids from 7 day old shoots than in those from 13 day old plants (Fig. 2). Moreover, when chloroplasts were isolated from each of four leaf stages of 12 day-old plants (see Fig. 3) those from the youngest leaves (stage 4) were 2 to 5 times more active in amino acid synthesis (Table 1) than those from the oldest leaves (stage 1).

TABLE 1. Influence of leaf age on homoserine biosynthesis in isolated intact chloroplasts.

Index	Relative Activity (% of maximum) at Leaf Stage			
	1st	2nd	3rd	4th
Chlorophyll	19	10	38	100
Protein	68	34	100	83
Plastid Number	38	15	69	100

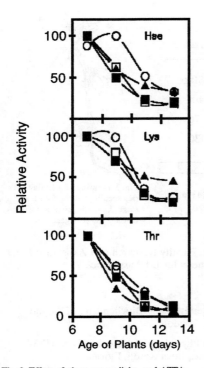

Fig. 2. Effect of plant age on light- and ATP/NADPH-dependent biosynthesis of aspartate-derived amino acids by both intact chloroplasts and plastid extracts. Activity in plastids from 7 day old plants exressed as nmol/mg chlorophyll/hour were as follows: light control; (O) hse, 20; lys, 1.8; thr, 1.4; light plus ATP/NADPH; (□) hse, 23.8; lys, 2.1; thr, 1.7; dark plus ATP/NADPH; (▲) hse, 14.8; lys, 1.3; thr, 0.9; lysed plus ATP/NADPH; (■) hse, 21.6; lys, 1.9; thr, 1.2.

When conducting developmental studies with isolated chloroplasts, it is difficult to find an appropriate index for comparison. For example, rates of CO_2 photoassimilation and photosynthetic O_2 evolution have traditionally been expressed on a chlorophyll basis (micromole/mg chl/hr); yet, it is well known that as leaf tissues mature, the amount of chlorophyll per plastid increases several fold [9]. Thus, one might get a flawed view of developmental variation in synthetic activity by utilizing chlorophyll as the sole index. However, this does not appear to be the case here since a similar pattern was observed regardless of whether chlorophyll, protein or plastid number was used as the basis of comparison (Table 1).

The basis for this variation in amino acid formation in isolated chloroplasts is not yet clear. However, there are several factors which could influence synthesis, including: 1) developmental variation in photosynthetic activity, 2) changes in chloroplast envelope permeability and 3) fluctuations in the activity of key regulatory enzymes.

CO_2-dependent O_2 evolution by leaf discs and isolated plastids [10] does vary markedly with pea leaf stage (see Table 2), and photosynthetic electron transport is known to decrease as leaf tissues age [11,12]; this obviously could influence light-dependent amino acid synthesis. However, this does not appear to be the case as both light- and ATP/NADPH-driven (dark) amino acid synthesis vary in similar ways (Fig. 2); since activity in darkness does not require photosynthesis, changes in incorporation cannot be due simply to a decline in photosynthetic activity.

Changes in plastid membrane permeability during development also have been noted [13]. Generally, there is more rapid uptake of amino acids early followed by a decline as tissues mature; this in turn could influence [14C]aspartate incorporation rates seen in intact plastids. Again, this appears unlikely, since amino acid production by Triton X-100 disrupted plastids (which would not be subject to permeability effects) varies in a similar fashion to light-driven activity (Fig. 2).

As noted, another possiblity is that the changes in essential amino acid synthetic capacity in isolated plastids are due to fluctuations in the catalytic activity [1] of key regulatory enzymes (see Fig. 1). Indeed, in preliminary experiments we have found aspartate kinase [14] and homoserine dehydrogenase [15] activity in plastids from 8 day old pea plants to be 2-6 times greater than in those from 14 day old plants (data not shown). Nonetheless, additional purification and immunological studies will be required to confirm these results.

TABLE 2. Influence of leaf age on CO_2-dependent
O_2 evolution in chloroplasts and leaf discs.

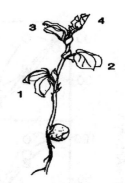

Sample	Relative Activity[a] (% of maximum) at Leaf Stage			
	1st	2nd	3rd	4th
Chloroplasts	39	68	100	76
Leaf discs	50	74	100	30

[a]Maximum activity (micromole/mg chl/hr) ranged from 45 to 143 in
isolated chloroplasts and from 31 to 55 in leaf discs.

Fig. 3. Drawing of a 12-day old
pea seedlings at the four leaf
stage. Leaf 1 is the oldest while
leaf 4 is the youngest.

4. ADDENDUM

4.1 Supported by NSF (PCM 8314328) and UH-CL Faculty Research and Assistance Fund.
We thank S. Hemenway-Cropp for the artwork and F. Matthews for DTP assistance.

REFERENCES

1 Lea, P.J., Wallsgrove, R.M. and Miflin, B.J. (1985) in Chemistry and Biochemistry of Amino acids, (G.C. Barrett, ed) pp 197-226, Chapman and Hall, London.

2 Mills, W.R., and Wilson, K.G. (1987) in Models in Plant Physiology and Biochemistry, (D.W. Newmann and K.G. Wilson eds) pp 19-24, CRC Press, Inc., Boca Raton, Florida.

3 Mills, W.R., Lea, P. J. and Miflin, B.J. (1980) Plant Physiol. 65, 1166-1172.

4 Atkins, C.A., Pate, J.S., Peoples, M.B. and Joy, K.W. (1983) Plant Physiol. 71, 841-848.

5 Mills, W.R. and Joy, K.W. (1980) Planta 148, 75-83.

6 Wintermans, J.E.G.M., and De Mots, A. (1965) Biochim. Biophys. Acta 109, 448-453.

7 Bradford, M.M. (1976) Anal. Biochem. 72, 248-254.

8 Lawrence, J.M. (1973) Phytochemistry 12, 2207-2209.

9 Leech, R.M. (1984) in Chloroplast Biogenesis, (N.R. Baker and J. Barber eds) pp 1-21, Elsevier, Amsterdam.

10 Robinson, S.P. and Wiskich, J.T. (1976) Plant Physiol. 58, 156-162.

11 Holloway, P.J., Maclean, D.J., and Scott, K.J. (1983) Plant Physiol. 72, 795-801.

12 Woolhouse, H.W. (1987) in Plant Senescence: Its Biochemistry and Physiology, (W.W. Thompson, E.A. Nothnagel, and R.C. Huffaker, eds), pp 132-142. ASPP, Rockville, Maryland.

13 Hampp, R., and Wellburn, A.R. (1976) J. Exp. Bot. 27, 778-784.

14 Lea, P.J., Mills, W.R. and Miflin, B.J. (1979) FEBS Lett. 98, 165-168.

15 Matthews, B.J., and Widholm, J.M.. (1978) Planta, 315-321.

ACTIVITIES OF CARBONDIOXIDE FIXING ENZYMES IN MAIZE TISSUE CULTURES
IN COMPARISON TO YOUNG SEEDLINGS

ASHWANI KUMAR, SHIKHA ROY AND K.-H.NEUMANN[*]
DEPARTMENT OF BOTANY,UNIVERISTY OF RAJASTHAN,JAIPUR,INDIA
AND INSTITUT FÜR PFLANZENERNÄHRUNG DER JUSTUS LIEBIG
UNIVERSITÄT, ABT: GEWEBEKULTUR, GIESSEN,F.R.GERMANY[*]

1. INTRODUCTION

Most callus cultures excised from higher plants turn green under
proper physico-chemical, nutritional and hormonal regimes. Some of
these cultures are reported to have mixotrophic and autotrophic mode of
nutrition(1-3). Photoautotrophic cell cultures provide a system for
studying the physiological and biochemical aspects of photosynthesis
at cellular level. There has been considerable speculation about the
connection between "Kranz" anatomy and physiology of C_4 plants.
There are increasing number of reports which suggest that less of a
dependence exists on "Kranz" anatomy than has long been believed (4).
Present investigations were undertaken with the objective to study the
enzyme patterns during different stages of leaf development and callus
cultures, by characterising the PEPC and RuBISCO.

2. PROCEDURE

2.1. Materials and methods

2.1.1. Material: Maize callus isolated from the apical portion of
young seedlings was raised on modified MS medium(5). Around
8 weeks old callus material was used for enzyme assay.
The maize seedlings raised in plastic pots containing 6Kg of
soil with 13 g of NPK mixture were used for present investigations. The plants were maintained in a growth chamber at
$27 \pm 2^{\circ}C$ and 30 W m^{-2} fluorescent light. After 15 days of
sowing the plants were excised for estimations. The outer-
most first leaf was carefully removed along with the leaf
sheath and excised into 4 portions (i)lower base (sheath)
(ii) lower middle (sheath) (iii) lower leaf blade(iv) upper
leaf blade. The third leaf was also excised into 4 portions
(i) lower base (ii) lower middle (iii) upper middle and (iv)
top. The fourth leaf (youngest leaf of the 4 leaf stage)
was carefully excised after removing the surrounding leaves
and was cut into (i)lower and (ii) upper halves of almost
equal size. The size of the leaves varied from 10 to 27 cm.

2.1.2. Enzyme assay of callus: Freshly harvested green callus
material of maize was ground in 30 ml of modified

M. Baltscheffsky (ed.), Current Research in Photosynthesis, Vol. IV, 275–278.
© 1990 *Kluwer Academic Publishers. Printed in the Netherlands.*

Breidenbach et al(6) ice cold grinding medium containing
0.15 M tris- HCl buffer (pH 7.5), 0.01 M EDTA, 0.01 M KCl,
0.001 M $MgCl_2$, 0.01 M dithiothreitol, 0.5 M sucrose and
0.4 M sodium ascorbate. RuBP carboxylase-oxygenase(RuBISCO)
was assayed by measuring the incorporation of ^{14}C into acid
stable compounds. The assay solution contained 80 mM Tris
(pH 7.5), 8 mM $MgCl_2$, 0.8 mM EDTA, 1.4 mM RuBP and 50 mM
$NaH^{14}CO_3$ (2μCi)(2). The reaction mixture for measuring
Phosphoenolpyruvate carboxylase(PEPC) activity 80 mM Tris
HCl (pH, 7.8), 1μm mercaptoethanol, 10 μM Glutamic acid,
1 μM PEP, 50 mM $NaH^{14}CO_3$ and 100 μl enzyme extract, in a total volume of 650 μl.The reaction was started by adding PEP.
Subsequesnt steps to measure $^{14}CO_2$ incorporation were the
same as for RuBP carboxylase.

2.1.3. Enzyme assay of the plant material: Approximately 5 g of each
leaf portion was grinded in grinding medium and assayed following the methods given above. The estimations were carried
out at, zero degree centrigrade.

3. RESULTS AND DISCUSSION

3.1. Maize callus cultures showed over eleven fold activity of PEPC
in the three week old callus cultures to that of RuBISCO(Table-1).
Apparently the C_4 callus cultures showed higher levels of PEPC
over RuBISCO which is in correlation with the enzyme pattern of
the non green or partially green portions of young leaves from
the basal region. However the different portions of the leaves
showed variable pattern. Lower portions of 1st leaf showed
greatest activity of PEPC which declines in the second portion.
After a slight increase in third portion the activity of PEPC
again showed a decline in the apical region. In contrast to this
the RuBISCO activity showed a gradual increase from basal portion
to the third portion i.e. lower leaf blade, then declined in apical portion. The non-green basal leaf sheath had lowest amount
of RuBISCO while it increased in the upper green portions (Table-
1).

3.2. In the third leaf also the RuBISCO activity was lowest in the
basal portion but increased gradually from base to the upper
region. In contrast to this basal portion showed greater
amount of PEPC which however gradually declined in the upper
region.

3.3. The fourth leaf was pale green in the terminal portion and
whitish green in the basal portion. It showed maximum PEPC in
the lower portion which declined in the upper portion. However,
RuBISCO activity was relatively higher in the upper portion as
compared to the lower portion.

3.4. In general all the leaves showed higher activity of PEPC in the
basal portion which declined in the upper portion while RuBISCO
activity was not uniform in all the leaves. Apparently PEPC
activity was more in lowest non-green portions which represent

the meristematic regions. This is in direct agreement with the higher activity of PEPC in callus cultures.

3.5. Transition in the activities of the PEPC and RuBISCO has been observed in young developing callus cultures (2,7). Previous investigations on the activities of RuBISCO and PEPC in callus cultures of carrot (C_3) have shown higher activity of PEPC in mixotrophic phase (2). Likewise Hanson and Edelman (8) also reported the activity of PEPC in carrot tissue cultures 13 times higher in comparison to RuBISCO activity. In the present investigations the partially green callus cultures of maize a C_4 plant showed over eleven times greater activity of PEPC as compared to RuBISCO.

3.6. The activity of PEPC has been reported in both C_3, as well as, C_4 plants (9). One of the features of C_4 plants, is the presence of "Kranz" anatomy . There is compartmentalization of enzymes in "Kranz" anatomy viz PEPC in the cytosol of mesophyll cells and RuBISCO in the chloroplasts of the bundle sheath cells(11). Accordingly in the present study, predominent activity of PEPC in the partially green maize callus cultures and lowest portion of young leaf lacking well developed chloroplasts can be explained.

3.7. The developing leaf of maize is reported to show several stages of development of chloroplasts, starting from base which does not have well defined "Kranz" anatomy but still has bundle sheath and mesophyll cells(12). The actively growing basal region of the leaf has undifferentiated plastids and thus might exhibit mixotrophic mode of nutrition. The mixotrophic cultures are shown to have higher activity of PEPC in general (2). This can also be compared to large extent to the callus cultures during the process of greening which pass through a heterotrophic, mixotrophic and autotrophic phase. Thus in general mixotrophic cells of actively growing leaf base or callus cultures exhibit PEPC activity in preponderance over that of RuBISCO. The activity of which enhances during the process of greening. The PEPC might paly a role in anaplerotic fixation of CO_2 to meet out the growing demand for carbon skeleton for amino acids in the actively growing cells.

4. ACKNOWLEDGEMENT
4.1. Award of USDA-ICAR project to Dr. Ashwani Kumar, and valuable suggestions of Professor R.A.Kennedy, USA, are gratefully acknowledged.

TABLE 1. Activities of PEPC and RuBISCO in the maize callus and different portions of various leaves from maize seedlings.

S.No.	Plant material	Portions	Enzyme activities (mU/ g Fr. Wt.)	
			PEPC	RuBISCO
1.	Maize callus	Entire callus	43.16	3.81
2.	1st leaf (Outermost)	(i) Lower base (Sheath)	28.11	10.94
		(ii) Lower middle (Sheath)	19.67	27.18
		(iii) Lower leaf blade	21.04	42.48
		(iv) Upper leaf blade	13.93	33.57
3.	3rd leaf	(i) Lower base	28.99	14.75
		(ii) Lower middle	29.27	49.55
		(iii) Upper middle	27.83	50.51
		(iv) Top	20.47	63.44
4.	4th leaf	(i) Lower portion	53.77	32.86
		(ii) Upper portion	21.55	37.75

REFERENCES
1   Neumann, K.H. ànd Raafat, A. (1973) Plant Physiol.51,685–690.
2   Kumar ,A. Bender,L. Pauler,B. Neumann, K.-H. Senger,H and Jeske,C. 1983a. Plant cell tissue and organ culture. 2, 161–177.
3   Kumar, A. Bender, L. and Neumann, K.-H.(1987)in Progress in Photosynthesis research. J.Biggins (eds) Martin Nijhoff Publishers, The Netherlands III (4), 363–366,
4. Kennedy, R.A. (1976). Plant Physiol. 58, 573–575.
5. Roy, S and Kumar, A. (1986) In Proc. VI International Congress of plant tissue and cell culture. Minneapolis, USA pp 400.
6. Breidenbach,W. Kahn, A. and Beavers, H.(1968) Plant Physiol. 43, 704–713.
7. Kumar, A. Bender, L. and Neumann, K.-H. (1983b) Plant Physiology and Biochemistry. 10, 130–140.
8. Hanson, A.P. and Edelman, J. (1972). Planta. 102, 11–25.
9. Davies, D.D.(1979). Annual Rev. Plant Physiol. 30:131–158.
10. Laetsch, W. M. (1974) Ann. Rev. Plant Physiol. 25, 27–52.
11. Edwards ,G.E. and Huber, S.C. (1979) in Encyclopedia of plant Physiology vol 6. ed M. Gibbs and E. Latzko) pp 102–112. Springer Verlag Berlin.
12. Miranda, V. Baker, N.R. and Long, S.P. (1981) New Phytol.88,595–605.

Measurement of Photochemical and Non-photochemical quenching: Correction for turnover of PS2 during steady-state photosynthesis[1].

THERESE MARKGRAF AND JOE BERRY
Carnegie Institution of Washington, Department of Plant Biology, Stanford, CA 94305

An empirical expression that could be used to predict the quantum efficiency of PS 2 during steady-state photosynthesis from measurements of chlorophyll fluorescence quenching was proposed by Weis and Berry [1], and several subsequent papers have presented evidence corroborating this approach [2–7]. However, there is disagreement between studies regarding the form of the relationship (i.e. linear or non-linear) and the value of empirical constants, making it difficult to address the fundamental underlying mechanisms. We note that this analysis is very sensitive to the reliability of measurements of the coefficients for photochemical and non-photochemical quenching (q_P and q_N, respectively), and in this paper, we describe an alternative method for estimating these coefficients.

Ideally, the quenching coefficients are estimated from changes in the yield of variable fluorescence of the tissue in three states: a) under steady-state illumination, $F_V = F_S - F_0$; b) when Q_A is fully reduced from the steady-state, $F_V^* = F_M - F_0$, and c) when Q_A is fully reduced after permitting the tissue to become dark-adapted, $(F_V^*)_R$. The attenuation of steady-state F_V^* relative to that in the dark-adapted state is attributed to non-photochemical quenching ($q_N = 1 - F_V^*/(F_V^*)_R$), and the attenuation of F_V at steady-state relative to the corresponding F_V^* is attributed to photochemical quenching ($q_P = 1 - F_V/F_V^*$), [8].

In practice, the value of F_V^* in either in the dark-adapted state or during photosynthesis is estimated by manipulations of the light regime intended to cause the primary acceptor of PS 2, Q_A to go fully oxidized (the F_0 level — a pulse of far red light only [1]) or fully reduced (the F_M level — application of a short (1–3 s) pulse of light of an intensity that is more than sufficient to saturate steady-state photosynthesis [9]). If these treatments do not result in the expected changes in the redox level of Q_A, then it follows that estimates of the quenching coefficients may be in error. Of particular concern here is the possibility that turnover of PS 2 linked to electron transport may prevent complete reduction of Q_A.

Theory. To examine the possibility that a light pulse does not result in complete reduction of Q_A, consider that the quantum yield for photochemistry must approach zero as Q_A approaches the fully reduced state. Therefore, it is only possible to maintain the fully reduced state if there is no simultaneous reoxidation of Q_A. Since there is electron transport during steady-state photosynthesis and since this presumably continues or may even be stimulated during the pulse, it follows that it is not theoretically possible to achieve full reduction of Q_A under conditions that permit normal photosynthesis — even with a very intense pulse. We will use the term F_V^* to refer to the yield of variable fluorescence with Q_A fully reduced, and F_V' to refer to the actual measured value. In this paper we develop a procedure to estimate the value of F_V^*.

Our approach is based upon consideration of the course of the electron transport during the pulse used to probe quenching. We assume that the rate of electron transport (after an initial transient phase) will come to a stable value which is determined by the capacity of some reaction downstream from the photoact, and that this rate should be constant at any

---

[1]CIW-DPB Publn. No. 1058

steady-state condition, provided I_P is sufficient to saturate this capacity. We may write using the electron transport rate equation derived by Malkin and Kok [10] that

$$(1) \qquad\qquad J_p = I_p \times (1 - \frac{F'_V}{F^*_V}) \times \phi_P,$$

where J_p is the stable rate of electron transport and F'_V the maximum level of variable fluorescence, respectively reached near the end of the pulse, and ϕ_P is the photochemical yield of "open" PS 2 centers at the steady-state. By solving for F'_V we may write a linear equation of the form $y = b - m \cdot x$, (2) where $x = 1/I_p$, $b = F^*_V$ and $m = F^*_V \times J_P/\phi_P$. The latter is constant at any steady-state. This equation can be solved graphically for F^*_V from a plot of F'_V observed vs. $1/I_P$ at different levels of I_P.

Materials and Methods. Intact attached leaves of *Helianthus annuus, Phaseolus vulgaris, Xanthium strumarium, Piper acquale* and *Alnus rubra* were mounted in a leaf chamber equipped to measure gas exchange and fluorescence as described in [1]. Chlorophyll fluorescence was measured with a PAM fluorometer [8] (PAM-101, H.Walz, D-8521 Effeltrich, F.R.G.) as described in [1] except that a xenon arc lamp (300 Watt, ILC Inc. Sunnyvale, CA) and neutral density filters provided the high intensity pulses (maximum intensity at the leaf surface $ca.$ 12,000 μmol photons (< 650 nm) m^{-2}s^{-1}). All of the experiments reported here were light response curves conducted at normal ambient CO_2 concentrations in 2 or 21% O_2. Values of F'_V were calculated as the difference between the F_0 level (measured in a brief dark interval following a pulse of far red light) and the F_M level observed at each pulse intensity. Successive pulses at the same steady-state were spaced at intervals > 2 min. The reference level of fluorescence was determined after 15 min dark-adaptation following the experiment.

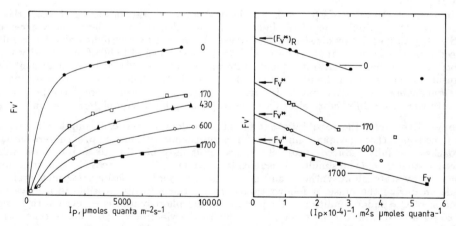

Fig. 1. (left) Influence of the pulse light intensity, I_p, on variable fluorescence, F'_V, obtained from sunflower leaves. The numbers to the right indicate different levels of steady-state illumination in μmol photons m^{-2}s^{-1}.

Fig. 2. (right) Data of Fig. 1 plotted vs. $1/I_P$ to obtain F^*_V by extrapolation

Results. Figure 1 shows a plot of the value of F'_V observed in an experiment with sunflower as a function of the intensity of light during the pulse, I_P. The value of F'_V decreased as the level of steady-state illumination increased, but in each case F'_V continued to increase up to the highest values of I_P that could be provided by our optical system — indicating that Q_A was not being completely reduced.

Figure 2 shows the same data plotted according to Eqn. 2. The data points at levels of $I_P > 3000$ μmol photons m^{-2}s^{-1} fall along straight lines that can be extrapolated to obtain the y-intercept as $1/I_P \to 0$. This is F$_V^*$, the fluorescence yield at infinite pulse intensity, and it is significantly higher than F$_V'$ measured with the highest values of I_P that could be obtained. Consequently, the values of q_N and q_P calculated using F$_V^*$ differ from the "apparent coefficients" estimated using any finite value of I_P. Similar experiments were conducted with each of the 5 species included in this study (data not shown). The responses differed among species with shade-plants (such as *Piper acquales*) approaching "saturation" at a lower pulse intensity than sun plants (such as *Helianthus annuus*) with high photosynthetic capacity. However, in each case the values of q_N and q_P estimated by extrapolation differed significantly from the "apparent values" estimated using finite values of I_P.

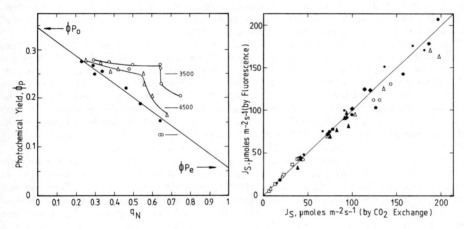

Fig. 3. (left) The dependence of the quantum yield of "open" PS 2 centers, ϕ_P, on the level of q_N calculated using F$_V^*$ (•) and from F$_V'$ at $I_P = 3500$ (○) or 6500 μmol photons m^{-2}s^{-1} ($\triangle$), respectively.

Fig. 4. (right) A comparison of rates of electron transport calculated from gas exchange measurements and from fluorescence quenching using Eqn. 3.

Following Weis and Berry [1] the effect of non-photochemical quenching on PS 2 photochemical efficiency may be quantified by a two step procedure. First the observed steady-state quantum yield, ϕ_s, is corrected for incomplete photochemical quenching giving the "intrinsic quantum efficiency," with all of the PS 2 traps in the "open" configuration ($\phi_P = \phi_s/q_P$). ϕ_P is then plotted versus q_N (Figure 3). The data presented here are based on q_N and q_P calculated directly from F$_V'$ at $I_P = 3500$ or 6500 μmol quanta m^{-2}s^{-1}, and these are compared with an analysis based on the extrapolated values of F$_V^*$ obtained as in Fig. 2. The latter set of data fall along a straight line, while the former describe curved lines with a tendency to be bi-phasic. Nevertheless, each set of data could be approximated by a linear regression — with increasing values of ϕ_{Pe} as the pulse intensity decreases. Pooled data for all species examined gave values of $\phi_{Po} = 0.33$ and $\phi_{Pe} = 0.05$ when based on the extrapolation to infinite pulse intensity, while analysis based on a finite intensity yielded different values for each set of measurements.

Using the empirical equation similar to Weis and Berry [1], we may calculate the electron transport rate, J, at any absorbed quantum flux, I, from estimates of the quenching coefficients as,

$$(3) \qquad J = I \times \phi_{Po} \times q_P(1 - \xi q_N)$$

where $\xi = 1 - \phi_{Pe}/\phi_{Po}$ or 0.85 using the values obtained above. Rates of electron transport calculated according to Eqn. 3 using these constants are compared (Figure 4) with independent measurements of electron transport calculated from CO_2 exchange. We conclude that the kinetic properties of the mechanisms that regulate non-photochemical quenching are similar in these, and probably most other C_3-plants.

Conclusions. The experiments reported here demonstrate the application of extrapolation to *infinite* pulse intensity in analysis of the control of electron transport by non-photochemical quenching in several species. The results are significantly different from inferences based on direct analysis of fluorescence responses at a single, *finite* pulse intensity. In particular, a single set of parameters fit equally well to all members of a group of species selected to have diverse photosynthetic properties.

This observation should simplify application of fluorescence methods to the estimation of steady-state electron transport rates by eliminating the need to conduct an empirical calibration for each plant studied. However, it is necessary to use a more complex experimental protocol, and in some instances it may be preferable to use a pulse of constant intensity and conduct empirical calibration experiments with that particular tissue. The present work does not preclude such an approach. However, it should be recognized that the values of q_P and q_N, so obtained, do not provide an accurate indication of the quenching of absorbed photons, and that the apparent dependence of electron transport on these parameters (Eqn. 3) may differ from leaf to leaf and may be non-linear.

The dependence of quantum efficiency on q_N estimated by extrapolation was approximately linear and nearly proportional to $1-q_N$ (Eqn. 3). If the value of ϕ_{Pe} were 0, these data would conform to the original three-state hypothesis put forward by Duysens and Sweers [11] — that PS 2 centers are reversibly transformed to a form that performs non-photochemical quenching of absorbed quanta rather than photochemistry. The significant non-zero intercept may be real, as accommodated by the four-state model of Weis and Berry [1], or it may be related to curvature originating, for example, from excitation transfer between PS 2 pigment–reaction center complexes [1].

References.
1. Weis, E. and Berry, J.A. (1987) Biochim. Biophys. Acta 894, 198–208.
2. Horton, P. and Hague, A. (1988) Biochim. Biophys. Acta 932, 107–115.
3. Sharkey, T.D., Berry, J.A. and Sage, R.F. (1988) Planta 176, 415–424.
4. Peterson, R.B, Sivak M.N. and Walker, D.A. (1988) Plant Physiol. 88, 158–163.
5. Weis, E. and Lechtenberg, D. (1988) in: Application of Chlorophyll Fluorescence (H.K. Lichtenthaler, ed.) pp. 71–76, Kluwer Academic Publishers.
6. Weis, E. and Berry, J.A. (1988) in: Plants and Temperature (S.P. Long & F.I. Wood-| ward eds.) pp. 329–46, The Company of Biologists Ltd.
7. Schäfer, C. and Björkman, O.E. (1988) Planta 178, 376–76.
8. Schreiber, U., Schliwa, U. and Bilger, W. (1986) Photosyn. Res. 10, 51–62.
9. Dietz, K.-J., Neimanis, S. and Heber, U. (1984) Biochim. Biophys. Acta 767, 444–450.
10. Malkin, S. and Kok, B. (1966) Biochim. Biophys. Acta 767, 444–450.
11. Duysens, L.N.M. and Sweers, H.E. (1963) in: Microalgæ & Photosynthetic Bacteria (Edited by the Japanese Society of Plant Physiologists) pp. 353–372, University of Tokyo press.

REGULATION OF CO_2 ASSIMILATION DURING PHOTOINHIBITION

Marie DUJARDYN and Christine H. FOYER

Laboratoire du Métabolisme, INRA, 78026 Versailles, France

1. INTRODUCTION

At high irradiance photosynthesis is limited by CO_2 assimilation and more light is absorbed than can be effectively used to drive photosynthesis. Dissipation of surplus excitation energy is essential because excessive excitation leads to the light-induced loss of thylakoid efficiency called photoinhibition. When the rate of carbon assimilation limits the overall rate of photosynthesis the capacity of ATP and NADPH production exceeds that of demand by the Benson-Calvin cycle and photosynthetic control of electron transport would be expected (1, 2). Photosynthetic control processes could favour photoinhibition since restriction of the oxidation of reduced plastoquinone at high transthylakoid ΔpH would favour over-reduction of PS II and over-oxidation of PS I. Previous studies on the effects of photoinhibition on the activity of the Benson-Calvin cycle have suggested that it is the rate of regeneration of RuBP that limits carbon assimilation and that this was caused by oxidation of redox-modulated enzymes (3, 5). In this study we investigated the responses of the Benson-Calvin cycle to changes in irradiance and photoinhibition.

2. MATERIALS AND METHODS

Hordeum vulgare var cytris was grown a low light regime (280 μE m^{-2} s^{-1}) until the fourth leaf was well-developed (28 $\pm$ 1 day old). In all the following experiments the 4th leaf only was used. Net CO_2 assimilation was measured using infra-red gas analysis and the transpiration rate was assessed with a hygrodynamic sensor. Leaves were allowed to equilibrate in air for 2 h in the assimilation chamber at the growth irradiance and temperature. The plants were than exposed to high irradiance (1400 μE m^{-2} s^{-1}) for a 2 1/2 h period and then returned to 280 μE m^{-2} s^{-1}. For metabolite measurements the frozen samples were ground with frozen $HClO_4$ (1 M) and neutralised with K_2CO_3. Ribulose-1,5-bisphosphate (RuBP), PGA, triose phosphate, ATP and fructose-1,6-bisphosphate (FBP) were measured as described previously (6).

For the enzyme assays the frozen leaf samples were ground with frozen extraction buffer consisting of 0.1 M Tricine-KOH buffer (pH 8.0) containing 1 mM dithiothreitol, 10 mM $MgCl_2$, 50 mM KCl, 1 mM EDTA and 0.1 % Triton X100. NADP-malate dehydrogenase was measured spectrophotometrically (7). FBPase was assayed spectrophotometrically at 340 nm in a reaction mixture containing 100 mM Tricine-KOH buffer (pH 8.0), 10 mM $MgCl_2$, 10 mM dithiothreitol, 0.2 mM NADP, 0.1 mM FBP and phosphoglucose isomerase (2.5 U ml^{-1}) and glucose 6-phosphate dehydrogenase (3.5 U ml^{-1})

M. Baltscheffsky (ed.), Current Research in Photosynthesis, Vol. IV, 283–286.
© 1990 *Kluwer Academic Publishers. Printed in the Netherlands.*

in a total reaction volume of 1 ml. RuBP carboxylase was measured as described by Parry *et al.* (8).

3. RESULTS AND DISCUSSION

Upon the transition from the growth irradiance (280 μmol m^{-2} s^{-1}) to a photoinhibitory irradiance (1400 μmol m^{-2} s^{-1}) the CO_2 assimilation rate of the leaves doubled within minutes (fig. 1) but high irradiance rapidly caused a reduction in quantum efficiency (table 1). Following exposure to high light the activities of NADP-malate dehydrogenase and FBPase obtained near maximum values and the activation state of ribulose-1,5-bisphosphate carboxylase increased. The activity of the latter remained constant throughout the period of photoinhibitory irradiance but the increase in the activities of FBPase and NADP-malate dehydrogenase was transient decreasing once more to much lower values (fig. 2). This suggests that immediately following the transition to high light reduction and activation of redox-modulated enzymes occured but then the stroma became relatively oxidised as a result of photoinhibition.

Photoinhibition was measured by the decrease in the ratio of variable chlorophyll a fluorescence (Fv) to maximum chlorophyll a fluorescence (Fm) and was accompanied by a decrease in the quantum yield of CO_2 assimilation (table 1). The Fv/Fm ratio and quantum yield both declined within minutes following the transition to high irradiance, reaching a minimum value after 1 h 30 min exposure. The Fv/Fm ratio and quantum yield subsequently remained at the constant lower level throughout the remaining period of high irradiance (table 1). The reduction in quantum yield resulted in a significant loss of capacity for CO_2 assimilation at low irradiance. Rates of CO_2 assimilation at high irradiance were much less effected (fig. 1).

Table 1. The effect of high light (1400 μE m^{-2} s^{-1}) on chlorophyll a fluorescence and the quantum yield of carbon assimilation.

Duration of high irradiance (min)	Fv/Fm	Quantum yield $\left(\frac{\mu\text{mol } O_2 .}{\mu\text{mol quanta}} ^{-1} \right)$
0	0.80	0.095
10	0.78	0.093
30	0.70	0.071
45	0.69	0.073
60	0.66	0.055
90	0.64	0.052
180	0.62	0.046

As the period of photoinhibitory irradiance progressed the RuBP pool rapidly fell while the PGA pool increased three-fold. This suggests that the carboxylation rate was greater than the rate of PGA reduction in these circumstances.

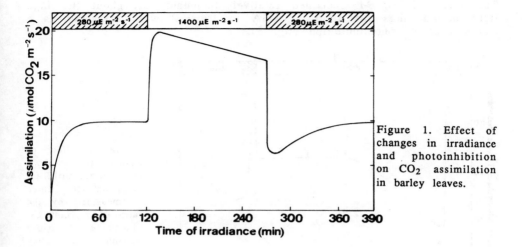

Figure 1. Effect of changes in irradiance and photoinhibition on CO_2 assimilation in barley leaves.

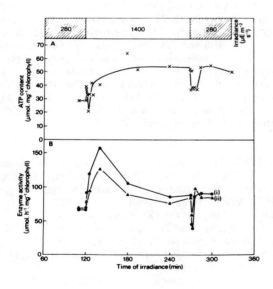

Figure 2. Effect of changes in irradiance and photoinhibition on the ATP content (A) and NADP-malate dehydrogenase (i) and fructose -1,6-bisphos- phatase (ii) activities (B) of barley leaves.

The level of triose-P remained relatively constant throughout the high light period, thus the ratio of PGA to triose-P was increasing as a consequence of photoinhibition (fig. 3).

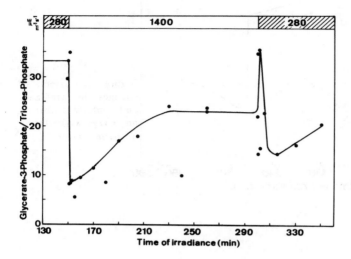

Figure 3. Effect of changes in irradiance and photoinhibition on assimilatory force as measured by the ratio of glycerate 3-phosphate to triose phosphate in barley leaves.

The change from low to high light caused an increase in the ATP pool of the leaf (fig. 2). This suggests that the ability to synthesise ATP was not impaired by photoinhibition. A high transthylakoid ΔpH together with a high ATP level would provide metabolic conditions that favour photosynthetic control of electron transport (2). Following photoinhibition the Benson-Calvin cycle is clearly limited by the capacity for non-cyclic electron flow which results in a reduction in assimilatory force as determined by the PGA/triose-P ratio (fig. 3) and oxidation of thiol modulated enzymes (fig. 1). Oxidation of the stroma may be the result of photosynthetic control exerted over thylakoid electron flow. Photoinhibitory loss of PS II capacity may be viewed as a manifestation of the operation of photosynthetic control processes.

REFERENCES
1. Weis R, JR Ball, J Berry (1987) In : Progress in Photosynthesis Research (Biggins J ed.) Vol 2, pp. 553-556, Martinus-Nijhoff Publishers, Dordrect.
2. Foyer C., R Furbank, Harbinson J, P Horton (1989) Photosyn Res, in press
3. Giersch C, SP Robinson (1987) Aust J Plant Physiol 14: 439-449
4. Miginiac-Maslow M, G Cornic, JP Jacquot (1988) Planta 173: 468-473
5. Powles SB, KSR Chapman, FR Whatley (1982) Plant Physiol 69: 371-374
6. Furbank RT, CH Foyer (1986) Arch Biochem Biophys 246: 240-244
7. Foyer CH, R Furbank, DA Walker (1989) Arch Biochem Biophys 268: 687-697
8 Parry MAJ, AJ Keys, CH Foyer, RT Furbank, DA Walker (1988) Plant Physiol 87: 558-561

INTERMEDIATES, CATALYTIC COMPONENTS AND LIGHT AND DARK REGULATION OF ALA AND CHLOROPHYLL FORMATION IN THE GREEN ALGA *SCENEDESMUS*

Dieter Dörnemann, Volker Breu, Kiriakos Kotzabasis, Peter Richter and Horst Senger, Fachbereich Biologie/Botanik der Philipps-Universität Marburg, Lahnberge, D-3550 Marburg, FRG

INTRODUCTION

The nature of the intermediates of the C_5-pathway has been a matter of controversy for a long time. Although the involvement of glutamate-1-semialdehyde (G-1-SA) (1) is widely accepted, the role of 4,5-dioxovalerate (DOVA) (2) as a catalytic component in the C_5-pathway is still challenged (3). Well established is yet the activation of glutamate for the formation of 5-aminolevulinate (ALA) by a tRNA[glu] as demonstrated for barley (4), *Chlamydomonas* (5), *Chlorella* (6), *Methanobacterium* (7), *Euglena* (8), *Cyanidium* (9), *Synechocystis* (9) and spinach (9).
The regulation of the C_5-pathway and the subsequent chlorophyll biosynthesis is even less understood. The yellow mutant C-2A' of the unicellular green alga *Scenedesmus obliquus* forms ALA and chlorophyll only after transfer to light. It is therefore an excellent tool for studies on the intermediates of the C_5-pathway and the regulation of chlorophyll biosynthesis.

MATERIAL AND METHODS

The X-ray induced mutant C-2A' was cultured and harvested as described earlier (10). DOVA-transaminase was purified as demonstrated in (11). The preparation of tRNA-fractions and the corresponding ligase preparation as well as the run-off fraction, containing the transaminases, ALA-dehydratase and porphobilinogenase were performed following (12). G-1-SA-pyrrole was formed by the condensation of the compound with ethylacetoacetate as described in (13). Protochlorophyllide (Pchlide) was isolated following (14). The separation into divinyl- and monovinyl-Pchlide was performed as described in (15).

RESULTS AND DISCUSSION

Meisch et al. criticized (3) that the isolated 2,3-diaminonaphthalene derivative of DOVA (DOVA-DAN) does not derive from DOVA itself, but rather from the disproportioning of the dihydrobenzoquinoxaline of ALA. In contrast, we demonstrated that in the complete absence of ALA DOVA-DAN could be isolated, when tetrapyrrole biosynthesis was inhibited by levulinic acid (LA) (2). The ratio of ALA to DOVA was 1:180 in *Scenedesmus* and 1:220 in barley. This suggests that in green algae, as well as in higher plants (2), DOVA is an intermediate in the C_5-pathway. This finding is supported by the fact that DOVA-transaminase could be purified to apparent homogeneity from *Scenedesmus* (11).

M. Baltscheffsky (ed.), Current Research in Photosynthesis, Vol. IV, 287–290.
© 1990 *Kluwer Academic Publishers. Printed in the Netherlands.*

When labelled glutamate was incubated with enzyme preparations containing all components for the formation of ALA it turned out that the label in ALA was diluted to about 50 % in the presence of 1 mM DOVA. This can only be varified if DOVA is an intermediate in the formation of ALA. The pool of labelled DOVA formed from ^{3}H-glutamate is then in competition with the added, unlabelled DOVA. These results could be confirmed with unlabelled substrates and their optical determination. The incubation with additional 1 mM DOVA did not show an additive effect, but revealed again a competition between the pool in the pathway and the additional DOVA, leading to about 80 % of the additive value.

Experiments with (aminooxy)-acetate and gabaculine showed different inhibition effects. Starting from glutamate, both inhibitors were very effective. However, with DOVA as substrate, gabaculine was much less effective, suggesting that two different transamination reactions must be involved in the formation of ALA. When the enzyme preparation was incubated with glutamate in the presence of gabaculine, a product could be isolated by its condensation with ethylacetoacetate which co-chromatographed with the corresponding derivative of chemically synthesized G-1-SA (13, 16). In the presence of 1 mM DOVA again G-1-SA accumulated as a consequence of the competition between the external DOVA and that formed from glutamate via G-1-SA. From these results the participation of both, G-1-SA and DOVA, in the C_5-pathway has to be concluded.

Furthermore it could be shown that in the presence of RNase the formation of ALA from glutamate decreased drastically, confirming the participation of an RNA in the C_5-pathway in *Scenedesmus* (16). From these results a new reaction scheme for the C_5-pathway was developed as shown in Fig. 1.

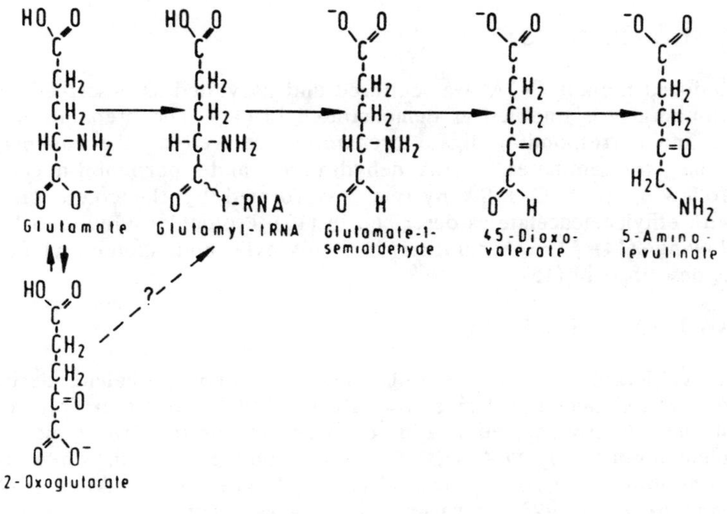

Fig. 1:
A new reaction scheme for the synthesis of 5-aminolevulinic acid, considering the RNA dependent formation of G-1-SA from glutamate, deamination to DOVA and transamination to ALA.

Little is known about the regulation of the C_5-pathway and subsequent chlorophyll biosynthesis in light and darkness. When a tRNA^{glu}-ligase preparation and a corresponding tRNA-fraction were incubated with glutamate in the presence of protochlorophyllide (Pchlide), the loading of the tRNA decreased drastically (14). With separated mono- and divinyl-Pchlide the K_i-value was determined to be < 0.5 μM. Similar inhibition kinetics could be shown for mono- and divinyl-Pchlide in the light dependent greening mutant C-2A' *Scenedesmus*, whereas in barley only monovinyl-Pchlide showed comparable kinetics. The divinyl-compound was much less effective which is in agreement with the finding that in etiolated barley only monovinyl-Pchlide accumulates. From these results a regulation scheme for plants with light-dependent greening during etiolated growth was developed as shown in Fig. 2.

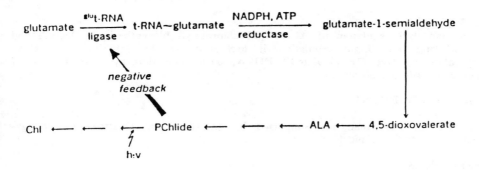

Fig. 2:
The regulation of ALA- and subsequently protochlorophyllide formation in dark grown mutant C-2A' of *Scenedesmus* and etiolated barley seedlings.

During light-growth, however, no Pchlide accumulates and thus cannot be effective in the regulation of the C_5-pathway. By feeding ALA to dark-grown cultures of mutant C-2A' the amount of accumulated Pchlide could be increased up to 20 to 30-fold. When, however, DOVA, the direct precursor of ALA, was fed, the Pchlide amount declined to its detection limits (17). When DOVA was added to greening cultures of mutant C-2A', chlorophyll biosynthesis stopped after the first, rapid phase of biosynthetic activity, when all C_5-precursors were readily consumed. When the rate of chlorophyll formation ceases, the surplus of DOVA which is a substrate analogue of LA acts as competitive inhibitor on ALA-dehydratase and thus prevents further formation of chlorophyll precursors. After DOVA was washed out from the culture and replaced by ALA, chlorophyll biosynthesis immediately commenced. The K_i-value of DOVA on an ALA-dehydratase preparation (16) was determined to be 60 ±5 μM, which is 10 % of the K_m-value of DOVA for DOVA-transaminase. Thus we conclude that DOVA is enzyme-bound under physiological conditions. It is, however, released to the chloroplast stroma when chlorophyll biosynthesis is finished or for other reasons an overflow of C_5-compounds is formed (17). From these results a regulation scheme including dark-regulation is proposed as shown in Fig. 3.

IV.16.**290**

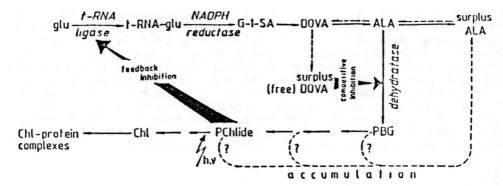

Fig. 3:
Light- and dark-regulation of ALA- and chlorophyll biosynthesis by DOVA and protochlorophyllide. Light regulation is archieved by the inhibition of ALA-dehydratase by free ("accumulated") DOVA, dark regulation by a feed back of accumulated protochlorophyllide.

ACKNOWLEDGEMENTS

This research was financially supported by grants of the Deutsche Forschungs-gemeinschaft to D. D. and H. S.

REFERENCES

1   Kannangara, C.G. and Schouboe, A. (1985) Carlsberg Res. Commun. <u>50</u>, 179-191
2   Breu, V, Kah, A. and Dörnemann D. (1988) Biochim. Biophys. Acta <u>964</u>, 61-68
3   Meisch, H.-U., Reinle, W. and Wolf, M. (1985) Biochim. Biophys. Acta <u>841</u>, 319-322
4   Kannangara, C.G., Gough, S.P., Oliver, R.P. and Rasmussen, S.K. (1984) Carlsberg Res. Commun. <u>49</u>, 417-437
5   Huang, D.-D., Wang, W.-Y., Gough, S.P. and Kannangara, C.G. (1984) Science <u>225</u>, 1482-1484
6   Weinstein, J.D. and Beale, S.I. (1985) Arch. Biochem. Biophys. <u>239</u>, 87-93
7   Friedmann, H.C., Thauer, R.K., Gough, S.P. and Kannangara, C.G. (1987) Carlsberg Res. Commun. <u>52</u>, 363-371
8   Weinstein, J.D., Mayer S.M. and Beale, S.I. (1986) Plant Physiol. <u>82</u>, 1096-1101
9   Schneegurt, M.A. and Beale S.I. (1988) Plant Physiol. 497-504
10 Bishop, N.I. and Senger, H. (1972) Plant Cell Physiol. <u>13</u>, 937-953
11 Kah, A., Dörnemann, D. and Senger, H. (1988) Z. Naturforsch. <u>43</u>c, 563-571
12 Wang, W.-Y., Gough, S.P. and Kannangara, C.G. (1981) Carlsberg Res. Commun. <u>46</u>, 243-257
13 Breu, V., Richter, P. and Dörnemann, D. (1989) Z. Naturforsch. (submitted)
14 Dörnemann, D., Kotzabasis, K., Richter, P., Breu, V. and Senger, H. (1989) Botanica Acta <u>102</u>, 112-115
15 Kotzabasis, K. and Senger, H. (1986) Z. Naturforsch. <u>41</u>c, 1001-1003
16 Breu, V. and Dörnemann, D. (1988) Biochim. Biophys. Acta <u>967</u>, 135-140
17 Kotzabasis, K., Breu, V. and Dörnemann, D. (1989) Biochim. Biophys. Acta

ADAPTATION OF PHOTOSYSTEM STOICHIOMETRY IN OXYGEN-EVOLVING THYLAKOID
MEMBRANES

ANASTASIOS MELIS, Division of Molecular Plant Biology, 313 Hilgard
Hall, University of California, BERKELEY, CA   94720, USA

1. INTRODUCTION
     Isolated thylakoid membranes can be poised electrochemically in
the dark so that a subsequent illumination will induce primary charge
separation in the reaction centers of photosystem I (PSI) and photosystem II (PSII). The ensuing oxidation-reduction reactions can be
monitored spectrophotometrically in a wavelength region specific to
the molecule undergoing the redox transition. Figure 1 provides
examples of the light-induced absorbance difference spectra generated
upon the photoreduction of the specialized quinone acceptor Q_A of
PSII (Fig. 1A), upon the photoreduction of the primary electron
acceptor pheophytin of PSII (Fig. 1B) and upon the photooxidation of
the reaction center P700 of PSI (Fig. 1C). From the known differential extinction coefficients [1-4] and from the amplitude of the
absorbance change at the peak wavelength (320 nm for Q_A^-, 685 nm for
$Pheo^-$ and 700 nm for $P700^+$), it is possible to calculate the concentration of each chemical species in the thylakoid membrane, assuming
that illumination of thylakoid membranes will result in the generation of 1 Q_A^- and 1 $Pheo^-$ per PSII center, and in the generation of 1
$P700^+$ per PSI center. Hence, it is possible to provide a direct
estimate of the photosystem concentration in thylakoid membranes [5-7].

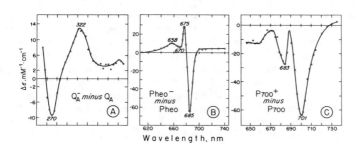

FIGURE 1. Light-induced absorbance difference spectra (A) of the
reduced minus oxidized forms of the primary quinone acceptor of PSII
(Q_A^- minus Q_A), (B) of the reduced minus oxidized form of the primary
electron acceptor pheophytin of PSII (Pheo$^-$ minus Pheo), and (c) of
the oxidized minus reduced forms of the reaction center P700 of PSI
($P700^+$ minus $\overline{P700}$).

M. Baltscheffsky (ed.), Current Research in Photosynthesis, Vol. IV, 291–298.
© *1990 Kluwer Academic Publishers. Printed in the Netherlands.*

The result of measurements with thylakoid membranes from diverse photosynthetic species indicated variability in the ratio of PSII to PSI reaction centers. Cyanobacteria and red algae commonly displayed photosystem stoichiometry PSII/PSI ratios between 0.3 and 0.7 (Table 1) [5,8-10]. Vascular plant chloroplasts from spinach and from other species grown under direct sunlight have PSII/PSI = 1.8:1.0 [6,11]. The chlorophyll (Chl) b-less chlorina f2 mutant of barley [12] and other virescent mutants [13] displayed PSII/PSI greater than 2 (Table 1).

TABLE 1. Chlorophyll ratios and photosystem stoichiometry in cyano-bacteria, mature vascular plant chloroplasts, and a Chl b-less mutant. Component quantitation (mol:mol) is based on the Chl (a+b) content.

	$\dfrac{\text{Chl a}}{\text{Chl b}}$	$\dfrac{\text{Chl}}{\text{PSI}}$	$\dfrac{\text{Chl}}{\text{PSII}}$	$\dfrac{\text{PSII}}{\text{PSI}}$
Synechococcus 6301	---	160	370	0.43
wild type chloroplasts	2.8	600	350	1.7
Barley chlorina f2	oo	300	100	3.0

The experimental evidence that photosystem stoichiometry ratios (PSII/PSI) differed from "strict unity" (and showed large variations among different photosynthetic membranes) was contrary to the conventional assumption based on the Z-scheme. Inevitably, the question was raised whether these variations in photosystem stoichiometry constituted a random phenomenon or a specific adaptation response of the plants. Examination of different aspects of this phenomenon argues strongly in favor of the latter.

2. ADAPTATION OF PHOTOSYSTEM STOICHIOMETRY IN RESPONSE TO MUTATIONS
There are developmental mutants in which the accumulation of Chl b and the development of the thylakoid membrane is retarded. Such mutants are commonly referred to as "virescent" or "Chl b-deficient". They possess fully functional photochemical reaction centers and other electron-transport intermediates. However, they show Chl a/Chl b ratios that are significantly higher than the corresponding wild type and often show altered thylakoid membrane ultrastructure. Since up to 80% or more, of the Chl antenna of PSII is associated with the Chl a-b LHC II [7,14] whereas only about 30-40% of the Chl antenna of PSI is associated with the Chl a-b LHC I [7,15], it follows that in Chl b-deficient mutants the light-harvesting capacity of PSII will be lower than that of PSI. Typical among the Chl b-deficient mutants are the Nicotiana tabacum (tobacco) yellow-green Su/su and the yellow Su/su var. Aurea [16], the soybean Cy9y9 and CY̅11y̅11 [17,18], the No. PBI line LMG mutant of sugar beet [19], and the OY-YG mutant of maize [20].

One common feature in these mutants is the smaller photosynthetic unit size, as measured both by the Chl/P700 and Chl/Q_A ratios (Table 2). The important common feature, however, is the elevated PSII/PSI ratio in the mutants (Table 2). Since the mutation reduced primarily the light-harvesting capacity of PSII, elevated PSII/PSI ratios may be thought of as a response of the plant in restoring the

TABLE 2. Photochemical apparatus organization in virescent mutants

Chloroplast type	Chl a / Chl b	Chl / P700	Chl / Q_A	PSII / PSI
Wild type	2.8	600	350	1.7
Tobacco Su/su	4.7	330	120	2.7
Tobacco Su/su, Aurea	5.7	300	75	4.0
Soybean y_9y_9	5.0	500	200	2.5
Soybean $Y_{11}y_{11}$	5.5	480	170	2.8
Sugarbeet No. PBI, LMG	5.2	410	170	2.4
Maize OY-YG	5.6	540	230	2.4

balance of electron flow between PSII and PSI. This response is similar to that of the Chl b-less chlorina f2 mutant of barley (Table 1). The rationale for this response is that a mutation caused a disproportionate reduction in the number of the antenna Chl molecules of PSII and the plasticity of the organelle (chloroplast) allowed an elevated PSII/PSI ratio in the thylakoid membrane, in essence countering the effect of the mutation.

3. ADAPTATION OF PHOTOSYSTEM STOICHIOMETRY IN RESPONSE TO CHANGES IN LIGHT-QUALITY

Early work on the stoichiometry of system I and system II reaction centers in spinach [5] provided subtle indications of a seasonal variation in the PSII/PSI ratio in the thylakoid membrane. It was suggested that oxygen-evolving plants may change the ratio of their photosystems in response to environmental light conditions. A more

TABLE 3. Photosystem stoichiometry under different light qualities

Chloroplast type	Chl a / Chl b	Chl / P700	Chl / Q_A	PSII / PSI
Pisum sativum				
PSII-light	3.0	530	430	1.2
Sun light	2.8	640	360	1.8
PSI-light	2.5	750	330	2.3
Synechococcus 6301				
PSII-light	--	155	580	0.27
Sun light	--	160	355	0.45
PSI-light	--	170	240	0.70

vigorous test of this assertion occurred when pea plants and cyano-bacteria were grown under illumination absorbed preferentially by PSI or by PSII [6,9,21-23]. These studies revealed that a principal response of the photosynthetic membrane to differential sensitization of PSI and PSII is the adjustment of the reaction-center stoichiometry (Table 3): Both in the phycobilisome-containing prokaryotic Synecho-coccus 6301 and in higher plants chloroplasts, the relative PSII/PSI ratio is low under conditions of PSII excitation (PSII-light) and substantially higher under conditions of PSI excitation (PSI-light). Thus, the quality of light during plant growth exerts a specific control on the thylakoid membrane organization and function. The response of the plant is meaningful since the adjustment of the PSII/PSI ratio restores an optimized (balanced) electron-transport between the two photosystems. This adjustment of the photochemical apparatus organization is a long-term but fully reversible response. Figure 2 shows the results of an experiment in which pea plants were grown under PSI-light (PSII/PSI = 2.5:1). At zero time, they were switched to PSII-light conditions (Fig. 2, left panel). The PSII/PSI stoichiometry ratio was decreased as a function of time until it reached a new steady-state of about 1.3:1 with a half-time of about 20 h. Upon transition to PSI-light conditions, (Fig. 2, right panel), the PSII/PSI ratio gradually increased to the value typical for PSI-light grown plants [24]. Similar results were

FIGURE 2. Chromatic acclimation of photosystem stoichiometry in pea plants following transfer of PSI-light grown peas to PSII-light (left panel) and of PSII-light grown peas to PSI-light (right panel).

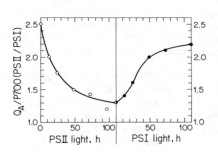

also obtained with cyanobacteria [25]. These results suggested the existence of a highly conserved mechanism in photosynthetic organisms designed to sense and correct imbalance in light absorption by the two photosystems through adjustment and optimization of the PSII/PSI stoichiometry ratio. The long-term response of photosystem stoichiometry adjustment should not be confused with short-term responses, such as state transitions [26] which may reflect changes in the steady-state fluorescence yield and rate of oxygen evolution but not in the basic composition of the photochemical apparatus.

4.   ADAPTATION OF THYLAKOID MEMBRANE COMPOSITION AND FUNCTION IN RESPONSE TO CHANGES IN LIGHT-INTENSITY
    A substantially different response is elicited when plants are grown in a light environment of constant quality but of variable intensity. A number of investigators reported substantial difference

in the Chl a/Chl b ratio among "high-light" grown plants and "low-light" grown plants [6,27-30].

Light intensity changes during plant growth induce changes in the size and composition of the light-harvesting antenna of the photosystems. This contention is supported by the variable Chl a/Chl b ratio and by direct measurements of the functional light-harvesting Chl antenna size of sun and shade plants [31], of "high-light" and "low-light" algae [29,32,33], and of "high light" and "low light" vascular plant chloroplasts [34-36]. In general, low light intensity conditions promote larger Chl antenna size for both PSII and PSI (larger photosynthetic unit size). High light intensity promotes a smaller Chl antenna size. This adjustment in the Chl antenna size of the photosystems comes about because of light-induced changes in the auxiliary Chl a-b LHC II and LHC I of PSII and PSI, respectively [34-36]. This response appears to be well conserved in all photosynthetic systems examined. The regulation of this phenomenon at the molecular and membrane levels is currently unknown.

In addition, a change in the light intensity during plant growth elicits stoichiometric changes between the cytochrome b_6-f complex and the two photosystems. Of considerable interest is the observation of variable Cyt b_6-f/PSI ratios: Under "high-light" conditions, the rate of light absorption by each photosystem is not limiting, and overall electron-transport is then limited by the intermediate electron transport steps. The high content of Cyt b_6-f in "high-light" plants (Cyt f/PSI = 1.5) is a response of the plant that improves overall electron-transport capacity. The converse is true in "low-light" plants and obligate shade species in which the rate of light absorption becomes the limiting factor and, under such conditions, the chloroplasts scale down the biosynthesis of Cyt b_6-f complex to a low level (Cyt f/PSI = 0.8) [27,28]. This observation is consistent with the proposal by Wilhelm and Wild [30] that overall electron-transport capacity, under both light-limiting and light-saturating conditions, could be accurately defined by the relative Cyt b_6-f complex content in the chloroplast. Interestingly, obligate shade species are examples of adaptation both to low light-intensity and to altered light-quality since a shade environment is dominated by PSI-sensitizing (far-red) wavelengths of low intensity.

The response of the photosystem stoichiometry to variation in light-intensity appears to depend on the plant species examined. In Anacystis nidulans [8], Chlamydomonas reinhardtii [32], and vascular plant chloroplasts from several species [6,37,38], low-light growth conditions result in low PSII/PSI ratios and high-light growth conditions elicit higher PSII/PSI ratios.

In diatoms and brown algae, however, the response of the cells to the light intensity during growth is opposite to the response of cyanobacteria, green algae and vascular plants [33,39]. There is one report suggesting invariable photosystem stoichiometry in the green alga <u>Dunaliella</u> <u>tertiolecta</u> [40]. Clearly, the cause and effect relationship between light intensity and photosystem stoichiometry is not adequately understood at present.

5. A MOLECULAR FEEDBACK MECHANISM FOR THE ADAPTATION OF PHOTOSYSTEM STOICHIOMETRY

The foregoing are evidence of the ability of oxygenic photosynthesis to sense imbalance in the electron-transport rate between individual thylakoid membrane complexes (PSII, Cyt b_6-f and PSI) and of the ability to regulate the relative concentration of these complexes. The molecular mechanism for the adjustment of photosystem stoichiometry would include a "sensing" and a "response" component. The similarity of the response of the PS stoichiometry to three independent "signals" (Chl b-deficiency, light-quality, and light-intensity) would eliminate the role of any specialized photoreceptor (i.e., phytochrome) in the signal identification process. Rather, it is proposed that the first step in signal identification occurs in the thylakoid membrane directly, as imbalance in the rate of electron-transport between individual intermediates (Fig. 3, [11]).

FIGURE 3. Schematic of a molecular mechanism for the regulation of photosystem stoichiometry in the thylakoid membrane of oxygenic photosynthesis.

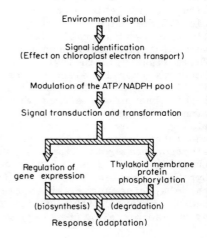

By necessity, signal identification (for example, an imbalance in electron-transport between PSII and PSI in the thylakoid membrane) must be "communicated" to other metabolic processes in the chloroplast to enable a meaningful response. The nature of the "signal transduction and transformation" process is unknown, although chloroplast-generated metabolites, such as ATP and NADPH, might play a role in this process [11].

The "response" of the plant probably involves selective regulation of the biosynthesis/assembly and disassembly/degradation of complexes in the thylakoid membrane. Preliminary evidence suggested a strong correlation between the PSI content in the thylakoid membrane and the steady state level of psaA (PSI) gene transcripts in chloroplasts grown under PSII or PSI-light [41,42]. Moreover, the process of thylakoid membrane protein phosphorylation has been implicated in the regulation of disassembly/degradation of surplus complexes in the thylakoid membrane (Fig. 3, [43]).

In summary, light quality and light intensity may exert different effects in terms of chloroplast structure, organization and function. The quality of light (balance of light absorption between PSII and PSI) during plant growth apparently controls the differentiation of the thylakoid lamella into grana and stroma thylakoids and the stoichiometric amounts of PSI and PSII complexes. Thus, plant growth under PSI excitation results in a greater concentration of PSII in the thylakoid membrane. The converse is also true. In both cases of light adaptation, the net result is optimization of the overall electron-transport process resulting in efficient use of the prevailing environmental light conditions. Light intensity apparently controls the chloroplast Chl $\underline{a}$ and Chl $\underline{b}$ content, the stoichiometry of the cytochrome $\underline{b_6}$-$\underline{f}$ complex relative to PSI and PSII complexes and the overall electron-transport capacity of the thylakoid membrane. Why plants respond with a PSII/PSI stoichiometry adjustment versus a Chl antenna size change is not understood at present. Clearly, more research is needed to delineate the interplay between different plant responses to irradiance variation (light-quality vs. light-intensity) and to address the question of environmental signal transduction and transformation in the cell.

REFERENCES

1 Van Gorkom, H.J. (1974) Biochim. Biophys. Acta 347, 439-442.
2 Ke, B., Inoue, H., Babcock, G.T., Fang, Z.X., and Dolan, E. (1982) Biochim. Biophys. Acta 682, 297-306.
3 Demeter, S., Neale, P.J. and Melis, A. (1987) FEBS Lett. 214, 370-374.
4 Hiyama, T. and Ke, B. (1972) Biochim. Biophys. Acta 267, 160-171.
5 Melis, A. and Brown, J.S. (1980) Proc. Natl. Acad. Sci. USA 77, 4712-4716
6 Melis, A. and Harvey, G.W. (1981) Biochim. Biophys. Acta 637, 138-145
7 Melis, A. and Anderson, J.M. (1983) Biochim. Biophys. Acta 724, 473-484
8 Kawamura, M., Mimuro, M. and Fujita, Y. (1979) Plant and Cell Physiol. 20, 697-705.
9 Myers, J., Graham, J.R. and Wang, R.T. (1980) Plant Physiol. 66, 1144-1149.
10 Manodori, A., Alhadeff, M., Glazer, A. and Melis, A. (1984) Arch. Microbiol. 139, 117-123
11 Melis, A., Manodori, A., Glick, R.E., Ghirardi, M.L., McCauley S.W. and Neale, P.J. (1985) Physiol. Veg. 23, 757-765
12 Ghirardi, M.L., McCauley, S.W. and Melis, A. (1986) Biochim. Biophys. Acta 851, 331-339.
13 Thielen, A.P.G.M. and Van Gorkom, H.J. (1981) Biochim. Biophys. Acta, 635, 111-120
14 Lam, E., Baltimore, B., Ortiz, W., Chollar, S., Melis, A. and Malkin, R. (1983) Biochim. Biophys. Acta 724, 201-211
15 Anderson, J.M., Brown, J.S., Lam, E. and Malkin, R. (1983) Photochem. Photobiol. 38, 205-210

16   Okabe, K., Schmid, G.H., and Straub, J. (1977) Plant Physiol.
     60, 150-156
17   Eskins, K., Delmastro, D. and Harris, L. (1983) Plant Physiol.
     73, 51-55
18   Ghirardi, M.L. and Melis, A. (1988) Biochim. Biophys. Acta 932,
     130-137
19   Abadia, J., Glick, R.E., Taylor, S.E., Terry, N. and Melis, A.
     (1985) Plant Physiol. 79, 872-878.
20   Greene, B.A., Staehelin, L.A. and Melis, A. (1988) Plant
     Physiol. 87, 365-370
21   Melis, A. (1984) Cell. Biochem. 24, 271-285.
22   Fujita, Y., Ohki, K. and Murakami, A. (1985) Plant Cell Physiol.
     26, 1541-1548
23   Manodori, A. and Melis, A. (1986) Plant Physiol. 82, 185-189
24   Glick, R.E., Larsson, U.K. and Melis, A. (1987) In, Progress in
     Photosynthesis Research, Biggins, J. (ed.), Vol. II, 253-256,
     Martinus Nijhoff Publishers, The Netherlands
25   Allen, J.F., Mullineaux, C.W., Sanders, C.E. and Melis, A.
     (1989) Photosynth. Res., in press
26   Wang, R.T. and Myers, J. (1974) Biochim. Biophys. Acta 347,
     134-140
27   Bjorkman, O., Boardman, N.K., Anderson, J.M., Thorne, S.W.,
     Goodchild, D.J. and Pyliotis, N.A. (1972) Carnegie Inst.
     Yearbook 71, 115-135
28   Boardman, N.K., Anderson, J.M., Bjorkman, O., Goodchild, D.J.,
     Grimme, L.H. and Thorne, S.W. (1974) Portug. Acta Biol. 14,
     213-236
29   Ley, A.C. and Mauzerall, D.C. (1982) Biochim. Biophys. Acta 680,
     95-106.
30   Wilhelm, C. and Wild, A. (1984) Plant Physiol. 115, 125-135
31   Malkin, S. and Fork, D.C. (1981) Plant Physiol. 67, 580-583
32   Neale, P.J. and Melis, A. (1986) J. Phycol. 22, 531-538
33   Smith, B.M. and Melis, A. (1988) Plant Cell Physiol. 29, 761-769
34   Lichtenthaler, H.K., Kuhn, G., Prenzel, U., Buschmann, C. and
     Meier, D. (1981) Z. Naturforsch. 37c, 464-475
35   Leong, T.-A., Anderson, J.M. (1984) Photosyn. Res. 5, 105-115
36   Larsson, U.K., Anderson, J.M., Andersson, B. (1987) Biochim.
     Biophys. Acta 894, 69-75
37   Wild, A., Hopfner, M., Rühle, W. and Richter, M. (1986) Z.
     Naturforsch. 41, 597-603
38   Anderson, J.M. (1986) Ann. Rev. Plant Physiol. 37, 93-136
39   Falkowski, P., Owens, T., Ley, A. and Mauzerall, D. (1981) Plant
     Physiol. 68, 969-973
40   Sukenik, A., Bennett, J. and Falkowski, P. (1987) Biochim.
     Biophys. Acta 891, 205-215
41   Glick, R.E., McCauley, S.W., Gruissem, W. and Melis, A. (1986)
     Proc. Natl. Acad. Sci. USA 83, 4287-4291
42   Deng, X.W., Tonkyn, J.C., Peter, G., Thornber, J.P. and
     Gruissem, W. (1989) The Plant Cell 1, 645-654
43   Glazer, A.N. and Melis, A. (1987) Annu. Rev. Plant Physiol. 38,
     11-45.

FACTORS DETERMINING LIGHT RESPONSE CHARACTERISTICS OF LEAF PHOTOSYNTHESIS

ICHIRO TERASHIMA[1] and AKIO TAKENAKA[2], Department of Botany, Faculty of Science, University of Tokyo, Hongo, Bunkyo-ku, TOKYO 113, JAPAN[1] and National Institute for Environmental Studies, Onogawa, Tsukuba, IBARAKI 305, JAPAN[2]

1. INTRODUCTION

A light response curve of leaf photosynthesis can be divided into four regions; (i) A part below the inflexion of the Kok effect (Kok effect region), (ii) a linear part, the slope of which is proportional to the quantum yield of photosynthesis (quantum yield region), (iii) a non-linear part above the initial slope but below the light saturation (transitional region) and (iv) the light-saturated region (1).

In this paper, we consider factors controlling photosynthetic parameters characterising these regions, in particular, focusing on those for transitional and the light-saturated regions. Since factors responsible for the Kok effect are still very ambiguous (2), this region is not dealt with.

2. QUANTUM YIELD REGION

The slope of the initial linear part of the light response curve (quantum yield region) is proportional to both absorptance of a leaf and the quantum yield. Absorptance of a leaf is affected by the pigment content and the structure of the leaf tissues. Normally, healthy green leaves absorb 75 to 95% of incident quanta of white light.

The quantum yield is expressed as the number of moles of O_2 evolved (or CO_2 fixed) per mole absorbed quanta of photosynthetically active radiation (400-700 nm). Obviously the quantum yield is constrained by biophysical/biochemical processes. Healthy leaves of C_3 plants show almost identical quantum yields for O_2 evolution at a saturating partial pressure of CO_2, irrespective of taxa and habitats of the materials, which approach the theoretical maximum of around 0.11 mol O_2 mol^{-1} absorbed quanta (2,3). Compared with this, the quantum yield is considerably lower at the CO_2 partial pressure of around 350 µbar due to photorespiration. Nevertheless, variation in the quantum yield among various C_3 plants remains small also at this CO_2 partial pressure. Thus, initial slopes of the light response curves are not markedly different among "healthy" C_3 plants.

3. TRANSITIONAL REGION

Provided that the cost of sharpening the transitional region is not substantial, the leaf having a light response curve with a sharper transitional region is advantageous in terms of raising photosynthetic productivity (4,5). Even though the light response curve of individual chloroplasts is claimed to be very sharp (1,6), the transition at the whole leaf level is not necessarily sharp. Since there is a marked gradient of light environment across a leaf, a situation can arise in which chloroplasts near the irradiated side of the leaf are light-saturated, while those near the opposite side require more light to be saturated. This causes a much blunter transitional region in the light response curve of photosynthesis in the whole leaf as compared with that of individual chloroplasts. However, "structural" heterogeneities have been found in light absorption characteristics and in the photosynthetic properties of chloroplasts, both of which would contribute to a sharper transition. The in situ absorption coefficient of chlorophyll is greater in spongy tissue than in palisade tissue (4,7). This is primarily due to the fact that light is scattered more intensively in spongy tissue than in palisade tissue, and the scattering increases the length of light-path (7). When the leaf is irradiated from the adaxial side, therefore, light absorption in palisade tissue tends to be moderated, while light absorption in spongy tissue is enhanced. This situation results in more homogeneous light environment across the leaf than would otherwise occur.

However, in spite of this moderating effect, the actual light gradient in the leaf is still marked (4,8,9). On a chlorophyll basis, chloroplasts in the uppermost layer of mesophyll absorb more light than those in the lowermost layer. Photosynthetic properties of chloroplasts appear to be adjusted to such an intra-leaf gradient of light environment : Chloroplasts in the uppermost layer of mesophyll are the most sun-type ones with high light-saturated rate, and with the increase in distance from the adaxial surface, they gradually change into shade-type ones with lower light-saturated rate (5,10-12).

It has long been known that the shape of the light response curves of dorsiventral leaves varies depending on whether the leaves are irradiated from the adaxial (upper) side or from the abaxial (lower) side (13-17). When a leaf is irradiated from the abaxial side, which rarely occurs in nature, light is absorbed mainly by spongy tissue chloroplasts, which are saturated at low light. On the other hand, palisade tissue chloroplasts with high light-saturated rate are irradiated with diminished light filtered through the spongy tissue, resulting in a very blunt transitional region (see Fig. 1).

Isobilateral dicot leaves, conifer needles, and many monocot leaves, receive light on both surfaces. The light response curves of photosynthesis of such leaves have sharper transition when the leaves are irradiated from both sides simultaneously than when irradiated unilaterally (18-20). This may also be ascribed to the differentiation of tissues in terms of optical properties and the gradient in properties of chloroplasts. Thus, it can be generalised that the leaf is constructed so as to maximise the sharpness of the transient region under natural light conditions.

The gradient in properties of chloroplasts is formed in response to the intra-leaf light gradient. For example, artificial irradiation of the first leaves of Glycine max (L.) Merrill from the abaxial side for 8 days during the period of leaf expansion could induce a completely reversed gradient in chloroplast properties (5,21).

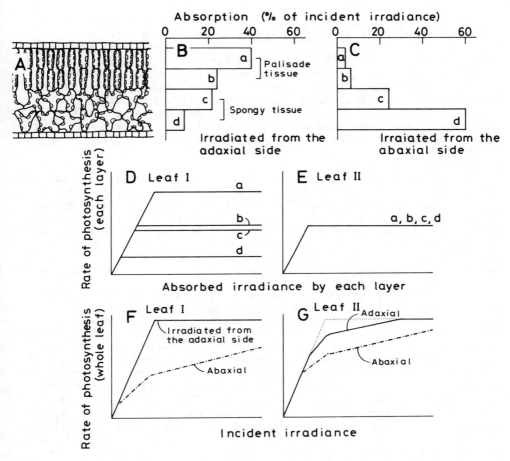

FIGURE 1. Light response curves of two model leaves I and II. Mesophyll
of these leaves are composed of four cell layers, each of which contains
an equal amount of chlorophyll. Among these four layers, two adaxial
ones form palisade tissue, and two abaxial ones spongy tissue. A layer
in palisade tissue absorbs 40% of available light while a layer in
spongy tissue absorbs 60%. A) A diagram of a cross-sectional view of a
dorsiventral leaf. B) The gradient of light absorption when these model
leaves are irradiated from the adaxial sides. C) The gradient of light
absorption when these leaves are irradiated from the abaxial sides. D)
Light response curves of respective layers in the model leaf I. Four
light response curves, expressed on a basis of absorbed irradiance, have
identical initial slopes but different light saturated rates. The ratio
of light-saturated rates is identical with the ratio of light absorption
among layers shown in B. E) Light response curves for four layers are
identical in the model leaf II. F) Light response curves of the model
leaf I. G) Light response curves of the model leaf II.

The light environments to which chloroplasts can be adjusted are limited. In leaves of <u>Spinacia oleracea</u> L. grown under 15% of sun light, the number of thylakoids per granum was around 8 throughout the leaf (22), indicating that in sun plants the intra-leaf gradient of properties of chloroplasts is not formed under such low light conditions. As expected, in these leaves, two light response curves obtained by irradiation from the adaxial and abaxial sides were similar to each other and blunt (10). In a shade tolerant plant, <u>Alocasia macrorrhiza</u> (L.) G. Don, the intra-leaf gradient was still evident even when leaves were grown under irradiance at 10 μmol quanta m^{-2} s^{-1} (23).

4. LIGHT-SATURATED REGION

Steady state level of photosynthesis under saturating light has been postulated to be limited by RuBP carboxylation, RuBP regeneration, or triose-phosphate utilization (24). At a usual ambient partial pressure of CO_2, photosynthesis is, in most cases, limited by RuBP carboxylation. At a saturating partial pressure of CO_2, it is usually RuBP regeneration process that limits photosynthesis. However, under certain conditions, triose-phosphate utilization process limits photosynthesis in both CO_2 regimes. Thus, the light-saturated rates would potentially be limited by several key processes.

There are good correlations between light-saturated photosynthetic rate of leaves and amounts and/or activities of photosynthetic components such as RuBP carboxylase (rubisco), thylakoid ATPase and cytochrome $\underline{f}$. Especially, there are many reports claiming a very strong linear correlation between the amount or "extractable" activity of rubisco and light saturated photosynthetic rate measured at an ambient CO_2 partial pressure of ca. 350 μbar (for a review, see 25). However, careful re-examination of such relationships often reveals curvilinear relationships rather than linear ones (25). This may be attributed to the fact that chloroplasts containing large amounts of rubisco tend to be fat. It is expected that the path for the diffusion of CO_2 is longer and the the partial pressure of CO_2 at the carboxylation site is lower in fat chloroplasts than in thin chloroplasts (22,26). Although the available data are limited, activity of thylakoid ATPase and the amount of cytochrome $\underline{f}$ appear to be more linearly correlated with light-saturated rate of photosynthesis than the amount or extractable activity of rubisco.

Environmental stresses also affect the light-saturated rate of leaf photosynthesis. Many stress factors reduce photosynthesis through stomatal closure, first, and then gradually cause damages to photosynthetic machinery in mesophyll. Chronic damages to photosynthetic machinery are often observed in nature (17).

5. OPTIMAL LIGHT-SATURATED RATE (= PHOTOSYNTHETIC CAPACITY) IN TERMS OF UTILISING A VARIABLE LIGHT ENVIRONMENT

In the previous sections, we have seen that light response curves of "healthy" leaves have similar initial slopes and similar sharpnesses, when the leaves are irradiated appropriately. This is quite reasonable because the higher the quantum yield and the sharper the transition are, the more efficient the leaf photosynthesis is, provided that there are no substantial costs of raising these values. On the other hand, the photosynthetic capacity of a leaf is known to vary over a wide range, i.e., by nearly two orders of magnitude (27,28). It varies not only among species, but also within individual species. Generally, plants adapted or acclimated to habitats with environmental conditions favorable for growth show high photosynthetic capacity. Such a correlation between photosynthetic capacity and habitat conditions suggests that the environmental conditions surrounding the plant determine the leaf photosynthetic capacity.

A conceptual framework of cost–benefit relations of photosynthetic capacity has been presented (27). It is argued that low photosynthetic capacity is advantageous in a resource-poor environment because high investment into photosynthetic systems would not be paid back due to the resource limitation. However, the specific characteristics of the cost and benefit as functions of the photosynthetic capacity still remain conjectural (29).

Here, we present a simple mathematical model to investigate the optimal photosynthetic capacity of a leaf maximising net photosynthetic production under variable light conditions (30). The model predicts the optimal photosynthetic capacity as a function of the relative frequency distribution of photon irradiance on a leaf.

In the present model, all income and expenditure of energy and materials are converted into the common currency, carbon flow. The cost to construct and maintain a leaf and the benefit it earns are averaged over the leaf lifetime and expressed as the flow of carbon per unit leaf area per unit time.

Let the light response curve of gross photosynthetic rate ($\underline{P}$) of a leaf be represented by the Blackman limiting-factor response curve, consisting of two linear parts, quantum yield and light-saturated regions. Light-saturated rate of photosynthesis, which we define as the photosynthetic capacity in the present model, is designated as $\underline{P}_{max}$ and the slope of the light response curve at the quantum yield region, ϕ. The value of $\underline{I}$, photon irradiance, at the breaking point of the curve is designated as $\underline{I}_s$ and given by $\underline{I}_s = \underline{P}_{max}/\phi$.

As description of temporally variable light environment, let us consider the relative frequency distribution of photon irradiance on a leaf during its lifetime. Let $\underline{F}(\underline{I})$ be the normalised cumulative distribution function of $\underline{I}$. By definition, $\underline{F}(0)$ represents relative time duration of night and $\underline{F}(\infty) = 1$. The benefit a leaf obtains, or the integration of gross photosynthesis averaged over the leaf lifetime, under given light environment, $\underline{F}(\underline{I})$, is given by

$$\underline{A}_g = \int_0^\infty \underline{P}(\underline{I})\, \underline{F}'(\underline{I})\, d\underline{I} \qquad (i)$$

where $\underline{A}_g$ is the gross photosynthesis and $\underline{F}'(\underline{I})$, the derivative function of $\underline{F}(\underline{I})$. Taking the derivative of $\underline{A}_g$ with respect to $\underline{P}_{max}$, we obtain

$$d\underline{A}_g/d\underline{P}_{max} = 1 - \underline{F}(\underline{I}_s) \qquad (ii)$$

(see 30 for details).

The right side of equation (ii) is the relative time duration when

$I > I_s$, i.e., P is light-saturated. Because I_s gets larger with increasing P_{max}, the time duration when $I > I_s$ decreases with increasing P_{max}. Thus, dependency of A_g on P_{max} is convex as shown in Fig. 2.

Consider the cost, C, to construct and maintain a leaf averaged over its lifetime. It is generally assumed that a leaf with a high photosynthetic capacity requires large construction and maintenance costs (24,28,29). Let C be proportional to P_{max} for simplicity (Fig. 2) and r denote C/P_{max} ratio ($r > 0$).

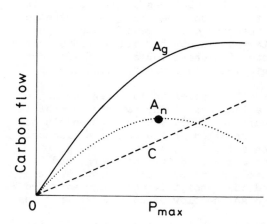

FIGURE 2. Schematic illustration of the dependencies of gross photosynthesis (A_g), cost(C) and net photosynthesis (A_n) on P_{max}. C increases linearly with P_{max}, while the increase of A_g with P_{max} is convex. A_g reaches the plateau when the light saturation point of photosynthesis gets to the peak irradiance. The maximum A_n (●) is realised when the difference between A_g and C is maximal.

Let us define net gain a leaf obtains during its lifetime as the averaged net photosynthetic production of a leaf, which is denoted by A_n. It is the difference between benefit (A_g) and cost (C). Since dependency of A_g on P_{max} is convex while C is a linear function of P_{max}, there would be an optimal P_{max} maximising A_n, as illustrated in Fig. 2. The derivative of A_n with respect to P_{max} is given by

$$dA_n/dP_{max} = dA_g/dP_{max} - dC/dP_{max}$$

$$= 1 - F(I_s) - r. \qquad \text{(iii)}$$

The maximum A_n is realised when $dA_n/dP_{max} = 0$, or,

$$1 - F(I_s) = r. \qquad \text{(iv)}$$

Equation (iv) shows that photosynthesis of a leaf with the optimal P_{max} is light-saturated for r fraction of time, because $1 - F(I_s)$ represents the relative time duration when the leaf is in the light-saturated condition. Noting that P_{max} is proportional to I_s, we can conclude from the above consideration that high photon irradiance during a large fraction of the total time favours high photosynthetic capacity, and low photosynthetic capacity is favoured if high photon irradiance occurs for only a small fraction of time. In other words, the relative frequency of I rather than its average or peak irradiance was shown to be the most critical feature of the light regime affecting the optimal photosynthetic capacity.

Another prediction drawn from the present model is the decrease in the optimal P_{max} with the increment of r: Plants would have lower photosynthetic capacity in habitats where the environmental constraints make the leaf cost higher. Nutrient deficiencies, drought, and high predation pressure can increase the cost to construct and maintain a leaf (27,32,33). The low photosynthetic capacities found in plants growing under nutrient-poor conditions (27,33) agree with the above prediction. For detailed discussion using this model, see (30).

6. PHOTOSYNTHETIC RESPONSES TO TEMPORAL FLUCTUATION OF LIGHT

In the previous sections, we have focused on photosynthetic characteristics obtained under steady-state light conditions. However, in nature, light environments are dynamically fluctuating and processes such as photosynthetic induction, responses of stomata and responses to very fast change in irradiance should be also sought. Recently, detailed analyses of photosynthetic response to brief sunflecks in shade plants have been made (34-37). For example, an understorey plant in tropical rain forest, _Alocasia macrorrhiza_ grown in the shade can fix up to 60% more CO_2 in response to a 5 s light fleck than would be predicted from measurements of steady state rates of photosynthesis. However, the fixation of CO_2 in response to 5 s light fleck in _A. macrorrhiza_ plants grown under high-light was much closer to the predicted values (35,37).

Detailed analyses of metabolites of photosynthesis revealed that in shade plants the build-up of triose-phosphate rather than RuBP during the light-fleck prevents inhibition of electron transport. Utilisation of the triose-phosphate for postillumination CO_2 fixation would require significant postillumination ATP synthesis. It is hypothesised that the extensive grana stacking and large intrathylakoid space relative to exposed surface of thylakoids to stroma could be an important contributing factor to the postillumination ATP formation (34). This may be the adaptive significance of conspicuous grana stacking in shade plants.

We thank Professor S. Katoh for his critical reading of the manuscript.

REFERENCES
1 Leverenz, J.W. (1987) Physiol. Plant. 71, 20-29
2 Walker, D.A. (1988) The Use of the Oxygen Electrode and Fluorescence Probes in Simple Measurements of Photosynthesis, 2nd ed., pp.188, University of Sheffield, Sheffield
3 Björkman, O. and Demmig, B. (1987) Planta 170, 489-504
4 Terashima, I. and Saeki, T. (1985) Ann. Bot. 56, 489-499
5 Terashima, I. and Takenaka, A. (1986) in Biological Control of Photosynthesis (Marcelle, R., Clijsters, H. and Van Poucke, M. eds.), pp.219-230, Martinus Nijhoff, Dordrecht
6 Leverenz, J.W.(1988) Physiol. Plant. 74, 332-341
7 Terashima, I. and Saeki, T. (1983) Plant Cell Physiol. 24, 1493-1501

8 Vogelmann, T.C. (1986) in Photomorphogenesis in Plants (Kendrick, R.E. and Kronenberg, G.H.M., eds.), pp. 307-337, Martinus Nijhoff, Dordrecht

9 Knapp, A.K., Vogelmann, T.C., McClean, T.M. and Smith, W.K. (1988) Plant Cell Environ. 11, 257-263

10 Terashima, I. (1989) in Photosynthesis (Briggs, W. ed.) Alan R. Liss, New York, in press

11 Terashima, I. and Inoue, Y. (1985) Plant Cell Physiol. 26, 781-785

12 Anderson, J.M. (1986) Annu. Rev. Plant Physiol. 37, 93-136

13 Moss, D.N. (1964) Crop Sci. 4, 131-136

14 Oya, V.N. and Laisk, A.Kh. (1976) Sov. Plant Physiol. 23, 381-386

15 Terashima, I. (1986) J. Exp. Bot. 37, 399-405

16 Pospíšilová, J. and Solárová, J. (1987) Photosynthetica 21, 349-356

17 Adams, W.W.III., Terashima, I., Brugnoli, E. and Demmig, B. (1988) Plant Cell Environ. 11, 173-181

18 Kirschbaum, M.U.F. (1987) in Progress in Photosynthesis Research (Biggins, J., ed.), Vol. IV., pp.IV 5:261-264, Martinus Nijhoff, Dordrecht

19 Leverenz, J.W. and Jarvis, P.G. (1979) J. Appl. Ecol. 16, 919-932

20 Wong, S.C., Cowan, I.R. and Farquhar, G.D. (1985) Plant Physiol. 78, 826-829

21 Terashima, I., Sakaguchi, S. and Hara, N. (1986) Plant Cell Physiol. 27, 1023-1031

22 Terashima, I. and Evans, J.R. (1987) Plant Cell Physiol. 29, 143-155

23 Chow, W.S., Qian, L., Goodchild, D.J. and Anderson, J.M. (1988) Aust. J. Plant Physiol. 15, 107-122

24 Sharkey, T.D. (1985) Bot. Rev. 51, 53-105

25 Evans, J.R. (1989) Oecologia 78, 9-19

26 Evans, J.R. and Terashima, I. (1988) Plant Cell Physiol. 29, 157-165

27 Mooney, H.A. and Gulmon, S.L. (1979) in Topics in Plant Population Biology (Solbrig, O.T., Jain, S., Johnson, G.B. and Raven, P.H., eds.) pp. 316-337. Columbia Univ. Press, New York

28 Larcher, W. (1983) Physiological Plant Ecology, pp. 252, Springer, Berlin

29 Field, C. and Mooney, H.A. (1986) in On the Economy of Plant Form and Function (Givnish, T.J., ed.) pp. 22-55. Cambridge Univ. Press, Cambridge

30 Takenaka, A. (1989) J. Theor. Biol. in press

31 Mooney, H.A. and Gulmon, S.L. (1982) BioSci. 32, 198-206

32 Chapin, F.S. III, Bloom, A.J., Field, C.B. and Waring, R.H. (1987) BioSci. 37, 49-57

33 Pearcy, R.W., Björkman, O., Caldwell, M.M., Keeley, J.E., Monson, R.K. and Strain, B.R. (1987) BioSci. 37, 21-29

34 Sharkey, T.D., Seemann, J.R. and Pearcy, R.W. (1986) Plant Physiol. 82, 1063-1068

35 Pearcy, R.W. (1988) Aust. J. Plant Physiol. 15, 223-238

36 Kirschbaum, M.U.F. and Pearcy, R.W. (1988) Planta 174, 527-533

37 Chazdon, R.L. (1988) in Advances in Ecological Research (Begon, M., Fitter, A.H., Ford, E.D. and Macfadyen, A., eds.), Vol. 18, pp. 1-63, Academic Press, London

PHYSIOLOGICAL CONTROL OF PRIMARY PHOTOCHEMICAL ENERGY CONVERSION IN
HIGHER PLANTS.

ENGELBERT WEIS, DOROTHEA LECHTENBERG & ANJA KRIEGER,
Botanisches Institut, Univ. Düsseldorf, D-4000 Düsseldorf, FRG

ABSTRACT

*During light-saturated photosynthesis electron transport to PSI
is controlled by the ΔpH ('photosynthetic control'). Accumulation
of oxidized PSI centers (P_{700}^{+}) which act as efficient quenchers
for singlet excited states is a consequence of this control. Photosynthetic control is accompanied by 'down-regulation' of PSII (high
energy quenching). The relationship between ΔpH-dependent and redox-
dependent control of light-reactions and its significance for
metabolic regulation of photosynthesis will be discussed.*

1.   INTRODUCTION

Upon absorption of light singlet excited states are created in the
pigment antennae system. When excitons reach an 'open' reaction
center of either PSI or PSII, excitation energy is used for a
primary photochemical process. It is generally accepted that about
one light quantum is consumed for each primary charge separation and
about 9.5 quanta are absorbed per evolved O_2 during steady state
photosynthesis in intact C3 plants [1]. It indicates that during
light-limited photosynthesis *in vivo* each photoreaction operates
close to the maximum of its theoretical quantum efficiency.
Obviously, this is only possible if the stable products of light
reactions, ATP and NADPH+H$^+$ are efficiently consumed by metabolic
reactions and electron transport reactions are well displaced from
its thermodynamic equilibrium [2]. Light dependent *ferredoxin-
thioredoxin* activation of enzymes [3] provides efficient *feed-
forward* control to adjust the rate of metabolic reactions to the
potential rate of energy conversion at the two photosystems.

Since photochemical reactions are exergonic processes large gradients of its primary products would be built up when the rate of
electronic excitation exceeds that of electron consumption by
biochemical reactions. Therefore, absorption of light energy not
used by biochemical reactions would perturb the photosynthetic
metabolism. Under extreme conditions, overexcitation of pigment
systems may even cause irregular photodynamic side reactions and
photooxidative damage to pigment systems [10]. Thus, *feedback*
mechanisms are expected to adjust the potential rate of primary
photochemical energy conversion to the rate of biochemical reactions. Recent work suggests that plants have actually developed very

M. Baltscheffsky (ed.), Current Research in Photosynthesis, Vol. IV, 307–312.
© 1990 *Kluwer Academic Publishers. Printed in the Netherlands.*

efficient control mechanisms to 'quench' excess singlet excited
states in the pigment system *via* pathways for non-photochemical and
non-radiative de-excitation [4,5,6,7,8,9, and others].

In this paper, we will discuss mechanisms of ΔpH-dependent control
of PS*I* and PS*II* and we present a quantitative analysis of the
contribution of 'quenching' processes to the overall control of
steady state photosynthesis *in vivo*. We will also discuss the
relationship between ΔpH-dependent feedback control of light-
reactions and thioredoxin-dependent 'light-activation' of enzymes.

2.   MATERIALS AND METHODS

Gas exchange of attached leaves of *Phaseolus vulgaris*, steady state
chlorophyll fluorescence and 820 nm absorbance changes (monitoring
the redox-state of P_{700}) were measured simultaneously (using a
pulse-modulated PAM fluorimeter/photometer from Walz), basically as
described in [4,5,6]. To keep the rate of photorespiration low,
O_2 in the atmosphere was reduced to 2% and net photosynthetic
electron transport within a leaf was calculated from gas exchange.

3.   RESULTS AND DISCUSSION

Control of PS*I* and thioredoxin-dependent enzyme activation.

When photosynthesis in leaves or intact chloroplasts is limited by
light, most reaction centers of PS*I* and PS*II* are in the photochemically active ('open') form [4-6], while 'reductive' enzyme activation (*via* the thioredoxin system) already saturates at very low
light, far below light-saturation of electron transport [11].
In principle, the thioredoxin system competes for electrons with
the ferredoxin-NADP-reductase (FNR) reaction, but also, to some
extent, with other electron consuming reactions such as NO_2^--
reduction and (pseudo)cyclic reactions. Efficient distribution of
electrons to the thioredoxin-system may require regulation of

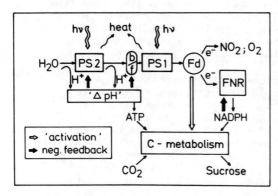

*Figure 1: Scheme of
feedback control of light-
dependent reaction and of
ferredoxin-thioredoxin-
dependent 'light-acti-
vation of the carbon
metabolis. Explanations
are given in the text.*

electron transfer from PSI to NADP. Since ferredoxin has a fairly
negative redox potential, significant electron-'backpressure' to
ferredoxin is unlikely to occur unless the NADPH/NADP ratio is very
high. However, there is indication that the ferredoxin-NADP-reductase (FNR), the most important 'electron gate' between PSI and
the stroma is efficiently controlled by allosteric feedback: NADPH
inhibits the FNR activity at low concentration (50% inhibition at
about 0.1 mM NADPH; [11]). It suggest that efficient electron flux
from PSI to NADP is only possible if the NADPH/NADP ratio is low.
When NADPH begins to pile up (because enzymes in the stroma are not
activated or ATP is in deficit) it feeds back and 'closes' the
electron gate through the FNR (by allosteric inhibition), before the
NADP-pool is fully reduced. Electrons are then delivered from the
'closed' ferredoxin side to the thioredoxin system (and, perhaps, to
a proton pumping cyclic reaction around PSI), which, in turn, serves
to activate NADPH-consuming reactions. As a consequence the NADPH/
NADP-ratio drops and the FNR-'gate' opens again (see also scheme,
Fig. 1). Thus, feedback control of FNR by NADPH may be regarded as a
mechanism to keep the stroma fairly oxidized and to establish an
appropriate electron 'resistance' between PSI and NADP which allows
distribution of electrons between competing pathways.

When NADPH- and ATP-consuming reactions become limiting for CO_2-
assimilation and light is in excess, the reaction center pigment of
PSI, P_{700} accumulates in the photochemically inactive, oxidized
form, P_{700}^+ (as detected by a new non-invasive optical approach)
while plastoquinone becomes more reduced [4,6,11]. This *redox-
crossover* is thought to be a consequence of pH-dependent control
of electron donation to PSI: When the acidification of the inner-
thylakoid space exceeds a certain threshold, re-oxidation of reduced
plastoquinone at the cytochrome b/f complex is inhibited and electron donation to PSI is slowed down. It has been referred to as
'photosynthetic control' (PC) [14], but its exact mechanism is not
well characterized. When PC takes place during steady state assimilation, PSI-activity is limited by a shortage of electron donation
and P_{700}^+ accumulates. Because of its absorbance properties, the
radical P_{700}^+ 'traps' excitation energy from the antenna as efficiently as the photochemically active center does, but the energy
is 'quenched' by a fast non-photochemical decay process [15]. Thus
PC and related formation of P_{700}^+-centers may be regarded as a mechanism to protect PSI against formation of long-living excited
states (which may cause photodamage) and to adjust the potential
rate of PSI photochemistry to the electron demand by biochemical
reactions. As a consequence of PC the ferredoxin side of PSI is kept
oxidized, even in high light. Fig. 2 (right side) shows the
actual distribution of energy absorbed by PSI in intact leaves
between different pathways for de-excitation during different steady
state conditions. The fraction of energy consumed by net electron
transport, $\delta_s(I)$ is calculated from gas exchange and light flux.
$\delta_d(I)$ denotes the fraction of total energy absorbed by PSI which is
dissipated at P_{700}^+ ($\delta_d(I) = [P_{700}^+]/[P_{700}+P_{700}^+]$), δ_r represents

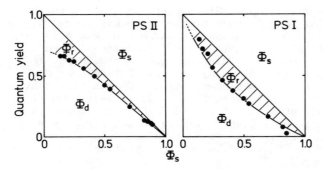

Figure 2: Distribution of energy absorbed by PSII (left) and
PSI (right) between different pathways for de-excitation. ꝗ is
a fractional coefficient (0<ꝗ<1). ꝗ$_s$ is a coefficient for
net photochemical energy consumption, obtained from a light-
response curve of CO_2 uptake (300 ppm CO_2, 2% O_2). Coefficients
for non-photochemical de-excitation, ꝗ$_d$ and ꝗ$_r$ were calculated from
fluorescence (PSII) and 820 nm change (PSI) as in refs. 6 & 11.

the 'residual' fraction of energy neither used for net electron
transport nor absorbed by P_{700}^+. It may include energy used for
(pseudo)cyclic reactions and/or energy absorbed from PSI centers
with 'closed' acceptor side (reduced ferredoxin). In any case,
ꝗ$_r$ may indicate the relative contribution of 'acceptor-side control'
of PSI. The figure demonstrates that most energy is either consumed
by net electron transport or 'quenched' at P_{700}^+-centers. Particularly when photosynthesis was strictly limited by CO_2 the coefficient ꝗ$_r$ could remain very small (< 0.1), even in high light, indicating strict donor-side limitation. ꝗ$_r$ increased, however, when
sucrose synthesis began to contribute to the overall limitation of
photosynthesis [6,11]. Despite of such variations, it is evident,
that PSI activity is mainly controlled by PC and that most quanta
not used for photosynthesis are 'quenched' by P_{700}^+-centers.

Non-balanced, excessive photosynthetic control, however, would bring
about 'overoxidation' of ferredoxin and would cause a collaps of
thioredoxin-dependent 'reductive' activation of enzymes. During CO_2-
fixation, allosteric feed-back control of FNR (see above) may help
to avoid such over-oxidation and to keep an appropriate 'electron
resistance' between ferredoxin and NADP, when photosynthetic control
is in effect (for further discussion, see [11]; see also Fig.1).

'High energy quenching' (HEQ) at PSII.

Recently, evidence has been presented that during steady state
photosynthesis energy absorbed by PSII and not used for electron
transport is dissipated via non-photochemical and non-radiative
'quenching' of excitation energy [5] and that this 'high energy

quenching', HEQ (which is reflected by quenching of fluorescence,
[16]) operates simultaneously with PC [4,6]. A model has been proposed which is based on the assumption that PS*II* can be converted
from a photochemically high efficient (high fluorescent) state,
PS*II*$_0$ to a low-efficient (low-fluorescent) 'quenching' state, PS*II*$_e$
(which operates as a non-photochemical trap), depending on the
energetic balance of the leaf, and that this conversion is mediated
by acidification of the inner thylakoid space: PS*II*$_0$ + H$^+$ <-->
PS*II*$_e$ [5,6]. The observations have been basically confirmed by
others [7.8,9,17 and others], but different suggestions about the
mechanism of HEQ have been made. In a separate paper, we discuss
that in the HEQ-state excitation energy is dissipated *via* fast internal charge recombination [12]. HEQ may be regarded as a control
process to match the rate at which electrons enter the electron
transport chain to the actual demand for electrons and to keep the
redox-system downstream to PS*II* relatively oxidized, even in high
light. Fig. 2 (left side) shows the distribution of energy absorbed
by PS*II* between different pathways for de-excitation during steady
state photosynthesis in a leaf, as calculated from electron transport and chlorophyll fluorescence (for more details of the analysis
see [6,11]. δ_d denotes the fraction of energy absorbed by PS*II* and
dissipated by HEQ, δ_r is the fraction of energy absorbed by 'closed'
centers (with reduced Q$_A$). The analysis demonstrates that over a
wide range of conditions less than 10 % of energy is absorbed by
closed centers while most energy not used for electron transport is
dissipated *via* HEQ. Obviously, during light-saturated photosynthesis, *both* photoreactions are mainly controlled by the proton
gradient, while electron backpressure and related 'closure' of
photosystems contributes to a minor extend to the overall control
(see also scheme in Fig. 1). By conversion of both photosystems to
'thermal' traps, excess excitation energy is taken away from the
photochemical path-way and the rate of primary energy conversion is
matched to the rate at which their products are consumed by
biochemical reactions.

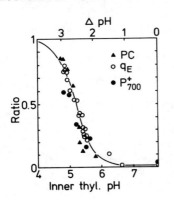

*Figure 3: Dependence of (normalized)
photosynthetic control (PC), high-
energy quenching of fluorescence, qE
and steady state level of oxidized
P700 on the pH and the pH in the
inner thylakoid space, respectively.
Methyviologogen was an electron
acceptor, light was saturating. pH
was calculated from 9-aminoacridine
fluorescence. Measurements in presence of 0.2 mM ADP and different
level of control have been obtained
by different level of Pi. PS =
controlled/uncoupled electron
transport.*

pH-dependent control of PS*I* and PS*II* and 'proton motive force'.

The main conclusion from the analysis presented here is that primary photochemical energy conversion at both photosystems is mainly controlled by the proton gradient across the thylakoid membrane. Since this gradient is thought to operate as a driving force for ATP-synthesis, it is important to understand the relationship between proton motive force (pmf) and pH-dependent control. Fig. 3 shows PC of electron transport, steady state level of P_{700}^+ and high energy quenching of fluorescence versus the ΔpH and the internal pH, respectively. It is seen that PC and related accumulation of oxidized PS*I* centers, P_{700}^+, and HEQ at PS*II* (indicated by the coefficient for non-photochemical fluorescence quenching, qE) appeared in a narrow pH-range (pH 5.5 to 4.8) while between 5.5. and 7.8 control was low, i.e., control did not appear until a ΔpH of more than 2 was built up. We could show that a ΔpH of about 2 (on the basis of the pH-determination used in this study) was sufficient to support a high rate of photophosphorylation (not shown). Apparently, pH-dependent control of light-reactions is not simply connected to the pmf. Only beyond a threshold any small increase in ΔpH (and in pmf, respectively) causes a large increase in control. Basically, the steepness of the pH-response of feedback control shown in Fig. 3 demonstrates how sensitive control mechanisms respond to a critical imbalance between energy converting and energy consuming reactions.

4.   REFERENCES

1   Demmig B & Bjorkman O 1987 PLANTA 171, 171-184
2   Heber U, Neimanis S, Dietz, KJ & Viil J 1986 BIOCHIM BIOPHYS ACTA 852, 144-155
3   Cseke C & Buchanan B 1986 BIOCHIM BIOPHYS ACTA 853, 43-63
4   Weis E, Ball T & Berry JA 1987 in: PROGRESS IN PHOTOSYNTHEIS RESEARCH, vol 2 (Biggins J, ed), pp 553-556, Martinus Nijhoff
5   Weis E & Berry JA 1987, BIOCHIM BIOPHYS ACTA 894, 198-208
6   Weis E & Lechtenberg D (1989) PHIL TRANS R SOC Lond B 323, 253
7   Horton P & Hague A 1988 BIOCHIM BIOPHYS ACTA 932, 107-115
8   Peterson RB, Sivak MN & Walker DA 1988 PLANT PHYSIOL 88, 158-163
9   Schäfer C & Björkman O 1988 PLANTA 178, 376
10 Kyle DJ 1987 in: TOPICS IN PHOTOSYNTHEIS vol 9 (Kyle DJ, Osmond CB & Arntzen CJ eds) pp 197-223, Amsterdam, Elsevier
11 Lechtenberg D, Voss B & Weis E 1989 in: PROGRESS VIIIth INTERN CONGRESS PHOTOSYNTHESIS, Stockholm, in press
12 Krieger A & Weis E 1989 in: PROGRESS VIIIth INTERN CONGRESS PHOTOSYNTHESIS, Stockholm, in press
13 Woodrow IE & Berry JA 1988 ANN REV PLANT PHYSIOL 39, 533-594
14 West KR & Wiskich JT 1968 BIOCHEM J 109, 533-594
15 Nuijs AM, Shuvalov VA, von Gorkom HJ, Plijter JJ & Duysens LNM 1986 BIOCHIM BIOPHYS ACTA 850, 310-318
16 Krause GH, Vernotte C & Briantais J-M 1982, BIOCHIM BIOPHYS ACTA 679, 116-124
17 Krause GH, Laasch H & Weis E 1988 PL PHYSIOL BIOCHEM 26, 445-452

TRANS–Δ^3–HEXADECENOIC ACID, LHCII AND LOW TEMPERATURE DEVELOPMENT IN
HERBACEOUS PLANTS

N.P.A. Huner, M. Krol, S. Boese, V. Hurry, Dept. of Plant Science,
University of Western Ontario, London, Canada N6A 5B7, J.P. Williams,
Botany Dept., University of Toronto, Toronto, Canada M5S 1A1 and G.
Oquist, Dept. of Plant Physiology, University of Umea, Sweden S-90187.

1. INTRODUCTION

    For cold tolerant herbaceous plants it has been documented that
the capacity to exhibit maximum low temperature tolerance requires
prolonged exposure of seedlings to low, non-freezing temperatures
(0C-5C)(1,2). Pre-exposure to a low temperature regime induces a cold
hardened state which imparts a particular level of freezing resistance
to the plant (Fig. 1).

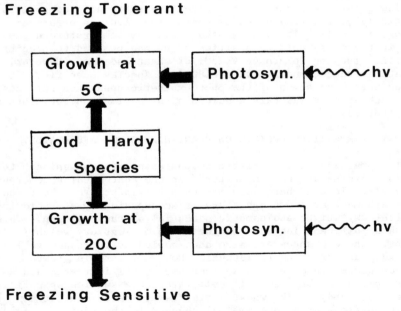

FIGURE 1.   A generalized scheme to illustrate the effect of growth
            temperature on the development of freezing tolerance in
            cereals.

M. Baltscheffsky (ed.), Current Research in Photosynthesis, Vol. IV, 313–320.
© 1990 *Kluwer Academic Publishers. Printed in the Netherlands.*

The extent of freezing tolerance acquired during this time is dependent upon many factors such as the temperature regime to which the seedlings have been exposed, the time of exposure to that low temperature, photoperiod, light intensity as well as the genetic potential of the plant species or cultivar to cold hardening in response to growth and development at the low temperature (1,2). Thus, for cold tolerant herbaceous plants such as rye, wheat, spinach and pea growth and development at low temperature is a prerequisite for the expression of maximum freezing resistance. Since photosynthesis provides the energy for this growth and development, my lab has been interested in understanding the effects of prolonged exposure to growth and development on the structure and function of the photosynthetic apparatus. The primary goal has been to determine to what extent a low temperature induced limitation on the photosynthetic process may limit the cold tolerance and the subsequent winter survival of the plant.

Data are presented which indicate that cold hardy cereals are more resistant than non hardy cereals to inhibition of photosynthesis incurred upon growth and development at low temperature. Ultrastructural as well as biochemical data are presented which indicate that cold hardy monocots modulate the organization of PSII-LHCII units in response to growth temperature with no changes in the gross pigment and polypeptide composition or content. Although lipid content is not affected, low growth temperature does alter the fatty acid composition of phosphatidylglycerol (PG) which is correlated with the organizational change in LHCII. It is shown that this low temperature dependent change in the fatty acid composition of PG can be used to predict accurately the freezing tolerance (LT50) of wheat and rye. However, low temperature induced modulation of LHCII is species specific. It is suggested that modulation of the photosynthetic apparatus reflects, in part, a mechanism to maintain conditions for optimal photosynthesis at low temperature.

2. LOW GROWTH TEMPERATURE EFFECTS ON PLANT MORPHOLOGY AND ANATOMY

Table 1 summarizes characteristic responses of rye and spinach to growth at low cold hardening temperatures at the anatomical and morphological levels. In cold hardy species such as winter rye, wheat and spinach, development at low temperature is accompanied by a 3-fold increase in leaf dry weight and osmotic potential of the cell sap. This results in a significant increase in the ratio of leaf dry weight/fresh weight. These changes are also accompanied by increases in leaf thickness and plant freezing resistance. However, certain growth responses to low temperature such as an increase in Chl/leaf area and an increase in the number of mesophyll cell layers are species specific. In contrast, non hardy spring wheat varieties typically exhibit a reduction in Chl/leaf area, and minimal changes in the ratio of leaf dry weight/fresh weight and freezing tolerance (LT50 = -5 to -7C).

TABLE 1. Summary of effects of low growth temperature on leaf morphology, anatomy and physiology.

Characteristic	Rye	Spinach
Dry wt/area	3X increase	3X increase
Leaf thickness	1.5X increase	1.5X increase
Mesophyll layers	no change	increase
Osmotic potential	2X increase	2X increase
Chl/leaf area	1.4X increase	no change
LT50	increase from -4C to -29C	increase from -3C to -9C

3. SUSCEPTIBILITY TO LOW TEMPERATURE INDUCED INHIBITION OF PHOTOSYNTHESIS

Do cold hardy and nonhardy cereals exhibit a differential susceptibility to low temperature induced inhibition of photosynthesis? In vivo room temperature fluorescence can be used as an indicator of photoinhibitory damage (3). Fv/Fm can be used to assess damage to PSII (4,5). Recently, it was shown that changes in Fv/Fm are directly proportional to changes in the apparent quantum yield for O_2 evolution in rye leaves (6). Upon exposure of RNH plants to successive increases in light intensity at 5C, the Fv/Fm decreased by 90% (Table 2). In contrast, the Fv/Fm decreased by only 35% when RH plants were exposed to the same photoinhibitory regime at 5C. No significant decrease in the Fv/Fm was observed when either RH or RNH plants were exposed to the same increase in light intensity at 25C. Thus, rye appears to become resistant to low temperature induced photoinhibition after growth to 5C. Similar results have been reported for cold

TABLE 2. Effect of exposure of RH and RNH plants to light at 5C on in vivo Fv/Fm.

Light Intensity (umol m^{-2} s^{-1})	Exposure Time (h)	Fv/Fm	
		RH	RNH
Control		0.61	0.72
100	18	0.69	0.70
230	24	0.60	0.59
400	74	0.40	0.06

hardened and nonhardened spinach (5). However, nonhardy cereals such as barley did not exhibit the capacity to increase resistance to low temperature induced photoinhibition upon growth at low temperature (6). In addition, it has been shown that nonhardy spring wheats are more susceptible to low temperature induced photoinhibition than cold hardy winter wheats as measured by a reduction in the apparent quantum yield for CO_2 fixation (Hurry and Huner, unpublished). Thus, it appears that cold hardy and nonhardy species of cereals do exhibit a differential susceptibility to low temperature induced inhibition of photosynthesis.

4. EFFECTS OF GROWTH TEMPERATURE ON RYE THYLAKOID COMPOSITION AND STRUCTURE

Low temperature induced organizational changes in rye thylakoids can be detected at various levels (Table 3). First, RH thylakoids require higher osmoticum to prevent uncoupling of electron transport

TABLE 3. Summary of effects of low growth temperature on properties of rye thylakoids.

Property	Growth temperature	
	20C	5C
Chla:b	2.90 +/- .15	2.96 +/- .19
Osmotic conc. required to prevent H^+ leakage	0.4M	0.8M
77K Fluorescence (F685/F742)	1.10	1.42
$H_2O \longrightarrow MV$	90 +/- 11	158 +/- 9
$H_2O \longrightarrow DCPIP$	235 +/- 20	225 +/- 15
$DPC \longrightarrow DCPIP$	480 +/- 25	500 +/- 25
Asc/DCPIP $\longrightarrow MV$	210 +/- 16	325 +/- 11
PSI Unit Size (Chl/$P700^+$)	505 +/- 47	530 +/- 53

due to proton leakage and to protect the O_2 evolving side of PSII (7). Second, titration of RH tylakoids with nonionic detergents such as Triton X-100 or B-octylglucoside results in the differential extraction of thylakoid components compared to RNH thylakoids (8). This was observed even though the microviscosity of the bulk lipid of RH and RNH thylakoids exhibited no change based on differential scanning calorimetry, rotational correlation times of the electron spin probe 16-doxylstearic acid and fluorescence polarization of diphenylhexatriene (9).

However, differential scanning calorimetry of isolated rye thylakoids did show a significant reduction in the heat capacity of the endotherms for the denaturation of PSII-LHCII upon development at low temperature (9). Similarly, 77K fluorescence emission spectra obtained during the conversion of rye etioplasts to chloroplasts under continuous light indicated a marked increase in the F685/F724 during biogenesis at 5C compared to thylakoid biogenesis at 20C (10, Table 3). These structural alterations in RH and RNH thylakoids did not have any effect on the apparent quantum yield for PSII electron transport or light saturated rates of PSII electron transport measured at 25C as $H_2O \longrightarrow DCPIP$ or $DPC \longrightarrow DCPIP$ (11, Table 3). The observed

increase in light aturated rates of whole chain electron transport in
RH thylakoids was due to an increase in light saturated rates of DCMU
insenstive electron transport associated with PSI (11, Table 3).

Ultrastructural examination of leaf cross sections indicated that
RH chloroplasts exhibited smaller grana than RNH chloroplasts (10,
Table 4). Freeze fracture of isolated thylakoids indicated that RNH
thylakoids exhibited the typical bimodal distribution of EFs particles
whereas RH thylakoids exhibited a unimodal particle size distribution.
However, no change in particle density was observed (10, Table 4).

TABLE 4. Summary of effects of low growth temperature on rye
chloroplast ultrastructure.

Characteristic	Growth Temperature	
	20C	5C
Chloroplast dia. (um)	3.5	3.5
Thylakoids/granum	40% > 10	15% > 10
EFs particle distribution	bimodal (100A and 160A)	unimodal (136A)
EFs particles/um^2	562 +/- 100	510 +/- 98

However, these structural alterations observed in situ and in
vitro occurred with no apparent changes in the Chla:b, carotenoid
content, thylakoid protein/Chl, thylakoid lipid/Chl or the thylakoid
polypeptide complement (9,12).

PG is the major phospholipid present in thylakoid membranes (9,
13). When present in higher plant thylakoids, this and only this
phospholipid is characterized by the presence of trans-Δ^3-hexadecenoic
acid (trans-16:1) esterified to carbon-2 of the glycerol backbone
(13). Although no change in overall thylakoid lipid content was observed between RH and RNH thylakoids, growth at low, cold hardening temperatures did result in a specific, 72% lower level in the trans-16:1
content associated with PG and a concomitant increase in the hexadecenoic acid (16:0) content of PG (9). This in vivo, low growth temperature induced change in the level of trans-16:1 was directly proportional to the ratio of oligomeric LHCII: monomeric LHCII (LHCII1:
LHCII3) observed in vitro. A lower level of trans-16:1 was correlated
with a predisposition of RH thylakoids to form monomeric LHCII in
vitro compared to a predominance of the oligomeric form in RNH
thylakoids. This linear relationship between the trans-16:1 and the
in vitro organization of rye LCHII exhibited an R^2 value of 0.93 (9).
Low growth temperature did not affect the fatty acid composition of
the other major rye thylakoid lipids MGDG, DGDG, SQDG and PC (9,14).

The light dependent synthesis of trans-16:1 (10,13) was examined
during the conversion of rye etioplasts to chloroplasts at 5C and 20C
under continuous light (CL) as well as intermittent light (IML) (10,

15). It was shown that maximization of trans-16:1 content in PG was
required to observe maximum oligomeric LHCII in vitro at 20C under CL.
In contrast, thylakoid biogenesis at 5C resulted in the maintenance of
a low level of trans-16:1 and the predisposition to form monomeric
LHCII in vitro. Furthermore, IML conditions allowed the accumulation
of trans-16:1 with no accumulation of LHCII (15). Prior accumulation
of PG high in trans-16:1 in rye thylakoids enhanced the in vitro stability of oligomeric LCHII. These results are consistent with a
sequential process for the accumulation of trans-16:1 and the stabilization of rye oligomeric LHCII in vitro.

Such a strong correlation between the in vitro organization of rye
LCHII and the fatty acid composition of PG indicated that PG may be an
integral component involved in the stabilization of LCHII. This has
been supported since purified RNH and RH LCHII exhibited a 5-fold enrichment in PG (16). Although thylakoid SQDG and PC are also charged
these lipids did not exhibit any enrichment during purification. The
composition of RH and RNH LHCII differed only with respect to the
level of trans-16:1 in PG (16, Table 5). Thus, development of rye at
low temperature may modulate the organization or packing of LHCII-PSII
units within the thylakoid membrane by altering the trans-16:1 content
of PG such that, in vitro, the oligomeric form of LCHII predominates
in RNH thylakoids whereas the monomeric form predominates in RH thylakoids (16).

TABLE 5. Trans-16:1/16:0 in PG of RH and RNH preparations.

Preparation	Trans-16:1/16:0		
	RNH	RH	RH:RNH
Whole leaf Extracts	0.86	0.21	4.1
Purified Thylakoids	1.06	0.18	5.8
Purified LHCII	1.48	0.32	4.6

5. TRANS-16:1 AND FREEZING TOLERANCE

The generality of this low temperature response with respect to
trans-16:1 and LCHII organization was investigated in several cold
tolerant monocots and dicots exhibiting a range of freezing resistance
(14). Pea, spinach, broadbean (Table 6) and periwinkle (14) grown at
low temperature did not exhibit any reduction in the level of trans-
16:1 nor any change in the organization of LHCII-PSII units. In
contrast, all 8 varieties of wheat and rye examined did exhibit a
lower level of trans-16:1 after growth at 5C (14, Table 6).

More important, the extent to which these monocots could lower the
level of trans-16:1 in response to low growth temperature was correlated (R^2 = 0.95) with the freezing tolerance of rye and wheat
cultivars. In addition, those monocots which exhibited the lowest

TABLE 6. Effect of growth temperature on the trans-16:1/16:0 in some cold tolerant species.

Plant Species	Growth Temperature	
	20C	5C
Winter rye	1.0	0.21
Winter wheat	1.6	0.63
Broadbean	1.5	1.8
Spinach	1.6	1.5
Pea	1.3	1.4

capacity to change the level of trans-16:1 also exhibited the least modulation of LCHII organization in vitro (14). This information has been employed successfully to predict the freezing tolerance (LT50) of wheat and rye cultivars (14). These results represent the first clear demonstration of a specific molecular change associated with LT50 in several cereal cultivars exhibiting a range of freezing tolerance. It is emphasized that the proposed role for PG in modulating the organization of LCHII as a function of growth temperature manifests itself to varying degrees in different plant species.

6. CONCLUSIONS

Winter cereals exhibit the capacity for increased resistance to low temperature induced photoinhibition. In contrast, nonhardy spring cereals developed at cold hardening temperatures remain sensitive to low temperature induced photoinhibition. Thus, light, in combination with low temperature, may be an important factor limiting the cold hardening process and the acquisition of maximum freezing tolerance in cereals (Fig. 2). Alterations in leaf anatomy and morphology as well as modulation of the thylakoid membrane may have important roles in overcoming this limitation in cereals.

REFERENCES
1 Levitt, J. (1980) Responses of Plants to Environmental Stresses, Vol. 1, Academic Press, New York.
2 Fowler, D.B. and Gusta, L.V. (1977) Can. J. Plant Sci. 57, 751-755.
3 Powles, S.B. (1986) Ann. Rev. Plant Physiol. 35, 15-44.
4 Bjorkman, O. and Bemmig, B. (1987) Planta 170, 489-504.
5 Somersalo, S. and Krause, G.H. (1989) Planta,
6 Oquist, G. and Huner, N.P.A. (1989) Planta, in press.
7 Huner, N.P.A. and Hopkins, W.G. (1985) Physiol. Plant. 64, 468-476.
8 Griffith, M., Huner, N.P.A. and Hayden, D.B. (1986) Plant Physiol. 81, 471-477.

9   Huner, N.P.A., Krol, M., Williams, J.P., Maissan, E., Low, P.S.,
    Roberts, D. and Thompson, J.E. (1987) Plant Physiol. 84, 12-18.
10 Krol, M., Huner, N.P.A., Williams, J.P. and Maissan, E. (1988)
    Photosyn. Res. 15, 115-132.
11 Huner, N.P.A. (1985) Can. J. Bot. 63, 506-511.
12 Huner, N.P.A., Krol, M., Williams, J.P., Maissan, E. and Krupa,
Z. (1989) in Low Temperature Stress Physiology in Crops (Li, P.H.,
    ed.), pp. 53-65, CRC Press, Baco Raton.
13 Harwood, J.L. (1980) in Biochemistry of Plants (Stumpf, P.K. and
    Conn. E.E., eds.), Vol. 4, Chapter 1, Academic Press, New York.
14 Huner, N.P.A., Williams, J.P., Maissan, E.E., Myscich, E.G.,
    Krol, M., Laroche, A. and Singh, J. (1989) Plant Physiol. 89,
    144-150.
15 Krol, M., Huner, N.P.A., Williams, J.P. and Maissan, E.E. (1989)
    J. Plant Physiol., in press.
16 Krupa, Z., Huner N.P.A., Williams, J.P., Maissan, E. and James,
    D.R. (1987) Plant Physiol. 84, 19-24.

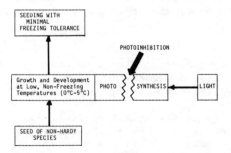

FIGURE 2.   Generalized scheme illustrating the possible role of
            photoinhibition in limiting low temperature development
            and subsequent freezing tolerance in cereals.

CHROMATIC ADAPTATION IN *PORPHYRIDIUM CRUENTUM* EXPRESSED IN THE DISTRIBUTION OF EXCITATION ENERGY AND IN THE THYLAKOID HIGH-ENERGY FLUORESCENCE QUENCHING

Ora Canaani[a], Sandra Driesenaar[a], Shmuel Malkin[a] and Elizabeth Gantt[b]

[a]Biochemistry Department, Weizmann Institute of Science, Rehovot, 76100 Israel and [b]Botany Department, University of Maryland, College Park, MD 20742, U.S.A.

1. Introduction

In many red algae and cyanobacteria a phenomenon of chromatic adaptation occurs, in which there are no significant changes in the phycobiliprotein ratios but mostly in the chlorophyll pigments, their synthesis and organization (1,2). From low temperature fluorescence studies in *P. cruentum* grown in white or green lights it was indirectly estimated that PSI contained about 95% while PSII contained about 5% of the total chlorophyll and that the phycobilisomes transferred their excitation energy to PSII units (1). However, in *P. cruentum* grown in red or blue light PSII contained about 40% of the total chlorophyll. The yield of energy transfer from PSII to PSI was estimated for cells grown in white light in states 1 and 2 (1). The state 1 - state 2 transitions and energetics of the electron transport chain in *P. cruentum* undergoing chromatic and intensity adaptation are still unknown.

2. Materials and Methods

P. cruentum was grown in an artificial sea water medium (3) at 20°C under lighting from high intensity fluorescence lamps. Part of the cultures were exposed to a full intensity of about 180 $\mu E/m^2sec$ ("High" cells), while some were grown under medium light intensity of about 20 $\mu E/m^2sec$ ("Medium" cells) and some were grown under red light, obtained by using a long-pass cellophane sheet (> 650 nm), of an intensity about 20 $\mu E/m^2sec$ ("Red" cells). Algal samples were inserted in special spectrofuorometric cuvettes of .1 mm thickness (for homogenous spread and optical transparency at freezing temperatures). Fluorescence emission spectra were measured with a MPF-44 Perkin-Elmer spectrofluorometer. The cuvette was placed in a glass dewar and aligned 45° to the incident light and to the direction of the emitted light. Samples were preilluminated at room temperature *in situ* for 10 min. with either blue light (440 nm, 20 nm bandwidth, ~40 $\mu E/m^2sec$) or green light (530 nm, 20 nm bandwidth, ~90 $\mu E/m^2sec$), to establish state 1 or state 2, respectively. After preillumination the sample was frozen to -196°C during illumination.

Light induced chlorophyll fluorescence quenching was measured at room temperature with a pulse modulation chlorophyll fluorometer (PAM, Walz, Effeltrich, FRG) (4). The non-photochemical fluorescence quenching, ascribed mainly to energy quenching (q_E), was calculated as in (4).

M. Baltscheffsky (ed.), Current Research in Photosynthesis, Vol. IV, 321–324.
© 1990 *Kluwer Academic Publishers. Printed in the Netherlands.*

3. Results and Discussion

Changes in the fluorescence emission of PSI and PSII, excited with either 440 nm (absorbed by chlorophyll) or 550 nm (absorbed by the phycobilins), were studied after short adaptation to either green or blue light.

"Medium" cells, preilluminated at 440 nm, frozen to liquid nitrogen temperature and excited at 440 nm, showed two emission peaks: 696 nm (PSII) and 713 nm (PSI) (Fig. 1, left). With 550 nm preillumination, however, there was a large emission decrease at 696 nm, such that the whole 696 nm band was not resolvable, while the 713 nm band increased. These experiments are consistent with a higher yield of energy transfer from PSII to PSI with green light adaptation, compared to blue light adaptation and hence "Medium" cells exhibited state 1 - state 2 transitions. For this conclusion one has to assume that there is a non-negligible fraction of the chlorophyll in PS II (at least as much as the extent of the changes). "Red" cells (Fig. 1, middle), preilluminated with blue light, showed only a small increase in 713 nm, compared to green light preilluminated cells. This may reflect more 440 nm light reaching PSI and emitted as fluorescence. In "High" cells a small fluorescence increase at 713 nm was observed with green light preillumination as compared to blue light preillumination (Fig. 1, right). In both "Red" and "High" cells, the 696 nm peak is hardly resolved from the 713 nm peak, consistent with very efficient energy transfer from PSII to PSI, independent of previous irradiation.

Similar experiments were conducted as above with 550 nm excitation. The fluorescence emission of "Medium" cells is shown in Fig. 2 (left). The major emission peak is at 695 nm (PSII) with shoulders at 658 nm, assigned to short emitting Allophycocyanin (APC), 683 nm, assigned to a mixture of long emitting Allophycocyanin B (APC-B) plus chlorophyll (in unknown proportions), and 710 nm, due to PSI. Preillumination with blue light resulted in an increase of both F695 and F710 emissions, compared to preillumination with green light. The 710 nm shoulder cannot be well separated from the dominating 695 nm peak, which by its changes indicates increased energy transfer from PSII to PSI after green light adaptation, as was concluded above. In "Red" cells (Fig. 2, middle) preillumination with green light, caused a small ($\sim$5%) decrease of PSII emission at 695 nm accompanied by a larger ($\sim$10%) increase in the emission of PSI at 710 nm. A still larger decrease ($\sim$16%) was observed at 682 nm after green light preillumination compared to blue light preillumination. This experiment suggests that "Red" cells, as compared to "Medium" cells, exhibit smaller changes in the yield of excitation transfer from PSII to PSI and hence of the extent of state 1 - state 2 transitions. On the other hand, the larger change observed in the emission at 682 nm (APC-B and/or Chl) indicates that the 682 nm emitting molecules transfer directly part of their excitation energy to PSI in the "Red" cells and participate in the state transitions. In "High" cells (Fig. 2, right), green light preillumination did not change F695 relative to blue light preillumination, while increasing all short wavelength emissions: F685 (due to APC-B and/or Chl) F658 (APC) and F642 (due to phycocyanin (PC)). At the same time it slightly decreased the F710 emission of PSI. This experiment suggests that the "High" cells do not undergo state transitions and that the adaptation to green light probably results in partial decoupling of the phycobilisomes, as reflected by the higher fluorescence emission from the phycobiliproteins. In Fig. 3 a more detailed spectrum of "Medium" cells is shown. With 530 nm excitation an emission doublet assigned to phycoerythrin is observed at 575 and 585 nm (while PE *in vitro* has only one peak at 580 nm). The much smaller emission peak of PC at

642 nm and APC at 654 nm, are followed by the emissions of 682 nm (APC and/or Chl), 692 nm (PSII) and 712 nm (PSI).

Recently, a phycobilisome (PBS) dissociation model was proposed (5) in which state 2 reflects both a dissociation of PBS from PSII and an increase of energy transfer from PSII chlorophyll to PSI chlorophyll. This model predicts that a large decrease in the amount of excitation energy reaching PSII will occur in state 2. Only PSII Chl excitation but not PBS excitation will result in the increase of the PSI emission. In "Medium" cells we observed indeed a complementary decrease in PSII emission and increase in PSI emission for excitation of Chl (Fig. 1, right) as well as a decrease in both PSII and PSI fluorescence emission in state 2 for excitation of the PBS (Fig. 2, right). according to this model. Another model, the mobile PBS previously proposed (5), involves the dissociation of the PBS from PSII and its subsequence association with PSI. This model predicts complementary changes in PSI and PSII effective absorption cross-sections in state 1 - state 2 transitions in wavelength where PBS contributes. In wavelengths where chlorophyll absorbs there would be no change. In "Red" cells, we observed small complementary changes in the fluorescence yields of PSII and PSI for excitation of the PBS at 550 nm (Fig. 2, middle) and no changes upon excitation of Chl at 440 nm, (Fig. 1, middle) presumably in agreement with a mobile PBS model. In "High" cells, the increase in the emission of phycobilins upon green light adaptation could reflect a dissociation of the PBS as a protection mechanism against excess light in PSII, which otherwise could lead to photoinhibition.

In order to investigate the high energy state of the thylakoid membrane in these three types of acclimated algae, we analyzed the relaxation of the energy dependent quenching of Chl fluorescence (3). Table I shows the extents of total non-photochemical quenching (which was largely uncoupler sensitive) in each type of cells after adaptations to either green light (580 nm) or far-red light (706 nm). In "High" and "Medium" cells similar extents of total non-photochemical quenching were observed after adaptation to green light. After adaptation to far-red light a larger non-photochemical quenching was observed in both types of these cells. In contrast, "Red" cells exhibited an opposite trend. The total non-photochemical quenching was higher after green light adaptation than after far-red adaptation. These results indicate that the energetics of "Red" cells in response to various spectral light qualities differs from the energetics of "High" and "Medium" cells.

References

1. Ley, A.C. and Butler, W.L. (1980) Biochim.Biophys.Acta *592* 349-363.
2. Ley, A.C. and Butler, W.L. (1980) Plant Physiol. *65* 714-722.
3. Provasoli, L.J., McLaughlin, J.A. and Droop, M.R. (1957) Arch. Microbiol. *25* 392-428.
4. Schreiber, U., Schliwa, U. and Bilger, W. (1986). Photosyn. Res. *10* 51-62.
5. Mullineaux, C.W. and Allen, J.F. (1988) Biochim. Biophys. Acta *894* 96-107.
6. Allen, J.F., Sanders, C.E. and Holmes, N.G. (1985) FEBS Lett. *193*, 271-275.

Acknowledgement

This research was supported by BSF No. 84-00269. We thank Miss Ilanit Gornik, Mr. Shlomo Gershon and Mrs. Anat Bromberg for excellent technical assistance.

Table I.

Extent of the non-photochemical fluorescence quenching, calculated as in (4), following 580 nm or 706 nm preillumination.

Type of Cells	580 nm	706 nm
"High"	0.28	0.49
"Medium"	0.20	0.33
"Red"	0.59	0.28

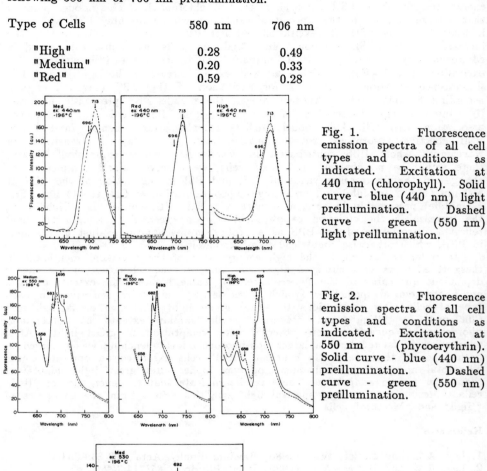

Fig. 1. Fluorescence emission spectra of all cell types and conditions as indicated. Excitation at 440 nm (chlorophyll). Solid curve - blue (440 nm) light preillumination. Dashed curve - green (550 nm) light preillumination.

Fig. 2. Fluorescence emission spectra of all cell types and conditions as indicated. Excitation at 550 nm (phycoerythrin). Solid curve - blue (440 nm) preillumination. Dashed curve - green (550 nm) preillumination.

Fig. 3. Fluorescence emission spectrum of "Medium" cells under conditions as indicated. Excitation at 530 nm (phycoerythrin)

THE INVOLVEMENT OF LHC 2 PHOSPHORYLATION IN THE ADAPTATION OF HIGHER PLANTS TO CHANGING LIGHT INTENSITIES AND SOME RESULTS ON THE REGULATION OF LHC 2 PHOSPHORYLATION IN VIVO

HOLGER DAU*, ORA CANAANI, Dept. of Biochemistry, Weizmann Institute of Science, REHOVOT 76100, ISRAEL
* present address: Inst. fuer Angewandte Physik, Universitaet Kiel, Leibnizstr. 11, 2300 KIEL, FRG

1. INTRODUCTION

Light adaptation of plants from previous dark periods has been subject to various studies. In contrast, little is known about the adaptation to changing light intensities. Dau and Hansen (1) have recently conducted a kinetic analysis of the photoacoustically measured oxygen evolution and chlorophyll fluorescence. The purpose of this research was to give a survey of the adaptation processes, occuring within the time-scale of seconds to minutes. In the present study further experimental support is provided for the idea (1) that changes in LHC 2 phosphorylation are of importance in the adaptation to changing light intensities. Evidence is given that in vivo LHC phosphorylation is controlled neither by the redox-state of the plastoquinone pool nor by the thylakoid pH-gradient.

2. MATERIALS AND METHODS

The measurements were performed on intact leaves or freshly cut leaf discs of spinach (Spinacia olacera L.), barley (Hordeum vulgare L.), and chlorophyll-b-less mutants of barley (Chlorina-f-2).

The modulated fluorescence f, f_m, and f_0 were measured as described elsewhere (2). The photoacoustic signal was measured by using a measuring light (halogen bulb + Corning 4(96)) modulated by a chopper with 13 Hz. The thermal component of the photoacoustic signal was eliminated by phase adjustment as described in (1). The remaining signal is assumed to be a measure of the yield r of oxygen evolution (3). Additional nonmodulated background light was provided by a halogen bulb + filter Corning 4(96).

3. RESULTS AND DISCUSSION

3.1. Response to an increase in light intensity. Leaves were adapted to the light intensity I_a of the measuring light. Then light intensity was increased by addition of nonmodulated light for about one hour. Complex transients of oxygen yield r (fig. 1A) and fluorescence yield f (fig. 1B) were induced. The initial decrease of r indicates a diminished efficiency of photosynthetic oxygen evolution. It consists of four phases (1). The three faster phases (1-5s) reflect the adjustment of a new redox poise, th fourth (5-30s) originates from the generation of a higher pH-gradient across the thylakoid membrane (1). Following this decrease, the oxygen signal increases for about 20 minutes, often by more than 100%, until a new steady state is reached. The extent of the increase points to an adaptational mechanism of considerable physiological importance also found to occur in spinach, dandelion, and Aegopodium podagraria. In leaves

M. Baltscheffsky (ed.), Current Research in Photosynthesis, Vol. IV, 325–328.

adapted to higher light intensities (I_a greater than 40 Wm^{-2}) the extent of the increase is much smaller.

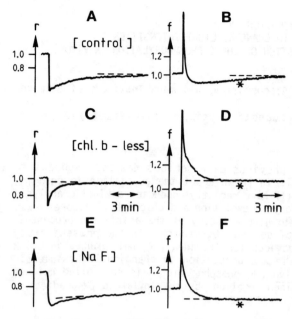

FIGURE 1: Responses of oxygen yield r and fluorescence yield f of leaves adapted to a light intensity of 10 Wm^{-2} (13Hz) to an additional light of 20 Wm^{-2}.
A,B: barley - wild type
C,D: chlorophyll-b-less barley mutant
E,F: spinach leaf incubated for 20 min in solution of 100 $\mu Mol/l$ NaF + 10 $mMol/l$ Tris Buffer (pH 8)
In B the increasing phase of fluorescence which parallels the slow phase of the increase in oxygen evolution is marked by an asterisk. In D and F this slow fluorescence increase was not observed.

3.2. The two components of the increase in oxygen evolution. A kinetic analysis reveals that the increase in oxygen evolution is biphasic (fig. 2). The fast phase ($T_{1/2}$ = 0.5 to 2 min), which corresponds to τ_5-component of (1), is coupled to a decrease in fluorescence yield (fig 1,2) indicating a control of photochemical efficiency of PS 2 by the redox-states of the primary acceptors (1). The most likely explanation is that it is due to a partial reoxidation of the electron transport chain as a consequence of a higher activity of the Calvin-Cycle. In contrast, the slower phase ($T_{1/2}$ = 3 to 10 min), which corresponds to the τ_6-component of (1), is characterized by a parallel increase of fluorescence. Recent investigations led to the hypothesis that the slow component of the oxygen increase is caused by changes of the LHC 2 mediated energy distribution, similar to a State 2 - State 1 transition (1, see below).

3.3 Evidence that the slow component of the oxygen increase originates from LHC 2 dephosphorylation (State 2 - State 1 transition)
3.3.1 The slow component of the oxygen increase is absent from chlorophyll-b-less mutants of barley lacking LHC. (fig. 1C,D and fig 2B)
3.3.2 The slow component is inhibited by the phosphatase inhibitor NaF (inhibition of LHC-dephosphorylation - (4)). (fig. 1E,F)
3.3.3. The slow component of the oxygen increase is coupled to a significant increase in the f_0- and f_m-fluorescence (data not shown).
  In conclusion, in vivo LHC 2 (de)phosphorylation is involved in the adaptation to changing light intensities. The physiological role might be the adjustment of cyclic electron transport. Now the question arises of how the observed dephos-

phorylation of the LHC is induced and controlled or, in other words, what is the "sensor" for the regulation of LHC 2 phosphorylation.

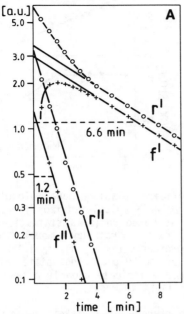 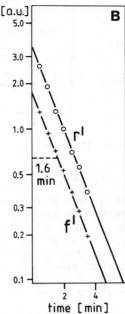

time [min]   time [min]

FIGURE 2: Kinetic analysis of the responses of oxygen yield and chlorophyll fluorescence to an increase in light intensity. A. Barley (wild type): Detection of two components (T_{fast}= 1.2min, T_{slow}= 6.6min, r' and f' give the deviations from steady state values, r'' and f'' give the deviations from the straight line). B. Chlorophyll-b-less barley mutant: Absence of the slow component.

3.4. Putative "sensors" of the LHC 2 kinase: the plastoquinone pool redox-state and the thylakoid pH-Gradient

3.4.1. In contrast to the suggested stimulation of LHC kinase by a reduced PQ-pool (5) we observe a dephosphorylation (slow phase of oxygen increase) despite of a more reduced pool (fig. 3).

3.4.2. According to (6) an increased thylakoid pH-gradient leads to a dephosphorylation of the LHC 2. In untreated leaves an increase in light intensity causes an increase in the thylakoid pH-gradient within about 10s (1). However, diminishing of the changes of thylakoid pH-gradient by the uncoupler nigericin (Fig. 4A) has no effect on the amplitude of the slow oxygen increase up to 80 μmol/l nigericin. At high nigericin concentrations the extent of the increase in thylakoid pH-gradient tends to vanish (as reflected by ΔqE $\rightarrow$ 0), however, the amplitude of the slow component of the oxygen increase is only slightly diminished. Thus, the increased thylakoid pH-gradient does not induce the LHC dephosphorylation which causes the slow phase of the oxygen increase.

In conclusion, neither the redox-state of the plastoquinone pool (5) nor the extent of thylakoid pH-gradient (6) control the LHC 2 phosphorylation. In vivo other or additional "sensors" are involved.

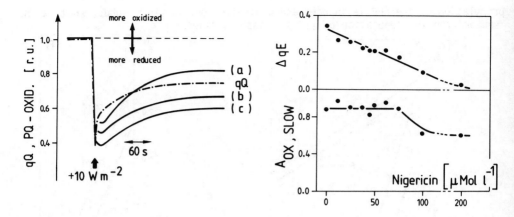

FIGURE 3 (left side): Relative amount of oxidized plastoquinone molecules after an increase in light intensity from 10 to 20 Wm^{-2} calculated from f, f_m, f_0 and oxygen yield r data (7). The calculation is based on (a) a statistical matrix model of PS 2, (b) a connected unit model, (c) a separate unit model. The dotted line gives the qQ quenching factor of fluorescence (= $(f_m-f)/(f_m-f_0)$) which is quite often assumed to be closely related to the PQ-pool redox-state. All curves – no matter what PS 2 structure is assumed – indicate clearly a more reduced state of the PQ-pool after the increase in light intensity.

FIGURE 4 (right side): Comparison of the changes of thylakoid pH-gradient as measured by the changes of f_m and the amplitude $A_{ox,slow}$ of the slow phase of the oxygen increase (normalized to the oxygen yield measured 20s after the increase light intensity). Freshly cut leaf discs of spinach had been incubated for 40 minutes in a solution of nigericin and 10 mMol/l Tris Buffer (pH 8). f_m values were determined by application of saturating light before ($f_{m,0}$) and 12s after ($f_{m,12}$) the increase in light intensity from 10 to 20 Wm^{-2}.
A: $\Delta qE = (f_{m,0}-f_{m,12})/f_{m,0}$. B: $A_{ox,slow}$.

Acknowledgement. These investigations were supported by the Deutsche Forschungsgemeinschaft (Ha 712/7-4), by Grant No. 84-00269 from USA-Israel Binational Science Foundation to Dr. O. Canaani and a Minerva stipend to H. Dau. We are grateful to Prof. U.-P. Hansen and Prof. S. Malkin for helpful discussions and to Mrs. E. Goetting for drawing the figures.

REFERENCES
(1) Dau, H. and Hansen, U.-P. (1989) Photosynth. Res. 20, 59-83
(2) Dau, H. and Hansen, U.-P. (1988) BBA 934, 156-159
(3) Poulet, P., Cahen, D. and Malkin, S. (1983) BBA 724, 433-446
(4) Canaani,O., Barber, J. and Malkin, S. (1984) Proc. Natl. Acad. Sci. (USA) 81, 1614-1618
(5) Allen, F.A., Bennet, J., Steinback, K.E. and Arntzen, C.J. (1981) Nature 291, 25-29
(6) Fernyhough, P., Foyer, C.H. and Horton, P. (1984) FEBS Lett. 176, 133-138
(7) Dau, H. and Canaani, O. (1990) submitted

THYLAKOID PROTEIN PHOSPHORYLATION IN AN ALGAE WITH
CHLOROPHYLL A/C/FUCOXANTHIN LIGHT HARVESTING ANTENNA.

PAMELA GIBBS AND JOHN BIGGINS, DIVISION OF BIOLOGY AND
MEDICINE, BROWN UNIVERSITY, PROVIDENCE R.I., 02912, U.S.A.

1. INTRODUCTION

Mechanisms for the regulation of excitation energy distribution between PS2 and PS1 have been proposed for higher plants (mobile antenna hypothesis) and for red algae cyanobacteria (spillover). These organisms utilize Chl b and phycobilins respectively as accessory light harvesting pigments. The Chromophytic algae encompass a taxonomically diverse group of phyla which are very successful competitors and contribute substantially to net global photosynthesis. These algae are characterized by their use of Chl c and carotenoid (fucoxanthin or peridinin) as accessory light harvesting pigments and by the arrangement of their thylakoids into extended bands of three. Despite their obvious importance, there has only been one prior report on the regulation of energy transfer in Chromophytic algae in which Owens (1) reported only intensity dependent changes. We have previously shown that the Chromophyte *Ochromonas danica* shows wavelength dependent changes in chlorophyll fluorescence (both 77K and room temperature) which are diagnostic for a re-distribution of excitation energy (2). We report here on the antenna polypeptide composition of *O. danica* as well as the *in vitro* protein kinase activity.

2. MATERIALS AND METHODS

2.1. *O. danica* cells were grown and fluorescence spectra were acquired as previously described (2).

2.2. For the in vitro protein kinase assay, *O. danica* cells were broken by sonication in 5.0 ml buffer containing 100 mM Sorbitol, 50 mM Tricine-NaOH, pH 7.8, 5 mM $MgCl_2$, 1 mM EDTA, 0.25 mg/ml BSA and protease inhibitors. Sonicated cells were further resuspended up to 30.0 ml in the above buffer (- BSA) and cells and large cell fragments were removed by centrifugation for 2 minutes at 120 x g. The supernatant was recentrifuged at 43,000 x g to obtain a crude membrane pellet. These membranes were resuspended by stirring on ice and then used for kinase assays. Membranes (~ 400 ug protein) were incubated in buffer with 10 mM NaF, 0.1% TX-100 and γ^{32}P-ATP (2,000 dpm/picomole ATP) to a final concentration of 100 uM ATP. At the specified time, aliquots were withdrawn and the reaction terminated by boiling for one minute in SDS buffer. Samples were then run on SDS-PAGE (12%), stained with Coomassie Blue-R for protein, dried and exposed to X-ray film. For in vivo labelling studies, cells (100.0 ml) were grown in 1,000 Microcuries of ^{32}Pi for 1 day and crude membranes were obtained as above with NaF (10 mM) being included in all buffers.

M. Baltscheffsky (ed.), Current Research in Photosynthesis, Vol. IV, 329–332.
© 1990 *Kluwer Academic Publishers. Printed in the Netherlands.*

3. RESULTS AND DISCUSSION

3.1. Typical 77K chlorophyll fluorescence emission spectra of *O. danica* cells are shown in Fig. 1 in which 2 emission peaks at 692 nm and 722 nm can be seen. These peaks most likely correspond to fluorescence emission from PS2 and PS1 respectively. When *O. danica* cells are pre-illuminated in red (640 nm) or far-red (700 nm) light of equal absorbed intensity, reversible changes in the 77K spectra occur which are consistent with a re-distribution of excitation energy. Room temperature fluoroescence changes have also been observed (Fig. 2) which are consistent with previous results regarding energy re-distribution (3) and are kinetically consistent with the changes in the 77K spectra.(2).

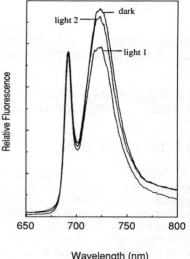

Fig. 1 Chlorophyll fluorescence emission spectra (77K) of *O. danica* . Cells were pre-illuminated for 10 minutes with light 2 (640 nm) or light 1 (700 nm) (5.5 mW m$^{-2)}$ or dark adapted. Excitation was 500 nm and spectra were normalized at the 692 nm maximum.

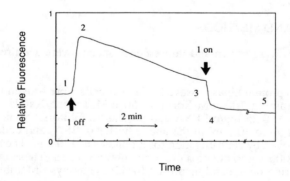

Fig. 2 Room temperature fluorescence trace of *O. danica* cells showing the fast and slow fluorescence changes at 680 nm. Cells were initially brought to State 1 in response to modulated light 2 (500 nm, 1.5 mW m^{-2}) and continuous background light 1 (720 nm, 65 mW m^{-2}). Removal and restoration of light 1 are indicated by the arrows.

3.2. The membranes of *O. danica* contain a major polypeptide(s) of 20 kD which is consistent with the MW of the major light harvesting antenna polypeptide(s) reported for other Chromophyte species (Fig 3, lane B) (4). (For comparison, the SDS-PAGE pattern of a crude spinach chloroplast membrane prep is also shown, lane D.) In addition to this 20 kD polypeptide, *O. danica* cells appear to contain a second antenna protein which binds predominantly Chl a (although some Chl c and carotenoid may also be present) and has an apparent MW of ~31 kD (lane C). The 20 kD antenna polypeptide(s) is unlikely to be a degradation product of the 31 kD polypeptide as 1) the 20 kD component is present in substantial quantities in acetone and 5% TCA extracts of whole cells and 2) the 20 kD component showed some cross-reactivity to antisera to spinach light harvesting complex while the 31 kD polypeptide showed none (data not shown). It is possible that the 31 kD polypeptide shares some homology with an intrinsic, chlorophyll binding protein of similar MW observed in Prochloron and Cyanobacteria (5, 6). Details of the isolation and characteristics of this protein will be reported elsewhere.

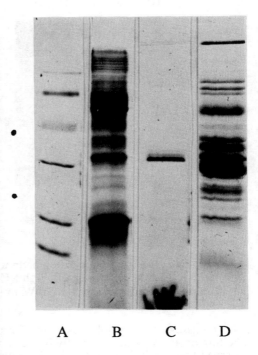

A   B   C   D

Fig. 3 Coomassie-stained SDS-PAGE pattern of polypeptides from *O. danica* and spinach. Lane A, MW marker proteins; lane B, crude membranes from *O. danica* ; lane C, 31 kD pigment-binding protein; lane D, crude spinach chloroplast membranes. The 20 and 31 kD polypeptides are indicated by the circles.

3.3. Recent work has been aimed at elucidating the possible role of a protein phosphorylation event in the regulation of excitation energy distribution between PS2 and PS1 analogous to that reported for higher plants. When crude membranes are incubated with γ^{32}P-ATP, several polypeptides are phosphorylated (Fig. 4). Although a significant amount of label is incorporated into high MW bands, the major phosphoprotein which is well resolved by this system is in the 20 kD range and most likely corresponds to the major light harvesting antenna polypeptides. In addition, there are two phosphoproteins in the 30 - 34 kD range, one of which co-migrates with the 31 kD antenna protein. Although the kinase is active under these conditions, activity was light independent and 20 mM dithionite inhibited rather than stimulated activity. Therefore, the *in vitro* regulation of the protein kinase appears to be significantly different to that reported for higher plants and green algae (7, 8) but similar to that reported for organisms with phycobilisomes (9) and Prochloron (6).

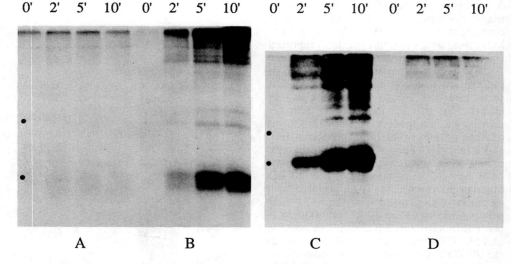

| 0' | 2' | 5' | 10' | 0' | 2' | 5' | 10' | 0' | 2' | 5' | 10' | 0' | 2' | 5' | 10' |

A   B   C   D

Fig. 4 *In vitro* phosphorylation pattern of crude membranes of *O. danica.* A, light + 20 mM Dithionite; B, light; C, dark; D, dark + 20 mM Dithionite. Illumination intensity was 1.2 mW m^{-2}. The 20 and 31 kD polypeptides are indicated by the closed circles.

3.4. To assess the physiological role of protein phosphorylation in the cell, in vivo labelling experiments are currently being conducted. Using this technique, it has been observed that the 20 kD and the 31 kD polypeptides are substrates for kinases in vivo. Further details regarding the in vivo regulation of protein phosphorylation will be presented elsewhere.

REFERENCES

1. Owens TG (1986), Plant Physiol, 80:739 - 746.
2. Gibbs PB and Biggins J (1989), Photosyn Res, 21:81 - 91.
3. Bonaventura C and Myers J (1969), Biochim Biophys Acta, 189:366 - 383.
4. Larkum AWD and Barrett J (1985), Adv in Bot Res, 10:1 - 210.
5. Riethman HC and Sherman LA (1988), Biochim Biophys Acta, 935:141 - 151.
6. Schuster G, Owens GC, Cohen Y and Ohad I (1984), Biochim Biophys Acta,767:596 - 605.
7. Allen JF, Bennett J, Steinback KE and Arntzen CJ (1981), Nature, 291:25 - 29.
8. Owens GC and Ohad I (1982), Journal of Cell Biology, 93:712 - 718.
9. Biggins J and Bruce D (1989), Photosyn Res, (1989), 20:1 - 34.

We would like to acknowledge the support of NSF (DMB-8603586) through a grant to JB and NIH (fellowship to P.G.).

CHARACTERISATION AND PURIFICATION OF POLYPEPTIDES UNDERGOING LIGHT-DEPENDENT PHOSPHORYLATION IN THE CYANOBACTERIUM SYNECHOCOCCUS 6301.

MICHAEL HARRISON AND JOHN F ALLEN
Department of Pure and Applied Biology, University of Leeds, Leeds LS2 9JT, England

1. INTRODUCTION

Chloroplasts and cyanobacteria contain thylakoids which differ greatly in their architecture and composition. Both are, however, able to perform state 1-state 2 transitions, an adaptation mechanism controlling relative distribution of excitation energy between the two photosystems, which permits the optimisation of photosynthetic quantum yield under incident light of varying spectral quality (1,2). In chloroplasts transition to state 2 is induced by phosphorylation of the chlorophyll a/b-binding protein, (LHCII), the mobile antenna of photosystem II, by a kinase the activity of which is controlled by the redox state of plastoquinone (3,4). Phosphorylation induces a decoupling of LHCII from PSII, effecting a decrease in absorbance cross-section for PSII (5,6).

The subject of state transitions in cyanobacteria is controversial (see (7)) but the mechanism is apparently under redox control in a way analogous to that in chloroplasts (8). The role of protein phosphorylation in state transitions in phycobilisome-containing organisms is unclear. Here we report conditions under which three species of polypeptide of M^r 18.5, 15 and 13kDa are phosphorylated in the cyanobacterium Synechococcus 6301.

2. METHODS

Culture and in vivo labelling of Synechococcus 6301 (mutant AN112) were performed as in (9) under light regimes specific for excitation of photosystem II and photosystem I defined by filters described in detail in (10). In vitro phosphorylation of thylakoids with [^{32}P]ATP was performed as in (11), (with modifications) under conditions described in the legend to Figure (1).

3. RESULTS AND DISCUSSION

Figure (1) shows the autoradiogram subsequent to SDS-PAGE analysis of Synechococcus 6301 thylakoid proteins incubated with [^{32}P]-ATP under various conditions (described in the figure legend). From Figure (1) it is

M. Baltscheffsky (ed.), Current Research in Photosynthesis, Vol. IV, 333–336.
© 1990 *Kluwer Academic Publishers. Printed in the Netherlands.*

clear that two polypeptides of M_r 18.5kDa and 15kDa are phosphorylated _in vitro_ in a light-dependent fashion in _Synechococcus_ 6301 thylakoids and that this reaction is inhibited by DCMU as described in (11). In addition, both are phosphorylated in the presence of duroquinol in the dark, conditions which would be expected to give slow reduction of the plastoquinone pool. Light incubation in the presence of duroquinone or methyl viologen, which could be expected to give oxidation of plastoquinone, induces essentially no phosphorylation of the 15kDa polypeptide, although labelling of the 18.5 kDa polypeptide, a putative phycobilisome component (9), remains. Presence of duroquinol or methyl viologen _in vivo_ in cyanobacteria has been shown to induce state 2 and state 1 respectively (Mullineaux, CW and Allen, JF, in press).

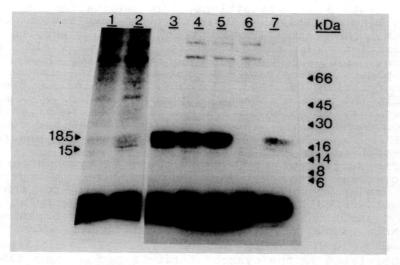

Figure (1) Incubation of _Synechococcus_ 6301 (AN112) thylakoids with [^{32}P]-ATP. Washed thylakoids were incubated under various conditions, subjected to SDS-PAGE and the resulting gel was autoradiographed. The autoradiogram is shown in the figure. In the interests of brevity the gel is not shown, but tracks showed identical loading (3ug Chl _a_ equivalent thylakoids). Positions of molecular mass markers are shown (kDa). Incubation conditions were: Track (1) Light + 20uM DCMU (2) Light (3) Pretreatment in the light with 20uM DCMU, then light + 0.5mM duroquinol (4) light + 50uM methyl viologen (5) light + 0.5mM duroquinone (6) Dark (7) Dark + 0.5mM duroquinol

We have also observed differential phosphorylation $\underline{in}$
$\underline{vivo}$ of both the 18.5kDa polypeptide and another, 13kDa,
polypeptide in cells adapted to light regimes which have
been found to induce state 1 or state 2 as short term
adaptations and also, as longer term adaptations,
photosystem stoichiometry changes (10,12). Figure (2)
shows SDS-PAGE analysis of polypeptides derived from cells
incubated for 30 minutes under light specific for
excitation of the phycobilisome ,and therefore for PSII,
(emission maximum 590nm) or light specific for excitation
of PSI (emission maximum 700nm) in the presence of $[^{32}-P]$
orthophosphate. Autoradiography of the same gel shows
labelling of the 18.5 and 13kDa polypeptides almost
exclusively under light 2 illumination, conditions known
to give state 2 in the short term and to increase the
PSI/PSII ratio as a long term adaptation (10,12).

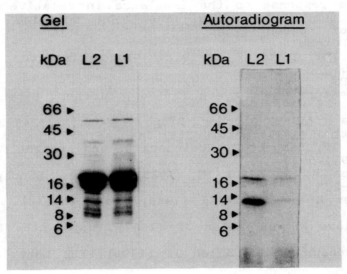

Figure (2) SDS-PAGE analysis of Synechococcus 6301
polypeptides derived from cells labelled $\underline{in}$ $\underline{vivo}$ with
$[^{32}P]$ orthophosphate and incubated under PSII light (L2)
or PSI light (L1). Left hand figure shows gel of total
cell polypeptides. Right hand shows autoradiogram of the
same gel.

We have purified and sequenced the 13kDa polypeptide
and determined that it has 63% identity with the P_{II}
protein of E.coli (13), a protein which is uridylylted as
part of a mechanism regulating both the activity of
glutamine synthetase and the transcription of its gene,

glnA (14). Details of purification, sequencing and sequence analysis will be published elsewhere (Harrison, MA, Keen, JN, Findlay, JBC and Allen, JF, submitted).

Of the three polypeptides undergoing light-dependent phosphorylation, it is apparent that the 15kDa thylakoid polypeptide at least is substrate for redox-controlled phosphorylation reaction broadly analogous to that for LHCII in chloroplasts. This protein is therefore a likely component for any protein phosphorylation model for the mechanism of state transitons in cyanobacteria.

The intriguing possibility also arises that a P_{II}-type protein in cyanobacteria is a component of a mechanism integrating efficiency of photosynthetic electron transport with nitrogen assimilation, or may even have an effect on transcription of photosynthetic genes, inducing alterations in photosystem stoichiometry as a long-term response to the imbalance in relative turnover of the two photosystems caused by changing spectral quality of incident light (15).

ACKNOWLEDGEMENTS

We are grateful to A.N. Glazer for the gift of cultures.

REFERENCES

1   Bonaventura C and Myers J (1969) Biochem. Biophys. Acta 189: 366-383
2   Murata N (1969) Biochem. Biophys. Acta 172:242-251
3   Bennett J (1977) Nature 269: 344-346
4   Allen JF, Bennett J, Steinback KE and Arntzen CJ (1981) Nature 291:25-29
5   Horton P and Black MT (1983) Biochem. Biophys. Acta 722: 214-218
6   Hodges M and Barber J (1983) Plant Physiol. 72:1119-1122
7   Williams WP and Allen JF (1987) Photosynth. Res. 13: 19-45
8   Mullineaux CW and Allen JF (1986) FEBS Lett. 205:155-160
9   Sanders CE and Allen JF (1987) Progress in Photosynthesis Research Vol.II (Biggins J, Ed.) Martinus Nijhoff, Dordrecht
10   Allen JF, Mullineaux CW, Sanders CE and Melis A Photosynth. Res., in press
11   Allen JF, Sanders CE and Holmes NG (1985) FEBS Lett. 193: 271-275
12   Melis A, Mullineaux CW and Allen JF (1989) Z. Naturforsch. 44c:109-118
13   Son HS and Rhee SG (1987) J. Biol. Chem. 262:8690
14   Magasanik B (1988) Trends Biochem. Sci. 13:475
15   Fujita Y, Murakami A and Ohki K (1987) Plant Cell Physiol. 28: 283-292

FUNCTIONAL ANALYSIS OF THE PHOTOSYNTHETIC APPARATUS
IN A CHLOROPHYLL-DEFICIENT MUTANT OF COWPEA

DIMAH HABASH, BERNARD GENTY AND NEIL R.BAKER, Dept. of
Biology, University of Essex, Colchester, CO4 3SQ, U.K.

1. INTRODUCTION

Mutations that depress total chlorophyll content such as
found in barley[1], maize[2], pea[3], soybean[4] and
tobacco[5] generally result in an increased chlorophyll a:b
ratio. Mutants of pea [3] and tobacco [5] have a decreased
capacity for CO_2 assimilation, and the change in the chla:b
ratio in a mutant of maize [2] reflects a reduction in
LHC2. Recently a single, temperature-sensitive, recessive
nuclear gene mutation of cowpea (Vigna unguiculata (L.)
Walp) has been found which results in a reduced leaf
chlorophyll content [6] but which exhibits similar vigour
and productivity in the field compared to the parent (A.E.
Hall personal communication). This study examines the
changes induced by this single gene mutation in the LHC2
and PS2 contents of thylakoids and assesses their
consequences for photosynthetic electron transport and
carbon fixation.

2. MATERIALS AND METHODS

Cowpea (Vigna unguiculata (L.) Walp) plants were grown
from seed in a glasshouse under a mean supplemented PPFD of
500 $\mu molm^{-2}s^{-1}$, day/night average temperatures were
$26/18^{\circ}C$. Thylakoid preparation from mature plants and
electrophoretic separation of chlorophyll-protein complexes
[7] and polypeptides were performed as described previously
[8]. O_2 evolution, at saturating CO_2 concentrations, was
measured using a leaf disc oxygen electrode and CO_2 gas
exchange was measured using infra-red gas analysis
essentially as described in [9]. Calculations of the number
of ^{14}C DCMU binding sites of PS2 and the binding constant
were determined using a modification of a previously
described method for labelled herbicides [10]. The
determination of the quantum efficiency of PS2 electron
transport in vivo was achieved by fluorescence measurements
as described before [11] simultaneously with measurements
of light-induced absorbance changes at 820nm in leaves [12]
to assess the quantum efficiency of PS1 in vivo.

RESULTS AND DISCUSSION

The cowpea mutant exhibits a substantial reduction (41%)
in total chla+b content per unit leaf area basis compared
to the parent. This decrease was associated with a reduced

M. Baltscheffsky (ed.), Current Research in Photosynthesis, Vol. IV, 337–340.

thylakoid chl:protein ratio, and an elavated chl a:b ratio and a decrease in leaf absorptivity (Table 1).

TABLE 1. Changes induced by the mutation in cowpea in chlorophyll characteristics, leaf absorptivity and the characteristics of DCMU-binding to thylakoids. Standard errors of means are given in paranthesis.

	Parent	Mutant
Chla+b/leaf area (g/m^2)	0.423(0.07)	0.249(0.03)
chla:b	2.68(0.53)	3.62(0.56)
chl: thylakoid protein (w/w)	0.234	0.164
Leaf absorptivity (%)	86.5(2.8)	76.9(3.4)
^{14}C DCMU binding capacity		
per chl (nmol/mg chl)	5.93(1.16)	9.88(1.93)
per leaf area (μmol/m^2)	2.52	2.36
DCMU binding constant (μM)	0.34(0.09)	0.49(0.08)

SDS-PAGE analysis of thylakoid proteins showed a large proportional decrease in polypeptides around 26-28 kDa in the mutant compared to the parent (Fig.1), suggesting a loss of LHC2 polypeptides in the mutant. Non-denaturing green gels confirmed this; in the mutant the oligomeric form of LHC2 (CPII*) was substantial reduced, while the monomeric LHC2 (CPII) species was reduced to a lesser extent (Fig.2).

Fig.1. Fig.2.

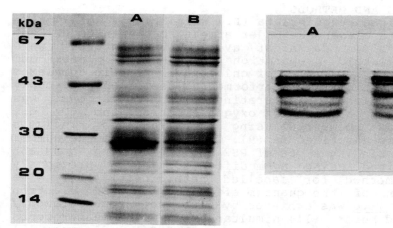

FIGURE 1. SDS-PAGE profiles of thylakoid proteins isolated from parent (A) and mutant (B) cowpea leaves. **FIGURE 2.** Unstained, non-denaturing gel showing chlorophyll-protein complexes of parent (A) and mutant (B) thylakoids. CPI*=P700+LHCI ; CPI=P700 ; CPII*=LHCII oligomer; PSII=CP47+CP43 ; CPII= LHCII monomer, band includes CP29.

The loss of LHC2 could have consequences for photosynthetic yield. Determination of the apparent quantum yields of CO_2 fixation showed a lowered value for the mutant (Table 2), while the true quantum yield showed very little difference between the two plants indicating that the decreased apparent quantum yield of mutant leaves is attributable to their decreased absorptivity. The same pattern of change was obtained for the quantum yields of O_2 evolution, however, the magnitude of differences between mutant and parent was less than that obtained for CO_2 fixation.

Table 2. The apparent ("Qy") and absolute (Qy) quantum yields of CO_2 fixation and O_2 evolution. The apparent quantum yields were obtained from slopes of the linear part (50-150 μmolm^{-2}s^{-1} PPFD) of light response curves then corrected to the absolute quantum yield using leaf absorptivity.

		Parent	Mutant
CO_2	"Qy"	0.052	0.043
CO_2	Qy	0.059	0.057
O_2	"Qy"	0.078	0.074
O_2	Qy	0.091	0.092

Determinations of DCMU-binding to the D1 reaction centre protein of PS2 in isolated thylakoids showed the mutant to have a greater number of binding sites per chlorophyll, but lowered DCMU-binding affinity when compared to the parent (Table 1). However, when the number of binding sites is expressed on a leaf area basis, the difference between the mutant and parent is only 6% (Table 1), suggesting there is little difference in the PS2 content per leaf area in the two plants.

FIGURE 3. The relationship between the quantum efficiencies of PS1 and PS2 for (●) parent and (▲) mutant leaves. These efficiencies were measured over a PPFD range of 0 - 3000 μmol m^{-2} s^{-1}.

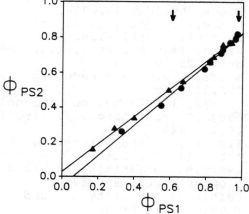

The efficiency of electron transport was studied in vivo using fluorescence and absorbance measurements. Plots of PS1 quantum efficiency versus that of PS2 yields a linear correlation for a range of light levels with very little difference being observed between the mutant and the parent (Fig.3) . This linear correlation indicates that at steady state photosynthesis at a range of PPFDs, below 1500 μmolm^{-2}s^{-1} PPFD between the arrows in Fig.(3), both the mutant and parent leaves maintain a similar balance between the efficiencies of PS1 and PS2 (9).

In conclusion, the chlorophyll deficiency in the cowpea mutant is attributable to a substantial loss of LHC2, which results in a decreased absorptivity of the leaves and a consequent decrease in the apparent quantum yield of CO_2 assimilation and O_2 evolution . However, despite this loss of LHC2 the absolute quantum yield of CO_2 assimilation , O_2 evolution and the ability to balance the efficiencies of PS1 and PS2 electron transport are similar in both the mutant and parent . This implies that the substantial decrease of LHC2 in the mutant does not lead to a loss in the efficiency with which its leaves can utilize absorbed light for photosynthesis, and implies that the parent can be considered to have an excess of LHC2 .

ACKNOWLEDGEMENTS

This work was supported by the AFRC (LRG 98) . We thank A.E Hall for supplying the seeds, and D. Hayden for assistance with the green gels.

REFERENCES

1. Nielsen,N.C., Smillie,R.M., Henningsoen,K.W., Wettstein, D.V. and French, C. (1979) Plant Physiol. 63,174-182
2. Green,B.A., Allred,D.R., Morishige, D.T. and Staehelin, L.A. (1988) Plant Physiol. 87, 357-364.
3. Highkin,H.R., Boardman,N.K., Goodchild,D.J. (1969) Plant Physiol. 44,1310-1320.
4. Keck,R.W., Dilley,R.A., Allen,C.F. and Biggs,S. (1970) Plant Physiol. 46,692-698.
5. Okabe,K., Schmid,G.H. and Straub,J. (1977) Plant Physiol. 60,150-156.
6. Kirchhoff,W.R., Hall, A.E. and Thomson, W.W. (1989) Crop Sci. 29,109-115.
7. Waldron, J.C. and Anderson, J.M. (1979) Eur. J. Biochem. 102,357-362.
8. Chua,N. (1980) Methods Enzymol. 69,434-446.
9. Bongi,G. and Long,S.P. (1987) Plant Cell Environment 10,241-249.
10.Tischer,W. and Strotmann, H. (1977) Biochim. Biophys. Acta 469,113-125
11.Genty,B., Briantais,J-M., and Baker,N.R. (1989) Biochim. Biophys. Acta 990,87-92.
12.Harbinson,J. Genty,B. and Baker,N.R. (1989) Plant Physiol., in press.

SLOW FLUORESCENCE TRANSIENTS IN PHOTOSYNTHETIC BACTERIA

Ivan ŠETLIK[1], Michaela WALDBURGER-SCHLAPP[2] and Reinhard BACHOFEN[2]
1 Institute of Microbiology, Czechoslovak Academy of Sciences, CS 37981, Třeboň, Czechoslovakia; 2 Institute of Plant Biology, University of Zurich, Zollikerstrasse 107, CH-8008 Zurich, Switzerland.

1. INTRODUCTION

Slow fluorescence transients in leaves and chloroplasts are being increasingly used as an efficient tool in analyzing thylakoidal events and their interaction with the stroma compartment (1). For phototrophic bacteria only a preliminary communication gives some records of fluorescence transients (2). Although the variable fluorescence in phototrophic bacteria has been studied (3,4) transient phenomena have not been further analyzed. Here we describe the application of the modulated light fluorimeter (5) to photosynthetic bacteria and show that slow fluorescence transients are similar to those characteristic of oxygenic photosynthesis.

2. MATERIAL AND METHODS

Rhodobacter sphaeroides wild type and mutant strain GA and *Rhodospirillum rubrum* wild type and mutant strain G9 were grown in Sistroms medium in 250ml flasks at 50 $W.m^{-2}$ and 30°C or in a fermentor at 200 $W.m^{-2}$ and 30°C. For the measurements cells from the exponential growth phase were centrifuged and resuspended in buffer (MOPS, pH 7.0) or fresh Sistrom medium (pH 6.8).

The Hansatech modulated fluorescence measuring system was connected to a recorder (Labograph E 586, METROHM) and a storage Oscilloscope (MSO-1270, MEGURO). To minimize stray light and to adapt the system for measuring the fluorescence of phototrophic bacteria the following filters were inserted into the various light paths: LED emitting measuring light 3 mm short pass filter Calflex (BALZERS) and 1 mm BG18 (SCHOTT), PIN photodiode detector 8 mm long pass filter with a cutting edge at 720 nm, actinic light from INTRALUX tungsten-iodine lamps 2 mm of Calflex (BALZERS) and 2 mm BG18 (SCHOTT) concentrated to fibre optics by a system of lenses accomodating a photographic shutter with a diaphragm for control of light intensity.

The first measurements were performed with a bacterial suspension in a cuvette stirred by bubbles of gas from a capillary. The transients in this suspension were found to be consistently simpler than under unstirred conditions (Fig.2). Mechanical mixing yielded similar, though less pronounced effects, possibly due to some concentration gradient close to the surface of the bacterial cells.

The stirring effect was eliminated and the bacteria maintained in a constant and well defined environment in a measuring chamber with an immobilized layer of cells as depicted in Fig.1. A thin layer (down to 0.5 mm) of a dense bacterial suspension is separated by a dialysis

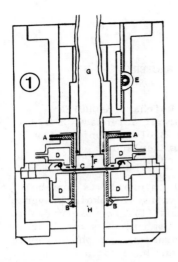

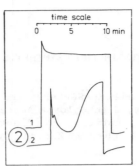

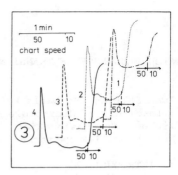

FIGURE 1: Schematic drawing of the measuring chamber. Inlet and outlet for (A) the bacterial suspension, (B) the circulating medium, (C) dialysis membrane, (D) cavities for thermostat water, (E) drive to adjust the thickness of the suspension layer, (F) bifurcated fibre optics connected to (G) the LED and photodiode detector and to (H) the two actinic light sources.

FIGURE 2: Fluorescence transients measured in a cell suspension with (1) and without (2) bubbling with N_2+CO_2. *R. rubrum* S1, MOPS buffer, 25°C, 100 $W.m^{-2}$.

FIGURE 3: Light transients measured in the cell layer chamber at various suspension densities (in μg $Bchl.ml^{-1}$): (1) 51, (2) 96, (3) 130, (4) 186. Cell layer 1 mm. *Rb. sphaeroides* GA in PO4 buffer, 25°C, 200 $W.m^{-2}$.

membrane from the circulating medium. Although the transients measured were perfectly reproducible with samples from the same suspension, the shape of the transient is influenced by the density of the suspension (Fig.3). In all experiments cell densities used were around 80 μg $Bchl.ml^{-1}$.

3. RESULTS AND DISCUSSION

Fig.4 and Fig.5 show the characteristic pattern of light and dark transients in *Rb. sphaeroides* and their variation with irradiance and temperature. Complicated oscillations were observed with cells from a fast growing culture characterized by a high ratio of electron carriers to Bchl, in contrast to slow growing cells. The transients display similar characteristics as described for oxygenic photosynthesis. Immediately upon illumination a peak appears which is followed by one or several sinks and maxima before a steady state is reached. Transients recorded with cells in buffer in the absence of organic substrate (-SU) are more articulated than in the presence of electron donors (+SU). Moreover, for (-SU) cells the steady state fluorescence is high, tending to move to the F_{max} value at higher irradiances. With (+SU) cells a low fluorescence level is approached which often lies at or below the F_0 value. F_0 is the level of fluorescence without actinic light for a time long enough to attain a steady state. Fig.6 shows the transition from (-SU) to (+SU)

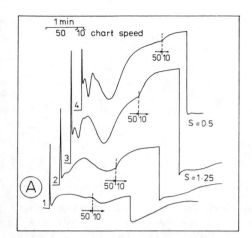 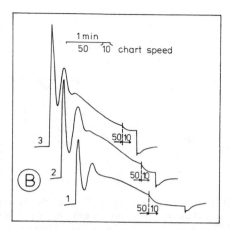

FIGURE 4: Transients at various irradiances (in $W.m^{-2}$): (1) 50; (2) 100; (3) 200; (400). *Rb. sphaeroides* GA, 30°C, N_2+CO_2. (A) MOPS buffer; recorder sensivity S: 1,2,3 : 1.25, 4: 0.5 $mm.mV^{-1}$ and (B) Siström medium.

condition during the measurement. The addition of succinate to the circulating medium suppresses the high fluorescence (curve 2) and later the pattern typical for (+SU) is recorded (curve 3).

Light transients after switching off the actinic light for increasing dark intervals (Fig.7) show that the order in which the individual sinks and maxima emerge differs, possibly linked with different rates of dark

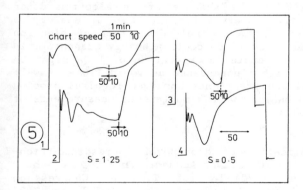 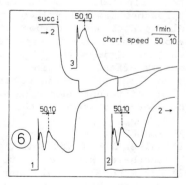

FIGURE 5: Transients at various temperatures: (1) 12°C, (2) 23°C, (3) 30°C, (4) 36°C. *Rb. sphaeroides* GA, MOPS buffer, N_2+CO_2 , 400 $W . m^{-2}$. (S) in $mm.mV^{-1}$.

FIGURE 6: Effect of succinate: (1), (2) cells in MOPS buffer; succ ↓ : succinate added to final concentration of 15 mM; (3) curve recorded 20 min after succinate addition.

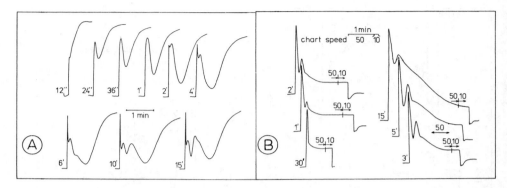

FIGURE 7: Light transients following dark intervals of varying length as indicated at the start of each curve. *Rb. sphaeroides* GA, 400 W.m^{-2}, 30°C, N_2+CO_2. Cells were suspended in MOPS buffer (A) or in Siström medium (B).

adaption of electron transfer and proton translocation steps.

The pattern of the transients and their response to various factors are similar to those described for chloroplasts and leaves. The mechanism of their generation, however, might differ in view of the differences between the bacterial and oxygenic photosynthetic membrane, bacteria having only a cyclic photoinduced electron flow leading to the formation of Δp. For the dissipation of Δp several competing pathways are present. Apart from the ATP synthetase Δp drives the reversal of the NADH dehydrogenase and the transhydrogenase reaction. Interestingly the steady state fluorescence with cells in the absence of an electron donor approaches maximal values, a fact observed long ago (6). In analogy to chloroplasts when carbon assimilation is halted by lack of electron donor, a high Δp is expected to build up causing energy quenching. In (-SU) conditions the high steady state concentration of P+QA might be equally effective in inducing high fluorescence as would P+QA-. A well founded interpretation of all the transients observed requires probing of the different quenching mechanisms with simultaneous measurements of the energetic state of the cells.

REFERENCES
(1) Walker D.A. (1988) In: Applications of Chlorophyll Fluorescence (Lichtenthaler H.K., ed.), pp. 13-20, Kluwer Academic Publ., Dordrecht.
(2) Hoffmann W. and Metzner H. (1972) in Proc. IInd Int. Congress on Photosynthesis, Stresa 1971 (Forti G. et al. eds.), Vol.1, pp. 369-371, Dr. W.Junk, The Hague
(3) Vredenberg W.J. and Duysens L.N.M. (1963) Nature 197,355-357
(4) deKlerk H., Govindjee, Kamen M.D. and Lavorel J. (1969) Proc. Natl. Acad. Sci. USA 62, 972-978
(5) Schreiber U. (1983) Photosynth. Res. 4, 361-364
(6) Wassink E.C., Katz E. and Dorrestein R. (1942) Enzymologia 10, 285-354

THE INFLUENCE OF LIGHT INTENSITY ON THE ORGANIZATION OF THE PHOTOSYN-
THETIC APPARATUS RHODOPSEUDOMONAS PALUSTRIS STRAIN AB

Yu.E.EROKHIN, Z.K.MAKHNEVA, I.R.PROKHORENKO, Institute of Soil Science
and Photosynthesis, USSR Acad. Sci., Pushchino, 142292, USSR

1.   INTRODUCTION
     The light intensity affects the organization of the photosynthetic
apparatus (PSA) of purple bacteria, inducing changes in the quantity of
pigment containing membranes, proteins, reaction centres (RC), and in
the size of photosynthetic units /1/. However, little is known about
changes in the organization of the basic components and their state in
membranes during adaptation of PSA to varying light intensities. It has
been the aim of the present work to study the state of pigments and
pigment-binding proteins in complexes and lamellae isolated from Rhodopseudomonas palustris st.AB grown at different light intensities under
the action of a nonpenetrating oxidizer potassium ferricyanide,
$K_3Fe(CN)_6$ and pronase E.

2.   MATERIALS AND METHODS
     The cells of Rps.palustris st.AB (the collection of Moscow State
University) were grown for 4 days at 30°C /2/ under anaerobic conditions
and the light intensity 300 and 30000 lx. The cells were disintegrated
at 4°C for 10 min in a homogenizer with glass beads (8000 rpm) in
0.05 M tris-HCl buffer, pH 7.4. The lamellae were isolated by fractional centrifugation. Pigment-protein complex B8000-850 and RC-B875 were
isolated by electrophoresis in PAAG after a incubation of lamellae with
3.3% Triton X-100.

3.   RESULTS AND DISCUSSION
3.1. Effect of light intensity on PSA Rps.palustris st.AB.
     The comparison of Rps.palustris st.AB cells grown at high and low
light intensities, as well as of the isolated lamellae and complexes revealed considerable differences in the composition of PSA
components (Table 1).
     The analysis of the spectra of lamellae and isolated complexes
showed that the high light intensity favours the formation of
membranes and LHII of Type I ($A_{850} \geqslant A_{800}$). At the low light intensity there appear membranes and LHII of Type II, ($A_{800} \geqslant A_{850}$)
(Fig.1), which is in accord with the earlier described results /2/.

M. Baltscheffsky (ed.), Current Research in Photosynthesis, Vol. IV, 345–348.
© 1990 Kluwer Academic Publishers. Printed in the Netherlands.

TABLE 1. Content of PSA components of Rps.palustris at different
light intensities

Object	Light intensity	
	300 lx	30000 lx
Cells:		
BChl, mol/cell	15.2×10^6	2.0×10^6
RC per cell	84.9×10^3	41.5×10^3
PCU (mol.BChl/RC)	179.5	47.7
Lamellae:		
RC (nmol)/mg protein	0.22	0.12
BChl (nmol)/mg protein	49.2	21.5
Complexes:		
B800-850; BChl (nmol)/mg prot.	77.3	38.5
RC-B875; BChl (nmol)/mg prot.	32.9	30.8

In view of the above said, the bacterium Rps.palustris st.AB has
been chosen as a convenient object to study the adaptational rearrangements in PSA.

3.2. Effect of potassium ferricyanide on the pigment system.
Potassium ferricyanide is able to accept electrons from P890 as
well as irreversibly oxidize different forms of BChl in the LHI
and LHII at concentrations as much as E_h +600 mV /3/. This ability
was used to asses the availability of different pigment forms in
lamellae and complexes of Types I and II.
In Type I lamellae, the oxidation of pigments was observed at
$K_3Fe(CN)_6$ concentrations of $10^{-3}M$, while in Type II, to register
the fact of BChl oxidation during the same period of time, it was
necessary to increase the concentration to $5 \cdot 10^{-3}M$. All this
points out to significant differences in the organization of
pigments in both types membranes.
The oxidation of BChl 800 in lamellae of both types went slowly
and after 2 h only 10% BChl were oxidized. Longwave forms of BChl
were oxidized very rapidly, and in Type II lamellae they were not
in the spectrum 10 min later, while in Type I, up to 20% of the
long-wave form were oxidized within the same time interval. The
rates of oxidation of BChl 800 and BChl 865 become comparable
when the ratio $A_{800}/A_{865}=1$ (Fig.2). The analysis of the absorption
spectra of the complexes, isolated from the lamellae which under-
gone the action of the oxidizer, reveals the predominant oxidation
of long-wave forms of BChl 850 in B800-850, and of BChl in RC-B875,
their maxima being shifted by 10 nm in B800-850 and by 35 nm in
RC-B875 (Fig.3a,b). It is noteworthy that more rapidly are oxidized the pigments of the LHII in case of the lamellae Type I and
the pigments of the LHI in case of the lamellae Type II.

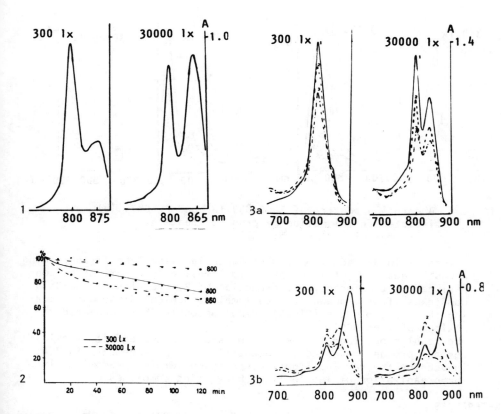

FIGURE 1. Absorption spectra of the lamellae of Rps.palustris.

FIGURE 2. Oxidation of different BChl forms in the lamellae of
Rps.palustris

FIGURE 3. Absorption spectra of B800-850 (a) and RC-B875 (b)
isolated from lamellae treated by $K_3Fe(CN)_6$:
1) - control: 2) - 10 min; 3)- 2 h.

3.3. Effect of pronase on the pigment binding proteins.
Pronase was used to reveal distinctions in the organization of
pigment binding proteins of the lamellae and complexes B800-850
of Type I and II. Type II lamellae were characterized by the predominant destruction of BChl800, while in Type I both BChl800 and
BChl875 degraded at similar rates. The spectral analysis of complexes B800-850 and RC-B875 released during the hydrolysis of
Type I and II lamellae showed an equal drop in the absorption in
the LHII of both forms (Fig.4a,b) which was accompanied by the
appearance of free BChl.

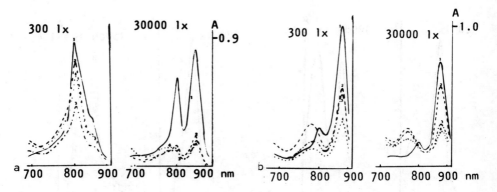

FIGURE 4. Absorption spectra of B800-850 (a) and RC-B875 (b)
isolated from lamellae by pronase treatment:
1) - control; 2) - 1 h; 3) - 2 h; 4) - 4 h.

A more rapid degradation of BChl800 in lamellae Type II containing
a double quantity of RC compared to lamellae Type I might be conditioned by the foregoing destruction of RC proteins. In RC-B875
complexes, from pronase treated lamellae BChl800 disappeared during the first minutes (Fig.4), simultaneously there appeared the
maximum of free BChl.
The results obtained in the present study on the effect of oxidizer and pronase revealed the adaptational rearrangements in PCA,
induced by the varying light intensity concerning predominantly
the organization of labile light harvesting complexes.

REFERENCES
1 Golecki, J.R., Schumacher, A. and Drews, G. (1980) Eur. J. Cell Biol.
23, 1-5
2 Hayashi, H., Miyao, M. and Morita, S. (1982) J.Biochem. 91, 1017-1027
3 Kuntz, J.D.,Jr., Loach, P.L. and Calvin, M. (1964) Biophys. J. 4,
227-249

EFFECTS OF GROWTH IRRADIANCE ON THE PHOTOSYNTHETIC APPARATUS OF THE
RED ALGA *PORPHYRIDIUM CRUENTUM*

Francis X. Cunningham, Jr., Ronald J. Dennenberg[*], Laszlo Mustardy,
Paul A. Jursinic[*] and Elisabeth Gantt

Department of Botany, University of Maryland, College Park, MD 20742;
[*]USDA-ARS, Peoria, IL 61604

1. INTRODUCTION

The unicellular red alga *Porphyridium cruentum* may be regarded as
a "shade" plant, growing best at light intensities much less than that
of full sunlight. Yet it is able to acclimate to higher growth
irradiance as evidenced by an increased photosynthetic capacity (1).
We are examining the acclimation process by quantifying various
components of the photosynthetic apparatus and certain key photosynthetic enzymes in order to understand the physiological changes which
underlie the enhancement in photosynthetic performance. The present
study is an investigation of changes in the light-harvesting apparatus
of *P. cruentum* as a function of growth irradiance.

2. MATERIALS AND METHODS

Porphyridium cruentum (ATCC 50161) was grown in batch culture at
18°C under continuous light provided by daylight fluorescent lamps (1)
and harvested in the log phase of growth. Thylakoids were prepared
and chlorophyll (Chl) and phycoerythrin (PE) were assayed as described
previously (1). Phycobilisome (PBS) numbers were calculated from the
PE levels. For HPLC analysis, Chl and carotenoids were extracted in
acetone:water (100:17, vol:vol) from cells which had been broken in a
French press. Pigments were separated on an Altex Ultrasphere ODS
column using a mobile phase gradient of increasing acetone in water.
They were identified by absorption spectra and retention time, and
quantified by integrated peak area in comparison with standards. P_{700}
and Q_A were quantified according to Dennenberg et al (2). Cell and
plastid volumes were determined from electron micrographs of central
sections of cells.

3. RESULTS AND DISCUSSION
3.1. Cell Growth and Morphology

Cultures of *Porphyridium cruentum* were grown under four different
intensities of continuous white light which together encompass nearly
the entire growth range. Generation time decreased with increasing
light intensity to a minimum of about 18 hours under 180 $\mu E \cdot m^{-2} \cdot s^{-1}$,
but a further increase in light intensity inhibited growth (Table 1).
Cell volume increased with increase in growth light intensity such
that cells under the highest light intensity had three times the
volume of cells grown under low light (Table 1).

M. Baltscheffsky (ed.), Current Research in Photosynthesis, Vol. IV, 349–352.

TABLE 1. Properties of the *Porphyridium cruentum* Cultures

Growth Irradiance ($\mu E \cdot m^{-2} \cdot s^{-1}$)	6	35	180	280
Generation time (h)	150	36	18	22
Cell volume (μm^3)	54 ± 14	102 ± 28	140 ± 32	156 ± 37
Plastid volume (μm^3)	38 ± 8	55 ± 12	37 ± 14	41 ± 12
Thylakoid area (μm^2/cell)	630 ± 190	580 ± 180	300 ± 150	250 ± 100

Volumes and Areas are mean ± SD of twenty separate measurements.

3.2. Chlorophyll and Carotenoids

Chl *a*, zeaxanthin, and β-carotene are the major pigments in *P. cruentum*, with a lesser amount of cryptoxanthin and trace amounts of other carotenoids (Table 2). Cells grown under the two higher light intensities had only one-third of the Chl and one-half of the β-carotene and cryptoxanthin found in cells grown under the two lower light intensities (Table 2). In contrast, zeaxanthin is not appreciably affected by the growth light intensity. The lack of any correlation of the level of zeaxanthin with Chl (Table 2), thylakoid membrane area (Table 1), or growth irradiance (Table 2) suggests that this carotenoid is not a component of the light-harvesting antenna.

TABLE 2. Cell Content of Chlorophyll and Carotenoids

Growth Irradiance ($\mu E \cdot m^{-2} \cdot s^{-1}$)	6	35	180	280
		mol/10^{17} cells		
Chlorophyll	192 ± 21	203 ± 17	62 ± 5	66 ± 4
Zeaxanthin	42 ± 7	52 ± 2	44 ± 4	57 ± 13
β-Carotene	32 ± 4	34 ± 2	17 ± 1	15 ± 3
Cryptoxanthin	3.0 ± 0.5	4.1 ± 1.2	1.9 ± 0.2	1.8 ± 0.6
Unidentified Carots.	2.7 ± 0.3	3.5 ± 0.6	2.2 ± 0.2	3.4 ± 1.2
Total Carotenoids	80 ± 11	93 ± 3	64 ± 6	76 ± 18

All values are mean ± SD of 3 to 5 independent experiments.

3.3. Cell Content and Stoichiometry of PSI, PSII, and Phycobilisomes

Cells grown under higher light intensities exhibited up to a three-fold reduction in PSI, PSII, and PBS, but the relative numbers of these components changed little with growth irradiance (Table 3). The ratio of PSII to PSI (measured as Q_A and P_{700}) remains in a narrow range between 0.43 and 0.54 (Table 3). PBS, which serve as the major light-harvesting antenna for PSII, maintain a relatively fixed stoichiometry with PSII. We found about three PSII centers per PBS. Values of Chl/P_{700} and Chl/Q_A both decrease by about 20% as photon flux density increases from 6 to 280 $\mu E \cdot m^{-2} \cdot s^{-1}$ (Table 3), indicating that the Chl antenna size of PSI or PSII (or both) becomes smaller.

TABLE 3. Phycobilisome and Reaction Center Content and Stoichiometry

Growth Irradiance ($\mu E \cdot m^{-2} \cdot s^{-1}$)	6	35	180	280
	mol/10^{19} cells			
PSI (P_{700})	107 ± 16	118 ± 7	41 ± 3	44 ± 2
PSII (Q_A)	57 ± 4	52 ± 12	18 ± 1	23 ± 1
PBS	20 ± 2	19 ± 2	6.0 ± 1.1	5.8 ± 0.7
	mol/mol			
Q_A/P_{700}	0.54 ± 0.06	0.45 ± 0.11	0.43 ± 0.02	0.53 ± 0.01
Q_A/PBS	2.9 ± 0.1	2.8 ± 0.4	3.0 ± 0.7	3.9 ± 0.4
Chl/P_{700}	181 ± 8	172 ± 13	152 ± 7	148 ± 1
Chl/Q_A	339 ± 33	405 ± 67	352 ± 33	281 ± 2

All values are mean ± SD of 3 to 5 independent experiments.

3.4. Phycobilisome Size Reduction Under High Light

Unlike those in cyanobacteria, the PBS of red algae are widely regarded as invariant in size and composition. However, the absorption spectrum of PBS isolated from cells of *P. cruentum* varies with the growth irradiance (Fig. 1). When normalized at the absorption peak of allophycocyain (APC; 650 nm), isolated PBS have equivalent absorbance at the peak of phycocyanin (PC; 625 nm), but those grown under higher light intensities exhibit a much lower absorbance in the range 480 to 580, where PE has its absorption maximum (Fig. 1). Based on the difference at 545 nm, PBS isolated from cells grown under 180 or 280 $\mu E \cdot m^{-2} \cdot s^{-1}$ contain only about 75% of the PE found in PBS isolated from cells grown under 6 or 35 $\mu E \cdot m^{-2} \cdot s^{-1}$ (Fig. 1 and data not shown). This reduction in PE is not due to a loss during purification of the PBS or to a bleaching or alteration in the chromophore content of PE. Immunoquantitation of the apoproteins of PE, PC, and APC in whole cells (not shown) indicates a comparable reduction (20-25%) in PE relative to PC and APC. Since APC is a core component while PE is more peripheral (3), we conclude that PBS in cells grown under high light intensities are deficient in PE compared to those grown under low light (Fig. 2).

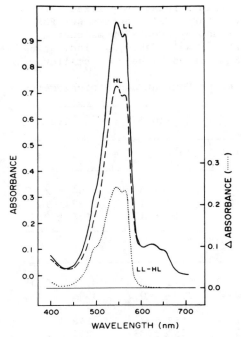

Low Light

PE

PC

APC

High Light

Figure 1. Absorption spectra and difference spectrum of PBS (in 0.5 M NaPO$_4$ at pH 7.0) from cells grown under 6 (LL) or 280 (HL) μE·m^{-2}·s^{-1}. Normalized at 650 nm.

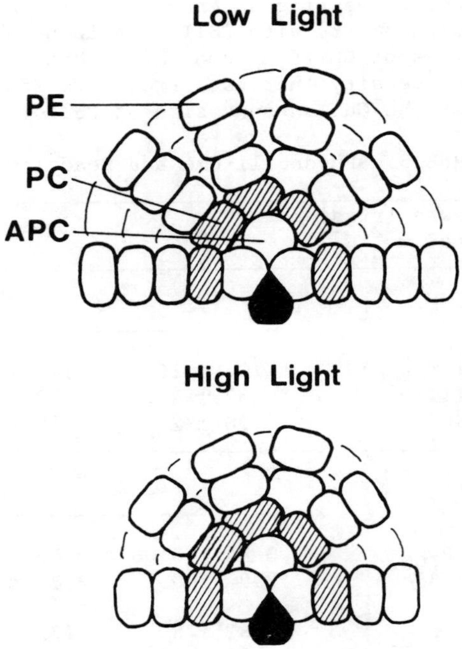

Figure 2. Schematic diagram of PBS grown under high or low intensity white light. PE content is reduced under the high light intensity.

4. SUMMARY

Acclimation of *P. cruentum* to an increase in irradiance involves:
1. No appreciable change in the stoichiometries of PSI, PSII, and phycobilisomes.
2. Up to a three-fold reduction in numbers of PSI, PSII, and phycobilisomes with a concomitant reduction in Chl, β-carotene, and thylakoid membrane area.
3. A decrease in phycobilisome size due to a reduction in phycoerythrin content by 20-25%.
4. No appreciable change in the cell content of zeaxanthin, the major carotenoid of this organism.

REFERENCES

1 Levy, I. and Gantt, E. (1988) J. Phycol. 24: 452-458
2 Dennenberg, R.J., Jursinic, P.A. and McCarthy, S.A. (1986) Biochim. Biophys. Acta 852: 222-233
3 Gantt, E., Lipschultz, C.A. and Zilinskas, B. (1976) Biochim. Biophys. Acta 430: 375-388

RED LIGHT ENHANCES Q_A RELATIVE TO P_{700} AND PHYCOBILISOMES IN THE RED ALGA *PORPHYRIDIUM CRUENTUM*

Francis X. Cunningham, Jr., Ronald J. Dennenberg[*], Laszlo Mustardy, Paul A. Jursinic[*] and Elisabeth Gantt

Department of Botany, University of Maryland, College Park, MD 20742; [*]USDA-ARS, Peoria, IL 61604

1. INTRODUCTION

In photosynthetic organisms which contain phycobilisomes (PBS), PSI and PSII have very different, almost complementary, absorption spectra. Most of the red and blue light-absorbing Chl *a* is in the light-harvesting antenna system of PSI (1-5). The green and orange light-absorbing phycobiliproteins are associated with and transfer absorbed light energy predominantly to PSII (1-5). In this study we examine the effects of growth under PSI light (red) or PSII light (green) on the photosynthetic light-harvesting apparatus of the unicellular red alga *Porphyridium cruentum*. The influence of light intensity is examined in a companion paper (6).

2. MATERIALS AND METHODS

Batch cultures of *Porphyridium cruentum* (ATCC 50161) were grown under 15 $\mu E \cdot m^{-2} \cdot s^{-1}$ (between 400 and 700 nm) of continuous red (RL) or green light (GL), or 6 $\mu E \cdot m^{-2} \cdot s^{-1}$ of white light (WL), so that all cultures had comparable generation times of about one week. Spectra of the red and green light fields are shown in Figure 1. White light was provided by daylight fluorescent bulbs. Cultures were harvested in the exponential phaseof growth at a density of 3-4 x 10^6 cells/ml. Other materials and methods are described in a companion paper (6).

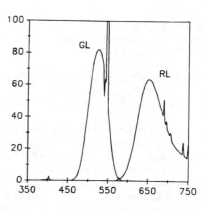

FIGURE 1. Spectra of the red and green light fields.

3. RESULTS AND DISCUSSION

3.1. Chlorophyll and Carotenoid Pigments

The pigment content of *P. cruentum* varies little whether cultures are grown under low intensity RL, GL, or WL (Table 1). Total amounts of Chl *a* and carotenoids are somewhat lower in the smaller GL cells, but the relative amounts of Chl *a* and the three major carotenoids

M. Baltscheffsky (ed.), Current Research in Photosynthesis, Vol. IV, 353–356.

(zeaxanthin, β-carotene, and cryptoxanthin, which together account for 94-98% of the total carotenoid) are remarkably constant (Table 1).

In cultures grown under GL, much of the absorbance at 650 nm in acetone extracts is due to compounds other than Chl a (see "Unidentified Chl" in Table 1). GL cells contain increased amounts of a component which elutes near the front (as expected for Chlide a or Pchlide a) when pigments are separated by HPLC on an ODS column (6). They also have substantial amounts of other compounds which are not detected, or only in trace amounts, in cultures grown under RL or under a broad range of WL intensities (6 to 280 $\mu E \cdot m^{-2} \cdot s^{-1}$; data not shown).

TABLE 1. Chlorophyll and Carotenoids

Growth Light	Green	Red	White
	$mol/10^{17}$ cells		
Chlorophyll a	146 ± 18	164 ± 23	183 ± 21
Unidentified Chl*	37 ± 18	7 ± 2	9 ± 1
Total Chlorophyll	183 ± 9	171 ± 26	192 ± 21
	$mol/100$ mol Chl a		
Zeaxanthin	23 ± 3	24 ± 1	23 ± 1
β-Carotene	20 ± 2	16 ± 1	18 ± 1
Cryptoxanthin	2.0 ± 0.2	1.5 ± 0.4	1.6 ± 0.1
Unidentified Carotenoids	0.8 ± 0.1	2.5 ± 0.8	1.5 ± 0.3
Total Carotenoids	45 ± 5	44 ± 2	44 ± 2

* Peaks in HPLC elution profiles other than Chl a, which absorbed at both 650 and 442 nm.
Data are mean ± SD of 3 to 4 independent experiments.

3.2. Cell Content and Stoichiometry of PSI, PSII, and Phycobilisomes

The spectral quality of the growth light greatly affects the cell content and stoichiometry of PSI, PSII, and PBS in $P.$ $cruentum$ (Fig. 2). PSII centers (measured as Q_A) are three times as numerous in RL cells than in GL cells (Table 2). WL cells contain an intermediate amount. Conversely, PSI centers in RL cells (measured as P_{700}) are only two-thirds as numerous as in GL or WL cells (Table 2). Cell content of PBS is about the same whether cultures are grown under continuous low intensity red, green or white light (Table 2), and their size and composition are constant (based on a fixed stoichiometry of PE, PC, and APC in whole cells and on comparable absorption spectra for isolated phycobilisomes; data not shown).

The ratio of PSII to PBS has been reported by Ohki et al (7) to be invariant irrespective of the spectral quality of the growth light both in cyanobacteria and in red algae, including $P.$ $cruentum$. Our data, which indicate a large variation in the ratio of PSII to PBS (Table 2), are in apparent conflict with this report, but are

TABLE 2. Phycobilisome and Reaction Center Content and Stoichiometry

Growth Light	Green	Red	White
	mol/10^{19} cells		
PSI (P_{700})	114 ± 8	75 ± 15	107 ± 16
PSII (Q_A)	29 ± 5	91 ± 22	57 ± 4
PBS	17 ± 1	20 ± 2	20 ± 2
	mol/mol		
Q_A/P_{700}	0.26 ± 0.04	1.26 ± 0.01	0.54 ± 0.06
Q_A/PBS	1.7 ± 0.3	4.4 ± 0.6	2.9 ± 0.1
Chl/P_{700}	158 ± 5	227 ± 8	181 ± 8
Chl/Q_A	628 ± 93	188 ± 22	339 ± 33
Chl/PBS	1050 ± 10	820 ± 50	980 ± 60

PBS numbers were calculated from spectral assays of phycoerythrin.
Data are mean ± SD of 3 to 5 experiments.

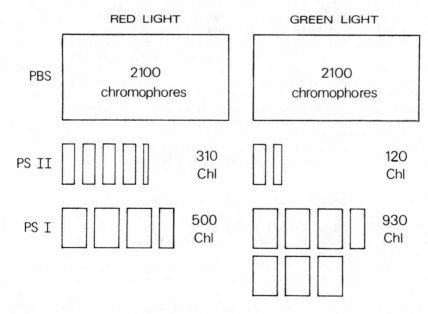

FIGURE 2. Schematic illustration of the relative numbers of PSI and
PSII per phycobilisome in cells grown under RL or GL. Each is drawn
to scale according to Chl content (70 Chl/PSI and 140 Chl/PSI) or
phycobilin chromophore content (PBS), and the approximate numbers of
PSI and PSII Chl per PBS are listed.

consistent with the earlier work of Ley and Butler on *P. cruentum* (2). They reported that cells grown under RL apportion 40% of their Chl to PSII compared to only 5% in GL, an eight-fold increase (2). Under the same conditions, PE increased only 1.6-fold (2). Our data indicate that PSI, PSII, an PBS maintain constant Chl and PE antenna sizes. Thus, these changes in Chl and PBS imply a five-fold change in the stoichiometry of PSII and PBS in GL and RL cells.

3.3. Chlorophyll Antenna Sizes of PSI and PSII

Chl antenna sizes of PSI and PSII were calculated from data in Table 2. Since RL cultures have 1.00 more Q_A per P_{700} than GL cultures (1.26 - 0.26 = 1.00), then each PSII is associated with 69 ± 16 Chl (227 Chl/P_{700} in RL minus 158 Chl/P_{700} in GL = 69 Chl per Q_A). Comparisons of RL and GL cultures with WL cultures give comparable estimates with mean values of 70 Chl/PSII and 140 Chl/PSI. From these we calculate that PSII has about 40% of the Chl in RL, 20% in WL, and 11% in GL-grown cultures of *P. cruentum* (See Fig. 2).

4. SUMMARY

Growth of the red alga *Porphyridium cruentum* under light absorbed primarily by PSI (red light) or by PSII (green light) resulted in compensatory changes in the light-harvesting apparatus:

1. The ratio of PSII to PSI increased five-fold in cultures grown under PSI light compared to those grown under PSII light. Cell content of both PSI and PSII is variable.
2. Chlorophyll antenna sizes of the photosystems remained constant at about 70 Chl per PSII and 140 Chl per PSI.
3. The proportion of the total Chl associated with PSI increases from only about 11% under PSII light to 40% under PSI light.
4. Phycobilisome size and composition remain constant, and their number per cell varies little with spectral quality.
5. Carotenoid content and composition are little affected by spectral quality.
6. Our most important finding is that the number of PSII per phycobilisome is not fixed but varies between two and four.

REFERENCES

1 Chereskin, B.M., Clement-Metral, J.D. and Gantt, E. (1985) Plant Physiol. 77: 626-629
2 Ley, A.C., Butler, W.L. (1980) Plant Physiol. 65: 714-722
3 Manodori, A., Alhadeff, M., Glazer, A.N. and Melis, A. (1984) Arch. Microbiol. 139: 117-123
4 Mimuro, M. and Fujita, Y. (1977) Biochim. Biophys. Acta 459: 376-389
5 Wang, R.T., Stevens, C.L.R. and Myers, J. (1977) Photochem. Photobiol. 25: 103-108
6 Cunningham, F.X. Jr., Dennenberg, R.J., Mustardy, L., Jursinic, P.A. and Gantt, E. (1989) In Proc. VIIIth Intl. Cong. Photosyn., Stockholm, Sweden
7 Ohki, K., Okabe, Y., Murakami, A. and Fujita, Y. (1987) Plant Cell Physiol. 28: 1219-1226.

REGULATION OF LHC II mRNA LEVELS DURING PHOTOADAPTATION IN DUNALIELLA
TERTIOLECTA (CHLOROPHYCEAE)

Julie LaRoche, Anne Mortain-Bertrand, John Bennett and
Paul G. Falkowski

Brookhaven National Laboratory, Upton, NY 11973

INTRODUCTION
    Many photosynthetic organisms adapt to growth irradiance changes by
adjusting the absorption cross-section of their photosynthetic apparatus
(1,2). Alteration of the effective absorption cross-section results in
part from changes in cellular abundance of pigment protein complexes.
The capability to photoadapt is especially pronounced in unicellular
algae which are well suited to the study of light intensity regulation.

We have previously studied physiological aspects of photoadaptation in
the marine chlorophyte Dunaliella tertiolecta (3,4,5) in which biochemical, and biophysical aspects of photoadaptation occurs on a time scale
of a few hours to tens of hours, depending on the photosynthetic component studied (6,7). Sukenik et al. (7) characterized the sequence of
events leading to a steady-state photosynthesis and growth in cells
which are shifted from high to low light. Their kinetic analysis revealed that LHC II apoprotein synthesis occurs prior to the synthesis
of reaction center proteins, or membrane lipids. Here we examine light
dependent regulation of the LHC II apoproteins at the molecular level.
We have sequenced a cDNA clone encoding a D. tertiolecta cab gene
(LaRoche et al., unpubl.) and use it here as a probe to assess the
complexity of the cab gene family in D. tertiolecta and to follow the
expression of LHC II mRNA during shifts from high to low irradiance
levels.

MATERIALS AND METHODS
    D. tertiolecta (Woods Hole clone DUN) was grown at $18^{\circ}C$ in a
turbidostat with artificial sea water (3) and at a cell density of
5×10^5/ml. Continuous light was provided by VHO fluorescent tubes. For
the kinetic studies, growth irradiance was shifted in a single step from
700 (HL) to 70 (LL) µmole quanta $m^{-2}s^{-1}$. Pigment determination and
thylakoid membrane preparation were as previously described (5). Whole
cell protein extracts were separated on 12% polyacrylamide gels, transferred to nitrocellulose and the levels of LHC II apoproteins were
determined by immunodetection using anti-LHC II raised against pea (5).
High molecular weight DNA was prepared from D. tertiolecta using the
method of Grant et al. (8). One µg of DNA was digested with the
restriction enzyme Hind III or Bgl II according to manufacturer's

M. Baltscheffsky (ed.), Current Research in Photosynthesis, Vol. IV, 357–360.

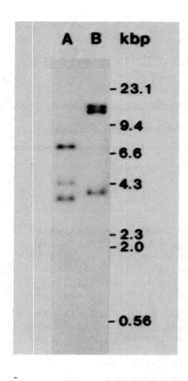

Fig. 1. Autoradiogram of genomic DNA
digested with: A) Hind III, and B) Bgl II
and hybridized to a short restriction
fragment (110 bp) at moderate stringency.

instructions, electrophorized on 0.7% agarose gels and transferred to
nitrocellulose (9). A short restriction fragment (110bp) encompassing
part of the second trans-membrane span of the D. tertiolecta cab gene
was radio-labelled with ^{32}P using random primers and used as a probe on
the genomic DNA. RNA was extracted from D. tertiolecta following the
method of (10). Two to five µg total RNA were electrophoresed on denaturing formaldehyde agarose gels, transferred to nitrocellulose, and
probed with nick-translated whole cDNA insert encoding for the cab gene
(9).

RESULTS AND DISCUSSION

Hybridization of a restriction fragment from the Dun Cab 1 containing part of the 2nd transmembrane span, to genomic DNA digested with
Hind III and Bgl II showed three distinct bands, suggesting the presence
of the same number of cab genes in D. tertiolecta (Fig. 1). Hybridization with the entire cDNA insert (not shown) suggests 4 to 7 genes.
However, short probes, usually yield more realistic results when estimating the size of a gene family (11). The number of cab genes in
higher plants ranges between 10 to 20 (12), Arabidopsis being an exception with three genes only (13). Although we have no data on the
complexity of genomic DNA from D. tertiolecta, we assume that the genome
is similar to that of C. reinhardtii and lacks almost entirely the
repetitive DNA regions (14) thus suggesting the presence of fewer

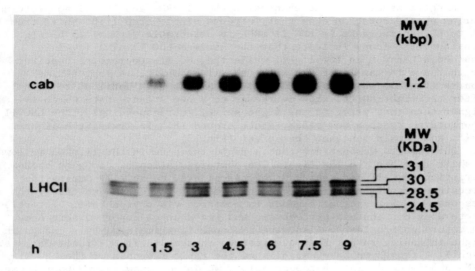

Fig. 2. Autoradiogram showing the increase in LHC II mRNA and apoprotein after a shift from high to low light at 0 hr. Total RNA
hybridized to ^{32}P-labelled cab cDNA insert (top) and whole cells
protein extract (bottom) challenged with anti-LHC II raised against pea.

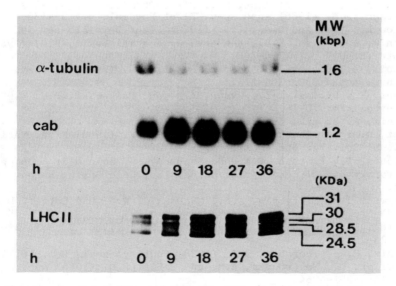

Fig. 3. Changes in α-tubulin and LHC II mRNA (top) and LHC II apoproteins (bottom) after a shift from high to low light at 0 hr.

rather than more cab genes in this species.

Kinetic studies of the changes in LHC II mRNA and LHC II apoproteins during photoadaptation show that, after a single step light shift from HL to LL, an increase in LHC II mRNA is detectable within 1.5 h (Fig.2). Densitometric scans indicate that the maximum LHC II mRNA level is reached after 6 h in low light, while the LHC II apoproteins continue to increase for at least 9 h after the light shift. A longer time course (Fig. 3) shows that LHC II mRNA remains high until up to 18 h after the light shift, then decreases to a new steady-state which is higher than that prior to the light shift. Correspondingly, the LHC II apoproteins reach a new steady-state around 18 h following the light shift and remain constant thereafter (Fig. 3).

Our results demonstrate that a rapid increase in LHC II mRNA follows a shift from high to low light. The photoregulation of cab gene transcription is well documented in higher plants, especially during the greening response of etiolated chloroplasts (12). In these cases, the response of photosynthetic genes is mediated via phytochrome. D. tertiolecta does not contain phytochrome and the changes reported here occur in mature chloroplasts. Also, the response is stimulated by a change in light intensity rather than qualitative changes in light (i.e., dark vs. light). Although we have established the rapid response of the LHC II mRNA abundance during photoadaptation, we do not know yet whether these changes reflect an increase in the rate of transcription of the cab genes or result from an increase in the stability of these RNA species. In addition, it is not clear whether this RNA level increase is essential or sufficient for the LL induced increase in LHC II.

REFERENCES
1. Boardman, N.K. (1977) Annu. Rev. Plant Physiol. 28: 355-377.
2. Anderson, J.M. (1986) Annu. Rev. Plant Physiol. 37: 93-136.
3. Falkowski, P.G. and Owen, T.G. (1980) Plant Physiol. 66: 592-595.
4. Sukenik, A., Wyman, K.D., Bennett, J. and Falkowski, P.G. (1987) Nature (Lond.) 327: 704-707.
5. Sukenik, A., Bennett, J. and Falkowski, P.G. (1988) Biochem. Biophys. Acta. 932: 206-215.
6. Berner, T., Dubinsky, Z., Wyman, K.D. and Falkowski, P.G. (1989) J. Phycol. 24: 70-78.
7. Sukenik, A. et al., in prep.
8. Grant, D.M., Gillham, N.W. and Boynton, J.E. (1980) Proc. Natl. Acad. of Sci. 77: 6067-6071.
9. Maniatis, T., Fritsch, E.F. and Sambrook, J. Molecular cloning. A laboratory manual Cold Spring Harbor Lab, Cold Spring Harbor, NY 1982.
10. Chirgwin, J.M., Przybyla, A.E., MacDonald, R.J. and Rutter, W.J. (1979) Biochemistry 18: 5294-5299.
11. Spoerel, N., Nguyen, H.T. and Kafatos, F.C. (1986) J. Mol. Biol. 190: 23-25.
12. Chitnis, P.R., Thornber, J.P. (1988) Photosynthesis Res. 16: 41-63.
13. Leutwiler, L., Meyerowitz, E.M. and Tobin, E.M. (1986) Nuc. Acids Res. 14: 4051-4064.
14. Howell, S.H. and Walker, L.L. (1976) Biochem. Biophys. Acta 418: 249-256.

FLUORESCENCE RESPONSES ON STEP CHANGES IN IRRADIANCE BY PLANTS FROM DIFFERENT LIGHT HABITATS

GILES JOHNSON[1], PETER HORTON[1], JULIE SCHOLES[1] AND PHILIP GRIME[2], [1]Robert Hill Institute, [2]N.E.R.C. Unit for Comparative Plant Ecology, University of Sheffield, SHEFFIELD, S10 2TN, UK

1. INTRODUCTION

Plants growing in different natural habitats experience light conditions that vary considerably in intensity, spectral quality and dynamic properties. Plants growing in the open will receive full sun for much of the time, with relativly little short term temporal variation. Leaves within a plant canopy will be exposed to rapidly fluctuating irradiance varying, both in quality and quantity, with leaf movement (1). Plants growing in an understorey will mainly receive light that has been leaf-filtered but this ambient low light will be punctuated by sunflecks as the sun passes over gaps in the canopy. These will vary in length from a few seconds to several minutes being affected by the density of tree cover and air movement (2).

Light, though a necessity for plants, can in excess damage the photosynthetic apparatus (3). Plants adapted to shaded habitats are particulary vulnerable to such photoinhibitory damage (4). Processes are known to exist that can help to protect against excess irradiance by enhancing the dissipation of light energy as heat (5,6). These processes are reflected in the non-photochemical quenching (qNP) of chlorophyll fluorescence seen on illuminating leaves.

Typically three different components of qNP are identified, being distinguished by half times for their relaxation in the dark (7). High energy-state quenching (qE) has a half time for relaxation of about 30 seconds and is believed to be associated with the trans-thylakoid pH gradient. State transition (qT) relaxing with a half time of 5-10 minutes is thought to be responsible for maintaining balanced excitation of the two photosystems. Photoinhibitory quenching (qI), with a half time of 30 minutes or more is thought to reflect both photodamage and the occurrence of longer term protective mechanisms.

Plants growing in light limiting situations need to maximise their efficiency of light capture and use whilst at the same time minimising photodamage during sunflecks. Protective mechanisms will help prevent damage during sunflecks but will, if they persist after the high light has ceased, lead to a decrease in the efficiency of photosynthesis. For plants of full sun habitats efficient use of light will be less important than the prevention of photodamage. Given the varying requirements of plants from different habitats it is of interest to ask whether differences can be seen in their use of the various dissipative processes. In this study a variety of species native to the region of Sheffield, England were examined in order to

M. Baltscheffsky (ed.), Current Research in Photosynthesis, Vol. IV, 361–364.
© 1990 *Kluwer Academic Publishers. Printed in the Netherlands.*

investigate whether there is any difference in their fluorescence response to step changes in irradiance.

2. MATERIALS AND METHODS.

Plants used in this study were either grown from seed collected locally or were themselves collected. In either case material was grown on under one of two artifical regimes. Light was provided by metal-halide lamps supplemented with tungsten filament light bulbs. "High light plants" were grown directly under these lights (intensity 200-500 μE m^{-2} s^{-1}). "Low light plants" were grown under filters selected to imitate natural understorey conditions. Plants were grown using an 14 hour day 8 hour night cycle.

Measurments were made on the youngest fully expanded leaf. Leaf discs were taken directly from the light and placed in Hansatech leaf disc O$_2$ electrode chamber (Hansatech Ltd, Kings Lynn, U.K.). Fluorescence was measured using a PAM 101 modulated fluorimeter (Heinz Walz, Effeltrich, W. Germany). White actinic light was provided by a Schott KL 1500 light.

Samples were dark adapted, in the chamber, for ten minutes before a saturating 1.5 second light pulse (intensity 2000-4000 μE m^{-2} s^{-1}) was given to establish the maximum fluorescence level (F$_m$). Actinic light was then switched on and further saturating pulses given as required. The quenching coefficients qQ (photochemical quenching) and qNP were calculated as described in (6).

In experiments where light increases were studied leaves were illuminated at the lower light intensity until a steady state had been reached (10-15 minutes) before the first saturating pulse was given. The actinic light was then increased to the higher intensity and pulses continued at 45 second intervals. Where responses to light decreases were investigated saturating pulses were started with the actinic light. Actinic light was then decreased after 10-15 minutes and saturating pulses continued at the lower intensity.

3. RESULTS AND DISCUSSION.

Figure 1. shows the response of two different species to a step increase in irradiance from 50 to 500 μE m^{-2} s^{-1}. There is a clear difference observable in the kinetics with which qNP builds up with the maximum level being reached much more rapidly in *Digitalis purpurea*, a plant of semi-shaded situations, than in *Chenopodium album* a full sun plant. This difference is seen in plants grown in either high or low light. In both species shown, as in all others studied studied qQ initally drops rapidly before recovering to a variable extent. The final level reached by both qQ and qNP was dependent on the high light intensity used. The kinetics of the rise of qNP was, however, found to be only partially dependent on the irradiance. Figure 2. shows data for *C. album* following an increase from 50 to 1500 μE m^{-2} s^{-1}. Whilst the final level of qNP is the same as seen in figure 1. for *D. purpurea*, the rate at which this level is reached is still slower. The use of a higher light appears to introduce a fast element in qNP rise whilst leaving a slower phase.

Figure 3. shows data for *C. album* and *D.purpurea* in response to a step decrease in irradiance from 500-50 μE m^{-2} s^{-1}. Again there is a difference in the kinetics of qNP change with relaxation being slower in *C. album* than in *D. purpurea*.

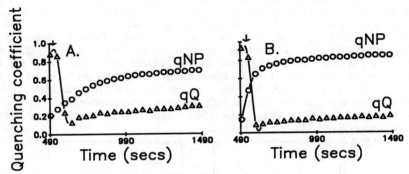

FIGURE 1 *Response of qQ (△) and qNP (○) in C. album (A.) and D. purpurea (B.) to a step increase in irradiance from 50 to 500 μE m^{-2} s^{-1}.*

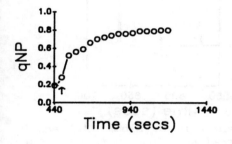

FIGURE 2 *Response of qNP in* C. album *to a step increase in irradiance from 50 to 1500 μE m^{-2} s^{-1}.*

Figure 4. shows part of the fluorescence data from which figure 3. was calculated. Whilst in *D. purpurea* there is a significant dip in the fluorescence (F_S) following the decrease in irradiance before the level recovers, this dip is absent in *C. album*. Such a dip can be induced by using a more intense high light but is never seen to the same extent as in *D. purpurea*.

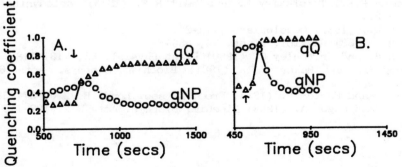

FIGURE 3 *Response of qQ (△) and qNP (○) in* C. album *(A.) and* D. purpurea *(B.) to a step decrease in irradiance from 500 to 50 μE m^{-2} s^{-1}.*

The processes responsible for non-photochemical quenching are still too poorly understood for any conclusions to be drawn as to the nature of the differences described here. It does seem reasonable to suppose that these differences are indicative of variation in the way in which the two species described deal with excess irradiance. The ecological significance of these data is unclear. The type of behaviour seen in *D. purpurea* is typical of plants from a wide variety of different habitats, including plants from full sun. The slow kinetics of *C. album* was only seen in two other species, both of full sun. The use of more persistent quenching processes by sun plants is consistant with their known habitat as is the use of rapidly induced and relaxing mechanisms by plants of dynamic environments. It is not possible to conclude from this data that there is a correlation between habitat and quenching characteristics.

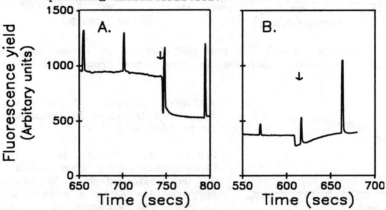

FIGURE 4   Response of fluorescence yield in C. album *(A.) and* D. purpurea *(B.) on a step increase in irradiance from 50 to 500 µE m⁻²* s^{-1}.

REFERENCES.
1. Kriedemann P.E., Torofkalvy E. and Smart R.E. (1973) Photosynthetica 7 (1) 18-27.
2. Pearcy R.W., (1983) Oecologia 58, 19-25.
3. Krause H. (1988) Physiol. Plant. 74, 566-574.
4. Powles S.B. and Critchley C. (1980) Plant Physiol. 65, 1181-1187.
5. Bradbury M. and Baker N.R. (1981) Biochim. Biophys. Acta 653, 542-551
6. Quick W.P. and Horton P. (1984) Proc. R. soc. Lond. B. 220, 371-382
7. Horton P. and Hague A. (1988) Biochim. Biophys. Acta 932, 107-115

THE RELATIONSHIP BETWEEN THE RELATIVE QUANTUM EFFICIENCIES OF PHOTOSYSTEMS IN LEAVES. EFFICIENCY OF PS2 IN RELATION TO NON-PHOTOCHEMICAL FLUORESCENCE QUENCHING.

B. Genty[1], J. Harbinson[2], J.M. Briantais[3], N.R. Baker[1], Dept of Biology, Univ. of Essex, Colchester, CO4 3SQ, U.K.[1], John Innes Inst., Norwich, NR4 7UH, U.K.[2], Lab. Ecologie Végétale, Univ. Paris Sud, Orsay, 91405 Cedex, France[3].

1.   INTRODUCTION

Recently the development of techniques capable of measuring in vivo simultaneously the photochemical (qQ) and non-photochemical (qNP) components of chlorophyll fluorescence quenching, absorbance changes at 820 nm and photosynthetic gas exchange of leaves have allowed quantitative estimation of the quantum efficiencies of photosystems 2 (ϕPS2) and 1 (ϕPS1) and non-cyclic electron transport in leaves (1-6). These studies have provided evidence that non-photochemical processes associated with qNP could explain the observed reduction of quantum yield of open PS2 reaction centres as light intensity is increased (1-3,5,6).

In this study, we show   a linear relationship between ϕPS1 and ϕPS2 and the quantum yield of non-cyclic electron transport in leaves when photosynthetic efficiency varies with light intensities. The results confirm that both the concentration of open PS2 reaction centres and their photochemical efficiency, which is modulated by non-photochemical processes associated with the antenna, determine ϕPS2.

Experiments with wild type and a chlorophyll b-less barley mutant are used to demonstrate that the amplitude of qNP depends upon the size and composition of the antenna. Analyses of light dosage response curves of the fluorescence yield increase induced by a single turnover flash in background continuous light of variable intensity are used to quantitate the decrease of the relative effective absorption cross section of PS2 units associated with qNP.

2.   MATERIALS AND METHODS

Intact leaves were obtained from plants of pea (Pisum sativum var. BC1), barley (Hordeum vulgare var. Clermont) and chlorophyll b -less barley (H. vulgare, chlorina F2 mutant) grown as previously described (3). Steady state measurements of modulated fluorescence emission yield were made simultaneously with modulated 820 nm absorbance change and CO2 gas exchange measurements as shown previously (5). Fo, Fs, Fm, qQ, qNP, the photochemical efficiency of open PS2 centres ϕexc estimated by Fv/Fm and the quantum efficiency of PS2 photochemistry ϕPS2 were determined as previously presented (3,5,6). The relative amount of non oxidised P700 in leaves was determined from 1-Δ820/Δ820max and was used to estimate the quantum efficiency of PS1, ϕPS1 (5,6).

Single turnover flash-induced fluorescence yield changes were

M. Baltscheffsky (ed.), Current Research in Photosynthesis, Vol. IV, 365–368.

recorded 170μs after the flash using a similar pulse amplitude fluorimeter as above (PAM 101, Walz). A xenon flash tube (15J, EG and G) in conjunction with a Schott BG39 glass filter produced a blue green flash with a half peak with of 3μs. The flash-induced changes in fluorescence yield were expressed as ΔFf (ΔFf=Ff-Fs) where Ff is the fluorescence yield induced by a single turnover flash and measured after 170us delay and Fs is the steady state fluorescence yield before the flash. Consequently ΔFf is defined as the flash-induced fluorescence yield change at 170μs after flash.

3. RESULTS AND DISCUSSION

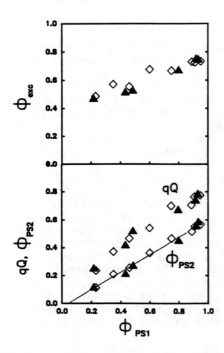

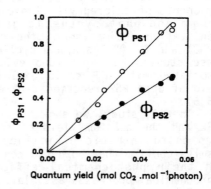

Quantum yield (mol CO_2 .mol $^{-1}$photon)

FIGURE 2. The relationship between the quantum efficiencies of PS1 and PS2, ΦPS1 and ΦPS2, and the steady state quantum yield of CO2 assimilation for a barley leaf in 2% O2 air.

FIGURE 1. The relationship between qQ, the photochemical efficiency of open PS2 reaction centres (Φexc), the quantum efficiency of PS2 (ΦPS2) and the quantum efficiency of PS1 (ΦPS1) for a barley leaf exposed to 2 (◊) and 20% (▲) O2 in air. Determination of these parameters were made at steady state over a range of irradiances from 0-1600 umol.m^{-2}.s^{-1}. Φexc was determined from Fv/Fm, ΦPS2 from ΔF/Fm (the product of qQ and Fv/Fm) and ΦPS1 from the size of the non oxidised P700 pool.

Increases in irradiance were used to modulate the photosynthetic activity of leaves and ΦPS1 and ΦPS2. The relationship between the PS2 parameters (qQ, Φexc, ΦPS2) and ΦPS1 for barley leaves in air or 2% O2 air observed under several light intensities (range 0-1600 umol.m^{-2}.s^{-1})

is presented in Fig.1. The linear correlation, passing almost through the origin of ΦPS1 and ΦPS2 demonstrates that over a wide range of irradiances barley leaves, at steady state photosynthesis, maintain a balance between ΦPS1 and ΦPS2. This balance is maintained under both photorespiratory and non-photorespiratory conditions. In low photorespiration conditions (2% O2), the changes of ΦPS1 and ΦPS2 correlate with the decrease of the quantum yield of CO2 assimilation (see Fig.2.) suggesting that a proportional relationship exists between quantum yield of non-cyclic electron transport and efficiency of the two photosystems.

These data imply a predominant regulatory role for non-cyclic electron transport under these conditions. They support the hypothesis that the quantum yield of non-cyclic electron transport is determined by both the concentration of open PS2 centres and the photochemical efficiency of these centres, Φexc which is estimated by Fv/Fm (3). They also suggest that processes associated with qNP modify the efficiency with which PS2 centres can capture and utilise excitation energy within the matrice of PS2 complexes.

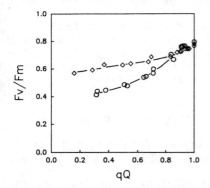 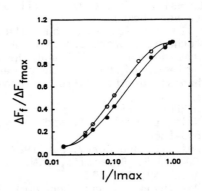

FIGURE 3. The relationship between the photochemical efficiency of open reaction centres as measured by Fv/Fm and qQ in wild type (o) and chlorophyll b less mutant (◊) barley leaves at steady state. Measurements were made in 2500 ppm CO2 and 1% O2 in N2 over a wide range of irradiances.

FIGURE 4. Single turnover flash energy saturation curves for the fluorescence yield increase in pea leaves exposed to continuous actinic background light of 45 (O) and 677 (●) $umol.m^{-2}.s^{-1}$. Fluorescence yield variations are expressed as ΔFf/ΔFfmax, where ΔFf is the flash induces increase above the steady state fluorescence yield Fs produced by an attenuated flash and ΔFfmax the fluorescence yield increase by a non-attenuated flash. I/Imax defines the relative intensity of the flash.

The comparative effects of increasing light intensity on qQ and Fv/Fm for leaves of wild type barley and a chlorophyll b -less mutant which lacks functional LHC2 and exhibits a substantially reduced antenna size of PS2 (7) show that for an equivalent decrease of ΦPS2, a smaller decrease of Fv/Fm in the mutant, compared to the wild type, is compensated by a larger decrease in qQ (see Fig.3.). Since in both plants, the quantum yield of electron transport determines ϕPS2 (3), it can be concluded that the size or composition of the antenna determines the amplitude of Fv/Fm and consequently that processes responsible for the major component of qNP are operative in the PS2 antenna.

Single turnover flash energy saturation curves for the fluorescence yield increases ΔFf were measured for pea leaves at two continuous background irradiances (45 and 677 $umol.m^{-2}.s^{-1}$), which produced qQ, qNP, Fv/Fm values respectively of 0.94, 0.17, 0.78 (45 $umol.m^{-2}.s^{-1}$) 0.77, 0.76, 0.54 (677 $umol.m^{-2}.s^{-1}$). Over this range of background light the ΔFf, produced by an unattenuated flash, which decreased by about 72%, was used to normalise the ΔFf obtained following the attenuation of the flash. Fig.4. shows that half-saturation of ΔFf requires a higher flash intensity (1.35 fold) with the greater light intensity revealing a decrease of the relative effective absorption cross section of PS2 units, as defined Mauzerall et al. (8,9), concomitant to the decrease of Fv/Fm. This phenomena is unlikely to be a consequence of a state 1-state 2 transition since this will occur even at the low light level used (data not shown).

In conclusion, this study has provided evidence that non-photochemical processes associated with qNP can quench excitation energy in the antenna of PS2 and therefore reduce significantly the quantum efficiency of PS2. Such a mechanism clearly offers a regulatory mechanism for the control of non-cyclic electron transport.

4.   REFERENCES
1 Weis, E. Ball, J.T. and Berry, J. (1987) Progress Photosynth. Res. 2, 553-556
2 Weis, E. and Berry, J. (1987) Biochim. Biophys. Acta 894, 198-208
3 Genty, B. Briantais, J.M. and Baker, N.R. (1989) Biochim. Biophys. Acta 849, 183-192
4 Harbinson, J. and Woodward, F.I. (1987) Plant Cell and Environ. 10, 131-141
5 Genty, B. Harbinson, J. and Baker, N.R. Plant Physiol. Biochim. in press
6 Harbinson, J. Genty, B. and Baker, N.R. Plant Physiol. in press
7 Ghirardi, M.L. McCauley, S.W. and Melis, A. (1986) Biochim. Biophys. Acta 851, 331-339
8 Mauzerall, D.C. (1972) Proc. Natl Acad. Sci. USA 69, 1358-1362
9 Falkowski, P.G., Wyman, K. Ley, A.C. and Mauzerall, D.C. (1986) Biochim. Biophys. Acta 849, 183-192

ADAPTATION OF THE LIGHT HARVESTING APPARATUS TO SHADE IN SILENE DIOICA (L.): RELATIONSHIP BETWEEN PSI AND PSII EFFICIENCIES

Marc McKiernan, Bernard Genty, and Neil R. Baker, Dept. of Biology, University of Essex, Colchester, Essex,U.K., CO4 3SQ.

INTRODUCTION
The capacity to grow in a range of light conditions, which may vary in both spectral composition and intensity as a result of shading by vegetative structures, is a major determinant of plant distribution in the natural environment. The lower, shaded leaves of many crop species are also subject to shading for a large part of their development. Changes in the spectral composition and intensity of the incident light are known to alter the stoichiometries of the pigment-protein complexes in the thylakoid membranes of higher plants, and these alterations are presumed to confer an optimising benefit between the extremes of adaptation to different light environments to which any one species is able to adapt. In this study consideration of changes in light intensity and light quality is integrated using a growth system which truly mimics the natural environment. Using Silene dioica, a species with a high degree of plasticity for adaptation to sun and shade light environments, sun and shade adapted plants are compared in two respects. Firstly, the stoichiometric alterations to membrane composition are quantified for PSI, PSII, and LHCII. Secondly, in intact leaves, using simultaneous measurements of chlorophyll fluorescence and changes in absorbance at 820nm, the relative efficiencies of PSI (ΦPSI) and PSII (ΦPSII), functioning in the context of sun and shade stoichiometries, were assessed in intact leaves at steady state rates of CO_2 assimilation. The stoichiometric studies and photosystem efficiency measurements are discussed in relation to the maintainance of balanced electron flow between PSI and PSII in the sun and shade light environments in which the plants developed.

M. Baltscheffsky (ed.), Current Research in Photosynthesis, Vol. IV, 369–372.
© 1990 Kluwer Academic Publishers. Printed in the Netherlands.

MATERIALS AND METHODS

Shade plants of S. dioica were grown in a glasshouse under a perspex tank containing a layer of the aquatic plant Lemna minor. The spectral composition of light beneath this canopy was similar to that in a dense deciduous wood. Sun plants were grown next to the tank. Stoichiometric measurements were made on isolated thylakoids from sun and shade leaves. The number of PSII's was assessed using binding of [^{14}C]atrazine to the herbicide binding site on the D1 protein of PSII (1). PSI levels were determined from chemically induced oxidised-reduced difference spectra at 701nm (2). LHCII was assessed from densitometric scans of SDS-PAGE profiles, and using fluorescence emission at 77K to to measure the relative rate of reduction of Q_A in sun and shade leaf discs. PSII efficiency was derived from fluorescence measurements according to the model of Genty et al (3). PSI efficiency was derived from measurements of changes in absorbance at 820nm (4, 5).

RESULTS AND DISCUSSION

Table 1 shows increases in PSII and LHCII , and a decrease in PSI content of shade thylakoids relative to sun. The similar increase in LHCII and PSII is in accordance with 77K fluorescence emission experiments which showed the same rate of PSII trap closure in sun and shade leaf discs, indicating that the antenna to reaction centre proportions remain the same for sun and shade plants of S. dioica when exposed to sun and shade light regimes which are the same as those in the natural environment.

Table 1: Changes in stoichiometries of LHCII, PSII and PSI of sun and shade leaves of S. dioica (S.E.'s):

	SUN	SHADE	$\Delta\%$
PSII: Chl/atrazine	472 (42)	390 (34)	21
PSI : Chl/P700	317 (23)	355 (21)	12
LHCII/protein(%)	100 (9)	125 (11)	25

Relative quantum efficiency of photosystems was assessed at light intensities which are similar to those found in the plant's natural environment. Fig.1 shows q_Q, the photochemical component of fluorescence quenching, and a measure of the number of open PSII traps, F_v/F_m, a measure of the efficiency of excitation capture by open PSII reaction centres (3), and ΦPSII, the product of q_Q and F_v/F_m (3), as a function of light intensities which are limiting for CO_2 assimilation. It is shown that the initial increase in light intensity causes a larger drop in q_O in shade than in sun plants. This indicates that for any given low light intensity, more PSII trap closure is effected in shade leaves than sun. As F_v/F_m is essentially the same for sun and shade leaves, it is shown that the number of open centres is the main component determining the difference in efficiency between sun and shade leaves. Fig.2 shows a decrease in PSI efficiency, concomitant with that of PSII, in shade plants relative to sun. Fig.3 plots q_O, F_v/F_m, and ΦPSII as a function of ΦPSI. For any given efficiency of PSI, particularly those found at light intensities below 100 umol $m^{-2}s^{-1}$ (Fig.2) ΦPSII in the shade leaves is relatively lower than the sun. F_v/F_m is the same for each leaf type as a function of ΦPSI, and it is therefore the number of open traps which is the main contributor to the relatively lower ΦPSII in the shade leaves. The more reduced PSII relative to PSI in shade plants implies an increased photon capturing cross section area of PSII relative to PSI in shade plants. The shade leaves of S. dioica were adapted to overall lower light intensities than the sun leaves.

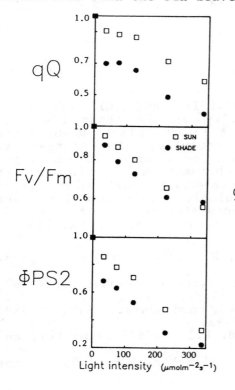

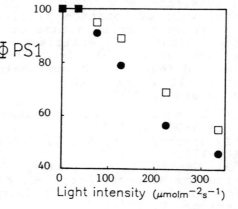

Fig.1: q_O, F_v/F_m, ΦPSII as a function of light intensity in leaves of S. dioica. (□) sun (●) shade.

Fig.2: ΦPSI as a function of light intensity in leaves of S. dioica. (□) sun (●) shade.

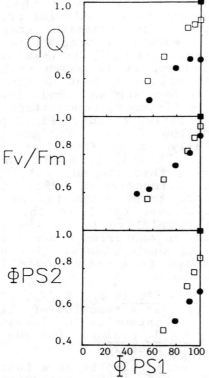

Fig.3 q_Q, F_v/F_m, and ΦPSII as a function of ΦPSI in leaves of S. dioica. (□) sun (●) shade.

The increases in amounts of PSII and LHCII (Table 1) presumably improve the capacity of the shade plant to harvest light relative to the sun plant when light intensities are low. Consequently, the changes in thylakoid composition initiated by changes in the light environment are such that the photosynthetic performance of the plant is optimised for that particular light environment. This is particularly significant for shade adapted leaves which must balance electron flow through PSI and PSII using light which is deficient in wavelengths absorbed by PSII.

(1) Tischer, W. and Strotmann, H. (1977) Biochim. Biophys. Acta 460, 113-125.
(2) Hiyama, T and Ke, B. (1972) Biochim. Biophys. Acta 267, 160-171.
(3) Genty, B, Briantais, J-M, and Baker, N.R. (1989) Biochim. Biophys. Acta 990, 87-92.
(4) Harbinson J., and Woodward, F.I. (1987) Plant Cell and Environ 10, 131-140.
(5) Harbinson, J., Genty, B., and Baker, N.R. (1989) Plant Physiol. (in press)

DIFFERENT AMINO ACID EXCHANGES IN THE D1 PROTEIN CAUSE DIFFERENT
DEGREES OF SHADE TYPE APPEARANCE IN HERBICIDE TOLERANT ANACYSTIS.

FRIEDERIKE KOENIG
Botanisches Institut der J.W. Goethe-Universität,
D-6000 Frankfurt am Main, West Germany

1. INTRODUCTION
    Different herbicide tolerant mutants of Anacystis R2, obtained via
    exchange of the susceptible versus a resistant psbA gene (1-4),
    show different phenotypes when grown in high light intensity. Con-
    cerning the architecture of the photosynthetic apparatus, some of
    the mutants have the appearance of wildtype cells grown either in
    low light in the absence or in high light in the presence of DCMU-
    type inhibitors (5,6). It will be demonstrated that site and mode
    of amino acid exchange in the D1 protein strongly influence the
    intensity of shade type appearance in the mutants.

2. PROCEDURE
2.1. Material and methods
    2.1.1. Cultures and culture conditions: Anacystis nidulans (Syn-
            echococcus spec. (PCC 7942) and mutants Di1, Di22, D5, Tyr5
            and G264 of this strain (1-4), kindly provided by Dr. J.
            Hirschberg, Jerusalem, were grown in standard mineral media
            (Allen's) at 32°C. Batch cultures were harvested after six
            days growth in continuous white light (110 μE m^{-2}s^{-1}).
    2.1.2. Determination of pigment contents: Molar ratios of phycocy-
            anin to chlorophyll and chlorophyll concentrations were de-
            termined as described earlier (5,6). Results are given in
            molar ratios of chromophores (Fig. 1. and Table).
    2.1.3. Observation of O$_2$ evolution: Light saturation curves of O$_2$
            evolution were measured in white light at the growth tempe-
            rature of the cultures by means of a Clark type electrode.
    2.1.4. Radioactive labelling (^{35}S) of Anacystis proteins: To 30 ml
            batch cultures in fresh sulphate containing media ^{35}S methi-
            onine was added. Growth in the presence of labelled sulphur
            source under otherwise original conditions of light and tem-
            perature was stopped after 6, 12, 18, 24 and 30 min. by addi-
            tion of cold methionine (final concentration 1 mol m^{-3}).
    2.1.5. Electrophoretic separation of whole cell proteins in the
            presence of sodium dodecyl sulphate and 2-mercaptoethanol
            was done according to Machold et al. (7), System II. Cells
            were disrupted before by ultrasonic treatment.

M. Baltscheffsky (ed.), Current Research in Photosynthesis, Vol. IV, 373–376.
© 1990 Kluwer Academic Publishers. Printed in the Netherlands.

2.1.6. <u>Quantitation of D1 protein</u>: Gels were dried after treatment
with 2,5-diphenyloxazol and exposed to X-ray film which was
later scanned by means of a densitometer.

3. RESULTS AND DISCUSSION
Herbicide tolerant mutants of <u>Anacystis</u> with different amino acid
exchanges in the D1 protein in positions 255 and/or 264 (Table,
refs. 1-4) were grown in strong light.
3.1. Compared to the wildtype, some of the mutants have a remarkably
higher ratio of phycocyanin (PC) to chlorophyll (chl) (Table and
Fig.1.). Obviously, site as well as mode of amino acid exchange in
the D1 protein strongly influence the intensity of shade type appearance in the mutants.

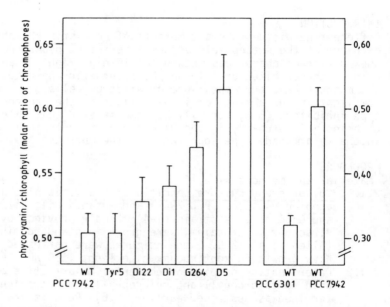

FIGURE 1. Comparison of <u>Anacystis</u> wildtypes (PCC 7942 and 6301)
with herbicide tolerant mutants derived from strain PCC
7942, concerning the ratio of phycocyanin to chlorophyll.
Molar ratio of chromophores is given on the ordinate.

The highest PC/chl ratio (0.615) is observed in mutant D5 in which
Ser 264 is exchanged for Ala and, in addition, Phe 255 for Tyr
(1,3). Mutant Tyr5 with only the exchange of Phe 255 versus Tyr (3)
has wildtype character (0.504). Exchange of only Ser 264 for Ala
(1,3) yields a mutant (Di1) with intermediate character concerning
the PC/chl ratio (0.540). Mutant G264 (4) with Gly in position 264
in contrast to Ala of Di1 appears more shade adapted (0.570) than
the latter (0.540). Double mutant Di22 (3) with Ala in position
264 and Leu in position 255 was found to be intermediate between

the single mutants Di1 (Ala 264) and Tyr5 (Tyr 255). Apparently, there is no clear correlation between the degree of tolerance to a certain herbicide and the degree of shade type appearance.

3.2. Electron transport, measured as O_2 evolution, appears strongly impaired in mutant D5 (by about 50%), while the other mutants were found to be nearly as fast as the wildtype.

3.3. Light dependent turnover of the D1 protein which can be influenced by DCMU-type inhibitors has been demonstrated to occur also in cyanobacteria (8,9). For the mutants Tyr5, Di22 and G264 Amir-Shapira et al. could show that this breakdown is accelerated compared to the wildtype to different extents (10).

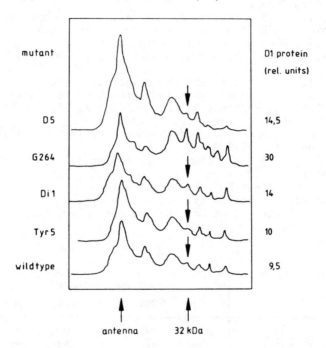

FIGURE 2. Comparison of <u>Anacystis</u> wildtype (PCC 7942) with herbicide tolerant <u>mutants</u> concerning the rate of synthesis of the D1 protein. Distribution of radioactivity in the polypeptide pattern of whole cells after 18 min. exposure to ^{35}S methionine.

The present paper presents preliminary evidence that the rate of synthesis of the herbicide binding protein (D1, M_r 32 kDa) is also accelerated to different degrees as compared to the wildtype (Fig. 2.), mutant G264 being the fastest, followed by mutants D5 and Di1. Again, mutant Tyr5 behaves like the wildtype.

With respect to this phenomenon, the mutants obtained via amino acid exchange in the D1 protein are markedly different from cells with shade character obtained either by growth in low light in the absence or in strong light in the presence of DCMU-type inhibitors (Koenig, to be submitted for publication).

ACKNOWLEDGEMENTS
Dr. J. Hirschberg, The Hebrew University, Jerusalem, kindly provided the herbicide tolerant mutants of Anacystis (refs. 1-4). Financial support of the Deutsche Forschungsgemeinschaft is gratefully acknowledged.

REFERENCES
1 Hirschberg, J., Ohad, N., Pecker, I. and Rahat, A. (1987) Z. Naturforsch. 42c, 758-761
2 Hirschberg, J., Ben Yehuda, A., Pecker, I. and Ohad, N. (1987) in Plant Molecular Biology (v. Wettstein, D. and Chua, N.-H., eds.), pp. 357-366, Plenum Publishing Corporation
3 Horowitz, A., Ohad, N. and Hirschberg, J. (1989) FEBS Letters 243, 161-164
4 Hirschberg, J. et al. (1989) Photosynthesis Research, in press
5 Koenig, F. (1987) in Progress in Photosynthesis Research (Biggins, J. ed.) IV.1.95-98, Martinus Nijhoff Publishers, Dordrecht
6 Koenig, F. (1987) Z. Naturforsch. 42c, 727-732
7 Machold, O., Simpson, D.J. and Lindberg Møller, B. (1979) Carlsberg Res. Commun. 44, 235-254
8 Koenig, F. (1987) Biol. Chem. Hoppe Seyler 368, 1260, abstract
9 Goloubinoff, P., Brusslan, J., Golden, S.S., Haselkorn, R. and Edelman, M. (1988) Plant Mol. Biol. 11, 441-447
10 Amir.Shapira, D., Poplawsky, R., Hirschberg, J. and Ohad, I. (1988) II. Intern. Congr. Plant Mol. Biol., Jerusalem, Nov. 1988, abstract 389

TABLE

		herbicide tolerant mutants					wildtype
		D5	G264	Di1	Di22	Tyr5	
amino acid in position	255 264	Tyr Ala	Phe Gly	Phe Ala	Leu Ala	Tyr Ser	Phe Ser
rel. resistance to (refs. 1-4)	diuron	167	10	100	1500	1.5	
	metribuzine	2000		5000	175	0.8	
	atrazine	200	2000	30	1.3	25	
	terbutryne	670	450	17	1.3	13	
phycocyanin/chlorophyll (molar ratio of chromophores)		0.615	0.570	0.540	0.528	0.504	0.504
mean errors		0.027	0.020	0.016	0.019	0.015	0.015

CHARACTERIZATION OF THE LIGHT DEPENDENT REGULATION OF THE
APPARENT QUANTUM YIELD OF PS I

A.M.REHM AND A.RIED.BOTANISCHES INSTITUT DER J.W.GOETHE-
UNIVERSITÄT, 6000 FRANKFURT/MAIN, SIESMAYERSTR. 70, FRG.

1. INTRODUCTION
In a recent paper (1) we have shown that in some red algae
a change in the wavelength of the exciting light may
produce a strong modulation of the apparent quantum yield
of PS I. This regulation cannot be explained by an altered
energy distribution between the two photosystems or an altered reduction rate of P-700 (via linear electron-transport from PS II to PS I or via DBMIB sensitive cyclic pathway around PS I). It was thought to depend on the redox
state of a redox-component associated with plastoquinone. A
similar modulation was also found in higher plants (2).

2. MATERIAL AND METHODS
Porphyridium purpureum and Porphyra yezoensis were cultured
as described elsewhere (1). Rhodella violacea was grown in
a modified Jones-medium (3).
      Cytochrome f- and P-700-turnover were estimated as
described previously (1).
      Fluorescence spectra were obtained with an O-SMA diode-
array detector system (Spectroscopy Instruments GmbH).
      The isolation procedure of PBS-vesicles described by
Dilworth and Gantt (4) was modified.
      $DCPIPH_2$-oxidation of the vesicles by PS I was moni-
tored at 597nm at 10°C. The redox potential was calculated
from the ratio of $DCPIPH_2/DCPIP$.

3. RESULTS AND DISCUSSION
The ability to reduce the apparent quantum yield of PSI in
Ll as described for Porphyridium purpureum and Porphyra
yezoensis (1) was found as a general phenomenon in many red
algae (Porphyra umbilicalis, Porphyridium aerugineum,
Rhodella violacea, Palmaria palmata and Chondrus crispus).

In P. purpureum the diminution of the rate of cytochrome f
photooxidation was saturated at fairly low light intensities (Fig. 1). Half-saturation was obtained with
$3-5 \cdot 10^{-11}$ mol photons $\cdot cm^{-2} \cdot s^{-1}$ of incident light (694nm) or
with $9 \cdot 10^{-11}$ mol photons $\cdot cm^{-2} \cdot s^{-1}$ of 699nm, corresponding
to the ratio of absorption at these two wavelengths.

M. Baltscheffsky (ed.), Current Research in Photosynthesis, Vol. IV, 377–380.
© 1990 *Kluwer Academic Publishers. Printed in the Netherlands.*

FIGURE 1. Rate of
cyt. f oxidation as
a function of the
L1-intensity during
preillumination.
Evaluation of the
same experiment in
two different ways
(O , ●).

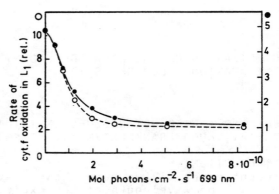

In all objects,the reversion of the reduction of the
apparent quantum yield of PS I in L2 needed substantially
more time than the induction by L1. For P. purpureum the
kinetics of these processes are shown in figure 2.

FIGURE 2. Rate
of cyt. f oxida-
tion in L1
(699nm) as a
function of the
time of preillu-
mination with
L1 (△) or
L2 (○) or of
incubation in
darkness (●).
Each individual
pretreatment was
preceded by
10min illumina-
tion with L1
(O ,●) or
L2 (△).

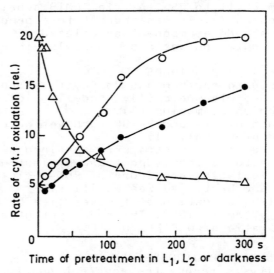

The ability of P. purpureum to regulate the quantum yield
of PS I was strongly influenced by temperature, with a
distinct maximum at 18°C (Fig. 3). Higher temperatures
(above 20°C) reduced the ability for regulation of the
PS I-quantum yield mainly by reducing the quantum yield of
PS I in L2. At about 30°C the PS I-quantum yield became
independent on the wavelength of preillumination.
    In Porphyra yezoensis the apparent quantum yield of
PS I after L1 and L2 preillumination showed a similar
temperature-dependence.

FIGURE 3.
Apparent
quantum
yield of
cyt. f oxi-
dation in
Ll (694nm)
after pre-
illumination
with Ll (△)
or L2 (○)
as a func-
tion of the
temperature
during pre-
treatment.

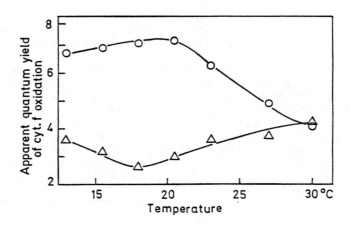

Gross and Grenier (5) found a functional decoupling of
PS I-antenna and reaction center in Mg^{2+}-deficient thylakoids. If such a mechanism would be responsible for the
regulation of the apparent quantum yield of PS I we should
find differences in the quantum yield of cyt.f-oxidation
after Ll-preillumination when the oxidation-rate of cyt. f
is measured in actinic Ll of different wavelength. As previously mentioned, we found no differences with Ll of 694nm
and 699nm (1). Even in Ll of 720nm we detected a strong reduction of the apparent quantum yield of cyt.f-oxidation
after Ll-preillumination, and the calculated ratios of
maximum and minimum quantum yield of PS I were the same
(error = 7%) in Ll of 694nm, 699nm and 720nm (not shown).
      No correlation was observed between a reduced quantum
yield of PS I in Ll and a change of the fluorescence emission of PS I at 77K in P. purpureum and R.violacea.
      So we conclude that a possible decoupling of PSI-an-
tenna and reaction center is not responsible for the observed reduction of the apparent quantum yield of PS I in Ll.

PBS-vesicles of P. purpureum were able to regulate the
quantum yield of PS I in the same manner as intact cells.
Ll (699nm) reduced the apparent quantum yield of PS I to
46.5% compared to dark pretreatment. In contrast to intact
cells, preillumination with L2 also causes a reduction, although only to 75%. This difference may be explained by the
fact that in PBS-vesicles the water-splitting system was
partly impaired. Therefore the L2 preillumination has resulted in a partial oxidation of the electron transport
chain as it is obtained in intact cells by irradiation with
Ll of low intensity. The effect of Ll-illumination on the
quantum yield of PS I was strongly diminished after addition of ascorbate (2-10mM) to the thylakoids. PS I-quantum

yield could be reduced to 30% after Ll-preillumination in
the absence of ascorbate. In the presence of ascorbate however, the quantum yield of PS I was reduced only to 82%.

To confirm that a redox component regulates the apparent
quantum yield of PSI we studied the dependence of PS I-
activity on the redox-potential of the medium. Thy-lakoids
were kept in the dark for 5-10 min and it was taken care,
that the redox-potential of the medium was constant prior
to the measurement. The plots of two experiments shown in
figure 4 were fitted by a Nernst-curve of a titration with
an one-electron step (n=1). The calculated midpoint-
potential was +140mV (pH 7,8) in both experiments.

FIGURE 4.
PS I-activity
(DCPIPH$_2$ oxida-
tion) as a func-
tion of the re-
dox potential of
the medium.

Two independent
experiments
(△ , ○).

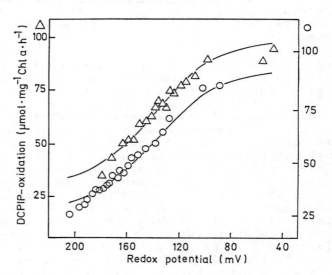

These experiments show that a redox-component (midpoint‐
potential + 140mV, pH 7,8) located in the thylakoid membrane
regulates the apparent quantum yield of PS I.

ACKNOWLEDGEMENT: This work was supported by a grant from
              the Deutsche Forschungsgemeinschaft.

REFERENCES
1 REHM, A.M., GÜLZOW, M. and RIED, A. (1989) Biochim.
   Biophys. Acta 973, 131-137
2 WEINZETTEL, A., RÜHLE, W., MARZINZIK, K. and WILD,A.
   (1989) Photosynth. Res., in press.
3 JONES, R.F., SPEER, H.K. and KURY, W. (1963) Plant
   Physiol. 16, 636-643.
4 DILWORTH, M.F. and GANTT, E. (1981) Plant Physiol. 67,
   608-612.
5 GROSS, E.L. and GRENIER, J. (1978) Arch.Biochem.
   Biophys. 187, 387-398.

ALTERATION IN THYLAKOID COMPOSITION AND STRUCTURE OF BRASSICA
RAPA SSP. OLEIFERA DURING AGEING IN HIGH AND LOW LIGHT

ARJA NURMI, DEPT. OF GENERAL BOTANY; UNIVERSITY OF HELSINKI
SF-00710 HELSINKI, FINLAND

1. INTRODUCTION

The organization and function of thylakoid proteins are greatly
affected by environmental conditions. Under changing environmental
conditions, many protein complexes are involved in shaping the
thylakoid architecture, the final structure depending on the
balance between different thylakoid complexes. In this study the
organization of membrane proteins was examined in plant material
ageing under different environmental conditions. Freeze-fracture,
electron microscopic and electrophoretic studies were made of
protein complexes in the chloroplast thylakoid of Brassica rapa
ssp. oleifera grown in high and low light.

2. PROCEDURES
2.1. Materials and methods
Brassica rapa ssp. oleifera was grown in the greenhouse the day/
night temperature range was $15^{\circ}C - 29^{\circ}C$, the average temperature
being $22^{\circ}C$. During growing period B, the natural daylight was
short, only 9 hours. Supplementary illumination was given for
18 h. The temperature range was $13^{\circ}C - 25^{\circ}C$, the average being
$19^{\circ}C$. The quantum flux density during experiment A was 800 umol
m-2 sec-1 (high light), and during experiment B 80 umol m-2 sec-1
(low light; Lamba Instruments, Quantum Sensor). The material for
the experiments was taken 13 (I), 20 (II) and 28 (III) days
after sowing.

For freeze-fracturing, the leaf material (second and third full
open leaf accepted) was homogenized in a Buchner blender in
50 mM K-phosphate buffer, 0.5 M sucrose, 10 mM KCl, 2% HEPES,
4 mM $MgCl_2$ (Tris to pH 7.4). Glycerol was added as cryoprotectant
to the suspensions to a final concentration of 30% (v/v). The
collected pellets were frozen in liquid nitrogen. The fracturing
was carried out in a Balzers apparatus at the stage temperature
of $-120^{\circ}C$. For the freeze-fracture analysis, the particle size
measurements were made with a digitizer-computerplotter system.

3. RESULTS AND DISCUSSION
In older low light plants, more light-harvesting capacity was
available compared with photosystem II core complex (Table 1),

M. Baltscheffsky (ed.), Current Research in Photosynthesis, Vol. IV, 381–384.
© 1990 *Kluwer Academic Publishers. Printed in the Netherlands.*

in contrast to the amount of PFs particles per square micron, which decreased during ageing (Table 2). Fewer but larger EFs particles were present in older plants in low light (Table 3). These represent larger units of tightly bound light-harvesting complex around photosystem II core complex (1).

TABLE 1. Percentage distribution of chlorophyll among chlorophyll-protein complexes in chloroplast thylakoids of _Brassica_ grown under high (HL) and low light (LL).

chlorophyll protein complexes	HL		LL	
	I	III	I	III
CPI a2	2		1	
CPI a1	3	2	2	3
CPI	23	24	21	22
LHCII* - 1	4	3	4	2
- 2	4	1	6	7
- 3	1		24	22
CP47	4	1	15	8
CP43	5	8		
CP29	20	19		
LHCII	10	14	18	26
CP24	11	13		
FP	13	15	9	10

* listed in order of increasing electrophoretic mobility

Ageing in low light was accompanied by some decrease in photosystem I protein complexes but an increase in light-harvesting proteins around PSI in non-appressed membranes on the PFu face (2). The increase in number of PFu particles might be due to migration of peripheral LHCII to non-appressed regions, since PFs particles decreased, though the amount of LHCII protein complexes was still high (Tables 1, 2; Fig. 1.).

In high light plants, chlorophyll-protein complexes were more heterogeneous and labile under high light intensities. Under long-term exposure to high light, a dramatic decrease in particle size and density occurred in the PFu, EFs and EFu faces. In developing plants, the amount of chlorophyll in LHC complexes first increased and then declined during ageing.

TABLE 2. Freeze-fracture particle densities of the chloroplast thylakoid in _Brassica_

Development stage		Density No./um^2				
HL		EFu	EFs	PFu	PFs	PFs/EFs
I		394	1345	6385	6108	4.5
II		139	722	5000	5962	8.3
III		153	574	6064	6422	11.2
LL		EFu	EFs	PFu	PFs	PFs/EFs
I		507	2452	6686	6954	2.8
II		472	2118	6987	6348	3.0
III		405	1793	6933	5940	3.3

TABLE 3. Average sizes of freeze-fracture particles of chloroplast thylakoid in Brassica rapa ssp. oleifera

Development stage	Average sizes			
	HL			
	EFu	EFs	PFu	PFs
I	106	128	93	78
II	85	116	87	71
III		103	89	68
	LL			
	EFu	EFs	PFu	PFs
I	102	118	80	63
II		117	80	70
III	72	123	76	66

This might indicate partly dissociation of LHCII from PSII, free LHCII remaining in the appressed regions (PFs) and the rest of PSII and LHCII migrating to the non-appressed regions, where degradation of membrane particles take place (3). In plants developing in high light, the reorganization of thylakoid components occurred in chlorophyll a/b -protein complexes rather than in PSII core units. A very small number of photosystem II particles on EFs face was observed in ageing thylakoids (Table 2). This might point to a change in the surface charges of membrane (4) proteins enabling the smaller photosystem II core complex alone or tightly bound antennae of PSII to cleave with the PFs face instead of the EFs face (Fig. 1.).

In older plants the grana area increased with a decrease in the relative amount of light-harvesting protein in smaller chloroplasts. The relative amount of total light-harvesting complexes and the density of PFs particles did not directly reflect the size of grana in ageing plants. Some other components than LHCII, represented by the PFs face particles especially, are also involved in membrane stacking in ageing and low light plants.

In addition, the occurrence decreasing amount of smaller PSII units, evident in non-appressed thylakoids as the EFu particles, might also have an influence on stacking of thylakoids while more inactive PSII is stored in larger grana (5). And the decreasing total amount of LHCP complexes in older chloroplasts (Table 1.) might reflect a decrease in photosystem I light-harvesting complex. Owing to the extensive heterogeneity of chlorophyll a/b -proteins, flexible light-harvesting units are needed to control organization. Therefore, the ratio of different antennae complexes, like CP29 and LHCII, may have a very important role in the compartmentation of thylakoids.

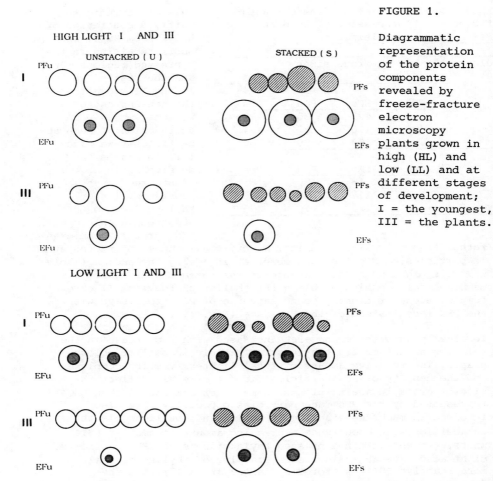

FIGURE 1.

Diagrammatic representation of the protein components revealed by freeze-fracture electron microscopy plants grown in high (HL) and low (LL) and at different stages of development; I = the youngest, III = the plants.

REFERENCES
1 Allen, K.D., Duysen, M.E. and Staehelin, L.A. (1988) J. Cell Biol. 107, 907-919
2 Greene, B.A., Staehelin, L.A. and Melis, A. (1988) Plant Physiol. 87, 365-370
3 Larsson, U.K., Sundby, C. and Andersson, B. (1987) Photosystem II, Biochim. Biophys. Acta 894, 59-68
4 Barber, J. (1988) in Encyclopedia of Plant Physiology (Staehelin, L.A. and Arntzen, C.J., eds.) pp. 653-664

CHANGES IN THYLAKOID SURFACE AREA WHEN SHADE ACCLIMATED HELIANTHUS ANNUUS L. CHLOROPLASTS ARE EXPOSED TO HIGH P.F.D.

Wayne R. Fagerberg. Department of Plant Biology. University of New Hampshire. Durham, NH. USA. 03824

INTRODUCTION   Mature mesophyll cells in sunflower (Helianthus annuus L.) are capable of dynamic alterations in cell and tissue structure in response to changes in light environment [1,2] and as a normal part of diel behavior [3]. Many of these rapid alteration in cell structure are related to changes in irradiance levels and are presumably adaptive [1,2].

In previous studies we have found when irradiances were reduced to approximately 200 μmols M^{-2} S^{-1} thylakoids in palisade cells underwent a rapid increase in surface area (approx. 30% at 1 hr post shading, Fagerberg, unpublished, and 1,2). Both granal and stromal thylakoids increased surface area but the increase was most rapid in granal thylakoids. We have also shown that stromal/granal responses were independent of each other and there was little interconversion of one type to the other [1,2]. The mechanisms by which plants detect changes in irradiance and effect various responses have not been determined although they may involve electron flow between PS II and I, changes in NADP/NADPH ratios, and/or gene activation by cryptochrome/phytochrome pigments [4,5,6,7,8].

The present work addresses the consequences of exposing shade acclimated chloroplasts to high irradiance levels in order to determine: 1. If chloroplast exhibit a loss of thylakoid membrane during sun acclimation (opposite of shade acclimation). 2. The time necessary for significant loss to occur. 3. Whether the sun acclimation response is simply a reverse of the shade acclimation response.

MATERIALS AND METHODS
    Potted plants (Helianthus annuus L.) were grown in UNH glasshouses and received normal summer irradiances (approx. 1000+ μmols M^{-2} S^{-1}, 12+ hrs light/day).
    Mature leaves from several plants were removed and returned to the laboratory, surface sterilized, cut into strips (13 X 70 mm) and placed in culture vessels on filter paper in such a way that the strips were perpendicular to incident irradiance. The bottom 10 mm of the strips was immersed in a dH_2O media throughout the study period.

M. Baltscheffsky (ed.), Current Research in Photosynthesis, Vol. IV, 385–388.
© 1990 Kluwer Academic Publishers. Printed in the Netherlands.

Leaf strips were first exposed to high irradiances (900 μmols M^2 S^{-1}) from 300W Halogen lamps for 6 hrs then ND shade screens placed over the culture vessels (200 μmols M^{-2} S^{-1}) for 6 hrs. Shade screens over <u>TEST</u> vessels were removed exposing leaf strips to high irradiances. These were sampled at time periods of; 30 sec, 5,15,30 min and 24 hr following screen removal. (Note: the 24 hr sample= 6 hrs light-12 hrs dark- 6hrs light).

Samples were fixed for EM with 3% GTA and 2% OsO_4 in 100 mols M^3 Cacodylate buffer, pH 7.2 (2). Morphometric analysis was performed on the leaf samples as described in Fagerberg (2).

Samples: Leaf strips from 3 separate leaves (a single strip from each of three different leaves) were placed into 6 different flasks (4 test and 2 control). Each flask contained three strips. All test and control strips were from the same population of leaves.

RESULTS AND DISCUSSION

Shade acclimated chloroplasts exposed to high irradiance showed a significant decrease in the surface density (S_v) of the granal thylakoids after 15 min post re-exposure (Table 1).

TABLE 1. SURFACE TO VOLUME RATIO VALUES FOR CHLOROPLAST THYLAKOIDS AND MITOCHONDRIAL MEMBRANES

Sample	CHLOROPLAST stroma	grana	g/s[1]	MITOCHONDRIA exterior	cristae	e/c[2]
Shade control	15.2	34.9	2.3	3.2	23.4	7.3
Sun control	13.1	31.1	2.4	4.15	23.4	5.6
30 sec test	14.4	38.9[b]	2.7	8.1[ab]	23.6	2.9
5 min test	13.3[a]	38.3[b]	2.9	3.3	23.7	7.2
15 min test	14.3	29.2[a]	2.1	6.3[ab]	18.2	2.9
30 min test	13.7	28.6[a]	2.1	6.2[ab]	21.6	3.5
1 hr * test	13.8[ab]	28.9[ab]	2.1	4.3[b]	14.5	3.3
6 hr* test	9.8[ab]	28.1[ab]	2.9	5.3	16.8	3.2
24 hr test	10.5[ab]	22.9[ab]	2.2	5.5[b]	26.5	4.9

[a] Significantly different than shade control p> .05.
[b] Significantly different than sun control p> .05.
* Data taken from previous study (Fagerberg, unpublished)
[1] g/s granal/ stromal thylakoid surface area ratio
[2] e/c exterior/cristae mitochondrial membrane surface area ratio

Changes in the surface density of the stromal thylakoids did not exhibit a statistically definable change compared to the sun or shade control chloroplasts until 1 hr post re-exposure (Table 1). After 1 hr and until 24 hr the surface density of both granal and stromal membranes was significantly different from both sun and shade control chloroplasts.   The proportion of granal vs. stromal thylakoids (g/s, Table 1) was variable but no light dependent pattern was evident (R^2= 0.18, P> .5 NS). This change in the relative proportion of granal and stromal thylakoids was reflected in the g/s ratios between 5 and 15 min samples (Table 1). In both sun and shade acclimation events the relative proportion of stromal thylakoids decreased indicating that the granal membranes respond more quickly than stromal thylakoids to changes in irradiance. In previous work (Fagerberg, unpublished) when stromal and granal thylakoid S_v were regressed against short and long term (integrated) change in irradiance the stromal thylakoids showed higher R^2 values (.84 vs. .70) with integrated light levels while grana showed higher R^2 values (.43 vs. .17) with short term changes in irradiance. The results of this study generally support earlier observations that grana were most responsive to changes in irradiance. Mitochondrial membranes showed no discernible irradiance related changes (Table 1).

Calculation of the volume density (V_v) for organelles showed they were not significantly altered during this experiment (Fagerberg, unpublished). The exception was the starch compartment of the chloroplast which required 24 hrs (two 6 hr light exposure periods) to accumulate enough starch to reach the volume found in the sun control chloroplasts.

No quantitative changes in relationships of leaf tissue compartments were detected during this experiment (Fagerberg, unpubl.). However, because differences in the size of mesophyll cells, tissue compartments for the different sample periods varied. On a per unit of leaf surface (100 mm^2) basis shade recovery leaves had larger palisade tissue compartments than fully shaded leaves.

Thylakoid packing ratios showed a significant loss of actual thylakoid surface area following exposure to high irradiance (Table 2). Presumably the potential efficiency with which photons might be captured by the palisade tissue would also decrease, thus acting as one mechanism to protect the chloroplast from photo-damaged membranes.

CONCLUSIONS

The results of this study indicate that: 1. Shade acclimated chloroplast rapidly lose thylakoid membrane in response to re- exposure to high irradiance. 2. Response time for decreasing membrane surface density differed for grana and stromal thylakoids. Granal thylakoids showed significant decreases between 5-15 min post H.I.E. while stromal thylakoids appeared to require 1 hr. The granal thylakoids were more responsive than stromal thylakoids in both rapidity and extent. 3. The pattern and trends in the sun acclimated response are similar to those of the shade acclimation response but in the opposite direction. Thus, we conclude that sun acclimation is simply the reverse of shade acclimation process at the structural level.

TABLE 2. PALISADE THYLAKOID PACKING RATIO. THYLAKOID SURFACE AREA (MM^2) PER MM^2 OF LEAF SURFACE

Packing Ratio

	STROMAL	GRANAL
Shade control	262	536
Sun control	246	585
30 sec test	315	851
5 min test	244	704
15 min test	251	515
30 min test		
24 hr test	92	200

REFERENCES
1. Fagerberg, W.R. 1983. Annals of Botany. 52: 117-126.
2. Fagerberg, W.R. 1987. American Journal of Botany. 74: 822-828.
3. Fagerberg, W.R. 1988. Botanical Gazette. 149: 295-302.
4. Miller, M.M. and P.S. Nobel. 1972. Plant Physiology 49: 535-541.
5. Glick, R.E., S.W. McCauley and A. Melis. 1985. Planta 164: 487-494.
6. Staehelin, L.A. 1986. pp. 1-72. In: (L.A. Staehelin and C.J. Arntzen eds) Photosynthesis III. Photosynthetic membranes and light harvesting systems. Springer-Verlag. New York.
7. Smith, H. 1981. pp 159-173. In:(C.B. Johnson ed). Physiological processes limiting plant productivity. Butterworths, Boston.

Effect of cold-hardening on the quantum yield of spinach leaves

K.J. van Wijk and P.R. van Hasselt, University of Groningen, Department of Plant Physiology, P.O.Box 14, 9750 Haren, The Netherlands

Introduction

Cold-acclimation concerns the decrease of the optimum temperature for photosynthesis [1,2] and a decreased susceptibilty for cold-induced photoinhibition [3]. Plants which are not acclimated to low temperature are, at low temperatures, easily damaged by light. The primairy site of damage is Photosystem II (PSII) [4]. Cold-acclimation might therefore concern the modification of PSII and might lead to a diminished chance of overreduction of PSII by a decrease of the light absorption cross-section or an increase of the capacity of Calvin cycle activity at low temperatures.

In this study we have tried to characterize changes in the photosynthetic apparatus and photosynthetic activity of spinach (- Spinacia oleracea L. cv. estivato) during a 14-days period of cold acclimation; most attention was payed to the role PSII.

Materials and Methods

Three weeks old spinach plants were cold-treated for 15 days at 7°C/4°C, 12 h light/12h dark and a PFD of 135 uE.m-2.s-1. Control plants were kept at 19°C/17°C and at the same light conditions as the cold-grown plants.

Measurements were performed on leaf discs (14.0 mm diameter) from the 3rd and 4th leaf. The chlorophyll a, b and the total carotenoids were measured according to [5].

Photosynthetic oxygen production and chlorophyll a fluorescence were measured simultaneously in a temperature controlled leaf chamber (Model LD-2; Hansatech, Kyngs Lynn, Norfolk, UK); the top section was modified to enable insertion of a glass fibre. The measurements were performed at different light intensities in the presence of 5% CO_2 and 2-5% [O_2]. Under these conditions photorespiration was almost absent and stomatal regulation was avoided [6].

Chlorophyll fluorescence was measured using a pulse amplitude modulation fluorometer (PAM, Heinz Walz, Effeltrich, FRG) as described by [7]. The methods and definitions from [7] were employed to calculate the quenching components qQ, qNP and qTot, which are respectively photochemical quenching, non-photochemical quenching and total quenching of variable fluorescence, all corrected for Fo-quenching (qFo). At each light intensity level, the leaf disc was allowed to achieve steady state of O_2-production and fluorescence and then Fs, Fv and Fo' were measured.

M. Baltscheffsky (ed.), Current Research in Photosynthesis, Vol. IV, 389–392.

Fo' was measured as in [8].

Photosynthetic oxygen production was measured polarographically with a Clark-type leaf disc electrode (Hansatech). The dark respiration, Rd, was measured in the dark adaptation period and was assumed not to be influenced by PDF.

The quantum efficiency of linear electron transport was calculated from the oxygen measurements (Φsi) as in [9] and from fluorescence measurement (Φsf) as in [10]:
Φsi = J/I in umol electrons.m-2.s-1;
with: J = electron transport
      I = incident light in uE.m-2.s-1
Φsf = (Fvs-Fv)/Fs

The quantum efficiency of open reaction centers (Φp) was calculated according to [8]: Φp=Φs/qQ

Results and discussion

The relation between PFD and the quenching components qFo, qQ, qNP and qTOT

During the temperature treatment period the relations between the quenching components and PFD were followed for control and cold-grown plants. Figure 1a,b shows qFo, qQ, qNP and qTot at a measuring temperature of respectively 7°C (a) and 19°C (b) at a PFD of 241 μE m-2 s-1 (PAR) for control and cold grown-plants during the period of temperature treatment.

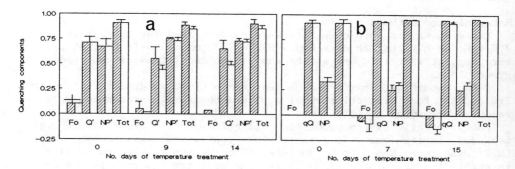

Fig 1a,b. The steady state values of the quenching components at an incident PFD of 241 μE m-2 s-1 at a measuring temperature of 7°C (a) and 19°C (b) during the 15-days temperature-treatment period. ([cold-grown], [control]) (I = std)

The cold-grown plants showed an increased qQ at low temperature, compared with control plants. This can be interpreted as an increased ability to perform linear electron transport at low temperature and as an adaptation to low temperature, diminishing the danger of photoinhibition. At 19°C measuring temperature, this relative increase

in qQ only occurred at high PFD, which again illustrates a diminished
risk of photoinhibition.
    At a measuring temperature of 7°C and low PFD, qNP was slightly lower
for the cold-grown plants compared with the control plants; at high PFD,
qNP was slightly higher. At a measuring temperature of 19°C, qNP was
lower for the cold-grown plants compared to the control plants,
reflecting a lower proton gradient over the thylakoid membrane due to
less cyclic electron transport.
The quantum yield of open PSIIrc, Φp, as function of qNP
    Representative examples of the relationship between qNP and Φp are
shown in fig. 2a,b. Extrapolated maximal (Φpo and qNP=0) and minimal
(Φpe and qNP=1) values of Φp were (not significantly) lower in the cold-
grown plants compared to control. The direction coefficient was not
significantly influenced by growth-temperature treatment.

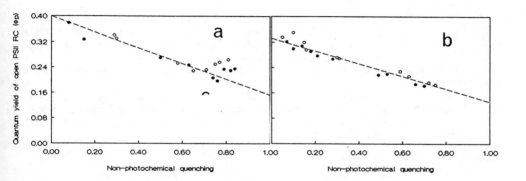

Fig. 2a,b. The quantum yield of open PSIIrc (Φp), as function of qNP
measured at 7°C after 9 days of temperature treatment (a) and at 19°C
after 7 days of temperature treatment (b). (● cold-grown plants, ◎
control plants)

    At 7°C Φp decreased linearly uptill qNP values of 0.7 and Φp of 0.2;
at higher qNP Φp increased again. In the cold-grown plants this
deviation from linearity occurred at slightly higher qNP values. The
sudden increase of Φp could be explained by an underestimation of qQ and
could be caused by:
1. A deviation from linearity of the relation between the fraction of
open PSIIrc and qQ, due to energy transfer between the PSIIrc, causing
the photochemical activity to be higher than estimated by qQ. From model
simulations it was shown (J. Snel, personal communication) that the
position of the upward bend due to energy transfer between the reaction
centers depended on the value of the coefficient for heat dissipation
(kd) in the 'energized' PSIIrc; an increased kd shifted this bend to
higher values of qNP. As a consequence, it can be be concluded that the
energy transfer is deminished in the cold-grown plants or that kd was

higher in the cold-grown plants. This corresponds with previous experiments, which showed that in cold-grown winter-rye the PSIIrc were less connected [11] and that 4 days chilling in the light of (chilling sensitive) pumpkin had increased the ratio PSIIß/PSIIα [12].
2. The occurrence of other non-photochemical components besides qE. It was shown that at a PFD, which was saturating for qE, a slow relaxing non-photochemical quenching component, qI, became increasingly important [13,14]. This component was shown not to decrease the light-saturated oxygen evolution rate, but did decrease the quantum yield. In high light the fall in qQ was found to provide good correlation with the rise in qI [14]. In our measurements a small contribution of qI to non-photochemical quenching could completely explain the deviation from linearity in the relationship qNP (qE) and Φp. The third non-photochemical component, qT, can not explain the increase in Φp as this component was shown to decrease under conditions of strong energetization [14].
3. The fact that the oxygen evolving complex, OEC, did not have sufficient capacity to donate electrons to reduce Qa completely at this temperature. However, this does not seem to be likely because the light pulse was sufficiently long to reach maximal fluorescence.

The steady state overall quantum efficiency, Φsi and Φsf, as function of the PFD
    The steady state overall quantum efficiency, Φsi, and Φsf, measured at 7°C and 19°C after one and two weeks of temperature treatment, were not affected by the growth temperature. sf showed the same pattern of dependence on PFD as Φsi.

Acknowledgements
This study was supported by the Foundation for Fundamental Biological Research (BION), subsidised by the Netherlands Organization for the Advancement of Pure Research (NWO).

References
1. Oquist G (1983). Plant, Cell and Environm 6: 281-300
2. Berry J and Björkman O (1980). Ann Rev Pl Phys 31: 491-543
3. Somersalo S and Krause GH (1989). Planta 177: 409-416
4. Krause GH (1988). Physiol. Plant. 74: 566-574
5. Lichtenthaler HK (1987). In: Methods in Enz 148: 350-382
6. Delieu JT and Walker DA (1983). Plant Physiol 73:534-541
7. Schreiber U, Schliwa U and Bilger W (1986). Phot Res 51: 51-62
8. Peterson RB, Sivak MN and Walker DA (1988). Plant Physiol 88: 158-163
9. Weis E and Berry JA (1987). BBA 894: 198-208
10. Genty B, Briantais JM and Baker NR (1989). BBA 990: 87-92
11. Griffith M, Huner NPA, Kyle DJ (1984). Plant Physiol 76: 381-385
12. Mäenpää P, Aro EM, Somersalo S, Tyystjärvi E (1988). Plant Physiol 87: 762-766
13. Horton P, Oxborough K, Rees D and Scholes JD (1988). Plant Physiol Biochem 26 (4): 453-460
14. Horton P and Hague A (1988). BBA 932: 107-115

ENVIRONMENTAL AND HORMONAL DEPENDENCE OF INDUCTION OF CRASSULACEAN
ACID METABOLISM IN *MESEMBRYANTHEMUM CRYSTALLINUM*.

Gerald Edwards, Shu-Hua Cheng, Chun Chu, and Maurice Ku.
Department of Botany, Washington State University, Pullman, Washington
99164-4230 USA

1. INTRODUCTION

   Mesembryanthemum crystallinum changes its mode of carbon
assmilation from C_3 photosynthesis to CAM when water stressed by high
soil salinity (1). Such a shift in photosynthetic pathway is
accompanied by marked increases in extractable activities of several
enzymes including PEP carboxylase and NADP-malic enzyme.

   During salinity induction, young leaves of *M. crystallinum* were
found incapable of performing CAM until they become mature (2).
Laboratory studies with this species demonstrated that the induction
of CAM by high salt only occurred after 6 weeks of growth (3). In
natural habitats, the onset of CAM induction occurs 3 months after
germination and the life cycle (from seed to seed) covers 7 to 8
months (1). In this study, we have accelerated the growth and, thus,
shortened the life cycle of *M. crystallinum* by growing the plants in
prolonged photoperiods under relatively high light. Evidence was also
obtained that abscisic acid could substitute for the induction of CAM
in the species by saline conditions..

2. MATERIALS AND METHODS
2.1 Plant materials.
   2.1.1. Photoperiod treatments: Plants of *M. crystallinum* were
         grown in growth chambers on 16 h/8 h, 20 h/4 h light/dark
         cycles or under continuous illumination without a dark
         period. The photosynthetic photon flux density (PPFD) was
         500 to 600 μmol quanta m^{-2} s^{-1} and the temperature was
         30°C. Plants were irrigated daily, once with one-fifth
         strength modified Hoagland's solution (with 1 mM NaCl) in
         the morning, and once with distilled water in the evening.
   2.1.2. Abscisic acid treatment: For abscisic acid treatments
         plants were grown on a 16/8 h photoperiod at 30°C/18°C. The
         PPFD was 400-600 μmol quanta m^{-2} s^{-1}.
2.2. Enzyme extraction and assays.
     Leaves were sampled at the end of the light period (e.g. for
     plants with a diurnal dark period) or under light (e.g. for
     plants grown under continuous light). The activities of
     phosphoenolpyruvate carboxylase (PEPC) and NADP-malic enzyme
     (ME) were assayed according to Holtum and Winter (4) with
     slight modifications.

M. Baltscheffsky (ed.), Current Research in Photosynthesis, Vol. IV, 393–396.
© 1990 *Kluwer Academic Publishers. Printed in the Netherlands.*

2.3. Titratable acidity and total malate content.
Leaf extracts were prepared by boiling leaf discs (8.5 mm in diameter) in 20% (v/v) ethanol. Titratable acidity was determined by addition of 5 mM KOH to pH 7.0 (photoperiod study) or pH 8.0 (hormone study). Malate in the supernatant was determined spectrophotometrically with NAD-malate dehydrogenase.

3. RESULTS AND DISCUSSION
3.1. Life cycle of *M. crystallinum*
Under all three growth conditions, one pair of leaves were produced from the main axis each week (excluding cotyledons). However, the onset of secondary growth was earlier in plants with longer light periods. Furthermore, a longer photoperiod also induced flowering at an earlier age: 5, 6, or 7 weeks for plants with 24 h/0 h, 20 h/4 h or 16 h/8 h photoperiods, respectively. During reproductive growth, plants branched rapidly and extensively. The overall growth pattern was like that in the natural environment (1), except that the initiation of flowering was shortened from about 5 months to 5-7 weeks, depending on the photoperiod.
3.2. Evidence for induction of CAM during development.
Under prolonged photoperiods, there was evidence for induction of CAM even without water or salinity stress. Two weeks after germination, the activities of NADP-ME and PEPC began increasing with further growth (results not shown). Both titratable acidity and total malate content increased along with the activity of PEPC during growth in continuous light.
This indicates that PEPC was functioning in the light. However, the apparent operation of CAM was evident only in plants grown on 16 h/8 h light/dark cycle, as reflected by significant diurnal fluctuations of both titratable acidity and malate

Table I. Titratable acidity, total malate content, and PEPC in *M. crystallinum* as influenced by photoperiod. Leaves (third node) were harvested at the end of light or dark periods except those grown in continuous light.

Photoperiod	Titratable acidity			Malate content			PEPC
	Light	Dark	Dark-light	Light	Dark	Dark-Light	
	μeq/g fr wt						μmol mg chl^{-1} min^{-1}
3-week-old							
24/0	8.1	-	-	71.3	-	-	4.2
20/4	9.9	8.8	-1.1	50.6	45.6	5.0	2.3
16/8	5.9	8.7	2.8	40.3	47.8	7.5	2.5
4-week-old							
24/0	13.1	-	-	91.7	-	-	10.3
20/4	14.1	16.1	2.0	33.7	30.7	-3.0	4.6
16/8	11.0	22.6	11.6	25.8	33.7	7.9	3.6

content (Table I). Plants from all three photoperiods, particularly those grown in continuous light, accumulated very high levels of malate. However, the malate content was much higher than the titratable acidity (μeq/g fr wt basis), suggesting that much of the malate exists as a salt. A high level of sodium has been observed in *M. crystallinum* even when plants were growing with extremely low sodium in the soil (5). Based on analyses of photosynthetic products, the accumulation of malate appears to be due to a secondary carboxylation using PGA as a precursor. When plants were salt stressed after 3 weeks of growth, there was a large increase in activities of PEPC and NADP-ME (not shown), indicating that CAM can be induced earlier than when plants are grown under a 12 h/12 h photoperiod (3).

3.3. Induction by Abscisic Acid (ABA).
   After 5 weeks of growth at 16 h/8 h, 30°C/18°C, polyethylene glycol (PEG) and NaCl were tested for induction of CAM in *M. crystallinum*. As shown in Fig. 1, ABA added to the nutrient solution was also very effective in inducing increased activities of PEPC and NADP-ME. Six days after treatment, the diurnal fluctuations in titratable acidity and malate content were similar in the abscisic acid treated and the salt or PEG treated plants. SDS-PAGE of the soluble protein from leaf extracts showed the appearance of a major polypeptide band at approximately 100 kD with ABA, salt and PEG treatment. This band corresponds to PEPC and is consistent with the large increase in activity observed after 6 days.

In conclusion, it is clear that developmental factors play a role in the expression of CAM in non-stressed plants. The simplest interpretation is that prolonged photoperiods allow more growth over a given time, hence plants reach a certain developmental stage earlier which allows an earlier induction of CAM. The dependence of induction on environment may be mediated through abscisic acid, which serves as a functional linkage between environmental stress and biochemical adaptation.

REFERENCES
1 Winter, K. (1985) in Photosynthetic Mechanisms and the Environment (Barber, J. and Baker, N.R., eds.), pp. 329-387, Elsevier, Amsterdam
2 von Willert, D.J., Kirst, G.O., Treichel, S., and von Willer, K. (1976) Plant Sci. Lett. 7, 341-346
3 Ostrem, J.A., Olson, S.W., Schmitt, J.M. and Bohnert, H.J. (1987) Plant Physiol. 84, 1270-1275
4 Holtum, J.A.M. and Winter, K. (1982) Planta 115, 8-16
5 Winter, K., Luttge, U., and Winter, E. (1978) Oecologia 34, 225-237

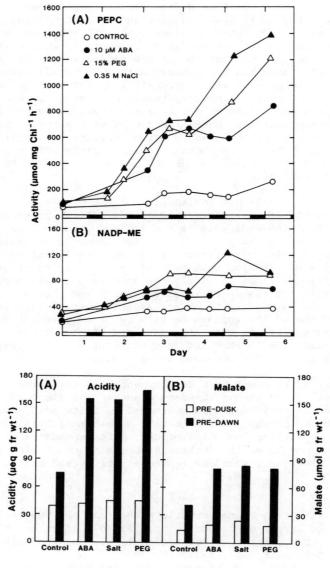

Fig. 1. Induction of CAM in *M. crystallinum* by abscisic acid, polyethylene glycol, and NaCl. After 5 weeks of growth in soil (day zero), plants were watered daily with nutrient media (control), or nutrient media containing 10 μM ABA, 15% PEG, or 0.35 M NaCl. The acidity and malate content of leaf extracts were measured after the sixth day.

CONTROL OF OXIDATIVE PHOSPHORYLATION IN THE ADAPTATION
OF Medicago sativa, Phaseolus aureus AND Phaseolus
vulgaris TO SALINITY

González, M.S., Quintanar, Z.R., Vázquez, M.J.
and Velasco, G.R. Lab. de Bioquímica. UMF
ENEP Iztacala. UNAM Apdo 314 Admon Tlalnepantla
Edo. de México. México

INTRODUCTION

Using the theory of metabolic control developed by
Kacser and Burns (1), and Heinrich and Rapoport (2,3),
it has been observed that in mammalian mitochondria, -
adenine nucleotide translocator, ATP synthase, b-c complex
and in other cases dicarboxylate carrier and cytochrome
oxidase have the principal contribution in flux control
of oxidative phosphorylation (4,5). In addition, the levels
of Ca^{2+} and Pi in mitochondria change the flux control -
coefficients (Ci) exerted by ATP/ADP carrier and ATP synthase (6). In that respect there is not information about
plant mitochondria. However, it has been described that
mitochondrial oxidative phosphorilation was depressed in
plants grown in medium salinized either with NaCl or Na_2SO_4
or by addition of both salts to the reaction mixture (7).
The present study examines the contribution of all steps
involved in the regulation of mitochondrial oxidative phosphorylation from three vegetal species with different salt
tolerance and the changes in the flux-control coefficients
induced by NaCl in the growth medium or in the reaction
mixture.

MATERIALS AND METHODS

Alfalfa (Medicago sativa), mungo bean (Phaseolus aureus)
and bean (Phaseolus vulgaris v. ojo de cabra) seeds, were
surface-sterilized 15 min in a 1% sodium hypochlorite solution and washed several times with water and remained in
imbibition 12 hours. Then, they were germinated at 30°C
in the dark. Alfalfa seeds were arranged in a lattice of
bronze (0.8 mm mesh) inside of a black acrilic cabinet with
circulating water impulsed with a submersible pump. Bean
seeds were arranged and germinated inside of a black plastic case. The etiolated shoots in each lattice were transferred to plastic boxes containing Hoagland solution with
0 or 75 mM NaCl and maintained 5 days in the dark.

M. Baltscheffsky (ed.), Current Research in Photosynthesis, Vol. IV, 397–400.
© 1990 Kluwer Academic Publishers. Printed in the Netherlands.

Alfalfa and bean etiolated shoots (100g) were cutted in
small pieces and the preparation of mitochondria performed
as described by Bonner ( ).
O_2 uptake was determinated polarographically using a Clark
type electrode in 1 ml of a medium containing 0.3 M mannitol, 5 mM $MgCl_2$, 10 mM KH_2PO_4 and 10 mM KCl brought to
pH 7.2 with Trisma-base.
Protein was estimated by the method of Bradford ( ).
Flux control coefficients were calculated according to –
Groen et al (4). Carboxyatractyloside, oligomycin and
antimycin were considered irreversible inhibitors (4).
Ki used for the calculations: cyanide (NC), 10 μM; N-ethylmaleimide (NC) 60 μM; phenylsuccinate (C), 0.71 mM; n-butyl
malonate (C), 0.35 mM. Km succinate, 1.17 mM.

RESULTS

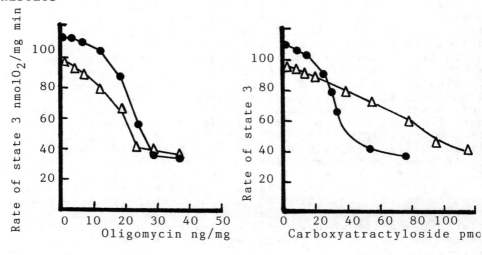

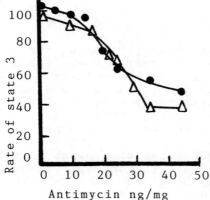

Fig 1. Inhibition of the rate
of state 3 respiration at –
different enzymatic steps in
isolated mitochondria from
Medicago grown at 0 and 75
mM NaCl.
Mitochondria were incubated
with the indicated inhibitors
in the conditions described in
methods.
State 3 was induced by the
addition of 100 UM ADP.

● 0 NaCl   Δ 75 mM NaCl

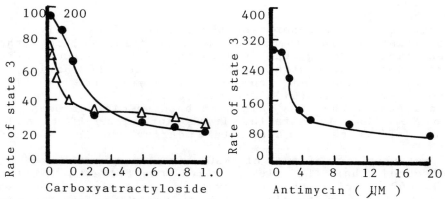

Inhibition of the rate of state 3 respiration at o and
80 mM NaCl at different enzymatic steps in mitochondria
isolated from Phaseolus vulgaris and Phaseolus aureus.
Conditions as described in fig 1. ● ONaCl ▲ 80 mM NaCl

Rate of state 3 (n mol O_2/mg prot min)

Enzyme	Ci					
	Medicago s		Phaseolus a		Phaseolus v	
	mM NaCl					
	0	75	0	80	0	80
ATP/ADP carrier	0.18	0.31	0.39	0.48	0.96	0.39
ATP synthase	0.13	0.31	0.62	0.56	0.28	0.33
b-c complex	0.18	0.13	0.88	0.50	0.70	0.54
Cytochrome oxidase	0.04	0.08	0.09	0.03	0.10	
Pi carrier	0.03	0.04	0.16	0.26	0.04	0.12
Dicarboxylate carrier	0.07	0.03	0.09	0.03	0.13	0.52
Ci =	0.63	0.90	2.23	1.86	2.21	

Flux-control coefficients of various steps in oxidative
phosphorylation of Medicago sativa, Phaseolus aureus
and Phaseolus vulgaris.
Flux control coefficients were calculated from the date
of fig 1,2 and other titration curves obtained with the
indicated inhibitor as described in methods.

DISCUSSION

In agreement with reports on the control of oxidative phosphorylation in mammalian mitochondria (4,5,6,),the present findings show that in alfalfa and bean mitochondria the most important control steps are the ATP/ADP carrier, ATP synthase and b-Cl complex, according to the flux control coefficients (Ci's) calculated.

In all steps, the Ci's values in both species of bean are higher than in alfalfa. It is not clear if this is due to differences on ion uptake during germination and growth.

In relation to effect of NaCl in the growth medium, we observed that the flux control coefficients exerted by ATP/ADP carrier and ATP synthase were increased two and three times respectly. The addition of NaCl to the reaction mixture decresead the control coefficient exerted by ATP/ADP carrier in P. vulgaris and b-Cl complex in both species of bean.

In mammalian mitochondria it has been shown that the control coefficients of the ATP/ADP carrier (ranged between 0.23-0.48) and ATP/synthase (0.57-0.50) were modified in a reciprocal way by Ca^{2+} and Pi concentrations (8).

It was also observed that the effect of $Ca2+$ on oxidative phosphorylation is modified by the concentration of Pi and the amount of intramitochondrial adenine nucleotides is affected by the internal concentrations of $Ca2+$.

The variations in the level of endogenous ions ($Ca2+$, $Mg2+$, Na+,Pi) or other components produced by effect of Na+ may account for the presently described observations.

According to others studies on mammalian mitochondria, in both species of Phaseolus there is not concordance with the summation theorem of the Metabolic Control Theory.

Three explanations had been proposed.[8]a) The equations proposed by Groen et. al.(4) using specific inhibitors may overestimate the Ci, b) some reactions could be draining the main flux (alternative respiratory pathway) and c) partial channeling of some intermediate metabolites.

LITERATURE CITED

1 Kacser,H. and Burns,J.(1973) Symp Soc Exp. Biol. 27, 65-104.
2 Heinrich,R. and Rapoport, T.(1974) Eur.J.Biochem 42,89-95
3 Heinrich,R. and Rapoport, T.(1974) Eur.J.Biochem42,97-105
4 Gröen,A., et al (1982) J. Biol Chem. 257,2754-2757.
5 Tager,J., et al (1983) FEBS Lett 151,1-9.
6 Moreno,R. (1985) J. Biol. Chem. 260,12554-12560.
7 Hasson,E. and Poljakoff,A.(1971) Plant Physiol 47,109-113
8 Moreno,R.(1988) in Integration of mitochondrial function (Lemasters,J. ed.) 297-304.Plenum Publishing Corporation.

SALINITY AND THE REGULATION OF PYRUVATE Pi DIKINASE.

DELILA MOUALEM-BENO AND ADIVA SHOMER-ILAN.
Dept. of Botany, Tel Aviv University, Tel Aviv 69978, Israel.

1. INTRODUCTION

Phosphoenolpyruvate (PEP), at concentrations higher than 1.0mM, was found to stabilize PEP carboxylase and pyruvate kinase and to prevent inactivation by NaCl invitro (1,2,3). Salt sensitivity or tolerance of other enzymes, e.g. glutamine synthetase and malate dehydrogenase were also found to be substrate dependent. Further, endogenous levels of PEP were found to increase, in different C_4 plants, to concentrations enabling insitu enzyme protection, when grown under saline conditions (2).

In certain C_4 plants, pyruvate-Pi-dikinase (PPDK) is the enzyme responsible for the regeneration of PEP. Accordingly, the aim of the present paper was to analyze the effect of salinity on the regulation of PPDK activity.

2. MATERIALS AND METHODS

Plant material: Plants of Jouvea pilosa (Poaceae, C_4, NAD-ME type, halophyte) were grown in a sand culture under controlled conditions, in a growth chamber., and irrigated with 50% Hoaglands' solution plus different concentrations of NaCl (J_0, J_{200}, J_{300}).

Enzyme assay: Crude extract, from young leaves, was desalted on sephadex G-25 coloumn. Enzyme was kept in incubation medium containing 20% glycerol or 300 mM glycine betaine and then assayed according to Hata and Matsuoka(3). Finnal concentration of glycerol in the assay was 7.5% and that of glycine betaine – 300 mM. The assay medium contained 2.5 mM pyruvate, 1.5 mM ATP and 2.5 mM Pi.

3. RESULTS AND DISCUSSION

3.1 Effects of salinity in the irrigation medium

Optimal growth of J. pilosa plants was observed when plants were irrigated with 200 mM NaCl (J_{200}). Under these saline conditions, the level of the compatible solute – betaine, an osmolite and a non specific protecting agent, had increased up to approximately 500 mM (Table 1). In paralel, the level of the specific ligand – PEP showed a three times increase (Table 1).

M. Baltscheffsky (ed.), Current Research in Photosynthesis, Vol. IV, 401–404.
© 1990 *Kluwer Academic Publishers. Printed in the Netherlands.*

The increase in the specific activity of PPDK - the enzyme regenerating PEP, under saline conditions (table 1), seems to be the main contributer to the higher level of PEP in saline environment.

Table 1: Effects of different concentrations of NaCl in irrigation medium (J_0, J_{200}, J_{300}) on the specific activity of PPDK, and the endogenic level of PEP and betaine. It was assumed that the cytosol was 7% of the water volume.

NaCl mM	PPDK activity	PEP		Betaine	
	$\frac{n\ mol}{min.\ mg\ protein}$	$\frac{n\ mol}{G.F.W.}$	mM estimated	$\frac{\mu\ mol}{G.F.W.}$	mM estimated
J_0	27.07	122	2.5	10.3	205
J_{200}	51.8	345	7.04	19.8	430
J_{300}	66.04	422.4	8.6	20.8	510

3.2 Salinity and PPDK activity in a cell free system.

3.2.1 Effects of compatible solutes and substrates.

The activity of PPDK in the desalted crude extract decreased with time. Stabilization was gained when glycerol (20%) or glycine-betaine (300mM) was added to the incubation medium.

NaCl inhibited the enzyme activity. The presence of compatible solutes - glycerol and glycine-betaine, in the saline assay medium, caused a partial protecting effect (table 2). While, the substra ts pyruvate (5; 10 mM) or ATP (2.5 mM) did not protect PPDK activity from inhibition by NaCl.

Table 2: Effects of compatible solutes and specific effectors on the relative activity (%) of PPDK in the presence of various concentrations of NaCl (The activity without protecting agents was denoted as 100% = 29.1 n mol/min. mg protein).

NaCl Agents	0	100 mM	200 mM	300 mM
0	100%	53 ± 7	27.5 ± 3	
betaine 300 mM	137.5± 9	83.9 ± 5	48.1 ± 9	28.8 ± 4
glycerol 7.5 %	178 ± 26	92.5 ± 10	40 ± 9	17.8 ± 2
F-1,6-P 0.5 mM (G 7.5%)	191 ± 12	112.1 ± 4	67.8 ± 9	27.4 ± 1
F-1,6-P 2.5 mM (G 7.5%)	240 ± 7	146 ± 12	74.8 ± 10	37.4 ± 2
G-6-P 2.5 mM (G 7.5%)	197.6± 5	119.3 ± 15	65.9 ± 9	33.8 ± 1
F-6-P 2.5 mM (G 7.5%)	185.1 ± 10	102.5 ± 9	51.6 ± 7	34.3 ± 5

3.2.2 Regulation and relative protection by effectors

Fructose-1,6-phosphate (0.5, 2.5 mM) and glucose-6-phosphate (2.5 mM), in the presence of glycerol, were found to activate PPDK (table 2) and thus might be endogenic regulators of PPDK activity. Further more, in their presence, the inhibition by NaCl is decreased (table 2). These tested concentrations of Fructose-1,6-phosphate and glucose-6-phosphate seem to be in the physiological range (5). Thus, these effectors could contribute to a change in the enzyme conformation and enable its stabilization and higher activity even in a saline environment.

4. CONCLUSIONS

4.1 Growth under saline environment caused a three times increase in the endogenic level of PEP in the leaves.

4.2 The increase in the specific activity of PPDK seems to be the main contributer to the higher level of PEP in saline environment.

4.3 Salinity caused increase in the level of endogenic betaine (up to 500 mM).

4.4 The compatible solute betaine seems to produce only a partial protection against inhibition of PPDK by NaCl.

4.5 The substrates pyruvate or ATP, at high concentrations, did not protect PPDK from salt inactivation.

4.6 The activators frutose-1,6-phosphate and glucose-6-phosphate behave also as protecting agents against inactivation of PPDK by salt.

4.7 Specific effectors might be a new group of salt protecting agents that together with the non specific agents e.g., the compatible solutes and the specific agents - the substrates, enable insitu enzyme activity in the presence of high ion concentrations.

REFERENCES

1. Shomer-Ilan, A., Moualem-Beno, D., Waisel, Y. (1985). Physiol. Plantarum 65, 72-78.
2. Shomer-Ilan, A., Waisel, Y. (1986). Physiol. Plantarum 67, 408-414.
3. Shomer-Ilan, A., Moualem-Beno D., (1987) in Prog. in Photosynthesis Res. IV, 185-188, Martinus Nijhoff Pub.
4. Hata, S., Matsuoka, M. (1987). Plant Cell Physiol. 28, 635-641.
5. Stitt,M., Heldt, H.W. (1985). Planta 164, 179-188.

NITROGEN DEPRIVATION AND THE PHOTOSYNTHETIC APPARATUS OF THE GREEN ALGA CHLORELLA FUSCA

MICHAEL H. RIEß, INGO DAMM and L. HORST GRIMME
Dept. of Biol./Chem., Univ. of Bremen, D-2800 Bremen, FRG

1. INTRODUCTION

Chlorosis, the decrease of photosynthetic pigments due to the deficiency of N, P, S, Si, Mg, Fe or K, is probably the most general response of algae to nutrient deprivation (1). Some like the green alga Chlorella fusca concomitantly turn red due to the synthesis of secondary-carotenoids. The loss of pigments has been studied, but the consequences of N-deprivation for the photosynthetic apparatus and its functioning are not well understood.

Several algal groups undergo a dramatical transformation of the structural and functional integrity of their photosynthetic apparatus under nitrogen starvation. This includes ultrastructural changes of thylakoid membranes leading to the loss of O_2-evolution (2), major reductions in the level of PS II-polypeptides (3), the preferential loss of chloroplast proteins (4) and the deficiency in the chlorophyll a/b light-harvesting complex (LHC) (5).

Along with the earlier studies on the effects of N-starvation on the green alga C. fusca (6-8) we investigated structural and functional features of the photosynthetic apparatus during the transformation of this alga from its autotrophic to its anabiotic status. Here we analyze the oxygen evolving capacity of cells, the PS I-activity of thylakoid membranes and the chlorophyll content during the first ten days.

2. MATERIALS AND METHODS

Synchronized C. fusca (9) (strain 211-15) was grown in an N-reduced (320 µmol KNO_3/l) medium for one cell cycle. After transfer to continous light (10-15 klux) the cells were cultivated for ten days without any nitrogen. Chlorophylls were determined by rp-HPLC according to (10). O_2-evolution of cells was measured using a CLARK-electrode under saturating white light and enrichment with HCO_3^-. PS I-activity of isolated thylakoid membranes from mechanically broken cells was measured polarographically as O_2-consumption in the presence of 150 µmol/l DCPIP, 1 mmol/l ascorbate, 10 µmol/l methylviologen and 10 µmol/l DCMU under saturating white light.

3. RESULTS

Fig. 1 shows the time course of the chlorophyll breakdown over a period of ten days in cells of C. fusca under N-deprivation. The chl a content of 265.7 pmol/10^6 cells is reduced to 30.5 pmol/10^6

M. Baltscheffsky (ed.), Current Research in Photosynthesis, Vol. IV, 405–408.
© 1990 *Kluwer Academic Publishers. Printed in the Netherlands.*

cells, representing a loss of 89 %, while the chl b content shows a reduction of 86 % from 75 to 10 pmol/10^6 cells. The chl a/b-ratio decreases from 3.3 to 2.5 within eight days of N-deprivation due to a preferential breakdown of chl a (Fig. 1). But after ten days the origional value is reached again and maintained afterwards.

Fig. 2 demonstrates the decline of the photosynthetic O_2-evolution calculated on the basis of the actual chlorophyll content during ten days of N-deprivation. It can be seen that the capacity of Chlorella to evolve oxygen is lost faster than both chlorophylls. The decrease is most dramatical within the first day of N-deprivation with a loss of 43 % of the O_2-evolving capacity, which totally declines during ten days of N-deprivation from 329 to 89 umol O_2/h x mg chl. This shows that the ability of the photosynthetic membrane to evolve oxygen is inhibited prior to the loss of chlorophylls under N-deprivation.

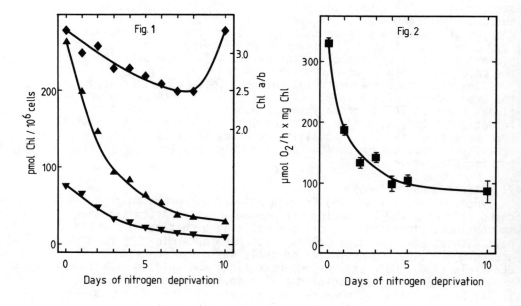

FIGURE 1.) Breakdown of chlorophyll a (▲) and b (▼) and the chl a/b-ratio (◆) in cells of Chlorella during a period of ten days of N-deprivation.

FIGURE 2.) Photosynthetic O_2-evolution on the basis of the actual chl content of Chlorella during a period of ten days of N-deprivation.

The analysis of the in vitro activity of PS I and PS II in thylakoid membranes of C. fusca during N-deprivation gave the following results: PS I-activity (Fig. 3) is stable over the period of ten days indicating that the drop in the photosynthetic oxygen evolution (Fig. 2) may result from the impairment of reactions around PS II. Indeed the analysis of PS II-HILL-activity reveals an immediate and complete loss during the first day of N-deprivation (data not shown), but this may be caused by the more drastic method of membrane preparation of N-deprived cells.

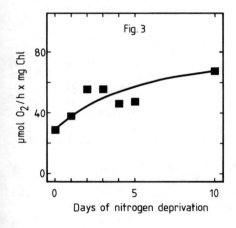

FIGURE 3.) PS I-activity of isolated thylakoid membranes from Chlorella during ten days of N-deprivation, measured polarographically as O_2-consumption of the reaction DCPIP/ascorbate to methylviologen

4. DISCUSSION

The decreasing chl a/b-ratio (Fig. 1) of C. fusca under N-deprivation leads to the conclusion that the different pigment-protein complexes of thylakoid membranes are selectively affected. This idea is supported by the analysis of pigment-protein complexes of Chlorella by SDS-PAGE, which reveals a preferential loss of PS I- and PS II-complexes in contrast to LHCP[3] (data not shown). This also has been suggested by LEVENKO and coworkers (11) from the selective bleaching of long wavelength-forms of chl a during N-starvation of Chlorella. Although ultrastructural investigations of N-deprived Cryptomonas maculata (2) show a decreasing amount of PS II-LHC complexes, this change was suggested to be the result of the decoupling of PS II and LHC, and not to be due to their degradation. N-limited Chlamydomonas reinhardtii, on the other side, is deficient in the LHC (5).

The inhibition of the photosynthetic oxygen evolving capacity prior to the loss of chlorophylls (Fig. 2) and the stability of in vitro PS I-activity (Fig. 3) of N-deprived C. fusca suggests an enhanced sensitivity of PS II towards N-deprivation. This close relationship has also been demonstrated by the analysis of room temperature fluorescence induction characteristics of PS II in Cryptomonas maculata (2) and the almost linear dependence of the photosynthetic oxygen evolution from N-supply in Phaeodactylum tricornutum (12). The increased sensitivity of PS II in Chlorella may be due to the change in the level of D1 and CP47 of PS II, as it was shown for five strains of uni-cellular marine algae grown under N-limitation, which leads to the suggestion that N-limitation may increase sensitivity to photo-inhibition (3, 4).

Photoinhibition preceeds any detectable photobleaching of chlorophylls and the presently discussed mechanism involves the light induced damage of D1 thereby leading to the impairment of the electron trans-port function of PS II (13). It remains to be demonstrated whether the observed inhibiton of the oxygen evolving capacity in Chlorella is due to an irradianve dependent inhibition of the photochemistry of PS II.

REFERENCES
1 Healey, F.P. (1973) Crit. Rev. Microbiol. 3, 69-113
2 Rhiel, E., Krupinska, K. and Wehrmeyer, W. (1986) Planta 169, 361-369
3 Kolber, Z., Zehr, J. and Falkowski, P. (1988) Plant Physiol. 88, 923-929
4 Coleman, L.W., Rosen, B.H. and Schwartzbach, S.D. (1988) Plant Cell Physiol. 29, 1007-1014
5 Plumley, F.G. and Schmidt, G.W. (1989) Proc. Natl. Acad. Sci. USA 86, 2678-2682
6 Grimme, L.H., Porra, R.J., Pyliotis, N.A., Thorne, S.W., Argyroudi-Akoyunoglou, J. and Akoyunoglou, G.A. (1974) Port. Acta Biol. Ser. A 14, 153-164
7 Pyliotis, N.A., Goodchild, D.J. and Grimme, L.H. (1975) Arch. Microbiol. 103, 259-270
8 Grimme, L.H., Fawley, M. and Brown, J.S. (1982) Carnegie Inst. Wash. Year Book 81, 37-38
9 Grimme, L.H., Damm, I., Steinmetz, D. and Scheffczyk, B. (1987) in Progr. Photosynth. Res. (Biggins, J., ed.) Vol. II, pp. 347-350, Nijhoff Pub., Dordrecht
10 Knoetzel, J., Braumann, T. and Grimme, L.H. (1988) J. Photochem. Photobiol. B: Biol. 1, 475-491
11 Levenko, B.A., Chemeris, K.Y. and Venediktov, P.S. (1985) Biochem. Physiol. Pflanz. 180, 157-162
12 Osborne, B.A. and Geider, R.J. (1986) Plant Cell Environ. 9, 617-625
13 Kyle, D.J. and Ohad, I. (1986) in Photosynthesis III (Staehelin, L.A. and Arntzen, C.J., eds.) Encycl. Plant Physiol. (New Series) Vol 19, pp 468-475, Springer, Heidelberg

GAS EXCHANGE, CHLOROPHYLL A FLUORESCENCE, AND METABOLITE LEVELS IN
LEAVES OF TRIFOLIUM SUBTERRANEUM DURING LONG-TERM EXPOSURE TO
ELEVATED CO_2

T. BETSCHE, F. MORIN, F. COTE, F. GAUGAIN, and M. ANDRE

DEPARTEMENT DE BIOLOGIE, CEN CADARACHE, F 13108 ST-PAUL-LEZ-DURANCE,
FRANCE

INTRODUCTION

   In many C_3-plants, the initial stimulation by high CO_2 of photosynthesis declines during long-term exposure to high CO_2. This is accompanied by excessive starch accumulation, and in some species chloroplast
distortion has been observed (1). It has been suggested that the breakdown of the thylakoid proton gradient causes the decline of photosynthesis or, alternatively, that "feedback" because of insufficient sink
or transport capacity for sucrose stimulates starch formation and finally inhibits photosynthesis (2). This communication reports of experiments with whole plants or attached leaves which were transferred to
high CO_2 or to high light and kept under these conditions for one to
two weeks.

MATERIALS AND METHODS

   Plants. Trifolium subterraneum was germinated in the greenhouse in
soil. Before use, six-week-old plants were re-potted in Perlite and kept
in the gas exchange chamber for another week.

Gas exchange measurements. Net CO_2-uptake was determined in closed systems as described in (3). Light/dark rhythm was 14h / 10 h, $25°$/ $20°C$,
and humidity was 82 % (whole plants). The leaf chamber was thermoregula-
ted to $20°C$.

Biochemical analysis. Sample preparation and metabolite determinations
were done essentially as described in (6). Ribulose-1,6-bisphosphate was
determined by CO_2-incorporation catalyzed by rubisco (7) and ATP by
luciferase. Glucose 6-phosphate or carbohydrates were extracted and determined after (6) or (8), respectively.

Chlorophyll a fluorescence was measured as described in (4). For definitions of energy quenching (qE), quinon reduction state (1-qQ), and
Fo-quenching refer to (4) and (5).

M. Baltscheffsky (ed.), Current Research in Photosynthesis, Vol. IV, 409–412.
© 1990 *Kluwer Academic Publishers. Printed in the Netherlands.*

RESULTS AND DISCUSSION

Net CO_2-uptake of whole Trifolium plants increased about twofold after transfer to 1000 $\mu l \cdot l^{-1}$ or 4000 $\mu l \cdot l^{-1} CO_2$. Thereafter, during growth, the daily increments of net CO_2-uptake were about equal in air and in high CO_2 (Fig. 1). This suggests that leaf area-based CO_2-uptake rates declined during long-term exposure to high CO_2. Many mature-old (not senescent) leaves yellowed in high CO_2 as it has been observed previously by other workers (1,2).

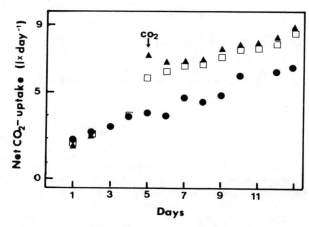

FIGURE 1.
Net CO_2-uptake by 10 Trifolium plants in air ● , (days 1 to 12), or after transfer to 1000 $\mu l \cdot l^{-1}$ □ , or 4000 $\mu l \cdot l^{-1}$ CO_2 ▲ , at 400 $\mu E \cdot m^{-2} s^{-1}$

After transfer of mature,attached leaves to high CO_2, the initial stimulation of photosynthesis declined as of the second day (Fig. 2A), and the leaves began to yellow. Chlorophyll a fluorescence induction kinetics of "energy quenching" (qE) indicate more rapid activation of the Calvin-cycle in high CO_2. qE was then stronger in high CO_2 than in air (Fig.2B). qE was also determined during the whole photoperiod, and Fig. 2C shows that when photosynthesis declined and yellowing occurred, qE and Fo-quenching (Qo= 0.34 at day 6) increased to very high values. 1- qQ (quinon reduction state) did not increase. One can conclude from the strong qE in high CO_2, that the decline of CO_2-uptake by Trifolium leaves does not result from limitation of CO_2-fixation by the transthylakoid proton gradient. This result does not conflict with the observation that excessive starch accumulation can cause physical damage to chloroplasts (1), and it supports results from light-scattering measurements (9) suggesting that high CO_2 disturbes the regulation of photosynthetic carbon metabolism (or carbon export) from the leaf.

In order to investigate this, we determined levels of photosynthetic metabolites and of end products in leaves after transfer to high CO_2 and in other leaves which were presumably acclimatized to either high CO_2 or high light. Under the latter conditions, net CO_2-uptake of the whole plants was identical. Table 1 shows that the levels of photosynthetic metabolites were higher in high CO_2 than in air (same irridiance). Sucrose increased equally in air and high CO_2 during the first halves of the days. Then substantially more sucrose accumulated in high CO_2. Starch

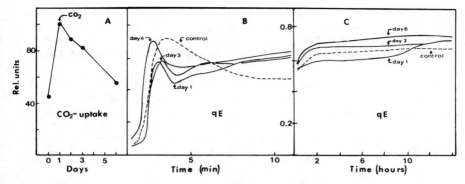

FIGURE 1. CO_2-uptake (A), chlorophyll a fluorescence induction kinetics of "energy quenching" (B), and time courses of qE during the day (C) after exposure of attached leaves to 4000 $\mu l \cdot l^{-1} CO_2$. Control: 340 $\mu L \cdot l^{-1} CO_2$, day before the increase of CO_2. Units: A, $1U = 0.51$ ml CO_2 day^{-1}

accumulation occurred more rapidly in high CO_2 as of the very beginning of the day (Table 1). It appears that more carbon is diverted into starch in high CO_2 than in air without heavy accumulation of sucrose. When net CO_2-uptake was equally stimulated by increasing either CO_2 or light, the accumulation of sucrose and hexose was equal (Table 2). Nevertheless, 2 to 3 times more starch, depending upon leaf age, accumulated in high CO_2 (Table 2). PGA/triose-P ratios were higher whereas ATP/ADP ratios and levels of glucose-6P were lower in high CO_2 (Table 2). Ribulose-P_2 was similar (data not shown). These results demonstrate that at the same rate of carbon supply the partitioning between starch (storage) and sucrose (export) is different in high CO_2 or high light although there is no evidence for "feedback" and sink limitation of photosynthesis in high CO_2. The observed high PGA/triose-P ratios together with the strong accumulation of starch support the suggestion that photosynthesis is limited by Pi in high CO_2 (10, 11). The strong qE in high CO_2 corroborates whereas

TABLE 1. Metabolite and carbohydrate levels in Trifolium leaves. Irradiance was 400 $\mu E \cdot m^{-2} \cdot s^{-1}$ Values are nmoles mg^{-1}phaeophytin for metabolites (10 leaves sampled after transfer) or μmoles hexose equivalents g^{-1} DW for carbohydrates (4 days after transfer).

Conditions	4000 $\mu l \cdot l^{-1} CO_2$		340 $\mu l \cdot l^{-1}$ CO_2	
Time of illum.	1.5 h	7 h	1.5 h	7 h
PGA	332	426	303	236
Gluc-6P	150	135	73	93
Time of illum.	4 h		4 h	
Hexose	56		49	
Sucrose	60		60	
Starch	1350		525	

TABLE 2. Metabolite and carbohydrate levels in leaves of different age when wole plant photosynthesis was equally stimulated by high CO_2 or by high light. Samples were taken 12 days after transfer to the respective conditions and 6 h after the onset of the light. For units see table 1.

Conditions	4000 µl·l⁻¹CO_2 400 µE·m⁻²·s⁻¹		340 µl·l⁻¹CO_2 800 µE·m⁻²·s⁻¹	
Leaf age	mature	old	mature	old
Sucrose	60	88	72	92
Starch	610	945	294	278
Gluc–P	128	107	154	157
PGA/ Triose–P	4,4	34	2.5	10
ATP/ ADP	1.5	2.2	2.5	3.1

the lower level of esterified phosphate (so far measured) in high CO_2-leaves is seemingly conflicting (data not shown). It is possible, however, that only stromal Pi is low perhaps because of the supression of photorespiration in high CO_2. This means that no P-glycolate is cleaved within the chloroplast. It is also plausible to assume that because of the absence of photorespiration, the phosphorylation potential is low in the cytosol. Recent work supports this suggestion (12). The low phosphorylation potential in the cytosol would be unfavorable for the synthesis of sucrose and so perhaps stimulate starch formation (10).

In conclusion, it appears that in Trifolium leaves photosynhesis is perturbed by CO_2 directly, and therefore excess starch accumulates. It is an open question whether all C_3-plants can acclimate to elevated CO_2 in such a manner that the plant supports continuing high rates of photosynthesis and that all extra-fixed carbon is approprately metabolized and exported from the leaves.

REFERENCES

1 Cave, L.N., Tolley, L.C., and Strain, B.R. (1981) Physiol. Plant. 51 171-174
2 Delucia, E.H., Sasek, T.W., and Strain, B.R. (1985) Photosynthesis Res., 7, 175-184
3 Andre, M., Massimino, D. and Daguenet, A. (1978) Physiol. Plant. 38, 1421-1431
4 Schreiber, U, Schliwa, U., and Bilger, W. (1986) Photosynthesis Res. 10, 51-62
5 Bilger, W., and Schreiber, U. (1986) Photosynthesis Res., 10, 303-308
6 Leegood, R.C. and Furbank, R.T. (1984) Planta 162, 450-456
7 Sharkey, T.D. and Badger, M.R. (1982) Planta 156, 199-206
8 Rufty, T.W. and Huber, S.C. (1983) Plant Physiol 72, 474-480
9 Dietz, K.J., Neimanis, S., and Heber, U. (1984) Biochim. Biophys. Acta 767, 444-450
10 Stitt, M., Huber, S. and Kerr, P. (1987) in The Biochemistry of Plants (Preiss J., ed.), Vol. 10, pp. 327-455, Academic Press
11 Foyer, C.H. (1987) Plant Physiol. Biochem. 25, 649-657
12 Gardeström P. (1987) FEBS Letters 212: 114-118

CHLOROPHYLLOUS CALLI FROM PSORALEA BITUMINOSA L. - ADAPTATION TO PHOTOMIXOTROPHISM

J. Diamond, A. Casimiro, M. S. Pais, Dept. de Biologia Vegetal,F.C.L., Bloco C2 Campo Grande, 1700 Lisboa, Portugal

1. INTRODUCTION

Photoautotrophic plant cell cultures provide a useful material for studies on the metabolism and physiology of autotrophic cells and can also be important for the knowledge of the metabolic pathways of the synthesis of natural products.

Some authors[1,2,3] have been using calli culture for the transition from heterotrophic to photomixotrophic and autotrophic cell culture. Chlorophyllous calli from a large number of species (tobacco, potato, carrot, tomato) were sucessfully established[4,5]. The growth rate and the chlorophyll content during the transition phase were compared in several studies[6,7]. However, very few information is available about physiological parameters during adaptation to photomixotrophism. According to Sato et al.[8], chlorophyll content and photosynthetic activity were not necessarily correlated.Furthermore in other studies it was described how important it is to reduce sucrose content, in the medium, in order to increase photosynthetic activity in calli[9].

The aim of this work was to select stable chlorophyllous and friable calli, in order to obtain photoautotrophic cell cultures from Psoralea bituminosa L.. Two sucrose concentrations were tested and physiological and biochemical parameters were studied.

2. MATERIALS AND METHODS

Portions of petioles of full developed leaves were used as primary explants from Psoralea bituminosa L.and were induced to form calli on a modified Murashige[10] and Skoog medium suplemented with naphtalene acetic acid (NAA) 2mg l^{-1} and benzyladenine, 1mg l^{-1}.   Two   sucrose concentrations (8g l^{-1} and 20g l^{-1}) were used.The pH of the medium was adjusted to 5.6. Calli were grown at 23°C $\pm$ 1 under a photosynthetic active radiation (PAR) of 100-120μE m^{-2} s^{-1},and with a photoperiod of 12 hours. Subcultures were performed every two weeks.

Chlorophyll content were determined in methanol extracts.

Sucrose concentrations in the medium and in calli were measured by a colorimetric method using the resorcinol reaction. The assays were performed after acid hydrolisis.

Oxygen evolution was estimated with a Clark type electrode (Hansatech Ltd.) in dark conditions for respiration and under saturating light for photosynthesis. Calli material (0.2g) was dispersed in 1ml liquid medium. Temperature was maintained at 25°C.

M. Baltscheffsky (ed.), Current Research in Photosynthesis, Vol. IV, 413–416.
© 1990 *Kluwer Academic Publishers. Printed in the Netherlands.*

Enzymatic activities of RuBP carboxylase and PEP carboxylase were determined according to Machler[11] and Nosberger and Price[12] and Hedley.
All the assays were made on the first and second week of each subculture. The results are means of five assays.

3. RESULTS AND DISCUSSION

Calli grown on medium with 20g l^{-1} sucrose concentration showed a visual darker green intensity when compared with calli of 8g l^{-1} sucrose concentration. This observation was confirmed by determinations of chlorophyll content. The results shown in Fig.1 suggest that chlorophyll content was correlated to the sugar content of the medium. High sugar concentration did not promote calli growth. In similar conditions it was verified lower growth rate and higher chlorophyll content[13].

CHLOROPHYLL CONTENTS

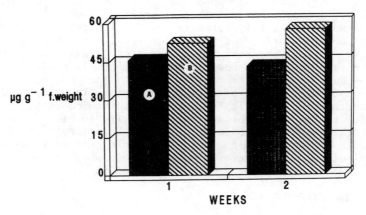

FIGURE 1. Chlorophyll contents in calli grown on medium A (8g l^{-1} sucrose) and B (20g l^{-1} sucrose).

The results of the assays of sugar determination in the medium and in the calli are summarized in Table 1.

TABLE 1. Sugar concentration in the medium and in the calli. A-8g l^{-1} sucrose medium. B-20g l^{-1} sucrose medium.

Time (weeks)	Medium (g l^{-1})		Calli (mg g^{-1} fresh weight)	
	A	B	A	B
1	1.83 ± 0.4	4.78 ± 1	1.81 ± 0.23	4.83 ± 0.36
2	1.6 ± 0.8	1.5 ± 0.5	1.78 ± 0.19	2.39 ± 0.09

At higher sucrose concentrations the sugar content in one week aged calli was directly correlated. However aged calli did not reveal a similar correlation. Calli grown on lower sucrose, maintain high sugar levels during culture, wich agree with other authors[14].

Respiratory and photosynthetic rates are shown in Fig. 2.

RESPIRATORY AND PHOTOSYNTHETIC RATES

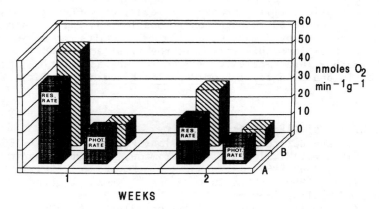

WEEKS

FIGURE 2.   Respiratory and photosynthetic rates of calli grown on medium A ($8g$ 1^{-1} sucrose) and B ($20g$ 1^{-1} sucrose)

In calli grown on $8g$ 1^{-1} sucrose medium it is particularly evident the lower respiratory rates and the higher photosynthetic activity. These results are in concordance with data shown in Fig. 3.

ACTIVITY OF PEP CARBOXYLASE

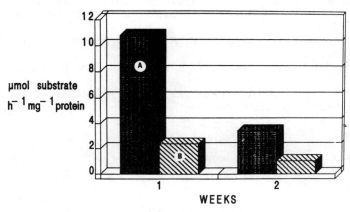

WEEKS

FIGURE 3.   Activity of PEP carboxylase in calli cultured on conditions A ($8g$ 1^{-1} sucrose) and B ($20g$ 1^{-1} sucrose).

Our data are in agreement with previous results[15] showing that chlorophyll content and photosynthetic activity were not necessarily correlated.

The increased PEPC activity in <u>calli</u> cultured on medium with lower sucrose contents confirmed the results obtained for photosynthetic rates.

It was not detected enzymatic activity of RuBP carboxylase. Being <u>Psoralea bituminosa</u> L. a C_3 plant it was then expected that RuBP would be the main enzymatic activity present. However, only PEPC activity was detected in <u>calli</u> cultured in both conditions (8 and 20g l^{-1} sucrose). As previously reported by Yamada et al.[16] these results may suggest that in mixotrophic conditions this enzyme is the first activated.

High PEP carboxylase activity may be a characteristic of the photomixotrophic phase in <u>calli</u> from <u>Psoralea bituminosa</u> L.

REFERENCES

1 Cordman, G. (1970) Planta 91, 752-756.
2 Berlyn, M. B. and Zelitch, I. (1975) Plant Physiol. 56, 752-756.
3 Sato, F., Nakagawa, M., Tanio, T. and Yamaoa, Y. (1981) Agric. Biol. Chem. 45, 2463-2467.
4 Gautheret,R. J. (1959) in "La Culture des Tissues Végétaux. Techniques et Réalisation" pp.341-343. Masson, Paris.
5 Vasil, I. K. and Hildebrandt, A. C. (1966) Planta 68, 69-82.
6 Dalton, C. C. (1980) J. Exp. Bot. 31, 791-804.
7 La Rosa, P. C., Hasegawa, P. M. and Bressan, R. A. (1984) Physiol. Plant. 61, 279-286.
8 Sato, F., Asada, K. and Yamada, Y. (1979) Plant and Cell Physiol. 29, 193-200.
9 Dalton, C. C. and Street, H. E. (1977) Pl. Sci. Lett. 10, 157-164.
10 Murashige, T. and Skoog, F. (1962) Physiol. Plant. 15, 473-497.
11 Machler, F. and Nosberger, J. (1980) J. Exp. Bot. 31, 1485-1491.
12 Price, D. N. and Hedley, C. L. (1980) Ann. Bot. 45, 283-294.
13 Davey, M. R., Fowler, M. W. and Street, H. E. (1971) Phytochemistry 10, 2555-2575.
14 Hardy, T., Chaumont, D., Wessinger, M. E. and Bournat, P. (1978) J. Plant. Physiol. 128, 11-19.
15 Sato, F., Asada, H. and Yamada, Y. (1979) Plant and Cell Physiol. 20, 193-200.
16 Yamada, Y., Sato, F. and Watanabe, K. (1982) in "Plant Tissue Culture 1982" pp. 249-250. Maruzen, Tokyo.

PHOTOSYNTHESIS IN FLOWERS OF PETUNIA HYBRIDA:
LOW CO_2 FLOW AND COORDINATED REDUCTION BETWEEN PHOTOSYNTHETIC SYSTEMS

David Weiss[1], Adiva Shomer-Ilan[2] and Abraham H. Halevy[1] Dept of Horticulture, The
Hebrew University of Jerusalem, Rehovot 76100, Israel[1]
Dept of Botany, Tel Aviv University, Tel Aviv 69978, Israel[2]

1. INTRODUCTION

In a previous paper (1) we reported on the presence of chloroplasts in the
corollas of Petunia hybrida, in all stages of their development. Chloroplasts
isolated from mature pink corollas carried out electron transport at only one
quarter of the rate of chloroplasts from green leaves. The aim of the present work
was to further characterize the photosynthetic systems of the Petunia corolla.

2. MATERIALS AND METHODS

Petunia hybrida plants (cv. Hit Parade Rosa) were used. Flower development was
divided into 7 stages. The corolla at stages 1 through 3 is green. Stage 4 through
6 is characterized by a sharp increase in growth rate and accumulation of
anthocyanin. Anthesis occurs at the end of stage 6. At stage 7 the flower is open
and exhibits two parts; the greenish tube and the pink limb. The flower at stage 6
was used to characterize the photosynthetic systems. Total chlorophyll and
chlorophyll a were determined by the method of Arnon (2). Chlorophyll a
fluorescence was measured as described by Beer et al (3). Stomatal aperature
measurement was done according to Scharwz et al (4). Leaf conductance was measured
with a steady state promoter Li 1600 (Li-Cor. Inc). $^{14}CO_2$ light fixation and the
activity of RuBP-case were measured as described by Weiss et al (5).

3. RESULTS AND DISCUSSION

Depsite the apparently normal structure of the corolla chloroplasts they were
able to carry out only 25% of the rate of electron transport as compared to
leaf-chloroplast (1). Their light carbon fixation rate was only 21% per unit
chlorophyll than that of the leaf (table 1). An attempt was made to elucidate the
factors determining this low light fixation efficiency.

M. Baltscheffsky (ed.), Current Research in Photosynthesis, Vol. IV, 417–419.
© 1990 Kluwer Academic Publishers. Printed in the Netherlands.

TABLE 1. Characteristics of different photosynthetic systems in green leaves and corollas (stage 6) of _Petunia hybrida_

	Stomatal conductance cm/s	light fixation $dpm^{14}CO_2/$ mg chl x min	RuBP-case $\mu mol\ CO_2/$ mg chl x min	electron transport [1] neq/mg chl x min
corolla	0.04 ± .004	6×10^3 ± 0.8	1.7 ± .11	417 ± 50
leaf	0.32 ± .03	28.3×10^6 ± 1500	6.6 ± .64	1767 ± 33
corolla/ leaf	0.121	0.21	0.27	0.24

Type of pathway: detached corollas (stage 6) and green leaves were pulsed with $^{14}CO_2$ for 6 seconds and the soluble metabolites extracted and analysed. The light fixation products were typical to C_3 plants in both leaves and corollas.

The activity of the key enzyme in the carbon reducing cycle was analysed. It was found that the activity of RuBP-case extracted from the corollas (stage 6) was only 27% of that extracted from the green leaves (Table 1). Thus, there seems to be a similar relative rate of electron transfer (25%) and RuBP-case activity (27%) with a little lower relative rate (21%) of the carbon fixation in the light. It seems that the systems in the corolla are well coordinated and potentially can function only at a lower rate. What could be the limiting factor?

TABLE 2. Number of stomata and stomatal aperature, in the dark and in the light, of fully expanded green leaf and corolla at stage 6 of _Petunia hybrida_

	No. of stomata per mm^2	stomatal aperature (μm) dark	light
corolla	18 ± 0.8	0.75 ± 0.1	0.8 ± 0.2
Leaf	93 ± 6.0	0.20 ± 0.08	11.8 ± 0.5

FIGURE 1. Epidermal strips of Petunia green leaf (A) and corolla at stage 6 (B) after two hours exposure to light, showing the stomatal aperature.

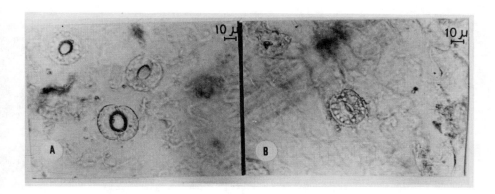

Gas flow through the various tissues was measured. Gas conductance of the corolla tissue (Stage 6) was only 12% that of the mature green leaf (Table 1). The number of stomata in the corolla (Stage 6) was only 19% of that found in the green leaf (Table 2).
The corolla stomata were non functioning; they had a fixed apperature with a very small opening, both in light and in dark (Table 2, Fig. 1). Thus, the CO_2 flow is slow and seems to be the limiting factor of CO_2 fixation.

4. CONCLUSIONS
1. Corollas of Petunia hybrida were able to fix CO_2 under both light and dark conditions.
2. Light fixation products were typical to C_3 plants in both leaves and corollas.
3. There was a similar relative decrease, between 70%-80%, in the activity of all the photosynthetic systems measured (light CO_2 fixation; RuBP-case activity and electron transport) in the corolla as compared to the green leaf. The systems seem to be well coordinated.
4. It is possible that the reduced efficiencies of these photosynthetic parameters are related to the low stomatal conductance of the corolla.

REFERENCES
1. Weiss, D., Schonfeld, M. and Halevy, A.H. (1988) Plant Physio. 87, 66-670.
2. Armon, D.I. (1949(Plant Physiol. 24, 1-15
3. Beer, S., Stewart A.J., Wetzel, R.G. (1982) Plant Physiol. 69. 54-57
4. Scharwz, A., Ilan N. and Gratz, D.A. (1988) Plant Physiol. 87, 583-587
5. Weiss, D., Shomer-Ilan, A., Vainstein, A. and Halevy, A.H. (1989) Physiol Plantarum (in press)

THE REVERSIBLE PHOTOCHEMISTRY OF PHYCOERYTHROCYANIN

SIEBZEHNRÜBL, S., LIPP, G., FISCHER, R., SCHEER, H. Botanisches Institut der Universität, Menzinger Str. 67, D-8000 MÜNCHEN 19, FRG

1. INTRODUCTION

Plant and algal biliproteins have two major functions: The phycobili-proteins are light-harvesting pigments for photosynthesis (1); the phytochromes are the photoreceptors of plant photomorphogenesis. Many cyanobacteria also show responses suggesting photoreversibly photo-chromic pigments as photoreceptors (see 2,3,4,5). The putative pigments have been termed adaptochromes and phycomorphochromes. Isolation attempts (review in 2) resulted in the spectral characterization of at least four different fractions termed phycochromes a-d; but in no case has there been conclusive evidence, that these are the putative photo-receptors.

The absorption spectra of all phycochromes suggest that they are biliproteins, too. These pigments may then combine both functions of light harvesting and photomorphogenesis induction in one molecule. Phycochrome b has indeed been shown to be most likely the α-subunit of the antenna pigment phycoerythrocyanin (PEC) (6). PEC is present in several species of cyanobacteria (7). It carries an unusual phycoviolo-bilin chromophore on its α-subunit (Fig. 1) (8), which is responsible for its photochromic response. Here we want to give further (9) results on the photochemistry of PEC from two cyanobacteria, e.g. *Mastigocladus* (*M*). *laminosus* and *Chroococcidiopsis* (*Ch.*) *spec.*. We have characterized the photochemistry of the pigment in different states of aggregation, and the mutual interdependence of its phototransformation and aggre-gation.

2. MATERIALS AND METHODS

Phycoerythrocyanin (PEC) of *M. laminosus* and *Ch. spec.* were prepared by the method of Füglistaller et al. (10). The subunits of PEC were obtained by isoelectric focusing (11) under anaerobic conditions. Absorption and absorption difference spectra were measured in split beam mode with thermostated cell holders. Irradiation was done in the photo-meter (150 W, light guide and suitable interference filters). The aggre-gation state of PEC was studied by sucrose-density gradient centrifu-gation at 238,000 x g (12). In the reactions relating irradiation with aggregation, a PEC (*M. laminosus*) stock solution (A 570 = 0.6 cm^{-1}) was irradiated alternately with green and orange light. Before the first and after each subsequent illumination an aliquot (0.2 ml) was applied to the sucrose gradient (5 ml, 7 to 17 % w/w).

3. RESULTS AND DISCUSSION
3.1. Characterization of photochemistry

When PEC or its α-subunit isolated from the blue-green algae *M. laminosus* or *Ch . spec.* were irradiated either with orange (600 nm; 575

M. Baltscheffsky (ed.), Current Research in Photosynthesis, Vol. IV, 421–424.
© 1990 *Kluwer Academic Publishers. Printed in the Netherlands.*

nm for *Ch. spec.*-α-subunit) or green light (500 nm), a typical photochemistry was observed. Irradiation with orange light leads to an
absorption difference spectrum with a maximum at 502-504 nm and a negative extremum at 565-570 nm. Illuminating the sample with green light
reverts the spectrum fully to the original. The amplitudes of the difference spectra are strongly dependent on the state of the pigment (Table
1). It is maximum in the presence of 4 M urea, whereas it is lower in
the fully denatured pigment (8 M urea) and very small in high aggregates
and phycobilisomes. Upon addition of increasing amounts of urea, the
difference extrema of the reversible reaction remain stationary up to
denaturant concentrations of 4 M (Table 1). At the same time, the amplitudes increase. At higher urea concentrations, the amplitudes decrease
again, and the extrema shift gradually to 510 and 600 nm. Reversible
photochemistry is retained up to 8 M urea, when the polypeptide chains
are fully unfolded. The photochemistry is very similar in PEC isolated
from the two different organisms, e.g. *M. laminosus* and *Ch. spec.* .
Reversible photochemistry is also retained in denatured PEC at low pH.

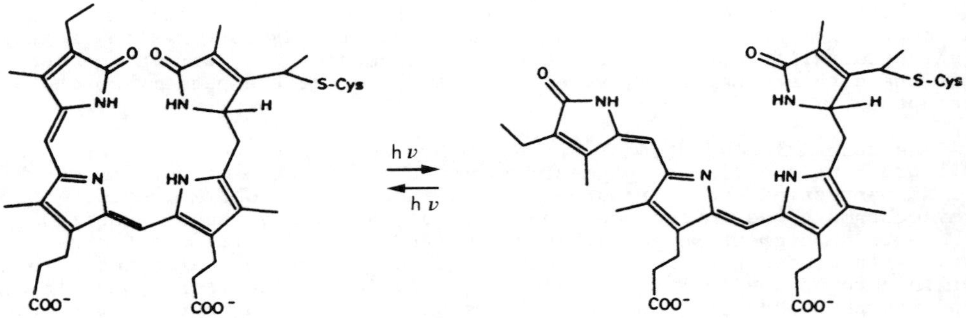

Fig. 1: Structures of phycoviolobilin chromophores in their 10Z,15Z
(left) and 10Z,15E-configuration (right). Schematic, native
chromophores have extended geometries.

The ß-subunit of PEC shows no reversible photochemical effects.
However the two phycocyanobilin chromophors of this subunit are very
sensitive against irradiation, and bleach rapidly to colorless pro-
duct(s) (viz. by 60 - 70 % within 12 min). This rapid bleaching contrasts with the relative stability of the phycocyanin ß-subunit (11).

The reversible photochemistry of PEC and its α-subunit is probably
related to a Z⇌E isomerisation of the phycoviolobilin chromophore
(Fig.1). Of the different chromophore types of phycobiliproteins, it is
the only one which shows a reversible photochemistry in its native **and**
denatured state. We suggest that isomerization takes place in the
α-subunit of PEC at the Δ15-double bond, similar to the phytochrome
primary reaction.

3.2. Interrelations of photochemistry and aggregation
Aggregation not only strongly influences the photochemical activity
of PEC (Table 1), but the inverse is also true, e.g. pre-irradiation

Table 1 : Absorption difference extrema and amplitudes of different PEC
samples or samples subjected to different pre-treatments.

Sample	C_{buffer} [mM] [a]	C_{urea} [M]	pH	Difference extrema [nm] orange	green	$\Delta\Delta A$ [%] [b]
PEC	100	0	7.0	570	503	18
PEC	100	1	7.1	569	503	32
PEC	100	4	7.3	567	502	35
PEC	100	6	7.5	600	510	12
PEC	100	8	7.0	599	515	6
PEC	100	8	3.0	598	507	13
PEC-monomer	100	c)	7.0	565	504	36
α-Subunit	100	0	7.0	569	504	50

a) Buffer — potassium phosphate buffer.
b) Amplitude (Min-max) of difference spectra.
c) 1 M KSCN, no urea.

Table 2 : Comparison of photochemistry of PEC between *Mastigocladus
laminosus* and *Chroococcidiopsis* spec.

Pigment	*Mastigocladus laminosus*	*Chroococcidiopsis* spec.
native Pigment [a]		
λ_{max}	573	574
Δ_{max}	(+) 503 / (-) 570 [b]	(+) 507 / (-) 576 [b]
$\Delta\Delta A$ [%]	18 %	26 %
denatured Pigment [c]		
λ_{max}	603 / 661 [e]	604 / 661 [e]
Δ_{max}	(+) 507 / (-) 598 [b]	(+) 506 / (-) 597 [b]
$\Delta\Delta A$ [%]	13 %	10.4 %
denatured Pigment [d]		
λ_{max}	587	597
Δ_{max}	(+) 515 / (-) 600 [b]	(+) 507 / (-) 595 [b]
$\Delta\Delta A$ [%]	6 %	2.4 %
α-Subunit (native) [a]		
λ_{max}	562	561
Δ_{max}	(+) 504 / (-) 569 [b]	(+) 501 / (-) 563 [b]
$\Delta\Delta A$ [%]	50 %	15 %

a) Green irradiated form in 100 mM phosphate buffer, pH 7.
b) Difference extrema (orange irradiated vs. green irradiated sample),
   (+) — positive, (-) — negative.
c) Green irradiated form in 8 M urea, 100 mM phosphate buffer
   acidified with HCl to pH 2.
d) Green irradiated form in 8 M urea + 100 mM phosphate buffer, pH 7.4.
e) Double maximum in the acidified state.

with different light qualities influences the aggregation of PEC (9).
A sample of PEC was irradiated alternately with orange and green light.
Aliquots of the original sample were then analyzed for aggregate distribution by ultracentrifugation. In every case, the sample is a mixture of mono- and trimeric PEC, but the amount of higher aggregates is
always increased after irradiation with green light, and decreased after irradiation with orange light. A reversible dissociation as
response to different light qualities would principally offer indirect
routes for signal transduction, since a direct effect of the phycobiliproteins may be questioned on the basis of the small size of the PEC
molecule primarily(?) optimized for light-harvesting.

An indirect route could be based on e.g. photodynamic effects of free
biliproteins (13) or the release of linker peptides (14-16).

Acknowledgement: This work was supported by the Deutsche Forschungsgemeinschaft, Bonn (SFB 143).

REFERENCES
1 MacColl, R. and Guard-Friar, D. (1987) Phycobiliproteins,CRC Press,
   Boca Raton
2 Björn, L. O. and Björn, G. S. (1980) Photochem. Photobiol. 32, 849-852
3 Bogorad, L. (1975) Ann. Rev. Plant. Physiol. 26, 369-401
4 Scheer, H. (1987) in Progress in Photosynthesis Research (Biggins, J.,
   ed.), Vol.I, pp. 143-149, Martinus Nijhoff Publishers
5 Tandeau de Marsac, N. (1983) Bull. Inst. Pasteur 81, 201-254
6 Kufer, W. and Björn, G.S. (1989) Physiol. Plant. 75, 389-394
7 Bryant, D.A. (1982) J. Gen. Microbiol. 128, 835-844
8 Bishop, J. E., Rapoport, H., Klotz, A. V., Chan, C. F., Glazer, A. N.,
   Füglistaller, P. and Zuber, H. (1987) J. Am. Chem. Soc. 109, 875-881
9 Siebzehnrübl, S., Fischer, R., Kufer, W. and Scheer H. (1989)
   Photochem. Photobiol. 49, 753-761
10 Füglistaller, P., Widmer, H., Sidler, W., Frank, G. and Zuber H.
   (1981) Arch. Microbiol. 129, 268-274
11 Schmidt, G., Siebzehnrübl, S., Fischer, R. and Scheer, H. (1988) in
   Photosynthetic Light-Harvesting Systems. Organization and Function
   (Scheer, H. and Schneider, S., eds.), pp. 77-88, W. deGruyter, Berlin
12 Martin, R.G. and Ames, B.N. (1961) J. Biol. Chem. 236, 1372-1379
13 Morcos, N. C., Berns, M. and Henry, W. L. (1988) Lasers Surg. Med. 8,
   10-17
14 Bryant, D.A. (1988) in Photosynthetic Light-Harvesting Systems.
   Organization and Function (Scheer, H. and Schneider, S., eds.), pp.
   217-232, W. DeGruyter, Berlin
15 Glazer, A.N. (1985) Ann. Rev. Biophys. 14, 47-77
16 Rümbeli, R. and Zuber, H. (1988) in Photosynthetic Light-Harvesting
   Systems (Scheer, H. and Schneider, S., eds.), pp. 61-70, W. deGruyter,
   Berlin

QUANTITATIVE ANALYSIS OF THE CHLOROPHYLL FLUORESCENCE INDUCTION
CURVE : FACTS AND ARTEFACTS

S. MAURO and R. LANNOYE.
Laboratoire de Physiologie végétale, Université Libre de Bruxelles,
Av. Paul Heger 28 (CP.169) - 1050 Bruxelles, Belgique.

1. INTRODUCTION

The sensitivity of PSII and its associated redox reactions to abiotic stresses has greatly stimulated the interest in the potential use of chlorophyll fluorescence as an intrinsic probe to assess the deleterious effects of extreme growth conditions.

In particular, quantitative analysis of the fluorescence induction curve obtained from DCMU inhibited systems has been shown to give usefull informations on the energy transfer (1), quantum efficiency (2), size (3) and heterogeneity of PSII photosynthetic units (4).

The present investigation was aimed at assessing the reliability of the fluorescence interpretation when measured from DCMU infiltrated leaves.

2. MATERIALS AND METHODS

Maize seedlings were grown in a phytotron programmed for a 16 hr photoperiod (300 μE $m^{-2}s^{-1}$) and a 25°C/15°C day/night temperature.

Fluorescence induction curves were obtained from DCMU infiltrated leaves (3) using a laboratory-made fluorimeter. The actinic light was from an array of 30 light emitting diodes (HLMP 3850) operated at 100 mA per couple. In order to provide an homogeneous illumination of the sample, the actinic light was processed by two lenses as described in (5).

The wavelength of maximum emission of the LED was 592 nm. The maximum light intensity was reached in $\sim$ 100 usec.

M. Baltscheffsky (ed.), Current Research in Photosynthesis, Vol. IV, 425–428.
© 1990 *Kluwer Academic Publishers. Printed in the Netherlands.*

3. RESULTS
Calculations on the kinetics of the fluorescence rise require an homogeneous illumination of the sample under investigation.
When dealing with leaves such a condition is not usually met as the pigment concentrations encoutered in vivo are usually very high. The kinetic analysis is further complicated because the photosynthetic apparatus will adapt to the light conditions prevailing at different depths in the leave. However the fluorescence from the uppermost cell layers can be measured selectively using an appropriate choice of the excitation and emission wavelengths (3). Fig. 1 shows a typical fluorescence induction curve measured from a DCMU inhibited leave. The fluorescence reached its maximal value in essentially 100 msec. Contrary to what has been observed with thylakoids the fast rise was not followed by a secondary slow rise (6) so that F_{Max} remained constant for at least 10 sec.

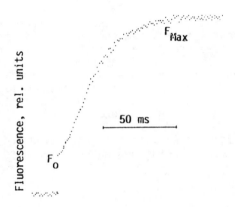

Fig. 1. Fluorescence transient exhibited by a DCMU-inhibited leave. The sample was inflitrated with 100 uM DCMU.
The paramater $1 - F_0/F_{Max}$ was 0.82 and the induction time (or complementary area) was 30.5 ms.

Fluorescence measurements were first intended to investigate the effects of a cold treatment on PSII organisation. The variations in the rate parameters derived from the fluorescence signal were so large that any realistic conclusion could be drawn. That situation prompted us to analyse the effect of F_0 and F_{Max} determinations on the fluorescence analysis.
The semilog plot of the fluorescence deficit appeared to be extremely dependant of the F_{Max} value (Fig. 2). However when F_{Max} was taken as the mean of 30 data points the semilog plot was reduced to a single, rapidly decaying, phase.

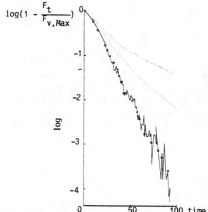

Fig. 2. Semilogarithmic plots of the fluorescence deficit.
The curves were calculated for different F_{Max} values.
The amplitude of F_{Max} changes was within the noise level
of the fluorescence signal.
The continuous line is for F_{Max} taken as the mean of 30
data points. The open circles are representative of the
semilog analysis when F_0 is taken as the fluorescence
intensity measured after 3 milliseconds of illumination.

Consequently the plot of the normalized F_v against the normalized
complementary area shifted from the typical shape obtained from a
mixture of α and β centers to the hyperbolic relationship specific to
the α type centers.
While the kinetic analysis was fairly insensitive to the F_0
determination (Fig. 2,3) the value of the complementary area was
reduced by 10 % when F_0 was taken as the fluorescence intensity
measured after 3 milliseconds of illumination (not shown).

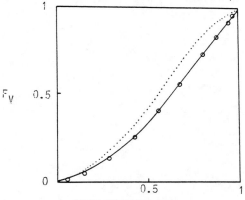

Fig. 3. Relationship between fluorescence increase and complementary
area for different F_{Max} and F_0 values.

4. CONCLUSION

We would like to add to the accumulating evidence (6,7) that the fluorescence induction curve is not a well suited measurement to analyse the heterogeneity of PSII photosynthetic unit.

We are aware that our analysis doesn't unambiguously invalidate the $\alpha.\beta$ hypothesis. But we do not easily understand how 30 to 50% of the active PSII units would escape fluorometric detection.

The outcome of our analysis is that quantitative analysis reduces to the measure and interpretation of the complementary area, energy transfer probability and quantum yield of photochemistry.

REFERENCES
1. Joliot, A. and Joliot P. (1964) C.R. Acad. Sci. Paris 258, 4662-4625.
2. Kitajima, M. and Butler, W.L. (1975) Biochem. Biophys. Acta 376, 105-115.
3. Malkin, S., Armond, P.A., Mooney, H.A. and Fork, D.C. (1981) Plant Physiol. 67, 570-579.
4. Melis, A. and Homann, P.H. (1978) Arch. Biochem. Biophys. 190, 523-530.
5. Sear's Optic (1981) Fondamental of optics. Addison Wesley.
6. Bell, D.M. and Hipkins, M.F. (1985) Biochem. Biophys. Acta 807, 255-262.
7. Sinclair, J. and Spence, S.M. (1988) Biochem. Biophys. Acta 935, 184-194.

PHYSIOLOGICALLY ACTIVE PRODUCTS OF CHLOROPLAST COMPONENTS DEGRADATION

I.A.Tarchevsky, A.N.Grechkin, S.I.Pankratova, A.U.Yarin, J.E.Andrianova

Kazan Institute of Bioology, USSR Academy of Sciences, P.O. Box 30, Kazan, 420084, USSR

1. INTRODUCTION

Acyl residues of lipid components in chloroplast membranes are represented mainly by linolenate (18:3) and linoleate (18:2) [1]. The lipoxygenase pathway of polyenoic fatty acid oxidation, which is well known in plants, leads to formation of traumatin and jasmonic acid [4,5]. These compounds was shown to be growth regulators [4,5]. Several new oxygenated fatty acids, particularly 12-hydroxy-9(Z)-dodecenoic and (9,10),(12,13)-diepoxioctadecanoic ones, were found in our laboratory during the biosynthetic experiments with pea seedlings [5,6]. The existing data about the regulatory activity of many natural oxygenated fatty acids allow to assume that above mentioned compounds can also be physoilogically active. The effects of several compounds on growth function of plant tissues was studied in present work to elucidate this question.

2. PROCEDURE

2.1. Materials and methods

2.1.1. Materials: 12-hydroxy-9(Z)-dodecenoic acid was prepared biosynthetically. (9,10),(12,13)-diepoxyoctadecanoic and 12-hydroxy-9-dodecynoic were prepared by partial and total chemical synthesis, respectively. 12-hydroxydodecanoic acid was obtained from Aldrich (Milwaukee, USA).

2.1.2. Callus cultures and other test-systems: Experiments were carried out on young (the 8-th passage) and long passaged callus (the 23-d passage) of soybean epycotyl as well as on the seeds and seedlings of radish. Primary callus was obtained from the steam segments of aseptically grown 4-d seedlings of soybean (var.Volna). Explants of 3mm were placed on media composed of the following: mineral salts according to Murashige – Skoog, nicotinic acid (PP)– 0.5 mg/1, pyridoxine HCl (B6)– 0,5 mg/1, thiamine HCl (B1)– 0.1 mg/1, meso-inositol – 100 mg/1, glycine– 2 mg/1,NAA– 2 mg/1, BAP– 1 mg/1, sucrose – 30 g/1, agar – 9 g/1, pH–5.6–5.8. The culture was grown in the dark at 26 C and passaged every three weeks.

2.1.3. Studies of the effects of oxygenated fatty acids:

M. Baltscheffsky (ed.), Current Research in Photosynthesis, Vol. IV, 429–432.
© 1990 *Kluwer Academic Publishers. Printed in the Netherlands.*

Test compounds with concentration of 10^{-3} M – 10^{-7} M were layered on the surface of agarified nutrient medium (2 ml/Petri
dish, 90 mm diameter) using 0,2 m membrane filters (Flow)
The growth intensity was determined by fresh and dry weight
of cells.
    2.1.4. Studies of the influence of exogenous carotene
and its degradation products on the photosynthesis intensity
of wheat seedlings: Photosynthesis intensity was determined
by radiometric method at 1% concentration of CO_2 and saturating light intensities.

3. RESULTS AND DISCUSSION
    It was found that oxygenated fatty acids with concentra-
tion of 10^{-5} – 10^{-6} M considerably stimulate an increase of
soybean epycotyl callus biomass when grown in the complete
nutrient medium (Table 1). The greatest effect was observed
under the influence of the most reduced metabolite, 12-hyd-
roxydodecanoic acid.
    It should be noted that these metabolites don't have
the same positive effect on the growth of long passaged soybean callus (the 18-th, the 23-d passages) as on young cal-
us (Table 2). In the medium without BAP and NAA stimulating
effect oxygenated linoleate derivatives manifested itself on
the 10-th day after callus treatment. Later the necrosis of
callus tissue was observed . At the same time when growing
callus in complete nutrient medium the effectiveness of the
action of these compounds (after their one time addition)
was preserved at rather high level (130% of control) during
subsequent passages too (tested till the 125-th day).
    Chlorophyll synthesis of initially etiolated soybean
callus considerably increases under the influence of oxyge-

TABLE 1. Effects of oxygenated fatty acids (10^{-5} M) on
        the increase of soybean epicotyl biomass.

Substance	Biomass increase	
	Relative, g/g fresh weight	Relative, in % to control
Control	1.77	100
12-hydroxy-9(Z)- -dodecenoic acid	4.77	253
(9,10),(12,13)-diepo- xyoctadecanoic acid	4.1	232
12-hydroxy-9-dodec- ynoic acid	4.5	254
12-hydroxydodecanoic acid	4.84	273

TABLE 2. Effect of 12-hydroxy-9(Z)-dodecenoic acid (10^{-5}M) on increase of soybean epicotyl callus as funtion of passage duration.

Additions to growth medium	Relative increase of callus biomass (in g/g fresh weight)		
	8th passage	18th passage	23th passage
No (control)	9.0 (100%)	2.6 (100%)	2.5 (100%)
12-hydroxy-9(Z)-dodecenoic acid	19.4 (216%)	3.3 (129%)	3.1 (125%)

nated fatty acids in the light (Table 3). In this case, however, biomass values remain at the control level or even is partially inhibited. It is necessary to note, that traumatic acid has larger effect on chlorophyll accumulation during the greening of initially etiolated callus, than 12-hydroxy-9(Z)-dodecenoic acid. And, on the contrary, 12-hydroxy-9(Z)-dodecenoic acid stimulates biomass increase of dark culture of soybean epicotyl callus more strongly, than traumatic acid.

Besides, under the influence of these compounds the going out of seeds from rest is accelerated during first 24 hours after soaking; the rate of seed germination increases, and the growth of main root and new formation of lateral roots enhance.

It is found that in the studied range of exogenous carotene consentrations (10^{-3}-10^{-6}M), 10^{-5}M is a stimulating concentration. At the deviation from these concentration both to the side of larger and smaller values the decrease of optimizing effect up to inhibition is observed. It should be noted that carotene action develops in time preserving the same concentration dependence (on the 3rd day optimizing effect decreases up to 0, and inhibitory action increases).

TABLE 3. Effects of 12-hydroxy-9(Z)-dodecenoic and traumatic acids (10^{-5} M) on chlorophyll accumulation during greening of initially etiolated soybean callus.

Additions to growth medium	Chlorophyll content in greening soybean callus (in % to control)
No (control)	100
12-hydroxy-9(Z)-dodecenoic acid	170
Traumatic acid	325

It is possible that in plant tissues products of β-carotene metabolizatin take part in the development of this effect. With this purpose the seedlings were exposed to β-carotene preliminarily illuminated in the solution at the intensity of 100-ths lx during 30 min. The resulting *cys-trans*-isomers have an enhancing effect only at the stimulating concentration of 10^{-5} M.

REFERENCES
1 Mazliak, P. (1977) in Lipids and Lipid Polymers in Higher Plants (Tevini, M. and Lichtenthaler, H.K., eds), pp.48--74, Springer, Berlin, Heidelberg, New York
2 Vick, B.A. and Zimmerman, D.C. (1983) Biochem. Biophys. Res. Communs 111, 470-476
3 Yamahe, H., Tagaki, H., Abe, H., Yokota, T. and Takahashi, N. (1981) Plant Cell Physiol. 22, 689-697
4 Sembdner, G. Klose, C. (1985) Biol. Rdsch. 23, 29-40
5 Grechkin, A.N., Korolev, O.S., Kuramshin, R.A., Yefremov, Y.J., Musin, R.M., Ilyasov, A.V., Latypov, S.K. and Tarchevsky, I.A. (1987) Dokl. Akad. Nauk SSSR (Proc. Acad. Sci. USSR) 297, 1257-1260
6 Grechkin, A.N., Kuramshin, R.A., Kukhtina, N.V., Safonova, E.Y., Yefremov, Y.J. and Tarchevsky, I.A. (1989) Dokl. Akad. Nauk SSSR (Proc. Acad. Sci. USSR) 305, 740-742
7 Pankratova, S.I., Yarin, A.U., Grechkin, A.N. and Tarchevsky I.A. (1988) Deponated Manuscript of VINITI, N 7591-1988

PHOTOSYNTHETIC INORGANIC CARBON TRANSPORT AND ACCUMULATION IN MACROALGAE

F. BRECHIGNAC, European Space Research & Technology Centre, Postbus 299,
2200 AG NOORDWIJK, THE NETHERLANDS

1. INTRODUCTION
   The study of photosynthetic inorganic C acquisition in marine and
freshwater macroalgae shows the ubiquitous ability of most of them to
use exogenous HCO_3 (as well as CO_2) as a C source. In microalgae, this
feature has often been connected to the further ability to internally
accumulate DIC, and then, sustain high rates of photosynthesis in conditions where the external CO_2 concentration is far too low given the
kinetics of the Rubisco carboxylase. Indeed, any internal DIC accumulation needs to be promoted by some active transport mechanism. As a
consequence, the nature of the mechanism of HCO_3 uptake has strong
implications on the putative existence of DIC accumulation.
   These features are still poorly known for macroalgae. Therefore, we
examined both the HCO_3 uptake/transport and the internal DIC accumulation, in *Chara corallina* and *Chondrus crispus*. A strong emphasis was
dedicated to *C. corallina* which presents to date the most advanced
proposed models for its HCO_3 uptake mechanism. One model involves a
plasmalemma-bound H^+-HCO_3 cotransport, while the other one relies on the
facilitated CO_2 diffusion which is locally provoked by an acid-mediated
dehydration of HCO_3 within the boundary layer of the charasomes (complex
network of plasmalemma invaginations). Both use a plasmalemma H^+-trans-
locating ATPase, as a driving force. A correlation between charasome
development and HCO_3 uptake recently favoured the last mechanism, put-
ting forward an important role of external carbonic anhydrase (1).
   In contrast to this early finding, the present study demonstrates
that charasomes are not essential for photosynthetic HCO_3 transport.
This reinforces the relevance of models based on active inorganic carbon
transport mechanisms. In addition to the CO_2 transport previously postulated (2) preliminary results indicate that HCO_3 transport also drives
DIC accumulation in HCO_3-grown *Chara* cells, a feature similarly observed
in *C. crispus*. A preliminary basis for an updated model is proposed for
Chara, integrating the previous kinetic features of photosynthesis (2).

2. MATERIALS AND METHODS
2.1 Material, culture conditions and photosynthesis measurements.
   Gametophytic thalli of the carrageen red macroalga *Chondrus cripus*
   (Rhodophyta, Gigartinales) were obtained from CECA S.A. (Carentan,
   France) and cultivated in natural filtered seawater, and in a
   closed loop aerated assimilation chamber as previously described
   (3). Male plants of *Chara corallina* Klein were cultured in the

M. Baltscheffsky (ed.), Current Research in Photosynthesis, Vol. IV, 433–440.
© 1990 *Kluwer Academic Publishers. Printed in the Netherlands.*

laboratory in illuminated nalgene tanks containing 60 litres of CPW (1.0 mM NaCl, 0.2 mM KCl, 0.2 mM CaSO$_4$). With respect to the inorganic carbon content of the medium, two different types of cultures were conducted. HCO$_3$–grown cells were cultured in stagnant conditions in CPW, after adding 1.0 mM NaHCO$_3$ (CPW/B, pH=8.2). CO$_2$–grown cells were cultivated in CO$_2$–enriched CPW (CPW/CO$_2$, pH=5.5), using a 4 % CO$_2$ gas stream and the further addition of 3 mM MES. Investigation of the kinetics of charasome and HCO$_3$ uptake inductions was carried out after transferring apical CO$_2$–grown shoots, consisting of 4 to 6 internodes, into CPW/B for various times. Photosynthetic O$_2$ evolution was measured polarographically, under 150 μmol photon. m^{-2}.s^{-1} of photon fluence rate, in a chamber specially designed for *Chara* branch cells complexes, (2).

2.2 Transmembrane potential measurements.

The electric potential between the vacuole of an internodal cell and the bathing solution was measured by using glass microelectrodes (approx. 10 μm tip diameter) filled with a 3 mM KCl solution (pH=2), using a WPI (Model 750) amplifier with a differential input, (4). The internodal cell was kept horizontal in an illuminated (100 μmol photon m^{-2}.s^{-1}) plexiglas chamber (10–1–2 cm, length–width–depth), which could be filled with the appropriate solutions, and sealed to minimize air exchanges with the atmosphere. The microelectrode was positioned at the half–length of the cell, and quickly inserted into the vacuole by means of a high–precision Narishige micromanipulator. This procedure, performed with the aid of a binocular microscope, did not alter the cytoplasmic streaming.

2.3 Techniques for electron microscopy observations.

The procedures used for preparation and fixation of internodal and "whorl" cells of *Chara* were similar to those previously reported (5). Thin sections were examined and photographed using a JEOL (Tokyo, Japan, model JEM 100S) transmission electron microscope.

3. RESULTS
3.1 EZ effects on *C. corallina* photosynthesis.

At pH=5.5, when photosynthesis was CO$_2$–supported, HCO$_3$–, as well as CO$_2$–grown cells, were insensitive to this CA inhibitor, irrespective of the CO$_2$ concentration (Table 1).

TABLE 1. EZ (20 μM) effects on the rate of CO$_2$–supported net photosynthetic O$_2$ evolution in HCO$_3$– and CO$_2$–grown *Chara* cells (pH=5.5).

Culture conditions	HCO$_3$–grown		CO$_2$–grown
CO$_2$ conc. (μM)	40	500	40
% inhib. ± SD (n)	1.0±7.8 (4)	−0.4±3.8 (2)	−5.3±1.7 (2)

This confirms that, at acidic pH: 1) CA is not required for the photosynthetic uptake of exogenous CO_2, 2) the rate of subsequent CO_2 reduction at the chloroplast level is not enhanced by CA. At pH= 8.2, when photosynthesis was HCO_3-supported, the HCO_3 grown cells exhibited a clear inhibition of photosynthesis, which was maximum (50 % inhibition) at limiting DIC concentrations (Fig. 1). Increasing DIC greatly reduced the extent of this inhibition, which could have been overcome above 5 mM. Surprisingly, when placed in the same conditions, freshly cut CO_2-grown cells were still capable of low, but significant, rates of HCO_3-sustained photosynthesis (Figure 1, insert). (The CO_2 contained in the medium at limiting DIC concentrations was far too low to explain such rates). These rates were also sensitive to EZ, but to a lesser extent than in HCO_3-grown cells, the maximum inhibition amounting to 20 % only (Figure 1).

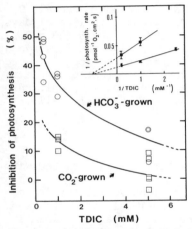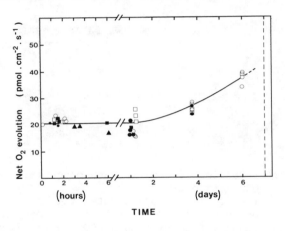

FIGURE 1. HCO_3-supported photosynthesis inhibition by 20 µM EZ in HCO_3 and CO_2-grown *Chara* cells.

FIGURE 2. Establishment of HCO_3-supported photosynthesis in CO_2-grown *Chara* cells (CPW/B, pH=8.2).

3.2 Establishment of HCO_3-supported photosynthesis in CO_2-grown cells.
When transferred to HCO_3 assimilating conditions (CPW/B, pH=8.2), and after having allowed them to consume all their internal CO_2 (due to recent extraction from CO_2-enriched medium), mature CO_2-grown cells still produced O_2 at a net rate of 20 pmol O_2.cm^{-2}.s^{-1} (Figure 2). This corresponded to 35 % of control rates currently observed in HCO_3-grown cells. Stable during 48 hours, this rate then started to increase, doubling after 6 days and approaching the control rates.

3.3 Plasticity of charasomes and kinetics of their synthesis.
Figure 3 shows the influence of CO_2-enriched medium (CPW/CO_2, pH= 5.5) on the structure and the development of the charasomes. The typical control cytological features of HCO_3-grown whorl or internodal cells are shown in Figure 3A. CO_2-grown cells were completely devoid of charasome (Figure 3B). An investigation of the induction

of new charasomes in such cells has been driven by transferring them into HCO₃-containing medium (CPW/B, pH=8.2), and harvesting them for fixation and further observation, on a schedule of 2, 6, 12 and 24 hours, and then daily for 10 days. These cells did not form new charasomes before 7 days after their transfer into CPW/B. A typical example of such young charasomes is illustrated on Figure 3C.

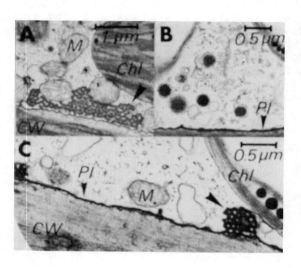

FIGURE 3. Influence of culture medium conditions on charasome development. A, HCO³-grown cell, illustrating the typical normal charasome development; B, CO₂-grown cell devoid of any charasome material; C, CO₂-grown cell after 7 days culture in CPW/B (pH = 8.2), illustrating the first young charasomes to appear in such conditions. (Pl: plasmalemma, M: mitochondrion, Chl: chloroplast, CW: cell wall).

3.4 Induction of the membrane potential characteristics associated with HCO₃ assimilation.

The resting membrane potential and its transient variations in response to light/dark transitions have been previously shown to be sensitive to exogenous HCO₃ (6,7). Figure 4 illustrates a typical example showing that the dark-induced hyperpolarization (D.H.) of recently cut CO₂-grown cells exposed to exogenous HCO₃ was much smaller than in HCO₃-grown cells. Furthermore, the transient hyperpolarization of the membrane potential elicited at the onset of reillumination (L.H.) was absent. Then, the time course in which CO₂-grown cells, after exposure to HCO₃-containing medium, induced the normal electrophysiological features observed in HCO₃-grown cells has been investigated. Figure 5 shows that control HCO₃-grown cells exhibited a constant resting membrane potential at −180 ± 9.9 mV during 5 days. In contrast, the initial resting potential of CO₂-grown cells was less negative, −130 mV, but it returned to the above control value within 1 hour after exposure to exogenous HCO₃. Figure 6 A and B show that the transient hyperpolarizations of CO₂-grown cells, elicited both by dark and reillumination treatments converged on those obtained in HCO₃-grown cells with a time course shorter than the 7 days period required for initiating charasome neoformation. When cells were cut 1 day prior to the measurement, thus eliminating perturbations associated with cutting and handling, a similar trend was observed (Figure 6A).

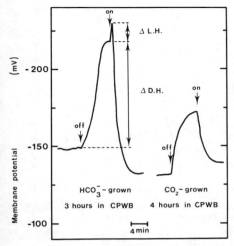

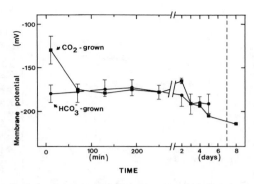

FIGURE 5. Plasmalemma resting potential of HCO3− and CO2−grown *Chara* cells as a function of time exposure to CPW/B (pH=8.2).

FIGURE 4. Typical dark/light transients observed on HCO3−and CO2−grown *Chara* cells after few hours exposure to CPW/B.

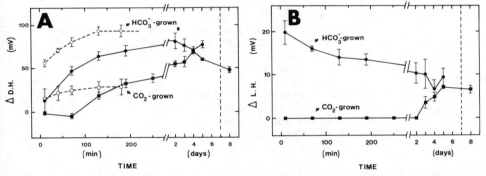

FIGURE 6. Inductions of the dark−induced Δ D.H. (A) and light− induced ΔL.H. (B) hyperpolarization of the membrane potential in HCO3 and CO2−grown cells as a function of the time exposure to CPW/B (pH=8.2).

3.5 DIC accumulation in HCO3 assimilating conditions.

In *C. crispus*, using the quantitative gas exchange technology previously described (3), including continuous dissolved CO_2 measurements, the sum of C disappearance in the closed measurement loop exceeded that of O_2 appearance during about 2 hours after the onset of illumination (Fig. 7). Using a similar technology adapted to the size of *C. corallina*, a 30 min post-illumination CO_2 burst has been detected in HCO3 assimilating conditions (Figure 8), which cannot be attributed to a photorespiratory CO_2 release, because photorespiration was previously shown not to occur in such conditions (2). The pH varied consistently with this burst. In contrast, O_2 was evolved linearly after the offset of light.

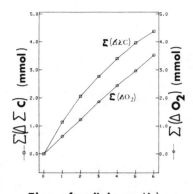

Time after light on (h)

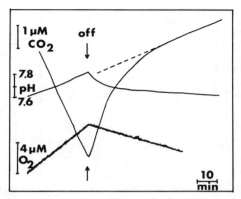

FIGURE 7. Comparison between the cumulated DIC uptake Σ(ΔΣC) and O₂ evolution Σ(ΔO₂) elicited by *C. crispus* in seawater after the onset of illumination.

FIGURE 8. Post-illumination CO₂ burst elicited by *C. corallina* in HCO₃ assimilation conditions at the offset of illumination as compared with net O₂ evolution.

4. DISCUSSION

4.1 Charasomes and HCO₃ transport.

This study confirms the plasticity of the charasome development in response to the pH of the culture medium. Since photosynthetic HCO₃ use at various pH values varied consistently with 1) the corresponding HCO₃/CO₂ ratios, and 2) the charasome development, it has been postulated that these organelles played a central role in the acquisition of exogenous HCO₃ (1). However, the present CO₂-grown cells obtained in conditions of low pH *and* high CO₂ were completely devoid of charasome (Fig. 3C), but they still exhibited substantial rates of HCO₃-supported photosynthesis as soon as 10 minutes after introducing HCO₃ in the medium (insert Fig. 1, Fig. 2). This demonstrates that the mechanism of HCO₃ acquisition remains functional in the absence of charasome. Furthermore, the rates observed with longer exposure to HCO₃ had raised up to 70 % of the control value after 6 days, time at which charasome development was still not initiated. It is therefore concluded that charasomes are not essential for the acquisition of exogenous HCO₃. This conclusion is also supported by the experiments which demonstrated that, when exposed to exogenous HCO₃, the membrane potential of CO₂-grown cells exhibited trends which converged on those observed in control HCO₃-grown cells before the initiation of charasome development (Fig. 3-7).

4.2 Carbonic anhydrase and the boundary layer problem

The model of HCO₃ acquisition via a periplasmic external CO₂ production is based on the existence of a boundary layer, extending within the charasomes, where exogenous HCO₃ is converted into CO₂. A central role for external CA activity within the charasomes has therefore been postulated to increase the efficacy of this mechanism (1). Since such a model cannot fully apply to CO₂-grown cells which have no charasomes, the significant inhibition of photosynthesis elicited by EZ at limiting DIC and pH=8.2 (Fig. 1) indicates that either, HCO3 acquisition is not restricted to the charasomes, and/or its CA-dependent step is internal rather than external. Interpreting the differential inhibition by EZ in HCO3-and CO2-grown cells as a charasome-associated step of CA-dependent HCO3 uptake results only in a maximum of 20-30 % of the whole photosynthetic DIC uptake. Therefore, the major part of HCO3 uptake capability does not appear to be sustained by a specific role of CA within the charasomes. Previous investigations which examined the influence of varying the boundary layer thickness on the HCO3 uptake capability have already questioned this model (8,9). All the above-mentioned results tend to indicate that the CA-dependent step of exogenous HCO3 acquisition occurs internally rather than in the periplasmic space. Indeed, a recent study concluded that *Chara* does not possess significant external CA activity (10).

4.3 Internal DIC accumulation

The excess of DIC taken up by *C. crispus* in comparison with its CO2 fixation indicated by the linear net O2 evolution (Fig. 7), suggests the build up of an internal DIC pool. Since the concept of an active HCO3 transport has been deduced from the usual observation of a photosynthetic depletion of HCO3 in comparison to CO2 (11), this carbon excess is concluded to represent an accumulation driven by HCO3 transport.

In *Chara*, an unexpected internal DIC accumulation has already been demonstrated to occur when photosynthesis was CO2-supported, from quantitative depletion experiments driven on HCO3-grown cells at pH=5.5, (2). This was further confirmed by the $K_m(CO_2)$ of Rubisco which exceeded the $K_{\frac{1}{2}}(CO_2)$ of whole cells, at a same O2 concentration. These results suggested the existence of either, a CO2 transport mechanism, or a HCO3 transport mechanism located at the chloroplast envelope level. The corresponding accumulation factor, however, which can be estimated at approximately 2 from the comparison of the kinetics of isolated Rubisco (12) and whole cells (2) in response to CO2, was far less than the current observations in microalgae. Since photosynthesis of such HCO3-grown cells was insensitive to EZ (Table 1), it is proposed that this accumulation is performed via an active CO2 transport, presumably at the plasmalemma level, and not via a HCO3 transport at the chloroplast envelope, which would have involved EZ-sensitive HCO3/CO2 interconversions.

The present study further establishes that at pH=8.2, HCO3-supported photosynthesis also drives an internal DIC accumulation which is revealed by a post-illumination CO2 release (Fig. 8). Therefore, the HCO3 transport in operation at pH=8.2 should be located in the plasmalemma.

4.4 Preliminary model for inorganic carbon transport in *Chara*

The present results suggest that inorganic carbon transport mechanisms are involved independently from charasomes. In an attempt to reconcile this feature with the photosynthetic kinetics previously observed in response to CO2 and HCO3 (2), it is proposed that *Chara* possesses 1) a HCO3 pump at the plasmalemma level, which is functional in both types of cells, 2) a CO2 pump, which is induced only when cells are cultured in HCO3 (low CO2) conditions (Fig. 9). Although the maximum HCO3-supported photosynthetic capacity was slower in CO2-grown cells following their exposure to exogenous HCO₃, the apparent affinities for this ion in both types of cells were similar (Fig.1, insert), suggesting a reduced number of functional HCO₃ transport sites in CO_2-grown cells. Longer exposure to exogenous HCO₃ in the medium would trigger the elaboration of additional functional transport sites, finally raising the V_{max}(HCO₃) to the control value observed in HCO₃-grown cells (Fig. 2).

The basic accumulation system of *Chara* would be driven by the plasmalemma HCO₃ pump. Rather than driving a significant accumulation, the CO_2 pump would enhance the efficacy of the HCO₃ pump by preventing CO_2 leakage back to the bulk medium. This would contribute to explain why, in conditions of HCO₃-supported photosynthesis, freshly CO_2-grown cells did not exhibit photosynthetic rates as fast as HCO₃-grown cells.

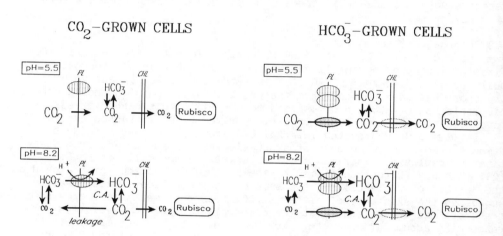

FIGURE 9. Preliminary model for inorganic carbon transport in *Chara*.
(Pl: plasmalemma, Chl: chloroplast envelope).

REFERENCES
1 Price, G.D., Badger, M.R., Basset, M.E. and Whitecross, M.I. (1985) Aust. J. Plant Physiol. 12, 241–256
2 Bréchignac, F. and Lucas, W.J. (1987) Plant Physiol. 83, 163–169
3 Bréchignac, F. and André, M. (1985) Plant Physiol. 78, 551–554
4 Keifer, D.W. and Lucas, W.J. (1982) Plant Physiol. 69, 781–788
5 Franceschi, V.R. and Lucas, W.J. (1980) Protoplasma 104, 253–271
6 Nishizaki, Y. (1968) Plant Cell Physiol. 9, 377–387
7 Lucas, W.J. (1982) Planta 156, 181–192
8 Lucas, W.J. (1985) in Inorganic carbon uptake by aquatic photosynthetic organisms (Lucas, W.J., Berry, J.A., eds.) pp. 229–254, ASPP
9 Lucas, W.J., Keifer, D.W. and Sanders, D. (1983) J. Membrane Biol. 73, 263–274
10 Shiraiwa, Y. and Kikuyama, M. (1988) Plant Cell Physiol. in press
11 Bréchignac, F. and André, M. (1986) Plant Physiol. 80, 1059–1062
12 Yeoh, H., Badger, M.R. and Watson, L. (1981) Plant Physiol. 67, 1151–1155

PHOTOSYNTHETIC ACCLIMATION TO LOW CARBON CONCENTRATIONS IN CHLAMYDOMONAS REINHARDTII.

Göran Samuelsson, Kristin Palmqvist, Zakir Ramazanov* and Lars-Göran Sundblad.
Dept. of Plant Physiology, University of Umeå, S-901 87 Umeå, Sweden.
* Inst. of Plant Physiology, Academy of Sciences, Moscow, USSR.

1. INTRODUCTION

Microalgae, have developed a CO_2 concentrating mechanism which enables them to accumulate inorganic DIC inside the cells to concentrations far above those outside [1]. This increases the ratio of CO_2/O_2 inside the chloroplasts and the apparent affinity for CO_2 of intact cells.

In green microalgae, light dependent accumulation of DIC [2] and increased extracellular CA-activity [3] are induced by lowering the external DIC concentration of the growth medium, to levels in equilibrium with air or below.

The biochemical modifications of the photosynthetic apparatus caused by transfer to low DIC, cause a physiological acclimation which can be measured as an increased affinity for DIC [4].

Figure 1. CO2-response in C.reinhardtii.

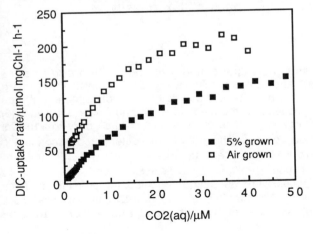

M. Baltscheffsky (ed.), Current Research in Photosynthesis, Vol. IV, 441–448.
© 1990 Kluwer Academic Publishers. Printed in the Netherlands.

This is illustrated in figure 1, where photosynthesis in cells of *C. reinhardtii* acclimated to high (5%) and low (≈350 ppm) $CO_2(g)$ is plotted as a function of the external $CO_2(aq)$ concentration. The figure illustrates that cells which have been growing under air conditions have a much more efficient photosynthesis at a $CO_2(aq)$ concentrations below 50 μM, than have high CO_2 grown cells. According to current theory, figure 1 illustrates the difference between accumulating and non-accumulating algae as expressed in whole cell photosynthesis.

In the present study, we suggest, that in green algal cells different parts of the DIC transporting/accumulating system are activated in order to optimize DIC uptake under varying environmental conditions. In other words, there are a range of acclimative steps that can be taken by the algal cell, each step or combination of steps aimed at optimizing DIC uptake under each specific condition. We are aiming to get a better understanding of how this acclimation is expressed on the the intact cell level.

By measuring photosynthetic DIC uptake, induction of extracellular CA activity and luminescence kinetics under varying external DIC conditions valuable information was obtained about the coordination of the different acclimation phases during the acclimation to low DIC and under steady state low DIC conditions.

ABBREVIATIONS

A- alkalinity; AZ- acetazolamid; CA- carbonic anhydrase; DIC- dissolved inorgainc carbon; PFD- photon flux density.

2. MATERIALS AND METHODS

Algal material; All experiments were performed with both *Chlamydomonas reinhardtii* 137 c+(wild-type) and CW.92 (cell wall-less mutant). **Culturing conditions;** The algae were grown in continuous light in a phosphate buffered medium(pH 7.5). The major components of the medium was as in Solter and Gibor [5] and the trace elements as in Surzycki [6]. The cultures were diluted daily to <1μgChl ml^{-1} and grown in 1 l cultivation vessels. Chlorophyll was determined according to MacKinney [7]. The temperature was 25⁰ C and the incident PFD was 120 μmol m^{-2}s^{-1}, obtained from fluorescent tubes (Philips TL 40 W/55S).

High-DIC grown cells were supplied with 5% $CO_2(g)$ bubbled through the medium. Air-grown cells were supplied with 400 ppm $CO_2(g)$ and "low-DIC grown cells" were supplied with 40 ppm $CO_2(g)$. **Measurements of inorganic carbon uptake;**

Uptake of inorganic carbon was calculated from high precision pH measurements as previously described [4].
For experimental use algal cells were transferred from their growth medium to the experimental cuvette by a light centrifugation, 1000 g for 1 min, and washed twice in the experimental medium. The experimental nutrient solution was equilibrated with 367 ppm $CO_2(g)$ and buffered with CO_3^{2-} to an alkalinity of 130 µM, giving a medium of an exactly known composition with respect to A, pH and DIC.
Acclimation from 5% $CO_2(g)$ to 10 and 1 µM $CO_2(aq)$ was followed in the experimental cuvette, by measurements of DIC-uptake rates. The $CO_2(aq)$ concentration during the experiments was held constant by additions of conc. $CO_2(aq)$, as previously described [9]. CO_2-response curves for 400 and 40 ppm grown algae were measured between 25-0 µM $CO_2(aq)$. The algae were added at the $CO_2(aq)$ concentration of 25 µM and allowed to consume $CO_2(aq)$ below 1 µM. The procedure was repeated 3-4 times by new additions of conc. $CO_2(aq)$ [4]. During experiments the chlorophyll concentration was 1 µg ml^{-1}. Saturating white light (290 µmol m^{-2} s^{-1}) was supplied by 3 metal halogen projector lamps.
Extracellular CA activity; was measured on harvested and washed intact cell samples in ice-cold phosphate buffer, as has been described elsewhere [8,9].
Luminescence measurements; All luminescence measurements were carried out in a modified Hansatech O_2-electrode (Hansatech, Norfolk,UK) allowing dark additions of HCO_3^-. 2 ml samples of algae ($\approx$10 µgChl ml^{-1}) were excited for 30 s with white light of a PPFD of 600 µmol m^{-2} s^{-1}, guided to the O_2 electrode by an optical fiber. A metal halogen lamp (Atlas 250 W, 24 V) was used as light source. Luminescence was detected with a Hamamatsu R 374 photomultiplier tube placed on top of the transparent lid of the O_2 electrode. HCO_3^- additions were made to a final concentration of 2.5 mM at times indicated in fig 4. The temperature during measurements was 20°C.

3. RESULTS AND DISCUSSION

Figure 1 illustrated that cells of *C. reinhardtii* had a more efficient photosynthesis at low DIC concentrations when the culture had been acclimated to air compared to high CO_2 acclimated cells. A similar pattern was found in *S. obliquus* and in *C. vulgaris* and also in the cell wall-less mutant CW.92. In all these algae 1/2 V_{max} was below 5 µM compared to about 50 µM in high CO_2 grown algae (data not shown).
Those results were obtained from cells under steady state conditions, i.e. they had been growing for at least 24 h in low CO_2. In experiments where cultures of *C. reinhardtii* and *S. obliquus* were suddenly transferred from high (5%) to 10 µM CO_2, an immediate acclimation to the lower DIC concentration started [4]. The induction phase was terminated within 90 minutes in both

species after which a steady state photosynthesis level was obtained.

What does this dramatic increase in photosynthesis reflect? Does it reflect the onset of a pumping mechanism or does it reflect the activity of extracellular CA, or both?

In other experiments, a culture of *C. reinhardtii* was acclimated to even lower CO_2 concentrations (≤ 1-2 μM CO_2). At this extremely low CO_2 concentration the induction phase was slower (figure 2) compared to the acclimation to 10 μM, and terminated after 3-4 hours. This can either be explained by the fact that much less carbon is available to support reorganization of the cells and therefore the process becomes slower but it might also indicate that a different mechanism is induced. The latter idea finds some support from CO_2 response curves (figure 3).

Figure 2.   Acclimation to low CO2 in C.reinhardtii

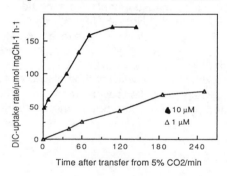

Time after transfer from 5% CO2/min

Figure 3.   Low-CO2 response in C.reinhardtii

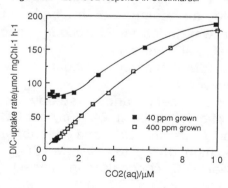

The results in figure 3 illustrates a comparison of photosynthetic carbon uptake between *C. reinhardtii* cells grown with 400 ppm $CO_2(g)$ (≈ 10 µM $CO_2(aq)$) and 40 ppm $CO_2(g)$ (≈ 1 µM $CO_2(aq)$), respectively.

Cells grown with 40 ppm and thereby acclimated to a $CO_2(aq)$ concentration of about 1 µM show a higher affinity for CO_2 below 10 µM, and the difference beeing approximately 10 fold at $CO_2(aq)$ concentrations below 1-2 µM.

We suggest that these results indicate a qualitatively different acclimation between *C. reinhardtii* cells acclimated to the two low-DIC concentrations. Especially notable is the high photosynthetic DIC uptake at ≈ 0 µM $CO_2(aq)$ in the 40 ppm grown cells. It should further be mentioned that these two "states" are partly diffuse and dependent on light and cell densities during growth. It is therefore important that the growth conditions are correctly defined, as acclimation to "air conditions" obviously can produce cells with different affinity for DIC.

However, there is a clear difference between cells of *S. obliquus* and *C. reinhardtii* in this respect as *S. obliquus* cells acclimated to 10 and 1 µM DIC have identical CO_2 response curves, beeing very similar to *C. reinhardtii* acclimated to 1 µM CO_2.

It is tempting to ascribe the two different acclimation states in *C. reinhardtii* different mechanisms,with one of them being relatively more dependent on the activity of CA and the other, relatively more dependent on active transport and accumulation of DIC into the cells.

In order to study the involvement of CA in the two acclimation states, we measured the induction of extracellular CA activity in intact cells of *C. reinhardtii* after transfer to 40 and 400 ppm CO_2 respectively, in order to see if we could correlate the increase in CA activity to the increased affinity for DIC.

The total increase in CA was about 10 times in *C. reinhardtii (WT)* after transfer to 10 µM $CO_2(aq)$ but no further increase appeared in cells acclimated to 1 µM. This tells us that acclimation to10 µM DIC is parallelled by an increased CA activity but that the further increase in DIC affinity after acclimation to 1 µM is not accompained by any further increase in extracellular CA activity. This could imply that acclimation to intermediately low $CO_2(aq)$ (10µM) is mainly maintained by an increased extracellular CA activity. The fact that an inhibitor of extracellular CA (AZ) caused an approximately 70% inhibition of photosynthesis in *C. reinhardtii* at 10 µM CO_2(aq) supports this idea [4]].

However, the increase in CA activity is much slower than the photosynthetic acclimation to 10 µM CO_2. The induction of photosynthesis is terminated within 90 minutes while full CA activity is not reached before 12 hours.

Another annoying fact, is that the cell wall-less mutant CW.92 which shows an identical acclimation pattern as the wild type cells, both to 10 and 1 µM CO_2, has only got one tenth of the extracellular CA activity of the wild type.

Unless very little extracellular CA is required to facilitate DIC transport into the cells and thereby to increase photosynthesis, our result indicates that the extracellular CA plays a minor role for the DIC transporting mechanism. The fact that AZ inhibits photosynthesis in *C. reinhardtii* acclimated to 10 µM, is easily explained by the fact that AZ has been shown to inhibit intracellular CA, as well as extracellular.

It seems though that extracellular CA is produced mainly to ensure that enough CO_2 is available outside the plasma membrane for active transport or diffusion into the cell.

A similar conclusion was also drawn in a recent paper by Sültemeyer, et al [10].

We know from our own experiments, and others, that there is an induction of intracellular CA activity, as well [11]. A rapidly induced CA, bound or associated to the plasma membrane is one probable explanation for the acclimation to the 10 µM CO_2(aq) level. The increased photosynthesis, in *C. reinhardtii* , could then be caused by a facilitated diffusion of CO_2 as has been shown to occure in many other biological systems. In a recent review on DIC transport [12], Smith concludes that when DIC is required by the cell it is "transported" by facilitated diffusion. Active transport is only used when the cells need to regulate the internal pH. This conclusion supports our data on the photosynthetic acclimation to low DIC concentrations in *C. reinhardtii*..

The above documented physiological differences between algal cells supplied with 400 and 40 ppm CO_2(g), respectively, are also consistent with the luminescence characteristics from the two acclimation states.

A decay component of luminescence apparent as a peak or shoulder, after about 10-20 s of darkness, was more clearly expressed in algae supplied with 40 than with 400 ppm CO_2(g) (fig 4 a b). This component of luminescence decay has earlier been suggested to reflect a decrease in internal [DIC] of the algae [13].

Figure 4. Luminescence decay for (a) 400 ppm grown cells and for (b) 40 ppm grown cells of *C.reinhardtii*.

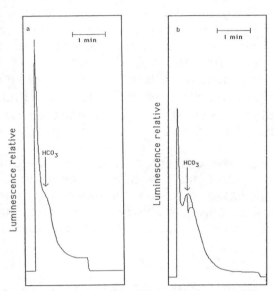

According to this hypothesis the concentration of internal [DIC] will decrease after excitation, since photosynthetically transduced energy will no longer be available for maintaining the DIC concentration gradient between the cell and the external medium. It has been shown on intact barley leaves that a decrease of $[CO_2$(g)$]$ results in a partial reduction of Q_A and a consequent stimulation of luminescence [14]. Based on these observations and interpretations, the more pronounced luminescence peak appearing, after a sudden light/dark transition, in 40 ppm CO_2(g) grown algae would indicate a more dramatic change of internal [DIC] than in 400 ppm grown cells.

This interpretation is strengthened by the different luminescence responses of HCO_3^- additions to algae of the two acclimation states. When HCO_3^- was added to 40 ppm grown cells, at the relative maximum of luminescence, a rapid quenching followed by a slower stimulation of luminescence was observed (fig 4 b). This effect was probably caused by a rapid uptake of DIC (causing oxidation of Q_A) followed by a slower release of DIC (causing reduction of Q_A) when the postillumination energy ceased. When HCO_3^- was added to 400 ppm grown cells, at the same phase of luminescence decay, no effect on luminescence was observed (fig 4 a). In this context it should be noted however, that also 400 ppm grown algae responded to HCO_3^- if the addition was made after only a few seconds of darkness (not shown), which is probably explained by the fact that more postillumination energy will be present for DIC uptake after a shorter period of darkness.

Taken together, the different decay patterns of luminescence between 40 and 400 ppm grown cells and the effect of HCO_3^- addition to the two acclimation states, might be interpreted as a proportionally higher accumulation of DIC inside the cells in 40 ppm acclimated algae.

Our final conclusion of the above presented results is therefore that at "higher" low CO_2 concentrations the CO_2 concentration at RubisCO is kept high by faciliated diffusion mediated via extra- and/or intracellular CA and that only cells experiencing extremely low CO_2 concentrations activates a "pumping" mechanism for accumulation of DIC.

REFERENCES.
[1] Berry, J., Boynton, J., Kaplan, A. and Badger, MR. Carnegie Inst Wash Year Book 75, 423-432.
[2] Spalding, MH. and Ogren WL. (1982) FEBS lett 145, 41-44.
[3] Coleman, JR., Berry, JA., Togasaki, RK. and Grossman AR. (1984) Plant Physiol 76, 472-477.
[4] Palmqvist, K., Sjöberg, S. and Samuelsson, G. (1988) Plant Physiol 87, 437-442.
[5] Solter, KM. and Gibor, A. (1977) Plant Sci Lett 8, 227-231.
[6] Surzycki, SJ. (1971) Methods Enzymol 23, 67-73.
[7] MacKinney, G. (1941) J Biol Chem 140, 315-322.
[8] Pronina, NA., Ramazanov, ZM. and Semenenko, VE. (1981) Fiziol Rast 28, 494-502.
[9] Williams, TG and Turpin DH. (1987) Plant Physiol 83, 92-96.
[10] Sültemeyer, DF., Miller, AG., Sepie, GS., Fock, HP. and Canvin, DT. (1989) Plant Physiol 89, 1213-1219.
[11] Moroney, JV, Togasaki, RK., Husic, HD. and Tolbert NE. (1987) 84, 757-761.
[12] Smith, RG. (1988) In Comp. Biochem. Physiol. Vol 90B, pp. 639-654. Printed in Great Britain.
[13] Sundblad, L-G., Samuelsson, G., Wigge, B. and Gardeström P. (1989) submitted to Photosynthesis Research.
[14] Sundblad, L-G. (1988) BBA 936, 429-434.

PROTEINS SYNTHESIZED DURING INDUCTION OF THE CO_2 CONCENTRATING MECHANISM IN *CHLAMYDOMONAS REINHARDTII*

JAMES V. MORONEY, Department of Botany, Louisiana State University, Baton Rouge, Louisiana 70803 USA

1. INTRODUCTION

The unicellular green alga, *Chlamydomonas reinhardtii*, can grow photoautotrophically at very low CO_2 concentrations. *C. reinhardtii* can grow under these conditions because it has the capacity to concentrate inorganic carbon, (C_i), internally to levels much higher than could be obtained by diffusion (1). This ability to concentrate C_i has been seen in many microalgae, both eukaryotic and prokaryotic (2-6). The CO_2 concentrating mechanism of algae is a major photosynthetic adaptation that is still poorly characterized.

In *C. reinhardtii*, the CO_2 concentrating mechanism is inducible, if the alga is grown on elevated CO_2 (1% (v/v) in air or higher), it exhibits a relatively low affinity for external C_i (1,7,8). If however the alga is grown on low CO_2 concentrations, it acquires a very high affinity for C_i (1) and now has an extremely low CO_2 compensation point (7,8). We have taken advantage of the inducible nature of the CO_2 concentrating system to determine which cellular components are important in the acquisition of CO_2 by *C. reinhardtii*. When this alga is switched from an environment high in CO_2 to one low in CO_2 the cells apparent affinity for CO_2 increases over a period of 3 to 5 hours. In addition, protein synthesis is required for this physiological change (9-11). We have labeled cells with $^{35}SO_4^{-2}$ to detect proteins that are preferentially synthesized under low CO_2 conditions. We have also isolated mRNA from cells undergoing this induction, made and screened a cDNA library, and selected for transformed colonies that contain DNA that preferentially hybridizes to RNA from low CO_2-grown cells.

2. MATERIALS AND METHODS

Algal Strains and Culture Conditions The wild-type strain of *Chlamydomonas reinhardtii* 137 mt^+, has been maintained in R.K.Togasaki's laboratory. CIA-5 was selected and characterized as previously described (12) and PMP-1 (7) was a gift of Dr. M.H. Spalding. The cell-wall deficient mutant, CC-400 cw-15 mt^+ was obtained from the Duke University *Chlamydomonas* Culture Collection. The cultures were maintained on plates of yeast-acetate medium until a few weeks before use. In liquid culture, the strains were grown in minimal media (13), aerated with 5% CO_2 in air and illuminated with 300 $\mu E\ m^{-2}s^{-1}$ of white light. For $^{35}SO_4^{-2}$ labeling, algal cells were switched to media with 1/10 the normal amount of sulfur 48 hours prior to the experiment.

^{35}S **labeling of wild-type and CC-400 cells** Cells that had been growing in minimal media with 1/10 sulfur (14) and aerated with 5% CO_2 were harvested by centrifugation at 1100×g (2500 rpm) in a Beckman JA-10 rotor for 5 minutes. The cells were resuspended in

M. Baltscheffsky (ed.), Current Research in Photosynthesis, Vol. IV, 449–454.
© 1990 *Kluwer Academic Publishers. Printed in the Netherlands.*

minimal media lacking sulfate (Min-S) and centrifuged again. The pellet was resuspended again in Min-S (3 mL) and chlorophyll concentration was determined spectrophotometrically. The cells were adjusted to 25 μg Chl/mL and divided into six 150-mL flasks. Three flasks were bubbled with air, and three with air supplemented with 5% CO_2. After a 30 minute adaptation in the light to the low and high CO_2 regimes, the cultures were labeled by adding carrier-free $^{35}SO_4^{-2}$ (1000 Ci/mmol), and illuminated for three hours for wild-type cells (four hours for CC-400).

Cell Fractionation All steps were carried out at 0-4°C. After incubating the cells for the appropriate time, the triplicate samples were combined and 100 mL was withdrawn from each (air vs. CO_2). These samples (Total Air and Total CO_2) were harvested by centrifugation at 4000 rpm for 10 minutes in a JA-14 rotor. The pellet was then washed twice with 50 mL ice-cold 20mM Tris-HCl (pH 7.5), collected by centrifugation and resuspended in 250 μL 20mM Tris-HCl (pH 7.5). The samples were quick-frozen in a dry ice/methanol bath and stored at -20°C.

The remaining 350 mL of each sample was then collected by centrifugation in a JA-10 rotor at 2800×g (4000 rpm) for 10 minutes. For CC-400 cells, the supernatant was reserved, and brought to 70% saturation with $(NH_4)_2SO_4$ and stirred for one hour. The samples were allowed to stand without stirring for an additional thirty minutes, then were collected by centrifugation in a JA-20 rotor at 27,000×g (15000 rpm) for 15 minutes. The pellet was taken up in 1 mL 20 mM Tris-HCl(7.5) and dialyzed overnight against 20 mM Tris-HCl (7.5). The resulting dialysate (extracellular soluble fraction) was quick-frozen as above.

The pelleted cells from the 350 mL harvest were washed twice with 100 mL ice-cold 20mM Tris-HCl (7.5) and recollected by centrifugation. The pellets were taken up in 12 mL cold fractionation buffer (20mM Tris-HCl (7.5), 150mM sucrose, 50mM NaCl, 0.4mM benzamidine, and 0.4mM aminocaproic acid) and were passed two times through a cell disruption bomb (Paar 4639), using a breakage pressure of 1800 psi for wild-type cells, and 1000 psi for cc-400, maintaining the pressure for four minutes for each pass. Unbroken cells were pelleted by centrifugation in a Sorvall Hb-4 rotor for two minutes at 670×g (2000rpm). The pellet was discarded and the supernatant was again centrifuged in a JA-20 at 6800×g (7500 rpm) for 10 minutes. The pellet was taken up in 250 μL 20mM Tris-HCl (pH 7.5) and quick-frozen (low speed membrane fraction). The supernatant was then centrifuged in a Sorvall T-875 rotor for two hours at 156,000×g (40000 rpm) and the pellet taken up in 250 μL 20mM Tris-HCl (pH 7.5) and quick-frozen (high speed membrane fraction). The supernatant was brought to 70% saturation with $(NH_4)_2SO_4$, and centrifuged at 27,000×g (JA-20 rotor, 15000 rpm, 15 minutes). The pellet was resuspended in 1 mL 20mM Tris-HCl (pH 7.5) and dialyzed overnight (intracellular soluble fraction).

mRNA isolation and cDNA Synthesis mRNA was isolated from *C. reinhardtii* cultures by a modification of the method of Cashmore (15). Briefly total RNA was purified by extraction of broken cells (two passes of cells through a Paar Bomb at full pressure) with chloroform:methanol:isoamyl alcohol (25:25:1) followed by repeated ethanol and $LiCl_2$ precipitations. The mRNA fraction was then purified by chromatography over a poly-U sepharose column twice. This resulted in an mRNA fraction essentially free of ribosomal RNA. cDNA using mRNA isolated from low CO_2-grown, wild-type cells as a template was made using a Pharmacia cDNA kit following the manufacturer's instructions.

cDNA Cloning and Screening cDNA was cloned into the EcoRI site of pUC18 using *E. coli* strain JM83 as the vector (16). Transformed colonies were selected for by ampicillin resistance and the formation of white colonies when grown on media containing X-gal indicating the interruption of the *lac-z* gene of pUC18. These colonies were then screened by differential hybridization to labeled mRNA isolated from low CO_2-grown wild-type cells and high CO_2-grown CIA-5 cells. CIA-5 cells were used in the screen as this strain has never shown induction of the low CO_2-specific polypeptides (reference 12 and figure 2).

Other Methods SDS-PAGE was performed according to Laemmli (17). The immunoblot assay was performed according to the protocol from Bio-Rad Laboratories using anti-*C. reinhardtii* periplasmic CA antibody as the primary antibody. *In vitro* translations were performed using the rabbit reticulocyte lysate system from Stratagene. Protein and chlorophyll concentrations were determined spectrophotometrically.

3. RESULTS AND DISCUSSION

Earlier work has established that *C. reinhardtii* synthesizes at least 4 polypeptides preferentially when grown under limiting CO_2 (11,14,18). One of the labeled polypeptides had a molecular weight of 37 kD, similar to the molecular weight of the periplasmic carbonic anhydrase (19,20). Surprisingly when fractionation studies were done with ^{35}S-labeled *C. reinhardtii* the 37 kD protein was found in the membrane fraction and not the soluble fraction where the periplasmic carbonic anhydrase activity was found. Spalding and Jeffrey (18) had done fractionation studies on cw-15 mt+ cells and reported a membrane-associated protein with molecular weights of 35 and 36 kD. We therefore performed cell fractionation experiments on CC-400 cells and recovered both the periplasmic carbonic anhydrase from the cell supernatant and isolated membrane fractions from the cell. Using immunoblot analysis we established that the membrane-associated ^{35}S-labeled band is distinct from the periplasmic carbonic anhydrase (Figure 1). These experiments demonstrate that at least one membrane associated protein is synthesized under limited CO_2 condition and that at least 5 distinct proteins, both soluble and membrane-bound are made under these conditions.

A.

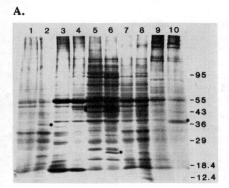

B.

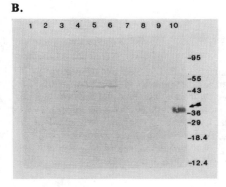

Figure 1. ^{35}S-labeled protein and immunoblot analysis of protein fractions from CC-400 cells. Labeled cells were subjected to SDS-PAGE and autoradiography (Figure 1A) or blotted and probed with an antibody raised against the periplasmic carbonic anhydrase (Figure 1B). In lanes 1, 3, 5, 7, and 9 are from cells grown on high CO_2, while lanes 2, 4, 6, 8, and 10 were from cells grown on low CO_2. Lanes 1 and 2, low speed membrane fraction; lanes 3 and 4, high speed membrane fraction; lanes 5 and 6, intracellular soluble protein fraction; lanes 7 and 8, total cellular protein fraction; lanes 9 and 10, extracellular protein fraction.

CIA-5 is a high CO_2-requiring mutant of *C. reinhardtii* that is unable to make any of the low CO_2-specific polypeptides (12). Figure 2 shows an autoradiograph of CIA-5 cells and wild type cells labeled under both low CO_2 and high CO_2 conditions. None of the polypeptides associated with low CO_2 growth are seen in this mutant. Figure 2 also shows the polypeptide pattern of the high CO_2 requiring mutant PMP-1. This mutant is missing at least two of the polypeptides associated with growth on low CO_2. These mutants further suggest that these polypeptides are important in the acquisition of CO_2 in *C. reinhardtii*.

To confirm the absence of the periplasmic CA in CIA-5, immunoblots were performed using antibodies to the purified periplasmic CA (Figure 3). Additionally, mRNA was isolated from low CO_2-grown, wild-type cells and from high CO_2-grown, CIA-5 cells. These mRNA preparations were then used as templates for *in vitro* translation experiments using the rabbit reticulocyte system. Figure 4 shows that the low CO_2-grown wild-type mRNA coded for two polypeptides with molecular weights of 36 kD and 42 kD. These polypeptides were greatly diminished in the *in vitro* translation using the CIA-5 mRNA. This experiment as well as the immunoblot (Figure 3) and the autoradiography (Figure 2) suggest that the mutation in CIA-5 is regulatory in nature.

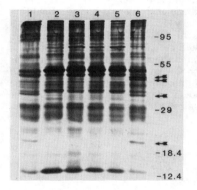

Figure 2. ^{35}S-Labeled polypeptides from wild type and mutant strains of *C. reinhardtii*. Labeled cells were subjected to SDS-PAGE and autoradiography. Lane 1, PMP-1 low CO_2; lane 2, CIA-5 low CO_2; lane 3, PMP-1 high CO_2; lane 4, CIA-5 high CO_2; lane 5, lane 6, WT low CO_2.

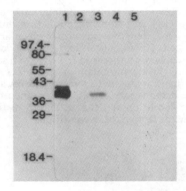

Figure 3. Immunoblot analysis of wild type and CIA-5 cells. CIA-5 and wild type cells (100 μg / lane) were subjected to SDS-PAGE, blotted and probed with anti-periplasmic CA antibodies. Lane 1, periplasmic CA (3 μg); lane 2, WT high CO_2; lane 3, WT low CO2; lane 4, CIA-5 low CO_2; lane 6, CIA-5 high CO_2.

The mRNA from the low CO_2-grown wild-type cells was then used to make a cDNA library. The cDNA was then cloned into the EcoRI site of the pUC-18 plasmid and these recombinant plasmids were used to transform *E. coli* strain JM83. Colonies carrying *C. reinhardtii* DNA that is expressed under low CO_2 conditions were screened for by differential hybridization to ^{32}P-polyadenylated mRNA from both low CO_2-grown, wild-type cells and high CO_2-grown, CIA-5 cells (Figure 4). Transformants that preferentially hybridized to the wild type mRNA have been selected and will be further characterized.

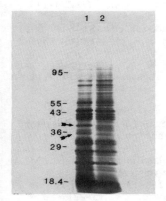

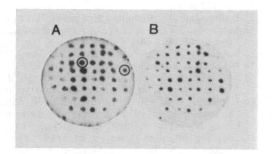

Figure 4. *In vitro* translations of mRNA purified from low CO_2 grown wild type cells (lane 1), or high CO_2 grown <u>CIA-5</u> cells (lane 2).

Figure 5. cDNA screening. *E. coli* transformants grown in duplicate were hybridized to either ^{32}P-labeled mRNA from low CO_2 grown wild type cells (A) or high CO_2 grown <u>CIA-5</u> cells (B).

4. SUMMARY

Chlamydomonas reinhardtii possesses a CO_2 concentrating mechanism that involves at least 5 inducible proteins. At least one of these proteins is membrane-associated. The CA isozyme located in the chloroplast is also required for growth on low CO_2 but it is made constitutively (21). The *in vitro* translations support the earlier suggestions that the induction process is at least in part transcriptionally controlled (9,11). We used the regulatory mutant, <u>CIA-5</u>, to screen a cDNA library for messages induced by low CO_2. This provides a promising approach to select for and characterize the genes and proteins involved in the CO_2 concentrating mechanism of *C. reinhardtii*. We are currently investigating the intracellular localization of these polypeptides. Past work has argued that C_i transport might occur at the chloroplast envelope (23,24), plasmalemma (25), or both (26). Now that some of the polypeptides involved in C_i transport have been identified, we can address this question.

5. ACKNOWLEDGMENTS

I thank Renu Jain, Livingston J. Manuel, and Catherine B. Mason for their expert experimental work and their valuable discussions. The support of the National Science Foundation grant DMB 8703462 and Louisiana Board of Regents Contract LEQSF (86-89)-RD-A-03 is also acknowledged.

6. REFERENCES

1 Badger, M.R., Kaplan, A., and Berry, J.A. (1980) Plant Physiol. 66, 407-413
2 Aizawa, K. and Miyachi, S. (1986) FEMS Microbiol. Rev. 39, 215-233
3 Burns, B.D. and Beardall, J. (1987) J. Exp. Mar. Biol. Ecol. 107, 75-86
4 Palmqvist, K., Sjöberg, S. and Samuelsson, G. (1988) Plant Physiol. 87, 437-442

5 Yagawa, Y., Muto, S. and Miyachi, S. (1987) Plant Cell Physiol. 28, 1253-1262
6 Kaplan, A., Badger, M.R., and Berry, J.A., (1980) Planta 149, 219-226
7 Spalding, M.H., Spreitzer, R.J., and Ogren, W.L. (1983) Plant Physiol. 73, 273-276
8 Moroney, J.V. and Tolbert, N.E. (1985) Plant Physiol. 77, 253-258
9 Coleman, J.R. and Grossman, A.R. (1984) Proc. Natl. Acad. Sci. USA 81, 6049-6053
10 Coleman, J.R., Berry, J.A., Togasaki, R.K. and Grossman, A.R. (1984) Plant Physiol. 76, 472-477
11 Bailly, J. and Coleman, J.R. (1988) Plant Physiol 87, 833-840
12 Moroney, J.V., Husic, H.D., Kitayama, M., Manuel, L.J., Togasaki, R.K. (1989) Plant Physiol. 89, 897-903
13 Sueoka, N. (1960) Proc. Natl. Acad. Sci. USA 46, 83-91
14 Manuel, L.J. and Moroney, J.V. (1988) Plant Physiol. 88, 491-496
15 Maniatis, T., Fritsch, E.F. and Sambrook, J. (1982) Molecular Cloning, a Laboratory Manual, Cold Spring Harbor Laboratory Cold Spring Harbor, pp567
16 Laemmli, U.K. (1970) Nature 227, 680-685
17 Cashmore, A.R. (1982) in Methods in Chloroplast Molecular Biology (Edelman, M., Chua, N.-H.and Hallick, R.B. eds) pp.387-392, Elsevier, Amsterdam
18 Spalding, M.H. and Jeffrey, M. (1989) Plant Physiol. 89, 133-137
19 Toguri, T., Muto, S. and Miyachi, S. (1986) Plant Cell Physiol. 27, 215-221
20 Yang, S.-Y., Tsuzuki, M. and Miyachi, S. (1985) Plant Cell Physiol. 26, 25-34
21 Husic, H.D., Kitayama, M., Togasaki, R.K., Moroney, J.V., Morris, K.L. and Tolbert, N.E. (1989) 89, 904-909
22 Moroney, J.V., Husic, H.D. and Tolbert, N.E. (1985) Plant Physiol. 79, 177-183
23 Moroney, J.V., Kitayama, M., Togasaki, R.K. and Tolbert, N.E. (1987) Plant Physiol 83, 460-463
24 Beardall, J. (1981) J. Phycol. 17, 371-373
25 Marcus, Y., Volokita, M. and Kaplan, A. (1984) J. Exp. Bot. 35, 1136-1144
26 Williams, T.G. and Turpin D.H. (1987) Plant Physiol. 83, 92-96

THE MOLECULAR BIOLOGY OF CARBONIC ANHYDRASE EXPRESSION
IN CHLAMYDOMONAS REINHARDTII

JOHN R. COLEMAN, Centre for Plant Biotechnology, Dept.
of Botany, University of Toronto, Toronto, Ontario
CANADA   M5S 3B2

1.   INTRODUCTION
     The inorganic carbon (C_i) concentration experienced
by the eukaryotic green alga Chamydomonas reinhardtii
during growth has a great impact on the photosynthetic
characteristics of this organism. When grown at air
levels of CO_2 (0.035%), the cells have a much higher
affinity for C_i than cells that have been grown at
elevated levels of CO_2. It is now apparent that the
presence of both carbonic anhydrase (CA) activity and
active C_i transport systems result in the formation of a
large, photosynthetically available pool of
intracellular C_i. This pool appears to be able to
eliminate much of the oxygen inhibition of
photosynthesis and also permits high rates of carbon
fixation at low external C_i concentrations. In
contrast, cells grown at elevated levels of CO_2 exhibit
little CA or C_i transport activity and require high
external concentrations of C_i to achieve maximal rates
of photosynthesis. An important consideration is that
the high and low C_i phenotypes exhibited by the alga are
in fact end points of an acclimation process. Cells are
able to acclimate to the prevailing external C_i
concentrations and this process involves the induction
or repression of a number of proteins including CA. We
have shown previously that acclimation of the alga to
low, external concentrations of C_i results in the de
novo synthesis of an externally-localized CA (1).
Composed of 37 kDa glycosylated monomers, the expression
of the extracellular CA is regulated at the
pretranslational level and the polypeptide is
synthesized as a 44 kDa precursor on 80S cytoplasmic
ribosomes (2). We have continued our studies of the
regulation of CA expression by Chlamydomonas and are
particularly interested in the molecular events
associated with the induced variation in CA activity.

M. Baltscheffsky (ed.), Current Research in Photosynthesis, Vol. IV, 455–462.
© 1990 *Kluwer Academic Publishers. Printed in the Netherlands.*

2. MATERIALS AND METHODS

Chlamydomonas reinhardtii 2137mt$^+$ and the cell wall-less mutant CW-15 were cultured axenically in minimal medium or minimal medium containing 10mM Na acetate as described previously (1). All bacteria and phage strains were maintained and cultured as generally described (4). Methods for Chlamydomonas genomic DNA isolation, construction of the expression library in the phage vector gt11, and screening protocols are described in Bailly and Coleman (3). Northern and Western blotting techniques were used to determine CA transcript and protein abundance (3,4). DNA from both strands was sequenced by the dideoxy-chain termination method (5) following supplier's instructions (U.S. Biochem. Corp.) The isolation of the extracellular CA from Chlamydomonas and generation of a polyclonal antibody have been described (1,2). For immunolocalization studies, air grown Chlamydomonas cells were fixed in 2% glutaraldehyde and the imbedded sections blocked by incubation with 1% BSA in PBS buffer. The sections were then incubated with a 1:500 dilution of the CA antibody in the same buffer at 37°C for 2 h and washed with 0.05 M Tris-HCl containing 0.5 M NaCl and 1% BSA. The sections were then incubated with a 1:10 dilution of gold-conjugated goat anti-rabbit IgG and washed with PBS prior to staining with uranyl acetate and lead citrate. Control experiments were performed with preimmune or with the omission of rabbit serum.

3. RESULTS AND DISCUSSION

It has been shown previously that the transfer of high CO_2 grown cells to air levels of C_i results in the rapid increase in total CA activity (1,6,7). The majority of the CA in air adapted cells is located outside of the plasma membrane and was thought to be either in the periplasmic space or associated with the cell wall. Using a polyclonal antibody raised against the 37 kDa CA monomer and electron microscopy, we have confirmed the extracelluar localization of CA in Chlamydomonas (Figures 1 and 2). Preliminary analysis of the data suggest that CA is associated with the inner surface of the cell wall itself rather than the periplasmic space. The removal of extracellular CA activity by autolysin treatment and the leakage of CA from the cell wall-less mutant Chlamydomonas CW-15, support the immunogold labelling data (8).

The polyclonal antibody was also used to isolate a 2.5 kb fragment containing a portion of the gene coding for CA from a Chlamydomonas genomic DNA expression

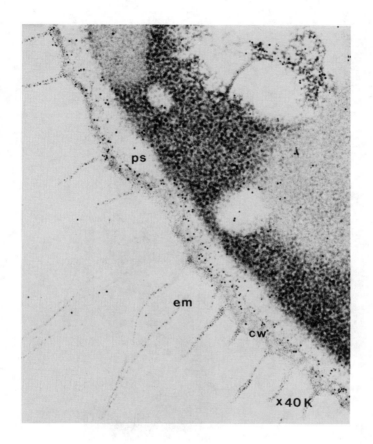

Figure 1.   Immunogold labelling of carbonic anhydrase.
Fixed and sectioned cells of <u>Chlamydomonas</u>, grown at
levels of CO_2, were incubated with a polyclonal antibody
directed against the extracelluar CA, washed and then
incubated with gold-conjugated goat anti-rabbit IgG
prior to staining with uranyl acetate and lead citrate.
Note the position of the majority of the small gold
particles on the inside of the cell wall (cw) as well as
some staining of the periplasmic space.   The long
projections from the cell surfacea are probably
extracellular mucilage (em).

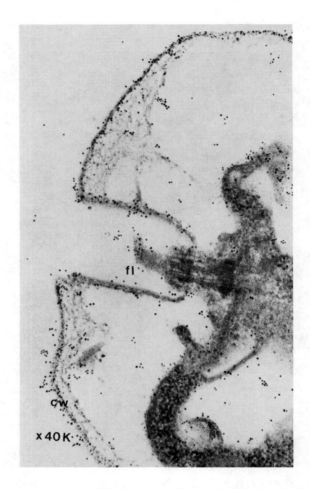

Figure 2. Immunolocalization of carbonic anhydrase. Sections of the anterior region of <u>Chlamydomonas</u>, prepared as described previously, show the same pattern of gold particle distribution. Significant staining of the cell wall (cw) even in the region of flagella (fl) attachment is apparent. Some non-specific staining of the starch grains was also found to occur with either pre-immune serum or with the polyclonal antibody directed against carbonic anhydrase.

library constructed in the phage gt11 (3,9). Using this
DNA fragment as a probe, Southern blot analysis of the
chromosomal DNA indicated that only a single copy of the
gene is present. The 2.5 kb genomic fragment has been
sequenced and contains several open reading frames
(ORF), the longest of which is 264 amino acids (data not
shown). The presence of introns within the sequence is
suggested by a number of termination codons and what
appear to be consensus sequences for Chlamydomonas mRNA
processing (10).

Northern blot analysis was used to determine
changes in CA transcript abundance in response to C_i
concentration, light and acetate availability. Transfer
of high CO_2 grown cells to air levels of CO_2 results in
the rapid appearance of a 1.4 kb transcript that shows
maximal abundance after 3 h air exposure followed by a
decline to levels found in fully air adapted cells
(Figure 3). Transfer of air adapted cells to high CO_2
conditions results in elimination of the CA transcript
after 60 min exposure to the elevated C_i (data not
shown). The rapid elimination is in direct contrast
with the reported slow turnover of both CA activity and
polypeptide abundance when air grown cells are
transferred to high CO_2 conditions (11).

Although light has been shown to be required for
the induction of CA activity after transfer of
Chlamydomonas from high to low C_i concentrations (12),
the CA transcript was found to be present (although
reduced in abundance) when high CO_2 grown cells were
transferred to air in the absence of light (Figure 4).
Similarly, air grown cells were able to eliminate the CA
transcript even when transferred to high CO_2 conditions
in the dark (Figure 4). As CA activity induction
depends on the operation of the photosynthetic
apparatus, the intermediates of photosynthesis or
photorespiration have been implicated as inducers of the
low CO_2 syndrome (12,13). Our observation that the
induction or repression of the CA transcript levels can
occur in the dark suggests that other regulatory
molecules may be involved.

Air adapted cells, grown on acetate in the light,
have been shown to have reduced levels of CA activity
however the extent of repression appears to be variable.
CA transcript abundance was found to decline after the
addition of 10 mM acetate to air grown cultures in the
light with a significant reduction visible after 6 h
acetate exposure and elimination of the transcript
within 15 h (Figure 5). Similar reports of acetate
repression of transcripts of photosynthetic proteins,
such as rbcS and cabII have been reported however a
mechanism has not been described (14,15). For carbonic

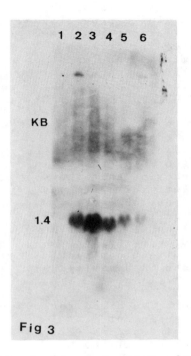

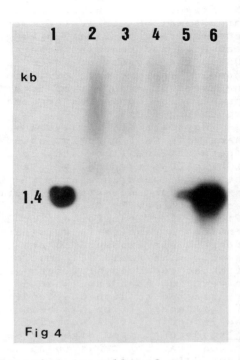

Figure 3. Induction of CA transcript in cells of
Chlamydomonas adapting to air levels of CO_2. The figure
shows the autoradiogram generated by hybridization of
the ^{32}P-labelled CA gene to total RNA isolated from 5%
CO_2 grown cells (lane 1) or from high CO_2 cells
transferred to air for 1 h (lane 2), 3 h (lane 3), 5 h
(lane 4), 8 h (lane 5),and 24 h (lane 6). The size (kb)
of the hybridization signal is indicated.

Figure 4. Autoradiogram showing the effect of light on
the induction or repression of the CA transcript. Total
RNA was isolated from air grown Chlamydomonas
transferred to darkness for 3 h (lane 1), transferred to
darkness and high CO_2 (lane 2), or maintained in the
light and exposed to air levels of CO_2 for 3 h (lane 3).
In a reciprocal experiment, RNA was isolated from high
CO_2 grown cells transferred to darkness for 3 h (lane
4), exposed to darkness and air levels of CO_2 for 3 h
(lane 5) or maintained in the light but exposed to air
for 3 h (lane 6). Following electrophoresis, a Northern
blot of the gel was probed with the ^{32}P-labelled CA
gene.

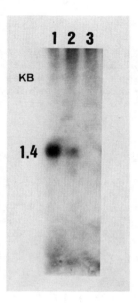

Figure 5. Effect of acetate on CA transcript abundance.
Total RNA was isolated from air grown cells (lane 1) and
from cells exposed to 10 mM Na acetate in the light for
6 h (lane 2) and 15 h (lane 3).   Following
electrophoresis on a 1.1% agarose gel, the RNA was
transferred to Biodyne A nylon membrane (ICN) and probed
with the ^{32}P-labelled CA gene.   Hybridization was
performed at 42° C and 50% formamide for 18 h.   The
blots were subsequently washed for three 5 min periods
in 2 x SSC and 0.1% SDS at room temperature followed by
a 20 min wash at 42° C in 0.1 x SSC and 0.1% SDS.   The
size of the CA transcript is indicated and was
determined by comparison with a synthetic RNA ladder
(BRL Corp.)

anhydrase, it possible that the stimulation of Krebs cycle activity by the addition of acetate, and the subsequent generation of intracellular respiratory CO_2, may result in repression of CA transcript accumulation or synthesis. This hypothesis is currently being studied.

Acknowledgements
    I am grateful to Dr. N. Benhamou, Dept. de Phytologie, Universite de Laval, Quebec, for preparation of the electron micrographs and N. Majeau, W. Yoshida, and G. Sunohara for research assistance. This research was supported by a grant to J. Coleman from NSERC (Canada).

REFERENCES
1.   Coleman, J.R. et al. (1984) Pl. Physiol. 74, 472-477
2.   Coleman, J.R. and Grossman, A.R. (1984) P.N.A.S. USA 81, 6049-6053
3.   Bailly, J. and Coleman, J.R. (1988) Pl. Physiol. 87, 833-840
4.   Maniatis, T. et al. (1982) Cold Spring Harbour Lab, N.Y.
5.   Sanger, F. et al. (1977) P.N.A.S. USA 74, 5463-5467
6.   Berry, J.A. et al. (1976) Carn. Inst. Wash. Yrbk. 75, 423-432
7.   Moroney,J.V. et al. (1985) Pl. Physiol. 79, 177-183
8.   Kimpel, D.L. et al. (1983) Pl. Cell Physiol. 24, 255-259
9.   Young, R.A. and Davis, R.W. (1983) P.N.A.S. USA 80, 1194-1198
10.   Franzen, L-G. et al. (1989) Pl. Molec. Biol. 12, 463-474
11.   Yang, S. et al. (1985) Pl. Cell Physiol. 26, 25-34
12.   Spalding, M.H. and Ogren, W.J. (1982) FEBS Lett. 145, 41-44
13.   Marcus, Y. et al. (1983) Pl. Physiol. 71, 208-210
14.   Kindle, K. (1987) Pl. Molec. Biol. 9, 547-563
15.   Steinbiss, H.J. and Zetsche, K. (1986) Planta 167, 575-581

Mutations in the 5' flanking region of rbcL inhibit the growth of Synechococcus PCC7942 in air-level of CO$_2$ and alter the carboxysome structure.

D. Friedberg, A. Kaplan, R. Ariel, R. Schwarz,
E. Sadovnick, M. Kessel, and J. Seijffers
Institute of Life Sciences   The Hebrew University of
Jerusalem, 91904 Jerusalem, Israel

1.   INTRODUCTION.

Cyanobacteria undergo a syndrome of changes during adaptation from high to low-CO$_2$ concentration in their environment. As a result they can concentrate inorganic carbon (Ci) within the cell and grow photoautotrophically under air level of CO$_2$ (1). To elucidate the molecular basis of the adaptation process we have used mutants of Synechococcus PCC7942, which do not grow in air-level of CO$_2$ but grow normally at 5% CO$_2$ in air (2,3).

2.   PROCEDURES.

The high-CO$_2$-requiring (hcr) mutants E1 and 0221 were isolated from Synechococcus PCC7942 and grown as described (2,3). Escherichia coli strains MV1190 and JM109 and the plasmids pUC118 and pUC119 were used for molecular cloning. DNA procedures were performed by know procedures.

3.   RESULTS AND DISCUSSION.

3.1. Cloning of putative hcr wild type genes which tranforms the hcr mutants 0221 and E1 to WT phenotype.

The hcrWT locus was cloned using the altered phenotype of the mutants, without the aid of known heterologous genes, as follows: WT DNA was partially digested with SauIIIA, and fragments of about 10 kb were isolated and ligated with BamHI-linearized pBRK (a modified pBR322 in which we have inserted a kanamycin resistance (Km^r) cartridge).

Transformation of mutant 0221 by the genomic library resulted in colonies growing at air-level of CO$_2$ (WT phenotype), in the presence of Km. The integration of the insert DNA into the transformant's genome was confirmed by Southern hybridization, using pBRK as a probe (not shown).

A recombinant plasmid comprising pBRK and a 10 Kb insert was rescued from a 0221 transformant following digestion of the chromosomal DNA by SalI and transformation of E. coli by the religated DNA (Fig. 1). The regenerated plasmid pE12 and its derivative, 8kb EcoRI fragment transformed both 0221 and E1 mutants, enabling them to grow at air-level of CO$_2$ in

M. Baltscheffsky (ed.), Current Research in Photosynthesis, Vol. IV, 463–466.

the presence of Km at a high frequency, indicating that pE12
contain an hcrWT locus.

3.2. Subcloning, mapping and insertional inactivation of
the hcrWT locus. Subcloning of the hcrWT locus from the 8 kb
EcoRI fragment was performed by transformation experiments
with 0221. A 3.5 kb ClaI fragment and its subclones BstEII-
BstXI, BclI-ClaI and PstI-BstXI (1.8 kb, 2.1 kb and 0.23 kb,
respectively) transformed 0221 to the WT phenotype (Fig. 2).
This implies that the mutation in the respective hcrWT locus
is located within the 0.23 kb PstI-BstXI restriction
fragment. The 3.5 kb ClaI fragment did not transform EI to
the WT phenotype, suggesting that the hcrEI mutation is
located within a distance of 7 kb from hcr0221. It is also
possible that EI contains more than one hcr mutation.

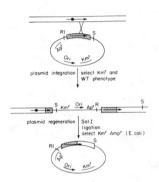

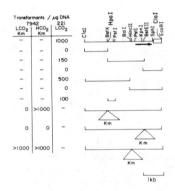

Fig. 1. Schematic presentation of the integration of the
wild type DNA library into the 0221 genome and subsequent
rescue of the recombinant plasmid pE12. (Left).

Fig. 2. Subcloning and insertional inactivation of the hcrWT
locus. Restriction fragments derived from pE12 were used to
transform 0221. The arrow represents the 5' end of rbcL, the
open bars represent pBRK DNA. (Right).

Sequence analysis of the BstEII-BstXI fragment (not
shown) revealed over 90% homology with the reported sequence
of the rbcL and its 5' flanking region from Synechococcus
PCC6301 (4). The BstXI site was mapped -1464 nucleotides
upstream rbcL thus mapping the hcr locus between this
nucleotide and the next PstI in a distance of 232
nucleotides (Fig. 2). The identification of the hcr locus in
the flanking sequence, 5' to rbcL, was confirmed by Southern
analysis (Fig. 3). BstEII-BstXI, ClaI, EcoRI and HindIII
digests of DNA from 0221 and from the 0221/ClaI 3.5 kb
transformant showed respective DNA fragments of 1.8, 8.0,
9.5 and 5.0 kb when the BstEII-BstXI fragment was used as a
probe (Fig. 3A). The same size of fragments were apparent

with WT DNA (not shown) and also when the blot was probed
with a 2.3 Kb PstI fragment carrying the rbc operon of
Synechococcus PCC6301 (5) (Fig. 3B).

Insertion of the Km^r cartridge into the BstXI site and
transformation of the recombinant construct to WT cells
(Fig. 2) resulted in a new high-CO_2 requiring mutant
(hcrBX1). This data further indicates the importance of this
DNA region for growth in low-CO_2. Insertional inactivation
of the BclI site did not affect the CO_2 requirement. On the
other hand, interruption of the BstEII site was lethal, as
expected, since this site is within the rbcL coding region.

3.3. The hcr mutants contain aberrant carboxysome
structures. The failure of the hcr mutants 0221 and EI to
adapt to air-level of CO_2 has been attributed to
inefficient utilization of the internal Ci pool (2,3). The
hcr0221 and hcrE1 mutations do not seem to affect the
kinetic parameters of RuBP carboxylase (2,3), nor do they
alter the intracellular location of the enzyme, which is
mainly confined to the carboxysomes (6). We analyzed their
ultrastructure in the WT and mutants. Stained electron
micrographs of WT cells show typical polyhedral bodies (Fig.
4a). None of the many 0221 cells examined contained normal
carboxysomes but, instead, exhibited non-geometric, less
dense inclusions (Fig. 4b). The hcrBX1 mutant, also
exhibited difused inclusions similar to the 0221 mutant. On
the other hand, 0221 transformed with the BclI-ClaI fragment
exhibited normal carboxysomes. Our finding that the mutants
0221 (Fig. 4b), EI and hcrBX1 (not shown) contain abnormal
carboxysome structure is consistent with the model
suggesting that the carboxysomes are involved in efficient
CO_2 utilization (7). This model proposes that carbonic
anhydrase and RuBP carboxylase are located within the
carboxysomes; the HCO_3^- actively accumulating in the
cytoplasm, enter the carboxysome, dehydrated to CO_2 by
carbonic anhydrase and fixed by the RuBP carboxylase.

It might be hypothesized that the hcr mutations leads to
an altered association between RuBP carboxylase and other
carboxysome components, impeding the availability of CO_2
to the enzyme in vivo, and thus results in high-CO_2
requirement. The results showing that our chemically induced
and genetically engineered mutants possess aberrant
carboxysomes, and that upon transformation both the
carboxysome structure and the physiological functions were
restored to normal, suggest that the 5' flanking region of
rbcL might be involved in controlling carboxysome structure.
The significance of the carboxysomes for growth under low-
CO_2 has also been observed in a Synechocystis PCC6803
mutant, in which the native rbcL was replaced by the rbcL
gene from Rhodospirillum rubrum. This mutant requires high-
CO_2 for growth, and is devoid of microscopically
observable carboxysomes (J. Pierce, personal communication).

Fig. 3. Southern analysis of DNA
from 0221/ClaI transformant
hybridized with BstEII-BstXI
fragment (A) and with pCS75
arbouring the rbc operon of
strain 6301 (B). DNA digested
with BstEII/BstXI, ClaI, EcoRI
and HindIII (a to d); 0221 DNA
digested with the same enzymes
(e to h).

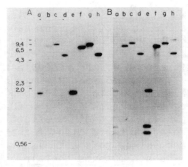

Figure 4. Electronmicrographs of wild type (a) and 0221 (b)
cells grown at 5% CO_2 in air. The bar represents 0.5 μm.

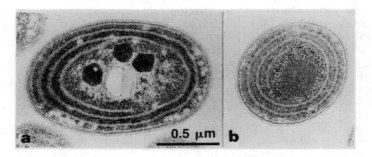

ACKNOWLEDGMENT.
Supported by grants from the Israeli Academy of Sciences;
National Council for Research and Development Israel and the
Bundesministerium for Forschung un Technologie (BMFT)
Germany; U.S.-Israel Binational Science Foundation (BSF).
REFERENCES.
1. Kaplan, A. (1985) In Inorganic Carbon Uptake by Aquatic
Organisms (Lucas, W.J. and Berry, J.A. eds.) pp. 325-338
American Society Plant Physiologist, Rockville, MD.
2. Marcus, Y. Schwarz, R. Friedberg, D. and Kaplan, A.
(1986) Plant Physiol. 82, 610-612.
3. Schwarz, R. Friedberg, D. Reinhold, L. and Kaplan, A.
(1988) Plant Physiol. 88, 284-288.
4. Shinozaki, K. and Sugiura, M. (1985) Gen. Genet. 200,
27-32.
5. Tabita, F.R. and Small, C.L. (1985) Proc. Natl. Acad.
Sci. USA 82, 6100-6103.
6. Codd, G.A. and Marsden, W.J.N. (1984) Biol. Rev. 59,
389-422.
7. Reinhold, L. Zviman, M. and Kaplan, A. (1987) In
Progress in photosynthesis research, (Biggins, J. ed.),.
Vol. 4, p. 289-296, Martinus Nijhoff Publ. Dordrecht.

IDENTIFICATION OF THE GENOMIC REGION WHICH COMPLEMENTS A TEMPERATURE-SENSITIVE, HIGH-CO$_2$ REQUIRING MUTANT OF THE CYANOBACTERIUM, SYNECHOCOCCUS PCC7942.

Eiji Suzuki, Hideya Fukuzawa, Toshihiko Abe[*] and Shigetoh Miyachi Institute of Applied Microbiology, University of Tokyo, Bunkyo-ku, Tokyo 113, Japan [*]Present address: Faculty of Marine Science and Technology, Tokai University, Orido 3-20-1, Shimizu, Shizuoka 424, Japan

1. INTRODUCTION

For the purpose of understanding the nature of inorganic carbon (C$_{inorg}$) transport system, several mutants of Synechococcus PCC7942 (Anacystis nidulans R2) that require high-CO$_2$ concentration for growth have been isolated (1-4). A temperature-sensitive mutant, C3P-O, was reported to be impaired in concentrating C$_{inorg}$ into the cells (4). However, as will be shown in the present study, the lesion caused in this mutant is rather in the ability to utilize the intracellular C$_{inorg}$ pool. The genes that are defective in these mutants remain to be defined. We report here the identification of the wild type genomic region which complements the mutant, C3P-O. The genetic location of the cloned segment relative to rbcLS genes encoding subunits of ribulose-1,5-bisphosphate (RuBP) carboxylase/oxygenase, and the transcription from the cloned genomic region will also be described.

2. MATERIALS AND METHODS

Uptake and fixation of C$_{inorg}$ in the cyanobacterium were determined by silicone oil centrifugation method (4). Transformation of the mutant C3P-O was performed as in (5). The cells were grown in a flat flask (50 ml) with aeration of 5% CO$_2$ at 30°C and harvested with the turbidity at 720 nm of 0.1 to 0.2. They were washed with and resuspended in the culture medium. The suspension was divided into 400 μl, to which 1 to 10 μg of the donor DNA was added. The mixture was shaken in the dark for 20 hours at 30°C. Portions (150 μl each) of the suspension were spread on agar plates and incubated at 42°C in ordinary air with continuous illumination. Discrete colonies became visible in 10 days of incubation.

3. RESULTS AND DISCUSSION

3.1. Photosynthetic characteristics of the mutant C3P-O: Previously, it was reported that the rates of intracellular C$_{inorg}$ accumulation and of photosynthetic CO$_2$ fixation in the mutant C3P-O were reduced to 1/6 and 1/200 that in the wild type, respectively, in

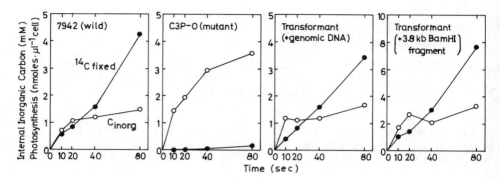

FIGURE 1. Intracellular inorganic carbon accumulation and CO_2 fixation in Synechococcus PCC7942 (wild), C3P-O (mutant) and transformants determined by silicone oil centrifugation method. Culture and assay were performed at 41°C. $NaH^{14}CO_3$ (50 μM) was added at pH 7.8.

the presence of 55 μM $NaH^{14}CO_3$ (4). The ability to take up and fix C_{inorg} was re-examined with wild and the mutant strains at 41°C, the non-permissive temperature (Fig. 1). The decreased level of intracellular C_{inorg} in the mutant was not reproducible. In contrast, the severe impairment of fixing the intracellular C_{inorg} was consistently observed. The rate of CO_2 fixation in the mutant was 1/30 that in the wild type. The observed level of intracellular C_{inorg} concentration in the mutant was nearly 2 times higher than in the wild type, possibly due to the blockage of C_{inorg} consumption for its fixation. Therefore, it is much more likely that the mutant C3P-O is deficient in utilizing intracellular C_{inorg} pool for CO_2 assimilation. It is possible that the mutant phenotype resulted from the defective RuBP carboxylase with higher K_m for CO_2. Thus, the extracts from the mutant and the wild strains were assayed for the enzyme activity at 41°C. However, the RuBP carboxylase activity at different concentrations of added $NaHCO_3$ was similar between the mutant and the wild strains.

3.2. Cloning of the wild type genomic region which complements the mutant: Genomic DNA of the wild strain was digested with EcoRI, size-fractionated by electrophoresis on a 0.5% low melting point agarose gel, and used to transform the mutant to the wild phenotype (capable to form colonies at 42°C under ordinary air). A fraction containing ≥20 kb EcoRI fragments which gave the maximum frequency of transformation was ligated to a shuttle plasmid vector, pECAN8 (6) to construct a sub-genomic library in Escherichia coli JM109. Among 107 recombinant plasmids, 3 independent clones were found to complement the mutant. The same restriction pattern was observed with these 3 clones. One of them, designated as pEC36, had an insert of approximately 36 kb

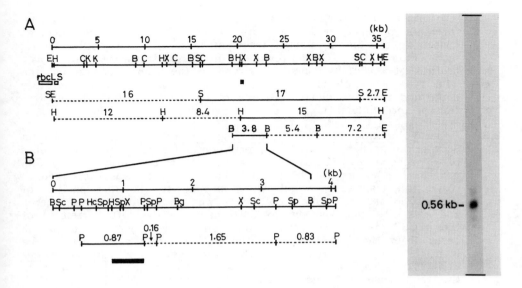

FIGURE 2. (left) Physical maps of the pEC36 insert (**A**) and of the 3.8 kb BamHI fragment (**B**). Restriction fragments were subcloned as indicated. Numbers represent lengths of the subclones in kb. Subclones depicted with solid lines were capable of transforming the mutant, while those depicted with broken lines were not. Closed boxes: the region which was defective in the mutant. Open boxes: location of rbcLS genes. Restriction sites were abbreviated as follows: B=BamHI, Bg=BglII, C=ClaI, E=EcoRI, H=HindIII, Hc=HincII, K=KpnI, P=PstI, S=SmaI, Sc=SacI, Sp=SphI, X=XhoI.

FIGURE 3. (right) Transcription of the cloned genomic region as analyzed by Northern hybridization. RNA (10 μg) was electrophoresed on a 1% agarose gel containing 0.7 M formaldehyde, transferred to Zeta-Probe (BioRad) and hybridized with the ^{32}P-labeled 0.87 kb PstI fragment. The RNA was prepared from cells exposed to low-CO_2 for 2 hours.

in length (Fig. 2). Restriction fragments derived from pEC36 were subcloned into pUC19. Transformation of C3P-O was observed with the subclones containing 17 kb SmaI-, 15 kb HindIII-, 3.8 kb BamHI- and 0.87 kb PstI-fragments. The transformant colonies were not obtained with the other subclones. Among the positive subclones, the 15 kb HindIII fragment overlapped only the right portion of the 0.87 kb PstI fragment by approximately 0.4 kb. The result indicated that the mutation in C3P-O resided in the genomic region corresponding to 0.4 kb HindIII-PstI fragment.

Uptake and fixation of C_{inorg} were determined in the transformants obtained with the total genomic DNA or the subclone containing the 3.8 kb BamHI fragment (Fig. 1). The ability to fix intracellular C_{inorg} was restored in these transformants. The profiles of the time courses observed in the transformants and the wild type were closely analogous to one another. It is therefore confirmed that the cloned genomic region is involved in the utilization of intracellular C_{inorg} pool in Synechococcus PCC7942.

3.3. Genetic location of the cloned segment relative to rbc operon: Southern hybridization with a probe containing rbcL and rbcS genes of Synechococcus PCC6301 (7) showed that the insert of pEC36 contained a portion of rbc genes. The rbc probe was hybridized to restriction fragments, which were mapped to the left portion of the pEC36 insert. One EcoRI site was found in the rbc operon and this site was thought to correspond to the left extremity of the pEC36 insert. The nucleotide sequence was determined for 43 bases from the EcoRI site on the pEC36 insert and shown to be identical to that found in the rbc genes of Synechococcus PCC6301. The 43-base segment started near the 3' terminus in the rbcL gene and ended within the spacer region between rbcL and rbcS genes. The genetic region which complements C3P-O was therefore located approximately 20 kb downstream from the rbc operon (Fig. 2).

3.4. Transcription from the cloned genomic region: Total RNA prepared from the wild type of Synechococcus PCC7942 was analyzed by Northern hybridization with the 0.87 kb PstI fragment of the cloned genomic region as the probe (Fig. 3). Messenger RNA of about 560 bases was detected as the almost single species. Thus, the cloned genomic region was actually transcribed in these cells.

REFERENCES

1 Marcus, Y., Schwarz, R., Friedberg, D. and Kaplan, A. (1986) Plant Physiol. 82, 610-612
2 Ogawa, T., Kaneda, T. and Omata, T. (1987) Plant Physiol. 84, 711-715
3 Schwarz, R., Friedberg, D. and Kaplan, A. (1988) Plant Physiol. 88, 284-288
4 Abe, T., Tsuzuki, M., Kadokami, Y. and Miyachi, S. (1988) Plant Cell Physiol. 29, 1353-1360
5 Golden, S.S., Brusslan, J. and Haselkorn, R. (1987) Methods Enzymol. 153, 215-231
6 Lau, R.H. and Straus, N.A. (1985) FEMS Microbiol. Lett. 27, 253-256
7 Shinozaki, K., Yamada, C., Takahata, N. and Sugiura, M. (1983) Proc. Natl. Acad. Sci. USA 80, 4050-4054

MOLECULAR ANALYSIS OF MUTANTS OF <u>SYNECHOCYSTIS</u> PCC6803 DEFECTIVE IN INORGANIC CARBON TRANSPORT

Teruo Ogawa[1], John G.K. Williams[2] and Tatsuo Omata[1]
[1]Solar Energy Research Group, The Institute of Physical and Chemical Research(RIKEN), Wako, Saitama 351-01, Japan and [2]E173/108 Central Research and Development Department, E.I. DuPont de Nemours & Company, Wilmington, DE 19898.

1. INTRODUCTION

Cyanobacteria possess a CO_2-concentrating mechanism which involves active transport of inorganic carbon (C_i). The molecular mechanism of the C_i-transporting system is not yet understood but it might be studied with the aid of mutants defective in C_i transport. Several mutants of <u>Synechococcus</u> PCC7942 which require high CO_2 for growth have been reported [1-3]. All of these mutants, however, showed the activity of C_i transport comparative to that in the wild type (WT) cells. To date, mutants of cyanobacteria defective in C_i transport have not been obtained.

We have succeeded in isolating mutants (RKa and RKb) of <u>Synechocystis</u> PCC6803 which are defective in C_i transport. One of these mutants, RKb, was transformed with a genomic library of WT <u>Synechocystis</u> DNA and a clone capable of restoring the ability of the mutant to grow under low CO_2 conditions was isolated from the library. A mutant (M9) defective in C_i transport was constructed following insertion of an aminoglycoside 3'-phosphotransferase gene at the site very close to the mutation site in the RKb mutant. Analysis of nucleotide sequence of the WT gene in the region of the mutation revealed an open-reading frame coding a protein which may be essential for C_i transport.

2. MATERIALS AND METHODS

Wild type (WT) and mutant cells of <u>Synechocystis</u> PCC6803 were grown at 30°C in BG-11 medium [4] supplemented with 10 mM Tes-NaOH buffer (pH 8.0) under aeration with 3% CO_2 in air. High CO_2-requiring mutants of <u>Synechocystis</u> were isolated following mutagenesis by N-methyl-N'-nitrosoguanidine (MNNG) and ampiciline enrichment as previously described [2].

A clone which complements the RKb mutant was isolated from a genomic library of WT <u>Synechocystis</u> DNA constructed in PUC18, by the

M. Baltscheffsky (ed.), Current Research in Photosynthesis, Vol. IV, 471–474.

aid of observation that cloned DNA in liquid applied directly onto the lawn of the mutant led to recovery of its ability to grow under low CO_2 conditions [5]. The cloned gene fragment was interrupted by the aminoglycoside 3'-phosphotransferase gene [the "kanamycin resistance (K_m^r) cartridge" that originated from the bacterial transposon Tn5]. The nucleotide sequences were determined using a DuPont DNA analysis system (Genesis^{TM} 2000).

3. RESULTS AND DISCUSSION
3.1 **Mutants Defective in C_i Transport**

High CO_2-requiring mutants were isolated from Synechocystis PCC6803 following MNNG treatment and their CO_2 uptake was measured using a mass spectrometer. Out of 70 mutants examined, two mutants (RKa and RKb) showed very low activity of CO_2 uptake; the rest of the mutants showed the activity as high as that in WT and appear to be the mutants similar in their physiological properties to those of Synechococcus [1-3]. Under high CO_2, the growth rate of RKa and RKb was

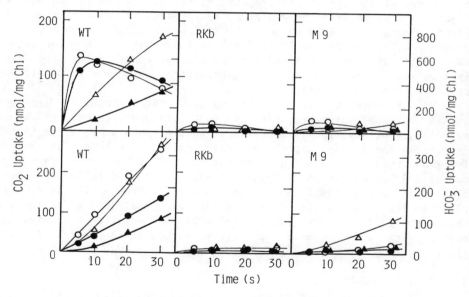

Fig. 1. Changes in intracellular C_i pool (upper panels) and photosynthetic products (lower panels) of WT, RKb and M9 cells with incubation time in the light, measured by the silicone-oil centrifugation method. ●,▲: high-CO_2 cells; ○,△: cells exposed to low CO_2 for 20 h; ●,○: $^{14}CO_2$ (9.9 μM, final concentration) was added; ▲,△: $H^{14}CO_3^-$ (149 μM) was added.

similar to that of WT. The growth of these mutants was very slow under low CO_2. Measurements of $^{14}CO_2$ and $H^{14}CO_3^-$ uptake into intracellular C_i pool (acid-labile ^{14}C) or photosynthetic products (acid-stable ^{14}C) indicated that the activities in the RKb mutant were less than 5% of those in WT (Fig. 1). Similar results were obtained with the RKa mutant. Thus, RKa and RKb are the mutants defective in C_i transport. Further studies were done with the RKb mutant.

3.2 A Region of a <u>Synechocystis</u> Genome Required for C_i Transport

The clone which complemented the RKb mutant contained a 5.2-kbp DNA insert. Fig. 2 shows the restriction map of a part of this DNA insert. Deletion of 591-bp nucleotides from the Hind III site led to the loss of the clone to complement the mutant while deletion of 450-bp nucleotides had no effect. Thus the site of mutation in RKb is in the range between 450 and 591-bp nucleotides from the Hind III site.

A K_m^r cartridge was inserted to the cloned gene at the site between two Spe I sites and the construct was used to transform WT <u>Synechocystis</u> PCC6803 into kanamycin resistance. Growth rate of the transformant (M9) in the presence of kanamycin was high under high CO_2 conditions but was very low under low CO_2 conditions. The transformants obtained following insertion of K_m^r at the site of either Nhe I, Bal I/Bal I or Pst I were able to grow under low CO_2 as well as under high CO_2 conditions. The activities of $^{14}CO_2$ and $H^{14}CO_3^-$ uptake into acid-stable and acid-labile products were very low with the M9 transformant (Fig. 1). Thus, M9 is the mutant which has similar characteristics to RKb. These data indicates that the clone contains DNA sequence in the region of two Spe I sites which is essential for C_i transport.

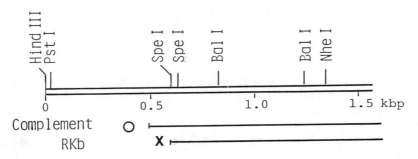

Fig. 2. Restriction map of a part of the 5.2-kbp Hind III/Pst I fragment cloned into PUC18. There was a Pst I site which was undigested during construction of the gene library. The DNA fragments which did or did not complement the RKb mutant are shown by the bars.

Nucleotide sequence between the Hind III and Bal I sites was analyzed and the sequence in the region of the Spe I sites is shown in Fig. 3. There is an open reading frame in this region which codes a protein consists of 80 amino acids. The protein is highly hydrophobic and, therefore, seems to be membrane-bound. The role of this protein is not known. The presence of residual activity of C_i transport in the M9 mutant (Fig. 1) suggested that the protein is not a C_i transporter but is an essential component to drive the C_i-transporting system.

```
cccgtcttcagaatgtgaggcccattattcttccgaataacaatcatttctgtagataat    362
aaattccttccttgctttagcaggcaagattggttcacaatttgattgggccattgcccc    422
attaccctaaccccgccaggattatggaagatttattaggtttgctactttctgaaacc     482
                  M  E  D  L  L  G  L  L  L  S  E  T
ggtttattggcgataatttatctaggcctaagcctagcctatctattggttttttccagcc   542
 G  L  L  A  I  I  Y  L  G  L  S  L  A  Y  L  L  V  F  P  A
cttttgtattggtatttgcaaaagcgttggtacgtggctagttccgtcgaaagactagtc    602
 L  L  Y  W  Y  L  Q  K  R  W  Y  V  A  S  S  V  E  R  L  V
atgtattttttggtctttctcttcttccctgggttactagtgctcagtccggtgctgaat   662
 M  Y  F  L  V  F  L  F  F  P  G  L  L  V  L  S  P  V  L  N
ctacgaccccgccgccaggctgcctagattttgcttttgtttagtctctaactgagtcgg   722
 L  R  P  R  R  Q  A  A  *
ctgttactccagacccagttgccgtgttttttttgttgcccattgttcccattgtcatcc   782
```

Fig. 3. Nucleotide sequence of a part of a 821-bp fragment from Synechocystis PCC6803 DNA, in the region of mutation in the RKb mutant. Nucleotides are numbered from the Hind III site. The deduced amino acid sequence from the open reading frame between nucleotides 447 and 687 is included. The Spe I sites are underlined.

REFERENCES

1. Marcus, Y., Schwarz, R., Friedberg, D. and Kaplan, A. (1986) Plant Physiol. 82, 610-612.
2. Ogawa, T., Kaneda T. and Omata, T. (1987) Plant Physiol. 84, 711-715.
3. Schwarz, R., Friedberg, D. and Kaplan, A. (1988) Plant Physiol. 88, 284-288.
4. Stanier, R.Y., Kunisawa, M., Mandel, M. and Cohen-Bazire, G. (1971) Bacteriol. Rev. 35, 171-205.
5. Dzelkalns, V.A. and Bogorad, L. (1988) EMBO J. 7, 333-338.

Is Carbonic Anhydrase Required for Photosynthesis?

C.A. Roeske[1], J.M. Widholm[2], and W.L. Ogren[3], [1]Department of Plant Biology and [2]Agronomy at the University of Illinois, and [3]USDA-ARS, Urbana, IL 61801

1. Introduction
Despite the isolation and biochemical characterization of plant carbonic anhydrase, understanding of its physiological role lags far behind that of the vertebrate enzyme. The hypothetical functions of carbonic anahydrase in plants include facilitated diffusion of CO_2 across membranes, supplying CO_2 to ribulosebisphosphate carboxylase when there is a local depletion, and catalysis of buffering by HCO_3^- or CO_2. Photoautotrophic cell suspension cultures which exhibit the photosynthetic properties of leaf cells generally have been found to contain little or no carbonic anhydrase, whether grown at 660 ppm or 5% CO_2(C.A. Roeske, unpublished). The exception is a soybean cell culture that has leaf-like levels of the enzyme (2670 IU/mg Chl). The location of isozymes of carbonic anhydrase, activity *in vivo*, and CO_2 response curves of the two cell lines are presented below.

2. PROCEDURE
2.1. Materials and Methods
   2.1.1. Photoautotrophic cells were grown at 660 ppm or 5% CO_2 under continuous light in a modified MS medium (1,2).
   2.1.2. CO_2 response curve. Cells were suspended in 30 mM MOPS, pH 7.0, with 200 IU/ml carbonic anhydrase. The sealed vials were flushed with 21% O_2 for 10 min in the light. Reactions were initiated with $NaH^{14}CO_3$ and quenched with 3N formic acid in methanol.
   2.1.3. ^{18}O-exchange. Cells were suspended in 10 mM HEPES, pH 7.35, over a membrane inlet to a gas analyzer(2). Reactions were initiated with $H^{13}C^{18}O_3^-$. The final concentration was 0.5 mM C_i. Data was analysed as described previously (3).
   2.1.4. Immunoblots. Cells were homogenized in liquid N_2 in 30 mM Tris, pH 9.0; 14 mM β-mercaptoethanol, 2 μM leupeptin, 2 μM antipain, and 100 μM benzamidine. Proteins in the crude extract or in an 80% acetone precipitate of the extract were separated by polyacrylamide gel electrophoresis. Immunoblots were prepared with antibodies to spinach carbonic anhydrase or *Chlamydomonas reinhardtii* phosphoribulokinase. Antibody bands were purified by selective elution off nitrocellulose (4).

M. Baltscheffsky (ed.), Current Research in Photosynthesis, Vol. IV, 475–478.
© 1990 *Kluwer Academic Publishers. Printed in the Netherlands.*

2.3.5. Carbonic anhydrase activity in native gels. Enzyme activity was visualized with bromothymol blue (5). Protein was extracted with 30 mM Tris, pH 9.0, 14 mM β-mercaptoethanol and 1% SDS.

2.3.6. Chloroplast isolation. Photoautotrophic cells were digested with 0.2% pectinase and 2% cellulase. Chloroplasts were isolated from ruptured protoplasts (6). Chloroplasts were isolated from homogenized leaves by centrifugation on a Percoll gradient (7).

3. RESULTS AND DISCUSSION

3.1. The levels of carbonic anhydrase in photoautotrophic cell suspension cultures (See Introduction) were verified by immunoblotting. Extracts of photoautotrophic soybean cells, containing 2 μg protein, gave 2 bands at about 30 kD. Two similar bands were observed in extracts of soybean leaves. Extracts of cotton cells, containing 20 μg protein, showed a single very faint band.

3.2. Despite the large difference in amount of carbonic anhydrase, the cotton and soybean cells have about the same $K_{1/2}(CO_2)$ for photosynthesis, 37 ± 3 μM and 39 ± 5 μM CO_2, respectively.

3.3. Enzyme activity in photoautotrophic cotton cells and soybean leaf cells was measured by ^{18}O-exchange form $^{13}C^{18}O_2$. The equations describing the exchange in the model in Figure 1 were used to derive the rate constants given in Table 1.

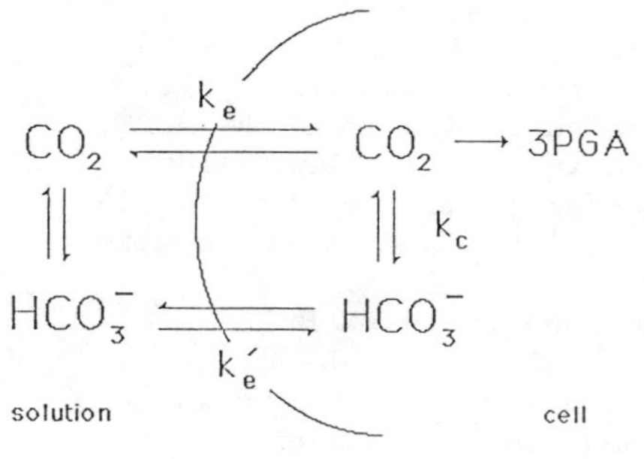

Figure 1. Model for CO_2, HCO_3^- interconversion in a cell.

TABLE 1. Rate constants for ^{18}O-exchange in cells.

	k_c (sec^{-1})	k_e (sec^{-1})	k_e' (sec^{-1})
Cotton cells (n=3)	39±6	0.54±0.13	1.0±0.3x10^{-2}
Soybean leaf cells	2500	2.4	1.2x10^{-2}

These rate constants indicate that CO_2 is the major form of inorganic carbon entering the cells. The rate of CO_2, HCO_3^- interconversion at $10\mu M$ CO_2 in the low-carbonic anhydrase cotton cells is 3600 $\mu mol/mg$ Chl·h, about 60 times faster than the rate of CO_2-fixation. This model cannot be used to determine the relative extent of ^{18}O-exchange in different locations within the cell.

3.4. The existence of isozymes in photoautotrophic soybean cells, and in soybean and pea leaves, was verified by polyacrylamide gel electrophoresis. Two high molecular weight bands of active enzyme were visualized with bromothymol blue in a native gel and correspond to the bands visible in the immunoblot. Only the lower band was visible in protein from isolated chloroplasts. In addition, the two bands visible on the immunoblot of an SDS gel were shown to both be carbonic anhydrase. Antibodies bound to each of the two bands of carbonic anhydrase (CA) were eluted and found to cross-react. Chloroplasts isolated from pea leaf and photoautotrophic soybean cells contained only the lower molecular weight band on both native and SDS gels. The lower band was shown to contain only the chloroplast enzyme by using a gel scanner to compare the amount present with the amount of phosphoribulokinase (PRK). The ratio of CA to PRK in 2-10 μg chloroplast protein was 7.3 ± 0.9, the same as 6.8 ± 0.6 measured in cell protein. Immunoblots of of protein from the low-carbonic anhydrase cotton suspension culture cells, which possess activity, showed a weak band corresponding to the one band of cotton leaf carbonic anhydrase. Chloroplasts isolated from these cells also contain the enzyme.

3.5. The cotton suspension cells examined contained only a low amount of carbonic anhydrase activity, at least some of which, and perhaps all, appeared to be associated with the chloroplast. Thus, there may be a requirement for this low amount of chloroplast carbonic anhydrase in photoautotrophic cell suspension cultures. Whether the enzyme is directly involved in supplying CO_2 to ribulosebisphosphate carboxylase is unclear. The higher levels of carbonic anhydrase found in leaves may be required to deal with transitory changes not found under the growth conditions of the cells, or may aid in CO_2 diffusion in the more complex morphology of the leaf.

4.REFERENCES
1 Blair, L.C., Chastain, C.J. and Widholm, J.M. (1988) Plant Cell Reports 7, 266-269
2 Horn, M.E., Sherrard, J.H., and Widholm, J.M. (1983) Plant Physiol. 72, 426-429
3 Tu, C.K., Wynns, G.C., McMurray, R.E., and Silverman, D.N. (1978) J. Biol. Chem. 253, 8178-8184
4 Werneke, J.M., Zielinski, R.E., and Ogren, W.L. (1988) Proc. Nat. Acad. Sci. USA 85, 787-791

5 Atkins, C.A., Patterson, B.D., and Graham, D. (1972) Plant Physiol. 50, 218-223
6 Robinson, S.P. (1987) Methods in Enzymology 148, 188-194
7 Robinson, S.P., and Porits, Jr., A.R. (1988) Plant Physiol. 86, 293-298

5. ACKNOWLEDGEMENTS
^{18}O-exchange experiments were done with C.K. Tu and D.N. Silverman at the University of Florida. Antibodies for carbonic anhydrase and phosphoribulokinase were gifts of C.R. Somerville, University of Michigan, and K.R. Roessler, University of Illinois.

This work was funded in part by the McKnight Foundation.

CARBONIC ANHYDRASE ACTIVITY IN BARLEY LEAVES AFTER TREATMENT
WITH ABSCISIC ACID AND JASMONIC ACID

L.P. Popova, G. N. Lazova
Institute of Plant Physiology, Bulgarian Academy of Sciences
1113 Sofia

1. INTRODUCTION

It is well established that ABA inhibits the rate of
photosynthetic CO_2 fixation and of O_2 evolution (1,5,6,8,10)
raises the rate of photorespiration (9) and changes the
activity of some enzymes of carbon and nitrogen metabolism
(2,8,12).
A similar mode of action on the above photosynthetic
parameter has been reported about another growth regulator-
Jasmonic acid (JA) (10). To a certain extent the action of
JA is similar to the inhibiting effect of ABA on the processes of germination and ageing, and also similar in the maner
of effect on the stomata and on the protein hydrolysis (14,
17). In its chemical structure and methods of synthesis JA
is very close to the group of the prostanoids which, in the
case of animals are known to belong to the class of stress-
related hormones (19).
It is also known that ABA is produced in the leaves of
plants under a variety of stress conditons, on account of
which it has been included in the group of stress phytohor-
mones (20). The assumption is that the common link between
enviromental stress and reductions in photosynthetic capacity may be ABA (15).
The common response of plants to a variety of enviromental stress and to exogenous application of ABA and JA is
closing the stomata and reduction the intercellular $CO_2(C_i)$.
This may be only one of the reasons for observed decrease in
the capacity for photosynthetic CO_2 assimilation. At both
types of effect there appears a decrease in the activity of
RuBPCase, whereas the activity of PEPCase in some cases was
stimulated, while in others it remains unaffected (13,8,11).
It is possible to assume that under these conditions
the atmospheric CO_2 is fixed initially in the cytoplasm by
PEPCase. Since the substrate of PEPCase is HCO_3^-, the expectation is that hydration of CO_2 will take place with the participation of Carbonic Anhydrase (CA) which will provide
the entry of CO_2 into the cytoplasm and its transfer to the

M. Baltscheffsky (ed.), Current Research in Photosynthesis, Vol. IV, 479–483.
© 1990 Kluwer Academic Publishers. Printed in the Netherlands.

site of RuBPCase action in chloroplasts. These reactions
will operate as an adaptive mechanism for CO_2 assimilation
in C_3 plants.
   This assumption determines our interest in the investigation of CA activity under conditions of exogenous treatment of barley seedling with ABA and JA.
2.   MATERIALS AND METHODS
   Plant material - The experiments were out with barley
(Hordeum vulgare, L.var.Alfa) cultivated for 7 days on water solutions of ABA and JA in concentrations of 10^{-6}M, 10^{-5}
M and 10^{-4}M. The seedlings grew in a growth chamber as dis-
cribed in 9 and 10.
   Preparation of leaf extracts - Leaf tissue from the
middle section of the leaf was ground in a mortar with 10
volumes of 0.01 M Tris-glycine buffer, pH 8.3 and 5% sucrose at 4°C. After centrifugation at 8.000 g for 20 min., the
supernatant was removed and used for assay of enzyme activities.
   Isolation of cfloroplasts - Chloroplasts were isolated
according to the method of James and Das (1957). The percentage of intact chloroplasts was determined by measuring O_2-
evolution with $K_3Fe(CN)_6$ before and after osmotic shock. The ex-
trachloroplasts fractions were centrifuged at 20.000 g for
20 min and supernatants were used for CA activity determination. To distrupt the chloroplasts they were placed in hypo-
tonic buffer (without sucrose) for 10 min. The suspensions
were centrifuged at 20.000 g. for 20 min and supernatant solutions containing the solube components from chloroplasts
were used for determination of CA activity.
   Carbonic Anhydrase assay - CA activity was assayed according to the method of Rickli et al.(1964), with a certain
modification. The reaction mixture contained 2.5 ml of 0.025
M KH_2PO_4 buffer, pH 8.3 and phenol rot (2.5 mg.per 100 ml.).
Enzyme solution 0.1 ml. of appropriate concentration (0.15-
0.20 mg.for cytoplasmic CA and 0.06-0.10 mg.for stromal CA)
was added and 2.5 ml of cold $KHCO_3$ was injected into the assay mixture. The rate of non-catalyzed reaction was recorded
from the moment of injection on $KHCO_3$ to a change in the colour of the indicator form yellow to orange. The enzyme activity was calculated as difference in the seconds between
the control and the catalitic reactions and was expressed as
μM CO_2min-1. mg.pr.$^{-1}$.
   Protein was determined by the method of Lowry et al.
(1951) with BSA as standard.
3.   RESULTS AND DISCUTION
   The results obtained indicate that the extractable activity of CA is higer in plants cultivated on ABA and JA solutions, in relation to the control plants (Table 1).
   The percentage of stimulation for ABA is best expressed at 10^{-5}M, while in the case of JA the three investigated
concentrations have a positive effect without any essetial

Table 1: Carbonic Anhydrase activity in leaf extracts of barley after treatment with Abscisic acid and Jasmonic acid.

Concentration (M)	Activity (μM $CO_2 min^{-1} mg.pr^{-1}$)-% of control				
	Abscisic acid		Jasmonic acid		
H_2O(controls)	3906 ± 282	100.0	4224 ± 67	100.0	
10^{-6}	4382 ± 234	112.2	6108[***] ±375	144.6	
10^{-5}	6088[**] ± 280	155.9	5729[***] ±493	135.6	
10^{-4}	5102[**] ± 178	130.6	5616[**] ±406	132.9	

Data are averages of four experiments ± SE
([*] $P < 0.05$,[***]) $P < 0.01$

concentration dependence.
It has been recorgnized from a number of studies that CA is localized in the chloroplasts of C_3 plants where its percentage content ranges according to the plant species, from 86% to 95% (16). In C_4 plants CA is localized in the cytoplasm of mesophyll cells, there is only a little CA activity in bundle sheath cells (4). In this type of plants the function of CA is hydration on the atmospheric CO_2 to HCO_3^- in cytoplasm where it is directly used by PEPCase. Since CA is responsible for the reversible hydration of CO_2 and for regulating the equilibrium between CO_2 and HCO_3^- , in both types of plants the enzyme can efficiently provide carbon substrate for the carboxylase reactions.
That is was necessary to investigate the intracellular compartmentation of CA in barley leaves and to establish which one of the two forms is influenced by ABA and JA.
Our results show that about 95% of barley CA localized in the chloroplast stroma (Table 2).

Table 2: Effect of Abscisic acid and Jasmonic acid on the activity and distribution of Carbonic Anhydrase in barley leaves.

Concentration (M)	Activity (μM $CO_2 min^{-1} mg.pr^{-1}$)		% of distr.	
Abscisic acid	cytoplasm	stroma	cytoplasm	stroma
H_2O (controls)	284 (100.0)	4629(100.0)	5.8	94.2
10^{-6}	384 (135.2)	6334(136.8)	5.7	94.3
10^{-5}	666 (234.5)	5376(116.1)	11.0	89.0
10^{-4}	664 (233.8)	4087(88.3)	14.0	86.1
Jasmonic acid				
H_2O(controls)	250 (100.0)	4915(100.0)	4.8	95.1
10^{-6}	666 (266.4)	6766(137.7)	9.0	91.0
10^{-5}	874 (349.6)	5171(105.3)	14.4	85.5
10^{-4}	1146 (458.4)	6242(127.0)	15.5	84.5

The activity of cytoplasmic CA is much higer in plants

cultivated on ABA and JA solutions. The stimulating effect
of ABA is between 135% and 235% depending on the concentration, while for JA it ranges from 266% for 10^{-6}M to 458%
for 10^{-4}M. On that background the stimulation observed on
the stromal CA is insignificant. One possible assumption to
explain the observed effect of ABA and JA is that these
plant grouwth regulators induced de novo synthesis of CA.
Acording to CA protein was synthesized in the cytoplasm by
a nuclear gene transported into chloroplasts. Our data abou
the percentage distribution of CA in the two fractions (Table 2) show an increase of the relative share of cytoplasmic
CA, and are to a certain extent in support of the assumptio
about induced de nóvo synthesis of this form of CA under th
influence of ABA and JA. These data are only an indirect
confirmation of the idea which needs to be proved by additional experiments.

As regards the function of CA upon exogenous treatment
with ABA and JA (and probably also upon stress cQnditions),
in may be assume that it participates in the adaptation of
C_3 plants to low CO_2 concentrations. We assume that the
reactions taking pláce are the following:

$$CO_2 \xrightarrow{\text{Carbonic Anhydrase}} HCO_3^- \xrightarrow{\text{PEPCase}} \text{Oxalacetic acid}$$

In chloroplasts oxalacetic acid could be reduceꞁ to malic
acid (by NADP-malate dehydrogenase) and this acid could be
decarboxylated and will regenerate the substrate for PEPCase
Another reaction is also possible - oxalacetic acid to be
directly decarboxylated by oxalacetate decarboxylase. In
either case the decarboxylase reactions will strengthen the
flow of CO_2 to RuBPCase and will contribute to the better
operation of Calvin cycle.

REFERENCES

1. Bauer, R., Huber, W.and Sankhla, N.,(1976), Z. Pflanzenphysiol., 77, 237-246,
2. Huber, W., and Sankhla, N., (1974), 116, 55-64.
3. James, W.C., and Das, V.S.R., (1957), New Photobiologist,
   56, 325-329.
4. Ku, S.B., and Edwards, G.E., (1975), Z. Pflanzenphysiol.
77, 16-32.
5. Maslenkova, L.T., Zanev, Yu., and Popova, L.P., (1989),
   Photosynth.Research, 21, 45-50.
6. Mittelheuser, C.J., and Van Stevinski, R.F.M.,(1971), Plant
   97, 83-86.
7. Okabe, K., Yang, S.Y., Tsuzuki, M., Miyachi, S., (1984),
   Plant Sci.Lett., 33, 145-153.
8. Popova, L.P., Dimitrova, O.D., and Vaklinova, S.G.,
   (1982), C.R.Acad.Bulg.Sci, 35, 1291-1294.
9. Popova, L.P., Tsonev, T.D., and Vaklinova, S.G.,(1987),

Plant Physiol., 83, 820-824.
10. Popova, L.P., Tsonev, T.D., and Vaklinova, S.G., (1988),
    J.Plant Physiol., 132, 257-261.
11. Salcheva, S.G., and Popova, L.P., (1982), C.R.Bulg.Acad.
Sci, 35, 973-976.
12. Sankla, N., and Huber, W.,(1974), Phytochemistry, 13,
    543-546.
13. Sankhla, N., and Huber, W., (1975), Z. Pflanzenphysiol.,
    74, 267-271.
14. Satler, S.O., and Thimann, T.V., (1981), C.R.Acad.Sci.
    Paris, Serie 3, 293, 735-740.
15. Seemann, J.R., and Sharkey, T.D., (1987), Plant Physiol.
    84, 696-700.
16. Tsuzuki, M., Miyachi, S., and Edwards, G.E., (1985),
    Plant Cell Physiol., 26, 881-891.
17. Weidhase, R.A., Lehmann, J., Kramell, H., Sembdner, G.,
    and Partheier, H., (1987), Physiol.Plant., 69, 161-166.
18. Rickli, E.E., Gharanfar, S.A.S., Gibbon, B.H.,ᵛEdsall,
    J.T., (1964), J.Biol.Chem., 239, 1065-1078.
19. Wolff, L.P., (1982), J.Neurochem., 38, 1-14.
20. Zeevaart, J.A., (1988), Ann.Rev.Plant Physiol., 39,
    439-473.

ISOLATION OF CARBONIC ANHYDRASE FROM THE HIGHER PLANT
PISUM SATIVUM.

NATHALIE MAJEAU AND JOHN R. COLEMAN, Centre for Plant
Biotechnology, Dept. of Botany, University of Toronto,
Ontario, CANADA M5S 3B2

1. INTRODUCTION
     The enzyme carbonic anhydrase is considered to be
one of the more abundant proteins in the C_3 plant
chloroplast, second only to ribulose-1,5-bisphosphate
carboxylase (Rubisco) in concentration (1,2). Its role
in photosynthesis however, has remained somewhat
elusive. Functionally, the enzyme is capable of rapidly
interconverting the major forms of inorganic carbon
(C_i), and therefore speeds the formation of CO_2 from
HCO_3^- as the CO_2 is consumed by Rubisco. In the absence
of carbonic anhydrase (CA), the dehydration of the HCO_3^-
in the alkaline interior of the stroma would be so slow
that the maximal rate of photosynthesis would be impeded
(3). It is also thought that the rapid hydration of the
CO_2 molecule immediately after diffusion across the
chloroplast membrane facilitates the the movement of CO_2
into this organelle. The catalysis of the hydration
reaction maintains the gradient for CO_2 diffusion at a
maximimum. The absolute magnitude of the gradient is a
function of the activity of Rubisco and the pH gradient
across the chloroplast membrane. Other proposed roles
for this polypeptide have been more concerned with its
ability to maintain the ionic balance between the
various compartments of the chloroplast by catalysis of
the CO_2/HCO_3^- exchange reaction (2). The localization
of CA activity to non-photosynthetic regions of the
plant, such as root and nodule tissue, are perhaps
indicative of this additional role (2,4). Little is
known about the regulation of CA expression in higher
plants. Some studies have suggested that higher plant
CA activities are regulated by CO_2 concentrations (5) as
has been shown for cyanobacteria and various eukaryotic
algae (6). As an initial step in the study of CA
expression in plants, we have isolated a cDNA clone
coding for the CA polypeptide in pea leaves.

M. Baltscheffsky (ed.), Current Research in Photosynthesis, Vol. IV, 485–488.
© 1990 *Kluwer Academic Publishers. Printed in the Netherlands.*

2. MATERIALS AND METHODS

Leaves and stems of 3-week old peas (Pisum sativum var.Little Marvel) were homogenized in 0.3 M Tris-SO$_4$, pH 8.3 with a Waring blender for 1 min, filtered through Miracloth and then clarified by centrifugation at 30,000 x g for 40 min. The supernatant was collected and subjected to (NH$_4$)$_2$SO$_4$ fractionation. The 30-60 % saturation precipitate was resuspended and dialyzed against 5 mM Tris-SO$_4$, pH 9.5 and then charged onto an affinity column (p-methylaminobenzene sulphonamide substituted Sepharose 4B) as previously described (11). Sephadex G-200 chromatography (8) native and SDS polyacrylamide electrophoresis (8), fluorescence detection of CA activity (12) and Western transfers and staining (7) were all performed as previously described. Following collection of the preimmune serum, rabbits were immunized with the purified CA using a standard immunization schedule (7). Polyclonal antisera against the pea CA was tested using Western blotting techniques and was then used to screen a pea leaf cDNA library constructed in the phage gt11 (13). The protocols for screening the library, immunodetection of positive clones and isolation of recombinant phage DNA have been described (7,9).

RESULTS AND DISCUSSION

Carbonic anhydrase from Pisum sativum has been purified by affinity chromatography and SDS-PAGE. In Fig. 1, the series of purification steps are described and the polypeptide profiles of the active fractions are shown. For comparison, the polypeptides eluted from a section of a native PAG exhibiting CA activity are also shown. CA activity in all purification steps was found to be associated with a polypeptide doublet of 25.5 kDa and 27.5 kDa which is similar to other reported CA monomeric weights (2). The two bands may be the product of proteolytic cleavage during the isolation (even though inhibitors were present) or may represent two distinct monomeric species. Previous studies have suggested that both chloroplastic and cytosolic forms of CA exist in pea (2,10). A polyclonal antibody generated against the CA doublet cross-reacts with the 25.5/27.5 kDa proteins (Fig. 1, lane I) and was used to screen a pea leaf cDNA expression library constructed in the phage gt11 (Fig. 2). Twelve positive signals were found to be true immuno-positive clones after rescreening at lower plaque densities. One of these clones was amplified and the 0.95 kb EcoRI insert into the vector pBS and subjected to restriction endonuclease mapping. Southern analysis, using this clone as a probe of the 11 other immuno-positive clones revealed that 9 have strong

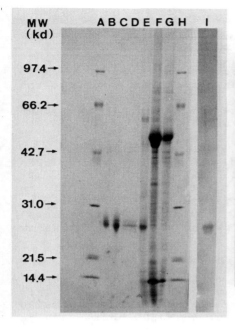

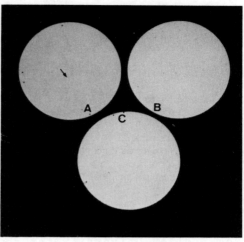

Figure 1. Purification of pea carbonic anhydrase. The figure shows a Coomassie Blue stained, 7-15% linear gradient, SDS polyacrlyamide gel (PAG) loaded with: total soluble protein (lane G), 30-60% $(NH_4)_2SO_4$ precipitate (lane F), eluate from the affinity column chromatography (lane E) and after excision and electroelution from an SDS-PAG of the affinity column eluate (lane D). Lane C contains the polypeptides found in fractions exhibiting CA activity after Sephadex G-200 chromatography of the affinity column eluate and lane B contains polypeptides electroeluted from a section of a native PAG stained for CA activity. A Western blot of the total soluble protein (lane G) probed with the CA polyclonal antisera is shown in lane I. Molecular weight markers (Bio-Rad Inc.) are shown in lanes A and H

Figure 2. Screening of a pea cDNA library for CA immunopositive clones. Nitrocellulose filters prepared from 86 mm plates containing approximately 10,000 recombinant plaques were incubated with the CA antisera. Specifically bound antibody was detected with horseradish peroxidase conjugated goat anti-rabbit IgG. A positive signal on a primary plate is shown (A) as well as the tertiary stage of plaque purification (B). A control filter with no positive signals is also presented (C).

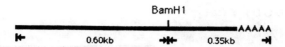

Figure 3. Restriction endonuclease map of the 0.95 kb immunopositive cDNA clone. Enzymes that did not cut the DNA include: <u>Acc</u>I, <u>Hind</u>III, <u>Pst</u>I, <u>Sac</u>I, <u>Sma</u>I, <u>Ava</u>I, <u>Cla</u>I, <u>Pvu</u>I, <u>Pvu</u>II. Partial sequence analysis has been used to identify the position of the poly A tail.

sequence homology with the 0.95 kb insert and we have initiated sequence analysis of two of the positive cDNA clones, the 0.95 kb insert and a larger 1.3 kb cDNA. We are particularly interested in extending this study to include measurements of variation in CA transcript abundance in response to changing environmental parameters such as CO_2 concentration and light intensity and quality.

Acknowledgements
       The authors would like to thank Dr. Gloria Coruzzi, Rockefeller University for the pea leaf cDNA bank. This research was supported by a grant to J.R.C. from NSERC (Canada). N.M. is a recipient of an NSERC post-graduate scholarship.

REFERENCES
1.   Tsuzuki, M. <u>et al</u>. (1985) Pl. Cell Physiol. 26,881-891
2.   Reed, M. and Graham, D. (1981) Prog. Phytochem. 7, 47-94
3.   Cowan, I. (1986) in Economy of Plant Form and Function (Givnish, T.J., ed.), pp.133-170, Cambridge U. Press, Cambridge
4.   Atkins, C.A. (1974) Phytochem. 13, 93-98
5.   Porter, M.A. and Grodzinski, B. (1984) Pl. Physiol. 74, 413-416
6.   Lucas, W.J. (1983) Ann. Rev. Pl. Physiol. 34, 71-104
7.   Bailly J. and Coleman, J.R. (1988) Pl. Physiol. 87, 833-840
8.   Coleman, J.R. and Grossman, A.R. (1984) P.N.A.S. USA 81, 6049-6053
9.   Davis, L.G. <u>et al</u>. (1986) Basic Methods in Molecular Biology, Elsevier Press, New York
10.   Atkins, C.A. <u>et al</u>. (1974) Pl. Physiol. 50, 218-223
11.   Yang, S-Y. <u>et al</u>. (1985) Pl. Cell Physiol. 26, 21-34
12.   Patterson, B.D. <u>et al</u>. (1971) Anal. Biochem. 44, 388-391
13.   Tingey, S. <u>et al</u>. (1987) EMBO J. 6, 1-9

MEMBRANE-BOUND CARBONIC ANHYDRASE TAKES PART IN CO_2 CONCENTRATION IN ALGAE CELLS

NATALIA A. PRONINA, VICTOR E. SEMENENKO, Plant Physiology Institute, USSR Academy of Sciences, Botanicheskaya,35, Moscow, USSR

INTRODUCTION

The concentration of CO2 restricts the photosynthetic productivity of microalgae because of the low partial pressure of the CO2 in the atmosphere and the low rate of diffusion of CO2 in water. As a result of biochemical adaptation the microalgae cells developed a CO2-concentration mechanism, the details of which remain unknown. On the other hand biochemical,physiological and genetic investigations leave no doubt that such a mechanism exists (1-3).

It is assumed that CA participates in the CO2-concentration mechanism, its activity being higher in L-cells than in H-cells. In microalgae Ci is concentrated, possibly,as a result of HCO_3^- being additionally transported along with CO2. HCO_3^- is transported either by active transfer into the cell or by dehydration of HCO_3^- to CO2 catalyzed by CA(3-5).In the latter case the activity of extracellular CA should be high in L-cells.In this connection we investigated the localization of CA in Chlorella cells,the photosynthetic characteristics of the culture under various conditions of CO2 supply and also the variation of these properties in the presence of CA inhibitors. On the basis of the result the mechanism of CO2-concentration in Chlorella cells is considered.

MATERIALS AND METHODS

The microalga (IPPAS) was grown photoautotrophicaly under bubling of ordinary air or air enriched with 2% CO2. Photosynthetic oxygen evolution was determined with an oxygen electrode .The CA activity was determined in cell suspended(CA intact cells),soluble fraction(sCA) and fraction of membranes(mbCA).Fractionation of the alga membranes carried out in sucrose density gradient (6).

RESULTS AND DISCUSSION

CA-localization. A mbCA has been found in cells of Chlorella, Chlamydomonas and Dunaliella which are not solubilized by many

---

Abbreviations: Ci,inorganic carbon; H-cells,cells grown under high CO2; L-cells,cells grown under low CO2; CA,carbonic anhydrase; mbCA,membrane-bound CA; sCA, soluble CA; AZ, acetazolamide; EZ, ethoxzolamide

M. Baltscheffsky (ed.), Current Research in Photosynthesis, Vol. IV, 489–492.
© 1990 *Kluwer Academic Publishers. Printed in the Netherlands.*

detergents of the anion and non-ion type (6) (fig.1). It has been possible to solubilize only partially a mbCA with a mass of 30 KD from Dunaliella cells. A mbCA is present in both L- and H-cells of Chlorella and Dunaliella (3). Fractionation of Chlorella membranes showed that the mbCA is located in the chloroplast membrane (20%) and cell wall fraction including plasmalemma elements (80%) (fig.2) (6).

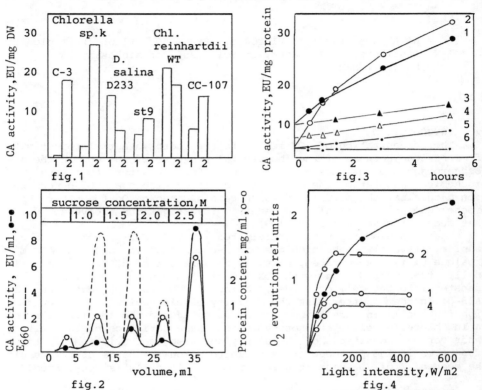

fig.1

fig.3   hours

fig.2

fig.4

FIGURE 1. Localization of CA in the soluble(1) and membrane(2) fractions of Chlorella, Dunaliella, (H-cells) and Chlamydomonas (cells grown on acetate medium).

FIGURE 2. Distribution of chlorophyll, protein and CA after fractionation of Chlorella sp.K cells membranes in sucrose density gradient.

FIGURE 3. Changes in CA activity Chlorella C-3 when H-cells transferred to 0,03% CO2. Homogenate (1); soluble fraction (2); membrane fraction (3); intact cells (4); soluble fraction + 20 μg/ml α-amanitin (5); soluble fraction + 5 μg/ml cycloheximide (6).

FIGURE 4. Photosynthetic O2 evolution in Chlorella sp.K when H-cells were transferred to 0,03% CO2 after 0 hr (1); 2,5 hr (2); 4,5 hr (3) in the absence or presence of 0,05 mM EZ (4).

At lower CO2 concentration (fig.3) sCA is synthesized de novo in Chlorella cells (3). The synthesis of sCA is suppressed by cycloheximide and α-amanitin. Synthesis of sCA is dependent on the light intensity and is absent in the dark in L-cells (3,6). A study of the mechanism of induction of sCA revealed that products of the glycolate pathway of carbon metabolism are involved in the synthesis of sCA.Glyoxylate is the inductor (7).

Thus a comparatively complex carbonic anhydrase system which includes mbCA in plasmalemma and chloroplast membrane and sCA in cytoplasm is observed in Chlorella cells. Resently periplasmic, cytoplasmic and chloroplast CA was found in Chlamydomonas (8).

Photosynthetic characteristics of Chlorella L-cells. The activity of CA and particularly of sCA increases in Chlorella cells transferred to low CO2 conditions (fig.3). A gradual increase of the height of the photosynthesis light curve plateau is also observed; this signifies that Chlorella L-cells assimilate Ci more efficiently than H-cells(fig. 4). It can be seen that the concentrating mechanism and the activation of sCA synthesis are more manifest at saturating light intensities and less pronounced at lower intensities. The plateau for L-cells does not increase in the presence of the CA inhibitor EZ which ca enter the cell. The CA inhibitor AZ which cannot enter the cell does not decrease the productivity of Chlorella L-cells (fig.5).

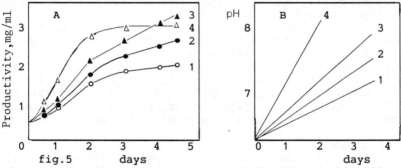

FIGURE 5.Changes of productivity (A) and pH values(B) of Chlorella sp.K when H-cells were transferred to 0.03% CO2 (1) in the presence of 40 mM NaCl(2);40 mM KCl(3); 40 mM NaCl+1 mM AZ

Functional role of the carbonic anhydrase system. The results obtained by employing CA inhibitors show that only internal CA forms (cytoplasmic sCA and chloroplast mbCA) play a significant role in the CO2 concentrating mechanism. The mbCA of the outer membranes do not participate in concentrating Ci, as assumed previously, by producing and additional flux of CO2 from dehydrated HCO (5,9). Apparently, the concentration of Ci is due to the active transport of HCO_3^- in addition to the CO2 flux to the cells. It is possible that the extracellular CA participates in the transport of Ci only for acidic pH values in L-cells thus ensuring a flow of HCO_3^- . The increase of the productivity of L-cells in the presence of millimolar concentration of NaCl and KCl may be due to the facilitation of HCO_3^- transfer via the HCO_3^- /CL-pump. The increase of the productivity of L-cells on inhibition of the extracellular CA can be attributed to a decrease in the reverse CO2 flow from the cell during the concentration of Ci.

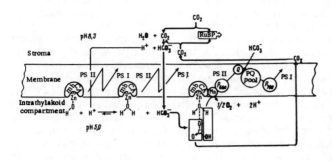

FIGURE 6. A model for concentration of CO2 in the carboxilation centre

What is the function of the mbCA in the chloroplast? As noted above the main form of Ci penetrating the L-cells is HCO_3^- and the same form accumulates at alkaline pH values within the cell. The substrate for RuBPC is CO2 for which the Km is high. The function of mbCA of the chloroplast may consist in the concentrating of molecular CO2 in the carboxylation zone. Two mechanisms of concentration of CO2 in the chloroplast are considered. One is the dehydration of HCO_3^- in the carboxylation zone and the other the dehydration of HCO_3^- in the thylakoid in which an acidic pH is created at the expense of energy-dependent H+ transport. The latter hypothesis is supported by data on the presence of CA in the thylakoid membrane (6) and also in photosystem 1 and 2 particles(10,11) and by the appreciable decrease in the mbCA activity in Chlamydomonas reinhardtii mutants deprived on photosystem reaction centers (N.A.Pronina, V.G.Ladigin unpublished).

REFERENCES
1   Pierce, J. and Omata, T. (1988) Photosynthesis Research 16, 141-154
2   Moroney, J.V., Husic, H.D., Tolbert, N.E.,Kitayama, M., Manuel,L.J, Togasaki, R.K. (1989) Plant Physiol. 89, 897-903
3   Pronina, N.A., Avramova, C., Georgiev, D., Semenenko, V.E. (1981) Sov. Plant Physiol. 28, 32-40
4   Moroney,J.V.,Husic, H.D.,Tolbert,N.E.(1985) Plant Physiol.79,177-183
5   Miyachi, S.,Tsuzuki, M.,Avramova, S.T.(1983)Plant. Cell Physiol. 24, 441-451
6   Pronina, N.A., Semenenko, V.E. (1988) Sov.Plant Physiol. 35, 38-46
7   Ramazanov,Z.M., Semenenko,V.E.(1986) Sov.Plant Physiol. 33,864-871
8   Husic, H.D., Kitayama, M., Togasaki, R.K., Moroney, J.V., Morris, K.L., Tolbert, N.E. (1989) Plant Physiol. 89, 904-909
9   Sultemeyer, D.F., Miller, A.G., Espie, G.S., Fock, H.P.,Canvin, D.T. (1989) Plant Physiol. 89, 1213-1219
10 Jursinic, P., Stemler, A. (1988) Photosynthesis Research,15,41-56
11 Pronina, N.A., Allachverdiev, S.I,, Klyachko-Gurvich, G.L., Klimov, V.V.,Semenenko, V.E. (1989) Fisiol. Rast. in press.

CHEMICAL CROSS-LINKING OF PERIPLASMIC CARBONIC ANHYDRASE FROM CHLAMYDOMONAS REINHARDTII

H. David Husic, Department of Chemistry, Lafayette College, Easton, PA 18042

INTRODUCTION

In *Chlamydomonas reinhardtii*, carbonic anhydrase (CA) is part of an inorganic carbon (C_i) concentrating system which enhances the efficiency with which these algae utilize low levels of C_i. The predominant form of the enzyme is extracellular (1,2) and accelerates the interconversion of CO_2 and HCO_3^- to facilitate the transfer of CO_2 into the cell (3). Previous studies have indicated that the enzyme has a molecular weight (M_r) in the range of 97-115 kDa and is comprised of subunits of 35-37 kDa (4,5), indicating that the native protein is trimeric. I have utilized a bifunctional chemical cross-linking agent to further evaluate the subunit composition of both the isolated enzyme, and of the enzyme *in vivo*, to investigate whether the enzyme is associated with other cellular proteins.

MATERIALS AND METHODS

Enzyme Isolation and Antiserum Preparation.   Periplasmic CA was prepared from air-grown *Chlamydomonas reinhardtii* (137 mt$^+$) by p-methylaminobenzenesulfonamide affinity chromatography as described by Yang *et al.* (6). Antiserum against the isolated enzyme was prepared in rabbits as we described previously (7). Chemically deglycosylated CA was prepared by trifluoromethanesulfonic acid hydrolysis (8,9).

Electrophoresis and Immunoblotting.   SDS-PAGE was carried out with linear 6-15% gradient polyacrylamide gels using the buffer system of Laemmli *et al.* (10). 2-Mercapto-ethanol was omitted from all electrophoresis solutions, except the sample preparation solution where indicated in the Results. Gels were transferred to nitrocellulose and CA was detected with antiserum against the enzyme (7) that had been preabsorbed with extracts of a CA-deficient mutant of the algae (cia-5). M_r values were estimated following immunoblotting by comparison to pre-stained standards (Bio-Rad).

Chemical Cross-Linking of Isolated Carbonic Anhydrase.   CA was dialyzed extensively against 50 mol·m^{-3} Na-borate, pH 8.5, and solutions of 60 μg CA·cm^{-3} were utilized for cross-linking experiments. The bifunctional cross-linker, ethylene glycolbis(succinimidyl-succinate) (EGS, from Pierce), was dissolved in dimethylformamide (DMF) and 5 μl of appropriate dilutions of a 10 mol·m^{-3} solution were added to the CA solution (50 μl) to give the desired final concentrations of EGS. After 2 h at 25°C, the reaction was quenched by the addition of 5 μl of 1.5 X 10^3 mol·m^{-3} Na-glycine, pH 8.5, and after a 10 minute incubation at room temperature, the samples were prepared for electrophoresis. CA and its cross-linked forms were detected by immunoblotting; the derivitized proteins were poorly detected in gels by either Coomassie blue or silver staining.

M. Baltscheffsky (ed.), Current Research in Photosynthesis, Vol. IV, 493–496.
© *1990 Kluwer Academic Publishers. Printed in the Netherlands.*

In Vivo Chemical Cross-Linking. Cells were harvested by centrifugation, and washed three times with H_2O, once with 50 mol·m^{-3} Na-borate, pH 8.5 and resuspended in the borate buffer to make a suspension containing about 0.5 mg Chl·cm^{-3}. To 0.5 ml of the suspension was added 15 μl of 125 mol·m^{-3} mM EGS in DMF, and the mixture was stirred at 25°C for 2 h in the dark. Controls contained 15 μl DMF and no EGS. The reactions were quenched by the addition of 25 μl of 1.5 X 10^3 mol·m^{-3} Na-glycine, pH 8.5 and the samples were frozen at -20°C until prepared for electrophoresis. Thawed samples were lysed in a cell disruption bomb (1500 psi, 5 min) and the electrophoretically separated proteins were detected by immunoblotting.

RESULTS

SDS-PAGE of Carbonic Anhydrase under Reducing and Non-Reducing Conditions. Following the electrophoretic separation of CA under non-reducing conditions, the predominant species has a M_r of 80 kDa, with less intense bands of 37 and 36 kDa (Fig. 1, lane A). When the samples were not boiled prior to electrophoresis under non-reducing conditions (Fig. 1, lane B), a faint band was observed with a M_r of 105 kDa, corresponding to that of a trimeric species of the enzyme. Under reducing conditions, a doublet at 36 and 37 kDa is observed (Fig. 2, lane A), although these polypeptides are often poorly resolved. The 37 kDa polypeptide was generally of greater intensity than that at 36 kDa. Following chemical deglycosylation, the 36-37 kDa doublet is reduced to a single 32 kDa polypeptide under reducing conditions (Fig. 2, lane B), indicating that the 36 and 37 kDa subunits may differ only in the extent of glycosylation. These data indicate that pairs of monomeric (36-37 kDa) subunits are joined by disulfide bonds, and that some monomers may not be disulfide bonded to the disulfide bonded pair.

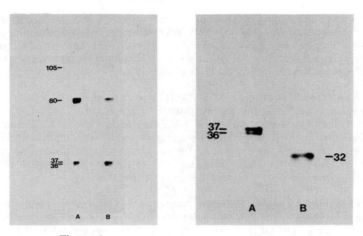

Figure 1.   Figure 2.

Figure 1. SDS-PAGE of CA under Non-Reducing Conditions. A, Boiled 1 minute prior to electrophoresis; B, Not boiled prior to electrophoresis.

Figure 2. SDS-PAGE of CA under Reducing Conditions. A, Untreated CA; B, Deglycosylated CA.

Chemical Cross-Linking of Isolated Carbonic Anhydrase. To further assess the subunit composition of the enzyme, CA subunits have been cross-linked with EGS prior to electrophoretic separation. With increasing concentration of EGS (Fig. 3, lanes A–D), there is a decrease in the 36-37 kDa species and an increase of a diffuse band of about 105 kDa corresponding to a trimer of 36-37 kDa monomeric units, as was observed when the enzyme was not boiled prior to electrophoresis under non-reducing conditions (Fig. 1, lane B). Significant levels of cross-linked dimers were not observed. At the highest concnetration of EGS tested, no significant cross-linking was observed if the enzyme was dissociated with SDS and 2-mercaptoethanol prior to treatment with the EGS (Fig. 3, lane E), indicating that there is no intermolecular cross-linking of CA under these conditions.

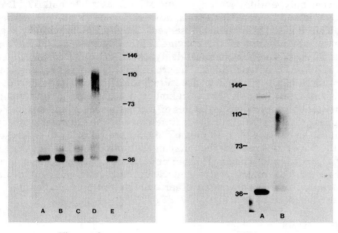

Figure 3.　　　　Figure 4.

Figure 3. SDS-PAGE of Purified CA Treated with EGS. A, No EGS; B, 0.01 mol·m^{-3}; C, 0.1 mol·m^{-3}; D, 1 mol·m^{-3}; E, CA dissociated with 1 % SDS and 100 mol·m^{-3} mercaptoethanol prior to cross-linking with 1 mol·m^{-3} EGS. Indicated are the expected migrations of monomers (36 kDa), dimers (72 kDa), trimers (110 kDa), and tetramers (146 kDa) of the 36-37 kDa subunits.

Figure 4. Immunoblot of Cell Extract after EGS Treatment. Control cells (A) or cells treated with 3.6 mol·m^{-3} EGS (B) were probed with anti-CA antiserum following SDS-PAGE.

In Vivo Chemical Cross-Linking of Carbonic Anhydrase. Because the majority of the cellular CA in *C. reinhardtii* is extracellular (1,2), it is susceptible to cross-linking by adding EGS to intact cells. Cells were treated with EGS under conditions similar to the utilized for the cross-linking of the isolated enzyme, the electrophoretically separated extracts transferred to nitrocellulose, and the CA detected with antiserum against the enzyme. The predominant cross-linked species had a molecular weight approximately corresponding to a trimer, as was observed with the isolated enzyme (Fig. 4, lane B). There was no evidence for higher molecular weight immunoreactive species unique to cells treated with EGS as might be observed if the enzyme was associated with proteins in the cell wall or plasma membrane. EGS treatment under these conditions resulted in only about a 10% reduction of extracellular CA activity, despite near complete cross-linking of the enzyme. The cross-linked enzyme retained a high affinity for sulfonamides, and the affinity purification of the cross-linked enzyme revealed some trimeric species, and also provided no evidence for the cross-linking of the enzyme to other polypeptides (not shown).

DISCUSSION

The results presented here indicate that *C. reinhardtii* CA is a trimer composed of monomeric units with a polypeptide chain of 32 kDa, and that these polypeptides are glycosylated to reveal polypeptides with apparent M_r values of 36 and 37 kDa. Pairs of subunits appear to be joined by disulfide bonds, however, some monomers are not disulfide bonded. No disulfide bonded trimers are observed. Bundy has previously reported that disulfide bonds may join subunits of the enzyme (11). Toguri *et al.* (9) have previously observed a 32 kDa polypeptide upon chemical deglycosylation of *C. reinhardtii* CA, but did not resolve the 36 and 37 kDa polypeptides. The cross-linking experiments indicate that the native enzyme is predominantly trimeric in structure, indicating that two subunits are joined by disulfide bonds and a third is not. The assignment of a trimeric subunit composition to the enzyme is consistent with previous estimates of the native M_r of the enzyme (4,5). The disulfide bonds appear to be essential for the maintenance of the oligomeric structure of the enzyme; treatment of the enzyme with 10 $mol \cdot m^{-3}$ dithiothreitol prior to cross-linking with EGS prevented the cross-linking of the enzyme subunits, indicating that they have dissociated (Berrier, A.L. and Husic, H.D., unpublished). The *in vivo* cross-linking experiments indicate that the enzyme is also trimeric in intact cells, and provide no evidence for the close association of the enzyme to other cellular proteins, indicating that CA is freely soluble in the periplasmic space.

ACKNOWLEDGEMENTS

This research was supported by NSF grant DCB-88-18845 and a Cottrell College Science Grant from Research Corporation. I thank Allison Berrier and Lisa Poritz for their assistance with some of this work.

REFERENCES

1 Coleman, J.R., Berry, J.A., Togasaki, R.K., and Grossman, A.R. (1984) Plant Physiol. 76, 472–477.
2 Kimpel, D.L., Togasaki, R.K., and Miyachi, S. (1983) Plant Cell Physiol. 24, 255–259.
3 Moroney, J.V., Husic, H.D., and Tolbert, N.E. (1985) Plant. Physiol. 79, 177–183.
4 Yagawa, Y., Muto, S. and Miyachi, S. (1988) Plant Cell Physiol. 29: 185–188.
5 Husic, H.D., Moroney, J.V., and Tolbert, N.E. (1987) in Progress in Photosynthesis Research (Biggins, J., ed.), Vol. 4, pp. 317–324, Martinus-Nijoff Publishers, Dordrecht.
6 Yang, S.-Y., Tsuzuki, M., and Miyachi, S. (1985) Plant Cell Physiol. 26, 25–34.
7 Husic, H.D., Kitayama, M., Togasaki, R.K., Morris, K.L., Moroney, J.V., and Tolbert, N.E. (1989) Plant Physiol. 89, 904–909.
8 Edge, A.S.B., Faltynek, C.R., Hof, L., Reichert, L.E., Jr. and Weber, P. (1981) Anal. Biochem. 118, 131–137.
9 Toguri, T., Muto, S. and Miyachi, S. (1986) Eur. J. Biochem. 158, 443–450.
10 Laemmli, U.K. (1970) Nature 222, 360–369.
11 Bundy, H.F. (1986) Comp. Biochem. Physiol. 84B, 63–69.

THE ROLE OF CARBONIC ANHYDRASE IN REGULATING PHOTOSYNTHETIC CO$_2$ FIXATION IN HIGHER PLANTS

Gao Yuzhu, Zhang Zhenlin, Guo Minliang, Wang Zhong
Lab of Crop Photosynthesis, Jiangsu Agricultural College, Yangzhou, Jiangsu Province, The People's Republic of China

1. INTRODUCTION

Carbonic anhydrase (CA, EC4.2.1.1), which catalyzes the reversible reaction between HCO$_3^-$ and dissolved CO$_2$, is widely distributed throughout the plant as well as animal kingdoms. It has relation to photosynthetic CO$_2$ fixation, which can be inferred from its intracellular distribution. There have been several reports indicating that CA is mainly localized in the chloroplasts of C$_3$ plants and in the cytoplasm of C$_4$ plants [1,2,3], which is in accordance with the localization of Rubisco in C$_3$ plants and PEPCase in C$_4$ plants. So far the role of CA in higher plants has been less studied than in algae.

In this paper we provide evidence that CA facilitates inorganic carbon (IC) diffusion and increases the substrate concentration in surroundings of the active site in Rubisco and PEPCase, thus enhancing the activities of the carboxylase. CA activity in response to environmental factor is also demonstrated.

2. MATERIALS AND METHODS

CA activities in crude spinach leaf extract was determinated with pH—meter system.

Infrared CO$_2$ analyzer was used to measure the rates of photosynthesis and photorespiration in detached wheat leaves.

PEPCase was purified from maize leaves. Malic dehydrogenase and acetazolamide (* Diamox, a potent inhibitor of CA) was made in Sigma Chemical Co., St Louis. CA (from bovine erythrocytes), NADH (sodium salt) and PEP was purchased from Shanghai biochemical institute of the Chinese Academy of Science. PEPCase activities were analyzed on a spectrophotometer at 340nm. The reaction was started by injecting 24mM, 0.1ml PEP solution into the colorimetric vessel holding 2.9ml reaction mixture which contained 3.3mM Barbitone—H$_2$SO$_4$(pH9.2), 3.3mM MgSO$_4$, 0.6mM NaHCO$_3$(unless otherwise indicated), 0.17mM NADH, 10μg Malic dehydrogenase, 6.2 μg protein / ml PEPCase, 10μg CA and 0.3 mM Diamox (as control treatment). PEPCase activity was monitored by NADH—dependent absorbance.

* Acknowledgements Dr. S. Miyachi provided us with Diamox.

3. RESULTS AND DISCUSSION

3.1 A Role of CA in the C$_3$ and C$_4$ Plants

It has been reported that CA not only increases RuBPCase activity but also decreases RuBPOase activity [4], which was supported by our experiments with C$_3$ plants [table 1].

M. Baltscheffsky (ed.), Current Research in Photosynthesis, Vol. IV, 497–500.
© 1990 *Kluwer Academic Publishers. Printed in the Netherlands.*

Table 1. Effect of Diamox on the Rates of Photosynthesis
and Photorespiration in C_3 Plants[a]

Materials	Apparent photosynthesis ($mgCO_2 \cdot dm^{-2} \cdot h^{-1}$)			Potorespiration[b] ($mgCO_2 \cdot dm^{-2} \cdot h^{-1}$)		
	Controls	Treatment with Diamox	Diminution (% of control)	Controls	Treatment with Diamox	Increment (% of control)
Wheat	8.6	6.9	21	2.3	3.3	43
Barley	7.2	6.0	17	1.6	2.1	31

[a] All values are means of six or more determinations from six or more samples.

[b] The data are calculated from postillumination CO_2 burst in CO_2-free air.

Fig.1 shows that CA obviously increased PEPCase activity, with the reaction mixture containing 0.6mM HCO_3^- (under equilibrium state at pH9.2). This effect was gradually enhanced by increasing [CA] until [CA] reached 10μg / vessel.

The effect of CA on PEPCase depended upon [HCO_3^-] [Fig.2]. At lower [HCO_3^-] (0.6mM) the effect of CA was the most marked, while at higher [HCO_3^-] (1.4mM) the effect disappeared. The effect also became more pronounced as carboxylation reaction carried on, especially in the presence of low [HCO_3^-] [Fig.3]. The phenomenon that CA promoted PEPCase actity was shown by another experiment in which photosynthetic rate of maize leaves was higher than that treated with Diamox.

Above results indicate a possible role of CA in regulating the photosynthetic carbon metabolism, i. e. CA participates in the acceleration of IC transport to supply substrate to the active centers of carboxylase where [IC] approaches scarcity after the start of reaction.

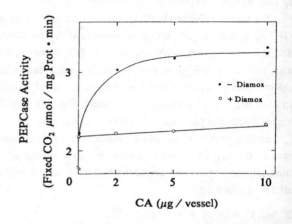

Fig.1   Effect of CA on PEPCase Activity

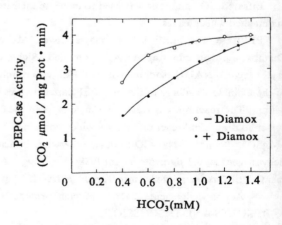

Fig.2   Effect of CA on activities of PEPCase in the Presence of varied [HCO_3^-]

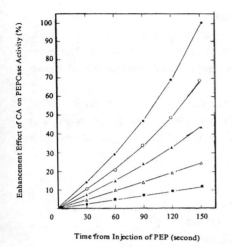

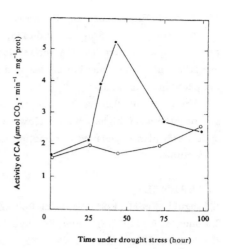

Fig.3 Effect of CA on PEPCase activity increases with reaction carrying on at various [HCO$_3$]: 0.6mM(•), 0.8mM(o), 1.0mM(▲), 1.2mM(△), and 1.4mM(■)

Fig. 4 Effect of drought stress on CA activity in wheat seedling •, treatment; o, control

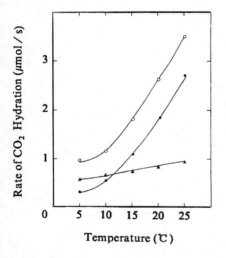

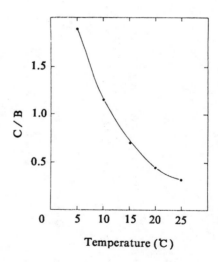

Fig. 5 Effect of temperature on rate of CO$_2$ hydration
A(o), gross rate of CO$_2$ hydration;
B(•), chemical rate of CO$_2$ hydration;
C(▲), net catalytic rate of CA (A−B).

Fig. 6 Relation between CA catalytic efficiency and temperature

3.2 Special Enviroment of Enhanced CA Effect

According to our previous studies [5], under CO_2−limiting conditions such as drought stress and low temperature, CA shows even higher activity [Fig. 4, 5, 6] so that during the regulation of IC−assimilation capacity to withstand unfavourable environmental factors CA plays an essential part.

From all of the results, authors suggest that CA plays an important role in photosynthesis in higher plants. However, its role may differ from that in algae and underwater plants. Detailed information about the function of CA in higher plants needs more studies.

REFERENCES

1. Tsuzuki M et al. (1985) Plant Cell Physiol. 26, 881−891
2. Poincelot Rp (1972) Biochim. Biophys. Acta 258, 637−642
3. Srivastava JP and Rathore VS (1985) Plant Physiol. 28, 259−263
4. Keiichiro Okabe, Angela Lindlar, Mikio Tsuzuki and Shigetoh Miyachi (1980) FEBS Letters 114, 142−144
5. Guo Minliang, Gao Yuzhu, (1988) International Symposium on Regulation and Efficiency of Photosynthesis, 48

EXPRESSION OF A CYANOBACTERIAL GENE REGULATED BY CO_2 CONCENTRATION

DANA CHAMOT AND JOHN R. COLEMAN, Centre for Plant Biotechnology, Dept. of Botany, University of Toronto, Ontario, Canada M5S 3B2

INTRODUCTION

Cyanobacteria, a large diverse group of photosynthetic prokaryotes, are known to possess an inducible inorganic carbon (C_i) concentrating mechanism which allows them to photosynthesize efficiently under the CO_2 limitations of their environments (1). The accumulation of a large body of physiological evidence has led to the postulation that this mechanism is comprised of several components including a CO_2 pump, a HCO_3^- pump, and the enzyme carbonic anhydrase (CA), which function in concert to supply Rubisco with saturating levels of CO_2 when C_i levels in the external medium are limiting (2). This study explores the molecular biology of the cyanobacterial response to low C_i by attempting to clone and characterize the expression of a gene which appears to be regulated by CO_2 concentration in the medium.

MATERIALS AND METHODS

The cyanobacterial strain <u>Anabaena variabilis</u> PCC 29413 was maintained as described (3) on solid and liquid media supplemented with 10 mM HEPES pH 8.0. High CO_2 cultures were stirred and bubbled with 2-5 % CO_2 in air while low CO_2 cultures were aerated with air alone (0.035 % CO_2). The bacterial strains <u>E. coli</u> HB101 and JM101 were maintained as described (4). Cyanobacterial genomic DNA and bacterial plasmid DNA was isolated essentially as described (5) with some modifications. Southern hybridization of restriction endonuclease fragments was performed with nitrocellulose membranes using ^{32}P-labelled heterologous probes according to the manufacturer's specifications (S & S). Total RNA isolation from <u>Anabaena</u> cells was performed as described (6) with some modifications. Northern hybridization was performed with nitrocellulose membranes using ^{32}P-

labelled homologous probes. In vitro transcription/
translation using an E. coli DNA-directed system was
performed as per the manufacturer's instructions
(Amersham). ³⁵S-labelled polypeptides were separated by
SDS-PAGE (7) on 7-15 % gradient gels and the newly
synthesized proteins visualized by autoradiography.

RESULTS AND DISCUSSION

Genomic digests of Anabaena DNA probed with the
Chlamydomonas reinhardtii CA gene (8) revealed strong
hybridization to a 4.4 kb Cla I fragment which was
subsequently cloned (Fig. 1). A much larger, weakly
hybridizing Cla I fragment was also visualized. This
may represent a gene which shares less DNA similarity
with Chlamydomonas CA but is still associated with the
carbon acquisition system and therefore has a "CA-like"

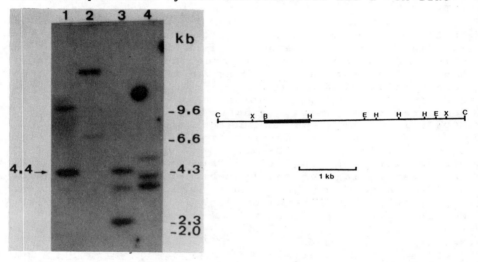

FIGURE 1. Autoradiogram of Southern blot of Anabaena
genomic DNA endonuclease digests probed with the ³²P-
labelled Chlamydomonas CA gene. Anabaena DNA was
digested with Cla I (lane 1), Eco RI (lane 2), Hind III
(lane 3) and Xba I (lane 4). Hind III digested lambda
DNA molecular size markers are indicated. The strongly
hybridizing 4.4 kb Cla I fragment is indicated.

FIGURE 2. Restriction endonuclease map of cloned
Anabaena 4.4 kb Cla I fragment. Restriction enzymes
which cut inside the fragment were: Xba I (X), Bgl I
(B), Hind III (H) and Eco RI (E). The smallest region
which hybridized to the Chlamydomonas CA gene is
indicated by a thick bar.

active site or C_i binding region. It could also represent another copy of the gene although this is unlikely in light of the relative signal intensity. Restriction endonuclease mapping revealed that the region hybridizing to the <u>Chlamydomonas</u> gene is internalized on a 0.85 kb <u>Bgl</u> I-<u>Hin</u>d III fragment (Fig. 2).

Figure 3 shows the autoradiogram of a Northern blot of equal amounts of total RNA isolated from 3 different cell types. The presence of an approximately 0.3 kb transcript in low CO_2 cells and in cells transferred to air for 12 hr suggests that transcription of a gene encoded within the 1.7 <u>Cla</u> I-<u>Hin</u>d III probe is regulated

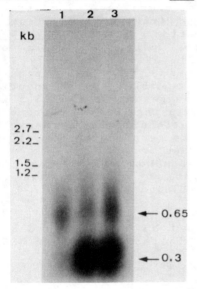
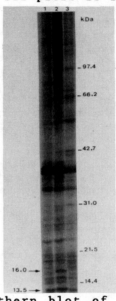

FIGURE 3. Autoradiogram of Northern blot of <u>Anabaena</u> total RNA probed with the ^{32}P-labelled 1.7 kb <u>Cla</u> I-<u>Hin</u>d III <u>Anabaena</u> fragment. RNA was isolated from cells grown under high CO_2 (lane 1), cells grown under high CO_2 and transferred to air for 12 hr (lane 2) and cells grown under low CO_2 (lane 3). Ribosomal RNA bands are indicated as molecular size markers. Two transcripts of 0.65 kb and 0.3 kb are indicated by arrows.

FIGURE 4. Autoradiogram of newly synthesized ^{35}S-labelled polypeptides separated by SDS-PAGE after <u>in vitro</u> transcription/translation of the plasmid pUC18 containing the 4.4 kb <u>Cla</u> I <u>Anabaena</u> fragment cloned in both orientations (lanes 1 and 2) and pUC18 alone (lane 3). Molecular weight standards are indicated. A 16 kDa and a 13.5 kDa polypeptide are indicated by arrows.

by CO_2. This is further evidence, in addition to the
Southern hybridization, that the <u>Anabaena</u> fragment codes
for a CA-like gene. It has been shown previously that
the expression of <u>Chlamydomonas</u> CA is similarly
regulated by CO_2 and that exposure to air levels of CO_2
results in a similar accumulation of the CA transcript
(8). The presence of a very low level of the 0.3 kb
transcript in high CO_2 cells suggests that there is a
basal level of transcript in all cell types. The
presence of a 0.6 kb transcript in all cell types
suggests that there is an additional gene encoded by the
same fragment of genomic DNA, either adjacent to the
CO_2-regulated gene or on the opposite strand (Fig 3).
     Additional evidence that there are 2 distinct
coding sequences on the <u>Anabaena</u> fragment comes from <u>in</u>
<u>vitro</u> transcription/ translation of the <u>Anabaena</u>
fragment in both orientations (Fig. 4). In one
orientation a single polypeptide of approximately 13.5
kDa was synthesized, however, in the opposite
orientation both a 16 kDa and the 13.5 kDa polypeptide
were synthesized. These data suggest that the 13.5 kDa
polypeptide may be capable of using its own promoter
since it appears in both orientations, while conversely,
the 16 kDa polypeptide appears to require the <u>E. coli</u> B-
galactosidase promoter for expression. We are
continuing our studies by sequence analysis of the
cyanobacterial DNA and attempts to generate high CO_2
requiring mutants by insertional inactivation.

ACKNOWLEDGEMENTS
     This research was supported by a grant to J.R.C.
from NSERC (Canada). D.C. is the recipient of an NSERC
post-graduate scholarship.

REFERENCES
1.   Aizawa, K. and Miyachi, S. (1986) FEMS
     Microbiol.Rev.39, 215-233.
2.   Price, G. D. and Badger, M. R. (1989) Pl. Physiol.
     89, 37- 43.
3.   Allen, M. M. (1968) J. Phycol. 4, 1-4.
4   Maniatis, T., Fritsch, E. F. and Sambrook, J.
     (1982) Cold Spring Harbour Lab.
5.   Marmur, J. (1961) J. Mol. Biol. 3, 208-218.
6.   Golden, S. S., Brusslan, J. and Haselkorn, R.
     (1987) Meth. Enzomol. 153, 215-237.
7.   Piccioni, R., Bellemare, G. and Chua, N. -H. (1982)
     in Methods in Chloroplast Molecular Biology
     (Edelman <u>et al</u>. eds), pp.985-1014, Elsevier,
     Amsterdam.
8.   Bailly, J. and Coleman, J. R. (1988) Pl. Physiol.
     87, 833- 840.

ADAPTATION OF *CHLAMYDOMONAS REINHARDTII* HIGH CO_2-REQUIRING MUTANTS TO LIMITING CO_2

MARTIN H. SPALDING[1], KENSAKU SUZUKI[2] AND ANNE M. GERAGHTY[1]

[1]Botany Department, Iowa State University, Ames, Iowa 50011, USA, and [2]Institute of Biological Sciences, University of Tsukuba, Tsukuba, Ibaraki 305, Japan.

1. INTRODUCTION

Chlamydomonas reinhardtii and other unicellular green algae use an energy-requiring, CO_2-concentrating system, inducible by limiting inorganic carbon (C_i) concentrations, to increase intracellular CO_2 concentrations (1). Operation of the CO_2-concentrating system results in a high affinity for C_i in photosynthesis. Increased intracellular CO_2 also reduces photorespiration and O_2 inhibition of photosynthesis by competitive inhibition of RuBP oxygenase. The CO_2-concentrating system involves active transport of C_i and includes CA as a component. This system apparently is only fully functional when cells adapt to low CO_2 (air-adapted cells), since cells exhibit much lower affinity for C_i when grown at 5% CO_2 (CO_2-enriched cells).

Exposure of CO_2-enriched *Chlamydomonas* to limiting CO_2 results in induction of the CO_2 concentrating system as exemplified by increased affinity for C_i and an increase in C_i transport (2). Several authors have identified polypeptides possibly involved in the CO_2-concentrating system of *Chlamydomonas* by their induction at limiting CO_2 (3, 4, 5, 6). One of these polypeptides, a 37 kD M_r, soluble polypeptide, has been identified as a periplasmic CA (4) which may be required for conversion of bicarbonate to CO_2 at alkaline pH (7).

Mutational analyses have defined two components of this system genetically, C_i transport (8) and intracellular CA (9). The defined loci, *ca-1* and *pmp-1* are represented by mutants *ca-1-12-1C*, *ca-1-cia-1*, *ca-1-cia-2*, *ca-1-cia-3*, *ca-1-18-6A*, *ca-1-18-7C* and *pmp-1-16-5K* (8, 9, 10, 11). Although general functions affected by these genetic lesions are known, the defective components have not specifically been identified.

2. MATERIALS AND METHODS

Wild-type *C. reinhardtii* strain 2137, cell-wall-less, wild-type strains CW-15 and CC1615, CO_2R mutants *ca-1-12-1C*, *ca-1-18-6A*, *ca-1-18-7C*, *pmp-1-16-5K*, and cell-wall-less, CO_2R strains *ca-1-12-1C-112*, *ca-1-18-6A-173* and *ca-1-18-7C-72* were cultured as described (11). Other methods used have been described (6, 11).

3. RESULTS AND DISCUSSION

Characteristics associated with the CO_2-concentrating system were compared for air-adapted and CO_2-enriched cells of wild type and CO_2R mutants (Table 1). In wild type, $K_{0.5}(C_i)$ of photosynthesis at 21% O_2 decreased dramatically after exposure to limiting CO_2, but the $K_{0.5}(C_i)$ was not significantly changed in any of the mutants and was much higher even than that of CO_2-enriched wild-type. Since the $K_{0.5}(C_i)$ of CO_2-enriched mutants is much higher than that of CO_2-enriched wild type, a lesion in either locus results in greatly reduced affinity for C_i even in CO_2-enriched cells. If genes corresponding to the loci *ca-1* and *pmp-1* were expressed only in air-adapted cells, photosynthetic characteristics of the mutants and wild type should be similar in CO_2-enriched cells. Therefore, the genes representing both loci must be expressed at least in part constitutively.

In addition, a lack of change in the C_i affinity of the mutant cells following induction was observed. In spite of the lack of change in C_i affinity, all mutants exhibited changes associated with induction of the CO_2-concentrating system (Table 1). All four mutants exhibited an induction of specific polypeptides (see below, 5) as observed with wild-type cells exposed to limiting CO_2 (5, 6) and an increase in CA activity. The C_i accumulation ratio increased in air-adapted cells of the *ca-1* mutants, although over-accumulation of C_i occurred in both air-adapted and CO_2-enriched cells. In *pmp-1-16-5K*, on the other hand, C_i was not accumulated into either cell type. However, this mutant apparently is deficient in C_i transport so an increase in C_i transport would not be expected. Although other components of the CO_2-concentrating system were induced in these mutants, the defective component in each was sufficient to prevent any significant increase in the affinity for C_i. Therefore, all components of the CO_2-concentrating system may be required to significantly affect the affinity for C_i when cells adapt to limiting CO_2.

TABLE 1: Photosynthetic characteristics of wild type (2137) and four CO_2R mutants of *C. reinhardtii*.

strain	growth	$K_{0.5}C_i$[1]	C_i[2]	CA[3]
2137	24h air	25	16.5	177.2
	5% CO_2	200	2.6	14.0
16-5K	24h air	600	1.9	106.9
	5% CO_2	550	1.6	4.7
12-1C	24h air	635	88.2	136.9
	5% CO_2	640	49.3	3.4
18-6A	24h air	620	75.4	112.8
	5% CO_2	740	35.8	5.6
18-7C	24h air	900	69.4	127.0
	5% CO_2	810	48.8	5.9

[1]$K_{0.5}$ of photosynthesis for C_i at 21% O_2 (μM).
[2]Ratio of [C_i] (internal/external).
[3]Carbonic anhydrase activity (units/mg Chl).

A distinctive characteristic of *ca-1* mutants is over-accumulation of intracellular C_i, thought to represent bicarbonate accumulation from C_i transport in the absence of intracellular CA (6, 9, 12). Such over-accumulation was observed in both CO_2-enriched and air-adapted cells of *ca-1* mutants, although it was less extreme in CO_2-enriched cells (Table 1). These results suggest that active C_i transport occurs in both cell types, although at a lower rate in CO_2-enriched cells. C_i transport in both air-adapted and CO_2-enriched cells would be consistent with the C_i affinity of CO_2-enriched *pmp-1* cells being lower than wild type, since this mutation apparently affects C_i transport. The data also indicate that C_i transport increases during induction. Thus, the wild-type allele of the *pmp-1* locus might be up-regulated under limiting CO_2.

Several authors have reported polypeptides induced *Chlamydomonas* cells by limiting CO_2 (3, 4, 5, 6). Because their appearance correlates with induction of the CO_2-concentrating system, the induced polypeptides are candidates for involvement in this system. The mutations at *ca-1* and *pmp-1* are inherited as nuclear-encoded genes (8, 9). When labeled polypeptides induced in response to limiting CO_2 were examined

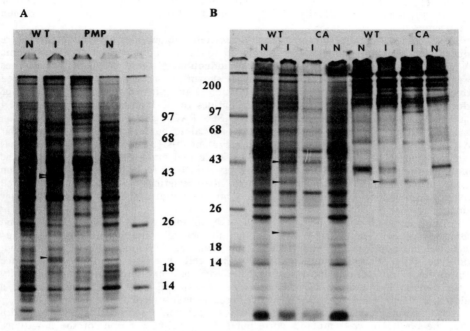

FIGURE 1. Fluorographs of SDS-PAGE gels of A) soluble proteins from CO_2-enriched (N) and 4h air-adapted cells (I) of C. reinhardtii wild type 2137 (WT) and pmp-1-16-5K (PMP) and B) total cellular protein (first four lanes) and extracellular protein (next four lanes) from CO_2-enriched (N) and 4h air-adapted cells (I) of C. reinhardtii wild type CC1615 (WT) and ca-1-12-1C-112 (CA). Arrows indicate polypeptides induced in wild type, including periplasmic CA (B, lane 6).

in the presence of CHI or CAM, induction of two membrane-associated polypeptides of 36 and 21 kD and three soluble polypeptides, two of 45 to 50 kD and one of 21 kD, was inhibited by CHI but not CAM (data not shown). These results indicate that the induced polypeptides are probably encoded by nuclear genes and possibily correspond to the defective components of these nuclear gene mutants.

Comparison of induced polypeptides from the *pmp-1* mutant and wild type indicated no differences except an apparent lack of induction of two soluble polypeptides of 45 to 50 kD (Fig. 1). Two polypeptides of the same M_r were observed in air-adapted mutant cells and CO_2-enriched cells of both the mutant and wild type, but with lower relative abundance than in air-adapted wild type. Manuel and Moroney (5) reported lack of induction in this mutant of two polypeptides similar in size to those reported here. However, the observations above suggest the polypeptides are up-regulated rather than induced *de novo*. If so, the *pmp-1* mutant lacks up-regulation, although the polypeptides are not absent. If there is simply a lack of up-regulation it is unlikely the *pmp-1* locus represents the structural gene for either of the polypeptides. Since the wild-type allele of the *pmp-1* locus may be up-regulated during induction, lack of up-regulation of polypeptides seems to fit the *pmp-1* mutation. However, the *pmp-1* mutation reduces the C_i affinity of CO_2-enriched cells (see above). If the defect caused by the *pmp*-1 mutation were lack of up-regulation of these polypeptides the C_i affinity of CO_2-enriched cells of wild type and *pmp*-1 should be the same.

In *ca*-1-12-1C-112 the membrane-associated polypeptides (36 and 21 kD) were induced only weakly, although the soluble 45 to 50 kD polypeptides and periplasmic CA were induced normally (Fig. 2). Weak induction of these polypeptides also was observed with two other *ca*-1 alleles (data not shown), so it is unlikely that the altered induction resulted from a second site mutation. In spite of the apparent lack of induction of the membrane-associated polypeptides in *ca*-1 mutants during the first 4 h, the polypeptides were observed in stained SDS-PAGE gels after 24 h of induction (data not shown). Mutants in the *ca*-1 locus appear to be deficient in an intracellular CA (9, 12), so a missing polypeptide could represent this enzyme. Intracellular CA has been reported to be present in both CO_2-enriched and air-adapted cells (12), and the functional defect in the *ca*-1 mutants is expressed in both (see above). Weak induction of the intracellular CA is inconsistent with these findings. Therefore, the altered polypeptide induction is associated with *ca*-1 mutations but probably not as the primary lesion.

Exposure of wild-type cells to the CA inhibitor EZA, which gives a good phenocopy of *ca*-1 mutants (9, 12), resulted in lack of induction of the membrane-associated polypeptides but no effect on the membrane fraction from CO_2-enriched, wild-type cells or other fractions from either cell type (data not shown). Since suppression of polypeptide induction by EZA treatment exhibited the same specificity as the genetic lesion at *ca*-1, it is probable the altered polypeptide induction is a pleiotropic effect, possibly resulting from altered metabolism of the mutant.

It seems unlikely that the alterations in polypeptide induction observed with either the *pmp*-1 or *ca*-1 mutants correspond to the primary lesions of the mutations. These results also serve to illustrate the need for caution in interpretation of polypeptide changes found to be associated with genetic defects.

Abbreviations: CA, carbonic anhydrase; EZA, ethoxyzolamide; CO_2R, high CO_2 requiring; CAM, chloramphenicol; CHI, cycloheximide.

This research was supported by NSF grant DMB-8500835 and USDA-CRGO grant CRCR-1-1591.

REFERENCES

1. Badger, M.R. (1987) In The Biochemistry of Plants, a Comprehensive Treatise (Hatch, M.D., Boardman, N.K., eds.), Vol 10, Photosynthesis., pp 219-274, Academic Press, San Diego.
2. Badger, M.R., Kaplan, A. and Berry, J.A. (1980) Plant Physiol. 66,407-413
3. Bailly, J. and Coleman, J.R. (1988) Plant Physiol. 87,833-840
4. Coleman, J.R., Berry, J.A., Togasaki, R.T. and Grossman, A.R. (1984) Plant Physiol. 76,472-477
5. Manuel, L.J. and Moroney, J.V. (1988) Plant Physiol. 88,491-496
6. Spalding, M.H. and Jeffrey, M. (1989) Plant Physiol. 89,133-137
7. Moroney, J.V., Husic, H.D. and Tolbert, N.E. (1985) Plant Physiol. 79,177-183
8. Spalding, M.H., Spreitzer, R.J. and Ogren, W.L. (1983) Plant Physiol. 73,273-276
9. Spalding, M.H., Spreitzer, R.J. and Ogren, W.L. (1983) Plant Physiol. 73,268-272
10. Moroney, J.V., Tolbert, N.E. and Sears, B.B. (1986) Mol. Gen. Genet. 204,199-203
11. Suzuki, K. and Spalding, M.H. (1989) Plant Physiol. 90,1195-1200
12. Moroney, J.V., Togasaki, R.K., Husic, H.D. and Tolbert, N.E. (1987) Plant Physiol. 84,757-761

A PHOSPHOGLYCOLATE PHOSPHATASE MUTANT OF *CHLAMYDOMONAS REINHARDTII*

Kensaku Suzuki[a], Laura Fredrick Marek[b] and Martin H. Spalding[b] Inst of Biological Sciences[a], Univ Tsukuba, Tsukuba, Ibaraki 305, Japan; Dept of Botany[b], Iowa State Univ, Ames IA 50011 USA

INTRODUCTION

High-CO_2 requiring mutants of *Chlamydomonas reinhardtii* have been isolated and used to study the CO_2 concentrating mechanism which is induced in this unicellular green alga during growth under air levels of CO_2 (1). One of the high-CO_2 requiring mutants, 18-7F, has shown some characteristics that indicate it is not a mutant of some component of the CO_2-concentrating mechanism but a mutant deficient in phosphoglycolate phosphatase, the first enzyme specific to the photorespiratory metabolic pathway.

MATERIALS AND METHODS:

Physiological analyses: *Chlamydomonas reinhardtii* wild type strain 2137 (mt+) and the high-CO_2-requiring mutant 18-7F (mt+) were grown photoautrophically in liquid medium with 5% CO_2 in air ("CO_2 enriched" cells) (2). "Air-adapted" cells were obtained by aerating CO_2 enriched cells with air for about 24 hours before use.

Photosynthetic O_2 exchange was measured at 25C in a Rank O_2 electrode using cells suspended in CO_2-free MOPS-NaOH (20 mM pH 7.0) (3). ^{14}C labelling of photosynthetic products was done as described in (2) with these changes. Cells were equilibrated in a Rank O_2 electrode in the dark, ^{14}C-bicarbonate added, (100 μM or 2.5 mM initial concentration) and photosynthesis initiated by turning on the light (500 μE m^{-2} min^{-1}). Soluble cell extracts were fractionated on a cation exchange column of Bio-Rad AG 50W-8X, H+. Separation and quantification of the neutrals + acids cation exchange fraction was done by anion exchange HPLC using a Spheresorb 5/25 SAX column from Phasesep.

Phosphoglycolate phosphatase activity was determined by measuring phosphoglycolate dependent inorganic phosphate release (4) in MES-KOH (pH 6.3). Inorganic phosphate was determined as described by Ames (5). Non-specific phosphatase activity was determined by the same method using nitrophenylphosphate as substrate (4). Cell enzyme extract was obtained by disrupting cells by sonication or by pressure cell. Carbonic anhydrase activity was measured by monitoring the pH change at 2C in 25 mM barbital buffered solution (6). Enzyme units were calculated as described in (6).

Genetic Analyses: Gametogenesis, mating, zygote maturation and germination were performed as described by Sears et al (7). 18-7F was crossed with wild type CC801 (sp*r-1*) for tetrad analysis and with CC1930 (arg-2) and 186A81 (arg-7) for complementation analyses (8,9). Phenotypes of tetrads and diploids were determined with spot tests on agar plates (10).

M. Baltscheffsky (ed.), Current Research in Photosynthesis, Vol. IV, 509–512.
© 1990 *Kluwer Academic Publishers. Printed in the Netherlands.*

RESULTS AND DISCUSSION

The data in Table 1 show that 18-7F, like wild type, induces the CO_2 concentrating mechanism. Both external carbonic anhydrase activity and apparent photosynthetic affinity for CO_2 increase dramatically in air-adapted cells. In spite of induction of the concentrating mechanism, 18-7F shows both oxygen and light inhibition of photosynthetic O_2 evolution (Fig 1).

Photosynthetic O_2 evolution was inhibited in air-adapted cells when the cells were incubated in the light to deplete internal DIC prior to the addition of bicarbonate (Fig 1). The lowest photosynthetic rates were obtained under conditions which also favored maximum RuBP-oxygenase activity (21% O_2, high CO_2 grown cells = no induction of CO_2 concentrating mechanism), which suggested that a photorespiratory metabolic product might be accumulating and inhibiting photosynthesis.

Table 1. Photosynthetic characteristics in *C. reinhardtii* 2137 and the high-CO_2R mutant 18-7F

Strain	Cell type	$K_{1/2}$ DIC[a]	CA[b]
2137+	24h air	25	70.4
	5% CO_2	200	12.3
18-7F+	24h air	55	24.9
	5% CO_2	450	5.3

a: at 21% O_2

b: carbonic anhydrase activity of intact cells

Fig 1. Photosynthetic O_2 evolution as a function of added $NaHCO_3$ in 24h air-adapted cells of C. reinhardtii mutant 18-7F. O_2 evolution measured under 2% ($\circ$,$\bullet$) or 21% ($\triangle$,$\blacktriangle$) O_2. O_2 evolution measured after incubation of cells in the light to deplete internal C_i concentration, photosynthesis initiated by the addition of $NaHCO_3$ (L-L; $\circ$,$\triangle$). O_2 evolution measured without prior light incubation; $NaHCO_3$ was added and photosynthesis initiated by turning on the light (D-L; $\bullet$,$\blacktriangle$).

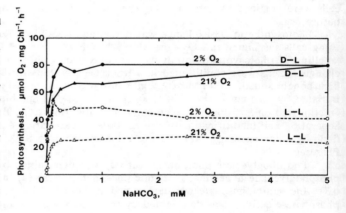

Analysis of acid-stable ^{14}C-labelled photosynthetic products from 18-7F (Table 2) showed a large accumulation of label in phosphoglycolate. 34% of the total label incorporated accumulated in P-glycolate after 5 min of photosynthesis in CO_2 enriched 18-7F cells labelled in low bicarbonate. No glycolate was detected. In wild type cells labelled under the same conditions, P-glycolate was barely detectable although appearance of a significant proportion of the ^{14}C in glycolate indicated flow of carbon into the photorespiratory pathway. Glycolate was never detectable in 18-7F but P-

Table 2. Percent of total acid-stable ^{14}C incorporated by *C. reinhardtii* 2137 and the high CO_2R mutant 18-7F after 5 min photosynthesis (pH 7.0, 25C). Cells were labelled with 100 μm or 2.5 mM $NaH^{14}CO_3$ initial concentration

| | 100 μM NaHCO$_3$ | | | | 2.5 mM NaHCO$_3$ | | | |
| | 5% CO$_2$ | | 24 h air | | 5% CO$_2$ | | 24h air | |
	WT	18-7F	WT	18-7F	WT	18-7F	WT	18-7F
insoluble	46.6	46.0	61.5	52.0	58.4	61.8	50.3	51.5
neutrals	1.3	1.1	2.1	4.6	2.7	5.9	2.5	8.5
acids								
glycolate	6.4	-	-	-	-	-	-	-
mono-P	11.1	4.6	16.2	4.1	17.0	3.6	10.7	6.9
PGA	3.9	-	2.4	-	3.5	3.9	10.8	5.5
P-glycolate	0.4	34.0	-	19.5	-	5.0	-	3.3
RuBP	6.1	-	12.2	1.1	-	-	1.4	0.3
basic	11.0	8.0	15.5	10.3	7.6	10.1	12.3	13.5

glycolate accumulation was always seen. P-glycolate accumulation was lowest in air-adapted cells. An accumulation of P-glycolate would be expected to inhibit triose phosphate isomerase (11) which would interfere with regeneration of RuBP. The O_2 and light inhibition of photosynthesis in 18-7F probably result form RuBP limitations to photosynthesis.

Phosphoglycolate phosphatase activity in 18-7F was 15% of the activity measured in wild type (data not shown). This amount of activity could be due to non-specific phosphatase activity which was estimated in the cell extracts using nitrophenylphosphate as the substrate. Non-specific phosphatase activity was the same in wild type and in the mutant. Mixing experiments indicated that the reduced enzyme activity in the mutant was not due to the presence of an inhibitor (data not shown).

Analysis of tetrads derived from the crossing of 18-7F with wild type CC801 (*spr*-1) showed that the low activity of phosphoglycolate phosphatase always co-segregated with the high CO_2 requiring phenotype (data not shown) and that the segregation pattern was 2:2. Activity of phosphoglycolate phosphatase in a heterozygous diploid strain was intermediate between the activity measured in a homozygous wild type diploid and in a homozygous 18-7F diploid. These data indicate a recessive mutation that results from a lesion in a single nuclear gene. Complementation analysis (data not shown) indicated that the lesion in 18-7F was not allelic to the lesions in 2 mutants defective in the CO_2 concentrating mechanism which also have high-CO_2 requiring phenotypes.

The physiological and genetic evidence described above indicate that the high-CO_2 requiring phenotype in the mutant 18-7F results from a deficiency in the photorespiratory metabolic pathway, not from a lack of the CO_2 concentrating mechanism.

REFERENCES

1. Spalding, M.H., Spreitzer, R.J. and Ogren, W.L. (1985) in Inorganic Carbon Uptake by Aquatic Photosynthetic Organisms (Lucas, W.J. and Berry, J.A., eds.), pp. 361-375, Am. Soc. Plant Physiol., Rockville
2. Spalding, M.H., Spreitzer, R.J. and Ogren, W.L. (1983) Plant Physiol. 73,268-272
3. Suzuki, K. and Spalding, M.H. (1989) Plant Physiol. 90,1195-1200
4. Husic, H.D. and Tolbert, N.E. (1985) Plant Physiol. 79,394-399.
5. Ames, B.N. (1966) Methods Enzymol. 8,115-118
6. Spalding, M.H. and Ogren, W.L. (1982) FEBS Let. 145,41-44
7. Sears, B.B., Boynton, J.E., and Gillham, N.W. (1980) Genetics 96,95-114
8. Loppes, R. and Matagne, R. (1972) Genetica 43,422-430
9. Loppes, R., Matagne, R. Strijkert, P.J. (1972) Heredity 28,239-251
10. Spreitzer, R.J., and Mets, L. (1981) Plant Physiol. 67,565-559
11. Anderson, L.E. (1971) Biochim. Biophys. Acta 235,237-244

This research was supported by NSF grant DMB-8500835 and USDA-CRCR-1-1591.
Abbreviations: CO_2R, CO_2 requiring phenotype

SELECTIVE INHIBITION OF CO_2 TRANSPORT IN A CYANOBACTERIUM

George S. Espie, Anthony G. Miller and David T. Canvin, Department of Biology, Queen's University, Kingston, ON, Canada K7L 3N6

1. INTRODUCTION

Accumulation of a large intracellular pool of DIC (CO_2+HCO_3^- +CO_3^{2-}) by cyanobacteria is mediated by mechanisms for the active transport of CO_2 and HCO_3^- and is essential for efficient photosynthetic assimilation of CO_2 (1). During steady-state photosynthesis CO_2 and HCO_3^- are transported simultaneously and continuously in light dependent processes (2). When the extracellular pH is alkaline and the [DIC] low, however, HCO_3^- transport is the predominant means of DIC acquisition (2,3,4). With air-grown cyanobacteria Na^+ at millimolar concentrations is required for HCO_3^- transport (3,4,5). Thus, by omitting Na^+ from the medium CO_2 transport may be studied without the complications of ongoing HCO_3^- transport. The ability to selectively inhibit CO_2 transport would be equally valuable. In this paper we report that carbonyl sulfide (COS) and hydrogen sulfide (H_2S) selectively and reversibly inhibit active CO_2 transport in Synechococcus UTEX 625.

2. MATERIALS AND METHODS

The unicellular cyanobacterium Synechococcus UTEX 625 was grown with air bubbling in unbuffered Allen's medium at 30°C (3). For experiments, cells were washed 3 times and suspended in Na^+- and CO_2-free Bis Tris Propane buffer, pH 8.0, at 30°C. The concentrations of dissolved O_2, H_2S, $^{12}CO_2$ $^{13}CO_2$ and COS (m/e = 32, 34, 44, 45, 60) were measured with a magnetic sector mass spectrometer equipped with a membrane inlet (6). Simultaneous measurements of Chl a fluorescence quenching associated with CO_2 and HCO_3^- transport (7) were made with a pulse amplitude modulation fluorometer. Actinic light to drive DIC transport and photosynthesis was provided by a quartz-halogen projector lamp at 210 $\mu E.m^{-2}.s^{-1}$. The ability to transport CO_2 was determined in two ways. The first method involved measuring CO_2 disappearance from illuminated suspensions following the addition of a "pulse" of CO_2. The second method involved measuring the increase (if any) in [CO_2] when cells were provided with a known [DIC] at the compensation point.

3. RESULTS AND DISCUSSION

Light dependent CO_2 uptake by Synechococcus UTEX 625 was progressively inhibited by increasing [Na_2S] or [COS] (Fig. 1). The inhibition of CO_2 transport was readily reversed following removal of H_2S or COS by gassing the suspension with N_2. Typically, 85 to 95%

M. Baltscheffsky (ed.), Current Research in Photosynthesis, Vol. IV, 513–516.
© 1990 Kluwer Academic Publishers. Printed in the Netherlands.

of the activity could be recovered. Inhibition of CO_2 transport occurred both in the absence and presence of Na^+ concentrations capable of supporting HCO_3^- transport. At constant $[Na_2S]$, it was found that CO_2 transport was inhibited to a much greater extent at pH 7, where 45% of the Na_2S exists as H_2S, compared to pH 8 where HS^- predominates. This result indicates that H_2S is the inhibitory sulfide species.

The hydrolysis of COS results in H_2S (and CO_2) formation. It is thus possible that COS inhibition of CO_2 transport was due solely to the presence of H_2S. However, the time course of COS inhibition was much more rapid (15-30 s) than COS hydrolysis (ca 5-8 min for 2 µm COS). In addition the [COS] required for maximum inhibition was about 3.5-fold lower than for Na_2S (Fig. 1).

The observed quenching of Chl $\underline{a}$ fluorescence when 25 µM DIC was added to illuminated cells at the compensation point (Fig. 2) was due primarily to HCO_3^- transport as little quenching occurred in the absence of 25 mM NaCl (not shown) and CO_2 transport was greatly limited by the CO_2 supply rate. Uptake of HCO_3^- was also indicated by the observation that photosynthesis exceeded the CO_2 supply rate by 11.7 fold. (Fig. 2). That CO_2 transport occurred, however, was shown by the fact the extracellular $[CO_2]$ remained near zero and well below the anticipated equilibrium concentration.

When 25 µM DIC was added to cells in the presence of 150 µM Na_2S, the $[CO_2]$ rose to a level considerably in excess of the anticipated equilibrium (Fig. 2) and indicated that CO_2 transport was greatly impaired. However, as judged by fluorescence quenching or photosynthetic O_2 evolution (Fig. 2) HCO_3^- transport was much less affected. Similar effects were also observed for COS (not shown). Using the silicone fluid filtering centrifugation technique (6) it was found that neither the initial rate of HCO_3^- transport nor CO_2 fixation was greatly reduced by COS.

The Na_2S (Fig. 2) or COS induced rise in $[CO_2]$ above the equilibrium level required Na^+ concentrations sufficient to support HCO_3^- transport. When $K_2^{13}CO_3$ was used to initiate similar experiments, the CO_2 arising in the medium was predominantly ^{13}C labelled indicating that the added DIC was the source of this CO_2. It appears then that the active transport and accumulation of HCO_3^- followed by intracellular conversion to CO_2 and leakage back to the medium is the mechanism responsible for the rise in extracellular $[CO_2]$. Once in the medium, CO_2 will be converted to HCO_3^- but presumably at a rate which is initially lower than the CO_2 efflux rate. Normally, leaked CO_2 is efficiently transported back into the cells keeping $[CO_2]$ near zero.

Carbonyl sulfide is structurally similar to CO_2 and for this reason may serve as a substrate for the CO_2 transport system. Fig. 3 shows that COS was, in fact, taken up by $\underline{Synechococcus}$ UTEX 625 cells and that the process is light dependent. Uptake of COS was inhibited by CO_2 (Fig. 3A) and by Na_2S (Fig. 3B).

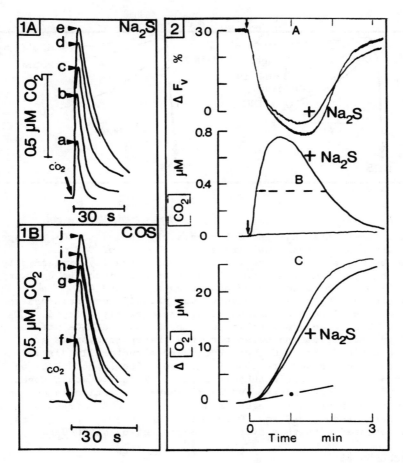

Figure 1. CO_2 transport was examined by pulsing illuminated cells with CO_2 contained in small aliquots of acidified water saturated with 5% v/v CO_2 at 0 C. Cells were suspended in buffer, pH 8, with 25 mM NaCl containing (a) 0, (b) 60, (c) 90, (d) 180 µM Na_2S or (f) 0, (g) 13, (h) 26, (i) 39 µM COS. Curves e and j are dark controls (no CO_2 transport).

Figure 2. Time dependent changes in Chl a fluorescence yield (A), $[CO_2]$ (B) and photosynthetic O_2 evolution (C) in buffered cell suspensions (pH 8), containing 25 mM NaCl, following the addition (↓) of 25 µM DIC in the absence and presence of 150 µM Na_2S. Dashed line (---) indicates $[CO_2]$ in equilibrium with 25 µM DIC. Broken line (—·—) is maximum CO_2 supported photosynthesis.

Figure 3. Light dependent uptake of COS in the absence or presence of various concentrations of DIC or Na$_2$S.

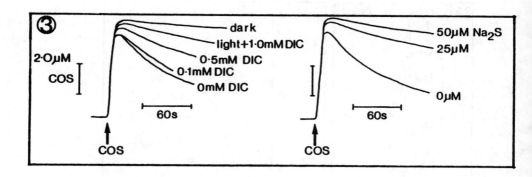

The data showed that H$_2$S and COS reversibly inhibited CO$_2$ transport but had little effect on HCO$_3^-$ transport. Uptake of COS was inhibited by CO$_2$ and H$_2$S. These data are most readily explained by assuming that CO$_2$ competed with COS for transport into the cell and that H$_2$S directly blocked the uptake of both CO$_2$ and COS. In previous studies (2,4,6,7) we have shown that Li$^+$, monensin and the lack of Na$^+$ inhibited HCO$_3^-$transport without greatly affecting CO$_2$ transport. The selective inhibition of both CO$_2$ and HCO$_3^-$ transport in this cyanobacterium indicates that the transport systems are separate entities. Since CO$_2$ and HCO$_3^-$ are structurally dissimilar the transport mechanisms are also likely to differ. Both H$_2$S and COS inhibit the enzyme carbonic anhydrase (CA). Thus, it would appear that the CO$_2$ transport system and CA may have properties in common, in agreement with earlier suggestions (1). That HCO$_3^-$ transport was largely unaffected by H$_2$S and COS suggest that CA-like properties may not be associated with this system. (Supported by NSERC Canada).

4.   REFERENCES

1.   Badger, M.R. (1987) in the Biochemistry of Plants Vol. 10 pp. 219-274, Academic Press.
2.   Espie, G.S., Miller, A.G. Birch, D.G. and Canvin D.T. (1988) Plant Physiol. 87: 551-554.
3.   Espie, G.S. and Canvin, D.T. (1987) Plant Physiol. 84: 125
4.   Miller, A.G. and Canvin, D.T. (1985) FEBS Lett. 187: 29-32.
5.   Kaplan, A. Volokita, M. Zenvirth, D. Reinhold L. (1984) FEBS Lett. 176: 166-168.
6.   Miller, A.G., Espie, G.S., Canvin, D.T. (1988) Plant Physiol. 86: 677-683
7.   Miller, A.G., Espie, G.S., Canvin, D.T. (1988) Plant Physiol. 86: 655-658.

CO₂ STORAGE AND CO₂ CONCENTRATING IN BROWN SEAWEEDS
I. OCCURRENCE AND ULTRASTRUCTURE

Hans Ryberg[1], Lennart Axelsson[3], Sonja Carlberg[2,3], Christer Larsson[2,3] and Jarmo Uusitalo[2,3]. Dept of Plant Physiology[1]; Dept of Marine Botany[2], Botanical Institute, Univ. of Göteborg, S-413 19 Göteborg, Sweden. Kristineberg Marine Biological Station[3], S-450 34 Fiskebäckskil, Sweden.

1. INTRODUCTION

Certain littoral brown seaweeds, notably of the family Fucaceae, are able to produce O_2 without any concomitant uptake of inorganic carbon (Ci), suggesting a 'CO₂ storing' capacity, similar to that of crassulacean plants (1,2). These algae also have properties suggesting the operation of a CO_2 concentrating mechanism, ie extremely low CO_2 compensation levels (3), O_2 insensitive photosynthesis (3,4) and high rates of photosynthetic carbon uptake both from gas phase (3,5) and from high pH seawater (2,6). In this paper, attempts have been made to correlate the occurrence of CO_2 storing and CO_2 concentrating in brown seaweeds with the occurrence of a specific ultrastructural organization, which has been described for this algal family (2,7). Other papers in this series describe in more detail the properties of the CO_2 concentrating system in relation to red and green algae (3) and make an attempt to describe the systems in metabolic terms (8).

2. MATERIALS AND METHODS

Most of the algae were collected at the Kristineberg Marine Biological Station, at the west coast of Sweden. *Himanthalia elongata* was collected at the west coast of Norway and *Hormosira banksii* at the south coast of Australia. Marine algae accumulate fairly high amounts of nitrate, which might give rise to O_2 production, independent of Ci uptake. By keeping the algae in a vigorously aerated aquarium, at a photon flux density of c 0.3 $mmol/m^2$ s, it was possible to greatly reduce this nitrate content (from c 5-10 down to 0.5-1 µmol/g fw for *Ascophyllum nodosum*).

Steady state photosynthesis was measured in a flowthrough system, both as rates of O_2 production and as rates of Ci uptake (ie CO_2 + kH⁺ uptake rates, calculated from the pH changes of the passing seawater; 1,2). Seawater free from Ci was prepared in barrels of 0.2 m³ by adding HCl, flushing with CO_2 free air, and adjusting the pH to a desired level with NaOH. This water, which contained less than 10 mmol m⁻³ of Ci, was used directly in the flowthrough system. By checking the total Ci content of the 'Ci-free' seawater (9) before and after the passage of the algae, it was possible to conclude that any increase in pH was almost exclusively caused by a proton uptake by the algae. The relation between the pH changes and the changes in alkalinity of the 'Ci-free' seawater (from which the rates of proton uptake could be derived) was obtained through calibrations (1,2).

3. RESULTS AND DISCUSSION

When *A. nodosum* was placed in a flowthrough system with 'Ci-free' seawater (<10 mmol m⁻³), there was an initially high rate of O_2 production, which during the following 24 h gradually decreased from 110 to 10 nmol/g fw min (Fig 1A;□). During this period, a total amount of c 48 µmol O_2/g fw was produced. The nitrate content of the algae was low, and the uptake of nitrate and Ci from the seawater was very small (maximal contribution to the O_2 production = 6 nmol/g fw min, ie 9 µmol/g fw during 24 h). Thus the major part of the

M. Baltscheffsky (ed.), Current Research in Photosynthesis, Vol. IV, 517–520.

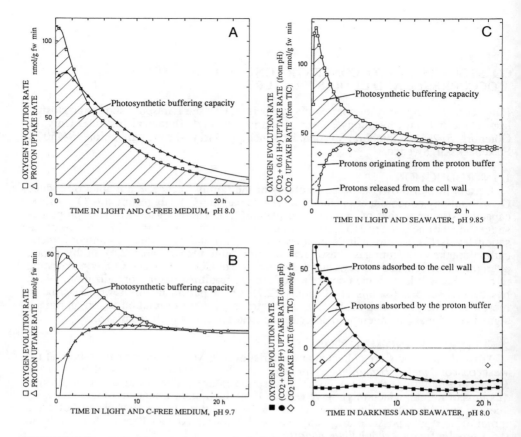

FIGURE 1. Rates of exchanges between *A. nodosum* and the passing medium in a flowthrough system. Before the measurements in A, B and C the alga was pretreated in darkness and normal seawater. D was measured directly after the treatment in C.

O_2 production (in the figure referred to as 'photosynthetic buffering capacity') must depend on an internal pool of photoreducible substances, most probably CO_2, derived from C-4 acids or amino acids, involved in the light independent CO_2 fixation of brown algae (1, 2, 10, 11). Accompanying the O_2 production, there was a pronounced proton uptake (△) of almost the same magnitude. This supports the suggestion that the CO_2-binding acids in *A. nodosum* occur as deprotonized anions, and that external protons are needed for a complete use of this CO_2-buffer (1, 2).

In high pH seawater free from Ci, the proton uptake was prevented (Fig 1B;△). At the same time there was a pronounced reduction in the total amount of O_2 produced (from 48 to 18 µmol/g fw). This reduced O_2 production in 'Ci-free' high pH seawater, is of a similar magnitude as the integrated transient O_2 production rate (photosynthetic buffering capacity) in high pH seawater of normal (c 2 mM) Ci content (Fig 1C). In both cases, the use of the bound CO_2 is probably restricted by protons derived from an internal pool (1). Consequently, when *A. nodosum* from Fig 1C was returned to darkness, and normal seawater

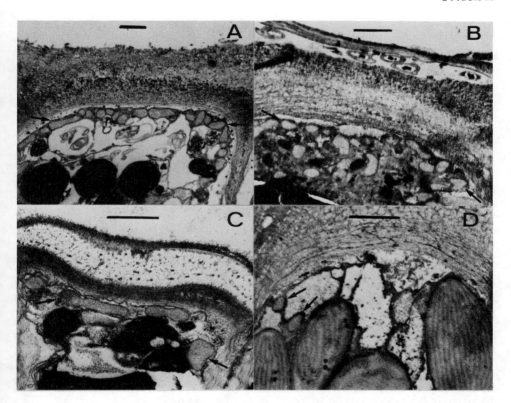

FIGURE 2. Electron micrographs at outer cell wall. A, *F. vesiculosus*; B, *A. nodosum*; C, *H. elongata*; D, *L. saccharina*. Arrows show mitochondria. The bars indicate 1 µm.

(pH 8.0), an uptake of totally 20 µmol H^+/g fw took place (Fig 1D;●). The protons were probably used to restore this proton pool, and the amount of protons absorbed is a measure of the size of this proton pool (1).

Ultrastructural investigations have revealed a specific organization of the meristo-dermal cells of members of the littoral brown algal family Fucaceae (2,7). A layer of mitochondria was localized close to the outer cell wall (Fig 2A,B), while the chloroplasts were localized towards the inner and side walls of the cells. Between the mitochondria and the chloroplasts there was a dense layer of physodes (cf 8). A similar organization was found in the littoral brown alga *Himanthalia elongata* (Fig 2C). The degree of mitochon-drial coverage at the outer cell membrane of several brown algae was quantified (Fig 3A). This property can be compared with the CO_2 compensation level in air (Fig 3B; measured as described in 3), with the Ci uptake (Fig 3C),and with different properties of the algae derived from experiments as these presented in Figs 1A,B (Fig 3D).

From this comparison, it appears to be a correlation between high density of mitochon-dria at the outer cell wall (Fig 3A) and properties related to a CO_2 concentrating mecha-nism, ie low CO_2 compensation levels (fig 3B), efficient HCO_3^- utilization at high pH (Fig 3C; ●) and high rates of CO_2 uptake from gas phase (Fig 3C;o). Such a correlation is understandable, and might indicate that ATP derived from mitochondrial respiration is

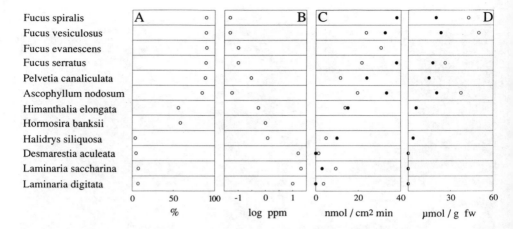

FIGURE 3. Some properties of different brown algae. A, per cent of the outer cell membrane area of the meristoderm covered by mitochondria; B, CO_2 compensation level in air; C, CO_2 uptake from air ($\circ$) and HCO_3^- uptake from seawater at pH 9.85 ($\bullet$; scale enlarged 20 times); D, photosynthetic buffering capacities in 'Ci-free' seawater at pH 8.0 ($\circ$) and at pH 9.7 ($\bullet$).

important for the CO_2 concentrating in these algae. There is also a correlation between occurrence of surface mitochondria and the different 'buffer capacities' presented in Fig 3D.

The best explanation to this situation is probably that the CO_2 concentrating and CO_2 storing systems are at least partly depending on the same metabolic systems. This is discussed in (8), where a tentative model for this integration has been worked out.

REFERENCES
1 Axelsson, L., Carlberg, S. and Ryberg, H. (1989, I) Plant Cell Envir. 12, in press
2 Axelsson, L., Carlberg, S. and Ryberg, H. (1989, II) Plant Cell Envir. in press
3 Uusitalo, J., Axelsson, L., Carlberg, S., Larsson, C. and Ryberg, H. (1989) These Proceedings
4 Johnston, A.M. and Raven, J.A. (1987) Phycologia 26, 159-166
5 Kremer, B.P. and Schmitz, K. (1973) Z. Pflanzenphysiol. 68, 357-363
6 Larsson, C., Axelsson, L., Carlberg, S., Ryberg, H. and Uusitalo, J. (1989) These Proceedings
7 McCully, M.E. (1968) J. Cell Sci. 3, 1-16
8 Axelsson, L., Carlberg, S., Larsson, C., Ryberg, H. and Uusitalo, J. (1989) These Proceedings
9 Axelsson, L. and Uusitalo, J. (1988) Mar. Biol. 97, 295-300
10 Akagawa, H., Ikawa, T. and Nisizawa, K. (1972) Bot. Mar. 15, 119-125
11 Kremer, B.P. (1981) Z. Naturforsch. 36c, 840-847

Supported by the Swedish Natural Science Research Council.

CO$_2$ STORAGE AND CO$_2$ CONCENTRATING IN BROWN SEAWEEDS II. FUNCTION IN GAS PHASE

Jarmo Uusitalo[1,2], Lennart Axelsson[1], Sonja Carlberg,[1,2], Christer Larsson[1,2] and Hans Ryberg[3]. Kristineberg Marine Biological Station[1], S-450 34 Fiskebäckskil, Sweden. Dept of Marine Botany[2]; Dept of Plant Physiology[3], Botanical Institute, Univ. of Göteborg, S-413 19 Göteborg, Sweden.

1. INTRODUCTION

CO$_2$ concentrating occur in a great number of vascular plants, both limnetic and terrestric, as well as in several both limnetic and marine microalgae. Using the terminology of Raven et al. (1), biochemical CO$_2$ concentrating predominates in vascular plants, while biophysical CO$_2$ concentrating is the only kind hitherto found in microalgae. Very few direct measurements of CO$_2$ concentrating have been carried out on marine macroalgae (2). HCO$_3^-$ is frequently utilized by several littoral marine macroalgae (3,4), and biophysical CO$_2$ concentrating is probably widespread in green macroalgae (5,6). Although evidence for HCO$_3^-$ uptake has been presented for *Rhodymenia palmata* (7), the mechanism for HCO$_3^-$ utilization in red macroalgae is very little investigated. In general, HCO$_3^-$ utilization, on a surface basis, appears to be much less efficient in littoral red macroalgae than in littoral brown and green macroalgae (8). Also from the results of pH drift experiments (3) different mechanisms for HCO$_3^-$ utilization between littoral red, green and brown macroalgae has been suggested. These data as well as recent investigations on *Chondrus crispus* (9), may be interpreted as if red algae rely on carbonic anhydrase (CA) for their HCO$_3^-$ utilization rather than on any CO$_2$ concentrating mechanism, at least their CO$_2$ concentrating is different from that of green and brown macroalgae. A biochemical CO$_2$ concentrating mechanism similar to that of the C$_4$ metabolism of certain terrestrial plants, has repeatedly been suggested for littoral algae (10,11), but has not been possible to verify in pulse chase experiments (12).

Reports on low CO$_2$ compensation levels using an infrared gas analyzer (IRGA), have been criticized for insufficient analytical precautions (13). An O$_2$ insensitive CO$_2$ uptake in gas phase has rewoken the idea of some kind of CO$_2$ concentrating (14) in the brown algal family Fucaceae, although the CO$_2$ concentrating in algal fragments of *Ascophyllum nodosum* was rather low (J.A. Raven, personal communication). The possibility that these algae may possess a biochemical CO$_2$ concentrating mechanism operating with one single enzyme (PEP-carboxykinase) and operating only during carbon limitation (15), and the discovery of a specific ultrastructure which might be connected to CO$_2$ concentrating (16) could perhaps to some extent explain the diverging results in this question.

In this paper, CO$_2$ compensation levels and CO$_2$ uptake in gas phase has been investigated for several brown, green and red macroalgae. In order to get a better understanding of their systems for photosynthetic uptake of inorganic carbon (Ci), the measurements were carried out at different O$_2$ concentrations.

2. MATERIALS AND METHODS

Most of the algae were collected at Kristineberg Marine Biological Station at the west coast of Sweden. *Pelvetia canaliculata* was collected at the west coast of Norway. *Himanthalia elongata* and *Alaria esculenta* were collected at the Faeroe islands and *Hormosira banksii* from the south coast of Australia. The experiments were carried out during the

M. Baltscheffsky (ed.), Current Research in Photosynthesis, Vol. IV, 521–524.
© 1990 *Kluwer Academic Publishers. Printed in the Netherlands.*

winter period (Nov-April).

CO$_2$ compensation levels at 10 C were measured in a closed loop system of circulating gas, with an IRGA, (ADC 225 Mark 3), using atmospheres with different O$_2$ tensions (0, 21 and 100 % O$_2$). The algal mass was kept fairly high (5-10 g fw) in order to avoid interference from small amounts of CO$_2$ leaking into the system. The zero level could be obtained at any time during the measurements by introducing a CO$_2$ absorber into the system.

The flowthrough system for measurements of CO$_2$ uptake in gas phase by the algae at different CO$_2$ concentrations allowed a rapid change in the O$_2$ content of the atmosphere, without affecting the CO$_2$ concentration. The effect of O$_2$ pressure on the CO$_2$ uptake could thus be detected with high accuracy (in fact much higher than can be discerned in Fig 4).

3. RESULTS AND DISCUSSION

A survey of all the measured CO$_2$ compensation levels (Fig 1) reveals the extremely low values for the members of the family Fucaceae (down to 0.05 ppm, left part of figure). The highest of the CO$_2$ compensation levels of *Pelvetia canaliculata* was obtained on specimens which had been kept in spray culture for some weeks. These specimens could be induced to show much lower values by repeated drying alternated with soaking in running seawater for several hours. As a further tendency, littoral algae as the Fucaceae (brown), *Ulva lactuca* (green) and *Porphyra umbilicalis* (red) appear to have the lowest CO$_2$ compensation levels within each taxonomical group, and among the littoral algae, the brown algae appear to be more efficient than the green, which in turn were more effective than the red. Many of the algae had much lower CO$_2$ compensation levels than the two limnetic C$_3$-plants. This could be interpreted as an indication of CO$_2$ concentrating mechanisms in these algae, especially since marine algae are assumed to have a Rubisco with a comparatively low affinity for CO$_2$ (17). The changes in CO$_2$ compensation levels as an effect of changing the atmosphere from

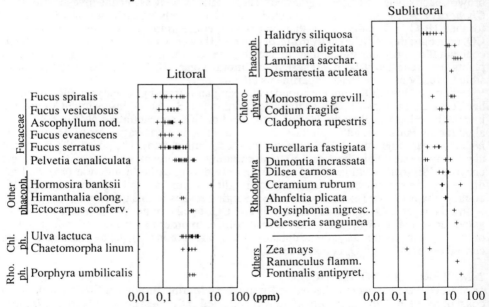

FIGURE 1. CO$_2$ compensation levels in air for brown, green and red macroalgae. For comparison CO$_2$ compensation levels for a C$_4$ (*Zea mays*) and two limnetic plants are shown.

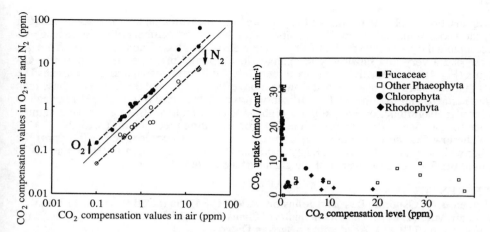

FIGURE 2. Effects on CO_2 compensation levels when changing from air (——————) to N_2 (O) or from air to O_2 (●).

FIGURE 3. CO_2 uptake in air vs CO_2 compensation levels for some marine macroalgae.

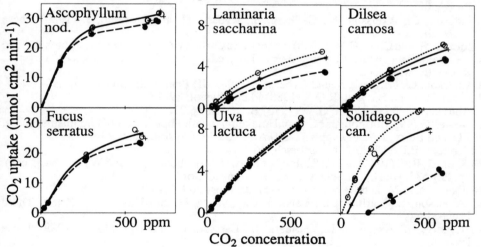

FIGURE 4. CO_2 uptake in gas phase at different partial pressures of CO_2 for five macroalgae and one terrestrial C-3 plant. The uptake was measured in a flow through system, in N_2 (O), air (+) and O_2 (●). Note the different scales.

air to N_2 or O_2 are best revealed on a logarithmic scale (Fig 2). From this plot, it appears that the effect (on a percent basis) is similar for all algae investigated. These data may be taken as evidence for the accuracy of the measuring system even down to the level of 0.1 ppm .

The data are not consistent with reports about low O_2 sensitivity of CO_2 compensation levels as a criterium for CO_2 concentrating systems (7,18). A comparison between the CO_2

compensation levels and the rate of CO_2 uptake in air measured on the same specimen (Fig 3), showed that the rather low CO_2 compensation levels for members of the Fucaceae was accompanied by a rather efficient CO_2 uptake from a gas phase. The CO_2 uptake from gas phase had a very low sensitivity to changes in O_2 partial pressure, as compared to C_3-plants (Fig 4). The sensitivity was extremely low for littoral brown and green algae. The fact that members of Fucaceae had a much more efficient CO_2 uptake from gas phase than *Ulva lactuca*, and that the HCO_3^- utilization (on a surface basis) in high pH seawater is of similar magnitude, or even slightly higher for *Ulva lactuca* (6) might have a significance for the location and nature of the CO_2 concentrating mechanisms (5,15,19).

The low CO_2 compensation levels for members of the Fucaceae (c 0.2-0.3 ppm) fits rather well with the values obtained by Surif and Raven (19; 2-4 ppm at pH 8.0 and 20-30 ppm at pH 5.5), assuming a pH of the algal surface close to 9.7 (cf 3).

REFERENCES

1 Raven, J.A., Osborne, B.A. and Johnston, A.M. (1985) Plant Cell Envir. 8, 417-425
2 Badger, M.R. (1987) *in* The Biochemistry of Plants (Hatch, M.D. and Boardman, N.K., eds), Vol. 10, pp.219-274, Academic Press, San Diego
3 Axelsson, L. and Uusitalo, J. (1988) Mar. Biol. 97, 295-300
4 Wheeler, W.N. (1982) *in* CRC Handbook of Biosolar Resources (Zabrosky, O. and Mitsui, A., eds), Vol. 1, pp.157-184, CRC Press, Florida
5 Carlberg, S., Axelsson, L., Larsson, C., Ryberg, H. and Uusitalo, J. (1989) These Proceedings
6 Larsson, C., Axelsson, L., Carlberg, S., Ryberg, H. and Uusitalo, J. (1989) These Proceedings
7 Colman, B. and Cook, C.M. (1985) *in* Inorganic Carbon Uptake by Aquatic Photosynthetic Organisms (Lucas, J.L. and Berry, J.A., eds) pp.97-110, Am. Soc. Pl. Physiol., Rockville, Maryland
8 Axelsson, L., Carlberg, S. and Ryberg, H. (1989, II) Plant Cell Envir. in press
9 Smith, R.G and Bidwell, R.G.S (1988) Plant Physiol. 89, 93-99
10 Karekar, M.D. and Joshi, G.V. (1973) Bot. Mar. 16,216-220
11 Bowes, G. (1985) *in* Inorganic Carbon Uptake by Aquatic Photosynthetic Organisms (Lucas, J.L. and Berry, J.A., eds) pp.187-210 Am. Soc. Pl. Physiol., Rockville
12 Kremer, B.P. (1981) Z. Naturforsch. 36c, 840-847
13 Kremer, B.P. (1981) *in* The Biology of Seaweeds (Lobban, C.S. and Wynne, M.J., eds), pp.493-533, Blackwell Scientific Publications, Oxford
14 Johnston, A.M. and Raven, J.A (1986) Oecologia 69, 288-295
15 Axelsson, L., Carlberg, S., Larsson, C., Ryberg, H. and Uusitalo, J. (1989) These Proceedings
16 Ryberg, H., Axelsson, L., Carlberg, S., Larsson, C. and Uusitalo, J. (1989) These Proceedings
17 Smith, R.G. (1988) Comp. Biochem. Physiol. 90B:4,639-654
18 Cook, C.M., Lanaras, T. and Colman, B. (1986) J. Exp. Bot. 37, 977-984
19 Surif, M.B. and Raven, J.A. (1989) Oecologia 78, 97-105

Supported by the Swedish Natural Science Research Council.

CO$_2$ STORAGE AND CO$_2$ CONCENTRATING IN BROWN SEAWEEDS III. A TENTATIVE WORKING MODEL

Lennart Axelsson[1], Sonja Carlberg[1,2], Christer Larsson[1,2], Hans Ryberg[3] and Jarmo Uusitalo[1,2]. Kristineberg Marine Biological Station[1], S-450 34 Fiskebäckskil, Sweden. Dept of Marine Botany[2]; Dept of Plant Physiology[3], Botanical Institute, Univ. of Göteborg, S-413 19 Göteborg, Sweden.

1. INTRODUCTION

The occurrence of some kind of CO$_2$ concentrating mechanism in marine macroalgae, and especially in the littoral brown algal family Fucaceae, has for some time been a matter of debate (1,2,3,4, cf 5). In spite of heavy labelling of malate and aspartate during ^{14}CO$_2$ photosynthesis (1), the ^{14}C incorporation pattern seems to exclude the operation of any mechanism similar to that of terrestrial C-4 plants (4,6). Some extent of inorganic carbon (Ci) concentrating obviously occurs during photosynthesis in the Fucaceae (c 4 times; J.A. Raven, personal communication). These algae also appear to possess external carbonic anhydrase (CA) activity (4).

Reinvestigations of the CO$_2$ compensation levels have revealed values down to 0.05 ppm (5). Thus, among the marine macroalgae, the fucacean family single out themselves by having extremely low CO$_2$ compensation levels (about one order of magnitude lower than that of any other alga measured), and a rather high CO$_2$ uptake rate from gas phase (about five times higher than that of the most efficient other algae; 5).

Other indications of CO$_2$ concentrating within this algal family is the fact that the photosynthetic CO$_2$ uptake in gas phase, over a wide range of CO$_2$ levels, is very little affected by changes in the O$_2$ partial pressure (5,7). They also have a very efficient HCO$_3^-$ utilization in high pH seawater (10). However, the fucacean algae share these two last properties with many littoral green algae, eg *Ulva lactuca* (5,8), which are also believed to have an efficient CO$_2$ concentrating mechanism (8,9).

In this paper, a metabolic scheme has been constructed, where an attempt has been made to connect the 'C-4' system with the CO$_2$ concentrating ability of the algae. The scheme also involves the biochemical CO$_2$ storing properties and a system for storage of protons, which are presented in part one of this series (10).

2. MATERIALS AND METHODS

Most of the algae were collected close to Kristineberg Marine Biological Station, at the west coast of Sweden, and immediately used for experiments (10). Steady state rates of photosynthesis were measured in a flowthrough system as changes in O$_2$ content and pH of the passing seawater (10,11). A closer description of calculations and preparation of 'Ci-free' seawater are presented in the first part of this series and references therein (10).

3. RESULTS AND DISCUSSION

The schematic drawing illustrates the possibility of a dual function (CO$_2$ storing and auxiliary CO$_2$ fixation) of the 'C-4 system' of the littoral brown algal family Fucaceae (Fig 1). The main entry for Ci will be along path I, where photosynthetically generated ATP is consumed in the photosynthetic carbon reduction cycle (PCRC).

M. Baltscheffsky (ed.), Current Research in Photosynthesis, Vol. IV, 525–528.
© 1990 *Kluwer Academic Publishers. Printed in the Netherlands.*

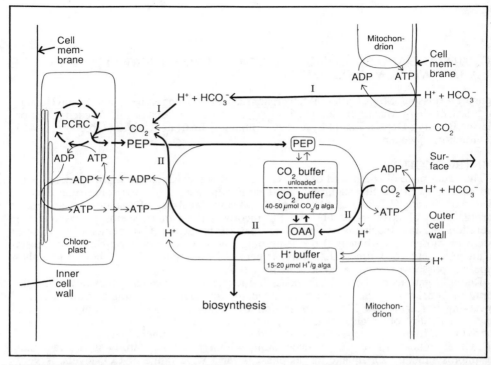

FIGURE 1. Working model for the CO_2 storing and the CO_2 concentrating in the littoral brown algal family Fucaceae

Lack of Ci at PCRC will cause an increased ATP export out of the chloroplast, initiating a transformation of oxalo acetic acid (OAA) into phosphoenol puruvic acid (PEP) and CO_2. OAA can be generated either from the CO_2 buffer or from PEP and CO_2. This generation may occur either at the outer cell membrane, thus completing a CO_2 concentrating along path II, or in the mitochondria using CO_2 preferentially from the respiration (cf Fig 2). Any use of the CO_2 buffer requires protons, either from the proton buffer or from the outside of the cell. The enzyme PEP carboxy kinase is assumed to have a key function both in the storage and the auxiliary fixation of CO_2.

Although most investigators report 100% incorporation of ^{14}C in phosphoglyceric acid (PGA; 6, J.A. Raven, personal communication) these investigations do probably not exclude a CO_2 transport along path II during conditions of severe CO_2 shortage. In fact, the results in (6) may suggest a limited (c 6%) ^{14}C incorporation in aspartate and malate for *Fucus serratus* already at the start of the fixation, while the corresponding value for *Laminaria saccharina* was close to zero.

The function of the C_4-system in Fucaceae is probably intimately connected with the specific ultrastructural organization of the meristodermal cells (Fig 2, cf 10). The very specific localization of most of the mitochondria close to the outer cell membrane is probably in some way important for the CO_2 concentrating system (Fig 3).

At the onset of incorporation, 100% of the ^{14}C activity of aspartate is derived via CO_2 fixation in the PCRC cycle (members of the Laminariaceae; 6). If

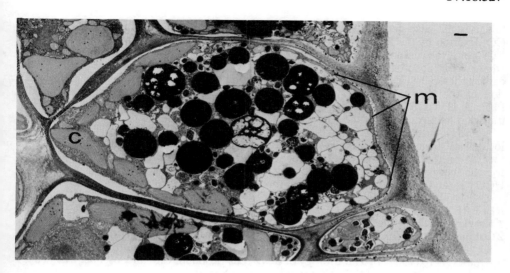

FIGURE 2. Electron micrograph of a
meristodermal cell of *Fucus vesiculosus*.
The membrane at the outer cell wall is
almost completely covered by mitochondria (m). Note the separation of the
mitochondria and the chloroplasts (c) at
the inner cell membrane. The bar indicates 1 μm.

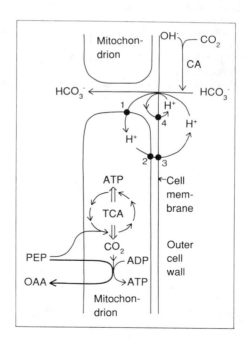

FIGURE 3. A possible model for the
C-4 system and the CO_2 concentrating in
Fucaceae, implying a specific role of
the mitochondria at the cell surface.
Possible locations for the ATP driven H^+
pump have been indicated (●).

this is valid also for the Fucaceae, which seems likely (cf 6), this implies that the CO_2 fixation by the PEP formed in the PCRC must be separated from the main entry of $^{14}C_i$ into the chloroplast. This situation fits well with the suggestion in Fig 3, where PEP absorbs respiratory CO_2 primarily and also provides fuel for the tricarboxylic acid (TCA) cycle. The model also comprise some suggestions for the operation of the Ci transporting system, which is driven by ATP, generated from or via PEP. A H^+/HCO_3^- symport is suggested for the Ci entry (4) driven by an active H^+ transport located at any of the places indicated in the figure.

It may be noted that CA will interfere with the H^+/HCO_3^- import if the pump is located at the cell membrane. This situation will not occur if the active H^+ pump is located on the 'end' parts of the mitochondria (position 1). CA is probably necessary for the very rapid CO_2 assimilation by these algae when emersed (5), at least if HCO_3^- is the Ci species crossing the cell membrane as suggested (4).

REFERENCES
1 Karekar, M.D. and Joshi, G.V. (1973) Bot. Mar. 16,216-220
2 Colman, B. and Cook, C.M. (1985) *in* Inorganic Carbon Uptake by Aquatic Photosynthetic Organisms, 97-110, Am. Soc. of Plant Physiologists, Rockville Maryland USA.
3 Kremer, B.P. (1981) *in* The Biology of Seaweeds (Lobban, C.S. and Wynne, M.J., eds), pp.493-533, Blackwell Scientific Publications, Oxford
4 Surif, M.B. and Raven, J.A. (1989) Oecologia 78, 97-105
5 Uusitalo, J., Axelsson, L., Carlberg, S., Larsson, C. and Ryberg, H. (1989) These Proceedings
6 Kremer, B.P. (1981) Z. Naturforsch. 36c, 840-847
7 Johnston, A.M. and Raven, J.A (1986) Oecologia 69, 288-295
8 Larsson, C., Axelsson, L., Carlberg, S., Ryberg, H. and Uusitalo, J. (1989) These Proceedings
9 Carlberg, S., Axelsson, L., Larsson, C., Ryberg, H. and Uusitalo, J. (1989) These Proceedings
10 Ryberg, H., Axelsson, L., Carlberg, S., Larsson, C. and Uusitalo, J. (1989) These Proceedings
11 Axelsson, L. (1988) Mar. Biol. 97, 287-294

Supported by the Swedish Natural Science Research Council.

INDUCIBLE CO₂ CONCENTRATING MECHANISMS IN GREEN SEAWEEDS I. TAXONOMICAL AND PHYSIOLOGICAL ASPECTS

Sonja Carlberg[1,2], Lennart Axelsson[1], Christer Larsson[1,2], Hans Ryberg[3] and Jarmo Uusitalo[1,2]. Kristineberg Marine Biological Station[1], S-450 34 Fiskebäckskil, Sweden. Dept of Marine Botany[2]; Dept of Plant Physiology[3], Botanical Institute, Univ. of Göteborg, S-413 19 Göteborg, Sweden.

1. INTRODUCTION

Following its discovery, CO_2 concentrating has been found to be fairly widespread among microalgae (1). Since the marine environment should be very suitable for the development of CO_2 concentrating mechanisms it has for some time been suspected that the very efficient HCO_3^- utilization by some green macroalgae (2,3) should depend on a CO_2 concentrating ability (3,4). In spite of this, there are no reports about CO_2 concentrating in green macroalgae (1). This is probably due to the fact that the method for demonstrating CO_2 concentrating, ie silicon oil centrifugation, was developed for microalgae (5). So far we know only of two attemps to adapt this method to cell clusters of fragmented macroalgae, and only two marine algae have been tested, the brown alga *Ascophyllum nodosum*, which had a limited CO_2 concentrating ability (6), and the red alga *Chondrus crispus*, where no CO_2 concentrating ability was found (7). One prominent feature of the CO_2 concentrating mechanism in microalgae is its absence when the algae have been grown in media with good supply of CO_2 (bubbled with 5% CO_2), and its ability to gradually develop during some 4-8 hours, when the algae have been transferred to a medium with low CO_2 content (bubbled with normal air; 1,8). The development of a flowthrough system for steady state photosynthesis in high pH (ie low CO_2) seawater (9, 10), resulted in the discovery of a gradually increasing HCO_3^- utilization by *Ulva lactuca* (11), very similar to the induction of CO_2 concentrating described for green microalgae (cf 1,8). Encouraged by this, we initiated a thorough investigation of the occurrence of inducible HCO_3^- utilization in other green seaweeds.

2. MATERIALS AND METHODS

All algae were collected at the west coast of Sweden, and in most cases used directly in the experiment. *U. lactuca* was kept in culture in vigorously aerated seawater, in perspex cylinders of 20 l, continuously supplied with seawater from 35 m depth. *Codium fragile* and *Chaetomorpha linum* were kept in spray culture in a greenhouse (12). Rates of steady state photosynthesis were measured in a flowthrough system as changes in pH and O_2 content of the passing seawater (9). The pH changes were recalculated directly into rates of inorganic carbon (Ci) uptake (10), neglecting the small contribution to pH changes caused by proton uptake (cf 9).

3. RESULTS AND DISCUSSION

When cultivated *U. lactuca* was exposed to high pH seawater, the pH changes of the passing seawater indicated an initially low rate of HCO_3^- utilization (<50 nmol/g fw min) which gradually (during c 10 h at c 16 C) approached a higher steady state level (c 700 nmol/g fw min; Fig 1). The similar shape of the curve illustrating the changes in the O_2 production rate is a strong support for the assumption that the major part of the pH changes are caused by an uptake of Ci. An experiment carried out in April on several

M. Baltscheffsky (ed.), Current Research in Photosynthesis, Vol. IV, 529–532.

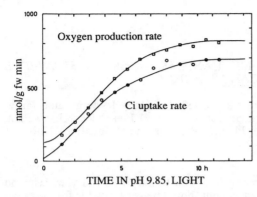

| | Rate of HCO$_3^-$ utilization | | Temp |
Alga	nmol / g fw min	nmol / cm^2 min	C
Ulva lactuca cultiv.	387	2.4	6-7
Ulva lactuca cultiv.	419	2.7	10
Ulva lactuca cultiv.	691	4.9	16-17
Enteromorpha linza	514	4.6	16-17
E. compressa	407	3.6	6-7
Monostroma grevillei	648	2.0	10
Acrosiphonia centralis	408	0.6	6-7
Cladophora rupestris	133	0.2	6-7
Chaetomorpha linum	84	0.1	6-7
Codium fragile	0	0	6-7

FIGURE 1. Gradual increase in O$_2$ production rate and inorganic carbon (Ci) uptake rate (calculated from pH changes), for *Ulva lactuca* photosynthesizing in a flowthrough system with high alkalinity seawater. Temperature 16-17 C, light intensity c 0.3 mmol m^{-2} s^{-1}.

TABLE 1. Maximal rates of HCO$_3^-$ utilization in high alkalinity (pH 9.85) seawater for some green macroalgae. Light intensity c 0.3 mmol m^{-2} s^{-1}.

species of green algae collected from the sea, revealed the same pattern of induced HCO$_3^-$ utilization and O$_2$ production for most of the littoral algae (Fig 2).

From this and similar experiments, it was concluded that the littoral green algae *Acrosiphonia centralis, Enteromorpha compressa, E. linza* and *Monostroma grevillei* had about the same capability to gradually enhance their HCO$_3^-$ utilization in high pH seawater, and also about the same HCO$_3^-$ utilization efficiency when activated, calculated on a fresh weight basis (Table 1). *Cladophora rupestris* and *Chaetomorpha linum*, which are typical "undergrowth" algae showed a considerably lower HCO$_3^-$ utilization efficiency (calculated on a fresh weight basis), although the time needed to complete their activation appeared to be similar (about 24 h at this temperature, ie 6-7 C).

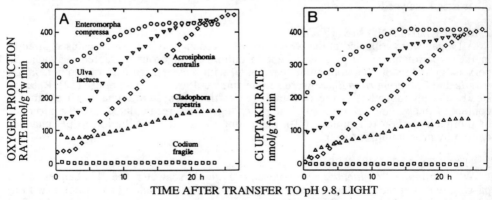

FIGURE 2. Gradual increase in O$_2$ production rate (A) and Ci uptake rate (B) for green macroalgae collected in late winter (cf Fig 1). Temperature 6-7 C.

If calculations were carried out on a surface basis, the efficiency of the very fine-threaded *A. centralis* was much lower than that of the more leafshaped littoral green algae *Ulva, Enteromorpha* and *Monostroma* (Table 1). The Ci uptake rate from the seawater by these algae amounted to at least 0.6 mol/m³s, which is considerably higher than the maximal rate of CO_2 formation in seawater of pH 9.8 and 2 mM Ci (cf 6), thus implying a direct utilization of the HCO_3^- pool of the seawater. The low CO_2 content of the seawater (<20 nM) and the comparatively high Ci uptake rate (c 3 nmol/cm²min) is a strong indication that the HCO_3^- utilization is accompanied by a CO_2 concentrating at Rubisco. The activation of the HCO_3^- utilization was temperature dependent, with a Q10 >4 (Figs 1 and 2). Taking into account the temperature dependency, the activation time agrees well with that reported for green microalgae (4-8 h, usually at 25-28 C; 1, 8).

By inserting *U. lactuca* in a closed loop connected to an IRGA (cf 13) it was possible to measure both the CO_2 uptake rate (Fig. 3) and the CO_2 compensation level in gas phase. No difference could be detected between specimens with and without activated HCO_3^- utilization. At the same time the extremely low O_2 sensitivity of the CO_2 uptake by *U. lactuca* in gas phase (13) is a strong indication that the CO_2 concentrating is working also in these conditions. One outcome of these results is that green seaweeds probably modify their HCO_3^- use by regulating their carbonic anhydrase (CA) activity in the cell wall, and that the CO_2 concentrating is always activated. This should agree with a preliminary report by Bowes (4), who failed to detect any changes in properties associated with CO_2 concentrating ability in *Udotea* and *Codium* as a response to different growth conditions. The results also seem to exclude the possibility that the CO_2 concentrating in *U. lactuca* (and probably other littoral green algae) is working through some kind of HCO_3^- utilization in the periplasmatic space (14). If it is located at the plasmalemma, it has to be an active CO_2 uptake. The Ci pump may also be located at the chloroplast membrane. It does not appear to be enough 'room' for any biochemical CO_2 concentrating between the plasmalemma and the chloroplasts (cf. Fig 5B). The induction of HCO_3^- use is not a simple process, as exemplified by *Chaetomorpha linum* (Fig 4). The first time this alga was exposed to high pH seawater, there was a pronounced lag period before the induction started . After deactivation for three weeks, the reaction occurred without lag and at a faster rate. The significance of this has yet to be evaluated.

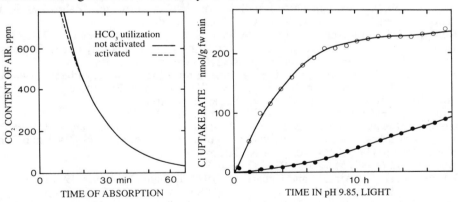

FIGURE 3. CO_2 absorption by *Ulva lactuca* from a closed volume of CO_2 enriched air.

FIGURE 4. Activation of the HCO_3^- utilization in lowlight grown *C. linum* for the first time (●) and reactivation after 20 days in normal seawater (○). Conditions as in fig 2.

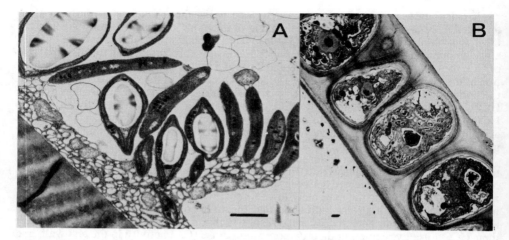

FIGURE 5. Electron micrographs of *Codium fragile* (A) and *Enteromorpha compressa* (B). The bars indicate 1 μm.

Only one of the green algae investigated, *C. fragile*, completely lacked the capacity to induce HCO_3^- utilization at high pH (Fig. 2). This alga has a very peculiar ultra-structural organization (Fig 5A), with very small connections between the main cytoplasm and the chloroplasts. This might suggest that a well established cytoplasm connection from cell membrane to chloroplast, as in *E. compressa* (Fig 5B), is necessary for the function of the inducible HCO_3^- utilization of green seaweeds.

REFERENCES
1 Badger, M.R. (1987) *in* The Biochemistry of Plants (Hatch, M.D. and Boardman, N.K., eds), Vol. 10, pp.219-274, Academic Press, San Diego
2 Wheeler, W.N. (1982) *in* CRC Handbook of Bisolar Resourses (Zabrosky, O. and Mitsui, A., eds), Vol 1, pp.157-184, CRC Press, Florida
3 Kerby, N. W. and Raven, J. A. (1985) Advances in Botanical Research 11, 71-123
4 Bowes, G. (1985) *in* Inorganic Carbon Uptake by Aquatic Photosynthetic Organisms (Lucas, W.J. and Berry, J.A., eds), pp.187-210, Waverly Press, Baltimore
5 Raven, J.A. (1985) *in* Inorganic Carbon Uptake by Aquatic Photosynthetic Organisms (Lucas, W.J. and Berry, J.A., eds), pp.67-82, Waverly Press, Baltimore
6 Surif, M.B. and Raven, J.A. (1989) Oecologia 78, 97-105
7 Smith, R.G. and Bidwell, R.G.S. (1987) Plant Physiol. 83, 735-738
8 Coleman, J.R., Green, L.S., Berry, J.A., Togasaki, R.K. and Grossman A.R. (1985) *in* Inorganic Carbon Uptake by Aquatic Photosynthetic Organisms (Lucas, W.J. and Berry, J.A., eds), pp.339-360, Waverly Press, Baltimore
9 Axelsson, L. (1988) Mar. Biol. 97, 287-294
10 Axelsson, L., Carlberg, S. and Ryberg, H. (1989, I) Plant Cell Envir. 12, in press
11 Axelsson, L., Carlberg, S. and Ryberg, H. (1989, II) Plant Cell Envir. in press
12 Lignell, Å. and Pedersén, M. (1986) Bot. Mar. 29, 509-516
13 Uusitalo, J., Axelsson, L., Carlberg, S., Larsson, C. and Ryberg, H. (1989) These Proceedings
14 Lucas, W.J. (1985) *in* Inorganic Carbon Uptake by Aquatic Photosynthetic Organisms (Lucas, W.J. and Berry, J.A., eds), pp.229-254, Waverly Press, Baltimore

INDUCIBLE CO₂ CONCENTRATING MECHANISMS IN GREEN SEAWEEDS II. ECOLOGY AND FIELD OBSERVATIONS

Christer Larsson[1,2], Lennart Axelsson[1], Sonja Carlberg[1,2], Hans Ryberg[3] and Jarmo Uusitalo[1,2]. Kristineberg Marine Biological Station[1], S-450 34 Fiskebäckskil, Sweden. Dept of Marine Botany[2]; Dept of Plant Physiology[3], Botanical Institute, Univ. of Göteborg, S-413 19 Göteborg, Sweden.

1. INTRODUCTION

In a majority of green seaweeds investigated, an inducible HCO_3^- utilization has been found, in some aspects similar to the inducible CO_2 concentrating described for several green microalgae (1,2,3). Investigations on field collected algae soon revealed that in some of the collected specimen, a certain activation of this HCO_3^- utilization must have been present already at the time of collection and also that the degree of activation varied between specimens collected from different localities. This paper describes the basis for the calculation of the activation degree on field collected green algae, and also presents data on some specimens collected during the late summer.

2. MATERIALS AND METHODS

All algae were collected close to Kristineberg Marine Biological Station at the west coast of Sweden, and in most cases used directly in the experiment. *Ulva lactuca* was kept in culture in vigorously aerated seawater, in perspex cylinders of 20 l, continuously supplied from the deep water system of the station (from 35 m depth). *Chaetomorpha linum* was kept in spray culture in an outdoor greenhouse (4). Rates of steady state photosynthesis were measured in a flowthrough system as changes in pH and O_2 content of the passing seawater (5). The pH changes were recalculated directly into rates of inorganic carbon (Ci) uptake (6), neglecting the small contribution to pH changes caused by proton uptake (cf 5).

3. RESULTS AND DISCUSSION

The gradual activation of the rate of HCO_3^- utilization for three different seaweeds, photosynthesizing in high pH seawater in the flowthrough system is shown in Fig. 1. Assuming the same proportion of H^+ to CO_2 uptake throughout the measurements, the exact degree of induction of the HCO_3^- utilization at the start of the experiment should be given by the expression 100a/b which is in per cent of the final rate of utilization. The possibility of small transients in the rate of proton uptake at the start of the experiment, results in an uncertainty of this value. The figure illustrates how this uncertainty was handled for three slightly differently shaped induction curves, ie how the curves were drawn and how this uncertainty was estimated. Thus, in Fig. 1, the initial activation for *Enteromorpha compressa* was between $100a_1/b$ and $100a_2/b$, ie 53-58%. The initial activation for *U. lactuca* was 20-28% and that for *Acrosiphonia centralis* 0-6%.

Since some period (less than 1 h) elapsed between the collection of the algae and the measurements, it was necessary to get some measure of the rate of deactivation of the HCO_3^- utilization. Thus six samples of *U. lactuca*, which had reached full activation (cf Fig 1), were returned to normal seawater at 14 C for 48 h. When reexamined according to the standard method (Fig 1), all samples still retained more than 60% activation, with little difference between samples kept in light or in darkness during the deactivation

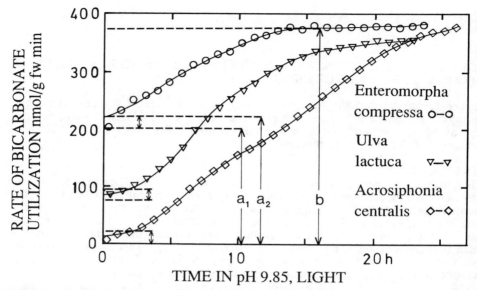

FIGURE 1. Gradual increase in HCO₃⁻ utilization for some green macroalgae exposed to high pH seawater in a flowthrough system. The values used to determine the initial activation degree (in per cent of final activation) are indicated by arrows (cf text).

(mean value $\pm$ SE = 63 $\pm$ 2.9%). The deactivation probably reflects the gradual disappearance of extracellular carbonic anhydrase (CA; 1,2) and, like the deactivation of the CO_2 concentrating in green microalgae, appears to occur at a much slower rate than the activation (cf 2,3). It can be noted that while the deactivation of the CO_2 concentrating in green microalgae usually is complete after c 24 h (cf 3), complete deactivation of the HCO₃⁻ utilization of *U. lactuca* appears to require some 3 days. Thus assuming a deactivation rate of less than 1% per h the deactivation during the time between the collection of the algae and the measurements of the activation degree was probably very small.

    U. lactuca, *E. compressa* and *E. linza*, collected from different localities of the sea in the afternoon on a sunny day in August, all had a certain degree of activation (Fig 2).

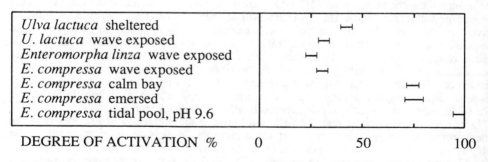

FIGURE 2. Initial activation of the HCO₃⁻ utilization system of field collected green macroalgae according to measurements as in Fig. 1.

The activation was lowest for specimen from wave exposed localities (c 30%), increased sharply in calm water (40-70%) and was highest in tidal pools (c 100%). No difference could be detected between submersed and emersed *E. compressa* (c 75%). For comparison, *E. compressa* collected from a tidal pool in late winter (April) showed an initial degree of activation of 55%, while *A. centralis*, collected at a depth of 0.5 m showed a very low degree of activation (cf Fig 1).

A comparison between *U. lactuca*, the most efficient of the green algae investigated (1), and the most efficient of the brown algae (the littoral family Fucaceae; 7) and the most efficient red alga (*Porphyra umbilicalis*), reveals some ecological aspects of their HCO_3^- utilization and CO_2 concentrating systems (Figs 3,4).

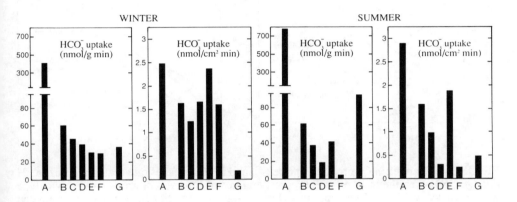

FIGURE 3. HCO_3^- utilization capacity for some littoral algae in winter (measured at 7-10C) and in summer (measured at 17-20 C). A, *Ulva lactuca*; B, *Fucus spiralis*; C, *F. vesiculosus*; D, *F. serratus*; E, *Ascophyllum nodosum*; F, *Pelvetia canaliculata*; G, *Porphyra umbilicalis*.

On a fresh weight basis, the HCO_3^- utilization capacity of *U. lactuca* is superior to that of brown and red algae, both in winter and in summer. The HCO_3^- utilization for both *U. lactuca* and *P. umbilicalis* is more efficient in summer, probably as a direct consequence of the higher temperature. For the brown algae, the HCO_3^- utilization is more efficient in winter, especially for *Pelvetia canaliculata* and *Fucus serratus* (Fig. 3), suggesting a seasonal adaptation in the HCO_3^- utilization of these algae, compensating for effects of the lower temperature. Thus at a sudden decrease in Ci availability, eg due to low rates of water exchange (exemplified by the high pH seawater in Fig. 4), the CO_2 buffer (cf 6) as well as the activated HCO_3^- utilization of *F. spiralis* results in highest possible photosynthetic capability even in cold water.

For *U. lactuca* both the maximum HCO_3^- utilization rate (Fig 3) and the induction of HCO_3^- utilization (Fig. 4) occur at a much lower rate in colder water (Q10 for the activation is c 4; 1), suggesting that the HCO_3^- utilization system of green algae is less suitable for colder regions of the sea.

4. CONCLUSION

HCO_3^- utilization can vary considerably between specimens of green algae collected at different localities.

This variation can be used to get a better insight into the ecological conditions, ie the importance of such factors as water motion, temperature, irradiation and nutrient status of the water.

The Ci handling systems of brown algae seem to be better adapted to colder regions of the sea than the HCO_3^- utilization system of green algae.

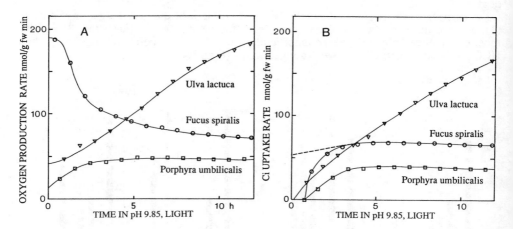

FIGURE 4. Changes in O_2 production rate (A) and in 'Ci uptake' rate (calculated from pH changes; B) when the most efficient representatives of littoral red, green and brown algae were exposed to high pH seawater in a flowthrough system. For *F. spiralis* a pronounced proton excretion during the first 3 h makes the value for 'Ci uptake rate' in the figure less representative of the true rate of the Ci uptake. During this period, the Ci uptake rate is better represented by the broken line (cf 6).

REFERENCES
1 Carlberg, S., Axelsson, L., Larsson, C., Ryberg, H. and Uusitalo, J. (1989) These Proceedings
2 Badger, M.R. (1987) *in* The Biochemistry of Plants (Hatch, M.D. and Boardman, N.K., eds), Vol. 10, pp.219-274, Academic Press, San Diego
3 Kaplan, A. (1985) *in* Inorganic Carbon Uptake by Aquatic Photosynthetic Organisms (Lucas, W.J. and Berry, J.A., eds), pp.325-338, Waverly Press, Baltimore
4 Lignell, Å. and Pedersén, M. (1986) Botanica Marina 29, 509-516
5 Axelsson, L. (1988) Mar. Biol. 97, 287-294
6 Axelsson, L., Carlberg, S. and Ryberg, H. (1989, I) Plant Cell Envir. 12, in press
7 Axelsson, L., Carlberg, S. and Ryberg, H. (1989, II) Plant Cell Envir. in press

Supported by the Swedish Natural Science Research Council.

SUBSTRATE BINDING TO NADP-MALIC ENZYME FROM MAIZE LEAVES AS DETERMINED BY INTRINSIC FLUORESCENCE QUENCHING

CARLOS S. ANDREO, FLORENCIO E. PODESTA AND ALBERTO A. IGLESIAS
CENTRO DE ESTUDIOS FOTOSINTETICOS Y BIOQUIMICOS (CONICET, F.M.LILLO, U.N.R.), Suipacha 531, 2000 ROSARIO, ARGENTINA

1. INTRODUCTION

NADP-malic enzyme catalyzes the decarboxylating step of the C_4 pathway of photosynthesis at the bundle-sheath chloroplasts in maize leaves (1). The enzyme purified from different C_4 plants exhibits a homotetrameric structure, although variations in the oligomeric state have been reported (2).

A divalent cation (presumably Mg^{2+} *in vivo*) is essential for the enzyme activity (3). The decarboxylase is specific for NADP and uses preferentially the L-isomer of malate (3). The binding patterns for the different effectors of the plant enzyme have been determined by means of kinetic measurements (3).

This work reports on studies on the binding of NADP to the maize malic enzyme, performed through intrinsic fluorescence quenching under conditions where the emission spectra were obtained by preferentially exciting triptophanyl residues (4). The results, compared with those of kinetic studies, are discussed in terms of the role of L-malate and Mg^{2+} in the binding of NADP to the malic enzyme.

2. PROCEDURE

2.1. Materials and Methods

2.1.1. <u>Enzyme purification and assay</u>. NADP-malic enzyme was purified to apparent electrophoretic homogeneity from *Zea mays* leaves as previously described (3). Enzyme activity was spectrophotometrically assayed at 30°C and pH 7 by following NADP reduction at 340 nm as in (3). One unit (U) of enzyme is defined as the amount that catalyzes the formation of 1 μmol of NADPH per minute.

2.1.2. <u>Fluorescence measurements</u>. Intrinsic fluorescence was determined in a Perkin-Elmer 650-40 fluorescence spectrophotometer thermostated at 30°C, using excitation and emission wavelengths of 295 and 336 nm, respectively. A buffer solution of 50 mM Hepes at pH 7 was used for enzyme desalting and for fluorescence measurements. ΔF is defined as $F_0 - F$ where F_0 and F are the fluorescence intensity of the protein in the absence or presence of the quencher,

M. Baltscheffsky (ed.), Current Research in Photosynthesis, Vol. IV, 537–540.
© 1990 *Kluwer Academic Publishers. Printed in the Netherlands.*

respectively. Final absorbance at 336 nm of each sample was maintained below 0.020, making unnecessary any correction for the inner filter effect. All solutions were previously filtered through Millipose HAWP 0.45 μm poresize filters.

2.1.3. Chemicals. All reagents used were of analytical grade.

3. RESULTS AND DISCUSSION

Excitation of NADP-malic enzyme at 295 nm revealed a broad fluorescent peak in the range of 305 to 360 nm (Figure 1). The addition of 5 mM L-malate and/or 10 mM MgCl₂ did not alter the fluorescence spectrum. For this reason, an arbitrary wavelength (in this case 336 nm) was chosen to follow the fluorescence changes (4), thus avoiding the interference produced by the Raman band of water at 308 nm (Figure 1).

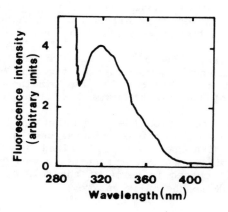

FIGURE 1. Corrected intrinsic fluorescence spectrum of NADP-malic enzyme obtained with an excitation light of 295 nm. Protein concentration was 10 μg x ml^{-1}.

The fluorescence quenching was dependent on NADP concentration, allowing the study of its binding to the protein. Figure 2A shows a double reciprocal plot of ΔF against the NADP concentration obtained at pH 7 in the absence (line a) or in the presence of 10 mM MgCl₂ (line b) or 5 mM L-malate (line c).

The non-linear plots shown in Figure 2A suggest a rather complex way for the binding of NADP to the enzyme, which is also influenced by the presence of either MgCl₂ or L-malate.

Hill plots of the data from Figure 2A evidenced the existence of cooperativity in the nucleotide binding. As shown in Table 1, in the absence of MgCl₂ and L-malate, a positive cooperativity (n_H of 1.50) and a relatively low affinity (K_d = 1.28 mM) were observed, indicating the existence at least two sites for the binding of NADP.

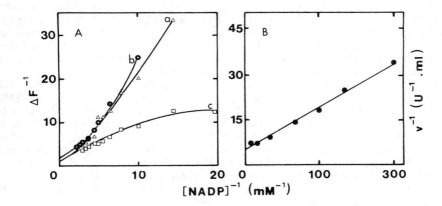

FIGURE 2. A: Double-reciprocal plots of ΔF versus NADP concentration in the absence ($\triangle$) or the presence of 10 mM MgCl$_2$ ($\bigcirc$) or 5 mM L-malate ($\square$). B: Double reciprocal plot of enzyme activity versus NADP concentration. MgCl$_2$ and L-malate concentrations were 10 and 5 mM, respectively.

TABLE 1.   NADP-binding parameters of maize leaf malic enzyme, obtained from Hill plots from Figure 2A (lines a, b, c) or from Figure 2B (line d) data.

Condition	K_d (mM)	K_m (mM)	n_H
a. No additions	1.28	–	1.50
b. + 10 mM MgCl$_2$	0.38	–	1.57
c. + 5 mM L-malate	0.11	–	0.18
d. b + c	–	0.020	1.00

MgCl$_2$ (10 mM) markedly increased the affinity of malic enzyme for NADP (K_d = 0.38 mM), without significant change in the cooperativity (n_H = 1.57). L-malate not only highly decreased the K_d value to 0.11 mM but also notoriously affected the allosteric behavior, as revealed by an n_H value of 0.18 (Table 1). Contrarily to this findings, cooperativity was absent in saturation isotherms for NADP obtained from kinetic studies (Figure 2B). From these hyperbolic patterns (n_H = 1) a K_m value for NADP of 0.020 mM was calculated (Table 1).

The fluorescence quenching technique allows performing binding studies under non-catalytic conditions. Thus, it is possible to independently characterize the interactions of the protein with its substrates and/or effectors. The results presented herein strongly suggest that the binding of NADP to the malic enzyme occurs at more than one site, exhibing positive cooperativity. No information was obtained for the interaction of Mg^{2+} and/or L-malate since these ligands did not alter the intrinsic fluorescence of the protein. However, the presence of either $MgCl_2$ or L-malate significantly affected the binding pattern of NADP, although in different manners: both effectors highly increased the affinity for NADP of the malic enzyme, but L-malate, besides, also sharply changed the cooperativity degree (n_H decreased from 1.50 in the absence to 0.18 in the presence of hydroxyacid).

In agreement with previous reports concerning the C_4 plants NADP malic enzyme (3,5) an absence of cooperativity in the binding of NADP and a K_m value in the range of 0.020 mM was seen under catalytic conditions. These data are considerably different when compared with those obtained by fluorescence quenching. The interpretation of the difference suggests that Mg^{2+} and L-malate favour the binding of NADP and change the whole allosteric behavior of the enzyme. However, it should be noted that the distinct binding patterns could be the consequence of the different techniques employed. A more accurate comparison could be achieved by using substrate analogues (providing cuasi-catalytic conditions) in fluorescence measurements.

ACKNOWLEDGEMENTS
     This work was supported by grants from the Consejo Nacional de Investigaciones Científicas y Técnicas (CONICET, Argentina) and from the Third World Academy of Sciences (BC 898-125). CSA and AAI are members of the Investigator Career from CONICET and FEP is a Fellow of the same Institution. C.S. Andreo is a recipient of a fellowship from the John Simon Guggenheim Memorial Foundation.

REFERENCES
1 Edwards, G. and Walker, D.A. (1983) in C_3, C_4: Mechanisms, and Cellular and Environmental Regulation of Photosynthesis, pp 299-325, Blackwell Scientific Publications, Oxford, London.
2 Thorniley, M.S. and Dalziel, K. (1988) Biochem. J. 254, 229-233
3 Iglesias, A.A. and Andreo, C.S. (1989) Plant Cell Physiol. 30, 399-406
4 Lehrer, S.S. and Leavis, P.C. (1978) Methods Enzymol. 49, 222-236
5 Asami, S., Inoue, K., Matsumoto, K., Murachi, A. and Akazawa, T. (1979) Arch. Biochem. Biophys. 194, 503-510

THE CO_2 CONCENTRATING FUNCTION OF C_4 PHOTOSYNTHESIS

R.T. Furbank, C.L.D. Jenkins and M.D. Hatch, CSIRO Division of Plant Industry, P.O.Box 1600, Canberra 2601, AUSTRALIA.

INTRODUCTION

C_4 plants suppress photorespiration by concentrating CO_2 at the site of ribulose-1,5-bisphosphate carboxylase (Rubisco). During photosynthesis in C_4 leaves an inorganic carbon pool develops which is up to 10 x that expected by simple equilibration with external CO_2 (1). The effective concentration of CO_2 in bundle sheath cells requires that the mesophyll-bundle sheath cell interface be resistant to CO_2 diffusion. The more "leaky" this interface is to CO_2 the more energy must be expended by "overcycling" of the C_4 cycle relative to net $CO2$ assimilation to maintain a high bundle sheath CO_2 concentration. The work presented here quantitatively examines the permeability of the bundle sheath-mesophyll interface to CO_2 and its implications for C_4 photosynthesis.

PROCEDURE

We examined the conductance of bundle sheath cells to CO_2 by determining the permeability coefficient for CO_2 diffusion into the bundle sheath compartment (P_{co2}). P_{co2} is defined as:

$$P_{co2} = CO_2 \text{ flux} / CO_2 \text{ gradient} \qquad (1)$$

The flux of CO_2 into bundle sheath cells was determined by measuring photosynthetic $CO2$ fixation, using Rubisco as a "coupling" enzyme. At strictly limiting CO_2 concentrations and saturating levels of RuBP, the rate of CO_2 fixation by Rubisco is equal to CO_2 flux into the bundle sheath cells. The CO_2 concentration in the cells, $[CO_2]_{IN}$, was calculated according to equation 2:

$$v = \frac{V_{MAX} [CO_2]_{IN}}{[CO_2]_{IN} + K_c (1 + [O_2]/K_o)} \qquad (2)$$

M. Baltscheffsky (ed.), Current Research in Photosynthesis, Vol. IV, 541–544.
© 1990 *Kluwer Academic Publishers. Printed in the Netherlands.*

where v is the rate of CO_2 fixation, K_c is the K_m for CO_2 and K_o the K_i for O_2 of Rubisco and V_{MAX} is the maximum activity of Rubisco extracted from the tissue used in this study.

RESULTS AND DISCUSSION

Two experimental systems were used in this study. Firstly, isolated bundle sheath cells were illuminated in the presence of limiting CO_2, and P_{CO_2} was calculated according to equations 1 and 2. Secondly, intact leaves of C_4 plants were treated with DCDP, an inhibitor of PEP-carboxylase (2), and then induced to fix CO_2 directly into the bundle sheath by providing high levels of CO_2 to the mesophyll gas phase. Leaves treated in this way were found to fix CO_2 predominantly by the C_3 pathway (as determined by analysis of radio-labelled products). P_{CO_2} was calculated from the known external CO_2 concentration required to partially restore photosynthesis and the rate of photosynthetic O_2 evolution.

The range of P_{CO_2} values obtained for five C_4 plants by both methods is shown in the following table. P_{CO_2} values determined for C_3 cells from *Xanthium strumarium* and literature values for C_3 leaves (3) are shown for comparison.

	P_{CO_2}	
Plant type and experimental system	μmol min^{-1} mg Chl^{-1} mM^{-1}	cm s^{-1}
C_4 leaves	6-21	$1.6\text{-}5.6 \times 10^{-3}$
C_4 cells	6-30	$1.6\text{-}4.5 \times 10^{-3}$
C_3 leaves	1595-3190	$71\text{-}140 \times 10^{-3}$
C_3 cells	510-3000	-

Where possible, values are given both as flux per unit gradient and as cm s^{-1}, calculated from published values for cell surface area per unit chlorophyll. These data show that bundle sheath cells of C_4 plants are 1 to 2 orders of magnitude less permeable to CO_2 than C_3 cells.

Using the derived values of P_{CO_2}, the leakage of CO_2 out of the bundle sheath during photosynthesis and consequent overcycling can be quantified. However, this is possible only if the pool size, composition and compartmentation of bundle sheath inorganic carbon are known. Of these parameters, only the size of the bundle sheath inorganic carbon pool has been measured (1). As carbonic anhydrase (CA) activity is extremely low in the bundle sheath cells (4), inorganic carbon equilibrates slowly in this compartment. The proportion of CO_2 and HCO_3^- present depends not only on pH but on rates of carbon leakage out of the cells, the rate of C_4 acid decarboxylation and the rate of CO_2 incorporation. Taking the bundle sheath inorganic carbon pool to be 55 nmol mg^{-1} Chl and the net photosynthesis rate as $6.5\,\mu$mol min^{-1}mg Chl^{-1} (from ref. 1), and the volumes and pHs of cell compartments (taken from electron micrographs and literature determinations) we modelled the concentration of CO_2 and HCO_3^- throughout the bundle sheath cell of a "typical" C_4 plant as a set of simultaneous equations. The solution to this model at air levels of CO_2 is shown in Figure 1.

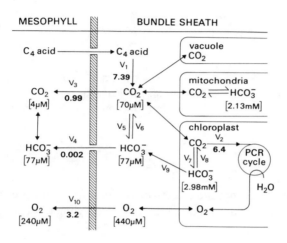

FIGURE 1

We previously examined the response of total bundle sheath inorganic carbon in *Urochloa panicoides* leaves to varying external CO_2 (1). This data was used in conjunction with the above P_{CO_2} values and our model of inorganic carbon composition to predict bundle sheath CO_2 concentration, the bundle sheath $[CO_2]/[O_2]$ ratio and the rate of overcycling (Figure 2). The model predicts that overcycling would remain a constant proportion of net photosynthesis over a wide range of photosynthetic fluxes. $[CO_2]/[O_2]$ in the bundle sheath would remain high enough to suppress photorespiration to between 3% and not more than 8% of carbon assimilation as net photosynthesis declines from 7 to $2\,\mu$mol min^{-1} mg Chl^{-1}. C_4 acid overcycling would be required to exceed net photosynthesis by 10-15% to maintain the calculated bundle sheath CO_2 pool in these experiments.

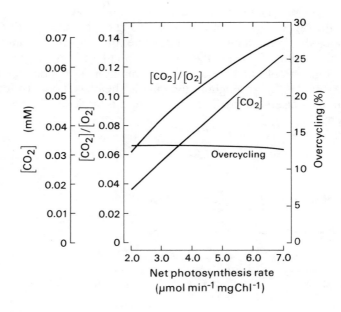

FIGURE 2

This model demonstrates that the effective elimination of photorespiration in C_4 plants within energetically acceptable limits of overcycling is an exercise in optimisation.

REFERENCES

1 Furbank, R.T. and Hatch, M.D. (1987) Plant Physiol. 85, 958-964.
2 Jenkins, C.L.D., Harris, R.L.N. and McFadden, H. (1987) Biochem. Int. 14, 219-226.
3 Evans, J.R., Sharkey, T.D., Berry, J.A. and Farquhar, G.D. (1986) Aust. J. Plant Physiol. 13, 281-292.
4 Burnell, J.N. and Hatch, M.D. (1988) Plant Physiol. 86, 1252-1256.

REGULATION OF CO_2 FIXATION IN THE CAM PLANT KALANCHOE PINNATA (L.) Pers. BY CELLULAR NITRATE

BALAKUMAR, T., SIVAGURU, M., MOORTHY, P., JAMES, M.R. AND ANBUDURAI, P.R., Unit of Stress Physiology and Plant Biochemistry, Department of Botany, The American College, Madurai 625 002, India.

INTRODUCTION

Voluminous reports (1) have appeared to elucidate the physiology and biochemistry of the Crassulacean Acid Metabolism (CAM). Nevertheless, its mechanism of regulation still continues to be a curiosity. Little information is available on nitrate (NO_3^-) assimilation in CAM tissues or on its coincidence or coordination with the other cycles which are characteristic of CAM, such as malate production in the dark. In the present paper we report a possible relationship between the efficiency of nitrate assimilation and CO_2 fixation (malate production) in the CAM plant **Kalanchoe pinnata**.

PROCEDURE

Plants of **Kalanchoe pinnata** (L.) Pers. growing in natural clones in our college premises show polymorphic (simple, transitionary and trifoliate) leaves (Plate 1a and 1b). Each form of leaf was chosen from the same nodal position and analyses were made. Efficiency of CO_2 fixation in the leaves was measured in terms of titratable acidify and chl a fluorescence transients were monitored. Further, cellular nitrate content and in vivo nitrate reductase (NR) activity in the leaves were also determined. The index of nitrate utilization (assimilation) efficiency was expressed as NR/NO_3^- ratio.

RESULTS AND DISCUSSION

Polymorphic leaves of **Kalanchoe pinnata** show marked difference in their ability to fix CO_2 (Fig.1). The trifoliate leaves are more efficient compared to the other two forms of leaves.

The higher level of 'M' peak of chl a fluorescence transients (Fig.2) also indicates that malate production (CO_2 fixation) is more in the trifoliate leaves.

Even though the cellular nitrate content and in vivo NR activity are lower in the trifoliate leaves as compared to the simple and transitionary ones, NO_3^- assimilation efficiency estimated as NR/NO_3^- ratio reveals that the trifoliate leaves only have greater efficiency over the other two (Fig.3).

M. Baltscheffsky (ed.), Current Research in Photosynthesis, Vol. IV, 545–548.
© 1990 *Kluwer Academic Publishers. Printed in the Netherlands.*

PLATE 1a

Kalanchoe pinnata in natural habitat.

PLATE 1b

Polymorphic leaves of **Kalanchoe pinnata** (Simple, Transitionary & Trifoliate).

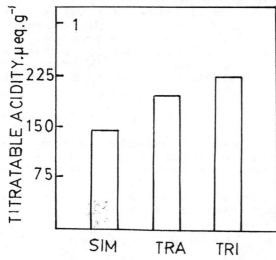

FIGURE 1

Titratable acidity (malate production) in the polymorphic leaves of **Kalanchoe pinnata.**
sim – simple;
tra – transitionary;
tri – trifoliate.

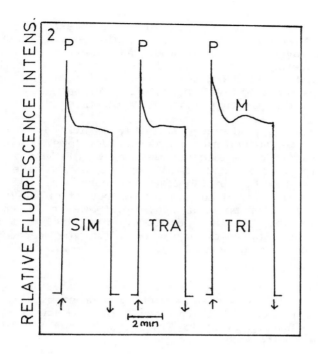

FIGURE 2 Room temperature chl a̲ fluorescence transients of the polymorphic leaves of **Kālanchoe pinnata.**

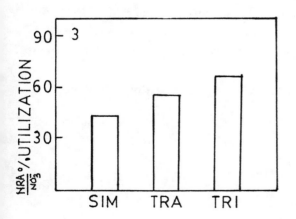

FIGURE 3

Nitrate utilization (assimilation) efficiency (NR/NO$_3^-$) of the polymorphic leaves of **Kalanchoe pinnata**.

Recently, it has been shown that exogenous supply of nitrate plays a crucial role in CO_2 fixation in the CAM plant **Kalanchoe blossfeldiana** (2). The most surprising feature of our data is the correlation that is found between NR/NO_3^- ratio and the quantum of malate production, which reveals that nitrate assimilation efficiency, rather than availability of nitrate, may be an important factor in CO_2 fixation in the CAM plants.

Nitrate reductase activity, which is the rate-limiting step in nitrate assimilation in plants, develops to a maximum in a CAM plant canopy before either RuBPCase, or PEPCase or CAM(3). It has been shown earlier that nitrate-grown plants have higher malate accumulation and higher PEPCase and dark CO_2 fixation(4). Therefore, from the findings of our studies the role of nitrate metabolism in the regulation of CAM appears possible, however, it may be indirect. Despite this, more specific studies are needed from other CAM plants also to conclusively establish the mechanism of regulation of CAM by nitrate metabolism.

Acknowledgement

This work was supported by a grant by the Research and Development Committee of the American College, Madurai 625 002, India. The authors are grateful to Prof. Sam George for the help rendered in taking photographs.

REFERENCES

1   Ting, I.P.(1985) **Ann. Rev. Plant Physiol. 36**, 595-622

2   Ota, K., Tezuka, T. and Yamamoto, Y. (1988) **Plant Cell Physiol. 29**, 533-537

3   Chang, N.M., Vines, H.M. and Black, C.C.(1981) **Plant Physiol. 68**, 464-468

4   Schweizer, P. and Erismann, K.H.(1985) **Plant Physiol. 78**, 455-458

EFFECTS OF STRESS ON PHOTOSYNTHESIS

Thomas D. Sharkey, Francesco Loreto, Terry L. Vassey, Department of Botany, University of Wisconsin, Madison WI 53706 USA

1. INTRODUCTION

Stress describes one part of the interaction between plants and their environment. The environment also provides resources and information. The distinctions between stress, supply of resources, and information are not always well defined.

Studies of the effects of stress on photosynthesis are usually undertaken to increase our understanding the interaction between photosynthesis and the vagaries of the environment. Stress was viewed as reducing the plant's capacity to attain its genetic potential. It was common to hear that the lesion in photosynthesis caused by a particular stress was sought so that we could engineer or somehow manipulate the plant to overcome the stress effect.

This underlying view of stress as preventing the full expression of the photosynthetic process has given way to a new viewpoint or paradigm. Now it is believed that plants respond to the vagaries of their environment with a myriad of coping mechanisms which promote survival. In the past these mechanisms have been arbitrarily divided into adaptive strategies and stress effects. As our understanding of the various mechanisms have increased, we have realized that many of the behaviors observed in response to stress are not easily categorized as either adaptive coping mechanisms or deleterious effects of stress on the photosynthetic apparatus.

In this paper, we will describe studies of the rate of photosynthesis in leaves of C_3 plants and how water-related stresses affect the rate of photosynthesis. What we shall see is that there is a specific enzyme in photosynthesis whose activity is severely restricted by even mild water stress. However, these changes in enzyme activity fall into the category of sensing information rather than the category of deleterious consequences of stress. To get to this conclusion we shall first describe methods used in studying the biochemistry of photosynthesis in intact leaves.

2. METHODS

2.1. **Analytical gas exchange** is the study of photosynthetic responses to perturbations

M. Baltscheffsky (ed.), Current Research in Photosynthesis, Vol. IV, 549–556.
© *1990 Kluwer Academic Publishers. Printed in the Netherlands.*

designed to diagnose which component processes limit or control the overall rate of photosynthesis. The justification of this approach can be seen by considering the following three statements, which progress from simple and specific to complex and general. Consider the statement that the rate of photosynthesis in intact leaves is light limited if and only if it responds to changes in light level. The same logic underlies the statement that the processes which limit the rate of photosynthesis affect the characteristics of intact leaf photosynthesis. Given the second statement, we can say that the characteristics of intact leaf photosynthesis can be used to diagnose which process limits photosynthesis. This is the justification for analytical gas exchange measurements.

The response of the rate of photosynthesis to CO_2 and O_2 has been most useful for diagnosing what limits photosynthesis. Two classes of limitation have been identified. They are rubisco and RuBP regeneration. The rate of photosynthesis in rubisco limited leaves responds strongly to CO_2 both because it is a substrate and because it suppresses photorespiration. The response to O_2 is also very strong. If rubisco alone limits the rate of photosynthesis, then no light response is observed. The limitation by RuBP regeneration can be subdivided. If the availability of light energy or the calvin cycle enzymes limit the rate of RuBP regeneration, then RuBP will come available at a constant rate. The proportion of RuBP used for carboxylation will depend on the ratio of O_2 to CO_2 and so photosynthesis will respond to changes in the CO_2 level. This is an important point. Sensitivity of photosynthesis to CO_2 is not proof that rubisco is limiting or colimiting photosynthesis. At the same time, a lack of response of photosynthesis to CO_2 when the CO_2 level is below 1000 μbar, cannot be explained by having saturating levels of rubisco.

The other way that RuBP regeneration can be limited turns out to be the most relevant to studies of stress effects on photosynthesis. Walker and Herold pointed out over 10 years ago that photosynthesis in intact leaves required some reactions in the cytosol, specifically sucrose synthesis. These reactions regenerate inorganic phosphate, which is needed by the chloroplast. The rate of these reactions do not depend upon either CO_2 or O_2 or the rate of photorespiration. Given our earlier statement that photosynthesis of intact leaves takes on characteristics of the limiting processes, we can, with benefit of hindsight, "predict" that when the rate of sucrose (plus starch) synthesis limits the rate of photosynthesis, photosynthesis will take on the characteristics of sucrose and starch synthesis and become insensitive to CO_2 and O_2. So CO_2 and O_2 sensitivity of photosynthesis serve as diagnostic tools predicting when sucrose and starch synthesis limit photosynthesis.

2.2. **Chlorophyll fluorescence quenching** has become one of the most important tools for studying photosynthesis in intact leaves. The important advance is the ability to measure two different ways that chlorophyll fluorescence can be quenched. Photochemical quenching is the reduction of fluorescence which occurs when more of the light energy is used for electron transport. When CO_2 is supplied to a CO_2 starved leaf, the flow of electrons to CO_2 causes less light energy to be lost as fluorescence; this is photochemical quenching. It has been found that much of the quenching of fluorescence which can routinely be observed is not related to increased use of light energy in electron transport. This is called nonphotchemical quenching and is caused by a number of different mechanisms. Chief among these is a quenching that is correlated with the energy gradient across the thylakoid membrane necessary for ATP synthesis. When this energy gradient is high, fluorescence is quenched, and this is designated q_E.

The energy dependent quenching is in some way related to the quantum efficiency of photosynthesis. As energy dependent quenching increases, quantum efficiency goes down. Provided measurements are made in a certain way, the rate of electron transport can be calculated by knowing the photochemical quenching, the energy dependent quenching, and the photon flux density. This gives an independent, biophysical method for testing the predictions made based on analytical gas exchange measurements.

Another component of nonphotochemical quenching recovers very slowly. This component is usually called photoinhibition. This photoinhibition can require hours to days for reversal. It is considered a stress response.

3. INTERPRETING THE CHARACTERISTICS OF PHOTOSYNTHESIS IN LEAVES

Three classes of limitation of the rate of photosynthesis can be demonstrated by combining analytical gas exchange with fluorescence quenching measurements (Fig. 1). At low CO_2 and moderate to high light, the rate of photosynthesis and electron transport increase with CO_2. This indicates that the increasing CO_2 is providing more acceptors for the light reactions and that the light reactions can increase. Hence, the regeneration rate of RuBP was not maximum. At low light, photosynthesis increases with CO_2 but the rate of electron transport does not. This indicates that the rate of RuBP regeneration is unaffected by the increasing availability of CO_2 and so must be at a maximum allowed by the incoming light energy. The increasing rate of photosynthesis is caused by diversion of RuBP from oxygenation to carboxylation. At high light and high CO_2, the rate of electron transport falls with increasing CO_2. The interpretation of this behavior is that the rate of photosynthesis is limited by the rate of starch plus sucrose synthesis. This limitation will be called feedback limitation of the rate of photosynthesis.

When the feedback limitation of photosynthesis occurs, high CO_2 leads to reduced electron transport

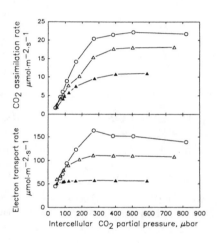

Figure 1. Response of photosynthetic CO_2 assimilation and electron transport rates to CO_2. The plant species was *Phaseolus vulgaris* var. Linden. Light levels were: o, 950; Δ, 380; ▲, 175 μmol photons m^{-2} s^{-1}. Leaf temperature was 25°C. Data from Sharkey et al. 1988.

rates. Therefore, we reasoned, high CO_2 should exacerbate photoinhibition in plants which suffer feedback. Photoinhibition was induced by holding leaves at 1000 μmol photons m^{-2} s^{-1} for five hours at 24°C. The growth light intensity was 500 μmol m^{-2} s^{-1}. Photoinhibition was detected as chlorophyll fluorescence quenching still apparent after one hour of darkness. The results of this experiment are shown in table 1. One hour after the end of the stress, the chlorophyll fluorescence was quenched and photosynthesis was reduced in both treatments. After 24 hours, photosynthesis recovered but chlorophyll fluorescence did not fully recover. At both time points the chlorophyll fluorescence was more quenched in the leaf that had been held in 1500 μbar CO_2 than the leaf held in 330 μbar.

Table 1. Photoinhibition is exacerbated at high CO_2

CO_2 during high light	Photosynthesis in 330 μbar CO_2			Photoinhibition (q_I)	
	before	after			after
hr		1 hr	24 hr	1 hr	2 4
μbar	$\mu mol\ m^{-2}\ s^{-1}$			%	
330	16.9	15.4	17.6	32	12
1500	18.4	17.2	18.0	43	23

4. EFFECTS OF WATER STRESS ON PHOTOSYNTHESIS

For the past 15 years it was believed that chloroplast metabolism was adversely affected by relatively mild leaf water deficits. However, in recent years a number of investigators have come to the conclusion that water stress does not affect the biochemical reactions of the chloroplast until well after other plant growth processes are affected (1-3).

How could such a dramatic error have arisen? As might be expected there are several reasons. One contributing factor is the difficulty in comparing results from isolated systems to intact, photosynthesizing organs. In fact there were indications for many years that much more severe osmotic stress was required to reduce the rate of photosynthesis in chloroplasts or cells than in intact leaves. For example Sharkey and Badger (4) found no reduction in photosynthesis of osmotically stressed, isolated cells of Xanthium strumarium at 1.5 MPa, but nearly complete inhibition of photosynthesis in leaves. These discrepancies were overlooked as problems associated in relating osmotic stress to water stress of intact leaves. Another contributing factor was the recently recognized problems in estimating the CO_2 partial pressure inside the leaf. We have learned that inhomogeneities across leaves, especially water stressed leaves, can interfere with the estimate of the partial pressure of CO_2 inside the leaf. Finally, changes in the response of photosynthesis to CO_2 inside the leaf were interpreted as deleterious consequences of stress rather than adaptive responses of photosynthesis to stomatal closure which was caused by water stress.

4.1. The problem of patchy stomatal closure

The problem of patchy stomatal closure was originally invoked to explain the apparent effect of abscisic acid on the biochemical reactions of photosynthesis. From the work of Terashima et al. (5), Downton et al. (6), and Ward and Drake (7), we now know that the apparent effect of abscisic acid results from patchy stomatal closure. Stomata over some patches of the leaf close so tightly that no gas exchange is possible while other parts of the leaf still engage in gas exchange. The estimate of partial pressure inside the leaf will be dominated by those sections of leaf still engaging in gas exchange. If stomates covering half of the leaf close completely, but the rest do not close at all, then the rate of photosynthesis will be cut in half, but the estimate of intercellular CO_2 will be unchanged. This is interpreted as an effect on the biochemistry of photosynthesis (8), when in fact it is a purely stomatal phenomenon. Patchiness has been demonstrated in water-stressed leaves (3).

Once made sensitive to the problem of patchiness, it is the homogeneity of photosynthesis across the leaf under most conditions which is surprising. A variety of stresses will in fact give rise to inhomogeneous photosynthesis across the leaf. Figure 2 shows some of these conditions. In all pairs the leaf on the left is a control

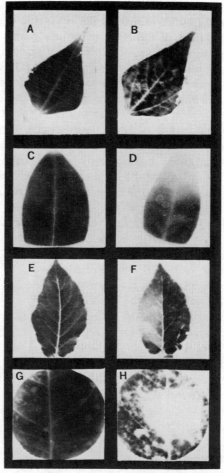

Figure 2. **Autoradiograms of leaves fed** $^{14}CO_2$ for 3 min. Control (A) and water stressed (B) *Phaseolus vulgaris*, control (C) and humidity stressed (D) olive, control (E) and *Verticillium* infected (F) potato, and control (G) and photoinhibited (H) orange leaf pieces.

for the treated leaf on the right. The top pair of autoradiographs (A,B) shows the effect of water stress on photosynthesis in leaves of *Phaseolus vulgaris*. The next pair (C,D) shows the effect of low humidity on young leaves of olive. In this case photosynthesis in the tip of the leaf was reduced. The next pair (E,F) shows an effect of infection of potato plants by *Verticillium*, a fungus which can block xylem elements. In this case one half of the leaf was affected, while the other half was not. The last pair (G,H) shows the effect of excess light on photosynthesis. This pattern was found in leaf pieces which had been used to determine fluorescence quenching parameters. The middle of the leaf, which had been exposed to super-saturating light flashes, necessary to determine the level of saturated variable fluorescence, lost all capacity for photosynthesis. What is easy to overlook in this figure is that in all cases the control leaf exhibits remarkable homogeneity of photosynthesis across the leaf. While patchiness explains all of the apparent effects of abscisic acid on photosynthesis, it does not explain all of the effects of water stress on photosynthesis.

4.2 The biochemical response to stomatal closure

As early as the experiments of von Caemmerer (1981) (see [9]), it was noticed that water stress not only reduced the rate of photosynthesis, it also changed the nature of the response of photosynthesis to CO_2. The effect can be seen in Figure 3. Several days of withholding water often led to reduced or even reversed sensitivity of photosynthesis to CO_2 and O_2. The O_2 insensitivity is a sure sign that patchy stomatal closure is not limiting photosynthesis. In fact, photosynthesis should be hypersensitive to O_2 when patchy stomatal closure is limiting photosynthesis because CO_2 limited photosynthesis is very sensitive to O_2. I have

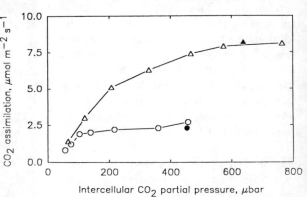

Figure 3. Response of photosynthetic CO_2 assimilation to CO_2 for a leaf of *Phaseolus vulgaris* var Tendergreen. The triangles are data from a well watered plant, the circles data from a mildly water-stressed plant. Filled symbols are data obtained in 18 mbar O_2, all other data obtained in 200 mbar O_2.

seen hypersensitivity to O_2 in *Phaseolus vulgaris* var. Linden which also exhibits patchy stomatal closure. However, *Phaseolus vulgaris* var. Tendergreen does not exhibit hypersensitivity to O_2 and does not readily exhibit patchiness. Flanagan and Jefferies (10) also observed hypersensitivity to O_2 in plants exposed to saline water and demonstrated that patchy stomatal closure was limiting photosynthesis in salinized plants.

So the CO_2 and O_2 insensitivity observed in water stressed plants indicates an effect on the biochemistry of photosynthesis, and from the analytical gas exchange analysis presented above, it is predicted that the effect is on sucrose or starch synthesis, or both. Vassey and Sharkey (11) found that the extractable activity of sucrose-phosphate synthase (SPS) was reduced by nearly 70% by mild water stress (Figure 4).

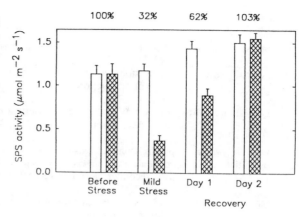

Figure 4. Extractable activity of sucrose-phosphate synthase from control (open bars) and mildly water stressed leaves of *Phaseolus vulgaris* var Linden. Data from Vassey and Sharkey 1989).

We have made a number of additional tests and have been able to demonstrate the following: 1. SPS in water stressed plants recovers when the plant is placed in high CO_2 (1 mbar) even though the stress is not relieved. 2. Unstressed plants held in a low CO_2 (75 μbar) environment for one hour exhibit reduced SPS activity. 3. The recovery of SPS activity in water stressed plants requires one to five hours and can be prevented by feeding cycloheximide.

From these investigations we conclude that water stress causes stomatal closure which restricts the CO_2 supply to photosynthesis. This is the primary effect of water stress. When photosynthesis is limited by low CO_2, the activity of SPS falls. However, this is a response to information about the prevailing conditions (low rates of photosynthesis) rather than a deleterious effect of water stress. The reduced activity of SPS leads to feedback limited photosynthesis at high CO_2 until protein synthesis can restore the activity of SPS.

5. CONCLUSION

Table 2 is a summary of effects of water-related stresses on photosynthesis. Water-related stresses appear not to affect the chloroplast reactions until well after the growth of plants has been affected. Photosynthesis is reduced and lack of photosynthate could limit plant growth. However, the reduced rate of photosynthesis results from stomatal closure, a response of plants to information about their environment. Evidence indicates that there is no weak link in photosynthesis which if reengineered, would allow water-stress-sensitive plants to become water-stress-tolerant.

Table 2

Stress	Effect on intact-leaf photosynthesis	References
Abscisic acid	patchy stomatal closure, no effect on chloroplast reactions	(5-7)
Low air humidity	patchy stomatal closure, no effect on chloroplast reactions	
Low soil-water potential	patchy stomatal closure, ion concentration effects as volume is lost, secondary loss of SPS activity	(2,3,11)
Salinity	patchy stomatal closure, no effect on chloroplast reactions	(10)

REFERENCES

1 Dietz, K.-J. and Heber, U. (1983) Planta 158, 349-356
2 Kaiser, W.M. (1987) Physiol. Plant. 71, 142-149
3 Sharkey, T.D. and Seemann, J.R. (1989) Plant Physiol. 89, 1060-1065
4 Sharkey, T.D. and Badger, M.R. (1982) Planta 156, 199-206
5 Terashima, I., Wong, S.-C., Osmond, C.B. and Farquhar, G.D. (1988) Plant Cell Physiol. 29, 385-394
6 Downton, W.J.S., Loveys, B.R. and Grant, W.J.R. (1988) New Phytol. 108, 263-266
7 Ward, D.A. and Drake, B.G. (1988) J. Exp. Bot. 39, 147-155
8 Farquhar, G.D. and Sharkey, T.D. (1982) Annu. Rev. Plant Physiol. 33, 317-345
9 Von Caemmerer, S. and Farquhar, G.D. (1984) Planta 160, 320-329
10 Flanagan, L.B. and Jeffries, R.L. (1989) Planta 178, 377-384
11 Vassey, T.L. and Sharkey, T.D. (1989) Plant Physiol. 89, 1066-1070

NITRATE REDUCTION IN LEAVES IS COUPLED TO NET PHOTOSYNTHESIS

WERNER M. KAISER, BOTANISCHES INSTITUT DER UNIVERSITÄT, MITTLERER DALLENBERGWEG 64, D-8700 WÜRZBURG

1. INTRODUCTION

Fast-growing herbaceous plants assimilate carbon and nitrogen at a ratio of about 10. With nitrate as the nitrogen source, formation of NH_3 consumes $8e^-$ / N, and $4e^-$ / C are needed for reduction of CO_2 to carbohydrate. Thus, up to 20% of total reductants produced by the photosynthetic light reactions are consumed for nitrate reduction. Especially when electron flow is limited by low photon flux density, both reactions might compete for reductants (1, but compare ref.2). On the other hand, an inhibition of CO_2 assimilation by stomatal closure at high photon flux (e.g. under water stress) might lead to an accumulation of potentially toxic NH_3, if nitrate reduction would continue at high rates. Therefore CO_2-and NO_3^--reduction are assumed to be well synchronized under a variety of environmental conditions.

In leaves of higher plants, photosynthesis is subjected to large diurnal fluctuations depending mainly on changes in photon flux density and in water availability. The latter is certainly the most important environmental factor which limits plant productivity. Photosynthesis is known to respond very sensitively to water stress (3,4). According to the above considerations, nitrate reduction should be adapted to the changing rates of photosynthesis.

In the following it is shown that light-dependent nitrate reduction in leaves is in fact strictly coupled to net photosynthesis. When CO_2 is not available, or when stomata close under water stress, nitrate reduction decreases drastically. This explains many earlier reports on a high sensitivity of nitrate reduction to water stress (5, and literature), and of nitrate accumulation in leaves under drought (5,6).

2. MATERIALS AND METHODS

Spinach was grown in a green house at a 10h light/14h dark cycle, at a photon flux density of 300 $\mu E \ m^{-2} sec^{-1}$.

M. Baltscheffsky (ed.), Current Research in Photosynthesis, Vol. IV, 557–563.
© 1990 *Kluwer Academic Publishers. Printed in the Netherlands.*

Nitrate reduction was measured by following the decrease
of the nitrate level in detached leaves. Nitrate and other
anions were measured in aqueous leaf extracts by isocratic
anion chromatography (Biotronik, Maintal, FRG).

NADH-dependent nitrate reductase activity in crude
leaf extracts was determined by following the formation of
nitrite (NO_2^-), with NADH (0.5mM) and NO_3^- (1mM) as
substrates (7). Leaf extracts were obtained by grinding
0.5g of leaf material in liquid nitrogen. The frozen powder
was suspended in 2.5ml of buffer solution (20mM HEPES-KOH
pH 7.8, FADH 10μM, leupeptin 0.05mM and $MgCl_2$ or EDTA as
indicated in the legends. After desalting by gel filtration,
the solution was stored on ice prior to use.

3. RESULTS AND DISCUSSION
It is a common observation that under water stress,
photosynthesis decreases. In air, water deficits smaller
than 10% often cause a 90% inhibition of photosynthesis
(Fig.1, ref.8). However, at external CO_2-concentrations
high enough to completely overcome stomatal resistance
(10 to 15%), photosynthesis is rather insensitive to even
severe dehydration (Fig.1, also compare 9,10). The
conclusion is that under water stress photosynthesis is
limited mainly by stomatal resistance to CO_2 diffusion.
The contribution of so-called non-stomatal effects appears
to be negligible (9,10).
Other metabolic processes such as PEP-carboxylation in
the cytosol appeared to be as insensitive to dehydration
as photosynthesis (11). It is therefore difficult to
interprete reports pointing to a rather high sensitivity to
water stress of nitrate reduction or nitrate reductase
activity (NRA) in leaves. E.g.,it was shown that a 35% water
deficit caused a more than 80% inhibition of NRA in
cucumber leaves (5, and literature). Such a water deficit
has practically no effect on photosynthesis at high
external CO_2 (compare Fig.1). Therefore it seemed possible
that the inhibition of the nitrate reducing system by
water stress was a consequence of decreased photosynthesis
rates, and not an independent event. This is in fact
suggested by the following observations.
In detached spinach leaves with the petiole in nitrate-
free solution, the nitrate level decreased during illumination. Most of that nitrate is located in the vacuole,
and obviously it was exported to the cytosol and reduced
rapidly. In spinach leaves, the initial rate of nitrate
reduction was 5 to 10μmoles mg^{-1} chlorophyll h^{-1} (Fig.2.).
There was hardly any nitrate reduction in the dark.

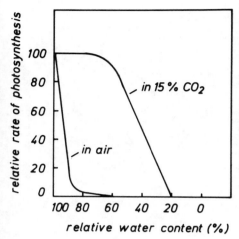

Fig. 1: Schematic presentation of photosynthesis of spinach leaves in air or in 15% CO_2 as a function of the relative water content. Leaves or leaf discs were wilted at dim room light in air until the desired water content was reached. Photosynthesis in air was measured as CO_2 gas exchange (data from ref.8), or as O_2 evolution in a leaf oxygen electrode chamber flushed with 15% CO_2 (data from ref.9,10).

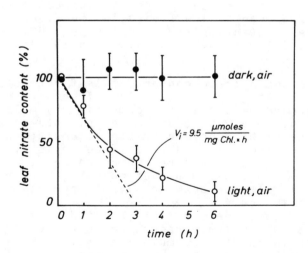

Fig. 2: Nitrate content of detached spinach leaves in the dark or in the light (300 w m^{-2} sec^{-1}) in air, as a function of time. Leaves were kept with their petiole in destilled water. The gas stream was humidified by passage through destilled water. At various time intervalls, discs were cut out, homogenized in liquid nitrogen and extracted with water for ion analysis (see Materials and Methods). Bars give SD (n=4).

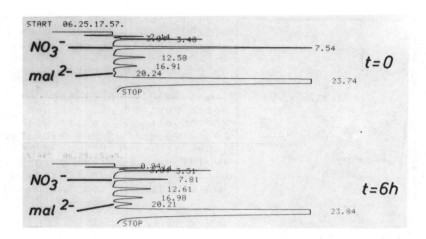

Fig. 3: Original anion chromatograms from extracts of
spinach leaves, which were either freshly harvested (t=0)
or illuminated (300 w m^{-2} sec^{-1}) for 6h (t=6h). Note that
after illumination, the nitrate peak had decreased and
the malate peak had increased. All other ion concentrations
were constant. Ions can be identified in the figure
according to their retention times (chloride 3.48;
phosphate 12.58; sulfate 16.91; oxalic acid 23.74).

By measuring the nitrate content of leaf extracts
through anion chromatography, we accidently observed that
nitrate disappearance was always accompanied by malate
accumulation (Fig.3). Since reduction of nitrate to NH_3
produces OH$^-$, one might consider malate accumulation as a
compensatory acid production. However, the ratio of malate
formed to nitrate reduced appeared to be rather variable,
and at present our data allow as yet no clearcut conclusions on a causal relation between nitrate reduction and
malate formation in leaves.

When spinach leaves were slightly wilted to a water
deficit of about 10%, nitrate reduction in air ceased
(Fig.4), and so did malate accumulation (not shown).
However, when the external CO_2 concentration was
drastically increased to 15%, nitrate reduction was
restored, as was photosynthesis (compare Fig.1 and 4).
Thus, the inhibition of nitrate reduction by mild water
stress in air appeared to be a consequence of stomatal
closure, just like the inhibition of photosynthesis.

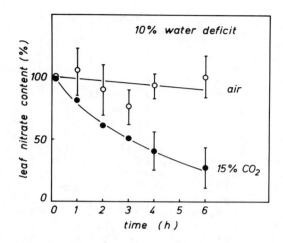

Fig. 4: Nitrate content of slightly wilted detached leaves during illumination in air or in 15% CO_2 (n=8).

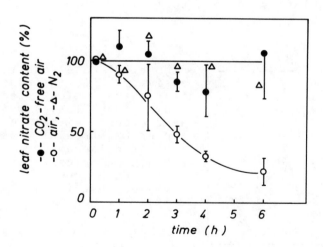

Fig. 5: Nitrate content of turgid spinach leaves illuminated in air, CO_2-free air or nitrogen (n=3-4).

When turgid leaves were illuminated in CO_2-free air or in nitrogen, nitrate reduction was also very low (Fig.5). Obviously, nitrate reduction in leaves was strictly coupled to net photosynthesis. Similar results were obtained when leaves were kept in a closed cuvette at the CO_2 compensation point (not shown).

The chemical or physical nature of the coupling of nitrate reduction to net photosynthesis is not clear. Attempts to find a regulatory intermediate of carbon or nitrogen metabolism were so far unsuccessful (Kaiser, unpublished). We found, however, that NRA decreased rapidly when leaves were kept in CO_2-free air, and it increased again when CO_2 was added (Fig.6). The half time for deactivation / activation was about 20 min. The deactivation / activation was much more pronounced when nitrate reductase was assayed in buffer containing Mg^{++}. In presence of a Mg-chelator (EDTA), the difference in extractable enzyme activity obtained by CO_2 removal or CO_2 addition was very small (Fig.6). Similar results were obtained for dark inactivation / light activation (not shown here). It is suspected that cytosolic free Mg^{++} might play a role in the regulation of NRA. It has been suggested earlier that a protein factor is involved in the regulation of NRA (12,13). Preliminary experiments (not shown here) have so far established this opinion. One might imagine Mg^{++} to be required for a binding of the postulated regulatory protein to nitrate reductase.

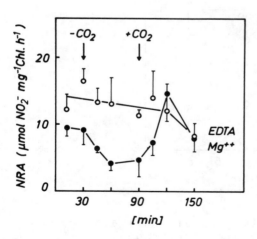

Fig. 6: Nitrate reductase activity (NRA) in crude leaf extracts (desalted) from spinach leaves which were exposed either to air or CO_2-free air, as indicated (arrows). Extraction or assay buffer contained either $MgCl_2$ (5mM) or EDTA (5mM). (n=4)

$MgCl_2$ (-●-)
EDTA (-o-)

4. CONCLUSIONS

In spinach leaves, nitrate reduction depends on net photosynthesis. Accordingly, it is affected by environmental conditions (e.g. water stress) in a similar way as CO_2 assimilation. The regulation apparently involves a modulation of NRA. There is no indication that one of the classical metabolites acts as an effector of the enzyme.

5. ACKNOWLEDGEMENTS

The skilled technical assistance of E. Brendle-Behnisch is greatfully acknowledged.

REFERENCES
1 Larsson, M. Olsson, T.,Larrson, C.M. (1985) Planta 164, 246-253
2 Robinson, J.M. (1988) Plant Physiol. 88, 1373-1380
3 Schulze, E.D. (1986) Annu. Rev. Plant Physiol. 37, 247-274
4 Bradford, K.J. and Hsiao, T.C. (1982) in Encyclopedia of Plant Physiology, Vol 2A,pp. 264-324, Physiological Plant Ecology II (Lange, O.L., Nobel, P.S., Osmond, C.B., Ziegler, H., eds.), Springer, Berlin
5 Sinha, S.K. and Nicholas, J.D. (1981) in The Physiology and Biochemistry of Drought Resistance in Plants (Paleg, L.G. and Aspinall, D., eds.). pp. 145-169, Academic Press Sydney
6 Leclerc, M.C. (1985) Acta Oecologia 6, 87-106
7 Hageman, R.H. and Reed, A.J. (1980) in Methods in Enzymology (San Pietro, ed.) Vol. 69, Part C, pp. 270-280, Springer, Berlin
8 Schwab, K.B., Schreiber, U. and Heber, U. (1989) Planta 177, 217-227
9 Kaiser, W.M. (1987) Physiol. Plant. 71, 142-149
10 Cornic, G., Le Gouallec, J.L., Briantais, J.M. and Hodges, M. (1989) Planta 177, 84-90
11 Kaiser, W.M., Schwitulla, M. and Wirth, E. (1983) Planta 158, 302-308
12 Wallace, W. (1974) Biochim. Biophys. Acta 341, 265-276
13 Omata Jolly, S. and Tolbert, N.E. (1978) Plant Physiol. 62, 197-203

ANALYSIS OF CHILL-INDUCED DEPRESSIONS OF PHOTOSYNTHESIS IN MAIZE

N.R. BAKER[1], G.Y. NIE[1], A. ORTIZ-LOPEZ[2], D.R. ORT[2,3] & S.P. LONG[1].
Dept. of Biology, University of Essex, Colchester CO4 3SQ, UK[1]; Dept.
of Plant Biology[2] and USDA Agricultural Research Service[3], University
of Illinois, Urbana, Illinois 61801, USA.

1. INTRODUCTION

Many crop species of tropical and sub-tropical origin exhibit a
chilling-induced depression of photosynthetic performance (1), which is
often considered to be an important factor in limiting the growth and
productivity of such plants in temperate regions (2).   Recent studies
on a maize crop in North-East Essex, UK, have demonstrated that the
quantum yields (∅) and the rates, close to light saturation, of carbon
dioxide assimilation of the youngest mature leaves were depressed
during May and June, compared to values in July and August (3).   Such
depressions in photosynthetic activity can, in part, be associated with
chill-induced, photoinhibition of PS2, which has been shown to occur in
maize in the field when the temperature falls below $12^{o}C$ and high light
levels are present (3).   However, it is unlikely that photoinhibition
of PS2 can account totally for the magnitude of the chill-induced
depressions in photosynthetic activities of maize during the early
growing season in the UK.   Low temperatures have been shown to result
in altered maize chloroplast ultrastructure (4) and the accumulation of
a 31kDa polypeptide in thylakoids (5), that has been identified as the
unprocessed precursor of the 29 kDa chlorophyll-protein, CP29(6).
Such low temperature-induced modifications are indicative of a
perturbation of chloroplast biogenesis, which could impair the
attainment of optimal photosynthetic activities in the maize leaf.
  The objectives of this study are twofold.   Firstly, to resolve the
factors determining the depression of ∅ when mature maize leaves are
chilled in the light.   Secondly, to examine the perturbations in
thylakoid development that may be associated with the loss of
photosynthetic ability when maize leaves are grown at low temperatures.

2. MATERIALS AND METHODS

2.1.Plant material: Maize plants (Zea mays L. cv. LG11) were grown
   from seed in potting compost in controlled environment cabinets at
   25, 17 or 14°C under a 16h photoperiod at a PPFD of 250
   $\mu mol\ m^{-2}\ s^{-1}$.   In chilling experiments on mature leaves 25°C-grown
   plants were transferred to a chilling cabinet at 5°C and exposed to
   a PPFD of 1000 or 50 $\mu mol\ m^{-2}\ s^{-1}$ for 6h.   Recovery of chilled
   leaves was followed on return to the controlled environment cabinet
   at 25°C.   All measurements were made on second leaves.
2.2.Measurements of carbon dioxide assimilation: Determinations of the
   absolute quantum yield of carbon assimilation were made in a light-
   integrating sphere using infra-red gas analysis as described

M. Baltscheffsky (ed.), Current Research in Photosynthesis, Vol. IV, 565–572.
© 1990 Kluwer Academic Publishers. Printed in the Netherlands.

previously (7). Carbon assimilation of detached leaves was measured as described previously (8) for determinations of light dosage response curves.

2.3. Measurements of photoinhibition of PS2: The ratio of variable to maximal fluorescence, Fv/Fm, was determined using a modulated fluorimeter. Leaves were dark-adapted for 15 min before being exposed to the weak, yellow modulated beam (PPFD 2 μmol m^{-2} s^{-1}) that produced F_o. White actinic light (PPFD 2500 μmol m^{-2} s^{-1}), which was saturating for Fv, was used to determine Fm. The atrazine-binding capacity of isolated thylakoids was determined using a previously described method (9). Thylakoids were isolated from mesophyll cells as described previously (10).

2.4. Measurements of in vivo photophosphorylation and membrane energization: The flash-induced electrotromic absorption band shift in attached leaves was measured as described previously (11).

2.5. PS1 and PS2 electron transport assays: PS1 electron transport in isolated mesophyll thylakoids from reduced tetramethyl-p-phenylene diamine to methyl viologen and PS2 electron transport from water to phenylenediamine in the presence of ferricyanide were determined essentially as described previously (12).

2.6 Labelling and analysis of thylakoid proteins: The labelling of thylakoid polypeptides with radiolabelled S-methionine was performed essentially as described previously (13). Leaf tissue was incubated with ^{35}S-methionine for 3h and then rinsed with 'cold' 1mM methionine prior to isolation of the thylakoids. Thylakoid polypeptides were fractionated by electrophoresis on linear 10-18% polyacrylamide gels and stained essentially as described previously (14). Labelled polypeptides were identified by fluorography as described previously (13). Immunoblotting of fractionated polypeptides was performed as described previously (5,15).

3. RESULTS AND DISCUSSION

Exposure of 25°C-grown maize leaves to 5°C for 6h at a PPFD of 1000 μmol m^{-2} s^{-1} (high light) resulted in a decrease of ca. 50% in the quantum yield of carbon dioxide assimilation, $\emptyset$ (Fig.1). The efficiency by which excitation energy harvested by the PS2 antennae is transferred to and utilised by PS2 reaction centres for photochemistry can be estimated from Fv/Fm (16). The ca. 40% decrease in Fv/Fm after the high light, chill treatment (Fig. 1) indicates a decrease in the efficiency of the photochemical reduction of Q_A, the primary quinone acceptor of PS2. The concomitant loss of about 60% of the capacity of the thylakoids to bind atrazine (Fig. 1) indicates that major modification or damage had occurred to the plastoquinone binding site of the PS2 reaction centre complex. The timecourses for the biphasic recovery of $\emptyset$ and Fv/Fm were similar when leaves were returned to the 25°C controlled environment cabinet, with almost complete recovery acheived after 48h (Fig.1). However, the recovery rate of atrazine binding was notably slower during the initial 10h of recovery (Fig. 1).

When leaves were chilled at 5°C for 6h at a PPFD of 50 μmol m^{-2} s^{-1} (low light) $\emptyset$ was depressed about 20%, but no significant changes were

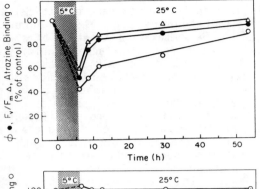

FIGURE 1. Timecourse of recovery at 25°C of Ø (●), Fv/Fm (△) and atrazine binding (○) following a 6h chill at 5°C and PPFD of 1000 µmol m^{-2} s^{-1}. The 100% prechill values were : Ø, 0.061±0.001; Fv/Fm, 0.79±0.01; atrazine binding, 2.1±0.1 mmol mol chl^{-1}.

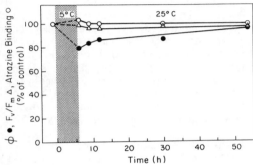

FIGURE 2. Timecourse of recovery at 25°C of Ø (●), Fv/Fm (△) and atrazine binding (○) following a 6h chill at 5°C and PPFD of 50 µmol m^{-2} s^{-1}. Other details are as given for Fig. 1.

observed in Fv/Fm or in the atrazine binding capacity (Fig.2). This depression of Ø at 5°C is clearly not associated with damage or inhibition of PS2 reaction centres. However, it is light-dependent, since chilling at 5°C in the dark produced no significant change in Ø. It is possible that chilling may impair the ability of thylakoids to synthesize ATP and consequently reduce Ø.

Energization of thylakoid membranes and coupling factor activity in intact leaf tissue can be assessed from analysis of the flash-induced

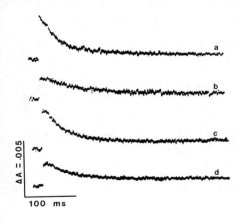

FIGURE 3. The effect of chilling in high and low light on the ΔA_{518} relaxation kinetics of leaves. Traces a-c are signal averages of 16 saturating flashes at 330ms intervals. (a) Control; (b) leaves chilled at 5°C for 6h at PPFD of 1000 µmol m^{-2} s^{-1}; (c) leaves chilled at 5°C for 6h at PPFD of 50 µmol m^{-2} s^{-1}. In (d) the intensity of the flashes was attenuated to produce a ΔA_{518} in control leaves of similar magnitude to that obtained in trace (b) from leaves chilled in high light.

electrochromic bandshift measured as the absorption change at 518 nm
(11). The magnitude of the flash-induced thylakoid membrane electrical
potential can be judged from the amplitude of the flash-induced
absorption change at 518 nm (ΔA_{518}).   The relaxation kinetics of the
absorption change provide information about coupling factor activity
and ATP formation since the proton efflux which drives ATP synthesis is
the dominant ionic current involved in thylakoid membrane
depolarization (17).   For maize leaves a 90s preillumination with a
PPFD of 300 μmol m^{-2} s^{-1} followed by a 2 min dark interval prior to the
actinic flash ensured activation of the coupling factor; no significant
reoxidation (deactivation) of the coupling factor occurred during the 2
min dark interval (A. Ortiz-Lopez, G.Y. Nie, D.R. Ort, N.R. Baker
submitted), consequently this protocol was used in all experiments.
Chilling leaves at 5°C for 6h at high light (PPFD 1000 μmol m^{-2} s^{-1})
produced a large decrease in ΔA_{518} (Fig. 3).   Analysis of the
exponential decays of the ΔA_{518} signals revealed an increase in the
time constant from 28ms for control leaves to 51ms upon chilling in
high light.   Chilling leaves at 5°c for 6h under low light (PPFD 50
μmol m^{-2} s^{-1}) produced negligible change in either the amplitude of the
ΔA_{518} or the time constant for the decay kinetics (Fig.3), implying
that chilling under low light does not impair thylakoid energization or
coupling factor activity.   Consequently, the low light, chill-induced
decrease in $\emptyset$ cannot be attributed to decreases in photophosphorylation
capacity.

The recovery timecourse of the flash-induced amplitude of the ΔA_{518}
when high light, chilled leaves are returned to 25°C appeared somewhat
slower than the recovery of the relaxation time constant for the decay
of ΔA_{518} (Fig.4).   The amplitude of the ΔA_{518} exhibited a biphasic
recovery, which was similar to the recovery of the atrazine capacity of
the thylakoids (Fig. 1), suggesting that modification or damage to the
PS2 reaction centres is directly related to the decrease in thylakoid
energization after chilling under high light.

It is evident that photoinhibition of PS2 is an important
contributing factor limiting $\emptyset$ in maize chilled under high light.
However, dysfunction of PS2 is not the sole cause of the depressed $\emptyset$,
since leaves chilled under low light exhibit a 20% decrease in $\emptyset$ with
no significant change in Fv/Fm, atrazine-binding capacity or flash-
induced membrane energization.   The basis of this depression of $\emptyset$ is
unclear.   It is possible that chilling interferes with the capacity or

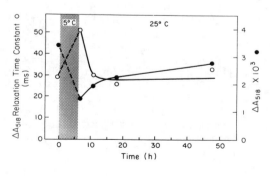

FIGURE 4.   Timecourse for the
recovery of the ΔA_{518}
amplitude ($\bullet$) and relaxation
kinetics following chilling
(5°C, 6h) at high (1000 μmol
m^{-2} s^{-1}) and low (50 μmol m^{-2}
s^{-1}) PPFD

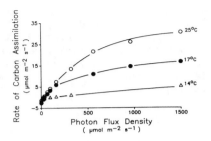

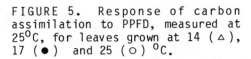

FIGURE 5. Response of carbon assimilation to PPFD, measured at $25^\circ C$, for leaves grown at 14 ($\triangle$), 17 ($\bullet$) and 25 ($\circ$) $^\circ C$.

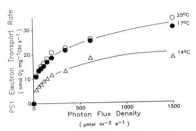

FIGURE 6. Response to PPFD of PS1 electron transport rate for mesophyll thylakoids isolated from leaves grown at 14 ($\triangle$), 17 ($\bullet$) and 25 ($\circ$) $^\circ C$.

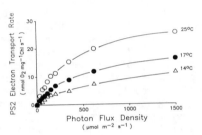

FIGURE 7. Response to PPFD of PS2 electron transport rate for mesophyll thylakoids isolated from leaves grown at 14 ($\triangle$), 17 ($\bullet$) and 25 ($\circ$) $^\circ C$.

efficiency of key enzymes of photosynthetic metabolism; e.g. in tomato, chilling at high light interferes with the reductive activation of stromal fructose bisphosphatase (18). Alternatively, chilling perturbation of the complex regulatory controls on energy transduction may be a candidate. However, stomatal patchiness does not appear to be important in this phenomenon in maize (A. Ortiz-Lopez and D.R. Ort, unpublished; 2).

The effect of growth temperature on the attainment of photosynthetic competence was examined by growing maize at 25, 17 and $14^\circ C$ under a PPFD of 250 μmol m^{-2} s^{-1}. The response of carbon dioxide uptake to incident PPFD at $25^\circ C$ for mature leaves grown at 25, 17 and $14^\circ C$ (Fig. 5) demonstrates that growth temperature has a marked effect on carbon assimilation over a wide PPFD range. PPFD dosage response curves for PS1 and PS2 electron transport of mesophyll thylakoids isolated from leaves grown at 14, 17 and $25^\circ C$ indicate that growth temperature can influence electron transport capacities severely (Figs. 6 and 7) with PS2 being more affected than PS1. A growth temperature of $17^\circ C$ had negligible affect on PS1 activity but produced a large decrease in PS2

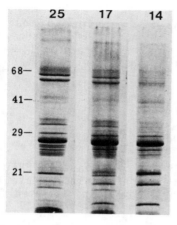

FIGURE 8. Polypeptide profiles of thylakoids isolated from mature leaves grown at 25, 17 and 14°C. Molecular masses of marker proteins are given in kDa. The tracks were loaded with equal amounts of total membrane protein.

activity, which was similar to the depression of carbon assimilation at this growth temperature.

With depression of growth temperature differences were observed in the thylakoid polypeptide profiles (Fig. 8). At 14°C there is a major loss of polypeptides in 55-70 and 30-35 kDa ranges, which could include, respectively, CP1 apoprotein, α and β subunits of CF_1 and the D_1 and D_2 PS2 reaction centre polypeptides. Also, a number of lower molecular mass polypeptides (10-22 kDa) appear as growth temperature is lowered. To determine how a number of known thylakoid proteins were affected by growth temperature, polypeptide profiles were transferred to nitrocellulose sheets and challenged with antibodies specific to polypeptide components of PS1, PS2, LHC2, cytochrome b_6/f complex and CF_1 (Fig.9). Depression of growth temperature reduces the amount of CP1 apoprotein, subunit II of PS1, D_1, cytochrome f, subunit IV of the cytochrome b_6/f complex and α and β sub-units of CF_1 as a proportion of the total thylakoid protein (Fig. 9). All of these polypeptides are products of chloroplast genes. The nuclear encoded polypeptides

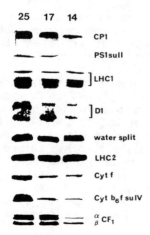

FIGURE 9. Immunoblot analyses of polypeptides of thylakoids isolated from mature leaves grown at 25, 17 and 14°C. Polypeptide profiles were probed with antibodies specific to CP1 apoprotein (65-70kDa), PS1 subunit II (22kDa), LHC1 (20-26kDa), D_1 (32kDa), extrinsic water splitting protein (33kDa), LHC2 (26-28kDa), cytochrome F (33kDa), cytochrome b_6/F subunit IV (17kDa) and α and β sub-units of CF_1 (58 and 57 kDa).

examined, i.e. LHC1, LHC2 and the 33 kDa extrinsic water splitting protein, did not show a decrease in the membranes with decreasing growth temperature (Fig.9). These data would suggest that lowered growth temperature inhibits selectively the accumulation of chloroplast, but not nuclear, encoded polypeptides in the thylakoids. To examine whether lowered growth temperatures inhibited synthesis of chloroplast encoded proteins developing leaves approximately half way through expansion were infiltrated with ^{35}S-methionine and after 3h thylakoids isolated. Fluorography of the polypeptide profiles showed that although, as expected protein synthesis was reduced at 17 and 14^{0}C compared to 25^{0}C, de novo synthesis of many polypeptides did occur (Fig. 10). It is of note that proteins in the 32-34 and 58-70 kDa range, which could include chloroplast encoded polypeptides associated with PS2, PS1 and CF_1, were synthesized at 14^{0}C. This might imply that the low temperature inhibition of the accumulation of chloroplast gene products in the thylakoids may be mediated at the level of protein stabilization in the membrane and not at the transcriptional and translational levels, although further studies are required to substantiate this contention.

Clearly it is important, with respect to the productivity of maize in temperate climates, that a growth temperature of 17^{0}C and below produces a large depression in the capacity for carbon assimilation over a PPFD range of 200-1500 μmol m^{-2} s^{-1} (Fig. 5). Such temperature and light conditions would be experienced regularly in the field during the development of the crop. Although the molecular basis of this low temperature-induced depression of carbon assimilation has not been resolved, the observed perturbation of the accumulation of chloroplast

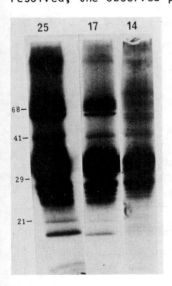

FIGURE 10. Fluorographs of polypeptide profiles of thylakoids isolated from developing leaves grown at 25, 17 and 14^{0}C. Leaves approximately half way through expansion were incubated with ^{35}S-methionine for 3h at their growth temperature. Molecular masses in kDa are indicated.

encoded proteins in the thylakoids at low temperatures would appear to be an important candidate for the depression of photosynthetic activity. In conclusion, this study has demonstrated that the reduced photosynthetic productivity induced in a maize crop by exposure to low temperatures can be attributed to perturbation of both the photosynthetic processes of the mature leaves and the development of the photosynthetic apparatus during leaf growth. The relative contributions of these two types of perturbation to the loss in photosynthetic productivity of the crop have still to be resolved.

4. ACKNOWLEDGEMENTS

This work was supported by grants from the AFRC (AG 84/5) and USDA (87-CRCR-1-2381). GYN received a scholarship from the British Council and NRB a Fellowship from OECD (Project on Food Production and Preservation). We are grateful to J. Barber, R. Malkin and J.P. Thornber for supplying the antibodies used in this study.

REFERENCES

1. Powles, S.B., Berry, J.A. and Bjorkman, O. (1983) Plant Cell Environ. 6, 117-123.
2. Baker, N.R., Long, S.P. and Ort, D.R. (1988) in Plants and Temperature (Long, S.P. and Woodward, F.I., eds.), pp. 347-375, The Company of Biologists Ltd., Cambridge.
3. Baker, N.R., Bradbury, M., Farage, P.K., Ireland, C.R. and Long, S.P. (1989) Trans. Roy. Soc. Lond. B. 323, 295-308.
4. Taylor, A.O. and Craig, A.S. (1971) Plant Physiol. 47, 719-725.
5. Hayden, D.B., Baker, N.R., Percival, M.P. and Beckwith, P.B. (1986) Biochim. Biophys. Acta 851, 86-92.
6. Hayden, D.B., Covello, P.S. and Baker, N.R. (1988) Photosynth. Res. 15, 257-280.
7. Ireland, C.R., Long, S.P. and Baker, N.R. (1990) Plant Cell Environ. in press.
8. Ireland, C.R., Baker, N.R. and Long, S.P. (1987) Biochim. Biophys. Acta 893, 434-443.
9. Tischer, W. and Strotmann, H. (1977) Biochim. Biophys. Acta 460, 113-125.
10. Hayden, D.B. and Hopkins, W.G. (1976) Can. J. Bot. 54, 1684-1689.
11. Wise, R.R. and Ort, D.R. (1989) Plant Physiol., in press.
12. Allen, J.F. and Holmes, N.G. (1986) in Photosynthesis, Energy Transduction - A Practical Approach (Hipkins, M.F. and Baker, N.R., eds), pp 103-141, IRL Press, Oxford.
13. Cooper, P. and Ort, D.R. (1988) Plant Physiol. 88, 454-461.
14. Chua, N-H. (1980) Methods Enzymol. 69, 434-446.
15. Montano, X. and Lane, D.P. (1984) J. Virol. 51, 760-767.
16. Butler, W.L. and Kitajima, M. (1975) Biochim. Biophys. Acta 376, 116-125.
17. Witt, H.T. (1979) Biochim. Biophys. Acta 505, 355-427.
18. Sassenrath, G.F., Ort, D.R. and Portis, Jr., A.R. (1987) in Progress in Photosynthesis Research, (Biggins, J., ed.), Vol. IV, pp 103-106, Martinus Nighoff Publishers, Dordrecht.

SPATIAL AND TEMPORAL HETEROGENEITIES OF PHOTOSYNTHESIS DETECTED
THROUGH ANALYSIS
OF CHLOROPHYLL-FLUORESCENCE IMAGES OF LEAVES

Klaus Raschke, Jürgen Patzke, Paul F. Daley, and Joseph A. Berry

Pflanzenphysiologisches Institut der Universität Göttingen, Untere
Karspüle 2, 3400 Göttingen, West Germany (K.R., J.P.); University of
California, Lawrence Livermore National Laboratory, Environmental
Sciences Division, P.O. Box 5507/L-524, Livermore, CA 94550 (P.F.D.);
Carnegie Institution, Department of Plant Biology, 290 Panama
Street, Stanford, CA 94305 (J.A.B.)

Short-term water stress, as well as an application of the
phytohormone, abscisic acid (ABA), can reduce the photosynthetic
capacity of leaves. In many cases, the rate of CO_2 assimilation
declines while the partial pressure of CO_2 in the intercellular
spaces remains constant. At the VIIth International Congress on
Photosynthesis, Farquhar et al. (1) suggested that such depressions
of photosynthesis were caused by closure of stomata in groups. Laisk
(2) had already shown that changes in the distribution function of
stomatal aperture can affect the rate of CO_2 assimilation of whole
leaves, without a direct impairment of the photosynthetic apparatus.
Starch prints and 14C-autoradiograms of ABA-treated leaves provided
evidence for correlated stomatal closure in some alveoli of the
leaves, while stomata remained open in other areas (3, 4). Thus, in
whole leaves, the rate of CO_2 assimilation, A, can decline because
the effective assimilating area decreases. If intercellular partial
pressures of CO_2, ci, are computed from the gas exchange of these
leaves, they are correct only for those areas where stomata are open.
For an assessment of the status of the photosynthetic apparatus in
the whole leaf, a way must be found to determine A and ci in all
parts of a leaf.
    The way stomata respond to stress is also important with respect
to the water cost of assimilation. Stomata can control gas exchange
either by all of them varying their aperture in parallel
("proportional control") or by varying the share of the closed
stomata among their total number ("binary control"). Proportional
control would allow an improved water use efficiency (5).

We derived spatial and temporal patterns of the nonphotochemical
fluorescence quench coefficient, qN, from video images of leaves (6).
From them, we computed topographies of ci, A, and stomatal
conductance, g.

M. Baltscheffsky (ed.), Current Research in Photosynthesis, Vol. IV, 573–578.
© 1990 *Kluwer Academic Publishers. Printed in the Netherlands.*

PROCEDURE

Fluorescence images of 8x8 or 13x14 mm^2-areas were recorded on various leaves at the ends of 1 sec-flashes of saturating light. For each picture element of each image, values of qN were computed according to Schreiber et al. (7, there "qE"); Fo was assumed to be have been nearly constant at 0.2 of the maximum fluorescence of the dark-adapted leaf. The results were scaled to 256, to exploit the eight-bit pixel matrix.

Relationships among qN, A, and ci were determined by measuring the gas exchange of the leaves, before they were subjected to the treatments, and while they were homogeneous in qN (Fig. 1). Regressions were derived, from which variations in qN could be converted into variations in ci and A; stomatal conductances for water vapor, g, were computed from leaf conductance $\bar{g}$ = 1.6 A/(ca - ci), where ca is the partial pressure of CO_2 in the atmosphere, and then taking the boundary layer conductance into account. It has been determined that the activity of ribulose-1,5-bisphosphate carboxylase was not affected by a treatment with ABA (<u>Xanthium strumarium</u>, 8) or by mild water stress (<u>Phaseolus vulgaris</u>, 9).

RESULTS

<u>Spatial distributions of qN among species.</u> Heterogeneities in qN appeared within few minutes of ABA application or exposure to dry air (Fig. 2). In <u>X. strumarium</u>, areas of high qN and low photosynthetic activity (dark) were enclosed by the minor veins and thus coincided with alveoli. In <u>Z. mays</u>, photosynthesis was inhibited in spots limited by the parallel venation along the leaf and apparently by the anastomosing minor veins perpendicular to them. Leaves of <u>A. unedo</u> showed large compartments and gradients of (1-qN) within them, indicating lateral diffusion of CO_2.

<u>Heterogeneous and homogeneous spatial responses to ABA or drought.</u> Stomatal responses to both, ABA (3,4,5) and wilting (9, 10), were reported to have been heterogeneous. In the examples shown in Fig. 3, both, application of 10 µM ABA or withholding water for a day caused reductions of assimilation by one-half. In ABA-treated leaves, this was the result of heterogeneous stomatal closure; but in the slowly wilting leaf, stomatal closing was homogeneous, in contrast to reports on other species (9, 10). (Note the difference in gradations between the two frames.) Figure 3 demonstrates that depressions of photosynthesis of comparable average magnitudes can have been caused either by predominantly heterogeneous "binary" responses of the stomata, or by all of them responding "proportionally".

<u>Compensatory spatial and temporal stomatal variations in a leaf operating at constant average ci, A, and g.</u> Local variations in responses to ABA extending over 30 min have already been demonstrated (6). Now we view a period of longer duration (Fig. 4). ABA was

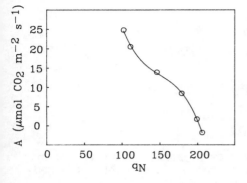

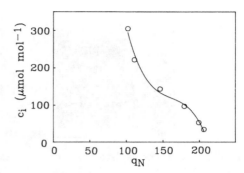

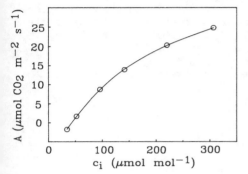

FIGURE 1. Relationships among rate of CO_2 assimilation, A, intercellular partial pressure of CO_2, ci, and the nonphotochemical quench coefficient, qN, of a non-stressed leaf of <u>Helianthus annuus</u> exhibiting homogeneous chlorophyll fluorescence. Divide qN values by 255 to obtain quench coefficients. Computed from area-averaged fluorescence and gas exchange.

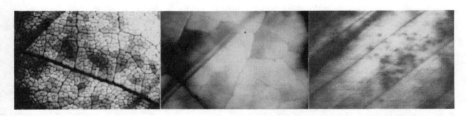

FIGURE 2. Images of (1-qN) (brightness proportional to photosynthetic activity) after application of 100 µM ABA to leaves of <u>Xanthium strumarium</u> (left) and <u>Zea mays</u> (right), or of dry air to <u>Arbutus unedo</u> (center), In each case, the width of the frame corresponded to 8 mm on the leaf.

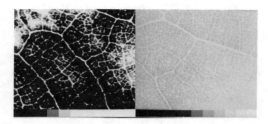

FIGURE 3. Topographies of qN on leaves of <u>H. annuus</u> after treatment
with 10 µM ABA (detached leaf, left) or one day's drought (attached,
right), resulting in similar reductions of A from about 20 to 10
µmol m^{-2} s^{-1}; quantum flux 1 mmol m^{-2} s^{-1}, 21% O2. In these examples,
brightness is proportional to inhibition of photosynthesis. qN scale
(black, increment, white) left: 0.625, 0.05, 1.025; right: 0.679,
0.05, 1.079. Area averages (ABA/drought): qN = 0.72/0.94;
A = 9.5/10.4 µmol m^{-2} s^{-1}; g = 87/122 mmol m^{-2} s^{-1}.
Left frame: 8 x 8 mm^2, right frame 13 x 14 mm^2 on the leaf.

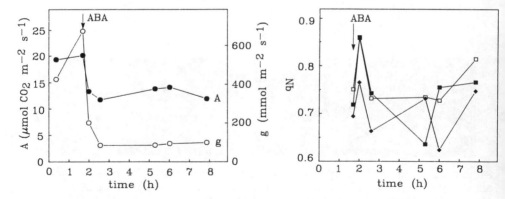

FIGURE 4. Decline in CO_2 assimilation, A, and stomatal conductance,
g, after application of 10 µM ABA to a leaf of <u>H. annuus</u>.
Compensatory variations of qN in three 0.22 mm^2 -windows, indicating
that stomata oscillated in groups.

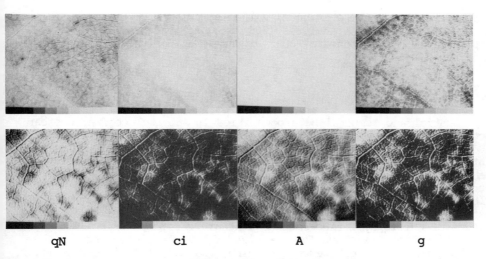

FIGURE 5. Images of qN and computed topographies of the partial
pressure of CO_2 in the intercellular spaces, ci, rate of CO_2
assimilation, A, and stomatal conductance for water vapor, g, of a
leaf of <u>H. annuus</u> before (upper row) and after (lower row)
application of 10 µM ABA . Grey scales (black, increment, white):
qN = 0.515, 0.025, 0.765,; ci = 0, 40, 400 µbar; A = −5, 3, 25
µmol m^{-2} s^{-1}; g (before ABA) = 0, 100, 1000 mmol m^{-2} s^{-1}; g (after
ABA) = 0, 20, 200 mmol m^{-2} s^{-1}. Experiment in 1.5 % O_2, quantum flux
500 µmol m^{-2} s^{-1}, partial pressure of CO_2 in the atmosphere
327 − 345 µbar. Frame : 13 x 14 mm^2 on the leaf.

applied to a leaf of <u>H. annuus,</u> and changes of qN were followed in
several windows on the leaf, each measuring 0.22 mm^2. Whereas overall
A and g declined to steady states; qN fell and then increased again,
depending on location. Changes of qN compensated each other among
windows; they disclose synchronized stomatal behavior in the patches.

<u>High-resolution topographies of qN, ci, A, and g.</u> Fluorescence
images can be used to compute zonations of qN, ci, A, and g on leaves
(6). Here we show images with increased resolution (Fig. 5). They
were obtained by evaluation of the fluorescence images pixel by pixel
based on relationships such as shown in Fig. 1. The average
assimilation rate was 22 µmol m^{-2} s^{-1} before the treatment of the
leaf with ABA, and ci was uniformly distributed. The variations in g
present had no effect on ci or A. However, after application of ABA,
stomata closed in patches, causing ci there to decline below 50 µbar
and A to drop close to zero. The image of A shows that in other parts
of the leaf photosynthesis proceeded at high rates. Computed from qN,
the overall rate of photosynthesis was 21 µmol m^{-2} s^{-1} before and 8
µmol m^{-2} s^{-1} after treatment; gas analysis had given rates of 22 and
12 µmol m^{-2} s^{-1} , respectively.

Before the treatment, average ci values computed from qN agreed with those derived from gas analysis (268/262 ubar); after ABA application, qN indicated a lower ci than that derived from gas analysis (50/141 ubar).

CONCLUSION

Spatial and temporal heterogeneities in stomatal conductance can occur in leaves under water stress and in response to applications of ABA; they cause heterogeneities in the partial pressure of CO_2 in the intercellular spaces and in photosynthesis. Therefore, area-averaging measurements of gas exchange cannot resolve unequivocally whether a decline in photosynthesis was caused by heterogeneous stomatal closure or by a direct impairment of the photosynthetic apparatus. Heterogeneities in photosynthetic activity can be recognized in images of chlorophyll fluorescence that are recorded during saturating light flashes. Topographies of the coefficient of nonphotochemical fluorescence quenching, qN, can be derived from such images which, in combination with measurements of gas exchange, allow the computation of spatial and temporal distributions of the partial pressure of CO_2 in the intercellular spaces, ci, rate of CO_2 assimilation, A, and stomatal conductance for water vapor, g. This procedure provides the information necessary to decide whether a particular inhibition of photosynthesis was direct or caused by stomatal closure.

REFERENCES

1 Farquhar, G.D., Hubick, K.T., Terashima, I., Condon, A.G. and Richards, R.A. (1987) in Progress in Photosynthesis Research (Biggins, J., ed.), Vol. IV, 209-212, Martinus-Nijhoff-Publishers, Dordrecht
2 Laisk, A., Oja, V. and Kull, K. (1980) Journal of Exp. Bot. 31, 49-58
3 Terashima, I., Wong, S.-C., Osmond, C.B. and Farquhar, G.D. (1988) Plant Cell Physiol. 29, 385-394
4 Downton, W.J.S., Loveys, B.R. and Grant, W.J.R. (1988) New Phytol. 108, 263-266
5 Raschke, K. (in press) in Plant Growth Substances 1988 (Pharis, R.P. and Rood, S., eds.) Springer-Verlag, Heidelberg
6 Daley, P.F., Raschke, K., Ball, J.T., and Berry, J.A. (1989) Plant Physiology, in press
7 Schreiber, U., Schliwa, U. and Bilger, W. (1986) Photosynthesis Res. 10, 51-62
8 Arretz, M. (1987) Thesis (Diplomarbeit), U. Göttingen
9 Sharkey, T.D. and Seemann, J.R. (1989) Plant Physiol. 89, 1060-1065
10 Downton, W.J.S., Loveys, B.R. and Grant, W.J.R. (1988) New Phytol. 110, 503-509

STRUCTURE AND POSSIBLE FUNCTION OF CHLOROPLAST HEAT-SHOCK
PROTEINS AND THE EFFECT OF CYCLIC HEAT-SHOCK ON PLANT MOR-
PHOGENESIS AND CIRCADIAN RHYTHMICITY

GABY KNACK, BEATE OTTO, PETER OTTERSBACH, ROLAND ALEXANDER,
ZHONGLAI LIU AND KLAUS KLOPPSTECH, INSTITUT FÜR BOTANIK,
HERRENHÄUSER STR. 2, 3000 HANNOVER 21, FEDERAL REPUBLIC OF
GERMANY.

1.   INTRODUCTION
    The heat-shock response is a very general phenomenon,
shared by eukaryotic and prokaryotic organisms. Based on experimental evidence it has been well established that heat-
shock proteins protect against damage during the exposure to
high temperatures (1). Exposure of the organisms to temperatures about 10°C above the optimal growth temperature leads
to rapid transcription of a number of genes. The gene products concerned are divided into two groups. The high molecular mass proteins, ranging from 50 to 100 kDa, display
considerable homology in both groups of organisms. The low
molecular mass proteins (17 to 30 kDa) are predominantly
found in plants (2).
We investigated whether plant chloroplasts, considered as
procaryotic in origin, might possess heat-shock proteins of
their own possibly with chloroplast specific functions. In
vivo labeling as well as posttranslational transport of in
vitro labeled translation products of poly(A)RNA from heat-
shocked cells provided evidence for nuclear coded heat-shock
proteins of 22 and 25 kDa, respectively, in the plastids of
soybean, pea and Chlamydomonas (3,4,). Cloning and sequencing of the mRNA of pea, soybean and Chlamydomonas 22 kDa
proteins (5,6,) indicated considerable homology with the
multigene families of the small cytosolic heat-shock proteins of the same organisms.
Quantitative studies of the transcriptional capacity of
heat-shock genes during the day, performed under otherwise
constant conditions, showed a circadian rhythmicity in their
expression (7). Since the effect of light as "Zeitgeber" for
the induction of circadian rhythm of mRNA levels has been
shown earlier (8) we asked whether a daily heat-shock, given
at the same time each day might function as Zeitgeber, too.

M. Baltscheffsky (ed.), Current Research in Photosynthesis, Vol. IV, 579–586.
© 1990 *Kluwer Academic Publishers. Printed in the Netherlands.*

These results indicate a surprising influence of heat-shock on morphology and gene expression of etiolated pea plants.

2. MATERIALS AND METHODS
    2.1. Plant growth
    Peas (c.v. Rosa Krone) were germinated and heat-shock-ed as described (6). For studies of developmental control the germlings were isolated at the indicated times, (the co-tyledos removed) and immediately frozen. For cyclic heat-shock plants were kept in dark at 25°C and shocked at 40°C from 7 to 8 a.m.. Alternatively plants were grown at a 12:12hrs rhythm at 25:15°C. The Chenopodium cell culture was maintained as described by Hüsemann et al. (9). Cell were collected by centrifugation and heat-shocked in one tenth of the original volume.
    2.2. Transport of in vitro translation products
    Transports were performed according to published proto-cols (10) either into chloroplasts of the untreated controls or of heat-shocked pea plants. After transport the chloroplasts were isolated, treated with proteases and frac-tionated into stroma and membrane fractions.
    2.3. Messenger RNA isolation and quantification
    These pocedures have been described in detail elsewhere (11).
    2.4. cDNA cloning and sequencing
    Cloning of the pea and Chenopodium heat-shock mRNA was done according to Gubler and Hoffman (12)into pMG 5 or bluescript,respectively. Sequence determination was done by the method of Sanger (13) as outlined in (6).

3. RESULTS AND DISCUSSION
    3.1. Plastid heat-shock proteins
    3.1.1. Characterization of heat-shock clones from pea and Chenopodium
    Cloning of cDNA from pea and differential colony hybri-dization yielded about 70 heat-shock-specific clones which were further characterized by means of hybrid-release trans-lation. Out of these the clones coding for proteins of 26 and 30 kDa,respectively, were further characterized as puta-tive candidates for precursors of plastid heat-shock prot-eins. To establish a precursor-product relationship the pro-ducts obtained by hybrid-release translation were studied in a transport assay with isolated chloroplasts from pea. The results are shown in fig. 1. Both products were transported into chloroplasts and processed into proteins indistinguish-able in onedimensional polyacrylamide gel. These two clones, furtheron described as P 30-22 and P 26-22, were sequenced. The sequence of P 30-22 turned out to be identical with that from Vierling et al. (5) except for amino acid 225 which is changed from Thr to Arg (not shown). Clone P 26-22 codes for a new plastid protein (Fig. 2). Sequence comparison

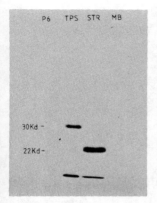 

Fig. 1: Posttranslational transport of in vitro products obtained with hybrid-release RNA from clones P 30-22 and P26-22 into isolated pea chloroplasts

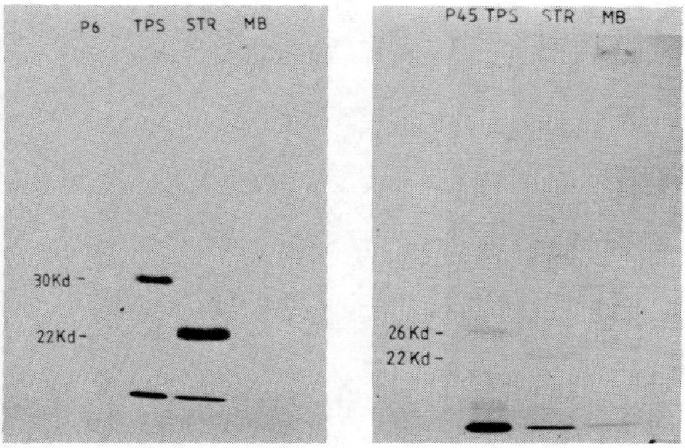

```
MSLKPLNMLL  VPFLLLILAA  DFPLKAKGSL  LPFIDSPNTL  LSDLWSDRFP
DPFRVLEQIP  YGVEKHEPSI  TLSHARVDWK  ETPEGHVIMV  DVPGLKKDDI
KIEVEENRVL  RVSGERKKEE  DKKGDHWHRV  ERSYGKFWRQ  FKLPQNVDLD
SVKAKMENGV  LTLTLHKLSH  DKIKGPRMVS  IVEEDDKPSK  IVNDELK
```
Figure 2. Derived amino acid sequence of HSP 26-22

```
KFTEPSSNLL  SFSIVTSIMA  SMALRRLASR  NLVSGGIFRP  LSVSRSFNTN
AQMGRVDHDH  ELDDRSNRAP  ISRRGDFPAS  FFSDVFDPFR  ATRSVGQLMN
LMDQLMENPF  MAASRGSGRA  MRRGWDVRED  EEALELKVDM  PGLAKEDVKV
SVEDNTLIIK  SEAEKETEEE  EQRRRYSSRI  ELTPNLYKID  GIKAEMKNGV
LKVTVPKIKE  EEKKDVFQVM  VD
```
Figure 3. Derived amino acid sequence of HSP Chen 30

indicated that this sequence is incomplete at its 5'end. Similarly, a cDNA clone, Chen 30, has been isolated from a photoautotrophic Chenopodium cell culture which codes for a protein of 32 kDa. This sequence is given in Fig. 3. and compared with pea HSP P 30-22 and HSP P 26-22, Chlamydomonas HSP 22 and cytosolic HSPs of soybean in fig. 4. A 50% homology with HSP P 30-22 can be observed over the entire length of the proteins indicating homology between Chenopodium and HSP P30-22, consistent with the observation of proteins of 25 kDa and 22 kDa in the cell culture after heat-shock and in vivo labeling. Final proof for homology should be obtained by in vitro transport. From fig. 4 it can be seen that regions of considerable homology over a stretch of 120 amino acids exist between all plant small HSPs at the carboxy terminal region. Towards the amino terminus a region C is found in which homology is higher among the plastid proteins than between the two groups of organellar and cytosolic proteins. Finally, in D similarity can only be observed between the 4 plastid proteins decreasing from HSP P 30-22 via HSP P26-22 to HSP Chlamydomonas 22. This rather striking similarity between plant small HSPs may indicate that about 50% of the sequence of the plastid protein serves a similar function in both compartments. Based on this com-

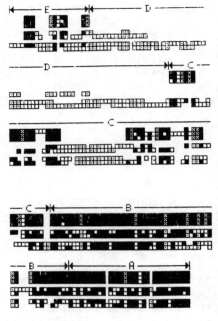

FROM TOP TO BOTTOM:

HSP 17.5 (soybean), HSP 18.5 (soybean), HSP 17.6 (soybean)

HSP 22 (Chlamydomonas), HSP 26-22 (pea), HSP 30-22 (pea)

HSP 30 (Chenopodium)

Fig. 4: Sequence comparison of HSP

Fig. 6: Pea morphology after cyclic heat-shock. From left: etiolated; etiolated and heat-shocked, and green pea

parison the amino terminal parts D and E might serve transport into the chloroplasts and possibly plastid-specific functions.

3.1.2. Membrane binding of heat-shock proteins

We asked whether heat-induced changes in the plastids might influence protein import. This seemed not the case. After a conditioning pre-heat-shock a considerable part of the imported proteins migrated with the membrane fraction. The change in the membrane properties is established within 15 min, lasts for up to 6 hrs and can be reinduced the next day. High light intensities during the conditioning heat-shock abolish the membrane binding (13). Unpublished data of Neumann and Nover with antibodies against HSP 22 (comparable to HSP P 26-22) and HSP 21 (HSP P 30-22) show localization of HSP 21 in the stroma and of HSP 22 in the grana region. The latter is consistent with the localization of HSP 22 from Chlamydomonas in the grana fraction (Ish-Shalom, unpublished) and with the observation that the functioning of PS II is partially protected against the combined effects of light and heat by a conditioning pre-heat-shock about 2 hrs prior to the experiment (14). The rapidity with which membrane binding occurs seems to argue against the idea that heat-shock granula might be the binding entities.

3.1.3. Effects of light on induction of heat-shock proteins

While in Chlamydomonas light seems an essential factor for transcription of heat-shock proteins (Ish-Shalom, unpublished) this is not the case in pea. Heat-shock mRNAs are induced in etiolated plants in the dark as well as in the light in a pattern comparable to that of green plants. Under these conditions the precursor to HSP P 30-22 was visible in 1-D gels while in green plants it was hidden by the precursor to LHC II. In the photoautotrophic cell cultures of Chenopodium the temperature necessary for the induction of mRNAs for heat-shock proteins, especially of HSP Chen 30, was decreased by up to 4°C under high light intensities. This effect can be interpreted as a protection against the combined effects of heat and light which are harmful for the photosynthetic apparatus.

3.1.4. Heat-shock and cellular development

Variable expression of heat-shock proteins during embryogenesis has been reported (15). We asked whether during germination and cell differentiation the expression of heat-shock proteins might underlie developmental regulation. During cellular development differential gene expression has been described in the barley leaf (16). When after a 2 hour heat-shock 7-day old barley leaves were divided into 6 segments slight differences in protein composition were detected between the most apical segment 6 and the basal segment 1 (not shown). The general pattern was, however, very similar; even the plastid heat-shock proteins P 30-22 and 26-22 were present although the chloroplast is not fully developed in the lower third of the leaf.

In contrast, developing pea sprouts, when separated from the cotyledos, show regulation of heat-shock expression. During the first 2 days of germination a response to heat-shock was not observable. Only after 3-4 days of development, at a time when the mRNA for the precursor of LHC II is expressed, a massive induction of heat-shock mRNAs was observed both by translation as well as by dot hybridization.

3.2. The effect of cyclic temperature treatment on gene expression in pea

When pea seeds were germinated in the dark and exposed daily to a 1 hr heat-shock the morphology of the plantlets was altered in a remarkable way. Leaves were expanded, hooks opened, stems shortened and second leaves already visible by

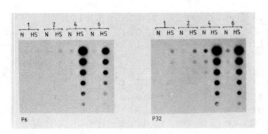

P6   P32

Fig. 5: Development
of the heat-shock re-
sponse in pea. Left:
P 30-22 and right:
clone for a 21 kDa
cytosolic protein.
Numbers: days of cul-
ture. N and HS: con-
trol and heat-shock

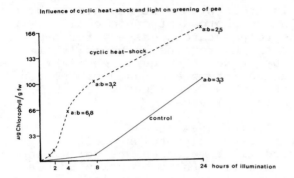

Influence of cyclic heat-shock and light on greening of pea

Fig. 7: Light-induced
accumulation of chlo-
rophyll in
control
and cyclic heat-
shocked
peas

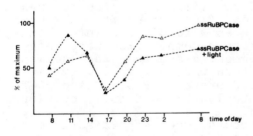

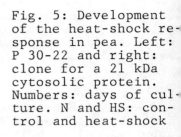

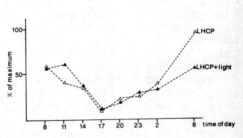

Fig. 8: Circadian os-
cillation of mRNA in
cyclic heat-shocked
pea after 7 d culture
in the dark, harvest-
ed directly or after
1 h illumination at
10.000lx. A: ssRuBP-
Case, B: LHC II, C:
ELIP

the 7th day (Fig.6). In addition the leaves appeared heavily yellow. At least the morphological changes are characteristics of photomorphogenesis (17). Since unexpected, the experiments were also repeated with plants that were exposed to a 12 h:12 h temperature change alternating between 25°C:15°C. The result was about the same.

Electron microscopy confirmed the morphological findings. The plastids in the heat-shock treated cells were of the same size as the chloroplasts of green plants and were considerably enriched in membranes which were, however, unstacked as to be expected in a plant that lacks chlorophyll.

When exposed to light the plantlets turned green within 2-4 hrs i. e. without the typical lag of etiolated plants of the same age (Fig. 7). Greening seemed to occur even advanced. The other remarkable property was a tremendous change in carotenoid contents. Analyzed by thin layer chromatography the content of lutein in heat-shock plantlets grown in the dark is 50% of that found after 8 hrs of illumination while in the etiolated controls only traces of lutein were found even after 8 hrs of illumination.

The levels of the mRNAs for LHC II and the small subunit of ribulose-1,5-bisphosphate carboxylase (ssRuBPCase) were highly elevated in the dark in comparison with the controls. Although greening can be observed already after 1 hr the same period of time was not sufficient to increase the mRNAs for LHC II or ssRuBPCase. In sharp contrast the mRNA for the early light-inducible protein (ELIP) of pea (18) remained strictly light-dependent.

In order to prove whether the cyclic temperature treatments could act as "Zeitgebers", plants that had been growing for 7 days under a 25:15 hr cyclic temperature regimen were collected every 3 hrs either directly or after 1 hr of illumination, frozen in liquid N_2 and stored at -80°C. The illumination was essential to increase the mRNA levels for ELIP. As can be seen in fig. 8. the levels for all three mRNAs fluctuate during the day with a minimum at around 17°° i. e. 10 hrs after the temperature shift. Although the curves are somewhat different from those reported (7) there is a clear fluctuation of mRNA levels during the day. In order to exclude mistakes in the quantification of mRNAs the filters were also hybridized as internal standard to an actin probe (19) which does not oscillate during the day.

The following hypothesis could explain the data: The photomorphogenetic response is controlled via the photoreceptor phytochrome. Phytochrome acts also as the receptor for the synchronization of the circadian clock via the light signals of the environment as shown by phase shift experiments (8). Phytochrome, however, should not occur in the activated form in the dark-grown heat-shocked plants as confirmed by the ELIP mRNA levels which are low during all phases of the day. Since we have shown that temperature sig-

nals can act as additional Zeitgebers which start or syn-
chronize the circadian clock in the etiolated plants phytochrome cannot be the relevant element. We suggest that it is
the setting of the circadian clock which brings about the
morphogenetic effects indistinguishable of photomorphogenesis. If this assumption holds true light would merely
act as synchronization signal for the circadian clock in its
connection with photomorphogenesis and not directly on gene
expression.

ADDENDUM
We are greateful to Dr. Ilse Barthelmess for critical reading the manuscript, to Dr. R.B. Meagher, Athens, Georgia,
for providing us with the actin clone and to Deutsche
Forschungsgemeinschaft, Bonn for financial support.

REFERENCES
1 Lindquist, S. and Craig, E.A. (1988) Annu. Rev. Genet.
   22, 631-677
2 Lyn, C-Y., Roberts, J. and Key, J.L. (1984) Plant
   Physiol. 74, 152-160
3 Kloppstech, K., Meyer, G., Schuster, G. and Ohad, I.
   (1985) EMBO J. 4, 1901-1909
4 Vierling, E., Mishkind, M.L., Schmidt, G.W. and Key, L.
   (1986) Proc. Natl. Acad. Sci. USA 83, 361-365
5 Vierling, E., Nagao, R.T., DeRocher, A.E. and Harris,
   L.M. (1988) EMBO J. 7, 575-581
6 Grimm. B., Ish-Shalom, D., Even, D., Glaczinski, H.,
   Ottersbach, P., Ohad, I. and Kloppstech, K. (1989) Eur.
   J. Biochem., in press
7 Otto, B., Grimm, B., Ottersbach, P. and Kloppstech, K.
   (1988) Plant Physiol. 88, 21-25
8 Tavladoraki, P., Kloppstech, K. and Argyroudi-
   Akoyunoglou, J. (1989) Plant Phsiol, in press
9 Hüsemann, W. and Barz, W. (1977) Physiol. Plant 40, 77-81
10 Grossman, A.R., Bartlet, S.G., Schmidt,G.W., Mullet, J.E.
   and Chua, N.H. (1982) J. Biol. Chem. 257, 1558-1563
11 Kloppstech, K. (1985) Planta 165, 502-506
12 Gubler, U. and Hoffman, B.J. (1983) Gene 25, 263-269
13 Glaczinski, H and Kloppstech, K. (1988) Eur. J. Biochem.
   173, 579-583
14 Schuster, G., Even, D., Kloppstech, K. and Ohad, I.
   (1989) EMBO J. 7, 1-5
15 Zimmerman, J.L., Petri, W.L. and Meselson, M. (1983) Cell
   32, 1161-1170
16 Viro, M. and Kloppstech, K. (1980) Planta 150, 41-45
17 Mohr, H. (1972) Photomorphogenesis, Springer, Berlin
18 Meyer, G. and Kloppstech, K. (1984) Eur. J. Biochem. 138,
   201-207.
19 Shah, D.M., Hightower, R.C. and Meagher, R.B. (1982)
   Proc. Natl. Acad. Sci USA 79, 1022-1026

CAROTENOIDS AND OXIDATIVE STRESS

Andrew J. Young and George Britton, Department of Biochemistry, University of Liverpool, P.O. Box 147, Liverpool, L69 3BX. U.K.

1.   INTRODUCTION

Carotenoids have two important functions in the higher plant chloroplast; first they act as accessory light-harvesting pigments and secondly they protect the photosynthetic apparatus from photooxidative damage. Protection is afforded by quenching of the triplet state of chlorophyll, thereby preventing the formation of harmful oxidative species such as $^1O_2$, and also by direct quenching of these activated oxygen species once formed. If this protective mechanism either fails or becomes overloaded then oxidative species will be formed, lipid peroxidation may occur and this ultimately leads to bleaching of the plant tissue.

2.   PROCEDURE

First-leaves of 7-day old seedlings of Hordeum vulgare (grown at $20^{\circ}C$, $150.molm^{-2}s^{-1}$) were removed and floated on   i) distilled water at a light-intensity of $4000.molm^{-2}s^{-1}$ and ii) lmM rose-bengal at $150.molm^{-2}s^{-1}$. Pigment extraction and high performance liquid chromatography of carotenoids and chlorophylls were performed according to [1]

3.   RESULTS AND DISCUSSION

3.1   The effect of high light.

Exposure to very high light intensities results in a faster loss of carotenoids than of chlorophylls (Fig. la). In general these and similar oxidative conditions result in chlorophyll a being degraded more rapidly than chlorophyll b (data not shown). Of the carotenoids it is the reaction-centre carotenoid ß-carotene which is most susceptible to these conditions and the major light-harvesting carotenoid, lutein, the most resistant. The rate of loss of the other major chloroplast carotenoids, namely neoxanthin and the violaxanthin-cycle carotenoids (violaxanthin, antheraxanthin and zeaxanthin) is intermediate between that of ß-carotene and lutein (Fig. lb). This pattern of pigment loss is almost identical to that seen in illuminated chloroplasts. Even a short exposure to high light results in the rapid de-epoxidation of violaxanthin to zeaxanthin (Fig. lc). It appears that no more than 50-60% of the violaxanthin is available for de-epoxidation under these conditions, confirming the observation that two separate pools of this xanthophyll exist, only one of which is available for conversion in to zeaxanthin [2]. Similar data have been obtained under a number of stress conditions (unpublished). Some workers [3] have recently reported that it is possible to achieve almost total conversion of violaxanthin in to zeaxanthin in certain higher plant species.

M. Baltscheffsky (ed.), Current Research in Photosynthesis, Vol. IV, 587–590.
© 1990 Kluwer Academic Publishers. Printed in the Netherlands.

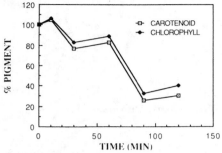

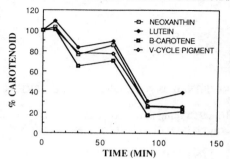

HIGH LIGHT-TREATED BARLEY LEAVES: VIOLAXANTHIN CYCLE

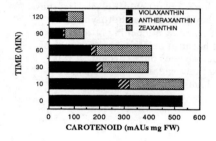

Figure 1.   The effect of high light on the pigment composition of barley leaves. Each point is the mean of 3 determinations, the standard error bars are not shown for clarity but never exceeded + 5%.

3.2   The effect of an exogenously applied photosensitizer

Rose-bengal is a well known $^1O_2$ sensitizer which when applied to leaf tissue or isolated chloroplasts leads to rapid; light-dependent, bleaching of chlorophylls and carotenoids [4]. There is a more rapid loss of chlorophylls than carotenoids during treatment with rose-bengal, so that after only 24 hours treatment almost 20% of the carotenoid and 40% of the chlorophyll are destroyed (Fig. 2a).

During the first two days of treatment both neoxanthin and ß-carotene are quite susceptible to $^1O_2$ treatment, whilst the violaxanthin-cycle pigments are much more resistant (Fig. 2b). Violaxanthin has been found to be intrinsically more resistant to oxidative conditions than the other chloroplast carotenoids and this may, at least in part, account its relative stability. In the later stages of treatment the pattern of pigment loss is quite different; the rate of loss of ß-carotene is much reduced (probably because of stabilisation of this carotenoid in the plastoglobuli formed in the more advanced stages of treatment) and large amounts of xanthophyll acyl-esters are formed. These esters may account for up to 60% of the total carotenoid present in the treated leaves. Compared to high light and other stress treatments the amount of zeaxanthin formed through de-epoxidation from violaxanthin is very small (Fig. 2c) presumably as there is little direct interaction between the $^1O_2$ and the photosynthetic processes.

4.   CONCLUSIONS

In this study the effects of a number of conditions that lead to bleaching of plant tissue have been investigated. Two different sources of activated oxygen species have been used, one extrachloroplastic and the other in which the oxidising species are produced at specific sites in the thylakoid membrane. These resulted in very different patterns of pigment photobleaching, as summarized in Table 1. Comparison with other forms of oxidative stress (e.g., atmospheric pollutants, senescence and 'contact and burn' herbicides) shows that the behaviour of chlorophylls and carotenoids during bleaching is largely governed by the site of production of the oxidative species. The nature of these species involved (eg. $^1O_2$, $\cdot OH$, $O_2^{\cdot}$) appears to be less important.

TABLE 1.   Carotenoid composition of untreated and partially-bleached leaves. The data are expressed as a percentage of total carotenoid (-, not detected).

	Control	High-light treatment (120 mins)	Rose-bengal treatment (96 hours)
Neoxanthin	12.0%	11.9%	4.6%
Violaxanthin	18.7%	8.1%	9.9%
Lutein-5,6-epoxide	0.3%	-	-
Antheraxanthin	-	11.0%	3.1%
Lutein	38.9%	48.0%	13.8%
Zeaxanthin	-	8.6%	2.0%
ß-Carotene-5,6-epoxide	-	1.6%	-
ß-Carotene	30.1%	20.7%	23.3%
Xanthophyll-acyl esters	-	-	42.9%
Ratio of Carotenoid:Chlorophyll	0.455:1	0.336:1	0.971:1
Ratio of Lutein/ß-Carotene	1.030:1	2.319:1	0.594:1
Ratio of Chl.a/Chl.b	2.090:1	1.940:1	2.890:1

Common to all conditions in which there is an extrachloroplastic source of oxidising species, are both the production of xanthophyll acyl esters and the relative stability of ß-carotene particularly in the latter stages of treatments. This is a consequence of conditions prevalent in the cell once the pigments have been released into the cytosol. These are not seen in photoinhibitory or other conditions that lead to pigment destruction in which the source of damage is closely associated with photosynthesis itself. Similarly the production of a photooxidative product of ß-carotene, ß-carotene-5,6-epoxide, is associated with the latter and has not been seen under the former conditions.

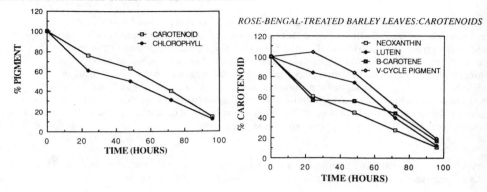

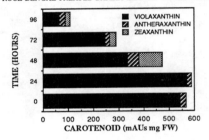

Figure 2. The effect of rose-bengal on the pigment composition of barley leaves.

ACKNOWLEDGEMENTS

This work was supported by the Science and Engineering Research Council of Great Britain.

REFERENCES

[1]   Price, A., Young, A.J., Beckett, P., Britton, G. and Lea, P.J. (1980) in Proceedings of the VIIIth International Congress on Photosynthesis, Stockholm. Kluwer Academic Publishers, Dodrecht.
[2]   Siefermann-Harms, D. (1984). Photochem. Photobiol. 40(4), 507-512.
[3]   Demmig, B. Winter, K. Kruger, A. and Czygan, F-C. (1987) Plant Physiol. 84, 218-224.
[4]   Percival, M.P. and Dodge, A.D. (1983) Plant Sci. Lett. 29, 255-264.

ANALYSIS OF THE MECHANISMS OF OZONE DAMAGE TO PHOTOSYNTHESIS IN VIVO

P.K. FARAGE[1], S.P. LONG[1], E. LECHNER[2] and N.R. BAKER[1], Department of Biology, University of Essex, Colchester, U.K.[1], Institut für Pflanzenphysiologie Universitat Wien, Austria[2]

1. INTRODUCTION

Ozone is now recognised as a serious air pollutant capable of significantly reducing crop yields. Considerable attention has been given to the inhibitory effects of ozone on leaf gas exchange (1) yet the underlying mechanisms have still to be resolved. Correlations between decreased stomatal conductance and CO_2 uptake have frequently failed to separate cause from effect. However, investigations at the subcellular level have shown that both chloroplast ultrastructure and activity are affected (2). The current investigation sought to identify the initial events which are responsible for the inhibitory effect of ozone on photosynthetic activity in vivo.

2. MATERIALS AND METHODS
Ozone fumigation:
Attached leaves of Triticum aestivum plants were inserted into a water-jacketed, stirred leaf chamber maintained at 22°C with a photosynthetic photon flux density of 300 μmol m^{-2} s^{-1}. Ozone concentrations of 200 and 400 nmol mol^{-1} were produced from an ultra violet source incorporated in a combined generator/analyser (1008-PC, Dasibi Inc. USA).

Leaf gas exchange measurements:
Carbon dioxide uptake (A) and transpiration were measured after fumigation in a separate leaf section chamber (LSC, ADC Ltd. UK) using the gas analysis system described previously (3). The CO_2 concentration was varied with a gas blender (series 850, Signal Ltd. UK) using cylinders of N_2, O_2 and CO_2.

Quantum yield and chlorophyll fluorescence measurements:
The quantum yield of CO_2 uptake for absorbed light (ϕ) was measured in an integrating sphere leaf chamber following the procedure of Idle & Proctor (4). A leaf disc electrode (LD2, Hansatech Ltd. UK) was used for measuring the quantum yield of oxygen evolution as described previously (5). The ratio of variable (F_v) to maximum (F_m) chlorophyll fluorescence was determined using a modulated fluorimeter (MFMS, Hansatech Ltd. UK) after dark adapting leaves for 30 minutes (6).

M. Baltscheffsky (ed.), Current Research in Photosynthesis, Vol. IV, 591–594.
© 1990 Kluwer Academic Publishers. Printed in the Netherlands.

3. RESULTS AND DISCUSSION

Following O_3 exposure leaf gas exchange was markedly reduced with both the light-saturated (A_{sat}) and light-limited rates of CO_2 uptake being affected.

Light-saturated photosynthesis:
The light-saturated rate of CO_2 uptake was progressively decreased as the concentration of O_3 and duration of exposure were increased (Fig. 1). This inhibition could result from a reduction in either the stomatal or mesophyll conductances to CO_2. The stomatal conductance did show a decline similar to that of A_{sat} (Fig. 1). However the stomatal limitation to CO_2 uptake, determined from the response of A to the internal CO_2 concentration (c_i, 7) only increased during the first 8 hours at 400 nmol mol^{-1} O_3; there was no significant change (t, P > 0.05) for any of the other treatments (Fig. 2a, b).

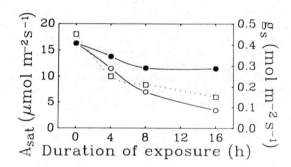

FIGURE 1. The effect of ozone concentrations of 200 nmol mol^{-1} (●) and 400 nmol mol^{-1} (○) on the light saturated rate of CO_2 uptake (A_{sat}) of <u>Triticum aestivum</u> leaves and on the stomatal conductance to CO_2 (g_s) for 400 nmol mol^{-1} (□).

Ozone fumigation decreased the initial slope of the A/c_i curve which is dependent on the efficiency of ribulose bisphosphate carboxylase. Carboxylation efficiency declined to 20% of the control value after 16 hours at 400 nmol mol^{-1} O_3 (Fig. 2). Conversely, regeneration of the primary CO_2 acceptor, i.e. RubP, was not severely affected by O_3 because at elevated levels of c_i the CO_2 saturated rate of photosynthesis was inhibited by no more than 30%. The capacity for regeneration of RubP relates to the maximum rate of coupled electron transport <u>in vivo</u> providing it is not restricted by the balance of chloroplast sugar phosphate export and inorganic phosphate import.

The A/c_i results therefore show that thylakoid processes are less susceptible to O_3 than the primary carboxylase. The sulphydryl groups associated with this enzyme would be expected to be particularly susceptible to oxidation. Previous investigations have found that both the amount (8) and activity (9) of RubisCO decrease following O_3 treatments.

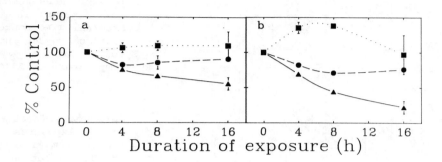

FIGURE 2. The effect of increasing ozone exposures of a) 200 and b) 400 nmol mol^{-1} on the stomatal limitation to CO_2 uptake (■), CO_2 saturated rate of CO_2 uptake (●) and carboxylation efficiency (▲) of <u>Triticum</u> <u>aestivum</u> leaves. Measurements were made at 20°C with a saturating photosynthetic photon flux density of 1200 μmol m^{-2} s^{-1}.

Light limited photosynthesis:
The limited susceptibility of the chloroplast thylakoids demonstrated under light-saturating conditions was confirmed under light-limiting conditions. The quantum yield of CO_2 uptake for absorbed light was not affected by the 200 nmol mol^{-1} O_3 treatments (Fig. 3a). Only after 8 hours at 400 nmol mol^{-1} O_3 did ∅ begin to decline, falling to 46% of the control value after 16 hours. Recently it has been shown that apparent reductions in ∅ can result if non-uniform stomatal closure occurs (10). However, this is unlikely to have happened here, because measurements made in the elevated CO_2 environment of the oxygen electrode, where stomatal limitation should be overcome, produced a very similar pattern of quantum yield results (Fig. 3b).

The fluorescence data similarly showed very little change with only a small but significant (t, $p < 0.05$) drop in F_v/F_m occurring after the most severe treatment (Fig. 3c). However the relative reduction in F_v/F_m was much less than for ∅ and implies that the decline in ∅ was not a consequence of photo-inhibitory damage to PSII.

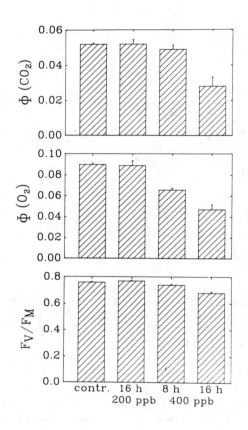

FIGURE 3a. The effect of ozone exposures on the quantum yield (ϕ) of CO_2 uptake for absorbed light of <u>Triticum aestivum</u> leaves. Measurements were made in an external CO_2 concentration of 340 µmol mol^{-1} at a leaf temperature of 20°C.

3b. The effect of ozone exposures on the quantum yield (ϕ) of O_2 evolution of <u>Triticum aestivum</u> leaves. Measurements were made in 5% CO_2 at 20°C.

3c. Changes in the fluorescence parameter F_V/F_m measured for <u>Triticum aestivum</u> leaves which had received differing ozone exposures.

4. REFERENCES
1. Darrall, N.M. (1989) Plant Cell Environ. 12, 1-30.
2. Guderian, R., <u>et al</u>. (1985) in Air Pollution by Photochemical Oxidants (Guderian, R., ed), pp. 132-169, Springer-Verlag, Berlin.
3. Bongi, G. and Long, S.P. (1987) Plant Cell Environ. 10, 241-249.
4. Idle, D.B. and Proctor, C.W. (1983) Plant Cell Environ. 6, 437-439.
5. Walker, D. (1987) The Use of the Oxygen Electrode and Fluorescence Probes in Simple Measurements of Photosynthesis, Oxgraphics Ltd., Sheffield.
6. Ogren, E. and Baker, N.R. (1985) Plant Cell Environ, 8, 539-547.
7. Farquhar, G.D. and Sharkey, T.D. (1982) Annu. Rev. Plant Physiol. 33, 317-345.
8. Pell, E.J. and Pearson, N.S. (1983) Plant Physiol. 73, 185-187.
9. Nakamura, H. and Saka, H. (1978) Jpn. J. Crop Sci. 47, 707-714.
10. Terashima, I. <u>et al</u> (1988) Plant Cell Physiol. 29, 385-395.

THE EFFECT OF OZONE ON PLANT PIGMENTS

ADAM PRICE(1), ANDY YOUNG(2), PHIL BECKETT(1), GEORGE BRITTON(2) and PETER LEA(1).
1 Division of Biological Sciences, University of Lancaster, LA1 4YQ, UK.
2 Department of Biochemistry, University of Liverpool, L69 3BX, UK.

1. INTRODUCTION

Ozone is the most economically important airborne pollutant in the USA, and perhaps Europe (1). Produced photochemically, concentrations can reach over 200 ppb (parts per billion) in heavily industrialised areas (2).

Ozone is known to reduce plant yield and its toxicity is largely due to its oxidising potential. Upon dissolving in water, activated oxygen species such as hydrogen peroxide and the superoxide and hydroxyl radicals are formed (3). It is predominantly through these reactive intermediates that ozone toxicity is thought to be expressed.

A symptom of several forms of oxidative attack is leaf chlorosis which occurs widely when plants are stressed. For example, loss of pigments can occur as a result of diuron (PSII inhibitor) or paraquat treatment (4), drought (5), chilling (6) and senescence (7), which all cause an increase in the concentration of activated oxygen species. Chlorosis is also a symptom of ozone injury. The site of radical production may vary between specific stresses, which has important implications for resistance. By studying the pattern of pigment destruction in ozone fumigation and comparing it with other stresses, an appreciation of the mechanism of radical damage, and in particular the location of radical production can be obtained. This presentation describes the use of simultaneous pigment analysis in elucidating the action of ozone toxicity.

2. METHODS

Barley plants were grown in a greenhouse for 11 days. They were then transferred to fumigation chambers (3) with a 16 hr., 20°C day, 8 hr., 15°C night, 180 µmol/s/m^2 light intensity and 60% humidity. Treated plants received 7 hrs. of 200ppb ozone from 9.00 am., controls receiving ambient air (10-20ppb ozone). Samples of the first leaf were taken every second day and stored under liquid nitrogen.
Samples were homogenised in redistilled ethanol, total lipids

M. Baltscheffsky (ed.), Current Research in Photosynthesis, Vol. IV, 595–598.
© 1990 *Kluwer Academic Publishers. Printed in the Netherlands.*

transfered to distilled diethyl-ether and dried under nitrogen. For HPLC analysis, lipids were redissolved in ethyl-acetate and injected onto an ODS 2 reverse-phase column (5um, 250x14.6mm) with a mobile phase of 0-100% ethyl-acetate in acetonitrile-water (9:1, containing 0.1% triethylamine). Detection was carried out by diode array spectrophotometry.

3. RESULTS

Ozone fumigation caused a loss of pigments after only 6 days treatment (Figure 1a). By the end of the 12th day, treated plants contained approximately 60% of the chlorophyll and 80% of the carotenoids compared to controls. The rate of destruction of chlorophylls a and b appeared similar except that in the first 4 days there was an indication of a preferential loss of the a form (Figure 1a). By the end of the experiment, the major carotenoids all decreased in concentration (Figure 1c). Compared to controls, there was a 20% loss of B-carotene, a 30% loss of violaxanthin, a 35% loss of lutein and a 40% loss of neoxanthin by Day 12. In addition, from Day 6 onwards carotenoid acyl-esters were detected (Table 1). These are not normally present in green barley leaves but accounted for 14% of the total carotenoid composition in the fumigated leaves at the end of the experiment.

TABLE 1. Composition of individual leaves of ozone-fumigated and untreated (control) barley. The carotenoid values are % of total carotenoid.

Carotenoid or Ratio	Day 0 control	Day 10 control	Day 4 ozone	Day 10 ozone
Neoxanthin	11.5%	11.8%	11.8%	9.1%
Violoxanthin	21.8%	19.4%	17.1%	13.3%
Lutein-5,6-epoxide	0.2%	0.2%	-	-
Antheraxanthin	1.7%	0.4%	0.6%	0.6%
Lutein	33.4%	35.6%	35.9%	30.5%
Zeaxanthin	-	-	0.3%	0.6%
B-Carotene	31.2%	32.5%	34.1%	39.2%[*]
Chlorophyll a:b	1.55:1	1.48:1	1.68:1	1.75:1
Carotenoid:chlorophyll	0.47:1	0.49:1	0.46:1	0.58:1
Lutein:B-carotene	1.07:1	1.09:1	1.05:1	0.78:1

(- = not detected)
[*] Xanthophyll-acyl-esters accounted for 6.6% of total carotenoids present.

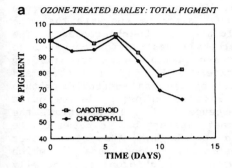

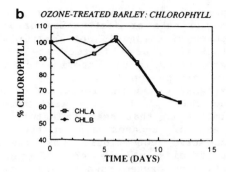

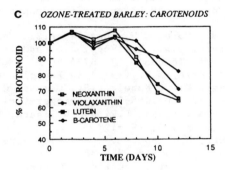

FIGURE 1. Pigment composition of fumigated leaves as % of same day control. a; Total pigments, b; Chlorophyll, c; Carotenoids.

4. DISCUSSION

   Ozone has been shown to inhibit photosynthesis (8-10) and cause changes in the chloroplastic activated oxygen scavenging system (3, 11) implying action at the chloroplast level.

   In this study, we have noted three factors which suggest that the primary events of ozone toxicity are located outside the chloroplast. Firstly, the production of xanthophyll-acyl-esters was evident in the later stages of fumigation. These have only been detected in barley leaves which have been subjected to oxidative degradation from sources thought to be extra-chloroplastic (eg application of the singlet oxygen-sensitiser, rose-bengal, or the herbicide acifluorofen). Interestingly, these acyl-esters have not been detected in conditions where electron flow has been impaired. Secondly, the effect of ozone on the rate of destruction of individual pigments suggests that the source of damage is not specifically located in the chloroplast. The observation of a faster rate of chlorophyll destruction compared to carotenoids is the opposite to the pattern in many other stresses, eg diuron-type or paraquat type herbicides. PS II inhibitors and paraquat cause the formation of singlet oxygen and superoxide within the chloroplast. The fast rate of loss of chlorophylls is quite similar to that seen in natural senescence (12). In addition, the level of B-carotene, usually the most susceptible carotenoid to oxidative conditions, was found to be higher than the other carotenoids at the end of the experiment, Conditions in which activated oxygen species are formed within the chloroplast generally lead to both a faster rate of loss of carotenoids than chlorophylls and a very rapid loss of B-carotene (13).

These observations, taken together, suggest that the major site of ozone damage is extra-chloroplastic and the observed effects of ozone on chloroplast function may be an indirect phenomenon.

1 Heck, W.W., Adams, R.M., Cure, W.W., Heagle, A.S., Heggestad, H.E., Kohut, R.J., Kress, L.W., Rawlings, J.O. and Taylor, O.C. (1983) Environ. Sci. Technol. 17, 573A-581A
2 Lendzian, K.J. and Unsworth, M.H. (1983) in Encyclopedia of Plant Physiology (Lange, O.L., Nobel, P.S., Osmond, C.B. and Ziegle, H., eds.), Vol 12d, pp.465-502, Springer-Verlag, N.Y.
3 Melhorn, H., Cottam, D.A., Lucas, P.W. and Wellburn, A.R. (1987) Free Rad. Res. Comms. 3, 193-197.
4 Farrington, J.A., Ebert, M., Land, E.J. and Fletcher, K. (1973) Biochim. Biophys. Acta 314, 372-381
5 Price, A.H. (1988) Ph.D. Thesis, Sheffield University, U.K.
6 Wise, R.R. and Naylor, A.W. (1987) Plant Physiol. 83, 278-282
7 Thompson, J.E., Legge, R.L. and Barber, R.F. (1987) New Phytol. 105, 317-344
8 Heath, R.L. (1980) Ann. Rev. Plant Physiol. 31, 395-431
9 Atkinson, C.J., Robe, S.V. and Winner, W.E. (1988) New Phytol. 110, 173-184
10 Rowland, A, Bamford, A.J., Coghlan, S. and Lea, P.J. (1989) Environ. Pollution 59, 129-140
11 Tanaka, K, Saji, H. and Kondo, N. (1988) Plant Cell Physiol. 29, 637-642
12 Britton, G and Young, A.J. (1989) In Proceeding of the National Seminar on Photosynthesis (Britton, G and Biswal, U.C. eds.), pp 208-224, Agro Botanical Publishers, India
13 Young, A.J. and Britton, G. (1989) In Proceedings of the 8th International Congress on Photosynthesis, Kluwer Academic Publishers, Netherlands, in press

EFFECTS OF SO_2 ON PHOTOSYNTHETIC CARBON METABOLISM IN LEAVES OF WINTER BARLEY (*Hordeum vulgare* CV. IGRI).

[1] PEDRO O. MONTIEL-CANOBRA, [1] J. W. BRADBEER, [2] N. M. DARRALL.
[1]Division of Biosphere Sciences, King's College London, Campden Hill Rd, LONDON W8 7AH, UK.
[2]Life Sciences Section, Central Electricity Research Laboratories, Kelvin Avenue, LEATHERHEAD, SURREY KT22 7SE, UK.

INTRODUCTION.
Research into the effects of air pollutants on plant growth and metabolism has moved towards the study of plant responses to low levels of pollutants ("chronic injury") and the interactions with environmental conditions. Plant growth and crop yield are known to be affected after exposure for long periods to low pollutant levels (1). For example, exposure to SO_2 and NO_x resulted in increased leafiness and reductions in root growth (2,3,4), while in barley overwinter reductions in crop growth have been reported (5,6). These effects on plant growth have been related to photosynthesis and the distribution of photoassimilate, the processes that sustain dry matter production in plants (7).

Following exposure to SO_2 under certain conditions, inhibition of assimilate distribution has been observed without changes in photosynthesis(8,9).This suggests that the primary effect was on translocation. However, alterations in the pattern of growth (not necessarily a reduction in growth) cannot be explained by inhibition of translocation alone, because translocation must be maintained for redistribution of assimilate to occur (10).

Clearly there is a need to further investigate the interaction, as well as individual pathways, of the metabolic processes which sustain plant growth under realistic conditions, of both pollutant regime and environment. The Littlehampton open-air fumigation experiment provided the opportunity to assess some enzymes and metabolites of photosynthetic carbon metabolism in leaf material from a commercially grown barley crop .

MATERIALS AND METHODS.
Winter barley cv. Igri was sown and grown according to the local farming practices at the Institute of Horticultural Research, Littlehampton, West Sussex, UK. The open-air fumigation system has been previously described (11). The crop was continuously exposed to SO_2 target concentrations by addition of 0.03 and 0.06 μl l^{-1} to the background levels (less than 0.01 μl l^{-1}) in the case of the two highest SO_2 treatments. The "low" SO_2 treatment corresponded to concentrations (0.02 μl l^{-1}

M. Baltscheffsky (ed.), Current Research in Photosynthesis, Vol. IV, 599–602.
© 1990 *Kluwer Academic Publishers. Printed in the Netherlands.*

target annual mean) taken from measurements at a rural site in Central England. The research reported here took place during the growing seasons of 1985/6 and 1986/7.

Particular attention was given to the flag leaf because of its important contribution to grain filling. Leaf samples for the measurement of leaf area and dry weight were sampled at midday, stored in polyethylene bags and assessed on the same day. Leaf material for the assaying of enzymes and metabolites were stored in liquid nitrogen immediately after sampling. The following enzymes were assayed in crude extracts: phosphoribulokinase (PRK, EC 2.7.1.19), NADP-dependent glyceraldehyde P-dehydrogenase (GPD, EC 1.2.1.13), phosphoglycerate kinase (EC 2.7.2.3) and cytosolic fructose 1,6 bisphosphatase (FBPase, EC 3.1.3.11). Photosynthetic products and metabolites assayed included total non-structural carbohydrates (TNC), soluble sugars (including sucrose), inorganic phosphate (Pi) and fructose 2,6 bisphosphate ($F2,6P_2$).

RESULTS AND DISCUSSION.

Both the leaf area and the dry weight of the flag leaf were significantly reduced ($P<0.05$) in the highest SO_2 treatment when compared with the ambient control, as shown in Table 1. Similar results had been found in the previous season.

Table 1 - Flag leaf measurements of plants from the ambient, medium and high SO_2 treatments at GS 69 (1986-7).

PARAMETER		$0.005 \ \mu l \ l^{-1}$	$0.028 \ \mu l \ l^{-1}$	$0.038 \ \mu l \ l^{-1}$	
Dry weight :	Treated (T)	43.26	41.27	34.58	
(mg)	Control (C)	47.31	40.06	44.7	
	Ratio (T/C)	0.91	1.03	0.77	* *
Leaf area	Treated (T)	9.27	8.98	7.65	
(cm^2)	Control (C)	10.28	8.72	9.64	
	Ratio (T/C)	0.90	1.03	0.79	* *

* $P<0.05$, ** $P<0.01$
Statistical analysis by One-Way ANOVA.

A smaller flag leaf has the potential to affect grain filling in cereals because on a leaf basis there is less photosynthate available for export from the particular source. In the same season delays in the emergence and senescence of the flag leaf were also recorded in the highest two SO_2 treatments (data not shown, 11). Similarly there were also reductions in above-ground crop growth during the winter months in the higher SO_2 treatments (A. R. McLeod, personal communication). These changes in the growth pattern of the crop may have been related (and are in agreement with previous research) to alterations in assimilate allocation and competition between sinks.

Significant differences (for the highest SO_2 treatment, $P<0.05$) in extractable enzymatic activity were found only for the cytosolic FBPase (Fig.1) which was reduced in the SO_2 treated material during the post-anthesis period in both seasons.

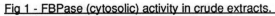

Fig 1 - FBPase (cytosolic) activity in crude extracts.
A - Crop season 1986-7   (n=8)

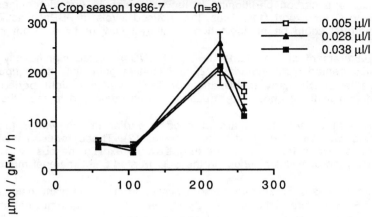

	0.005 µl/l
	0.028 µl/l
	0.038 µl/l

B - Post-anthesis period 1985-6   (n=5)

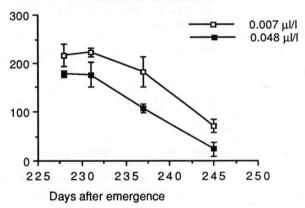

| | 0.007 µl/l |
| | 0.048 µl/l |

Days after emergence

Table 2 - Total non-structural carbohydrate gain during the photoperiod.
(µmol Glu eq./h/ mg Chl.)   at GS 32. (26-27 March 1987).

SO2 Treatment	Day 1	Day 1 to 2	Day 2
	10.00-16.30 h	16.30-9.00 h	9.00-16.00
0.005 µl l-1	2.46	-1.63	4.54
0.028 µl l-1	2.33	-1.65	4.05
0.038 µl l-1	2.12 ***	-1.02 **	3.54 ***

** P<0.01,   *** P<0.001. One-way ANOVA was performed on the individual sets of
data per daytime point comparing SO2 treatment vs. ambient control.

Cytosolic FBPase is part of the elaborate chloroplastic/cytosolic regulation of sucrose synthesis and carbon partitioning in leaves, which in turn determines the availability of fixed C for export (11). Thus, the reduced levels of FBPase activity in SO_2 treated material could be an indication of altered flow of fixed C out of the chloroplast.

The measurement of the diurnal levels of TNC revealed significantly lower levels in the SO_2 treated plant material (12) and smaller gain of C throughout the photoperiod (Table 2). Similarly mobilization of TNC over the night period was significantly reduced in the highest SO_2 treatment when compared to the other two treatments.

Measurement of soluble sugars at midday earlier in the winter (January 1986-7) coincided with this finding (data not shown, 12). These reduced levels of fixed C available for export from the mature leaves would explain the observed lower growth rates during the overwinter period in the SO_2 treated plant material mentioned above.

The diurnal levels of $F2,6P_2$ were also assessed in the same plant material. The diurnal levels of $F2,6P_2$ were higher in the SO_2 treated leaf material (data not shown, 12) which would imply reduced sucrose synthesis and would be in agreement with the reduced levels of soluble sugars and TNC found in the same material, revealing an adjustment of leaf metabolism to the presence of the pollutant.

Further work is required to elucidate the metabolic response of crops to these kind of stresses in the natural environment, particularly about the role played by the regulatory processes of photosynthesis and carbon partitioning in source leaves with regard to growth responses at the whole plant level.

REFERENCES.
(1)   Roberts, T.M., Darrall N.M., Lane P. (1983) Adv. Applied Biology 9, 1-142.
(2)   Jones, T. and Mansfield, T.A. (1982) Environ. Pollut. Ser. A 28, 199-207.
(3)   Whitmore, M.E. and Mansfield, T.A. (1983) Environ. Pollut. Ser. A, 217-35
(4)   Murray, F. (1985) J. Exp. Bot. 36(164), 449-57
(5)   Pande,P.C. and Mansfield, T.A. (1985) Environ. Pollut. Ser. A 39, 281-91
(6)   Baker C.K., Colls J.J., Fullwood A.E., Seaton G.G.R. (1986) New Phytol. 104, 233-41
(7)   Mooney, H.A.and Winner, W.E (1987) in Air pollution and Plant Metabolism (Schulte-Hostede S., Darrall N.M., Blank L.W., Wellburn A.R., Eds)Elsevier Applied Science, London.
(8)   Noyes, R.D. (1980)Plant Physiol. 63, 142-5
(9)   Teh, K.H. and Swanson, C.A. (1982) Plant Physiol. 69, 88-92
(1 0) McLeod , A.R., Fackrell, J.E., Alexander, K. (1985) Atmos. Environ. 19, 1639-49
(1 1) Montiel-Canobra, P.O., Darrall, N.M., Bradbeer, J.W. (1989) Agric. Ecosystems Environ. (submitted)
(1 2) Montiel-Canobra, P.O., Darrall, N.M., Bradbeer, J.W. (1989). In preparation.

(This paper is published with the permission of the Central Electricity Generating Board.)

INFLUENCE OF PHOTOSYNTHETIC CAPACITY, IRRADIANCE AND SO_2
FUMIGATION ON SHOOT GROWTH OF AZALEA (<u>RHODODENDRON</u>) CULTIVARS

David J. Ballantyne
        Department of Biology
        University of Victoria
        Victoria, B.C. Canada V8W 2Y2

1. INTRODUCTION

Azalea (<u>Rhododendron</u>) shoot growth is of considerable concern to
commercial growers, because it requires considerable cultural time.
Ceulemans et al. (2) found a positive relationship between photosynthesis and shoot growth of closely related greenhouse cultivars.
The studies reported here have utilized a method of determining oxygen
evolution of leaf segments in carbon dioxide saturation developed by
Steffen & Palta (6), to investigate a possible relationship between
photosynthesis and shoot growth of distantly related outdoor azalea
cultivars. Badger (1) considered such determination to be net oxygen
flux. The effect of SO_2 on post-fumigation photosynthesis and shoot
growth of 2 cultivars has been investigated. Lorenc-Plucinska (3)
found that Scots pine seedlings with a high photosynthetic rate were
more susceptible to SO_2. Because Pettersen (5) reported on the
stimulating effect of long days on azalea shoot growth at high
temperatures, the effect of photoperiod on net oxygen flux was
investigated. Also the effect of leaf position and PPFD on net oxygen
flux of leaf segments were determined.

2. MATERIALS AND METHODS

Two weeks after plants were pruned in the greenhouse (night
temperature 16 ± 1°C), they were placed in the growth chambers.
Usually the growth chambers were under 15-hr days, PPFD of 300 µE
$m^{-2}s^{-1}$, 22°C days and 13°C nights. In one experiment an additional
growth chamber PPFD of 100 µE $m^{-2}s^{-1}$ was used. In the SO_2 experiment
a median concentration of 35 pphm SO_2 and a maximum concentration of
40 pphm were maintained over 9 hours, with a photoperiod of 10 hours,
PPFD of 300 µE $m^{-2}s^{-1}$, 22°C days and 16°C nights. In the photoperiod
experiment both long day and short day plants received 10 hours of
130 µE $m^{-2}s^{-1}$, plus 14 hours of 10 µE $m^{-2}s^{-1}$ in the case of long day
plants, all at 22°C.

M. Baltscheffsky (ed.), Current Research in Photosynthesis, Vol. IV, 603–606.
© 1990 *Kluwer Academic Publishers. Printed in the Netherlands.*

To carry out determinations of net oxygen flux, 16 leaf discs, 4 mm in diameter, were cut in half and segments were placed in the medium of Steffen & Palta (6), i.e. 50 mM HEPES, 0.5 mM $CaSO_4$, pH 7.2, and infiltrated with an aspirator twice for 3 minutes at a time. After a 10 minute pre-irradiation at the same PPFD as the subsequent reaction PPFD, $NaHCO_3$ was added to the reaction vessel to a concentration of 20 mM. (The only exception to the above was a pre-irradiation of 1400 μE $m^{-2}s^{-1}$ when the reaction PPFD was 2000 μE $m^{-2}s^{-1}$.) Then O_2 uptake in the dark, O_2 evolution in the light, and again O_2 uptake in the dark were determined, all at 30°C. Chlorophyll was extracted with 96% EtOH as indicated by Steffen & Palta (6).

3. RESULTS AND DISCUSSION

Leaf segments from leaves of the middle and lower regions of the stems of the cultivar 'Fashion' had a lower photosynthetic capacity than did upper leaves. Segments from middle and lower leaves of 'Fashion' had a lower photosynthetic capacity than did segments of leaves from 'Hinocrimson' (Table 1).

Table 1. Net oxygen flux at carbon dioxide saturation and shoot dry weight of azalea cultivar 'Fashion' compared with values for other azalea cultivars. Data presented as per cent of the value for 'Fashion'.[1]

Leaf Position on shoot	Growing PPFD μE $m^{-2}s^{-1}$	Reaction PPFD μE $m^{-2}s^{-1}$	Per cent value for 'Fashion'						
			Net O_2 flux μ mol O_2 * (mg chlor)$^{-1}$hr^{-1}			Shoot dry weight mg(shoot)$^{-1}$ mg cm^{-1}			
			HC[2]	VS[3]	RW[4]	HC	VS	HC	VS
Top	300	2000	124	-	100	-	-	-	-
Middle	300	2000	160*	-	107	-	-	-	-
Bottom	300	2000	173*	-	140	-	-	-	-
Top	100	100	155	178*	-	92	183*	143*	221*
Top	300	300	136*	136*	-	87	153*	96	178*

[1]All shoots had grown for 2 months in 15hr days, 22°C day, 13°C night. Segments prepared from fully expanded leaves for oxygen flux assay.
[2]Cultivar 'Hinocrimson'.
[3]Cultivar 'Vuyk's Scarlet'.
[4]Cultivar 'Red Wing'.
*Asterisk indicates value is significantly different than the value for 'Fashion' at the 5% level.

Three potential stress factors have been at least partially investigated--irradiance, SO_2 and photoperiod. In the case of irradiance, a low PPFD reduced net oxygen flux and shoot dry weight.

At a low PPFD (100 μE $m^{-2}s^{-1}$) 'Fashion' had a lower net oxygen flux
and shoot dry weight than did 'Vuyk's Scarlet', and a lower shoot dry
weight than 'Hinocrimson' (Table 1). At a higher PPFD (300 μE $m^{-2}s^{-1}$)
all 3 cultivars had higher net oxygen flux and shoot dry weight, but
the difference between 'Fashion' and 'Vuyk's Scarlet' remained. SO_2
may have had a direct effect on photosynthesis, but no post-fumigation
effects could be detected. However, SO_2 did decrease shoot dry weight
of 'Hinocrimson' but not of 'Fashion' (Table 2). In long days
'Fashion' had a lower net oxygen flux than did 'Hinocrimson', but this
was not reflected in decreased shoot dry weight. Short days did
reduce shoot dry weight of the three cultivars investigated (Table 2).
Mousseau (4) found that under short days <u>Chenopodium</u> had a higher
photosynthetic rate.

Table 2. Net oxygen flux at carbon dioxide saturation and shoot dry
weight of azalea cultivar 'Fashion' compared with values for
other azalea cultivars when treated with sulfur dioxide and
photoperiod. Data presented as per cent of the value for
'Fashion'.[1]

Photoperiod	SO_2	Per cent value for 'Fashion'					
		Net O_2 flux μ mol O_2 (mg chlor)$^{-1}$hr^{-1}		Shoot dry weight			
				mg (shoot)$^{-1}$		mg cm^{-1}	
		HC[2]	RW[3]	HC	RW	HC	RW
Short[4]	–	106	–	102	–	100	–
Short	+[5]	121	–	72*	–	70*	–
Short[6]	–	130*	117	94	100	100	175*
Long[7]	–	86	75*	70	108	108	142*

[1] All shoots had grown for 3 months. Segments prepared from fully
expanded leaves for oxygen flux assay.
[2] Cultivar 'Hinocrimson'.
[3] Cultivar 'Red Wing'.
[4] Short days were 10 hr; 22°C day, 16°C night; PPFD of 300 μE $m^{-2}s^{-1}$.
[5] Median SO_2 conc. of 35 pphm, maximum conc. of 40 pphm for 9 hr/day.
[6] Short days were 10 hours; PPFD of 130 μE $m^{-2}s^{-1}$; 22°C constant temp.
[7] Long days were 10 hours of 130 μE $m^{-2}s^{-1}$ plus 14 hours 10 μE $m^{-2}s^{-1}$;
22°C constant temp.
*Asterisk indicates value is significantly different from the value
for 'Fashion' at the 5% level.

Net oxygen flux of leaf segments was influenced by cultivar, leaf
position, photoperiod and reaction PPFD. Shoot dry weight was
influenced by cultivar, probably by photosynthesis, as well as growing
PPFD, SO_2 and photoperiod. In each case, there were numerous
interactions between these factors.

4. REFERENCES

(1) Badger, M.R.   (1985) Ann. Rev. Plant Physiol. 36, 27–53.

(2) Ceulemans, R., Heursel, J., Ibrahim, N and Impens, I.   (1984)
     Scientia Hortic. 13, 147–155.

(3) Lorenc-Plucinska, G.   (1982) Photosynthetica 16, 140–144.

(4) Mousseau, M.   (1981) Photosynthesis Research 2, 85–94.

(5) Pettersen, H.   (1972) J. Amer. Soc. Hort. Sci. 97, 17–24.

(6) Steffen, K.L. and Palta, J.P.   (1986) Physiol. Plantarum
     66, 353–359.

5. ACKNOWLEDGEMENT

Funds for these studies were provided by the Faculty Research
Fund of the University of Victoria.

SIMULTANEOUS MEASUREMENTS OF CHLOROPHYLL FLUORESCENCE AND CO_2-GAS EXCHANGE ON SPRUCE UNDER FUMIGATION WITH PEROXIDES

S. DRENKARD[1], J. MAGUHN[2], A. ZIEGLER-JÖNS[3], D. KNOPPIK
[1] Lehrst.Physik-Weihenstephan,TU München,D-805 Freising 12
[2] GSF-Institut für Ökologische Chemie, D-8042 Neuherberg
[3] Senator für Bildung, Wissenschaft & Kunst, D-2800 Bremen

INTRODUCTION:
Peroxides are thought to be among the causes of forest decline (1). Therefore the effect of fumigation with several
peroxides on the photosynthesis of spruce needles *(picea
abies)* was studied.

MATERIAL and METHODS:
Single twigs of 5-year-old spruce trees of the same clone
were enclosed in gas-exchange cuvettes and fumigated with
peroxides. Gas exchange and chlorophyll fluorescence were
recorded simultaneously before, during and after fumigation. CO_2-response curves were measured in order to obtain
more detailed information. Records of chl. fluorescence
were taken by the method described in (2) using a PAM
fluorometer (Walz,Effeltrich,FRG). Gas-exchange measurements and the interpretation of the CO_2-response curves
were done according to (3). Net photosynthesis rate, A,
stomatal conductance, g^c, and ATP turnover, U_{ATP}, were
calculated from measured photosynthesis rates according to
(4) and (5). The concentration of ozone *inside* the cuvette
was measured with a Dasibi 1009-CP UV-spectrometer and
that of H_2O_2, PAN and homologs with a toxic-gas analyser
(Antechnika TGM 555,Ettlingen,FRG). The peroxide concentrations were between 200 and 750 ppb; the needle temperature in the cuvette was $25^{O}C$ and the PPFD 1100 μE $m^{-2}s^{-1}$
approximately. As a control an equivalent twig of another
tree was also enclosed in a gas-exchange cuvette and treated in the same way except for the fumigation. For the
purpose of clarity, only results obtained by ozone fumigation are shown here; others will be published elsewhere.

RESULTS and DISCUSSION:
The effect of fumigation with ozone was first investigated
at natural CO_2 partial pressure (Fig.1). While there is
only a slight and insignificant change in A and g^c of the
control, A and g^c of the fumigated twig begin to decrease
simultaneously after one hour of fumigation. One hour after the end of fumigation, A and g^c stabilize at 50 % and
30 % of the initial value, respectively.

M. Baltscheffsky (ed.), Current Research in Photosynthesis, Vol. IV, 607–610.
© 1990 *Kluwer Academic Publishers. Printed in the Netherlands.*

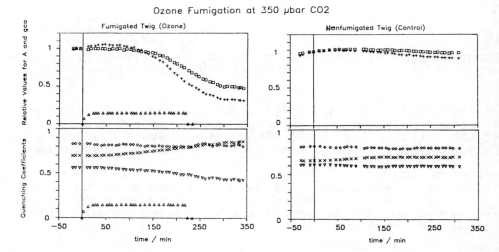

Fig. 1: Time course of gas exchange (above) and chlorophyll fluorescence (below) of an ozone-fumigated and a
nonfumigated spruce twig at 350 μbar CO_2.
($\triangle$:[Ozone]/ppm·5 (~750ppb); $\square$: net photosynthesis rate A;
+ :stomatal conductance g^c; $\diamond$:q_O (photochemical quench);
× : q_N (nonphotochemical quench); $\triangledown$: $1-F_O/F_S$

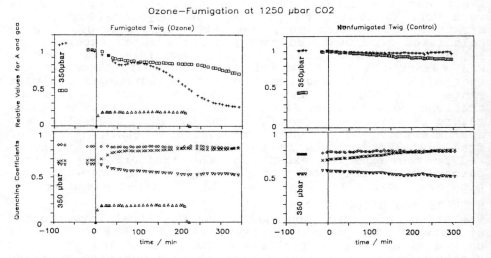

Fig. 2: Time course of gas exchange (above) and chl. fluorescence (below) of an ozone-fumigated and an unfumigated
spruce twig at 1250 μbar CO_2; symbols as in Fig. 1.

The time course of fluorescence is rather similar. For the control there is no change in the photochemical quench coefficient qQ (= percentage of open PS II reaction centers) and only a small increase of the nonphotochemical quench coefficient qN, indicating an increase in the transthylacoidal pH gradient. Whereas qQ of the fumigated twig remains unaffected, 1h after the start of fumigation qN begins to increase, reaching a maximum value of about 0.88 1h after the end of fumigation.

As a third parameter, $1-F_o/F_S$ is plotted, where F_o is the *actual* fluorescence when nearly all reaction centers (RC) are open and F_S is the fluorescence during a light saturation pulse and represents the situation when all RC are closed. For a dark-adapted twig this parameter is identical with $1-F_o/F_{max}=F_{vm}/F_{max}$, for which a correlation with the quantum yield of photosynthesis has been shown (6). Whether the parameter $1-F_o/F_S$ is also quantum-yield-correlated is not yet established. But it is a good tool for differentiating two aspects indicated by a qN-change: 1. a correlation between qN and the ΔpH over the thylakoid membrane; 2. the feed back of a high ΔpH (=high qN) to a change in the antenna structure causing a reduction of the quantum yield both for fluorescence and photosynthesis; now indicated in a $1-F_o/F_{max}$ change, also.

To determine whether the reduction of A (Fig.1) is caused by stomatal closure, the fumigation was repeated with CO_2 in excess (Fig.2). A and qN show a rapid change of about 15%, which could not be explained by a stomatal effect. Only at the end of the fumigation is the reduction of A likely to be the result of stomatal closure. The initial 'damage' thus indicates biochemical changes followed by stomatal effects. It should be mentioned that these results can be observed in spring but not in autumn.

Fumigation with ozone reduces the initial slope of the $A(p^C)$ curve (Fig.3) as well as the saturation rate, the latter slightly more than the former, so that saturation occurs at lower p^C after fumigation. The increase in A at higher-than-atmospheric CO_2 is not accompanied by an increase in ATP consumption, U_{ATP}; to the contrary, U_{ATP} shows a slight decrease at high CO_2. Below normal atmospheric CO_2, U_{ATP} decreases, but more slowly than the net CO_2 uptake, A. Both effects can be explained by the fact that less ATP is required for carboxylation than for oxygenation of RuBP. This also reflects the CO_2 response of qN, which increases at both low and high CO_2 because of a lower rate of ATP consumption and hence a higher ΔpH. In qQ there is no significant change. It is only lower for very small p^C, possibly because of an e^- accumulation caused by the lack of NADPH consumption.

After fumigation there is a significant loss of structure of the CO_2 response of qN and $1-F_o/F_S$ due to the decreased

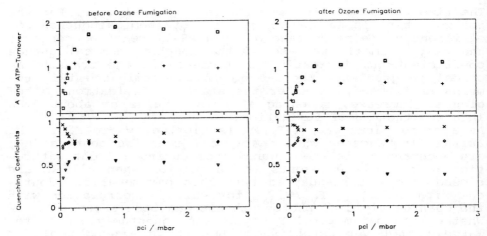

Fig. 3: CO_2-response curves of a spruce twig before (left) and after (right) ozone fumigation (3.5 h, 750 ppb). Above: net photosynthesis rate A ($\square$) and ATP turnover (+); below: quenching coefficients: q_O (photochemical, $\diamond$), q_N (nonphotochemical, x) and $1-F_O/F_S$ ($\triangledown$).

range of A and U_{ATP}. The changes in the value and structure of $1-F_O/F_S$ could be referred to a reduced quantum yield and a reduced regulatory capacity, respectively, due to the behavior of ΔpH after fumigation as indicated by the absolute value of qN.

SUMMARY:
1. Gas exchange and chl. fluorescence vary similarly with time as well as with CO_2, and they correlate in regard to U_{ATP} and q_N.
2. Ozone damage could be separated into two effects: one fast, smaller and nonstomatal and the other slower, but larger and (mainly) stomatal.
3. CO_2-response curves show a nearly proportional reduction in A over the whole CO_2 range, while the fluorescence data indicate an increased transthylacoidal pH gradient and probably a reduced quantum yield after fumigation.

REFERENCES:
1 Prinz,B.; Krause,G.H.M.; Stratmann,H.(1982);LIS-Berichte <u>28</u>, Landesanstalt für Immissionsschutz, Essen (FRG)
2 Weis,E.; Berry,J.A.(1987);Biochim.Biophys.Acta <u>894</u>, 198f
3 Ziegler-Jöns,A. (1989); Planta <u>178</u>, 84-91
4 Caemmerer,S.v.;Farquhar,G.D. (1981); Planta <u>153</u>, 376-387
5 Farquhar,G.D.;Caemmerer,S.v.(1982) in Encyclop. of Plant Physiol.(Lange,O. et al;eds),Vol 12B,549,Springer,Berlin
6 Demmig,B.; Winter,K.; Krüger,A.; Czygan,F.C.(1987);Plant Physiol. <u>84</u>, 218-224

THE EFFECT OF PROLONGED EXPOSURE TO AIR-BORNE POLLUTANTS ON THE PHOTOSYNTHESIS OF DOUGLAS FIR (*Pseudotsuga menziesii*) STUDIED WITH *in vivo* CHLOROPHYLL FLUORESCENCE

Olaf van Kooten[1], Lambert W.A. van Hove[2] and Wim J. Vredenberg[1]
Dept. Plant Physiol. Res[1]; Dept. Air Pollution[2]; Agricultural University Wageningen, Gen. Foulkesweg 72, NL-6703 BW Wageningen, the Netherlands.

1. ABSTRACT

Two year old douglas firs were exposed to moderate concentrations of SO_2, NO_2, NH_3 or combinations of these gases. The effect on photosynthesis of young needles (age between 20 and 135 days, which had sprouted during the fumigation treatment) was determined with Pulse Amplitude Modulated chlorophyll fluorescence (1). The electron transport rate was inferred from the fluorescence measurements by a method described by Genty et al. (2), which was found to be more appropriate for douglas fir than the method described by Weis and Berry (3). The light response curves were fitted to a formula described by Leverenz (4) from which the maximal electron transport rate, the quantum yield and a measure of the convexity of the light response curve can be deduced. All treatments resulted in a reduced rate of electron transport at saturating illumination as compared to the control (exposed to filtered air). But the most severe reduction (>50%) was observed in the plants exposed to a combination of SO_2 and NO_2. Firs exposed to NO_2 alone revealed an enhanced chlorophyll content, which was concluded from a significant decrease in the convexity of the light response curve. The plants exposed to SO_2 revealed a slightly enhanced quantum yield, similarly as has been observed before in poplar shoots (5). The reduced maximal electron transport rate in fir needles fumigated with NH_3 was in marked contrast to previous measurements in poplar shoots and broad beans (6-8).

2. MATERIALS AND METHODS

2.1 **Plant material**: two year old seedlings of Douglas fir (*Pseudotsuga menziesii* (Mirb.) Franco provenance Arlington 202) were planted in plastic 3 liter pots in earth consisting of 30% frozen peat, 30% composted bark, 20% fiber, 20% finn peat, to which lime and fertilizer was added. The seedlings were kept at 15°C and 50 μmol m^{-2} s^{-1} (PAR) for 2 weeks and at 20°C and 180 μmol m^{-2} s^{-1} for 4 weeks in the phytotron respectively, before they were transferred to the fumigation chambers. The relative humidity was about 70%. Each fumigation chamber contained 10 seedlings selected on uniformity. The environmental conditions in the fumigation chambers were: day and night temperature 20 °C and 18 °C respectively, relative humidity 60-80%, light intensity 320 μmol.m^{-2}.s^{-1} (PAR) during a 16h photoperiod.

M. Baltscheffsky (ed.), Current Research in Photosynthesis, Vol. IV, 611–614.
© 1990 *Kluwer Academic Publishers. Printed in the Netherlands.*

The soil of each pot was covered with teflon film in order to exclude effects of the exposure treatments via the soil. The air between the soil and the teflon film was exchanged by a small continuous flow of filtered air. Each sprouting shoot during the exposure period was dated.

2.2 **The exposure treatments:** the fumigation chambers are described elsewhere (5). The concentration of pollutants in the chambers were as follows:

$$\begin{array}{llll}
\text{filt. air (FA)}:NH_3 = & 15(\pm5) & \mu g\ m^{-3}, & NO_x = 16(\pm3)\ \mu g\ m^{-3} \\
NH_3:NH_3 = & 83(\pm7) & \mu g\ m^{-3}, & NO_x = 24(\pm4)\ \mu g\ m^{-3} \\
NH_3+NO_2:NH_3 = & 80(\pm5) & \mu g\ m^{-3}, & NO_2 = 79(\pm14)\ \mu g\ m^{-3} \\
SO_2:SO_2 = & 79(\pm7) & \mu g\ m^{-3}, & NO_x = 16(\pm3)\ \mu g\ m^{-3} \\
SO_2+NO_2:SO_2 = & 112(\pm9) & \mu g\ m^{-3}, & NO_2 = 93(\pm10)\ \mu g\ m^{-3} \\
NO_2: & & & NO_2 = 87(\pm12)\ \mu g\ m^{-3}
\end{array}$$

2.3 **Chlorophyll fluorescence measurements:** the measurements were performed with a slightly modified PAM fluorometer (Walz, FRG) described elsewhere (9). The intensity of the actinic light source could be varied between 0 and 616 μmol.m^{-2}.s^{-1} using a carousel of neutral density filters (KL 1500, Schott) and a filter to cut off light above 700 nm. A specially developed cuvette was used, in which a part of the leaf could be clamped. The cuvette provided access on the upper side to the fiberoptics bundle of the measuring system. The distance between the needles and fiberoptics was 3 mm. A gas mixture, at a rate of 100 ml.min^{-1}, containing 350 μl.l^{-1} CO_2 and 2% O_2 (v/v) was led through the cuvette. The low O_2 concentration was meant to minimize corrections for O_2-reducing reactions. A fluorescence measurement was immediately started at the highest light intensity, i.e. 616 μmol m^{-2} s^{-1}, and continued until both the variable (F_v) and the saturated (F_s) fluorescence remained constant. This was repeated at lower light intensities, i.e. 429, 219, 115, 63 and 30 μmol m^{-2} s^{-1}. After a 10 minute dark interval and 30 s of far red light (25 W m^{-2}, $\lambda>715$ nm) the minimal F_o and the maximal F_m fluorescence are determined. From this last measurement the photochemical quantum yield is determined F_v/F_m as described by Björkman and Demmig (10). The electron transport rate at every light intensity is calculated from pfd·$(F_s-F_v)/F_s$, where pfd is the photon flux density (2). This is an overestimation of the actual electron transport rate since the absorption cross section σ_A is not accounted for in this formula. The resulting electron transport rates J_{pfd} are fitted to a light response curve (4):

$$J_{pfd} = (\ pfd \cdot qy + J_m - \sqrt{((pfd \cdot qy + J_m)^2 - 4pfd \cdot qy \cdot J_m \cdot M))}/2M$$

where J_m is the maximum electron transport rate, J_{pfd} is the electron transport rate at the current photon flux density, qy is the quantum yield at limiting light intensity and M is the convexity of the light response curve and inversely related to the chlorophyll density.

3. RESULTS AND DISCUSSION

In fig. 1 representative light response curves are shown of 4 plants with different treatments. Electron transport rates were calculated from chlorophyll fluorescence measurements and are represented by the symbols (circles = FA, triangles = SO_2, diamonds = NO_2 and squares = NH_3). The curves are the result of a least squares fit to the light response curve described in the materials and methods. To have an indication of the validity of the fit the resulting qy was compared to the measured F_v/F_m. These two values are supposed to be equal. The average difference between qy and F_v/F_m was <5%. It is clear that the electron transport rates in the fumigated plants is reduced in comparison with the control plant. This can also be inferred from the averaged values from ten plants per treatment (see table 1). Fig. 2 reveals a slight correlation between needle age and the maximum electron transport rate J_m. However an analysis of covariance revealed that it was sufficient to use a one way analysis of variance to test for significant differences in table 1. Neither M nor qy correlates with needle age (data not shown). The effect of a decreased M value, as in the case of the NO_2 treatment, can be seen in fig. 1. In addition the decrease in M could be correlated to a rise in chlorophyll content (4) and thus to a rise in the absorption cross section σ_A. Consequently the net electron transport rate (e.g. deduced from O_2 evolution measurements) will be higher than expected. It is very well possible that the maximum net photosynthesis rate P_m of NO_2 treated plants is comparable to the control FA. In this way a decrease in photosynthesis capacity in the chloroplasts can be compensated by a rise in chlorophyll content. The significant rise in M in the NH_3 treated

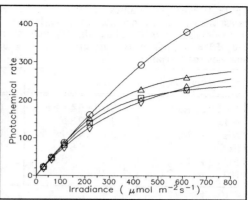

Figure 1: Light response curves in 4 different plants. O=FA, J_m=559, M=0.88, qy=0.77; △=SO_2, J_m=317, M=0.81, qy=0.81; ◇=NO_2, J_m=361, M=0.46, qy=0.75; □=NH_3, J_m=263, M=0.84, qy=0.76

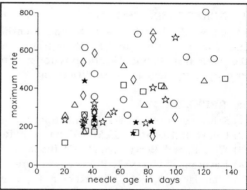

Figure 2: Maximum electron transport rates versus needle age from light response curve fits of 6 treatments and 10 plants per treatment. Open stars= NH_3+NO_2, filled stars= SO_2+NO_2, other symbols as in fig. 1

plants indicates a decrease in chlorophyll content. Both the decrease in chlorophyll content and J_m is in sharp contrast with the results obtained previously in poplar shoots (6,7) and bean plants (8). This difference might be related to a difference in nitrogen demand between these plant species (5). The slight rise in qy in the SO_2 treated plants has been observed before in poplar shoots (5). So far no explanation

Table 1: averaged values (n=10) of light response curves fitted to electron transport rates measured in needles of Douglas fir. Needles of different age were used for these measurements. The values given after ± is the standard error of the mean. ⊕, ⊕⊕, ⊕⊕⊕, significantly different at P = 0.05, 0.01 and 0.001 respectively (one way analysis of variance)

treatment	Jm	M	qy
filt. air	500±54⊕⊕⊕	0.66±0.08	0.79±0.008
NH$_3$	279±38⊕	0.80±0.03⊕⊕	0.77±0.008
NH$_3$ + NO$_2$	316±42	0.76±0.04	0.78±0.013
SO$_2$	372±46	0.61±0.06	0.80±0.012⊕⊕
SO$_2$ + NO$_2$	230±23⊕⊕⊕	0.77±0.05	0.77±0.010
NO$_2$	379±51	0.54±0.08⊕⊕⊕	0.78±0.018

can be given for this result. The dramatic decrease in J_m of plants exposed to SO_2 + NO_2 is in accordance with results of others (11). However the inhibition of photosynthesis does not have to be a consequence of a direct interaction of the pollutant with components of the chloroplast. For instance damage to stomata could lead to increased transpiration and induce a similar effect. Gas exchange measurements are performed at present to clarify this question.

4. ACKNOWLEDGEMENTS

We would like to thank Manon Mensink for her help with the plant treatments and Wilma Versluis for the fluorescence measurements. This work was financed by the Natl. Inst. Public Health Environm. Protection (RIVM) and is part of the Dutch Priority Programma on Acidification.

5. REFERENCES

(1) Schreiber U., Schliwa U. and Bilger W. (1986) Photosynth. Res. 10, 51-62.

(2) Genty B.,Briantais J.-M.and Baker N.R. (1989) Biochim. Biophys. Acta 990, 87-92.

(3) Weis E. and Berry J.A. (1987) Biochim. Biophys. Acta 894, 198-208.

(4) Leverenz J.W. (1987) Physiol. Plantarum 71, 20-29.

(5) Van Hove L.W.A., Van Kooten O., Van Wijk K.J., Vredenberg W.J., Adema E.H. and Pieters G.A. (1989) Plant Cell Environm., submitted.

(6) Van Hove L.W.A., Van Kooten O., Adema E.H., Vredenberg W.J. and Pieters G.A. (1989) Plant Cell Environm., in press.

(7) Van Kooten O, Van Hove L.W.A. and Van Wijk K.J. (1988) In: Applications of Chlorophyll Fluorescence (Lichtenthaler H.K. ed.), pp. 203-209, Kluwer Acad. Publ., Dordrecht.

(8) Van Kooten O. (1988) Report to the Dutch Priority Programme on Acidification (Natl. Inst. Public Health Environm. Protection) pp. 23, Bilthoven, the Netherlands.

(9) Van Kooten O. and Van Hove L.W.A (1988) In: Air Pollution and Ecosystems (Mathy P. ed.) pp. 596-601, D. Reidel Publ. Co., Dordrecht.

(10) Björkman O, and Demmig B. (1987) Planta 170, 489-504.

(11) Mansfield T.A., Lucas P.W. and Wright E.A. (1988) In: Air Pollution and Ecosystems (Mathy P. ed.) pp. 123-141, D. Reidel Publ. Co.

PROPERTIES OF SELENIUM-INDUCED GLUTATHIONE PEROXIDASE IN LOW-CO_2-GROWN CHLAMYDOMONAS REINHARDTII

Shigeru Shigeoka[1], Toru Takeda[1], Tsuyoshi Hanaoka[1], Akiho Yokota[2], Shozaburo Kitaoka[2] and Yoshitomi Iizuka[1]
Department of Food and Nutrition, Kinki University, Nara 631[1];
Department of Agricultural Chemistry, University of Osaka Prefecture, Sakai, Osaka 591[2], Japan

1. INTRODUCTION

Organisms have catalase, L-ascorbate peroxidase (AsAPOD), and glutathione peroxidase (GSHPOD) capable of scavenging H_2O_2, one of the toxic forms of O_2. Catalase with a low affinity for H_2O_2 is found only in peroxisomes and cannot decompose the lipid hydroperoxides. Thus, AsA- and GSHPODs detoxify such active oxygens in energy-generating organelles. While both peroxidases have the same function in protection of the cell from oxidative damage, the distribution of the peroxidases is apparently distinct: AsAPOD occurs only in plant tissues, protozooa, and algae, while GSHPOD is only present in animal tissues (1).

We had reported that culture of the green algae Chlamydomonas reinhardtii in a medium containing sodium selenite caused the activity of AsAPOD to disappear and GSHPOD to appear, and suggested that since natural fresh water contains a small amount of selenium, C. reinhardtii was originally an organism that required selenium (2). In this study we purified GSHPOD from Chalamydomonas reinhardtii grown in the presence of sodium selenite and studied the characterizations and immunological properties of the enzyme.

2. MATERIALS AND METHODS

Chalamydomonas reinhardtii Dangeard was cultured in Allen's medium with sodium selenite (3 mg l^{-1}) at 26°C for 6 days under illumination at 240 $\mu Em^{-2} s^{-1}$ with bubbling with sterile air.

Assays of GSHPOD and AsAPOD were done as described previously (2,3).

The algal cells (14.5 g wet weight) were washed with 100 mM Tris-HCl buffer, pH 8.3, containing 0.3 M sucrose and 5 mM GSH and disintegrated by passing them through a cooled French pressure cell at 400 kg cm^{-2} and the cell homogenate was centrifuged at 10,000 x g for 20 min. The obtained supernatant was put onto a DEAE-cellulose column (2.2 x 40 cm) equilibrated with the above Tris-HCl buffer. The column was eluted with a 500 ml linear gradient (0-0.6 M) of KCl. Active fractions were brought to 30-70% saturation of ammonium sulfate. The precipitate was dissolved in the above buffer and then chromatographed on a Sephadex G-150 column (2.2 x 90 cm). The active fractions were put onto a column

M. Baltscheffsky (ed.), Current Research in Photosynthesis, Vol. IV, 615–618.

(1.6 x 10 cm) of DEAE-Sepharose CL-6B and the column was eluted with a
300 ml linear gradient (0-0.4 M) of KCl. The active solution was concentrated in dialysis tubing with poly(ethylene glycol) 20,000 powder
for 12 hr and subjected to a Sephadex G-15 column (1.1 x 15 cm) to remove KCl. Enzyme fractions were chromatographed on a hydroxyapatite
column (1.6 x 10 cm) equilibrated with 10 mM potassium phosphate buffer,
pH 7.8, and eluted with a 160 ml linear gradient (10-100 mM) of the
above phosphate buffer. The purified enzyme was collected and dialyzed
for 5 hr against Tris-HCl buffer, pH. 8.3.

Estimation of molecular weight by gel filtration on a Sephadex G-
150 column and SDS-PAGE were done as described previously (4).

For selenium analysis, Chlamydomonas GSHPOD subunit was excised
from a slab gel in SDS-PAGE and measured fluorometrically using 2,3-di-
aminonaphthalene after digestion with nitric and perchloric acids (5).

GSHPOD from bovine erythrocytes (Toyobo) was emulsified with an
equal volume of Freund's complete adjuvant and subcutaneous injections
of 100 μg to rabbit were done four times at one week intervals. One
week after the last booster, the serum was collected, purified by chromatography on Protein A-Sepharose CL-4B, and stored at -20°C. Immunoblots were done by a modification of the procedure of towbin et al (6).

3. RESULTS AND DISCUSSION

Table 1 summarizes the purification of GSHPOD from Chlamydomonas
reinhardtii by a six-step procedure. The enzyme preparation had been
purified 323-fold over the crude enzyme, giving finally a 10% recovery
of the peroxidase activity. Polyacrylamide gel electrophoresis of the
purified enzyme showed only one detectable protein band.

The enzyme retained full activity up to 18°C between pH 7.8 and
8.7. GSH was the best electron donor, giving a specific activity of
193.6 μmol of GSH oxidized mg protein^{-1} min^{-1}; L-ascorbic acid, NADPH,
NADH, guaiacol, pyrogallol, and o-dianisidine could not substitute for
GSH. The peroxidase reduced cumene hydroperoxide and t-butyl hydroperoxide with the specific activities 86.1 and 150.6 μmol mg protein^{-1}
min^{-1}, respectively. These values correspond to 44.5 and 77.8%, respectively, against the value found when H_2O_2 was reduced by the enzyme,

TABLE 1. Purification of GSHPOD

Step	Total protein (mg)	Total activity (μmol min^{-1})	Specific activity (μmol min^{-1} mg protein^{-1})	Yield (%)
1. Crude extract	225.0	135.0	0.6	100
2. DEAE-cellulose	20.7	47.6	2.3	35.3
3. (NH$_3$)$_2$SO$_4$ (30-70%)	3.14	21.7	6.9	16.1
4. Sephadex G-150	0.64	19.3	30.1	14.3
5. DEAE-Sepharose CL-6B	0.16	15.4	96.4	11.4
6. Hydroxyapatite	0.07	13.6	193.6	10.1

suggesting that <u>Chlamydomonas</u> GSHPOD works for the protection of cell membrane, like the peroxidases in animal tissues, by reducing the peroxide compounds generated endogenously from unsaturated fatty acids.

By using double reciprocal plots of GSH concentration versus reaction velocity, the enzyme systems gave parallel lines, suggesting that the reaction proceeds by a ping-pong Bi Bi mechanism as shown in mammalian GSHPODs. Secondary plots of intercepts allowed us to calculate the kinetic constants; the Km values for GSH and H_2O_2 were 3.70 mM and 240 μM, respectively. The values for GSH and H_2O_2 are comparable with the values reported for the other GSHPODs (7).

The <u>Chlamydomonas</u> GSHPOD had a molecular weight of 67 kDa by gel filtration and 17 kDa by SDS-PAGE, suggesting that GSHPOD exists as a tetramer in its native state, similar to those seen for bovine (21 kDa subunit) and rat (21 kDa) erythrocytes, and rat liver (19 kDa).

Since AsAPOD in plants and <u>Euglena</u> is a hemoprotein (1,3), it is inhibited by cyanide and azide, the inhibitors specific for heme-containing enzymes. These compounds completely inhibited AsAPOD from <u>C. reinhardtii</u> grown without selenium, but had no effect on selnium-induced GSHPOD. Selenium was detected in the <u>Chlamydomonas</u> GSHPOD subunit, which corresponds to a molecular weight of 17 kDa by SDS-PAGE, indicating that the peroxidase is a selenoprotein.

Table 2 summarizes the properties of GSHPOD based on the results reported here.

Figure 1 shows immunoprecipitation of various amounts of antibody to bovine GSHPOD with GSHPODs from several sources. After incubation, the insoluble complex was removed by centrifugation and the remaining activity of supernatant was measured. GSHPODs from <u>Chlamydomonas</u> and erythrocytes of rat, human, and bovine were precipitated and their activities were inhibited 90, 60, 70, and 80%, respectively, by antibody to bovine GSHPOD. As shown in Figure 2, the antiserum reacted with the purified <u>Chlamydomonas</u> GSHPOD subunit with a molecular weight of 17 kDa

TABLE 2. Properties of GSHPOD

pH stability	7.8-8.7
Thermal stability	18°C >
Molecular weight	
Gel filtration	67 kDa
SDS-PAGE	17 kDa
Km values	
GSH	3.70 mM
H_2O_2	0.24 mM
GSH	3.13 mM
t-BuOOH	0.26 mM
Inhibition	
KCN	none
NaN_3	none
Reaction mechanism	Ping-pong Bi Bi

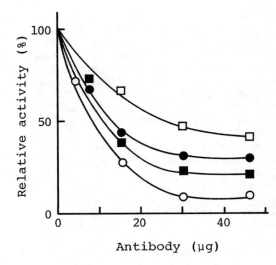

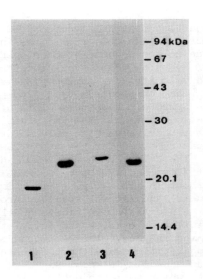

FIGURE 1. Immunoprecipitation of antibody to bovine GSHPOD with GSHPODs from several sources. (O) Chlamydomonas; (□) rat; (●) human; (■) bovine.

FIGURE 2. Immunoblot analysis of antibody to bovine GSHPOD. Lane 1, Chlamydomonas; lane 2, bovine; lane 3, human; lane 4, rat.

(lane 1) and with the enzymes from bovine (lane 2), human (lane 3) and rat (lane 4) erythrocytes.   These results on immunological properties indicate Chlamydomonas GHSPOD is similar to molecular species like animal enzymes in molecular structure.

The experimental results reported here have clearly shown that selenium-induced GSHPOD from Chlamydomonas reinhardtii resembles peroxidases from animal sources that contain selenium in enzymological, physicochemical, and immunological properties.

REFERENCES
1. Halliwell, B. and Gutteridge, J. M. C. (1985) Free Radicals in Biology and Medicine, Oxford
2. Yokota, A., Shigeoka, S., Onishi, T. and Kitaoka, S. (1988) Plant Physiol. 86, 649-651
3. Shigeoka, S., Nakano, Y. and Kitaoka, S. (1980) Arch. Biochem. Biophys. 201, 121-127
4. Shigeoka, S., Onishi, T., Nakano, Y. and Kitaoka, S. (1987) Biochem. J. 242, 511-515
5. Bayfield, R. F. and Romalis, L. F. (1985) Anal. Biochem. 144, 569-576
6. Towbin, H., Staehelin, T. and Gordon, J. (1979) Proc. Natl. Acad. Sci. USA 76, 4350-4354
7. Wendel, A. (1981) Methods Enzymol. 77, 325-333

MOLECULAR PROPERTIES OF ASCORBATE PEROXIDASE FROM TEA LEAVES

Gong-Xiang Chen and Kozi Asada, The Research Institute for
Food Science, Kyoto Univ., Uji, Kyoto 611, Japan

SUMMARY
   Ascorbate (AsA) peroxidase scavenges hydrogen peroxide in chloroplasts. Two isozymes were purified from tea leaves. Amino acid sequence
of the isozyme II showed little homology with those of guaiacol peroxidases. Further, AsA peroxidase was distinct from guaiacol peroxidase
with respect to the prosthetic group, the specificity of electron
donor, inhibitors, stability in the AsA-depleted medium and
carbohydrate. Hydroxylamine, hydroxyurea, p-aminophenol and p-cresol
inactivated AsA peroxidase in the presence of hydrogen peroxide, which
is caused by their radicals produced by the enzyme. AsA scavenges these
radicals and protects the enzyme from the inactivation.

1.   INTRODUCTION
   Superoxide radicals are inevitably photoproduced in chloroplasts,
and hydrogen peroxide is formed from superoxide. Hydrogen peroxide not
only inhibits the enzymes for the cycle of carbon dioxide fixation, but
also produces the hydroxyl radical by metal-catalyzed Haber-Weiss reaction (1). AsA peroxidase takes an important part in scavenging hydrogen
peroxide in chloroplasts (1), which lack catalase and glutathione peroxidase (2). We have purified two types of AsA peroxidase from tea
leaves (3), and one of them (isozyme II) is localized in chloroplasts
(4, Chen and Asada, unpublished).
   We have characterized the molecular properties of AsA peroxidase
(3). AsA peroxidase is distinct from guaiacol peroxidase with respect
to the following properties. a) AsA peroxidase is not a glycoprotein,
but guaiacol peroxidase is. b) AsA peroxidase is inactivated in the
absence of electron donor. c) AsA peroxidase seems to contain non-heme
iron in addition to protoheme. d) AsA peroxidase is inhibited by thiol
reagents, but guaiacol peroxidase is not. e) AsA peroxidase shows a high
specificity to AsA as the electron donor but low or no activity for
other electron donors such as guaiacol, glutathione and NAD(P)H. f)
Little homology of the amino acid sequences between AsA peroxidase
isozyme II and guaiacol peroxidase has been found.
   In this presentation, we report the inactivation of AsA peroxidase
by hydroxylamine (HA), hydroxyurea (HU), p-aminophenol (AP) and p-
cresol (CR) in the presence of hydrogen peroxide. Actual molecular
species of inactivation is their radicals produced by the enzyme, and
thus these electron donors are the suicide inhibitors of AsA
peroxidase, but not of guaiacol peroxidase.

M. Baltscheffsky (ed.), Current Research in Photosynthesis, Vol. IV, 619–622.
© 1990 *Kluwer Academic Publishers. Printed in the Netherlands.*

2. MATERIALS AND METHODS
    Isozymes I and II of AsA peroxidase were purified from tea leaves
as described previously (3). Guaiacol peroxidase B purified by Asada et
al. (5) was used. AsA peroxidase and guaiacol peroxidase activities
were determined as described previously (3). Hydrogen peroxide was
determined by the amounts of dioxygen evolved upon the addition of
bovine catalase (Sigma), using an oxygen electrode. ESR signal was
recorded with a JES-RE2X ESR spectrometer. The ESR spectra were simulated by an isotropic program using ESPRIT ESR data system 330.

3. RESULTS AND DISCUSSIONS
    The oxidation rate of AsA by AsA peroxidase decreased in the pre-
sence of HU with time and with an increase of the HU concentration
(Fig. 1). The inhibition of AsA peroxidase by HU was observed also
when the AsA peroxidase activity was determined by the reduction rate
of hydrogen peroxide. The reduction rate of hydrogen peroxide decreased
by the increase of HU added, but, increased with an increase of the
concentration of AsA (Fig. 3) indicating that AsA protects AsA peroxidase from the inactivation by HU.
    Preincubation of AsA peroxidase in the absence of either hydrogen
peroxide or HU showed no effect on the enzyme activity. However, if
hydrogen peroxide was added, AsA peroxidase was inactivated even after
the concentration of HU in the assay medium was lowered to the level at
which only negligible effect of HU on the enzyme activity was observed.
Preincubation with a stable oxidation product of HU also showed no
effect on the enzyme activity. These results suggest that the oxidized
intermediate of HU participates in the inactivation of AsA peroxidase.
    The one-electron oxidation product of HU by AsA peroxidase was
detected by ESR spectrum (Fig. 2). This signal was not observed if
either HU, hydrogen peroxide or AsA peroxidase was omitted from the
reaction mixture. The observed signal showed the same spectrum as the
simulated aminoxy radical of HU assuming two fine coupling constants to
be a_N=0.82 and a_H=1.18 mT. Thus, the radical produced by AsA peroxidase
is identified to be the aminoxy radical of HU. The signal of the HU
radical disappeared upon the addition of AsA, and in place of it the
signal of monodehydroascorbate (MDA) was observed, indicating the uni-
valent oxidation of AsA by the HU radical.
    The inhibition of AsA peroxidase by HU is implied by a mechanism
that AsA peroxidase univalently oxidizes HU to produce the HU aminoxy
radicals, and the radicals inactivate the enzyme. AsA scavenges the
radicals and then protects the enzyme from inactivation (Fig. 4). Thus,
HU is a suicide inhibitor of AsA peroxidase.
    AsA peroxidase I was also inactivated by the HU radical, but the
inactivation rate was slower than the isozyme II was. The signal of HU
radical was detected by incubation of HU with guaiacol peroxidase and
hydrogen peroxide (Fig. 2), but guaiacol peroxidase was not inactivated
by the HU radicals.
    In addition to HU, HA, AP and CR also were found to be the suicide
inhibitors of AsA peroxidase, but urea, hydroquinone and resorcinol
showed no effect on the AsA peroxidase activity.

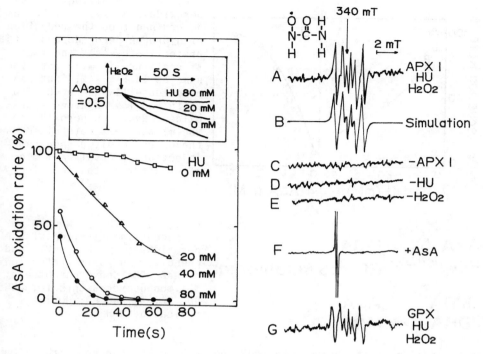

Fig. 1 (left). Time course of inactivation of AsA peroxidase II by hydroxyurea. The assay mixture contained AsA peroxidase II (0.15 unit) and HU at the indicated concentrations. The reaction was started by the addition of hydrogen peroxide, and change of the oxidation rate of AsA with time was determined from the time course of absorbance decrease at 290 nm (insert).

Fig. 2 (right). ESR spectrum of the aminoxy radical of HU produced by AsA peroxidase and its suppression by AsA. A: The reaction mixture (0.1 ml) contained 50 mM potassium phosphate (pH 7.0)/AsA peroxidase I (0.15 unit)/50 mM HU/10 mM hydrogen peroxide. ESR signals were recorded 60 s after the start of the reaction upon the addition of hydrogen peroxide or peroxidase. B: The simulation of the aminoxy radical of HU as described in the text. C: AsA peroxidase was omitted from A. D: HU was omitted. E: Hydrogen peroxide was omitted. F: 10 mM AsA was added to A. G: Same as A, but 100 mM HU and spinach guaiacol peroxidase (6 unit) were added instead of AsA peroxidase. Instrument conditions: modulation amplitude, 0.32 mT for A, C, D, E and G, and 0.05 mT for F.

The radicals produced by the enzyme would site-specifically react with the target site, resulting in the inactivation. The SH group is necessary for AsA peroxidase activity (3), and the phenoxy radical is able to oxidize thiols (6). Therefore, the enzyme thiol is a

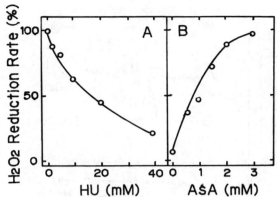

Fig. 3 . Inhibition of AsA peroxidase activity by HU as determined from the reduction of hydrogen peroxide and its protection by AsA. The reaction mixture (1 ml) was the same as in Fig. 2, but AsA peroxidase II was used and contained 1 mM hydrogen peroxide. Hydrogen peroxide in the mixture was determined as the oxygen evolved upon the injection of catalase 1 min after start of the reaction.

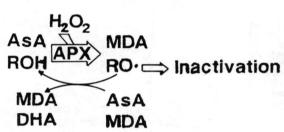

Fig. 4. The mechanism-dependent inactivation of AsA peroxidase by HA, HU, and phenols, and their protection by AsA. DHA:dehydroascorbate; MDA:monodehydroascorbate; ROH: HU, HA, AP and CR; RO·: radical of ROH.

possible site of the target, in addition to heme and non-heme iron. On the other hand, HU and HA are scavengers of the tyrosine radical in ribonucleotide reductase (7) and of PS II membranes (8). Although it is unclear whether any one of the four tyrosine residues in AsA peroxidase participates in the reaction, the tyrosine residue is another possible target site of the inactivation.

REFERENCES
1   Asada, K. and Takahashi, M. (1987) in Photoinhibition, (Kyle, D. J., Osmond, C. B., and Arntzen, C. J., ed.), pp. 227-287, Elsevier, Amsterdam.
2   Newcomb, E. H. and Fredrick, S. E. (1971) in Photosynthesis and Photorespiration, (Hatch, M. D., Osmond, C. B. and Slatyer, R. O., ed.), pp. 442-457, Wiley-Interscience, New york. NY.
3   Chen, G-X. and Asada, K. (1989) Plant Cell Physiol. 30, in press.
4   Nakano, Y. and Asada, K. (1981) Plant Cell Physiol. 22, 867-880.
5   Asada, K. and Takahashi, M. (1971) Plant Cell Physiol. 12, 361-375.
6   Ross. D., Norbeck, K. and Moldeus, P. (1985) J. Biol. Chem. 260, 15028-15032.
7   Larsen, K. I., Sjorberg, B-M. and Thelander, L. (1982) Eur. J. Biochem. 125, 75-81.
8   Chen, G-X. and Asada, K. (1989) This Proceedings, Serial No. 294

RECOVERY OF PHOTOSYNTHESIS IN WINTER STRESSED SCOTS PINE.

CHRISTINA OTTANDER, GUNNAR ÖQUIST, DEPT. OF PLANT PHYSIOLOGY, UNIV. OF UMEÅ, S-901 87 UMEÅ, SWEDEN.

INTRODUCTION:

During winter, high light and freezing temperatures interact to cause damage to photosynthesis of pine (1). The photochemical efficiency of photosystem II (PS II), the quantum yield and the rate of light saturated photosynthesis are severely inhibited during natural winter conditions. Strand and Öquist (2, 3) have shown that winter stress of Scots pine involve both photoinhibition of photosystem II and frost inhibition of the enzymes in the Calvin cycle or the photophosphorylation. In the field it may take several months before full photosynthetic efficiency is restored after the winter (4, 5).

In this study, chlorophyll fluorescence at room temperature and light dependent O_2-evolution were used to assess the recovery of photosynthesis in winter stressed pine. The aim was to reveal the relations between the recovery of Fv/Fm, the quantum yield and the light saturated O_2-evolution in order to determine the limiting steps during recovery. The potential for recovery, the actual recovery of photosynthesis in the field and the light dependence of the photochemical recovery were investigated.

MATERIAL AND METHODS.

Plant material.
Scots pine (*Pinus sylvestris* L.) shoots from exposed branches of a tree growing on campus (63° 50′N, 20°20′E) were studied during the winters of 1988 and 1989. The latest developed needles were used in the measurements.
The outdoor temperature regimes were quite different for the two years. From -4 to -26 and -1 to -7 °C in February and March 1988, respectively and 4 to -11 and 1 to -4 °C in February and March 1989, respectively (SMHI-report, Umeå airport, Norrköping, Sweden).
Prior to experiments the shoots were thawed at 4 °C recut and placed in water. The shoots were placed at 18 °C, and a photon flux density of 100 μmol m^{-2}s^{-1} with a photoperiod of 18 h. Needles were collected at different times and the recovery of photosynthesis was studied. During the mild winter of 1989 we standardized the frost treatment by keeping the shoot in a freezer at -18 °C over night before thawing.

Fluorescence measurement.
The photochemical efficiency of photosystem II was measured as the Fv/Fm ratio using a Plant Stress Meter (Bio Monitor S.C.I. AB, Umeå, S) (6).The photon flux density of the actinic light was 400 μmol m^{-2}s^1 and the time of excitation was 5 s. The needles were dark adapted at room temperature for 30 min before measuring.
Q-quenching (qQ) and energy-dependent quenching (qE) were determined, during induction of photosynthesis, at room temperature according to (7, 2).

M. Baltscheffsky (ed.), Current Research in Photosynthesis, Vol. IV, 623–626.

Measurement of O_2-evolution.

O_2-evolution of 10 intact needles, fastened side by side on a strip of transparent tape, were measured with a leaf disc electrode at 25 °C and under 5 % CO_2 in water saturated air (LD 2; Hansatech Ltd., Kings Lynn, UK) as described by (8, 9). Apparent quantum yield was determined because no correction for absorption was made.

RESULTS AND DISCUSSION.

The photochemical efficiency, expressed as Fv/Fm, of an outdoor pine was about 0.2 when the investigation started in 1988 and about 0.3 in 1989. Figure 1 shows the time course of the recovery of Fv/Fm in intact needles of *Pinus sylvestris* at 18 °C in a PFD of 100 μmol m^{-2}s^{-1} and in darkness. In 1988, when the photochemical efficiency was most deeply depressed the recovery of Fv/Fm showed a lag-phase of 2-3 h (fig.1), which was absent during the mild winter of 1989. Recovery was rapid within the first 10 h followed by a slower phase of recovery. After 24 h the photochemical efficiency had recovered 87 ± 7 % (mean ± SD, n=10). Both Fo and Fm increased during recovery. The recovery under darkness was slow and incomplete, but was stimulated by light when applied after 48 h of dark recovery (fig.1).

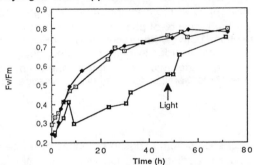

FIGURE 1.
Time course and light dependence of recovery of room temperature fluorescence emission, expressed as Fv/Fm, from intact needles of *Pinus sylvestris*. Recovery in (♦) 1988 and in (▫) 1989. The shoots were kept at 18 °C, in light (100 μmol m^{-2}s^{-1}) and in darkness (▪). Arrow indicates transfer to light (100 μmol m^{-2}s^{-1}). Needles were dark adapted for at least 30 min prior to fluorescence measurements.

The light dependence of photochemical recovery was studiey at photon flux densities of 6, 36, 120 and 300 μmol m^{-2}s^{-1}. No difference in the rate of recovery was observed at these light levels (data not shown). A photon flux densitiy of 6 μmol m^{-2}s^{-1} was below the light compensation point of photosynthesis in all measurements. Still that light level was enough to induce a rapid recovery. The recovery of the photochemical efficiency therefore seems to be a light activated rather than a light driven process.

In an attempt to reveal the relative rates of recovery of partial steps of photosynthesis, the time course of recovery of light limited and light saturated O_2-evolution were determined. After 48 h, the apparent quantum yield had increased from less than 0.008 to 0.057 (fig 2). No further recovery of the apparent quantum yield occurred under conditions used for recovery. The recovery of the light saturated rate of O_2-evolution was measured at a PFD of 1700 µmol $m^{-2}s^{-1}$. The time course of the recovery of light saturated O_2-evolution followed that of the quantum yield (fig. 2).

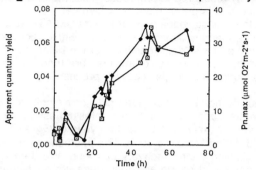

FIGURE 2.

The time course of the recovery of the quantum yield (▣) and the rate of light saturated O_2-evolution (◆) in *Pinus sylvestris* in March (light saturating=1700 µmol $m^{-2}s^{-1}$). O_2-evolution was measured at 25 °C and 5% CO_2 in water saturated air. The recovery took place at 18 °C and a photon flux density of 100 µmol $m^{-2}s^{-1}$.

Greer et al. (10) showed that recovery from photoinhibition needs *de novo* synthesis of photodamaged proteins. The lag-phase preceding the Fv/Fm increase may be due to transcription and translation of the genes for photodamaged proteins, e.g. the Q_B protein. Recovery did not affect the chlorophyll content or the chlorophyll *a* to *b* ratio (data not shown).

The modulated fluorescence technique was also used in an attempt to reveal if the limitation of photosynthesis was in the photochemical or in the enzymatic part of photosynthesis during the course of recovery. The first 10 h of recovery showed a very low variable fluorescence and a quenched F_0 level. Figure 3 shows the effect of the recovery on the kinetics of photochemical (qQ) and energy dependent quenching (qE). During the first hours of recovery, qQ was relatively high during initial induction of photosynthesis indicating that Q_A was relatively oxidized. After 10 h, qQ decreased during induction of photosynthesis indicating a significant transient

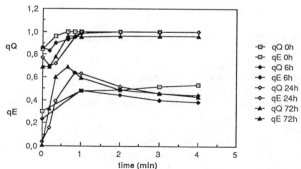

FIGURE 3.

The time course of the kinetics of photochemical (qQ) and energy dependent quenching (qE) during the recovery.

reduction of Q_A. This is in agreement with the recovery of the photochemical efficiency of PS II as shown by recovered Fv/Fm ratios. The rate of development of qE was retarded during the first hours of recovery which can be due to a bad connection between Q_B and the plastoquinone pool, or a damaged ATP:ase. However, the steady state qQ and qE reminded largely constant during the whole recovery process, indicating that the "light reactions" and the "dark reactions" are in balance. One can assume that the level of activation of the Calvin cycle enzymes are tuned by the light driven processes in the thylakoids during the whole recovery process.

In order to reveal if photoinhibition does play any significant ecological role during recovery from winter stress, recovery of photosynthesis in the field was studied. Figure 4 shows the recovery of the quantum yield of O_2-evolution and the recovery of Fv/Fm in the field during March to June. The photochemical efficiency of PS II does not seem to be rate limiting during recovery in spring. We therefore conclude that the photoinhibition component of winter stress does not limit photosynthesis in pine during the course of spring recovery of photosynthesis. Photoinhibition appears to down regulate photosystem II to prevent further damage to the photosynthetic apparatus during the winter (11). Photoinhibition in pine does probably not limit plant growth and development under natural growth conditions since photoinhibition occurs during autumn and winter when low temperature causes a natural cessation of growth and development (11).

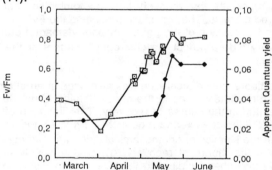

FIGURE 4.
The course of recovery of the quantum yield of O_2-evolution (♦) and of the recovery of Fv/Fm (▫) in the field during March to June.

This work was supported by the Swedish Natural Science Research Council.
REFERENCES.
1. Öquist, G., 1983. Plant Cell and Environ. 6; 281-300.
2. Strand, M., Öquist, G., 1988. Plant Cell Environ. 11:231-235.
3. Strand, M., Öquist, G., 1985. Physiol. Plant. 65:117-123.
4. Leverenz, J.W. and Öquist, G., 1987. Plant, Cell and Environ. 10, 287-295.
5. Lundmark, T., Hällgren, J.E. and Hedén, J., 1988. Trees 2: 110-114.
6. Öquist, G. and Wass, R., 1988. Physiol. Plantarum, 73: 211-217.
7. Schreiber, U., Schliwa, U. and Bilger, W., 1986. Photosynthesis Research 10: 51-62.
8. Delieu, T. and Walker, D.A., 1981. New Phytol. 89, 165-178.
9. Ögren, E., 1988. Planta 175: 229-236.
10. Greer, D.H., Berry, J.A., Björkman, O., 1986. Planta 168, 253-260.
11. Öquist, G. and Huner, P.A. 1989. Manuscript.

CHILLING-INDUCED ALTERATIONS IN THE PHOTOSYNTHETIC CAPACITY OF CHILLING-TOLERANT AND CHILLING-SENSITIVE CULTIVARS OF ZEA MAYS

C.S. Ting[1], T.G. Owens[2] and D.W. Wolfe[1], [1]Department of Vegetable Crops and [2]Section of Plant Biology, Cornell University, Ithaca, N.Y. 14853

An inhibition of photosynthetic capacity is commonly observed when plants of tropical and subtropical origin are subjected to temperatures between 0°C and 15°C. Chilling-induced alterations in photosynthetic processes are one of the first manifestations of chilling stress and have often been characterized by declines in the rate of CO_2 uptake over time (1-3). This inhibition of photosynthetic capacity appears to be the result of many different interacting factors and the contribution of these factors varies among plant species and with the light intensity, relative humidity, and oxygen partial pressure during chilling. Our primary objective was to examine the effects of short-term chilling stress (5°C, 48 h) on photosynthesis in chilling-sensitive (CS) and chilling-tolerant (CT) cultivars of Zea mays using leaf gas exchange and chlorophyll fluorescence measurements. In addition, recovery from chilling stress was examined.

MATERIALS AND METHODS
Z. mays cultivars BR102 (CS, common to New York state) and YF8-4 (CT, grown in the Mexican highlands) were grown in growth chambers at 23/11°C (475 uE m^{-2} s^{-1}, 14 h thermo/photoperiod). When plants reached the stage at which their fourth leaf was fully expanded (determined by the presence of a ligule at the base of the fourth leaf), they were chill stressed at 5°C (200 uE m^{-2} s^{-1}, 14 h photoperiod) for 48 hours. Following chilling stress and after 24, 48 and 72 hours of recovery at 23/11°C, leaf gas exchange and chl fluorescence were measured on replicate samples from several control and stressed plants.
Leaf gas exchange was measured at 660 uE m^{-2} s^{-1} using a Beckman 315A infrared gas analyzer and an open steady state system. Chl fluorescence was measured at 20°C using a pulse amplitude modulated fluorometer (4). Fluorescence measurements were made after leaves used in the gas exchange studies were dark adapted for 90 min. Changes in the ratio of the maximum variable fluorescence (Fvm) to initial fluorescence (Fo) were evaluated in terms of increases in Fo/chl resulting from uncoupling of PSII antenna (5) and decreases in Fvm/chl due to photoinhibition (6).

M. Baltscheffsky (ed.), Current Research in Photosynthesis, Vol. IV, 627–630.
© 1990 Kluwer Academic Publishers. Printed in the Netherlands.

The fraction of uncoupled PSII antenna was calculated from changes in Fo/chl using an equation based on the relative contribution of coupled and uncoupled PSII antenna to total fluorescence emission (0.37 and 1.82, respectively, from time-resolved fluorescence measurements of wild-type and PSII-minus <u>Chlamydomonas</u> (7)). The following equation was used:

$$0.37[1 + FD] = 1.82X + 0.37[1 - X]$$

where FD is the fractional difference in Fo/chl between control and stressed plants and X is the fraction of uncoupled PSII antenna.

Fluorescence induction was measured at 72 uE m^{-2} s^{-1}. Photochemical (qQ) and non-photochemical (qN) fluorescence quenching were measured with 250 ms pulses (2000 uE m^{-2} s^{-1}) and calculated as described in (8). Two sample-t tests were conducted at the .05 and .10 alpha levels and their results are reported as p-values.

RESULTS AND DISCUSSION

Following chilling stress at 5°C for 48 hours, only BR102 exhibited significant decreases (51%) in net photosynthetic rates per unit leaf area (Table 1). The 25% decrease observed in this parameter in YF8-4

Table 1. Photosynthetic rates (Pnet) per unit leaf area (umol m^{-2} s^{-1}) and per unit chlorophyll ($mgCO_2$ $g^{-1}chl$ s^{-1}), stomatal and mesophyll conductances (cm s^{-1}), and internal CO_2 concentrations (ppm) for BR102 and YF8-4 grown at 23/11°C and following chilling stress and recovery. Values in parentheses represent p-values calculated in tests of significance between mean values of a parameter for stressed and unstressed plants.

Treatment	Pnet/leaf area	Pnet/chl	Stomatal Conductance	Mesophyll Conductance	Internal CO_2 Concentration
BR102					
23/11°C	23.2 ± 3.7	2.2 ± .7	.42 ± .09	.33 ± .03	161 ± 4
23/11°C + 5°C 48 hrs	11.5 ± 1.9 (.04)	1.3 ± .1 (.13)	.20 ± .06 (.04)	.22 ± .00 (.11)	142 ± 18 (.38)
5°C + 24 hrs recovery	19.3 ± 1.5 (.23)	2.1 ± .6 (.78)	.32 ± .10 (.29)	.35 ± .13 (.90)	158 ± 38 (.93)
YF8-4					
23/11°C	21.4 ± 2.4	1.8 ± .6	.39 ± .15	.40 ± .06	144 ± 22
23/11°C + 5°C 48 hrs	16.0 ± 3.5 (.11)	1.5 ± .1 (.45)	.29 ± .13 (.46)	.30 ± .01 (.27)	150 ± 10 (.80)
5°C + 24 hrs recovery	22.0 ± 2.6 (.79)	2.3 ± .5 (.32)	.39 ± .20 (.97)	.45 ± .12 (.69)	139 ± 36 (.89)

was not significant. Neither BR102 nor YF8-4 exhibited decreases in chlorophyll per unit leaf area after chilling (data not shown). Chilling-induced changes in fluorescence parameters were also significant only in BR102 (Table 2). The 11% decrease in Fvm/Fo is due solely to a 44% increase in Fo/chl (no decrease in Fvm/chl) and indicates that chilling stress resulted in about 11% of the PSII antenna being uncoupled. The absence of decreases in Fvm/chl suggests that photoinhibition did not occur. Following chilling, BR102 also lost the S to M rise in its fluorescence induction curve (data not shown) and exhibited a 44% decrease in steady state fluorescence (F_T - Fo). This decrease is attributable to the 16% increase in qN observed in this cultivar (Table 2). Although YF8-4 exhibited a chill-induced decrease in fluorescence levels, increases in qQ and qN and decreases in F_T were not statistically significant.

Table 2. Initial (Fo) and maximum (Fmax) fluorescence levels per ug chlorophyll a, Fvm/Fo, steady state fluorescence levels (F_T), qQ, and qN for BR102 and YF8-4 subjected to chilling stress and recovery. Values in parentheses represent the parameter value for control plants. The results of significance tests between control and stressed plants are reported as p-values.

Cultivar & Treatment	Fo/chl	Fmax/chl	Fvm/Fo	F_T	qQ	qN
BR102						
5°C 48hrs	.46 +.04	2.0 +.2	3.3	.05 +.02	.80 +.02	.80 +.03
	(.32+.02)	(1.5+.1)	(3.7)	(.09+.01)	(.74+.07)	(.69+.01)
	p=.018	p=.046		p=.05	p=.31	p=.032
5°C + 24hrs Recovery	.41 +.02	1.7 +.1	3.2	.05 +.02	.85 +.05	.73 +.03
5°C + 48hrs Recovery	.38 +.06	1.7 +.3	3.5	.07 +.02	.77 +.06	.71 +.01
	(.32+.06)	(1.7+.3)	(4.3)	(.11+.02)	(.72+.01)	(.68+.04)
	p=.43	p=1		p=.12	p=.26	p=.49
YF8-4						
5°C 48hrs	.39 +.06	1.5 +.1	2.8	.07 +.03	.84 +.08	.64 +.07
	(.35+.11)	(1.6+.3)	(3.6)	(.09+.02)	(.75+.09)	(.71+.03)
	p=.56	p=.62		p=.44	p=.40	p=.24
5°C + 24hrs Recovery	.37 +.10	1.7 +.1	3.6	.07 +.03	.84 +.05	.62 + .05
5°C + 48hrs Recovery	.37 +.04	1.7 +.2	3.6	.06 +.02	.84 +.05	.69 +.02
	(.28+.02)	(1.5+0)	(4.4)	(.06+.01)	(.82+.01)	(.68+.03)
	p=.08	p=.31		p=.83	p=.72	p=.72

These changes in fluorescence parameters permit analysis of processes contributing to the 41% chilling-induced reduction in photosynthesis per unit chl in the CS cultivar BR102. Because the light intensity used to measure photosynthetic rates was limiting, the 11% uncoupling of PSII antenna can account for about one-fourth of the reduction in photosynthesis. In addition, assuming that qN is inversely proportional to photochemical yield in open PSII reaction centers (9,10), the 16% increase in qN can account for more than half of the remaining decrease in photosynthesis. Because there was no indication of photoinhibition, this increase in qN was most likely due to an increase in qE (fluorescence quenching due to the establishment of the trans-thylakoid pH gradient). Increases in qE may have resulted from chilling-induced decreases in pyruvate orthophosphate dikinase activity (11,12). Declines in the activity of this enzyme may result in a decreased demand for ATP in both the synthesis of phosphoenol pyruvate and the Calvin Cycle; these decreases in ATP demand may lead to a decrease in the rate of pH gradient dissipation via CF_o/CF_1, and an increase in qE. Under our experimental conditions, the insensitivity of internal CO_2 to chilling (Table 1) indicates that decreased stomatal conductance did not contribute to the increase in qN or the decline in photosynthetic rates.

The recovery data (Tables 1,2) for YF8-4 must be interpreted with caution due to the 20% decrease in Fo/chl observed in control plants over the experimental period. Interpretations must take into account that control plants continued to grow rapidly and develop over the experimental period. Recovery data for BR102 indicate that although significant changes were observed in photosynthetic and fluorescence parameters after chilling, these were not indicative of permanent damage to the photosynthetic apparatus.

REFERENCES
1) Taylor, A.O., J.A. Rowley (1971) Plant Physiol. 47, 713-718
2) Long, S.P., T.M. East, N.R. Baker (1983) J. Exp. Bot. 34, 177-188
3) Powles, S.B., K.S.R. Chapman, C.B. Osmond (1980) Aust. J. Plant Physiol. 7, 737-747
4) Schreiber, U. (1986) Photosyn. Res. 9, 261-272
5) Bilger, W., U. Schreiber, O.L. Lange (1984) Oecologia 63, 256-262
6) Powles, S.B., K.S.R. Chapman, C.B. Osmond (1980) Aust. J. Plant Physiol. 7, 737-747
7) Hodges, M., I. Moya (1987) Photosyn. Res. 13, 125-141
8) Schreiber, U., W. Bilger (1985) NATO Advanced Research Workshop, Portugal
9) Krause, G.H., U. Behrend (1986) FEBS Lett. 200, 298-302
10) Weis, E., J.A. Berry (1987) Biochim. Biophys. Acta 894, 198-208
11) Sugiyama, T. (1973) Biochemistry 12, 2862-2867
12) Hatch, M.D. (1979) Aust. J. Plant Physiol. 6, 607-619

PHOTOINHIBITION AND RECOVERY IN ISOLATED MESOPHYLL CELLS OF
HARDENED AND NON-HARDENED RYE.

Line Lapointe and Norman Huner, Dept of Plant Sciences; University of Western
Ontario, London, Canada.

1. INTRODUCTION

Low temperature has been shown to increase photoinhibition under moderate to
high light intensities (1). Even cold tolerant species can show photoinhibition if the
light intensity or the duration of the treatment is sufficient (2). But cold hardening
increases the resistance of certain species like spinach (3) or rye (öquist and Huner,
submitted) to photoinhibition under low temperature conditions. To further investigate
the source of this increased resistance to photoinhibition in cold hardened rye, isolated
cells have been submitted to photoinhibitory treatment and recovery.

2. MATERIAL AND METHODS

Mesophyll cells were isolated according to the technique of Servaites and Ogren
(4) from leaves developed at 20 °C (RNH) or at 5 °C (RH) . Viable cells were
separated by Percoll gradient centrifugation (5) and resuspended in a medium
containing: 0.1 M HEPES at pH 7.8, 0.25 M sorbitol, 2 mM $CaCl_2$, 1 mM $MgSO_4$, 5
mM KNO_3, 0.5 mM KH_2PO_4, 0.01 mM $CuSO_4$, and 0.2% BSA.

CO_2 fixation rates were evaluated by measuring the incorporation of $^{14}CO_2$
(supplied as $NaH^{14}CO_3$ in the medium) into the cells after a preincubation period of 5
minutes at the same light intensity and temperature as the measurement conditions.

Susceptibility to photoinhibition was analyzed at 5 °C and 20 °C, by pre-exposing
the cells to 3500 μmol m^{-2} s^{-1}. Recovery occurred in dim light (30 μmol m^{-2} s^{-1}) at the
same temperature as the photoinhibitory treatment.

3.0 RESULTS

3.1 Photoinhibition

The time course of photoinhibition measured at 25 °C under light limiting
conditions (29 μmol m^{-2} s^{-1}) indicates a linear decrease in photosynthetic activities at
both 5 and 20 °C over a 30 minute period (figure 1). Photoinhibitory rates are not
significantly different between RH and RNH cells even after 30 minutes of treatment
(60 % photoinhibition), nor between the 20 and the 5 °C treatment. No significant
effect was noticed when antibiotics (chloramphenicol or cycloheximide) were added

M. Baltscheffsky (ed.), Current Research in Photosynthesis, Vol. IV, 631–634.

during 5 and 20 °C photoinhibitory treatment for both RH and RNH cells (data not shown).

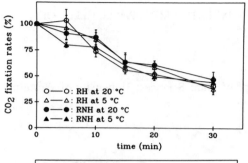

Figure 1: Time course of photo-inhibition of rye cells. CO_2 fixation rates were measured at 25 °C, under 29 μmol m^{-2} s^{-1}.

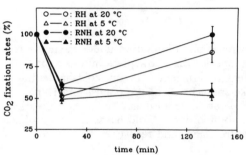

Figure 2: Recovery rates following a 20 minute photoinhibitory treatment for rye cells.

3.2 Recovery

Figure 2 illustrates the recovery of photosynthesis of rye cells measured at 25 °C under light limiting conditions. The recovery rates were significantly slower at 5 °C than at 20 °C, but RH and RNH cells show similar rates of recovery.

The addition of antibiotics had no significant effect on the first 40 minutes of recovery following a 20 minute photoinhibitory treatment (figure 3). However after 2 hours of recovery at 20 °C, the antibiotic treatments resulted in a significant decrease in the recovery of rye cells.

The recovery rates of RH and RNH cells at 5 °C were very slow and not significantly affected by the presence of antibiotics over the 2 h time course period (data not shown). Since the recovery rates are practically nil at 5 °C the effect of antibiotics can not be satisfactory tested with that method.

4.0 DISCUSSION

4.1 Photoinhibition

Previous results on intact rye leaves indicated that RH and RNH plants exhibited no photoinhibition after treatment at 20 °C at 400 μmol m^{-2} s^{-1} (öquist and Huner, submitted). In addition, RH plants exhibited a significant resistance to photoinhibition at 5 °C in contrast to RNH plants. The results for isolated RH and RNH indicated a similar susceptibility to photoinhibition at either 5 or 20 °C. Furthermore, RH and RNH mesophyll cells did not exhibit a differential resistance to the photoinhibitory treatment. Clearly, isolated rye mesophyll cells respond quite differently to photoinhibitory treatment than intact leaves. The anatomical and morphological changes observed in RH leaves (6) may play an important role in the overall response to photoinhibition. However, this does not explain the lack of a temperature dependence in the susceptibility of isolated mesophyll cells to photoinhibition. Further work is required to explain this phenomenon.

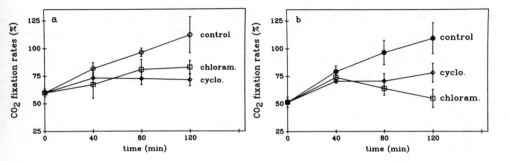

Figure 3:   Recovery rates of a) RH and b) RNH cells in the presence or abscence of chloramphenicol or cycloheximide.

4.2 Recovery

The recovery rates are faster at 20 than at 5 °C which suggests a possible metabolic requirement, such as protein synthesis. Greer (7) has also shown an increase in recovery rates with increased temperature in a kiwi plant. RNH cells recover at the same rate as RH cells both at 20 °C and at 5 °C. Whole leaf study with fluorescence kinetics have also shown similar recovery rates for RH and RNH plants after a photoinhibitory treatment at 5 °C (öquist and Huner, submitted) suggesting that differential photoinhibitory response between RH and RNH plants are not related to differential recovery rates.

The absence of antibiotic effect during the first minutes of recovery are in contradiction with previous studies (8,9). Recovery can also be dependent upon other mechanisms, such as decrease in non-radiative decay, once the stress is over (10,11). Non-radiative decay has been shown to be inhibited at 5 °C in pea leaves (11), which could explain the differential response of rye cells at 5 and at 20 °C during the first minutes of recovery.

Antibiotic effects over longer periods of recovery at 20 °C suggests the presence of protein synthesis as part of the repair mechanism. At 5 °C the effect of antibiotics are less noticeable than at higher temperatures as noticed by Greer *et al* (8). Both chloramphenicol and cycloheximide appear to be efficient in reducing the recovery suggesting that synthesis of chloroplastic and nuclear encoded proteins take part in the recovery process.

5.0 REFERENCES
1 Van Hasselt, P.R. and Van Berlo, H.A.C. (1980) Physiol. Plant. 50, 52-56.
2 Ogren, E., öquist, G. and Hallgren, J.-E. (1984) Physiol. Plant. 62, 181-186.
3 Somersalo, S. and Krause, G.H. (1989) Planta 177, 409-416.
4 Servaites, J.C. and Ogren, W.L. (1977) Plant Physiol. 59, 587-590.
5 Singh, J. (1981) Plant Physiol. 67, 906-909.
6 Huner, N.P.A. (1985) Amer. J. Bot. 72, 1290-1306.
7 Greer, D.H. (1988) Aust. J. Plant Physiol. 15, 195-205.
8 Greer, D.H., Berry, J.A. and Björkman, O. (1986) Planta 168, 253-260.
9 Lidholm, J., Gustafsson, P. and öquist, G. (1987) Plant Cell Physiol. 28, 1133-1140.
10 Buschmann, C. (1987) Photosynth. Res. 14, 229-240.
11 Havaux, M. (1989) Plant Physiol. 89, 286-292.

PHOTOINHIBITION AND RECOVERY OF PHOTOSYNTHESIS IN ANTARCTIC BRYOPHYTES UNDER FIELD CONDITIONS.

Adele Post[1], Erica Adamson [2] and Heather Adamson[1],
1.Biological Sciences, Macquarie University, NSW 2109, Australia
2.Antarctic Division, Kingston, Tasmania 7050, Australia

INTRODUCTION.

Antarctic bryophytes survive frozen over winter and grow fully exposed to sunlight in summer. Preliminary observations of quantum yields, light saturated photosynthetic rates and variable fluorescence of bryophytes suggested that photoinhibition was a major factor limiting productivity of Antarctic ecosystems (1). Although the combination of low temperature and bright light are potentially damaging to the photosynthetic apparatus of plants and detrimental effects have been observed for bryophytes (2,3,4) the phenomenon of photoinhibition has not been systematically investigated in polar environments (5). This paper documents daily changes in photosynthetic capacity of an endemic Antarctic bryophyte, Grimmia antarctici Card., growing in the field over late summer. Environmental variables, light and temperature, were continuously monitored, while chlorophyll fluorescence and oxygen evolution rates were determined on samples collected every few hours from the field.

METHODS.

The study was carried out at Casey , 66°17'S 110°32'E, between 2-19 February 1989. Light was monitored using a Li-Cor (LI-1000) datalogger with a quantum radiation sensor. Temperature was measured using a Squirrel meter-logger (-40 to +20°C) with a Grant minithermistor probe inserted just below the surface of the moss. Grimmia turf was sampled using a 2cm diameter cork borer and the cores immediately taken to the laboratory.

Moss cores were allowed to dark adapt in the laboratory at 20°C for 15 (and 70 minutes, results not shown) before fluorescence was measured using a Brancher SF-10 plant productivity fluorometer connected to a fast transient chart recorder. Excitation light intensity used was $15\mu E\ m^{-2}\ s^{-1}$. The ratio of variable fluorescence (F_v) to peak fluorescence (F_p) was calculated from six transients at each harvest time.

Rates of oxygen evolution were measured over a range of light intensity, progressing from darkness to $1500\mu Em^{-2}s^{-1}$, using a Rank aqueous oxygen electrode. The photosynthetic leaves at the tips of the moss were prepared by slicing the top 3mm from the core. A known weight of tissue was placed in the electrode chamber with 20mM HEPES pH 7.6 and 20mM carbonate, equilibrated at 20°C.

M. Baltscheffsky (ed.), Current Research in Photosynthesis, Vol. IV, 635–638.
© 1990 Kluwer Academic Publishers. Printed in the Netherlands.

RESULTS.

The midday depression of photosynthetic activity is shown in Fig 1 (and is confirmed by measurements over 17 days, not shown). The fluorescence ratios are low (maximum 0.250) compared to those found for higher plants (6,7,8,9). On sunny days the fluorescence ratios are particularly low with only a slight midday depression. After a series of overcast days the fluorescence ratio increases and the midday depression becomes more marked. Light saturated oxygen evolution rates show a similar trend.

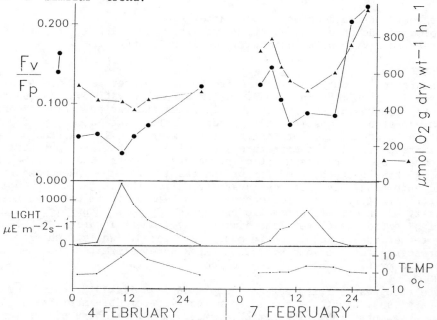

Fig 1: The photosynthetic capacity (fluorescence ratio and light saturated photosynthetic rates at 20°C) of _Grimmia_ at different times on typical bright and cloudy days.

Fig 2:
Relationship between the fluorescence ratio and light saturated photosynthetic rates, derived from data obtained from 2-19 February. Fluorescence ratios were grouped: 0-0.69 (n = 22), 0.07-0.139 (n = 22) and >0.14 (n = 9), and the mean and std error plotted.

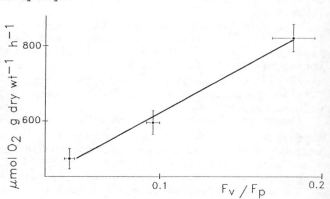

Fig 2 shows that the decrease in the fluorescence ratio reflects decreased photosynthetic rates. This is consistent with photoinhibitory damage to the photosynthetic pathway.

Fig 3: The effect on the fluoresence ratio of light or darkness at low temperature (mean and std error, n=3).

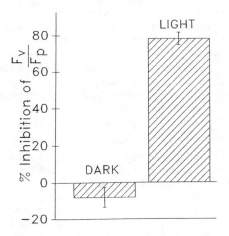

Fig 4: The relationship between light intensity and photoinhibition (expressed as % reduction in the fluorescence ratio) for field samples collected from 2-19 February. The % reduction in the fluorescence ratio was calculated as the difference between the mean ratio obtained in darkness overnight and the fluorescence ratio obtained in the light. Fluorescence ratios were then grouped according to light intensity ($\mu Em^{-2}s^{-1}$): 1-99 (n = 6), 100-199 (n = 7), 200-499 (n = 10), 500-899 (n = 9), >900 (n = 10) and the mean and std errors plotted.

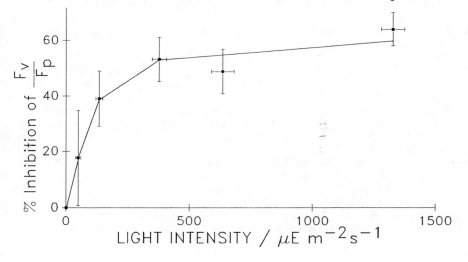

Fig 3 confirms that it is light at low temperature rather than low temperature alone, which is responsible for the reduction in variable fluorescence. A control sample of <u>Grimmia</u> maintained in the laboratory, 20° and $50\mu m^{-2}s^{-1}$, showed reproducibly high fluorescence ratios after 15 minutes dark adaption. This sample was exposed to ambient temperature ($1-2^{\circ}C$) in the dark followed by exposure to sunlight. Fluorescence was measured immediately after the dark exposure and following 15 minutes dark adaption after the light exposure. Exposure to light levels $>200\mu Em^{-2}s^{-1}$ resulted in 78% decrease in the fluorescence ratio.

Photoinhibition was observed at extremely low light levels (Fig 4). <u>Grimmia</u> in the field experienced maximum inhibition at light levels above $500\mu Em^{-2}s^{-1}$, while half the maximum inhibition of the fluorescence ratio is observed at a light level of only $100\mu E\ m^{-2}\ s^{-1}$. We estimate (from Fig 3) that above $500\mu Em^{-2}s^{-1}$ (i.e. maximum inhibition of photosynthesis by light) photosynthetic capacity (light saturated oxygen evolution at $20^{\circ}C$) is reduced by about 40%.

DISCUSSION.

This study shows that photoinhibition is experienced daily by an Antarctic bryophyte growing in the field over summer. Inhibition was observed even at low light levels and must significantly reduce the potential growth of the moss. After bright days recovery overnight was reduced compared to cloudy days, suggesting that the damage caused by light is greater and leads to an accumulated drop in the photosynthetic rate of the moss. A few cloudy days, still bright enough to cause photoinhibition with daily sunlight maxima $<750\mu E\ m^{-2}\ s^{-1}$, result in raised levels of photosynthesis indicating increased recovery and suggests that acclimation to lower light over a period of days is occurring (6).

REFERENCES.
1 Adamson, H., Wilson, M., Selkirk, P., Seppelt, R. (1989) Polarforschung (in press)
2 Rastorfer, J.R. and Higinbotham, N. (1968) Amer. J. Bot. 55, 1225-1229
3 Rastorfer, J.R. (1970) The Bryologist 73, 544-556
4 Kallio, P. and Valanne, N. (1975) in Fennoscandian Tundra Ecosystems. Part 1., (Wielgolaski, F.E., ed.), pp.149-162, New York, Springer-Verlag
5 Longton, R.E. (1988) in Biology of Polar Bryophytes and Lichens, (Longton R.E.), pp.141-210, Cambridge University Press
6 Leverenz, J.W. and Oquist, G. (1987) Plant, Cell and Environment 10, 287-295
7 Ogren, E. (1988) Planta 175, 229-236
8 Demmig-Adams, B., Adams, W.W.III, Winter, K., Meyer, A., Schreiber, U., Pereira, J.S., Kruger, A., Czygan, F-C. and Lange, O.L. (1989) Planta 177, 377-387
9 Somersalo, S. and Krause, G.H. (1989) Planta 177, 409-416
10 Krause, G.H. (1988) Physiol. Plant. 74, 566-574

PHOTOSYNTHESIS IN <u>GRIMMIA ANTARCTICI</u>, AN ENDEMIC ANTARCTIC
BRYOPHYTE, IS LIMITED BY CARBON DIOXIDE.

Erica Adamson, Adele Post and Heather Adamson,
Antarctic Division, Kingston 7050 and Biological Sciences,
Macquarie University, 2109, Australia.

INTRODUCTION

Terrestrial vegetation on the Bailey and Clark Peninsulas, East
Antarctica ($66^\circ 17'S$, $100^\circ 32'E$), consists entirely of algae, lichens
and bryophytes. Ground cover is sparse and low productivity so
easily attributed to the combined effects of water and nutrient
stress, short growing season and low summer temperatures that other
environmental factors capable of limiting growth in Antarctic
ecosystems are often overlooked (1,2). Elsewhere in these
proceedings we have described damaging effects of light leading to
chronic photoinhibition. This paper describes the effect of carbon
dioxide concentration on photosynthesis in an abundant Antarctic
moss (<u>Grimmia antarctici</u>) and, for comparison, a shade adapted C3
monocot, widely distributed in temperate latitudes (<u>Tradescantia</u>
<u>albiflora</u>). Results from three measuring systems are presented:
aqueous (Rank) and gas phase (Hansatech) oxygen electrodes and
infrared gas analysis (IRGA).

PROCEDURE

During the summer of 1988/89 cushions of <u>Grimmia</u> <u>antarctici</u> Card.
were collected from a moist site and rates of gas exchange
determined on green shoot tips approximately 3mm in length. The cut
tips were moistened, blotted in a consistent manner, subsampled and
fresh and dry weights determined ,before and after each
photosynthesis measurement, respectively. Hydration was relatively
constant around 300% (25% dry weight). Tissue was prepared in the
same way for all measurements. Photosynthetic rates were determined
as net CO_2 uptake from air in an ADC Series 2, closed recirculating
IRGA system, with gas flow through a small airtight Erlenmyer flask,
past shoot tips which were constantly agitated to ensure gas mixing,
or, as net O_2 production in Rank and Hansatech oxygen electrodes (3).
Known weights of tissue were placed in 4ml 20 mM Hepes buffer (pH
7.6) containing 20mM potassium bicarbonate in the Rank electrode or
in the Hansatech chamber over carbonate/bicarbonate buffer mixtures
(4) providing a range of sustainable CO_2 concentrations. Gas
exchange measurements were carried out at $20^\circ C$. Light was provided
by a slide projector (Rank) or Bjorkman lamp Light intensity was
controlled by neutral density filters and was measured using a Li-
Cor (LI-1000) datalogger with a quantum radiation sensor.

M. Baltscheffsky (ed.), Current Research in Photosynthesis, Vol. IV, 639–642.
© 1990 Kluwer Academic Publishers. Printed in the Netherlands.

Photosynthetic rates determined on replicate samples from the same moss cushion were generally highly reproducible (standard error of mean <10%). Comparative measurements on Tradescantia were made under identical conditions.

RESULTS AND DISCUSSION

Photosynthetic rates of Grimmia and Tradescantia at atmospheric CO_2 levels and a range of light intensities are shown in Fig.1. They are consistent with other evidence that photosynthetic rates of mosses measured using an IRGA system are substantially lower than those of higher plants (1). The light saturated rate of 22-29 umol O_2/ g dry weight/ h for Grimmia is in the range found for bryophytes (1,2). The light saturated rate for Tradescantia of 132 umol CO_2/ g dry weight/ h is low for an angiosperm but is in the range expected for shade plants (5).

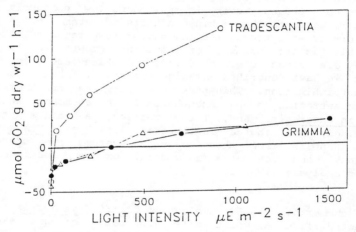

Fig. 1. Net photosynthesis as a function of light intensity for Grimmia and Tradescantia determined by IRGA.

When photosynthetic rates of Grimmia and Tradescantia are compared using a Rank oxygen electrode, the light saturated rates are much higher than in the IRGA (15-30 and 3-6 times respectively) and there is no difference between the two species (Tab. 1). This indicates that low photosynthetic rates of Grimmia in field situations (ambient CO_2 / approx. 340 ppm)) are not due to an inherently low photosynthetic capacity, as has been suggested for other bryophytes (6). As shown in Fig. 2, they are due to limited availability of CO_2.

Fig. 3 compares light saturated photosynthesis of Grimmia and Tradescantia at different CO_2 concentrations in a Hansatech chamber. Both plants responded to increasing CO_2 levels above atmospheric concentration, but the effect was significantly more pronounced in

Grimmia. The maximum rate of photosynthesis achieved by Grimmia at CO_2 saturation was nearly 3 times the rate at ambient concentration: the CO_2 saturated rate for Tradescantia was only 10% higher than the ambient rate.

Tab. 1. Typical light saturated photosynthetic rates of Grimmia, Tradescantia determined at high CO_2 using a Rank oxygen electrode (umol O_2 g DW $^{-1}h^{-1}$)

Grimmia	Tradescantia
450-1000	400-800

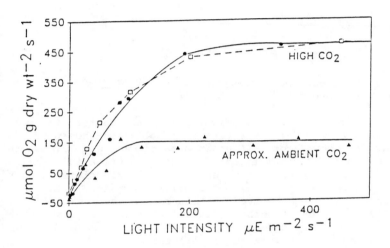

Fig. 2. Net photosynthesis as a function of light intensity for Grimmia at approx. atmospheric and high CO_2. (Hansatech, closed symbols; Rank, open symbols).

Tab.2 compares the photosynthetic performance of Grimmia and Tradescantia at atmospheric and substantially elevated CO_2 levels. The ratios of light saturated Grimmia / Tradescantia rates indicate that the difference is least when CO_2 is present in excess.

Tab. 2. Comparative photosynthetic performance of Grimmia and Tradescantia at elevated and near atmospheric CO_2 concentrations (Figs. 1 and 3).

	Atmospheric CO_2		Elevated CO_2
	Hansatech	IRGA	Hansatech
Light saturated photosynthetic rate Grimmia/Tradescantia	0.12	0.16	0.38

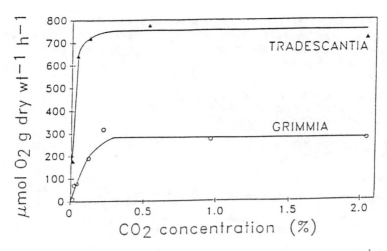

Fig. 3. Net light saturated photosynthesis of <u>Grimmia</u> and <u>Tradescantia</u> at different CO_2 concentrations.

CO_2 is not generally seen as a primary limiting factor in most terrestrial ecosystems (7). The present results and those of (8) suggest that bryophyte communities in Antarctica and elsewhere might be exceptions. Maximum rates of oxygen evolution in <u>Grimmia</u> were achieved at CO_2 concentrations approximately ten times higher than present atmospheric levels. Similar increases in net photosynthesis have been observed in temperate mosses exposed to excess CO_2 (9). Taken together, these findings suggest that availability of CO_2 at the chloroplast may be a major factor affecting bryophyte productivity at all latitudes.

REFERENCES

1 Kallio,P.and Karenlampi,L.(1975) In: Photosynthesis and Productivity in Different Environments (Cooper,J.P. ed) Cambridge Univ Press. Cambridge. U.K.
2 Longton, R.E.(1989) The Biology of Polar Bryophytes and Lichens. Cambridge Univ. Press. Cambridge, U.K.
3 Allen,J. and Holmes,N. (1986) In Photosynthesis Energy Transduction (Hipkins,M. Baker,N. eds), pp 103-141 IRL Cambridge
4 Umbreit,W.,Burris, R.and Stauffer,J. (1945) Manometric Techniques, Burgess, Minneapolis
5 Bjorkman,O., and Holmgren,P. (1963) Physiol Plant 16, 889-914
6 Valanne,N. (1984) In The Experimental Biology of Bryophytes (Dyer,F. and Ducket, J. eds) pp 257-273, Academic Press, London
7 Shugart.H.and Emanuel,W. (1985) Plant, Cell, Envir. 8, 381-386
8 Silvola, J. (1985) Lindbergia 11, 86-93
9 Aro,E., Gerbaud, A. and Andre, M. (1984) Plant Physiol. 76, 431-435

PHOTOSYNTHETIC CHARACTERIZATION OF SPINACH DEVELOPED AT COLD HARDENING AND
NON HARDENING TEMPERATURES

BOESE, S.R. AND N.P.A. HUNER, Dept. of Plant Sci., University of Western
Ontario, LONDON, ONTARIO, CANADA N6A 5B7.

1. INTRODUCTION

Various aspects of spinach have been studied both from the prospective
of cold acclimation and cold hardening (1). Hardening protocols are
often short (10 to 14 days) thus they can not involve long
developmental processes.

We were interested in determining if leaf expansion and development at
different temperatures would alter the structure and the function of
the photosynthetic apparatus. Further, we were interested in
determining if the temperature of leaf development would limit; the
ability of the leaf to respond to photosynthesis under a new
temperature condition as is the case for rye (2).

2. PROCEDURE
2.1. Materials and methods
   2.1.1. Growth Conditions: Spinach (Spinacia oleracea L.) plants were
      grown at 5 or 16C under 250 uE PAR with a 16 hour photo-period.
      Only fully expanded leaves from the second leaf pairs were
      utilizeed. Plants grown at 16C reached this stage 32 to 36 days
      after planting while 5C plants required 88 to 96 days to reach
      the same stage. For some experiments, the plants grown to this
      stage were then subjected to a temperature shift. Again, only
      the second leaf pairs were utilized.
   2.1.2. Measurements: Leaf area was determined using a Li-Cor portable
      area meter (LI-3000). Dry weights were determined following 48
      hours of drying at 80C. Leaf thickness were measured at 100X
      under a light microscope. Chlorophyll concentrations were
      determined from acetone extracts according to Arnon (3).
      Carotenoids were separated using TLC plates as previously
      described (4). Concentrations were determined spectrophoto-
      metrically according to Davies (5). Electorphoretic separation
      of chlorophyll-protein complexes and thylakoid polypeptide was
      accomplished as described by Huner (6). Whole leaf CO_2 uptake
      was determined using a Li-Cor 6200 portable photosynthesis
      system. Thylakoid preparations and PS1 (ASC/DCPIP to MV)
      reaction buffers were as described by Huner (7) with final
      chlorophyll concentrations of 10 ug per ml. Samples were
      prepared for 77K fluorescence by diluting thylakoid preparations
      to 3.5 ug/ml with a 1:1 mixture of tricine buffer and glycerol.
      Samples were then frozen overnight at -70C.

M. Baltscheffsky (ed.), Current Research in Photosynthesis, Vol. IV, 643–646.

3. RESULTS AND DISCUSSION

3.1. LEAF MORPHOLOGY

The second leaf pair was selected for study. Comparative growth kinetics were used to determine the relative physiological age of 5 and 16C expanded leaves. Leaves expanded at 5C had greater fresh weight, dry weight, and leaf area than leaves expanded at 16C. Leaves expanded at 5C had dry weight/area ratios of 10 mg/cm^2 while 16C leaves had a ratio of 4.4 mg/cm^2. Concomitantly, 5C expanded leaves had a greater leaf thickness (670 $\pm$ 105 um) than 16C leaves (446 $\pm$ 68 um). This appeared to be due to an increase in the number of palisade layers associated with growth at 5C. Temperature of leaf expansion did not alter the chl a/b ratio (2.81 for 16C; 2.88 for 5C) or the chlorophyll/carotenoid ratios. Total chlorophyll or carotenoid contents of the 5C leaves was 60% lower than 16C leaves when based on dry weight. However, pigment contents were similar when calculated on an area basis. Chlorophyll contents of 64 ug/cm^2 and carotenoid contents 9.5 ug/cm^2 were measured for both 5 and 16C expanded leaves. Further, chlorophyll-protein complexes and thylakoid polypeptides resolved by gel electrophoresis indicated no compositional differences between the 5 and 16C leaves.

3.2. CO$_2$ FIXATION

Neither temperature of leaf expansion or the measurement temperatures (5 and 16C) affected the apparent quantum efficiency or light saturated rates of whole leaf CO$_2$ uptake measured as umol CO$_2$ m^{-2}s^{-1} (Table 1). Apparent quantum efficiencies ranged from 0.037 to 0.043 $\pm$ 0.004 umol CO$_2$/uE m^{-2}s^{-1} PPFD and light saturated rates of about 23 umol CO$_2$ m^{-2}s^{-1}. In other experiments, leaves fully expanded at 5C were shifted to 16C or visa versa and held for 12 days at the new temperature before quantum efficiency and light saturated rates of CO$_2$ uptake were measured. Controls were leaves expanded at 5 or 16C and held there for an additional 12 days. Leaves shifted to 5C and controls maintained at 5C showed no loss of quantum efficiency or light saturated rates relative to non shifted leaves regardless if measured at 5C or 16C. Contrary, leaves shifted to 16C or controls maintained there showed a loss of quantum efficiency to 0.027 $\pm$ 0.004 umol CO$_2$/uE m^{-2}s^{-1} PPFD at both measurement temperatures with no associated loss in light saturated rate of CO$_2$ uptake. This loss of quantum efficiency is likely due to the faster aging at 16C and not a result of the temperature shift as it also occurred in control leaves not subjected to a temperature shift. Temperature optima for CO$_2$ uptake yielded very broad profiles between 3 and 20C with no significant differences between 5 and 16C leaves.

TABLE 1. Quantum efficiencies and light saturated rates of CO_2 uptake by 5 or 16C expanded leaves measured at 5 and 16C.

Sample	n	r^2	slope	$\pm$	sat. rate
16C at 16C	5	.988	.037	.002	22.7
5C at 16C	5	.977	.04	.004	24.5
16C at 5C	5	.995	.044	.002	19.9
5C at 5C	5	.993	.042	.002	22.7

3.3 ELECTRON TRANSPORT

Light saturated rates of PS I were consistently higher for preparations from 5C expanded leaves. Average rates of 264 and 152 umol O_2 consumed mg $Chl^{-1}h^{-1}$ were measured for 5 and 16C expanded leaves respectively. We were interested to see if this difference in rate was a reflection of energy distribution between the photosystems and thus would be reflected in the 77K fluorescence eemission spectra. Emissions were scanned between 650 and 800 nm. Preliminary results indicate a greater 695:730 ratio for preparations from 5C expanded leaves as compared to 16C preparations. No differences in the wavelengths of maximum emmissions were observed for control 5 and 16C preparations (fig. 1). Preparations from leaves exposed to a temperature shift showed both a reduction in the 695:730 ratio and a 3 nm shift to the red in the wavelengths of maximum emissions.

4. CONCLUSIONS:

1. It is evident that low temperature during leaf expansion results in a modification of the leaf morphology and components of the photosynthetic apparatus. Changes in morphology include increased dry weight, dry weight/area, leaf thickness and number of palisade layers. Leaf expansion at 5C resulted in increased PSI activity and greater 695:730 ratios for 77K fluorescent emissions spectra.
2. Pigment contents/area, chlorophyll-protein complex profiles, thylakoid polypeptide profiles and CO_2 uptake are not affected by the temperature of leaf expansion.
3. Tissues grown at one temperature and subsequently exposed to a new temperature regime were not adversely affected photosynthetically.

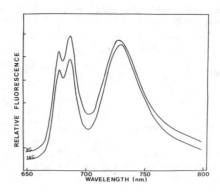

FIGURE 1.   Steady-state 77K fluorescence emission spectra of thylakoid
preparations from 5 or 16C expanded leaves. Final chlorophyll
concentration was 3.5 ug/ml.

REFERENCES

1 Krause, G.H., Klosson, R.J., and Troster, U. (1982) in Plant Cold
Hardiness and Freezing Stress Mechanisms and Crop Implications (Li, P.H.,
and Sakai, A. ed), Vol. 2, pp. 55–75, Academic Press, New York
2 Krol, M., Griffith, M., and N.P.A. Huner (1984) Can. J. Bot. 62, 1062–1068
3 Arnon, D.I. (1949) Plant Physiol. 24, 1–15
4 Hager, A., and Berthenrath, T. (1962) Planta 58, 564–5684
5 Davies, B.H. (1965) in Chemistry and Biochemistry of Plants (Goodwin,
T.W., ed.), Vol. 1, pp. 489–532, Academic Press
6 Huner, N.P.A., Krol, M., Williams, J.P., Maissan, E., Low, P.S., Roberts,
D., Thompson, J.E. (1986) Plant Physiol. 84, 12–18
7 Huner, N.P.A. (1985) Can. J. Bot. 63, 506–511

FROST RESISTANCE OF WHEAT AND CHL a IN VIVO FLUORESCENCE INDUCTION KINETICS

Lin Shiqing, Yang Dianan, Zhang Jide, Li Tongzhu, Tang Chongqing, Lou Shiqing and Kuang Tingyun.

Photosyn Lab, Institute of Botany, Academia Sinica, 100044 Beijing, China

1. INTRODUCTION

In recent years more and more studies have shown that physiological status of a living plant under different environmental conditions can be revealed by signals of chlorophyll a in vivo fluorescence induction kinetics, such as low temperature, heat, water stress and polution etc (1) (2). A screening method for chilling torlerance has been established (3) . But the application is restricted in plants with chilling susceptibility or with morderately chlilling torlerance (above 0'C). This paper is designed to study detailed changes of fluorescence induction kinetics of winter wheat with different frost torlerant cultivars over wintering period and try to confirm a procedure and conditions which can be used for comparison of relative frost resistance of cultivars (below 0'C).

2. METERIAL AND METHOD

6 winter wheat cultivars with already known frost resistance were selected for comparison of their fluorescence induction kinetics over wintering period. They were Yanda 1817, Nongda 183, Nongda 139, Taishan No 1, Fengchan No 3 and No 7023 designated as W-1...W-6, resp. and arranged in the order of decreasing frost resistance. They were sown in the field in the late of Sep. One day before each experiment some of the whole plants were kept in darkness at 0-5'C for 15-20 hr. Then 3 developing young leaf sections were cut off at the same position from the centre of 3 individual plants and placed on a plastic plate as a measuring sample. The excitation light was emitted from a projective halogen lamp through a SFR 11 filter. The intensity at the sample was $1.4*10^4$ erg cm^{-2} sec^{-1}. Fluorescent signal was received by a PMT (EMI 9558) protected with a short-cut red filter. The photometer was controlled by a computer (NEC PC-8001 MKII) through triggering an

Abbr : Fo, Fm, Fs and Fv: constant, maximum, quasi-stationary and variable fluorescence. ^Fv: quenching of Fv (e.g. Fm-Fs). T: time for quenching from Fm to Fs. ^Fv/T: quenching rate of Fv. T1/2: half time for fluorescence rise. CA: complementary area of rise.

M. Baltscheffsky (ed.), Current Research in Photosynthesis, Vol. IV, 647–650.
© 1990 Kluwer Academic Publishers. Printed in the Netherlands.

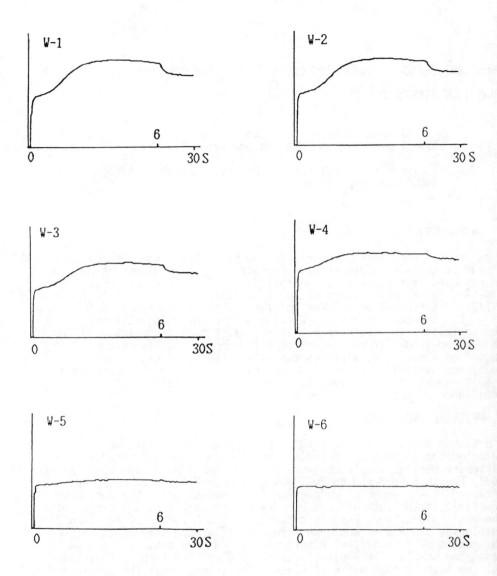

Fig 2. Comparison of Chlorophyll fluorescence induction kinetics parameters-(A) CA/Fo, (B) Fm/Fo, (C) Fs/Fo, (D) ^Fv/Fo, (E) ^Fv/^T and (F) t1/2 among wheat cultivars (W-1...W-6). These data were calculated from Fig 1.

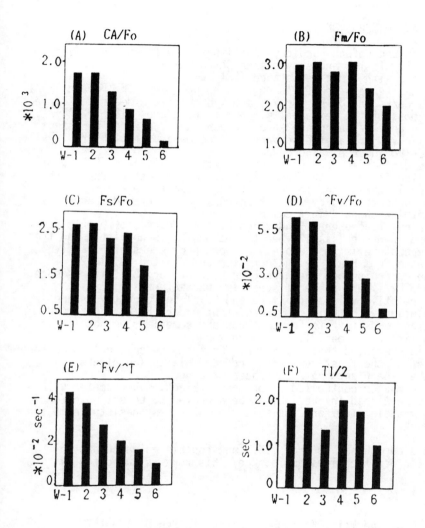

Fig 1. Comparison of Chlorophyll fluorescence induction kinetics
curves of 6 wheat Cultivars (W-1...W-6) in the order of decreasing
frost resistance. Each curve was plotted after accumulation and
average from 10 measurements. 3 leaf sections for one measurement.

electronic shutter (Uniblitz SD-1000) (opening time < 1.3 ms) and through operating an A/D/A converter (AMDEK ADA-200).
All fluorescence data were normalized by Fo. The experiments were repeated for 3 years.

3. RESULTS AND DISCUSSION

3.1. In autumn before hardiness cultivars with frost sensitivity (W-5, W-6) grow faster and show higher CA/Fo, Fm/Fo, ^Fv/Fo and ^Fv/T than cultivars with frost resistance (W-1, W-2).
3.2. As the temperature falls down in autumn first ^Fv/Fo and ^Fv/T than Fm/Fo, Fs/Fo and CA/Fo for W-5 and W-6 cultivars decrease. By the middle ten days of the next Jan (minimum tempereture: -18— -22'C) their ^Fv/Fo and ^F/T approach zero. In contract for frost resistant cultivars (W-1, W-2), as the tempereture decreases their ^Fv/Fo, ^Fv/T, Fm/Fo and CA/Fo inversely increase.
3.3. The death time for the frost susceptive cultivars (W-5, W-6) in North China is not in the severely cold Jan, but after the tenth of Feb as Fv is diminished to zero. At that moment the weather in Beijing is characterized by draught, strong sun light and frequently freezing-thawing changes in a day-night cycle.
3.4. Typical fluorescence induction kinetics curves of 6 cultivars are recorded in March (Fig 1) when the hardening is completed and the average temperature is just above 0'C. Some parameters of 6 cultivars are calculated from Fig 1 by the computer and plotted in Fig 2.
3.5. The quenching and the quenching rate of variable flworescence (^Fv/Fo and ^Fv/T) are the most sensitive parameters in Fig 2. The relative values of ^Fv/Fo and ^Fv/T for 6 cultivars are in good correlation with their frost resistant order. Fm/Fo, Fs/Fo and CA/Fo are less sensitive to frost stress and sometimes do not always correlated with the order. T1/2 is even worse.
3.6. It is suggested that ^Fv/Fo and ^Fv/T be the critical parameters for the test of the frost resistant order of plants (cultivars) provided that the plants have just heen hardened.
3.7. The computer-controlled fluorescence kinetics photometer with its program developed in our lab has been proved to be suitable for both photosynthsis study and the selcetion of stress-resistance in the breeding work.

We express our thanks to Prof P.S. Tang for his guidance and to Mrs Xu Li for her technical assistance. This work is supported by NNSFC.

REFERENCES

1. Krause, G.H. and Weis, E. (1984) Photosynth Res 5: 139-157
2. Renger, G. and Schreiber, U. (1986) in Light emission by plants and bacteria (Govindjee et al.eds.), pp.587-619, Academic Press, New York.
3. Smillie, R.M. and Hetherington, S.E. (1984) in Advances in photosynth Res (Sybesma, C. ed.) Vol. IV. pp.471-474, Martinus Nijhoff / Dr. W. Junk Publishers.

CHANGES OF PHOTOSYNTHETIC MEMBRANE AND CELL RESISTANCE OF
A LEAF OF WHEAT SEEDLINGS DURING TEMPERATURE ACCLIMATION

FILIMONOV A.A., VIROLAINEN V.A., SHERUDILO E.G.,
TITOV A.F.

I.   INTRODUCTION
     Temperature acclimation of plants is known to be con-
nected with the increased resistance of numerous cellular
structures and functions (1,2). But if some authors think
that adaptation is based on temperature induced conformational rearrangements of macromolecules (1), the others see
its reason in a quantitative and qualitative changes observed in the protein complex of a cell (3). We believed
(4), that both above mechanisms function in plants mutually supplemeting each other. It is assumed that a real contribution of each of them is dependent on the intensity
and duration of temperature effects, biological characteristics of the object and on occumpanying conditions (illumination, humidity, etc).
     The aim of the present report was to study some cha-
racteristics of adaptive reactions of winter wheat at the
level of an intact cell and membrane structure of the photosynthesis apparatus.
2.1. MATERIAL AND METHODS
     Seven-day old wheat seedlings (v. Mironovskaya 808)
grown in factorostatic conditions (25°C) were used in the
experiments. They were subjected to heat hardening for 1
day at 40°C and to cold hardening for 7 days at 2°C. One
day before hardening some plants were placed on the solutions of actinomicin D (ACT, 5 mg/l), cycloheximide (CH,
10 mg/l), choramphenicol (CP, 200 mg/l) or 1-(chlormetyl)
silatran (mival, M, 0,15%) or the mixture of the latter
with CP or CH.
     Leaf cuttings were tested for heat resistance by 5
min heating in an aquatic ultra-thermostat (5), for cold
resistance they were frozen for 5 min in a micro-refrigera-
tor (6). Temperature inducing cytoplasmic coagulation in
50% of the palisade cells (LT_{50}) was taken as the value of
thermoresistence. The value of thermostability of PSA membranes was the temperature ($T_{0.5}$) corresponding to the 50%

M. Baltscheffsky (ed.), Current Research in Photosynthesis, Vol. IV, 651–654.
© 1990 *Kluwer Academic Publishers. Printed in the Netherlands.*

(in comparison with the maximum level) decrease of the intensity of delayed fluorescence of leaf chlorophyll heated at a rate of 1-2°/min.

3.   RESULTS AND DISCUSION
The experiments have shiwn a pronounced increase of $T_{0.5}$ and LT_{50} levels in wheat exposed to 40°C. It is essential that the increase of PSA thermostability was greater than the rise of cell heat resistance (Fig.1).

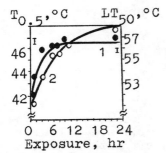

Fig.1. Dynamics of heat resistance of PSA membranes (1) and leaf cells (2) at 40°C. Here and hereafter in Figures 2-5: $T_{0.5}$ - thermostability of PSA membranes; LT_{50} - heat(cold) resistance of cells

It is noteworthy that a change of heat resistance was also observed in hypothermal conditions. Thus at 20°C an increase was observed both of cold- and heat resistance of the above also of thermostability of PSA membranes. But the dynamics of the above values has its own characteristics: if the cold resistance of cells increased monotonically during the whole experiment, the other two reached their maximum on the 2-3d day and then decreased.

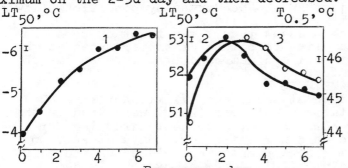

Figure 2. Dynamics of cold (1) and heat (2) resistance of leaf cells and thermostability of PSA membranes (3) of wheat at 2°C

In order to answer the question on the identity of the mechanisms causing an increase of heat resistance of PSA components at low and high hardening temperatures we used a method consisting of alternating the regimes of heat and cold hardening: 2°C x 2 days ⇌ 40°C x 1 day. It turned out that a consrcutive exposure of plants to low and to high temperatures did not result in any additional increase of PSA membrane thermostability. A change of heat to cold (40° → 2°) did not cause an additional increase of $T_{0.5}$ or its fall either. But longer exposure to 2°C resulted in a decrease of $T_{0.5}$ in plants preadapted to heat though it was not so rapid as a change of the LT_{50} level (Fig.3).

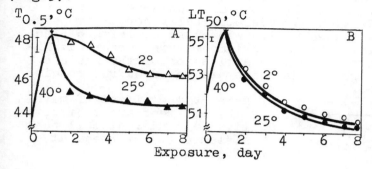

Figure 3. Dynamics of thermostability of PSA membranes (A) and leaf cell heat resistance (B) of wheat with a change of temperature regimes (the moment of change of temperature is indicated with an arrow)

In our opinion the characteristics of the dynamics of $T_{0.5}$ and LT_{50} values found in these experiments allow to speak of the functional autonomy of the mechanisms determining the level of PSA membrane thermostability and cell heat resistance.

The additional evidence to support this conclusion comes from the experiments with inhibitors of RNA and protein synthesis. All the inhibitors used blocked effectively the increase of the cell resistance at plant hardening, while the $T_{0.5}$ values in the control seedlings (hardening without inhibitors) and experimental variants were practically the same (Fig.4).

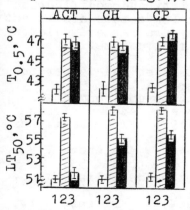

Figure 4. The effect of inhibitors of protein biosynthesis on PSA membrane thermostability (A) and leaf cell heat resistance (B) of wheat at 40°C
1 - control (the initial level);
2 - hardening without inhibitors;
3 - hardening with inhibitors

It is noteworthy that specific weight of different mechanisms involved in the development of the increased resistance is strongly dependent on the character of external effects. Thus if at heat hardening, to all appearance, the process of protein synthesis (mainly on 80S ribosomes) are of prime importance, then when affected by mival a large increase of $T_{0.5}$ and LT_{50} was also observed in the presence of CH or CP even at physiologically normal temperature (Fig.5). At the same time was no summarising of the effects of mival and hardening temperatures observed. Mival seemed to favour complete activation of the whole complex of adaptive reactions which did not require protein synthesis de novo.

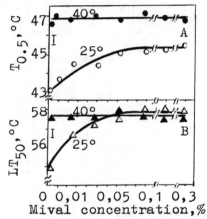

Figure 5. The effect of mival on the PSA membrane thermostability (A) and leaf cell heat resistance (B) of wheat at 25°C and 40°C

The results obtained and their comparison with literature data allows to say that the development of plant thermoresistance is a complicated cooperative process uniting the whole complex of reactions. If the growth of cell heat resistance is mostly resulted from protein synthesis de novo, the increase of thermostability and modification of functional properties of the main PSA components is not connected with this process, but they are rather mediated by the effect of temperature on their structure.

4.   References

1 Alexandrov V.Ya. (1977) Cells, molecules and temperature, 330p., Berlin etc: Springer-Verl.
2 Levitt J. (1980) Responces of plant to environmental stresses, Vol. 1, 497 p., New York etc, Academ. Press
3 Guy C.L., Niemie K.J., Brambt R. (1985) Proc. Natl. Sci. USA, Vol. 82, pp.3673-3677
4 Titov A.F., Drozdov S.N., Kritenko S.P., Talanova V.V. (1983) Soviet Plant Physiol., Vol. 30, pp.544-551
5 Alexandrov V.Ya. (1963) Botanica Experimentalis (U.S.S. R.), Vol. 4, pp.234-274
6 Drozdov S.N., Titov A.F., Talanova V.V., Kritenko S.P., Sherudilo E.G., Akimova T.V. (1984) Exp. Bot., Vol. 35, pp.1595-1602

EFFECT OF HEAT STRESS ON INTACT WHEAT LEAVES AND ITS RECOVERY STUDIED BY FLUORESCENCE INDUCTION KINETICS

Ranjit Kishore Mishra and Gauri S. Singhal
School of Life Sciences, Jawaharlal Nehru University,
New Delhi-110067 INDIA.

1.   INTRODUCTION
     Photosystem II is known to be one of the most susceptible complexes of the higher plant chloroplasts. Heat stress is reported in cause a blockage of the PSII reaction centres and a functional separation of the light harvesting Chl a/b complex (LHC) from the rest of the PSII core (1,2,3). The cause for this functional disruption is given as a migration of the PSII core complex together with some tightly bound LHC from the non-appressed to the appressed grana lamellae which is called stateI-stateII transition (4). High temperature dependent separation of PSII from the bulk of LHC is considered to be a mechanism to prevent overexcitation and photodamage to PSII when subjected to high light and high temperature (5).

     In this report we have examined the effect of high temperature on the fluorescence induction kinetics of attached wheat leaves. In addition, we have also studied the extent of recovery of the leaves after heat stress at various temperatures.

2.   PROCEDURE
     Wheet seeds (HD 2329, IARI, New Delhi) were germinated on petri plates and were grown at 25°C in 14-10 h light/dark cycles. 8-Days old wheat seedlings were subjected to heat treatment for 30 minutes at desired temperatures in dark. The fast and slow fluorescence transients of dark adapted attached leaves were recorded on a SF-30 Plant Productivity Fluorometer (Richard Brancker, Ottawa, Canada) with a timebase of 10 sec and 4 minutes respectively. The exciting light centered upon 670 nm was provided by a LED at 75dW per meter square. All the readings were corrected for light scattering by recording the fluorescence transient of a bleached leave which did not contain any chlorophyll. In a separate experiment, fluorescence was plotted versus light intensity which gave a straight line. Fo was determined by this curve by taking the fluorescence level at 2 percent of the measuring light intensity.

     Damage and recovery of the leaves were monitored by the changes in variable fluorescence (Fv) and the ratio of variable to maximum

M. Baltscheffsky (ed.), Current Research in Photosynthesis, Vol. IV, 655–658.
© 1990 *Kluwer Academic Publishers. Printed in the Netherlands.*

fluorescence (Fv/Fm). All the heat treatments and recovery experiments were done in dark to avoid the effects of photoinhibition and leaves were dipped in water for 1 min after heat treatment to avoid any change due to water stress.

3. RESULTS AND DISCUSSION

A decrease in the ratio of Fv/Fm was observed as the temperature was raised from 25 to 44°C. The decrease was, however, slow up to 39°C, beyond which it decreased sharply and the ratio remained only about 15 percent of the control at 43.5°C (Fig.1A). The reduction in Fv/Fm ratio was mainly due to decrease in Fv which resulted from

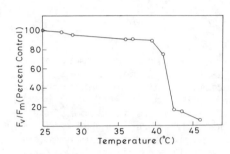 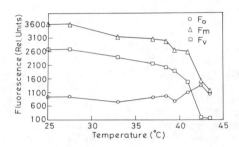

Fig.1 Effect of heat shock on Fv/Fm (A) and Fo, Fm and Fv (B) of dark adapted intact wheat leaves relative to the controls.

a decrease in Fm and an increase in Fo (Fig.1B). Physiologically, the decrease in Fv/Fm ratio and an increase in Fo indicates a decrease in the photochemical efficiency of PS II which could be due to ineffi- ciency of energy transfer from antenna to the reaction centre of PSII, or due to a damage to the functions of the reaction centre itself (6). The decrease in Fm could be due to structural alterations of PSII causing an increase in the radiationless internal conversion of excited states (7). Studies on the rise of fluorescence from

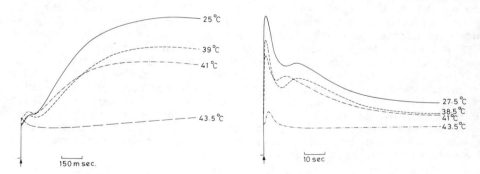

Fig.2 Room temperature fluorescence induction kinetics of heat stressed intact wheat leaves.

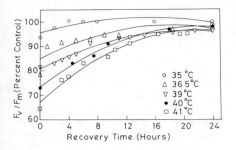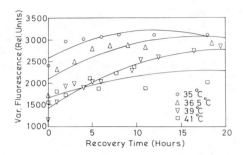

Fig.3 Recovery of Fv/Fm (A) and Fo, Fm and Fv (B) at room temperature in dark after heat treatment of intact wheat leaves at different temperatures.

Fo to P have attributed the I-D transient to oxidation of the primary quinone electron acceptor Q_A by an electron acceptor, probably Q_B located between Q_A and the plastoquinone pool (B). Fig.2A shows a decrease in the rate of rise of fluorescence from Fo to P indicating a decrease in the rate of Q_A reduction. This could be explained by a weaker association of the antenna with the PSII reaction centre. It could also be a result of migration of LHC from the appressed grana region to the non appressed stroma lamellae resulting from stateI-stateII transitions.

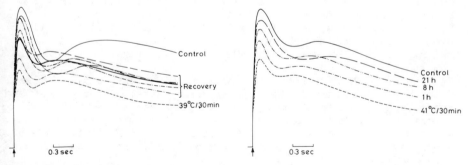

Fig.4 Room temperature fluorescence induction kinetics of dark adapted intact wheat leaves after different times of recovery in dark at room temperature subsequent to heat shock at different temperatures for 30 minutes.

In addition to the reduction in Fm (the P-peak) a gradual disappearance of the M-peak was also observed as the temperature was raised from 25 to 44°C (Fig.2B). The disappearance of M-peak could be correlated with a decreased rate of carbon assimilation on heat treatment.

Recovery of the fast as well as slow fluorescence transients were studied in separate sets of experiments. A restoration of Fv/Fm ratio (Fig.3A), variable fluorescence (Fig.3B) and the M-peak was observed when the plants were kept at 25°C in dark after heat treatment at various temperatures (Fig.4). The recovery was less as the treatment temperature was increased and 5 percent recovery was observed in case of plants which were stressed at 42°C. Although the Fv/Fm ratio recovered almost to 100 percent in case of treatments at lower temperatures, but in no case the value of Fm and Fo recovered back to the control levels. Another important feature of the fluorescence transients was the appearance of both the P and M-peaks at an early time after heat treatment of the plants. A reason for shift in the P-peak could be faster quenching of the fluorescence by Q_B in oxidized state due to dark adaptation of the leaves. However, the dominance of oxidized Q_B over reduced Q_A could also be a reason which may result from weaker association of the LHC with the PSII reaction center thereby decreasing the rate of photoreduction of Q_A.

4. ACKNOWLEDGEMENT

Ranjit K. Mishra gratefully acknowledges the award of SRF from CSIR, India. This work was supported in part by the USDA Project grant No. FG-In-678.

REFERENCES

1. Schreiber, U. and Armond, P.A. (1978) Biochim. Biophys. Acta 502, 138-151.
2. Armond, P.A., Bjorkman, O. and Staehelin, L.A. (1980) Biochim. Biophys. Acta 601, 433-442.
3. Gounaris, K., Brain, A.P., Quinn, P.J. and Williams, W.P. (1984) Biochim. Biophys. Acta 766, 198-208.
4. Sundby, C., Melis, A., Maenpaa, P. and Andersson, B. (1986) Biochim. Biophys. Acta 881, 478-483.
5. Melis, A. and Homann, P.H. (1976) Photochem. Photobiol. 23, 345-350.
6. Briantais, J.-M., Vernott, C., Krause, G.H. and Weis, E. (1986) Chlorophyll a Fluorescence of Higher Plants: Chloroplasts and Leaves. In "Light Emission by Plants and Bacteria" (eds. Govindjee, Amesz, J. and Fork, D.C.) pp. 539-583. Academic Press, Orlando.
7. Klosson, R.J. and Krause, G.H. (1981) Planta 151, 347-352.
8. Jennings, R.C. and Forti, G. (1975) Biochim. Biophys. Acta 396, 63-71.

SYNTHESIS OF SUCROSE AND FRUCTANS IN WHEAT LEAVES: THE EFFECTS OF
TEMPERATURE

C. PAULINO and M. C. ARRABAÇA
Departamento de Biologia Vegetal, Faculdade de Ciências da
Universidade de Lisboa, Portugal

ABSTRACT
    The activities of FBPase, UDPG-pyrophosphorylase, SPS and SS
enzymes involved in sucrose biosynthetic pathway were measured at 10
and 25°C in order to explain the accumulation of F6P and G6P at 10°C,
without concomitant increase in sucrose content, previously found. The
activities of all enzymes were lower at the lower temperature, and
could not explain the variation in sucrose. However, this can be
explained by an increase, of about three times, on the content in
fructans at 10°C.

INTRODUCTION
    In wheat leaves, sucrose is the major storage carbohydrate and its
concentration changes rapidly at the beginning of both the light and
dark periods [1]. Sucrose synthesis occurs in the cytosol of mesophyll
cells [2], from triose-phosphates generated within the chloroplast and
exported by way of the phosphate translocator [3].
    In the sucrose biosynthetic pathway, the first irreversible step is
catalyzed by cytosolic fructose-1,6-bisphosphatase (F1,6BPase: EC
3.1.3.11). The resulting fructose-6-phosphate (F-6-P) originates
sucrose-phosphate, by reacting with uridine-5'-diphosphoglucose (UDPG),
through the enzyme sucrose-phosphate synthase (SPS, EC 2.4.1.14). The
esther bond is hydrolyzed by the enzyme sucrose-phosphate phosphatase
(EC 3.1.3.24), which has little or no regulatory function [4]. UDPG is
synthesized by UDPG pyrophosphorylase (EC 2.7.7.9), with UTP and
glucose-1-phosphate. The latter is formed from F6P, by the sequential
 activities of phosphoglucomutase and phosphoglucoisomerase.
    Sucrose synthase (SS, EC 2.4.1.13) is involved in sucrose synthesis
and breakdown; however, in wheat, a sucrose storer, invertase is the
main hydrolytic enzyme [5].
    Previous work with photosynthesizing wheat leaf segments [6]
indicated that, at low temperatures, there was an accumulation of F6P
and G6P, which was not accompanied by an increase in sucrose, as should
be expected.
    The aim of the present work is to determine, in leaf extracts, how
the activities of the enzymes involved in sucrose synthesis change with
temperature. The content in fructans, which is formed from sucrose [7],

M. Baltscheffsky (ed.), Current Research in Photosynthesis, Vol. IV, 659–662.
© 1990 *Kluwer Academic Publishers. Printed in the Netherlands.*

was also measured in leaf segments, adapted to low (10°C) and to high (25°C) temperatures.

MATERIAL AND METHODS
Plant material:
   Triticum aestivum, var. nazareno-Strampelli, was used. Nine day old seedlings were grown in a growth chamber, with a photoperiod of 16 hours, a day/night temperature of 22/15°C and a light intensity of 90 $\mu E.m^{-2}.s^{-1}$.
   For enzymatic assays, leaves were collected after 2 or 8 hours illumination. The enzymatic activities were measured at 10 and 25°C.
   For the measurement of fructan content, the first leaves were collected at the end of the dark period. One segment (4 cm long) was cut from each leaf and illuminated at 650 $\mu E.m^{-2}.s^{-1}$, for 1.5 hours, after which they were quickly killed in boiling 50% ethanol. Soluble sugars were then extracted, as previously descibed [8].
Enzymatic activities:
   To measure the activities of SPS, SS and UDPG pyrophosphorylase, leaves (about 1 g FW) were ground in a chilled mortar with 5 ml medium, containing 50 mM HEPES-NaOH, pH 7.5, 5 mM $MgCl_2$, 1 mM EDTA, 2% PEG 4000, 5 mM DTT, 1% BSA and sand. The brei was centrifuged at 20 000 x g, for 15 minutes and the supernatant used for the assays, according to [9], at 10 and 25°C. The activity of F1,6BPase was measured as in [10].
Fructan content:
   Fructan in leaves was measured according to [11].

RESULTS AND DICUSSION
   The effect of temperature on the activities of sucrose biosynthetic enzymes was studied after 2 hour (Table 1) or after 8 hour (Table 2) illumination of plants.
   The activities of FBPase and of SPS appear to control sucrose formation, as in spinach leaves [12]. These enzymes, as well as UDPG pyrophosphorylase and SS, have lower activities at 10°C. The activity of FBPase decreases about 6 times whereas the activity of UDPG pyrophosphorylase is about 4 times lower (Table 1). These changes cannot explain the increase in F6P and G6P at low temperatures. Also, the small drecrease in the activities of SPS and SS, observed at 10°C, do not explain the decrease on sucrose, previously reported [6, 8].

TABLE 1: Enzyme activities after 2 hour illumination of plants

	Enzyme Activity ($\mu mole.mg^{-1}$ chlorophyll.h^{-1})	
	10°C	25°C
FBPase	14.1±1.5(5)	85.4±2.8(5)
UDPG pyrophosphorylase	260.4±19.2(5)	965.8±44.6(5)
SPS	13.3±0.3(5)	23.1±1.8(5)
SS	16.1±1.5(6)	18.5±0.8(6)

The results are means ±SD. In parenthesis are the number of replicates.

Comparing Tables 1 and 2, it can be seen that, at either temperature, the activities of SPS and UDPG pyrophosphorylase do not change, during

daytime, as in soybean plants [9], but contrary to what has been found
in maize [13]. Also, the activity of SS did not change during daytime.
Cytosolic FBPase activity, at 25°C, decreases significantly after 8
hour illumination, contrary to what has been reported for soybean [9].

TABLE 2: Enzyme activities after 8 hour illumination of plants

	Enzyme Activity (μmole.mg^{-1} chlorophyll.h^{-1})	
	10°C	25°C
FBPase	11.1±1.3(6)	55.1±3.1(6)
UDPG pyrophosphorylase	268.5±25.4(4)	894.8±31.5(6)
SPS	16.1±2.1(6)	24.3±1.4(7)
SS	18.1±1.7(6)	19.0±1.4(6)

The results are means ±SD. In parenthesis are the number of replicates.

Table 3 shows that the content in fructans increases by about three
times, and can explain the decrease in sucrose [6], at the lower
temperature. The synthesis of fructans is linked to the availability
of sucrose, and it can be regarded as an extension of the sucrose
storage pool [7]. Low starch and high sucrose contents are generally
associated with fructan accumulation in leaves. It has been reported
[14] that the activities of some of the enzymes involved in fructan
biosynthesis, in *Lolium temulentum* L., increase following chilling.

TABLE 3: Temperature dependent fructan content

Temperature (0°C)	Fructan content (mg.g^{-1} FW)
10	13.2±0.3(2)
25	4.6±0.4(2)

Fructan is expressed as fructose, after hydrolysis, in leaf
segments illuminated for 1.5 hours

The results are means ±SD. In parenthesis are the number of replicates.

Thus, it seems that the decrease in sucrose content of wheat leaves,
found when temperature is decreased from 25 to 10°C, can be explained
by a concomitant increase in the content of fructan.

REFERENCES
[1] Sicher, R. C., Kremer, D. F. and Harris, W. G. (1984) Plant.
    Physiol. 76, 165-169
[2] Bird, I. F., Cornelius, M. J., Keys, A. J. and Whittingham, C. P.
    (1974) Phytochemistry 13, 59-64
[3] Heber, U. (1974) Ann. Rev. Plant. Physiol. 25, 383-421
[4] Sicher, R. C. (1986) Physiol. Plant. 67, 118-121
[5] Akasawa, T. and Okamoto K. (1980) in The Biochemistry of Plants
    (Stumpf, P. K. and Conn, E. E., eds), Vol 3, 199-220, Academic
    Press, New York
[6] Arrabaça, M. C., Keys, A. J. and Whittingham, C. P. (1981)
    Photosynthesis IV. Regulation of Carbon Metabolism (Akoyunoglou, G.,
    ed), 463-470, Balaban International Science Services, Philadelphia
[7] Pollock, C. J. (1986), Current Topics in Plant Biochemistry and

Physiology (Randall, D. D., Miles, C. D., Nelson, C. J.,Blevins, D.
   G. and Miernyk, J. A.,eds), Vol 5, 1-16, Univ. of Missouri
[8] Arrabaça, M. C. (1981) Ph.D. Thesis, University of London, UK
[9] Rufty Jr., T. W., Kerr, P. S. and Huber S. C. (1983) Plant Physiol.
   73,428-433
[10] Kobza, J. and Edwards, G. E. (1987) Plant Physiol. 83, 69-74
[11] Beutler, H. O. (1981) in Methods in Enzymatic Analysis, 3rd ed.
   (Bergmeyer, H. U., ed), Vol VI, 41-45, Verlag Chemie, Weinheim
[12] Habron, S., Foyer, C. and Walker, D. (1981) Arch. Biochem.
   Biophys. 212, 237-246
[13] Kalt-Torres, W. and Huber, S. C. (1987) Plant Physiol. 83, 294-298
[14] Pollock, C. J. (1984) New Phytol. 96, 527-534

ACKNOWLEDGEMENTS
   This work was supported by Instituto Nacional de Investigação
Científica, Portugal (CEB, Linha de Acção Nº 6).

THE EFFECT OF TEMPERATURE ON PHOTOSYNTHESIS AND AMOUNTS AND TRANSPORT OF ASSIMILATE IN SUNFLOWER AND RAPE.

M.J. PAUL and D.W. LAWLOR, Biochemistry and Physiology Department, AFRC Institute of Arable Crops Research, Rothamsted Experimental Station, Harpenden, Herts, AL5 2JQ, U.K.

1. INTRODUCTION

Cool temperatures limit plant productivity, but the exact nature of this constraint and the temperature-dependent relationship between photosynthesis and consumption of photosynthate is not well understood.

In the cold photosynthesis may be limited by a decreased supply of Pi caused by slow sucrose synthesis (1). This is demonstrated by a smaller stimulation of photosynthesis by 2kPa O_2 compared to 21kPa O_2 with decreasing temperature, and by eventual insensitivity to 2kPa O_2 at a temperature dependent on species (2). Carbohydrate accumulates in the cold (3), and feedback inhibition of photosynthesis caused by accumulation of carbohydrate due to low sink demand may occur at low temperatures (4). The rate of export of photosynthate from leaves, can be estimated by monitoring ^{14}C efflux from $^{14}CO_2$—fed leaves (5), and in conjunction with measurements of amounts of carbohydrate, indicates carbohydrate utilisation and sink demand.

The present study describes the effect of temperature on photosynthesis and photosynthate utilisation in sunflower and rape — species known to differ in response to temperature (6) — and assesses the relationship between these processes and biomass production in the cold.

2. PROCEDURE

Plant material: Sunflower (*Helianthus annuus* L.) and oilseed rape (*Brassica napus* L.) were grown at 30°C (warm) and 13°C (cold).

Photosynthesis: Rates of photosynthesis of individual leaves were measured using an open—circuit gas—exchange system at between 5°C and 35°C after equilibration for 15 minutes and for periods of 4 hours under constant conditions at the growth temperature.

Carbohydrates and phosphorylated intermediates were estimated at the growth temperature and after transfer to 13°C or 30°C. Soluble carbohydrates were analysed by gas chromatography, and starch measured enzymically after amyloglucosidase digestion. Phosphorylated intermediates were also estimated enzymically.

Labelling with $^{14}CO_2$: Entire attached leaves were exposed to $^{14}CO_2$ for 15 minutes. The amount of ^{14}C remaining in these leaves was

M. Baltscheffsky (ed.), Current Research in Photosynthesis, Vol. IV, 663–666.

monitored at the growth temperature and after transfer to 13°C and 30°C by attaching a Geiger-Muller tube to the underside of the fed leaf. The amount of ^{14}C remaining in the fed leaves was expressed semi-logarithmically against time and used to estimate carbon export from the fed leaf.

3. RESULTS AND DISCUSSION

Photosynthetic rate was at a maximum at higher temperatures in sunflower than rape grown at both temperatures. Photosynthetic rates in rape were greater at cool temperatures than in sunflower (Figure 1). Hence, it is surprising to find that sunflower but not rape was sensitive to 2kPa O_2 in the cold (Figure 2). Continuing stimulation of photosynthesis in the cold may be due to greater Pi recycling due to a faster rate of sucrose synthesis or to a greater capacity to maintain cytosolic Pi at the expense of the vacuolar pool.

Maintenance of a constant photosynthetic rate over 4 hours (it increased by 1%) in warm-grown sunflower at 30°C contrasts with the 9.5% decline in photosynthetic rate at 30°C in warm-grown rape over the same period. At higher temperatures the movement of triose phosphate towards sucrose synthesis may be too rapid in rape depleting Calvin cycle pools and depressing photosynthetic rate. In cold-grown plants of sunflower and rape photosynthetic rate declined over 4 hours by 7.4% and 3.6% respectively. The decline in photosynthetic rate in the cold may be due to a progressive diminuition of Pi caused by slow consumption of triose phosphate. The accumulation of carbohydrates in the cold (Table 1), may also depress photosynthesis by feedback inhibition.

In sunflower, in marked contrast to rape, the disappearance of ^{14}C from $^{14}CO_2$-fed leaves was immediately affected by temperature transfers (Figure 3). Export in sunflower was far slower at 13°C than at 30°C in warm- and cold-grown plants, but in rape there was little difference in export rates at 13°C and 30°C between warm- and cold-grown plants. The suppression of export in warm-grown sunflower at 13°C is too quick to be explained by a reduction in sink demand. The inhibition of export at 13°C in cold-grown sunflower suggests a lesion of the transport mechanism not alleviated by acclimation to cool temperatures.

In conclusion: photosynthesis and growth function optimally at lower temperatures in rape than in sunflower. Utilisation of assimilate seems to control photosynthetic rate which is at a maximum when temperature-dependent sink demand is greatest. The maintenance of photosynthesis in excess of sink demand in the cold until storage carbon pools are full, prevents photodamage and provides a reserve of carbohydrate for use when conditions become more favourable for growth. The inhibition of photosynthesis in the cold due to carbohydrate accumulation and Pi sequestration will only limit biomass production if it prevents storage pools being filled to capacity. We conclude that at low temperatures biomass production is limited by assimilate utilisation.

(Research supported by Commission of the European Communities).

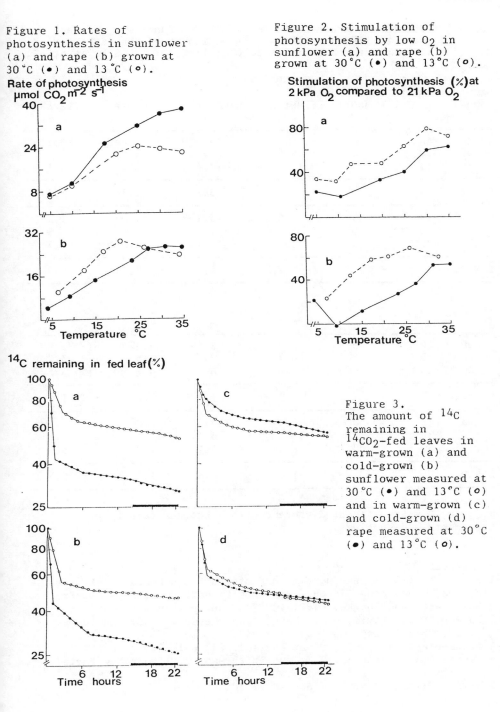

Figure 1. Rates of photosynthesis in sunflower (a) and rape (b) grown at 30°C (•) and 13°C (○).

Figure 2. Stimulation of photosynthesis by low O_2 in sunflower (a) and rape (b) grown at 30°C (•) and 13°C (○).

Rate of photosynthesis μmol CO_2 m^{-2} s^{-1}

Stimulation of photosynthesis (%) at 2 kPa O_2 compared to 21 kPa O_2

^{14}C remaining in fed leaf (%)

Figure 3. The amount of ^{14}C remaining in $^{14}CO_2$-fed leaves in warm-grown (a) and cold-grown (b) sunflower measured at 30°C (•) and 13°C (○) and in warm-grown (c) and cold-grown (d) rape measured at 30°C (•) and 13°C (○).

Table 1 Amounts of carbohydrate (mmol m^{-2}) in sunflower and rape grown at 30°C and 13°C at the beginning of the light period (0) and after 8 hours at 30°C or 13°C (8). L.S.D. is at 5%.

Sunflower

Growth Temperature °C	Transfer	Hours	Fructose	Glucose	Sucrose	Starch
30	30	0	5.0	10.0[xo]	5.6[xo]	2.7[x]
30	30	8	5.6	9.9	5.6	3.2
30	13	8	11.7	17.4	22.3	5.1
L.S.D.			3.6	3.1	1.3	1.1
13	13	0	4.0	13.7[xΔ]	12.8[x]	1.5[xΔ]
13	13	8	5.1	12.7	15.4	1.9
13	30	8	3.8	12.1	11.0	1.7
L.S.D.			1.7	4.8	1.8	0.3

Rape

Growth Temperature °C	Transfer	Hours	Fructose	Glucose	Sucrose	Starch
30	30	0	6.2	3.2[o]	3.2[□o]	2.9[□]
30	30	8	6.7	2.7	3.5	3.2
30	13	8	5.6	4.1	4.7	3.5
L.S.D.			3.1	1.2	1.2	1.3
13	13	0	3.8	2.1[Δ]	11.7[□]	7.4[□Δ]
13	13	8	13.5	9.4	17.0	6.8
13	30	8	6.5	4.7	11.7	6.8
L.S.D.			1.7	4.8	1.8	0.3

L.S.D. at 5%
x, Δ, o, □ = Significant differences (5%) between temperature treatments and species.

REFERENCES
1 Stitt, M. (1987) in Progress in Photosynthesis Research (Biggens, J., ed.) Vol. 3 pp.685-692, Martinus Nijhoff Publishers, Dordrecht.
2 Sage, R.F. and Sharkey, T.D. (1987) Plant Physiol. 84, 658-664.
3 Lawlor, D.W., Boyle, F.A., Keys, A.J., Kendall, A.C. and Young, A.T. (1988) J. Exp. Bot. 39, 329-343.
4 Azcon-Bieto, J. (1983) Plant Physiol. 73, 681-686.
5 Owera, S.A.P., Farrar, J.F. and Whitbread, R. (1983) New Phytol. 94, 111-123.
6 Warren-Wilson, J. (1966) Ann. Bot. 30, 753-761.

EFFECTS OF LOW TEMPERATURE ON CHLOROPHYLL PROTEIN COMPLEXES AND REGULATION CAPACITY OF EXCITATION ENERGY DISTRIBUTION IN CHLOROPLAST MEMBRANE OF CUCUMBER

C.H.Xu, F.H.Zhao, K.B.Wang, D.H.Yang and Y.L.Dai
DEPARTMENT OF PHOTOSYNTHESIS, INSTITUTE OF BOTANY, ACADEMIA SINICA, 100044 BEIJING, CHINA

1. INTRODUCTION

It has been demonstrated that photosynthetic organisms have the ability of regulating the distribution of excitation energy between PSII and PSI to balance the photochemical events within them in order to maintain maximal rates of photosynthesis.The distribution of excitation energy between the two photosystems can be altered by adding cations, which control the spillover of energy from PSII to PSI [1].Recently it was shown that phosphorylation of the light harvesting chlorophyll a/b protein (LHC−II) was thought to be reversibly related to an increase in the energy distributed to PSI and a decrease in the distributed to PSII [2].Increasing evidences have been presented in indicating that the regulation of excitation energy distribution between PSI and PSII is attributed to the movement of the LHC between grana and stroma [3, 4, 5].

In this paper, we report that the Chl−protein complexes are disintegrated and the mechanisms of regulation of the excitation energy distribution can be perturbed in leaves of cucumber submitted to chilling stress conditions.

2. MATERIALS AND METHODS

Cucumber plants (Cucumis sativus L.) of var.Jilinmici were grown in a greenhouse (Ca.27℃ / 22℃ day/night).Detached leaves, usually the most recently expanded ones, were chilled at 0℃ 16 hours in the dark.Chloroplasts were isolated according to Dai et al.[6].For Mg^{2+}−treatment experiment, 5mM $MgCl_2$ was added to the chloroplast suspension.Chl−protein complexes were resolved at 4℃ by SDS−PAGE.Profile of Chl−protein complex bands was determined by scanning gel coloums at 675nm on a Shimadzu mode CS−910 TLC scanner.The 4th derivative absorption spectra were measured by a Shimadzu model UV−3000 recording spectrophotometer. Fluorescence emission spectra at 77K were recorded by using a Hitachi model MPF−4 fluorescence spectrophotometer.LHC−II phosphorylation was referred to Kyle et al. [4].

3. RESULTS AND DISCUSSION

3. 1. Effects of chilling pretreatment on chlorophyll absorption species and Chl−protein complexes

No visible injury was observed on the chilling treated cucumber leaves.There was also no distinct differance between the absorption spectra of the chloroplasts from the control and from the chilling treated leaves.However the 4th derivative absorption spectra (Fig. 1) revealed that the relative proportion of Chl a absorption species at 670nm (A670) decreased in the chilled chloroplasts. As show in table 1, the ratio of an absorption species at 683nm (A683) to an absorption species at 651nm (A651) in the chilled chloroplasts was unchanged by comparing with that in the control.But the ratios of A670 / A651 and A670 / A683 of chilled chloroplasts decrease from 0.57 to 0.44 and from 0.2 to 0.15 respectively.This result indicates that chilling induced the change of the chorophyll components of chloroplast.

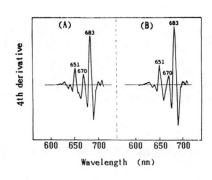

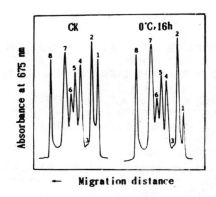

← **Migration distance**

FIGURE 1.The 4th derivative absorption spectra of chloroplasts of control (A) and chilling (0℃ 16h, in darkness) pretreated (B) cucumber leaves

FIGURE 2.The effect of chilling pretreatmeat on cucumber Chl−protein complexes 1−CPI$_a$; 2−CPI; 3−LHCII$_{1a}$; 4−LHCII$_1$; 5−LHCII$_2$; 6−CP$_a$; 7−LHCII$_3$; 8−FP

TABLE 1.The 4th derivative absorption spectra components of chtoroplasts from control and chilling temperature treated cucumber leaves

Treatment	A670 / A683	A683 / A651	A670 / A651
Control	0.20	2.8	0.57
0℃,16h	0.15	2.8	0.44

The Chl−protein complexes resolved by SDS−PAGE from chloroplast thylakiod membrane isolated separately from chilling (0℃ 16h, in the dark) pretreated and untreated cucumber leaves are shown in Fig.2. The resolved bands in the order of increasing mobility are designated as CPI$_a$, CPI, LHC−II$_{1a}$, LHC−II$_1$LHC−II$_2$, CP$_a$, LHC−II$_3$, and finally free pigments band.

The most significant change in Chl−protein complexes induced by chilling pretreatment was that CPI$_a$decreased whereas CPI increased. As shown in table 2, CPI$_a$was 10.2% for the control and 5.1% for the chilling pretreated ones.It is known that, CPI$_a$is the reaction center complex of PSI associated with LHC−I, whereas CPI is the reaction center complex of PSI.The decreasing of CPI$_a$while increasing of CPI implied that some LHC−I may be seperated from PSI reaction center and some of them may move to PSII.

TABLE 2.Distribution of chlorophyll (%) among the chlorophyll−protein complexes and free pigments in thylakoids of cucumber leaves

Treatment	CPI a	CPI	LHCII$_{1a}$	LHCII$_1$	LHCII$_2$	CP$_a$	LHCII$_3$	FP
Control	10.2	16.7	2.0	14.2	12.7	9.0	22.0	13.2
0℃,16h	5.1	17.2	2.0	12.3	12.8	9.1	26.0	15.5

LHC–II$_1$ which is considered to represent the oligomeric form of LHC–II$_3$ was also found to be less (12.3%) in the chilling pretreated leaves than that in the control leaves (14.2%) .Correspondingly, LHC–II$_3$ significantly increased from 22% in the control leaves to 26% in the chilling pretreated leaves.It is considered that LHC–II was easily dissociated in chilling pretreated leaves.Because LHC plays an important role in the distribution of excitation energy between PSI and PSII, therefore these structural changes of Chl–protein complexes induced by chilling treatment should alter the distribution of excitation energy between the two photosystems.

3. 2. Effect of chilling pretreatment on the regulation of Mg^{2+}on excitation energy distribution

It is well–known that the changing of concentration or valency of cationsin the medium can control the excitation energy distribution between the two photosystems.Table 3 shows that the addition of Mg^{2+}in the control chloroplasts suspension increased both F687 and F695 signals, originating from PSII, relative to that of F735, raising from PSI.It was interesting to find that Mg^{2+}induced changes in the ratios of F685 / F735 and F695 / F735 of the chloroplasts from the chilling treated leaves were high (by 32% and 25% respectively) compared to that (21% and 16% respectively) in the control one.This indicates that Mg^{2+}induced more excitation energy transfer towards PSII in the chilling pretreated leaves.

TABLE 3.The effect of Mg^{2+}on fluorescedce emission (at 77K) of chloroplasts isolated seperately from control and chilling temperature treated (0℃,16h) cucumber leaves

Treatment		F687 / F735		F695 / F735	
Control	−Mg^{2+}	1.98	100%	1.80	100%
	+Mg^{2+}(5mM)	2.41	121%	2.10	116%
0℃,16h	−Mg^{2+}	1.57	100%	1.30	100%
	+Mg^{2+}(5mM)	2.08	132%	1.63	125%

It has been suggested that LHC–I and LHC–II are able to move from stroma lamellae to grana lamellae, this can adjust the distribution of excitation energy more towards PSII.It seems that the cation–induced significant change in F685 / F735 ratio under chilling condition is due to the easy seperation of LHC–I from PSI reaction center and moved to PSII by low temperature pretreatment.

3. 3. Effect of chilling pretreatment on the LHC II phosphorylation–controlled distribution of excitation energy .

It is now clearly establish that another mechanism of the regulation and control of the excitation energy distribution is the phyosphorylation of LHC–II , by which the excitation energy distribution is reversibly favourable to PSI and decrease in PSII as proved by the analysis of PSII fluorescence decrease upon phosphorylation. Table 4 shows that the ratio F687 / F735 at 77K greatly decreased from 1.74 to 1.05 by the phosphorylation of LHC–II in the chlorophasts from control leaves, but in the chloroplasts from chilling pretreated leaves the ratio was almost unchanged (1.13) compared to that (1.18) under nonphosphorylation condtion.This indicates that chilling induced the decline of the regulation capacity of the excitation energy ditritution towards PSI upon phosphorylation.It has been suggested that protein phosphorylation can afford partial protection to chloroplasts exposed to photoinhibitory [7], so our results citated above implied that chilling can increase the sensitivity of chloroplast thylakoid to photoinhibition.We consider that this may be due to the structure changes of Chl—protein complexes induced by chilling, so it causes the damages to the detachment of a fraction of LHC—II from PSII and the functional association of this fraction of LHC—II with PSI.

TABLE 4.The effect of phosphorylation on fluorescence emission characteristics (at 77K) of chloroplasts isolated from control and chilling treated (0℃,16h) cucumber leaves

Treatment		F687 / F735		F695 / F735	
Control	Non—phosphorylated	1.74	100%	1.51	100%
	phosphorylated	1.05	60%	1.21	80%
0℃,16h	Non—phosphorylated	1.18	100%	1.08	100%
	phosphorylated	1.13	96%	1.16	107%

It was found that in the chloroplasts from chilling pretreated leaves LHC which was disintegrated into more monomeric form would be less effective in funnelling light energy to the reaction centers, and the excitation energy might be distributed more towards PSII caused by the damage of the LHC—II phosphorylation—controlled mechanism and by more pronounced action of the valence of cation.

This work is supported by NNSFC.

References
1.Murata, N. (1969) Biochim. Biophys. Acta.172, 242—257
2.Bennette, J. (1983) Biochem.J. 212, 1—13
3.Barber, J. (1983) Photobiochem. Photobiophys. 5, 181—190
4.Kyle, D.J., Kuang, T.Y., Watson, J.L.and Arntzen, C.J. (1984) Biochim.Biophys.Acta 765, 89—96
5.Kuang, T.Y., Yuan, J.G., Tang, C.Q., Zhang, Q.D., and Lin, S.Q. (1987) in : Progress in Photosynthesis Research (Biggins, J., ed.), Vol.II, pp.729—732, Martinus Nijhoff, Dordrecht
6.Dai, Y.L., Xu, C.H., zhao, F.H. (1987) Ibid, Vol.IV, pp.99—102
7.Horton, P.and Lee, P. (1985) Planta 165, 37—42

GENETIC VARIATION AND DIVERSITY OF LOW TEMPERATURE INDUCED DAMAGES IN
MAIZE SEEDLINGS AS ASSESSED BY CHLOROPHYLL FLUORESCENCE INDUCTION CURVES.

M-F. SCHARLL, R. LANNOYE AND S. MAURO.
Laboratoire de Physiologie Végétale ULB, av. P. Héger n°28, CP169,
B-1050 Bruxelles. Belgium.

1. INTRODUCTION

In North Europe, the combination of low temperatures and high light
intensities experienced by maize in the fields represents the major
environmental constraint to the expansion of its culture.
Therefore breeders tend to incorporate different cold resistance tests
in their breeding programs.
Different screening techniques based on prompt and delayed fluorescence
measurements have been proposed. We have focused our attention on the
fluorescence induction curves from stressed leaves. The technique looked
attractive since it has been shown to give useful informations on energy
tranfer (1), quantum efficiency (2), size and heterogeneity of the PSII
photosynthetic units (3,4).
Our objective was twofold. We intended to assess the reliability of the
measure as a ranking technique. We also tried to identify the nature of
the reactions primarily affected by the cold stress and thus to introduce
physiological criteria in cold breeding programs.

2. MATERIALS AND METHODS

Maize seedlings were grown in a phytotron programmmed for a 16hr
photoperiod (300 $\mu E.m^{-2}.s^{-1}$) and a 25°C/15°C day/night temperature.
Fluorescence induction curves were obtained from DCMU infiltrated leaves
using a laboratory-made fluorometer. The wavelength of maximum emission
was 592 nm. The fluorescence was measured at 685 nm.
Thylakoids were isolated as described in 5. Quantification of the
apopeptides of LHCII was done by two-dimensional gel electrophoresis.
For the first dimension chlorophyll-protein complexes were resolved by
mild SDS-polyacrylamide gel electrophoresis. For the second dimension the
green band corresponding to LHCII was excised and reelectrophoresed under
denaturing conditions (5).

M. Baltscheffsky (ed.), Current Research in Photosynthesis, Vol. IV, 671–674.

3. RESULTS

The principles of the quantitative analysis of the fluorescence curve
obtained from DCMU infiltrated leaves have been described by Malkin et
al.(3). They demonstrate that the surface concentration of PSII reaction
centres could be calculated according to :

$$RCII = \alpha_2 \quad \phi_2 \quad I \quad t$$

where RCII is the quantity of reaction centres (mol),
$\quad \alpha_2$ is the fraction of the actinic light absorbed by PSII,
$\quad \phi_2$ is the maximal efficiency of photochemistry in PSII,
$\quad$ I is the rate of light absorption,
$\quad$ t is the induction time.

A good quantitative correlation between the maximal photosynthetic rates
has been demonstrated for different species (6).
The fluorescence transients were similar in the different inbreds
(Fig.1.a). The yield of photochemistry, as estimated by the parameter
$1 - F_o/F_{max}$, and the induction time were respectively 0.8 ± 0.03 and 36.4 ± 0.02 ms.

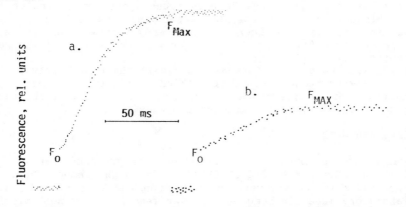

Fig.1 Fluorescence induction curves of control (a) and photoinhibited (b)
leaves.

Chilling the plants for 8 hours in the dark revealed significant
differences in the cold sensitivity of our inbreds. The cold treatment
left unaffected two inbreds (1873, 2751) while inducing a decrease in
yield of photochemistry of 1194 and 1061. The changes in the induction
time were complementary to those observed for the quantum efficiency
(Table 1).

Table 1: genetic variation in cold sensitivity.
(t is in ms; the light intensity was 300 $\mu E/m^2.s$)

	1194		1061		2751		1873	
	t	O_2	t	O_2	t	O_2	t	O_2
2°C, dark	47.8	0.71	48.6	0.74	30.4	0.78	36.0	0.80
3°C, light	122.7	0.41	-	-	-	-	67.3	0.57

The changes in the induction time were complementary to those observed
for the quantum yield so that the product of $O_2.t$ was constant.
The reduced quantum efficiency can, a priori, result from either a
reduced connectivity between the reaction centre and its associated
antennae or from an inhibition of the electron flow between the water
splitting system and P_{680}^+. As the F_0 level was not changed by the
treatment(not shown), we tend to favour the second hypothesis. The
increase in the induction time reflects the additional amount of photons
required to reduce all Q_A present in the illuminated area. Thus the cold
treatment does not seem to affect the amount of light absorbed by PSII.
Plants were than compared after an additional treatment of 7 hours in
the light at 3°C. The light treatment resulted in a large, although more
pronounced for 1194, reduction of the variable fluorescence (Fig.1b) in
both inbreds.
However, in the case of 1194, the increase in the induction time could
not be accounted for by the decrease in the quantum yield of the PSII
photochemistry (Table 1).
To test the possibility that the amount of light absorbed by PSII was
affected, we analysed the distribution of the LHCII complexes (Fig.2).
As expected, the light induced a quantitative as well as a qualitative
change in the composition of the stromal derived membranes. After 7
hours in the light at 25°C, the stromal membranes were enriched with
LHCII proteins apparently derived from the grana. The same changes were
essentially observed when the plants were illuminated at 3°C. This
indicates that phosphorylation of LHCII still proceeds at low
temperature. However the drastic changes brought about by light and low
temperature in granal fraction indicate that the pigment organization in
the granal PSII is severely affected and thus support our interpretation
of a specific light induced increase of the induction time.

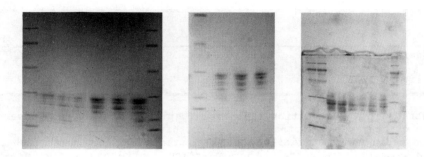

Fig.2 Two-dimensional electrophoresis for resolution of LHCII
apopolypeptides.
Lane 1: molecular weight standards, lanes 2, 11: dark adapted
stromal and granal membranes kept at 15°C; lanes 16, 18: granal
and stromal membranes after 7 hr in the light at 25°C; lanes 19,
22: stromal and granal membranes after 7 hr in the light at 3°C.

3. Conclusion.

Our preliminary results indicate that the fluorescence induction curves
obtained from stressed leaves infiltrated with DCMU can be used as a
ranking technique for cold resistance. We wish to emphasize that a
correct interpretation would help to define a set of physiological
criteria which may constitute the basis of breeding programs .

4. References.

1. Joliot, A. and Joliot, P. (1964) C.R. Acad. Sci. Paris 258, 4625-4662.
2. Kitajima, M. and Butler, W. (1975) Biochem. Biophys. Acta 376,
   150-115.
3. Malkin, S., Armond, P.A., Mooney, H.A. and Fork, D.C. (1981) Plant
   Physiol. 67, 570-579.
4. Melis, A; and Homann, P.H.   (1978) Arch. Biochem. Biophys. 190,
   523-530.
5. Larsson, U.K., Sundby, C. and Andersson, B. (1987) Biochem. Biophys.
   Acta 894, 59-68.
6. Morgan, C.L. and Austin, R.B. (1986) Photosynthesis Research 7,
   203-219.

The Effects Of Low Temperature On Activities Of Carbon Metabolism Enzymes In Zea mays L. Seedlings.

M.R. Hull,[1,2] S.P. Long,[1] and C.R. Raines,[1] Dept of Biology,[1] University of Essex, Colchester. CO4 3SQ. U.K.; Shell Research Ltd.[2], Sittingbourne. Kent. ME9 8AG. U.K.

Abbreviations: A_{sat}, light saturated rate of CO_2 uptake per unit leaf area; F16BPase, fructose 1,6-bisphosphatase (E.C. 3.1.3.11); NADP-MDase, NADP-dependent malate dehydrogenase (E.C. 1.1.1.82); PEPC, phosphoenolpyruvate carboxylase (E.C. 4.1.1.31); PPiDiK, pyruvate orthophosphate dikinase (E.C. 2.7.9.1); RPP, reductive pentose phosphate pathway.

1. INTRODUCTION.

Attempts to grow maize (Zea mays) in cool temperate countries have been hindered by (a) the slow growth rates under cool (c.a. 14°C) early season conditions and (b) its susceptibility to chilling (<12°C) dependent photoinhibition in high light. These effects are manifest as decreases in the potential for both light limited and light saturated CO_2 uptake. This injury of maize is significant in cool temperate climates since the period of seedling establishment will coincide with spells when prolonged periods of chilling temperatures may occur, sometimes combined with high light levels e.g. cold bright mornings (1). Chilling dependent photoinhibition has been shown to occur in maize crops in the field (2).

Changes in the levels of the enzymes of the C_4 pathway (PPiDiK, PEPC, NADP-MDase) and the RPP pathway (e.g. F16BPase) are one potential cause of decreased rates of CO_2 uptake at light saturation. This study examines the situation as follows: (a) Enzyme activities were compared between maize grown at 25°C (control conditions) with those in plants grown at 14°C. This was in order to determine which of the C_4 enzymes are potentially rate limiting steps in metabolism; and (b) The response of the enzyme activities when 25°C grown maize was subjected to a 6h, 5°C, 1500umolm^{-2}s^{-1} photoinhibition treatment and returned to control conditions.

2. PROCEDURES.

Maize Zea mays c.v. LG11, was grown at 340umolm^{-2}s^{-1}, 16/8 d/n photoperiod, 70% RH, temperature 25°C (control) or 14°C. For each enzyme, a section was taken from the oldest part of recently expanded second leaves, as it is known that this is the most susceptible to low temperature and

M. Baltscheffsky (ed.), Current Research in Photosynthesis, Vol. IV, 675–678.

photoinhibition (3). The leaf was frozen in liquid nitrogen and enzymes extracted in the relevant buffer solution. Preliminary studies showed no loss of activity following this freezing procedure.

Enzyme activities were measured as described previously: PPiDik(4), PEPC(5), NADP-MDase(6) and F16BPASE(7). All activities were assayed at 25°C. A_{sat} was measured at 25°C using an ADC, LCA 2 portable IRGA.

3. RESULTS AND DISCUSSION.

A preliminary study had shown that the enzyme PPiDiK gave the greatest in vitro decrease in activity with temperature reduction from 25°C to 5°C. The activity on a unit leaf area basis in vitro at 5°C was 3umolm^{-2}s^{-1}. This equals the assimilation rate in vivo at this temperature.

Fig.1. compares enzyme activities in Zea mays grown at 25°C with those in maize grown at 14°C. Activities were expressed on a leaf area basis (μmolm^{-2}s^{-1}) to allow comparison with A_{sat} of leaves grown at 25°C and 14°C.

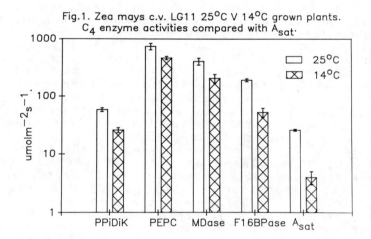

Fig.1. Zea mays c.v. LG11 25°C V 14°C grown plants. C_4 enzyme activities compared with A_{sat}.

Of the C_4 enzymes, PPiDiK was affected most by the treatments. Activity in 14°C grown leaves was reduced 55% compared to control leaves although this was still sufficient to support photosynthetic levels in vivo, the rate being six times greater than the assimilation rate of 14°C grown leaves. NADP-MDase activities were reduced by 49% and with PEPC, 38% reductions in activity in 14°C grown leaves were observed. The RPP pathway enzyme F16BPase had only 28% of control activity remaining in 14°C leaves equivalent to 52μmolm^{-2}s^{-1}. However, this would be more than sufficient to support observed rates of in vivo photosynthesis, since it was thirteen times greater than A_{sat}.

Although this study shows F16BPase activity to be the most decreased of the enzymes examined, as far as temperature during development is concerned, PPiDiK activity is again low compared to other enzymes at both high ($25^{\circ}C$) and low ($14^{\circ}C$) temperatures. This adds further evidence to its potential role in limiting maize photosynthesis at low temperature. The high substrate levels used in the assays are not likely to be found in-vivo therefore activities within the leaf might be expected to be even lower.

Fig.2. shows the response of the C_4 enzymes to a 6h, $5^{\circ}C$ photoinhibition treatment immediately after return to $25^{\circ}C$, and then 1,2,3,4 and 20h later.

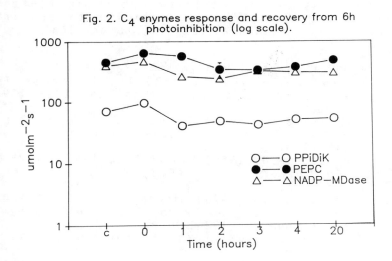

Fig. 2. C_4 enymes response and recovery from 6h photoinhibition (log scale).

After recovery at $25^{\circ}C$ for 1h, each enzyme showed a marked decrease in activity followed by a slow recovery. PPiDiK was reduced to $40 \, \mu mol \, m^{-2} s^{-1}$. However, recovery of this enzyme appeared incomplete. After 20h, activity was still 26% less than in controls. PEPC activity declined more slowly and recovered full activity after 20h. NADP-MDase decreased more sharply and as with PPiDiK appeared not to recover; however, the difference was not statistically significant ($t, p > 0.05$).

Interpretation can be made along two lines. First, changes in synthesis or degradation of the proteins. This is being investigated using gel electrophoresis (SDS-PAGE) and monoclonal antibody techniques. Preliminary results have indicated that some changes in amount do occur, in particular in the protein PPiDiK protein. Secondly, changes in the level of activation of these enzymes.

Activation mechanisms and regulation of these enzymes are diverse, both substrates and/or products having a critical influence on the level of enzyme activation (8). The effect of photoinhibition on each of these biochemical and physiological processes both during and after the chill/high light phase must therefore be clearly understood in order to interpret the significance of the enzyme changes. These results suggest that effects on enzymes of the C_4 pathway following a 6h chill in high light are secondary to changes at the level of the photosynthetic membrane (9). The reduced CO_2 fixation capacities of 14^oC grown plants and reduced C_4 and RPP pathway enzyme activities would be expected to render these more susceptible to chilling dependent photoinhibition. In particular, the loss PPiDik activity, which in control plants shows only just sufficient activity to support observed rates of CO_2 fixation at 5^oC, may be critical.

References.
1. Long, S.P. (1983) Plant Cell and Environ. 6,345-363.
2. Farage, P.K. and Long, S.P. (1987) In. Progress In Photosynthesis Research. (Ed. J. Biggins) Vol 12, 139-142.
3. Long, S.P., Nugawela, A., Bongi, G. and Farage, P.K. (1987) In. Progress In Photosynthesis Research. (Ed. J. Biggins) vol 4,131-138.
4. Andrews,T.J.and Hatch,M.D.(1969) Biochem. J. 114,117-125
5. Hatch, M.D. and Oliver, I.R. (1978) Aust. J. Plant. Physiol. 5,571- 580.
6. Johnson,H.S. and Hatch,M.D.(1970) Biochem. J. 119,273-280
7. Kelly, G.J., Zimmermann, C. and Latzo, E. (1976) Biochem. Biophys. Res. Commun. 70,193-199.
8. Edwards, G.E. and Nakamato, H. (1985) Ann. Rev. Plant. Physiol. 36,255-86.
9. Baker, N.R., East, T. and Long, S.P. (1983) J. Exp. Bot. 34,189-197.

CHILL-INDUCED MODIFICATIONS TO THE RELATIONSHIP BETWEEN THYLAKOID PROTEIN
PHOSPHORYLATION AND ENERGY DISTRIBUTION TO PHOTOSYSTEM 2 IN MAIZE

Jesús Val and Neil R. Baker, Dept. of Biology, University of Essex,
Colchester CO4 3SQ, U.K.

1. INTRODUCTION

Phosphorylation of LHC2 and PS2 proteins by membrane-bound kinases is
often considered to be an important factor in regulating excitation energy
distribution and electron transport (1,2). When maize leaves are chilled in
high light damage occurs to the D_1 reaction centre protein of PS2 (3) and a
31 kDa polypeptide, which is thought to be the unprocessed precursor of
CP29 (4), accumulates in LHC2 (5). Such perturbation to PS2 and LHC2 might
be expected to result in changes in the characteristics of phosphorylation
and its effects on PS2 electron transport. In this study the phosphorylation
characteristics and consequences for PS2 electron transport are examined
for thylakoids of maize leaves exposed to low temperature under high and
low light.

2. MATERIAL AND METHODS

Maize plants (*Zea mays* L. cv. LG 11) were grown at 25°C under PPFD of
250 μmol m^{-2}s^{-1} and 16 h photoperiod 10-12 days prior to treatment at
high (1500 μmol m^{-2}s^{-1}, HL) or low (250 μmol m^{-2}s^{-1}, LL) light at 5°C for
6 h.

Thylakoids were isolated from mesophyll cells of the second leaves
essentially as described previously (5). *In vitro* phosphorylation was
carried out at 25°C for 10 min in 50 mM Tricine, 10 mM KCl, 5 mM MgCl$_2$, 5
mM NaF and 200 μM ATP containing 40 μCi of γ-^{32}P-ATP mol^{-1} at pH 7.8 and
under a PPFD of 30 μmol m^{-2}s^{-1}. Membranes were solubilized in 4% (w/v) SDS,
60 mM dithiothreitol and 80% sucrose with an SDS:chlorophyll ratio of 40:1
prior to separation using polyacrylamide gel electrophoresis as described
previously (5). Phosphoproteins were visualized by autoradiography at -70°C.

PS2 electron transport from water to p-phenylene diamine in the
presence of ferricyanide (6) and chlorophyll fluorescence kinetics from
thylakoids in the presence of DCMU (7) were determined as described
previously.

Phosphorylation of thylakoid polypeptides *in vivo* was achieved by
growing plants in 20 cm^3 of Hoaglands solution containing 5 μCi cm^{-3} of
^{32}P-orthophosphate.

3. RESULTS AND DISCUSSION

The phosphoprotein profile of thylakoids isolated from control maize
leaves was similar to those previously published for pea and spinach (1)
with the 9, 32 and 42 kDa PS2 and the 27-29 kDa LHC2 polypeptides being

M. Baltscheffsky (ed.), Current Research in Photosynthesis, Vol. IV, 679–682.

most heavily phosphorylated (Fig. 1). Thylakoids isolated from leaves chilled for 6 h at 5°C in both high and low light contained the 31 kDa polypeptide, which was not present in significant amounts in control thylakoids (Fig. 1). The phosphorylation profile of thylakoids from HL-chill treated leaves was essentially the same as for control thylakoids (Fig. 1). However, LL-chill thylakoids exhibited a remarkably different-phosphoprotein profile with the PS2 polypeptides being considerably less phosphorylated than in control thylakoids, yet LHC2 phosphorylation was similar (Fig. 1)

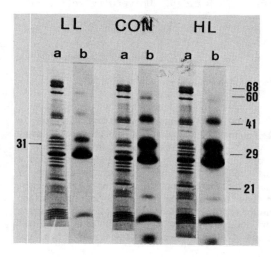

Fig.1. Polypeptide profiles (tracks labelled a) and their autoradiograms (tracks labelled b) of thylakoids isolated from leaves exposed to control (CON), chill in high light (HL) and chill in low light (LL) treatments after phosphorylation *in vitro*. The molecular masses of marker proteins are given in kDa

The kinetics of fluorescence induction in DCMU-poisoned thylakoids isolated from control, HL-chill and LL-chill treated leaves were measured and values of Fo, Fm, Fv and Fv/Fm determined (Table 1). HL-chill treatment produced a large decrease in Fv/Fm, which when considered in conjunction with the decrease in PS2 electron transport (Fig. 2) and the previously observed decrease in atrazine-binding capacity (3) is indicative of photoinhibitory damage to PS2.

TABLE 1. Effect of protein phosphorylation on fluorescence induction parameters of DCMU-poisoned thylakoids which had been isolated from leaves exposed to control, chill in high light (HL-chill) and chill in low light (LL-chill) treatments.

TREATMENT		Fo	Fm	Fv/Fm
Control	− ATP	2.63 (0.91)	7.82 (1.54)	0.67 (0.06)
	+ ATP	3.83 (1.06)	8.07 (1.40)	0.53 (0.04)
HL-chill	− ATP	0.68 (0.03)	0.96 (0.10)	0.29 (0.04)
	+ ATP	0.68 (0.04)	1.00 (0.05)	0.32 (0.02)
LL-chill	− ATP	3.90 (0.57)	7.56 (1.27)	0.48 (0.01)
	+ ATP	4.18 (0.41)	8.50 (1.40)	0.51 (0.01)

Standard errors of the means of 5 replicates are given

A small decrease in Fv/Fm was observed after LL-chill treatment, however this was attributable to an increase in Fo, not a decrease in Fm. Interestingly LL-chill treatment produced no effect on either the light-limited or saturated rates of PS2 electron transport (Fig. 2), and consequently this decrease in Fv/Fm is not associated with photoinhibition of PS2. Phosphorylation of thylakoid proteins produced the expected decrease in Fv/Fm for control membranes, but had little effect on Fv/Fm of both HL-chill and LL-chill thylakoids (Table 1). This was surprising since LHC2 was heavily phosphorylated in both HL-chill and LL-chill thylakoids (Fig. 1). Clearly LHC2 phosphorylation is not ubiquitously associated with a decrease in Fv/Fm.

Protein phosphorylation was found to reduce both the light-limited and saturated rates of PS2 electron transport in control and LL-chill thylakoids. This was not the case in HL-chill thylakoids were only a small decrease in the light-limited rate and no effect on the light-saturated rate was observed on phosphorylation (Fig. 2), although LHC2 was heavily phosphorylated (Fig . 1)

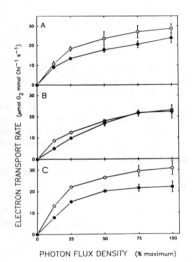

Fig. 2. Photosystem 2 electron transport from water to phenylene diamine as a function of photon flux density for thylakoids isolated from leaves exposed to control (A), chill in high light (B) and chill in low light (C) treatments. Rates are given for non-phosphorylated (O) and phosphorylated (●) thylakoids. Each point represents the mean of 4 replicates.

In order to evaluate the significance of the above data to a possible regulation of electron transport in the leaves, phosphoprotein profiles of thylakoids isolated from plants grown in ^{32}P-orthophosphate and exposed to control, HL-chill and LL-chill treatments were determined (Fig. 3). The phosphoprotein profile of control thylakoids *in vivo* was similar to that found on phosphorylation of membranes *in vitro* (see Fig. 1). This was not the case for HL-chill leaves, whose thylakoids showed no phosphorylation of LHC2, although the PS2 polypeptides were phosphorylated. The absence of phospho-LHC2 in HL-chill leaves *in vivo* supports the contention that phosphorylation of LHC2 is not a mechanism for the alleviation of photoinhibition *in vivo* (8). Interestingly in thylakoids in LL-chill leaves both LHC2 and PS2 polypeptides were more heavily phosphorylated than in control leaves. The significance of this is not clear. Presumably the reduced phosphorylation *in vitro* of PS2 polypeptides in thylakoids isolated from LL-chill leaves (Fig. 1) may be attributable to these polypeptides being heavily phosphorylated prior to incubation of the membranes with ATP.

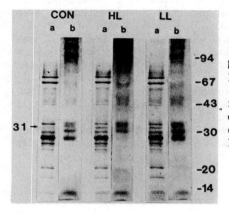

Fig. 3. Polypeptide profiles (tracks labelled a) and their autoradiograms (tracks labelled b) of thylakoid membranes isolated from leaves grown in ^{32}P-orthophosphate and exposed to control, chill in high light (HL) and chill in low light (LL) treatments

These data indicate that chilling maize leaves under both HL and LL does not modify significantly the ability of the isolated thylakoids to phosphorylate LHC2 and PS2 polypeptides, although *in vivo* under HL LHC2 is not phosphorylated. Chilling in HL, but not LL, results in an inability of LHC2 phosphorylation to reduce PS2 electron transport, whilst after chilling in both HL and LL LHC2 phosphorylation does not produce the expected decrease in Fv/Fm. Clearly these two chilling treatments produce different modifications to the membranes which results in changes in the relationships between phosphorylation and the changes it induces in excitation energy distribution to PS2 and PS2 electron transport.

ACKNOWLEDGEMENTS

This work was supported by a grant from the AFRC (AG84/4). J.V. received a fellowship from the Consejo Superior de Investigaciones Científicas.

REFERENCES

1 Barber, J. (1986) Photosynth. Res. 10,243-253
2 Anderson, J.M. (1986) Ann. Rev. Plant Physiol. 37,93-136
3 Percival, M.P., Bradbury, M., Hayden, D.B. and Baker, N.R. (1987) In Progress in Photosynthesis Research (Biggins, J., ed), Vol IV, pp. 47-50. Martinus Nijhoff Publishers, Dordrecht.
4 Hayden, D.B., Covello, P.S. and Baker, N.R. (1988) Photosynth. Res. 15,257-270.
5 Hayden, D.B., Baker, N.R., Percival, M.P. and Beckwith, P.B. (1986) Biochim. Biophys. Acta 851,86-92
6 Allen, J.F. and Holmes, N.G. (1986) In Photosynthesis: Energy Transduction-A practical Approach (Hipkins, M.F. and Baker, N.R., eds) pp.103-141, IRL Press, Oxford.
7 Percival, M.P., Webber, A.N. and Baker, N.R. (1984) Biochim. Biophys. Acta 767,582-589.
8 Demming, B. Cleland, R.E. and Björkman, O. (1987) Planta 172:378-385

CHILLING STRESS AND ACTIVE-OXYGEN ENZYMES IN Zea mays and Zea diploperennis.

Leland S. Jahnke[1], Mark R. Hull and Stephen P. Long Dept. of Biology, Univ. of Essex, Colchester, Essex CO4 3SQ, UK. [1]Permanent address: Dept. of Plant Biology, Univ. of New Hampshire, Durham, NH 03824, USA.

INTRODUCTION

Photosynthesis is one of the first processes affected when chilling-sensitive plants are exposed to chilling temperatures (1,2). The symptoms of chilling damage are particularly pronounced in the presence of light and dioxygen. Many workers have shown that decreasing oxygen partial pressures from air levels produces a significant decrease in the chilling inhibition of photosynthesis (3,4,5,6). This suggests that oxygen is a third stress factor which directly interacts with chilling temperatures and light in producing inhibition of the photosynthetic mechanism.

Photosynthetic organisms have enzymes and anti-oxidant substances to remove most highly reactive forms of oxygen as they are formed (7, 8). The active-oxygen scavenging system in plants consists of five enzymes: superoxide dismutase (SOD), glutathione reductase, dehydroascorbate reductase, monodehydroascorbate reductase, and ascorbate peroxidase (reviewed in 8).

We are looking for correlations between reduced enzyme activity and increased chilling susceptability, at room temperature and low temperatures in these enzymes extracted from chilling sensitive and chilling tolerant species of a single genus Zea, and the enzymic response of these plants to growth at low temperatures. Two Zea genotypes, Zea mays cv. LG11 and Z. diploperennis, known to differ in their susceptibility to chilling dependent photoinhibition were chosen (9).

PROCEDURE

Fourteen day old plants of Z. mays cv.LG11 were grown in a glasshouse. Second leaves were used for enzyme analyses. For enzymes assays, crude extracts were obtained in phosphate buffer using the procedures of (10) adding 5mM diethylene- triaminepentaacetic acid (DTPA). The assays for Ascorbate Peroxidase (11); Monodehydroascorbate Reductase (12); Glutathione Reductase (13); Superoxide Dismutase (14) were modified slightly: 0.2mM DTPA was used in all buffers instead of EDTA. Soluble protein was measured with the Coomassie Blue binding assay of (15).

RESULTS and DISCUSSION

The specific activities of four enzymes were measured at two

M. Baltscheffsky (ed.), Current Research in Photosynthesis, Vol. IV, 683–686.
© 1990 *Kluwer Academic Publishers. Printed in the Netherlands.*

temperatures (Table 1). Enzyme activity at "room temperature" ($19^{\circ}C$) was compared with activity at $5^{\circ}C$. With the exception of SOD which did not show loss of activity, the other enzymes showed significant reductions in specific activity. Ascorbate peroxidases lost from 30 to 40% of its activity. Nevertheless, the total activities of both superoxide dismutase (SOD) and ascorbate peroxidase (APX) are well in excess of likely rates of formation of reduced dioxygen species (reviewed in 8, 16), and that this excess of activity is maintained even at chilling temperatures, and in _Z. diploperennis_, the activities of these two enzymes were approximately double those of _Z. mays_ cv.LG11 (Table 1). This correlates to the markedly greater resistance of the former genotype to photoinhibition under chilling conditions (9).

Table 1. Specific activities (μmol [mg protein]$^{-1}$ h^{-1}) of enzymes involved in scavenging photoreduced species of dioxygen in _Zea mays_ and _Zea diploperennis_ leaves, assayed at 19 and $5^{\circ}C$. The plants had not been chill stressed. Mean values ±SE of triplicate samples are given. Figures in parenthesis indicate the percentage reduction in enzyme specific activity at $5^{\circ}C$ relative to $19^{\circ}C$.

Enzyme	Assay temp.	Z. mays	Z. diploperennis
GLUTATHIONE	$19^{\circ}C$	5.5 ±0.4	4.7 ±0.2
REDUCTASE	$5^{\circ}C$	1.2 ±0.1	1.7 ±0.3
		(78.4%)	(63.4%)
MONODEHYDRO-	$19^{\circ}C$	12.2 ±1.0	10.3 ±0.7
ASCORBATE REDUCTASE	$5^{\circ}C$	4.2 ±0.4	3.5 ±0.4
		(65.5%)	(66.5%)
ASCORBATE	$19^{\circ}C$	52.5±2.1	107.2±4.6
PEROXIDASE	$5^{\circ}C$	32.2±1.4	72.9±6.2
		(38.5%)	(31.9%)
SUPEROXIDE	$19^{\circ}C$	17.2±0.6[a]	39.5±3.3[a]
DISMUTASE	$5^{\circ}C$	15.0±1.3[a]	33.2±2.3[a]
		(13.4%)	(16.0%)

[a] Expressed as Units [mg protein]$^{-1}$ as defined by Beyer and Fridovich (1987).

Total activities of monodehydroascorbate reductase (MDHAR) and glutathione reductase (GTR) (Table 1) were less than the saturated rates of photosynthesis (data not shown), which may serve as an indication of the maximum likely rates of production of reduced dioxygen species. Measured oxygen reduction rates in leaves vary from 3 to 27% of electron transport rates (16).

The effects of chilling ($10^{\circ}C$) during growth on the activity of these enzymes were investigated in _Z. mays_ and _Z. diploperennis_. Nine day old _Z. mays_ and _Z. diploperennis_ plants (grown at $25^{\circ}C$, 340 μmol quanta m^{-2}s^{-1}) were transferred to $10^{\circ}C$, .pa340 μmol quanta m^{-2} s^{-1} (16:8 light:dark cycle). Enzymes were extracted during the middle of each photoperiod and measured at $25^{\circ}C$. Controls were obtained by using parallel samples of leaves maintained at $25^{\circ}C$ throughout. No statistically significant (t, p>0.05) changes in the activities of the four enzymes were observed in leaves of the control plants (i.e.

maintained at 25°C) over the 5 day period (data not shown). On chilling, extractable activities of APX changed minimally (Fig 1A,B).
But, activities of two of the scavenging enzymes are shown to change substantially. Here genotypic differences are apparent. When Z. mays is placed in chilling conditions a significant rise of ca. 60% in the extractable activity of MDHAR is apparent within 8 h, but there is no increase in GTR activity (Fig. 1B). By contrast, in the same experiment Z. diploperennis shows a significant (ca. 80%) increase in GTR activity within 24 h, but a decrease in MDHAR activity over the same period (Fig 1A). These results imply that the two genotypes may make different use of the two pathways for removing the monodehydroascorbate radical.

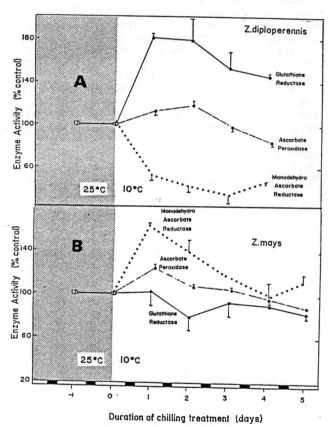

Fig. 1A, 1B. Percentage changes in the specific activity of ascorbate peroxidase, monodehydroascorbate reductase, and glutathione reductase in leaf extracts from chill-exposed Z. diploperennis and Z. mays assayed at 25°C.

REFERENCES:
1. Oquist, G., Greer, D.H., Ogren, E. (1987) In Photoinhibition, pp.67-88, Kyle, D.J., Osmond, C.B., Arntzen, C.J., eds. Elsevier Science Publishers. Amsterdam New York Oxford.
2. Long, S. P. (1983) Pl. Cell and Envir. 6,345-363.
3. Abelovich, A., Shilo, M. (1974) Photochem. Photobiol. 19,379-382.
4. Lindeman, W.(1979) Photosynthetica 13,175-185.
5. Powles, S., Berry J., Bjorkman, O. (1983) Plant Cell and Enivronment 6,117-123 .
6. Rowley J., Taylor, A. (1971) New Phytol. 71,477-481.
7. Halliwell, B. (1984) Chloroplast Metabolism. Revised edition Clarendon Press, Oxford.
8. Asada, K., Takahashi, M. (1987) In: Photoinhibition, pp.227-289.
9. Long, S. P., Nugawela, A., Bongi, G., Farage, P.K. (1987) Progress in photosynthesis research Vol IV, pp. 131-138, Biggins, J., ed. Martinus Nijhoff, Dordrecht, The Netherlands.
10. Foster, J.G., Hess, J.L. (1982) Phytochemistry 21,1527-32.
11. Nakano, Y., Asada, K. (1981) Plant and Cell Physiol. 22,867-880.
12. Hossain, M.A., Nakano, Y., Asada, K. (1984) Plant Cell Physiol. 25,385-395.
13. Schaedle, M., Bassham, J. A. (1977) Plant Physiol. 59,1011-1012.
14. Beyer, W.F., Fridovich, I. (1987) Analytical Biochemistry 161,559-566.
15. Sedmak, J.J., Grossman, S.E. (1978) Analytical Biochemistry. 79,544-552.
16. Badger, M., (1985). Ann. Rev. Plant Physiol. 36,27-53.

LOW TEMPERATURE PERTURBATION OF THYLAKOID PROTEIN METABOLISM DURING MAIZE LEAF DEVELOPMENT

Gui Ying NIE and Neil R. BAKER, Dept. of Biology, University of Essex, Colchester CO4 3SQ, Essex, UK.

1. INTRODUCTION

Low temperatures during the early growing season have long been considered to be a major factor limiting the productive cultivation of maize in temperate regions (1).   We have demonstrated recently that both the light-limited and light-saturated rates of carbon assimilation of mature leaves are severely reduced when maize is grown at $14^{O}C$, compared with $25^{O}C$ (2).   These depressions in photosynthetic abilities induced by low temperature coincided with decreases in PS1 and PS2 photochemical activities and a loss of specific proteins from the thylakoid membranes (2).   The proteins lost appear to be those encoded by the chloroplast genome;   nuclear encoded thylakoid proteins do not seem to be affected as severely by the low temperature stress (2).   It is likely that this imbalance between nuclear and chloroplast encoded proteins in the thylakoids occurring during chloroplast development at low temperatures is associated with the depression of photosynthesis and the consequent decrease in productivity.   Chilling has been shown previously to produce major perturbations of protein metabolism in another chilling-sensitive plant, tomato (3).   In this study we examine some effects of temperature on thylakoid protein metabolism in developing maize leaves grown at 25 and $14^{O}C$.

2. MATERIALS AND METHODS

Plants of maize (<u>Zea mays</u> L. cv. LG11) were grown from seed in controlled environment cabinets at 25 or $14^{O}C$ under a PPFD of 250 µmol m^{-2} s^{-1} and a 16h photoperiod.   Second leaves, which were ca. 50% fully expanded, were used in all experiments.

Leaves were fed ^{35}S-methionine whilst still attached to the plant, essentially using a method previously described (3), except that the whole leaf blade was painted with a solution containing 400 µCi ^{35}S-methionine cm^{-3} (specific activity <800 Ci $mmol^{-1}$) and 0.4% (v/v) Tween 20.   In some experiments this solution was supplemented with cycloheximide (20µg cm^{-3}) or chloramphenicol (200 µg cm^{-3}).   Leaves were labelled in the controlled environment cabinets for 3h. Thylakoids were isolated from mesophyll cells and their polypeptide profiles determined essentially as described previously (4).   Gel tracks were loaded on an equal chlorophyll basis, since the chlorophyll : protein ratios for thylakoids isolated from 25 and $14^{O}C$ grown plants were identical.   Radiolabelled proteins were identified by fluorography at $-70^{O}C$ after gels had been impregnated with Autofluor autoradiographic image enhancer.

M. Baltscheffsky (ed.), Current Research in Photosynthesis, Vol. IV, 687–690.
© 1990 *Kluwer Academic Publishers. Printed in the Netherlands.*

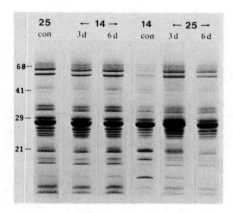

FIGURE 1. Polypeptide profiles of mesophyll thylakoids isolated from leaves grown at 25 (track 1) and $14^{o}C$ (track 4). Profiles are also shown for thylakoids from $25^{o}C$-grown leaves transferred to $14^{o}C$ for 3 (track 2) and 6 days (track 3), and from $14^{o}C$-grown leaves transferred to $25^{o}C$ for 3 (track 5) and 6 days (track 6). Molecular mass markers in kDa are indicated.

3.   RESULTS AND DISCUSSION

Polypeptide profiles of mesophyll thylakoids isolated from maize leaves grown at 25 and $14^{o}C$ exhibit differences; at $14^{o}C$ there is a marked loss of proteins in 55-70, 40-42, 30-34 and 10-14 kDa regions and an accumulation of 3 polypeptide bands between 15 and 22 kDa (Fig. 1).   Transferring $25^{o}C$-grown plants to $14^{o}C$ for a period of 6 days produced no large decreases in the thylakoid polypeptides, although some increased accumulation of polypeptides in the 15-22 kDa range was evident.   These data suggest that the repression of accumulation of thylakoid proteins at $14^{o}C$ is primarily an effect on chloroplast development mediated during the early phases of leaf expansion.   When $14^{o}C$-grown leaves were transferred to $25^{o}C$ a large accumulation of polypeptides in the 10-14, 30-34 and 55-70 kDa ranges occurred;   there was also a loss of the three polypeptides between 15-22 kDa, which

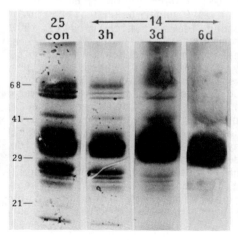

FIGURE 2.   Fluorographs showing thylakoid protein synthesis during a 3h pulse labelling with ^{35}S-methionine in $25^{o}C$-grown leaves at $25^{o}C$ (track 1) and on transfer to $14^{o}C$ for 3h (track 2), 3 days (track 3) and 6 days (track 4).   Molecular mass markers in kDa are indicated.

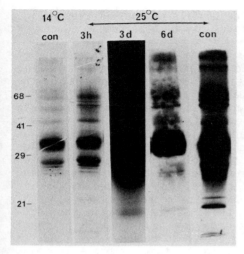

FIGURE 3. Fluorographs showing thylakoid protein synthesis during a 3h pulse labelling with ^{35}S-methionine in 14°C-grown leaves at 14°C (track 1) and on transfer to 25°C for 3h (track 2), 3 days (track 3) and 6 days (track 4). Data for a 25°C-grown leaf at 25°C (track 5) is also shown. Molecular mass markers in kDa are indicated.

accumulated at 14°C (Fig. 1). Clearly 14°C-grown leaves have the ability, on transfer to 25°C, to accumulate many of the thylakoid polypeptides which are lacking at 14°C, although after 6 days at 25°C the polypeptide profile of a 14°C-grown leaf is not identical to that of a 25°C-grown leaf.

When 25°C-grown leaves are transferred to 14°C there is a slight decrease in thylakoid polypeptide synthesis during the first 3h, but the general pattern of synthesis remains essentially similar to that at 25°C (Fig. 2). This suggests that an immediate decrease in leaf temperature to 14°C has no major direct effect on the pattern of thylakoid protein synthesis. However, over 6 days at 14°C, 25°C-grown leaves exhibit a large decrease in polypeptide synthesis except for proteins in the 30-34kDa range. This loss of polypeptide synthesis at 14°C over 6 days is to some extent determined, but is not totally accounted for, by the normal, developmental decrease in protein synthesis with leaf age (data not shown).

The rate of thylakoid protein synthesis in 14°C-grown leaves at 14°C is considerably less than in 25°C-grown leaves at 25°C (Fig. 3). On transferring 14°C-grown plants to 25°C an increase in synthesis is observed in 3h for polypeptides in the 10-24, 42-44 and 55-70 kDa range (Fig. 3). The rate of synthesis of polypeptides in 14°C-grown leaves after 3 days at 25°C increased enormously, as shown by the almost complete blackening of the fluorograph, and was considerably greater than that found in 25°C-grown leaves at 25°C (Fig. 3). After 6 days at 25°C protein synthesis had decreased, except for synthesis of proteins in the 30-34 kDa range (Fig. 3); this is probably indicative of a general decrease in total thylakoid protein synthesis with an increased turnover rate of the 32 kDa D_1 reaction centre protein of PS2. It is of note that the three polypeptides in the 15-22kDa range that accumulate in 14°C-grown leaves (see Fig.1) do not appear to be synthesized de novo, since no major bands in this region appear on the fluorograph of the thylakoid polypeptide profile of these leaves (Fig. 2). This implies that these polypeptides may be breakdown products of higher molecular mass proteins.

It is evident from these studies that a chilling temperature of $14^{\circ}C$ has severe effcts on thylakoid protein metabolism in maize, producing a decrease in the accumulation of many polypeptides in the membrane. This is attributable in part to a decrease in polypeptide synthesis. However, it has been shown that a preferential decrease in the accumulation of many chloroplast encoded, but not nuclear encoded, thylakoid proteins occur at $14^{\circ}C$ compared to at $25^{\circ}C(2)$. Infiltration of $14^{\circ}C$-grown leaves at $14^{\circ}C$ with chloramphenicol and cycloheximide have demonstrated that synthesis of thylakoid proteins can occur on both cytoplasmic and chloroplast ribosomes (data not shown), suggesting that the preferential decrease in chloroplast encoded thylakoid proteins at $14^{\circ}C$ may not be entirely due to decreased synthesis. The accumulation of three polypeptides in the 15-22kDa range in the $14^{\circ}C$-grown leaves, which are not synthesized de novo during a 3h pulse of ^{35}S-methionine at $14^{\circ}C$ and consequently appear to be breakdown products of higher molecular weight proteins, suggests that membrane proteins may be more rapidly degraded at $14^{\circ}C$ than $25^{\circ}C$. Factors involved with stabilization of polypeptides in the thylakoids, as well as polypeptide synthesis, may be involved with this phenomenon at $14^{\circ}C$ and warrant investigation. It is noteworthy also that developing $14^{\circ}C$-grown leaves placed at $25^{\circ}C$ do not attain thylakoid polypeptide profiles similar to $25^{\circ}C$-grown leaves even after 6 days, suggesting that low temperature perturbation of thylakoid protein metabolism cannot easily be overcome when the growth temperature is raised. This could have profound implications for photosynthetic performance of maize leaves that develop at low temperatures, even though they experience increased temperatures at a later date.

ACKNOWLEDGEMENTS
This work was funded by the AFRC (Grant PG84/10). GYN was the recipient of a British Council Scholarship.

REFERENCES
1. Bunting, E.S. and Wiley, L.A. (1957) J. Natn. Inst. Agric. Bot. 8, 364-377.

2. Baker, N.R., Nie, G.Y., Ortiz-Lopez, A., Ort, D.R. and Long, S.P. (1990) in These Proceedings.

3. Cooper, P. and Ort, D.R. (1988) Plant Physiol. 88, 454-461.

4. Hayden, D.B., Baker, N.R., Percival, M.P. and Beckwith, P.B. (1986) Biochim. Biophys. Acta 851, 86-92.

PERTURBATION OF THE MAIZE LIGHT-HARVESTING APPARATUS BY CHILLING

D.A.Campbell, D.B.Hayden, L.B. Johnson, (University of Western Ontario, London, Ontario, N6A 5B7 Canada) & N.R.Baker (University of Essex, Colchester, Essex, C04 3SQ, UK)

Introduction

Chilling maize leaves under high light levels results in the classical symptoms of photoinhibition of PS II related to damage to the D_1 protein (1). Also, a 31 kDa polypeptide accumulates in the thylakoids (2). Maximum accumulation of this polypeptide is achieved at light levels at and above 250 umol m^{-1} s^{-1} at 9°C (3). This chill-induced polypeptide co-extracts with LHC II particles and is immunologically related to the apoprotein of CP 29 (4).

Fluorescence emission spectra at 77K of LHC II particles from chilled leaves indicate that the energetics of the particles is perturbed (4). While the 31 kDa polypeptide present in the LHC II particles from chilled leaves disappears after only 1 hour upon return to non-chilling temperatures, the emission spectra do not return to normal (4).

In this report, we use mildly denaturing gel electrophoresis to examine the various pigment-protein complexes comprising LHC II, during chilling and recovery, in a effort to explain the spectral and other perturbations seen in the thylakoid.

Materials and Methods

Temperature treatment: Maize seedlings were grown at 24 °C, and a PPFD 350 umol photons m^{-2} s^{-1} (16 h/day) for ten days. Plants were shifted from dark to 5 °C, 350 umol m^{-2} s^{-1} for six hours, and then back to growing conditions. Leaves 3 or 4 were radiolabelled on control plants, during the chill and after 1, 24 and 48 h of recovery.

Radiolabelling: Leaves were gently abraded, labelled with 0.37 MBq aliquots of ^{3}H-lysine (NEN) in 0.4 % Tween-20 (Fisher) solution, incubated for 1 h, and then harvested onto ice. Thylakoids were prepared according to (4) and frozen. Labelled chlorophyll-protein complexes were separated by mildly denaturing electrophoresis 'green gels' using a b-octyl glucoside/SDS detergent system (4) or a deoxycholate/SDS detergent system (5).

Two dimensional analysis of chlorophyll-proteins: Light harvesting bands from deoxycholate 'green gels' were incubated in denaturing solution (6), and separated according to Laemmli (7).

Immunoblotting: Polypeptides were electrophoretically transferred from gels to Immobilon (Millipore) using the ABN Polyblot system. Blots were probed with antibodies against CP 29 (MLH2) and the large (ca. 28 kDa) LHC II polypeptide (MLH 1) (8).

M. Baltscheffsky (ed.), Current Research in Photosynthesis, Vol. IV, 691–694.
© 1990 *Kluwer Academic Publishers. Printed in the Netherlands.*

Results & Discussion

Chlorophyll-protein complexes from radiolabelled thylakoids were resolved using two mildly denaturing gel electrophoresis techniques. The first, employing SDS and octyl-glucoside as detergents, resolved three complexes associated with the light-harvesting apparatus of PS II: oligomeric and monomeric forms of the light-harvesting chlorophyll a/b pigment-proteins, and CP 29 (1). As shown in Fig. 1, label incorporation into these LHC II related complexes was markedly affected by the chill treatment.

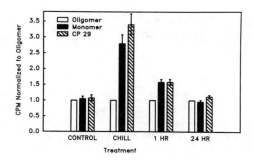

Fig. 1 ^{3}H-Lysine Incorporation Profile of Maize LHC II.
Octyl Glucoside/SDS 'green gel' separation of oligomeric & monomeric LHC II and CP 29 (1). Samples isolated during 5°C chill, after 1 and 24 h of recovery.
Radioactivity normalized to activity in oligomer band. Standard error of 3-5 replicates expressed as error bars.
Absolute incorporation declined to 1/3 control in during chill.

While incorporation into the three bands was approximately equal in control plants, relative incorporation into the oligomer in chilled plants was much reduced compared to the control level. Recovery to control levels was achieved after 24 h at non-chilling temperatures. Throughout the chill & recovery period the relative incorporation of label into the monomer & CP 29 remained approximately equal.

The second mildly denaturing gel electrophoretic technique, employing deoxycholate & SDS as detergents, yields three pigment-protein bands associated with LHC II (2). These are thought to be oligomer, dimer & monomer forms of the light-harvesting chlorophyll a/b pigment-proteins. To confirm the composition of the complexes resolved using this system, the polypeptides contained in the complexes were further denatured, electrophoretically transferred, and probed with antibodies to the major LHC II apoprotein (MLH 1) and the apoprotein of CP 29 (MLH 2) (3). As shown in Figure 2, immunoblotting indicates the presence of the major LHC II polypeptide in the oligomer, dimer and monomer. However, while the dimer and monomer are shown to contain CP 29, it is not apparent in the oligomer.

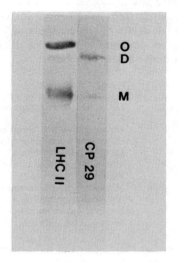

Fig. 2 Immunoblots of Deoxycholate 'Green Gel' of Maize Thylakoids.
Blots probed with antibodies against CP 29 apoprotein (MLH2) and LHC II major subunit apoprotein (MLH 1) (3).

Subsequent analysis of the polypeptides contained in the three complexes excised from the mildly-denaturing deoxycholate gel confirm these observations. In this system, the oligomer contains three polypeptides in the 25-27 kDa range (Fig. 3). The monomer contains a 27 kDa polypeptide, the apoprotein of CP 29, and only a trace of a 25 kDa species. The dimer contains these polypeptides as well as a number of contaminating polypeptides of both higher and lower MW. It is interesting to note that in chilled thylakoids, the 31 kDa polypeptide is present in both the monomer and dimer, paralleling the distribution of the related CP 29 apoprotein (Fig. 3).

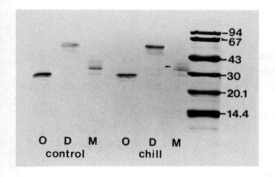

Fig. 3 Two Dimensional Analysis of LHC II Bands Separated on Deoxycholate/SDS 'green gel'.
Polypeptide profiles of oligomer, dimer and monomer forms of LHC II from control and chilled maize.

To avoid error introduced by label contained in the contaminating polypeptides comigrating with the dimer, only the oligomer and monomer were compared in Fig. 4. Consistent with the results shown in Fig. 1, chill stress results in an increase of ^{3}H-lysine incorporation into the monomer relative to the oligomer. Recovery is complete after 24-48 h. The chill-induced shift is not as dramatic as shown in the octyl-glucoside/SDS system, perhaps because the dimer has been omitted.

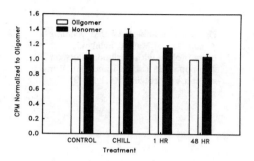

Fig. 4 ^{3}H-Lysine Incorporation Profile of Maize LHC II.
Deoxycholate/SDS 'green gel' separation of oligomeric & monomeric LHC II (2). Samples isolated during 5°C chill, and after 1 and 48 h of recovery. Radioactivity normalized to activity in oligomer band. Standard error of 5-7 replicates expressed as error bars. Absolute incorporation declined to 1/3 control in during chill.

The results in Figures 1 and 5 show that chilling in the light alters the relative incorporation of label into the pigment-protein complexes known to comprise LHC II. While the 31 kDa chill-induced polypeptide described earlier disappears with 1 h of recovery at non-chilling temperatures, the pattern of label incorporation does not return to control levels for 24 h. This time course more closely parallels the recovery seen in other parameters altered by chill stress.

A change in the relative rates of synthesis of even one of the constituent polypeptides could account for these results given that precise stoichiometries are presumably required for the assembly of the various pigment-protein complexes.

The data regarding polypeptide composition of the monomer, dimer and oligomer forms of the LHC II chlorophyll-proteins confirm their heterogeneity. In particular, CP 29 comigrates with dimer and monomer only, as does the 31 kDa polypeptide in chilled thylakoids.

References

1. Percival M.P., M. Bradbury, D.B. Hayden & N.R. Baker (1987) in Prog. Photosyn. Res. (Biggins J., ed.) Vol. 4, pp. 47-50, Martinus Nijhoff, Dordrecht
2. Hayden D.B., N.R. Baker, M.P. Percival & P.B. Beckwith (1986) Biochim. Biophys. Acta 851: 86-92
3. Covello P.S., D.B. Hayden & N.R. Baker (1988) Plant Cell Environ. 11: 481-486
4. Hayden D.B., P.S. Covello & N.R. Baker (1988) Photosynth. Res. 15: 257-270
5. Krol M., N.P.A. Huner, J.P. Williams & E. Maissan (1988) Photosynth Res 15: 115-132
6. O'Farrell P.H. (1975) J. Biol. Chem. 250: 4007-4021
7. Laemmli U.K. (1970) Nature 227: 680-685
8. Darr S.C., S.C. Somerville & C.J. Arntzen (1986) J. Cell Biol. 103:733-740

EFFECTS OF FIRE ON PHOTOSYNTHESIS AND TRANSPIRATION IN A MEDITERRANEAN ECOSYSTEM

FLECK,I., IÑIGUEZ,F.J., DIAZ,C, PASCUAL,M.
DEPARTAMENT DE BIOLOGIA VEGETAL. FACULTAT DE BIOLOGIA.
UNIVERSITAT DE BARCELONA.

1. INTRODUCTION
   This study was undertaken to determine the relationships between the rapid growth of vegetation after fire and the seasonal variations of some physiological factors in resprouts compared with unburnt material. Seasonal photosynthesis and transpiration measurements as well as leaf nitrogen content were conducted during the first post-fire year.

2. PROCEDURE
2.1. Materials and methods
   2.1.1. Plant material: The material studied was Arbutus unedo (evergreen) and Coriaria myrtifolia from a mediterranean-type forest (Quercetum ilicis galloprovinciale arbutetosum) located in Sant Llorenç de Munt, near Barcelona. The two stands chosen were of similar vegetation type, soil type, altitude and slope and measured 20 x 20 m^2 each (control and burnt area).
   2.1.2. Sampling: Samples of mature leaves of both areas were taken in the winter, spring, summer and autumn of the first post-fire year (1987). Fire had occurred in August 1986. Sampling was always carried out at the same time (2 p.m.) to avoid diurnal variations in the parameters. Photosynthesis and transpiration measurements were followed by liquid nitrogen freezing of the leaves and laboratory analysis.
   2.1.3. Methods: Photosynthesis and transpiration rates were measured with a portable A.D.C. Irga- porometer. The number of replicates was at least ten per plant and treatment. Nitrogen content of lyophyllized material was determined with a Carlo Erba Elemental Analyzer.

M. Baltscheffsky (ed.), Current Research in Photosynthesis, Vol. IV, 695–698.
© 1990 *Kluwer Academic Publishers. Printed in the Netherlands.*

3. RESULTS AND DISCUSSION
3.1. Differences in photosynthesis and transpiration during
the first post-fire year were observed between resprouts of the burnt area and control leaves. (Fig. 1 and
2). Resprouts of <u>Arbutus unedo</u> and <u>Coriaria myrtifolia</u>
showed higher rates in hot seasons whereas only slight
differences were observed in winter and autumn. This
effect was not due to ontogenic differences between
control leaves and resprouts since the response pattern was identical in the evergreen and the caducifo+
lia species.
Reports of enhanced photosynthesis have also been described during the first post-fire year in Californian
chaparral (Radosevich et al.,1977; Oechel and Hastings,
1983; Oechel and Reid, 1984).

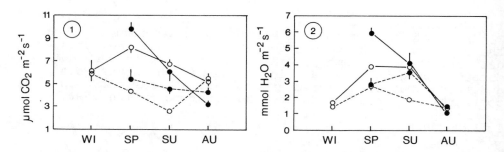

Fig.1 Photosynthesis rates and Fig.2 Transpiration
rates of <u>Arbutus unedo</u> (O) and <u>Coriaria myrtifolia</u>
(●) during the <u>first</u> post-fire year. (——— resprouts, - - - control leaves; WI= winter, SP= spring,
SU= summer, A= autumn).

3.2. Data of the Water Use Efficiency and Relative Water
Content of the leaves studied (Fig. 3 and 4) show
improved water relations of the resprouts. The stability of their water content, especially in hot
months, may account for the observed photosynthesis
enhancement in these leaves (Radosevich and Conard,
1980).

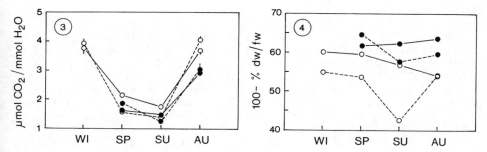

Fig. 3 Water Use Efficiency and Fig. 4 Relative Water Content of <u>Arbutus unedo</u> (O) and <u>Coriaria myrtifolia</u> (●) during the first post-fire year. (——— resprouts, - - - control leaves; WI= winter, SP= spring, SU= summer, AU= autumn).

3.3. Moreover, higher leaf nitrogen content in re-
     sprouts (Fig.5) may also lead to increasing pho-
     tosynthesis (2) by influencing the enzymes of
     photorespiratory and photosynthetic metabolism
     (Apel et al. 1985) or the stochiometry of the
     photorespiration pathway (Hák and Nátr, 1988).

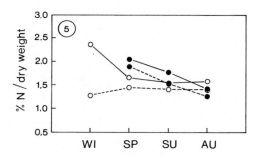

Fig. 5. Nitrogen content of <u>Arbutus unedo</u> (O) and <u>Coriaria myrtifolia</u> (●) during the first post-fire year. (——— resprouts, - - - control leaves; WI= winter, SP= spring, SU= summer, AU= autumn).

REFERENCES
1 Radosevich, S.R., Conard, S.G. and Adams, D.R. (1977) in Proceedings of the symposium on the environmental consequences of fire and fuel management in mediterranean ecosystems (Mooney, H.A., Conrad, C.E., eds) pp 378-382,US Department of Agriculture, Washington D.C.
2 Oechel, W.C. and Hastings, S.J. (1983) in Ecological Studies (Kruger, F.J., Mitchell, D.T. and Jarvis, J.U.M., eds) Vol. 43, pp 274-285, Springer Verlag, Berlin, Heidelberg, New York.
3 Oechel, W.C. and Reid, C.D. (1984). Bull. Soc. bot. Fr. 131, 399-409
4 Radosevich, S.R. and Conard, S.G. (1980) Amer. J. Bot. 67,1442-1447
5 Apel,P., Bauwe,H., Frank,R. and Peisker,M. (1985) Kulturpflanze 33, 41-72
6 Hák,R. and Nátr,L. (1988) Photosynthetica22,335-340

PROTECTIVE EFFECT OF PUTRESCINE AND SPERMIDINE ON THE THYLAKOID
MEMBRANE ACTIVITY AFTER HIGH TEMPERATURE TREATMENT

I.T.Yordanov*, V.Goltsev**, Lidia Kruleva*
Institute of Plant Phisiology, Bulgarian Academy of Sciences,
G.Bontchev str., bl. 21, 1113 Sofia, Bulgaria*
Sofia University, Biological Faculty, 1000 Sofia, Bulgaria**

. INTRODUCTION
Polyamines (PAs) are important factor regulating growth,
iosynthesis of protein, RNA, DNA (1-3) as well as stabilizing
hloroplast thylakoid membranes and retarding chlorophyll loss (4).
olyamine metabolism change may play a role in plant adaptation to
gents inducing biological stress and may serve as a homeostatic
uffering mechanism to stabilize cellular pH in stressed plant cells
1,5). Many of the biological functions of PAs appears to be attributed
o the cationic nature of these molecules, which are highly protonated
t physiological pH (6,7), and their electrostatic interactions with
egatively charged functional groups of membranes and enzymatic or
tructural proteins in the cells (5). Changes in the surface charge
ensity induce considerable conformational alterations and reorganiza-
ions of the pigment-protein complexes (8,9) which are sufficient for
he heat-induced inactivation of photosynthetic activity (10,11).
In this paper we attempted to clear up if two- and threevalent PAs -
utrescine (Put) and spermidine (Spd) exert protective effect on the
hylakoid membrane activity against high temperatures.

. MATERIALS AND METHODS
The experiments were carried out with young bean, Phaseolus vulga-
is L. cv. "Tcheren Starozagorski" plants grown at light flux 35-40 Wm^{-2}
nd temperature 23-26ºC. Three groups of plants were used in experiments:
ontrols (C), grown at 23-26°C, plants acclimated (A) according to our
cheme (12) and non-acclimated (NA) plants, subjected to a single 5h
reatment at 52.5°C.
The chloroplasts were isolated according to (13) and stored in
iquid nitrogen (14). Before the experiment chloroplasts were thawed
nd samples were kept at 0-4°C.
To evaluate the photosystem 2 (PS2) activity the parameters F_0 and
v of prompt fluorescence induction kinetics of leaf discs and isolated
hloroplasts were measured with chlorophyll fluorescence measuring
ystem, PAM (15). The chloroplasts were diluted with 10 mM Tricine buf-
er, pH 7.8, containing 330 mM sorbitol, 5 mM $MgSO_4$ and 1.6 mM of
orresponding PA to 60 µg/ml. The leaf discs were incubated 1h in

1. Baltscheffsky (ed.), Current Research in Photosynthesis, Vol. IV, 699–703.
© 1990 Kluwer Academic Publishers. Printed in the Netherlands.

distillated water or in 10^{-4} M solution of Put or Spd as in (16). Each sample was incubated and darck adapted 3 min (discs p 5 min) in fluorescent chamber at the given temperature. The fluorescence induction kinetics were recorded in the first 10 s of sample irradiation and F_0 and F_m values were determined. The measuring irradiance was 750 nmol $m^{-2}s^{-1}$ and excitation irradiance - 1000 µmol $m^{-2}s^{-1}$.

3. RESULTS AND DISCUSSION

The treatment of leaf discs with the both investigated PAs did not change considerably the induction kinetics pattern and the amplitude of the prompt fluorescence parameters at 25°C (Table 1). Lowered F_v values expressed by the parameters F_v/F_0 and F_v/F_m in NA plants in relation to these in C and A were slightly compensated after an incubation with Spd.

Table 1

Influence of PAs on the F_v/F_0 and F_v/F_m ratio in leaf discs and isolated chloroplasts from control, acclimated and non-acclimated plants

Variants		Leaf discs				Chloroplasts			
		F_v/F_0		F_v/F_m		F_v/F_0		F_v/F_m	
Put		-	+	-	+	-	+	-	+
C		5.69	5.17	0.85	0.84	1.77	3.19	0.64	0.76
A		4.26	4.30	0.81	0.81	3.86	4.85	0.79	0.83
NA		3.44	3.32	0.78	0.77	1.75	2.85	0.64	0.74
Spd		-	+	-	+	-	+	-	+
C		4.67	4.64	0.82	0.82	1.44	3.10	0.59	0.76
A		4.63	4.78	0.82	0.83	2.78	3.68	0.73	0.78
NA		3.96	4.19	0.80	0.81	1.85	2.85	0.64	0.74

Polyamines very strongly influenced the fluorescent parameters of isolated chloroplasts. That was especially characteristic for the parameter F_v/F_0. Put increased it with 80% in chloroplasts from C plants and with 63% - in NA. Analogous was Spd action, increasing the same parameters for these variants with 114% and 54% respectively. In the two cases PAs effect on chloroplasts from A plants was minimum. F_v/F_m changed in a similar way, but it was less sensitive to PAs action the F_v values of thylakoid membranes were relatively low, especially with C and NA plants due to a certain destabilization during their izolation and high temperature stress (14). PAs action compensated partially this instability and was an indication, that the lowered functional activity of thylakoid membranes was probably a result of structural modification (destacing) connected with its increased surface charge. The interaction of PAs with the membrane surface led to their stacking, to a separation of the photosystems and association of LHCP2 with PS2 core complex. The enhance F_v without a considerable change in F_0 was an indication for that.

The incubation of photosynthetic objects at high temperatures led to their inactivation, expressed also as changes in the pattern of the prompt fluorescence induction kinetics - F_O increase and a reciprocal decrease in F_V (17). PAs treatment of the investigated objects did not change the course of F_O temperature dependence, but considerably influenced F_V. The curve of high temperature inactivation of the ratio F_V/F_O (this parameter was the most sensitive to temperature action) was sigmoidal and the temperature of 50% inhibition (T50) indicated the thermostability of the object (Figs. 1,2).

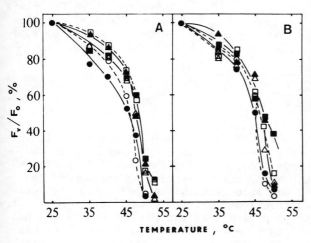

Fig. 1. Temperature dependence of F_V/F_O ratio in leaf discs from control (●,○), acclimated (▲,△) and non-acclimated (■,□) bean plants incubated 1h without (●,▲,■) and with (○,△,□) 10^{-4} M Put (A) and Spd (B).

Chloroplasts isolated from three groups of plants manifested a similar bahaviour to the temperature inactivation, but for A T50 was slightly increased. The addition of Put to chloroplast suspensions before the temperature treatment shifted the thermograms with about 3°C toward higher temperatures for every group of plants (Fig. 2A, Table 2). F_V temperature stability measured of leaf discs was considerably higher in comparison with the same in isolated chloroplasts.

Table 2

Influence of PAs on T50 of F_V/F_O ratio in leaf discs and isolated chloroplasts from C, A and NA plants

Variants	Leaf discs		Chloroplasts		Leaf discs		Chloroplasts	
	-Put	+Put	-Put	+Put	-Spd	+Spd	-Spd	+Spd
C	45.5	45.8	33.3	36.3	47.7	47.0	33.3	37.3
A	47.3	47.5	34.7	37.4	49.5	49.0	35.7	40.1
NA	48.3	48.0	33.7	35.8	50.0	49.0	32.9	36.5

That is why, a longer temperature treatment (5 min) of the objects was necessary. Under this conditions T50 in A plants increased with 1.8°C and 2.8°C respectively (Fig. 1A, Table 2). Leaf discs incubation in PAs solutions did not change considerably the temperature stability of the photosynthetic apparatus   (Fig. 1)

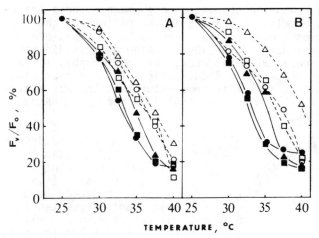

Fig. 2. Temperature dependence of Fv/F$_O$ ratio in
thylakoid membranes from
control (●,o), acclimated
(▲,△) and non-acclimated
(■,□) bean plants suspen-
ded in 10 mM Tricine buf-
fer, pH 7.8, containing
330 mM sorbitol, 5 mM
MgSO$_4$ and 60 μg Chl/ml in
absence (●,▲,■) and pre-
sence 1.6 mM Put (o,△,□)-
(A) and Spd (B).

     Polyamines effect on the thylakoid was predominantly due to its abi-
lity to bind with the negatively charged phospholipid head groups or
other anionic sites of membranes, thus altering the stability and permea
bility characteristics of such membranes. This binding influenced the
fluidity and, in this way PAs was able to modulate indirectly the activities of membrane associated reactions (5). The stabilization manifeste
an increase in both the membrane proton gradient (8) and Fv. It was best
expressed in the destabilized object - thylakoids from C and NA plants
and lower in A. Polyamines did not increase the photochemical activity
in well stacked membranes of intact tissues - leave discs. The membrane
temperature inactivation was prevented to a certain extent by PAs, but
only in the destabilized membranes of izolated chloroplasts and not in
the leaf discs. Probably, the thylakoid membrane in intact cells have
optimum conformatiom, both with regard to their functional activity and
to temperature stability.

REFERENCES
1 Smith,T.A. (1975) Annu.Rev.Plant Physiol. 36, 117-143
2 Bagni,N. (1986) Acta Horticulare 179, 95-103
3 Galsto, A.W, and Kaur-Sawhney,R. (1982) In: Plant Growth Substances
   (Wareing,P.F.,ed.), 451-461, Acad. Press
4 Cohen,A.S. et al. (1979) Plant Physiol. 64, 717-720
5 Slocum,R.D. et al. (1984) Arch.Biochem.Biophys. 235,283-303
6 Kimberly,M.M. and Goldtstein,J.H. (1981) Anal.Chem. 53, 789-793
7 Takeda,J. et al. (1983) Eur.J.Biochem. 130, 383-389
8 Sculley,M.J. et al. (1980) Arch.Biochem.Biophys. 201, 339-346
9 Rubin,B.T. and Barber,J. (1980) Biochim.Biophys. Acta 552, 87-102
10 Larson,U.K. et al. (1987) Biochim.Biophys.Acta 849, 59-68
11 Goltsev,V. et al. (1987) Planta 170, 478-488
12 Yordanov,I. (1981) In: Photosynthesis IV. Photosynthesis and
   Environment (Akoyunoglou,G.,ed.), 379-388, Balaban Sci.Servises
13 Fish,L.E. and Jagendorf,A.T. (1982) Plant Physiol. 70, 1104-1114

14 Yordanov,I. et al. (1987) Planta 170, 471-477
15 Schreiber,U. (1986) Photosynth.Res. 9, 261-272
16 Costa,G. and Bagni,N. (1983) HortSci. 18, 59-61
17 Yordanov,I. and Weis,E. (1984) Z.Pflantzenphysiol. 113, 338-395
18 Yordanov,I. et al. (1989) Photosynthetica, 23, (in press)

TWO SITES OF HEAT-INDUCED DAMAGE TO PHOTOSYSTEM II

David W. Becker, Gretchen Bain, Joanna Norman, Melissa
        Moholt-Siebert, Dept Biology, Pomona College,
        Claremont, CA 91711 USA

Introduction
        The photosynthetic apparatus of plants is particularly
susceptible to damage by exposure to elevated temperatures.
Heat treatment of isolated chloroplasts revealed that
Photosystem II is generally the most heat-labile component,
suffering loss of oxygen evolution capacity (1,2) following
brief (min) exposures to temperatures elevated, but still
experienced by plants in nature (40-50°C). Heat treatment of
intact plant tissue reveals similar alteration of the
photosynthetic apparatus(3,4). In addition to loss of PSII
function, membrane disorganization results in the
disconnection of LHCP from PS II centers (5). Loss of
chloride has been correlated to loss of O_2-evolving capacity
in heated PS II (6,7). Some loss of polypeptides from heated
thylakoid membranes has been reported (8). In addition to
the loss of water-splitting activity, a loss of PSII reaction
center function has also been observed in tissue heated *in
vivo* (3,4) and *in vitro* (1,2,9). The loss of PSII reaction
center function upon heat treatment is generally less severe
than the loss of water-oxidizing capacity. We have been
examining heat effects on PSII in wheat, and can distinguish
kinetically the loss of activity to the water-oxidizing
complex from the loss of reaction center function.
        Virtually all organisms respond to a brief exposure to a
normally damaging temperature or a more prolonged exposure to
elevated but not damaging temperature by synthesizing a small
number of highly conserved proteins, the heat-shock proteins
(10). In plants, several of these nuclear-encoded heat shock
proteins are localized in chloroplasts (11). We have found
that a heat-shock pretreatment confers some protection
against the heat-induced loss of PSII function.

M. Baltscheffsky (ed.), Current Research in Photosynthesis, Vol. IV, 705–708.
© 1990 *Kluwer Academic Publishers. Printed in the Netherlands.*

Wheat (*Triticum vulgare* var. Neeley or TAM 101) was
grown in vermiculite in plant growth chambers at 20°C day/14°C
night, 60% RH, 250 µEin/m^2/s^{-1}. Heat-shock pretreatment
consisted of placing plants in a growth chamber at 35°C for
2 h (60% RH, 100 µEin/m^2/s^{-1}). Control plants were placed in
an otherwise identical chamber at 20°C. Heat treatment was
carried out (in dark) by placing 3 g of 1-2 mm segments of
wheat leaves in beakers containing 20 ml of 20 mM tricine,
1 mM NaCl, pH 7.5. The heat treatment beakers and buffer
were pre-equilibrated in a water bath at the desired
temperature. Following the time of heat treatment, the
beakers were placed on ice and chloroplasts were isolated
(12) for assays of photosynthetic activity. Oxygen evolution
or uptake was measured polarographically with a Clark type
electrode in a 20°C reaction vessel at saturating or with sub-
saturating (neutral density filters), heat-filtered, red
light.   PSII reaction center function was measured
spectrophotometrically as the NH$_2$OH-dependent photoreduction
of DCIP. Light-limiting conditions were employed.

Results
        We observe no change in PSI activity in chloroplasts
isolated from heat-treated leaf segments, even at 50°C for 20
minutes. However, loss of oxygen evolution capacity is rapid
and dependent on the temperture and time of treatment (Figure
1). The damage at 50°C is complete in about 3 min of
treatment, while lower temperatures exert a slower
inactivation of the water-oxidizing capacity of PSII. Light
saturation studies of chloroplasts isolated from leaf
segments treated at 50°C for 0, 30 and 60 sec revealed that
the quantum yield declined for the heat-damaged samples but
that the saturated rate of oxygen evolution also declined.
The decrease in quantum yield is evidence of heat-induced
disconnection of LHCP from the PSII centers (5), resulting in
less efficient centers. The lower light-saturated rates in
the heat-treated samples (demonstrating 0, 35 and 75%
inhibition for the 0, 30 and 60 sec treatments, respectively)
indicate that in addition to the decrease in efficiency,
there is a decline in the number of functional centers.
        PSII donor activity also demonstrates a decline which is
dependent on temperature and time of treatment (Fig 2). A
comparison of the intial slopes of the curves in Fig 2 and
Fig 1 reveals that the rate of loss of PSII reaction center

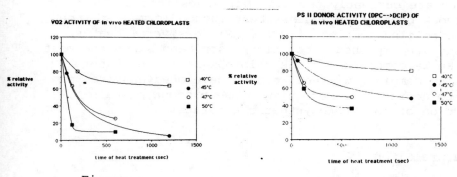

Figure 1.   Figure 2.

function is slower that the loss of water-oxidation capacity
at a given temperature. Additionally, the extent of loss of
PSII donor activity is less than the loss of oxygen
evolution. Thus there are at least two heat-induced sites of
damage in PSII: the water-oxidizing complex is inactivated
first and more completely, followed by the less extensive
inhibition of PSII reaction center. We are currently probing
further into the precise site(s) within the PSII reaction
center that is impaired by heat treatment.

Preliminary results demonstrate that a heat-shock
pretreatment (35°C for two hours in light) confers significant
protection against the heat-induced damage to the water-
oxidizing comples of PSII (Fig 3). In the experiment of
Figure 3 the heat-shock pretreatment provides 60% and 40%
protection against treatments for 2 and 10 min, respectively,
at 47°C.

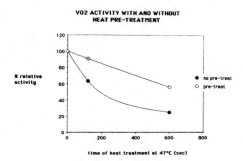

Figure 3.

We are currently pursuing our investigation into the heat-shock protection against heat-induced damage to the water-oxidizing complex of PSII. Since several heat-shock proteins are imported into chlorplasts, and since the most heat-labile component of the chloroplast is the water-splitting complex, we feel we have developed a system in which to address the mechanism of heat-shock protein protection of the photosynthetic apparatus.

Literature Cited

1. Katoh S, A San Pietro 1967 Arch Biochem Biophys 122: 144-152
2. Yamashita T, WL Butler 1968 Plant Physiol 43: 2037-2040
3. Mohanty N, SDS Murthy, P Mohanty 1987   Photosyn Res 14: 259-237
4. Al-Khatib K, GM Paulsen 1989 Plant Physiol 90: 1041-1048
5. Armond PA, O Bjorkman, LA Staehelin 1980 Biochim Biophys Acta 601: 433-442
6. Critchley C, RK Chopra 1988 Photosyn Res 15: 143-152
7. Coleman WJ, Govindjee, HS Gutowsky 1988 Photosyn Res 16: 261-276
8. Volger H, KA Santarius 1981 Physiol Plant 51: 195-200
9. Inoue H, T Kitamura, M Noguchi 1987 Physiol Plant 71: 441-447
10. Lindquist S 1986 Annu Rev Biochem 55: 1151-1191
11. Vierling E, ML Mishkind, GW Schmidt, JL Key 1986 Proc Natl Acad Sci, USA 83: 361-365
12. Callahan FC, GM Cheniae 1985 Plant Physiol 82: 261-269.

LIGHT REGULATION OF THE 22 KD HEAT-SHOCK PROTEIN IN
CHLAMYDOMONAS REINHARDTII

Dvorah Ish-Shalom, Anton Post, Klaus Kloppstech* and Itzhak Ohad
Dept of Biological Chemistry, The Hebrew University, Jerusalem, Israel and
*Institüt für Botanik, Universitat Hannover, Hannover, FRG

1.INTRODUCTION

Heat shock genes are specific genes which are turned on by sublethal temperature elevation. Heat shock proteins (HSPs) have been detected in every organism investigated so far (1). We and others have reported before that during heat shock, specific nuclear coded HSPs are transported into the chloroplast (2,3). One such protein is the 22 kD HSP of *Chlamydomonas reinhardtii*, which is localized in the grana thylakoids. As suggested by Schuster et al. (4) HSP 22 may prevent light damage to the photosystem II reaction center during heat shock. Our present work investigates the effects of light and the effect of the physiological state of the chloroplast on the regulation of the HS 22 gene.

2. RESULTS AND DISCUSSION

2.1. Heat shock at different light intensities

The photosynthetic electron flow, probed by variable fluorescence [(Fm-Fo)/Fo], was measured during heat shock of cells at different light intensities. Variable fluorescence was significantly reduced in cells exposed to heat shock at 2.5 or 5 Wm^{-2} (*Fig. 1*). Measurements of variable fluorescence during heat shock at 35 Wm^{-2} showed reduction during the first hour, followed by a transient recovery during the following 1.5-2.5 hours. This transient recovery previously termed "partial protection" (4) correlated with the appearance of HSP 22 as demonstrated by immunoblotting. The effect of light on the induction of HSP 22 was clear with an apparent threshold of ~ 10 Wm^{-2}.

In order to detect the step in which

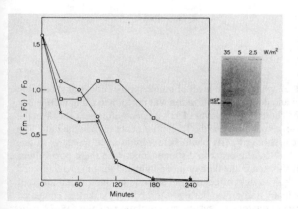

Fig. 1. Effect of different light intensities during heat shock on photosynthetic electron flow as correlated with the presence of HSP 22.
Cells were heat shocked for 4 hours at (x) 2.5 Wm^{-2}; (o) 5 Wm^{-2} and (□) 35 Wm^{-2}. Photosynthetic electron flow probed by variable fluorescence was measured at the times indicated (4). The right panel shows immunoblot (using anti HSP) of thylakoids prepared from the various samples after 4 hours of heat shock.

M. Baltscheffsky (ed.), Current Research in Photosynthesis, Vol. IV, 709–712.
© 1990 *Kluwer Academic Publishers. Printed in the Netherlands.*

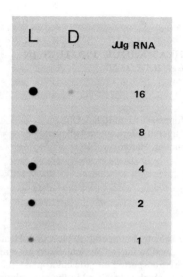

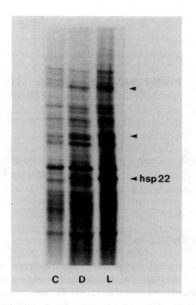

Fig. 2. Transcript level of HS 22 gene after heat shock in the light (L) or in the dark (D). Cells were heat shocked (42°C, 2 h) either in the light (10 Wm⁻²) or in the dark. After heat shock cells were harvested and total RNA was prepared as described (Chirgwin et al. Biochem. 18, 5294-5299). Different amounts of RNA were applied to a nitrocellulose filter using a dot blot apparatus. The immobilized RNA was probed with ^{32}P - labeled HS 22 cDNA clone. After hybridization and washing the dried filters were exposed to X-ray film.

Fig. 3. In vitro translation of poly (A)-rich RNA from control cells or light (L) and dark (D) heat shocked cells. Cells were heat shocked (42 °C, 2 h) either in the light (10 Wm⁻²) or in the dark. Control cells were induced at 25 °C, 10 Wm⁻². Poly (A)-rich RNA was prepared and translated in vitro (3). Arrows indicate 3 different heat shock proteins.

light interferes with the heat induction of HSP 22 we tested the level of transcript for cells heat shocked in light and dark. Poly(A)-rich RNA was isolated and dot blot hybridization was performed using pCHS62-a cDNA clone of HS 22 (5) as a probe (Fig. 2). The transcript level of HS 22 gene after heat shock in the dark is dramatically lower (15-20 fold decrease) as compared to the level after heat shock in the light. The reduced amount of transcript in the dark heat shocked cells could be common to all mRNAs in this condition or it could be specific for the HS 22 mRNA. In order to distinguish between these possibilities poly(A)-rich RNA was isolated from cells heat shocked in the dark or in the light and the in vitro translated products were analyzed by SDS-PAGE (Fig. 3). The light effect did not seem to be due to total arrest of RNA synthesis since two other HSPs were efficiently transcribed during heat shock in the dark as compared to heat shock in the light. Thus, light has a regulatory effect on accumulation of the HS 22 gene transcript.

The preferential translational expression of HS 22 mRNA at elevated temperatures that was demonstrated before (6) was confirmed for HS 22 mRNA that was induced either in the light or in the dark (data not shown). The resistance of HS 22 mRNA to translational inhibition by small cytosolic RNA (7) was also common to RNAs induced both in the light and in the dark. These results suggested that mRNAs induced in the dark or in the light did not differ in their translational properties.

2.2. Induction of HSP 22 during chloroplast development

Chlamydomonas reinhardtii (y-1) cells have been found to be particularly useful for investigating chloroplast participation in the biosynthesis of the photosynthetic apparatus. This is because chlorophyll synthesis in these cells is totally light dependent (8). Growth of these cells in the dark produces cells containing a plastid that lacks photosynthetic membranes (8). Membrane development can be induced by illumination of dark grown cells (9), a process named greening. Since HSP 22 is localized in the grana and believed to be involved in protection of photosystem II activity during heat shock in the light (5) it was interesting to study the accumulation of HSP 22 after heat shock at different stages of greening. Cells were grown in the dark for 5 days after which yellow cells were transferred to the light. Samples were taken at different time intervals during the greening process and were subsequently heat shocked for 1.5 hour (42 °C, 10 Wm^{-2}). As shown in Fig. 4 HSP 22 was not induced in either yellow cells or cells after 1.5 hours of greening. After 3 hours of greening, when chlorophyll concentration was apparently unchanged, the photosynthetic activity probed by fluorescence induction started to rise. At this stage induction of HSP 22 was observed. It is still unclear whether transcription and/or translation of the protein was blocked in yellow cells. Chloramphenicol added to the cells during greening blocked the repair of the photosynthetic activity and inhibited the induction of HSP 22 (data not shown). Plastid derived factors controlling transcription of nuclear genes have been described before (9,10). Such a factor, which is presumably light regulated, may affect the level of induction of the HSP 22 at the nucleus.

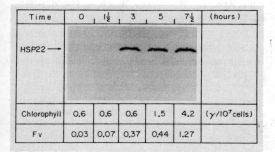

Time	0	1½	3	5	7½	(hours)
HSP22 →						
Chlorophyll	0.6	0.6	0.6	1.5	4.2	($\gamma/10^7$cells)
Fv	0.03	0.07	0.37	0.44	1.27	

Fig. 4. Induction of HSP 22 during greening. Cells were grown in the dark for 5 days (degreening). Yellow cells were exposed to light for the time indicated and subsequently heat shocked for 2 hours (42 °C, 10 Wm^{-2}). Thylakoids were isolated and fractionated by SDS-PAGE followed by immunodecoration with anti-HSP 22.

3. CONCLUSIONS

- The results presented indicate that the expression of the HS 22 nuclear gene is light dependent.

- Accumulation of HS 22 transcript is light dependent.

- Translational regulation of the HSP 22 is the same in light and dark.

- Induction of the HS 22 gene by heat is dependent on the physiological state of the chloroplast.

4. ACKNOWLEDGEMENTS

The work presented here was supported by a grant awarded by the Deutsche Forschungsgemeinschaft and by a grant awarded by the National Council for Research and Development Joint German-Israel Program in Biotechnology.

REFERENCES

1 Kelly, P. and Schlesinger, M.J. (1978) Cell 15, 1277-1286
2 Vierling, E., Mishkind, M.L., Schmidt, G.W. and Key, J.L. (1986) Proc. Natl. Acad. Sci. 83, 361-365
3 Kloppstech, K., Meyer, G., Schuster, G. and Ohad, I. (1985) EMBO J. 4, 1901-1909
4 Schuster, G., Even, D., Kloppstech, K. and Ohad, I. (1988) EMBO J. 7, 1-6
5 Grimm, B., Ish-Shalom, D., Even, D., Glaczinski, H., Ottersbach, P. and Ohad, I. (1989) Eur. J. Biochem. (in press)
6 Kloppstech, K. and Ohad, I. (1986) Eur. J. Biochem. 154, 63-68
7 Kloppstech, K., Lorberbaum, H., De Groot, N. and Hochberg A. (1987) Eur. J. Biochem. 155: 501-505
8 Ohad, I., Siekevitz, P. and Palade, G.E. (1967) J. Cell Biol. 35, 521-552
9 Ohad, I., Siekevitz, P. and Palade, G.E. (1967) J. Cell Biol. 35, 553-584
10 Batschauer, A., Mosinger, E., Kreuz, K., Dorr, I. and Apel, K. (1986) Eur J. Biochem. 154, 625-634
11 Burgess, D.G. and Taylor, W.C. (1988) Mol. Gen. Genet. 214, 89-96

RESPONSES OF SOME PHOTOSYNTETIC PARAMETERS IN C_3 AND C_4 CROP PLANTS UNDER WATER DEFICIT

M. Castrillo, D. Fernández, A.M. Calcagno and I. Trujillo
Dept. Biología de Organismos. Universidad Simón Bolívar. Aptdo. Postal 89000, Caracas 1080 A. Venezuela

1. INTRODUCTION

Some authors(1) concluded that photosynthesis at low Ψ_w was more limited by the loss of chloroplast activity than by increased difussive resistance. RBPC activity decreased in bean and cotton plants at water stress(2)(3)(4). PEPC and RBPC activities decreased at water stress in barley plants(5). In mesophyll cells from bean and tomato plants there was decreased in CO_2 fixation at fairly low osmotic potentials which simultaneous with stomatal closure(6). Recently it was reported(7) that in soybean leaves a non stomatal limitations of leaf photosynthesis under drought stress conditions appears to be due in part to a reduction in the in vivo activity of RBPC. On the other hand it has been reported that chlorophyll content(8)(9)(10) shows alterations due to water stress. In the present work we pretend to compare the responses of carboxylase activities and chlorophyl content to water deficit in two maize hybrids (C_4)(CPB2 and CPB8), two tomato cultivars (C_3)(Pera Quibor, PQ and Río Grande, RG) and two bean cultivars (C_3)(Tacarigua,T and VUL-73-401,V).

2. PROCEDURE

2.1.Materials and methods

  2.1.1.Plant Material:Seeds of two selected hybrids of maize(CPB2 and CPB8), two selected cultivars of beans (T and V) and two selected cultivars of tomato (PQ and RG) were used in this work. After germination, the seedlings were transferred to 5 l plastic pots (one plant per pot) except for tomato, where the seedlings were transferred to sand, and at the appearance of the cotyledons, the plants were as transferred as above indicated. The plants were mantained in a greenhouse. A thirty five days of average age the plants were used for experiments. Watering was witheld from 30-40 plants (water stressed plants) and another 30-40 plants were watered and mantained as control. Measurements were taken at 2-3 days intervals during a period of 2-3 weeks, using the third leaf from the apex of four replicates. All measurements were made on each replicated. A set of four replicates were used at each day-interval of measurements. The replicates were used to measure all parameters Ψ_w, Ψ_s, RWC, RBPC activity and PEPC activity (only in maize) and chlorophyl content.

  2.1.2.Water potential(Ψ_w), osmotic potential(Ψ_s), and relative water content(RWC): All measurements were made at predawn time. for Ψ_w measurements leaf discs of maize and bean from 4 replicates

M. Baltscheffsky (ed.), Current Research in Photosynthesis, Vol. IV, 713–716.
© 1990 *Kluwer Academic Publishers. Printed in the Netherlands.*

were measured in HR-33T Dew Point microvoltimeter using C-52
chambers, leaflets of tomato from 4 replicates were measured
using a L-44 sealed chambers (Wescor, Inc.). After measuring
the Ψ_w the leaf discs were frozen in liquid nitrogen and Ψ_s
was measured in the expressed sap using the HR-33T Dew Point
microvoltimeter attached to C-52 chamber (Wescor Inc.) The
method of Turner(1981)(11)was followed for RWC determinations.

2.1.3. <u>Leaf extraction</u>: The extraction medium contained 0.2 M. Tricine-NaOH, 20mM $MgCl_2$, 10mM $NaHCO_3$, 0.2mM Na-EDTA, 20m 2M-Mer-
captoethanol, $16g.l^{-1}$ PVPP at pH 8.3. Magnesium and bicarbonate were included in the extraction medium to obtain an
activated RBPC form(12). Illuminated leaves were used for
extraction and assays in order to obtain appropiate conditions
for enzyme activity assays (13)(14). Leaves without midvein
were ground in a mortar (1:5w/v). The homogenate was filtered
through 4 layers of muslin. The filtrate (leaf extract) was
kept a 0°C and used for assay and determinations. Leaf extraction and assays were performed at midday (13:00)(13).

2.1.4. <u>RBPC(EC 4.1.1.39) Assay</u>: The reaction medium contained, in a
final volume of 170µl: 150mM Tricine-NaOH, pH 8.2; 25mM $MgCl_2$;
50mM 2-ME; 2mM RuBP; 16mM $NaH^{14}CO_3$(3.7MBq/mmol, Amersham)(15).

2.1.5. <u>PEPC(EC 4.1.1.31)Assay</u>: The reaction medium contained in a
final volume of 170µl: 150mM Tricine-NaOH pH 8.2; 25mM $MgCl_2$;
50mM 2-ME; 6mM PEP; 6mM sodiumglutamate; 15mM $NaHCO_3$(3MBq/mmol,
Amersham)(15). All assays were performed within 5 to 15 min
after extraction. The reactions were performed at 27°C and
started with the addition of 30µl of leaf extract and was
allowed to run for 1min, after which they were stopped with
200µl 25% acetic acid. Radioactivity incorporated into the
acid-stable fraction was counted in a scintillation counter
(Packard Tricarb 3385). Calculations of the specific radioactivity took into account the $NaHCO_3$ brought into the reaction
mixture from the enzyme aliquot fraction.

2.1.6. Chlorophyll determination was undertaken according to Bruinsma
(1963)(16).

2.1.7. Statistic analysis. The Spearman rank correlation was used for
correlations (17).

3. RESULTS AND DISCUSSION

The minimum values of Ψ_w and Ψ_c reached by the water stressed plants
during the water deficit period are shown in Table 1. The activity of
RBPC expressed as percentaje of control plants decreased up to 58% for
PQ cv and 50% por RG cv tomato plants; up to 20% for T cv and 18% for V
cv bean plants and up to 60% for CPB2 and CPB8 hybrids of maize plants.
The PEPC activity expressed as percentaje of control plants decreased up
to 58% for CPB2 and up to 70% for CPB8 hybrids. The chlorophyll content
expressed as percentaje of control plants showed a decrease up to 90%
for PQ cv and 76% for RG cv of tomato plants; for beans plants the
decrease was up to 36% for T cv and 28% for V cv and for maize plants
the decrease was up to 62% for CPB2 and up to 80% for CPB8 hybrids.

TABLE 1. Minimum values of Ψ_W and Ψ_S reached by the water stressed plants.

Hybrid/cultivar		Ψ_W (MPa)	Ψ_S (MPa)
Maize (C$_4$)	CPB2	-1.58	-1.60
	CPB8	-1.98	-2.00
Tomato (C$_3$)	RG	-2.16	-2.30
	PQ	-2.45	-2.50
Bean (C$_3$)	T	-1.40	-1.45
	V	-2.20	-2.25

TABLE 2. Correlations among Ψ_W, Ψ_S, RWC and RBPC and PEPC activities and chlorophyll content in water stressed plants of two maize (C$_4$) hybrids (CPB2 and CPB8), two tomato cultivars (C$_3$)(PQ and RG) and two bean cultivars (C$_3$) (T and V). Spearman coefficient is significantly different (=0.05).

Measured Parameter	Hybrid/cultivar		Ψ_W (MPa)	Ψ_S (MPa)	RCW (%)
Chlorophyll content (g.kg^{-1}DW)	maize (C$_4$)	CPB2	0.71*	0.87*	0.86*
		CPB8	0.70*	0.40*	0.88*
	tomato (C$_3$)	RG	0.42*	0.34	0.41
		PQ	0.22	0.69*	0.26
	bean (C$_3$)	T	0.86*	0.89*	0.86*
		V	0.75*	0.71*	0.81*
RPBC activity (molCO$_2$ kg^{-1}DW.h^{-1})	maize (C$_4$)	CPB2	0.04	0.65*	0.45
		CPB8	0.40	0.64*	0.67*
	tomato (C$_3$)	RG	0.50*	0.50*	0.58*
		PQ	0.78*	0.87*	0.83*
	bean (C$_3$)	T	0.90*	0.79*	0.87*
		V	0.90*	0.92*	0.91*
PEPC activity (molCO$_2$ kg^{-1}DW.h^{-1})	maize (C$_4$)	CPB2	0.47	0.77*	0.49*
		CPB8	0.44*	0.55*	0.32*

The correlation coefficients among physiological variables and leaf water components in water stressed plants is shown in Table 2. The chlorophyll content was positively correlated with Ψ_W, Ψ_S and RWC in both hybrid of maize (C$_4$) and both bean cultivars, showing that it was not possible to establish any difference between photosyntetic group of plants. The RPBC activity was positively correlated with Ψ_W, Ψ_S and RWC

in C_3 plants; while in maize (C_4) was only Ψ_S. PEPC activity in maize
was correlated with Ψ_W, Ψ_S and RWC in CPB8 hybrid and with Ψ_S, and RWC in
CPB2 hybrid. The effects of water deficit in plants on the carboxylase
activities has been reported (2)(3)(4)(5)(7). Some authors (18) have
concluded that in plants under water deficit the Ψ_S decreases by
increase of solute concentration, which will be the cause of enzyme
inhibition. Kaiser(1987)(19) concluded that the concentration of some
critical anions could cause inhibition of RBPC. The above could be
associated with the observed decrease in enzyme activities correlated
with the decreased Ψ_S, although it is not known wether that anion
inhibition would persist in the enzyme activity measured in vitro unless
it is irreversible. The observed decrease in enzymes activities could be
due as well to a decrease in protein content (data no shown). Maize
plants (C_4) showed a significant positive correlation of RBPC, PEPC and
chlorophyll content with Ψ_S. Bean and tomato plants showed significantly
positive correlation of RBPC with Ψ_S in C_3 and C_4 plants could be due to
that the decreased Ψ_S, effects on enzyme activities and/or protein
content, but this effects could be more effective on the enzymes
involved in the C_4 plants.

Seeds were supplied by FONAIAP (Venezuelan National Fund for Agriculture and Animal Husbandry, Maracay, Venezuela). Financial support was
provided by CONICIT (Venezuelan Council for Science and Technological
Research). Project S1-1325 and by Decanato de Investigaciones, Universidad Simón Bolívar.

REFERENCES
1 Matheus M.A. and Boyer J.S.(1984) Physiol Plant 57.21-6
2 O'Toole J.C., Ozbun J.L. and Wallace D.H.(1977) Physiol Plant 40,111-4
3 O'Toole J.C., Crookston R.K., Treharne K.J. and Ozbun J.L.(1976) Plant
    Physiol.57.465-68
4 Jones H.G.(1973).New Phytol.72,1095-1101
5 Huffaker R.C., Radin T., Kleinkopf G.E. and Cox E.L.(1970).Crop Sci.
    10.471-74
6 Mawson B.T. and Coleman B.(1983).Physiol Plant. 57,21-27
7 Vu J.C.V., Allen L.H. Jr. and Bowes G.(1987).Plant Physiol.83,573-78
8 Maranville J.W. and Paulsen G.M.(1970) Agron. Jr. 62,605-08
9 Haspel-Horvatovic E. and Holubkova B.(1981).Phytopath Z. 100,340-46
10 Kao C.H.(1981)Plant Cell Physiol. 22,683-88
11 Turner N.C.(1981) Plant Soil 58, 339-66
12 Lorimer T.J.(1976) Biochemistry 15, 529-36
13 Servaites J.C., Parry M.A.J., Gutteridge S. and Keys A.(1986) Plant
    Physiol 82,1161-63
14 Doncaster H.D. and Leegood R.C.(1978) Plant Physiol.84,82-7
15 Castrillo M.(1978)D.Phil. Thesis. Botany Dept. Oxford University
16 Bruinsma J.(1983) Photochem. Photobiol. 2,241-49
17 Sokal R.R. and Rohlf F.J.(1981).Biometry.V.H.Freeman Co.S.Francisco
18 Kaiser W.M., Schroppel Meir G. and Wirth E.(1986) Planta 167,292-99
19 Kaiser W.M.(1978)Physiol Plant. 71, 142-49

A gas exchange procedure to evaluate non uniform stomatal
closure effects in single mesophyte evergreen leaves under
high vpd.

Guido BONGI, C.N.R. Centro Studi Olivicoltura, Madonna
Alta, 06100 Perugia, Italy.

1. INTRODUCTION
     Under stresses involving ABA it has been found
heterogeneous opening of stomata and heterogeneous CO_2
conductance (1, 2). Probably stomata acting as primary
target of this type of stress behave indipendently of
photosynthetic sites. This evenience produces large
variations in substomatal CO_2 partial pressure, p_i.
The slope of assimilation rate relationship with
conductance diminishes markedly in high conductances,
because the relationship between carboxylation and p_i is a
biphasic non rectangular hyperbola. This slope effect tends
to be great if very high conductances (g) and high
photosynthetic fluxes (A) are involved; leaf water
conductance and nitrogen density are potentially involved
in creating more or less pronounced effects on p_i
determinations.
     CO_2 p_i, is obtained from gas exchange collection of
mean values of A and g; in heterogenous conditions even the
notion of a mean value of p_i is without sense unless
knowing individual values and distribution of A and g
throught stomata. In a bimodal distribution no part of the
leaf is in the conditions of the mean.
The imaging of non photochemical quenching, qe, as been
developed (3), because it is related in part to ATP
production and hence to electron transport rate, J. In CO_2
pressures below the ambient J of a C3 plants is
potentially higher than carboxylation rate and J tends to
increase according to CO_2 p_i (4); within these conditions
qe senses p_i. Problems can be raised in hypostomatous
leaves, where it is usually seen the side without stomata
and in thick mesophyte evergreens a large part of the leaf
is receiving low light fluxes.
     Terashima (1) used O2 evolution in high CO_2 as check
for the existance of diffusional barriers and this approach
seems still now less affected from artifacts; we tried to
quantitate the significance of diffusional heterogeneity
using the same principle. We however subjected single
leaves to low humidity air and this fact generated an high
leaf-air H2O vapour pressure deficit (vpd). To mantain the

M. Baltscheffsky (ed.), Current Research in Photosynthesis, Vol. IV, 717–720.
© 1990 Kluwer Academic Publishers. Printed in the Netherlands.

condition in O2 evolution we had to develop a technique on attached leaves.

2. PROCEDURE

Intact leaves of mesophyte evergreens were clamped in a gas exchange cuvette with an inner volume of .6 mL and a surface of 6 cm2 was exposed to gas exchange. A small volume closed circuit comprising a micropump (LCA2-3/7 ADC, Hoddeston UK), micro valves and the body of an leaf segment O2 electrode (LD2 Hansatech, King's Linn, Norfolk UK) allowed O2 exchange measurements ; 8% CO2 was circulated when the system was set in this mode. Volume calibration was done increasing the pressure trought a T arm. Otherwise a open gas exchange system for CO2 and H2O was operating in the same cuvette and gas exchange parameters were calculated on line using a microcomputer and the procedure of S. von Caemmerer and G.D. Farquhar (5). Before and during stress were collected A(230 p_i), A(800 p_i) and electron transport rate, J. J was taken as O2 evolution rate x 4 in 8% CO2. We extimate a potential assimilation rate from J and NADPH limitation at pi of 800 ubar by modelling a potential photosynthetic flux as Am $= J(p_i - \Gamma^*)/(4p_i + 8\Gamma^*)$ - Rd, where eventually Γ^* and Rd can be evaluated by gas exchange on the same apparatus (6). Within these constraints we can compare Am values scaled to the Am of control and this should give the metabolic effect of the stress. The same comparison between CO2 gas exchange actual rates includes diffusional heterogeneity and one can quantitate its relative effect.

3. RESULTS and DISCUSSION

It this preliminary report we show only partial results obtained under high vpd (26 mbar bar-1, 28°C) condition wich generates p_i and conductance decrease. It does involve a feed foreward response of stomata to water vapour and differences in turgor pressure of epidermis and mesophyll have been observed; it is not clear were around stomata is located the water loss site but stomatal transpiration can modify localized water potentials and leaf metabolism via the ABA route. Stomatal heterogeneity can thus be produced. High vpd generated heterogeneous stomatal closure in Olive, Pistachio and Ilex, but the effect tended to vanish with progress in time. In Ilex there was the possibility of a persistance longer than 200 min (Tab 1).

TABLE 1. Effects of high vpd (26 mbar bar-1) on A at
230 p_i or in 8% CO2 ; # indicate signifiant differences
between Am relative decrease (Am/x) and A relative
decrease (x/A) and hence an high possibility of
heterogeneous stomatal closure.

time	t(20 min)	t(50 min)	t(200 min)
Olive (hom hyp)	-.15/-.29#	-.13/-.14	-.10/-.10
Pistachio (hom amp)	-.20/-.28#	-.17/-.17	-.16/-.16
Ilex (het hyp)	-.18/-.56#	-.16/-.30#	-.14/-.20#

The effects of vpd on A at 800 pi were much less evident
that at ambient CO2: this open a question wich involves or
larger heterogeneities at low CO2 or, perhaps more
probably, the existance of a transient diffusional barrier
internal to the mesophyll.

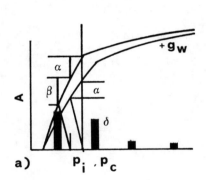 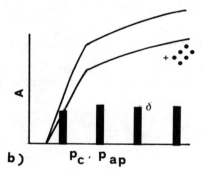

FIGURE 1.
.a) Model of an A-p_i,-p_C response (p_C is CO2 partial
pressure in chloroplasts) in presence of an internal
diffusive barrier g_{wl} of .150 mol m-2 s-1. The model
was obtained using a Rubisco activity of 90 umol m-2 s-
1 in relationships already published (6). α represent
the lowering of A due to stomata and ß is the lowering
throught internal walls; δ is the decimal reduction of
A among the two curves, the highest δ is .41. Note that
g_{wl} produces an apparent increase in the transition
point.   .b) as above but with heterogeneous stomata
instead of g_{wl}: the highest δ value is .34. To generate
A-p_{ap} response p_i was let to vary in 15 equally

weighted classes of stomatal conductance from
compensation, using the same biochemistry of fig. 1a.

An high evaporative demand can transiently increase
the thickness of the liquid barrier aroud cells and hence
create an decrease in a homogeneous component of internal
diffusive conductance, g_{wl}, wich is however easily removed
by an increase in p_i. g_{wl} effect is proportional to
assimilation rate relative variations, wich tend to be much
less important in CO2 partial pressures higher than 600
ubar. This is expected from the hyperbolic relation between
A and p_i wich tends invariably to flatten in high p_i. In
heterogenous leaves under stress a lot of cells won't ever
attain high p_i, and this effect should be absent.
In any case a reduction in relative Am (800) values is
present suggesting additional metabolic effects of vpd.

REFERENCES
1 Terashima I., Wong S.C., Osmond C.B., Farquhar G.D.
      (1988) Plant Cell Physiol. 29(3) 385-394
2 Cornic G., Le Gouallec J.L., Briantais J.M., Hodges M.
      (1989) Planta 177 84-90
3 Daley P., Raschke K., Ball T., Berry J. (1988)
      Photosynthesis Symposium July 12-22 Stanford (in
      press)
4 Sharkey T.D., Berry J.A., Sage R.F. (1988) Planta 176
      415-424
5 Brooks A. and Farquhar G.D. (1985) Planta 165 397-406
6 von Caemmerer S. and Farquhar G.D. (1981) Planta 376-387

DOES AIR RELATIVE HUMIDITY DURING GROWTH CONDITION PHOTOSYNTHETIC CHARACTERISTICS OF COFFEE LEAF ?

Maria A. Nunes and Paula S. Rijo
Centro de Estudos de Produção e Tecnologia Agricolas, Tapada da
Ajuda, Apartado 3014, Lisboa, Portugal

1. INTRODUCTION

Coffee grows naturally in the understory of the wet tropical forest
and bears some physiological characteristics of a shade plant (1).
Air humidity is certainly an important factor in the devellopment of
the plant, but the basic information on this topic is very short. In
sequence of previous work (2) this, presents more data showing
that low air humidity is a stress factor on photosynthesis and
suggests that it affects not only stomatal conductance but chemical
characteristics of the mesophyll related with photosynthesis.

2. PROCEDURE

2.1. Materials and methods

Plants of Coffea arabica L. from cvs. CATURRA, CATUAI, CATIMOR, S4
AGARO, KENT and GEISHA were used for the measurements of
conductance but only plants from cv CATURRA were used for the
chemical analysis and study of photosynthetic characteristics. The
plant material was about two years old and had grown, with good
irrigation ,either in the greenhouse (G) under natural light or in
a growth cabinet (C) .

TABLE 1. Environmental conditons during growth and measurements

	Cabinet	Greenhouse	Measurement
Irradiance ($\mu mol/m2/s$)	150	300-150	150
Temp. ºC	22/19	23/17	23
Air RH (%)	50	80	60

2.2 Instruments

A porometer LICOR 1600 and two IRGA (LEYBOLD-HERAUS and LICOR
LI 6200) were used.

2.3 Chemical analysis

Protein was determined using the method of Lowry (3) after
percipitation with 5% TCA solution. The percipitate was obtained by
using the TCA solution directly to grind a sample of 10 discs with
5mm diameter (total protein) and from an aliquota of the extract
prepared for measurement of the RUBP carboxylase activity.

M. Baltscheffsky (ed.), Current Research in Photosynthesis, Vol. IV, 721–723.
© 1990 *Kluwer Academic Publishers. Printed in the Netherlands.*

Chlorophyll was extracted by imersion of leaf discs in methanol during 5 days in dark and cool conditions.
RUBP carboxylase activity was measured using an adaptation of Brooks method (4) with labelled NaHCO3 with 50µC mmol^{-1} of specific activity in the assay solution.

3. RESULTS AND DISCUSSION

Leaf conductance under a range of light conditions was measured in several ocasions, in plants from cvs. Caturra, Catimor, Catuai, Kent, Geisha and S4 Agaro grown in the greenhouse . It was observed that values scatter between 120 to 280 mmol m^{-2} s^{-1}.
Under light <150µmol m^{-2} s^{-1} the conductance tends to be a little less, the highest frequency of points was between 150-220 mmol m^{-2} s^{-1}. Concurrent photosynthesis rates were also measured in cvs. Kent Geisha and Caturra. The most frequent rates of net photosynthesis were around 6µmol m^{-2} s^{-1} , values as high as 7.5 µmol m^{-2} s^{-1} were measured in the cv. CATURRA. Those values score among the highest found in the literature (5).

Values of conductance and photosynthesis measured in plants from different cvs. grown in the Cabinet were allways lower than 150 mmolm^{-2} s^{-1} and 3.5 µmol m^{-2} s^{-1} respectively .

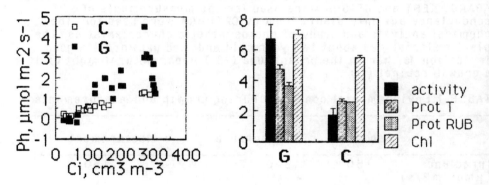

Figure 1. (left) Relationship between net photosynthesis rate (Ph) and internal CO2 concentration (Ci) in the tissue of leaves from the Greenhouse (G) and from the Cabinet C).

Figure 2. (right) Activity of the RUBP carboxylase, protein total and extracted with the RUBPC, and chlorophyll content. Units: activity- mmol m^{-2} s^{-1}, protein- g m^{-2}, chlorophyl- g m^{-2}.

In order to discriminate between stomatal and mesophyll components of photosynthesis (Ph) from leaves grown in G and C the photosynthesis dependence curves on conductance and internal CO2 (Ci) concentration were drawn. Stomatal control was good in the G but seemed poor in C leaves. Concerning the Ph/Ci relationship,

leaves from G had a higher slope suggestting a higher
carboxylation efficiency in the leaves grown in this environment
(Fig. 1).

Analysis of RUBPC activity, protein and clorophyll contents expressed
either on the leaf area or dry weight basis was significantly higher in
the G leaves (Fig.2). Gas exchange and chemical analysis agree in
supporting the higher values of Ph and g consistently found in θ
leaves and paralell what has been refered in contrasting sun and shade
environments (6). However, there was no important difference
between irradiance level of G and C, instead RH was the most stricking
and persistent difference . So, in the addition to the well known effects
of RH in the stomatal conductance, here also evident, we are inclined
to admitt that this factor affected mesophyll components that support
photosynthesis.

REFERENCES
1 Rhizopoulou S., Nunes M.A. (1981). in Components of
   productivity ofMediterranean Climate Region(Margaris N.S.,
   Mooney H.A. ,eds) . pp.85-89, Dr Junk Publ. The Hague.
2 Nunes M.A. (1988) Photosynthetica 22, 547-553.
3 Lowry O.H., Rozenburg N.J., Fare A.L. and Randall R.J.R. (1951)
   J Biol Chem 193, 265-275.
4 Brooks A. (1981) Aust J Plant Physiol 13, 221-237
5 Nunes M.A., Bierhuizen J.F., Ploegman, C. (1968) Acta bot neerl
   17, 93-102.
6 Bjorkman O. (1981).in Physiol Plant Ecology I(Lang,O.L., Nobel,
   P.S., Osmond,C.B. and Ziegler,H.,ed.),vol12A,pp.57-109,Springer-
   Verlag, Berlim.

THE EFFECT OF DROUGHT ON CHLOROPHYLL FLUORESCENCE IN TWO MAIZE LINES

LJubinko Jovanović, Vaskrsija Janjić and Sonja Veljović, University of Belgrade, INEP, Institute of Pesticides and Environmental Protection, 11080 Zemun Banatska 31b, Yugoslavia

1.INTRODUCTION

In addition to other photosynthetic processes, chlorophyll fluorescence can be a good indicator of the altered status of photosynthetic apparatus occurring due to dehydration of plant tissues (1). Chlorophyll fluorescence yield *in vivo* under normal physiological conditions is mostly a function of two types of fluorescence quenching, photochemical and non-photochemical (2).It was shown that contribution of photochemical and non-photochemical quenching to the total fluorescence quenching in the leaves tended to vary during drought and was likely to suggest the functional alterations incurred due to tissue dehydration (3). The present paper will concentrate on the investigations of water status and fluorescence quenching in two maize lines differing in drought resistance and abscisic acid accumulation (4).

2.PROCEDURE
2.1.Materials and Methods
The plants of two maize lines differing in drought susceptibility, ZPBL 1304 (resistant) and ZPL 389 (susceptible), were grown in the soil-filled pots under controlled conditions (12 h with PPFD 300 μmol m^{-2} s^{-1} at 25°C, and 12 h in the dark at 18°C). Drought treatment (dewatering) was commenced when the third leaf was fully developed. Samples for the determination of the relative water content (RWC) and osmotic water potential (ψ_s) were cut out from the third leaf which was first subjected to chlorophyll fluorescence measurement. Us was determined using psychrometric dew point method (5).Chlorophyll fluorescence was measured using a new type fluorometer with the modulated low intensity light source (PAM 101, H. Walz, Germany). The differentiation between the photochemical and non-photochemical quenching is possible by the application of saturation pulse method (3). PPFD of the actinic illumination and the saturating pulses was 134 μmol m^{-2} s^{-1}, and 8860 μmol m^{-2} s^{-1} respectively. Plants were dark adapted for 4 hours, before fluorescence induction curves were recorded. Leaves were measured in the air, if not indicated otherwise. Quenching coefficients qQ and qE were calculated as previously described (6).

3. RESULTS AND DISCUSSION
Figure 1. shows parameters of water status during drought treatment of the two maize lines. In both of them RWC decreases but faster and earlier in the susceptible line. The osmotic potential in the same line decreases to reach a maximum (-2.5 MPa) on the seventh day of the

M. Baltscheffsky (ed.), Current Research in Photosynthesis, Vol. IV, 725–728.
© 1990 *Kluwer Academic Publishers. Printed in the Netherlands.*

drought. The decline of both RWC and ψs pointed out to the passiveness
of the process in the susceptible line, suggesting that ψs decrease
resulted from a fast water loss from the leaf. In the resistant line,
though, a comparatively slower decrease of ψs than the RWC may be sug-
gestive of osmoregulation (Fig. 1.).

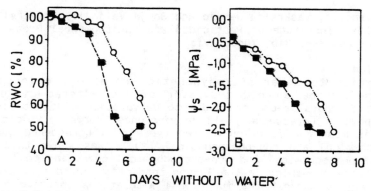

Fig. 1. Relative water content, RWC(A) and osmotic potential, ψs (B) in
two maize lines: (..) ZPBL 1304, and (---) ZPL 389, exposed to
drought. Each point is the mean of 3-5 measurements.

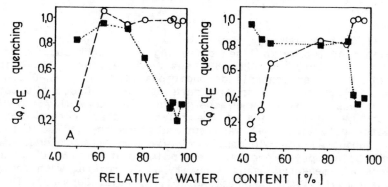

Fig. 2. Fluorescence quenching dependence on the relative water content in drought resistant line, ZPBL 1304 (A) and drought susceptible
line, ZPL 389 (B). qQ (---) and qE(...). Each point is the mean of
3-5 measurements.

The fluorescence quenching of two maize lines leaves was measured
under steady state illumination at different relative water content of
leaves. With decreasing relative water content the saturation pulse
fluorescence induction pattern is markedly affected especially in the
susceptible line. At 90% RWC Q-quenching decreases to become more
pronaunced with further dehydration whereas the relaxation of
E-quenching is strongly suppressed staying at the same level until 50%
RWC, whereupon it rises with the RWC drop to 45% (Fig. 2.A.). In the

resistant line the increase of membrane energization (qE) is more steep attaining maximum at 70% RWC. In the same time Q-quenching remains at an almost the same level. With further dehydration to 50% RWC Q-quenching and E-quenching decrease (Fig. 2.B).

The decrease of Q-quenching in the susceptible line becomes apparent on the second day of the drought, whereas the resistant line suffers alterations only on the day 6 (not shown). In the susceptible line already on the day 2 E-quenching reached a level to remain stable throughout the drought . In the resistant line, though, E-quenching reached such level only on the 6th day.

With aim to eliminate the effect of the closing stomata fluorescence measurements were made in an atmosphere with the increasing CO_2 concentrations (Fig.3.).

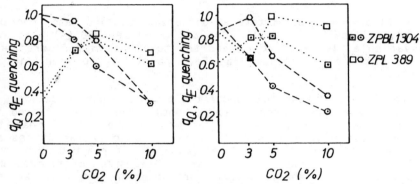

Figure 3. The effect of increasing CO_2 (3, 5, 10%) in the air in the measuring chamber on fluorescence quenching at 98% RWC (A) and 78% RWC (B). qQ (---) and qE (...). Each point is the mean of 3-5 measurements.

With the increase of CO_2 concentration Q-quenching in both lines decreased and E-quenching increased thus reflecting the inhibitory effect of CO_2 in these experimental conditions (Fig. 3.A). In the mild water stress (79% RWC) the same trend was maintained for both lines except the E-quenching was high also in the air (Fig. 3.B). Only in susceptible line the increase of CO_2 to 3% led to increasing qQ and decreasing qE reflecting the reversal of drought effect.

Previous reports have shown that the destructive effect of photosynthetic apparatus can be proved by measuring some fluorescence parameters (Fo, Fv/Fm) (7). In our experiment the Fv/Fm ratio was reduced from 0.8 in the control to 0.6 on the day 6 of the drought, and was similar in both maize lines (Fig. 4.A). In parallel with reduction of PSII photochemical efficiency under strong stress conditions (RWC=50%), basic fluorescence level decreased in both lines (Fig. 4.B). In addition to dehydration, some exogenous factors, such as a high intensity of the light, under normal drought conditions may also inhibit photosynthesis (8,9).

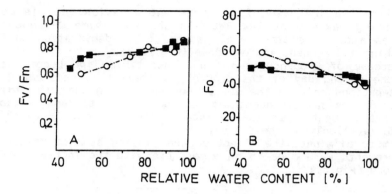

Figure 4. Fluorescence parameters at different relative water contents in two maize lines: (...) ZPBL 1304, and (---) ZPL 389.(A) The ratio of the variable fluorescence Fv and the total maximal fluorescence Fmax; (B) basic fluorescence, Fo. Each point is the mean of 3-5 measurements.

The results have shown that under the given drought conditions, in addition to the altered water capacity, both maize lines suffered the changed photosynthetic processes. It was further shown that the fluorescence may be a very sensitive parameter of water stress and thus be used successfully for the determination of plant drought susceptibility. Further investigations into relationships of fluorescence parameters and photosynthetic activity are necessary, so as to acquire a quantitative dimension of the photosynthesis by means of a fast and undestructive measurements of chlorophyll fluorescence *in vivo*.

REFERENCES
1 Wiltens, J.,Schreiber, U.,Vidaver, W.,(1978) Can. J. Bot. 56: 2787-2794.
2 Krause, G.H., Weis, E.(1988) In: HK Lichtenthaler (ed) Applications of Chlorophyll Fluorescence, Kluwer Academic Publ.
3 Renger, G., Schreiber, U., (1986) In: Govindjee,Amesz J,Fork DC(eds) Light Emission by Plants and Bacteria. Academic Press, Orlando New York London, 587-619.
4 Pekić, S., and Quarrie, S.A., (1987) J.Plant. Physiol.Vol. 127 pp 203-217
5 Neumann, H.H.,Thurtell, G.W.,(1973) In: Psychrometry in Water Relations Research, Brown & van Haven (eds)
6 Schreiber, U.,Schliwa, U.,Bilger, W., (1986) Photosynth. Res. 10: 51-62.
7 Demmig, B., Bjorkmann, O.,(1987) Planta 170: 489-504.
8 Kaiser, W.M., (1987) Physiol. Planatarum 71:142-149.
9 Havaux, M., Lannoye, R.,(1983) Irrig. Sci. 4:147-151.

DROUGTH EFFECT ON PHOTOSYNTHESIS AND PLANT PRODUCTION
OF TWO CONTRASTING *TRIFOLIUM* CULTIVARS

Vadell J., Cabot C., Medrano H.
Lab. de Fisiologia Vegetal. Dep. de Biologia i C.S. Institut d'Estudis
Avançats (UIB-CSIC). 07071, Palma de Mallorca, Spain.

1. INTRODUCTION

Water stress is the first cause of plant yield reduction in Mediterranean areas. Forage crops as subterranean clover, that maintain growth from September to June are widely affected by water deficit. (1,2). Photosynthesis rate is strongly reduced by water stress by lowering stomatal conductance and decreasing photosyntetic capacity of mesophyll cells (3,4). Intraespecific differential responses of photosynthesis to water stress has been reported in legumes such as soybean (5) and others under controlled conditions but rarely on field grown plants.

We are reporting here water defficit effects on photosynthetic and water economy characteristics under field conditions of two subterranean clover cultivars with contrasting yield capacity under drought.

2. PROCEDURE

2.1. Materials: Seeds from two commercial cultivars of subterranean clover
(*Trifolium subterraneum* L.), Clare and Seaton Park were used.
2.2. Methods: *Rhizobium trifolii* inoculated seeds were sown on a well fertilized calcareous soil in Palma de Mallorca (Spain) on October 31st. 1988.

Plants were grown in small plots (1.5 x 4 m), under irrigated (soil water potential $\geq$ -2.5 cbar) and non irrigated conditions. Treatments were set up in triplicate and measurements were carried out in January, on healthy, well developed plants. Twelve plants from each treatment were harvested and fresh and dry weight (after 24 h at 70°C) of roots, shoots and leaves were recorded.

Photosynthesis and transpiration rates as well as stomatal conductance and CO_2 mesophyll concentration were measured using an IRGA Licor 6200 on attached fully developed leaves in field conditions.

3. RESULTS AND DISCUSSION

3.1. Plant production and leaf status:

During the experiment (November to January) no rain was recorded, so, generous irrigation was supplied to all the treatments

M. Baltscheffsky (ed.), Current Research in Photosynthesis, Vol. IV, 729–732.
© 1990 *Kluwer Academic Publishers. Printed in the Netherlands.*

to promote germination and first growth after sown.Average day and night temperatures were around 10 and 17°C.

Under these conditions, plants started to grow achieving a size among 8-15 cm over the ground at the end of January.

Morphological modifications were coincident in water stressed plants in which respects to leaf number and leaf area reduction. However, the extend of this modifications clearly contrasted between the two cvars. Clare didn't reduce leaf number, but it showed 40% lower leaf area under water stress. Seaton Park leaf number under drought was to about half of under irrigation. Plant production under water stress was only little lower in Clare but it was 46% lower in Seaton Park (in respect to irrigated plants) (table 1).

Table 1: Plant characteristics as affected by drought.

	LEAF NUMBER	LEAF AREA (cm^2)	PLANT PRODUCTION (mg)			
			LEAVES	SHOOTS	ROOTS	TOTAL
CV. CLARE:						
Irrigated	8.3±0.7	31.3±2.1	108± 8.3	104.1± 7.7	73.4±12.6	285.5±26.8
Drought	9.4±0.9	21.0±2.3	104.9±11.6	92.9±11.0	68.0± 8.5	265.8±30.6
CV. SEATON PARK:						
Irrigated	12.3±1.1	18.4±1.6	62.7± 5.7	59.5± 6.6	66.4±10.3	185.9±20.9
Drought	6.2±0.7	8.1±0.6	35.8± 3.7	41.6± 4.1	21.6± 3.3	99.0±10.2

Leaf changes associated with water stress in both cultivars were reductions in leaf area, water content and water potential and an increase in leaf specific dry weight. Nevertheless, Clare showed a bigger modification in each one of this leaf characters except in water content (table 2)

Table 2: Leaf Parameters

	WATER CONTENT (% dw)	WATER POTENTIAL (bar)	L.A. (cm^2)	SDW (mg cm^{-2})
CV. CLARE:				
Irrigated	79.6±0.2	-2.0±0.3	3.8±0.1	3.3±0.1
Drought	67.6±0.6	-3.1±0.9	2.2±0.1	5.0±0.1
CV. SEATON PARK:				
Irrigated	79.7±0.2	-1.6±0.4	1.5±0.1	3.1±0.1
Drought	64.4±0.8	-2.1±0.7	1.3±0.0	4.3±0.2

3.2. Photosynthesis and stomatal conductance:

Under irrigation, photosynthesis rate and stomatal conductance at irradiation levels above 1000 μE $m^{-2}s^{-1}$ were higher than below this level (500-1000 μE $m^{-2}s^{-1}$). Increases in stomatal conductance were proporcionally much higher than photosynthesis rate in both cultivars reflecting that these irradiation levels are near the saturation ones.

Under both irradiation levels tested Seaton Park showed the higher values either in photosynthesis rate or stomatal conductance (table 3).

Photosynthesis rates in water stressed leaves showed a dramatic reduction respect to irrigated plants and stomatal conductance. Above and bellow 1000 μE $m^{-2}s^{-1}$ A and g values were similar in Clare. Seaton Park A and g values were clearly lower than Clare ones above 1000 μE $m^{-2}s^{-1}$.

Under drought Clare took a clear advantatge in photosynthesis rate with g values close to Seaton Park ones either bellow or above 1000 μE $m^{-2}s^{-1}$, so the superior A values must be atributed to nonstomatal effects that able Clare cvar to maintain higher CO_2 assimilation rates (table 3).

Table 3: Photosynthesis rates and stomatal conductance.

	A (μmol CO_2 $m^{-2}s^{-1}$)		g (mol $m^{-2}s^{-1}$)	
	≥ 1000 μE	≤ 1000 μE	≥ 1000 μE	≤ 1000 μE
CV. CLARE:				
Irrigated	21.8±0.5	17.7±1.2	0.53±0.03	0.40±0.02
Drought	7.1±1.3	6.8±0.2	0.07±0.02	0.08±0.01
CV. SEATON PARK:				
Irrigated	23.8±1.1	19.8±1.5	0.86±0.04	0.57±0.03
Drought	2.7±0.3	4.7±0.4	0.05±0.01	0.08±0.01

(A=CO_2 Assimilation; g=Conductance)

3.3. Plant water economy:

Consistent with conductance values, transpiration rates were much higher in Seaton Park under irrigation and closer to Clare ones under drought. Good agreement was presented between water economy indexes and photosynthetic parameters so transpiration efficiency and 1-Ce/Ca index values were always higher in Clare, both in water stressed and nonstressed plants at irradiation levels above and bellow 1000 μE $m^{-2}s^{-1}$ (table 4).

These data show that morphological and physiological modifications associated with water stress able cvar Clare to maintain higher rates of photosynthesis and plant production, but also that the water economy indexes were superior in this cultivar even under irrigation, showing the efficiency of this indexes and also the existence of intraespecific variability in photosynthesis rates under drought that able cultivar Clare to maintain better CO_2 assimilation rates by water stressed leaves.

Table 4: Water Economy.

	E (mol $m^{-2}s^{-1}$)		A/E		1-(Ci/Ca)	
	≥1000 µE	≤1000 µE	≥1000 µE	≤1000 µE	≥1000 µE	≤1000 µE
CV. CLARE:						
Irrigated	5.6±0.4	3.9±0.2	3.89	4.53	0.253	0.222
Drought	0.9±0.0	0.6±0.1	7.89	11.33	0.456	0.494
CV. SEATON PARK:						
Irrigated	9.1±0.5	4.9±0.2	2.62	4.04	0.198	0.203
Drought	0.8±0.0	0.7±0.03	3.38	6.71	0.236	0.290

4. REFERENCES

1. Turner N.C. and Begg J.E. (1981) Plant and Soil 58:97-131.
2. Taylor N. L. (ed.) (1985). Clover Science and Technology. Agronomy, 25.
3. Farquhar G.D. and Sharkey T.D. (1984) Ann. Rev. of Plant Physiol, 33: 317-345.
4. Kaiser W.M. (1987) Physiol. Plant, 71: 142-149.
5. Bunce J.A. (1988) Plant Physiol. and Biochem. 26 (4) 415-420.

WATER STRESS EFFECTS ON CANOPY PHOTOSYNTHESIS, TEMPEATURE, TRANSPIRATION AND SHEDDING OF LEAVES AND FRUIT IN COTTON.

Avishay Ben-Porath[1], Donald N. Baker[2] and Avishalom Marani[3]

MIGAL, Kiryat Shmona 10200, Israel[1]; USDA-ARS, C.S.R.U., Miss. State, USA[2]; The Hebrew Univ. of Jerusalem, Israel[3].

1. INTRODUCTION

As a result of water stress, plant growth rate is reduced and senescence processes are accelerated [1, 2]. The aging of leaves causes an additional reduction in canopy photosynthesis because solar radiation is intercepted by older leaves [3].
The purpose of this study was to quantify the accumulated effects of mild and severe water stress on cotton canopies grown under constant temperature, during the boll development stage.

2. MATERIALS AND METHODS

Cotton (Gossypium hirsutum L.) var. 'Stoneville 825' plants were grown outdoors, in 7 liter pots filled with sand, arranged in a field configuration (10 plants m^{-2}). The plants were drip-fertigated with nutrient solution 12 times per day. Soil water potential in the pots was maintained in the range of -5 to -40 kPa.
At the age of 77 days, 10 nursery plants were destructively harvested and other 30 plants were transferred to 3 sunlit growth chambers (32/20°C day/night) for water stress treatments. These consisted of 12, 8, and 4 irrigation pulses per day for the "C", "M", and "S" chambers, respectively (60 ml pot^{-1} in each pulse). The chambers have been described in detail elsewhere [3, 4, 5]. Each chamber formed a closed system, measuring 0.5 by 2.0 m and a height of 1.5 m, around the aerial parts of 10 plants.
Simultaneous observations of canopy photosynthesis, temperature (Tc-Ta) and transpiration (ET) were recorded automatically during 35 days. After 11 days of stress, plants of "S" chamber were harvested to provide dry weight (DW) partitioning data and were replaced by "fresh" nursery plants. Fallen leaves and fruit were collected daily from the chamber floor. Measurements and analysis of gross photosynthesis rate (PS) were carried out according to [5]. Essentially, PS was calculated every 15 min. by adding dark respiration rate to net photosynthetic rate. Solar radiation (Rad) data were used to produce daily curves of PS vs. Rad. Those curves were analyzed by fitting a rectangular hyperbola equation.

3. RESULTS AND DISCUSSION

During 35 recording days 1100 observations of concurrently measured parameters (Tc-Ta, PS, ET and Rad) were obtained. These data were pooled for all three treatments, and multiple linear regression equations were calculated:

M. Baltscheffsky (ed.), Current Research in Photosynthesis, Vol. IV, 733–736.
© 1990 Kluwer Academic Publishers. Printed in the Netherlands.

[1]   (Tc-Ta) = 0.336 + 4.957*10^{-3}(Rad) - 1.796(ET) - 0.0613(PS)

$[R^2 = 0.73]$

[2]   PS = 5.327 - 5.585(Tc-Ta) + 4.046*10^{-2}(Rad)

$[R^2 = 0.73]$

(Tc-Ta) is expressed in C, (Rad) in W m^{-2}, (ET) in mm hr^{-1}, and (PS) in μMole CO_2 m^{-2} ground area sec^{-1}.

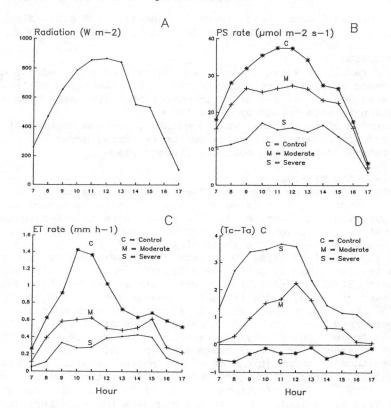

FIGURE 1. Average hourly values of chamber measurements on third stress day. (A) Solar radiation. (B) Canopy gross photosynthetic rate. (C) Evapotranspiration rate. (D) Canopy minus air temperature.

After 3 stress days midday leaf water potentials (LWP) were -1.5, -2.7 and -3.8 MPa for "C", "M" and "S" plants, respectively. Fig. 1 clearly indicates that PS rate of "S" plants was reduced to about one half of that of "C" plants. "S" plants reached their maximal PS rate at about 10 a.m. Leaves in "S" canopies were found to be warmer, with their Tc-Ta being raised by up to 5°C.

"M" and "S" plants adjusted their ET rates according to the reduced irrigation rates within 5 days of stress (Fig. 2). After that the daily PS rose to somewhat higher values (Fig. 3). ET reduction was larger than PS reduction in both treatments.

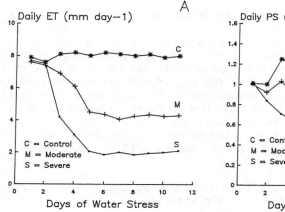

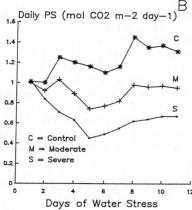

FIGURE 2. Daily totals of: (A) Evapotranspiration, and (B) Gross photo-
sinthesis in three growth chambers.

The shedding of old mainstem leaves helped to alleviate water
stress of the upper canopy, as indicated by midday LWP data (not
shown). Abscission of old leaves and young fruit was well correlated
to the degree of stress. "S" plants shed their leaves at an
accelerated rate, and "M" plants shed only a few leaves at a linear
rate (Fig. 3). "S" plants abscissed during 11 days of water stress
29%, 95% and 21% of their leaf DW, small fruit and large bolls,
whereas "C" plants, shed only 3%, 48% and 10%, respectively, of
these organs.

FIGURE 3. Cumulative leaf
abscission in three
growth chambers
during 11 stress days.

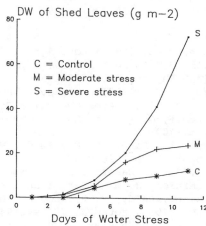

Comparison of DW distribution data, of plant before and after
severe water stress (Table 1), indicates that only 3 types of organs
grew during 11 day period: large bolls, small roots, and stems. From
the total gain of these organs (12 g DW plant^{-1}) about 33% was used

for large boll growth, 43% used for fine root growth, and 24% was used for stem suberization.

The initiation of new roots during water stress periods was observed in cotton [6] and corn [7]. The growth of large bolls can be easily explained, since developing bolls are the main sink of the plant during this stage [8, 9]. The significant growth of stem DW during the stress period, however, was quite unexpected. The increase in stem DW (16.5%) was larger than the increase in plant height (3.3%). It may therefore be concluded that the stem of the cotton plant probably serves as a sink for excess carbohydrates, not used by other plant organs whose growth rate was reduced by the water stress.

TABLE 1. Plant dry weight distribution before and after severe stress. Average and S.D. values of 10 plants.

Plant Character	Before water stress (77 day plants)	After water stress (88 day plants)	Difference
Height (cm)	89.6 ± 0.2	92.6 ± 0.4	+ 3.0
Leaves (#)	44.20 ± 1.98	34.70 ± 2.12	− 9.50
Small fruit (#)	16.20 ± 2.54	0.80 ± 0.64	− 15.40
Large bolls (#)	12.20 ± 0.28	8.70 ± 1.28	− 3.50
Leaf DW (g)	25.05 ± 0.56	18.18 ± 1.71	− 6.87
Stem DW (g)	17.18 ± 1.00	20.01 ± 0.23	+ 2.83
Taproot (g)	6.51 ± 0.89	7.07 ± 0.44	+ 0.56
Small root (g)	3.75 ± 0.44	8.91 ± 1.54	+ 5.16
Small fruit (g)	1.43 ± 0.28	0.04 ± 0.04	− 1.39
Large bolls (g)	25.29 ± 1.39	29.30 ± 1.10	+ 4.01

REFERENCES:
1. Turner, N. C. (1986) Adv. Agron. 39, 1-51
2. Berlin, J., Quisenberry, J. E., Bailey, F., Woodworth, M. (1982) Plant Physiol. 70, 238-243
3. Hsiao, T. C. (1973) Ann. Rev. Plant Physiol. 24, 519-570
4. Kreig, D. (1981) Proc. Beltwide Cotton Prod. Res. Conf. 41-42
5. Constable, G. A., and Rawson, H. M. (1980) Aust. J. Plant Physiol. 7, 89-100
6. Marani, A., Baker, D. N., Reddy, V. R. and McKinion J. M. (1985) Crop Sci. 25, 798-802
7. Phene, C. J., Baker, D. N., Lambert, J. E., Parsons, J. E., and McKinion, J. M. (1978) Trans. ASAE 21, 924-930
8. Acock, B., Reddy, V. R., Hodges, H. F., Baker, D. N., McKinion, J. M. (1985) Agron J. 77, 942-947
9. Malik, R. S., Dhankar, J. S., and Turner, N. C. (1979) Plant Soil 53, 109-115
10. Sharp, R. E., and Davies, W. J. (1985) J. Exp. Bot. 36, 1441-1456
11. Ashley, D. A. (1972) Crop Sci. 12, 69-74
12. Constable, G. A., and Rawson, H. M. (1982) Aust. J. Plant Physiol. 9, 735-747

WATER USE EFFICIENCY IN FIELD-GROWN MAIZE :
EFFECTS OF SOIL STRUCTURE

Olivier Bethenod[1] and Francois Tardieu[2]

Station de Bioclimatologie[1];
Laboratoire d'Agronomie[2];   INRA, 78850 THIVERVAL-GRIGNON, FRANCE

1. INTRODUCTION

Rain water use efficiency can be defined by the ratio of dry matter production (DMP) to rainfall (R). It can be written as the product of three ratios (i) the ratio of transpiration (E) to rainfall, (ii) that of CO_2 net assimilation to transpired water (An/E), (iii) that of the conversion of this photosynthesis into dry matter.

$$(DMP/ R) = (E/ R) (An/ E) (DMP/ An) \tag{1}$$

Growth and water status of maize have been followed by Tardieu[1,2] with either a favourable (O) or a compact (C) soil structure in the ploughed layer. Differences in DMP and in stomatal conductance (gs) were observed, and related to water uptake by roots (ratio i). This was ascribed to the spatial arrangement of roots [3]. The objective of this article is to present the second term of rain water use efficiency: leaf water use efficiency (WUE).

Gas exchanges at the leaf level are an indicator of the regulation between An and E when a stress appears[4]. Since E is the product of gs and of the water vapor difference between the leaf and the air (vdp), WUE could be split up into two components: vdp and the ratio of net assimilation to leaf CO_2 conductance (gc), (gc=gs/1.6).

$$An/E = (An/gc) (1.6/vdp) \tag{2}$$

We will, therefore, study the response of net assimilation (An) to leaf molar conductance for the two soil structures defined above.

2. MATERIALS AND METHODS

Maize (*Zea mays* L. F1 hybrid LG1) was sown on May 5, 1987 at Grignon, 40 km W of Paris, in a clay-loam field. Plant density was 85,000 ha^{-1}, the distance between rows being 80 cm. Two experimental treatments were compared. In the first (O), the ploughed layer was made of fine earth and small clods, the average bulk density of the layer being 1.35. In the second (C), the ploughed layer was continuously compacted to a bulk density of 1.6. The seed bed(0 - 10cm) was loosened by a rotating harrow in both treatments. The root system was characterized in both treatments using the method of root mapping on horizontal and vertical planes [3]. Examples of root maps on vertical planes are presented in Fig 1. The colonization in C was irregular: the seed bed was densely colonized, but roots penetrated in the ploughed layer only through shrinkage cracks. Conversely, root density was more even in treatment O.

Soil water content and soil water potential were measured with a neutron probe and tensiometers. Plant water potential was measured

M. Baltscheffsky (ed.), Current Research in Photosynthesis, Vol. IV, 737–740.
© 1990 *Kluwer Academic Publishers. Printed in the Netherlands.*

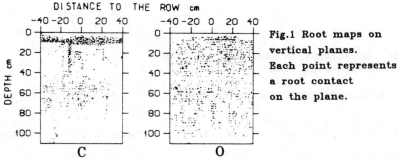

DISTANCE TO THE ROW cm

Fig.1 Root maps on
vertical planes.
Each point represents
a root contact
on the plane.

with a pressure chamber and averaged on six leaves. Comparison between
plants from (O) and (C) were made three times a day, at 9 a.m., 12noon,
and 3 p.m..

Measurements of the rate of CO_2 assimilation and stomatal conductance
were made in a transient open gas exchange system (LCA2 with Parkinson
Leaf Chamber, ADC), with the following modifications: The reference and
measure flow rates were regulated by mass flow controllers (Tylan).
Pressurized dry air from cylinders provided in the chamber a CO_2
concentration higher than in natural air. Mole fraction of water vapour
entering the chamber was measured by a blank after every 20 measurements
on (O) leaves, followed by 20 measurements on (C) leaves. For maize, An
reaches a plateau when CO_2 concentration is over 300 ppm [5]. We thus
measured the actual net assimilation in the chamber and the value of gc
before clamping the chamber. Internal CO_2 concentration (Ci), An, gc,
were calculated according to Caemmerer and Farquhar[6].

3. RESULTS AND DISCUSSION

3.1 Leaf and soil water status. Values of predawn water potentials
were lower in C compared with O (Fig.2). This was due to a rapid drop

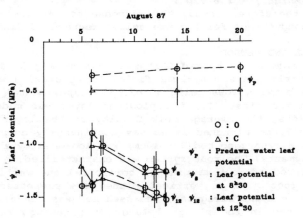

Fig.2 Leaf Water Potential of maize, Ψ_L and Ψ_P, for two soil
structures O and C. Mean values and confidence intervals on ten leaves.

in potential in the 0 - 10 cm soil layer in C, which was densely colonized, while this drop was slower in O. Conversely, subsequent layers were drier in O compared with C. Leaf water potentials were similar from 10 am to 2 pm.

3.2 Gas exchange. The two main results from the gs response curve against photosynthetic photon flux density (PPFD) are the following : the maximum values of gs in the (O) treatment is higher than in (C), and the data are less scattered in (O) than in (C) (Fig.3). Similarly, the net assimilation measurements versus PPFD show higher and less scattered data in the (O) than in the (C) treatment (Fig.4).

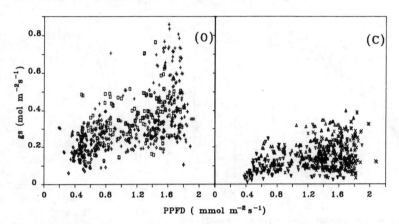

Fig.3 Stomatal conductance of maize vs. Photosynthetic Photon Flux Density for two soil structures "O" and "C" (see text). Each symbol corresponds to different leaves.

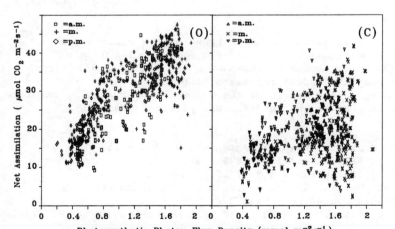

Fig.4 Net assimilation rate of Maize vs. Photosynthetic Photon Flux Density, for two soil structures: "O" and "C" (see text). Each symbol corresponds to different leaves.

Fig.5 exhibits the relationship between An, corrected by interaction between water and CO_2[6], and gc, for optimal conditions of temperature (T) and PPFD: $26<T<31°C$; $PPFD> 1$ $mmolm^{-2}s^{-1}$. This response curve is an hyperbola close to the two assymptotes: (i) one represents (Ca-Ci), (ii) the plateau (Pmm), maximum of net assimilation in optimal conditions for CO_2, T, and PPFD[7] for gc over 0.2 $molm^{-2}s^{-1}$. For the same range of gc, $0.1-0.2$ $mmolm^{-2}s^{-1}$, both O and C exhibit the same response curve, i.e. the same Ci. Nevertheless, the O treatment gives higher An and gc. For gc higher than 0.2 $molm^{-2}s^{-1}$, An reaches the plateau, Pmm.

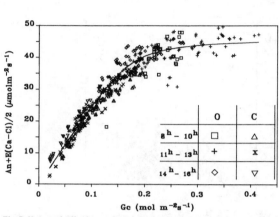

Fig.5 Net assimilation rate of maize, corrected by transpiration flux, vs. stomatal conductance, gc, for optimal conditions : $25<T<31°C$, $PPFD> 1mmolm^{-2}s^{-1}$. In eq.3 , Ca=340 ppm , (Ca-Ci)=258.7 ppm; Pmm=49 $\mu mol.m^{-2}.s^{-1}$; m=0.863

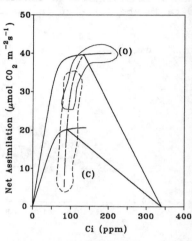

Fig.6 Scheme of the An/Ci response curve for maize on two soil structures (0) and (C).

The An/gc response curve can be written, with a concavity m :
$$[(Ca-Ci).An+Pmm-[((Ca-Ci).An+Pmm)^2-4.m.Pmm.(Ca-Ci)]^{1/2}]/2m =0 \qquad (3)$$
slight differences occur between morning, midday and afternoon: the slope of the response curves increases with vdp.

Figure 6 sums up the effect of the C treatment by showing the rate of CO_2 assimilation, An vs. Ci in different plants of Maize.

REFERENCES
1 Tardieu, F. Manichon, H (1987) Agronomie 7, 279 - 288
2 Tardieu, F. (1987) Agronomie 7, 279 - 288
3 Tardieu, F. (1988) Plant and Soil 107, 267-272
4 Prioul, J.-L.,Cornic, G. and Jones, H.G. (1984) Advances in Photosynthesis Rechearch 4, 375-378
5 Bethenod, O., Jacob, C., Rode, J.-C. and Morot-Gaudry, J.-F. (1982) Agronomie 2, 159-166
6 Caemmerer, S. von and Farquhar, G.D. (1981) Planta 153, 376-387
7 Chartier, P. and Bethenod O. (1977) in Les Processus de la Production Végétale Primaire (Moyse, A., ed.) pp.77-112, Gauthier-Villars, Paris

AN EVALUATION OF THE EFFECT OF SALINITY ON PHOTOSYNTHESYS

ENRICO BRUGNOLI AND MARCO LAUTERI
C.N.R. ISTITUTO PER L'AGROSELVICOLTURA, Via Marconi 2,
05010 Porano (TR), Italy

INTRODUCTION

Exposure to salinity causes large effects on higher plants, both halophytes and glycophytes. In glycophytes the rate of photosynthetic CO_2 assimilation (A) is generally reduced by salinity. This reduction has been partly attributed to stomatal closure (e.g.: 1, 2). Salt induced non-stomatal inhibition of photosynthesis has also been observed in several plant species (2, 3, 4, 5, 6). This inhibition has been attributed to a reduction in the activity of ribulose-1,5-bisphosphate (RuBP) carboxylase when RuBP is in limiting supply (6), to reduced RuBP regeneration capacity (5, 6), or to the sensitivity of photosystem II (PSII) to NaCl (7).

Recently it has been argued that some of the non-stomatal effects of salinity could be only apparent, being actually caused by spatial heterogeneity of stomatal aperture over the leaf. Terashima et al.(8) have demonstrated in ABA treated leaves that stomatal heterogeneity causes a systematic overestimation of intercellular CO_2 partial pressure (p_i) calculated from gas exchange. Similar effects have also been observed in water stressed plants (9, 10, 11).

The present study describes the effects of salinity on stomatal behaviour and photosynthesis of cotton taking into account possible consequences of heterogeneity of stomatal conductance. We present results which indicate that the non-stomatal effect of salinity is actually smaller than originally expected on the basis of conventional gas exchange studies.

MATERIALS AND METHODS

Plants of cotton (Gossypium hirsutum L.) were grown at three different salinity levels: 0, 50, 250 mM NaCl. Gas exchange was measured using an open system similar to that described by von Caemmerer and Farquhar (12). Spot gas exchange measurements were taken with a portable photosynthesis system (Analytical Development Company, U.K.). Light response curves of O_2 evolution were measured with a leaf-disc oxygen electrode as described previously (13) and according to Björkman and Demming (14). Carbon isotope composition of plant material was measured according to Brugnoli et al. (15). Chlorophyll content and Chl a/b ratio were determined according to

M. Baltscheffsky (ed.), Current Research in Photosynthesis, Vol. IV, 741–744.
© 1990 Kluwer Academic Publishers. Printed in the Netherlands.

Arnon (16).

RESULTS AND DISCUSSION

Growth of cotton was strongly affected by salinity. Total leaf area and shoot dry weight were reduced in both salt treatments, compared with control plants (data not shown).

Gas exchange characteristics of cotton plants grown at different salinity levels showed large variations. Stomatal conductance always decreased with increasing salinity. This reduction caused a restriction of CO_2 availability as indicated by the decline of p_i in salt stressed plants. Similar results were reported in several salt sensitive species (1, 2, 5).

The salt induced stomatal inhibition of photosynthesis was confirmed by the analysis of carbon isotope composition (δ) in plant material. Salt stressed plants were always enriched in ^{13}C with respect to control plants, indicating a strong decline of p_i/p_a (17). A strong correlation was found between δ and p_i/p_a calculated from gas exchange ($r^2=0.96$ in leaves and $r^2=0.90$ in cotton fiber), according to the theory (17).

The analysis of the assimilation as a function of intercellular CO_2 partial pressure suggests a decline of photosynthetic capacity with increasing salinity. The A (p_i) response curves of cotton plant grown under salinity condition showed a marked decline (Data not shown), both in the linear portion at low p_i and in the saturated region at high p_i. This would imply that non-stomatal limitations of photosynthesis also occur during salt stress, and they involve both rubisco activity and RuBP regeneration capacity (12). Non-stomatal inhibition of photosynthetic capacity has been reported for several salt sensitive species (2, 3, 6, 18). However, it could be possible that the salt induced depression of A(p_i) curves is overestimated to an extent which depends on the distribution of open stomata over the leaf (8).

This possibility was evaluated using an oxygen electrode at saturating CO_2 (CO_2 partial pressure of 100 mbar). It has been demonstrated that such very high CO_2 concentration can overcome the effect of heterogeneity of stomatal aperture (8, 10). Our results indicate that the apparent quantum yield of oxygen evolution was fairly insensitive to salinity (Table I), being about 0.08 (mol O_2 evolved/mol incident quanta) in all salinity treatments. This value is very close to that reported previously for cotton (14). We could not measure the quantum yield on the basis of absorbed photons. However, leaves didn't show any significant variations among salinity treatments, either in the total chlorophyll content or in Chl a/b ratio (data not shown). Therefore, possible changes in leaf absorptance among treatments would be caused by differences in leaf thickness and cuticolar or epidermal reflectance (14). We don't expect such possible effects to be large enough to cause marked variations of the quantum yield on the basis of absorbed photons.

The lack of decline of quantum yield seems to imply that the efficiency of energy conversion is not affected by salinity. It has been shown that PSII in isolated thylakoids, from both halophytes

(<u>Avicennia</u> <u>marina</u>) and glycophytes (<u>Pisum</u> <u>sativum</u>), is highly sensitive to NaCl (7). However, a direct effect of salinity on PSII would cause a decline of the quantum yield, not observed in the present experiment. This would mean that PSII is insensitive to salinity <u>in vivo</u>, or more likely that plants are able to keep a low level of toxic ions inside the chloroplast.

The light and CO_2 saturated rate of O_2 evolution showed a salt induced decline. This inequivocally demonstrates a non-stomatal effect of salinity on photosynthesis. However, the decline of the light saturated rate of O_2 evolution in salt stressed plants was smaller than expected on the basis of $A(p_i)$ relationship. These results seem to indicate that some of the non-stomatal effects, as detected by depression of $A(p_i)$ curves, are only apparent and could be attributed to patchy stomatal closure. Furthermore, the rate of O_2 evolution showed a significant enhancement increasing the partial pressure of CO_2 from 50 mbar to 100 mbar (data not shown). These evidences confirm for salt stress other previous observation on the effect of ABA (8, 10, 19) and on the effect of water stress (9, 10, 11, 20).

There are several possibility to explain the salt induced reduction of the light and CO_2 saturated rate of oxygen evolution. The carbon reduction pathway could be impaired by salinity. For example, such effect could result from a reduction of the maximum RuBP regeneration capacity. At low light this would be unimportant if the rate of RuBP formation is still enough to sustain photosynthesis. The effect would be only apparent at high light. A possible effect of salinity on photophosphorylation could explain the salt induced decline of the light saturated rate of O_2 evolution. Ben et al.(20) found a similar response of sunflower leaves to sustained mild water stress and suggested that the sensitivity of photophosphorylation to water stress (21, 22) could be responsible of such behaviour. We extend this hypotesis to the effect of salinity. If the ion level inside the chloroplast is kept lower than that of cytoplasm and/or vacuole, an osmotic gradient would rise between chloroplast and cytoplasm and/or vacuole. This could cause an osmotic stress similar to that originated by water stress.

TABLE I.   Apparent quantum yield of O_2 evolution (mol O_2 evolved/mol incident quanta) of cotton (<u>Gossypium</u> <u>hirsutum</u> L.) grown at different salinity concentration.

TREATMENT	APPARENT QUANTUM YIELD $\pm$ S.E.	
Control	0.082 ± 0.004	(n=5)
50 mM NaCl	0.080 ± 0.003	(n=5)
250 mM NaCl	0.080 ± 0.003	(n=5)

REFERENCES
1 Downton, W.J.S., Grant, W.J.R. and Robinson, S.P. (1985) Plant
   Physiol. 77, 85-88
2 Seemann, J.R. and Critchley, C. (1985) Planta 164, 151-162
3 Gale, J., Kohl, H.C.and Hagan, R.M. (1967) Physiol. Plant. 20, 408-
   420
4 Walker, R.R., Torokfalvy, E., Steele Scott, N. and Kriedemann, P.E.
   (1981) Aust. J. Plant Physiol. 8, 359-374
5 Ball, M.C. and Farquhar, G.D. (1984) Plant Physiol. 74, 1-6
6 Seemann, J.R. and Sharkey, T.D. (1986) Plant Physiol. 82, 555-560
7 Ball, M.C. and Anderson, J.M. (1986) Aust. J. Plant Physiol. 13,
   689-698
8 Terashima, I., Wong, S.C., Osmond, C.B. and Farquhar, G.D. (1988)
   Plant Cell Physiol. 29, 385-395
9 Downton, W.J.S., Loveys, B.R. and Grant, W.J.R. (1988) New Phytol.
   110, 503-509
10 Robinson, S.P., Grant, W.J.R. and Loveys, B.R. (1988) Aust. J. Plant
   Physiol. 15, 495-503
11 Cornic, G., Le Gouallec, L., Briantais, J.M. and Hodges, M. (1989)
   Planta 177, 84-90
12 von Caemmerer, S. and Farquhar, G.D. (1981) Planta 153, 376-387
13 Delieu, T. and Walker, D.A. (1981) New Phytol. 89, 165-175
14 Björkman, O. and Demming, B. (1987) Planta 170, 489-504
15 Brugnoli, E., Hubick, K.T., von Caemmerer, S., Wong, S.C. and
   Farquhar, G.D. (1988) Plant Physiol. 88, 1418-1424
16 Arnon, D.J. (1949) Plant Physiol. 24, 618-633
17 Farquhar,G.D., O'Leary, M.H. and Berry, J.A. (1982) Aust. J. Plant
   Physiol. 9, 121-137
18 Downton, W.J.S. (1977) Plant Physiol. 4, 183-192
19 Downton, W.J.S., Loveys, B.R. and Grant, W.J.R. (1988) New Phytol.
   108, 263-266
20 Ben, G.Y., Osmond, C.B. and Sharkey, T.D. (1987) Plant Physiol. 84,
   476-482
21 Keck, R.W. and Boyer, J.S. (1974) Plant Physiol. 53, 474-479
22 Sharkey, T.D. and Badger, M.R. (1982) Planta 156, 199-206

SALINITY INDUCED CHANGES IN LEAF EXPANSION, PHOTOSYNTHESIS AND K+ ACCUMULATION IN SUNFLOWER

JOHN M. CHEESEMAN and SWATI BASU, Department of Plant Biology, University of Illinois, Urbana IL 61801, USA

1. INTRODUCTION

It is well known that plants whose growth is environmentally limited are smaller that plants with sufficient or unlimiting resources, but the physiological causes and consequences of growth reductions are not always easily defined. Clearly, if plants are smaller, their total photosynthesis will be reduced in the long term. In the shorter term, the effects on photosynthesis, and the importance of those effects to growth, are more variable.

It is not unusual, however, to find that plant growth under "stress" is reduced more than would be expected based on changes in carbon metabolism, i.e. that growth is not carbon limited (c.f. ref. 1 for a brief review). In this paper, we examine the effects of mild salinization on growth of sunflower. We will discuss the results with respect to the integration of carbon metabolism and growth, and the possible role of K+ distributional processes in that coordination.

2. PROCEDURE

2.1. Materials and methods

2.1.1. Seeds of *Helianthus annus* L. cv. RHA 273, a dwarf variety supplied by Interstate Seed Co., Fargo ND USA, were soaked in aerated water overnight and germinated on moist vermiculite in the light. Approximately 6 days later, the seedlings were transferred to solution culture under growth chamber conditions (Conviron E15, 13 h photoperiod, 25°C/22°C, 50% r.h., > 680 μmol quanta m^{-2} s^{-1}). The culture medium was a modified HOaglands supplemented with 10 mM NaCl (2), and 8 plants were grown in each of 2-64 L containers. For higher salinity treatments, the NaCl concentration was increased to 50 and 100 mM on days 19 and 20 after germination.

2.1.2. Leaf areas were determined using blade width and lengths beginning 10 d after germination. Leaf Na+ and K+ were determined by flame photometry using 2-0.28 cm^2 leaf disks. Comparison with plants from which no disks were taken indicated that total projected leaf area was not reduced by this sampling procedure. Photosynthetic gas exchange studies were performed *in situ* using an ADC portable IRGA. Light response curves were determined on leaf disks using the Hansatech LD2 system. Carbohydrate analyses were performed using a procedure modified from ref. 3.

M. Baltscheffsky (ed.), Current Research in Photosynthesis, Vol. IV, 745–748.
© 1990 *Kluwer Academic Publishers. Printed in the Netherlands.*

3. RESULTS

3.1.   The initial indication that growth could be severely retarded in the RHA 273 cultivar of sunflower without effects on photosynthetic performance was that *in situ* CO_2 fixation and stomatal conductance were identical in plants at 10 and 100 mM NaCl after two weeks of treatment. Under growth chamber conditions, the average values for leaves 3 to 8 were 20 μmol CO_2 m^{-2} s^{-1} (P_{net}), and 1.2 mol m^{-2} s^{-1} (conductance). The similarity of performance was also indicated by O_2 electrode studies of quantum yield. For leaves 2 and 4, the apparent yields were 0.059 and 0.070 for the 10 and 100 mM NaCl treatments respectively.

3.2   Figure 1 shows the lack of treatment effects immediately following salinization as well. *In situ* gas exchange measurements were made daily in early afternoon. The plants at the higher salinity were increased from 10 to 50 to 100 mM NaCl over a period of 4 hours, and the first point taken immediately thereafter. Although stomatal conductance decreased markedly for several days, it did not result in limited carbon fixation.

3.3   It is possible, even if net photosynthesis is maintained through salinization, that the overall C budget is altered sufficiently to produce reduced growth. One method of considering this alternative is to compare the levels of carbohydrate in leaves of different ages in the two treatments. In Table 1, such a comparison is made for expanded, rapidly growing, and very young leaves, approximately 10 days after the final salinization. Though leaf expansion was reduced >30% and dry weight was affected similarly, there was little effect on the overall C status.

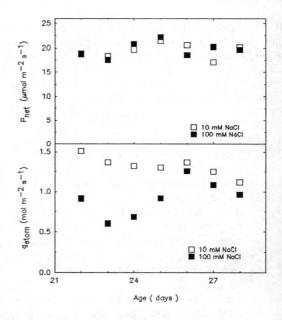

Figure 1. The response of P_{net} and g_{stom} to salinization from 10 to 100 mM NaCl in sunflower. Salinity was increased just prior to the first measurement.

Table I. Carbohydrates in leaves of sunflowers at low (10 mM NaCl) and high (100 mM NaCl) salinities. Concentrations during the late afternoon are followed (in parentheses) by the percent remaining at the end of the following dark period. Data are given for three stages of expansion.

		Sucrose	Hexose	Starch
		μmol/gFW		mg/gDW
"Fully expanded"	10	30(63)	14(81)	98(37)
	100	32(65)	20(75)	59(19)
"Rapidly expanding"				
	10	29(40)	16(50)	87(16)
	100	20(51)	26(64)	89(14)
"Young"	10	39(43)	24(48)	93(17)
	100	48(40)	29(70)	85(18)

Figure 2a shows the response of leaf expansion to the salinization treatment. Leaf 3 was ca. 50% expanded at the time of salinization and growth ceased immediately. Younger leaves (i.e. 4 to 6) which were rapidly expanding, slowed growth, eventually becoming no more than half the size of the low salinity leaves (data not shown). Leaves which had not begun expanding at the time of salinization also showed the growth reduction (Fig. 2a).

In a number of other types of growth studies (e.g. ref. 4,5), we had previously noted the tight coordination between growth and K^+ accumulation in leaves, regardless of the limitation imposed to reduce growth. Figure 2b shows that K^+ accumulation in sunflower leaves was affected similarly to area expansion. With the possible exception of leaf 4 which showed a net loss of K^+ in the week following salinization to 100 mM, there was no indication of net K^+ redistribution in these studies.

Though the data suggest that salinity decreased the capacity of the plants to accumulate nutrients, this is not the inevitable conclusion. As shown in Figure 2c, the adjustment of leaf growth and K^+ accumulation resulted in a nearly constant ratio of K^+ to leaf area. Analysis of leaves 3 to 8 confirmed that there were no salinity effects in any layer (data not shown).

DISCUSSION

The results presented here are consistent with a number of reports indicating that growth of plants under water and salt stress is not limited by the availability of fixed carbon (1). The results similarly indicate that the ability to acquire K^+ is not limiting to leaf expansion. The overall, organismal picture is, however, still far from clear. It may be that leaf expansion is

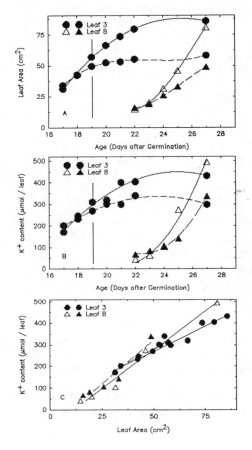

largely limited by K^+ (6), and thus that the process of transport across the roots is the key one to understand. On the other hand, it may be that leaf "demand", nebulous as the concept may be, controls the delivery of K^+ from the roots, in which case the commun- ications process is to be determined. It may, more reasonably, be expected that the answer comines these and other factors.

4.2 This leaves us with the less than satisfactory conclusion that there is an organismal level of integration of photosynthesis and other processes which determines growth and responses to environmental factors, about which we still no very little. It does, however, lead us to the realization that the control and integration of resource acquisition and allocation in plants deserves serious attention in the future.

5.0 Acknowledgement -- This research and the participation of JMC in this Congress were supported by grant Ag- 87-CRCR-1-2501 from USDA-CRGO.

Figure 2. Relationship between leaf area, K^+ content and age in sunflowers. Solid lines -- 10 mM NaCl; dashed lines -- 100 mM. Salinity was increased on day 19 (vertical bar).

REFERENCES
1. Cheeseman, J. M. (1988) Plant Physiol. 87, 547-550.
2. Lazof, D. B. and Cheeseman J. M. (1988) Plant Physiol. 88, 1279-1284.
3. Jones, M. G. K., Outlaw, W. H. Jr., and Lowry, O. H. (1977) Plant Physiol. 60, 379-383.
4. Wickens, L. K. and Cheeseman, J. M. (1988) Physiol. Plant. 73, 271-277.
5. Cheeseman, J. M. and Wickens, L. K. (1986) Physiol. Plant. 67, 15-22.
6. Van Volkenburgh, E., Cleland, R. E. and Björkman, T. (1989) Plant Physiol. 89S, 137.

EFFECT OF ENVIRONMENTAL STRESS ON PHOTOSYNTHESIS OF ISOLATED MESOPHYLL
CELLS FROM COWPEA LEAVES

Z. Plaut[*], C.M. Grieve[**] and E. Federman[*]
[*]INSTITUTE OF SPILS AND WATER, ARO, P.O.B.6, BET-DAGAN 50250, ISRAEL
[*]US SALINITY LAB., 4500 Glenwood Drive, RIVERSIDE CA.92501, U.S.A.

. ABSTRACT
   Mesophyll cells from leaves of cowpea (Vigna unquiculata (L.) Walp.)
lants, grown in salinized nutrient solution or under soil moisture
ensions, were isolated and used for the determination of photosynthe-
ic CO_2 fixation rate. Maximal CO_2 fixation was obtained when the
smotic potential of both isolation and CO_2 fixation assay media were
lose to leaf osmotic potential, yielding zero turgor pressure. No
ecrease in photosynthesis was obtained for NaCl concentrations up to
7 moles per cubic meter in the growing medium. However, a decrease of
ver 50% was obtained at a similar level of soil matrix potential. The
ight response curve of cells from low-salinity-grown plants was simi-
ar to the controls. Cells were close to CO_2 saturation at 5 mmol
aHCO3 in the medium, regardless of environmental conditions.

. INTRODUCTION
   A limitation in CO_2 uptake during photosynthesis by plants subjected
o water stress and salinity is a generally accepted phenomenon. Both
nvironmental stress conditions result in a distinct decrease of leaf
ater potential, stomatal closure and a drop in leaf diffusive conduct-
nce, leading to a decrease in CO_2 uptake. It was, however, shown that
n spite of the decrease in intercellular CO_2 concentration under water
tress, this was not the cause for the decrease in photosynthesis (1).
he response of intact leaf photosynthesis to water and salt stresses
ere, however, found to be not so similar (2). Water stress inhibited
O2 fixation more drastically than an equivalent intensity of salt
tress.
   The effect of stomatal conductance on photosynthesis can be by-
assed by studying photosynthesis of isolated mesophyll cells. Photo-
ynthetically active cells can be isolated from a variety of plant
pecies and this is much easier than the preparation of chloroplasts.
   The purpose of the present study was to develop adequate conditions
equired for CO_2 fixation in isolated mesophyll cells and to investi-
ate the effect of NaCl and water stress on photosynthesis of these
ells.

M. Baltscheffsky (ed.), Current Research in Photosynthesis, Vol. IV, 749–752.
© 1990 Kluwer Academic Publishers. Printed in the Netherlands.

3. MATERIALS AND METHODS

Cowpea (<u>Vigna</u> <u>unquiculata</u> (L.) Walp.) cv 'California Blackeye' seeds were germinated on paper towels saturated with 0.5 mol.m^{-3} CaSO$_4$. Seedlings were grown in continuously aerated modified half strength Hoagland solutions or in a prewetted sandy loam soil. Eight seedlings were grown per container filled with 15 L of nutrient solution or one seedling per pot filled with 2 kg of dry soil. The water withdrawn by transpiration was always replenished. Plants were grown in a naturally illuminated glasshouse, in which the temperature was maintained between 27°C during the day and 17°C at night. Nutrient solutions were gradually salinized to reach the final NaCl concentrations within three days. In the soil, water stress was applied by withholding irrigation water for different time periods reaching the predetermined soil moisture potentials at about the same day. The final level of both water and salt stress was obtained at the stage of full expansion of the first trifoliated leaf. Plants were then covered with transparent polyethylene bags and transferred to shade for 7 days to minimize transpiration and reach steady state.

The second trifoliated leaf which was fully expanded at this stage was harvested for the preparation of mesophyll cells. The preparation of cells and the assay of CO$_2$ fixation by these cells were conducted as described elsewhere (3).

RESULTS AND DISCUSSION

The optimal sorbitol concentration required for maximal rates of photosynthesis depends on leaf water and osmotic potentials (Ψ_w and Ψ_s). Fig. 1 shows linear relationships between leaf Ψ_w and Ψ_s and the osmotic potential of the nutrient solution, suggesting that the plants fully adjusted osmotically. We assumed that the leaves were at steady state and the cells would thus be at an identical Ψ_s to that of the intact leaf. In leaves of control plants the Ψ_s was about -0.7 MPa, and the highest CO$_2$ fixation rate was obtained when cells were prepared and assayed at 300 mol.m^{-3} sorbitol which is equivalent to this Ψ_s. This implies that maximal CO$_2$ fixation was implemented by zero turgor and that high turgor pressure on one side and plasmolysis on the other were inhibitory (Table 1). The requirement for a higher sorbitol concentration in cell preparation and CO$_2$ fixation assay media for higher salinity level is thus a result of leaf osmotic adjustment. This requirement is less evident in plants which were exposed to water stress as osmotic adjustment was not fully accomplished. The decrease in intact cell photosynthesis under conditions of shrinkage or plasmolysis is probably similar to that shown for chloroplasts (4,5,6). Such a decrease was achieved by reduced Ψ_s of the

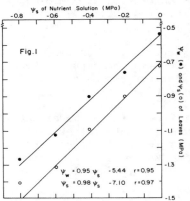

Fig. 1: Leaf water potential (Ψ_w) and osmotic potential (Ψ_s) as a function of external salinity level.

$\Psi_w = 0.95 \Psi_s -5.44$ $r=0.95$

$\Psi_s = 0.98 \Psi_s -7.10$ $r=0.97$

TABLE 1. Fixation rates (μmol mg.Chl^{-1}h^{-1}) of leaf cells from plants exposed to salinity or water stress.

Sorbitol concentration	NaCl in nutrient solution (mol.m^{-3})			
(mol.m^{-3})	0	43	87	130
200	39	5	1	0
300	92	97	63	34
500	48	74	98	62
700	19	22	36	53
	Soil moisture potential (KPa)			
	−50	−200	−400	−1200
300	86	84	18	1
500	64	85	38	9
700	42	37	26	12

media for a given cell population or by a decrease in soil moisture potential. The effect of salinity was much less as at 87 mol.m^{-3} NaCl in the growing media no decrease in CO_2 fixation was found, while at an equivalent soil moisture potential - −400 KPa - the decreae was marked.

The relation between initial cell Ψ_s and the external solution Ψ_s in controlling CO_2 fixation by cells implies that limited sorbitol was taken up by the cells causing water uptake and change in volume. We have determined that the uptake of sorbitol by intact cells was negligible and served mainly as an osmoticum to control water flow. This is in contrast to isolated chloroplasts as shown by Robinson (6).

The influence of NaHCO3 concentration on photosynthesis in isolated cells of salinity grown plants was determined at optimal sorbitol concentrations for each salinity level (Fig. 2). Cells were close to CO_2 saturation at 5 mol.m^{-3} NaHCO3 regardless of salinity in the growing medium. The NaHCO3 response curve were similar for all salinity levels and 50% of maximal activity was found at 0.98 mol.m^{-3} NaHCO3 (equivalent to 0.17% CO_2). Extrapolation of CO_2 fixation to a zero rate showed a similar value up to 130 mol.m^{-3} NaCl. The rate of CO_2 fixation was markedly inhibited at 173 mol.m^{-3} NaCl, and there was also a change in its zero extrapolation.

The lack of interaction between radiant flux density and salinity up to 130 mol.m^{-3} NaCl (Fig. 3) also suggest that the effect was not due to chloroplast activity.

Cells isolated from plants grown at 173 mol.m^{-3} NaCl and assayed at an appropriate sorbitol concentration were light saturated at 160 μEm^{-2}s^{-1} (Fig. 3). The response of CO_2 fixation was not much influenced by leaf age (Table 2). Cells of expanding leaves (L-4) were, however, less sensitive to salinity than cells from mature leaves.

It is concluded that the salinity adaptation of mesophyll leaf cells and the minimal inhibition of photosynthesis occurred up to a salt level which caused direct damage to cells. This was at 173 mol.m^{-3} NaCl which resulted in high concentrations of Na$^+$ and Cl$^-$ in the leaf.

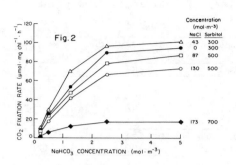

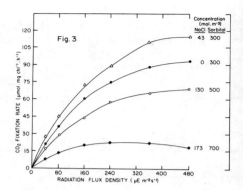

Fig. 2: CO_2 fixation rates of mesophyll cells from plants of different salinity levels as a function of $NaHCO_3$ concentration.

Fig. 3: CO_2 fixation rates of mesophyll cells from plants of different salinity levels as a function of radiant flux densities

TABLE 2. CO_2 fixation rates of mesophyll cells isolated from mature (L-1) and expanding (L-4) cowpea leaves.

NaCl ($mol.m^{-3}$)	Sorbitol ($mol.m^{-3}$)	CO_2 fixation rate ($\mu mol.mgChl^{-1}.h^{-1}$)	
		L-1	L-4
0	300	83	39
43	300	99	59
87	500	81	57
130	700	60	51
173	700	13	12

REFERENCES
1 Farqhuar, G.D. and Sharkey, T.D. (1982) Ann. Rev. Plant Physiol. 33:317-345.
2 Plaut, Z. (1989) in: Structural and Functional Responses to Environmental Stresses (Kreeb, K.H., Richter, H. and Hinckley, T.M., eds.), pp.155-163. SPB Academic Publishing, The Hague.
3 Plaut, Z., Grieve, C.M. and Federman, E. (1989) Plant Physiol. In press.
4 Berkowitz, G.A. and Gibbs, M. (1983) Plant Physiol. 72:1100-1109.
5 Ort, D.R. and Boyer, J.S. (1985) in: Changes in Eukaryotic gene expression in response to environmental stresses. Academic Press.
6 Robinson, S.P. (1985) Plant Physiol. 79: 996-1002.

ASSIMILATORY FORCE IN ILLUMINATED LEAVES GROWN IN SUN OR SHADE OR UNDER
MINERAL DEFICIENCY

KATHARINA SIEBKE, KARL-JOSEF DIETZ AND ULRICH HEBER
Lehrstuhl Botanik I, Mittlerer Dallenbergweg 64,
8700 WÜRZBURG, FEDERAL REPUBLIK OF GERMANY

1. INTRODUCTION

In photosynthesis, ADP is phosphorylated and NADP reduced at the
expense of light energy. The NADPH and ATP formed by the
chloroplast thylakoid system serve to reduce CO_2 in the
chloroplast stroma. The product of the phosphorylation potential
($ATP/ADP \cdot P_i$) and the redox ratio ($NADPH \cdot H^+/NADP^+$) is termed
assimilatory force (F_A). It is instrumental in driving carbon
reduction. The reaction

$$PGA+NADPH+H^+ +ATP \longleftrightarrow DHAP+NADP^+ +ADP+P_i \quad (1)$$

in which ATP is consumed and NADPH oxidized, is close to
thermodynamic equilibrium even when photosynthesis is fast[1]. It is
therefore possible to calculate F_A from the ratio of
dihydroxyacetone-phosphate (DHAP) to 3-phosphoglycerate (PGA):

$$\frac{ATP}{ADP \cdot P_i} \cdot \frac{NADPH}{NADP^+} = \frac{K}{H^+} \cdot \frac{DHAP}{PGA} = F_A \quad (2)$$

using the equilibrium constant K of (1). If it is sufficient to
compare relative values of F_A rather than to know absolute values,
measurements of PGA and DHAP in leaf homogenates can substitute
for chloroplast measurements, because changes in the concentration
of PGA and DHAP ocurring in the stroma are transmitted to the
cytosol over the chloroplast envelope[2].

F_A is not a thermodynamic driving force. The increase in the free
energy of the phosphorylation potential and of the NADP system
produced by illumination[3] is described by

$$\Delta G = -R \cdot T \cdot \ln(F_A \text{ light}/F_A \text{ dark}) \quad (3)$$

Since a chemical flux is proportional to a thermodynamic driving
force ΔG and inversely proportional to a kinetic flux resistance,
knowledge of photosynthetic fluxes and of F_A can give information
on flux limitations in photosynthesis.

2. ASSIMILATORY FORCE IN SUN FLOWER LEAVES (*Helianthus annuus*) GROWN
    IN SHADE OR SUNLIGHT

F_A increased on illumination. However it decreased with increasing
light intensity in sunflower leaves. Shade-grown leaves showed
higher F_A values than sun-grown leaves.

M. Baltscheffsky (ed.), Current Research in Photosynthesis, Vol. IV, 753–756.
© 1990 Kluwer Academic Publishers. Printed in the Netherlands.

However the latter did not reach the photosynthetic rate of the former. The flux resistance in the Calvin cycle was higher in shade- than in sun-grown leaves.

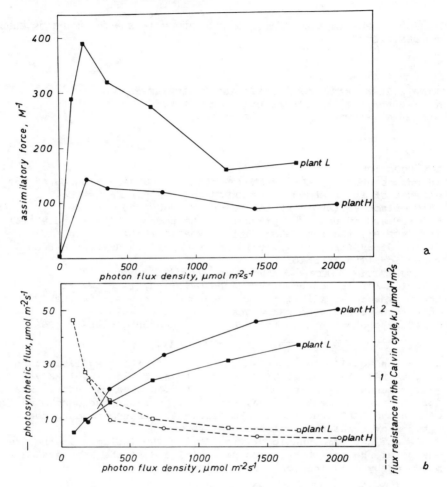

FIGURE .1 Sunflower leaves were grown at two different light
   intensities (leaves L: 400 μmol·m^{-2}·s^{-1},
   leaves H: 1700 μmol·m^{-2}·s^{-1})
   Photosynthesis was measured at various intensities of white light.
   The leaves were gassed with a CO_2-concentration of 1000 μl/l CO_2
   and a O_2-concentration of 2% O_2. After the steady state had been
   reached the leaves were rapidly frozen and used for determination
   of the PGA- and DHAP-concentrations.
a) Assimilatory force
b) Photosynthetic rate and flux resistance in the Calvin cycle

3.   COMPARISON OF F_A IN LEAVES OF *Asarum europaeum* GROWN IN SUN OR
     SHADE

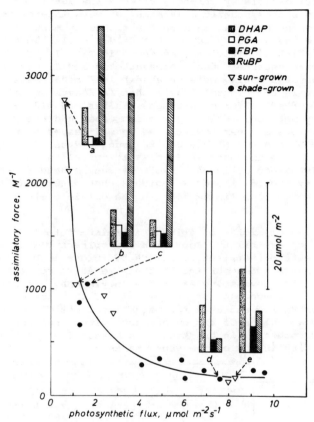

FIGURE   2. Leaves were detached from plants of *Asarum europaeum* grown
     either in the shade of beech trees or exposed to full sunlight
     until early afternoon. They were gassed with 1000 µl/l CO_2 and 2%
     O_2 and illuminated with 1000 $\mu mol \cdot m^{-2} \cdot s^{-1}$ white light until steady
     state was established.

In contrast to the data shown above for sunflower leaves (Fig. 1)
(cf also[4]), F_A in leaves of *Asarum* was not noticeably dependent on
the light regime during growth. It was high when carbon reduction
was slow owing to partially closed stomata. The highest F_A-values
were observed in sun grown leaves around midday when stomata were
closed and when reduced oxygen tension prevented significant
photorespiratory CO_2 turnover.
At comparable photosynthetic fluxes (see inset pairs b/c and d/e)
no significant differences in respect to leaf metabolites were
seen between sun- and shade- grown plants.

4.   EFFECTS OF MINERAL DEFICIENCY ON F_A IN *Spinacea oleracea*
Mineral deficiency strongly affects the development of leaves and
of the photosynthetic apparatus. We were interested to know
whether carbon flux is more restricted in mineral deficient leaves
by the thylakoid system or the Calvin cycle. Spinach was grown
under mineral deficiency as shown in Tab. 1. Leaves of different
age were detached and photosynthesis and F_A was measured. Rates
of photosynthesis were on a unit leaf area basis consistently
higher in the control leaves than in leaves deficient in
phosphorus, sulfur or nitrogen. Sulfur and old nitrogen deficient
leaves were chlorotic. F_A was increased under all deficiency
conditions and particularly so in old leaves of phosphate and
nitrogen starved plants and in young leaves of sulfur-deprived
plants. The increase in F_A clearly correlated with the development
of pronounced deficiency symptoms and reduced rates of
photosynthesis. The data indicate that mineral deficiency
introduces flux limitations in the Calvin cycle.

TABLE 1.
Assimilatory force of spinach in relation to leaf age and plant
nutrient avaibility. Four week old spinach plants were starved for
two weeks on nutrient solutions deficient in N, P or S. Leaves
were harvested according to their relative age (leaf # 1 was the
first leaf developing after the cotyledons), illuminated at a
photon fluence rate of 250 $\mu mol \cdot m^{-2} \cdot s^{-1}$ at ambient CO_2
concentration and used for metabolite determinations[5]. The results
are mean values of two experiments with three replicates each.
Photosynthesis (in brackets) was measured at saturating light
intensity in one of the experiments.

Leaves		F_A (M^{-1}), photosynthetic rate $(\mu mol \cdot m^{-2} \cdot s^{-1})$			
		Control	– phosphate	– sulfate	– nitrogen
1+ 2	old	152 (11.0)	299 (4.8)	311 (6.1)	721 (–)
3+ 4	↑	144 (12.3)	224 (9.9)	260 (4.9)	480 (3.9)
5+ 6		132 (15.4)	242 (11.0)	302 (4.4)	438 (–)
7+ 8	↓	153 (12.8)	195 (10.7)	560 (1.8)	363 (11.3)
9+10	young	192 (10.5)	–	–	–

5.   CONCLUSION
Photosynthetic carbon reduction can be highly efficient at low F_A
values. Under all conditions investigated, reduced photosynthesis
was accompanied by high F_A values. F_A increased, when stress
conditions limited photosynthesis.

REFERENCES
1 Dietz KJ, Heber U (1984) Biochim. Biophys. Acta 767, 432-43
2 Heber U, HW Heldt (1981) Ann. Rev. Plant Physiol. 32, 139-68
3 Dietz KJ, Heber U (1989) in Techniques and New Developments in
  Photosynthesis, (Barber J. ed.), Plenum Press, London: in press.
4 Sharkey TD, JR Seemann, RW Pearcy (1986) Plant Physiol. 82,   1063-68
5 Dietz KJ (1989) J. Plant Physiol. 134, 551-57

IRON DEFICIENCY-INDUCED MECHANISMS OF DISSIPATION OF EXCESS ENERGY IN HIGHER PLANTS.

ANUNCIACION ABADIA, FERMIN MORALES AND JAVIER ABADIA. Dept. Plant Nutrition, Aula Dei Exp. Sta. Apdo 202, 50080 ZARAGOZA, SPAIN.

1. INTRODUCTION

The most obvious effect of Fe deficiency in higher plants is the yellowness of the young leaves. It has been known for many years that this yellow aspect reflects a relative enrichment in carotenoids, namely xanthophylls (1). Recently it has been shown that three closely related xanthophylls are largely responsible for this enrichment in carotenoids (2). These pigments can undergo interconversions (epoxidations and de-epoxidations) within the xanthophyll cycle (thereafter referred to as VAZ cycle).These xanthophylls differ in the number of epoxide groups in the molecule: violaxanthin (2 epoxides), anteraxanthin (1 epoxide) and zeaxanthin (no epoxides). This cycle is known to be regulated by tight pH conditions associated with the stroma-exposed side of the membrane (epoxidase) or to the lumenal side (de-epoxidase).

2. PROCEDURE

2.1 Materials and methods

Pigments were analyzed by HPLC as described in de las Rivas et al. (3). Typical photosynthetic pigment separations from Fe deficient and control sugarbeet leaves are shown in Fig. 1. Fluorescence induction curves were obtained after 15 min dark adaptation of plants. Leaves were illuminated with saturating blue light (620 nm cut-off filter). The detector was protected with a RG665 filter and a 680 interference filter. The signal from the detector was fed to a digital storage oscilloscope. Modulated fluorescence was measured with the Hansatech apparatus. Absorptance was measured with the integration sphere of a Shimadzu UV-3000 spectrophotometer. Iron-deficient leaves were sampled from leaves of different species grown in different environments: Beta vulgaris (growth chamber in Spain), Phaseolus vulgaris and Zea mais (greenhouse in Colchester, U.K.) and Pyrus communis (field in Zaragoza, Spain).

3. RESULTS AND DISCUSSION

3.1 Iron deficiency causes characteristic changes in photosynthetic pigment composition. Iron deficiency decreases the amount of all photosynthetic pigments. However, the extent of this decrease depends on the specific pigment considered. Least affected were the three carotenoids within the VAZ cycle, violaxanthin, anteraxanthin and zeaxanthin. As a result of Fe deficiency, the

M. Baltscheffsky (ed.), Current Research in Photosynthesis, Vol. IV, 757–760.
© 1990 *Kluwer Academic Publishers. Printed in the Netherlands.*

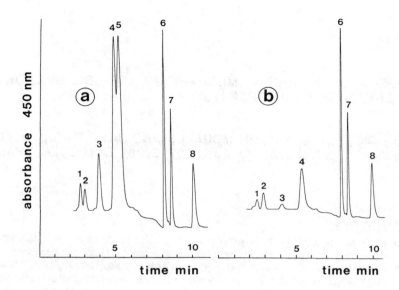

FIGURE 1. HPLC separation (3) of pigments from a Fe-deficient (A) and a control sugarbeet leaf (B). [1] neoxanthin, [2] violaxanthin, [3] anteraxanthin, [4] lutein, [5] zeaxanthin, [6] Chl b, [7] Chl a, [8] β-carotene.

molar ratios of VAZ pigments to 100 Chl a increase in several species from 5-10 in control plants up to 50 or even 200 (Fig. 2; ref 2). The molar ratios VAZ pigments / Chl a were linearly related to the absorptance per unit Chl (r^2=0.96 in sugarbeet, r^2=0.83 in pear).

3.2 <u>Transformations within the VAZ cycle and iron deficiency.</u> In other materials enriched in carotenoids, such as etiolated or senescent leaves, the VAZ pigments do not undergo interconversions within the cycle (not shown). However, VAZ pigments in Fe deficient plants undergo epoxidations and de-epoxidations within the VAZ cycle. The extent of these transformations may be roughly described by an index measuring the actual number of epoxides in the VAZ pigments vs. the maximum i.e. as if violaxanthin was 100% of VAZ pigments. A sugarbeet Fe deficient leaf (2 nmol Chl.cm^{-2}) had a VAZ epoxide content of 84% after several hours in the dark (Fig. 3). When the growth chamber light (350 μE.m^{-2}s^{-1}) was switched on, 95% of the violaxanthin was rapidly converted into anteraxanthin or zeaxanthin (Fig. 3). The half-time for the interconversion was less than 120 s, and the final VAZ epoxide content after 2 h of illumination was 13%.

3.3 <u>Iron deficient plants exhibit characteristic chlorophyll fluorescence induction curves and modulated fluorescence</u>
Iron deficient sugarbeet plants grown in nutrient solutions in the growth chamber exhibited increased levels of PSII (680 nm) Chl fluorescence. Levels of Fo,

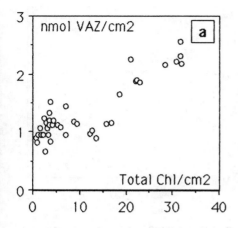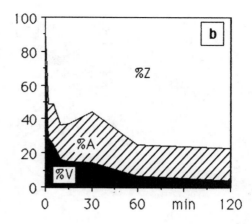

FIGURE 2.a) **VAZ pigments per unit leaf area** **vs** **total Chl per area. All pigments are given in nmol.cm^{-2}.** b) **Light-induced displacement of the VAZ cycle. V: violaxanthin, A: anteraxanthin, Z: zeaxanthin. A Fe deficient sugarbeet leaf was sampled in the growth chamber before and after switching on the chamber lights.**

Fi and Fp became progressively larger as the deficiency developed. These plants exhibited decreases in the ratios Fp/Fo and Fv/Fp, indicating a lowered efficiency of PSII photochemistry. A characteristic of the induction curves was the increased Fi/Fo ratios found in Fe deficient plants. These ratios were not significantly decreased by preillumination with far red light, indicating that they were not due to a reduced state of PQ in the dark. The O to I transient has been ascribed to impaired electron transport after Q_A (4) and to slowly turning over reaction centers (5). The possible relationship of the increase in Fi/Fo with a lack of the Fe-quinone included in the PSII core complex is currently under investigation. Modulated fluorescence indicated that in Fe-deficient bean and mais leaves Q_A was more reduced than in the control plants. However, Q_A was not totally reduced even in severely stressed leaves. Iron deficient leaves exhibited an increase in q_E, that may be related to an increased thylakoid ΔpH, in line with evidence showing that ΔA_{535} is large in these leaves (6).

3.5 <u>Relationship between the Chl fluorescence induction curve and the VAZ cycle.</u>
There was a good linear relationship ($r^2=0.60$ in sugarbeet, $r^2=0.80$ in pear) between the amount of total VAZ pigments per Chl a and the ratio Fv/Fp. However, the change from dark to light in Fe deficient plants displaces the VAZ cycle towards zeaxanthin but induces relatively minor changes in the fluorescence induction curve (Fo and Fp values were quenched by about 15 to 20%, and Fv/Fp decreased by 15%). Furthermore, these changes can be explained by changes in the Chl content during the first few minutes of illumination. This suggests that the cause of the decrease in Fv/Fp may be the increase in the total amount of VAZ carotenoids per Chl, rather than other mechanisms previously proposed, related to the displacement of the VAZ cycle towards zeaxanthin (7, 8). This displacement of the cycle may be just a consequence of two of the prevailing

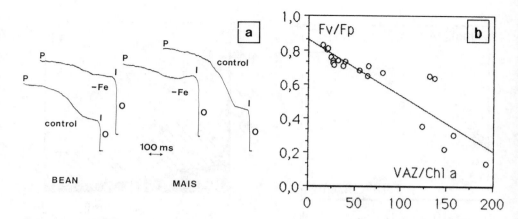

FIGURE 3. a) **Fluorescence induction curves from iron deficient and control bean and mais plants grown in the greenhouse.** b) **The ratio Fv/Fp in the fluorescence induction curve vs the amount of VAZ pigments per Chl in field grown pear leaves. The r^2 was 0.80.**

circumstances in the Fe deficient thylakoid (and also in other environmentally stressed leaves): the increased intrathylakoid ΔpH and/or the reduced state of Q_A.

3.6 _Iron deficiency and mechanisms for energy dissipation._ In Fe deficient leaves the amount of light absorbed per Chl can be very large. The data suggest that the amount of some carotenoids present in the Fe deficient leaf is linearly related to the amount of light absorbed by the leaf Chl. The amount of these carotenoids is linearly related to the ratio Fv/Fp in the fluorescence induction curve, suggesting they contribute to a decrease in PSII photochemical efficiency.

Acknowledgements. J.A. Is grateful to the OECD (Project on Food Production and Preservation) for a 1987 short term fellowship to study fluorescence techniques and to N.R. Baker and B. Genty (U. Essex, U.K.) for their help at the beginning of the experiments. Work partially supported by DGICYT grant PB 88/0084 to J.A.

REFERENCES

1. Terry N. and Abadía J. (1986) J Plant Nutr. 9, 609–646.
2. Abadía A., de las Rivas J., and Abadía J. (1989) J Plant Nutr. 12, in press.
3. de las Rivas J., Abadía A. and Abadía, J. (1989) Plant Physiol. 90, in press.
4. Melis A. (1985) Biochim Biophys Acta 808, 334–342.
5. Chylla R.A. and Withmarsh J. (1989) Plant Physiol. 90, 765–772.
6. Abadía J., Rao I.M. and Terry N. (1988) J Plant Nutr. 11, 423–434.
7. Demmig B., Winter K., Kruger A. and Czygan F.-C. (1988) Plant Physiol. 87, 17–24
8. Demmig B., Winter K., Kruger A. and Czygan F.-C. (1987) Plant Physiol. 84, 218–224

LOW-IRON STRESS IN THE CYANOBACTERIUM *ANABAENA VARIABILIS*

Birgit Michelsen, Mette Miller and Raymond P. Cox
Institute of Biochemistry, Odense University, Campusvej 55,
DK-5230 Odense M, Denmark.

1. INTRODUCTION
Iron is a constituent of a number of cellular compounds in
cyanobacteria, including several components of the photosynthetic
apparatus, and growth can be limited by low concentrations of available
iron in the medium. We report here studies of iron-limited growth and
siderophore production in the heterocyst-containing filamentous
cyanobacterium *Anabaena variabilis*.

2. EXPERIMENTAL
The cyanobacterial strain used was obtained from CCAP as *Anabaena
flos-aquae* 1403/13a and is the same as *Anabaena variabilis* ATCC 29413.
It was grown at 32-35°C under continuous illumination in a nitrogen-
free medium (BG-11o) or an iron-limited variant of BG-11o from which
citrate and EDTA were omitted. Iron-limited medium contained either
0.2 µM or 2.0 µM added $FeCl_3$. Fructose (10 mM) was added as carbon
source. Growth kinetics were measured using 50 ml volumes of culture in
100 ml shaken flasks. Cyanobacteria for the purification of siderophore
were grown in 300 ml batches in 1000 ml flasks. Growth was routinely
measured by apparent absorbance at 550 nm and converted to cell carbon
using a separate calibration curve for each iron concentration.

Siderophore production was determined using a chemical assay
for iron chelating agents (1). The siderophore was purified from the
culture supernatant essentially as described by Mullis et al. (2).

3. RESULTS AND DISCUSSION
3.1. Iron-limited growth
Fig. 1 shows the results of growth experiments in shaken flasks in
medium with different amounts of added iron. Growth of the control
culture showed two phases, presumably corresponding to the utilisation
of fructose (720 mg C/litre added) and then atmospheric CO_2. Growth in
the presence of 2 µM added Fe was clearly iron-limited. This was
confirmed by measurements of the iron content of the washed
cyanobacteria (not shown).

3.2. Siderophore production
An iron-chelating substance was detected in the supernatant of the
iron-limiting cultures. The purified compound was identified as
schizokinen from its proton NMR spectrum (2), in agreement with the
unpublished results of J. Hering and F.M.M. Morel (cited in ref. 3)

M. Baltscheffsky (ed.), Current Research in Photosynthesis, Vol. IV, 761–763.
© 1990 *Kluwer Academic Publishers. Printed in the Netherlands.*

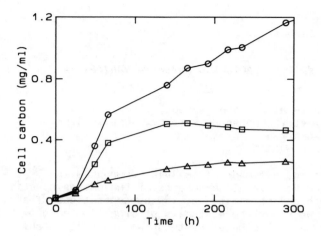

Fig. 1. Growth curves for *Anabaena variabilis* with different
concentrations of Fe added to a BG-11o base medium. Cultures
were started with a 4% innoculum of cyanobacteria grown with
2 μM added Fe for at least five successive subcultures.
Triangles, 0.2 μM Fe; squares, 2.0 μM Fe; circles, 20 μM Fe.

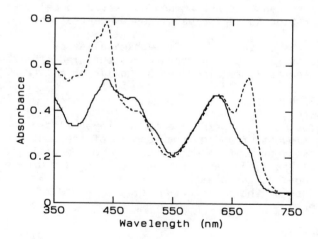

Fig. 2. Absorbance spectra of iron-limited cells grown with 0.2 μM
added Fe (solid line) and control cells (dashed line). The
spectra have been normalised to the same absorbance at 625 nm.

with the same strain from another culture collection (*Anabaena flos-aquae* UTEX 1444). Schizokinen was the first cyanobacterial siderophore to be detected (in *Anabaena* PCC 6411) (4) and has also been detected in paddy field soils (5). It is not confined to cyanobacteria, being also produced by *Bacillus megaterium* (2).

3.3. Composition of the photosynthetic apparatus

Fig. 2 shows a comparison of the absorbance spectra of iron-limited and iron-sufficient cells. The spectra show a much higher phycobilin to chlorophyll ratio in the iron-limited cells. This result is unexpected since several strains of unicellular cyanobacteria have the opposite response, showing breakdown of phycobilisomes as a response to iron-limitation (6). It is not clear whether these opposite results represent a general difference between unicellar and heterocystous cyanobacteria.

REFERENCES
1 Schwyn, B. and Neilands, J.B. (1987) Anal. Biochem. 160, 47–56.
2 Mullis, K.B., Pollack, J.R., Neilands, J.B. (1971) Biochemistry 10, 4894–4898.
3 Goldman, S.J., Lammers, P.J., Berman, M.S. and Sanders-Loehr, J. (1983) J. Bacteriol. 156, 1144–1140.
4 Simpson, F.B. and Neilands, J.B. (1976) J. Phycol. 12, 44–48
5 Akers, H.A. (1983) Appl. Environ. Microbiol. 45, 1704–1706
6 Riethman, H., Bullerjahn, G., Reddy, K.J. and Sherman, L.A. (1988) Photosynthesis Res. 18, 133–161.

VIOLAXANTHIN CYCLE AND FLUORESCENCE IN IRON-DEFICIENT MAIZE LEAVES

Jesús Val[1,2] and Emilio Monge[2]   [1]Depart. of Biology, Univ. of Essex, Colchester, CO4 3SQ, U.K., [2]EE Aula Dei (C.S.I.C.), Aptdo 202, 50080 Zaragoza, Spain

1. INTRODUCTION

Iron deficiency in plants induces alterations in thylakoid membranes. The more evident symptom of this stress is the yellowing of the leaves (chlorosis) which is the manifestation of the decrease of chlorophyll content in leaves relative to carotenoids (1). During iron deficiency a reduction in the stacking and in the amount of thylakoid membranes is found (2) which is accompanied by decreases in proteins, galactolipids, and all the light harvesting pigments (3).

There is evidence to suggest that a decrease in the effective antenna size of PS2 in iron deficient higher plants occurs (4). This also has been studied in iron deficient cyanobacteria by fluorescence kinetics (5) observing an increase in the initial fluorescence (Fo) and a depressed variable fluorescence (Fv). An increase in Fo is characteristic of PS2 inactivation whereas a decline in Fv may indicate the increase a non-photochemical quenching process at or close to reaction centre (6). The Fo level is known to be affected by environmental stress that causes structural alterations at the PS2 pigment level (7)

The exposure of plants to light intensity higher than during their growth, results in photoinhibitory damage of the photosynthesis. This process is manifested by a reduced quantum yield and alteration of the chlorophyll-fluorescence which is thought to be due to damage of the photochemistry of PS2 (8)

A regulatory mechanism to dissipate excess of excitation energy during high light exposure has been proposed to partially protect leaves from photoinhibition of PS2 photochemistry (9, 10). This mechanism is the non-radiative energy dissipation of excess excitation energy where the xanthophylls cycle may play an important role (11).

In this work we study the violaxanthin cycle and chlorophyll-a fluorescence in iron-deficient maize plants highly susceptible to photoinhibitory damage due to the low content of photosynthetic pigments.

2. MATERIAL AND METHODS

Maize plants (*Zea mays* L. cv. LG 11) were grown in a glasshouse at ambient temperature ($\approx 25^\circ C$) and a minimum PPFD of 500 $\mu mol\ m^{-2}s^{-1}$. The plants were developed in hydroponic culture with complete Hoagland's solution (C-plants) and in the same medium without iron (D-plants). All determinations were made in the second fully developed leaf.

Chlorophyll fluorescence was measured by a pulse amplitude modulation fluorimeter Hansatech.

M. Baltscheffsky (ed.), Current Research in Photosynthesis, Vol. IV, 765–768.

Photosynthetic pigments were separated and quantified by HPLC (Beckman System-Gold with a 15 cm stainless steel C_{18} column) essentially as described previously (12) except the flow (2 $cm^{-3}.min^{-1}$) and the mobile phase. This phase consisted in two isocratic steps: first (6 min) acetonitrile/ethylacetate (50/50 v/v) and second (10 min) dichloromethane/methanol/water/acetonitrile (1.75/1.75/2/94.5 v/v).

Prior 10 minutes of light treatment at 1500 μmol $m^{-2}s^{-1}$ (HL) the plants were submitted to 12 h of dark adaptation. After this treatment the plants were returned to dark and fluorescence measures and pigment analysis were determined regularly to study the recovery.

3. RESULTS AND DISCUSSION

The separation of photosynthetic pigments by HPLC was obtained by using the system described in material and methods which permitted the clear resolution of zeaxanthin and lutein (Fig. 1). This method allowed to study the changes produced in photosynthetic pigments, and in particular, those of the xanthophylls involved in the violaxanthin cycle.

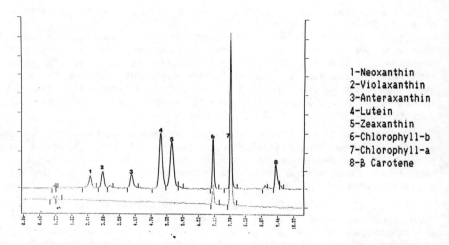

1-Neoxanthin
2-Violaxanthin
3-Anteraxanthin
4-Lutein
5-Zeaxanthin
6-Chlorophyll-b
7-Chlorophyll-a
8-β Carotene

Fig. 1. Chromatogram of photosynthetic pigment extracts from 12 h dark adapted iron deficient leaves after 10 minutes under 1500 μmol $m^{-2}s^{-1}$. Solid and dotted lines correspond to the chromatogram monitored at 440 and 650 nm respectively.

The pigment characteristics of the leaves from 12 h dark adapted D and C plants are given in table 1. The concentration of photosynthetic pigments in leaves from D-plants, as could be expected, was much lower than in C-plants. Although the total chlorophyll in D-plants was below 5 $\mu g.cm^{-2}$, the ratio of chlorophylls a and b was very similar to the observed for C-plants. This implies that the proportion of reaction centres, in which the main pigment is chlorophyll-a, and chlorophyll-b-containing light harvesting structures remained unchanged in contrast with other plant species in which this ratio increased (1). However, the ratio of chlorophyll/carotenoids decreased in D-plants as is typical in iron deficient leaves.

Table 1. Concentrations (µg.cm⁻²) and some relationships of photosynthetic pigments from 12 hours dark adapted control (C) and iron deficient (D) maize leaves

	Carotenoids	Chlorophylls	Ratio a/b	Chl/Carot	V+A+Z
C	6.36(0.67)	33.90(1.57)	3.17(0.12)	5.32(0.29)	0.85(0.11)
D	0.90(0.12)	2.19(0.16)	3.21(0.21)	2.43(0.30)	0.28(0.09)

Standard errors of the means of 3 replicates are given

The appearance of zeaxanthin and violaxanthin during the dark period after HL-treatment is shown in Fig. 2. Control leaves showed the maximum of zeaxanthin on illumination, although the leaves from D-plants developed the maximum level of this pigment following 5 minutes of recovery in the dark. These results demonstrate that in iron deficient leaves the enzyme de-epoxidase is still active, at least in the first minutes of dark after a period of high intensity illumination. Therefore the violaxanthin cycle seems to be not directly dependent on the light.

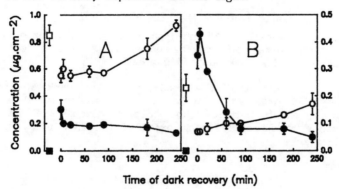

Fig. 2. Changes in violaxanthin (O) and zeaxanthin (●) in control (A) and iron deficient (B) plants during their recovery in the dark, after a treatment consisted in 12 h of dark adaptation and 10 minutes at 1500 µmol m⁻²s⁻¹. Squared symbols (□,■) correspond to 12 h dark adapted samples

As it was expected the xanthophyll cycle was enhanced in iron deficient leaves comparing with the control. It was observed a rapid disappearance of zeaxanthin between the 5 to 90 minutes of dark recovery, following by a slow phase. In contrast, violaxanthin showed a slow phase in the first 3 h of darkness, following a rapid increase, recovering the value found in 12 h dark adapted leaves. The same rapid and slow phases of the violaxanthin cycle were found for C-plants, except that the concentration of violaxanthin was always higher than that of zeaxanthin.

In order to confirm that the xanthophyll cycle acts even at low light in iron deficient plants, both D and C plants were submitted to low light (150 µmol m⁻²s⁻¹) during 1 hour. No variation in photosynthetic pigments was observed for control leaves, but in D-plants decreases in violaxanthin (from 0.25±0.10 to 0.08±0.01 µg.cm⁻²) corresponding with the appearance of significative amounts of zeaxanthin (0.15±0.01 µg.cm⁻²) were observed.

The recovery of the photochemistry of PS2 was studied by fluorescence measurements with the same criterion of light and dark treatments (Fig. 3). D-plants showed a dark value of Fo higher than in C-plants probably due to a deteriorate photochemistry of PS2, following illumination Fo in C-plants remain unchanged, but Fm is lower than in the dark. On illumination of D-plants Fo and Fm values were lower than the ones found in the dark, which could be due to an increase in the rate constant of non-radiative energy dissipation.

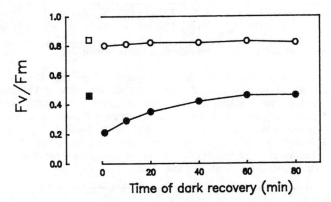

Fig. 3. Fv/Fm ratios in control (O) and iron deficient (●) plants during the recovery by darkness after 10 minutes under 1500 μmol $m^{-2}s^{-1}$. Squared symbols correspond to 12 h dark adapted samples

These results suggest that the recovery in the dark of the normal levels in pigments of violaxanthin cycle and fluorescence parameters follow different kinetics, which indicate that both processes are not directly related. This study is currently being extended to other plant species, in particular in C_3 plants

ACKNOWLEDGEMENTS
We are grateful to Professor N.R. Baker for providing laboratory facilities for part of this study, and also for, together with Dr. B. Genty for assistance with the study. J.Val received a fellowship from the Consejo Superior de Investigaciones Científicas. E. Monge received a short time fellowship from the Royal Society of Biology.

REFERENCES
1 Monge, E., Val, J. Heras, L. and Abadía, J. (1987) Prog. Photsynth. Res. IV, 4,201-204
2 Platt-Aloia, K.A., Thompsom, W.W. and Terry, N. (1983) Protoplasma 114,85-92
3 Nishio, J.N., Taylor, S.E. and Terry, N. (1985) Plant Physiol. 77,705-711.
4 Nishio, J.N., Abadia, J. and Terry, N. (1985) Plant Physiol. 78, 296-299.
5 Guikema, J.A. (1985) J. Plant Nutr. 8,891-908.
6 Baker, N.R. and Horton, P. (1987) In Photoinhibition (Kyle, D.J., Osmond, C.B. and Arntzen, C.J., eds) pp. 145-168, Elsevier Sci. Publ.
7 Krause, G.H. and Weis, E. (1984) Photosynth. Res.
8 Powles, S.B. (1984) Annu. Rev. Plant Physiol. 35,15-44.
9 Björkman, O. (1987) Prog. Photosynth. Res. 4,11-18
10 Demmig, B. and Björkman, O. (1987) Planta 171,171-184
11 Demmig, B., Winter, K., Krüger, A. and Czygan, F-C. (1987) Plant Physiol. 84,218-224
12 Val, J., Abadía, J. Heras, L. and Monge, E. (1986) J. Micronutr. Anal. 2:305-312

ACID RESISTANCE AND THE CO_2 - CONDUCTANCE OF THE PLASMA MEMBRANE OF *DUNALIELLA ACIDOPHILA*

C.Weiss, U.Weis, H.Kugel*, H.Gimmler, Lehrstuhl Botanik I, Universität Würzburg, and Fachbereich Chemie-Physik*, Universität Bremen, FRG.

1. INTRODUCTION

The acid resistant green alga *Dunaliella acidophila* exhibits optimal growth at pH 1.0, the lower limit being close to pH 0.3 (1.2,4,5). The cytoplasmic pH of this alga is about 7 (3), the H^+ concentration ratio outside to inside is about 10^6. The alga is more sensitive to *internal* H^+ stress than to *external* H^+ stress (6). Some problems for this alga may arise from the protean nature of dissolved inorganic carbon (DIC). DIC may enter the cell by diffusion of CO_2, as discussed for higher plant cells, or by carrier mediated uptake, as discussed for CO_2(7,11,12) and bicarbonate (10) for algae). In any case, the internal substrate for RUBISCO is CO_2. In respect to diffusion, CO_2 distributes like a weak acid between the medium and the cells according the Henderson-Hasselbalch equation. Permeation of CO_2 through the plasma membrane (PM) is followed by internal formation of bicarbonate and a stoichiometric liberation of H^+. The pK_a of 6.4 and the cytoplasmic pH of 7.2 predict a maximal 7fold accumulation at equilibrium in the dark. Because of light-induced alkalizations of both the stroma and the cytoplasm (3) the accumulation will be significantly higher in illuminated cells, but maximal twice as much as that in the dark. At low external CO_2, H^+ produced internally will be reexported into the medium by means of PM-ATPases. Internal pH will be stable and normal photosynthetic rates will we observed. In higher plants (isolated chloroplasts, mesophyll cells) high CO_2 causes acidifications which cannot be counteracted by the H^+ export capacity at the PM, resulting in an inhibition of photosynthesis. Does similar apply also to the acid resistant *D. acidophila*? At an external pH of 1.0, hardly any bicarbonate is available for uptake, eventhough the surface pH of the cells may be slightly higher than that of the medium because of the positive membrane potential. This implies that CO_2 rather than bicarbonate is the carbon species taken up by *D. acidophila*. The question arises, whether CO_2 is taken up by diffusion or by a catalyzed transport process, as considered already by several authors for other green algae (7,11). It is of interest to know, whether *D. acidophila* exhibits the same sensitivity against high external CO_2 concentrations as observed for higher plants or whether a low conductance of the PM for CO_2 minimizes internal acidifications and thereby inhibitions of photosynthesis.

2. MATERIAL AND METHODS

Dunaliella acidophila was grown at pH 1.0 (low π, gassing with air + 1.5 % CO_2) as described earlier (4,6). Photosynthesis was measured polarographically or by ^{14}C-fixation and the cytoplasmic pH by ^{31}P-NMR spectroscopy (3,4). The conductance of the PM for CO_2 was determined by the silicone oil–centrifugation technique (9). For the determination of total uptake silicone oil was underlayered with NaOH, for the determination of fixed carbon with trichloroacetic acid.

3. RESULTS AND DISCUSSION

The cytoplasmic pH of *D. acidophila* is scarcely influenced if cells are suspended for 1–3 h in media of different pH (fig.1). This demonstrates an efficient pH regulation. Illumination of cells causes a slight alkalization (0.1–0.3 pH units), whereas under anaerobiosis cytoplasmic pH drops by about 0.4–0.6 pH units (not shown). The dependence of photosynthesis of *D. acidophila* on external CO_2 is complex (fig.2). At lower concentrations Michaelis–Menten kinetics are observed

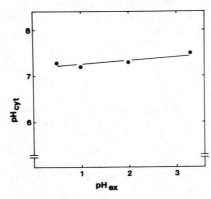

FIGURE 1. Cytoplasmic pH as function of external pH (dark, 25°C).

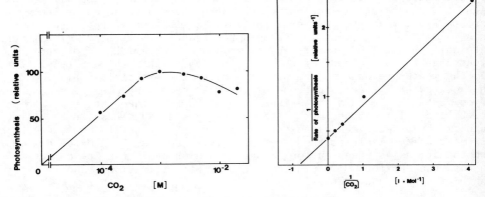

FIGURE 2. Photosynthesis of *D. acidophila*. A) Rate (rel. units) versus CO_2 concentration. B) Double reciprocal plot of (A) (lower CO_2 concentration, only) (pH_1 1.0, 20 min incubation, average of 10^2 experiments, 0.3 mE sec^{-1} m^{-2}). K_m for CO_2 = 0.125 mM, V_{max} = 0.5 μmol CO_2 m^{-2} sec^{-1}.

(apparent K_m for CO_2 = 0.125 mM, V_{max} = 500 nmol CO_2 m^{-2} sec^{-1}). The K_m value is higher than that found for *D.parva* (0.06 mM) under comparable growth conditions (air + 1.5 % CO_2), but still fits into the range determined for other microalgae. If photosynthesis of *D. acidophila* is measured at pH 7 (a pH at which no growth is observed), the apparent K_m for CO_2 was found to be 0.25 mM. Limitation of photosynthesis by CO_2 uptake is unlikely to be the reason for the fact that cells do not grow at pH 7.0. Concentrations higher than 10 mM CO_2 start to inhibit photosynthesis at pH 1 (fig.2a). Half maximal inhibitions are observed close to 30 mM CO_2. This is a much higher value than that observed for higher plants. The reason for the higher resistance against CO_2 could be a lower conductance of the PM for CO_2 and/or a higher H$^+$ export capacity

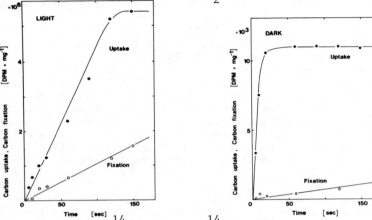

FIGURE 3. Uptake of $^{14}CO_2$ (●) and $^{14}CO_2$ fixation (o) in *D. acidophila* as function of time. A:light (0.3 mE m^{-2} sec^{-1}), B:dark (pH 1.0, 1 mM CO_2). Photosynthetic rate = 0.16 μmol CO_2 m^{-2}sec^{-1}. Note different scale!

of the intact cells (6). In order to determine the conductance of the PM for CO_2, short time uptake and incorporation experiments were carried out (fig.3). At 0.1 mM CO_2 the rate of CO_2 uptake was much higher in the light (A) than in the dark (B), whereas saturation was reached earlier in the dark than in the light. Photosynthetic $^{14}CO_2$ fixation and CO_2 fixation in the dark were significantly lower than the corresponding

TABLE 2. Conductance of the plasma membrane of *Dunaliella* for CO_2.

Species	Growth conditions	Experimental treatment	P_{S} (m sec^{-1})	Reference
D. acidophila	air + 1.5 % CO_2	light	3 x 10^{-6}	This paper
		dark	1 x 10^{-7}	This paper
		light, DCMU	4 x 10^{-7}	This paper
D. parva	air + 1.5 % CO_2	dark	2 x 10^{-6}	(9)
D. salina	air	dark	1 x 10^{-7}	(8)

rates of CO_2 uptake. Photosynthetic fluxes were lower (160 nmol CO_2 m^{-} sec^{-1}) under these conditions than measured in figure 2, perhaps due t a lower intensity of photosynthetic active radiation applied for th the short time incubation experiments. Nevertheless, the different up take of CO_2 in light and dark demonstrates that at 1 mM CO_2 in th light, CO_2 is taken up preferentially up via a catalyzed transpor process rather than by diffusion. CO_2 uptake was found to be inhibite by DCMU.

From the range of linear uptake the conductance of the PM for CO was calculated and compared with corresponding values of other *Duna liella* species. The conductance of the PM of *D. acidophila* for CO_2 i the dark is lower than that of *D. parva*, but similar to that of ai grown *D. salina* (table 1). A relatively low partition of CO_2 betwee octanol and the *D. acidophila* culture medium (K_r = 1.3), confirms a lo P_S value of the PM for CO_2. The "Collander plot" for *D. parva* (9) pre dicts for such a K_r a P_S value close to 4×10^{-7} m sec^{-1}, compared t an experimentally determined value of 10^{-7} m sec^{-1}.

Since the light/dark differences in CO_2 uptake hint to the exis tence of a carrier mediated CO_2 uptake (7,11), "P_S values" calculate for illuminated cells are not permeability coefficients in the classi cal sense. They reflect the conductance of a PM, in which a Michaelis Menten-type of carrier mediated uptake exists beside diffusional uptake It will depend on the applied external CO_2 concentration, whether th total uptake is determined by the carrier mediated uptake system (lo external CO_2, no saturation of the carrier) or by pure diffusion (hig CO_2, saturation of the catalyzed uptake). The conductance of the PM in the dark permits at 1 mM CO_2 a CO_2 influx of maximal 100 nmol CO_2 m^{-} sec^{-1}, which is incompatible with photosynthetic fluxes of 160 $\pm$ 50 nmol CO_2 m^{-2} sec^{-1}. Only the increase conductance in the light permit the experimentally determined photosynthetic fluxes.

ACKNOWLEDGEMENTS. This study was supported by the DFG (SFB 251).

REFERENCES
1 Fuggi,A., Pinto,G., Pollio,A., Taddei,R.(1988) Phycologia 27, 334-339
2 Fuggi,A., Pinto,G., Pollio,A., Taddei,R.(1988) Phycologia 27, 439-446
3 Gimmler,H., Kugel,H., Leibfritz,D., Mayer,A. (1988) Physiol. Plant. 7
521-530.
4 Gimmler,H., Weis, U., Weiss,C. (1989) New Phytologist 113 (in press).
5 Gimmler,H., Weis,U., Weiss,C. (1989) Proc. Internatl. Workshop o
Plant Membrane Transport, Venedig (in press).
6 Gimmler.H., Bental,M., Pick,U., Degani,H., Avron,M.(1989) Proc. VIIIt
Internatl. Congress on Photosynthesis, Stockholm (see this volume).
7 Marcus,Y., Volokita,M., Kaplan,A. (1984) J.Ex.Bot. 35, 1136-1144.
8 Zenverth,D., Kaplan,A., (1981) Planta 152,8-12.
9 Gimmler,H., Hartung, W. (1988) J.Plant Physiol. 133, 165-171.
10 Lucas,W.,J., Berry,J.A. (1985): Inorganic carbon uptake by aquati
photosynthetic organisms. Am.Soc.Plant Physiol., Rockville (USA).
11 Sültemeyer,D.F., Miller,A., Espie,G.S., Fock,H.P., Canvin,D.T. (1989
Plant Physiol. 89, 1213-1219.

THE H$^+$-EXPORT CAPACITY OF *DUNALIELLA ACIDOPHILA* AND THE PERMEABILITY OF THE PLASMA MEMBRANE FOR H$^+$ AND WEAK ACIDS

.Gimmler, M.Bental*, H.Degani*, M.Avron** and U.Pick**, Lehrstuhl otanik I, Universität Würzburg, FRG, and Isotope* and Biochemistry** epartments, The Weizmann Institute of Science, Rehovot, Israel.

1. INTRODUCTION

The acid resistant green alga *Dunaliella acidophila* tolerates H$^+$ oncentrations in the medium up to 0.3 M (1,2) without any significant hange of the cytoplasmic pH, which is kept close to pH 7 (3-6). Factors ontributing to this extreme acid resistance are a positive membrane po- ential, a positive surface charge, a low permeability coefficient (P$_S$ alue) of the plasma membrane (PM) for H$^+$ (4,5), and an efficient PM-H$^+$- TPase (Sekler, unpublished). In order to get some information regar- ing the H$^+$ transport capacity of intact cells, we exposed the algae to *nternal* H$^+$ stress by incubation with weak acids. When incubated at pH .0 the protonated species of weak acids (HAc) is expected to diffuse a- ross the PM into the cells along the chemical gradient. Inside the ells HAc dissociates into the anion (Ac$^-$) and H$^+$. Since the cytoplasmic H of *D. acidophila* is close to 7 and that of the medium is 1.0, inter- al accumulations of Ac$^-$ and H$^+$ are expected. To maintain cytoplasmic H, the protons are expected to be reexported by ATPases of the PM. This ill depend on the ATP-ase capacity in vivo and the extent of internal $^+$ stress. Monitoring the uptake of weak acids and simultaneously ytoplasmic pH by means of NMR techniques can provide an estimate for he minimal proton transport capacity, which is a measure for the cid resistance of intact cells.

2. MATERIAL AND METHODS

Dunaliella acidophila was grown at pH 1 and low osmotic pressure r) as described earlier (4,7). For NMR experiments cells were cultured nder continuous illumination with additional 0.2 M Na$_2$SO$_4$ (high π). hotosynthesis, P$_S$ values, ATP, K$^+$, the buffer capacity of the cells, nd cell volumes were measured as described elsewhere (3,4,9). Prepa- ation of cells for NMR experiments and the methods for maintaining them etabolically active during the measurements are described elsewhere 8). Uptake of acetic acid into the cells was followed by ^{13}C – NMR pectroscopy while the pH was monitored in the same sample by ^{31}P – NMR pectroscopy using a Bruker AM-500 spectrometer (8).

3. RESULTS AND DISCUSSION

Photosynthesis of *Dunaliella acidophila* is considerably less inhi- ited by strong acids (dissociated at pH 1.0) than by weak acids completely protonated at pH 1.0) (fig.1). This implies that external rotons are largely excluded from the cells, whereas the weak acids di- tribute between the cells and the medium according to the Henderson-

1. Baltscheffsky (ed.), Current Research in Photosynthesis, Vol. IV, 773–776.

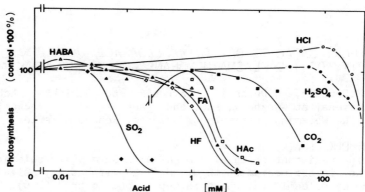

FIGURE 1. The effects of strong and weaks acids on the photosynthesis of
D. acidophila (pH 1.0, 25°C, low π, 20 min incubation).

Hasselbalch equation, resulting in a substantial accumulation of Ac^-.
Inhibition of photosynthesis could be due to internal acidification
(fig.2), osmotic stress (at low π) (fig.3a) and/or salt effects of the
investigated anions. In order to check whether the inhibition of photosynthesis can be correlated with internal acidification, an expected

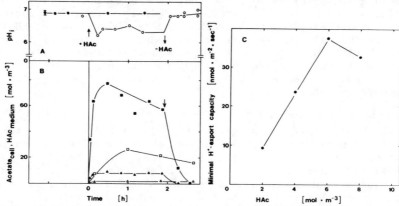

FIGURE 2. A) Cytoplasmic pH in cells incubated with medium containing
acetic acid (● 4 mM, o 8 mM) (^{31}P-NMR technique). B) Uptake of
^{13}C-acetic acid. Separate intracellular and medium ^{13}C-signals were
observed. HAc in the medium: △ 4 mM, ▲ 8 mM. Cytoplasmic Ac^-
(squares) at 4 (□), respectively 8 mM (■) HAc in the medium. C: Minimal H^+ export capacity of intact cells calculated from A and B.
Arrows indicate addition or removal of HAc from the medium.

acidification was calculated from the concentrations of weak acids
required for 50 % inhibition of photosynthesis, the P_S values of the PM
for these acids and the buffer capacity (table 1). For acetic acid,

TABLE 1. P_S values of the PM for weak acids, half maximal inhibition of photosynthesis (20 min incubation) and theoretical acidifications calculated from both parameters. P_S for HF is an overestimate, since it is determined for higher plant cells (10). The PM of *Dunaliella* exhibits a lower conductance than that of the PM of higher plant cells (9). P_S for SO_2 was assumed to be similar as that measured for CO_2, as found for *D. parva* (9).

Acid	pK_a	P_S value (m sec^{-1})	50% inhibition of photosynthesis D_{50} (mM)	Theoretical acidification (pH units 20 min^{-1})
Sulfuric acid	1.9	---	400	---
HCl	-7	---	350	---
HF	3.17	$<1 \times 10^{-7}$	1	<1.7
CO_2, light	6.37	3×10^{-6}	30	(1542)
dark		1×10^{-7}		(51.4)
ABA	4.8	3×10^{-11}	10	0.005
Acetic acid	4.8	6×10^{-9}	2	0.2
Formic acid	3.75	1×10^{-8}	2	0.34
SO_2	1.8	2×10^{-7}	0.08	0.27

formic acid and SO_2 internal acidifications during 20 min fall between 0.2 to 0.3 pH units. For CO_2, which exhibits an unexpectedly low inhibitory effect on photosynthesis, completely unrealistic values of internal acidifications are calculated. Values are higher than maximal possible accumulations calculated for the equilibrium. Therefore the equation relating P_S, flux and solute concentration gradients as driving force for uptake, cannot be applied for CO_2. The latter is true also for another reason: Different "P_S values" were measured for illuminated cells and cells kept in the dark, indicating a catalyzed transport of inorganic carbon into illuminated cells (table 1)(6). Such a transport process is expected to exhibit substrate saturation kinetics, whereas pure diffusional processes are strictly proportional to the driving forces. At low CO_2 concentrations the major part of inorganic carbon is taken up through an catalyzed transport mechanism and only a minor part by pure diffusion. This situation is reversed at high CO_2 concentration. Therefore at high CO_2 concentration the P_S value measured in the dark rather than that of the light should be applied even in the light. If done so, much lower, but still unrealistic theoretical acidifications are obtained (table 1).

From the uptake of acetic acid into the cells and the response of the internal pH under these conditions (fig.2a,b) a minimal H^+ export capacity in the dark was calculated (fig.2c). It was found to be at least 30 nmol H^+ m^{-2} sec^{-1}, corresponding to an alkalization of about 0.5 pH units per 20 min. This H^+ flux capacity in the dark is low (5 %) compared to photosynthetic fluxes, but high (25 %) compared to respiratory fluxes.

Internal H^+ stress by acetic acid is accompanied by a marked decrease in ATP and internal K^+ (fig.3b). This suggests that H^+ export

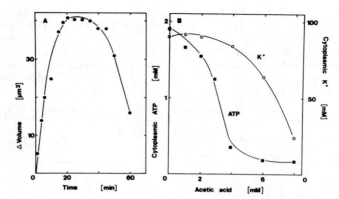

FIGURE 3. Osmotic volume as affected by 6 mM acetic acid (A) and the effect of acetic acid (1 h) on ATP and K^+ concentrations (B).

requires ATP. In addition, however, ATP is utilized to maintain a proper K^+ level.

The observed H^+ export capacity can easily account for the low calculated acidifications induced by SO_2, acetic acid, and formic acid at D_{50} of photosynthesis (table 1). It should be noted that the effect of photosynthesis was measured in the light while the H^+ export capacity was derived from measurements in the dark. For acetic acid however the pH was monitored in the dark and even 4 mM acetic acid did not cause a significant change of the cytoplasmic pH within an hour (fig.2a), thus confirming the prediction in table 1.

In conclusion, the data presented here suggest that in _D. acidophila_ inhibitions of photosynthesis by weak acids are predominantly not a result of acidifications but are mainly due to specific anion effects and at low π also due to osmotic effects.

ACKNOWLEDGEMENTS. This study was supported by the DFG (SFB 251).

REFERENCES

1 Fuggi,A., Pinto,G., Pollio,A., Taddei,R.(1988) Phycologia 27, 334-339.
2 Fuggi,A., Pinto,G., Pollio,A., Taddei,R.(1988) Phycologia 27, 439-446.
3 Gimmler,H., Kugel,H., Leibfritz,D., Mayer,A. (1988) Physiol. Plant.74, 521-530.
4 Gimmler,H., Weis, U., Weiss,C. (1989) New Phytologist 113 (in press).
5 Gimmler,H., Weis,U., Weiss,C. (1989) Proc. Internatl. Workshop on Plant Membrane Transport, Venedig (in press).
6 Weiss,C, Weis,U., Kugel,H., Gimmler.H. (1989) Proc. VIIIth Internatl. Congress on Photosynthesis, Stockholm (see this volume).
7 Albertano,P., Pinto.G., Santisi,S., Taddei,R. (1981) Gironale Botanico Italiano, 115, 65-76.
8 Bental,M., Pick,U., Avron,M., Degani,M. (1989)(submitted).
9 Gimmler,H., Hartung, W. (1988) J. Plant Physiol. 133, 165-172.
10 Kronberger,W. (1987) Phyton 27, 241-265.

VARIABLE FLUORESCENCE FOR MONITORING ALGAL ACTIVITY IN A
HIGH RATE PHOTOSYNTHETIC POND

B. EL HAMOURI, R. MOUNDIB. AND R. BERRADA, Laboratoire de
Biochimie, Institut Agronomique et Vétérinaire Hassan II,
BP 6202 Rabat-Instituts, Morocco

1. INTRODUCTION

The high rate photosynthetic pond, also called High rate
oxidation pond, is a powerful system for wastwater
treatment in hot climate. Algal photosynthesis is speeded
up by mixing the pond content and the depth is kept low
(0.45 cm) so the sun light may reach most of the algal
cells in the pond (1-3).
Oxygen supply to the oxidative bacteria for sufficient
organic matter and nutriments removal depends on the
rate of algal growth and the rate of photosynthesis.
However, many factors in the pond are acting as inhibiting factors for photosynthesis and algae growth (turbidity)
due to suspended solids and bacterial biofloc; high level
of ammonia and phosphorus; depletion of CO_2 and high pH.
Variable fluorescence induction measurements have been
found to be a useful tool for photosynthesis studies
under limiting environment conditions (stresses): high
light levels (photoinhibition) (4-6; high and low
temperatures (7-8) etc..
The objective of the present study is to gain further
insight in the understanding of the algal photosynthesis
in the high rate photosynthetic pond. The identification
of the limiting factors and their site of action on the
photosynthetic apparatus of the algae will allow a better
operating of the pond and the improvement of its waste
removal performances.

2. MATERIAL AND METHODS

Fluorescence measurements were done in a modified oxygen
electrode (Rank brothers) at 25°C.
Excitation light consisted of an array of 36 leds with a
nominal wavelength 660 nm (hansatech LS1 light source).

M. Baltscheffsky (ed.), Current Research in Photosynthesis, Vol. IV, 777–780.
© 1990 *Kluwer Academic Publishers. Printed in the Netherlands.*

Fluorescence signals were monitored using a photodiode system (Hansatech Fluorescence detector). Protected by a 740 nm filter. Amplified signals were directed simultaneously to an oscilloscope and a voltage recorder. Dissolved oxygen was measured using field oxymeter scött Gerate Model CG86.

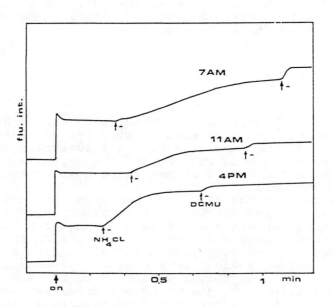

Fig. 1 Chla Fluorescence induction curves of dark adapted alga taken from the pond at 7,11 a.m. and 4 p.m. NH4cl and DCMU were added at indicated time for monitoring Qe and Qq respectively (Qe = energy dependent quenching and Qq = photochemical quenching of fluorecence)

3. RESULTS AND DISCUSSION

Fig. 1 depicts the chlorophyll fluorescence induction of the algal Cell in the pond at 7,11 a.m. and 4 p.m. NH4Cl was added for monitoring energy-dependent quenching (Qe) and DCMU for electron flow quenching (Qq). The part of energy-dependent quenching represents about 50% of the overall quenching of the fluorescence at 7 a.m. This part increases gradually to reach 75% of the overall quenching at 4 p.m. This would be interpreted as a CO_2 supply to the calvin cycle (9) during the time

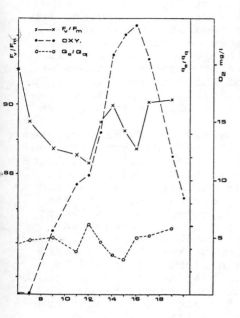

Fig. 2. Time course of dissolved
oxygen in the pond, FV/Fm and
calculated Qe/Qq. Dissolved
oxygen has been monitored at
mid-depth. Mixing of the pond
is continiously operated.
(FV = variable fluorescence and
Fm = maximum fluorescence).

Fig. 3. The same as Fig. 2
except the pond was not
mixed continiously. Mixing
was interupted between 11 a.
and 4 p.m.

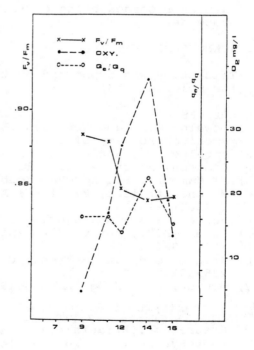

course of the day. The depletion of CO_2 becaming dramatic at the end of the day (4 p.m.) However, it is clear from Fig. 2 that the photosynthetic apparatus of algae is stressed as stated by FV/Fm decrease from 7 to 11 a.m. and by the low rate of oxygen evolution from 11 to 12 a.m. The reason of the increase of the energy-dependent quenching relatively to that of the electron flow could then be the occurence of photoinhibition (probably favoured by) or conjugated to a low CO_2 content in the pond (4-6; 9).
This explanation is supported by Fig. 3. FV/Fm decrease in this case is not reversed. The pond content being not mixed and samples were taken from the upper 10 cm. Algae at this layer are over exposed to high level of light (1600 u $Em^{-2}s^{-1}$) and the CO_2 is certainly all consumed in that area. The simultaneouse decrease of FV/Fm and increase in the energy dependent quenching relative to electron flow quenching in this case is pleading in favour of the occurence of photoinhibition in the pond. In all the cases, full reversion of the FV/Fm decrease is achieved during the following night this could be due to some repairs mechanism(s) (5) acting on the photosynthetic apparatus and also to some supply of CO_2 by the oxidative bacteria during the nights. The high temperatures recorded being certainly activating such a processes.

4. ACKNOWLEDGEMENT

This study was supported by the International Foundation for Science (IFS).

REFERENCES
(1) Oswald, W.J. and Gotaas, H.B. (1957) Transaction of the american society of civil engineering , 122,73-105.
(2) Moraine, R., Shelef, G., Meydan A. and Levi, A., (1979) Biotech, Bioen. 21,1191-1207.
(3) El Hamouri, B., Bouchabchoub, A., Rhallabi, N., Margich, M. and Ettalibi, M. (1987) Actes Inst. Agro. Vet., 7 (3&4)5-15.
(4) Powles, S.B., and Björkman, O.(1982) Planta, 156-97-107.
(5) Greer, D.H., Berry, J.A. and Björkman, O. (1986) Planta, 168,253-260.
(6) Krause, G.H. and Behrend, U. (1986) FEBS Letters 200(2) 298-302.
(7) Öquist, G. and Ögren, E. (1985) Photosy.Res.7,19-30.
(8) Hetherington,S.E.Smillie&M. malagamba&P. and Human Z. (1983) Planta 159,119-124.
(9) Krause,G.H.,Briantais,J.M. and Vernotte,C. (1981) in PhotosynthesisI (Akoyunouglou,G.ed.)pp 575-584,Balaban International Science Service, Philadelphia, Pa.

THE EFFECTS OF DICLOFOP-METHYL AND METHABENZTHIAZURON ON
PHOTOSYNTHETIC PARAMETERS IN VICIA FABA

VIDAL,D., MIRANDA, M.A., RODRIGUEZ, F. and SIMON, E.
DEPT. PLANT BIOLOGY, UNIV. BARCELONA, 08028 BARCELONA,SPAIN

1. INTRODUCTION

Methabenzthiazuron is a preemergence herbicide, urea
derivative and photosynthetic inhibitor that inhibits photosynthetic electron transport at the "diuron site". After
treatment with this herbicide, the wheat crop showed "physiological effects", such as a delayed senescence of leaves,
a "greening effect" and a decrease in carbohydrate content.
A high number of herbicides, whose only common attribute is
their photosynthetic electron transport action, give the
same kind of response (1).

Diclofop-methyl is a postemergence grass herbicide
whose action is not related to photosynthetic electron
transport. Its herbicidal effect, still not well known, probably involves an antagonism of auxin-mediated processes
and an increase in membrane permeability (1,2). Its "physiological effects" have not been described.

In this work, the effect of both herbicides on growth,
photosynthetic activity and pigments, and N_2 fixation in
Vicia faba have been studied. We have tried to find out:
a) whether methabenzthiazuron caused the same "physiological
effects" in V. faba as in cereals (3) and b) if both herbicides caused the same effects on V. faba in spite of their
different herbicidal action.

2. PROCEDURE
2.1. Material and methods
  2.1.1. Plant material: V. faba (cv. R. Blanca) was grown
         in a xerofluvent mollic soil under natural envi-
         ronment conditions at the Experimental Fields of
         the University of Barcelona (Spain). Each plot
         had 8 plants.m^{-2}. Plots were regularly irrigated.
  2.1.2. Treatments: Methabenzthiazuron was applied at
         two levels: 175 g.ha^{-1} (M1) and 220 g.ha^{-1} (M2),
         17 days after sowing, before plant emergence. Di-
         clofop-methyl at 360 g.ha^{-1} (D1) and 450 g.ha^{-1}
         (D2), 40 days after sowing (▼). There were four
         replicates per treatment.
  2.1.3. Methods: Photosynthetic O_2 evolution of leaf
         slices was determined with a Clark-type oxygen

M. Baltscheffsky (ed.), Current Research in Photosynthesis, Vol. IV, 781–784.
© 1990 Kluwer Academic Publishers. Printed in the Netherlands.

electrode at 24ºC under 700 μE.m^{-2}.s^{-1} (4). Leaf
discs were cut into small pieces and suspended in
a medium containing 0.35M sorbitol, 50mM NaH$_2$PO$_4$
and 0.2mM CaCl$_2$ at pH 6.8.
Chlorophyll and carotenoid content were estimated
in representative samples of fresh leaves homogenized in 85% aqueous acetone, using the spectrophotometric method of Lichtenthaler (5).
N$_2$ fixation was evaluated by the acetylene reduction assay of excised nodules (6).

3. RESULTS AND DISCUSSION
3.1. Both methabenzthizuron and diclofop-methyl cause simi-
     lar effects in V. faba on photosynthetic parameters,
     growth and N$_2$ fixation as is shown in Figures 1 to 5.

     FIGURE 1. Photosynthetic rate and N$_2$ fixation in V. fa-
              ba during the growth period after M1 and M2.

     FIGURE 2. Photosynthetic rate and N$_2$ fixation in V. fa-
              ba during the growth period after D1 and D2.

     FIGURE 3. Chlorophyll content in V. faba during the
              growth period. a) M1 and M2. b) D1 and D2.

     FIGURE 4. Chlorophyll a/b ratio in V. faba during the
              growth period. a) M1 and M2. b) D1 and D2.

     FIGURE 5. Leaf density thickness (LDT) during the
              growth period of V. faba. a) M1 and M2 treat-
              ments. b) D1 and D2 treatments.

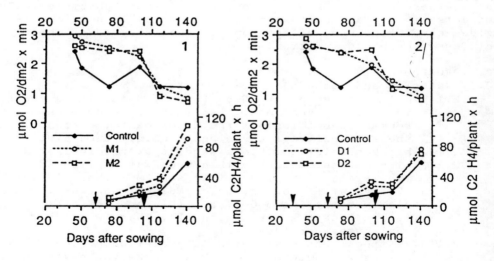

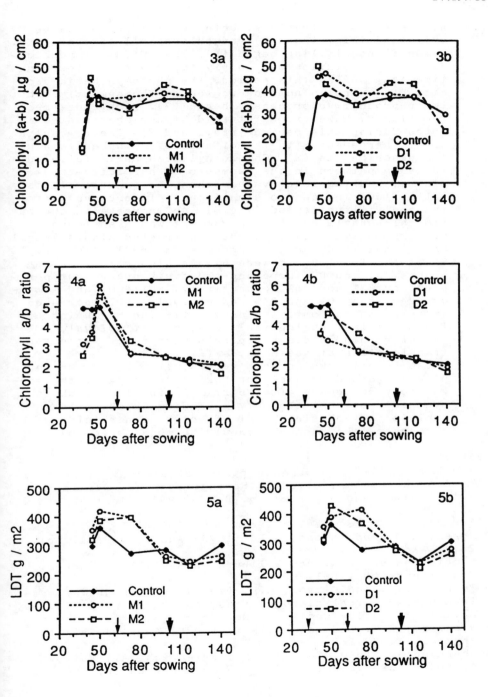

3.2. At tested concentrations, both herbicides increased O_2
     evolution (Fig. 1 and 2) and chlorophyll content (Fig.
     3) until pod filling began (↓). The effect of herbici-
     des on O_2 evolution was mainly important at flowering
     time (↓). During this period, the photosynthetic capa-
     city of control plants decreased at the same time that
     the reproductive processes began (7). Herbicide-trea-
     ted plants, however, maintained higher photosynthetic
     rates during this period (Fig.1 and 2). These results
     are in agreement with the effects of methabenzthiazu-
     ron described in (3). Chlorophyll a/b ratio followed
     the same pattern in the two sets of herbicide-treated
     plants, showing lower values than the control plants
     until flowering and no significant differences during
     the pod filling period (Fig.4). An increase in the ra-
     tio chlorophyll/carotenoid content was also found.
     N_2 fixation was always higher in treated plants (Fig.1
     and 2) mainly due to an increase in nodule biomass.
     Shoot and fruit yield were always higher in treated
     plants. D1 and D2 increased the fruit dry weight per
     plant by 23% and 38% respectively, while M1 and M2 in-
     creased it by 9% and 34% respectively. LDT increased
     in relation to control plants until the beginning of
     fruit setting. During fruit development LDT values we-
     re lower than in control plants because of a greater
     translocation of assimilates (Fig.5).
     These results, which show very similar behaviour for
     plants treated with either herdicide, suggest that re-
     gulatory responses after partial inhibition of photo-
     synthesis are not the only mechanism which would
     explain the "physiological effects" of herbicides, and
     a hormone-like response should be considered (8).

REFERENCES
1 Fedtke, C. (1982) Biochemistry and Physiology of Herbicide Action (Fedtke, C.,ed.), Springer-Verlag, Berlin
2 Wright, J.P. and Shimabukuro, R.H. (1987) Plant Physiol.
  85, 188-193
3 Fedtke, C. (1973) Pestic. Sci. 4, 653-664
4 Jones, H.G. and Osmond, C.B. (1973) Aust. J. Biol. Sci.
  26, 15-24
5 Lichtenthaler, H.K. and Wellburn, A.R. (1983) Biochem.
  Soc. trans. 603, 591-592
6 Turner, G.L. and Gibson, A.H. (1980) in Methods for evaluating biological nitrogen fixation (Bergersen, F.J. ed.)
  pp.111-131, Wiley and sons, New York
7 Woodward, R.G. and Rawson, H.M. (1976) Aust. J. Plant
  Physiol. 3,257-267
8 Chernyad'ev, I.I., Choojka, L., Friedrich, A., Volfova,
  A. and Brezinova, A. (1986) Photosynthetica 20, 196-203

INFLUENCE OF ENVIRONMENTAL STRESSES ON THE PHOTOSYNTHETIC CAPACITY OF S-TRIAZINE SUSCEPTIBLE AND RESISTANT BIOTYPE OF <u>SOLANUM NIGRUM</u>

A. Winterberg, P. Panneels and R. Lannoye. (Laboratoire de Physiologie Végétale ULB, av. P. Héger n°28, CP169, B-1050 Bruxelles. Belgium)

1. INTRODUCTION:

The photochemical activity of resistant biotype seems to be significantly affected by polypeptide D1 mutation. Resistant biotype is at a disadvantage in intra-species competition; indeed, without herbicide treatments, resistant biotype disappears from wild population. The decrease of the electron transfer kinetic constant between QA and QB seems to be one of the most important factor for resistant biotype competitiveness decrease.

In this work, we have studied the physiological difference between R and S biotypes in response to different light and temperature treatments, in the absence of herbicide.

2. RESULTS:

2.1. Without environmental stresses: QA- reoxydation rate:

QA- reoxydation kinetic can be studied by chlorophyll fluorescence leaf relaxation after illumination by saturating light. Resistant biotype <u>Solanum nigrum</u> has been characterized by a clear decrease of fluorescence relaxation rate. That indicates an inhibition of electron transfer between QA and QB. We can estimate the half time fluorescence decay graphically.

<u>Fig 1 :</u>

Kinetics of chlorophyll fluorescence relaxation induced by a single saturating flash in atrazine R and S Solanum nigrum leaves.

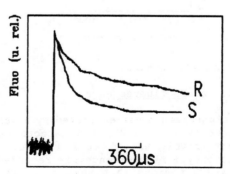

2.2. Under environmental stresses.

2.2.1. LIGHT STRESS:

It seems obvious that there is a difference between the two biotypes growth at different light intensity as show in figure 2 and 3.
Light growth treatments were: LL : Low Light , 10 $\mu E.m^{-2}.s^{-1}$.
                                HL : High Light, 80 $\mu E.m^{-2}.s^{-1}$.
under controlled conditions.

2.2.1.a. Photochemical quenching of chlorophyll fluorescence.

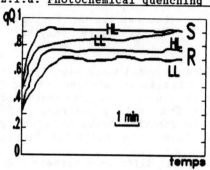

Fig 2 :

Photochemical (qQ) component of chlorophyll fluorescence decay in <u>Solanum nigrum</u> leaves grown under two light treatments.

2.2.1.b. Oxygen evolution rate in intact leaves:

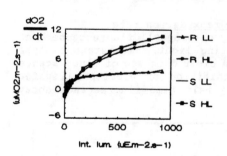

Fig 3 :

In vivo oxygen production, studied by LD2 (Clark electrode) at different light intensities on the two biotypes.

2.2.2. HEAT STRESS.

2.2.2.a. FO fluorescence.

FO fluorescence was estimated by a very dim 650 nm beam modulated at high frequency of 1.6 Hz, and detected by a photodiode. The leaves were progressively warmed at a rate of 1°C/min and the dark level FO of chlorophyll fluorescence was recorded simultaneously with temperature. It seems obvious that peak temperature is significantly higher in the susceptible biotype.(see fig 4.).

Peak temperature is a direct index of chloroplast thermostability and can be used to estimate the relative heat tolerance.

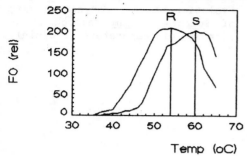

```
****************************
*                 peak temp. *
****************************
*  Susceptible  *   60°   *
*  Resistant    *   54°   *
****************************
```

Fig 4 :

Fluorescence temperature curves for the two biotypes of <u>Solanum nigrum</u>.

2.2.2.b. <u>Photochemical quenching of chlorophyll fluorescence.</u>

FO was induced by a very weak modulated light L1. Fv was induced by a second light L2, non-modulated and of an intensity of 450 µmol/s/m2. qQ can be used as an indicator of the rate of reduced QA.
The leaf was progressively warmed at a rate of 1°C/min. qQ was measured at every degree increase. A decrease of qQ in function of temperature was observed. This decrease is higher in resistant biotype.

Fig 5 :

Effects of heat stress on the quenching qQ of chlorophyll fluorescence in <u>Solanum nigrum</u> leaves.

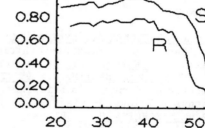

2.2.2.c. <u>QA- reoxydation rate</u>
A single flash was applied on a leaf at different temperatures.
The flash induces only one electron transfer. This method can be used to measure the rate of electron transfer between QA and QB.
T1/2 represents the half of the time to pass from the maximum fluorescence Fm to the minimum FO. We observed an increase ofthe half point (Fm-Fo)/2 decrease ($T_{1/2}$) with the temperature. That would indicate a lower rate of electron transfer between QA and QB. The electron transfer seems to be more affected by temperature in resistant biotype.

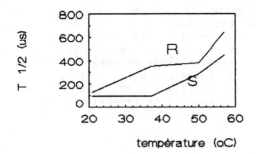

Fig 6 :

Evolution of QA- reoxydation rate
of _Solanum nigrum_ undergoing an
increase of temperature (1°c/min).

3. CONCLUSIONS

We have shown that there is a significant difference between resistant
and susceptible biotypes of _Solanum nigrum_ as well in the responses to
high temperatures and light treatments as in the absence of stresses.
The electron transfer between QA and QB seems to be slower in resistant
biotype; this difference is increased by types and values of stress. It
seems that D1 polypeptide mutation has a complex influence on chloroplast
photosynthetical activity. As showed by our F0 experiment that gives us
an indication of a drastic difference in the chlorophyll antenna
organization in the two biotypes.
These results suggest the effective weakness of the resistant biotype in
a wild population under natural conditions.

4. RERFERENCES

HIRSCHBERG J., BLEECKER A., KYLE D., Mc INTOSH L. & ARNTZEN C. (1984) The
molecular basis of triazine-herbicide resistance in higher-plant
chloroplasts. - Z.Naturforch. 39C : 412-420.
ORT D., AHRENS W., MARTIN B. & STOLLER E. (1983) Comparison of
photosynthetic performance in triazine-resistant and susceptible biotypes
of Amaranthus hybridus. - Plant Physiol. 72 : 925-930.
SCHREIBER U., SCHLIWA U. & BILGER W. (1986) Continuous recording of
photochemical and non-photochemical chlorophyll fluorescence quenching
with a new type of modulation fluorometer. - Photosyn. Res. 10 : 51-62.
SCHREIBER U. (1986) Detection of rapide induction kinetics with a new
type of high-frequency modulated chlorophyll fluorometer. - Photosyn.
Res. 9 : 261-272.

5. ACKNOWLEDGMENTS

This research was supported by "IRSIA" under contract n° D1/4 -
8497/5044A). A.W. thanks the FNRS for financial support.

INHIBITION OF PHOTOSYNTHESIS IN BARLEY (Hordeum vulgare L.) LEAVES BY PHOSPHINOTHRICIN (GLUFOSINATE). SHORT AND LONG-TERM EFFECTS.

M. Lacuesta[1], C. González-Murua[1], A. Muñoz-Rueda[1] and M. Sivak[2]
[1]Depto. Biol. y Ecol., Fac. Ciencias, Univ. del País Vasco, Apdo.644, 48080-Bilbao, Spain. [2]Research institute for Photosynthesis, Univ. of Sheffield, Sheffield S10 2TN, U.K.

INTRODUCTION

Several inhibitors of the GS (Methionine sulphoximine, MSO; Phosphinothricin, PPT) have been used in studies of the role of this key and the mechanism of its action. Both substances can inhibit GS "in vivo", cause a dramatic increase of ammonia and inhibit the rate of photosynthetic CO_2 uptake. Initially it was thought that the build-up of ammonia was the cause of photosynthetic inhibition; however, Sauer et al. (1987) postulated that aminoacid metabolism, disturbed by PPT, results in: a) Inhibition of synthesis of proteins,e.g. the Q_B protein causing eventually the collapse of electron transport;
b) Toxic accumulation of glyoxylate, an inhibitor of Rubisco
c) Depletion of the pool of intermediates of the RPPP via hidroxipiruvate derived from peroxisomal serine transamination.

In the present study we examine the response to this inhibitor of several aspects of photosynthesis of barley.

MATERIALS AND METHODS

Measurements were performed on intact barley leaves (12-14 cm long) or leaf segments supplied with water or with PPT solutions through the petiole. Chlorophyll fluorescence was measured using a pulse amplitude modulation (PAM) fluorometer (Schreiber et al. 1986) as described by Sivak et al. (1988). CO_2 exchange was measured by infrared gas analysis (ADC). Gases were mixed to obtain the required concentrations using a Signal Blender. The temperature was kept constant at 20°C In these conditions, the leaf-air water vapour concentration gradient was approximately 15 mbar. Light response curves of photosynthetic oxygen evolution by intact leaves were obtained using a leaf disc electrode (LD-2, Hansatech) in conjunction with a PAM.

RESULTS AND DISCUSSION

To study the effect of $[O_2]$ on photosynthesis, the leaves were first illuminated in the chamber in 1% $[O_2]$ and until steady-state photosynthesis was reached, then the effect of changes in the $[O_2]$ flowing over the leaf was examined by intermitent changes from 1 to 21 to 51%, as indicated in Fig 1.

M. Baltscheffsky (ed.), Current Research in Photosynthesis, Vol. IV, 789–792.
© 1990 *Kluwer Academic Publishers. Printed in the Netherlands.*

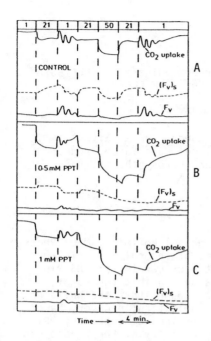

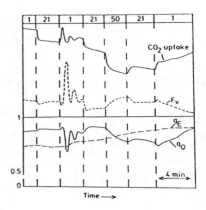

FIGURE 2. Photosynthetic CO_2 uptake, variable fluorescence kinetics and analysis of chlorophyll fluorescence quenching during changes of $[O_2]$ in the gas-phase surronding a leaf fed with 1 mM PPT.

FIGURE 1. Effect of PPT on the response to O_2 concentration. Characteristic responses of the kinetic of CO_2 uptake, associated chlorophyll fluorescence and the saturated variable fluorescence to changes in $[O_2]$ in leaves supplied with water (A) or with 0.5 (B) or 1 mM (C) PPT.

Leaves of the control (Fig 1A) showed the caracteristic reversibility of changes in photosynthesis, fluorescence and (Fv)s, the latter an in dicator of chloroplast energization and characteristic oscillations followed the decrease of $[O_2]$ to 1%. Energization increased when $[O_2]$ was increased from 21 to 50%, or decreased to 1%. PPT feeding modified these response, (Fig 1B,1C). Although in the treated plants, some oscillations (Fv) were aparent in the first transient back to 1% O_2, none were observed in the subsequent transients. In the leaf fed with the lower concentration of PPT, some relaxation of energization (increase in (Fv)s) could be observed after that same transient, but from then on energization kept increasing, and in the leaf treated with 1mM PPT, (Fv)s decreased from the first change to 21% O_2 and did not relax throught the duration of the experiment. With the lower concentration of the inhibitor, slow relaxation was eventually observed upon returning the leaf to 1% O_2, and this change was accompanied by the also slow recovery of the rate of CO_2 uptake. It must be noted that uncoupling of electron transport would be seen as a decrease in energization rather than the decreased observed as a result of PPT feeding.

Quenching coefficients can be calculated from data like illustrated in Fig 1, providing an estimation of how photochemical (q_Q) and non-photochemical quenching (q_E) affect the variable fluorescence Fv. From these, q_E is another way of expressing the information contained in the kinetics of $(Fv)_S$, shown in Fig 1, and q_Q is an indicator of the redox state of Q_A, the primary acceptor of photosystem II.

During changes in $[O_2]$ during illumination in constant $[CO_2]$, q_Q does not change very much in a control leaf (not illustrated but see Sivak et al. 1988), probably because the photosynthetic apparatus can adjust its redox status to the amounts of the different acceptors avai-lable, i.e. CO_2, O_2 (in the Mehler reaction), nitrite, etc. A PPT trea-ted leaf (Fig 2), however, shows a progresive fall in q_Q, indicative of a more reduced state, as the experiment progresses and the presence of high $[O_2]$ instead of increasing q_Q through the effect of O_2 as an alter-native electron acceptor, decreases it. A slow increase in q_Q followed the decrease of $[O_2]$ to 1%, and together with the slow decrease in ener-gization (increase in $(Fv)_S$, decrease in q_E) and the increase in CO_2 up-take can be taken as an indicator of recovery from illumination of the treated leaf in high $[O_2]$.

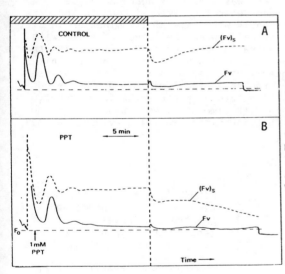

FIGURE 3. Chloroplast ener-gization during illumina-tion in high $[CO_2]$ and fo-llowing transfer to air. Kinetics of Fv and $(Fv)_S$ displayed by leaves illu-minated first in 0.7% CO_2 20% O_2, balance N_2.
A. Control. B. Feeding with 1 mM PPT.

FIGURE 4. Kinetics of Fv, q_E and q_Q.
The experiment was essentially as in Fig 3 but feeding with 1 mM PPT was continued for lon-ger before the change to air.

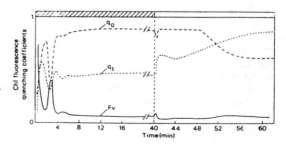

Photosynthesis was also measured at saturating CO_2 concentrations
(Fig 3). Upon illumination, the leaf displayed characteristic oscillations and eventually reached a steady-state rate of photosynthetisis,
the gas-phase was then changed to air. In these conditions, photosynthesis in the control leaf increased slowly and reached a new steady-state
rate after about 5 min (Fig 3A). A leaf fed with 1 mM PPT (Fig 3B), however, did not reach a new steady-state in air but the rate declined.
The long illumination in air during PPT feeding (Fig 4) allowed a larger
increase in energization (high q_E). In these circumstances, q_Q stayed
constant for some time but eventually fell, indicating an increased reduction of the primary acceptor q_A.

Illumination in air while feeding the leaf with 1 mM PPT affected
the fluorescence characteristics measured during the subsequent illumination under high $[CO_2]$. The "true" Fm could not be determined, i.e.
the leaf was not left for a long time in the dark, to avoid the possible complications of recovery from the treatment in this period. The
leaf therefore, was left in the dark for about 5 min before the determination of Fo and applying a single saturating flash. The value Fm/Fo
in the control (illuminated in water) was 4.6, very near the value of 5
typical of healthy barley leaves and determined after 1 hour in the dark.
This value did not change significantly with time of illumination in
air, in water, but decreased dramatically when the leaves were fed with
PPT during illumination in air. The ratiodecreased to 3.9 (after 1h) and
1.6 (5h), suggesting that photorespiratory damage had occur. This
was confirmed by the quantum requeriments, measured in the same leaves,
and that increased from 9.5, near the theoretical minimum 9, in the control, to 10.6 (1h) and 26.3 (5h). The rate of photosynthetic oxygen evolution at saturating CO_2 decreased with time of illumination in air and
exposure to PPT. Figure 5 shows that inhibition was also evident in the
maximum rate.

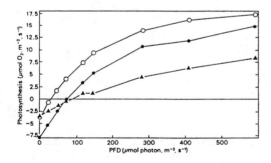

FIGURE 5. Effect of illumination in air of control and
PPT treated leaves on the subsequent photosynthesis oxygen
evolution at high $[CO_2]$. Light
response curves.
Quantum requirements were calculated from the slope at the
linear part of the curve:
Control(○); PPT: 1h(●), 5h(▲)

REFERENCES
Sauer, H.; Wild, A. and Ruehle, W. (1987) Z. Naturfos. 42, 270-278.
Schreiber, U.; Bilger, W. and Schliwa, U. (1986) Photos. Res.10, 51-62.
Sivak, M.N.; Lea, P.J.; Blackwell, R.D.; Murray, A.J.S.; Hall, N.P.;
    Kendall, A.C.; Turner, J.C. and Wallsgrove, R.M. (1988) J. Exp.Bot.
    39, 655-666.

EFFECT OF THE HERBICIDE SAN 6706 ON PIGMENT COMPOSITION IN BARLEY:
MEASUREMENTS USING HPLC

René Juhler and Raymond P. Cox
Institute of Biochemistry, Odense University, Campusvej 55,
DK-5230 Odense M, Denmark

1. INTRODUCTION
Higher plant chloroplasts contain a number of carotenoid pigments,
principally β-carotene and the xanthophylls lutein, violaxanthin,
neoxanthin and zeaxanthin. The herbicide SAN 6706 inhibits the
desaturation reactions involved in the synthesis of these compounds
from colourless precursors (1). High-performance liquid chromatograpy
(HPLC) provides a sensitive technique for the quantitative analysis of
the separate carotenoids together with chlorophylls a and b (2,3). We
describe here a novel procedure for HPLC analysis of pigments and
present results on the effect of treatment with SAN 6706 on the pigment
composition of barley seedlings grown in weak red light.

2. EXPERIMENTAL
2.1. Treatment with SAN 6706
The herbicide SAN 6706 (metflurazon) was kindly provided by Dr. J. Harr
and Dr. G. Schulke, Agro-biological Research Station, Sandoz AG, CH-4108
Witterswil, Switzerland.

Seedlings of barley (*Hordeum vulgare* cv. Svalovs Bonus) were grown for 8
days in a growth cabinet at 22°C with a cycle of 8 h darkness and 16 h
of weak red light (>630 nm, 15 nmol quanta/m^2.s between 630 and 700 nm).
Seeds (17 g) were added to 300 ml of water in aluminium trays (200 cm^2)
containing an inert matrix ("Leca"). SAN 6706 was added to the water
from a stock solution in ethanol (36 mM), and extra ethanol added if
necessary to bring the concentration to 0.3% v/v.

2.2. Extraction of pigments
Seedlings were harvested under dim red light, weighed and frozen in a
test tube with liquid N_2 before grinding with a spatula in the presence
of a solid equimolar mixture of KH_2PO_4 and Na_2HPO_4. Pigments from 2 g
plant material were extracted with 8 ml 100% acetone and then rextracted
twice with 2 ml 80% acetone, the residue being separated by
centrifugation after each extraction.

2.3. HPLC analyses
An HPLC system with 2 Kontron 420 pumps, a Kontron 432 UV/vis detector
with tungsten lamp set at 450 nm, and a Kontron 450 data system was
used. The column was 120 mm x 4 mm i.d. and was packed with octadecyl
silica (Shandon Hypersil 5 μm spherical particles). The column

M. Baltscheffsky (ed.), Current Research in Photosynthesis, Vol. IV, 793–796.
© 1990 *Kluwer Academic Publishers. Printed in the Netherlands.*

temperature was maintained at 30°C. A mixing chamber was inserted between the two pumps and the column.

Separation of pigments was acheived in a gradient of tetrahydrofuran and water. The flow-rate was 1 ml/min. At the time of injection the solvent was 47:53 THF:water. After 5.3 min at this composition, the THF content was increased linearly until the ratio was 90.4:9.6 after 13.3 min. During repetitive measurements the composition was then decreased linearly to 47:53 over the next 5 min, and then retained at this level for 3 minutes (total analysis time 21 min). Tetrahyrofuran was HPLC grade (Rathburn). Solvents were degassed by ultrasonic treatment under vacuum and bubbled with He during chromatography.

Calibration was carried out using pigments isolated from spinach using reverse-phase TLC. Concentrations were determined using data provided by Davies (4) and Lichtenthaler (4)

3. RESULTS AND DISCUSSION
3.1. Development of HPLC protocol
A typical chromatogram is shown in Fig. 1. Our method involves the use of a simple gradient system using a relatively non-toxic solvent and provides good separations in a reasonable analysis time. Unfortunately the isomers lutein and zeaxanthin are not unambigously resolved.

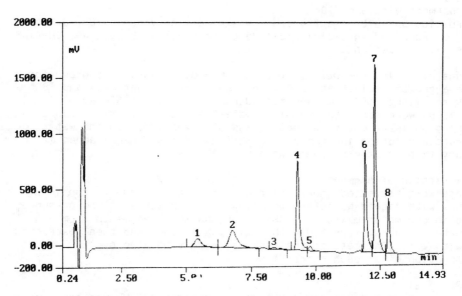

Fig. 1. Typical chromatogr: of extract of barley seedlings.
  1, neoxanthin; 2, violaxanthin; 3, unknown; 4+5, lutein + zeaxanthin; 6, chlorophyll b; 7, chlorophyll a; 8, ß-carotene.

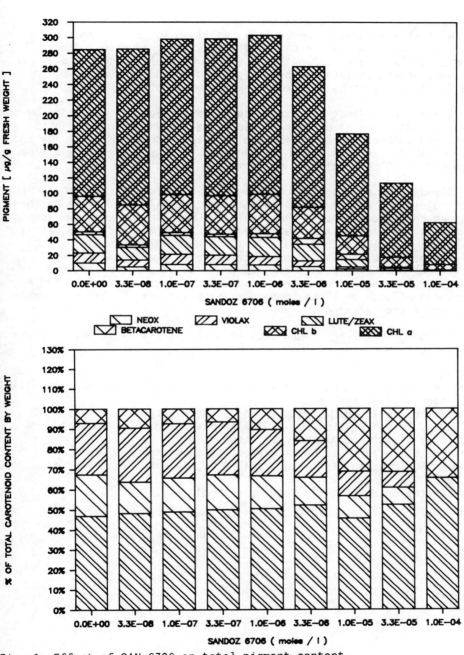

Fig. 2. Effect of SAN 6706 on total pigment content.
Fig. 3. Effect of SAN 6706 on relative proportions of carotenoids.

3.2. Effects of treatment with SAN 6706

Growth of barley seedings under weak red light in the presence of different concentrations of SAN 6706 allows the production of plant material containing chlorophyll but very low levels of carotenoids. In contrast, growth in intense white light led to the production of totally white seedlings with very low pigment contents.

Fig. 2 shows the effect of increasing concentrations of herbicide on the pigment composition of extracts of seedlings grown under red light. Carotenoid content was approximatelely halved with 10 µM herbicide and very low at 100 µM. The concentration of chlorophyll a and b was also decreased at 10 µM herbicide and above.

Fig. 3 shows the effect of increasing concentrations of SAN 6706 on the relative proportions of the different carotenoids. Lutein + zeaxanthin remained fairly constant at about half the total carotenoid, whilst neoxanthin and violaxanthin decreased and ß-carotene increased. It is noteworthy that neoxanthin (an allenic trihydroxy carotenoid) and violaxanthin (a dihydroxy, diepoxy carotenoid) are the most highly derivatised of the compounds considered. Thus it appears that the effects of the herbicide on the inhibition of desaturation has the most pronounced effects on those compounds which involve the largest number of biosynthetic reactions.

ACKNOWLEDGEMENT. The HPLC apparatus used was partially funded by a grant from the Carlsberg Foundation.

REFERENCES
1 Fedtke, C. (1982) Biochemistry and Physiology of Herbicide Action, Springer Verlag, Berlin.
2 Ruddat, M., Will, O.H., III, (1985) Methods Enzymol. 111, 189-200
3 Goodwin, T. and Britton, G. (1988) in Plant Pigments (Goodwin, T.W., ed.) pp. 61-132, Academic Press, London.
4 Davies, B.H. (1976) in Chemistry and Biochemistry and Plant Pigments, (Goodwin, T.W., ed.) Vol. 2, pp. 38-165, Academic Press, London
5 Lichtenthaler H.K. (1987) Methods Enzymol. 148, 350-382

CHANGES IN PHOTOSYNTHESIS OF WHEAT PLANTS INFECTED BY STEM RUST

G. SCHMITTMANN, B. MOERSCHBACHER, and H.J. REISENER, Institut für
Biologie III (Pflanzenphysiologie), Aachen University of Technology,
Worringer Weg, D-5100 AACHEN, FEDERAL REPUBLIC OF GERMANY

1. INTRODUCTION

Photosynthesis plays a vital role in a biotrophic parasite's life. It
represents the major source for the large amounts of substrates which the
pathogen needs for its numerous syntheses on the way to its successful
propagation. Originally, all plants were susceptible for newly existant
pathogens - but sometimes, plants reacted very efficiently by the development of resistant varieties. As a rule, infection of susceptible
plants by parasites and pathogens leads to decreased photosynthesis (1).
Often, investigations only concerned compatible interactions between
hosts and parasites or different cultivars with more or less effective
resistance mechanisms (2).

Because of its considerable importance to world nutrition, the investigation of the wheat stem rust interaction is of general interest. With
the breeding of so called near isogenic wheat lines which solely differ
in one gene locus crucial for resistance or susceptibility to the stem
rust fungus, it became possible to investigate exclusively resistance
specific reactions and to avoid measuring of variety specific reactions.

One of the most important questions is whether different resistant
wheat isolines only react quantitatively or if there are qualitatively
distinct mechanisms of resistance which lead to specific types of ans-
wers. To elucidate this, we measured net photosynthesis, chlorophyll
content, and DCMU sensitive Hill activity (H_2O -> ferricyanide) of a
susceptible, a moderately resistant, and a highly resistant near isogenic
line of the wheat cultivar Prelude following stem rust inoculation.

2. MATERIALS and METHODS

Plant and fungus: near isogenic lines of the wheat cultivar Prelude
(Triticum aestivum L.), carrying either the Sr5 gene for resistance, the
Sr26 or Sr24 gene for the moderately resistant reaction, or the corresponding srx allele for susceptibility were obtained from R. Rohringer,
Agriculture Canada Research Station, Winnipeg. Race 32 of the stem rust
fungus (Puccinia graminis Pers. f.sp. tritici Erikss. & E. Henn.) was
used in all experiments.

M. Baltscheffsky (ed.), Current Research in Photosynthesis, Vol. IV, 797–800.
© 1990 Kluwer Academic Publishers. Printed in the Netherlands.

Cultivation of wheat plants and inoculation with stem rust uredo-spores were performed as described in (3).

Net photosynthesis of whole detached secondary leaves was polarographically measured with a Clark type oxygen electrode during the first ten days of pathogenesis according to (2).

Chlorophyll content: after measuring oxgen evolution, the chlorophyll content of these leaves was determined according to (4).

Preparation of chloroplasts from healthy and infected secondary leaves was carried out following (5).

Determination of Hill activity: 10 µl of the chloroplast suspension (eq. ca. 30 µg chlorophyll for healthy plants) were added to 3 ml of reaction mixture (27 mM tricine-NaOH pH 8.0, 1 mM ferricyanide, 3.3 mM $MgCl_2$) and absorption at 420 nm was determined before and after illumination for 1 min. When indicated, methanol diluted dibromothymoquinone (DBMIB) and dimethyl-methylenedioxy-p-benzoquinone (DMMDBQ) (6) were added to a final concentration of 10^{-6} M and 10^{-4} M, respectively.

3. RESULTS AND DISCUSSION

Susceptible Isoline: Starting with the fifth day post inoculation net photosynthetic rate of the infected leaves falls below that of the noninfected control. In the last few days of the measuring interval, net photosynthesis stabilizes to a final level at 40-45 % of the controls (Fig. 1). Linked to the drop in photosynthesis, the chlorophyll content declines to 50-60 % of the control leaves (Fig. 2). Hill activity from H_2O to ferricyanide (PSII + PSI) of thylakoid suspensions isolated from infected leaves decreases to 60-70 % of that of healthy leaves (Fig. 3). DMMDBQ stimulated and DBMIB inhibited thylakoid suspensions (PSII solely) only show a small infection related change in activity (Fig. 3).

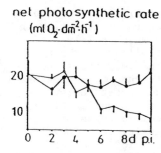
net photosynthetic rate
$(ml\,O_2 \cdot dm^{-2} \cdot h^{-1})$

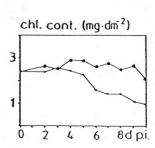
chl. cont. $(mg \cdot dm^{-2})$

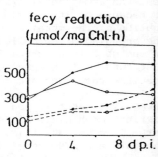
fecy reduction
$(\mu mol/mg\,Chl \cdot h)$

FIGURE 1. Net photosynthetic rate of secondary leaves of the susceptible isoline of the wheat cultivar Prelude. o: infected with stem rust; ●: control. Data are mean values of 6 leaves from one representative experiment.

FIGURE 2. Chlorophyll content of the same leaves as in Fig. 1. o: infected with stem rust; ●: control. Data are mean values of 2 extractions from 3 leaves each.

FIGURE 3. Hill activity of thylakoid suspensions of the susceptible isoline of the wheat cultivar Prelude. o: infected with stem rust; ●: control; —— : H_2O -> FeCy (PSII + PSI); --- : H_2O -> FeCy, + DBMIB + DMMDBQ (PSII).

The infection with wheat stem rust causes a considerable decrease in net photosynthesis and chlorophyll content, when the fungal mycelium has invaded large areas of the leaves and sporulation is going to start. This indicates a strong intervention in the plant metabolism by the fungus. Nevertheless, photosynthesis is still working at a reduced level in the last days of the measuring interval. Investigations of the fungus in axenic culture have shown that substrate limiting conditions are essential for the induction of sporulation (7). We conclude that the plant is incapable to recognize the fungus as a pathogen, or - alternatively - the stem rust maintains the substrate supply equivalent to its needs.

From the Hill measurements we deduce a predominant influence on photosystem I rather than on photosystem II by the infection. Presumably, the degradation is preceded by a depletion of the cytochrom b/f complex, linking the two photosystems, which will lead to a diminished ferricyanide reduction by photosystem I.

Moderately Resistant Isoline: During the initial days p.i., the changes in net photosynthetic rate are similar to that seen in the susceptible isoline. In the course of infection photosynthesis collapses completely, the infected leaves die (Fig. 4). Chlorophyll is degraded totally. Hill activity (PSII + PSI) declines to 60-70 % of the control (Fig. 5). PSII activity is slightly reduced to around 80 % of the non-infected leaves (Fig. 6).

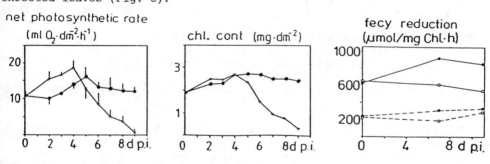

FIGURE 4. Net photosynthetic rate of the moderately resistant isoline. For further explanations see Fig. 1.
FIGURE 5. Chlorophyll content of the same leaves as in Fig. 4. For further explanations see Fig. 2.
FIGURE 6. Hill activity of thylakoid suspensions of the moderately resistant isoline. For further explanations see Fig. 3.

Likewise as in the compatible interaction we detect a decline in both photosynthesis and chlorophyll content, but it is much more drastic and both parameters decrease towards zero. This fact becomes clear, when we look macroscopically at the infected leaves. A few days after inoculation leaves are yellowing, desiccated and withered. At the same time, a very sparse sporulation sets in.

Possibly, plants react with declining photosynthesis to withdraw the necessary substrates from the fungus. In this moderately resistant way, the plant looses some leaves or leaf areas, but prevents a more successful sporulation and consequently a further propagation of the parasite.

   Chlorophyll degradation seems to proceed in a similar manner as in
the susceptible plant, because the decline in Hill activity is mainly
based on the loss of activity in photosystem I. In general, Hill activity these small amounts of chlorophyll is only detectable because its
value is related to mg chlorophyll.

   Highly Resistant Isoline: In the first days post inoculation, net
photosynthesis of the infected leaves increases (Fig. 7). Depending on
infection density there may later on be a slight decrease below the
controls (data not shown). The chlorophyll content remains nearly unaffected by infection (Fig. 8). Neither Hill activity from H_2O -> ferricyanide (PSII + PSI) nor PSII activity are influenced by the rust infection (Fig. 9).

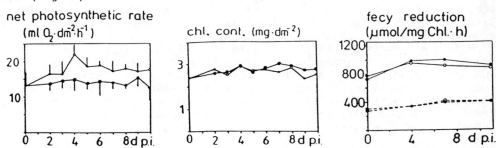

FIGURE 7. Net photosynthetic rate of the highly resistant isoline.
          For further explanations see Fig. 1.
FIGURE 8. Chlorophyll content of the same leaves as in Fig. 7.
          For further explantions see Fig. 2.
FIGURE 9. Hill activity of thylakoid suspensions of the highly resistant
          isoline. For further explantions see Fig. 3.

The mesophyll cells of highly resistant plants defend themselves against
the invading parasite by the very efficient hypersensitive reaction (8),
i.e. the infected cells lignify and collapse within some hours after
penetration. Thus, the fungus starves and just a few cells are affected
by infection. The minor chlorophyll losses due to the hypersensitive
reaction are compensated by a somewhat intensified photosynthesis and
the integrity of the thylakoid membranes and electron transfer are by
no means disturbed.

REFERENCES
1 Wood, R.K.S. (1967) in Physiology and Plant Pathology (Wood, R.K.S.,
  ed.), pp. 393-397, Blackwell Scientific Publ., Oxford
2 Berghaus, R. and Reisener, H.J. (1985) Phytopathol. Z. 112, 165-172
3 Moerschbacher, B.M., Noll, U., Flott, B.E. and Reisener, H.J. (1988)
  Physiol. Molec. Plant Pathol. 33, 33-46
4 Arnon, D.I. (1949) Plant Physiology 24, 1-15
5 Nelson, N., Drechsler, Z., Neumann, J. (1970) J. Biol. Chem. 245, 143
6 Trebst, A., Reimer, S., Dallacker, F. (1976) Plant Sci. Lett. 6, 21-24
7 Kuck, K.H., Reisener, H.J. (1985) Physiol. Plant Pathol. 27, 259-268
8 Tiburzy, R. (1984) Ph.D. Thesis, RWTH Aachen, FRG

DROUGHT EFFECT ON THE STRUCTURAL AND FUNCTIONAL CHARACTERIS-
TICS OF PHOTOSYNTHETIC APPARATUS
I.A.Tarchevsky,   Y.E.Andrianova, N.I.Safina, E.A.Philippova,
D.I.Babuzhina

Kazan Institute of Biology, USSR Academy of Sciences,
P.O. Box 30, Kazan, 420084, USSR

1.   INTRODUCTION
     The available method of estimation of photosynthetic
productivity by plant surface (leaf area index) has some restrictions caused by irregularity of chlorophyll distribution in plant .It has been shown in some publications [1,2,3]
that index based on total chlorophyll content in plant has
some advantages.

2.   PROCEDURE
     Chlorophyll photosynthetic potentials (CPP) may be cal-
culated as the area under the curve of chlorophyll dynamics
in the whole plant. Chlorophyll content was determined by
spectrophotometery method.

3.   RESULTS AND DISCUSSION
     Chlorophyll photosynthetic potentials and their struc-
ture for wheat and rye are shown on Fig. 1 .Chlorophyll
photosynthetic potentials allow to determine potential pho-

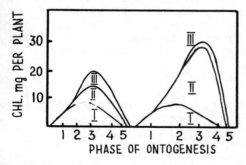

FIGURE 1.
The   structure of chlorop
photosynthetic   potential
(CPP)
   I - CPP of leaf lamina,
  II - the same of stem,
III - the same of ear
1- bushing ,2- stem-phase,
3-earing-phase,4-ripeness
milky, 5- ripeness wax

photosynthetic capacities of different parts of plant more
objectivly.For instance stem and leaf vagina contributions
predominating for rye in comparison with wheat..Fig. 2
shows chlorophyll photosynthetic potentials of buckwheat.
The shaded segment corresponds to a drought period .CPP of
buckwheat proves the high sensititivity of pigment apparatus to drought and its sort specificity.CPP correlates with

M. Baltscheffsky (ed.), Current Research in Photosynthesis, Vol. IV, 801–804.

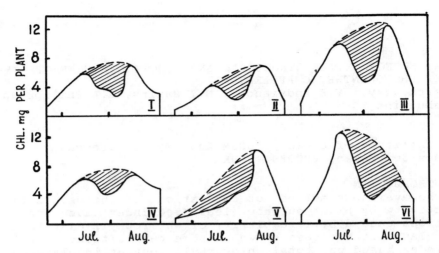

FIGURE 2   The somewhat chlorophyll photosynthetic potentials of buckwheat varietis (the shaded segment
shows the drought eaten away part of CPP):
I - Mayskaya,II- Kazanskaya crupnosernaya (2 mln
seeds on ga), III - Smolavicheskaya, IV - Kazanskaya crupnosernaya (1 mln seeds on ga), V - Ar-
oyashshkaya ,VI - Kazanskaya 3

photosynthetic productivity (correlation coefficient of CPP
with yield is 0.8 - 0.9). It is shown that drought conditions in reproductivity period change the structure of CPP so
that leaf contribution in total CPP decreases and "non-leaf"
parts contribution increases. This dependence is most clearly observed during dry wind influence as well as soil drought conditions. This regularity is characteristic of many
cultures. It is shown (Table 1) that in wheat for instance
the drought effect during earing results in the decrease of
leaf contribution in two times.

TABLE 1.   The contribution of different plant parts to the
chlorophyll potential of wheat*

Plant parts	Control	Drought
Ear	10	24
Leaf blades	29	14
Leaf vaginal	20	22
Stem	32	40

*The phase of milky ripeness of grain

Our results show that the specific changes of pigment apparatus in comparison with stem and ear are characteristic of leaves. At gradually increasing drought the adaptational splash followed by fast destruction of pigments is observed only in leaf blades of wheat (Fig. 3). In the

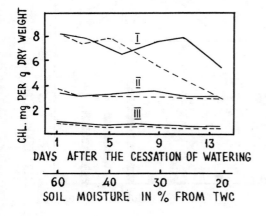

FIGURE 3.
The dynamics of chlorophyll content in different wheat organs at the dehydration
I - leaf blades, II- stem, III - ear
— - control, -- drought

stem with leaf vaginas as well as in ear the pigment system is more stable to drought effects. Apparently this is not connected with the particularities of water regime changes in different parts of plant, bacause as Japanese authors showed [4,5], water potentials of different parts of wheat reduced similarly. One can assume that the stability of pigment apparatus of "non-leaf" organs is connected with the particularities of chlorophyll structure organization.

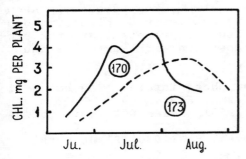

FIGURE 4.
Chlorophyll photosynthetic potentialof winter rye. Outlined values are chlorophyll photosynthetic potential in g chlorophyll per plant for vegetative season

A somewhat different picture of CPP structure is observed when drought occurs at early stages of ontogenesis. It is shown that in case of winter rye spring drought reults in the cease of growth and in the reduction of vegetation period (Fig. 4,5). In this case the CPP value remains in fact unchanged. Then the leaf contribution into the CPP of winter rye is greatly increased.

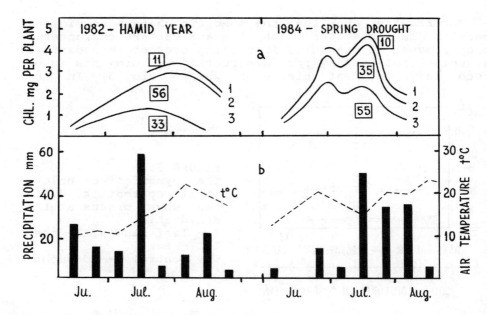

FIGURE 5.a) Chlorophyll photosynthetic potential of winter
             rye (average value for variety Rossiyanka, Ka-
             zanskaya korotkostebelnaya, Kamalinskaya 4)
             1 - ear, 2 - stem, 3 - leaf
             Outlined values are contribution of several plant
             part in CPP for vegetative season (%)
             b) Meteorological data

        In conclusion it should be noted that the changes of
chlorophyll potentials and their structures adequately show
the alteration of photosynthetic activity of plant in drought conditions.This method allows to prognosticate the productivity more reliably in comparison with surface account.

REFFERENCES
1 Tarchevsky I.A. (1971) Osnovi photosinteza, (The basis of
photosynthesis), pp.276-289, Kazan, KSU
2 Billore S.K. and Mall Z.P. (1975) Indian Bot.Soc., Vol.54,
  1-2, 75-77
3 Tarchevsky I.A. and Andrianova Y.E. (1980) Plant physiol.,
  Vol.27, 2, 341-348
4 Xu Hui-Jian, Yamagishi Tohru,Kumara Atsuhiko (1987) Jap.J.
  Crop. Sci., Vol.56, 4, 455-460
5 Xu Hui-Jian, Yamagishi Tohru,Kumara Atsuhiko (1987) Jap,J
  Crop .Sci., Vol.56, 4, 461-666

ISOLATION AND CHARACTERIZATION OF TWO ISOZYMES OF SUPEROXIDE DISMUTASE FROM SCOTS PINE

G. WINGSLE*, P. GARDESTRÖM**, J.-E. HÄLLGREN*

*Swedish University of Agricultural Sciences Department of Forest Genetics and Plant Physiology, S-901 83 UMEÅ, SWEDEN. ** Department of Plant Physiology, University of UMEÅ, S-90187 UMEÅ, SWEDEN.

INTRODUCTION

Superoxide dismutase (SOD; EC 1.15.1.1) is a metalloenzyme which catalyzes the disproportionation of superoxide radicals (O_2^-) to molecular oxygen and H_2O_2. Superoxide dismutases have been discovered in all aerobic organisms and seem to play an important role in protecting cells against oxygen toxicity (1). Three types of SOD have been found and they are distinguished by different metals in their catalytic center. Cu/Zn-SOD is inhibited by cyanide and H_2O_2, Fe-SOD by H_2O_2 and the Mn-SOD is insensitive to both reagents.

Here two isozymes of superoxide dismutase (EC 1.15.1.1) from Scots pine (*Pinus silvestris* L.) needles was purified and their sub-cellular location was determined.

PROCEDURE

Pine seedlings (approx. 5 g) were grown in darkness for 3 weeks and then exposed to light (300 μmol $m^{-2}s^{-1}$, RH 70-80%, photoperiod 18/6 and temperature 25 °C) and cut into small pieces and kept in tissue wash medium (0.5 M sorbitol, 1 mM $CaCl_2$, 1% PVP-25, 1mM ascorbate, 5mM Hepes, pH 7.2) on ice until all needles were cut. Protoplast isolation, sub-cellular fractionation and measurements of marker enzymes was done according to Gardeström and Wigge (2). For the enzyme purification current and one-year old needles (500 g) from 15-year old Scots pines (*Pinus silvestris* L.) were collected from field-grown trees in January. The enzyme purification was done according to Wingsle (3) with an additional gel filtration step with G-150 Sephadex chromatography prior to the Phenyl-Superose HR 5/5 chromatography step.

RESULT AND DISCUSSION

The distribution of the marker enzyme activities in the chloroplast (NADP-TPD), mitochondria (fumarase) and cytosolic fraction (PEPcase) obtained from protoplasts by differential centrifugation showed good correlation to the corresponding fraction (Tab. 1). Values of 65% or higher recovered activity were found for all enzymes. The distribution of SOD-1 and SOD-2, determined by gelscanning and active staining on polyacrylamide gels correlated with the cytosolic fraction (Fig. 1b) and SOD-3 correlated to the chloroplastic fraction (Fig. 1 c). The mitochondrial fraction is denominated d in the figure. It is concluded that SOD-1 and SOD-2 are cytosolic enzymes and SOD-3 is a chloroplast enzyme.

M. Baltscheffsky (ed.), Current Research in Photosynthesis, Vol. IV, 805–808.
© 1990 *Kluwer Academic Publishers. Printed in the Netherlands.*

TABLE 1. The distribution of marker enzyme activites in fractions obtained from pine protoplasts by differential centrifugation. The total activites (μmol (mg chl)$^{-1}$ h^{-1}) was 22 for PEPcarboxylase (PEPcase), 32 for fumarase, and 69 for NADP triosephosphate dehydrogenase (NADP-TPD), respectively. The values are the means from two separate fraction experiments.

Fraction	% of recovered activity		
	Fumarase	NADP-TPD	PEPcase
400 g P	23	66	6
11 000 g P	65	21	12
11 000 g S	12	13	82
Recovery %	153	106	95

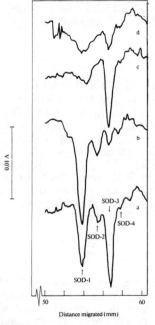

Fig.1 Gel scanning of SOD from Scots pine determined by active staining

The mol wt (Mw) of SOD-1 and SOD-3 were determined by gelfiltration on HPLC using two columns in serie, TSK-300 and Superose Hr 12 LKB-Pharmacia,

Sweden) equilibrated with 50 mM sodium phosphate, pH 7.0, containing 0.15 M NaCl. Ovalbumin (45 kDa), carbo anhydrase (30 kDa), chymotrypsinogen (25 kDa) and cytochrome c (12.4 kDa) were used as mol wt standards. In addition superoxide dismutase from bovine liver was used as an internal standard. SOD-1 and SOD-3 eluted at a position corresponding to a mol wt of approximately 35 kDa (Fig. 2). SOD from bovine liver eluted at a nearly identical position as the pine enzymes.

When SOD-1 and SOD-3 were runned on SDS-PAGE gels they appeared as single bands, indicating that the preparation was homogeneous (Fig. 3). The subunit size of SOD-1 and SOD-3 was 16.5 kDa and 20.4 kDa, respectively.

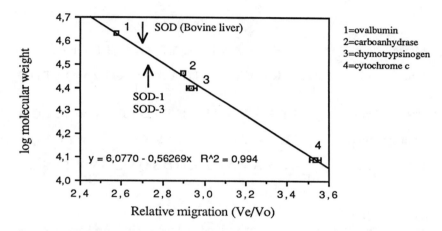

Fig. 2. Gelfiltration of SOD-1 and SOD-3 from Scots pine.

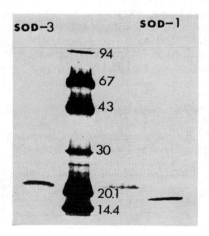

Fig.3 SDS-PAGE of SOD from Scots pine needles. Molecular weight calibration proteins: phosphorylase b (94 kDa); albumin (67 kDa); ovalbumin (43 kDa); carbonic anhydrase 30 (kDa); trypsin inhibitor (20.1 kDa); -lactalbumin (14.4 kDa).

The cytosolic (SOD-1) and chloroplastic (SOD-3) isozymes were determined of their NH_2-terminal up to 24 residues (Fig. 4). It is obvious that both SOD-1 and SOD-3 are evolutionally related to the compared SOD:s from other plant sources. Position 4, 5, 6, 7, 8, 9, 15, and 17 are highly conserved compared to SODs from spinach and pea chloroplasts (4, 5) and from maize cytosol (6). In addition SOD-1 are conserved in position 21 of the cytosolic enzyme compared to the other plants. The percentage homology of the NH_2-teminal sequence (residue 1-23) between pine and spinach and pea stromal enzyme was high, 83% and 87% respectively. However the percentage homology of the NH_2-teminal sequence (residue 2-23) between pine and maize cytosolic SOD:s was lower (41 %).

		5	10	15	20

Maize	(cyt)	V K A V A V L A G T D - V K G T I F F S Q
Pine	(cyt)	G L L K A V V V L N G A A - V K G V V Q F T D G
		(S)
Pea	(chl)	A A K K A V A V L K G T S E V E G V V T L T Q D
Spinach	(chl)	A T K K A V A V L K G T S N V E G V V T L T Q
Pine	(chl)	A A K K A V A V L K G D S Q V E G V V T L S Q E
		(E) (R)

CONCLUSION

Superoxide dismutases have been purified and the genes have been isolated, cloned and sequenced in several plant species. SODs related to the same subcellular compartment have been shown to be highly conserved. There is however, a lack of information from gymnosperms. Here isozymes of SODs from Scots pine has been purified and characterized. The two main bands, designated SOD-1 and SOD-3 were found to belong to the Cu/Zn SODs, and located in the cytosol and the chloroplast, respectively. The chloroplastic enzyme was found to be biochemically and genetically evolutionary related to the earlier described SODs from higher plants. The cytosolic enzyme showed less homology with earlier reported SODs.

REFERENCES
1. Fridovich , I. (1986). in Advances of Enzymology 58, 61-97.
2. Gardeström, P. and Wigge, B. (1988). Plant Physiol. 88, 69-76
3. Wingsle, G. (1988). Physiologia Plantarum 76, 24-30.
4. Kitagawa, Y., Tsunasawa, S., Tanaka, N., Katsube, Y., Sakiyama, F. and Asada, K. (1986). J Biochem. 99, 1289-1298.
5. Scioli, J. R. and Zilinskas, B. A. (1988). Proc. Natl. Acad. Sci. 85, 7661-7665.
6. Cannon, R., White, J. A. and Scandalios. (1987). Proc. Natl. Acad. Sci. 84, 179-183.

AN ASSESSMENT OF ETHYLENE AND CARBON DIOXIDE EXCHANGE IN PLANTS

BERNARD GRODZINSKI AND LORNA WOODROW, DEPT OF HORTICULTURAL SCIENCE, UNIVERSITY OF GUELPH, GUELPH, ONTARIO N1G 2W1 CANADA. Present address: Agriculture Canada, Research Station, Harrow, Ont N0R 1G0

1. INTRODUCTION

Current evidence indicates that ethylene is a volatile by-product of amino acid metabolism. Ethylene synthesis is linked with nitrogen metabolism through methionine and S-adenosylmethionine and as a volatile emission may serve as a non-destructive probe of amino acid turnover during photosynthesis and photorespiration. Very little is known about the relationship between ethylene and CO_2 gas exchange in photosynthetic tissue. CO_2 enhances the rate of ethylene release from leaf tissue in the light (1-5) and it has been proposed (3) that ethylene synthesis and/or metabolism may be moderated by photosynthetic and respiratory processes in photosynthetically competent leaves through changes in the internal CO_2 concentrations.

The effects of environmental CO_2 concentration on plant metabolism may be studied as short-term, immediate responses to changes in the CO_2 concentration, or as long-term effects as plants are allowed to grow at controlled CO_2 levels (6). The present report summarizes investigations into the magnitude of ethylene release from leaves during growth at elevated CO_2 as well as responses during short-term incubations at varying CO_2 concentrations. The effects of ethylene on photosynthetic carbon assimilation, partitioning, and growth have also been reviewed.

2. PROCEDURE

2.1. Plant Material: Tomato plants, Heinz TH 318, were grown in a greenhouse under daylight conditions in soil culture (7). Plants grown under CO_2 enrichment were housed in polyethylene chambers within the greenhouse (8).

2.2. Ethylene Release: Ethylene release from excised leaf discs during incubation in sealed flasks was quantified by gas chromatography. The CO_2 content of the flask headspace was maintained by inclusion of a centrewell containing filter paper and sodium bicarbonate in phosphate buffer. The CO_2 level was varied by changing the buffer pH and the bicarbonate concentration (9). Headspace CO_2 levels were monitored by infrared gas analysis.

2.3. Steady-state Leaf Gas Exchange: All gas exchange measurements and $^{14}CO_2$ feedings were conducted on attached leaves of intact plants using a continuous open gas exchange system (7). Extraction and analysis of metabolites was performed as described previously (7).

2.4. Ethephon Application: Continuous ethylene exposure was achieved by application of a 300 mg.l^{-1} ethephon solution to the plants. Ethephon degrades to ethylene in plant tissue and results in a continuous ethylene emanation extending over several days (7).

2.5. Whole Plant Gas Exchange and Carbon Gain: Whole plant CO_2 exchange and C gain was determined using a semi-open system (10).

M. Baltscheffsky (ed.), Current Research in Photosynthesis, Vol. IV, 809–812.
© 1990 Kluwer Academic Publishers. Printed in the Netherlands.

Plants were matched with respect to total leaf area, leaf number, and shoot height at the start of the experiment and the design followed that of Woodrow et al (11). Control and ethephon treated plants were always run in tandem. Initial diurnal gas exchange patterns were established for the plants prior to ethephon treatment. Carbon gain was calculated from the CO_2 exchange rates and the quantity of CO_2 metered into the system. Dry matter accumulation was calculated from C gain assuming a 40% C content (10).

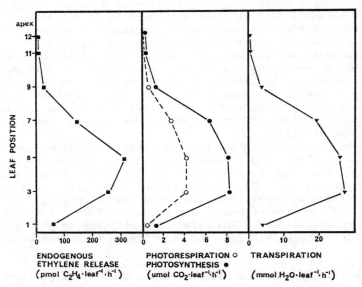

FIGURE 1. a) Endogenous ethylene release, b) phototosynthesis at 300 ubar CO_2 (●) and photorespiration (○), and c) transpiration rates expressed on a per leaf basis in tomato plants. Photorespiration is the difference between net CO_2 uptake at 210 and 20 mbar O_2.

3. RESULTS AND DISCUSSION

Leaf tissue sampled from odd numbered leaf positions of 12-leaf tomato plants was incubated at 350 umole quanta.m^{-2}.s^{-1} (PPFD 400-700nm) and 300 ubar CO_2. The youngest leaf tissue on the tomato plants exhibited the highest rates of ethylene evolution on a unit leaf area basis such that ethylene release in th eapical region was high. The rate of ethylene release decreased from 9.89+0.69 to 2.83+0.17 nmoles.m^{-2}.s^{-1} with leaf expansion and maturation (data not shown). However when ethylene evolution was expressed on a per leaf basis instead of a unit leaf area basis, the greatest contribution to plant release was made by the large expanded leaves (Fig. 1.a.) These source leaves also represent the major sites of CO_2 assimilation and transpiration in these plants (Figs. 1.a. and 1.b.). The following data examines the effects of CO_2 concentration on ethylene evolution in representative expanded source leaves at leaf position five.

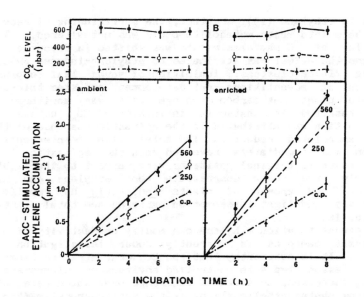

FIGURE 2. Time courses of ACC-stimulated ethylene release by leaf tissue from leaf position five of twelve leaf tomato plants grown under a) ambient (350 ubar) and b) enriched (1300) CO_2.

Ethylene release by leaf tissue incubated in the light is enhanced by increasing CO_2 concentration. Figure 1 illustrates time courses of ethylene release by leaf tissue excised from the fifth leaf of plants grown under ambient (350 ubar CO_2, Fig. 1.a.) and enriched (1300 ubar CO_2, Fig. 1.b.) conditions. The tissue was incubated in the light at CO_2 levels as indicated in the figure. The top quarters of the figure represent the actual CO_2 concentrations of the headspace as monitored during the experiment. The data show that long term growth of intact plants at elevated CO_2 concentrations results in higher rates of ethylene release from leaf tissue than from the tissue of plants grown at ambient CO_2 levels when incubated at the same CO_2 assay concentrations (Fig. 2). Short-term fluctuations in enviromental CO_2 concentrations may occur in plant canopies as well as in structures in which air exchange is restricted, such as greenhouses. Long-term exposure and growth under high CO_2 may occur in greenhouses supplemented with CO_2 and increasing global CO_2 levels may alter the magnitude of ethylene synthesis and/or release from photosynthetic tissue in the future.

Ethylene exposure typically reduces total plant growth and there have been reports suggesting that ethylene can exert a direct inhibitory effect on photosynthetic processes (12, 13). However studies in this laboratory have demonstrated that steady-state leaf photosynthesis, photorespiration, dark respiration, and transpiration are not affected by continuous ethylene exposure (7). These observations were in agreement with earlier studies of steady-state leaf gas exchange responses to ethylene (14). Further, the partitioning of recently fixed photosynthate into major metabolite pools was not altered. The spatial partitioning of ^{14}C-photoassimilate was shifted in favour of the root system and the effect was attributed to ethylene-induced abscission of developing flower clusters, inhibition of young leaf expansion, and stimulation of adventitious root development and stem thickening (7). When whole plant net carbon exchange rate was monitored, ethylene exposure resulted in substantial inhibition of CO_2 uptake (11, 15). This inhibition was attributed to the epinastic response of the plants and the associated reduction in total light interception. The inhibition was immediately reversed when the epinastic leaves were returned to their original positions with respect to the light source. Collectively the data demonstrate that ethylene can alter the development and growth of plants indirectly by modifying sink distributions and light interception patterns and total plant CO_2 uptake (7, 11, 15, 16)

The extent to which ethylene can modify productivity of natural and agricultural canopies is currently under investigation in this laboratory. It is noteworthy that the CO_2 concentration range from 0 to 1500 ubar, associated with controlled environment culture and predicted global CO_2 increases, constitutes the range over which rates of ethylene release from photosynthetic tissue is the most responsive (2-5, 9, 16).

REFERENCES

1. Dhawan, K.R., Bassi, P.K., and Spencer, M.S. (1981) Plant Physiol, 68, 831-4
2. Grodzinski, B. (1984) Plant Physiol, 74, 871-6
3. Grodzinski, B., Boesel, I., and Horton, R.F. (1982a) J Expl Bot, 33, 344-54
4. Grodzinski, B., Boesel, I., and Horton, R.F. (1982b) J Expl Bot, 33, 1185-93
5. Grodzinski, B., Boesel, I., and Horton, R.F. (1983) Plant Physiol, 71, 588-93
6. Bishop, P.M. and Whittingham, C.P. (1968) Photosynthetica, 2, 31-8
7. Woodrow, L., Thompson, R.G., and Grodzinski, B. (1988) J Expl Bot, 39, 667-684
8. Eng, R.Y.N., Tsujita, M.J., Grodzinski, B., and Dutton, R.G. (1983) HortSci, 18, 878-9
9. Woodrow, L. and Grodzinski, B. (1987) J Expl Bot, 38, 1224-32
10. Dutton, R.G., Jiao, J., Tsujita, M.J., and Grodzinski, B. (1988) Plant Physiol, 86, 355-8
11. Woodrow, L., Jiao, J., Tsujita, M.J., and Grodzinski, B. (1989) Plant Physiol, 90, 85-90
12. Kays, S.J. and Pallas Jr., J.E. (1980) Nature, 285, 51-2
13. Taylor, G.E. Jr and Gunderson, C.A. (1988) Plant Physiol, 86, 85-92
14. Pallaghy, C.K. and Raschke, K. (1972) Plant Physiol, 49, 275-6
15. Woodrow, L. and Grodzinski, B. (1989) J Expl Bot, 40, 361-8
16. Grodzinski, B. and Woodrow, L. (1989) In Biochemical and Physiological Aspects of Ethylene Production in Lower and Higher Plants (Clijsters, H., de Proft, M., Marcelle, R., and van Poucke, M., eds.), pp.271-8, Kluwer Academic, Dordrecht

RESPONSE OF AGING CHLOROPLASTS TO UV RADIATION

BASANTI BISWAL[1] AND G. KULANDAIVELU[2]
1. School of Life Sciences, Sambalpur University, Jyoti vihar, 768 019, Orissa, India.
2. School of Biological Sciences, Madurai Kamraj University, Madurai - 625 021, India.

1. INTRODUCTION
    Extensive reports are available on degradation of chloroplasts during leaf aging(1). Stress like water deficity(2), high temperature(3) and high light intensity (4,5, 6) are demonstrated to accelerate leaf aging, consequently a rapid degradation of chloroplasts. Ultaviolet(UV) radiation is known to produce extensive damages of thylakoid membranes(7,8). The objective of the present work is to investigate the kinetics of loss of pigments, specific changes in photochemical reactions associated with PS I and PS II during aging of detached maize leaves exposed to UV radiations. It is established that cellular DNA remains stable with conservation of all informations to control leaf aging(9). Since UV radiation is known to cause a significant damage to leaf DNA(10), it is important to investigate if UV exposed leaves will exhibit any differential kinetics of aging induced degradatiion. Since the plants are known to respond differently to different regions of UV spectrum, chloroplast degradation during aging has been investigated in the leaves exposed to UV-A, UV-B and UV-C radiations.

2. PROCEDURE
2.1. Materials and Methods
    2.1.1. Plant material and UV treatment :
           Maize (Zea mays L. CV. CO1) seeds were grown in soil-filled plastic trays in dark for 2 days. The pots were then transferred to continuous illumination (55µ mol m^{-2} s^{-1}) at 28 ±2°C. After 7 days of growth, 15 segments, each measuring 1 cm X 3 cm, were excised from the second leaf and incubated on 4 layers of moist filter papers at 28 ± 2°C. Detached leaf segments were allowed to age for 3 days. The leaf segments in separate petridishes were irradiated with either philips

black light, type 05 (UV-A emission maximum 365 nm) or philips 20W/12 Sun lamp (UV-B, 285-320 nm) filtered with cellulose acetate 5 ml filters or philips 15W germicidal lamp (UV-C, emission maximum 254 nm). The duration of exposure was 60, 30 and 15 min per day at the fluence rate of 75, 64 and 50μ mol $m^{-2} s^{-1}$ respectively for UV-A, UV-B and UV-C radiations. Under this treatment, the extent of inhibition of overall photosynthesis was same in all UV wave bands. The samples were taken for different measurements at every 24 h interval.

2.1.2. Biochemical analysis :
Pigments were extracted in 80% acetone. The content of total chlorophyll was estimated by the method of Arnon(11).

2.1.3. Isolation of chloroplasts :
Chloroplasts were isolated grinding the leaves with ice chilled 20 mM Tris-HCl buffer (pH 7.8) 5 mM $MgCl_2$, 300 mM sucrose, 10 mM NaCl and 1 mM EDTA. The homogenate was squeezed through 2 layers of nylon cloth and the filtrate was centrifuged by 5 min at 3000 X g. The pellet was washed and resuspended in isolation buffer for immediate use.

2.1.4. Measurement of electron transport activities :
The rate of PS II electron transport was measured as DCPIP(2,6-dichlorophenol indophenol) reduction using a Hitachi 557 spectrophotometer as described earlier(7). PS I electron transport from the artificial electron donor was assayed as O_2 uptake using a Hansatech O_2 electrode at 25°C under saturating white light from a slide projector fitted with a 150W Halogen lamp (Photophone Ltd., India).

3. RESULTS AND DISCUSSIONS

Comparative kinetics of pigment loss during senescence of detached maize leaves exposed to different UV radiations are shown in Fig. 1. Loss of pigment, however, is significantly enhanced when the detached maize leaves were exposed to UV radiation for a short period (Fig.1). Among the three radiations tried, UV-C caused the destruction of chlorophyll more rapidly than UV-A and UV-B. Disorganization of thylakoid membrane is suggested to activate membrane bound chlorophyllase for degradation of chlorophyll(12). Since UV light is known to cause membrane disorganization, the enhancing effect of chlorophyll loss could be attributed to stimulation of chlorophyllase activity induced by the radiation.

Table 1 shows the changes in the rates of PS I and

PS II reactions of chloroplasts isolated from aging leaves.

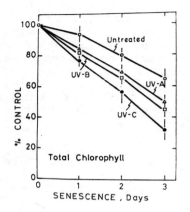

FIGURE 1 : Changes in the level of total chlorophyll of aging maize leaves. For condition of aging and UV treatment see materials and methods. Bars indicate ± SE (n=3). The 100% value for total chlorophyll was 2.09± 0.3 mg/g (FW) .

TABLE 1. Changes in the rate of PS II ($H_2O \longrightarrow$ DCPIP) and PS I (DCPIPH$_2 \longrightarrow$ MV) activity in control and UV-treated maize leaves 3 days of aging. Figures in parentheses represent percentage activity with reference to respective 0 time control activity. values represent ±SE(n=4).

Sample	$H_2O \longrightarrow$ DCPIP μ mol DCPIP mg chl^{-1} h^{-1}	DCPIPH$_2 \longrightarrow$ MV μ mol O$_2$ mg Chl^{-1} h^{-1}
0 Day control	76.3±6.8(100.0)	173.0±20.7(100.0)
3 Days control	62.8±6.3(82.3)	170.5±18.5(98.6)
3 Days + UV-A	51.4±7.1(67.4)	223.6±31.3(129.3)
3 Days + UV-B	40.9±5.9(53.6)	218.0±24.5(126.0)
3 Days + UV-C	20.8±3.1(27.3)	167.8±12.6(97.0)

The PS II mediated DCPIP reduction showed a 18% reduction during the 72h aging of detached maize leaves. The data on the loss in the electron transport efficiency of thylakoid membrane during leaf aging of maize corroborates with the earlier findings of Choudhury and Biswal(13). The photochemical reactions associated with PS I and PS II of thylakoid membrane exhibit differential susceptibility to aging. Aging induced declie in PS I activity is negligible, where as the PS II activity showed significant reduction. The observed high susceptibility of PS II mediated reaction could be attributed to a damage of oxygen evolving complex (1) or plastoquinine level(14). Treatment of leaves with UV radiations was found to enhance aging induced loss in the

DCPIP photoreduction. The extent of loss in the photochemical reaction, however, varied with different UV treatments, the loss being maximum with UV-C and minimum with UV-A. In contrast to PS II reactions, the PS I mediated reaction is markedly stimulated by UV-A and UV-B, while UV-C had no significant effect. It is plausible that UV radiation may reorganise PS I complexes in the thylakoid membranes contributing to their stability during aging. Further, the possibility of UV induced uncoupling of LHC from core complex of PS II and its subsequent migration to PS I region with consequent enhancement in its photochemical reaction can not be ruled out.

REFERENCES
1 Biswal, U.C. and Biswal, B. (1988) Int. rev. Cytol. 113, 270-321.
2 Sestak, Z. and Pospisilova, J. (1986) photobiochem. photobiophys. 12, 163-172.
3 DeLuca d' oro, G.M. and Trippi, V.S. (1987) Plant Cell Physiol. 28, 1389-1396.
4 Pjon, C.J. (1981) Plant Cell physiol. 22, 847-854.
5 Biswal, B.; Choudhury, N.K.; Sahu, P. and Biswal U.C. (1983) Plant Cell Physiol. 24, 1203-1208.
6 Biswal, B. and Choudhury, N.K. (1986) Plant Cell Physiol 27, 1439-1444.
7 Noorudeen, A.M. and Kulandaivelu, G. (1982a) Physiol. Plant. 55, 161-166.
8 Noorudeen, A.M. and Kulandaivelu, G. (1983) J. Biol. Res. 3. 71-77.
9 Woolhouse, H.W. (1982) In the Molecular Biology of Plant Development (Smith, H. and Grierson eds.), pp. 256-281, Oxford, Blackwells, ISBN.
10 Noorudeen, A.M. and Kulandaivelu, G. (1982b) Plant Physiol. Biochem. 9,33-40.
11 Arnon, D.I. (1949) Plant Physiol. 24, 1-15.
12 Lambers, J.W.J.; Verkleij, A.J. and Terpstra, W. (1984) Biochim. Biophys. Acta. 786, 1-8.
13 Choudhury, N.K. and Biswal, U.C. (1980) Physiol. Plant. 49, 43-48.
14 Kulandaivelu, G. and Senger, H. (1976) Physiol. Plant 36, 157-164.

ESTIMATING SO$_2$ STRESS BY CHLOROPHYLL FLUORESCENCE MEASUREMENTS WITH AN ACTIVE SYSTEM USED IN THE REMOTE SENSING MODE

CORNELIS KLIFFEN, Research Institute for Plant Protection; P.O. Box 9060, 6709 GW WAGENINGEN, THE NETHERLANDS

1. INTRODUCTION

By measuring the chlorophyll fluorescence induction kinetics and the fluorescence spectrum of an intact leaf or plant the condition and potential activity of the photosynthetic apparatus can be estimated (1, ed. H.K. Lichtenthaler). Solely two parameters namely the chlorophyll fluorescence ratio F685/F730 and the fluorescence life time are reliable to measure by remote sensing (2).
In this paper experiments are described in which fluorescence was excited by a blue laser beam positioned at a distance of 15 meters away from the plants and fluorescence spectra were subsequently recorded from the same distance.
Correlations are discussed between the chlorophyll fluorescence ratio F685/F730, the concentration of SO$_2$ which has been applied during fumigations of the plants and the rate of photosynthesis, chorophyll content and growth parameters like the dry matter production.

2. MATERIALS AND METHODS

2.1. Plants: Vicia faba (cv minica) plants were grown in climate chambers adjusted to 15$_2$C and 75% relative humidity (RH) for 24 hours, with 105 W/m^2 photosynthetic radiation (PAR) at the canopy for 14 hours per day. Two weeks after sowing the plants were placed in the climate chambers where fumigation took place.

2.2. Fumigation doses: The eight climate chambers were fumigated with respectively 0, 25, 50, 75, 100, 150, 200 and 300 μg/m^3 SO$_2$.

2.3. Chlorophyll fluorescence: For the measurements the IROE-FLIDAR-2 was used (3). The system consisted of a laser source producing a pulse every second with a wavelength of 480 nm and a duration of 15 ns; a telescope which collected the radiation from the canopy and an optical multichannel analyser (OMA) which analysed the collected radiation from the canopy at wavelengths over 540 nm to form a spectrum. The fluorescence spectrum was obtained by substracting the spectrum measured before the pulse from the one registered during the pulse. The fluorescence ratio F685/F730 was subsequently calculated from the averaged fluorescence spectrum.
In a relatively dark corridor a straight line of plants were

M. Baltscheffsky (ed.), Current Research in Photosynthesis, Vol. IV, 817–820.
© 1990 *Kluwer Academic Publishers. Printed in the Netherlands.*

situated 15 meters from the FLIDAR. The horizontal laser beam was launched through the axis of the telescope. The row was hit at an angle of 45 degrees at 3/4 of the height of the plants. During the measurement the plants were continuously illuminated by a 400 W HPI lamp horizontally placed one meter from the plants at right angles to the row. In each measurement 100 pulses were used. The plants has been fumigated for 7 weeks.

2.4. <u>CO_2 assimilation rate</u>: The net CO_2 assimilation rate (PN) was measured in a leaf chamber in which one of the leaves was clamped (4). Conditions inside the chamber were $23^{\circ}C$ and 50% RH. The measurements took place at six different light intensities, with 234 W/m^2 as a maximum. Calculated were: The rate of photosynthesis at light saturation (PMAX), the dark respiration rate (RD) and the efficiency of light utilisation (EFF).
Measurements took place on plants fumigated for 38 days on the 12th leaf from soil level.

2.5. <u>Chlorophyll content</u>: The leaves were extracted in 80% acetone; the chlorophyll content of the extract was calculated from the absorbances at 645, 652 and 663 nm (5).
Estimations took place after 6 to 7 weeks of fumigation.

2.6. <u>Dry matter production</u>: The dry matter of the above ground parts were weighed after 7 weeks of fumigation. For this purpose the plants were dried at $105^{\circ}C$ for 24 hours.

3. RESULTS AND DISCUSSION

3.1. <u>Chlorophyll fluorescence</u>: There excists a positive relationship between the fluorescence ratio F685/F730 and the SO_2 concentration (see Fig. 1.).
Light of 685 nm is more reabsorbed by chlorophyll than that of 730 nm (6) indicating a lower chlorophyll content of fumigated with the higher SO_2 concentrations.

3.2. <u>CO_2 assimilation rate</u>: A negative relationship is obvious between the EFF and the SO_2 concentrations (see Fig. 2.).
RD shows a slight positive correlation (see Fig. 3.) while effects of the fumigation on the AMAX can not be detected (see Fig. 4.).
These results point out that SO_2 causes some damage to the photosynthetic apparatus lessening its efficiency and causing repair respiration to appear. No clear change in the capacity per unit of leaf area of the system is found.

3.3. <u>Chlorophyll content and dry matter production</u>: The amount of chlorophyll per unit leaf area is not affected by the SO_2 fumigation (see Fig. 5.). The dry matter production (growth) is less in plants fumigated with higher concentrations SO_2 (see Fig. 6.).
Combination of these two results makes it plausible that the amount of chorophyll per plant decreases with increased SO_2 concentrations.

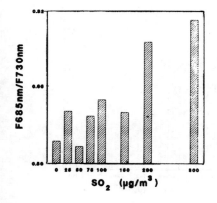

FIGURE 1.
Chorophyll fluorescence ratio
F685/F730 of Vicia faba plants
fumigated for 7 weeks with
different concentrations of SO_2.

CO_2 assimilation rate of leaves from Vicia faba plants fumigated for 38
days with different concentrations of SO_2:

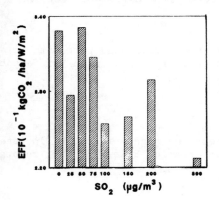

FIGURE 2 (left).
Efficiency of light utilisation.

FIGURE 3 (left below).
Dark respiration rate.

FIGURE 4 (right below).
Rate of photosynthesis at light
saturation.

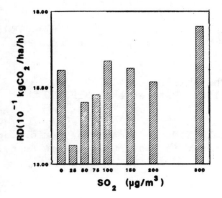

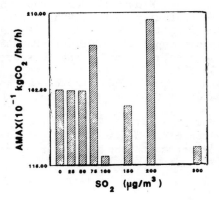

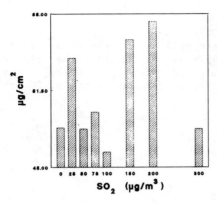 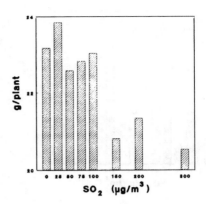

FIGURE 5 (left). Chlorophyll content of leaves from Vicia faba plants fumigated for 6 to 7 weeks with different concentrations of SO_2.

FIGURE 6 (right). Dry matter content of the above ground parts of Vicia faba plants fumigated for 7 weeks with different concentrations of SO_2.

4. CONCLUSIONS

SO_2 fumigation has injurious effects on plants resulting in less growth. By recording the fluorescence reatio F685/F730 by remote sensing these effects can be measured.

REFERENCES

1 Applications of Chlorophyll Fluorescence (Lichtenthaler, H.K., ed.), pp 1-366, Kluwer Academic Publishers, Dordrecht/Boston/London
2 Lichtenthaler, H.K. (1988) Reference 1, 287-297
3 Castagnoli, F., Cecchi, G., Pantani, L. and Radicati, B. (1987) IROE report, pp 1-11, IROE, Via Panciathichi 64, I 50127, Florence
4 Louwerse, W. and van Oorschot, J.L.P. (1969) Photosynthetica 3, 305-315
5 Bruinsma, J. (1963) Photochem. and Photobiol. 2, 241-249
6 Baret, F., Guyot, G. and Major, D. (1988) Reference 1, 319-323

ACKNOWLEDGEMENTS

The technical assistance by Ms. Annemieke W.N. Kooijman in performing the experiments and in preparing this paper is gratefully acknowledged.

PHOTOSYNTHESIS AND FIELD ENVIRONMENTAL PRODUCTIVITY INDICES

PARK S. NOBEL, DEPARTMENT OF BIOLOGY AND LABORATORY OF BIOMEDICAL AND
ENVIRONMENTAL SCIENCES, UNIVERSITY OF CALIFORNIA, LOS ANGELES, CA
90024, U.S.A.

SUMMARY
    Based on the effects of water status, temperature, and
photosynthetically active radiation (PAR) on net CO_2 uptake measured
over 24-h periods in the laboratory, net CO_2 uptake and productivity
have recently been predicted month-by-month in the field for agaves
and cacti using an environmental productivity index (EPI). EPI is
the product of a Water Index, a Temperature Index, and a PAR Index,
each of which can have a maximum value of unity when field values of
that environmental factor do not limit net CO_2 uptake. A Nutrient
Index, similarly ranging from 0.00 to 1.00, has recently been proposed
to handle edaphic limitations on net CO_2 uptake. In distinction to
other productivity indices that customarily focus on only one
environmental factor, EPI thus incorporates simultaneous effects of
water, temperature, PAR, and even nutrients. Using EPI, the
productivity of agaves, cacti, and potentially other species can be
predicted over wide geographical regions and under any environmental
conditions.

INTRODUCTION — COMPONENT INDICES
    Soil water status influences the daily pattern and the magnitude
of net CO_2 uptake by plants. Drought, defined as commencing when the
plant under consideration has a higher water potential than does the
soil and hence can no longer take up water, causes a decrease in the
maximal rate of net CO_2 uptake and in the total CO_2 uptake over 24 h.
Total uptake is determined by integrating the curves for the
instantaneous net rates of CO_2 uptake over a 24-h period; e.g., under
well-watered conditions, net CO_2 uptake over a 24-h period is 206 mmol
m^{-2} day^{-1} for Agave deserti, a common succulent from the Sonoran
Desert whose net CO_2 uptake over 24-h periods has been studied in
considerable detail under various environmental conditions (1-3). Net
CO_2 uptake over 24-h periods for A. deserti decreases 64% after 9 days
of drought and becomes zero after 33 days of drought (2).
    Based on the response of net CO_2 uptake to soil water status and
taking into consideration the water storage capacity of individual
plants, a Water Index was proposed and applied to data with A. deserti

M. Baltscheffsky (ed.), Current Research in Photosynthesis, Vol. IV, 821–825.
© 1990 Kluwer Academic Publishers. Printed in the Netherlands.

(2). The Water Index is the net CO_2 uptake over 24 h under a particular condition of water availability divided by the maximum net CO_2 uptake over 24 h when water is not limiting; i.e., it represents the fraction of maximal net CO_2 uptake due to water limitations. Hence, the Water Index is 1.00 under well-watered conditions. It becomes 0.36 after 9 days of drought for A. deserti and 0.00 after 33 days of drought (2). By measuring net CO_2 uptake over 24-h periods after various periods of drought, a functional relationship can similarly be obtained between days of drought and the Water Index for any species.

Indices were likewise proposed for two other environmental variables affecting the daily pattern and the magnitude of net CO_2 uptake — temperature and photosynthetically active radiation (PAR). Again, these two indices are unity when the environmental factor represented does not limit net CO_2 uptake over 24-h periods and are zero when net CO_2 uptake is completely abolished. Specifically, net CO_2 uptake in the laboratory is optimal for day/night air temperatures of 25°C/15°C for A. deserti, conditions under which the Temperature Index is therefore 1.00 (2). Net CO_2 uptake by a Crassulacean acid metabolism (CAM) plant such as A. deserti is influenced primarily by temperatures at night when nearly all net CO_2 uptake occurs, so in practice only average nighttime temperatures, or, alternatively, minimum daily temperatures, are needed to determine the functional relationship between temperature and the Temperature Index (3). For A. deserti, net CO_2 uptake over a 24-h period is reduced 16% at day/ night air temperatures of 15°C/5°C and 33% at 35°C/25°C compared with 25°C/15°C (2). Hence, its Temperature Index is 0.84 for average nighttime temperatures of 5°C and 0.67 for 25°C. To obtain the PAR Index, relationships were determined in the laboratory between net CO_2 uptake over 24-h periods and the total PAR incident on a particular leaf surface during the daytime. For A. deserti, the PAR Index is 0.00 at a total daily PAR of 3 mol m^{-2} day^{-1} (the light compensation level), 0.50 at 11 mol m^{-2} day^{-1}, 0.90 at 22 mol m^{-2} day^{-1}, and 1.00 at 37 mol m^{-2} day^{-1}, the latter representing PAR saturation (2).

ENVIRONMENTAL PRODUCTIVITY INDEX

The three component indices were combined into an Environmental Productivity Index (EPI), which quantifies the combined effect of these three environmental factors on net CO_2 uptake over a 24-h period (2-3):

$$EPI = \text{Water Index} \times \text{Temperature Index} \times \text{PAR Index}$$

EPI has its maximal value of unity for well-watered conditions, optimal temperatures for net CO_2 uptake, and saturating PAR — under other conditions, EPI represents the fraction of maximal net CO_2 uptake expected. To calculate EPI for some species in the field, its net CO_2 uptake over 24-h periods should be measured in the laboratory while varying one factor at a time, and the environmental conditions in the field should be specified, preferably on a daily basis. Models can be used to predict certain field conditions, such as soil water status as a function of rainfall and time, and monthly averages can sometimes be used, such as for calculating the Temperature Index (3).

Because all of the environmental factors represented by the component indices can simultaneously limit net CO_2 uptake, a multiplicative form is used for EPI. When one component index is zero, net CO_2 uptake will not occur no matter what the other indices are. For instance, if no stomatal opening occurs because of drought, then net CO_2 uptake over 24-h periods and hence EPI will be zero even when the temperature is optimal for net CO_2 uptake. Actually, second order interactive effects can occur among the environmental factors represented by the component indices, but such effects have proved to be small for agaves and cacti (3).

EPI has been successfully used to interpret various responses of Agave deserti and also has been determined month-by-month over 1-year periods for A. fourcroydes, A. lechuguilla, A. salmiana, A. tequilana, Ferocactus acanthodes, and Opuntia ficus-indica (3). For example, productivity estimates based on EPI for A. deserti over a 5-month period are within 4% of those based on dry weight obtained via destructive harvesting (2). EPI correctly predicted the resulting interactive effects of soil water status, temperature, and PAR on growth for A. deserti along a transect extending from an elevation of 300 m to one of 1200 m, for which rainfall increased 3-fold (4). Calculations based on the Temperature Index indicate that Agave fourcroydes, which is the main crop of the Yucatán Peninsula of Mexico, would have a higher productivity in regions with slightly lower nighttime temperatures (5). Calculations based on the PAR Index demonstrate that the spacing typically used for adult plants of this species are nearly optimal (4000 plants hectare^{-1}) but that greater distances between the young plants before they are transplanted into the final field spacing would enhance growth (6).

NUTRIENT INDEX

Although EPI has proved useful for interpreting and predicting the influences of environmental factors on net CO_2 uptake, growth, and productivity, the influences of various nutrients in the soil should also be considered. Therefore, a Nutrient Index was proposed as another multiplicative factor in EPI that accounts for the primary influences of such soil factors on net CO_2 uptake and hence productivity (7). Numerous observations indicate that nitrogen is the most important nutrient affecting CO_2 uptake, shoot volume increases, and dry weight gains of agaves and cacti and that these measures of productivity usually increase in a logarithmic fashion with the nitrogen level in the soil or in a hydroponic solution, leading to the form adopted for the Nitrogen Index (3). Growth also tends to be logarithmically related to the phosphorus level and the potassium level in the soil, so these indices also take a logarithmic form (7). The only other elements whose effects on growth have been documented for several species of agaves and cacti are boron and sodium, the former enhancing growth and the latter inhibiting it. The proposed Nutrient Index was therefore restricted to five elements.

Assuming that the various elements were co-limiting in the Nutrient Index, just as for environmental factors in EPI, and incorporating the empirical relationships between growth and the level of the five

elements considered, the following Nutrient Index was proposed for
agaves and cacti (7):

Nutrient Index = Nitrogen Index $\times$ Phosphorus Index $\times$ Potassium Index
$\times$ Boron Index $\times$ Sodium Index
= $(1.418 + 0.348 \ln N) \times [1 + 0.195 \ln (P/60)]$
$\times [1 + 0.117 \ln (K/250)] \times B^{0.213} \times (1 - 0.00288 Na)$

where N is in % of the soil by dry weight, and P, K, B, and Na are in
ppm of the soil by dry weight. A component index becomes unity when
the element in question no longer limits growth, which the preliminary
evidence indicates occurs for $N \geq 0.3\%$, $P \geq 60$ ppm, $K \geq 250$ ppm, and
$B \geq 1.0$ ppm; the Sodium Index is appropriate up to about 150 ppm Na
(7). Presently, the Nutrient Index is being tested, which should lead
to certain modifications and restrictions. In any case, it summarizes
the available nutrient data for agaves and cacti and indicates the
primary influences of edaphic factors on net CO_2 uptake, growth, and
productivity before idiosyncrasies of individual species and different
soils are taken into account.

USING EPI — OTHER INDICES
EPI times the maximal CO_2 uptake over 24 h equals the actual CO_2
uptake. Hence, values of EPI, including adjustments based on the
Nutrient Index, can be readily converted to net CO_2 uptake per unit of
photosynthetic surface. Using the leaf area index and/or the stem area
index as appropriate, CO_2 uptake can be expressed per unit ground area,
the usual area considered in productivity studies. CO_2 uptake
averaged over the shoot surface, when adjusted for root respiration
and growth, therefore indicates aboveground productivity. Moreover,
EPI allows for the extrapolation of productivity measured at some site
to other sites with different edaphic and environmental conditions.
Productivity can also be predicted for a new climate, such as the
changes in temperature and rainfall patterns associated with
"greenhouse" gases, particularly elevated atmospheric CO_2
concentrations (for this, net CO_2 uptake over a 24-h period needs
to be measured or estimated under elevated CO_2 for some specified
condition).
Although the development and the initial applications of EPI have
been for research on agaves and cacti (3), the approach is general and
can be applied to any species whose responses of net CO_2 uptake to
water, temperature, PAR, and soil nutrients are known or measured.
Moreover, EPI and especially its component indices are analogous to
other indices that have been proposed for quantifying growth and
productivity. Some productivity indices and yield predictions have
been based only on rainfall and evapotranspiration (8–12), although
productivity varies more from year to year at a particular site than
does rainfall (13). Indices for crop performance and forage yields
have also been based on the moisture supply and water-holding capacity
of soils (10, 14, 15). Growth indices are often based on the
accumulated time that the temperature is above some value, the
"degree-day" approach (16, 17). Also, crop growth has been indicated

to be proportional to intercepted radiation (18, 19), and considerable
modelling effort has been devoted to predicting radiation interception.
These single-factor approaches have proved extremely useful for
specific applications and indeed are simpler than EPI, which argues
in their favor. Yet an integrated approach, simultaneously
considering water status, temperature, PAR, and soil elements such as
embodied in EPI, seems much more realistic and pertinent to
quantitative predictions and interpretations of net CO_2 uptake,
growth, and productivity of plants.

ACKNOWLEDGMENT
    Financial support during the course of these studies was provided
by the Ecological Research Division of the Office of Health and
Environmental Research, U.S. Department of Energy.

REFERENCES
 1 Nobel, P.S. (1976) Plant Physiol. 58, 576-582
 2 Nobel, P.S. (1984) Oecologia 64, 1-7
 3 Nobel, P.S. (1988) Environmental Biology of Agaves and Cacti.
   Cambridge University Press, New York
 4 Nobel, P.S. and Hartsock, T.L. (1986) Oecologia 68, 181-185
 5 Nobel, P.S. (1985) J. Appl. Ecol. 22, 157-173
 6 Nobel, P.S. and Garcia de Cortázar, V. (1987) Photosynthetica 21,
   261-272
 7 Nobel, P.S. (1989) J. Appl. Ecol., in press
 8 Sneva, F.A. and Hyder, D.M. (1962) J. Range Management 15, 88-93
 9 Chang, J.-H. (1968) Climate and Agriculture: An Ecological Survey.
   Aldine, Chicago
10 Nix, H.A. and Fitzpatrick, E.A. (1969) Agric. Meteorol. 6, 321-337
11 Duncan, D.A. and Woodmansee, R.G. (1975) J. Range Management 28,
   327-329
12 Le Houérou, H.N. (1984) J. Arid Environ. 7, 1-35
13 Le Houérou, H.N., Bingham, R.L., and Skerbek, W. (1988) J. Arid
   Environ. 15, 1-18
14 Dahl, B.E. (1963) J. Range Management 16, 128-132
15 McBride, R.A. and Mackintosh, E.E. (1984) Soil Sci. Soc. Am. J. 48,
   1343-1350
16 Castonguay, Y. and Dubé, P.A. (1985) Agric. Forest Meteorol. 35,
   31-45
17 Long, S.P. and Woodward, F.I., eds. (1988) Plants and Temperature.
   Symposium XXXXII of the Society for Experimental Biology.
   Company of Biologists, Cambridge
18 Monteith, J.L. (1977) Phil. Tran. Roy. Soc., London, Ser. B, 281,
   277-294
19 Jones, H.G. (1983) Plants and Microclimate. Cambridge University
   Press, Cambridge

PHOTOSYNTHESIS OF PLANTS IN RELATION TO RESOURCE
AVAILABILITY IN THE FIELD

E.-D. SCHULZE, LEHRSTUHL PFLANZENÖKOLOGIE, UNIVERSITÄT
BAYREUTH, POSTFACH 101251, 8580 BAYREUTH, WEST GERMANY

1. INTRODUCTION

Photosynthesis is the process that provides energy to
all anabolic and catabolic processes in ecosystems. The
rate at which plants assimilate CO_2 in the field may be
quite different from optimal conditions in the test
tube or in growth cabinets. The rate depends on the
environmental conditions of the habitat which determine
to what extent the genetic capability of a plant can
actually be used for photosynthesis. The main factor
restricting photosynthesis in the field is the availability of light. But, other factors my become just as
rate limiting, such as atmospheric carbon dioxide
concentration, air humidity and temperature, and water
or nutrient supply from the soil. Time is an additional
important factor which influences the carbon balance
via plant age but also by deterimining the dose of
stress.

Plants are quite capable to adapt and to acclimate to
habitat conditions. In fact during evolution almost all
available habitats from the oceanshore to the alpine
ice, and from the dry desert to marshlands were inhabi-
tated by different plant species. In each situation the
plant has to cope with the variability of climatic and
edaphic conditions. There are long-term effects, which
generally cause non-reversible adaptations in the
plant, such as caused by light climate, nutrition and
water availability, and short-term reversible effects
such as caused by changing weather. It is the aim of
field investigations to identify relations between
plant response and habitat. This involves a quantification of adaptations of plants to given habitat conditions (physiological mechanisms) and of the actual carbon inputs into ecosystems (element cycling in ecosystems).

In the following I will discuss the effect of environment on plant performance with special emphasis on

M. Baltscheffsky (ed.), Current Research in Photosynthesis, Vol. IV, 827–834.
© 1990 *Kluwer Academic Publishers. Printed in the Netherlands.*

understanding of the variability in photosynthetic capacity.

2. DAILY COURSES OF PHOTOSYNTHESIS

Photosynthetic rates have been measured in the field since about 20 years. There is a fairly good understanding of the general photosynthtic response under most environmental conditions (e.g. Schulze and Hall, 1982, Lange, 1986).

Even within the same habitat daily courses of photosynthesis may be quite different depending on physiological pathways and plant type (Fig.1). In a desert habitat, one extreme are the lower plants, e.g. lichens. Following dew fall at night they may use only a short period in the morning for photosynthesis until they are dried by evaporation. The daily carbon gain of these plants is very low, because of respiratory losses of the hydrated thallus over night (Lange et al. 1970). In contrast, the main carbon gain of CAM plants may occur in the dark, while C_3 and C_4 plants photosynthesize during the day but differ in their response to light, temperature and humidity.

FIGURE 1. Diurnal CO_2 gas exchange of different plant species in a desert habitat (after Schulze and Hall, 1982).

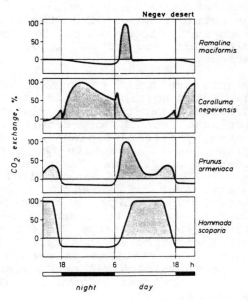

These daily patterns of CO_2 exchange may vary with seasons, which affects plant development. During a wet season daily courses of CO_2 uptake will be one-peaked, however with proceeding dry season, daily courses become progressively bi-modal. In addition distinct changes in maximal photosynthetic rates take place with leaf age. The actual weather conditions may reduce the photosynthetic rate substantially below the point which may be reached under otherwise optimal conditions, say in a growth cabinet.

Thus CO_2-assimilation in the field is determined by the constitution of the plant type (e.g. poikilohydrous versus homoiohydrous, CAM, C_4, C_3 type), by phenology (e.g. leaf age and development), by long term acclimation to the environment (e.g. light, nutrition) and by the actual habitat conditions (e.g. light, temperarture, water). Within this framework, we are mainly lacking measurements and models which explain the maximal rates of photosynthesis. However, these are nesessary for any predictions of plant and ecosystems carbon budgets.

3. MAXIMAL RATES OF PHOTOSYNTHESIS

When relating CO_2 uptake to CO_2 concentration the well known saturation curve emerges, which is determined by the initial slope of CO_2 uptake at low concentrations (the carboxylation efficiency) and the maximal photosynthetic capacity at CO_2 saturation. Within this range the plant operates below (often less than 60%) their capacity at a point which is determined by the actual CO_2 concentration and the degree of stomatal closure.

FIGURE 2. Photosynthetic capacity as related to maximum stomatal conductance in different leaf types (after Körner et al., 1979).

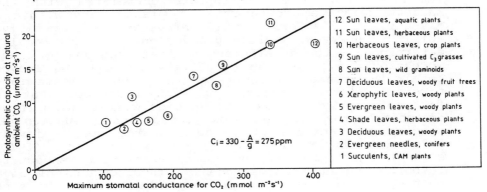

The problem with respect to photosynthesis in nature is not the underlaying biochemistry to explain the shape of this curve, but to understanding the observed large differences in capacity of different plant types which exist even within the same habitat (Fig. 2). The photosynthetic rates of coniferous needles and sun leaves of herbaceous plants may differ by factor 4 in favor of the herbaceous plant, but obviously the conifer will dominate the habitat.

FIGURE 3. CO_2-assimilation at ambient CO_2-concentrations of different species and plant life forms as related to light intensity and nitrogen contents of the leaves (after Schulze and Chapin, 1987).

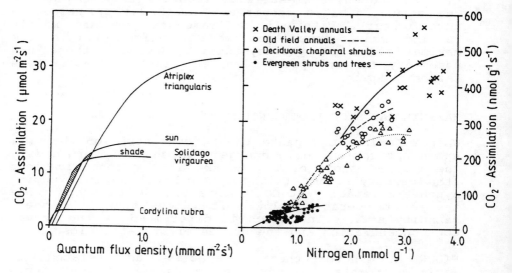

The maximum rate of CO_2 uptake correlates with the maximum relative growth rate of plants, and within a given plant life form it will influence its competitive ability. However, total production is additionally determined by the development of leaf area and by plant morphology, i.e. by the capability to exposing leaves to the environment (Schulze et al., 1986). These factors may become important to such a degree, that in fact only early successional species exhibit high rates of photosynthesis, but late successional species or species of habitats with low resource supply invest less into photosynthesis. Orians and Solbrig (1977) suggested that overlapping niches exist with respect to resource use and photosynthesis. Thus, plants of high photosynthetic rate are not capable to sustain such rate at low resource supply. In contrast plants of low resource habitats have a low rate at optimal conditions but maintain such low rate of photosynthesis even at low resource supply. A nich separation emerges (Fig. 2) when relating photosynthesis of different plant life forms to nitrogen contents in their tissue as a measure of nitrogen supply or to the prevailing quantum flux density of the habitat (Schulze and Chapin, 1987).

Resource supply over time (e.g. habitat conditions of nutrition) and resource supply within space (e.g. seasonal changes of nutrient or water availability) determine in concert with morphological features the distribution of plant life forms, and within each group the evolution of photosynthetic capacity.

4. PLANT INTERNAL CONTROL OF PHOTOSYNTHESIS

There is no conceptual understanding of how plants maintain or regulate their photosynthetic capacity. On the one hand it is the demand for carbohytrates in the cytosol and the regeneration of P_i and Ribulose-bi-phosphate which affect the actual photosynthetic rate. However, the carbon-cycle and the competitive demand for carbohydrate-structures in the chloroplast and the cytosol is only one aspect in this plant internal regulation (Stitt et al., 1987). There is increasing evidence, that photoinhibition may be another factor which eliminates overinvestments of light harvesting structures (Demig et al.,1987). The combination of both mechanisms may in fact determine the actual photosynthetic capacity. However, to my knowledge, this has not been studied in the field.

In addition to these plant internal biochemical controls, plants appear to reallocate resources within the plant such that maximum use is made of these resources with respect to photosynthesis. Field and Mooney (1986) suggested that plants reallocate their nitrogen content such that the most light exposed leaves reach the highest concentrations und thus reach the highest photosynthetic rates. Urtica dioica is an example for such a response type (Fig. 4). It forms a dense canopy which continually grows to greater hight, renwing its total foliage 3 to 5 times during a single growing season. At all leaf positions leaf conductance and CO_2 assimilation are linearly correlated. The difference in rates is determined by the nitrogen concentration in the leaves which changes in the plant such that always the top leaves reach the highest concentration. Reallocation of nitrogen in the plant is regulated such that it results in maximal photosynthtic rate with respect to available light in different canopy layers.

FIGURE 4. Maximal leaf conductance as related to CO_2 assimilation under optimal climnatic conditions and ambient CO_2, and CO_2 assimilation as related to leaf nitrogen content and leaf position. The leaf nodes are counted with the youngest developing leaf being node number 1.

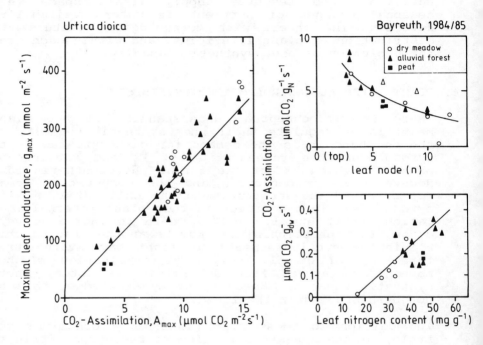

Besides light and nutrition, plant water status is an additional important environmental factor influencing the rate of CO_2 uptake. In general, the initial phase of this response is a response of stomata, which are more sensitive to water stress than the photosynthetic metabolism. If plant water status decreases further, also photosynthesis is reduced. In laboratory experiments it has been shown, that it is not the leaf water status but hormonal and ionic relations between root and shoot which regulate stomatal opening and photosynthesis under soil water stress (Gollan et al., 1988).

5. ARE PLANTS MAXIMIZING OR OPTIMIZING WATER USE DURING PHOTOSYNTHESIS?

Cowan and Farquahr (1978) hypothesized that plants should optimize water use by stomatal regulation such, that a maximum of daily photosynthesis is reached for a given daily water use. This hypothesis has not been approved or rejected in the field, because of the difficulty of measuring photosynthetic capacity and caboxylation efficiency changes during the day in concert with conductance and natural transpiration. Laboratory experiments on single leaves showed, that the response of stomata to humidity supports the concept of optimization (Schulze and Hall, 1982). However, whole plants did not (Schulze et al., 1983). In order to further test this hypothesis, woody species were grown in an arid climate with different amounts of available water per year (Fig. 5). If plants were to regulate stomata according to the optimization theory, it was expected, that plants with less available water would show an increase in production over water use. However, Fig. 5 shows a single linear response for all treatments of water supply during a 4 year growth experiment.

FIGURE 5. Total plant production of <u>Prunus dulcis</u> growing in large lysimeters. Plants were harvested after 1, 2, 3, and 4 years of growth. The lysimeters were watered with 2.5, 5, and 7.5 m^3 water per year.

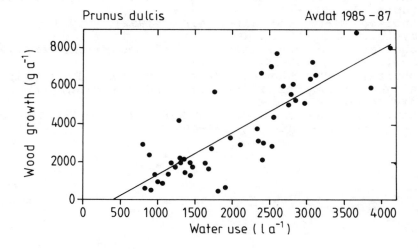

The result is interpreted, that plants do not optimize water use at the whole plant level, but rather use water when available at maximum rate. Annual production is eventually determined by the maximum rate of photosynthesis and the length of time for open stomata at high water consumption. The physiological responses of stomatal closure and restricted assimilation are rather a response towards ensuring survival rather than increasing water use and productivity.

REFERENCES

1 Cowan, I.R. and Farquhar, G.D. (1977) Soc. Exp. Biol. Symp. 31, 471-505
2 Demmig, B., Winter, E., Krüger, A. and Czygan, F.-C. (1987) Plant Physiol. 84, 218-224
3 Field, Ch. and Mooney, H.A. (1986) In: On the Economy of Plant Form and Function, Cambridge Univ. Press pp. 25-56
4 Gollan, T., Passioura, J.B. and Munns, R. (1986) Austr. J. Plant Physiol. 13, 459-464
5 Körner, Ch., Scheel, J.A. and Bauer, H. (1979) Photosynthetica 13, 45-82
6 Lange, O.L. (1987) Ecological Studies 61, 149-163
7 Lange, O.L., Schulze, E.-D. and Koch, W. (1979) Flora 159, 38-82.
8 Orians, G.H. and Solbrig, O.T. (1977) Am. Nat. III, 677-690
9 Schulze, E.-D. and Chapin III, F.S. (1978) Ecological Studies 77, 120-148
10 Schulze, E.-D. and Hall, A.E. (1982) Encyclop. Plant Physiol. 12 B, 181- 230
11 Schulze, E.-D. Schilling, K. and Nagarajah, S. (1983) Oecologia 58, 169-177
12 Schulze, E.-D., Küppers, M. and Matyssek, R. (1986) In: On the Economy of Plant Form and Function, Cambridge Univ. Press pp. 585-602
13 Stitt, M., Huber, S.C. and Kerr, P. (1987) The Biochemistry of Plants 10, 327-409

DAMAGE TO PHOTOSYNTHESIS DURING CHILLING AND FREEZING, AND ITS
SIGNIFICANCE TO THE PHOTOSYNTHETIC PRODUCTIVITY OF FIELD CROPS.

S.P. LONG, P.K. FARAGE, Q. GROOME, J.M.N. MACHARIA & N.R. BAKER
Department of Biology, University of Essex, COLCHESTER, CO4 3SQ, U.K.

1. INTRODUCTION

Exposure of Z. mays, and other chilling sensitive plants, to
high light during chilling (0 - 12°C) results in photoinhibition of
photosynthesis (1-4). This inhibition is manifest as decreased CO_2
uptake rates at both light saturation (Asat) and under light limiting
conditions - expressed as change in the maximum quantum yield (∅)
(1,2). This inhibition is not readily reversible and may persist for
several hours following return to non-chilling temperatures. In S.
England, i.e. near the northern limit of Z. mays cultivation in
Europe, chilling dependent photoinhibition of photosynthesis is
frequently observed in May and June. Exposure of the young crop to a
dawn temperature of 5°C coupled with clear sky conditions may result in
a 50% reduction in ∅. If this is followed by a period of dull weather,
recovery occurs within 3-4 days in the field (5). Z. mays might be
viewed as exceptional. It is a crop of tropical origin which would be
expected to be particularly susceptible to low temperature stress in
N.W. Europe. Many of the major arable crops of N.W. Europe and other
cool temperate climate zones are winter annuals which maintain a green
leaf canopy throughout the winter and spring. Might a form of
photoinhibition, similar to that observed in chilling susceptible crops
at chilling temperatures, occur in these chilling tolerant crops during
periods of freezing? This question is examined by field studies here
for Brassica napus (Winter Oil-seed Rape) and in a separate article for
Triticum aestivum (Winter Wheat) (6).

The study of photoinhibition during periods of sub-optimal
temperatures has so far been limited to effects at the leaf level.
Significance at the crop level will depend on the effect of
photoinhibition on canopy photosynthesis. Extrapolation from single
leaf to whole canopy effects is complicated by consideration of the
contributions of different parts of the canopy, light distribution
within the canopy and any compensating respiratory changes. By
integrating the effects of photoinhibition on the response of CO_2
uptake to light for indivdiual leaves with a model of light
distribution in Z. mays canopies, Baker et al. (7) showed that under
radiation levels typical of June in S. England a 50% decrease in ∅
would reduce canopy photosynthesis by ca. 40% in a crop with a leaf

M. Baltscheffsky (ed.), Current Research in Photosynthesis, Vol. IV, 835–842.
© *1990 Kluwer Academic Publishers. Printed in the Netherlands.*

area index (LAI) of 3. Dry matter production (dW_i) by a crop over an interval (i) is determined by three key factors, the sum of incident radiation over the period (Q_i), the efficiency with which this radiation is intercepted (E_{qi}) and the "efficiency" with which the intercepted radiation is converted into dry matter (E_{ci}) over the same period; equation 1:

$$dW_i = Q_i.E_{qi}.E_{ci} \quad .... \quad (1)$$

Previous studies of crop growth have suggested that environmental stresses commonly depress dry matter production primarily through decrease in E_q, rather than through changes in E_c, implying a subsidiary role for any depression of photosynthetic capacity. In a range of crops E_c was observed to be constant over most of the growth period and was also very similar between species of the same photosynthetic type (8). Whilst significant photoinhibition of photosynthesis occurred in Sorghum bicolor during water stress, its elimination had little effect on yield (9). If low temperature impairment of photosynthesis is of any significance to the dry-matter production of crops in the field then it would have to result in a decrease in the conversion efficiency (E_c).

The objectives of this study were: 1) to examine the possibility that photoinhibitory reduction of photosynthetic CO_2 assimilation occurs in over-wintering annual crops and 2) to examine whether photoinhibitory depression of photosynthesis at low temperatures in Z. mays and B. napus crops corresponds to significant depression of light conversion efficiency, and hence production, at the whole crop level.

2. METHODS

Crops of Z. mays (cv. LG11) and of B. napus (cv. Bienvenu) were sown on a clay-loam soil in N.E. Essex in early May and September, respectively. Plant densities, cultivation, fertilizer and pesticide treatments were as recommended to commercial growers in the region. Air, leaf and soil temperature were measured with shielded, miniature and soil thermistor probes, respectively (Grant Instruments, Cambridge, U.K.). All temperature probes were calibrated against a precision mercury-in-glass thermometer, previously calibrated against standard thermometers at the British Standards Institution. Light flux was measured by quantum sensors (LI-190SR, Li-Cor Inc., Lincoln, Nebraska). Tube solarimeters (TSL, Delta-t devices) were placed above and at the base of the canopy. Intercepted radiation was obtained from the difference in radiation received at these two canopy positions (10). All meteorological probes were interfaced to a data-logger (Squirrel, Grant Instruments, Cambridge, U.K.; or DL1, Delta-T devices, Burwell, U.K.).

At 1-3 day intervals throughout the early growth of the B. napus crop and at ca. 2 week intervals in the Z. mays crop, individual plants, selected by randomized block design, were removed and immediately transferred to the laboratory for determination of ϕ. Photosynthetic CO_2 uptake was measured for attached leaves enclosed in a controlled environment cuvette incorporated into an open gas exchange system as described previously (4). Quantum yield of CO_2 uptake ($\emptyset$) was determined either by direct illumination of the upper surface of the leaves in a leaf section cuvette, followed by correction for leaf reflectance and transmittance measured with a Taylor integrating sphere (4) or by direct measurement using a transparent cuvette inside and Ulbricht integrating sphere (11). All measurements of $\emptyset$ were made in normal air, using a series of photon flux densities in the range 50-150 μmol m^{-2} s^{-1}. Whilst, $\emptyset$ measured under these conditions may not represent the maximum $\emptyset$ that could be attained by the leaf, it ensures that the value reflects the capacity of the leaf under the actual field conditions.

To determine whether decreases in $\emptyset$ observed in the B. napus crop in the field were the result of photoinhibition, a sample of plants, selected by a randomized design, were shaded from direct sunlight each morning. Shades consisted of vertical screens of 66 cm square, covered in reflective aluminium foil. Each day at dusk, shades were placed on the eastern side of the selected individuals. This ensured that each of these plants would be shaded from direct sunlight at dawn and during the morning. A second treatment in which shades were positioned for 6 day periods was used at intervals from January to March to examine the effect of successive days of photoinhibition.

At 5-7 day intervals 12 - 16 plants were selected from both crops by a randomized block design. The whole plant was removed including the attached root system which was carefully excavated. In B. napus and during the first 80 days of growth of the Z. mays crop it was possible to remove most of the major roots of each individual, however in the later stages of growth of the maize crop significant quantities of the root system could not be completely extracted without damage to adjacent plants, leading to some underestimation of dry matter in the maturing crop. Leaf area of each plant was determined with an area meter (AM1, Delta-t Devices). After the roots had been washed free of soil, plants were dried to constant weight at 80°C in a forced-draft oven. Interception efficiency of the crop (E_q) was obtained as the ratio of intercepted to incident radiation over each period (equation 2), and conversion "efficiency" (E_q; g MJ^{-1}) as the ratio of dry matter increase to intercepted radiation over each harvest interval (equation 3).

$$E_{qi} = (Q_{ai} - Q_{bi})/Q_{ai} \dotsb (2)$$

Where Q_{ai} and Q_{bi} are integrals of radiation per unit ground area (MJ m^{-2}) received above and below the canopy, respectively, for the interval i.

$$E_c = dWi/(Qai - Qbi) \dotsb (3)$$

3. RESULTS

Fig. 1 shows the progression of the dry weight of a Z. mays crop with the accumulated quantity of intercepted solar radiation. The non-linearity of the actual relationship indicates that the efficiency of conversion is decreased in the early growth period when low temperature is most likely to cause a decrease in ∅. This is confirmed in Fig. 2 which shows a marked depression of E_c during the first 100 days of crop growth, coincident with the period in which ∅ is depressed.

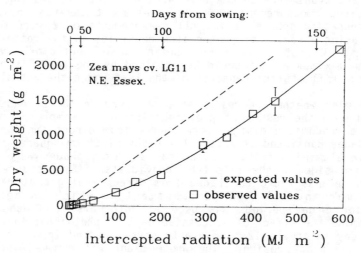

Fig. 1. The mean dry weight per unit ground area in relation to the cumulative quantity of visible radiation intercepted by a Z. mays crop in N.E. Essex, England. The broken line is the expected relationship in the absence of any depression in conversion "efficiency".

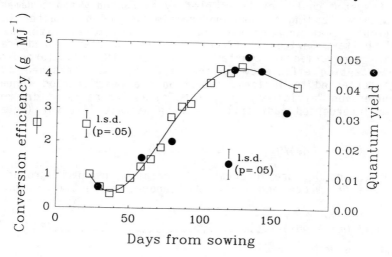

Fig. 2. The "efficiency" of conversion of intercepted light into dry matter (E_c), calculated from the moving average of dry weight over three adjacent harvests of the Z. mays crop. The mean quantum yield for leaves within the same crop is also indicated.

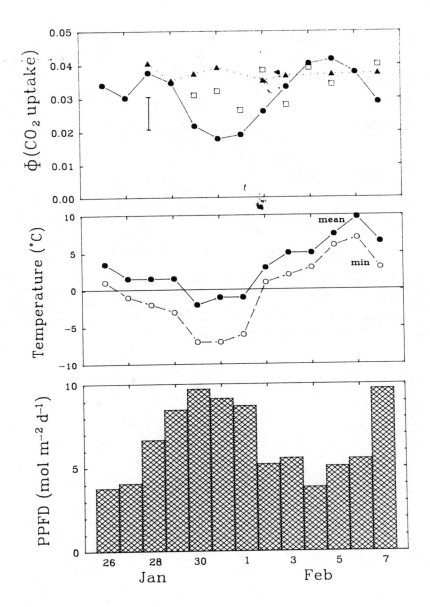

Fig. 3. The quantum yield of CO_2 assimilation (ϕ) for leaves of
Brassica napus on a field site in N.E. Essex during a 13 day period
during 1987. Plants were shaded for 6 days prior to the measurement
(▲); shaded for the morning prior to measurement only (□); or
unshaded (●). Each point is the mean of 5 - 10 replicates.

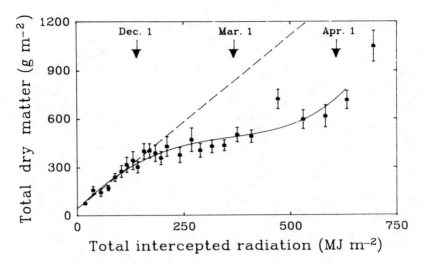

Fig. 4. The progression of crop dry weight (means + s.e.; n = 16) for the B. napus crop as a function of the accumulated quantity of total intercepted radiation. The broken line indicates the progression of dry weight per unit of intercepted radiation that could be expected in the absence of any depression of conversion "efficiency".

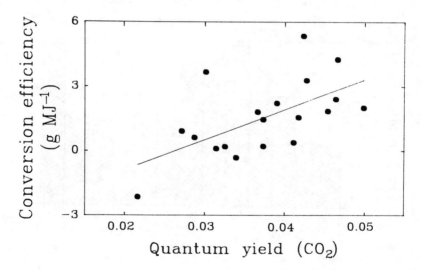

Fig. 5. The efficiency of conversion of intercepted solar radiation into dry matter (E_c) as a function of quantum yield ($\emptyset$) for the B. napus crop during the winter and early spring of 1987. The best-fit least squares linear relationship is illustrated.

Just as coincidence of chilling and high light has been shown to reduce ∅ in the chilling sensitive crop Z. mays (5), Fig. 3 shows that the coincidence of freezing temperatures (ca. -2°C) with high photon fluxes results in a ca. 50% decrease in ∅ in a B. napus crop, which recovers within 3 days of return to non-freezing and lower light conditions. In plants which are shaded from direct sunlight throughout this period, no decrease in ∅ is apparent, even though temperatures of the shaded leaves were found to be ca. 1 - 2°C lower during daylight hours. The observation that ∅ is higher in plants shaded throughout the 6 day period than in plants shaded only on the morning of measurement, demonstrates that 1 day was an inadequate period for recovery of ∅. The quantum yield of CO_2 assimilation was found to be depressed through most of the winter and early spring period. On most occasions during the months of January through March a decrease in ∅, relative to shaded controls, was observed (data not illustrated). From Jan. to March ∅ averages ca. 0.03, compared to an expected value of above 0.055 (8). Only during April did ∅ return to values approaching that expected for a C3 species. Fig. 4 shows the progressive increase in dry matter from emergence, plotted against the cumulative quantity of intercepted radiation. A sharp decrease in gradient (i.e. E_c) is apparent at the beginning of January coinciding with a decrease in ∅. The correlation of ∅ and E_c throughout the growth of this B. napus crop is illustrated in Fig. 5.

4. DISCUSSION

This study shows that coincidence of freezing and high light produces photoinhibition of an over-wintering stand of the chilling resistant crop, B. napus. Photoinhibition is evident as a decrease in the quantum yield for CO_2 assimilation. These decreases persist for 3-4 days when milder duller conditions occur. This contrasts to the situation in T. aestivum where complete recovery occurs within a few hours (6).

If depression of ∅ during periods of low temperature are of significance then a parallel decrease in E_c is expected. This expectation is fulfilled in both the chilling sensitive Z. mays crop and the chilling resistant B. napus crop. In Z. mays E_c shows a pattern of variation which closely parallels variation in ∅. In B. napus, decline in ∅ appears linearly related to decline in E_c (Fig. 5.). This indicates a decline in E_c to zero when ∅ declines to ca. 0.02. The absence of a zero intercept might be explained by the fact that a portion of the photosynthate will be lost in respiration. A ∅ of 0.02 may be the point below which CO_2 fixation by the canopy is insufficient to compensate respiratory losses. Canopy photosynthesis will be influenced by change in both ∅ and Asat, at the leaf level. The close correlation of ∅ with Ec might therefore seem surprising. There are two possible explanations of this. 1) That A_{sat} changes in parallel with ∅, as has been observed in laboratory studies of Z. mays (1,2). 2) That ∅ is the more important determinant of canopy photosynthesis. In overwintering crops, light levels will be low with peak photon flux densities of 300 - 900 μmol m^{-2} s^{-1} on clear days. In the B. napus crop examined here, LAI exceeded 3 throughout the winter period. This high LAI, coupled with the planophile architecture of the B. napus canopy will mean that at this time of year, most leaves will be in light limiting conditions for most of the day. The average depression of ϕ that could be attributed to photoinhibition for the period of Jan. 1 to Mar. 31 was ca. 0.006. Extrapolating from the relationship illustrated in Fig. 5 this would reduce E_c by ca. 2.1 g MJ^{-1}. This analysis also provides some indication of how important low temperature depression of photosynthesis may be to these crops. The dry matter production that would be attained without any depression of E_c may be projected by assuming a constant conversion efficiency. These are indicated in Figs. 1 and 4 which show that the final dry weight of the Z. mays silage crop, 2 200 g m-2 would have been attained ca. 40 days earlier in the absence of any inhibition. Similarly, in B. napus, the dry weight of ca. 800 g m-2 attained by April 1, would have been achieved 45 days earlier. These extrapolations are based on the use of a constant E_c and take no account of the fact that increased dry matter accumulation might accelerate leaf growth and hence simultaneously increase E_g (Equation 1). If this were to occur, then absence of a depression of E_c would lead to an even greater increase in dry matter production. It is uncertain as to whether increased economic yield would result if inhibition of conversion efficiency could be avoided in these crops. In the case of silage Z. mays, either an increased yield or earlier maturity date could be expected. The results suggest that low temperature dependent photoinhibition, possibly in contrast to photoinhibition under water stress (9), does have potential to significantly influence crop dry matter production.

REFERENCES

1. Long, S.P., East, T.M. & Baker, N.R. (1983) J. Exp. Bot. 34, 177-188.
2. Long, S.P., Nugawela, A., Bongi, G. & Farage, P.K. (1987) in Progress in Photosynthesis Research (Biggins, J., ed.), Vol. IV, pp. 131-138, Martinus Nijhoff, Dordrecht.
3. Powles, S.B. (1984) Ann. Rev. Pl. Physiol. 35, 15-44.
4. Bongi, G. & Long, S.P. (1987) Pl. Cell Env. 10, 241-249.
5. Farage, P.K. & Long, S.P. (1987) in Progress in Photosynthesis Research (Biggins, J., ed.), Vol. IV, pp. 139-142, Martinus Nijhoff, Dordrecht.
6. Groome, Q., Long, S.P. & Baker, N.R. (1989) This volume.
7. Baker, N.R., Long, S.P. & Ort, D.R. (1988) in Plants and Temperature (Long, S.P. & Woodward, F.I., eds.), Cambridge Univ. Press, pp. 347-376.
8. Beadle, C.L., Long, S.P., Imbamba, S.K., Hall, D.O. & Olembo, R.J. (1985) Photosynthesis in Relation to Plant Production in Terrestrial Environments. U.N.E.P./Tycooly Publishing, Oxford.
9. Ludlow, M.M. & Powles, S.B. (1988) Aust. J. Pl. Physiol. 15, 179-194.
10. Nobel, P.S. & Long, S.P. (1985) in Techniques in Bioproductivity and Photosynthesis (Coombs, J. et al., eds.), pp. 41-49, Pergamon, Oxford.
11. Ireland, C.R., Long, S.P. & Baker, N.R. (1989) Pl. Cell Env. (in press).

SOME FACTORS LIMITING PHOTOSYNTHESIS IN NATURE

Yun-Kang Shen, Shanghai Institute of Plant Physiology
Academia Sinica, 300 Fenglin Road, Shanghai, 200032, China

1. INTRODUCTION

In carefully arranged experiments the solar energy conversion efficiency of plants may reach 5%.   However, photosynthesis in nature is generally not so effective. This is due to the fact that photosynthesis in nature proceeds often under more or less unfavorable conditions.

Recently, we have studied this problem, and found some limiting factors in many cases acting upon the operation of photosynthetic apparatus . Here I would like to describe some parts of our results.

2. MATERIALS AND METHODS

2.1. Spinach, wheat, rice, soybean and cotton were grown in the field or in pots under normal conditions. Bamboo (<u>Phyllostachys</u> <u>pubescens</u>) were grown on the hill as a forest in the experimental station of the Institute of Subtropical Forestry, Fuyang, Zhejiang Provience.

2.2. Photosynthesis under natural conditions was measured with ADC portable Infra-Red Gas Analyzer Type LCA.

2.3. Photosynthesis under saturated CO_2 conditions was measured with Hansatech leaf disc oxygen electrode(1).

2.4. Photosynthesis of leaves after Vacuum infiltrated with phenazine methosulphate (PMS) was measured by aqueous-phase oxygen electrode(2).

3. RESULTS AND DISCUSSION

3.1. Photophosphorylation may limit photosynthesis

The precise stoichiometry of photophosphorylation (ATP:NADPH) is still uncertain, i.e. whether the ATP/2e or P/O ratio is 1.0,1.33 or 2.0. The importance of understanding the correct ratio is relevant to the mininum number of quanta to fix one molecule of CO_2(3). The reduction of one molecule CO_2 to carbonhydrate level requires 3 ATP and 2 NADPH(P/O ratio equals 1.5). Although it is still uncertain whether the P/O ratio of the completely coupled noncyclic photophosphorylation is higher or lower than 1.5, we have often found that

M. Baltscheffsky (ed.), Current Research in Photosynthesis, Vol. IV, 843–850.
© 1990 *Kluwer Academic Publishers. Printed in the Netherlands.*

the actual P/O ratio in vivo is significantly lower than 1.5, that is, the degree of coupling is not always complete and thus may limit the photosynthesis in nature. Two cases can illustrate this phenomenon.

First, when a low concentration of PMS was added to wheat, rice, soybean or spinach leaves to increase the ATP content in the leaves by increasing cyclic photophosphorylation, the rate of photosynthesis was often increased (Fig.1). This enhancement was higher in young spinach leaves, whose coupling efficiency, as measured in isolated chloroplasts, was lower than that of mature ones(2).

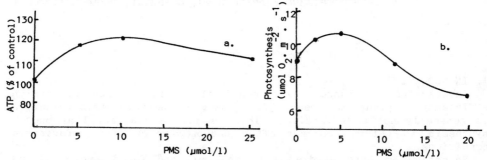

Fig.1 The effect of PMS on the ATP content (a) and photosynthesis (b) in the spinach leaves

Second, when wheat leaves were sprayed with aureomycin, the photosynthetic rate was higher than that in control for several days(Tab.1).

Table 1 The effect of aureomycin on the photosynthesis of wheat leaves

Date	Photosynthetic rate (μmol $CO_2 . m^{-2} . s^{-1}$)		
	Control	Aureomycin	Increase (%)
May 10*	8.8	10.7	21.4
May 12	12.2	13.8	12.9
May 20	12.7	12.5	-1.5

* 2 hours before measurement on May 10, spraying leaves with 50 ppm aureomycin.

Further studies showed that the main effect of aureomycin on isolated chloroplasts was to improve the P/O ratio(Tab.2) by acting on the coupling factor at the τ-subunit, making it dissipate less energy in a nonproductive way as determined by measuring the proton motive force by various methods(Fig.2)(4). Later, we found many reagents, such as polymyxin(5), polybasic acids(6),and the cytokinin-like substance 6-benzyladenine(7), to have a similar effect, though their modes of action on the coupling factor may differ somewhat in

detail(Fig.3).   Among them, the polybasic acids(malate, citrate,
bicarbonate and phosphate) and cytokinin deserve more attention
because they are present in vivo and may take part in regulating the
coupling efficiency under natural conditions.

Table 2 The effect of spraying wheat leaves with
aureomycin on photophosphorylation activity and P/2e value

| Date | Treatment | Noncyclic photophosphorylation | | |
		ATP μmol/ mg Chl·hr	Fecy μmol/ mg Chl·hr	P/2e
May 13	Control	167	320	1.04
	Aureomycin	272	379	1.44
May 15	Control	231	391	1.18
	Aureomycin	333	430	1.54

On May 12, spraying leaves with 50 ppm aureomycin.

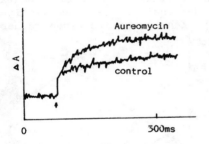

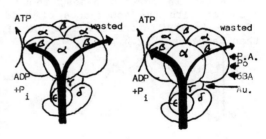

Fig.2 The effect of aureomycin on
the pH in the cavity of thylakoid
measured as the absorption change
of neutral red

Fig.3 Suggested scheme of the effect
of coupling efficiency improvers on
coupling factor(CF$_1$).
P.A., Polybasic acid; Po, polymyxin;
6-BA, 6-benzladenine; Au, Aureomycin.

3.2.Midday depression of photosynthesis often occurs in many C$_3$ plants
on fine days

Midday depression of photosynthesis is a well known phenomenon.
However, there are still debates about its mechanism. We found that
there are two main factors responsible for this phenomenon in nature.
Midday depression of photosynthesis in wheat leaves was well
correlated with partial stomatal closure and the lowering of internal
CO_2 concentration in many cases(Fig.4)(8). Increasing the humidity
in the ambient air could alleviate midday depression (Fig.5). The
yield might be raised by more than 10% by spraying fine water droplets
on leaves at noon after flowering stage(8).

Another important factor is photoinhibition caused by strong sunlight, which is often superimposed on the water vapor saturation
deficit problem mentioned above and is more subtle.

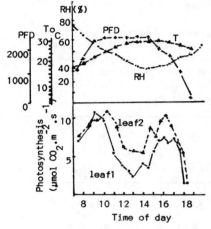

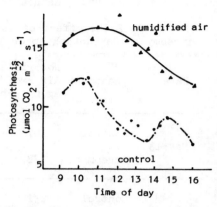

Fig.4 Diurnal variation of
photosynthesis in wheat leaves

Fig.5 The effect of increasing
humidity on diurnal variation of
photosynthesis in wheat leaves

However, in certain cases, though the partial closure of stomata
occurred with the appearance of midday depression, the concentration
of CO_2 in the intercellular space of the leaves was increased rather
than decreased(Fig.6.7).

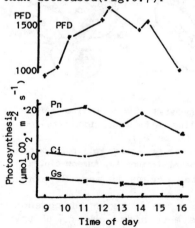

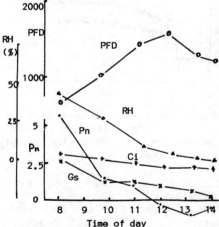

Fig.6 Diurnal variation of
photosynthesis in wheat leaves

Fig.7 Diurnal variation of photosynthesis in bamboo leaves

This speaks of the possibility that the midday depression in these
cases is due to the damage of the photosynthetic apparatus by photoinhibition and not to the decrease of stomatal conductance. The
diurnal change of the light response curve of bamboo photosynthesis
has been measured(Fig.8)(9). From Fig.8, it may be seen that not

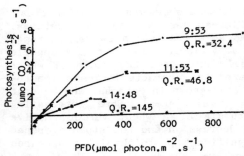

Fig.8 Diurnal variation of quantum requirement of photosynthesis in bamboo leaf

only the rate of photosynthesis under high light intensity but also the quantum efficiency under low light intensity are significantly decreased at noon, indicating the occurence of photoinhibition. A survey of diurnal variation of the quantum efficiency of photosynthesis in nature showed that photoinhibition is a common phenomenon for many plants,such as rice, wheat, soybean and cotton.(1) The relationship between the midday depression of quantum efficiency and photoinhibition was verified by measuring quantum efficiency of leaf discs under saturated CO_2 concentration with oxygen electrode (Tab.3).

Table 3 Diurnal variation of photosynthetic efficiency
in the soybean leaves measured in saturating CO_2 (Oct.19,1987)

Time of day	08:35 - 09:15	12:50 - 13:30
AQR (n=2)	21.0±0.7	36.3±6.0

CO_2 concentration 5%, Temterature 30 $^{\circ}$C

On cloudy days or when the plants were shaded in the morning, the diurnal variation of quantum efficiency disappeared. In the literature, photoinhibition is being studied intensively now. Many experiments were done under laboratory conditions and photoinhibition could be induced by very strong light under N_2 atmosphere. Our results showed that photosynthetic apparatus under ordinary natural environments also is liable to photoinhibition. Therefore, we are paying more attention to the study of the mechanism of photoinhibition under conditions similar to natural habitat. For example, we have found that in the presence of oxygen, the damage is not limited to the photosystem II, and oxygen has both accentuating and alleviating effects on photoinhibition(Fig.9)(10).

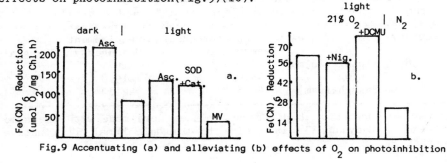

Fig.9 Accentuating (a) and alleviating (b) effects of O_2 on photoinhibition

3.3. Photosynthesis in Qinghai-Tibet Plateau shows some peculiarities.
 The environment on Qinghai-Tibet Plateau has many special features.
Due to the high elevation there, the solar radiation is very strong,
diurnal change of temperature is very large, and the atmospheric
pressure is rather low. When well irrigated, the yield of wheat
may reach 15T/ha or more. We compared the characteristics of photosynthesis of wheat grown there with that grown in Shanghai and brought
to Qinghai-Tibet Plateau in pots by airplane. Some interesting
results were found. The photosynthesis of a wheat variety native
to the Plateau showed little midday depression and the stomata opened
even wider at noon(Fig.10). No significant photoinhibition appeared
on fine days(Fig.11).

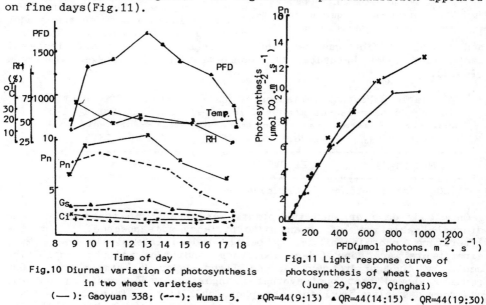

Fig.10 Diurnal variation of photosynthesis
in two wheat varieties
(——): Gaoyuan 338; (---): Wumai 5.

Fig.11 Light response curve of
photosynthesis of wheat leaves
(June 29, 1987. Qinghai)
×QR=44(9:13) ▲QR=44(14:15) •QR=44(19:30)

However, the quantum efficiency measured there was much lower than
that measured in Shanghai even with the same pot of wheat(Tab.4).

Table 4. The apparent quantum requirement of
photosynthesis measured at places of different altitude

Wheat variety	Place of growth	Apparent quantum requirement	
		Measured in Xining	Measured in Shanghai
Gaoyuan 338	Xining(2265m)	43.0	19.1
Wumai 5	Xining	44.0	19.8
Wumai 5	Shanghai(4m)	43.6	21.9

The two measurements at diffrerent places were made with the same
pot of wheat. Gaoyuan 338 is native to Qinghai, Wumai 5 is native
to Shanghai.

Imitation experiments in closed chamber with variable atmospheric pressure showed that this lowering of quantum efficiency owed mainly to the change of atmospheric pressure(Fig.12).

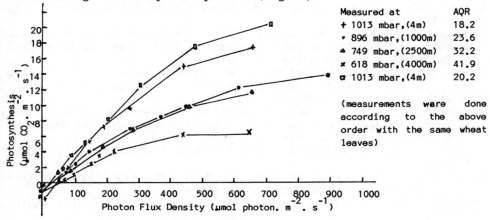

Fig.12 Light response curves of wheat leaf photosynthesis
at different atmospheric pressure

Table 5 The effect of atmospheric pressure and gas composition on
the apparent quantum requirement of photosynthesis in wheat leaves

Atm. Pressure (mbar)	Gas Composition $\mu mol.L^{-1}$	AQR
1013	N_2 98%, O_2 2%, CO_2 13.9	16.6± 2.4
1013	Air, CO_2 13.7	27.1± 6.5
749	N_2 98%, O_2 2%, CO_2 9.4	41.8± 6.8
749	N_2 98%, O_2 2%, CO_2 13.6	39.6± 4.7
749	Air, CO_2 9.3	59.3± 5.3
749	Air, CO_2 13.5	56.8±13.2

Increasing the concentration of CO_2 could increase the quantum efficincy. However, it was still lower than that measured under normal atmospheric pressure(Tab.5). It seems that low atmospheric pressure itself may affect the efficiency of photosynthesis. Further study of this problem is in progress.

REFERENCES
1 Xu,D.Q., Xu,B.J. and Shen,Y.K. (1989) Acta Phytophysiologia Sinica, 15, (in press)
2 Shen,Y.K. (1989) in Current Biochemical Research in China (Tsou,

C.L., ed.) pp.137-147, Academic Press, San Diego.
3 Hall,D.O. and Rao,K.K. (1987) Photosynthesis (4th ed.) pp 137-138, Edward Arnold, London.
4 Huang,Z.H., and Shen,Y.K. (1988) Acta Phytophysiologia Sinica, 14, 107-112
5 Wei,J.M., Shen,Y.K. and Li,D.Y. (1988) Abstracts of International Symposium on Regulation and efficiency of Photosynthesis (Organized by Chinese Soc. of Plant Physiol.) p.39
6 Shen,Y.K.(1987) in Bioenergetics and Biomembranes (Fleischer,S., King,T.E. and Papa,S. eds.) pp. 341-357, Vanderbilt University Printing Services, Tennessee.
7 Huang,Z.H., Shen,Y.K. and Qian,Y.Q.(1988) Abstracts of International Symposium on Regulation and Effeiciency of Photosynthesis(Organized by Chinese Soc. of Plant Physiol.) p.26
8 Xu,D.Q., Li,D.Y. and Shen Y.K.(1984) Acta Phytophysiologia Sinica 10,269-276
9 Shen,Y.K., Qiu,G.X., Huang,Q.M. and Yang,D.D. (1987) Report from China Regional Center of UNEP Project pp. 9-10
10 Wu,J.T. and Shen,Y.K. (1989) Acta Phytophysiologia Sinica 15,(in press).

This Work was supported by National Natural Science Foundation of China. The study concerning with bamboo was supported by UNEP Project on Bioproductivity and Photosynthesis of Grassland in Tropics and Subtropics.

PHOTOSYNTHETIC CAPACITY TO SOLVE THE CARBON DIOXIDE PROBLEM

STEFAN LEU AND ALLAN MICHAELS, DEPARTMENT OF BIOLOGY, BEN GURION UNIVERSITY OF THE NEGEV, BEER-SHEVA, ISRAEL

1. INTRODUCTION

The carbon dioxide content of the atmosphere has been rising constantly since the beginning of the industrial age, from about 280 ppm to the present level of about 350 ppm (1). This rise is caused by burning of fossil fuels and large scale burning of tropical forests. Parts of this carbon dioxide are absorbed by the oceans and other possible sinks, but about 55% of this carbon dioxide accumulates in the atmosphere every year.

Sources of carbon dioxide released into the atmosphere:	Billion tons of carbon per year
Fossil fuel combustion	5.3 ± 0.5
Tropical forest destruction (2)	1.7 ± 0.9
Tropical forest destruction (3)	1.0 ± 0.6
Carbon dioxide 'sinks':	
Atmospheric increase	2.9
Oceanic uptake	2.2 ± 0.2
Unknown 'sink' (2)	1.9 ± 1.5
Unknown 'sink' (3)	1.2 ± 1.3

Table 1: Fate of carbon dioxide released to the atmosphere by human activities (1980).

The increasing carbon dioxide content of the atmosphere is responsible for the "greenhouse effect", which causes a global temperature increase. A further increase of the atmospheric carbon dioxide concentration may have serious consequences within the next fifty years (4). Sea levels will rise, and global climatic changes may affect the productivity of major agricultural areas. No realistic solution has been found for this problem. Fast replacement of fossil fuels by solar energy or nuclear power is impossible due to enormous costs and ecologists concerns. Reduction in the use of fossil fuels is possible in the developed countries, but at the same time demand will rise in developing countries with 80% of the world population.

M. Baltscheffsky (ed.), Current Research in Photosynthesis, Vol. IV, 851–854.
© 1990 *Kluwer Academic Publishers. Printed in the Netherlands.*

2. PHOTOSYNTHETIC POTENTIAL OF FORESTS

The amount of carbon dioxide produced by human activities is small compared to the carbon turnover of the biosphere. The net primary productivity of forests alone is 6 times the amount of carbon released by human activities (5, 6). Per hectare, forests store up to 200 tons of carbon in biomass and up to 100 tons in the soil (2). Reforestation of two million square kilometers would incorporate 35% of the presently accumulating amount of carbon dioxide for the next fifty years (7). More careful managment of tropical forests would reduce or stop the carbon dioxide accumulation in the atmosphere (8). These options have never been considered seriously in recent discussions, probably because of the mistaken view that investments in reforestations are not sufficiently productive. But reforestations, forest protection and improved forest management are needed to solve other urgent problems and to supply sufficient wood to meet growing demand (9, 10).

3. DESERTIFICATION AND EROSION

The progressive biosphere destruction threatens the global economic, ecological and climatic balance and prevents the development of the third world. About 3 million square kilometers of former productive areas have been transformed to desert in the last 30 years, and to date another 5 million square kilometers of semi-arid areas are threatened by desertification (meaning that their vegetation cover is strongly damaged), due to human overuse. Mountain areas have been stripped of their protective forests leading to erosion and complete loss of productivity (9, 10). In addition to losses in productivity, these phenomena also regularly cause disasters like floods, droughts and famine.

To save desertifying and eroding areas, their biomass cover has to be restored. This can only achieved by reforestation (probably in the million square kilometer range), which will stabilize erosion, balance water circulation and supply firewood. The costs to stop erosion and desertification have been estimated to be 2.5 billion dollars per year (9). These measures would contribute significantly to the development of the poorest countries in the world, and at the same time about 20 % of the carbon dioxide accumulating in the atmosphere in the next fifty years could be bound into biomass and restored soil.

4. TROPICAL FORESTS AND THE CARBON DIOXIDE BUDGET

The amounts of carbon dioxide released to the atmosphere by burning of tropical forests is strongly disputed (2, 3, 8; see also recent discussion in Science, 241, p 1736 ff, 1988). Probably more than one billion tons of carbon per year are released to the atmosphere from forest burning (Table 1). Therefore, it is not possible to balance the carbon dioxide budget only using the known fluxes. An unknown carbon sink must remove the 'missing' carbon dioxide. This sink may be large enough to absorb most of the carbon dioxide accumulating in the atmosphere, if the contribution from forest burning is eliminated (Table 1).

In addition, the elimination of shifting agriculture would leave huge forest areas regrowing. At present, about 200,000 square kilometers of tropical forests per year are used in this way. The area is cultivated for a few years, and then abandonned for about 15 years for recovery. This technique creates an equilibrium between burning and regrowth (2). Establishing sustainable agriculture on part of this area would leave the remaining part regrowing. Complete regrowth of one million square kilometers of tropical forest, with a uptake potential of about 18,000 tons of carbon per square kilometer (2), could remove about 15% of the carbon dioxide accumulating in the atmosphere during the next fifty years.

5. SUBSTITUTION OF FOSSIL FUELS

In order to solve the carbon dioxide problem definitively, fossil fuels have to be replaced by renewable energy sources. The use of solar energy is complicated and expensive. However, a fast growing forestry plantation, transforms up to 1% of the incoming light into wood, a storable chemical energy form, at investment costs orders of magnitude lower than a similar solar energy plant. Wood produced under sustainable conditions is a renewable energy source, not causing a net carbon dioxide release to the atmosphere. Burning of wood in optimally closed systems avoids pollution and allows the recycling of minerals for fertilization.

About 15 - 20 billion tons of wood would be needed per year to substitute the present consumption of fossil fuels. Forests produce from 1000 to 5000 tons of wood per square kilometer and year (11). Intensive wood plantations can produce even more than 5000 tons per square kilometer, and modern forest management methods might double or triple the present productivity of forests within fifty years (6). Thus, the amount of wood needed to substitute the present fossil fuel consumption can be produced either by improved sustainable management of natural forests or by intensive tree cultivation on a few million square kilometers.

Installation of tree plantations for villages in developping countries is a major need to remove ecological pressures by woodgatherers (9). Intensive wood production is also an economically interesting alternative on surplus agricultural areas in overproducing developed countries.

6. CONCLUSIONS

The carbon dioxide accumulation in the atmosphere can immediately be stopped or significantly reduced by measures restoring and protecting the damaged biosphere. The same measures have many additional positive effects:

a) Stopping and reversing erosion and desertification by reforestation will: improve the ecological stability and agricultural productivity of the affected areas; and reduce floods and droughts or their consequences.

b) Stopping forest burning and improved agricultural techniques in the tropics will save rain forests from complete destruction and maintain its climatic balance.

c) Establishment of tree plantations will meet growing wood demand, prevent destruction of natural vegetation by woodgatherers and may be a production alternative for oversubsidized agricultures.

d) Future energy needs can be met by substitution of fossil fuels with wood grown under improved forest management. This will definitively solve the carbon dioxide problem.

The investments needed to realize these measures are orders of magnitude lower than those predicted for any technical alternative. Regrowing forests will immediately start to accumulate carbon dioxide, and will therefore immediately reduce the carbon dioxide accumulation in the atmosphere. No additional scientific progress, but worldwide political and social collaboration, are needed for the realization of these measures. Financial support from the industrialized countries is needed as well as the agreement of the third world countries. Even partial implementation of the measures summarized would reduce the carbon dioxide accumulation in the atmosphere much faster than any possible technical solution.

7. REFERENCES

1. A. Neftel, E. Moore, H. Oeschger, B. Stauffer, Nature 315, 45 (1985).
2. Houghton R.A. et al, Nature 316, 617 (1985).
3. R.D. Detwiler and C.A.S. Hall, Science 239, 42 (1988).
4. W. S. Broeckner, Nature 328 (1987).
5. R. T. Whittaker and B. E. Likens, The Biosphere and Man, Springer Verlag New York (1975).
6. S. H. Spurr, Sci. Amer. 240 (2) (1979).
7. Woodwell G.M., Science 241, 1736 (1988).
8. Woodwell G.M. et al, Science 222, 1081 (1983).
9. GAIA, an Atlas of Planet Management, Norman Myers ed., Anchor Press/Doubleday & Co (1984).
10. The Global 2000 Report to the President, Penguin (1982).
11. Physiological Plant Ecology IV: Ecosystem Processes, Springer Verlag, Berlin (1984).

WATER USE EFFICIENCY IN POTATO :
MODEL AND EXPERIMENTAL TEST OF CROP PHOTOSYNTHESIS

Olivier Bethenod[1], Jean-Paul Lhomme[2] and Nader Katerji[1],

Station de Bioclimatologie, INRA[1];
Lab. Chaire de Bioclimatologie, INA-PG[2]; 78850 THIVERVAL-GRIGNON, FRANCE

1. INTRODUCTION

CO_2 flux and H_2O flux pass through stomata. Stomatal aperture depends on both internal and external factors. As Wong *et al.*, 1979,[1] pointed out, the capacity of the mesophyll tissue to fix carbon allows the regulation of stomatal conductance (gc): For instance, DCMU, an inhibitor of photosynthetic electron transport, modifies both mesophyll CO_2 assimilation and stomatal conductance in such a way that the intercellular concentration of CO_2 (Ci) remains proportional to the air CO_2 concentration (Ca) :

$$Ci = k \cdot Ca \tag{1}$$

In a previous paper[2], we showed that, in field-grown potato (*Solanum tuberosum* L. cv. Bintje), (i) net photosynthetic rate (Pn) was proportional to leaf molar conductance (gc) up to 0.23 mol m^{-2} s^{-1} ; at this point Pn reached a plateau, (ii) as long as gc remained below 0.23 mol m^{-2} s^{-1}, the ratio k was constant thoughout the day under a net radiation flux (Rn) higher than 50 W m^{-2}, from day to day the mean ratio k remained constant but differed in two canopy layers: in the upper one (30-60 cm), k=0.79 and in the lower one k=0.84, (iii) the ratio k was constant when leaf water potential decreased from -0.8 to -1.3 MPa as well as when predawn leaf water potential varied between -0.2 and -0.5 MPa.

We use here a multi-layer model to calculate crop photosynthesis (An). Each layer is characterized by 4 main parameters: k, gc, the leaf area index (LAI$_i$) of each layer, and the aerodynamic conductance (ga) between two layers. Crop photosynthesis (An) is the sum of aerodynamic CO_2 flux, Φ , above the canopy, and soil CO_2 flux, ϕn. To test this model we compared Φ, to the aerodynamic fluxes measured above the canopy by a simplified aerodynamic method[3].

2. MATERIALS AND METHODS

2.1. *Plant materials*. Potato (*Solanum tuberosum* L. cv. Bintje) were grown in a field at Grignon, 40 km W of Paris (France). The crop was 60 cm high with a Leaf Area Index of 2.8. The crop was separated into two layers (0-30 cm and 30-60 cm).

2.2. *Leaf Gas exchange*. Measurements of the rate of CO_2 assimilation and stomatal conductance were made in a transient open gas exchange system (LCA2 with Parkinson Leaf Chamber, ADC) ,with the following modifications: The reference and measure flow rates were regulated by mass flow controllers (Tylan). Mole fraction of water vapour entering

M. Baltscheffsky (ed.), Current Research in Photosynthesis, Vol. IV, 855–858.
© 1990 *Kluwer Academic Publishers. Printed in the Netherlands.*

the chamber was measured by a blank after every 20 leaf measurements. The calculation of Pn,gc,Ci were made according to Caemmerer and Farquhar[4,2].

2.3. *Canopy Gas exchange*. The Carbon dioxide gradient (δCO_2) and the gradients of horizontal wind velocity (δU) and air temperature (δT) at two levels (δz) above the canopy were measured simultaneously. Then the aerodynamic CO_2 flux, Φ, was calculated as:

$$\Phi = f(\delta U, \delta T, \delta z) . \delta CO_2 \tag{2}$$

The f function depends on stability conditions above the canopy, and is described in the flow chart (fig. 1); during the experiment δz was fixed : $\delta z = 1$ m ,between 1.1 and 2.1 m above the soil.

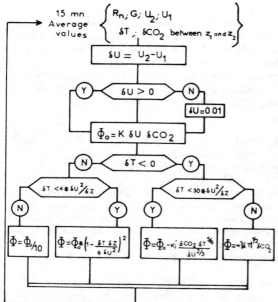

Fig. 1. Flow chart showing how to determine actual CO_2 flux using measurements of wind velocity at two levels (U_2, U_1), difference in air temperature, (δT), and in air CO_2 concentration. K is calculated according to ITIER[5] :

$$K = 192/Ln^2 (z_2/z_1)$$

$$K'_i = 7*K*((gz/\theta) Ln(z_2/z_1))^{5/6}$$
with : $z = (z_1 z_2)^{1/2}$; θ: potential temperature. Here $\theta = T$.

$$\alpha = 55(z_1^{-1/3} - z_2^{-1/3})3/2$$

2.4. *Model*. The discrete multi-layer model,according to Lhomme[6],is used to describe the CO_2 exchanges between canopy and atmosphere, Fig 2 and 3. The basic equations are those of the model originally devised by Waggoner and Reifsnider[7]. The crop canopy, considered as horizontally homogeneous, is divided into several parallel layers. Subscrit i refers to layer number, counted from 1 to n from the top of the canopy to the soil surface. LAI_i is the leaf area index of layer i per unit ground

Fig. 2. Electrical analogy showing the CO_2 diffusion process inside a crop layer.

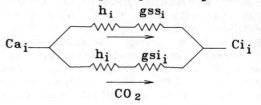

surface. The model is based on an electrical analogy where CO_2 fluxes replace current, and corresponding driving potentials are CO_2 concentrations, Ca_i and Ci_i. Ci_i is proportional to Ca_i: $Ci_i = k_i Ca_i$.

The CO_2 equivalent conductance for each layer is given by :
$$ge_i = [(1/h_i + 1/gss_i)^{-1} + (1/h_i + 1/gsi_i)^{-1}].LAI_i \qquad (2)$$
and the elementary CO_2 flux by :
$$\phi_i = ge_i.(Ca_i - Ci_i) \qquad (3)$$
where h_i is the leaf boundary layer , gss and gsi, the CO_2 conductance of the upper leaf surface and the lower one.

Crop photosynthesis (An) is calculated as the sum of elementary fluxes :
$$An = \Sigma\phi_i = \Sigma_{i=1}^{i=n} ge_i.Ca_i.(1-k_i) \qquad (4)$$
An is the sum of atmospheric, Φ , and soil, ϕ_n CO_2 fluxes
$$An = \Phi + \phi_n \qquad (5)$$
The recurrent expression for elementary fluxes gives a general expression of crop photosynthesis:
$$An = [A.Ca_o + \phi_n(A/Ga-B/ga_1)]/[1 + (A/Ga-B/ga_1)] \qquad (6)$$
where Ca_o represents CO_2 concentration at the reference height, Ga the aerodynamic conductance between the reference height and the top of canopy; A and B coefficients are functions of ge_i, ga_i and k_i.

For potato crop, parameters are given by Bethenod *et al.*[2].Stomatal conductances were measured by a porometer (Li-Cor 700). Porometer and Leaf Chamber responses were similar. Leaf water potentials are measured by a Pressure Chamber.

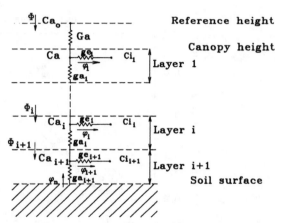

Fig.3. Electrical analogy of CO_2 exchange processes within the crop canopy.

To test the model leaf measurements are made on each layer and averaged every 45 min in order to compare measured and calculated CO_2 fluxes.

3. RESULTS AND DISCUSSION

Fig. 4 displays net assimilation Pn, corrected by the intermolecular collisions between CO_2 and water vapour[4], versus leaf conductance to CO_2 (gc). For example, data on august 1 are given: up to gc values between 0.2 and 0.23 mol m^{-2} s^{-1}, the gc dependence on Pn is almost linear and the slope of this line represents Ca-Ci. This justifies the model chosen. Canopy gas exchange and net radiation are given for the same day (Fig. 5). CO_2 aerodynamic fluxes measured, Φmes, and calculated, Φcal, by the model are shown.

The model was tested on six days (Fig. 6): Φcal are in good agreement with Φmes.

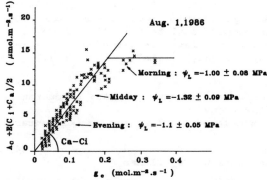

Fig.4 Net Assimilation rate, Ac, vs. stomatal conductance, gc, for a typical day. Each symbol corresponds to different leaves.

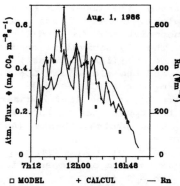

Fig.5 Modelled and calculated CO_2 gas exchanges of a Potato Crop, Net Radiation, for a typical day.

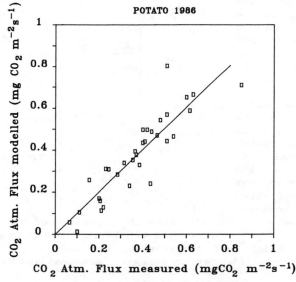

Fig.6 Test of Φ modelled on 6 days.

REFERENCES

1 Wong, S.C., Cowan, I.R., Farquhar, G.D. (1979) Nature 282, 424-426

2 Bethenod, O., Katerji, N., Quetin, P., Bertolini, J.-M., (1988) Photosynthetica 22, 491-501

3 Itier, B., (1980) J. Rech. Atmos. 14, 17-34

4 Caemmerer, S. von and Farquhar, G.D. (1981) Planta 153, 376-387

5 Itier, B., (1981) Agronomie 1, 869-876

6 Lhomme, J.-P. and Katerji, N., (1985) Agronomie, 5, 397-403

7 Waggoner, P.E. and Reifsnyder, W.E. (1968) J. Appl. Meteorol. 7, 400-409

PHOTOSYNTHETIC CHARACTERISTICS OF THE MANGROVE, BRUGUIERA PARVIFLORA, (ROXB.) WRIGHT & ARN., UNDER NATURAL CONDITIONS

D.R. CARTER[1], J.M. CHEESEMAN[1], B.F. CLOUGH[2], C. LOVELOCK[2], R.G. SIM [2] & ONG J.E[3]. Dept. Plant Biology, Univ. of Illinois, Urbana IL, USA[1]; Australian Inst. of Marine Sci., Townsville, Qld[2]; Sch. Biol. Sci., Universiti Sains Malaysia, Penang[3].

1. INTRODUCTION

In addition to salinity, mangroves must also endure prolong exposure to high irradiance and leaf temperature even when stomatal conductances and photosynthetic rates are extremely low (1). For these reasons, mangroves are often targeted for studies of photoinhibition (2). Björkman *et al.* (1) in describing mangrove photosynthesis have suggested that excessively high irradiances do not damage mangrove leaves because of their ability to dissipate excess excitation in the form of radiationless energy (3), albeit at the cost of lower photochemical efficiency. In this study, we have examined the photosynthetic characteristics of the mangrove, *Bruguiera parviflora*, under natural conditions in Queensland, Australia. The results suggest that rapid adaptation to extreme conditions can be accomplished without the loss of photosynthetic efficiency and that regulation of photosynthesis by rapid changes in carboxylation capacity may be important.

2. MATERIALS AND METHODS

The photosynthetic characteristics of *Bruguiera parviflora* (Roxb.) Wright & Arnold were investigated at a field site on the Daintree River (16°16'S, 145°25'E) in North Queensland during a 2-week period in October, 1988. A 17 m, multi-platform tower and adjoining boardwalk were temporarily constructed on site. *In situ* measurements of net photosynthesis and leaf absorptivity were made throughout the canopy using the LiCor Photosynthesis System (6200) and a portable integrating sphere/gas exchange apparatus (4).

For oxygen evolution and fluorescence measurements (Hansatech leaf disc system), the canopy was sampled in four height zones: top(15.5 m), 15-14 m, 12-9 m, 9-6 m. The times of day for sampling were early morning (0800-0900), mid-morning (1000-1100), early afternoon (1330-1430), and mid-afternoon (1600-1700). Over a four-day period, measurements were rotated so that each canopy zone was sampled once at each of the four time intervals.

3. RESULTS AND DISCUSSION

3.1 Field Observations. Approximately 85% of the PAR incident at the top of the canopy was attenuated within the first meter. Outlined in Table I are some of the photosynthetic characteristics which changed with the light

M. Baltscheffsky (ed.), Current Research in Photosynthesis, Vol. IV, 859–862.
© 1990 *Kluwer Academic Publishers. Printed in the Netherlands.*

extinction profile, though in a more gradual manner. In contrast, relative fluorescence (F_v/F_p) and half-times for $F_o \rightarrow F_p$ (Table II) were the same at all canopy levels. Since exposed leaves at the top of the canopy showed no loss of any photosynthetic capacity, the occurrence of photoinhibition was ruled out. This included leaves whose gas exchange had been monitored *in situ* throughout the day and were known to have photosynthetic rates and stomatal conductances which were virtually zero concommitant with prolonged exposure to high irradiance and leaf temperature. Because no decreases in photon yields or fluorescence were evident, we suggest that protection against photodamage was not associated with a reduction in photochemical efficiency.

Table I. A summary of the photosynthetic and respiratory O_2 exchange of leaves grown at different canopy positions. Data points were taken from a combination of four separate light curves per canopy level. Light saturation points were estimated visually, and maximum net photosynthesis values are based on rates at 1800 $\mu Ei \cdot m^{-2} \cdot s^{-1}$ PAR. Apparent quantum yields, light compensation points, and dark respiration rates were determined by a linear equation fitted to light intensity points ranging from 0 to 102 $\mu Ei \cdot m^{-2} \cdot s^{-1}$ (r > 0.9 in all cases). Absorbed photon yields can be estimated by dividing apparent quantum yields by the average leaf absorbancy.

CANOPY POSITION

	Top(15.5 m)	15-14 m	12-9 m	9-6 m
Light sat. (approx) ($\mu Ei \cdot m^{-2} \cdot s^{-1}$)	200	200	150	100
Max P_{net} ($\mu mol\ O_2 \cdot m^{-2} \cdot s^{-1}$)	15	11	10	7
Apparent photon yield	0.073	0.074	0.062	0.052
Leaf absorptivity (%)	74±2	78±5	75±4	75±4
Light comp. pt. ($\mu Ei \cdot m^{-2} \cdot s^{-1}$)	16	17	13	8
Dark respiration ($\mu mol\ O_2 \cdot m^{-2} \cdot s^{-1}$)	-1.2	-1.2	-.08	-.04

Table II. Room temperature fluorescence of leaf discs taken from the four canopy zones. Details: 5-minute dark adaptation, blue excitation (Schott BG18, 400 $\mu Ei \cdot m^{-2} \cdot s^{-1}$), fluor. probe filtered by Wratten 88A. Means ± s.e. (n=4).

CANOPY POSITION

	Top(15.5)	15-14 m	12-9 m	9-6 m
F_v/F_p	0.68±0.02	0.68±0.03	0.70±0.01	0.70±0.01
$t_{1/2}$ (F_o to F_p; ms)	510±10	520±30	480±30	480±40

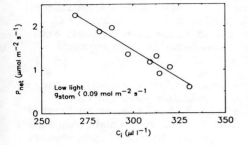

Figure 1. The negative relationship of P_{net} and C_i at low light (<50 $\mu Ei \cdot m^{-2} \cdot s^{-1}$) and low stomatal conductance (0.09 $mol \cdot m^{-2} \cdot s^{-1}$).

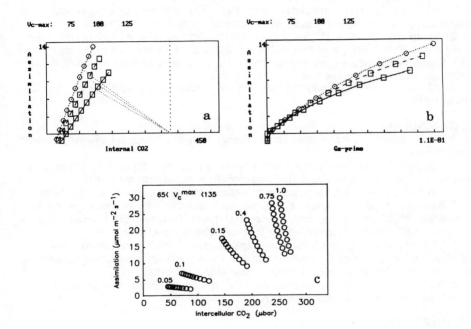

Figure 2. Results of simulation modeling to consider the causes of the negative P_{net} dependence on C_i. (a). Simulated net photosynthesis at three levels of V_c^{max}, centered around a "typical" C-3 value. The highest level of V_c^{max} is indicated by the open circles. The dotted lines indicate the conductances at the operating points, linking the curves with the ambient CO_2 value. (b). By sweeping the conductance lines in (a) along the curves, the P_{net} vs conductance ($G_{s\text{-prime}}$) relationship was simulated. For experimental purposes, it is effectively linear and independent of V_c^{max}. (c). By varying V_c^{max}, at different fixed conductances, a series of P_{net} vs C_i relationships were generated. At low g_{stom}, the relationships were negative. Conductance values were 0.05, 0.1, 0.15, 0.4, 0.75 and 1 $mol \cdot m^{-2} \cdot s^{-1}$.

Although normal relationships of net photosynthesis (P_{net}) $vs.$ stomatal conductance (g_{stom}) were obtainable by plotting the combined data from infrared gas analyzer studies, an unconventional relationship of P_{net} $vs.$ internal CO_2 concentration (C_i) was seen when individual gas exchange measurements were plotted (Fig. 1). The correlation of P_{net} $vs.$ C_i was negative when stomatal conductances were low (i.e. < 0.11 mol$\cdot$m$^{-2}\cdot$s^{-1}).

3.2 Computer Simulation. To determine what conditions might be required to produce a negative P_{net} $vs.$ C_i relationship, a simulation model of C_3 photosynthesis (JMC) was employed which essentially used the carbon fixation and photochemistry equations of Farquhar et $al.$ (5) and the stomatal response equations of Jarvis (6). Based on that analysis, an adjustment of carboxylation efficiency was implicated in the short term control of photosynthesis as follows:

1) Given different values for the maximum rate of carboxylation (V_c^{max}), P_{net} $vs.$ C_i relationships were predicted (Fig. 2a). The dotted lines represent conductances at operating points under normal ambient conditions.

2) From Fig. 2a, the P_{net} $vs.$ g_{stom} relationship can also be calculated based on constant CO_2 levels, i.e., the dotted lines can be swept along the curves (Fig. 2b). These relationships were practically linear and independent of V_c^{max} over the range of conductances used in the model.

3) At any given g_{stom}, varying the V_c^{max} will produce a negative P_{net} $vs.$ C_i relationship (Fig. 2c).

4. SUMMARY
* Each canopy zone was distinguishable based on general photosynthetic characteristics.
* Photoinhibition was not apparent even in leaves exposed to prolonged periods of high irradiance and leaf temperature concommitant with photosynthetic rates and stomatal conductances which were virtually zero.
* No loss of photon yield or fluorescence was seen in leaves exposed to excessively high irradiance, suggesting that protection against photoinhibition was not associated with a reduction in photochemical efficiency.
* The negative P_{net} $vs.$ C_i relationships observed in $B.$ $parviflora$ were simulated in a model of C_3 photosynthesis by adjusting the carboxylation capacity in combination with limiting stomatal conductances.
* An adjustment of the maximum rate of carboxylation was implied as a short-term control of photosynthesis in $B.$ $parviflora$.

REFERENCES
1 Björkman, O., Demmig, B., Andrews, T.J. (1988) Aust. J. Plant Physiol. 15:43-61.
2 Powles, S.B. (1984) Ann. Rev. Plant Physiol. 35:15-44.
3 Demmig, B. & Björkman, O. (1987) Planta 171:171-184.
4 Ireland, C.R., Long,S.P. & Baker, N.R. (1989) In press: Plant, Cell and Environment.
5 Farquhar, G.D., von Caemmerer, S. & Berry, J.A. (1980) Planta 149:78-90.
6 Jarvis, P.G. (1976) Phil. Trans. R. Soc. Lond. B. 273:593-610.
Supported by the National Sci. Fdn. and the Australian Inst. of Marine Science. Additional support to DRC was povided by the McKnight Fdn. through the Interdisciplinary Photosynthesis Research Program at the Univ. of Illinois-UC.

SOME PHYSIOLOGICAL ASPECTS OF PASPALUM DILATATUM GROWN UNDER FIELD
CONDITIONS

J. MARQUES DA SILVA, A. BERNARDES DA SILVA, D. COELHO REBELO*
and M. C. ARRABAÇA
Departamento de Biologia Vegetal, Faculdade de Ciências da
Universidade de Lisboa and *Departamento de Genética e
Melhoramento de Plantas, Estação Agronómica Nacional,
Oeiras, Portugal

ABSTRACT
     To study the adaptation of the C_4 plant, *Paspalum dilatatum*, to the
climate conditions of the centre of Portugal, some physiological
parameters, related to photosynthesis, were determined. Measurements
were made from January to July 1988. The rates of photosynthesis and
transpiration increased significantly during the summer, while the
chlorophyll content fluctuated from March to July. The activities of
PEPC and NADP-ME were measured at 32 and 15°C. At both temperatures,
there was a significant drop on the activity of PEPC, during the
hottest months. The activity of NADP-ME was constant during the study.

INTRODUCTION
     Grasses fixing atmospheric CO_2 through the C_4 pathway of
photosynthesis are able to grow with higher productivities than C_3
plants mainly under warm, dry conditions [1, 2]. The great agronomical
and economical interest of the C_4 pasture plant *Paspalum dilatatum* lies
in its ability not only to survive to the hot and dry conditions in
summer but also to survive to low temperatures and winter frosts [3,4].
Thus it is possible to have green meadows all the year round.
     The aim of this work was to study some photosynthetic related
parameters in plants grown under field conditions in order to understand
their adaptation to different weather conditions.

MATERIAL AND METHODS
Plant material
     Paspalum dilatatum cv Raki was grown under field conditions in
alkaline soil, in Oeiras, litoral centre of Portugal. Measurements
started two months after cutting.
Gas exchange measurements
     In winter and spring, photosynthesis was determined by $^{14}CO_2$
incorporation [5] and transpiration rates were measured using a ΔT
Devices MK 3 water diffusion porometer. In the summer both parameters
were measured with a portable Infra Red Gas Analyser (IRGA) (ADC LTD
England). Transpiration rates were determined according to [6].

M. Baltscheffsky (ed.), Current Research in Photosynthesis, Vol. IV, 863–866.
© 1990 *Kluwer Academic Publishers. Printed in the Netherlands.*

Enzymatic assays
Leaf samples were collected at 10.00 am and stored in liquid nitrogen. The frozen leaf segments (about 0.1 g FW) were quickly homogenized in a chilled mortar with sand in 5 ml of extraction medium containing 50 mM Tris-HCl pH 8.3, 1 mM EDTA, 5 mM $MgCl_2$, 5 mM DTT, 3% (w/v) of soluble polyvinylpirrolidone (PVP) and some grains of insoluble PVP.
Phosphoenolpyruvate carboxylase (PEPC) (EC 4.1.1.31) was assayed as described in [7].
NADP-Malic enzyme (NADP-ME) (EC 1.1.1.40) activity was measured as in [8].
Chlorophyll and protein content were determined according to MacKinney [9] and Bradford [10], respectively.

RESULTS AND DISCUSSION
Net photosynthetic rate increases significantly ($P < 0.05$) from winter to summer months (Fig. 1) as expected. *P. dilatatum* being a C_4 plant, it grows better under hot conditions and high light intensity [1].

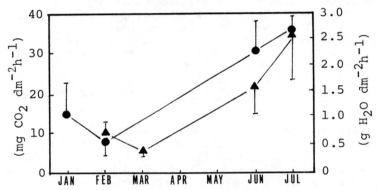

FIGURE 1. Rates of photosynthesis (●) and transpiration (▲) from January to July. The results are means ±SD of 7 samples for photosynthesis and of 20 for transpiration.

The rate at which water is lost from the leaf in transpiration (Fig. 1) is characteristically low, as in other C_4 plants [2], but increases significantly with temperature and radiation [11].
The chlorophyll content increases significantly (Fig. 2) from January to May, probably due to better climatic conditions and also to increased leaf expansion [12]. Changes in the content of chlorophyll from May to July can tentatively be related with the grain filling period. From its beginning in May, the pigment amount decreases, but increases again in July, at the end of the period.
PEPC activity was measured at 32°C, the temperature at which the activity was found to be maximal, (results not shown) and at 15°C (Fig. 3). The activities found in February and March at 32°C are in accordance with those obtained for maize [13]. The decrease in activity in May and June may be due to leaf ageing [14] and also

associated to grain development. For 15°C the differences in activity are not statistically significant. This may indicate that, under these conditions, temperature is the limiting factor in enzyme activity.

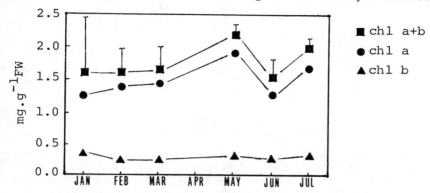

FIGURE 2. Chlorophyll content from January to July. The results are means ±SD of 3, 2, 7, 17, 8 and 10 samples for each month, respectively.

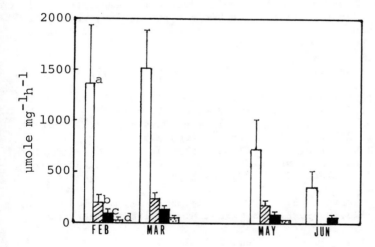

FIGURE 3. PEPC activity from February to June.
(a) and (b) expressed by chlorophyll at 32 and 15°C, respectively.
(c) and (d) expressed by protein at 32 and 15°C, respectively.
The results are means ±SD of 8 samples.

The activity of NADP-Malic enzyme was also measured at 32°C, temperature at which the activity was near maximal (results not shown), and at 15°C (Fig. 4). the values found are in accordance with those reported for maize [13]. Contrary to PEPC the activity of this enzyme did not change all the year round.

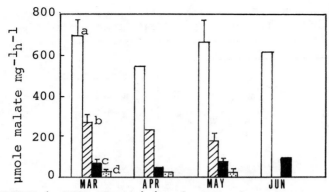

FIGURE 4. NADP-ME activity from March to June.
(a) and (b) expressed by chlorophyll at 32 and 15°C
respectively. (c) and (d) expressed by protein at 32 and
15°C, respectively. The results are means ±SD of 6 samples
for March and May. For April and June only one sample was
taken.

Results suggest that the plant is well adapted to temperate mildly
hot climates. In order to optimize the biomass production, we are now
studying plant response to periodical cutting and nitrogen feeding.

REFERENCES
[1] Rowley, J. A., Tunnicliffe, C. G. and Taylor, A. O. (1975) Aust. J.
    Plant Physiol. 2, 447-451
[2] Ludlow, M. M. (1985) Aust. J. Plant Physiol. 12, 557-572
[3] Rowley, J. A. (1976) Aust. J. Plant Physiol. 3, 597-603
[4] Taylor A. O. and Rowley, J. A. (1971) Plant Physiol. 47, 713-818
[5] Bravdo, B. A. (1972) Physiol. Plant. 27, 209-215
[6] Long, S. P. and Hallgren, J. E. (1985) in Techniques in
    Bioproductivity and Photosynthesis, 2nd ed. (Coombs, J., Hall,D. O.,
    Long, S. P. and Scurlock, J. H. O., eds.) pp 66-87, Pergamont
    Press, New York
[7] Donkin, M. and Martin E. S. (1980) J. Exp. Bot. 31, 357-363
[8] Edwards, G. E., Ku, M. S. B. and Hatch, M. D. (1982) Plant Cell
    Physiol. 23, 1185-1193
[9] MacKinney, G. (1941) J. Biol. Chem. 140, 315-322
[10] Bradford, M. M. (1976) Anal. Biochem. 72, 248-254
[11] Forde, B. J., Mitchell, K. J. and Edge, E. A. (1977) Aust. J.
     Plant Physiol. 4, 889-899
[12] Mae, T., Makimo, A. and Ohira, K. (1987) in Plant Senescence: Its
     Biochemistry and Physiology (Thomson, W. W., Northnagel, E. A. and
     Huffaker, R. C., eds) pp 123-131, Pub. by American Society of
     Plant Physiologists, Rockville, Maryland
[13] Usuda, H., Ku, M. S. B. and Edwards, G. E. (1985) Physiol. Plant.
     63, 65-70
[14] Thiagarajah, M. R., Hunt, L. A. and Mahon, J. D. (1981) Can. J.
     Bot. 59, 28-33.

IMMUNOGOLD LOCALIZATION OF RIBULOSE 1,5-BISPHOSPHATE CARBOXYLASE IN AMPHIBIOUS <u>ELEOCHARIS</u> SPECIES IN RELATION TO C3 AND C4 PHOTOSYNTHESIS

OSAMU UENO AND MUNEAKI SAMEJIMA
DEPARTMENT OF APPLIED PHYSIOLOGY, NATIONAL INSTITUTE OF AGROBIOLOGICAL
RESOURCES, TSUKUBA SCIENCE CITY, IBARAKI 305, JAPAN

1. INTRODUCTION
    The genus <u>Eleocharis</u> is a leaf-less sedge group growing in aquatic and wet environments. It includes some C_4 species and possibly C_3-C_4 intermediate species, although most species of the genus are C_3 (1). Recently, we found that <u>Eleocharis</u> <u>vivipara</u>, an amphibious plant, differentiated into the C_4 type under the terrestrial conditions and into the C_3 type under the submersed aquatic conditions (2). In order to elucidate the mechanisms of conversion of the photosynthetic metabolisms in <u>E</u>. <u>vivipara</u>, we attempt to study the inter- and intra-cellular localization of C_3 and C_4 photosynthetic enzymes. This study reports on the distribution of RuBP carboxylase/oxygenase (Rubisco) protein in the photosynthetic tissues of <u>E</u>. <u>vivipara</u> and <u>E</u>. <u>baldwinii</u>, another amphibious species which possesses the C_4 characteristics at least under the terrestrial conditions.

2. MATERIALS AND METHODS
2.1. <u>Plant</u> <u>materials</u> : Plants were collected from the field of Tampa, Florida. The terrestrial forms were grown in a greenhouse (25 C to 35 C during the day/20 C to 25 C at night) under sunlight. The submersed forms were maintained in aquaria in the greenhouse. The immunolabelling experiments were done for the samples fixed early in October, 1988. Plants for δ^{13}C determinations were grown in a growth chamber and a aquarium under the conditions indicated in Table 1.
2.2. <u>Antibody</u> : Rabbit antiserum raised against the large subunit of Rubisco from pea leaves was a kind gift from Dr. S.Muto, University of Tokyo. Western blotting analysis showed that the antiserum recognized specifically Rubisco (LSU) from the plants examined.
2.3. <u>Tissue</u> <u>preparation</u> <u>and</u> <u>immunolabelling</u> : In <u>Eleocharis</u> species, the leaf blades are reduced and the culms are the photosynthetic organ. Culm segments were fixed in 3 % glutaraldehyde in 50 $mol.m^{-3}$ sodium phosphate buffer (pH 7.2) or 4 % paraformaldehyde-0.2 % glutaraldehyde in the buffer for 3 hr at 4 C. They were embedded in Lowicryl K4M resin at -20 C. Sections were incubated in 0.5 % BSA in PBS containing 0.1 % Tween 20 and in diluted antiserum. For control, non-immune serum was used instead of the antiserum. They were treated with Protein A-

M. Baltscheffsky (ed.), Current Research in Photosynthesis, Vol. IV, 867–870.
© 1990 *Kluwer Academic Publishers. Printed in the Netherlands.*

TABLE 1. $\delta^{13}C$ values of culms of <u>Eleocharis</u> species grown in different conditions.

Growth condition	$\delta^{13}C$ (‰)	
	E. vivipara	E. baldwinii
Terrestrial condition		
Field, Florida	−13.5*	−12.7
35/30 C**, sunlight, for 4 months	−14.4, −14.6	−13.0, −13.8
Submersed condition		
Field, Florida	−25.9*	−25.9
35/30 C**, sunlight, for 4 months	−22.1, −24.1	−18.5, −19.7

* Data from Ueno <u>et al</u>. (1988).   ** Day/night temperature.

gold (15 nm, E.Y.Lab.Inc.) and stained with uranyl acetate and lead citrate.
2.4. <u>Carbon isotope analysis</u> : The carbon isotope ratios were determined as described in Ueno <u>et al</u>.(1).

3. RESULTS
The terrestrial forms of the two species possess erect, firm culms, while the submersed forms exhibit hair-like structure consisting of slender, soft culms. The terrestrial forms showed the $\delta^{13}C$ values typical of C4 plants. The submersed form of <u>E. vivipara</u> showed C3-like $\delta^{13}C$ values and that of <u>E. baldwinii</u> did C3-like or C3-C4 intermediate values (Table 1).
These two forms possessed anatomical structures of culms clearly differing from each other. The terrestrial forms had an unusual Kranz type of anatomy which is characterized by the presence of colourless mestome sheath cells intervening between the mesophyll cells and the Kranz cells (1,2,3). The chloroplasts with well-developed grana and many large mitochondria were <u>scattered</u> in the Kranz cells, although the terrestrial forms had biochemical features of the NAD-malic enzyme C4 subtype (2,3). The submersed forms possessed large spherical mesophyll cells and reduced vascular bundles, which are characteristic of submersed aquatic plants (2,4). Kranz cells contained relatively smaller chloroplasts than the Kranz cells of the terrestrial forms.
In C4 plants Rubisco is located exclusively in chloroplasts of the Kranz cells (5,6). Our immunolabelling study confirmed this distributional pattern of Rubisco in leaves of maize, <u>Chloris gayana</u> and <u>Eragrostis ferruginea</u>. In the terrestrial form of <u>E. vivipara</u>, Rubisco was distributed evenly in chloroplasts of the mesophyll cells as well as of the Kranz cells (Fig.1A,B). Similar labelling pattern of Rubisco was also observed in the chloroplasts of the two types of green cells in the submersed form of <u>E. vivipara</u> (Fig.1C). In the terrestrial form of <u>E. baldwinii</u>, on the other hand, Rubisco was distributed mostly in the chloroplasts of the Kranz cells and slightly in those of the mesophyll cells (Fig.1D,E). In the submersed form of <u>E. baldwinii</u>, the labelling densities in the two types of green cells were close to each other,

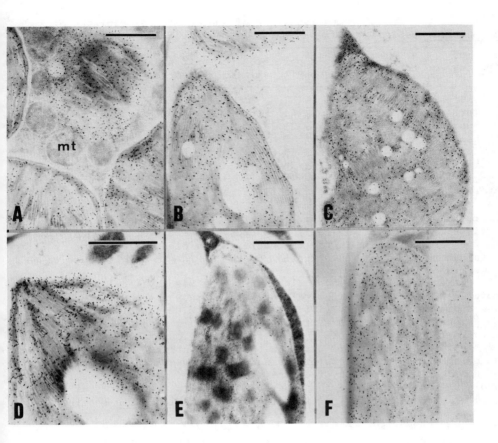

FIGURE 1. Immunogold labelling of chloroplasts of <u>Eleocharis</u> species by antibodies to Rubisco. A, B and C : <u>E. vivipara</u>, A : Kranz cell of the terrestrial form, B : Mesophyll cell of the terrestrial form, C : Mesophyll cell of the submersed form. D, E and F : <u>E. baldwinii</u>, D : Kranz cell of the terrestrial form, E : Mesophyll cell of the terrestrial form, F : Mesophyll cell of the submersed form. Scales : 1.0 μm. mt : mitochondria.

indicating the increment of Rubisco concentration in the chloroplasts of the mesophyll cells (Fig.1F and Table 2).

4. DISCUSSION
It is interesting to compare the distributional pattern of Rubisco with the physiological and biochemical data of <u>E. vivipara</u> previously reported (2). These data suggest that the C4 pathway is operating in the terrestrial form. In contrast with the location of Rubisco, PEP carboxylase appears to be distributed largely in the cytosol of the

TABLE 2. Density of immunolabelling of Rubisco in chloroplasts of Eleocharis species.

| Species and form | Gold particles per unit area (μm^2) | | Ratio |
	Mesophyll cell chlt	Kranz cell chlt	(MC/KC)
E. vivipara			
Terrestrial	86.0 ± 41.1 (6)	98.9 ± 11.5 (5)	0.87
Submersed	97.1 ± 23.1 (7)	145.9 ± 40.0 (6)	0.67
E. baldwinii			
Terrestrial	20.8 ± 10.6 (5)	256.0 ± 31.0 (6)	0.08
Submersed	132.1 ± 38.0 (5)	162.9 ± 45.0 (7)	0.81

Average ± standard deviation (sample number).

mesophyll cells(unpublished). Presently it is not clear whether the Rubisco in the mesophyll cells is photosynthetically functioned. There is the same situation in the terrestrial form of E. baldwinii as well, although the Rubisco concentration in the mesophyll cells appears to be lower than that of E. vivipara.

In the submersed forms of Eleocharis, the mesophyll cells are well developed whereas the Kranz cells generally show a trend of reduction. The submersed form of E. vivipara seems to fix CO_2 mainly through the C_3 pathway (2). Therefore, the Rubisco in the mesophyll cells may play a primarily important role for CO_2 fixation in contrast with the case of the terrestrial form. Although the photosynthetic metabolism in the submersed form of E. baldwinii is not presently examined, the increment of Rubisco in the mesophyll cells is noteworthy. Further research would be required before the understanding of the mechanisms of conversion of photosynthetic functions in amphibious Eleocharis species.

5. ACKNOWLEDGMENTS
Supported by a Grant-in-Aid from the Ministry of Agriculture, Forestry and Fisheries of Japan (Integrated Research Program for the Use of Biotechnological Procedures for Plant Breeding). We thank Drs. I.Matsuda, T.Terao, T.Murata and H.Nakamura for varied assistance.

6. REFERENCES
1. Ueno,O., Samejima,M. and Koyama,T. (1989) Ann. Bot. in press.
2. Ueno,O., Samejima,M., Muto,S. and Miyachi,S. (1988) Proc. Natl. Acad. Sci. USA 85:6733-7.
3. Ueno,O. and Samejima,M. (1989) Bot. Mag. Tokyo, in press.
4. Sculthorpe,C.D. (1967) The Biology of Aquatic Vascular Plants, Arnold, London.
5. Hattersley,P.W., Watson,L. and Osmond,C.B. (1977) Aust. J. Plant Physiol. 4:523-9.
6. Perrot-Rechenmann,C., Chollet,R. and Gadal,P. (1984) Planta 161: 266-71.

RELATIONSHIPS BETWEEN SOURCE LEAF PHOTOSYNTHESIS,
EXPORT AND GRAIN FILLING IN MAIZE.

Jean-Louis PRIOUL, Agnès REYSS, Nicole SCHWEBEL-DUGUE and Alain LECHARNY
Laboratoire Structure et Métabolisme des Plantes, Associé au CNRS (URA 1128),
Bâtiment 430, Université de Paris-Sud. 91405 ORSAY Cédex, France

1. INTRODUCTION
     Grain filling in Maize is mainly dependent on photosynthetic carbon fixed after
pollination[1]. However in spite of the high sink demand, photosynthetic rate tends
to decline because of leaf senescence[2]. This phenomenon is probably linked to N
remobilization needed for grain protein synthesis.
     We studied this problem by examining carbon metabolism in the ear and in the
adjacent leaf. In both organs carbohydrate pools were measured in relation to key
enzymes of this metabolism : sucrose-P-synthase, sucrose-synthase, invertase,
ADPglucose pyrophosphorylase.
     Carbon fixation was assessed from Rubisco activities, leaf N remoblization was
estimated from loss in soluble protein and Rubisco protein.

2. MATERIAL AND METHODS
2.1. Plant Growth and Sampling
     Maize plants (c.v. F7F2) were grown outdoors in a small experimental field at
     Orsay (11 May to 12 November 1987) at a normal sowing density (70 plants
     m-2). After pollination five plants were sampled every 10 days. The leaf
     adjacent to the ear was punched and discs (0.5 cm-2) were stored at -70°C
     until furtherbiochemical measurements. Similarly 25 grains/ear were
     sampled.

2.2. Methods
          Carbohydrates were extracted by Methanol, Chloroform, water (12/5/3,
     in 300 µl) and the water soluble fraction was analysed and quantified by HPLC.
     Starch was determined after treatment by 0.02 N NaOH, digestion by
     amyloglucosidase and enzymatic measurement of glucose.
          Rubisco activity was measured by radiochemical method and enzyme
     quantity by immunorocket as in [3]. Extracts for Sucrose-P-synthase were
     desalted on G-25 Sephadex column and the reaction was run as in [3],
     except that UDP glucose and Fructose 6 P were adjusted to 25 and 10 mM
     respectively.The spectrophotometric assay was used to measure ADPglucose
     pyrophosphorylase [3]. Sucrose synthase and neutral invertase were assayed
     as in [4].

3. RESULTS AND DISCUSSION
3.1. Grain fresh weight increased linearly for the first 40 days and then the rate
     slowed down until a plateau was reached by 60-80 days. Dry matter
     accumulation presented a 10-15 day lag and a regular increase between 20 to
     60 days. This kinetic of grain filling serves as a basis for comparison with time

M. Baltscheffsky (ed.), Current Research in Photosynthesis, Vol. IV, 871–874.

course of other parameters (fig. 1).

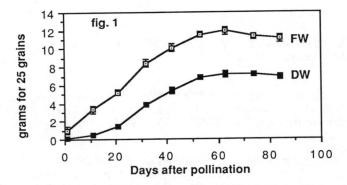

FIGURE 1. Fresh and dry matter accumulation in grain as a function of time

3.2. Rubisco activity peaked immediately after pollination, declined by half until day 42 and was nil at day 74 (fig. 2a). At that time chlorophyll was totally absent. Rubisco quantity varied similarly except that the initial decline was slower since 50 % of the protein was still present, at day 63. The fate of Rubisco-protein was different from that of total protein, the latter declined more rapidly but remained constant after day 74 (fig. 2b).

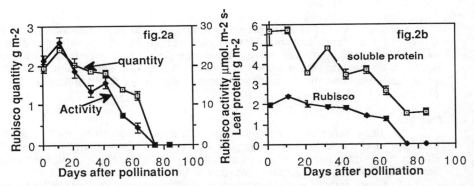

FIGURE 2. a) Rubisco activity and quantity, b) soluble protein and Rubisco quantity in ear-leaf as a function of time after pollination.

3.3. Leaf carbohydrates and enzymes of sucrose metabolism.

Soluble leaf carbohydrates (fig. 3a) presented two maxima separated by a marked drop corresponding to the beginning of rapid grain filling. A continuous decrease was observed after day 40. Sucrose usually represented more than 90% of soluble carbohydrates, except at the end (days 70-80) when hexoses were predominant. Sucrose-P synthase activity (fig. 3b) presented a broad peak which coincided with the rate of grain filling (cf. fig. 1). In contrast with SPS, the activity of sucrose degrading enzymes, namely sucrose-synthase and neutral invertase, were rather low during grain filling but a sudden increase occurred when leaf senesced (not shown).

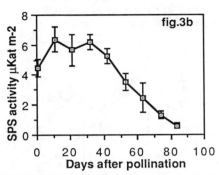

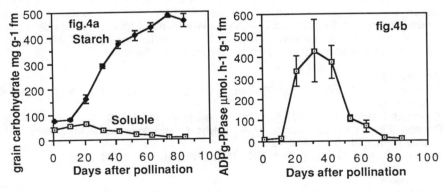

FIGURE 3. a) Total soluble carbohydrate and sucrose, b) sucrose-P-synthase activty in ear-leaf as a function of time after pollination.

3.4. Stem carbohydrates.

Carbohydrates increased in the pith of the internode adjacent to the ear, indicating partial storage of assimilates exported from the leaf. Sucrose was the major soluble carbohydrate and starch represented only 1-2 % of total (not shown).

3.5. Grain carbohydrates and enzymes.

Soluble carbohydrates were maximum at day 20 and declined thereafter (fig.4 a). At the beginning, sucrose represented only 34 % of soluble sugar indicating a rapid hydrolysis of imported sucrose. Starch was always the major carbohydrate even though the rate of accumulation lagged during the first 11 days. Accumulation was linear from 11 to 40 days (fig. 4a). Starch represented 60 % of grain dry matter at the beginning and nearly 80 % at final harvest. ADP glucose-pyrophosphorylase is a key regulatory enzyme in starch synthesis pathway. The variation of its activity was remarkably parallel to starch accumulation rate (fig. 4b).

FIGURE 4. a)Starch and soluble carbohydrate, b) ADPglucose-pyrophosphorylase in grain as a function of time after pollination.

3.6. Source-sink manipulation.

Leaf carbohydrate export and grain filling were altered by two ways : either ear excision at pollination = ear (-) or excision of all source leaves except the one above the ear = leaf (-).

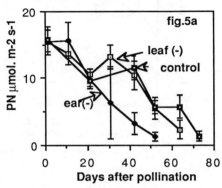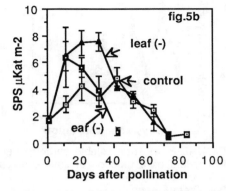

FIGURE 5. a) Net photosynthesis and b) Sucrose-P-synthase activity of the leaf above ear in plants subjected to ear excision or to elimination of all other leaves

Net photosynthesis rate of the medial part of the leaf above the ear was measured with a portable CO_2 analyser (ADC). Net CO_2 fixation was not affected during the first 20 days, then declined more rapidly in plants without ear (fig.5a). This corresponded to the onset of visible senescence in the plants.

Sucrose-P-synthase in the same leaf responded clearly to changes in assimilate demand. It increased rapidly in both treated plants at day 11 but declined below control in ear (-) plants whereas it remained high for 40 days in plants deprived of most of their leaves (fig. 5b).

4. CONCLUSION

The variation of sucrose-P-synthase in the leaf adjacent to the ear parallels the variation of assimilate demand by the ear. Carbon fixation capacities decreased continuously but the degradation of Rubisco is less rapid than other soluble proteins. A close agreement exists between the activity of grain ADP glucose pyrophosphorylase and rate of starch accumulation in the grain.

REFERENCES
1 Duncan, W.J. (1975) in Crop Physiology (Evans L.T., ed.), pp. 23-50, Cambridge University Press.
2 Crafts-Brandner, S.J. (1987) Plant Physiol. 84, 255-260
3 Rocher, J.P., Prioul J.L., Lecharny A., Reyss A. and Joussaume M. (1989) Plant Physiol. 89 : 416-420
4 Huber S.C. and Akazawa T. (1986) Plant Physiol. 81 : 1008-1013

THE DEPENDENCE OF SOME PHOTOSYNTHETIC PARAMETERS ON THE PHOSPHORUS CONCENTRATION IN A NUTRITION SOLUTION AND WHEAT GENOTYPE

SLOBODANKA ZATEZALO, ŽIVKO STANKOVIĆ and MILOJE R.SARIĆ
Institute of Biology, University of Novi Sad, Novi Sad, Yugoslavia

1. INTRODUCTION

Thorough utilization of nutrients is a method of obtaining maximum economically yields. This assumes the recognition of genetic specificity of mineral nutrition by plants (1, 2). Plant species and their cultivars differ in their ability to grow with low level of some nutrients (3). We drew attention to inorganic phosphorus which occurs in plants as a very important regulator of photosynthesis (4, 5, 6). Uptake, distribution and accumulation of this element in plants depend upon the environmental conditions and genetic traits of a plant species, cultivar or inbred line (7). Apart from the rate of photosynthesis and respiration, content of photosynthetic pigments and phosphorus in three wheat cultivars, we investigated also the activity of acid phosphatase as one of the factors connected with ability of plant adaption at low phosphorus level (8, 9, 1o).

2. MATERIALS AND METHODS

Experimental genetic material consisted of three cultivars of winter wheat (Žitnica, Jugoslavija and Novosadska rana 2). The plants were cultivated under natural illumination in the greenhouse by using the method of water culture with an exchange of the nutrient solution every 72 h. The culture solution was the Reid - York (11) with increasing phosphate concentration (0, 0.05, 0.1, 0.5, 1 and 2 mM Pi). The analyses were carried out after 28 days. The photosynthetic activity and respiration were determined by using a polarographic method (12), pigment and phosphorus content by spectrophotometry. The isolation and the determination of the acid phosphatase activity are described in detail by Kummerova (10). The results are mean values of two (phosphorus content and acid phosphatase activity) and three (rate of photosynthesis and respiration and pigment content) independent experiments. They were evaluated statistically by LSD - test

3. RESULTS AND DISCUSSION

The photosynthetic activity in all three cultivars increased as Pi concentration in nutrient solution increased (Fig. 1).

M. Baltscheffsky (ed.), Current Research in Photosynthesis, Vol. IV, 875–878.
© 1990 *Kluwer Academic Publishers. Printed in the Netherlands.*

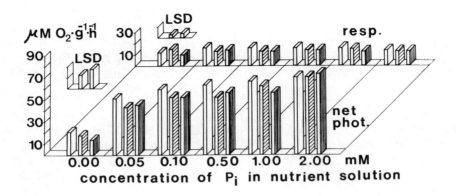

$\mu M\ O_2\cdot g^{-1} h^{-1}$

Fig. 1. Rate of photosynthesis and respiration in three wheat cultivars in relation to Pi concentration in nutrient solution $(mM\ O_2\ g^{-1} h^{-1})$

ŽITNICA

JUGOSLAVIJA

NS RANA 2

Highly significant differences in photosynthetic activity of all three cultivars between Po and all remaining Pi treatments were obtained.
Irespective of a treatment employed, the rate of photosynthesis in cultivar Žitnica was higher than in the remaining two cultivars, although the differences recorded were not significant in all cases analysed.

No significant differences were recorded in respiration rate between cultivars or individual Pi treatments (Fig. 1). Therefore, the genetic specificity of mineral nutrition by these three cultivars may be eliminated as one of the factors affecting net photosynthesis under given experimental conditions.

Phosphorus content in the aboveground part and root depended upon its concentration in nutrient solution and in all cultivars highly significant differences were recorded between individual treatments employed.
However, the obtained results show that cultivar Žitnica had a significantly higher ability for uptaking and accumulation of phosphorus from the solution than the remaining two cultivars (Fig. 2).

With regard to pigment content, no significant differences between cultivars as well as between Pi treatments were found.

The level of acid phosphatase activity in the aboveground part indicated differences between cultivars. Significant differences in activity were between cultivars Žitnica and Novosadska rana 2 in all Pi treatments except Po. An increase in acid phosphatase activity was determined in all cases with the decrease of Pi concentration in thenutrient solution in the aboveground part as well as in the root (Fig. 3).

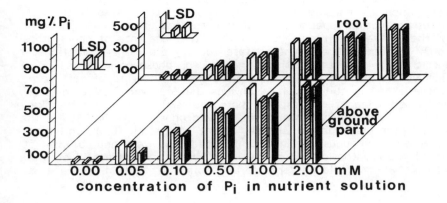

Fig. 2. Pi concentration in aboveground part and root in three wheat
cultivars in relation to Pi concentration in nutrient solution (mg%)

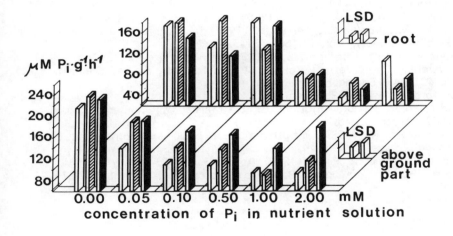

Fig. 3. The activity of acid phosphatase in aboveground part and root in
three wheat cultivars in relation to Pi concentration in nutrient
solution $(\mu M\ Pi\ .\ g^{-1}h^{-1})$

4. CONCLUSION

In this paper attention is payed to the study of those physiological and
biochemical processes that affect plant production and where genetic

markers can operate as selection criteria. It is desirable to idntify genotypes which are capable, even under conditions of limited Pi as nutrient,of producting superior level of biomass and grain yield. On the basis of the our results it may be concluded that the rate of photsynthesis, phosphorus content and acid phosphatase activity are rather conditioned by the genetic traits of wheat cultivars than by the phosphorus status (although we did not get significant differences in the rate of net photosynthesis among cultivars, it is obvious that cultivar Žitnica in all Pi treatments had a higher rate of net photosynthesis). Cultivar Novosadska rana 2 had a significantlly higher level of acid phosphatase activity in the aboveground part than cultivar Žitnica, but at the same time content of phosphorus was just opposite. Significant differences were not observed at the rate of photosynthesis. Our results may be put into effect in creating new cultivars which would be very useful in plant production.

REFERENCES

1 Natr, L., Apel, P., Fialova (1983) Biol. Plant. 25, 433-439
2 Sarić, M. R., Mišić, T., Vulić, B., Momčilović, V. (1986) Savremena poljoprivreda 34, 299-309
3 Clark, R. B. (1983) Plant Soil 72, 75-196
4 Santarius, K. A., Heber, U. (1965) Biochem. Biophys. Acta 102,39-54
5 Walker, D. A., Sivak, M. N. (1985) Physiol. Veg. 23, 829-841
6 Rao, I. M., Abadia, J., Terry, N. (1987) in Progress and Photosynthesis (Biggins, J., ed.), Vol. III, pp. 325-328
7 Bieleski, R. L., Ferguson, I. B. (1983) in Encyclopedia of Plant Physiology (New Series) Vol. 15 A (Ed. Läuchli, A. and Bieleski, R.L.) pp. 421-449. Springer-Verlag Berlin
8 Besford, R. T. (1980) Ann. Bot. 45, 225-227
9 Mc Lachlan, K. D., Elliot, D. E., De Marco, D. G., Garran, J. H. (1987) Austr. J. Agric. Res. 38, 1-13
10 Kummerova, M. (1983) Scripta Fac. Sci. Nat. Univ. Purk. Brun. 13, 343-348
11 Reid, P. H., York, E. T. (1958) Agron. J. 50, 63-67
12 Jones, H. G., Osmond, C. B. (1973) Australian J. Biol. Sci. 26,15-24

INFLUENCE OF MINERAL NUTRITION ON THE CONTENT OF
PHOTOSYNTHETIC PIGMENTS IN VARIOUS WHEAT CULTIVARS

MILOJE R. SARIĆ, ŽIVKO STANKOVIĆ, BORIVOJ KRSTIĆ and
SLOBODANKA ZATEZALO, Institute of Biology, University of Novi Sad,
Novi Sad, Yugoslavia

1. INTRODUCTION
It is known that numerous abiotic and biotic factors influence the
content of chlorophyll pigments. Among abiotic factors, the major role is
given to the influence of light, while the influence of elements of mineral
nutrition immediately follow. Therefore, up to now, great importance has
been given to investigations which refer to the importance of individual
elements of individual elements of mineral nutrition in the synthesis and
content of chloroplast pigments (1, 2, 3, 4). Since the chlorophyll molecule
contains nitrogen and magnesium in its structure, their influence is
regarded as dominant on the content of chlorophyll. It is proved that
certain elements have specific influence on the structure of chloroplasts
too, and this certainlly conditions their influence on the content of pigments
in them. Finally, it should be emphasized that the obtained results are,from
time to time, contradictory which can be interpreted by unequal conditions
under which experiments were performed, mainly the concentration of
elements in the nutritive medium and the genetic specificity of the plant
model, as well as their ontogenic development.
Therefore, we wanted to examine the influence of certain combinations
of N, P and K in three wheat cultivars, on the content of chloroplast
pigments leaving, all other conditions constant during the growth of plants.

2. METHODS AND TECHNIQUE OF WORK
In the greenhouse, under optimal temperature conditions and soil
humidity, three wheat cultivars were grown: Novosadska rana 2, Jugoslavija
and Žitnica. The given cultivars differed among each other geneticaly, but
were almost the same in their ontogenic development. Combinations of
nutrition were the following: control (without the use of N, P and K), the
usage of individual elements, that is, fertilizer N, P, K and double
combinations NP, NK and PK and finally, the usage of all three elements in
growing doses (NPK, $(NPK)_2$ and $(NPK)_3$) but with equal ratio's. In the
stage of earing, in the last two leaves (flag leaf and the one next to it),
the content of chlorophyll pigments was determined, by an acetone
solution according to the method of Wettstein (1957).

3. RESULTS AND DISCUSSION
Chlorophyll a (Fig. 1) On the average, regardless to the cultivar,

M. Baltscheffsky (ed.), Current Research in Photosynthesis, Vol. IV, 879–882.
© 1990 *Kluwer Academic Publishers. Printed in the Netherlands.*

the smallest content of chlorophyll **a** was found in individual use of P and K, then PK and in the control. A significantly higher content was found in combination in which N was used. By the usage of all three elements, the content of chlorophyll **a** increases with the increase of their concentration in the substratum. The same relations were obtained in the examined cultivars. On the average, regardless to the combination nutrients, significant differences between cultivars were not traced. Although, in certain combination of mineral nutrition, differences between cultivars were significant. Cultivar Žitnica has demonstrated a better effect when using N and K, while cultivar Jugoslavija by the influence of P.

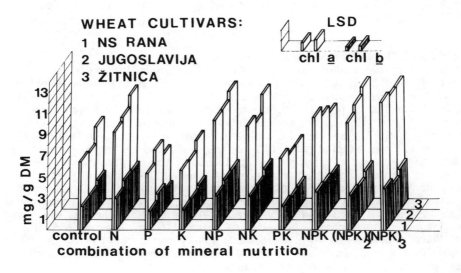

Figure 1.Content of chlorophyll **a** and **b** in three wheat cultivars depending on different combination of mineral nutrition

Chlorophyll b (Fig. 1) Mineral nutrition has also had influence on the content of chlorophyll **b.** Although, according to highly significant differences, there were only two groups: without and with the usage of N. It is characteristic that differences between nutritive combinations did not exist where N was added no matter of its combination. The same tendencies were obtained for individual examined cultivars. On the average, regardless to the nutritive combinations, cultivar Žitnica had a significantly higher content of chlorophyll **b** than the other two cultivars. It should be emphasized that in certain variants of nutrition, a significant difference existed between cultivars. Cultivar Žitnica had a significantly higher content of chlorophyll **b** under more favourable conditions of nutrition than the other two cultivars, especially by the use of N and K, while cultivar Jugoslavija had reacted much better to the use of P than the other two cultivars.

The content of chlorophyll a+b (Fig. 2) The total content of chlorophyll **(a+b)** also had the same tendencies as their individual contents.

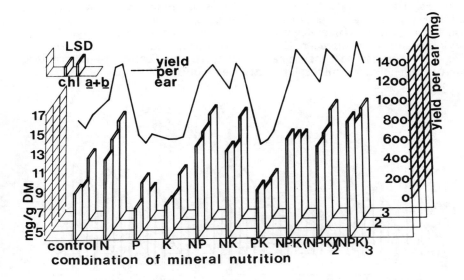

Figure 2. Content of chlorophyll **a+b** in three wheat cultivars depending on different combination of mineral nutrition

a : b chlorophyll ratio The ratio had varied depending on the mineral nutrition more than on the cultivar. In optimum conditions of nutrition, especially by usage of all three elements **a:b** ratio was higher,particulary in cultivar Jugoslavija. Although, by the use of N only, **a:b** ratio in this cultivar was the smallest. In general, ratio's are smaller under less favourable conditions of mineral nutrition.

Carotenoids (Fig. 3) The smallest content of carotenoids was obtained in all variants of nutrition in which N was not present and among these variants of nutrition there were no significant differences. Although, by the use of N, the content of carotenoids had significantly increased, especially by using medium and small doses of NPK between which, a significant difference was obtained. In the examined cultivars, the same tendency was traced although, between means in cultivars differences were not significant as well as the content of chlorophyll. Cultivar Žitnica had a better reaction to N and K than the other two cultivars while Jugoslavija reacted better to P.

4. CONCLUSION

The obtained results have shown that the content of chloroplast pigments had been different depending on the combinations of N, P, and K. Nitrogen has demonstrated a dominant significance in all cultivars. Although, there were definite cultivar specificity in relation to the pigment content by certain combinations of mineral nutrition.

Cultivar Žitnica had reacted stronger on the use of nitrogen in comparison to other two cultivars, and cultivar Jugoslavija on the use of phosphours. The content of chloroplast pigments might be an axceptable parametar for nitrogen plants needs. The automatically multiscanners measuring at any technical level may be used in an estimation for supplying plants with nitrogen (5, 6, 7). Also, it should be emphasized that kernel yield per ear had the same tendency as the content of chloroplast pigments depending on mineral nutrition as well.

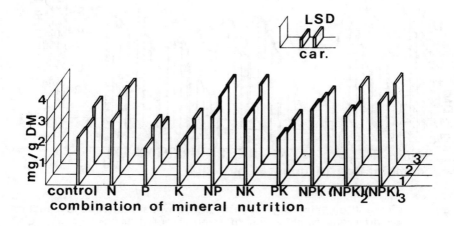

Figure 3. Content of chlorophyll **carotenoids** in three wheat cultivars on different combination of mineral nutrition

Acknowledgement. - These investigations are an integral part of the Project P-620, supported by J. B. Yugoslavia-USA

REFERENCES

1 Repka, J. (1986) Funkcia mineralych živin v regulacii fotosyntezy a rastu rastlin. Vidavateistvo SAV Veda, p. 187
2 Natr, L., Apel, P., Vialova, S. (1984) Biol. Plant. 28 (6),433-439
3 Pušnjak, L.F. (1987) in Mineralnoe Pitanie i produktivnost rastenii, 178-185, Naukova dumka, Kiev
4 Osman, A. M., Goodman, P. J., Cooper, J. P. (1977) Photosynthetica 11, 66-75
5 Baker, M. E. (1975) Adv. Argon. 27, 271-304
6 Richardson, A. J., Everitt, J. H. and Gausman, H. W. (1983) Remote Sensing Environ. 13, 179-184
7 O'Neill, E. J., Batey, T. and Crosser, M. S. (1984) Plant and soil 77, 315-326

DORSIVENTRALITY OF THE PHOTOSYNTHETIC-LIGHT RESPONSE IN NATURALLY
OCCURRING C_3 DICOTS

T.A. DAY, E.H. DeLUCIA[*], and W.K. SMITH[**]   *Department of
Plant Biology, University of Illinois, Urbana, Illinois 61801 USA,
**Department of Botany, University of Wyoming, Laramie, Wyoming 82071
USA

1. INTRODUCTION
     The photosynthetic response to irradiance is central to
comparative ecophysiology, yet our understanding of the natural light
environment on both leaf surfaces and the function of leaves as
light-harvesting organs is limited. In practice ecophysiologists
treat leaves as cosine-corrected light sensors, and photosynthetic
measurements are generally made with leaves oriented perpendicular to
incident irradiation. This is clearly not how most leaves function in
natural light regimes. Diurnal and seasonal changes in solar angle
coupled with variation in leaf orientation can result in substantial
irradiance on the abaxial (bottom) as well as adaxial (top) leaf
surface. This is especially true for species that have more vertical
leaf orientation.
     The few studies available for agronomic and native plants
indicate that leaves may be functionally bilateral or unilateral in
their ability to process light [1,2,3]. Photosynthetic rates are not
necessarily the same when leaves are illuminated on the adaxial versus
abaxial surface. The ecological significance of this asymmetry is
illustrated by the extreme case of a vertical east-west leaf. This
type of leaf receives equal daily irradiance on both leaf surfaces[4],
thus lower light harvesting capacity by the abaxial surface would
result in a substantial reduction in daily carbon gain. In this
preliminary study we compared the photosynthetic response to incident
irradiance for three native species that characterize the extremes in
leaf orientation and light environment.

2. METHODS
     Three common subalpine species were selected: Mahonia repens,
Rumex densiflorus and Populus tremuloides. Mahonia repens is a low
stature understory shrub with horizontal foliage. Rumex densiflorus
and Populus tremuloides, an open-growing herb and tree, respectively,
have primarily vertical leaf orientation. Plants grew in an
Artemisia-dominated forest opening and in the adjacent understory of
a dense stand of Pinus contorta at ca. 300 m in the Medicine Bow
Mountains, Wyoming. The forest opening and understory were selected

M. Baltscheffsky (ed.), Current Research in Photosynthesis, Vol. IV, 883–886.

as representative high and low irradiance habitat, respectively.
    Leaf angle (degrees from horizontal) and azimuth were measured
for all leaves on 10 plants of each species (4 for P. tremuloides) in
the open and understory habitat, except for Rumex densiflorus which
did not occur in the understory. The azimuths for Populus tremuloides
and Mahonia repens were random, and Rumex densiflorus had a slight
east-west orientation. The photosynthetic response to irradiance
incident on the adaxial or abaxial leaf surface was measured in situ
using a closed IR gas analysis system (LiCor LI-6200). Photosynthetic
measurements were made in the forest opening where light striking
foliage could be reduced with shade cloth. The ad- or abaxial leaf
surface was oriented perpendicular to the sun during the gas exchange
measurement, and the leaf surface opposite from the sun was shaded.
Three light-response curves were measured for each species and
representative data are presented.

3. RESULTS AND DISCUSSION

    For species that occurred in both light environments leaf angle
was considerably steeper in the open versus understory (Fig. 1). Mean
leaf angle for Populus tremuloides in the open and understory were
58.2° and 37.9°, respectively, and 33.9° and 16.9°, respectively, for
Mahonia repens. Rumex densiflorus did not grow in shaded habitats.
    Vertically oriented leaves of Populus tremuloides were
symmetrical with regard to photosynthetic light utilization (Fig. 2).
Net photosynthesis and conductance were the same regardless of
direction of illumination. In contrast, below irradiances of 1000
μmol m^{-2} s^{-1} leaves of Mahonia repens had markedly reduced
photosynthetic rates when illuminated on the abaxial surface (Fig. 3).
At high irradiances, however, photosynthesis became similar when
illuminated on the ad- or abaxial leaf surface. Light direction
appeared to have no effect on conductance for M. repens. Net
photosynthesis and leaf conductance were reduced at all irradiances
when leaves of Rumex densiflorus were illuminated on the abaxial
surface (Fig. 4). This was surprising given the vertical leaf
orientation for this species (mean leaf angle = 71.3°).
    Our preliminary results suggest at least three possibilities
regarding the functional symmetry of leaves. 1) Vertically oriented
leaves of Populus tremuloides are functionally bilateral, thus
contributing to maximum light capture as solar angle varies during the
day. 2) Horizontally oriented leaves of Mahonia repens are
functionally uilateral at low irradiances but become symmetrical as
irradiance increases, whereas 3) foliage of Rumex densiflorus is
functionally unilateral at all irradiances. Unilateral function of
understory leaves of M. repens may be associated with structural and
biochemical attributes that maximize photosynthesis at low irradiance.
    The physiological and anatomical basis of functional symmetry are
currently under investigation. Low stomatal conductance when leaves
of Rumex densiflorus were illuminated on the abaxial surface suggest
stomata on this surface may have greater sensitivity to light[5,6,7],
despite vertical leaf orientation, and thus limit gas exchange.
Photosynthetic asymmetry of M. repens, however, appears to be under

non-stomatal control and may result from differences in absorptance
and transmitance of ad- and abaxial tissues[8,9,10,11]. The effect of
leaf anatomy and pigment distribution on light penetration in foliage
is being investigated with recently developed fiber optic probes[11,12].

Traditional comparisons of photosynthetic performance of whole
leaves over the past thirty to forty years have relied almost
exclusively on data generated by leaves with adaxial sides oriented
perpendicularly to the light source. Projected area, or approximately
1/2 of total area for broad leaves, is typically used to express
photosynthesis on leaf area basis. Rarely has photosynthesis been
measured or estimated for natural leaf orientations in the field,
except for extrapolations using the cosine law for incident
direct-bean sunlight. The importance of sunlight at acute angles or
on abaxial leaf surfaces has not been evaluated. This is despite the
fact that many species become photosynthetically active at well below
perpendicular light levels, especially in more shaded habitats of
shaded positions in the canopy. Until the symmetry of the
photosynthetic response to light is understood, accurate estimates of
photosynthetic performance under natural conditions will not be
possible.

REFERENCES
1. Syvertsen, J.P. and Cunningham, G.L. (1979) Photosynthetica 13,
   399-405
2. Knapp, A.K., Vogelmann, T.C., McClean, T.M. and Smith, W.K.
   (1988) Oecologia 74, 62-67
3. Terashima, I. and Takenaka, A. (1986) in Biological Control of
   Photosynthesis (Marcelle, R., Clijsters, H., Van Poucke, M.,
   eds.), pp. 219-230, Martinus Nijhoff, Dordrecht
4. Novel, P.S. (1980) Oecologia 44, 160-166
5. Waggoner, P.E. (1965) Crop Sci. 5, 291-297
6. Turner, N.C. (1970) New Phytol. 69, 647-653
7. Smith, W.K. (1981) Oecologia 48, 353-359
8. Wolley, J.T. (1971) Plant Physiol. 47, 656-662
9. Terashima, I. and Inoue, Y. (1985) Plant Cell Physiol. 26, 63-75
10. Terashima, I. and Saeki, T. (1983) Plant Cell Physiol. 24,
    1493-1501
11. Vogelmann, T.C., Knapp, A.K., McClean, T.M. and Smith, W.K.
    (1988) Physiol. Plant. 72, 623-630
12. Vogelmann, T.C. and Bjorn, L.O. (1984) Plant Physiol. 60, 361-368

FIGURE LEGENDS
Figure 1. Frequency distributions of leaf angles (0° = horizontal) for
Populus tremuloides, Mahonia repens, and Rumex densiflorus.
Measurements were made on plants growing in the forest understory
(filled bars) or in an adjacent opening (striped bars).
Figures 2, 3, and 4. The response of net photosynthesis (A), stomatal
conductance (gL), and intercellular CO_2 concentration (C_i) to incident
irradiance when leaves were illuminated on the adaxial (solid line) or
abaxial (dashed line) leaf surface. Figure 2: Populus tremuloides;
Figure 3: Mahonia repens; Figure 4: Rumex densiflorus.

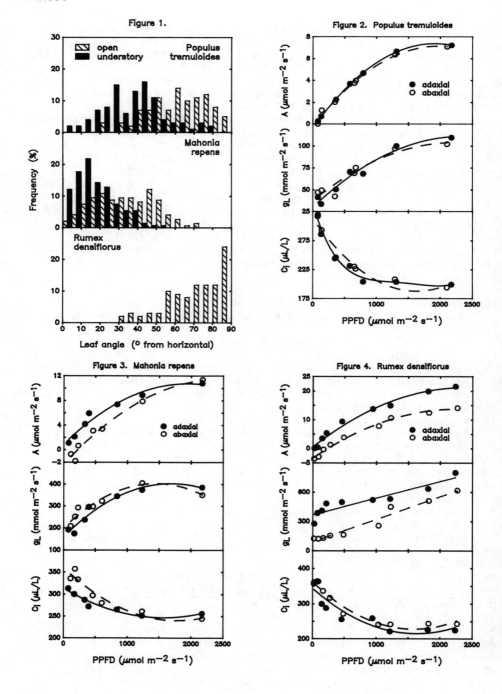

Figure 1.

Figure 2. Populus tremuloides

Figure 3. Mahonia repens

Figure 4. Rumex densiflorus

THE EFFECT OF CULTIVAR AND LEAF AGE ON THE CONTENT OF
PHOTOSYNTHETIC PIGMENTS IN WHEAT

ŽIVKO STANKOVIĆ, MILOJE R. SARIĆ, BORIVOJ KRSTIĆ and
SLOBODANKA ZATEZALO, Institute of Biology, University of Novi Sad,
21000 Novi Sad, Yugoslavia

1. INTRODUCTION

The synthesis of photosynthetic pigments is genetically controled (1).
The amount of pigment synthesied depends upon environmental conditions
(2) and the ontogenetic development of the plant (3, 4). The ratios and
stability of the pigments in photosynthetic tissue are also important in the
photosynthetic production of organic matter and the total yield (1, 5).
This paper shows the results obtained from the examination of the content
of chlorophylls **a** and **b**, and total carotenoids present in 15 wheat
cultivars which were grown in field conditions.

2. MATERIALS AND METHODS

The fifteen wheat cultivars: 1) Novosadska rana 2, 2) Partizanka,
3) Balkan, 4) Osječanka, 5) Super zlatna, 6) Kragujevačka 56, 7) Skopljanka,
8) Jugoslavija, 9) Posavka, 10) Zvezda, 11) Mačvanka, 12) Baranjka,
13) Zelengora, 14) Nizija and 15) Žitnica were grown in an experimental
field at the Insitute of Field and Vegetable Crops, Faculty of Agriculture
in Novi Sad, under optimum conditions of mineral nutrition and
agrotechniques. Selected cultivars were characterized by equal vegetation
periods. The largest difference between cultivars in the earing stage being
approcimately three days. The pigment content was determined
spectrophotometrically during the earing and milk-waxy maturity stages in
I, II and III leaves (number I indicates the flag leaf), after extraction in
absolute acetone (6).

3. RESULTS AND DISCUSSION

Tables 1, 2 and 3 show that there were significant differences between
the content of chlorophyll **a**, **b** and the total carotenoids amongst the
individual wheat cultivars. The content of the pigments varied more, on
average, during the milk-waxy maturity stage than during the earing stage.
So, on average, the variation factor for all of the leaves for chlorophyll **a**
amounted to 1.2 in the earing stage and 1.5 in the milk-waxy maturity
stage, for chlorophyll **b** 1.3 and 1.7, and for the carotenoids 1.2 and 1.4.
The content of all the pigments present in the analysed leaves I, II and
III were compared. Leaf II contained the highest content of pigments while

M. Baltscheffsky (ed.), Current Research in Photosynthesis, Vol. IV, 887–890.
© 1990 *Kluwer Academic Publishers. Printed in the Netherlands.*

TABLE 1. Chlophyll **a** content (mg.g^{-1}) dry mass)
Cultivar numbers refer to those given in Materials and Methods.

Cultivar No.	Earing Leaves			Milk-waxy maturity Leaves		
	I	II	III	I	II	III
1	9.29	9.47	9.91	7.52	7.71	5.11
2	8.55	8.72	7.22	7.95	7.70	6.71
3	8.81	9.37	7.62	6.70	8.15	5.89
4	10.23	11.32	5.97	8.24	9.48	6.07
5	8.24	9.16	9.57	7.62	7.69	5.09
6	9.84	10.00	6.93	8.34	9.70	7.23
7	9.48	10.55	9.36	8.74	8.04	5.78
8	9.73	9.99	8.53	8.24	8.68	7.02
9	8.53	9.82	7.96	8.15	9.62	5.98
10	8.40	9.55	7.50	7.46	8.30	6.24
11	8.87	9.99	8.40	7.54	7.56	5.13
12	9.07	9.29	9.10	7.66	7.92	7.20
13	8.63	9.58	8.97	8.28	8.24	6.26
14	9.04	8.83	6.30	6.40	6.40	3.43
15	8.65	9.42	8.81	5.76	6.97	5.76
LSD 0.05 / 0.01	0.75 / 1.00			0.72 / 1.97		

TABLE 2. Chorophyll **b** content (mg.g^{-1} dr mass)

Cultivar No.	Earing Leaves			Milk-waxy maturity Leaves		
	I	II	III	I	II	III
1	2.58	3.84	3.46	2.43	2.65	1.85
2	2.58	2.85	2.61	2.56	2.69	2.45
3	2.63	3.06	2.55	2.46	3.32	2.76
4	2.88	3.49	2.03	3.12	4.43	3.06
5	2.48	3.19	3.88	2.29	2.68	1.88
6	3.06	4.01	3.06	2.49	3.27	2.75
7	2.92	3.67	3.53	2.95	3.02	2.29
8	2.65	3.06	2.84	2.64	3.06	2.69
9	2.68	3.43	3.02	3.12	4.10	2.95
10	2.53	3.44	3.11	2.15	2.81	2.21
11	2.21	2.96	3.04	2.39	2.85	2.10
12	2.49	3.20	3.88	2.40	2.73	2.62
13	2.58	3.28	4.06	2.66	2.72	2.10
14	2.60	3.09	3.68	1.99	2.48	1.32
15	2.60	2.96	3.68	1.82	2.41	2.11
LSD 0.05 / 0.01	0.46 / 0.62			0.30 / 0.41		

TABLE 3. The total carotenoids content (mg.g^{-1} dry mass)
Cultivar numbers refer to those given in Material and Methods.

Cultivar No.	Earing Leaves			Milk-waxy maturity Leaves		
	I	II	III	I	II	III
1	3.40	3.03	3.21	2.72	2.82	1.90
2	3.06	3.11	2.64	2.91	2.59	2.48
3	3.19	3.30	2.69	2.33	2.67	1.85
4	3.19	4.02	2.15	2.72	3.02	1.91
5	2.92	2.98	3.06	2.70	2.66	1.78
6	3.56	3.51	2.53	3.06	3.33	2.52
7	3.49	3.70	3.22	3.06	2.89	2.10
8	3.57	3.58	3.06	3.04	3.12	2.56
9	3.13	3.43	2.76	2.76	3.16	1.93
10	3.04	3.36	2.55	2.79	3.02	2.33
11	3.33	3.64	3.06	2.85	2.70	1.82
12	3.33	3.18	3.08	2.78	2.73	2.49
13	3.04	3.16	2.81	3.00	2.84	2.22
14	3.20	3.03	2.20	2.44	2.33	0.38
15	3.11	3.23	2.97	2.09	2.48	2.08
LSD 0.05	0.32			0.29		
0.01	0.43			0.39		

TABLE 4. Chlorophyll **a/b** ratios

Cultivar No.	Earing Leaves			Milk-waxy maturity Leaves		
	I	II	III	I	II	III
1	3.6	2.5	2.9	3.1	2.9	2.8
2	3.4	3.1	2.8	3.1	2.9	2.7
3	3.4	3.1	3.0	2.7	2.4	2.1
4	3.6	3.2	2.9	2.6	2.1	2.0
5	3.3	2.9	2.5	3.3	2.9	2.7
6	3.2	2.5	2.3	3.3	3.0	2.6
7	3.2	2.9	2.6	3.0	2.7	2.5
8	3.7	3.3	3.0	3.1	2.8	2.6
9	3.2	2.9	2.6	2.6	2.4	2.0
10	3.3	2.8	2.4	3.5	3.0	2.8
11	4.0	3.4	2.8	3.1	2.6	2.4
12	3.6	2.9	2.3	3.2	2.9	2.9
13	3.3	2.9	2.2	3.1	3.0	3.0
14	3.5	2.9	2.5	3.2	2.6	2.6
15	3.3	3.2	2.4	3.2	2.9	2.7
Average	3.4	2.9	2.6	3.1	2.7	2.5

leaf III contained the lowest content, with leaf I intermediate. But, in certain cultivars, particularly during the earing stage. The content of pigments was approximately the same in all of the leaves. The chlorophyll **a/b** ratio is shown in table 4. From this table it can be seen that, in general, the highest chlorophyll **a/b** ratio was found in the youngest leaf (leaf I), and the lowest ratio was found in the oldest leaf (leaf III) during both stages of the investigation.

Our previous results (7), performed with plants grown under controled conditions, also indicate that the content of pigments differ significantly in the stated cultivars but those differences were not so prominent.

A large scale of variation in the content of pigments within leaves in certain cultivars indicates that the stability, or rate of degradation, differes. This can be attributed to a genetic specificity. From the results of the chlorophyll **a/b** ratio it can be concluded that chlorophyll **b** is more stable than chlorophyll **a** (7), but this could be a result of the photosynthetic apparatus becaming adapted to a lower light intensity (5, 8).

Acknowledgement. - These investigations are an integral part of the Project P-620, supported by J. B. Yugoslavia-USA

REFERENCES

1 Nasyrov, Yu, S. (1978) Ann. Rev. Plant Physiol. 29, 215-237
2 Silaeva, A. M. (1978) Struktura hloroplastov i faktori sredi. Naukova dumka, Kiev, p. 203
3 Gautam, O. P. (1963) Indian J. Plant Physiol. 1, 44-59
4 Herzog, H. and Stamp, P. (1982) Zeit. Pflanzenzuchtung 88, 127-136
5 Anderson, J. M. (1986) Ann. Rev. Plant Physiol. 37, 93-136
6 Wettstein, D. (1957) Exptl. Cell Res. 12, 427-433
7 Sarić, M. R., Stanković, Ž. S. and Krstić, B. (1987) in Progress in Photosynthesis Research (Biggins, J., ed.) vol. 4, pp. 395-398, Martinus Nijhoff Publishers, Dordrecht
8 Lichtenthaler, H. K. (1984) In Advances in Photosynthesis Research (Sybesma, C., ed.) vol. 4, pp. 241-244, Martinus Nijhoff/Dr W. Junk Publishers, the Hague

EFFECT ON NET CARBON ASSIMILATION AND ALLOCATION OF ASSIMILATES
UNDER ELEVATED CO_2 IN MUNGBEAN
Division of Plant Physiology, Indian Agricultural Research Institute,
New Delhi 110012, India

U.K. SENGUPTA AND ARUNA SHARMA

1.   INTRODUCTION
      Leaves in present atmosphere are not able to produce maximum
rates of photosynthesis due to limiting ambient CO_2 levels. With
increase in CO_2 concentration, photosynthesis increases until some
other factor, such as light becomes limiting (1). Linear increase
in photosynthesis has been shown in many crop species when concentrations is increased in the range of 0-600 ul l^{-1} CO_2 (2,3,4). The
response of individual leaves, at various positions and age or at
different growth stages of the plant, to increased CO_2 may not be
alike. Also, increased photosynthesis and thereby increased carbohydrate synthesis would affect carbon allocation and partitioning in
the source leaves. The present study reports photosynthesis and
translocation of assimilates as affected by CO_2 enrichment, in leaves
of mungbean, at different leaf positions and age.

2.   PROCEDURE
2.1   Materials and methods
      A mungbean cultivar was grown in pots under optimal conditions.
The 12 day old 2nd leaf (LPI-2) at vegetative stage, 12 day old
5th leaf (LPI-5I) and 18 day old 5th leaf (LPI-5II) at reproductive stage were treated for 5 h, with ambient air, 600 and 900
ul l^{-1} CO_2. One sink organ, a third leaf in case of LPI-2 and
axillary pod in case of LPI-5I and II, were retained and the
rest of the leaves and tip were removed 24 h before CO_2 enrichment. CO_2 air mixture of desired concentration was generated
by breathing into a 20 litre jar and diluting the mixture by
ambient air using vacuum pump. A steady state open system was
developed and the enriched CO_2 was passed through the leaf
enclosed in a chamber under a photon flux density of 1000 uE m^{-2}
s^{-1} at 30°C. NCER was measured for a period of 5 h by IRGA.
RuBP carboxylase activity was measured after 5 h enrichment.
Carbon allocation and partitioning was studied by introducing a
pulse of $^{14}CO_2$ generated from 10 u Ci $NaH^{14}CO_3$ at the beginning
of enrichment. Plants were kept in pot house after 5 h of
enrichment and harvested after 24 h. Samples were extracted as
described elsewhere (5). Total sugar and starch content of the
leaves were estimated by Somogyi's (6) method after hydrolysis
according to McCready et al'(7).

M. Baltscheffsky (ed.), Current Research in Photosynthesis, Vol. IV, 891–894.
© 1990 *Kluwer Academic Publishers. Printed in the Netherlands.*

3. RESULTS AND DISCUSSION

3.1 In ambient air, 2nd leaf (LPI-2) showed higher Net Carbon dioxide Exchange Rate (NCER) as well as RuBP carboxylase activity than the 5th leaf (LPI-5I) of the same age, while the 12 day old leaf had higher NCER and RuBP carboxylase activity than the 18 day old 5th leaf (LPI-5II). On enrichment with 600 and 900 ul l^{-1} CO_2 2nd leaf showed a much higher NCER than the 5th leaf of same age. Similarly, the younger 5th leaf showed more response than the older 5th leaf. It appears that leaf position as well as leaf age, both affect the response to elevated CO_2 but the leaf position is more effective of the two (Table 1).

TABLE 1: Effect of CO_2 enrichment on NCER and RuBP carboxylase activity

LPI	NCER (mg CO_2 dm^{-2} h^{-1})			RuBP carboxylase (CPM mg $protein^{-1}min^{-1}$ $1x10^5$)		
	2	5(I)	5(II)	2	5(I)	5(II)
CO_2conc (ul l^{-1})						
300	11.80	10.20	7.2	4.20	3.60	3.60
600	30.60	18.70	15.10	4.20	3.50	3.40
900	47.30	27.20	20.70	4.20	3.60	3.43

3.2 CO_2 enrichment did not show any increase in RuBP carboxylase activity in the treated leaf extracts at any of the stages, indicating that CO_2 has no regulatory effect on this enzyme and increased value of NCER are due to higher carboxylating efficiency in vivo due to increased availability of CO_2 as a substrate.

3.3 Comparison of carbon allocation and partitioning of allocated carbon into starch and sugars in the source leaves showed that leaf at 5th node was a better exporter (54%) than the leaf at 2nd node (32%) of same age (Table 2). This allocation of fixed carbon to the source leaf at a particular leaf position may be influenced by the nature of the sink and the sink demand. Sinks in these two cases were functionally and metabolically distinct.

3.4 At elevated CO_2, incorporation of label led carbon into the source leaf was higher. The partitioning of allocated carbon on the basis of actual label present in the source leaf showed that the amount of carbon retained in the fed leaf enriched with CO_2 was almost equal to that found in leaf under normal air in all the three stages. All the extra carbon incorporated as a result of CO_2 enrichment was translocated out of the source leaf, within 24 h. This suggests that carbon allocation to the source leaf is predetermined genetically and temporary external manipulation of carbohydrate pool does not affect this allocation.

TABLE 2: Effect of CO_2 enrichment on translocation of photosynthates and partitioning into starch and sugars

CO_2 concentration (ul 1^{-1})	300	600	900
		LPI -2	
Total ^{14}C in plants (dps)	98213	167618	209251
^{14}C retained in fed leaf (dps)	66784	67215	68216
	(68.0%)	(40.1%)	(32.6%)
^{14}C translocated (dps)	31428	100403	141035
	(32.0%)	(59.9%)	(67.4%)
Total sugars (mg g^{-1} fr wt)	7.92	12.12	12.98
Starch (" ")	20.20	21.60	23.60
		LPI-5(I)	
Total ^{14}C in plants	88210	158010	205586
^{14}C retained in fed leaf (dps)	40576	43611	45229
	(46.0%)	(27.6%)	(22.0%)
^{14}C translocated (dps)	47634	114399	160357
	(54.0%)	(72.4%)	(78.0%)
Total sugars (mg g^{-1} fr wt)	13.30	15.65	16.72
Starch (" ")	26.21	28.30	30.84
		LPI-5(II)	
Total ^{14}C in plants (dps)	74215	106711	107062
^{14}C retained in fed leaf (dps)	38294	107611	107062
	(51.6%)	(35.0%)	(30.5%)
^{14}C translocated (dps)	35921	69948	65843
	(48.4%)	(65.0%)	(61.5%)
Total sugars (mg g^{-1} fr wt)	12.65	13.09	14.12
Starch (" ")	24.15	25.24	30.12

3.5 There was substantial increase in sugars but not in starch content in 600 ul 1^{-1}. Under 900 ul 1^{-1} CO_2 sugar values were comparable to those seen under 600 ul 1^{-1} CO_2 but starch content increased (Table 2). It appears that there was greater synthesis of sucrose in 600 ul 1^{-1} CO_2 while in 900 ul 1^{-1} CO_2 sucrose synthesis might have reached a saturation and triose phosphate was diverted towards starch synthesis. Thus all extra carbon fixed is exported out either as current photosynthate or during dark mobilisation if starch is synthesised. Thus CO_2 enrichment increased NCER and carbohydrate pool but not the carbon allocated to the source leaf within one diurnal cycle. Sugar-starch partitioning was affected and depended on the amount of extra carbon synthesised.

REFERENCES
1 Tolbert, N.E. and Zelitch, I. (1983) In CO_2 and Plants (Lemon, E.R., ed.), pp 21-64, Westview Press Inc. Colorado
2 Brun, W.A. and Cooper, R.L. (1967) Crop Sci. 7, 451-454
3 Bhagsari, A.S. and Brown, R.H. (1976) Peanut Sci.3, 10-14

4   Sengupta, U.K. (1988) Curr. Sci. 57, 145-146
5   Sharma,Aruna., Reddy, K.J., Sirohi, G.S. and Sengupta, U.K. (1981) Indian J. Exp. Biol. 19, 250-252
6   Somogyi, M. (1952) J. Biol. Chem.195, 19-23
7   McCready, R.M., Guggloz, J., Silviera, V.and Owen, H.S. (1950) Anal. Chem.22,1156-1158

$\delta^{13}C$ ANALYSIS TO APPROACH THE MECHANISM OF VARIETAL DIFFERENCE OF PHOTOSYNTHETIC RATE IN RICE PLANTS

H.SASAKI, M.SAMEJIMA*, AND R.ISHII
(Faculty of Agriculture, The University of Tokyo, Bunkyo-ku, Tokyo 113, Japan; *National Institute of Agrobiological Resources, Tsukuba, Ibaraki 305, Japan)

INTRODUCTION

We have been so far conducting the research of varietal difference of apparent photosynthetic rate per unit leaf area (APS) in rice plants, aiming to clarify the mechanism of APS determination. APS is limited by the following two CO_2 diffusion resistances, stomatal (Rs), and mesophyll (Rm) one. However, the process limited by Rm involves so many different kinds of physical and chemical processes. The purpose of this paper is to divide Rm further to two resistances. One is the physical CO_2 diffusion resistance from the stomatal cavity to the CO_2 fixation site in the chroloplasts, and the other is the chemical reaction resistance at the site of ribulose-1,5-bisphosphate carboxylase/oxygenase (RuBisCO).

In the recent years, measurement of isotope composition ($\delta^{13}C$) in the leaf was attempted by several researchers, and it has been found that it can provide us with very useful informations to approach the mechanism in the difference of APS. $^{13}CO_2$, which exists in the atmospheric air, is discriminated in the process of CO_2 diffusion and fixation in a leaf, resulting in relative decrease of ^{13}C in the photosynthetic products. $\delta^{13}C$ is different with plant species, as between C3, C4, and CAM plants(1). It has recently been found that $\delta^{13}C$ is correlated with the ratio of intercellular and atmospheric CO_2 concentrations, and consequently with water use efficiency(2)(3)(4). Furthermore, the correlation of $\delta^{13}C$ with the dry matter and grain yields was observed(4)(5)(6). These findings suggest that $\delta^{13}C$ analysis can contribute to the approach to the mechanism of APS determination.

MATERIAL AND METHODS

Plant materials: Thirty one genetically related varieties of rice plants (Oryza sativa L.), which were bred in Japan in the last 100 years, were used for the experiment. The plants were grown in the paddy field by the normal cultivating methods.

Measurement of APS: APS and transpiration rate were simultaneously measured with the gas exchange rate measuring system, which was constructed by ourselves, and installed in a van-type car for the field use. A clip-typed leaf chamber was extended by teflon tubing from the

M. Baltscheffsky (ed.), Current Research in Photosynthesis, Vol. IV, 895–898.
© 1990 Kluwer Academic Publishers. Printed in the Netherlands.

car to the measuring spot. About 2 minutes was required for one measurement. The measurement of APS was conducted at the maximum tillering time on the uppermost fully expanded leaf, and at the heading, the ripening, and the harvesting time on the flag leaves. All the measurements were made under full sunlight.

Soluble sugars extraction: In order to obtain the values of $\delta^{13}C$ in the sugars formed at the time of APS measurement, the leaves for sugars extraction were sampled by the following procedure. The leaves at the same position as the APS measuring leaves, were covered with a black cloth in the field at 14:00 h, and they were exposed to the sun at 9:00 h in the next morning. The leaves were sampled at 12:00 h, from those plants, and served for the extraction of sugars. By this procedure, we could expect that the extracted sugars were de novo products. The sugars were extracted according to the method of Brugnoli et al. with a little modification(2).

Assay of carbon isotope discrimination and calculation of transportation resistance: The carbon isotope discrimination (Δ) is expressed by Eq.1, according to Hubick et al.(8).

$$\Delta = \frac{\delta a - \delta p}{1 + \delta p} \tag{1}$$

where δa and δp are the isotope compositions in the atmospheric air (= $- 8\%_o$), and in the photosynthetic product, sugars, respectively(7). On the other hand, Δ is also expressed from the gradients of CO_2 concentration between the two places in the process of CO_2 flux, by the following modified Farquhar's equation(3).

$$\Delta \times 10^3 = 4.4 \times \frac{[CO_2]atm - [CO_2]stc}{[CO_2]atm}$$
$$+ (1.1 + 0.7) \times \frac{[CO_2]stc - [CO_2]cht}{[CO_2]atm}$$
$$+ 27 \times \frac{[CO_2]cht}{[CO_2]atm} \tag{2}$$

where, [CO2]atm, [CO2]stc, and [CO2]cht are the CO_2 concentrations in the atmospheric air, in the stomatal cavity, and in the chloroplasts, respectively. The figures of 4.4, (1.1 + 0.7), and 27 are the discrimination coefficients of ^{13}C for stomatal passage, for the transfer from stomatal cavity to fixation sites, and for the CO_2 fixation, respectively. [CO2]atm was maintained constant as 340 $\mu l/l$, [CO2]stc was calculated from APS and transpiration rate. δp was determined with the extracted sugars by a mass spectrometer (MAT-250). From these values, we can calculate [CO2]cht by the above equations. Finally, transportation resistance of CO_2 (Rr) was obtained from APS, [CO2]stc, and [CO2]cht according to Ohm's law, and carboxylation resistance (Rc) was obtained by the subtraction of Rr from Rm.

RESULTS AND DISCUSSION
    Table 1 shows the APS, Rs, and Rm in the first three columns. If we calculate the relative magnitude of each resistance against total

TABLE 1. APS, Rs, Rm, Rr and Rc of the different varieties at the maximum tillering stage.

Variety	APS $mgCO_2/dm^2/h$	Rs(Rs/Rt) sec/cm	Rm sec/cm	Rr(Rr/Rt) sec/cm	Rc(Rc/Rt) sec/cm
Aikoku	38.1	1.62(.28)	4.01	0.45(.07)	3.56(.63)
Kameno-o	26.1	2.49(.30)	5.75	0.53(.06)	5.22(.63)
Ginbohzu	26.4	2.28(.28)	5.86	0.57(.07)	5.29(.64)
Asahi	28.9	1.86(.24)	5.68	1.00(.13)	4.68(.62)
Johshu	37.3	1.70(.29)	4.06	----(---)	----(---)
Sen'itsu	30.1	2.02(.28)	5.12	0.50(.07)	4.62(.64)
Rikuu 132	36.2	1.85(.30)	4.11	0.73(.12)	3.38(.56)
Tohsan 38	34.1	1.50(.23)	4.90	0.61(.09)	4.29(.67)
Kinki 33	27.8	2.05(.26)	5.75	----(---)	----(---)
Fujisaka 5	38.0	1.59(.27)	4.15	0.67(.11)	3.48(.60)
Nohrin 1	34.5	1.92(.30)	4.36	0.55(.08)	3.81(.60)
Nohrin 6	24.3	1.98(.22)	6.89	1.10(.12)	5.78(.65)
Nohrin 8	25.5	2.02(.23)	6.42	1.31(.15)	5.11(.60)
Nohrin 17	38.3	1.80(.31)	3.87	0.42(.07)	3.44(.60)
Nohrin 22	27.1	2.67(.33)	5.32	----(---)	----(---)
Nohrin 29	27.1	1.86(.23)	6.14	0.94(.11)	5.19(.64)
Hohnenwase	37.2	1.98(.34)	3.81	0.57(.09)	3.23(.55)
Koshihikari	35.2	2.03(.33)	4.09	0.27(.04)	3.82(.62)
Manryoh	23.0	2.06(.21)	7.39	1.27(.13)	6.12(.64)
Fujiminori	35.5	1.89(.31)	4.20	0.49(.08)	3.70(.60)
Nipponbare	23.9	1.91(.20)	7.18	----(---)	----(---)
Sasanishiki	39.4	2.03(.37)	3.42	0.26(.04)	3.16(.57)
Reimei	39.0	1.76(.31)	3.77	0.46(.08)	3.31(.59)
Toyonishiki	37.0	2.26(.38)	3.56	0.01(.00)	3.54(.60)
Kiyonishiki	38.2	1.68(.29)	4.02	0.58(.10)	3.43(.60)
Akihikari	39.8	1.70(.31)	3.73	0.30(.05)	3.42(.62)
Hatsunishiki	36.3	1.82(.30)	4.14	0.46(.07)	3.67(.61)
Sasashigure	35.8	1.98(.32)	4.03	0.42(.06)	3.61(.60)
Akinishiki	33.3	1.73(.26)	4.77	0.34(.05)	4.42(.67)
Oh-u 239	31.5	1.51(.21)	5.46	1.22(.17)	4.24(.60)
Sasaminori	37.7	1.71(.29)	4.01	0.66(.11)	3.35(.58)

resistance (Rt) , Rs, and Rm occupied 20-37, and 63-80 %, respectively, showing relatively large contribution of Rm to APS. To divide Rm into two resistances as mentioned before, the transportation (Rr), and carboxylation resistance (Rc) of CO_2 were calculated, according to the method described in MATERIL AND METHODS, and shown in the fourth and fifth columns of Table 1. Rr varied from 0.01 to 1.31 sec/cm, which occupied less than 17 % in Rt, while Rc occupied as much as 55 to 67 %. However, the values of Rr increased with the advance of plant growth; 0.40 to 2.05 sec/cm in the ripening stage, and 1.27 to 3.25 sec/cm in the harvesting stage, although their percentages against Rt were still unchanged at the level of less than 18 %. In these calculations, the following two points should be noticed. Firstly, the effects of dark respiration and photorespiration were ignored, because it was reported by Evans et al. that there were practically no effects of them on the values of Δ (8). Secondly, we took the value of 1.8×10^{-3} as the coefficient of discrimination of ^{13}C in the process between the stomatal cavity and the RuBisCO sites, although there is an argument for this value(9)(10).

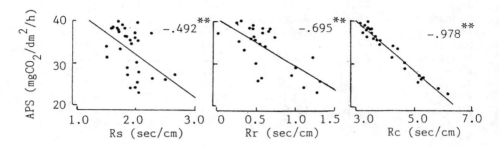

FIGURE 1. Correlation of APS with Rs, Rr, and Rc at the maximum tillering stage. **; significant at the 0.01 provability level.

Evans et al. also tried to calculate Rr in wheat plants, and they obtained the value of about 0.9 sec/cm(11). This value is almost in the same range as those in this paper. Here, it could be concluded that the main limiting step of APS should be CO_2 fixation process. However, we have to take account of the fact that Rr showed such a high negative correlation coefficient as -.695** with APS (Fig.1). This will suggest that Rr is also a factor determining the varietal difference of APS, although its contribution is not so much as Rs or Rc.

REFERENCES
1 Troughton, J.H. and Card, K.A. (1975) Planta 123, 185-190
2 Brugnoli, E., Hubick, K.T., von Cammerer, S., Wong, S.C. and Farquhar, G.D. (1988) Plant Physiol. 88, 1418-1424
3 Farquhar, G.D. and Richards, R.A. (1984) Aust. J. Plant Physiol. 11, 539-552
4 Hubick, K.T., Shorter, R. and Farquhar, G.D. (1988) Aust. J. Plant Physiol. 15, 799-813
5 Condon, A.G., Richards, R.A. and Farquhar, G.D. (1987) Crop Sci. 27, 996-1001
6 Wright, G.C., Hubick, K.T. and Farquhar, G.D. (1988) Aust. J. Plant Physiol. 15, 815-825
7 Hubick, K.T., Farquhar, G.D. and Shorter, R. (1986) Aust. J. Plant Physiol. 13, 803-816
8 Evans, J.R., Sharkey, T.D., Berry, J.A. and Farquhar, G.D. (1986) Aust. J. Plant Physiol. 13, 281-292
9 O'Leary, M.H. (1984) J. Phys. Chem. 88, 823-825
10 Vogel, J.C., Grootes, P.M. and Mook, W.G. (1970) Z. Physik. 230, 225-238
11 Evans, J.R. (1983) Plant Physiol. 72, 297-302

A NEW OPEN GAS-FLOW SYSTEM CONFIGURATION FOR MEASUREMENT OF PHOTOSYNTHETIC CO_2 RESPONSE CURVE

L. NÁTR, R. HÁK*and V. KOTVALT

*Dept. Plant. Physiol.,Fac. Sci. Charles Univ., Vinična 5,
CS-128 44, Prague 2, Czechoslovakia
*Dept. Plant Physiol., Res. Inst. Crop Prod., Ruzyně 507,
CS-161 06 Prague 6, Czechoslovakia*

INTRODUCTION

Gasometric methods employing an infra-red gas analyser (IRGA) have been widely used for determining photosynthetic CO_2 uptake, both in the laboratory and in the field. Generally, gas-exchange measuring systems may be classified into 3 basic types: closed, semi-closed and open (for more detailed description see [1] and [2]). A serious methodical objection to a closed system is that since CO_2 concentration continuously changes, steady-state observation cannot be obtained. On the other hand, this fact can be exploited in dynamic studies and modelling of photosynthesis [3]. Open system measurement have recently been commonly used, especially in studies based on the assumption of a steady-state condition [4].

MATERIALS AND METHODS

A new system has been developed (Fig.1) for easy and rapid measurement of the CO_2 dependence (P_N-CO_2 curve) of net photosynthetic rate. The continuous and precisely determined changes in CO_2 concentration in the air entering the assimilation cuvette are brought about by a mixing chamber. It is filled with air of c_0 concentration of CO_2 and at a precisely defined time $t=0$ a constant flow of the air with c_1 concentration enters the chamber. Assuring good mixing (i.e. supposing homogenous conditions inside the mixing chamber), the CO_2 concentration $c(t)$ coming out gradually changes from c_0 to c_1 according to an exponential function of time.

A glass cylinder with an inner volume (V) of 30 dm^3 was used as a mixing chamber with a flow rate of 120 dm^3 h^{-1}. Pure nitrogen and bottled air of 320 $cm^3(CO_2)m^{-3}$ were used in the first experiment (Fig.2), CO_2-free air and air artificially enriched with CO_2 [5] were used in the second experiment (Fig.3). Photosynthesis measurements were carried out with primary barley leaves (cca 30 cm^2 exposed leaf area) under conditions of quantum irradiance of 1000 μmol m^{-2} s^{-1}(PAR), a temperature of 25 C and a flow rate through the leaf cuvette of 30 dm^3 h^{-1}.

Acknowledgement: We thanks to Dr. **Z. Vedral** for construction of A/D convertor and writing the main data handling programm.

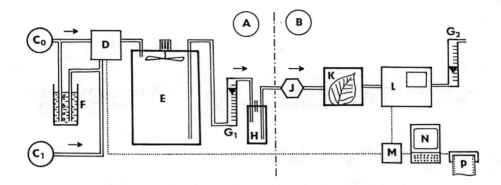

Fig. 1. The new input gas-mixing circuit (**A**) and conventional open gas-flow circuit (**B**): c_0 and c_1 are two gas stream channels with different CO_2 concentration, c_0 and c_1, respectively. The channels can be switched by two way sequential valve (**D**), so the mixing chamber (**E**) can be filled either by c_0 or c_1 concentration. The mixing chamber (**E**), functioning like the first-order-kinetics flow reactor, was realised by using a glass cylinder with perspex top sealed by silicon rubber. A fan with 12 V DC motor is used to stirr the air inside the cylinder. **F** is overflow pressure regulator, G_1 and G_2 are the float flow meters. Overflow chamber (**H**) permits different and mutually independent flows through the mixing chamber and leaf cuvette regarding to to pressure and flow rate conditions. In open gas-flow system (**B**) **J** denotes membrane pump, **K** is steel-perspex leaf cuvette and **L** is absolute-mode infra-red gas analyser (URAS 3G, Hartmann und Braun, F.R.G.). Data acquisition and data handling unit consists of an analog/digital convertor (**M**), microcomputer with disk drive units (**N**) and printer (**P**).

RESULTS AND DISCUSSION

The performance of the measuring circuit is shown in Fig. 2, which demonstrates the good reproducibility of the exponential CO_2-time function. Fig. 3 shows a comparison of data output with and without a leaf sample inside the system. Only primary data output is shown without processing and without estimating final P_N-CO_2 curve parameters The results cannot be obtained using simple open or closed-system formulae because of the non-steady-state process of photosynthesis and complicated processes of gas mixing and dilution in the circuit, hence measurement requires computer data acquisition and processing [Kotvalt, Sailerová and Janáček, in preparation]. A model derived for non-steady-state measurement of photosynthetic CO_2 uptake can be used for data evaluation [6].

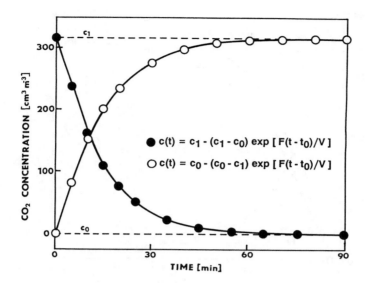

Fig. 2. Performance of the new-gas mixing equipment (shown in Fig. 1, part A). The change of CO_2 concentration measured in an open circuit (without leaf sample) follows exponential time function after switching from c_0 to c_1 and vice versa. Bottled nitrogen was used as CO_2-free air c_0 and bottled air of 320 cm^3 (CO_2) m^{-3} as c_1 air mixture. Each point represents mean of 3 values, the confidence intervals (95%) are smaller then circle symbols.

CONCLUSIONS

The new configuration of the gasometric circuit combines the advantages both of classical open and closed systems while avoiding their failings.

1. Using an open system with its typical advantages, P_N-CO_2 curves can be measured as simply and quickly as in a closed system.

2. The configuration of the system makes it possible to obtain P_N-CO_2 curves in both directions, upwards and downwards (i.e. from low CO_2 to high CO_2 concentration and vice versa).

3. The rate of CO_2 concentration changes may be regulated by the volume of the mixing chamber, by the flow rate or by the difference between c_0 and c_1 concentrations. In addition, the changes are independent of the measuring circuit arrangement, leaf cuvette volume and net CO_2 uptake rate itself.

4. The simplicity and versatility of the new open system configuration promises new approches, especially in studies of the transient processes in CO_2 exchange of the leaf.

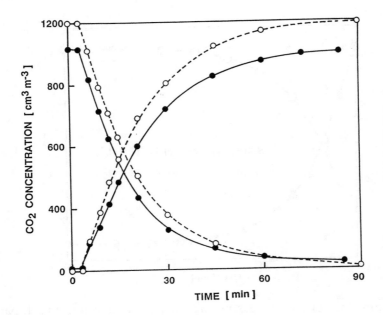

Fig. 3. Demonstration of CO_2 concentration changes in the new open system (shown in Fig.1) with leaf sample (barley, 1000 μmol m^{-2} s^{-1} PAR, 25°C - full symbols and line) in comparison with behaviour of the system without leaves (open symbols and broken line). CO_2-free air and CO_2-enriched air (according to [5]) were used as c_0 and c_1 mixtures (see Fig. 2). Each point represents the mean from 3 repetition, the confidence intervals (95%) are smaller than circle symbols.

REFERENCES
[1] **Šesták, Z., Čatský, J., Jarvis, P.G.** (1971) Plant Photosynthetic Production. Manual of Methods, Dr. W. Junk Publ., The Hague.
[2] **Sharkey, T.D.** (1989) in: Gases in Plant and Microbial Cells (Linskens, H.F., Jackson, J.F., eds.), pp. 73-93, Springer Verlag, Berlin, New York etc.
[3] **Kaitala, V., Hari, V., Vapaavuori, E., Salminen, R.** (1982), Ann. Bot. 50, 385-396.
[4] **von Caemmerer, S, Farquhar, G.D.** (1981) Planta 153, 376-387.
[5] **Apel, P.** (1966) Flora(A) 157, 330-333.
[6] **Palovský, R., Hák, R.** (1989) Photosynthetica 23, in press.

IMPAIRMENT OF CHLOROPLAST DEVELOPMENT AND SINK STRENGTH
BY BLOCKADE OF LIGHT IN CHLOROEMBRYOS OF *CYAMOPSIS
TETRAGONOLOBA* (L.) TAUB.

P. Kaladharan* and M. Vivekanandan, Department of Botany,
Bharathidasan University, Tiruchirapalli 620 024, INDIA
*Scientist S-1, Central Marine Fisheries Research Institute,
Cochin 31, INDIA

ABSTRACT
In many members of Fabaceae synthesis of chloroplast pigments takes place even when the embryo is deep inside the
fruit. Blockade of light totally etiolated the embryos of
developing *Cyamopsis* fruits upto 16-18 days after anthesis
(DAA), whereas the pigments of the mature embryos, when
shaded, were not significantly affected. Upon illumination,
resynthesis of green pigments by etiolated embryos occurred
both *in vivo* and *in vitro* more significantly during the
early stages of growth of the embryos (upto 18 DAA). Shading
of developing fruits at different growth stages of embryos,
reduced the growth of sink. The results are discussed in
relation to the importance of light on embryo greening and
dry matter production.

1.   INTRODUCTION
     'Chloroembryos' has been the subject of much curiosity
in recent times with regard to their location, development
and function (Ryczkowski and Szewczyk, 1975; Yakovlev and
Zhukova, 1980; Palanisamy and Vivekanandan, 1986; Kaladharan
and Vivekanandan, 1989). The present report explains the
vital role of photosynthetically active radiant energy on
the formation of chloroplast pigments and sink strength in
the developing chloroembryos of *Cyamopsis tetragonoloba* (L.)
Taub, although they reside deep inside the endosperm, seed
coat and pod wall.

2.   MATERIALS AND METHODS
     From the field-grown plants of *Cyamopsis tetragonoloba*
Cv. Nowbagar, flowers were tagged on the day of anthesis.
Developing pods were grouped into four stages based on the
DAA, viz., stage I: embryos of 8-10 DAA; stage II: 16-18
DAA; stage III: 26-28 DAA; stage IV: 36-38 DAA. Developing
intact pods of *Cyamopsis* were blocked from the radiant
energy by shading half the pod with light proof dark

M. Baltscheffsky (ed.), Current Research in Photosynthesis, Vol. IV, 903–906.
© 1990 *Kluwer Academic Publishers. Printed in the Netherlands.*

polythene sheet in the form of sleeves, while other half was
covered with sleeves of clear polythene sheet as control.
The shaded pods were left intact continuously for 8 days
sufficient to etiolate the embryos. Removal of sleeves
from the etiolated pods was done to facilitate *in vivo* regreening, and *in vitro* regreening was induced by exposing
the detached etiolated embryos to continuous white light of
150 W m^{-2} for 12 h in Petri-plates lined with Whatman No.1
paper wetted with sterile water. Chloroplast pigments were
determined by the method of Arnon (1949). Sink strength was
expressed as mg dry matter per gram fresh weight of embryos.

3. RESULTS AND DISCUSSION
    Formation of etiolated embryos as a result of shading
of fruits clearly proves that certain amount of radiant
energy passes through the fruit wall, seed coat and endosperm, and finally reaches the embryo confirming that chlorophyll synthesis in the embryos is by light-dependent pathway (Kaladharan and Vivekanandan, 1983). Further, blockade
of light in developing fruits of *Cyamopsis* containing green
embryos led to the breakdown of chlorophylls *a* and *b* in the
embryos (Table 1) suggesting that a continuous supply of
radiant energy is essential for maintenance of chloroplast
pigments. Breakdown of chloroplast pigments in mature
embryos (stage IV) is a slow process, whereas in younger
ones (stages I-III) the process is faster, which may be
attributed to faster turnover of pigments.

Table 1. Effect of shading of growing fruits of *Cyamopsis*
          tetragonoloba at various stages of growth on chlo-
          rophyll content of the embryos. (After 10 days of
          shading, the embryos were isolated from shaded and
          unshaded parts of the fruits and chlorophyll
          content was determined.)

Embryo		Chl. *a*	Chl. *b*	Carotenoids	Chl.*a/b*
		(μg gfw^{-1})			
Stage I	BS	205.54	106.27	104.86	1.93
	AS	4.62	3.55	15.94	1.30
Stage II	BS	534.80	252.01	211.40	2.12
	AS	12.70	9.12	12.09	1.39
Stage III	BS	411.57	271.11	210.17	1.52
	AS	31.04	25.37	19.04	1.22
Stage IV	BS	308.94	152.02	112.00	2.03
	AS	180.58	90.98	65.00	1.98

BS = Before Shading; AS = After Shading.

Removal of mask (dark sleeves) and reillumination of
the fruits to natural light resulted in regreening of the
etiolated embryos (Table 2) suggesting a normal light-induced
development of chloroplasts from etioplasts as regulated by
phytochrome (Lichtenthaler and Buschmann, 1978). Uponir-
radiation, more chloroplast pigments were formed in etiolated
stage III than stage II embryos. It appears as though the
embryos of *Cyamopsis* need to reach a certain stage of development to acquire optimum level of certain factor(s) in
light before they can be induced to regreen upon illumination.

Table 2.   Resynthesis of chloroplast pigments in *vivo* and
           in vitro by the embryos of *Cyamopsis tetragonoloba*
           shaded at different stages of growth

	Stage II		Stage III	
	Total chl.	Total carotenoids	Total chl.	Total carotenoids
	(μg gfw^{-1})			
Shaded embryos *In vivo*	8.17	15.94	21.82	12.09
5 days re-exposure *In vitro*	164.50	55.22	312.02	97.20
12 h after re-exposure	35.91	11.43	110.27	18.17

As shown in Fig. 1, shading young fruits of *Cyamopsis*
just a day after anthesis for 8 days caused 65% reduction
in drymatter of etiolated embryos than the green embryos of
the same half of the fruit covered by clear polythene sheet.
However, the etiolated part of fruitwall showed only 13%
reduction. Similarly in stage II fruits reduction was 40%
and 9% respectively in the embryos and fruitwall, and reduction of dry matter in the embryos of stages III and IV
was 16% and 7% respectively without causing significant reduction in dry matter of fruit wall. Prevention of shading
of fruit during early stages of development resulted in considerable reduction in dry matter of the embryos with only
marginal reduction in fruitwalls. Similarly Hole and Scott
(1981) observed that shading of pea fruits reduced yield in
terms of number and size of seeds per fruit by 24% over the
unshaded control.

Prevention of radiant energy in the black polythene-
shaded part of the fruit probably resulted in limited synthesis of assimilates in the embryo, whereas the other half
covered by clear polythene sheet under normal radiant
energy synthesized their own assimilates by the self-sustai-
ned chloroembryos (Kaladharan and Vivekanandan, 1989). It

can be surmised from the
present study that through
the chloroembryos are
deeply situated in the
fruit, they are capable
of utilising the diffused
light for chloroplast pigments formation and
synthesis of assimilates
suggesting the possibility
of a role for embryonal
chlorophyll in photosyn-
thesis as evidenced drastic
dry matter reduction in the
embryos of the shaded
fruits, whereas that of
fruit wall was least
affected.

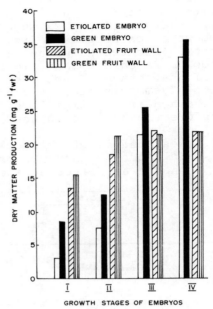

Fig. 1. Effect of shading of
fruits of *Cyamopsis*
on dry matter produc-
tion of fruit wall and
embryo

REFERENCES
1 Ryczkowski, M. and Szewczyk, E. (1975) Z. Planzen-
physiol. 75, 175-180
2 Yakovlev, M. S. and Ahukdva, G. Ya. (1980) Bot. Notiser,
133, 323-336
3 Palanisamy, K. and Vivekanandan, M. (1986) Plant Physiol.
123, 395-399
4 Kaladharan, P. and Vivekanandan, M. (1989) Plant Physiol.
(in press)
5 Arnon, D. I. (1949) Plant Physiol. 24, 1-15
6 Hole, C. C. and Scott, P. A. (1981) Ann. Bot. 48,
827-835

ESTIMATION OF THE LIGHT LIMITATION OF PHOTOSYNTHESIS

HAMLYN G JONES, AFRC INSTIUE OF HORTICULTURAL RESEARCH, WELLESBOURNE, WARWICK CV35 9EF, UNITED KINGDOM, AND ANGELO MASSACCI, CNR, VIA SALARIA KM 29,300, 00016 MONTEROTONDO SCALO, ITALY.

1. INTRODUCTION

Photosynthesis depends on a supply of light energy as well as a supply of the main substrate (CO_2) and of phosphate. The light energy is required to provide ATP and reducing power; therefore a light limitation of photosynthesis could occur either if irradiances are low, or if light harvesting is inefficient as a result, for example, of low levels of chlorophyll, or if there are deficiencies in the electron-transport system or its coupling to ATP or NADPH production. Localisation of photosynthetic limitations in any situation will be an important step in breeding better, more productive plants.

General approaches for describing and quantifying photosynthetic limitations have been reviewed by Jones (1). Perhaps the most useful is based on sensitivity analysis where the contribution of any component (x) to assimilation (A) is given by dA/dx. In its most general form, the process x could be anything from stomatal conductance (g_l), rubisco activity, or electron transport capacity, to a resource such as light or CO_2. It is convenient to normalise the sensitivity to obtain a relative limitation (L_x) as (dA/A)/(dx/x). This approach is formally equivalent to the metabolic control theory approach introduced by Kacser and Burns (2) where the relative limitation for any step in the photosynthetic pathway equates to the flux control coefficient (using the later terminology of Kacser and Porteous (3)). It is important to note that in this approach one can use controls which are either intrinsic to the system (eg g_l) or extrinsic (eg light). In this paper we consider ways in which one can estimate the light limitation to photosynthesis.

2. THEORETICAL APPROACHES
2.1 From light response curves

The most straightforward approach is to define an absolute sensitivity to light, $L_{l1} = dA/dI$, which at low light is the quantum yield, and is a measure of the efficiency of light utilisation by the photosynthetic apparatus.

M. Baltscheffsky (ed.), Current Research in Photosynthesis, Vol. IV, 907–910.
© 1990 *Kluwer Academic Publishers. Printed in the Netherlands.*

An alternative approach to the use of light response curves is to normalise this measure (1), and to define the 'light limitation' (L_{l2}) as:

$$L_{l2} \quad = \quad (dA/A)/(dI/I) \tag{1}$$

This limitation varies from unity when assimilation is proportional to irradiance (I) (and is therefore assumed to be entirely light limited), to zero at light saturation. This approach, which is similar to one previously proposed (4), includes embedded within it a component of the CO_2 limitation, because changing irradiance can alter either or both of g_l and A and hence affects the intracellular CO_2 partial pressure (c_i), which itself affects A. Therefore, although this method may give a true measure of the overall response to I, it is for many purposes useful to dissect this limitation further to obtain components related to the electron transport limitation and to CO_2 diffusion. It could therefore be possible to rewrite equation (1), which implicitly has ambient CO_2 concentration (c_a) maintained constant to one where c_i is maintained constant:

$$L_{l3} \quad = \quad (\partial A/A)/(\partial I/I) \tag{2}$$
$$c_i = const$$

Alternatively one could define a partial sensitivity with g_l maintained constant.

Other problems with the sensitivity approach occur when, as is usual, the light response curve does not cross both axes at zero. Furthermore, a linear photosynthetic response to light does not necessarily imply that the availability of light is the sole limiting factor, as two photosynthetic response curves with different quantum yields may both have L_l equal to one (Fig. 1).

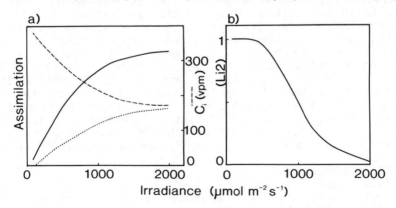

FIGURE 1. Light response curve for photosynthesis (solid), L_{l2} and the corresponding changes in c_i (dashed line). The response for a leaf with a very low quantum yield is shown dotted.

2.2. From assimilation bursts

An alternative approach might be to define the limitation in terms of the size of photosynthetic burst obtained in response to a brief flash of saturating light:

$$L_{i4} = \text{size of assimilation burst} \qquad (2)$$

In this analysis a large burst indicates a large light limitation, while no burst indicates light saturation. In principle, this approach might become less dependent on stomatal conductance with shorter flashes, and it avoids changes in stomatal aperture in response to the irradiance. It does, however, only give a relative measure of light limitation, as the absolute magnitude of the burst depends on many factors.

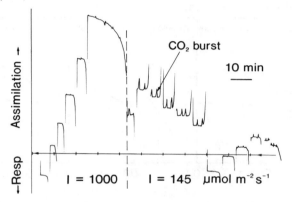

FIGURE 2. Assimilation burst size for different irradiances (145 or 1000 $\mu mol\ m^{-2}\ s^{-1}$) and different CO_2 concentrations.

2.3. From chlorophyll fluorescence quenching

Schreiber and Bilger (5) proposed the use of photochemical quenching (q_Q) as a measure of the light limitation of photosynthesis (L_{i5}), but this is affected by the degree to which molecular oxygen can act as an electron acceptor and might be expected to lead to anomalous results. The use of the non-photochemical component (q_N) of chlorophyll-a fluorescence quenching, may however, be more reliable as the components of q_N tend to increase as the light limitation drops. As the capacity to use ATP and reducing power declines, for example because CO_2 availability is limiting, there is a tendency for an increased thylakoid pH gradient and increased high energy-state quenching. Other responses such as photoinhibition and state transitions that occur in the presence of excess light also have a similar effect. All these effects tend to reduce the size of the fluorescence peak in response to a saturating flash, so peak height (which is approximately inversely related to q_N, e.g. 6) and could be used as an estimate of light limitation (L_{i6}).

3. MATERIALS AND METHODS

Gas-exchange (CO_2 and water vapour) and modulated fluorescence (using a Hansatech MFS1 system) were measured simultaneously using a porometer system (6). Response curves relating A to CO_2 and to light were obtained for outdoor-grown apple leaves in September 1987, and saturating pulses of light (approx. 2 s at 3000 μmol m^{-2} s^{-1}) were given at intervals to estimate the height of the fluorescence peak and the burst of assimilation. Measurements were made when an apparent steady state had been reached at between 5-10 min after changing conditions.

4. RESULTS AND DISCUSSION

The calculated dependence on irradiance and ambient CO_2 concentration of three measures of light limitation (L_{i6}, L_{i4} and L_{i2}) is shown in Fig. 3 for unstressed apple leaves. There are significant differences between these measures.

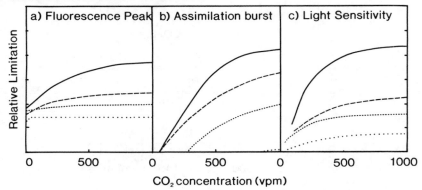

FIGURE 3. Comparison of estimates of light limitation obtained from the three approaches : a) fluorescence peak, b) burst of photosynthesis, c) light sensitivity.

The large errors in estimation of q_Q for the present data mean that it is not possible to evaluate L_{i5} as a measure of light limitation in this case. Of the methods in Fig. 3, the flourescence peak height is apparently the least sensitive measure, but this is partly related to the fact that there is a residual fluorescence peak at light saturation. It was not possible to obtain an estimate of the sensitivity analysis approach based on the sensitivity to light at constant c_i (L_{i3}), though one would expect such a correction to increase the calculated L_i.

REFERENCES
1 Jones, H.G.(1985) Plant, Cell & Env. 8, 94-104
2 Kacser, H. and Burns, J.A. (1973) Symp. Soc. Exp. Biol. 27, 65-107
3 Kacser, H. and Porteous, J.V. (1987) TIBS 12, 7-13
4 Dietz, K-J. (1986) Planta 167, 260-263
5 Schreiber, U. and Bilger, W. (1987) In Plant response to stress (Tenhunen, J.D. et al.,eds.) pp.27-53, Springer-Verlag, Berlin
6 Jones, H.G. and Massacci, A. (1989) in preparation

THE EFFICIENCY OF UTILIZATION OF PHOTOSYNTHETICALLY ACTIVE RADIATION
AND DISTRIBUTION OF ASSIMILATES IN SUNFLOWER (Helianthus annuus L.)

Zvonimir Sakač, Tomislav Ćupina, Institute of Field & Vegetable Crops,
University of Novi Sad, 21000 Novi Sad, Yugoslavia

1.   INTRODUCTION
    Photosynthetic basis of increased sunflower yield implies:
a) maximum absorption of light energy by the foliage, b) efficient conversion of the absorbed light energy in photosynthetic products, and
c) distribution of photoassimilates in economically valuable acceptors
(1). The most direct effect of solar radiation on the vegetative growth
and development sunflower plants is exercised via the quantity of light
energy absorbed by the crop (2,3). The amount of energy stored by sunflower plant in the form of chemically bound energy (0.2-5% of the global radiation) depends on the leaf area index (3,4).
    The aim of this investigation was to study the formation of leaf
area, dynamics of dry matter accumulation in leaves, and the distribution of total dry mass per plant and chemically bound energy in different plant parts in order to evaluate the efficiency of utilization of
photosynthetically active radiation in the course of growth and development of Novi Sad sunflower genotypes. Further aims were to study the
dynamics of accumulation of assimilates in the course of vegetative
growth and development and the transformation of carbohydrates in sunflower seed.

2.   PROCEDURE
2.1. Material and methods
    The experimental objects were 6 sunflower genotypes: the hybrid
NS-H-26 RM and its parent components CMS-Ha-V-8931-3-4 (female ♀)   and
RHA-58 (male ♂) and the hybrid NS-H-43 and its parent components
OCMS-22 (female ♀) and RHA-SNRF (male ♂). Grown in the stand of 45,000
plants per ha, they were scored for photosynthetically active radiation
(PAR, influx and reflected radiation) above and inside the stand. Each
day from May 15 to September 20, hourly (MJ m^{-2} $hour^{-1}$) and daily (MJ
m^{-2} day^{-1}) sums of absorbed energy were measured.
    Chemical energy of dry mass in the entire plant and individual
plant parts was measured calorimetrically (IKA-Calorimeter C-400).
    The efficiency of utilization of PAR was calculated as the quotient
of chemically bound energy in dry mass (in MJ) and absorbed photosynthetically active radiation (in MJ).
    Qualitative and quantitative analyses of carbohydrates were carri-
ed out on a HPLC system OPTILAB 5931 with a HSRI detector, protein content by Kjeldal, and oil content by an NMR analyzer.

M. Baltscheffsky (ed.), Current Research in Photosynthesis, Vol. IV, 911–914.
© 1990 *Kluwer Academic Publishers. Printed in the Netherlands.*

3.   RESULTS AND DISCUSSION
     Daily sums of PAR   (Figure 1) were obtained as the difference of
global and reflected radiation above the stand, adding up the hourly
energy sums. The average value of global radiation at the level of top
leaves was 17.914 MJ m^{-2} day^{-1}. The sums of PAR for individual phases
of development were obtained by adding up the daily sums of photosynthetically active radiation.

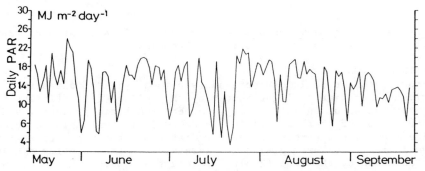

Fig. 1. Daily sums of photosynthetically active radiation (PAR, MJ m^{-2}
        day^{-1}) in sunflower crop at the experimental field Rimski Šan-
        čevi, Novi Sad.

     All genotypes reached maximum values of chemically bound energy
per leaf mass at the stage of flowering (Figure 2). Two underlying processes were observed in NS-H-26 RM: an accelerated accumulation of total chemically bound energy in dry mass of leaves, due to a dynamic
forming of leaf area, i.e., a dynamic accumulation of dry matter in
leaves, and reduction of average specific energy value of dry matter in
leaves (J g^{-1} of dry matter in leaves) to the stages of flowering and
seed filling.These processes seem to indicate that a major part of high
energy assimilates is rapidly transported from the foliage in the head
in the course of flowering and subsequent phases.
     The same phenomenon was observed in the parent lines, but on a
lower scale. Reductions in average specific energy of dry matter in leaves tended to stop at the stage of flowering the both parent components.
Nevertheless, the female line, although behind the male line in the dynamics of accumulation of dry matter in leaves, accumulated much more
chemically bound energy of dry mass in leaves due to a higher average
specific energy value of dry mass in its leaves.
     In the hybrid NS-H-43, the situation was somewhat changed. After
reaching the maximum values at the stage of flowering, the content of
chemically bound energy remained rather stady in the hybrid and its
male component. However, large drops in the average values of specific
chemically bound energy of dry matter in leaves had been registered at
the stage of intensive development of leaf area.
     To assess the efficiency of utilizing PAR in the forming of sunflo-
wer biomass, chemically bound energy of dry matter in plant was measured calorimetrically. The efficiency, expressed in percentage in relation to PAR, as well as the dynamics of accumulation of dry mass per

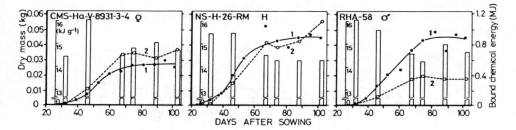

Fig. 2. Dry mass (1) and bound chemical energy (2) of leaves of sunflower hybrid NS-H-26 RM and its parental lines in different stages of plant development. Bars represent average bound chemical
energy in kJ per g dry mass of leaves.

plant parts and the entire plant are shown in Figure 3. Both hybrids
we·e more efficient users of PAR than their parents on account of larger area. While the hybrids reached the maximum values of the efficiency of utilization of PAR at the stage of grain filling, the male lines
reached the maximum values at the stage of flowering.

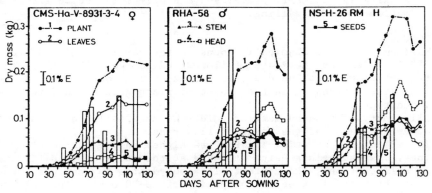

Fig. 3. Efficiency of PAR utilisation (bars) and dynamics of dry mass
accumulation and distribution among plant organs of sunflower
hybrid NS-H-26 RM and its parental lines in the course of plant
development.

The dominant carbohydrate forms transported from the leaves (mostly the top ones) were glucose, fructose and sucrose. High percentages
of carbohydrates, especially of sucrose, in seeds were recorded in all
genotypes at the beginning of the stage of seed filling (Figure 4). The
content of carbohydrates, especially of sucrose, kept dropping sharply
throughout the course of seed filling and conclusive with physiological
maturity while the contents of oil and proteins kept increasing. During
the period studied, the hybrids had higher percentages of sucrose and
rafinose within the total soluble carbohydrates than their parent components.

Throughout the period studied, the specific energy of dry mass in seeds increased in proportion with the percentage of oil in dry mass in seeds (bars in Figure 4.)

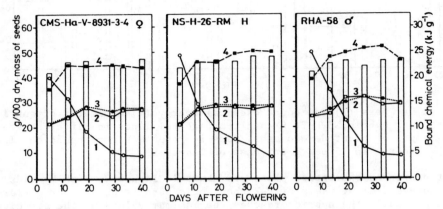

Fig. 4. Specific bound chemical energy in J per g dry mass of seeds (bars) and content of assimilates in sunflower seeds (sugars-1, total amino-acids-2, proteins-3 and oil-4) in the course of formation and seed filling.

4.   CONCLUSION

Maximum values of chemically bound energy per leaf shifted from the 10th-14th leaf at the stage of flower bud to the 20th-24th leaf at the stage of flowering. The chemically bound energy of dry mass in heads and stems kept increasing in the course of plant growth and development of all genotypes.

All genotypes reached maximum values of chemically bound energy of dry matter in leaves at the stage of flowering.

The efficiency of utilizing PAR was higher in the hybrids than in the lines, maximum values being achieved at the stage of seed filling.

In all genotypes, the content of carbohydrates in seed was reduced to 50% of the initial value in the period of 10-20 days after the stage of flowering while the contents of oil and proteins were increased proportionally. Sucrose and rafinose were prevalent carbohydrates.

REFERENCES

1. Gifford,R.M., Thorne,J.H., Hitz, W.D., Giaquinta,T., (1984) Science, 225, 801-808
2. Guiducci,M., (1988), Proceedings ot the 12th International Sunflower Conference, vol 1, 89-94
3. Marrien,A., (1986), Cahier Technique - Physiologie
4. Terbea,M., Tanase,V., Stoenescu,F.M., (1985) An.I.C.C.P.T., 52, 393-404

THE RELATION OF CHLOROPHYLL DELAYED FLUORESCENCE OF PLANT WITH PHOTOSYNTHESIS. LIGHT DEPENDENCE

V.Morgun, N.Znak, S.Doldjikov   Agricultural Inst.
Mira ave 88, Krasnoyarsk, 660049 USSR

Millisecond delayed fluorescence (DF) of PS 2 is one of delicate tools for investigation of photosynthetic energy conversion. Exponential relationship of DF with proton motive force has been shown. Also it is known that the nature of light-induced changes of DF is closely connected with development of energyzation of the thylakoids membranes (Wraight, Crofts, 1971; Evans, Crofts, 1973). In addition recently it was supposed that DP-rise of DF induction curve reflects the appearance of electric potential difference as a result of depletion of buffer capacity of thylakoids (ΔMg^{++}). Besides, during PS-decline of DF the increase of ΔpH simultaneously with Mg^{++} transport from thylakoids takes place (Grigor'ev et al., 1983; Morgun et al., 1989). In this paper the data about light-dependence of energyzation of native chloroplasts membranes, obtained by means of induction of integrated DF (time region 0,8 - 2,0 ms) is described. As objects leaves of pea, wheat, suspension of Chlorella vulgaris, Spirulina Platensis and leaves of some wild plants were used.

The logarithms of DF intensity on maximum (P) and stationary (S) levels of induction were used as indexes of energyzation of thylakoids. On fig. 1 the interrelation of ln P and ln S with energyzation is demonstrated in terms of proportionality of coupled electron transport and light-scattering with inner H^+ concentration. The indexes ln P and ln S was getting saturated with light growth, while ln S was saturated more slowly (see Fig. 2). The light curves of P/S-ratio, indicating energy consumption during induction of photosynthesis, were immonotoneous with maximum near half-saturating the photosynthesis light intensity. The removal of CO_2 abolished the ummonotone of the light the light curve of P/S-ratio (see Fig. 2) shifting it to the shape of the light curve of P/S-ratio of chloroplasts in ferricyonide-containing medium. At hight light the removal of CO_2 had no effect on the DF induction,

M. Baltscheffsky (ed.), Current Research in Photosynthesis, Vol. IV, 915–918.
© 1990 *Kluwer Academic Publishers. Printed in the Netherlands.*

but O_2-removal induced growing of S-level. Besides this O_2 removal provoked the decrease of P-level and slowed down the rate of DP-rise. The time of DP-rise got fully saturated at light intensity where P/S-ratio was maximum

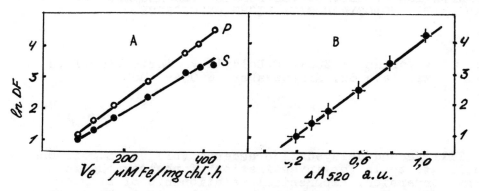

FIGURE 1. A - Interrelation of DF on P and S levels of induction and ferricyonide mediated electron transport of pea chloroplast at different light intensities. B - Interrelation of DF on S level of induction and steady-state changes of light scattering at 520 nm of pea leaf.

(see Fig. 2). In spite of this the time of DP-rise of variable fluorescence, the time of appearance of second maximum of DF (M) and steady-state kinetics of DF decay were not fully saturated at this and higher light intensities. In these conditions diuron stopped to stimulate variable fluorescence of Chlorella on P-level what implied the reduction of electron transport chain. It is possible that the decrease of P/S-ratio took place in conditions, when stationary electron transport rate was higher than the initial one and electron carriers were reduced. One may speculate that state 1 - state 2 transition is induced in these conditions.

Light curves of ln P, ln S, P/S of sun and shade plants grown at native habitats and of green and blue-green algae differed (see Fig. 3, 4). The same difference was observed between upper and lower sides of leaf (see Fig. 4). Changes of light optimum of P/S-ratio took place for Spirulina as a result of light and chromatic adaptation, and for Chlorella during light adaptation. These adaptation responses allowed to reach P/S-ratio near to maximum at light condition of growth. The process like this one has been observed for wheat DF for 4-5 days after the transition of a vegetation pot from power sunlight to weaker continuous lamp light. It is necessary to emphasize that the maximum of light curve of P/S-ratio of

plants grown at native light was wider than the one at
the continuous lamp light.

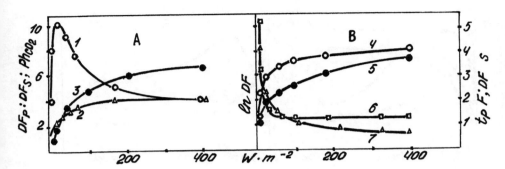

FIGURE 2. A - Light curves of DF induction levels P and
S ratio (1); the same in CO_2-free air (2) and
of CO_2 uptake (3). B - Light curves P (4) and
S (5) levels of DF induction, time of DF (6)
and of fluorescence (7) rises to P-level. All
parametres of pea leaf.

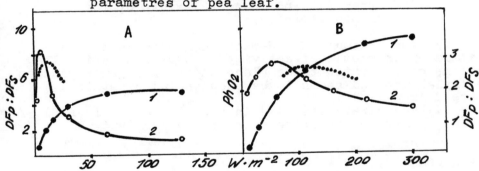

FIGURE 3. A - Light curves of O_2-evolution (1) and P/S-
ratio of DF (2) of Chlorella vulgaris.
B - The same of Spirulina platensis.
Algae were grown at white light (40 $W \cdot m^{-2}$).
Dotted lines: P/S maximum of DF of algae,
grown at 120 $W \cdot m^{-2}$.

The following conclusions have been made :
(1) The light curve of ln P indicates the growth of
energy stored as electric potentials difference during the
plastoquinone- and O_2-mediated electron transport,

(2) The light curve of ln S indicates the growth of
steady-state Δ pH during the electron flow to CO_2. At
hight light intensity the role of O_2 as ultimate electron
acceptor is increasing,

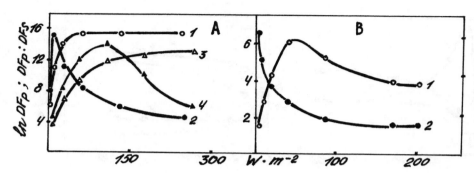

FIGURE 4. A - Light curves of ln P (1, 3) and P/S-ratio
(2, 4) of DF induction of Maianthemum bifolium
(1, 2) and Elytrigia repens (3, 4), grown at
shade and sun habitats, correspondently.
B - Light curves of P/S-ratio of DF induction
of upper (1) and lower (2) sides of leaf of
Peperomia globella.

(3) The maximum of P/S-ratio corresponds to the
maximum of energetic effectivity of photosynthesis. The
decline of P/S-ratio takes place under extra energyzation
of thylakoids and seems to be accompanied by state 1 -
state 2 transition,
(4) The parametres 1 - ln S/ln P and 1 - ln(P/S)$_{st}$/
/(P/S)$_{max}$ may characterize energetic effectivity of
photosynthesis.

REFERENCES
1 Wraight, C.A. and Crofts, A.R. (1971) Eur. J. Biochem.
19, 386-397
2 Evans, E.N. and Crofts, A.R. (1973) Biochem. et Biophys.
Acta. 292, 130-139
3 Grigor'ev, Y.S. et al. (1983) Biophysica 28, 779-783
4 Morgun, V.N. et al. (1989) Photosynthetica (in press).

INTERCEPTED IRRADIANCE LIMITS CARBON ASSIMILATION OF A COASTAL DUNE PLANT

N.W. PAMMENTER[1] and V.R. SMITH[2]. PNMRU, Department of Biology, University of Natal, Durban[1] and Department of Botany, University of the Orange Free State, Bloemfontein[2], South Africa

1. INTRODUCTION

Scaevola plumieri (L) Vahl. is a common primary coloniser of the coastal sand dunes of the east coast of southern Africa. The plant has an erect habit, up to 800mm tall, with 15 to 30 large (120 x 70mm) semi- succulent, sessile, elliptic to obovate leaves. Young leaves are orientated almost vertically with the old leaves being almost horizontal. In a recent review of the ecology of sand dune vegetation (1), the need for detailed ecophysiological studies was pointed out. This contribution reports some studies on the gas exchange characteristics of S. plumieri in the field, undertaken to identify the environmental parameters most important in controlling the rates of C assimilation.

2. MATERIALS AND METHODS

2.1. Field Site and Plant Material.

Studies were undertaken at the Mlalazi Nature Reserve (28° 58'S, 31° 47'E), 130 km north east of Durban, South Africa. Average annual rainfall and temperature for the area are approximately 1 200 mm and 22°C (I.F. Garland, personal communication). The plants studied were growing on a well established embryo dune and were estimated to be three to four years old. Measurements were made in late summer when midday temperatures can exceed 35°C and vapour pressure deficits can be as high as 2.5 kPa.

2.2. Gas Exchange Measurements.

Rates of net CO_2 assimilation (A), transpiration (E) and stomatal conductance to water vapour (g_s) were measured using portable equipment. A weighted average photosynthentic photon flux density (PPFD) incident upon each leaf was calculated by measuring the PPFD on both the shaded and unshaded portions of a leaf and estimating the relative shaded and unshaded areas. The influence of PPFD on A was measured on an unshaded leaf and varying irradiance using layers of grey shade netting. To measure the response of A to intercellular CO_2 concentration (c_i), air of high CO_2 concentration was passed from a gas cylinder through an ADC gas diluter prior to entry into the leaf cuvette. Excised stems were used in a laboratory based system that permitted the simultaneous measurement of gas exchange by each surface of the leaf independently.

M. Baltscheffsky (ed.), Current Research in Photosynthesis, Vol. IV, 919–922.

3.   RESULTS
    The data presented in this report are from the mature leaves of
a single stem measured hourly from sunrise to sunset. Correlation
analyses between A and environmental variables showed the highest
correlation coefficient between A and PPFD (R = 0.88). In the field,
light saturation of assimilation was not apparent (Fig. 1). By
integrating the areas under the diurnal time course plots of A and
PPFD, the total C assimilated and total photosynthetically active
radiation (PAR) intercepted by each leaf was calculated. Total C
assimilated by a leaf over the course of a day was linearly related to
the total PAR intercepted (Fig. 2).

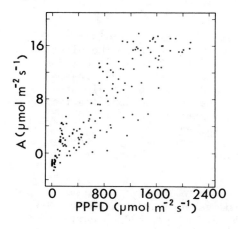

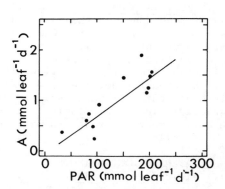

Figure 1. Relationship between
A and PPFD of several leaves

Figure 2. Total daily C fixed
related to PAR intercepted

    This apparent light limitation of C assimilation can be partly
explained by leaf orientation and mutual shading: at midday only half
of the leaves on a stem experience a weighted average PPFD in excess
of 1000 μmol m^{-2}s^{-1}. However, single leaves also show a lack of
saturation of A at high PPFD (Fig. 3). This is a consequence of leaf
anatomy. S. plumieri has a semi-succulent leaf that is almost
isobilateral in nature (Fig. 4). When gas exchange of each surface is
measured independently it is seen that when the upper surface is
illuminated, assimilation by that surface saturates at a PPFD of 800
μmol m^{-2}s^{-1} (Fig. 5). As incident PPFD increases, more light is
transmitted through the leaf to the lower surface, giving rise to an
almost linear increase in assimilation by this surface. The overall
effect is a non-saturating response of A by the whole leaf to PPFD.

    It could be suggested that the reduction in interception of
radiation consequent upon leaf orientation and mutual shading is a
water conservation mechanism. However, water use efficiency (WUE),
calculated as A/E, increases with PPFD (Fig. 6).

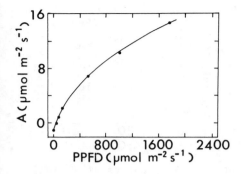

Figure 3. Response of A of a single leaf to PPFD

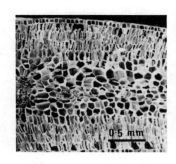

Figure 4. Scanning electron micrograph of a leaf cross section

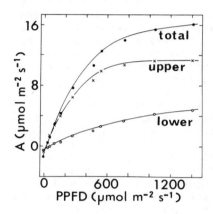

Figure 5. A of each surface and whole leaf in relation to PPFD

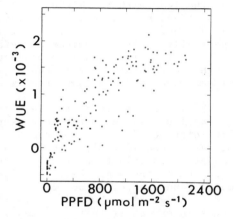

Figure 6. Relation between WUE and PPD of several leaves

The intersection of the supply function with the $A:c_i$ curve for a leaf of S. plumieri at high PPFD (Fig. 7) indicates a stomatal limitation (2) of 33%, which could be at variance with the suggestion of light limitation of C assimilation in the field. However, the shape of the $A:c_i$ curve changes with incident PPFD (Fig. 8), such that A increases with PPFD, despite high stomatal limitations.

4.   DISCUSSION

The data presented in Figs. 1 and 2 indicate that C assimilation by S. plumieri growing in an open, exposed habitat (leaf area index (LAI) of approximately 1) is limited by intercepted PAR. This is a consequence of both canopy architecture (leaf orientation and mutual shading) and leaf anatomy (Figs. 4 and 5). The reduced interception of radiation does not appear to be a water conservation mechanism as instantaneous values of WUE increase with PPFD (Fig. 6) and on a daily

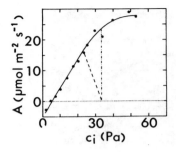

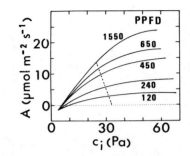

Figure 7. A:c_i curve at 1900 μmol m^{-2}s^{-1} PPFD

Figure 8. A:c_i curves of a single leaf at the indicated PPFDs

basis, the leaf with the highest WUE is the leaf that intercepts the most PAR (data not shown). In communities of high LAI, intercepted PAR is a major determinant of C assimilation (3). Communities of low LAI generally occur in semi-arid regions and less is known about the direct effect of irradiance on productivity in these communities, although photosynthesis by leaves of desert plants usually is not light saturated under midday irradiances (4).

The lower surface of the leaf appears to have as much chlorophyllous tissue as the upper surface although the average ratio of PAR intercepted by the upper and lower surfaces is 3.5:1 (this value varies considerably with leaf orientation and time of day). C assimilation is able to respond to irradiances in excess of those intercepted by the leaf (Fig. 3). Furthermore, even at infinite stomatal conductance, values of c_i are inadequate to saturate A at high PPFD (Fig. 7). Thus S. plumieri appears to have a photosynthetic capacity in excess of that realized in the field. A similar phenomenon has been reported for Cistus salvifolius, a semi-deciduous Mediterranean shrub (5). This implies a N investment in the photosynthetic apparatus in excess of that utilized. In a sand dune environment low in soil N (1), this poses interesting ecological questions.

REFERENCES
1   Barbour, M.G., de Jong, T.M. and Pavlik, B.M. (1985) in Physiological Ecology of North American Plant Communities (Chabot, B.F. and Mooney, H.A., eds.), pp.296–322, Chapman and Hall, New York, London
2   Farquhar, G.D. and Sharkey, T.D. (1982) Annu. Rev. Plant Physiol. 33, 317–345
3   Monteith, J.L. (1977) J. Appl. Ecol. 9, 747–766
4   Ehleringer, J. (1985) in Physiological Ecology of North American Plant Communities (Chabot, B.F. and Mooney, H.A., eds.), pp.162–180, Chapman and Hall, New York, London
5   Harley, P.C., Tenhunen, J.D., Beyschlay, W. and Lange, O.L. (1987) Oecologia (Berl.) 74, 380–388.

PHYTOPLANKTON PHOTOSYNTHESIS IN THE ATLANTIC OCEAN AS MEASURED FROM A
SUBMERSIBLE PUMP AND PROBE FLUOROMETER IN SITU.

PAUL G. FALKOWSKI and ZBIGNIEW KOLBER, Oceanographic
Sciences Division, Brookhaven National Laboratory, Upton, NY
11973, USA.

INTRODUCTION
    Photosynthesis by phytoplankton in the sea accounts for 40 to 50%
of the total global primary productivity. The assessment of
photochemical activity from variable fluorescence has conceptually
increased the potential for the measurement of photosynthesis under
natural conditions. Pulsed light fluorometers (1,2) or pump and probe
fluorometers (3,4) can measure photochemical and non-photochemical
quenching under ambient light. We report here on measurements of
variable fluorescence yields made in real-time, in situ, under ambient
irradiance in the northwest Atlantic Ocean. Using a submersible pump
and probe fluorometer, we measured the relative absorption cross
sections of PS II, the kinetics of electron transport, and components
which contribute to changes in variable fluorescence in natural
phytoplankton communities. From these measurements we calculated
ongoing photosynthetic rates and compared the results with concurrently
measured photosynthetic rates based on radiocarbon labeling.

MATERIALS AND METHODS
    Fluorescence was measured with a submersible, custom-built pump and
probe fluorometer interfaced with a conductivity, temperature, depth
(CTD) sensor. The instrument measures the change in the quantum yield
of fluorescence of weak probe flash preceding (F_o) and 70 μsec
following (F_s) a saturating pump flash. The flashes are provided by a
Hamamatsu L2453 flash tubes. The red light is isolated with two Corion
S10-69A0 interference filters and is detected by a Hamamatsu R1463 PMT.
Samples of seawater, containing phytoplankton, freely flow in and out
of the sample chamber and are exposed to the natural background
irradiance during the measurements. Irradiance was recorded with a
Biospherical Instruments 4π quantum sensor. Changes in the quantum
yield of fluorescence ($\Delta\phi$) are operationally separated into two
components, photochemical (qQ) and non-photochemical (qNP) quenching.
We calculated qQ and qNP from the expressions:

$$qQ = (F_s - F_a)/F_s \tag{1a}$$
$$qNP = (F_{smax} - F_s)/F_{smax} \tag{1b}$$

where F_s is the fluorescence yield immediately following the saturating
flash (all reaction centers closed), F_a is the fluorescence yield
preceding the saturating flash; both F_s and F_a are measured under
ambient irradiance. F_{smax} is the fluorescence yield with all the
reaction centers closed by the saturating flash, but measured in dark.
Chl a was measured on filtered samples after extraction with 90%

M. Baltscheffsky (ed.), Current Research in Photosynthesis, Vol. IV, 923–926.
© 1990 Kluwer Academic Publishers. Printed in the Netherlands.

acetone. Radiocarbon, provided as 5 μCi NaH^{14}CO$_3$, was measured after 4 to 6 h incubation on samples from selected depths. Samples were incubated in a deck—board incubator with flow—through seawater under natural light using neutral density screens to simulate light conditions at collection depths. Samples were filtered on Millipore HA filters, fumed for 60 s over conc. HCl and counted in a liquid scintillation spectrometer.

RESULTS AND DISCUSSION

Representative vertical profiles of the changes in photochemical quenching qQ and the components of fluorescence are shown in Fig. 1. During the night variations in F_o and F_s closely follow chlorophyll concentrations, qQ is maximal, and qNP is nil (Fig 1a). At mid—day qQ is lowest and qNP is highest in the upper water column, where sunlight is greatest. Both qQ and qNP gradually change with depth to their dark values. Because of these two effects, variations in F_a and F_s in the upper water column do not track chlorophyll. qQ is lowest near the surface, increases slowly to a maximum value, and remains relatively constant thereafter (Fig 1b).

Using Eq. 1 we calculated the rate of ongoing photosynthesis using a kinetic model thus:

$$\Phi_p = \sigma PSII * qQ * \Phi_{trans} *(1-a_i) \tag{2}$$

where σPSII is the absorption cross section of photosystem II, Φ_{trans} is the efficiency of electron transport from PS II to PS I and a_i is the fractional decrease in photosynthesis at superoptimal irradiance levels. Φ_{trans} is a function of the reduction level of the plastoquinone pool: Assuming that charge separation events follow a Poisson distribution (5), Φ_{trans} may be calculated as:

$$\Phi_{trans} = \sum_{i=0}^{N-1} (R_{cs}*\tau_{Pox})^i / \sum_{i=0}^{N} (R_{cs}*\tau_{Pox})^i \tag{3}$$

where N is the size of the plastoquinone pool, $R_{cs} = I_o*\sigma PSII*qQ$ is the calculated rate of charge separation and τ_{Pox} is the time constant for the oxidation of PQH$_2$. Φ_{trans} is relatively insensitive to N above values of 5. Photoinhibition was calculated as proportional to the probability of charge separation in a situation where QA is reduced and the primary donor to RC II is still oxidized, thus:

$$a_i = \frac{R_{cs}*\tau_{IIred}}{1+R_{cs}*\tau_{IIred}} * \frac{R_{cs}*\tau_{Qox}}{1+R_{cs}*\tau_{Qox}}, \tag{4}$$

where τ_{Qox} (400 μs) and τ_{IIred} (250 μs) are the average time constants for Q$_A$ oxidation and RC II reduction, respectively.

Application of Eq. 2 to the fluorescence data, such as those presented in Fig. 1 provides a basis for calculating photosynthetic electron transport rates in real time, non—destructively. We compared photosynthetic rates with those measured using radiocarbon during 6 h incubations (Fig. 2). Our results reveal that the fluorescence derived estimates of photosynthesis explain 79% of the variance in the photosynthesis predicted from radiocarbon fixation. Considering that photosynthesis calculated from variable fluorescence does not include respiratory losses, while that from radiocarbon has some respiratory

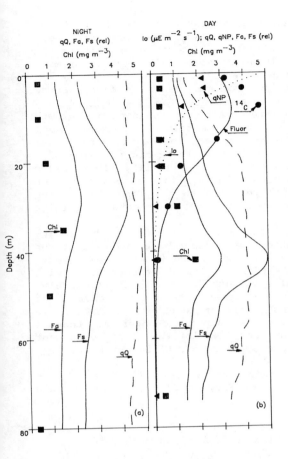

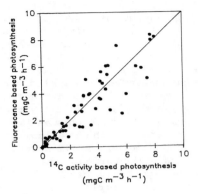

Fig. 1 (left) vertical profiles of qQ, qNP, F_a and F_s,
extracted Chl, ^{14}C incorporated and irradiance in March
1989 in the Atlantic Ocean
off the east coast of the
U.S. (a) Night time measurements and (b) the same
station at mid-day.

Fig. 2 (top). Correlation
between photosynthesis
measured by ^{14}C incorporation and that calculated
from variable fluorescence
signals using eq. 2
(n=51, r=0.897).

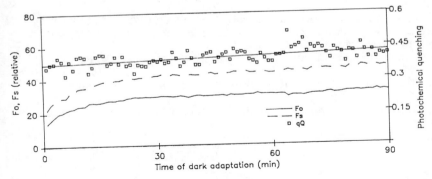

Fig. 3. Time course of changes in qNP in a natural phytoplankton
population. Note the initial, rapid change in F_o and F_s and the
slow rise in qQ.

component, the agreement is remarkable. Moreover, we stress that the fluorosensing measurements are made in real-time and are non-destructive, allowing for the effect of short term changes in irradiance (such as the passing of clouds across the sky) on primary photochemistry to be immediately assessed.

We have previously found that the maximum change in fluorescence yields measured in dark adapted samples, $\Delta\phi_{sat}$, ($\Delta\phi_{sat} = (F_{smax}-F_o)/F_o$) is 1.6 to 1.7 in nutrient replete cells, independent of growth irradiance (6). Under nitrogen limited conditions however, $\Delta\phi_{sat}$ decreases. We have observed variations in $\Delta\phi_{sat}$ in coastal waters that are related to the availability of dissolved inorganic nitrogen (7). This phenomenon is not associated with the availability of dissolved phosphate. We suggest that the decrease in $\Delta\phi_{sat}$ is due to a reduction in the synthesis of CP43 and CP47 relative to the light harvesting chlorophyll proteins under nitrogen, but not phosphorus, limiting conditions (6).

We are currently evaluating the effect of qNP on the energy dissipation in natural phytoplankton populations. The analysis of the qNP relaxation in the dark reveals at least two kinetic components, which affect F_s and F_o differently (Fig.3). The short component, with a time constant of about 5 min. affects both F_o and F_s proportionately, without changing $\Delta\phi_{sat}$. The long component with a time constant of about 1.5 h affects F_s more than F_o, leading to changes in $\Delta\phi_{sat}$. We suggest that the short component is due to changes in thermal deactivation within the pigment bed, while the long component represents either a xanthophyll cycle, or repair of D1, or both.

This research was supported by NASA grant UPN 161-35-05-08 and contracts from the U.S. Department of Energy, Office of Health and Environmental Research

REFERENCES
1. Ogren, E., Baker, N.R. (1985) Plant Cell Environ. 8:539-548.
2. Schreiber, U., Bilger, W. and Schliwa, U. (1986) Photosyn. Res. 10:51-62.
3. Mauzerall, D. (1972) Proc. Nat. Acad. Sci. USA (1972) 69:1358-1362.
4. Falkowski, P.G., Wyman, K., Ley, A.C. and Mauzerall, D. (1986) Biochim. Biophys. Acta 849:183-192.
5. Ley, A.C. and Mauzerall, D. (1982) Biochim. Biophys. Acta 680:95-106.
6. Kolber, Z., Zehr, J. and Falkowski, P.G. (1988) Plant Physiol. 88:923-929.
7. Kolber, Z., Wyman, K. and Falkowski, P.G. (1989) Limnol. Oceanogr. (in press).

COMPARISON OF GROWTH OF MICRO-ALGAE NOSTOC LINCKIA &
CHLORELLA SP. IN DILUTE CULTURE.

NOMITA SEN
GOVT. SCIENCE & M.H.COLLEGE OF HOME SCIENCE
246, GUPTESHWAR , PREMNAGAR, JABALPUR (INDIA)

INTRODUCTION : Dilute cultures mean starting the
experimental cultures with few individuals
of uniform inoculum. Cultures were grown in low light
when photosynthetic reactions are prevented. These were
grown in CHU.NO.10 medium (50 ml) in 150 ml Borosil
make conical flask at a light intensity of 200 lux
under ambient conditions.
CULTURES GROWN IN THE DARK :
            No growth was observed in cultures grown
in the dark with or without nitrate as nitrogen source
and with or without additions of organic substances.
CULTURES GROWN IN LOW LIGHT :
            Nostoc exhibited growth in nitrogen free
medium . In ammonium medium cultures were paler in colour
than those of nitrate and nitrogen free medium. In
ammonium medium heterocysts production was completely
suppressed.
            Chlorella did not grow in nitrogen free
medium. Culture media without nitrate but with ammonium
stimulated growth of Chlorella.
            To study the effects of various organic
substances on the final yield of these two algae, CHU.NO.10
medium has been used as the basal medium. The growth
behavior in low light appears to differ in nitrogen
fixing procaryotic alga Nostoc linckia and non-
nitrogen fixing eucaryotic alga Chlorella sp. Glucose did
not increase the final yield of Nostoc linckia but
Chlorella sp. showed increase in final yield in relation
to the control. Aspartic and citric acids did not support
growth in Nostoc linckia whereas oxalic acid increased
the final yield . In Chlorella citric acid had no effect
on growth whereas aspartic and oxalic acids decreased the
final yield (TABLE). Glutamic acid increased the final
in both . In cultures with glutamic acid Nostoc
filaments were without heterocysts.

M. Baltscheffsky (ed.), Current Research in Photosynthesis, Vol. IV, 927–930.

TABLE

EFFECTS OF VARIOUS ORGANIC SUBSTANCES ON THE FINAL YIELD
OF <u>NOSTOC</u> & <u>CHLORELLA</u>

Chlorella		Nostoc		Name of the
Control	with organic substance	Control	with organic substance	organic substance
0.25	0.40	0.17	0.17	GLUCOSE
0.06	0.06	0.08	0.00	CITRIC ACID
0.07	0.06	0.07	0.00	
"	0.16	"	0.12	GLUTAMIC ACID
	0.17		0.09	
0.08	0.03	0.08	0.10	OXALIC ACID
0.09	0.04	0.09	0.11	
"	0.01	"	0.00	ASPARTIC ACID
	0.03		0.00	

(Readings taken in Biochem Double Cell Colorimeter with
Red filter - 640 mu)

DISCUSSION AND CONCLUSION: If chloroplast DNA is similar
to bacterial DNA, then from the above experimental results
it can be concluded that in these micro-algae light and
suitable organic substance induce synthesis of nucleic
acids (OPERON) leading to protein synthesis which play
an important role in the synthesis of cell materials
during growth provided the concentration of the early
intermediates are kept low favouring the end products of
the metabolic reactions . Supporting evidence comes from
the work of Sen (Chowdhuri) and Fogg, 1966, on an obli-
gately phototrophic strain of <u>Chlorella pyrenoidosa</u> (Chick).
There was progressive reduction in the final yield of
this alga with increasing concentrations of glycollate,
an early intermediate of photosynthesis. Cultures were
yellowish suggesting protein deficiency. Nomita Sen
(refer T.S.Sadasivan) also stated that the increase in
final yield without any increase in respiration (Sen,
1966) seem to suggest that the alga could utilise
suitable organic substances directly in light for the
synthesis of nitrogenous substances leading to protein
synthesis. The following condition seems to prevail
during photoassimilation :-

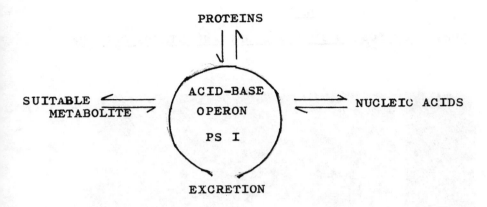

REFERENCES

Nalewajko,C.,Chowdhuri,N., and Fogg,G.E.1963. Excretion of glycollic acid and the growth of a planktonic Chlorella . In Micro-algae and Photosynthetic bacteria. pp. 171-83. Japanese Society of Plant Physiologists, Tokyo.
Roach,B.M.Bristol.1926. Ann.Bot.Lond.40: 149-201.
＿＿＿＿＿＿＿＿.1928. Ann.Bot.Lond.42: 317-45.
Sadasivan,T.S.1966.Summer School in Experimental Botany. Jour.of Scientific & Industrial Research. 25: 7-11.
Sen(Chowdhuri),Nomita., and Fogg,G.E.1966.Effects of glycollate on the growth of a planktonic Chlorella. J.Expt.Bot. 17:417-25.
Sen(Chowdhuri),Nomita.1966.Growth of a planktonic Chlorella and formation of glycine.J.Ind.Bot.Soc.45:175-87.
Sharma,A.K.1981.Evolution of cell and chromosome in Eucaryota. J.Ind.Bot.Soc.60:1-8.

PLATES

GROWTH OF NOSTOC IN LOW LIGHT AND DILUTE CULTURE

EFFECTS OF SUBOPTIMAL TEMPERATURE AND LIGHT CONDITIONS DURING GROWTH ON
TEMPERATURE DEPENDENT CHLOROPHYLL FLUORESCENCE OF TOMATO.

Luuk H. J. Janssen and Phillip R. van Hasselt, Dept. of Plant Biology;
Lab. of Plant Physiology, Univ. of Groningen, The Netherlands.

Introduction

Chilling sensitive plants like tomato (*Lycopersicon esculentum* L.)
are damaged by sudden exposure to suboptimal temperature. However, a
gradual change of growth conditions enables plants to adapt to less
favourable circumstances and maintain growth. The ability to perform an
adaptation differs between species and even between cultivars.
   In a previous paper (2) we reported the use of chlorophyll a
fluorescence to monitor adaptation to suboptimal growth conditions of
cucumber. Two breaks were observed in the curve of the first
fluorescence induction maximum Fv(p) plotted against temperature, which
were affected by suboptimal growth conditions.
   In this study tomato plants were used. As with cucumber two breaks
were observed. The effect of different temperature and light
intensities during growth on the breakpoint temperatures were studied.
Alteration of actinic light intensity and inhibition of electron
transport by DCMU was applied to reveal the mechanisms causing the
breaks in Fv(p) plotted against temperature.

Methods

Tomato plants were grown at 22 and 17°C under high ($300\mu E.m^{-2}.s^{-1}$) and
low ($100\mu E.m^{-2}.s^{-1}$) light intensity. Daylength was 12 hours; relative
humidity 80%.

Chlorophyll a fluorescence induction of tomato leaf discs ($\phi7mm$) was
measured at decreassing temperatures from 30 to 0°C with a newly
developed automatic, system which allows :

   - control of temperature and gas composition
   - fluorescence induction measurement of 100 leaf discs
   - data processing and storage

The actinic light intensity was 10 or $150\mu E.m^{-2}.s^{-1}$. The O_2 concentration
was kept at 2% (in N_2). Leaf discs were incubated with $50\mu M$ DCMU in
tap water during 2 hours in dim light.

M. Baltscheffsky (ed.), Current Research in Photosynthesis, Vol. IV, 931–934.
© 1990 *Kluwer Academic Publishers. Printed in the Netherlands.*

Results and Discussion

Relative changes in Fv(p) at decreasing temperature are shown in Fig.
1a. Fv(p) changed lineairly with temperature. At two temperatures a
sudden change in slope (break) occured. No breaks were observed in
constant fluorescence, Fo.

The effect of electron inhibition by DCMU on Fv(p) is shown in Fig.
1b. Only one breakpoint was observed around 23°C. It is suggested that
the low temperature breakpoint, absent with electron transport
inhibition, is caused by a low temperature induced decrease of the rate
of electron transport between photosystems I and II. Temperature
dependent inhibition of lateral diffusion of plastoquinone in the
chloroplast thylakoid membrane (3) could be an explanation for such a
decrease in electron transport rate. The increase of Fv(p), observed
from the low breakpoint temperature to 0°C in the absence of DCMU at
$10\mu E.m^{-2}.s^{-1}$, reflects an increase in Q_a reduction at Fv(p). Results
obtained with an increased actinic light intensity ($150\mu E.m-2.s-1$)
resembled the DCMU results. This higher actinic light intensity
strongly reduces Q_a at Fv(p). Further reduction of Q_a at low temperature
will be limited, and as a consequence, the low temperature breakpoint
was absent.

The high temperature breakpoint, which remains with electron
transport inhibition or high actinic light intensity, may be caused by
a change in light distribution between the photosystems. In spinach
leaves it was found that the dark adapted state of the leaf is State I
at low temperatures and State II at high temperatures (4). A State II-
State I shift could account for the increase in Fv(p) between 30°C and
the high temperature breakpoint. The state transition is assumed to be
completed at the high temperature breakpoint, resulting in a State I at
low temperatures.

The effect of growth condition on the temperature of both
fluorescence breakpoints is shown in table 1.
Growth temperature and light intensity had no significant effect on the
low breakpoint temperature suggesting that the temperature of electron
transport inhibition between the photosystems is not affected by the
growth conditions. Similar results were found earlier with cucumber
(1). It should be noted that the low breakpoint temperature equals the
low temperature limit of growth of tomato.
The data of table 1 show that the light intensity during growth had a
major effect on the high temperature breakpoint but the temperature
during growth had no significant effect. This indicates that the high
breakpoint temperature reflected mainly an adaptation of the
chloroplasts to light intensity. A change of the dark state of the
thylakoid membrane could be an important factor explaining the observed
adaptive change of temperature dependent Fv(p).

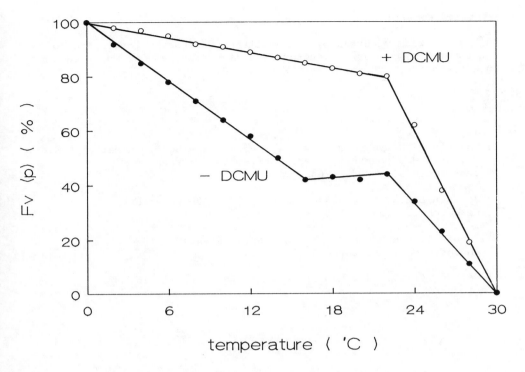

Figure 1. Fv(p) of tomato leaf discs at decreasing temperature.

The first maximum of fluorescence induction, Fv(p), is expressed in relative units. The minimal value is represented as 0%, the maximal as 100%.

growth condition	low	high
17°C, 100μE.m^{-2}.s^{-1}	12.9 (0.5)	19.5 (2.5)
17°C, 300μE.m^{-2}.s^{-1}	14.6 (1.3)	23.2 (0.5)
22°C, 100μE/m^{-2}.s^{-1}	12.9 (0.5)	20.0 (3.1)
22°C, 300μE/m^{-2}.s^{-1}	16.4 (0.8)	22.7 (1.4)

Table 1   Effect of temperature and light intensity during growth on the breakpoint temperatures of Fv(p) plotted against temperature of tomato leaf discs.

Acknowledgements

This study was supported by the Committee for Energy Consumption of the Dutch Ministry of Agriculture and Fisheries, and was carried out in cooperation with the IVT in Wageningen.

References

1) Hasselt P. R. van, Woltjes J., Jong F. de (1982), In Marcelle R., Clysters H., Poucke M., (eds), Effects of stress on photosynthesis, 257 - 265.

2) Janssen L.H.J., van Hasselt P.R. (1988), Photosynthesis Research 15: 153 - 162.

3) Scoufflaire R., Lannoye R., Barber J. (1985), Photosynthesis Research 6: 133 - 145.

4) Weis E. (1985), Biochim Biophys Acta 807: 118 - 126.

PHOTOTROPHIC BACTERIA THAT FORM HEAT RESISTANT ENDOSPORES

JOHN ORMEROD[1], TORE NESBAKKEN[2] AND YNGVE TORGERSEN[1], Biology Dept.[2] Oslo University[1] and Apothekernes Laboratorium A/S[2], OSLO, NORWAY.

INTRODUCTION

The Heliobacteriaceae are a newly discovered family of green anaerobic phototrophs which contain bacterio-chlorophyll (Bchl) g (absorption spectrum, Fig. 1) and have reaction centres probably similar to those of PS I (1, 2).

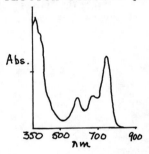

Fig.1. Absorption spectrum of Bchl g in methanol.

The first known representative of the group, Heliobacterium chlorum, was isolated by Gest & Favinger (3) from a garden soil enrichment culture. During examination of tropical soils for phototrophic bacteria we observed the dull green growth of helio-bacteria in enrichment cultures inoculated with soil from paddy fields. We have subsequently isolated a number of strains of these organisms from such soils and Beer-Romero and Gest (4) have also isolated a new heliobacterium from one of them.

The heliobacteria have been classified with the gram positive bacteria on the basis of their 16s RNA sequences (5) and on the same basis have close affinity with the clostridia (6). It was therefore not entirely surprising to discover that some of the heliobacterial strains now isolated form endospores.

MATERIALS AND METHODS Two types of enrichment media were used: 0.25 % (w/v) yeast extract in distilled water (YE) or malate medium (7) containing 0.1 % ammonium sulphate. These media were dispensed into 60 ml screw capped bottles 2/3 full, autoclaved and inoculated with a few g of dry soil. Usually the gas space was flushed with N_2. The caps were screwed down and the bottles incubated in the light (1 000 - 2 000 lux) at 32 - 38° C. Anaerobic chemoheterotrophic bacteria grew up first, but after a few days some of the cultures turned green. These were streaked on plates of YE

M. Baltscheffsky (ed.), Current Research in Photosynthesis, Vol. IV, 935–938.

agar in an anaerobic chamber (Forma Scientific) containing
$N_2:CO_2:H_2$ 85:10:5 and incubated in   the   chamber   in   the
light.   Greenish colonies were examined microscopically and
restreaked   until pure, when they were transferred to screw
cap tubes of YE medium and   incubated in the light. Growth
experiments   were carried out in screw cap tubes and growth
was estimated turbidimetrically.
    Cells for   electron microscopy   were fixed   in 3 % (w/v)
glutaraldehyde and postfixed with OsO_4 For thin sectioning
the   cells were   embedded in epoxy and the sections stained
with uranyl acetate and lead citrate. Negative staining was
with phosphotungstate. Preparations were examined in a Jeol
JEM 100C or   JSM   35C   electron   microscope.   X-ray microanalysis   of purified spores was carried   out in a Jeol JEM
100CX coupled to a LINK 860 series 2 X-ray detector.

RESULTS A large   spirillum, given   the   provisional   name
Heliobacterium gestii,in honour of Howard Gest, who with J.
Favinger discovered the Heliobacteiaceae, was isolated from
paddy   field   soil   from   Chainat,   Thailand.   It   measures
0.6-0.8   x 8-20   um and   is motile   with polar   or subpolar
flagella,   inserted at both ends (Fig. 2). Thin sections of
H.   gestii show neither   invaginations   of the cell membrane
nor chlorosomes (Fig. 3).

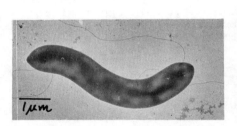
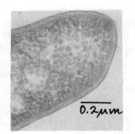

Fig. 2. H. gestii, negative   Fig. 3. Thin section of
           stain   H. gestii

The GC content   is 54.8%   (kindly determined   by Dr.   R. L.
Gherna,   ATCC) and the 16s RNA sequence data (determined by
Dr. C.R. Woese) show 96% homology with those of H. chlorum.
    H.   gestii   is   strictly   anaerobic   and   phototrophic,
requires biotin   and a   reduced sulphur   source and   uses a
number of   simple organic carbon sources.   It grows best at
pH 7-8,   35-38° C and high   light intensity. Ammonium salts
are   a good nitrogen source for   the organism, but   only at
low concentrations. Growth is as rapid on N_2 as on NH_4^+.
    The spores are subterminal, cylindrical, 0.9 x 2 um. They
are formed sporadically in old cultures but sediment and
clump   together   in   large   numbers,   making   quantitation
difficult.   Cultures containing such spore clumps were used
for determining heat resistance (Table 1).

TABLE 1. Heat resistance of H. gestii spores.

Treatment	No. of colonies
None	16
60°, 1 h	33
85°, 15 min	21
None	64
Boiled 3 x	18

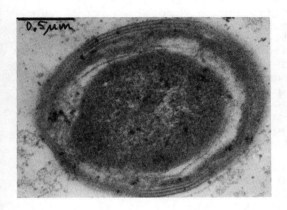

The spores were found to release dipicolinic acid on autoclaving, and to contain 5-6 x as much Ca^{2+} as vegetative cells, as determined by X-ray microanalysis. Fig. 4 shows a section of a spore. The surface layers are believed to be the protein layers of the spore coat. It is not known whether the spores contain Bchl.

Fig. 4. Section of spore of H. gestii.

Heliobacterium fasciculum (Latin fasciculus, bundle), was isolated from Tanzanian paddy field soil. The rods are 0.8-1 x 8-20 um, motile with thick, polar (?) flagella, and associate in parallel motile bundles (Fig. 5), which swim with a characteristic rolling motion and are phototactic.

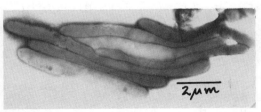

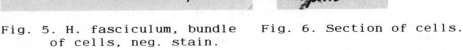

Fig. 5. H. fasciculum, bundle of cells, neg. stain.

Fig. 6. Section of cells.

The membrane structure of H. fasciculum is like that of H. gestii (Fig. 6). The organism is strictly anaerobic and grows best at high light intensity and 35 - 40° C. Little is known about its nutrition. After two or three transfers growth ceases but can be restarted by adding a small amount of sterile filtered spent enrichment medium.

H. fasciculum sporulates abundantly and the cylindrical endospores, measuring 1 x 2-3 um, distend the sporangium.

DISCUSSION

H. gestii and H. fasciculum have many features in common with the two earlier described heliobacteria (3,4). Absorption spectra, membrane structure, growth requirements and, where known, nucleic acid characteristics, are all very similar. The main differences appear to be morphological. A strong case can therefore be made for classifying all of the known heliobacteria in a single genus.

So far we have only obtained heliobacteria from dried or pasteurised tropical paddy field soil samples. Fresh, untreated soil gives cultures dominated by purple bacteria. These observations may explain why the heliobacteria remained undiscovered for so long (3).

Most heliobacteria seem to be adapted to tropical environments: seasonal flooding and drying out, high temperatures and light intensities. The fact that heliobacteria are avid nitrogen fixers (7) indicates that they may be important in rice nutrition.

It has been suggested that all the gram positive bacteria may have descended from photosynthetic ancestors and indeed that the ancestor of all eubacteria was photosynthetic (5). It is, therefore, important to search for other new types of photosynthetic bacteria in an effort to shed more light on the early evolution of photosynthesis. Our findings suggest that such organisms may not be ubiquitous and will require specific enrichment methods for their isolation.

REFERENCES

1 Fuller, R.C., Sprague, S.G., Gest, H. and Blankenship, R.E. (1985) FEBS Lett. 182, 345-349
2 Amesz, J. (1987) Photosynthetica 21, 225-235
3 Gest, H. and Favinger, J.L. (1983) Arch. Microbiol. 136, 11-16
4 Beer-Romero, P. and Gest, H. (1987) FEMS Microbiol. Lett., 41, 109-114
5 Woese, C.R. (1987) Microbiol. Revs. 51, 221-271
6 Woese,C.R., Debrunner-Vossbrinck, B.A., Oyaizu, H., Stackebrandt, E. and Ludwig, W. (1985) Science, 229, 762-765
7 Ormerod, J.G., Ormerod, K.S. and Gest, H. (1961) Arch. Biochem. Biophys., 94,449-463
8 Heda, G.D. and Madigan, M.T. (1987) in Green Photosynthetic Bacteria (Olson, J.M., Ormerod, J.G., Amesz,J., Stackebrandt, E. and Truper, H.G., eds) pp. 175-187, Plenum, New York.

Index of Names

944

III.9.9
Freiberg, A., **II.**4.157
Friedberg, D., **IV.**18.463
Friesner, R.A., **I.**1.93
Fromme, P., **III.** 9.15
Fronko, R.M., **I.**3.797
Füglistaller, P., **II.**4.93
Fujii, T., **II.**7.655
Fujimura, Y., **I.**2.403, **I.**3.957
Fujita, S., **III.**13.763
Fukuzawa, H., **IV.**18.467
Furbacher, P.N., **III.**10.221, **III.**10.271, **III.**13.799
Furbank, R.T., **IV.**18.541

Gaba, V., **I.**2.209,
Gabai, C., **III.**13.823
Gad'on, N., **II.**4.121
Gadal, P., **IV.**16.243, **IV.**16.247
Gal, A., **II.**8.779, **II.**8.783
Gale, J., **IV.**15.55
Gale, M.D., **III.**12.601
Galmiche, J.-M., **III.** 9.65
Gamble, P.E., **III.**12.423
Ganago, A.O., **I.**1.117
Gans, P., **IV.**15.43
Gantt, E., **IV.**17.321, **IV.**17.349, **IV.**17.353
Garab, G., **II.**7.667
Garbisu, C., **II.**7.699
Garcia-Véscovi, E., **II.**8.895
Gardeström, P., **IV.**15.9, **IV.**15.59, **IV.**19.805
Gardet-Salvi, L., **IV.**16.167
Garlaschi, F.M., **II.**5.313, **II.**5.317
Garnier, J., **II.**5.277
Gärtner, S., **I.**2.295
Gasparich, G.E., **II.**4.1
Gast, P., **I.**3.953
Gau, A.E., **I.**2.295
Gaugain, F., **IV.**17.409
Gaul, D., **I.**1.113
Geacintov, N.E., **I.**2.467, **II.**4.125
Geiken, B., **II.**6.373
Gennis, R.B., **III.**10.263
Genty, B., **IV.**16.259, **IV.**17.337, **IV.**17.365, **IV.**17.369
George, G.N., **I.**3.685
Georgi, S., **III.**11.385
Gepstein, S., **III.**11.411
Geraghty, A.M., **IV.**18.505
Gerhardt, V., **I.**3.853, **I.**3.857
Gerken, S., **I.**3.837
Gerrish, C., **III.**13.759

Geva, N., **III.**11.411
Ghanatry, J.A., **II.**4.73,
Ghanotakis, D.F., **I.**2.275, **I.**2.643
Ghirardi, M.L., **II.**8.733
Ghosh, R., **II.**4.77
Giacometti, G.M., **I.**2.339, **II.**6.419
Giardi, M.T., **I.**2.339, **II.**6.419
Gibbs, P., **IV.**17.329
Gillbro, T., **II.**4.11, **II.**4.117, **II.**4.181, **II.**5.301
Gillham, N.W., **III.**12.509
Gilmore, A.M., **II.**6.495
Gimenez, P., **IV.**15.95
Gimmler, H., **IV.**19.769, **IV.**19.773
Gingras, G., **I.**1.125
Giorgi, L.B., **I.**2.415, **II.**6.519
Girard-Bascou, J., **III.**12.437
Girault, G., **III.** 9.65
Girvin, M.E., **III.**10.271
Glaser, E., **III.**13.815
Glauser, M., **II.**4.89,
Gleason, F.K., **IV.**16.175
Gleiter, H.M., **I.**2.479, **I.**2.531
Gnanam, A., **III.**12.633
Godik, V.I., **II.**4.157
Goetze, D.C., **II.**7.691
Golbeck, J.H., **II.**6.401, **II.**7.531
Golden, S.S., **II.**6.431, **II.**8.863, **III.**12.445
Goldfeld, M.G., **III.**9.105, **III.**9.111
Goldschmidt-Clermont, M., **III.**12.437
Goltsev, V., **IV.**19.699
Gomez-Moreno, C., **II.**7.663
Gong, H., **II.**6.397
González, M.S., **IV.**15.47, **IV.**17.397
González-Murua, C., **IV.**19.789
Goodchild, D.J., **II.**8.803
Gorgé, J.L., **IV.**16.163, **IV.**16.251
Görlach, J., **III.**14.857
Gornicka, O., **II.**8.887
Gottstein, J., **II.**4.45,
Gough, S.P., **III.**12.585
Gounaris, K., **I.**2.223, **I.**2.327
Govindjee, **I.**2.451, **I.**2.459, **I.**2.511, **I.**2.515
Gräber, P., **III.** 9.15, **III.**9.33, **III.**9.37, **III.**9.217
Grandoni, P.A., **III.**9.145
Granok, H., **I.**2.367
Granot, G., **IV.**15.55
Gratton, E., **I.**2.459,
Grätzel, M., **I.**2.619,
Gravett, A.E., **II.**6.475
Gray, J.C., **III.**10.267, **III.**12.461, **III.**12.625

958